System of National Accounts 1993

Harry C. Trexler Library
Muhlenberg College

System of
National Accounts
1993

Prepared under the auspices of the
Inter-Secretariat Working Group on National Accounts

Commission of the European Communities—Eurostat

International Monetary Fund

Organisation for Economic Co-operation and Development

United Nations
Department for Economic and Social Information
and Policy Analysis—Statistical Division
Economic Commission for Europe
Economic and Social Commission for Asia and the Pacific
Economic Commission for Latin America and the Caribbean
Economic Commission for Africa
Economic and Social Commission for Western Asia

World Bank

Brussels/Luxembourg, New York, Paris, Washington, D.C., 1993

Office for Official Publications of the European Communities
Catalogue number CA-81-93-002-EN-C

International Monetary Fund
Publication Stock No. SNA-EA

Organisation for Economic Co-operation and Development
OECD Code 30 94 01 1

United Nations publication · Sales No.E.94.XVII.4,
document symbol ST/ESA/STAT/SER.F/2/Rev.4

World Bank Stock Number: 31512

ISBN 92-1-161352-3

Foreword

The revised *System of National Accounts* (SNA) presented in this volume has been undertaken under the joint responsibility of our five organizations. Through the mechanism of an Inter-Secretariat Group, the staff of our organizations have organized and managed the review process from the mid-1980s onwards. The resulting *System* is being published jointly by the five organizations.

The *System* is a comprehensive, consistent and flexible set of macroeconomic accounts intended to meet the needs of government and private-sector analysts, policy makers and decision takers. It is designed for use in countries with market economies, whatever their stage of economic development, and also in countries in transition to market economies. The *System* has been welcomed and unanimously approved by the Statistical Commission of the United Nations.

The revision process has required numerous meetings over several years in which experts in national accounts from countries throughout the world have participated. The revised *System* owes much to their collective advice and wisdom. The revision has been a major exercise in cooperation conducted at a world level between national and international statistical agencies. It serves as a model for future collaborative work on the development of improved statistical systems and standards, including national accounts. The SNA is intended for use by both national and international statistical agencies, and countries are advised to start to compile accounts utilizing the revised *System* as soon as possible.

Boutros Boutros-Ghali
Secretary-General
United Nations

Michel Camdessus
Managing Director
International
Monetary Fund

Jacques Delors
President
Commission of the
European Communities

Jean-Claude Paye
Secretary-General
Organisation for
Economic Co-operation
and Development

Lewis T. Preston
President
World Bank

Summary

Contents

---

*The detailed contents of the annexes including figures and tables may be found beginning on page 519.

Preface

The *System of National Accounts 1993* (1993 SNA) represents a major advance in national accounting. Adoption of the 1993 SNA was unanimously recommended to the United Nations Economic and Social Council by its Statistical Commission at its twenty-seventh session, held in New York from 22 February to 3 March 1993.[1] In its resolution 1993/5 of 12 July 1993, the Council recommends that member States consider using the 1993 SNA as the international standard for the compilation of their national accounts statistics, to promote the integration of economic and related statistics, as an analytical tool, and in the international reporting of comparable national accounting data. The Council further recommends that international organizations consider the 1993 SNA and its concepts when they review standards for particular fields of economic statistics and endeavour to achieve consistency with the 1993 SNA.

As another step in the evolution of national accounting, the 1993 SNA successfully maintains the proven strengths of the previous System[2] while satisfying the Statistical Commission's mandate to update the previous System to fit new circumstances, to clarify and simplify it, and to harmonize it more completely with other international statistical standards.

A. New features and the role of the System of National Accounts

The 1993 SNA embodies many new features. Many of the important ones can be summarized as aspects of updating, clarifying and simplifying, and harmonizing.

With respect to updating, economies have evolved in the 25 years since the 1968 SNA was published. Inflation has been a central policy concern. The role of government has changed in many countries, notably those now moving toward market economies. Service activities, especially business services such as communications and computing, have taken on increasing importance. Financial institutions and markets have become increasingly sophisticated, and financial instruments have spawned numerous hybrids. The environment's interaction with the economy has become a major and growing concern.

The 1993 SNA is responsive to these and other changes in the institutions and policy concerns of the world's economies in a number of ways.

It provides a separate account to record the revaluation of assets, a key impact of inflation. It also splits the holding gains recorded there into gains due to changes in the general level of prices and gains due to changes in relative prices.

It defines the aggregate actual final consumption for households, government, and non-profit institutions serving households. This aggregate sheds additional light on government activity.

It describes the treatment of services when their distinctive characteristics affect their recording in the accounts.

It establishes criteria for the delineation of the financial corporate sector and for the classification of financial instruments in light of the many innovations in this field.

It has opened toward environmental accounting in defining the asset boundary, in the classification of assets, and in other ways.

With respect to clarifying and simplifying, the 1993 SNA is meant to be applicable to economies that are increasingly complex or changing in other ways, but it aims to simplify the work of the economic accountant. First, it recognizes the wide range of conditions and institutional arrangements that may be found in developed and developing countries and in newly emerging market economies. Secondly, it provides the rationale for the treatments applied so that economic accountants can, by extension, decide on treatments for new conditions and institutional arrangements. Features of the publication itself that aim to help national accountants and other readers are described below in the "Reader's guide".

In addition to this general approach, the 1993 SNA provides clarification on a number of specific issues. By identifying the principles, it reduces the seeming complexity of such a comprehensive system. For example:

It identifies the rules of accounting—the principles of valuation, time of recording, and grouping by aggregation, netting and grossing—in a separate chapter.

It clearly states that illegality itself is not a reason for exclusion from the accounts.

It recommends a treatment for taxes of the valued-added type, which have been introduced in a number of countries since the 1968 SNA.

It recommends a treatment to be applied under official multiple exchange-rate systems.

It recommends that annual chain indices be used to compile an integrated set of prices and volume measures consistent with the concepts and accounting principles of the SNA (and that fixed base indices be used when the volume measures have to be additively consistent).

Finally, the 1993 SNA embodies the result of harmonizing the SNA and other international statistical standards more completely than in the past. The result, as of 1993, is most obvious for the balance of payments because, while working on the revision of the SNA itself, the International Monetary Fund was also revising its *Balance of Payments Manual*. Future readers will note that not only definitions, but even passages describing the concepts, are often the same in the two texts. Future Fund publications will show the greater harmonization between the SNA and the Fund's government finance and financial statistics. The SNA and the International Standard Industrial Classification (ISIC, Rev.3) were brought together in that the definitions of kinds of activities and of statistical units are the same. With respect to population and related measures, the SNA and the International Labour Organisation (ILO) will use the same production boundary and the same key definitions, such as the definition of employment. Further, the 1993 SNA notes and makes use of the distinction between the informal and formal sectors so that when the ILO has completed work on criteria for distinguishing the two, they can be used in conjunction with other breakdowns in the SNA.

In such a vast undertaking, it was, of course, impossible to satisfy the definitions and treatments preferred by all countries on all subjects. Reservations were expressed in the Statistical Commission on several topics: the treatment of research and development expenditures as current and of mineral exploration as capital; the exclusion of rent on buildings owned and occupied by government and non-profit institutions serving households; the treatment of armaments as current expenditures; the degree of detail with which the production accounts for households are presented; the need for the distinction between actual final consumption and final consumption expenditure; and lack of identification of "consumer" subsidies. Nevertheless, the Commission felt that a satisfactory balance had emerged and that the draft adequately represented a general consensus on most issues. (See the discussion of the research agenda in the section below, "Perspectives on the 1993 SNA: looking back and looking ahead".)

The adoption of the updated, simplified and clarified, and more completely harmonized SNA is one of the most important events in the field of official statistics in the past 25 years. That its adoption is so regarded is a reflection of the comprehensiveness of its coverage and the breadth of its applicability. Four points may be made about these features to highlight the role the SNA has come to play:

(a) The 1993 SNA provides a comprehensive view of an economy

It shows the economic behaviour of the economy's participants, their interrelationships and the results of their economic activity. It completes the integration of balance sheets, thus providing a full picture of the resources at the economy's disposal. It consolidates information on some important elements of the economy—for example, population and labour force, price and volume measures and purchasing power parities—that previously had been separate.

(b) The 1993 SNA is expected to provide guidance for national accounts almost universally

From the outset of the revision, it has been the express wish of developing countries that one framework be devised to be applicable to developed and developing economies alike. By the early 1990s, most of the countries with centrally planned economies that previously used the System of Balances of the National Economy (often called the Material Product System, or MPS) had announced their intent to move to the SNA. Throughout the revision, efforts had been made to harmonize MPS and SNA concepts and definitions, and in the final years special efforts were made to include explanations and clarifications that would ease these countries' move to the SNA.

(c) The 1993 SNA recognizes the need for flexibility

It incorporates flexibility as the means of facilitating international comparisons and of encouraging the use of SNA in economies that differ widely, given that analytical requirements and data availability will dictate the varying emphases as matters of national statistical policy. As one aspect of flexibility, the 1993 SNA provides a classification system and an accounting framework that may be used at different levels of detail. The 1993 report suggests how satellite accounts can be used to present concepts that are additional to or that differ from those in the central framework. It shows how alternative classifications, in the framework of a social accounting matrix, augment the tools for analysing poverty and other social concerns.

(d) The 1993 SNA reinforces the central role of national accounts in statistics

National accounts serve as a framework for statistical systems and as a point of reference in establishing standards for related statistics. In one dimension, harmonization, such as between the SNA and the balance of payments, makes efficient use of statistical resources in both countries and international organizations. It also increases the analytical power of the statistics available to the variety of users. Analytical power was a prime focus in the SNA's opening toward the environment, and developmental work is proceeding in recognition of the usefulness of having integrated economic and environmental accounting. In another dimension, the SNA will be the basis for elaborating national accounts for groups of countries, as evidenced by the expected consistency of the revised version of the European Communities' system of accounts with the SNA.

B. Acknowledgements

The *System of National Accounts 1993* is the result of a process that was notable for its breadth and openness. The decade-long, resource-intensive process took place under the auspices of the Inter-Secretariat Working Group on National Accounts (ISWGNA), comprised of Eurostat (the Statistical Office of the European Communities), the International Monetary Fund (IMF), the Organisation for Economic Co-operation and Development (OECD), the Statistical Division (UNSTAT) and regional commissions of the United Nations Secretariat, and the World Bank. The substantial achievements of the process were made possible through close cooperation among the five member organizations of ISWGNA and contributions, both in cash and in kind, from ISWGNA organizations, other international, regional and non-governmental organizations, a number of countries, and many individual experts in national accounting and related fields from all regions of the world.

Between 1982 and 1985, ISWGNA met several times to identify issues and group them together for discussion and to organize the subsequent revision process, and the individual member organizations of ISWGNA held a number of expert meetings to discuss issues. Between 1986 and 1989, one expert group meeting on the SNA structure and seven expert group meetings on specific subject areas were held (see annex VI). Sponsorship and finance were divided among the five ISWGNA member organizations. A core of five national accounts experts participated in all the subject-area expert group meetings to ensure consistency and continuity in decisions taken in different fields. These core experts were: Ms. Carol Carson (United States of America); Mr. Jagdish Kumar (India); Mr. Heinrich Lützel (Germany); Mr. Pablo Mandler (Argentina); and Mr. André Vanoli (France). Throughout the revision process, in addition to providing the secretariat for the various expert group meetings and seminars, the professional staff of the ISWGNA member organisations met together frequently to discuss substantive issues and make proposals and recommendations. The individuals who participated in most or all of these meetings were Mr. Derek Blades (OECD), Datuk Ramesh Chander (World Bank), Ms. Anne Harrison (OECD), Mr. Peter Hill (OECD), Mr. Brian Newson (Eurostat), Mr. Kevin O'Connor (IMF) and Mr. Jan van Tongeren (UNSTAT).

In 1989, the Expert Group on SNA Coordination was established. It consisted of the five core experts mentioned above plus the following experts who had participated in the eight previous expert group meetings: Mr. Eneas Avondoglio (Argentina); Mr. Jack Bame (United States of America); Mr. Adriaan Bloem (the Netherlands); Ms. Uma D. R. Choudhury (India); Mr. Youri Ivanov (Russia); Mr. Moffat Nyoni (Zimbabwe); Mr. Colin Pettigrew (United Kingdom); and Mr. René Rakotobe (Madagascar). Between 1989 and the first half of 1991, this Expert Group met five times to review the first set of draft chapters and to discuss outstanding issues. In all, 65 experts from 36 countries participated in one or more of these meetings, representing all regions and experience in a wide variety of specialized fields such as balance of payments, government finance, money and banking, labour statistics, input-output, household surveys, social accounting matrices, and environmental accounting. These experts, in addition to those already listed, were: Hans Adler (Canada), H.G. Akhniotis (Cyprus), Peter Al (Netherlands), Odd Aukrust (Norway), Michael Beekman (the Netherlands), Keith Blackburn (Australia), Cornelius van Bochove (the Netherlands), M. de Cartagena (Ecuador), Shirley Carter (United Kingdom), Margaret Costa (Brazil), Jean Courty (France), J.C. Dawson (United States of America), Pierre Demangel (Congo), Barbara Dunlop (Australia), Bernardo Ferrán (Venezuela), Alfred Franz (Austria), Rodolfo R.Fuentes (Cuba), M.E. Gomez-Luna (Mexico), Alan Heston (United States of America), Akinari Horii (Japan), Piroska Horvath (Hungary), P. Jayasundera (Sri Lanka), R.P. Katyal (India), Y. Kurabayashi (Japan), Kishori Lal (Canada), Marion Libreros (Colombia), José Lopez Pereda (Cuba), Devi Manraj (Mauritius), Salvador Marconi (Ecuador), M. Mouyelo-Katoula (Congo), M. van Nieuwkerk (Netherlands), Igor Pogosov (former USSR), Karin Polenske (United States of America), Graham Pyatt (United Kingdom), Boris Ryabushkin (former USSR), Jacob Ryten (Canada), K. Saleh (Indonesia), Gyorgy Sandor (Hungary), Stephan Schlosser (Czechoslovakia), Bogdan Sculz (Canada), John Shadlow (Papua New Guinea), Vaska Spasova (Bulgaria), Erkki Tassia (Finland), Bent Thage (Denmark), Seppo Varjonnen (Finland), Stewart Wells (Canada), C. Wibulswasdi (Thailand), John F. Wilson (United States of America), Liu Xiaofan (China), Sergio Zamora (Chile), and D. Zmanay (Mauritius).

A first set of 14 draft chapters and three draft annexes, based on the recommendations of these expert group meetings, was considered by the Statistical Commission at its twenty-sixth session in 1991. Most of these were prepared by Mr. Hill (on secondment from the OECD). Mr. Vanoli prepared an overview chapter and chapters on applications and on satellite accounts.

Additional technical meetings were organized by the five regional commissions of the United Nations (ECA, ECE, ECLAC, ESCAP and ESCWA), Eurostat, OECD, professional groups such as the International Association for Research in Income and Wealth (IARIW) and ISWGNA itself. Most meetings organized by ISWGNA were hosted by member organizations; the others were hosted by the national statistical offices of the former Soviet Union, Zimbabwe and Mexico. The last meetings were the Interregional Seminar on the Revision of the SNA, held in October 1992, and the sixth meeting of the Expert Group on SNA Coordination, which was held in conjunction with the Seminar. The Interregional Seminar provided the opportunity for over 80 country, regional and international experts from all over the world to express their views on the final draft SNA before its consideration at the twenty-seventh session of the Statistical Commission.

For the last critical years of the revision process, from 1989 to 1993, ISWGNA benefited from the coordination and management support provided by Ms. Carson of the United States Bureau of Economic Analysis (USBEA). With the assistance of Mr. Brian Grove, also from USBEA, she coordinated, monitored and tracked the many revisions to the various chapters and annexes and facilitated frequent communications among all the parties involved or interested in the revision process.

In the final revision process, from 1991 to 1993, Mr. Hill undertook additional drafting and revisions for chapters I, IV to X, the section of chapter XII dealing with the revaluation account, and chapter XVI. Mr. Vanoli undertook additional drafting and revisions for chapters II and XIX and the first three sections of chapter XXI. Other contributors in this final phase of drafting and revising were the following: Ms. Carson, assisted by Ms. Stephanie Howell (also of USBEA), major parts of the front matter, including the SNA history; Mr. Cor Gorter (the Netherlands, as consultant to Eurostat), in close collaboration with Mr. Newson (Eurostat), chapter III; Mr. O'Connor (IMF), chapter XI; Ms. Helen Stone Tice (USBEA), in close collaboration with Ms. Carson, the section of chapter XII dealing with other changes in the volume of assets account and chapter XIII; Mr. Bame (as consultant to IMF), chapter XIV; Mr. Erling Flottum (Norway, as consultant to Eurostat), in close collaboration with Mr. Newson, chapter XV; Mr. Ralph Turvey (United Kingdom, as consultant to OECD), chapter XVII; Mr. Blades (OECD), chapter XVIII; Mr. Steven Keuning (Central Bureau of Statistics of the Netherlands), chapter XX; Mr. van Tongeren (UNSTAT), the section of chapter XXI on environmental accounting; Ms. Cristina Hannig (UNSTAT), in close collaboration with Mr. van Tongeren, annex I; Mr. Mahinder Gill (IMF), assisted by Mr. Bame, annex II; Ms. Harrison (OECD), annexes III and IV.

The classifications and most accounts, tables and figures describing the System in the chapters and annexes were developed by Mr. Vanoli and Mr. van Tongeren, assisted by several UNSTAT staff members. Mr. van Tongeren, assisted by several UNSTAT staff, also prepared a list of SNA terms as a starting point for the index.

Numerous supporting papers and technical documents prepared for the expert group meetings by staff of ISWGNA member organizations and others, as well as the reports of the meetings and working drafts of chapters, were distributed for comments to over 200 experts all over the world. Their comments were valuable contributions at different stages of the revision process, particularly during the final stages.

In the last years of the process, in response to letters from ISWGNA seeking financial support for a number of tasks related to the revision work programme, contributions in cash and in kind were made by Australia, Austria, Canada, France, Germany, Netherlands, New Zealand, Norway, Sweden, Switzerland and the United States of America. IARIW acted as the administrator of contributions in cash. These contributions supplemented the very substantial contributions in cash and in kind made by the five member organizations of ISWGNA and allowed the process to move ahead on several critical tasks.

During the last stage of the revision process, ISWGNA dealt with several important policy issues. The senior officials representing the member organizations of ISWGNA at this stage were Mr. Yves Franchet (Eurostat), Mr. John McLenaghan (IMF), Mr. Louis Kincannon (OECD), Mr. William Seltzer (UNSTAT) and Datuk Chander (World Bank).

The following other staff members and consultants to international organizations also participated in one or more of the expert group meetings: Roberto B. Ibarra (Centro de Estudios Monetarios Latinoamericanos (CEMLA)); René Rakotobe (ECA); George Szilagyi (ECE); Raúl García Belgrano (ECLAC); Meng Kow Loh, Jagdish Kumar (ESCAP); Kotb Salem (ESCWA); Piero Erba, Alain Chantraine, D. Glatzel, Hugo K. Locker, J. Roman, R. Salvat, Werner Thon (Eurostat); Ralf Hussmans (ILO); Arie Bouter, Warner Dannemann, Mahinder Gill, Jonathan Levin, Chandrakant Patel, Samuel Pizer (IMF); Lourdes Urdaneta-Ferrán (International Research and Training Institute for the Advancement of Women (INSTRAW)); J.E. Chapron, I. Divoy, Jeff Owens, Erwin Veil (OECD); Y.R. Cho, B. Dissmann, S. Lyakh, G. Robyn, M. Usui, T. Yamada (UNIDO); Lazslo Drechsler, Vladimir Drjuchin, Guadalupe Espinosa, Cristina Hannig, Y. Kurabayashi, Curtis McSween, Irene Tsao, Viet Vu (UNSTAT); Ernest Lutz, John O'Connor, M. Ward (World Bank).

Final publication of the English version of the 1993 SNA was coordinated, with the involvement of ISWGNA member organizations, by Mr. Robert Johnston from UNSTAT, in close collaboration with Mr. van Tongeren and Ms. Hannig. The Office of Conference Services, Department of Public Information, Division of Economic and Social Affairs and Secretariat Services and Office of General Services of the United Nations Secretariat provided extensive design, editorial and support services for the production process.

Finally, mention should be made of the many staff members from all the member organizations of ISWGNA and from USBEA who, in addition to those already mentioned above, greatly contributed to the success of the revision process with their many professional, technical, administrative and secretarial skills that supported such a complex and long-term work programme.

Notes

1 *Official Records of the Economic and Social Council, 1993, Supplement No. 6* (E/1993/26), para. 62.

2 *A System of National Accounts,* Studies in Methods, Series F, No. 2, Rev.3 (United Nations publication, Sales No. E.69.XVII.3), often referred to as the 1968 SNA.

Perspectives on the 1993 SNA: looking back and looking ahead

With the 1993 SNA, significant advances in national accounting have been achieved. The significance of these advances is best appreciated in light of some historical background, provided in the first section below. The second section discusses a research agenda which looks ahead to the SNA's continuing evolution in the future.

A. Looking back

From a historical perspective, the content of the 1993 SNA and the review and revision process reflect the broadening of the experience and expertise underlying the SNA, the increasing harmony between the SNA and other international statistical standards, and the changing research agenda.

The history of the SNA combines two threads—the development of national accounting and the "internationalization" of statistical concerns. The accounting history is too broad a topic to cover comprehensively. Instead, reference will be made to several "development indicators", including the scope of the accounting structure, the number of countries reporting national accounting statistics internationally and the availability of practical guides. The internationalization history, in turn, encompasses two concerns relevant to the SNA—the comparability of economic statistics and the development of international standards and guidelines. These two threads will be traced by referring to official documents such as those of the United Nations Statistical Commission and publications of international organizations.

Forerunners of the System National Accounts

Official interest in the comparability of economic statistics dates back at least to 1928. In that year the League of Nations held an International Conference Relating to Economic Statistics to encourage the compilation of such statistics and the adoption of uniform presentation methods. The Final Act of the Conference stated that international comparability should be a goal, especially among countries with sophisticated statistical systems. It urged countries to consider extending the scope of official statistics to facilitate compilation of national income estimates at regular intervals.

Considerable impetus was given to the work on national income by the Great Depression of the 1930s, on the one hand, and by developments in macro-economic theory, on the other. In 1939 the League of Nations first published national income estimates. A table in its annual *World Economic Survey* shows estimates for all or part of the period 1929 to 1938 for 26 countries. Estimates for

about half the countries were compiled as official estimates, and estimates for the rest as academic or other private studies.

In the same year, the Committee of Statistical Experts of the League of Nations recognized the need for guidance in the measurement of national income. The Committee, which viewed its general task as improving statistics and increasing their comparability, was already conducting work on several kinds of statistics—for example, indices of industrial production, housing, international trade and balance of payments. Because a number of countries were compiling statistics on national income but were using different methods, the Committee decided, in accordance with the 1928 Conference, to add the measurement of national income to its work programme.

The years immediately following this decision were eventful in the field of national accounting. A growing recognition of the usefulness of national income estimates to fiscal and economic policy-making—especially for war-time mobilization in some countries—strengthened official interest in the field. Although international comparability of the reported estimates was not the focus of the most intense work, that goal was kept in sight. For example, in 1944 and 1945, representatives from the United States of America, Canada, and the United Kingdom of Great Britain and Northern Ireland discussed the problems of international comparability. The result was the first international agreement on the conceptual methods and presentation of national estimates.

As the Second World War ended there was an immediate need for comparable measures of national income as a basis for apportioning the expenses of international organizations. To help address this need, the Sub-Committee on National Income Statistics of the League of Nations Committee of Statistical Experts was formed. Consisting primarily of experts who were directing the compilation of national income and related estimates in countries of Europe, North America and Australia, the Sub-Committee met in December 1945, working from a memorandum prepared by Richard Stone.

The origins of the SNA trace back to the Sub-Committee's report, published in 1947.[1] The Sub-Committee hoped, according to the preface, that the guiding principles and recommendations in the report and its appendix would be applied to the widest possible extent in each country in the computation of national income and related accounts in order to secure greater international comparability than in the past.

The 1947 report and its appendix, "Definition and measurement of the national income and related totals", by Richard Stone, showed how to obtain national income and gross national product by selecting and combining the elementary transactions of an economic system and how to display the interdependence of these transactions. This approach, then called the social accounting approach, contrasted with an approach that focused on building up a single total, such as national income. It was viewed as a logical development of current work in the field and became the foundation for further work.

The report recommended a set of nine tables to present national income statistics. This set, adapted from the more detailed set of accounts outlined in Stone's appendix, was viewed as having great utility in practical economic analysis and as being capable of estimation. It featured the derivations of, and relationships among, analytically important income, expenditure, capital formation and saving aggregates. The set of 24 accounts in Stone's appendix was based on an underlying structure of current accounts (operating and appropriation) and capital accounts (capital and reserve) for five sectors—productive enterprises, financial intermediaries, insurance and social security agencies, final consumers and the rest of the world. Reflecting most of the experience to that time, the accounts were based on a model of an advanced industrial economy in which transactions in money dominated.

One chapter of the report, "Statistical sources and practical problems of implementation", included an item-by-item survey of the procedures then in use to prepare estimates for the nine recommended tables. Reference was made to publications in various countries for more detail.

The 1953 SNA

Experience in national accounting accumulated rapidly in the early post-war years. Totals and breakdowns by industry of origin, type of income and category of expenditure provided essential information for the analysis of current economic trends, inflationary or deflationary tendencies, effects of foreign aid and, in general, factors that determine the level of employment and economic activity. These statistics were increasingly useful for studies of economically under-developed countries, where estimates of income by industry of origin and of capital formation were of special importance. By 1950 the United Nations Statistical Office was able to assemble estimates from country sources, for *National Income Statistics, 1938-1948*, for several years from 41 countries. Half of these estimates were published in country publications within 12 months after the close of the year to which they referred. These estimates included the 13 sets that were prepared by countries that were using the social accounting approach.[2]

In Europe, the national accounts served as a framework for information about economic conditions and performance that was used to administer post-war aid and encourage economic growth. The Organisation for European Economic Co-operation (OEEC), in 1950, published a set of accounts prepared by its National Accounts Research Unit, a unit set up to promote comparable national accounts statistics among member countries.[3] This set of accounts was used to prepare a series of country studies, which provided a test of its practicability and convenience. This experience, supported by comments and further research, was the basis for *A Standardised System of National Accounts*,[4] published in 1952. The stated objectives were, first, to present a set of standard tables displaying the basic national accounting information that experience had shown to be useful in economic description and analysis and, secondly, to relate the entries in the tables in an articulated system of accounts and to define these entries and provide classifications for them. The Standardised System included for the first time detailed classifications of the main items of the accounts—for example, consumers' expenditures.

Meanwhile, the Statistical Commission of the United Nations recommended continued work toward a uniform reporting basis for the wider group of United Nations members. It stressed the need for establishing international standards as quickly as possible, and in 1951 it allocated high priority to this work. An expert group appointed by the Secretary-General of the United Nations met in 1952 in New York to formulate a standard system. The result was the 1953 report *A System of National Accounts and Supporting Tables*.[5]

The 1953 report presented a set of six standard accounts. They were based on an underlying structure of production, appropriation, capital reconciliation and external transactions accounts for three basic sectors—enterprises, households and private non-profit institutions, and general government. The entries were arranged and consolidated so that each of the six standard accounts related to one of the familiar and important aggregates, such as national income. A set of 12 standard tables presented details and alternative classifications of these flows in the accounts. Compared to the presentation in the 1947 report, the 1953 accounts were further elaborated with respect to capital transactions.

The preface to the 1953 report noted that the concepts and definitions and the tables of the 1953 system were applicable to most countries: "The purpose of this report ... is to set out a standard national accounting system in order to provide a framework for reporting national income and product statistics which is of general applicability." This objective was ambitious; in fact, some countries, in commenting on the 1953 report, questioned the appropriateness of establishing international standards in the field at the time.

Unlike the 1947 system, the 1953 system explicitly took the needs of developing countries into consideration. For example, the report noted that the separation of households from enterprises and the inclusion of production for home consumption in total product were major practical problems for developing countries. Accordingly, the report attempted to provide clearly defined rules for drawing the production boundary. Further, one of the 12 standard tables, showing the receipts and disbursements of the rural sector, was designed to provide developing countries with a separate account for a part of the economy in which non-monetary transactions play an important role.[6]

The 1953 report recognized the importance of harmonizing international statistical standards. Specifically, it recognized that the international guidelines on economic and financial statistics and on national accounts should be consistent and well integrated. It noted the care that had been taken in drawing up the SNA to ensure consistency with definitions and classifications used or recommended by others, notably the International Monetary Fund on international transactions and the OEEC.

The first chapter of the 1953 report was on the development and uses of national accounting. The outstanding use of national accounting statistics had been in connection with public policy. Countries that rely mainly on monetary and fiscal measures find national accounts useful because they provide a systematic framework for assessing the probable course of economic development and the adjustments needed in government policy. Countries, both developed and developing, that apply national budgeting—that is, the matching of supply and demand of productive resources and their finance—also can use a national accounts framework. Different claims on the productive system can be coordinated to meet certain general requirements, such as the stability of the economic system as a whole, which cannot be taken into account if each claim is considered in isolation.

In discussing the development of national accounting, the first chapter noted that efforts to systematize the increasing amount of economic information had led to distinct but partially related sets of statistics: national income and product, input-output, financial flows, balance sheets, and prices and quantities. It was viewed as unlikely, however, that these investigations, which had been done primarily for individual countries, would lead at that time to the construction of comprehensive accounting systems that embraced all the available statistics. Further, given the practical needs and resources, the construction of such a system was not an immediate objective for economic statisticians.[7]

The research agenda: a case study

One of these areas of statistics—prices and quantities, specifically constant-price measures—provides a case study of how a topic on the research agenda moves through the research and consensus-building stages to incorporation in international standards and guidelines. Constant-price measures are used as the case study because a high priority was assigned to this item on the research agenda. One indication is that a long paragraph placed prominently in the preface acknowledged that the 1953 report was confined to accounts in current money terms and recognized the need for constant-price measures.

Earlier, *National Income Statistics, 1938-1948* had included a section entitled "Intertemporal comparisons of real national income" in its chapter on conceptual problems. The section stated that for many purposes, particularly in periods of rapidly rising or falling prices, there was a need for statistics adjusted for fluctuations in the price level. An appendix presented national income in constant prices for 17 countries, noting that the methods used differed widely. It concluded that the series then published could be used for comparing intertemporal changes among countries "only with reservations".

In 1952, the OEEC, referring to work on accounts in current money values as the first stage of national accounting, had begun research on comparisons over time. The foreword to a 1956 report, a product of that research, said that, although substantial agreement on concepts and methods had emerged from two conferences of national accounts experts in 1952 and 1955, "opinion and practice had not yet reached the point which would make the adoption of international standards practicable".[8]

Work by the United Nations led to a report to the Statistical Commission in 1957.[9] By the mid-1950s, many countries were producing constant-price national accounts measures. They still differed widely, however, in scope and quality. The report was based on a survey of country practices but went beyond practice; it attempted to define a system of quantity indexes—including quantity indexes for non-commodity flows—drawn up within a comprehensive, but abridged, SNA framework. Characterized as tentative and exploratory, the report noted the ongoing nature of the work and referred to the upcoming (1959) conference of the International Association for Research in Income and Wealth. That conference included a session that was described on the jacket of the volume containing the published papers as "the highly controversial subject of national account deflation, which created lively discussion".

Lively discussion apparently continued into the 1960s. A draft of the proposals for revision of the SNA circulated in 1965 focused, in about 25 paragraphs, on constant-price measures of product flows. By 1967, widespread discussion—including three regional working groups devoted to national accounts at constant prices—led to a doubling in the number of paragraphs. Two new sections provided practical rules in specifying prices and quantities (for example, dealing with variations in quality and seasonal variation) and numerical illustrations. Foreshadowing the next section of this historical perspective, by the time of publication in 1968, the number of paragraphs had doubled again. A new section included a more explicit distinction between the approach of decomposing value into price and quantity to obtain constant-price measures and the approach of selecting a "basket" of items in terms of which to obtain purchasing power measures. It prominently explained why the results of obtaining quantity indexes within a balancing set of accounts—production, consumption and accumulation for a closed economy, much less with an external account—were not useful.

Subsequent editions

Subsequently, two slightly modified editions of the 1953 SNA were published. The second edition, published in 1960, reflected comments, invited by the Statistical Commission, on country experience in applying the 1953 SNA. A review of these comments in 1956 had led the Commission to conclude that, although no major changes were needed immediately, several minor modifications were needed to maintain or improve comparability with related international standards and to introduce clarifications and other adjustments. The Commission asked that proposals for amendments be formulated; most of the proposals were formulated by the United Nations jointly with the International Monetary Fund and OEEC at a meeting in 1956.

In looking toward a major review later, the 1958 Statistical Commission expressed the hope that a wider system could be established that would take account of the very considerable experience in the field by countries with planned economies. Such a system, the Commission noted, should also consider the differing requirements of countries at various levels of development, and for this purpose the system would need to be flexible.

The 1960 publication seems to reflect some move during the 1950s toward a more extended system; it was envisaged that the SNA would be extended at some future date to include, first, flow of funds and input-output tables and, as a longer-term objective, balance sheets. Countries were either already preparing or were considering preparing these extensions, and it was recognized that eventually international guidelines would have to be established.

The third edition of the 1953 SNA, published in 1964, improved consistency with the International Monetary Fund's *Balance of Payments Manual*, corrected or clarified the text at several points and updated references to other international guidelines.[10]

Manuals and the questionnaire

In the 1953 report no attention was given to the statistical problems of compiling and measuring the items entering the accounts. For help on practical problems, reference was made to other reports that the United Nations intended to issue in the future. In 1955, the United Nations completed a provisional manual on methods of estimating national income.[11] It was prepared with the needs of developing countries especially in mind. Even before the 1953 SNA, which was the basis for the exposition of methods, the Statistical Commission had repeatedly expressed interest in a report of this nature.

Using the 1953 SNA as a basis, the United Nations developed a questionnaire to be sent to member countries to collect national accounts information on a regular, systematic basis.[12] The questionnaire requested estimates for nine of the standard tables and information about differences between the country estimates and the SNA. The responses, supplemented by information from country statistical offices and publications, were published, beginning in 1958, in the *Yearbook of National Accounts Statistics*.[13] The first

Yearbook showed national accounts statistics for 70 countries and territories.

The 1968 SNA

Even as the third edition was being published, the United Nations convened an expert group to make proposals for the extension and revision of the SNA. The expert group met for two weeks in 1964, basing its discussion on a draft paper prepared by Richard Stone and supplementary papers on selected aspects prepared by the United Nations and the Organisation for Economic Co-operation and Development (OECD). The document produced after the meeting was the basis for discussion by working groups of national statistical authorities within the United Nations regional commissions and by the Statistical Commission. In addition, there were rounds of discussions in the International Association for Research in Income and Wealth and in similar regional associations. A second document was prepared as a result of these discussions and further study; it was considered by the expert group at its second session in 1966 and by the Statistical Commission. Subsequently, the regional working groups considered national accounting at constant prices and income distribution statistics, and studies were made of input-output and other selected aspects. A third document was considered by the expert group at its third session in 1967 and submitted, along with the expert group's conclusions, to the Statistical Commission.[14] In 1968 the Statistical Commission approved a revised SNA.[15]

The introduction to the 1968 SNA reported that two developments since the 1953 SNA helped make the new SNA possible and, at the same time, made it necessary, if international standards were to keep pace with work going on in countries. The first development was the elaboration and development of national accounting. Along one line, more detail was being added to the accounts to respond to the growing needs of economic analysis; in the absence of a comprehensive framework, the new detail tended to take variant forms in different parts of the world. Often the result was a new statistical endeavour. Many countries prepared input-output accounts, some prepared flow of funds accounts, and a few had moved in the direction of balance sheets. Along another line, more attention was being given to estimates at constant prices.

Intensive efforts were made to bring the SNA and the System of Balances of the National Economy (often called the Material Product System, or MPS) closer together. The MPS, long used in the Soviet Union, was elaborated, beginning in 1965, under the auspices of the Council for Mutual Economic Assistance as a standard for the use of its members. The Statistical Commission, in 1971, requested that the description of the MPS be published and circulated widely.[16]

The second development behind the *1968 SNA* was the construction of disaggregated economic models as an aid to economic analysis and policy. For many purposes, modelling in which the aggregates of output, consumption, investment and so on were subdivided exacerbated some problems that arose in building aggregate models and added certain others. First, the number of accounting identities was much larger. Secondly, subdivided aggregates needed to be classified in several ways according to the point of view taken in different parts of the analysis. Thirdly, general economic and accounting principles were no longer sufficient to resolve all the taxonomic problems; the needs of particular forms, such as input-output analysis, contributed to the choice of the solution.[17]

Accordingly, the 1968 SNA incorporated major extensions. These extensions with respect to the structure of the accounts were to (a) disaggregate the production account into input-output accounts; (b) disaggregate net lending or borrowing into sector financial flows; (c) divide the income and outlay accounts and capital accounts for the nation to show accounts for the sectors; and (d) add balance sheets for the sectors and the nation. The structure of the system was set out in a matrix. It represented each account—for opening assets, production, consumption, accumulation, the rest of the world, revaluations and closing assets—by a row and column pair. In addition, the 1968 SNA incorporated additional classifications for the activities of government and non-profit institutions and for transfers. Finally, reflecting the research and consensus-building previously described, the 1968 SNA integrated constant-price data for goods and services.

To incorporate these extensions, the 1968 SNA presented a set of 20 accounts, broken into three classes. Class I accounts are the consolidated accounts for the nation. They are an articulated set that summarizes the accounts on production, consumption expenditure, income and outlay, capital formation and capital finance and are closed by an account on the external transactions for the nation. Class II accounts relate to the production, consumption expenditure and capital formation accounts. They show the supply and disposition of goods and services, separately for commodities and other goods and services, and the production of goods and services, separately for the four classes of producers. Class III accounts relate to the income and outlay and capital finance accounts. They show these accounts for the institutional sectors into which resident transactors are divided—non-financial corporate and quasi-corporate enterprises, financial institutions, general government, private non-profit institutions serving households, and households.

A set of 26 standard supporting and supplementary tables exhibited detailed series that, although valuable and feasible to compile for national and international use, could not be shown in the form of accounts. A number of standard supporting tables presented the constant-price series. Others, such as the two tables on input-output, delineated the structure of the accounts as well as relevant detailed classifications. Yet others, such as the table on the income and outlay and the capital transactions of the socio-economic subsectors of the household sector, presented detailed classifications of selected accounts or an aspect of an account. These accounts and tables related to all aspects of the system except balance sheets.

The introduction to the 1968 SNA referred to the 1953 SNA's role as a standard—that is, a basis of international reporting—as the

system's "main purpose". It also noted its role as a guideline—that is, as an aid to countries wishing to work in the field. The *1968 SNA* was also expected to guide countries. But reflecting its extended coverage, the 1968 SNA went beyond the previously stated purpose of guiding countries in preparing national accounts; the preface explicitly mentioned guiding countries in developing their systems of basic statistics. In discussing the uses of national accounts, the introduction stated that practical experience had shown that the accounts provided an excellent framework for appraising actual and proposed plans for economic statistics. The increased emphasis on this aspect (it had also been mentioned in the 1953 report) is understandable considering the international organizations' concern with basic data development.

The 1968 SNA was seen as applicable to countries at every stage of economic and social development. However, the report provided a separate chapter to suggest ways in which developing countries might adapt the full system. The chapter was careful to note that its modified and supplementary presentations were not intended as international guidelines, but to suggest how the classifications and the tables and accounts might be adapted to the country.

The European System of Integrated Economic Accounts (ESA), prepared by the Statistical Office of the European Communities, represents another kind of adaptation of the 1968 SNA.[18] That Statistical Office had participated in work on the 1968 SNA. The foreword to the ESA described it as the Community version of the SNA, differing from the SNA in that it provided additional information about production and finance, detail on the distribution and redistribution of income, and more precise and rigorous concepts and definitions. These characteristics were expected to lead to more complete and detailed knowledge about the economies of member countries and to improve the comparability of the statistics. Assessments to support the Communities' organizations are based on a formula that includes gross national product.

Although the 1968 SNA extended national accounting substantially, the report noted that a number of topics remained for future discussion and research:

(a) In four fields work had been done: balance sheets; constant prices; statistics on the distribution of income, consumption and wealth; and elaboration of specific parts of the SNA by specialized agencies of the United Nations to provide links to such fields as agriculture, health and education (preparation of guidelines was listed as the next step for the first three);

(b) In two fields there had been general discussion but no work: regional accounting and human flows and stocks (a population matrix);

(c) In two other fields there had been little discussion: functional classification of inputs and the boundary between current and capital expenditure, including questions of extending the concept of capital expenditures to consumer durables, research and development, and education and health.[19]

The 1968 SNA provided a mix of conceptual and practical guidance. The accounts, it was said, were intended to delineate the basic features of the system. But the 1968 SNA went on to furnish practical guidance concerning the presentation of the main series of the system, including the periodicity and priority with which the accounts and tables might be used in presenting national accounting estimates. There were also short discussions of statistical discrepancies—the archetype practical problem—and of some major problems and techniques for showing estimates in constant prices. However, the extent of the practical guidance given in the 1968 SNA was limited, and supplemental manuals were planned.

Subsequently, several manuals came out about a decade after the 1968 SNA. These included the three that were listed as next steps in the research agenda: balance sheets; distribution of income, consumption and wealth; and constant prices.[20]

The 1993 SNA: the review and revision process

When the Statistical Commission approved the 1968 SNA, it requested a review and report on progress made by countries in applying the new system and difficulties encountered. By the early 1970s, about 120 countries and areas were reporting national account statistics to the United Nations for inclusion in the *Yearbook*, 40 more than a decade earlier.

In 1975, the United Nations undertook a review of country experience with the 1968 SNA. An early step was an inter-regional seminar in 1975 to review developing countries' experiences. Several other regional meetings followed during the next five years. After considering a preliminary report on the findings of these meetings, the Statistical Commission in 1979 directed the convening of an expert group. That expert group met in 1980 to discuss the status of work on the SNA and its future direction in the light of country experience and the changing analytic priorities and statistical capabilities. Following another report to the Statistical Commission, incorporating the expert group's views, the Commission asked that specific proposals be developed for short-term clarifications and updating of the SNA. The Commission emphasized the role of the SNA (as well as the MPS) as a point of reference in establishing standards for related statistics. National accounts, because of their comprehensiveness, ranked ahead of standards developed for particular fields of economic statistics.

An expert group meeting in 1982 recommended a review of the SNA designed to lead to a revision. The main objectives would be updating to fit new circumstances, clarification and simplification, and further harmonization with related statistical standards. The Statistical Commission, at its 1983 and 1985 sessions, accepted the expert group's recommendations, although it noted the importance of maintaining continuity by avoiding major changes in definitions and classifications. It assigned a high priority to topics relevant to the implementation of the SNA in developing countries.

At the 1985 session, the Statistical Commission entrusted the Inter-Secretariat Working Group on National Accounts—consisting of Eurostat (more formally, the Statistical Office of the European Communities), the International Monetary Fund, the Organisation for Economic Co-operation and Development, the Statistical Division and regional commissions of the United Nations, and the World Bank—with planning the work programme and arranging for adequate participation of experts from national statistical offices and interested international organizations. The resulting cooperative effort was evidence of the increasing recognition of the SNA as the framework for statistical systems in both developing and developed countries and as the basis for international standards. This recognition increased the scope of the work to be done by an order of magnitude and thus made it especially desirable to share the burden and avoid conflicting and duplicative efforts.

From 1982 to 1985, topics for discussion were identified and studies on these topics prepared by the international organizations, consultants or national statistical offices. These studies were circulated for comment to experts on the specific topics and thereafter discussed at regional meetings in which national statistical offices were represented. Two main documents—on the organization of the review and on the conceptual framework of the revised SNA—were assembled by the Inter-Secretariat Working Group as background for the next stage.[21]

From 1986 to 1989, expert groups met to discuss a wide range of issues grouped into eight topics: SNA structure, prices and quantity comparisons, external sector, household sector, public sector, production accounts and input-output tables, financial flows and balances, and reconciliation of SNA and MPS. In 1989 an Expert Group on SNA Coordination was established to deal with outstanding issues and to review draft chapters of the revised SNA; it met six times. Approximately 50 experts, representing expertise—in national accounting and in different field specialties—from about 40 countries in all regions of the world participated in one or more of the total of 14 meetings (of five to 10 working days each).

A round of meetings sponsored by the United Nations regional commissions was held in 1990 to obtain views on the draft chapters, which had begun to be available in 1989. A paper prepared by the Inter-Secretariat Working Group was the main guide for discussion.[22] A number of other meetings were held to discuss the draft chapters, especially in Europe. Accounting for the environment was of increasing interest in these later meetings, and it was the subject of a special conference of the International Association for Research in Income and Wealth.

A 582-page provisional draft of the revised SNA was available for the 1991 Statistical Commission.[23] Further refinements and elaborations were incorporated into a revised set of draft chapters and annexes by the summer of 1992. That draft was the basis of discussion for an interregional seminar in October 1992. The same draft was presented to the 1993 Statistical Commission along with the report of the seminar, which concluded, "The participants thought that the revised SNA was a vast improvement over the 1968 predecessor".[24] As noted in the preface, the Statistical Commission unanimously recommended the adoption of the 1993 SNA, and the United Nations Economic and Social Council urged its use by member States and international organizations.

xliii

B. Looking ahead: the research agenda

The 1993 SNA, like its predecessors, represents a stage in the evolution of national accounting. To continue that evolution, further research will need to be carried out. Consensus must be reached on certain topics before they can be incorporated into international guidelines and standards. Although there is substantial agreement on the topics to be addressed, a research agenda has emerged along several lines during the final steps of the revision process.

In 1993, the Statistical Commission agreed that the highest immediate priority was to develop practical guidelines for the explicit allocation of financial intermediation service charges indirectly measured to specific users. The Commission addressed the related issues in detail and accepted a proposal by the Inter-Secretariat Working Group on National Accounts to provide a flexible treatment in the SNA. This treatment would recognize the desirability of allocating such charges fully while allowing flexible implementation in particular countries or groups of countries.

The Inter-Secretariat Working Group had also recommended that certain other topics be placed on the research agenda.[25] The topics listed below were among those mentioned most often in the 1993 Statistical Commission:

(a) Cost of capital

The draft of the SNA completed in 1992 included imputations for rent on buildings owned and occupied by government and non-profit institutions serving households. However, this treatment presents certain conceptual and practical difficulties. For example, some have argued that the coverage of assets should be more extensive than the coverage of buildings if the concept of the cost of capital is to be used. These imputations were therefore deleted, and the topic was placed on the research agenda.

(b) Consumer subsidies

The 1992 draft maintained the treatment of subsidies found in the 1968 SNA. It has not been possible, despite considerable discussion, to agree on how to distinguish between payments to be treated as mainly benefiting consumers and those to be treated as mainly benefiting producers. Further research is needed, especially given the importance of the subsidies in some countries.

(c) Informal-formal distinction

The 1992 draft noted the difficulty in developing appropriate criteria to distinguish between informal and formal economic activities, a distinction that has been widely recognized as useful. The International Labour Organisation is the lead agency for this work, and the topic is on the national accounting research agenda to support continued collaboration with ILO in this field.

Three additional topics included in the 1993 SNA will require further research:

(a) Environmental accounting

The section of chapter XXI on environmental satellite accounts notes that it is presenting the state of the art, as of 1993, on the integration of economic and environmental accounting. However, the state of the art does not permit the introduction of environmentally adjusted aggregates in the central framework. The section is intended as a guide to countries wishing to design satellite accounts responsive to policy and analysis focused on environmentally sound and sustainable growth and development. It urges that cooperative research and methodological work by national accountants and environmentalists continue, a sentiment widely expressed in the reviews conducted in various forums.

(b) Classifications

Chapter XVIII (Functional classifications) notes that two of the classifications described—Classification of Individual Consumption by Purpose (COICOP) and Classification of Producers by Purpose (COPP)—are provisional. COPP, in particular, may need substantial revision. The Classification of the Functions of Government (COFOG) should be modified both to identify more precisely social transfers in kind and to identify more fully functions that are of increasing policy concern, such as repair and prevention of environmental damage.

(c) Matrix presentation

The annex to chapter II notes that the matrix presented there is provisional. Further work is needed to improve the matrix treatment of the accumulation accounts and balance sheets.

The interregional seminar, held jointly with the final expert group meeting in October 1992, devoted a session to updating and refining the SNA in the future. Many of the topics listed above were mentioned. Also cited were: scope of capital formation and stocks; output of services, including services produced within households; financial activities, including those associated with instruments such as derivatives; labour accounts; and regional accounts. The first topic includes two subtopics mentioned on the research agenda that emerged from the 1968 SNA. On one, research and development, substantial work was done during the review and revision toward treating relevant expenditures as capital formation. On the other, education and other aspects of human capital, not now treated as capital in the SNA, little progress has been made.

Finally, there is an interest in reviewing the purposes of the SNA. Two views have emerged on this question. One is that the national accounts are primarily an organizational scheme for economic statistics. The main value of the SNA, then, is in its consistent classifications and definitions and in its display of the interrelationships among the various parts of the economy. This view leads to an emphasis on the improvement of basic statistics, for the accounts will improve only as the basic statistics allow. A contrasting view is that the national accounts serve primarily to facilitate analysis of the economy and decision-making. The SNA, through its structure and definitions, not only determines the kind of analysis that can be carried out but also influences the way economic and social issues are considered. This view would lead to a review of the uses of national accounting, and research on this topic has also been suggested. The

upcoming fiftieth anniversary of international guidelines and standards for national accounts might provide the occasion for a review of the purposes and uses of the SNA along these lines.

Notes

1 United Nations, *Measurement of National Income and the Construction of Social Accounts,* Studies and Reports on Statistical Methods, No. 7, Report of the Sub-Committee on National Income Statistics of the League of Nations Committee of Statistical Experts, with an appendix, "Definition and measurement of the national income and related totals", by Richard Stone (Geneva: United Nations, 1947). The participants at the Sub-committee's meeting were Richard Stone, Chairman (United Kingdom), H.P. Brown (Australia), J.B.D. Derksen (Netherlands), C.M. Isbister (Canada), George Jaszi (United States of America), Hildegarde Kneeland (Inter-American Statistical Institute), Raul Ortiz Mena (Mexico), Arne Skaug (Norway) and Julius Wyler (Switzerland).

2 United Nations, *National Income Statistics, 1938-1948* (United Nations publication, Sales No. 1950.XVII.2).

3 Organisation for European Economic Co-operation, *A Simplified System of National Accounts* (Paris: Organisation for European Economic Co-operation, 1950).

4 Organisation for European Economic Co-operation, *A Standardized System of National Accounts* (Paris: Organisation for European Economic Co-operation, 1952). A second edition was published in 1958. The 1958 edition reflected experience with the 1952 text and interest in eliminating the differences between the United Nations and the OEEC systems of national accounts and in harmonizing those systems with the balance of payments. The 1958 and 1960 editions of the OEEC and the United Nations systems, respectively, were virtually identical.

5 United Nations, *A System of National Accounts and Supporting Tables,* Studies in Methods, Series F, No. 2 (United Nations publication, Sales No. 1952.XVII.4). The members of the Expert Group were Loreto M. Dominguez (Pan American Union) Kurt Hansen (Denmark), George Jaszi (United States of America), Moni Mohan Mukherjee (India) and Richard Stone (United Kingdom).

6 In addition, the United Nations Statistical Office prepared a somewhat consolidated and therefore simplified version of the accounting framework for the consideration of countries in which the scarcity of basic statistics precluded the use of the full system. This simplified system was consistent with the full 1953 SNA in terms of basic concepts, definitions and classification.

7 The 1968 SNA (paragraph 1.3) is more specific: "Although some work had been done in each of the fields mentioned, it was insufficient, except in the case of the national accounts

expressed in current money terms, to provide *an acceptable basis for international standards*" [emphasis added].

8 Richard Stone, *Quantity and Price Indexes in National Accounts* (Paris: Organisation for European Economic Co-operation, 1956).

9 "A system of price and quantity indexes for national accounts" (E/CN.3/L.46), 27 December 1957.

10 International Monetary Fund, *Balance of Payments Manual* (Washington, DC: International Monetary Fund, 1948). Subsequent editions were published in 1950, 1961 and 1977.

11 United Nations, *Methods of National Income Estimation,* Studies in Methods, Series F, No. 8 (United Nations publication, Sales No. 1955.XVII.5).

12 Beginning with 1972 edition of the questionnaire, the United Nations and the Organisation for Economic Co-operation and Development used a joint questionnaire.

13 United Nations, *Yearbook of National Accounts Statistics* (United Nations publication, Sales No. 58.XVII.3). This publication superseded *Statistics of National Income and Expenditures,* Statistical Papers, Series H, of which 10 issues were published. The *Yearbook* was renamed *National Accounts Statistics: Main Aggqregates and Detailed Tables* in 1982.

14 Abraham Aidenoff, on the staff of the United Nations Statistical Office, provided secretariat support throughout and drafted substantial parts of the three documents. The documents were "A System of National Accounts (proposals for the revision of SNA, 1952)" (E/CN.3/320) of 9 February 1965, which was submitted to the Statistical Commission at its thirteenth session; "Proposals for revising the SNA, 1952" (E/CN.3/345) of 28 June 1966, which was submitted to the Statistical Commission at its fourteenth session; and "Proposals for the revision of the SNA, 1952" (E/CN.3/356) of 14 August 1967, which was submitted to the Statistical Commission at its fifteenth session.

15 United Nations, *A System of National Accounts,* Studies in Methods, Series F, No. 2, Rev.3 (United Nations publication, Sales No. E.69.XVII.3). The Expert Group consisted of O. Aukrust (Norway), B. Ferrán (Venezuela), E. Hicks (International Monetary Fund), George Jaszi (United States of America), J.D. Mayer (France), M.D. McCarthy (Ireland), M. Mód (Hungary), C.A. Oomens (Netherlands), Richard Stone (United Kingdom) and S.G. Tiwari (India). Richard Stone served as Chairman for each of the expert group's three meetings. In addition, representatives from the statistical services of the Organisation for Economic Co-operation and Devel-

opment and the European Economic Community participated in the Group.

16 United Nations, *Basic Principles of the System of Balances of
the National Economy*, Series F, No. 17, Rev.1 (United Nations publication, Sales No. E.89.XVII.3). The MPS became,
beginning with the *Yearbook* for 1970, the standard for the national accounting statistics reported to the United Nations by
countries with centrally planned economies.

17 1968 SNA, paragraphs 1.4 to 1.10.

18 Statistical Office of the European Communities, *European
System of Integrated Economic Accounts* (Luxembourg: Statistical Office of the European Communities, 1970). A second
edition was published in 1980.

19 1968 SNA, paragraphs 1.83 to 1.98.

20 United Nations, *Provisional International Guidelines on the
National and Sectoral Balance-Sheet and Reconciliation Ac-
counts of the System of National Accounts,* Statistical Papers,
Series M, No. 60 (United Nations publication, Sales No.
E.77.XVII.10). United Nations, *Provisional Guidelines on
Statistics of the Distribution of Income, Consumption and Ac-
cumulation of Households*, Statistical Papers, Series M, No.
61 (United Nations publication, Sales No. E.77.XVII.11).

United Nations, *Manual on National Accounts at Constant
Prices*, Statistical Papers, Series M, No. 64 (United Nations
publication, Sales No. E.79.XVII.5).

21 "Organization of the SNA review" (ESA/STAT/AC.28/2), 17
March 1986, and "Conceptual framework of the revised
SNA" (ESA/STAT/AC.28/3), 9 February 1986. Both papers
include extensive bibliographies mentioning reports of meetings and topical papers.

22 "System of National Accounts (SNA) review issues", prepared by the Inter-Secretariat Working Group on National
Accounts, 22 March 1990.

23 "Revised System of National Accounts: draft chapters and
annexes" (ST/ESA/STAT/SER.F/2/Rev.4, Provisional).

24 "Report of the Interregional Seminar on the Revision of the
System of National Accounts (SNA)" (ESA/STAT/ AC.
43/8), 11 December 1992, paragraph 146.

25 Report of the Inter-Secretariat Working Group on
National Accounts on the revision of the SNA
(E/CN.3/1993/4), 30 December 1992, and its
recommendations on specific issues concerning the
revised SNA (E/CN.3/1993/4/Add.1 and 2).

Reader's guide

The goal of this publication is to describe the SNA as a conceptual system. This conceptual system is meant to be applicable to economies around the world. The publication therefore recognizes differing conditions and institutional arrangements that may be found in developed and developing countries and in newly emerging market economies. Further, it attempts to present the rationale for the treatments applied so that national accountants can, by extension, decide on treatments for new developments and new institutional arrangements in the future.

The publication does not attempt to provide guidance on how to make estimates, on the priority with which different accounts should be implemented, or on the frequency and format of their presentation. Instead, both practical guidance and specialized guidance are to be given in supplementary manuals and compilation guides that will receive increased attention now that the conceptual system is in place. Several manuals and guides are already in preparation. Publication of the handbook *Integrated Environmental and Economic Accounting* is expected in 1993. Work on the handbook on the application of the SNA in countries in transition has high priority in view of the urgent need for guidance to countries that previously had used the System of Balances of the National Economy. Preliminary discussions have taken place on a handbook dealing with application of the SNA in countries with high rates of inflation. The International Monetary Fund is developing its compilation guides in parallel with its conceptual manuals. The first of these is expected in 1993 to accompany the fifth edition of the *Balance of Payments Manual*.

The 21 chapters in this publication are in five groups. They are organized, first of all, to reinforce the structure of the SNA - for simplicity, called the System. Secondly, they are organized in recognition of the fact that not all chapters will be read by the same individuals or used in the same way. Some chapters, it can be expected, will even be used by the same individual in different ways at different times.

The chapters in group I provide information about the 1993 SNA designed to be of interest not only to national accountants but also to others, such as analysts who use national accounts statistics, economic journalists, statisticians in fields other than national accounts and government officials who make decisions that will affect resources available for the development of statistics. Chapter I describes the main features of the sequence of accounts in the System, its institutional sectors, and its concepts and classifications; the uses of national accounts; the harmonization between different statisti-

cal systems; the links with business accounting and with economic theory; and the roles the aggregates can and cannot serve. Chapter II gives a picture of the central framework of the SNA. As an overview it is selective in order not to be overwhelming, but references are made to the appropriate chapters that follow. It first sets out the elements that make up the skeleton of the system: institutional units and sectors; transactions and other flows; assets and liabilities; activities, establishments and products; and purposes. Next it summarizes the accounting rules. The chapter then describes the accounting structure within which flows and stocks, using these tools, are entered. The chapter introduces the several degrees of flexibility that are available to the user of the System.

Group II chapters deal with the basic "tools" with which national accountants work to construct a system of accounts. Chapter III, on flows, stocks and accounting rules, defines the nature of the entries in the System and explains the rules of accounting that underlie the ways those entries are made. The discussion is a general one; definitions of specific stocks and flows and specific applications of the accounting rules appear in later chapters. Chapter IV describes institutional units and the five institutional sectors into which the resident institutional units are grouped. Chapter V describes establishments and the industries, following the International Standard Industrial Classification, into which they are grouped.

Group III chapters are built around the accounts and tables of the central framework. Chapters VI through IX cover the current accounts of the full sequence of accounts for institutional units and sectors - the production account, the primary distribution of income account, the secondary distribution of income account, and the use of income account. Chapters X through XII cover the accumulation accounts—the capital account, the financial account, the other changes in volume of assets account, and the revaluation account. Chapter XIII covers the balance sheets of the full sequence of accounts for institutional units and sectors. Chapter XIV, on the rest of the world account, covers the transactions and other flows, and resulting stock of assets and liabilities, between resident institutional units and non-resident units in respect of all kinds of economic activity. Chapter XV covers the set of supply and use tables and input-output tables that provide a more detailed basis for analysing industries and products through a breakdown of the production account, generation of income account, and goods and services account.

Group IV chapters are about measures associated with stocks and flows that are entered into the accounts and tables described. Chapter XVI describes a set of interdependent measures that make it possible to carry out analyses of inflation and economic growth. It is mainly concerned with compiling price and volume measures for flows of goods and services, but it also examines the measurement of income in real terms—that is, income adjusted for changes in purchasing power—for the total economy. Chapter XVII discusses population, which is needed to express product and consumption expenditure in per capita terms, and labour inputs, which are needed to examine productivity.

Group V chapters deal with elaborations, applications and uses of complementary or alternative concepts. Chapter XVIII describes the classifications for certain transactions in products by producers and for three institutional sectors—households, general government and non-profit institutions serving households—that identify the "purposes" or "objectives" of the transactions.

Three other chapters in group V highlight the flexibility of the System. The central framework is consistent and integrated. However, its presentation in this manual does not imply any order of priority or frequency of compilation, nor does the accounting structure described imply that results are necessarily to be presented in this way. Chapter XIX, on the application of the integrated framework to various circumstances and needs, shows how the emphases may be varied by, for example, using the System's classifications and accounts at various levels of detail, by using different valuations, by rearranging the results and by introducing additional elements. The chapter provides recommendations for the treatment of multiple exchange rates and a parallel treatment of interest under significant inflation. Chapter XX, on social accounting matrices, illustrates the exploitation of flexibility to highlight special interests and social concerns such as poverty, featuring the display of interconnections, disaggregation of the household sector, and linkage of income generation and consumption. Chapter XXI describes how the System may be expanded for selected areas of concern by using classification schemes and concepts that are complementary or alternative to the one in the central framework. It describes a framework that may be used for functionally oriented satellite accounts, such as for tourism or social concerns such as health or education. It presents, as an example of satellite accounts that give more emphasis to alternative concepts, a framework in which natural resources are treated as capital and their using up is treated as the depletion or degradation of capital.

Several of the chapters have one or more annexes. These typically elaborate an aspect or a treatment specific to the chapter. For example, an annex to chapter II shows how the System can be presented in diagrammatic, equation and matrix form; an annex to chapter XII provides an example of how to calculate holding gains.

In addition, five of the annexes at the end of the manual pull together in one place significant information that draws upon several chapters. Annex I first describes the general features of the 1993 SNA that changed or received greater emphasis while retaining the basic theoretical framework of the 1968 SNA. Next, the annex mentions the specific changes, grouped into nine sections and with cross-references to the appropriate chapters and tables. This annex, together with the history of national accounting up through the 1968 SNA presented in the previous section, will help readers, especially those familiar with earlier systems, who wish to focus on the changes incorporated into the 1993 SNA.

Annex II lays out the relationship between the rest of the world account and the balance of payments accounts. Harmonization has been attained between the SNA and the balance of payments, as described in the fifth edition of the International Monetary Fund's *Balance of Payments Manual* with respect to issues such as the delineation of resident units, valuation of transactions and of assets and liabilities, time of recording transactions, conversion procedures and the coverage of major aggregates. There are, however, differences in the level of detail. These reflect differences in analytical requirements, the relative quantitative significance in international transactions in respect of some items, and constraints imposed by the internal structure of the two systems. The annex focuses on the relationship between the aggregates and details in the SNA rest of the world accounts and corresponding items in the *Manual* by using a series of reconciliation tables.

Annexes III and IV show the treatment of two kinds of transactions—those related to financial intermediation services indirectly measured and those related to insurance, social insurance and pensions—that cut across several accounts.

Annex V provides the classifications and accounts. The classifications shown are for institutional sectors, transactions and other flows, and assets. The hierarchy of the classifications and the codes are systematically laid out. A complementary classification of transactions and other flows facilitates additional presentations and analysis. It shows a number of transactions in kind explicitly, the components of certain flows, such as output, and certain observed transactions that are split into components for use in the System. In addition, the functional classifications described in chapter XVIII are provided for convenience. The sequence of accounts for institutional sectors and the rest of the world are presented in full detail.

Several features of the volume are designed specifically to aid the reader. First, the table of contents is very detailed, reproducing the headings used in each chapter. Thus, the reader can use the table of contents to place a particular topic in context—for example, to identify a component as one of several within an aggregate. Second, the accounts and tables throughout the volume have numerical entries so that the reader can sum to an aggregate, trace the interrelationships and carry out other operations that reinforce understanding. These data, and the references to them in the text, are purely illustrative and do not correspond to actual data in any country. Finally, the list of acronyms and abbreviations and the index are especially useful in a technical publication of this size.

List of abbreviations and acronyms

AGE-model	applied general equilibrium model
c.i.f.	cost, insurance, freight
COFOG	Classification of the Functions of Government
CPC	Central Product Classification
CPI	consumer price index
ECU	European currency unit
EDP	environmentally adjusted net domestic product
FIFO	first-in-first-out
f.o.b.	free on board
FISIM	financial intermediation services indirectly measured
GDP	gross domestic product
GFS	government finance statistics
GNI	gross national income
GNP	gross national product
ILO	International Labour Organisation
IMF	International Monetary Fund
ISIC	International Standard Industrial Classification of All Economic Activities

LIFO	last-in-first-out
NDP	net domestic product
n.e.c.	not elsewhere classified
NIFO	next-in-first-out
NNI	net national income
NPI	non-profit institution
NPISH	non-profit institutions serving households
OECD	Organisation for Economic Co-operation and Development
OTC	over-the-counter
PPP	purchasing power parity
R and D	research and development
SAM	social accounting matrix
SDR	special drawing right
SEEA	system of environmental and economic accounts
SNA	System of National Accounts
VAT	value added tax

I. Introduction

A. The SNA as a System

1.1. The System of National Accounts (SNA) consists of a coherent, consistent and integrated set of macroeconomic accounts, balance sheets and tables based on a set of internationally agreed concepts, definitions, classifications and accounting rules. It provides a comprehensive accounting framework within which economic data can be compiled and presented in a format that is designed for purposes of economic analysis, decision-taking and policy-making. The accounts themselves present in a condensed way a great mass of detailed information, organized according to economic principles and perceptions, about the working of an economy. They provide a comprehensive and detailed record of the complex economic activities taking place within an economy and of the interaction between the different economic agents, and groups of agents, that takes place on markets or elsewhere. In practice the accounts are compiled for a succession of time periods, thus providing a continuing flow of information that is indispensable for the monitoring, analysis and evaluation of the performance of an economy over time. The SNA provides information not only about economic activities, but also about the levels of an economy's productive assets and the wealth of its inhabitants at particular points of time. Finally, the SNA includes an external account that displays the links between an economy and the rest of the world.

1.2. The SNA may be implemented at different levels of aggregation: at the level of individual economic agents, or institutional units as they are called in the System; for groups of such units, or institutional sectors; or at the level of the total economy. Although traditionally described as a system of national accounts, for analytical purposes the SNA has to be implemented at lower levels of aggregation. In order to understand the workings of the economy, it is essential to be able to observe and analyse the economic interactions taking place between the different sectors of the economy. Certain key aggregate statistics, such as gross domestic product (GDP), that are widely used as indicators of economic activity at the level of the total economy, are defined within the System, but the calculation of such aggregates has long ceased to be the primary purpose for compiling the accounts.

1.3. The System is built around a sequence of interconnected flow accounts linked to different types of economic activity taking place within a given period of time, together with balance sheets that record the values of the stocks of assets and liabilities held by institutional units or sectors at the beginning and end of the period. Each flow account relates to a particular kind of activity such as production, or the generation, distribution, redistribution or use of income. Each account is balanced by introducing a balancing item defined residually as the difference between the total resources and uses recorded on the two sides of the account. The balancing item from one account is carried forward as the first item in the following account, thereby making the sequence of accounts an articulated whole. The balancing items typically encapsulate the net result of the activities covered by the accounts in question and are therefore economic constructs of considerable interest and analytical significance—for example, value added, disposable income and saving. There is also a strong link between the flow accounts and the balance sheets, as all the changes occurring over time that affect the assets or liabilities held by institutional units or sectors are systematically recorded in one or another of the flow accounts. The closing balance sheet is fully determined by the opening balance sheet and the transactions or other flows recorded in the sequence of accounts.

B. Accounts and their corresponding economic activities

1.4. The purpose of this section is to give a very brief summary of the main sequence of accounts in order to describe the main features of the System before discussing other related issues. It is impossible to do justice to the wealth of information contained in the System in a short section of this kind, and reference should be made to chapter II for a comprehensive overview of the System. Before summarizing the sequence of accounts, it should be noted that although it is necessary to present the accounts in a particular order, the activities they describe should not be interpreted as taking place sequentially in time. For example, incomes are generated continuously by processes of production, while expenditures on the outputs produced may also be taking place more or less simultaneously. An economy is a general equilibrium system in which interdependent economic activities involving countless transactions between different institutional units are carried out simultaneously. Feedbacks are continually taking place from one type of economic activity to another.

1. The sequence of accounts

Current accounts

1.5. These accounts record the production of goods and services, the generation of incomes by production, the subsequent distribution and redistribution of incomes among institutional units, and the use of incomes for purposes of consumption or saving.

Production account

1.6. The production account records the activity of producing goods and services as defined within the System. Its balancing item, gross value added, is defined as the value of output less the value of intermediate consumption and is a measure of the contribution to GDP made by an individual producer, industry or sector. Gross value added is the source from which the primary incomes of the System are generated and is therefore carried forward into the primary distribution of income account. Value added may also be measured net by deducting consumption of fixed capital.

Distribution and use of income accounts

1.7. These consist of a set of articulated accounts showing how incomes are:

Generated by production

Distributed to institutional units with claims on the value added created by production

Redistributed among institutional units, mainly by government units through social security contributions and benefits and taxes

Eventually used by households, government units or non-profit institutions serving households (NPISHs) for purposes of final consumption or saving.

1.8. The balancing item emerging from the complete set of income accounts is saving. The income accounts have considerable intrinsic economic interest in themselves. In particular, they are needed to explain the behaviour of institutional units as final consumers—that is, as users of the goods and services emanating from production for the satisfaction of the individual and collective needs and wants of households and the community. The balancing item, saving, is carried forward into the capital account, the first in the System's sequence of accumulation accounts.

Accumulation accounts

1.9. These are flow accounts that record the acquisition and disposal of financial and non-financial assets and liabilities by institutional units through transactions or as a result of other events:

The capital account records acquisitions and disposals of non-financial assets as a result of transactions with other units or internal bookkeeping transactions linked to production (changes in inventories and consumption of fixed capital).

The financial account records acquisitions and disposals of financial assets and liabilities, also through transactions.

A third account, the other changes in assets account, consists of two sub-accounts. The first, the other changes in volume of assets account, records changes in the amounts of the assets and liabilities held by institutional units or sectors as a result of factors other than transactions; for example, destruction of fixed assets by natural disasters. The second, the revaluation account, records those changes in the values of assets and liabilities that result from changes in their prices.

1.10. The link between the accumulation accounts and the income accounts is provided by the fact that saving—that is, disposable income that is not spent on consumption goods or services—must be used to acquire financial or non-financial assets of one kind or another, if only cash, the most liquid financial asset. When saving is negative, the excess of consumption over disposable income must be financed by disposing of assets or incurring liabilities. The financial account shows the way in which funds are channelled from one group of units to another, especially through financial intermediaries. Access to finance is a prerequisite for engaging in many types of economic activities.

Balance sheets

1.11. The balance sheets show the values of the stocks of assets and liabilities held by institutional units or sectors at the beginning and end of an accounting period. As already noted, the values of the assets and liabilities held at any moment in time vary automatically whenever any transactions, price changes or other changes affecting the volume of assets or liabilities held take place. These are all recorded in one or another of the accumulation accounts so that the difference between the values in the opening and closing balance sheets is entirely accounted for within the System, provided, of course, that the assets and liabilities recorded in the balance sheets are valued consistently with the transactions and other changes—that is, at current prices.

2. Activities and transactions

1.12. The accounts of the System are designed to provide analytically useful information about the behaviour of institutional units and the activities in which they engage, such as production, consumption and the accumulation of assets. They usually do this by recording the values of the goods, services or assets involved in the transactions between institutional units that are associated with these activities rather than by trying to record or measure the physical processes directly. For example, the accounts do not record the physical consumption of goods and services by households—the eating of food or the burning of fuel within a given time period. Instead, they record the expenditures that households make on final consumption goods and services or, more generally, the values of the goods and services they acquire through transactions with other units, whether purchased or not. Data on transactions provide the basic source material from which the values of the various elements in the accounts are built up or derived. The use of transactions data has important advantages. First, the prices at which goods and services are exchanged in transactions between buyers and sellers on markets provide the information needed for valuing, directly or indirectly, all the items in the accounts. Secondly, a transaction that takes place between two different institutional units has to be recorded for both parties to the transaction and therefore generally appears twice in a system of macroeconomic accounts. This enables important linkages to be established in the System. For example, output is obtained by summing the amounts sold, bartered or transferred to other units plus the amounts entered into, less the amounts withdrawn from inventories. In effect, the value of output is obtained by recording the various uses of that output by means of data on transactions. In this way, flows of goods and services can be traced through the economic system from their producers to their eventual users. Some transactions are only internal bookkeeping transactions that are needed when a single unit engages in two activities, such as the production and consumption of the same good or service, but the great majority of transactions take place between different units on markets.

C. The institutional sectors of the economy

1.13. The purpose of this section is to indicate very briefly what are the main sectors of the economy for which it is possible to compile the full sequence of accounts summarized in the previous section. Two main kinds of institutional units, or transactors, are distinguished in the System—households and legal entities. The latter are either entities created for purposes of production, mainly corporations and non-profit institutions (NPIs), or government units, including social security funds. Institutional units are essentially units that are capable of owning goods and assets, incurring liabilities and engaging in economic activities and transactions with other units in their own right. For the purposes of the System, institutional units that are resident in the economy are grouped together into five mutually exclusive sectors composed of the following types of units:

  Non-financial corporations

  Financial corporations

  Government units, including social security funds

  NPIs serving households (NPISHs)

  Households.

The five sectors together make up the total economy. Each sector is also divided into sub-sectors. For example, the non-financial and financial corporations sectors are divided to distinguish corporations subject to control by Governments or foreign units from other corporations. The System makes provision for a complete set of flow accounts and balance sheets to be compiled for each sector, and sub-sector if desired, as well as for the total economy. The total number of accounts that may be compiled is therefore potentially quite large, depending upon the level of disaggregation that is required and feasible. Only by disaggregation into sectors and sub-sectors is it possible to observe the interactions between the different parts of the economy that need to be measured and analysed for purposes of policy-making. The complete set of accounts at the level of the five main sectors is shown in annex V at the end of this manual.

1.14. Institutional units that are resident abroad form the rest of the world. The System does not require accounts to be compiled in respect of economic activities taking place in the rest of the world, but all transactions between resident and non-resident units have to be recorded in order to obtain a complete accounting for the economic behaviour of resident units. Transactions between residents and non-residents are grouped together in a single account, the rest of the world account.

D. Other features of the System

1.15. The SNA is a rich and detailed economic accounting system that extends well beyond the main sequence of accounts to encompass other accounts or tables that either contain information that cannot be included in the main accounts or present information in alternative ways, such as matrices, that may be more appropriate for certain types of analysis. It is not proposed to list all these various elements at this point, as they are described in chapter II, but it is useful to draw attention to two specific elements which play a major role in the System.

1. Supply and use tables

1.16. In addition to the flow accounts and balance sheets described earlier, the central framework of the System also contains detailed supply and use tables in the form of matrices that record how supplies of different kinds of goods and services originate from domestic industries and imports and how those supplies are allocated between various intermediate or final uses, including exports. These tables involve the compilation of a set of integrated production and generation of income accounts for industries—that is, groups of establishments as distinct from institutional units—that are able to draw upon detailed data from industrial censuses or surveys. The supply and use tables provide an accounting framework within which the commodity flow method of compiling national accounts—in which the total supplies and uses of individual types of goods and services have to be balanced with each other—can be systematically exploited. The supply and use tables also provide the basic information for the derivation of detailed input-output tables that are extensively used for purposes of economic analysis and projections.

2. Price and volume measures

1.17. The System also provides specific guidance about the methodology to be used to compile an integrated set of price and volume indices for flows of goods and services, gross value added and GDP that are consistent with the concepts and accounting principles of the System. It is recommended that annual chain indices should be used where possible, although fixed base indices may also be used when the volume measures for components and aggregates have to be additively consistent for purposes of economic analysis and modelling.

1.18. Rates of inflation and economic growth appropriately measured by price and volume indices for the main aggregates of the System are key variables both for the evaluation of past economic performance and as targets for the formulation of economic policy-making. They are an essential part of the System, especially given the emergence of inflation as an endemic economic problem in many countries. The System also recognizes that the growth in the volume of GDP and the growth of an economy's real income are not the same because of trading gains or losses resulting from changes in international terms of trade.

E. Concepts and classifications

1.19. The contents of the SNA depend not only on the accounting structure itself—that is, on the type and format of the accounts—but also on the ways in which the items included in the accounts are defined and classified. The issues involved are not simply of a technical nature but raise fundamental questions of economic theory and principles. The concepts and classifications used in the System have a considerable impact on the ways in which the data may be used and the interpretations placed on them.

1. The production boundary

1.20. The activity of production is fundamental. In the System, production is understood to be a physical process, carried out under the responsibility, control and management of an institutional unit, in which labour and assets are used to transform inputs of goods and services into outputs of other goods and services. All goods and services produced as outputs must be such that they can be sold on markets or at least be capable of being provided by one unit to another, with or without charge. The System includes within the production boundary all production actually destined for the market, whether for sale or barter. It also includes all goods or services provided free to individual households or collectively to the community by government units or NPISHs.

Household production

1.21. The main problem for defining the range of activities recorded in the production accounts of the System is to decide upon the treatment of activities that produce goods or services that could have been supplied to others on the market but are actually retained by their producers for their own use. These cover a very wide range of productive activities, in particular:

(a)   The production of agricultural goods by household enterprises for own final consumption;

(b)   The production of other goods for own final use by households: the construction of dwellings, the production of foodstuffs and clothing, etc.;

(c)   The production of housing services for own final consumption by owner occupiers;

(d)   The production of domestic and personal services for consumption within the same household: the preparation of meals, care and training of children, cleaning, repairs, etc.

All of these activities are productive in an economic sense. However, inclusion in the System is not simply a matter of estimating monetary values for the outputs of these activities. If values are assigned to the outputs, values have also to be assigned to the incomes generated by their production and to the consumption of the output. It is clear that the economic significance of these flows is very different from that of monetary flows. For example, the incomes generated are automatically tied to the consumption of the goods and services produced; they have little relevance for the analysis of inflation or deflation or other disequilibria within the economy. The inclusion of large non-monetary flows of this kind in the accounts together with monetary flows can obscure what is happening on markets and reduce the analytic usefulness of the data.

1.22. The SNA is a multi-purpose system. It is designed to meet a wide range of analytical and policy needs. A balance has to be struck between the desire for the accounts to be as comprehensive as possible and the need to prevent flows used for the analysis of market behaviour and disequilibria from being swamped by non-monetary values. The System therefore includes all production of goods for own use within its production boundary, as goods can be switched between market and non-market use even after they have been produced, but it excludes all production of services for own final consumption within households (except for the services produced by employing paid domestic staff and the own-account production of housing services by owner occupiers). These services are consumed as they are produced and the links between their production and market activities are more tenuous than for goods production, such as agricultural goods which households may produce partly for own final consumption and partly for sale, or barter, on the market. The location of the production boundary in the System is a compromise, but a deliberate one that takes account of the needs of most users. In this context it may be noted that in labour force statistics economically active persons are defined as those engaged in productive activities as defined in the SNA. If the production boundary were extended to include the production of personal and domestic services by members of households for their own final consumption, all persons engaged in such activities would become self-employed, making unemployment virtually impossible by definition. This illustrates the need to confine the production boundary in the SNA and other related statistical systems to market activities or fairly close substitutes for market activities.

Other production boundary problems

1.23. Certain natural processes may or may not be counted as production depending upon the circumstances in which they occur. A necessary condition for an activity to be treated as productive is that it must be carried out under the instigation, control and responsibility of some institutional unit that exercises ownership rights over whatever is produced. For example, the natural growth of stocks of fish in open seas is not counted as production: the process is not managed by any institutional unit and the fish do not belong to any institutional unit. On the other hand, the growth of fish in fish farms is treated as a process of production in much the same way that rearing livestock is a process of production. Similarly, the natural growth of wild, uncultivated forests or wild fruits or ber-

ries is not counted as production, whereas the cultivation of crop-bearing trees, or trees grown for timber or other uses, is counted in the same way as the growing of annual crops. However, the deliberate felling of trees in wild forests, and the gathering of wild fruit or berries, and also firewood, counts as production. Similarly, rainfall and the flow of water down natural watercourses are not processes of production, whereas storing water in reservoirs or dams and the piping, or carrying, of water from one location to another all constitute production.

1.24. These examples show that many activities or processes that may be of benefit to institutional units, both as producers and consumers, are not processes of production in an economic sense. Rainfall may be vital to the agricultural production of a country but it is not a process of production whose output can be included in GDP.

2. The consumption boundary

1.25. The coverage of production in the System has ramifications that extend considerably beyond the production account itself. The boundary of production determines the amount of value added recorded and hence the total amount of income generated by production. The range of goods and services that are included in household final consumption expenditures, and actual consumption, is similarly governed by the production boundary; for example, these expenditures include the estimated values of the agricultural products consumed by households that they have produced themselves and also the values of the housing services consumed by owner occupiers, but not the values of "do-it-yourself" repairs and maintenance to vehicles or household durables, the cleaning of dwellings, the care and training of children, or similar domestic or personal services produced for own final consumption. Only the expenditures on goods utilized for these purposes—e.g., cleaning materials—are included in household final consumption expenditures.

3. The asset boundary

1.26. Balance sheets are compiled for institutional units, or sectors, and record the values of the assets they own or the liabilities they have incurred. Assets as defined in the System are entities that must be owned by some unit, or units, and from which economic benefits are derived by their owner(s) by holding or using them over a period of time. Financial assets and fixed assets, such as machinery, equipment and structures which have themselves been produced as outputs in the past, are clearly covered by this definition. However, the ownership criterion is important for determining which naturally occurring—i.e., non-produced—assets are included in the System. Naturally occurring assets such as land, mineral deposits, fuel reserves, uncultivated forests or other vegetation and wild animals are included in the balance sheets provided that institutional units are exercising effective ownership rights over them—that is, are actually in a position to be able to benefit from them. Assets need not be privately owned and could be owned by government units exercising ownership rights on behalf of entire communities. Thus, many environmental assets are included within the System. Assets that are not included are those such as the atmosphere or open seas, over which no ownership rights can be exercised, or mineral or fuel deposits that have not been discovered or that are unworkable—i.e., incapable of bringing any benefits to their owners, given the technology and relative prices existing at the time.

1.27. Changes in the values of naturally occurring assets owned by institutional units between one balance sheet and the next are recorded in the accumulation accounts of the System. For example, the depletion of a natural asset as a result of its use in production is recorded in the other changes in volume of assets account, together with losses of fixed assets due to their destruction by natural disasters (floods, earthquakes, etc.). Conversely, when deposits or reserves of minerals or fuels are discovered or previously unworkable deposits become workable, their appearance is recorded in this account and they enter the balance sheets in this way.

F. Uses of the SNA

1.29. The SNA is a multi-purpose system, as stated above, designed for economic analysis, decision-taking and policy-making, whatever the industrial structure or stage of economic development reached by a country. The basic concepts and definitions of the System depend upon economic reasoning and principles which should be universally valid and invariant to the particular economic circumstances in which they are applied. Similarly, the classifications and accounting rules are meant to be universally applicable. There is no justification, for example, for seeking to define the components of a production account—output, intermediate consumption and gross value added—differently in less developed than in more developed economies, or in large relatively closed economies than in small open economies, or in high-inflation economies than in low-inflation economies. Certain definitions, or accounting rules, specified in the System may become superfluous in certain circumstances (e.g., when there is no inflation), but it is nevertheless necessary for a general system such as the SNA to include definitions and rules covering as wide a range of circumstances as possible.

1.30. The fact that data needs and priorities, and also statistical capabilities, may vary considerably between different kinds of countries does not justify the construction of different systems with different concepts, definitions, classifications or accounting rules. Some countries may be able, at least initially,

4. National boundaries

1.28. The accounts of the System are compiled for resident institutional units grouped into institutional sectors and sub-sectors. The concept of residence is the same as that used in the *Balance of Payments Manual* of the International Monetary Fund (IMF). An institutional unit is said to be resident within the economic territory of a country when it maintains a centre of economic interest in that territory—that is, when it engages, or intends to engage, in economic activities or transactions on a significant scale either indefinitely or over a long period of time, usually interpreted as one year. As an aggregate measure of production, the GDP of a country is equal to the sum of the gross values added of all resident institutional units engaged in production (plus any taxes, and minus any subsidies, on products not included in the value of their outputs). This is not exactly the same as the sum of the gross values added of all productive activities taking place within the geographical boundaries of the national economy. Some of the production of a resident institutional unit may take place abroad—for example, the installation of some exported machinery or equipment or a consultancy project undertaken by a team of expert advisers working temporarily abroad. Conversely, some of the production taking place within a country may be attributable to foreign institutional units.

to calculate only a small number of accounts and tables for the total economy with little or no disaggregation into sectors, but a reduced set of accounts or tables does not constitute an alternative system. It is not appropriate to try to lay down general priorities for data collection when economic circumstances may vary so much from one country to another. In practice, priorities can only be established country by country by economic analysts or policy-makers familiar with the economic situation, needs and problems of the individual countries in question. It is not useful, for example, to try to specify general priorities for developing countries when they constitute a very heterogeneous group of countries at a world level. Data priorities may vary as much between one developing country and another as between a developing and a developed country.

1. Specific uses

1.31. The main objective of the SNA is to provide a comprehensive conceptual and accounting framework which can be used to create a macroeconomic database suitable for analysing and evaluating the performance of an economy. The existence of such a database is a prerequisite for informed, rational policy-making and decision-taking. Some of the more specific uses of the SNA are described in the following sections.

Monitoring the behaviour of the economy

1.32. National accounts data provide information covering both different types of economic activities and the different sectors of the economy. It is possible to monitor the movements of major economic flows such as production, household consumption, government consumption, capital formation, exports, imports, wages, profits, taxes, lending, borrowing, etc., the flows of goods and services being recorded at both current and constant prices. Moreover, information is provided about certain key balancing items and ratios which can only be defined and measured within an accounting framework—for example, the budget surplus or deficit, the share of income which is saved, or invested, by individual sectors of the economy or the economy as a whole, the trade balance, etc. National accounts also provide the background against which movements of short-term indicators, such as monthly indices of industrial production or of consumer or producer prices, can be interpreted and evaluated. The monitoring of the behaviour of the economy may be significantly improved if at least some of the main aggregates of the System are compiled quarterly as well as annually, although many of the accounts, tables or balance sheets of the System are not usually compiled more frequently than once a year.

Macroeconomic analysis

1.33. National accounts are also used to investigate the causal mechanisms at work within an economy. Such analysis usually takes the form of the estimation of the parameters of functional relationships between different economic variables by applying econometric methods to time series of data at both current and constant prices compiled within a national accounting framework. The types of macroeconomic models used for such investigations may vary according to the school of economic thought of the investigator as well as the objectives of the analysis, but the System is sufficiently flexible to accommodate the requirements of different economic theories or models, provided only that they accept the basic concepts of production, consumption, income, etc. on which the System is based.

1.34. Advances in computer technology have made it possible for the econometric analysis of large macroeconomic models to be carried out on microcomputers. Many econometric software packages have been developed for this purpose so that this kind of modelling is no longer confined to a few government departments, research institutes or universities with large mainframe computers. It is increasingly being undertaken by private corporations or institutions with only limited resources available for these purposes.

Economic policy-making and decision-taking

1.35. Economic policy in the short term is formulated on the basis of an assessment of the recent behaviour and current state of the economy and a view, or precise forecast, about likely fu-

ture developments. Short-term forecasts are typically made using econometric models of the type just described. Over the medium or long term, economic policy has to be formulated in the context of a broad economic strategy which may need to be quantified in the form of a plan. Most of the elements which make up a medium- or long-term economic plan consist of national accounts flows, and it may be impossible to draw up such a plan without them. A good macroeconomic model which accurately reflects the past performance of the economy may be indispensable for planning as well as forecasting.

1.36. Economic policy-making and decision-taking take place at all levels of government and also within public and private corporations. Large corporations such as multinationals have the ability to build their own macroeconomic models tailored to their own requirements, for which they need national accounts data. The investment programmes of major corporations must be based on long-term expectations about future economic developments that require national accounts data. There are also, of course, specialist agencies that provide forecasts for individual clients in return for fees. Such agencies typically require very detailed national accounts data.

International comparisons

1.37. The SNA is the system used for reporting to international or supranational organizations national accounts data that conform to standard, internationally accepted concepts, definitions and classifications. The resulting data are widely used for international comparisons of the volumes of major aggregates, such as GDP or GDP per head, and also for comparisons of structural statistics, such as ratios of investment, taxes or government expenditures to GDP. Such comparisons are used by economists, journalists or other analysts to evaluate the performance of one economy against that of other similar economies. They can influence popular and political judgements about the relative success of economic programmes in the same way as developments over time within a single country. Databases consisting of sets of national accounts for groups of countries can also be used for econometric analyses in which time-series and cross-section data are pooled to provide a broader range of observations for the estimation of functional relationships.

1.38. Levels of GDP or, alternatively, gross national income (GNI) per head in different countries are also used by international organizations to determine eligibility for loans, aid or other funds or to determine the terms or conditions on which such loans, aid or funds are made available. When the objective is to compare the volumes of goods or services produced or consumed per head, data in national currencies must be converted into a common currency by means of purchasing power parities and not exchange rates. It is well known that, in general, neither market nor fixed exchange rates reflect the relative internal purchasing powers of different currencies. When exchange rates are used to convert GDP, or other statistics, into a common currency the prices at which goods and services in high-income countries are valued tend to be higher than in low-income countries, thus exaggerating the differences in real incomes between them. Exchange rate converted data must not, therefore, be interpreted as measures of the relative volumes of goods and services concerned. Levels of GDP, or GDP per head, in different countries are also used to determine, in whole or in part, the size of the contributions which the member countries of an international organization make to finance the operations of the organization.

1.39. Although international organizations use the SNA in order to be able to collect internationally comparable national accounts data, the SNA has not been created for this purpose. It has become the standard, or universal, system used with little or no modification by most countries of the world for their own national purposes. National statistical offices and government agencies have a strong vested interest in ensuring that the SNA meets their own analytic and policy requirements and have taken an active part in the development of the System for this reason.

2. Flexibility of implementation and use

1.40. The SNA is designed to be sufficiently comprehensive that individual countries, whatever their economic structures, institutional arrangements or level of development, can select from within it those parts of the System which are considered to be most relevant and useful to implement in the light of their own needs and capabilities. The SNA is meant to be implemented in a flexible manner and the accounts and tables, classifications and sectoring presented in this volume should not be regarded as fixed. In some cases, the System explicitly insists on flexibility. For example, two alternative methods of sub-sectoring the general government sector are proposed in chapter IV without either being assigned priority. Similarly, although the System suggests sub-sectoring the households sector on the basis of the household's principal source of income, it stresses that this is only one possible criterion for sub-sectoring. In some cases, it may be more appropriate to sub-sector on the basis of socio-economic criteria or the type of area in which the household is located or, indeed, to carry the disaggregation of the households sector further by using two or

more criteria together in a hierarchical manner.

1.41. Ways in which the System may be adapted to meet differing circumstances and needs are specifically addressed in chapter XIX. For example, classifications of institutional units, transactions and assets may be implemented flexibly in order to adapt them to the data availability and special circumstances of different countries. The flexible use of classifications does not change the basic concepts and definitions of the System. However, as explained in chapter XXI, flexibility may be taken a stage further by developing satellite accounts that are closely linked to the main System but are not bound to employ exactly the same concepts or restricted to data expressed in monetary terms. Satellite accounts are intended for special purposes such as monitoring the community's health or the state of environment. They may also be used to explore new methodologies and to work out new accounting procedures that, when fully developed and accepted, may become absorbed into the main System in the course of time, in the way that input-output analysis, for example, has been integrated into the System.

1.42. Another way in which the System may be implemented flexibly is by rearranging the data in the accounts in the form of a social accounting matrix in order better to serve particular analytical and policy needs. Such matrices should not be construed as constituting different systems but as alternative ways of presenting the mass of information contained in the System which many users and analysts find more informative and powerful for both monitoring and modelling social and economic development.

3. The SNA as a coordinating framework for statistics

1.43. The System also has a very important statistical function by serving as a coordinating framework for economic statistics in two different senses: first, as the conceptual framework for ensuring the consistency of the definitions and classifications used in different, but related, fields of statistics, and secondly, as an accounting framework for ensuring the numerical consistency of data drawn from different sources, such as industrial inquiries, household surveys, merchandise trade statistics, VAT returns and other administrative sources.

G. Harmonization between different statistical systems

1.44. The SNA and related statistical systems need to be as consistent as possible in respect of their basic concepts, definitions and classifications. National accounts have always occupied a central position in economic statistics because the data from more specialized systems, such as balance of payments or labour force statistics, typically have to be used in conjunction with national accounts data. Consistency between the different systems enhances the analytical usefulness of all the sta-

tistics involved. The harmonization of the SNA and related statistical systems, such as financial statistics or balance of payments statistics, has been one of the driving forces behind the revision of the System.

1.45. Revisions of other statistical systems have been conducted in parallel with, and in close collaboration with, that of the SNA in order to eliminate conceptual differences between them other than a few exceptions that can be specifically justified in terms of the special characteristics of different kinds of data, or the special requirements of different kinds of users. Harmonization between the SNA and other major systems has been largely successful and has been achieved by making changes to the SNA as well as to the other systems.

1.46. Because of the active involvement of IMF in the revision of the SNA, the harmonization process has been particularly effective in respect of balance of payments statistics, government finance statistics and money and banking statistics, for which IMF has responsibility. Revisions of each of these three systems are being undertaken by IMF in order not only to update these systems but also to make them consistent with the SNA to the fullest extent possible. Revised manuals on these systems are being published at about the same time as, or in the years immediately following, the 1993 SNA.

1.47. Various other revised international guidelines are being issued at about the same time as the revised SNA. These include, the third revision of the United Nations International Standard Industrial Classification of All Economic Activities (ISIC), the industrial classification that is used in the SNA. The establishment as described in ISIC is also the statistical unit used to

compile the production accounts by industry that make up supply and use tables of the SNA, the concept of the establishment being the same in both the SNA and ISIC. The International Labour Organisation (ILO) has issued revised standards on labour statistics that define employment in a way that is consistent with the boundary of production in the SNA, as summarized earlier in this chapter. An extract from the resolution of the Fifteenth International Conference of Labour Statisticians concerning the distinction between the formal and informal sectors is reproduced as an annex to chapter IV. Another example is provided by the revised *Handbook on Agricultural Accounts*, prepared by the Food and Agricultural Organization of the United Nations (FAO), which has been brought into line with the treatment of agricultural products and activities in the SNA. It is neither necessary nor feasible to list here all the revisions to international statistical systems and standards that are being undertaken or planned as it is the policy of all the various international agencies involved at a world level to harmonize these systems with each other and with the SNA to the fullest extent possible.

H. Implementation of concepts and classifications

1.48. The contents of the accounts are determined not only by the conceptual framework, definitions and classifications of the System but also by the ways in which they are interpreted and implemented in practice. However simple and precise concepts and classifications may appear in principle, there are inevitably difficult borderline cases which cannot easily be fitted into predetermined categories. These points may be illustrated by considering a fundamental distinction in economics and in the System, namely, the distinction between consumption and gross fixed capital formation (or gross fixed investment, as it is often described in other contexts).

1. Final consumption, intermediate consumption and gross fixed capital formation

1.49. Consumption is an activity in which institutional units use up goods or services. There are two quite different kinds of consumption. Intermediate consumption consists of inputs into processes of production that are used up within the accounting period. Final consumption consists of goods and services used by individual households or the community to satisfy their individual or collective needs or wants. The activity of gross fixed capital formation, on the other hand, is restricted to institutional units in their capacity as producers, being defined as the value of their acquisitions less disposals of fixed assets. Fixed assets are produced assets (mostly machinery, equipment, buildings or other structures but also including some intangible assets) that are used repeatedly or continuously in production over several accounting periods (more than one year).

1.50. The general nature and purpose of the distinction between gross fixed capital formation and consumption, whether intermediate or final, is clear. The distinction is fundamental for economic analysis and policy-making. Nevertheless, the borderline between consumption and gross fixed capital formation is not always easy to determine in practice. Certain activities contain some elements that appear to be consumption and at the same time others that appear to be capital formation. In order to try to ensure that the System is implemented in a uniform way decisions have to be taken about the ways in which certain difficult, even controversial, items are to be classified. Some examples are given below.

Training, research and development

1.51. Expenditures by enterprises on activities such as staff training or research and development are not the type of intermediate inputs whose consumption is determined by the level at which production is carried out in the current period but are designed to raise productivity or increase the range of production possibilities in the future, in much the same way as expenditures on machinery, equipment, buildings and other structures. However, expenditures on training and research or development do not lead to the acquisition of assets that can be easily identified, quantified and valued for balance sheet purposes. Such expenditures continue to be classified as intermediate consumption, therefore, even though it is recognized that they may bring future benefits. In fact, many other expenditures undertaken by enterprises may also have impacts in future periods as well as the current period—for example, market research, advertising and expenditures on health and safety that affect the well-being and attitudes of the workforce.

Education

1.52. It is often proposed that expenditures on education should also be classified as gross fixed capital formation as a form of investment in human capital. The acquisition of knowledge, skills and qualifications increases the productive potential of the individuals concerned and is a source of future economic benefit to them. However, while knowledge, skills and qualifications are clearly assets in a broad sense of the term, they cannot be equated with fixed assets as understood in the System. They are not produced because they are acquired through learning, studying and practising—activities that are not themselves processes of production. The education services produced by schools, colleges, universities, etc. are consumed by students in the process of their acquiring knowledge and skills. Education assets are embodied in individuals as persons. They cannot be transferred to others and cannot be shown in the balance sheets of the enterprises in which the individuals work (except in rare cases when certain highly skilled individuals are under contract to work for particular employers for specified periods). Education assets could possibly be shown in balance sheets for the individuals in which they are embodied, but individuals are not enterprises. They would be difficult to value, bearing in mind that the remuneration received by a skilled worker depends upon the amount of time and effort expended and is not simply a return payable to the owner of an asset.

1.53. It may also be noted that final consumption consists of the use of goods and services for the direct satisfaction of human needs or wants, individually or collectively. Education services are undoubtedly consumed in this sense. They increase the welfare and improve the general quality of life of those consuming them. Moreover, they are not the only services consumed by individuals to bring long- as well as short-term benefits. For example, the consumption of health services brings long-term benefits and even the consumption of basic items such as food and housing is necessary in order to keep an individual in good health—and good working order.

Repairs, maintenance and gross fixed capital formation

1.54. Another, less familiar, example of the intrinsic difficulty of trying to draw a dichotomy between consumption and gross fixed capital formation is provided by repairs and maintenance. Ordinary maintenance and repairs undertaken by enterprises to keep fixed assets in good working order are intermediate consumption. However, major improvements, additions or extensions to fixed assets, both machinery and structures, which improve their performance, increase their capacity or prolong their expected working lives count as gross fixed capital formation. In practice it is not easy to draw the line between ordinary repairs and major improvements, although the System provides certain guidelines for this purpose. Some analysts, however, consider that the distinction between ordinary repairs and maintenance and major improvements and additions is neither operational nor defensible and would favour a more "gross" method of recording in which all such activities are treated as gross fixed capital formation.

2. Interpretation of the distinction between consumption and gross fixed capital formation

1.55. The examples given above show that a simple dichotomy between consumption and gross fixed capital formation inevitably presents problems when dealing with flows of goods and services that do not fit comfortably under either heading. The issue is not simply how to classify certain flows, but also how to achieve an economically meaningful and feasible set of accounting procedures for the assets acquired through gross fixed capital formation within an integrated, coherent set of accounts encompassing past and future periods as well as the present.

1.56. Some care and sophistication is needed in using the accounts. For example, goods and services "consumed" by households—i.e., acquired for the satisfaction of their needs or wants—are not suddenly "used up" and do not "vanish" at the moment of acquisition. In particular, households "consuming" services such as health and education may continue to derive benefits over long periods of time. The "consumption" of such services therefore has some points of similarity with "investment" in assets. Similarly, enterprises may continue to benefit over long periods of time from the intermediate consumption of services such as maintenance and repairs, training, research and development, market research, etc. Thus, while the acquisition of fixed assets by enterprises—that is, gross fixed capital formation—is undertaken specifically to enhance future production possibilities, they are not the only types of expenditure that may be expected to bring future benefits.

1.57. The decision whether to classify certain types of expenditure by households or government, such as education or health services, as final consumption expenditures or gross fixed capital formation does not affect the size of GDP, as both are final expenditures. On the other hand, the decision to classify certain expenditures by enterprises as intermediate consumption rather than gross fixed capital formation does reduce the gross value added and operating surplus of the enterprise and hence GDP as a whole. However, treating certain expenditures as intermediate reduces not only gross fixed capital formation but also consumption of fixed capital in subsequent periods. It is therefore an open question as to how net value added and net domestic product (NDP) are affected in the longer term, depending upon the pattern of the relevant expenditures over time.

I. Links with business accounting and economic theory

1.58. The accounting rules and procedures used in the System are based on those long used in business accounting. The traditional double-entry bookkeeping principle, whereby a transaction gives rise to a pair of matching debit and credit entries within the accounts of each of the two parties to the transaction, is a basic axiom of economic or national accounting. For example, recording the sale of output requires not only an entry in the production account of the seller but also an entry of equal value, often described as the counterpart, in the seller's financial account to record the cash, or short-term financial credit, received in exchange for the output sold. As two entries are also needed for the buyer, the transaction must give rise to four simultaneous entries of equal value in a system of macroeconomic accounts covering both the seller and the buyer. In general, a transaction between two different institutional units always requires four equal, simultaneous entries in the accounts of the System—i.e., quadruple entry accounting—even if the transaction is a transfer and not an exchange and even if no money changes hands. These multiple entries enable the economic interactions between different institutional units and sectors to be recorded and analysed. However, transactions within a single unit (such as the consumption of output by the same unit that produced it) require only two entries whose values have to be estimated.

1.59. The design and structure of the System draws heavily on economic theory and principles as well as business accounting practices. Basic concepts such as production, consumption and capital formation are meant to be rooted in economic theory. When business accounting practices conflict with economic principles, priority is given to the latter, as the System is designed primarily for purposes of economic analysis and policy-making. The difference between business accounting and economic theory can be illustrated by the concept of cost of production used in the System.

1.60. Business accounts commonly (but not invariably) record costs on an historic basis, partly to ensure that they are completely objective. Historic cost accounting requires goods or assets used in production to be valued by the expenditures actually incurred to acquire those goods or assets, however far back in the past those expenditures took place. In the System, however, the concept of opportunity cost as defined in economics is employed. In other words, the cost of using, or using up, some existing asset or good in one particular process of production is measured by the amount of the benefits that could have been secured by using the asset or good in alternative ways. Opportunity cost is calculated with reference to the opportunities foregone at the time the asset or resource is used, as distinct from the costs incurred at some time in the past to acquire the asset. The best practical approximation to opportunity cost accounting is current cost accounting, whereby assets and goods used in production are valued at their actual or estimated current market prices at the time the production takes place. Current cost accounting is sometimes described as replacement cost accounting, although there may be no intention of actually replacing the asset in question after it has been used.

1.61. When there is persistent inflation, even moderate inflation, the use of historic costs tends to underestimate the opportunity costs of production in an economic sense so that historic cost profit may be much greater than the operating surplus as defined in the System. Profits at historic costs are liable to give very misleading signals as to the profitability of the production processes to which they relate by systematically undervaluing inputs compared with outputs. They can lead to mistaken decisions at both a microeconomic and macroeconomic level.

1.62. Current cost accounting has ramifications that permeate the entire System. It affects all the accounts and balance sheets and their balancing items. A fundamental principle underlying the measurement of gross value added, and hence GDP, is that output and intermediate consumption must be valued at the prices current at the time the production takes place. This implies that goods withdrawn from inventories by producers must be valued at the prices prevailing at the times the goods are withdrawn and not at the prices at which they entered inventories. This method of recording changes in inventories is not commonly used in business accounting, however, and may sometimes give very different results—especially when inventory levels fluctuate while prices are rising. Similarly, consumption of fixed capital in the System is calculated on the basis of the estimated opportunity costs of using the assets at the time they are used, as distinct from the prices at which the assets were acquired. When there is persistent inflation, the value of consumption of fixed capital is liable to be much greater than depreciation at historic costs, even if the same assumptions are made in the System and in business accounts about the service lives of the assets and their rates of wear and tear and obsolescence. To avoid confusion, the term "consumption of fixed capital" is used in the System to distinguish it from "depreciation" as typically measured in business accounts, just as the term "operating surplus" is used instead of "profit" or "operating profit".

1.63. Measuring consumption of fixed capital at current costs is equivalent to measuring the operating surplus from production after deducting the costs of maintaining intact the stock of fixed assets used in production—that is, after deducting the costs of replacing assets used up in production (as distinct from the costs of replacing assets destroyed by events not connected with production, such as earthquakes or other natural disasters, or acts of war, such losses being recorded elsewhere in the System in the capital accumulation accounts). Even when the fixed assets used up are not actually replaced, the amount of consumption of fixed capital charged as a cost of production should be sufficient to enable the assets to be replaced, if desired. Similarly, the concept of disposable income used in the System is based on the underlying idea that it represents the maximum amount available to a household for purposes of consumption after maintaining its net worth intact, i.e., its assets minus its liabilities valued at current prices. However, the System excludes from the calculation of income any assets received or disposed of as a result of capital transfers that merely redistribute wealth between different units, and also any assets received or disposed of as a result of "other volume changes" as described in chapter XII. It also excludes any real holding gains or losses on assets or liabilities due to changes in their relative prices. At a macro level, the aggregate income of a group of units is not changed by redistributing wealth within the group. The System takes account of capital transfers, other volume changes and real holding gains or losses by recording them in the accumulation accounts of the units concerned and not in their income accounts.

Micro-macro links

1.64. The sequence of accounts and balance sheets of the System could, in principle, be compiled at any level of aggregation, even that of an individual institutional unit. It might therefore appear desirable if the macroeconomic accounts for sectors or the total economy could be obtained directly by aggregating corresponding data for individual units. There would be considerable analytical advantages in having micro-databases that are fully compatible with the corresponding macroeconomic accounts for sectors or the total economy. Data in the form of aggregates, or averages, often conceal a great deal of useful information about changes occurring within the populations to which they relate. For example, economic theory indicates that changes in the size of distribution of income may be expected to have an impact on aggregate consumption over and above that due to changes in the aggregate level of income. Information relating to individual units may be needed not only to obtain a better understanding of the working of the economy but also to monitor the impact of government policies, or other events, on selected types of units about which there may be special concern, such as households with very low incomes. Micro-data sets also make it possible to follow the behaviour of individual units over time. Given the continuing improvements in computers and communications, the management and analysis of very large micro-databases is becoming progressively easier. Data can be derived from a variety of different sources, such as administrative and business records, as well as specially conducted censuses and surveys.

1.65. In practice, however, macroeconomic accounts can seldom be built up by simply aggregating the relevant micro-data. Even when individual institutional units keep accounts or records the concepts that are needed or appropriate at a micro level may not be suitable at a macro level. Individual units may be obliged to use concepts designed for other purposes, such as taxation. The accounting conventions and valuation methods used at a micro level typically differ from those required by the System. For example, as already noted, the widespread use of historic cost accounting means that the accounts of individual enterprises may differ significantly from those used in the System. Depreciation as calculated for tax purposes may be quite arbitrary and unacceptable from an economic viewpoint. In such situations, it is impractical to try to adjust the individual accounts of thousands of enterprises before aggregating them. It may be much easier to adjust the data after they have been aggregated to some extent. Of course, the data do not have to be aggregated to the level of the total economy, or even complete sectors or industries, before being adjusted and it is likely to be more efficient to make the adjustments for smaller and more homogenous groups of units. This may involve compiling so-called intermediate systems of accounts. At whatever level of aggregation the adjustments are made, the inevitable consequence is to make the resulting macro-data no longer equivalent to simple aggregations of the micro-data from which they are derived. When the micro-data are not derived from business accounts or administrative records but from censuses or surveys designed for statistical purposes, the concepts used should be closer to those required, but the results may still require adjustment at a macro level because of incomplete coverage (the surveys being confined to enterprises above a certain size, for example) and bias from response errors.

1.66. Most households are unlikely to keep accounts of the kind needed by the System. Micro-data for households are typically derived from sample surveys that may be subject to significant response and reporting errors. It may be particularly difficult to obtain reliable and meaningful data about the activities of small unincorporated enterprises owned by households. Aggregates based on household surveys have to be adjusted for certain typical biases, such as the under-reporting of certain types of expenditure (on tobacco, alcoholic drink, gambling, etc.) and also to make them consistent with macrodata from other sources, such as imports. The systematic exploitation of micro-data may also be restricted by the increasing concerns about confidentiality and possible misuse of such databases.

1.67. It may be concluded therefore that, for various reasons, it may be difficult, if not impossible, to achieve micro-databases and macroeconomic accounts that are fully compatible with each other in practice. Nevertheless, as a general objective, the concepts, definitions and classifications used in economic accounting should, so far as possible, be the same at both a micro and macro level to facilitate the interface between the two kinds of data.

J. The aggregates of the system as indicators of economic activity and welfare

1. Introduction

1.68. The SNA consists of a coherent, consistent set of macroeconomic accounts and tables designed for a variety of analytical and policy purposes. Nevertheless, certain key aggregates of the System, such as GDP and GDP per head of population, have acquired an identity of their own and are widely used by analysts, politicians, the press, the business community and the public at large as summary, global indicators of economic activity and welfare. Movements of such aggregates, and their associated price and volume measures, are used to evaluate the overall performance of the economy and hence to judge the relative success or failure of economic policies pursued by Governments.

1.69. GDP is a measure of production. The level of production is important because it largely determines how much a country can afford to consume and it also affects the level of employment. The consumption of goods and services, both individually and collectively, is one of the most important factors influencing the welfare of a community, but it is only one of several factors. There are also others, such as epidemics, natural disasters or wars, that can have major negative impacts on welfare, while others, such as scientific discoveries, inventions or simply good weather, may have significant positive impacts. These factors obviously do not enter into the measurement of GDP, which refers only to the flow of goods and services produced within a given period. Thus, movements of GDP on their own cannot be expected to be good indicators of changes in total welfare unless all the other factors influencing welfare happen to remain constant, which history shows is never the case. These points are elaborated further in this section because of common misunderstandings about GDP as an indicator of welfare.

1.70. There are two aspects that need to be separated. The first is the adequacy of the main aggregates of the System as summary indicators of economic activities taking place within the economy as a whole and flows of goods and services produced or consumed. The second is the more general question of the validity of using measures of aggregate production or consumption as indicators of welfare.

2. The coverage of GDP and the role of estimates and imputations

1.71. A distinction needs to be drawn between activities such as production and consumption taking place in the economy and the transactions associated with those activities that are recorded in the accounts. As noted, transactions are interactions between institutional units, such as the exchange of ownership of a good. The physical process by which a good is produced is quite separate from the subsequent transaction in which it may be sold or supplied to another unit.

1.72. When goods and services produced are sold in monetary transactions, their values are automatically included in the accounts of the System. Many goods or services are not actually sold but are nevertheless supplied to other units: for example, they may be bartered for other goods or services or provided free as transfers in kind. Such goods and services must be included in the accounts even though their values have to be estimated. The goods or services involved are produced by activities that are no different from those used to produce goods or services for sale. Moreover, the transactions in which the goods and services are supplied to other units are also proper transactions even though the producers do not receive money in exchange. It is misleading to describe such output as "imputed". For example, the services of financial intermediaries which are indirectly measured in the System are not imputed. However, their values have to be estimated.

1.73. When goods or services are retained for own use, no transactions with other units take place. In such cases, in order to be able to record the goods or services in the accounts, internal transactions have to be imputed whereby producers allocate the goods or services for their own consumption or capital formation and values also have to be estimated for them. Nevertheless, as in the case of non-monetary transactions between units, the goods and services themselves are not imputed.

1.74. Thus, estimates and imputations are needed in order to be able to record in the accounts productive activities whose outputs are not disposed of in monetary transactions with other units. Such estimates and imputations should therefore not be interpreted as introducing hypothetical activities or flows of goods and services into the System. Their purpose is the opposite—namely, to capture in the accounts major flows of goods and services actually taking place in the economy that would otherwise be omitted. In order to obtain comprehensive measures, values have to be estimated for all outputs of goods and services that are not sold but disposed of in other ways.

1.75. In practice the System does not record all outputs, however, because domestic and personal services produced and consumed by members of the same household are omitted. Subject to this one major exception, GDP is intended to be a comprehensive measure of the total gross value added produced by all resident institutional units. GDP is, of course, confined to outputs produced by economic activities that are capable of being provided by one unit to another. Not all activities that require the expenditure of time and effort by persons are productive in an economic sense—for example, activities such as eating, drinking or sleeping cannot be produced by one person for the benefit of another. Consistent with this principle, the activity of studying and learning also does not qualify as production, as already noted. Pupils and students are consumers of the educational services produced by teachers and educational establishments.

3. Changes in welfare

1.76. In a market economy, the prices used to value different goods and services should reflect not only their relative costs of production but also the relative benefits or utilities to be derived from using them for production or consumption. This establishes the link between changes in aggregate production and consumption and changes in welfare. However, changes in the volume of consumption, for example, are not the same as changes in welfare. The distinction between the quantity of some good or service and the utility derived from consuming it is clear enough at the level of an individual good or service. For example, the quantity of sugar consumed by households is measured in physical units. It is measured quite independently of any utility that the households may, or may not, derive from consuming it.

Interaction with non-economic factors

1.77. As already noted, total welfare depends on many other factors besides the amounts of goods and services consumed. Apart from natural events such as epidemics, droughts or floods, welfare also depends on political factors, such as freedom and security. Obviously, as a measure of production, GDP is not intended to embrace non-economic events, such as political revolutions, wars, natural disasters or epidemics.

1.78. Consider the effects of an exceptionally severe winter combined with an influenza epidemic. Other things being equal, the production and consumption of a number of goods and services may be expected to rise in response to extra demands created by the cold and the epidemic; the production and consumption of fuels, clothing and medical services will tend to increase. As compared with the previous year, people may consider themselves to be worse off overall because of the exceptionally bad weather and the epidemic, notwithstanding the fact that production and consumption may have increased in response to the additional demand for heating and health services. Total welfare could fall even though GDP could increase in volume terms.

1.79. This kind of situation does not mean that welfare cannot be expected to increase as GDP increases, other things being equal. Given the occurrence of the cold and the epidemic, the community presumably finds itself much better off with the extra production and consumption of heating and health services than without them. There may even be a general tendency for production to rise to remedy the harmful effects of events that reduce people's welfare in a broad sense. For example, production may be expected to increase in order to repair the damage caused by such natural disasters as earthquakes, hurricanes and floods. Given that the disaster has occurred, the extra production presumably increases welfare.

1.80. GDP may also be expected to rise in response to disasters other than natural ones. In particular, the production and consumption of goods and services typically rises as a result of wars.

The same reasoning applies as for natural disasters. Given that a state of war exists, any consequential increase in the production and consumption of armaments or defence services may well increase welfare by affording extra protection to the community. Whether such increased welfare is sufficient to compensate for the loss of welfare caused by the war itself is quite another matter. The fact that the volume of GDP may increase as a result of the outbreak of war when the consumption of individual goods and services by households may be falling does not expose a deficiency in national accounts concepts, as is sometimes maintained. It has been argued that collective defence services should be classified as intermediate rather than final consumption, but there are in fact no further processes of production in which such services are consumed. It is clear that the total level of production in the economy is likely to rise in response to the community's increased consumption of collective defence services, even though the community would presumably prefer the output to be used for other purposes if there were no war.

1.81. Similar considerations arise with respect to so-called "regrettable necessities" in general. When production and consumption increase in order to compensate for the loss of welfare created by damage or "bads" that did not previously exist, the community may be no better off than if the damage had not occurred. However, this should not be allowed to obscure the fact that without the extra production and consumption the community would actually be worse off still. The extra production and consumption, in itself, actually increases welfare. Goods and services are consumed by households to satisfy their needs and wants. Some of these needs or wants may be created or increased by factors or events over which households have little or no control and which they may resent—bad weather, natural disasters, pollution, etc.—but this in no way diminishes the fact that they do derive benefits from consuming the goods and services in question. Quite ordinary consumer goods such as food and drink could be characterized as "regrettable necessities" which merely satisfy the recurrent basic needs of hunger and thirst without leaving the individuals any better off than before the onset of the hunger and thirst. Pushed to its logical conclusion, scarcely any consumption improves welfare in this line of argument.

Welfare, economic analysis and policy-making

1.82. Although movements in GDP and other aggregates for the total economy can be useful indicators of changes in both economic activity and welfare, the calculation of such aggregates is not the main reason for compiling national accounts. The SNA is an integrated system of accounts embracing different kinds of activities and sectors. It is intended for purposes of economic analysis, decision-taking and policy-making. It is a multi-purpose system designed to meet the requirements of different kinds of users: governments, businesses, research institutes, universities, the press and the general public. No single user, or group of users, can take priority over all others. The use of one or two aggregates to gauge changes in welfare may be one of the more important uses of the System, but it is only one use. The System is primarily intended to provide data at different levels of aggregation to meet the needs of analysts and policy makers interested in the behaviour of the economy and the factors responsible for major market disequilibria, such as inflation and unemployment. The System is inevitably a compromise intended to yield the maximum benefits to different kinds of users and may not therefore be optimal for any one purpose taken in isolation.

II. Overview

A. Introduction

2.1. This chapter provides an overall picture of the central framework of the System of National Accounts (SNA). It introduces the main categories, which are in a sense the backbone of the System, and the rules of accounting to be followed when recording the various entries. It then describes the System's accounting structure and discusses some of the ways in which the central framework may be applied flexibly, depending on specific country requirements. These presentations are based on the point of view that national accounts are an integrated system of accounts for which complete consistency is required. This is the traditional point of view on national accounting and it remains the central one. Thereafter, the chapter proceeds from a second point of view, one that regards national accounts as a set of interrelated subsystems, each of which is fully consistent internally and all of which, although differing from one another in some aspects, are compatible in a loose sense. Satellite accounts are introduced. These are constructs that are semi-integrated with the central framework.

2.2. As stated in chapter I, the central framework describes the essential phenomena which constitute economic life: production, income, consumption, accumulation and wealth. It provides an understandable and simplified but complete representation of this set of phenomena and their interrelations.

2.3. The central framework is an integrated system. That is, the same concepts, definitions and classifications are applied to all accounts and sub-accounts. For example, all dwellings are treated as assets used to produce goods and services. As a consequence, all housing services, whether sold or consumed by the owners, are included within the production boundary, and all of the corresponding income originating from the production of housing services appears in the System in the same accounts using the same definitions and classifications.

2.4. Nevertheless, integrated does not mean restricted to a single point of view. The central framework includes several points of view—for example, stocks and flows, the nature of transactions and the purposes of transactions, institutional units and establishment-type units, market output, output produced for own final use and other non-market output, consumption expenditure and actual consumption. All of them are mutually consistent.

2.5. The central framework is also consistent. That is, each economic flow or stock is measured identically for the parties involved. This consistency is achieved by applying throughout the System the same concepts and definitions and also by using a single set of accounting rules for all entries in the System. Of course, the actual data coming from the accounts or statistics provided by elementary units will not be fully consistent for various reasons. In practice, achieving consistency in national accounts requires a large amount of additional work.

2.6. Integration and consistency are basic requirements originating from the fundamental characteristics of economic life and coherent accounting. These features allow the central framework to serve as a basis for the coordination of economic, and in part social, statistics.

1. Analysing flows and stocks

2.7. Basically, the purpose of a system of national accounts is to record economic flows and stocks. Economic flows can be thought of in various ways. Consider the question "Who does what?" "Who" refers to the economic agent engaged in doing something, the operator. "What" is connected with the kind of action this agent is undertaking. In a few cases, the answer to this simple question provides a good preliminary characterization of an economic flow.

2.8. But in general the question is too simple to provide even a rough economic description of a specific flow. Take the example of somebody buying a loaf of bread. In order to characterize the flow, it is necessary to consider from whom this loaf of bread is bought (a retailer or a supermarket) and what is given in exchange (a coin or a note). So the starting question is transformed into "Who does what with whom in exchange for what?" This rather simple flow involves two operators (a buyer, a seller), two main actions (a purchase, a sale), two secondary actions (a payment, a receipt) and two objects (bread, a coin or a note). Again, a complete description would require more information: at least the weight, kind and price of the bread.

2.9. The picture in the real world is still more complicated. Before this flow occurred, the seller had a certain quantity of bread in his shop; afterward he has less bread but more money. The buyer had a certain amount of money, now he has less money but some bread (before eating it). So the flow between them has changed their initial situations. This means that flows cannot be looked at in isolation; the situations before and after a flow occurs need to be considered. At those two points in time, one must ask the question "Who has what?" The baker not only has bread and currency, he also has a house with the shop, a kneading-trough, some flour, a deposit in a bank, a car, etc. In other words, he has (he owns) a certain stock of objects. The same is true for the buyer. In addition to what they are in themselves, flows modify stocks. Flows and changes in stocks are intrinsically connected. The previous question is again transformed into "Who does what with whom in exchange for what with what changes in stocks?"

2.10. However, the various ways of looking at this example have not yet been exhausted. Before the baker can sell bread, he has to bake it. He uses flour, water, electricity, a kneading-trough, etc. So, an additional question is "Who does what by what means?" What he does can also be characterized in two ways: his activity (to bake) and the result of it (a product: bread).

2.11. With respect to the buyer one can ask "Why does he buy bread?" The obvious purpose is for eating it, as food; however, it could be different— for giving it to a beggar, as charity. This raises the question "Who does what for what purpose?"

2.12. Mixing all the questions together results in a rather complex combination of simple links: "Who does what by what means for what purpose with whom in exchange for what with what changes in stocks?" Answering these questions for all economic flows and stocks and operators in a given economy would provide an enormous amount of information describing the complete network of economic interrelations. However, it would require an enormous amount of basic data, which are not always available, nor complete (i.e., they cover only certain aspects of the complex chain of questions). In addition, it is necessary to organize the recording of economic flows and stocks in an intelligible way, as discussed in the next section. It will become apparent that full articulation of all the questions raised by the analysis of economic flows is not necessary.

2. Recording flows and stocks

2.13. Users' needs set certain requirements for the accounting framework. First, it should provide a picture of the economy, but the picture, to be intelligible and manageable, must be simplified. Secondly, it should faithfully represent economic life by covering all important aspects in a balanced way without neglecting or giving too little emphasis to some aspects or giving others too much prominence. Finally, it should portray all significant economic behaviour, interrelations and the results of economic activity. Although meeting these requirements is necessary, they are contradictory to a certain extent. Achieving the right balance among them is not easy. Too great a simplification can lose sight of or neglect important aspects of economic life. Too close a portrayal of reality can overburden the picture and reduce insight. Too much sophistication can lower intelligibility and mislead some users, and so on.

2.14. To meet these requirements, the System uses, first, a limited number of basic categories to analyse and aggregate certain aspects (Who? What? What purpose? What stocks?) of the very numerous elementary flows. This is explained briefly in the next part of this chapter and in detail in the relevant chapters. Secondly, the System simplifies the picture it gives of the economic interrelations by not recording systematically the "who with whom?" question; that is, it does not depict the network of flows between the various types of operators. However, the "who with whom?" relation, which is not introduced in the accounting framework, is obvious in a number of cases and recommended in practice in some others. Also, the System does not record at all the "what in exchange for what?" question; that is, it does not indicate, for example, the specific nature of the financial counterpart (currency or deposit or short-term loan, etc.) of the purchases of goods and services or the payment of taxes.

2.15. Thus, in lieu of showing the network of direct economic relations between pairs of operators, the System is structured to avoid the need to record relations between pairs of operators and to make it sufficient to record each type of relation between a given operator (or group of operators) and all the other operators indiscriminately. The dummy, or screen, accounts that accomplish this objective are presented below in paragraphs 2.152 and 2.154 to 2.160.

2.16. The fact that the System is integrated, although not fully articulated, does not reduce its consistency requirements. In effect, the purpose of the System is to get national accounts that are as consistent as they would be if they were fully articulated; each economic flow or stock should be measured identically for both parties involved. The consistency in the System is achieved by applying throughout the same concepts and definitions and also by using a single strict set of accounting rules. These accounting rules are also presented briefly in section C below and more completely in chapter III.

2.17. The recording of flows and stocks is made in accounts, each account referring to a certain aspect of economic life. National accounts may be presented in several ways. The System mainly follows the classical presentation in the form of balancing statements with incomings on one side and outgoings on the other side. The accounts of the System are described in section D of this chapter and, with more detail, in each relevant chapter. The other main way of presenting the accounts is a matrix, in which each account is represented by a row and column pair. The matrix presentation is introduced in the annex to this chapter (and is used systematically in social accounting matrices, which are discussed in chapter XX). The annex also introduces presentations in the form of diagrams and equations.

B. Main categories

2.18. The SNA contains a number of classifications which in a sense constitute the skeleton of the System and permit various aspects of the questions raised above to be answered:

> Institutional units and sectors (who?)
>
> Transactions and other flows (what?)
>
> Assets and liabilities (what stocks?)
>
> Activities, establishments, products (other aspects of who and what?)
>
> Purposes (what for?).

They are presented in turn.

1. Institutional units and sectors

2.19. The fundamental units identified are the economic units which are capable of owning assets and incurring liabilities on their own behalf. They can engage in the full range of transactions. These units are called *institutional units*. In addition, being centres of legal responsibility, institutional units are centres of decision-making for all aspects of economic life. In practice, some institutional units control others and thus in such cases autonomy of decision is not total and may vary over time. Legally independent holding of assets and liabilities and autonomous behaviour do not always coincide. In the System, preference is generally given to the first aspect because it provides a better way to organize the collection and presentation of statistics even if its usefulness is limited in some cases.

Institutional sectors

2.20. The institutional units are grouped together to form institutional sectors, on the basis of their principal functions, behaviour, and objectives:

> *Non-financial corporations*: institutional units which are principally engaged in the production of market goods and non-financial services
>
> *Financial corporations*: institutional units which are principally engaged in financial intermediation or in auxiliary financial activities
>
> *General government*: institutional units which, in addition to fulfilling their political responsibilities and their role of economic regulation, produce principally non-market services (possibly goods) for individual or collective consumption and redistribute income and wealth
>
> *Households*: all physical persons in the economy, with the institutional unit in the household sector consisting of one individual or a group of individuals. According to the criteria given for defining the institutional unit, the household of the owner of an unincorporated enterprise in general includes this enterprise, which is not consid-

ered an institutional unit (except under certain conditions). The principal functions of households are the supply of labour, final consumption and, as entrepreneurs, the production of market goods and non-financial (possibly financial) services

> *Non-profit institutions serving households (NPISHs)*: legal entities which are principally engaged in the production of non-market services for households and whose main resources are voluntary contributions by households.

2.21. Each sector, except NPISHs, contains a number of sub-sectors (with various levels) distinguished according to a hierarchical classification (see chapter IV). A sub-sector comprises entire institutional units, and each institutional unit belongs to only one sub-sector. In addition, the distinction between public, national private and foreign controlled corporations and between various socio-economic groups of households is emphasized in the System in order to respond to policy concerns.

Delimitation of the total economy and the rest of the world

2.22. The total economy is defined in terms of institutional units. It consists of all the institutional units which are resident in the economic territory of a country. The economic territory of a country, although consisting essentially of the geographical territory, does not coincide exactly; some additions and subtractions are made (see chapter XIV). The concept of residence in the System is not based on nationality or legal criteria. An institutional unit is said to be a resident unit of a country when it has a centre of economic interest in the economic territory of that country—that is, when it engages for an extended period (one year or more being taken as a practical guideline) in economic activities on this territory. The institutional sectors referred to above are groups of resident units.

2.23. Resident units engage in transactions with non-resident units (that is, units which are residents of other economies). These transactions are the external transactions of the economy and are grouped in the account of the rest of the world. Strictly speaking, the rest of the world is the account of transactions occurring between resident and non-resident units, but it may also be seen as the whole of non-resident units that enter into transactions with resident units. So, in the System's accounting structure, the rest of the world plays a role similar to that of an institutional sector, although non-resident units are included only in so far as they are engaged in transactions with resident institutional units. Consequently, as far as coding of classifications is concerned, a specific item for the rest of the world is included at the end of the classification of sectors.

2. Transactions and other flows

2.24. Institutional units and their members fulfil various economic functions; that is, they produce, consume, save, invest, etc. They engage in various economic activities (agriculture, manufacturing, etc.) as entrepreneurs or wage-earners or suppliers of capital, or they are unemployed. In all aspects of their economic functions and activities, they undertake a great number of elementary economic actions. These actions result in economic flows, which, in addition to their specific nature (wages, taxes, fixed capital formation) create, transform, exchange, transfer or extinguish economic value; they involve changes in the volume, composition or value of an institutional unit's assets or liabilities. The economic value may take the form of ownership rights on concrete objects (a loaf of bread, a dwelling) or intangible assets (a film original) or of financial claims (liabilities being understood as negative economic value). In all cases, it represents a certain quantum of abstract economic value which is potentially usable to acquire goods or services, pay wages or taxes, etc.

2.25. Most economic actions are undertaken by mutual agreement between institutional units. They are either an exchange of economic value or a voluntary transfer by one unit to another of a certain amount of economic value without a counterpart. These actions undertaken by mutual agreement between two institutional units are called transactions in the System. The System also treats as transactions certain economic actions involving only a single institutional unit which are similar in nature to actions undertaken by mutual agreement by two different institutional units, such as own-account fixed capital formation. They are internal, or intra-unit, transactions.

2.26. However, not all economic flows are transactions. For example, certain actions undertaken unilaterally by one institutional unit have consequences on other institutional units(s) without the latter's consent. The System records such actions only to a limited extent, essentially when governments or other institutional units take possession of the assets of other institutional units, including non-resident units, without full compensation. In real life, unilateral economic actions bearing consequences, either positively or negatively, on other economic units (externalities) are much broader. However, such externalities are not recorded in the System. Also, human action may result in the transfer of natural assets to economic activities and the subsequent transformation of these assets. These phenomena are recorded in the System as economic flows, changing the amount of economic value. Moreover, non-economic phenomena, such as wars and natural disasters, may destroy economic assets, and this extinction of economic value must be accounted for. Also, the value of economic assets and liabilities may change during the time they are held as stocks, as a consequence of changes in prices. These and similar flows that are not transactions, which are called other economic flows in the System, are described in chapter XII.

2.27. The economic flows can be actual, observable flows or they can be built up or estimated for analytical purposes. Certain flows may be directly observed in value terms. This is the case for monetary transactions between two institutional units, such as a purchase/sale of a good or the payment of a tax. Other two-unit flows are observable but cannot be immediately valued. These flows include barter of goods and services or education services consumed by students and provided free of charge by government; a value in money terms has to be attributed to them. Both of these types of two-unit transactions may or may not involve a "quid pro quo"—that is, a flow in one direction is linked to a counterpart flow in the opposite direction. Barter is an example of a two-unit flow involving a quid pro quo; a social assistance benefit in cash is a two-unit flow that does not involve a quid pro quo. Another kind of flow involves only one institutional unit. They may be physically observable, as in the case of output, own-account consumption or capital formation, or destruction by natural catastrophes. A value has to be attributed to them (this may be fairly easy in certain cases, such as when output is mostly sold). Other intra-unit, or internal, flows may not be observable as such; accounting entries are then constructed for the sake of measuring economic performance correctly. This is the case for the consumption of fixed capital or the revaluation of assets and liabilities. Certain inter-units flows, like the reinvested earnings on direct foreign investment, are also accounting entries created for analytical purposes. Finally, some observable monetary transactions are not recorded as they are observed in practice because they are of a composite nature (nominal interest, total insurance premiums) or their legal nature does not correspond to their economic one (financial leasing). Consequently, for the System, they are split up into various components and/or their classification and routing is modified.

2.28. In modern market economies, most transactions are monetary and take place between different institutional units. They constitute the fundamental basis for valuing flows in national accounts. The relative importance of non-monetary transactions varies according to the type of economy and the objectives pursued by the accounting system. It is generally greater for less developed economies than for developed ones, in which, however, it is not negligible.

Main types of transactions and other flows

2.29. Elementary transactions and other flows are innumerable. They are grouped into a relatively small number of types according to their nature. The System's main classification of transactions and other flows includes four first-level types, with each subdivided according to a hierarchical classification. It is designed to be used systematically in the accounts and tables of the central framework and cross-classified with institutional sectors, industry and product, and purpose classifications.

2.30. *Transactions in goods and services (products)* describe the origin (domestic output or imports) and use (intermediate consumption, final consumption, capital formation or exports) of goods and services. By definition, goods and services in the System are always a result of production, either domestically or abroad, in the current period or in a previous one. The term products is thus a synonym for goods and services.

2.31. *Distributive transactions* consist of transactions by which the value added generated by production is distributed to labour, capital and government and of transactions involving the redistribution of income and wealth (taxes on income and wealth and other transfers). The System draws a distinction between current and capital transfers, with the latter deemed to redistribute saving or wealth rather than income (see chapter VIII).

2.32. *Transactions in financial instruments* (or financial transactions) refer to the net acquisition of financial assets or the net incurrence of liabilities for each type of financial instrument. Such changes often occur as counterparts of non-financial transactions. They also occur as transactions involving only financial instruments. Transactions in contingent assets and liabilities are not considered transactions in the SNA (see chapter XI).

2.33. *Other accumulation entries* cover transactions and other economic flows not taken into account before which change the quantity or value of assets and liabilities. First, they include consumption of fixed capital and acquisitions less disposals of non-produced non-financial assets. Then, they cover other economic flows of non-produced assets, such as discovery or depletion of subsoil resources or transfers of other natural assets to economic activities. They also cover the effects of non-economic phenomena such as natural catastrophes and political events (wars for example). Finally, they include holding gains or losses, due to changes in prices, and some minor items (see chapter XII).

Characteristics of transactions in the System

2.34. In order to provide more useful answers to the questions raised in the analysis of flows, some transactions are not recorded in the System as they might be directly observed. First, the System often uses categories which are more closely identified with an economic concept. For example, gross fixed capital formation, a sub-category of transactions in goods and services, is broader than the limited coverage thought of as "purchases of fixed assets". In order to be closer to an economic concept, it covers the acquisition of new and existing fixed assets, through purchases, barter transactions, own-account capital formation or investment grants received in kind, less the disposal of existing assets, through sales, barter transactions or investment grants made in kind.

2.35. Secondly, as the previous example shows, the System also often uses categories which are compacted, that is, are the result of combining a number of elementary transactions. "Changes in inventories", for example, is the difference be-

tween entries into and withdrawals from inventories and recurrent losses. The same netting happens for transactions in financial instruments. All transactions in an instrument held as an asset (or as a liability) are grouped under the heading of this instrument. The item "loans", for example, covers issuance of new loans, conversions, and redemptions or cancellations of existing loans. Finally, some categories of transactions in the System, such as distributive transactions concerning interest and net non-life insurance premiums, require an actual transaction to be split into parts.

2.36. Although monetary transactions have a basic role in the valuation of flows in the System, non-monetary transactions are also significant. They include flows of goods and services that take place between institutional units for which values have to be estimated and also some flows that are assumed to take place within units. It is often desirable, therefore, to show monetary transactions separately from non-monetary in the broad sense, with in-kind transactions as an additional sub-category.

Complementary classification of transactions and other flows

2.37. Since introducing all relevant distinctions throughout the classification of transactions and other flows would overburden the picture, the System provides a complementary classification to facilitate additional presentations and analysis. The complementary classification is not intended for regular use but for use when a more detailed analysis of certain accounts or of certain transactions is needed and when users need help in understanding the results. Moreover, it is not intended to limit the extension of national complementary classifications: the latter may indeed have a broader coverage, according to specific needs.

2.38. The complementary classification of transactions and other flows shows, first, a number of transactions in kind explicitly, such as own-account final consumption, barter transactions and wages and salaries in kind. Secondly, it shows the components of compacted flows, such as output and intermediate consumption. Also, it includes observed composite transactions, such as nominal interest or total insurance premiums, that are split into components for use in the System. Finally, it provides additional details and complements. As stressed in chapter XIX, countries are invited to use both the main and complementary classifications in a flexible way. In particular, they may want to subdivide some headings of the main classification to analyse specific transactions; the complementary classification provides a useful reference.

2.39. The main and complementary classifications are in annex V at the end of this manual.

3. Assets and liabilities

2.40. Assets and liabilities are the components of the balance sheets of the total economy and institutional sectors. In contrast to the accounts that show economic flows, a balance sheet shows the stocks of assets and liabilities held at one point in time by each unit or sector or the economy as a whole. However, stocks are connected with flows: they result from the accumulation of prior transactions and other flows, and they are modified by future transactions and other flows. Generally recorded at the point in time when an inventory is drawn up, they result in fact from a continuum of entries and withdrawals, plus some changes, either in substance or in value, occurring during the period a given asset or liability is held. Thus stocks and flows are closely related.

2.41. The coverage of assets is limited to those assets which are subject to ownership rights and from which economic benefits may be derived by their owners by holding them or using them in economic activity as defined in the System. Most consumer durables, human capital, culture as such and natural resources that are not capable of bringing economic benefits to their owners are outside the scope of assets in the System.

2.42. The classification of assets distinguishes, at the first level, financial and non-financial (produced and non-produced) assets (see chapter X). Most non-financial assets generally serve two purposes. They are primarily objects usable in economic activity and, at the same time, serve as stores of value. Financial assets are directly stores of value, although they may also fulfil other functions.

4. Producing units and products

Producing units

2.43. Institutional units such as corporations may produce various types of goods and services. These goods and services result from processes of production which may differ as regards materials and supplies consumed, kind of equipment and labour employed and techniques used. In other words, they may come from different economic activities.

2.44. To study production and production functions in detail, it is necessary to refer to more homogeneous units. The ideal solution would be to delineate, among institutional units, units which would be totally homogeneous—that is, engaged in only one economic activity—and observable. In practice, it is not always feasible to distinguish, inside multi-activity units, units of production engaged in a single activity and for which the necessary data are available so that some secondary activities that cannot be separated are covered. For that reason, the SNA uses for the detailed study of production a unit which, in addition to its principal activity, may cover secondary activities. As it is also necessary to give a picture of the distribution of production in space, this unit also has to be in a single location or nearby sites. This unit is the establishment.

2.45. Establishments that have the same principal activity are grouped in industries according to the International Standard Industrial Classification of All Economic Activities (ISIC, Revision 3).

2.46. Given the fundamental role played by the market in modern economies, the SNA distinguishes, as an essential feature of its structure, between establishments which are market producers, producers for own final use and other non-market producers. Market establishments produce mostly goods and services for sale at prices which are economically significant. Producers for own final use produce mostly goods and services for final consumption or fixed capital formation by the owners of the enterprises in which they are produced. Other non-market establishments supply most of the goods and services they produce without charge or at prices which are not economically significant.

2.47. There is a hierarchical relationship between institutional units and establishments. An institutional unit contains one or more entire establishment(s), either market, producers for own final use or other non-market. An establishment belongs to one and only one institutional unit.

2.48. For more refined analysis of the production process, use is made of an analytical unit of production. This unit, which is not always observable, is the unit of homogeneous production, defined as covering no secondary activities. These units constitute homogeneous activities.

Products

2.49. Goods and services, also called *products*, are the result of production. They are exchanged and used for various purposes: as inputs in the production of other goods and services, as final consumption or for investment. Here again the SNA makes a conceptual distinction between market, own final use and other non-market goods and services, allowing in principle any kind of good or service to be either type. In order to study transactions in goods and services in detail, the System uses the Central Product Classification (CPC).

5. Purposes

2.50. The concept of purpose, or function, relates to the type of need a transaction or group of transactions aims to satisfy or the kind of objective it pursues. Transactions are first analysed in the System according to their nature. Then, for certain sectors or kind of transactions, they are analysed from the expenditure side, by purpose, answering the earlier question "for what purpose?" In any analysis by purpose, the transaction or group of transactions is, in principle, the statistical unit to which a classification is applied. The classifications used in the System are described in chapter XVIII.

2.51. In the case of households, consumption expenditure and/or actual consumption are traditionally classified by purpose in household surveys and national accounts. Such analysis may cover other parts of household accounts, like fixed capital formation, interest paid and some transfers. All expenditure by NPISHs is broken down by purpose.

2.52. For government, the analysis by purpose applies to all transactions except, in most instances, to transactions in financial claims and interest on the public debt.

2.53. Normally, the analysis by purpose of market goods and services has to be made from the users' side. A market producer is normally not directly concerned with the purpose for which a purchase is made, even if the purpose is of interest for market

research. For market producers, the problem is different: in some instances producers may incur costs (intermediate, labour, capital) which contribute to market prices but serve a purpose that is different from the one the market good or service itself is destined to satisfy. This is the case, for example, for expenditures for environmental protection or employee training. The System provides for additional analysis in this connection.

C. Rules of accounting

1. Introduction

Terminology for the two sides of the accounts

2.54. The SNA utilizes the term *resources* for the side of the current accounts where transactions which add to the amount of economic value of a unit or a sector appear. For example, wages and salaries are a resource for the unit or sector receiving them. Resources are by convention put on the right side. The left side of the accounts, which relates to transactions that reduce the amount of economic value of a unit or sector, is termed *uses*. To continue the example, wages and salaries are a use for the unit or sector that must pay them.

2.55. Balance sheets are presented with *liabilities and net worth* (the difference between assets and liabilities) on the right side and *assets* on the left. Comparing two successive balance sheets, one gets changes in liabilities and net worth and changes in assets.

2.56. The accumulation accounts and balance sheets being fully integrated, the right side of the accumulation accounts is called *changes in liabilities and net worth* and their left side is called *changes in assets*. In the case of transactions in financial instruments, the changes in liabilities are often referred to as (net) incurrence of liabilities and the changes in assets as (net) acquisition of financial assets.

Double entry/quadruple entry

2.57. For a unit or sector, national accounting is based on the principle of double entry, as in business accounting. Each transaction must be recorded twice, once as a resource (or a change in liabilities) and once as a use (or a change in assets). The total of transactions recorded as resources or changes in liabilities and the total of transactions recorded as uses or changes in assets must be equal, thus permitting a check of the consistency of the accounts. Economic flows that are not transactions have their counterpart directly as changes in net worth, by construction. This is shown in section D below (and also in chapter XII, which describes the other changes in volume of assets account and the revaluation account).

2.58. The implications of the double entry principle are easy to

grasp in a number of cases: a household's purchase on credit of a consumer good will appear as a use under final consumption expenditure and as an incurrence of a liability under loans, for example. If this good is paid for in cash, however, the picture is less simple: the counterpart of a use under final consumption is now a negative acquisition of assets, under currency and deposits, for instance. Other transactions are even more complicated. Output of goods is recorded as a resource in the account of a producer, its counterpart among uses is recorded as a positive change in inventories. When the output is sold, there is a negative change in inventories—that is, a negative acquisition of assets—balanced by a positive acquisition of assets, for instance under currency and deposits.

2.59. In many instances, as explained earlier, the difficulty of seeing how the double entry principle applies is due to the fact that the categories of transactions in the System are compacted.

2.60. In principle, national accounts—with all units and all sectors—are based on a principle of quadruple entry, because most transactions involve two institutional units. Each transaction of this type must be recorded twice by the two transactors involved. For example, a social benefit in cash paid by a government unit to a household is recorded in the accounts of government as a use under the relevant type of transfers and a negative acquisition of assets under currency and deposits; in the accounts of the household sector, it is recorded as a resource under transfers and an acquisition of assets under currency and deposits.

2.61. The principle of quadruple entry does not imply that the relations between sectors (from whom to whom?) are directly shown in the accounts. Recording correctly the four transactions involved results in full consistency.

2.62. Although these accounting principles are the conceptual basis for the consistency of national accounts, national accounting cannot always take advantage of them in practice. The accounts of the nation are not kept in the same way as a business unit or government—that is, by actually recording all flows occurring in a given period. They rely on accounts of various units that are not always consistent, complete or even available. For household accounts in particular, other statistics such as those from household surveys have to be used. However, the quadruple entry principle remains fundamental.

2. Time of recording

2.63. One implication of the quadruple entry principle is that transactions, or other flows, when relevant, have to be recorded at the same point of time in the various accounts in question for both units involved. The same applies to stocks of financial assets and liabilities.

2.64. The general principle in national accounting is that transactions between institutional units have to be recorded when claims and obligations arise, are transformed or are cancelled—that is, on an accrual basis. Transactions internal to one institutional unit are equivalently recorded when economic value is created, transformed or extinguished. Generally speaking, all transactions, apart from their intrinsic nature, can always be viewed as dealing with economic value.

2.65. One has thus to distinguish carefully between a transaction and the corresponding cash movement which takes place, except for a transaction in kind, at a given point of time. Even when a transaction (a purchase/sale of a good, for example) and the payment/receipt are simultaneous, the two aspects exist. The purchaser is incurring a liability, the seller acquiring a claim as a counterpart of the delivery of the good. Then liability and claim are cancelled by the payment. In most cases there is a delay between the actual transaction and the corresponding payment/receipt. In principle, national accounts record actual transactions, not on a cash basis, but on an accrual basis. Conceptually they follow the same principle as business accounting.

2.66. If the principle is clear, its implementation is far from simple. Institutional units do not always apply the same rules. Even when they do, differences in actual recording may occur for practical reasons such as delays in communication. Consequently, transactions may be recorded at different times by the transactors involved, sometimes not even in the same accounting period. Discrepancies exist which national accounts must eliminate by after-the-fact adjustments. In addition, because the time at which a claim/liability arises is not always unambiguous, further implementation problems arise. The rules and conventions adopted in the System for particular transactions are specified in the relevant chapters (see also chapter III).

3. Valuation

General principles

2.67. Again, following the quadruple entry principle, a transaction must be recorded at the same value through all the accounts of both sectors involved. The same principle applies to assets and liabilities. It means that a financial asset and its liability counterpart have to be recorded for the same amount in the creditor and the debtor accounts.

2.68. Transactions are valued at the actual price agreed upon by the transactors. Market prices are thus the basic reference for valuation in the System. In the absence of market transactions, valuation is made according to costs incurred (non-market services produced by government) or by reference to market prices for analogous goods or services (services of owner-occupied dwellings).

2.69. Assets and liabilities are valued at current prices at the time to which the balance sheet relates, not at their original prices. Theoretically, national accounts are based on the assumption that assets and liabilities are continuously revalued at current prices, even if estimates are in fact made only periodically. The appropriate valuation basis for assets and liabilities is the price at which they might be bought in markets at the time the valuation is required. Prices observed in markets or estimated from observed market prices should preferably be used. Current prices may be approximated for balance sheet valuation in two other ways: by accumulating and revaluing transactions over time or by estimating the discounted present value of future returns expected from a given asset (see also chapter XIII).

2.70. Internal transactions are valued at current prices at the time these transactions occur, not at original prices. These internal transactions include entries in inventories, withdrawals from inventories, intermediate consumption and consumption of fixed capital.

Methods of valuation

2.71. Various methods of treating taxes on products, subsidies, and trade and transport margins in valuing transactions on products (goods and services) exist. For the sake of integrating the System, the same methods are followed in the institutional sector accounts and the central supply and use tables (see section D below).

2.72. The preferred method of valuation of output is at basic prices, although producers' prices may be used when valuation at basic prices is not feasible. The distinction is related to the treatment of taxes and subsidies on products. Basic prices are prices before taxes on products are added and subsidies on products are subtracted. Producers' prices include, in addition to basic prices, taxes less subsidies on products other than value added type taxes. This means, to be specific, that three valuations of output may be encountered: at basic prices, at producers' prices in the absence of value added type taxes, and at producers' prices in the presence of value added type taxes.[1]

2.73. In the same set of accounts and tables, all transactions on the uses of goods and services (like final consumption, intermediate consumption, capital formation) are valued at purchasers' prices. Purchasers' prices are the amounts paid by the purchasers, excluding the deductible part of value added type taxes. Purchasers' prices are the actual costs to the users.

2.74. The various methods of valuing output, with intermediate consumption always at purchasers' prices, imply consequences for the content and uses of value added (the difference between output and intermediate consumption) by a producer or a sector or an industry. In the same set of accounts and tables, uses of value added at basic prices include, besides primary incomes to labour and capital, only taxes less subsidies on production other than taxes less subsidies on products; uses of value added at producers' prices include, in addition, taxes, less subsidies, on products other than value added type taxes (which means all taxes, less subsidies, on products[2] when value added type taxes do not exist). A complementary definition of value added is at factor cost, which excludes taxes on production of any kind.

2.75. When looking at the economy as a whole, that part of taxes on products (less subsidies) not included in value added is added to the sum of value added of all producers (either institutional sectors or industries) in order to reach the main aggregate of product and income generated in the economy.

2.76. Other methods of valuation may be used in other versions of the supply and use tables and symmetric input-output tables. In particular, valuation at basic prices may be used for output, when not already done in the central supply and use tables, and for uses of goods and services detailed by product. (In the latter case, an additional row for taxes, less subsidies, on products is introduced to get, for each type of use, the total at purchasers' prices.) Another alternative valuation of uses by product excludes trade and transport margins, the latter being directly channelled to the users.

Volume measures and measures in real terms

2.77. To this point, only current prices have been described. In addition, the System emphasizes calculation at constant prices, that is, use of the system(s) of prices which prevailed in a past period(s). The changes over time in the current values of flows of goods and services and of many kinds of assets can be decomposed into changes in the prices of these goods and services or assets and changes in their volumes. Flows or stocks at constant prices take into account the changes in the price of each item covered. They are said to be in *volume* terms. However, many flows or stocks do not have price and quantity dimensions of their own. Their current values may be deflated by taking into account the change in the prices of some relevant basket of goods and services or assets, or the change in the general price level. In that case, flows or stocks are said to be in *real* terms (at constant purchasing power). For example, the System provides for the calculation of income in real terms.

2.78. Inter-spatial comparisons raise similar but even more complex problems than inter-temporal comparisons. The additional difficulty is due mainly to the fact that many countries are involved. Purchasing power parities (the ratios between prices prevailing in various countries) are calculated and indicators of relations in volume between various groups of items and national aggregates for different countries are obtained by using a great many elementary calculations at prices constant-in-space.

2.79. Both inter-temporal and inter-spatial measures are discussed in chapter XVI.

4. Consolidation and netting

2.80. Consolidation may cover various accounting procedures. In general, it refers to the elimination, both from uses and resources, of transactions which occur between units when the latter are grouped and to the elimination of reciprocal financial assets and liabilities.

2.81. For institutional units, normally only transactions with other institutional units are recorded. However, when it is necessary to give meaningful measures of economic phenomena, the System records internal flows. This is done for consumption of fixed capital and for output used for own final uses. As regards internal intermediate uses, the System follows a convention: deliveries among technical units of an establishment are consolidated with the corresponding output, but deliveries among establishments belonging to the same enterprise are not. Consequently, output and intermediate consumption, once measured at the establishment level, are not modified whatever level of aggregation is used.

2.82. For sub-sectors or sectors, flows between constituent units are not consolidated as a matter of principle. However, consolidated accounts may be built up for complementary presentations and analyses. This may be useful, for example, for the government sector as a whole, thus showing the net relations between government and the rest of the economy. Even then, transactions appearing in different accounts are never consolidated to avoid changing the balancing items.

2.83. Accounts for the total economy, when fully consolidated, give rise to the rest of the world account (external transactions account).

2.84. Consolidation must be distinguished from netting. For current transactions, netting refers, outside the context of consolidation of various units, to offsetting uses against resources. The System does this only in a few specific presentations; for example, taxes on products may be shown net of subsidies on products. For changes in assets or changes in liabilities, netting may be envisaged in two ways. First, various types of changes in assets (for example, entries in inventories and withdrawals from inventories) or various types of liabilities (for example, incurrence of a new debt and redemption of an existing debt) are netted. Secondly, by changes in financial assets and changes in liabilities (or, in the balance sheet, financial assets and liabilities themselves) related to a given financial instrument are netted. As a matter of principle, the System discourages netting beyond the degree shown in the classifications of the System. Netting financial assets (changes in financial assets) against liabilities (changes in liabilities) is especially to be avoided. Netting is discussed in chapters III and XI.

D. The accounts

1. Introduction

2.85. With the tools introduced in sections B and C above, all flows and stocks can be recorded. This is done in the accounts of the System. An account is a tool which records, for a given aspect of economic life, the uses and resources or the changes in assets and the changes in liabilities and/or the stock of assets and liabilities existing at a certain time.

2.86. Accounts can be built up for the categories presented in section B above:

Institutional units and sectors

Transactions

Rest of the world (external transactions)

Assets and liabilities

Establishments and industries

Products

Purposes.

2.87. For units (institutional units; establishments) or groups of units (institutional sectors and, by extension, the rest of the world; industries), different sub-accounts record the transactions or other flows which are connected to some specific aspect of the economic life (for instance, production). Such a set of transactions usually does not balance; the total amounts recorded as receivable and payable usually differ. Therefore, a balancing item must be introduced. Usually, a balancing item must also be introduced between the total of assets and the total of liabilities of an institutional unit or sector. Balancing items are meaningful measures of economic performance in themselves. When summed up for the whole economy, they constitute significant aggregates.

2.88. Before entering into the details of the accounts, it is useful to survey the structure of the central framework. This can be done by looking at figure 2.1. The central framework thus consists of the following:

(a) The integrated economic accounts in which are presented the full set of accounts of institutional sectors and the rest of the world, together with the accounts for transactions (and other flows) and the accounts for assets and liabilities; it is worth noting at this preliminary stage that the relations between sectors ("from whom to whom?") are not directly depicted in this table;

(b) The supply and use table in which are integrated the accounts of industries, according to kind of economic ac-

Figure 2.1. Survey of the central framework

Integrated economic accounts
Institutional sectors and rest of the world
×
Accounts
×
Transactions and other flows
×
Assets/liabilities

Supply and use table
Accounts of industries by kind of economic activity
. . .
Accounts of transactions in goods and services by type of products
. . .

Three-dimensional analysis of:
Financial transactions
Institutional sectors
×
Institutional sectors
×
Transactions in types of financial assets and liabilities
Stocks of financial assets and liabilities
Institutional sectors
×
Institutional sectors
×
Types of fiancial assets and liabilities

Functional analysis
Institutional sectors
×
Purposes
×
Transactions

Population and employment tables

Note—"×" indicates "cross-classified by".

tivity, and the accounts of transactions in goods and services, according to type of product;

(c) The three-dimensional analysis of financial transactions and stocks of financial assets and liabilities, in which the relations between sectors ("from whom to whom?") are directly depicted;

(d) The functional analysis, in which certain transactions of

Figure 2.2 Integrated economic accounts (simplified presentation)

Goods and services	Rest of the world	Total economy	Institutional sectors	Transactions balancing items, assets and liabilities	Institutional sectors	Total economy	Rest of the world	Goods and services
Current accounts								
Uses					Resources			
Accumulation accounts								
Changes in assets					Changes in liablities and net worth			
Balance sheets								
Assets					Liabilities and net worth			

institutional sectors are presented according to the purpose they serve;

(e)   The population and employment tables.

2.89. These various blocks, which altogether constitute the central framework, are interlinked in various ways that are described later. They are fully consistent because they use the same set of concepts, definitions, classifications and accounting rules.

2.90. Two sections are devoted successively to:

(a)   The integrated economic accounts and their components; and

(b)   The other parts of the accounting structure.

2. The integrated economic accounts and their components

2.91. This section starts with a preliminary view of the integrated economic accounts. Then it presents:

(a)   The full sequence of accounts for institutional units and sectors and their balancing items;

(b)   The transactions accounts;

(c)   The assets and liabilities accounts;

(d)   The rest of the world accounts;

(e)   The aggregates; and

(f)   The integrated economic accounts: a complete view.

A first glance at the integrated economic accounts

2.92. The integrated economic accounts are at the centre of the accounting framework. They provide an overall view of a given economy. It is useful to take a first glance at them through the simplified presentation in figure 2.2. They will be described

more completely after the various accounts have been introduced in detail.

2.93. Figure 2.2 shows that, in columns, the integrated economic accounts include the accounts of institutional sectors (on both sides, there is, of course, a column for each sector, which is not shown separately here). These accounts are structured in three sub-sets, for current accounts, accumulation accounts and balance sheets. The current accounts record production and the distribution and redistribution of income; they show how disposable income is used for final consumption; they end with saving. The accumulation accounts record all changes in assets and liabilities, and consequently all changes in the difference between assets and liabilities—that is, in net worth—which occur in a given period. Balance sheets record the stocks of assets and liabilities, and the difference between them, which exist at the opening and the closing of the accounting period. There is also a column for the rest of the world.

2.94. The central column includes the transactions, balancing items and assets and liabilities ordered according to the structure of the accounts referred to above. Thus, in a row for a given transaction, such as interest, the chart shows the payables and the receivables by the various institutional sectors and the rest of the world. Each account for a given transaction is in principle balanced: the sum of interest payable is equal to the sum of interest receivable. A transactions account is a dummy account. It does not show how much interest is payable/receivable by an institutional sector to/from each of the institutional sectors or the rest of the world, but only how much interest is payable and receivable in total by each sector. Transactions in goods and services are a special case, because there is a unique balance for all transactions in goods and services and not for each of them. For this reason, a special column corresponds to the goods and services account. As explained later, each transaction in goods and services (production, final consumption,

Figure 2.3. Synoptic presentation of the accounts, balancing items and main aggregates

Accounts				Balancing items	Main aggregates [1]
Full sequence of accounts for institutional sectors					
Current accounts	I. Production account [2]			B.1 Value added	Domestic product (GDP/NDP)
	II. Distribution and use of income accounts	II.1. Primary distribution of income accounts	II.1.1. Generation of income account [2]	B.2 Operating surplus; B.3 Mixed income	
			II.1.2. Allocation of primary income account — II.1.2.1. Entrepreneurial income account	B.4 Entrepreneurial income	
			II.1.2.2. Allocation of other primary income account	B.5 Balance of primary incomes	National income (GNI, NNI)
		II.2. Secondary distribution of income account		B.6 Disposable income	National disposable income
		II.3. Redistribution of income in kind account		B.7 Adjusted disposable income	
		II.4. Use of income account — II.4.1. Use of disposable income account		B.8 Saving	National saving
		II.4.2. Use of adjusted disposable income account			
Accumulation accounts	III. Accumulation accounts	III.1. Capital account		B.10.1 (Changes in net worth, due to saving and capital transfers) [3]; B.9 Net lending/Net borrowing	
		III.2. Financial account		B.9 Net lending/Net borrowing	
		III.3. Other changes in assets accounts	III.3.1. Other changes in volume of assets account	B.10.2 Changes in net worth, due to other changes in volume of assets	
			III.3.2. Revaluation accounts	B.10.3 Changes in net worth, due to nominal holding gains/losses	
			III.3.2.1. Neutral holding gains/losses	B.10.31 Changes in net worth, due to neutral holding gains/losses	
			III.3.2.2. Real holding gains/losses	B.10.32 Changes in net worth, due to real holding gains/losses	
Balance sheets	IV. Balance sheets	IV.1. Opening balance sheet		B.90 Net worth	National worth
		IV.2. Changes in balance sheet		B.10 Changes in net worth, total	Changes in national worth
		IV.3. Closing balance sheet		B.90 Net worth	National worth
Transaction accounts					
0. Goods and services account	0. Goods and services account				National expenditure
Rest of the world account (external transactions account)					
Current accounts	V. Rest of the world account	V.I. External account of goods and services		B.11 External balance of goods and services	External balance of goods and services
		V.II. External account of primary income and current transfers		B.12 Current external balance	Current external balance
Accumulation accounts		V.III. External accumulation accounts — V.III.1. Capital account		B.10.1 (Changes in net worth due to current external balance and capital transfers) [3]; B.9 Net lending/Net borrowing	
		V.III.2. Financial account		B.9 Net lending/Net borrowing	Net lending/Net borrowing of the nation
		V.III.3. Other changes in assets account	V.III.3.1. Other changes in volume of assets account	B.10.2 Changes in net worth, due to other changes in volume of assets	
			V.III.3.2. Revaluation accounts	B.10.3 Changes in net worth, due to nominal holding gains/losses; neutral holding gains/losses; real holding gains/losses	
Balance sheets		V.IV. External assets and liabilities account	V.IV.1. Opening balance sheet	B.90 Net worth	Net external financial position of the nation
			V.IV.2. Changes in balance sheet	B.10 Changes in net worth	
			V.IV.3. Closing balance sheet	B.90 Net worth	Net external financial position of the nation

1 Most balancing items and aggregates may be calculated gross or net.
2 Applies also to industries.
3 Not a balancing item, but plays a similar role.

etc.) appearing in the accounts of the institutional sectors is reflected in this column.

2.95. The integrated economic accounts also include a column for the sum of the (resident) institutional sectors, i.e., the total economy as a whole. Thus the aggregates for the total economy are directly visible. These aggregates are the sums of various transactions and, more importantly, of balancing items.

2.96. The detailed presentation of the elements which are shown in the integrated economic accounts is considered next. As this is a lengthy explanation, it is useful to refer to figure 2.3, which includes a synoptic presentation of the accounts, balancing items and main aggregates and shows how they are articulated. The various elements appearing in figure 2.3 are presented in the following sub-sections.

The full sequence of accounts for institutional units and sectors and their balancing items

2.97. Before presenting the full sequence of accounts for institutional units and sectors, some preliminary remarks are useful. The purpose of this sub-section is to explain the accounting structure of the System in general, not to show the precise content of the accounts for each specific unit or sector. The accounting structure is uniform throughout the System. It applies to all institutional units, sub-sectors, sectors and the total economy. However, some accounts may not be relevant for certain sectors. Similarly, not all transactions are relevant for each sector and, when they are, they may constitute resources for some sectors and uses for others. The precise content of the accounts for each sector is presented in the following chapters, dealing in detail with the various types of accounts.

2.98. Another remark relates to the way the classification of transactions is used when presenting the general structure of the accounts. Section B above shows only the main categories of transactions, not the detailed ones which are displayed in the relevant chapters of the manual. However, in order to make the accounts clear, it is necessary to include a number of transactions. This is done by using the actual classification of transactions in the System at a level of detail sufficient for a good understanding of the accounts. However, definitions of these transactions are not given at this stage, unless absolutely necessary.

2.99. It is also worth noting that balancing items can be expressed gross or net, the difference being the consumption of fixed capital. Conceptually, net balancing items are much more meaningful. However, gross concepts, specifically gross aggregates, are widely used and gross accounts are often estimated more easily, accurately and promptly than the net ones. In order to accommodate both solutions and to ease the integrated presentation of the accounts and aggregates, a double presentation of balancing items is allowed.

2.100. Finally, it has to be said that the sequence of accounts shows

the accounting structure of the System; it is not necessarily a format for publishing the results.

2.101. The accounts are grouped into three categories: current accounts, accumulation accounts, balance sheets.

2.102. Current accounts deal with production, income and use of income. Accumulation accounts cover changes in assets and liabilities and changes in net worth (the difference for any institutional unit or group of units between its assets and liabilities). Balance sheets present stocks of assets and liabilities and net worth.

> Current accounts: Production, distribution of income, use of income
>
> Accumulation accounts: Changes in assets and liabilities and changes in net worth
>
> Balance sheets: Stocks of assets and liabilities and net worth.

2.103. Accumulation accounts show all changes which occur between two balance sheets. Even when balance sheets are not compiled, a clear understanding of the conceptual relationship between accumulation accounts and balance sheets is necessary if the accumulation accounts themselves are to be correctly elaborated.

2.104. The relation between current accounts and accumulation accounts is a little more complex. All current transactions make net worth vary either positively (in the case of resources) or negatively (uses). The recording of a transaction as a current resource means an increase in the amount of economic value a unit or a sector has at its disposal; conversely, a transaction recorded as a current use means a decrease in this amount of economic value. The difference between all current uses and all current resources (saving) represents, for a given period, the change in net worth resulting from current transactions. However, the latter are not the only source of changes in net worth. These points are elaborated further below.

2.105. These three broad kinds of accounts are examined in turn.

Current accounts

2.106. Current accounts deal with production, distribution of income and use of income. Each account starts with the recording, as resources, of the balancing item of the previous one. The last balancing item is saving which, in the SNA context, is that part of income originating in production, domestically or abroad, which is not used for final consumption.

2.107. Production, distribution of income and use of income are considered successively.

Production account (Account I)

2.108. The production account (see table 2.1, Account I) is designed to emphasize value added as one of the main balancing items in the System. Consequently, it does not cover all transactions linked with the production process, but only the result of pro-

Table 2.1.   Account I: Production account

Uses			Resources		
P.2	Intermediate consumption		P.1	Output [1]	
B.1g	*Value added, gross* [2]				
K.1	Consumption of fixed capital				
B.1n	*Value added, net* [2]				

1 For the valuation of output, refer to chapter VI, paragraphs 6.210-6.227.

2 For the total economy this item corresponds to gross domestic product, net domestic product respectively. It is equal to the value added of the institutional sectors plus taxes less subsidies on products.

duction (output) and the using up of goods and services when producing this output (intermediate consumption). Intermediate consumption does not cover the progressive wear and tear of fixed capital. The latter is recorded as a separate transaction (consumption of fixed capital) making the difference between the gross and net balancing items. Thus:

$$\text{Production account} \rightarrow \text{value added}$$

2.109. Thus the production account shows only output as resources and intermediate consumption as uses; the balancing item is value added, which is measured both gross and net.[3] As already explained (see section C.3 above), different types of valuation of output may be used according to the choice made between basic prices and producers' prices and, in the latter case, the existence or absence of value added type taxes. Consequently, the extent to which taxes (less subsidies) on products are included in value added differs.

2.110. All institutional sectors have a production account. However, in the production account of institutional sectors, output and intermediate consumption are shown in total only, not broken down by products.

Distribution of income accounts

2.111. The process of distribution and redistribution of income is so important that it is worth distinguishing various steps and depicting them separately in different accounts. As long as all kinds of distributive current transactions included in the System are actually measured, increasing the number of accounts adds very little to the work already done, but it allows the introduction of balancing items that are meaningful concepts of income.

2.112. The distribution of income is decomposed into three main steps: primary distribution, secondary distribution and redistribution in kind. The first refers to the distribution of value added to factors of labour and capital and to government (through taxes, less subsidies, on production and imports). It measures the balance of primary incomes. The second covers redistribution of income through, essentially, transfers in cash.

It measures disposable income. The last one relates to further redistribution through transfers in kind. It measures adjusted disposable income, as shown below:

Distribution of income

Primary distribution of income $\rightarrow$ balance of primary incomes

Secondary distribution of income $\rightarrow$ disposable income

Redistribution of income in kind $\rightarrow$ adjusted disposable income

a. Primary distribution of income account
(Account II.1)

2.113. The primary distribution of income account shows how gross value added is distributed to factors of labour and capital, government and, where necessary, flows to and from the rest of the world. Its balancing item is the balance of primary incomes.

2.114. In fact Account II.1 is subdivided between two sub-accounts, in order to measure, in addition, operating surplus/mixed income, a balancing item which is important both for institutional sectors and industries.

2.115. The generation of income account (see table 2.1, Account II.1.1) records, from the point of view of producers, distributive transactions which are directly linked to the process of production. The resources consist of value added; its uses include compensation of employees, and taxes on production and imports, less subsidies, as far as they are included in the valuation of output (see paragraph 2.71). The balancing item is operating surplus/mixed income.[4]

2.116. The allocation of primary income account (see table 2.1, Account II.1.2) shows the remaining part of the primary distribution of income. It records, for each sector, property income receivable and payable, and compensation of employees and taxes, less subsidies, on production and imports receivable, respectively, by households and government. Since transactions of this kind may appear in the rest of the world account, these must be included also. Account II.1.2 has operating surplus/mixed income as resources and balance of primary incomes as a balancing item. Thus primary income covers

Table 2.1.   Account II.1:   Primary distribution of income account

II.1.1: Generation of income account

Uses		Resources	
D.1	Compensation of employees	B.1	*Value added* [1] [2]
D.2	Taxes on production and imports [3]		
D.3	Subsidies(-) [3]		
B.2/B.3	*Operating surplus/mixed income* [1]		

1 The operating and the closing balance item of this account can be expressed in gross or in net terms.
2 For the total economy this item corresponds to domestic product. It is equal to the value added of the institutional sectors plus taxes less subsidies on products.
3 For the contents of the items "taxes on production and imports and subsidies", refer to chapter VI, paragraphs 6.210 to 6.227

II.1.2: Allocation of primary income account

Uses		Resources	
D.4	Property income	B.2./B.3	*Operating surplus/mixed income*[1]
		D.1	Compensation of employees
		D.2	Taxes on production and imports
		D.3	Subsidies (-)
		D.4	Property income
B.5	*Balance of primary incomes* [1] [2]		

1 The opening and the closing balancing item of this account can be expressed in gross or in net terms.
2 For the total economy this item corresponds to national income.

operating surplus/mixed income, net property income, compensation of employees and taxes, less subsidies, on production and imports receivable.

2.117. For sectors which are important market producers—that is, for non-financial and financial corporations, and households—the allocation of primary income account is further subdivided in order to show an additional balancing item, entrepreneurial income, which is closer to the concept of current profit familiar in business accounting. This balancing item and the related sub-accounts are shown in chapter VII.

b. Secondary distribution of income account (Account II.2)

2.118. The secondary distribution of income account, (see table 2.1, Account II.2) covers in principle redistribution of income through transfers in cash only, in order to distinguish two steps in the redistribution process, one through transfers in cash, the other through transfers in kind. This distinction is made in the relations between households from one side, general government and NPISHs from the other. However, it is not significant in the case of corporations and the rest of the world. For this

reason, transfers in kind to and from corporations or the rest of the world are recorded in the secondary distribution of income account, as if they were in cash. This does not prevent showing them separately.

2.119. This account records as resources, in addition to balance of primary incomes, current taxes on income, wealth, etc. and other current transfers except social transfers in kind. On the uses side, the same types of transfers are also recorded. Since these transfers are resources for some sectors and uses for others also, their precise content varies from one sector to another.

2.120. It is worth explaining in some detail here the way social contributions are recorded in the System. Although employers normally pay social contributions on behalf of their employees directly to the social insurance schemes, in the System these payments are treated as if they were made to employees who then make payments to social insurance schemes. In terms of the accounts, this means that they first appear as a component of compensation of employees in the use side of the generation of income account (Account II.1.1) of employers and the resource side of allocation of primary income ac-

Table 2.1.   Account II.2: Secondary distribution of income account

Uses			Resources		
D.5	Current taxes on income, wealth, etc.		B.5	*Balance of primary incomes* [1][2]	
D.61	Social contributions		D.5	Current taxes on income, wealth, etc.	
D.62	Social benefits other than social transfers in kind		D.61	Social contributions	
D.7	Other current transfers		D.62	Social benefits other than social transfers in kind	
			D.7	Other current transfers	
B.6	*Disposable income* [1]				

1   The opening and the closing balancing item of this account can be expressed in gross or in net terms.
2   For the total economy this item corresponds to national income.

count (Account II.1.2) of households (adjusted of course for external flows in compensation of employees). Then they are recorded as uses in the secondary distribution of income account (Account II.2) of households (and possibly of the rest of the world), and as resources of the sectors managing social insurance schemes (essentially government). All employers' social contributions follow this route. This way of recording transactions as if they followed another course is often called "rerouting".

2.121. The balancing item of Account II.2 is disposable income. This is the income which can be used for final consumption expenditure and saving. Disposable income is mainly in cash. However it also involves an in-kind component. The latter includes compensation of employees in kind, transfers in kind from the rest of the world and corporations (if any), own final consumption, own-account fixed capital formation and that part of output which has not yet been sold or otherwise disposed of and is recorded under changes in inventories. For non-financial and financial corporations, disposable income is income after tax not distributed to owners of equity.

c. Redistribution of income in kind account (Account II.3)

2.122. The redistribution of income in kind account (see table 2.1, Account II.3) shows two more elements in the description of the redistribution process. First, it records social benefits in kind, which include both benefits for which the recipient household does not incur the expense and benefits for which the household makes the initial outlay and is later reimbursed. Secondly, it records the transfer of individual non-market goods and services, such as education, not included in social benefits in kind. All these transactions are included under the heading of social transfers in kind in the classification of distributive transactions.

2.123. Account II.3 records as resources disposable income and, for households, social transfers in kind. Then, on the uses side, social transfers in kind appear for government and NPISHs. The balancing item is adjusted disposable income.[5] Because of the

nature of the transactions concerned, this account is significant only for government, households and NPISHs.

2.124. The purpose of this account is fourfold. First, it aims at giving a clearer picture of the role of government. Secondly, it delivers a more complete measure of household income. Thirdly, it facilitates international comparisons and comparisons over time when economic and social arrangements differ or change. Fourthly, it gives a more complete view of the redistribution process between sub-sectors or other groupings of households. Redistribution of income in kind is a tertiary distribution of income.

d. Use of income account (Account II.4)

2.125. The use of income account (see table 2.1, Account II.4) shows, for those sectors which have some final consumption, how disposable income or adjusted disposable income is allocated between final consumption and saving. In the System, only government, NPISHs and households have final consumption. In addition, the use of income account includes, for households and for pension funds, an adjustment item (D.8 Adjustment for the change in net equity of households on pension funds) which relates to the way transactions between households and pension funds are recorded in the System. This adjustment item, which is explained in chapter IX, is not discussed here. There are two variants of Account II.4.

2.126. The use of disposable income account (see table 2.1, Account II.4.1) records disposable income as resources and final consumption expenditure as uses, as well as the adjustment item referred to above, when relevant.

2.127. Final consumption expenditure covers transactions on final consumption of goods and services for which a sector is the ultimate bearer of the expense. Government and NPISHs produce non-market goods and services in their production account, where intermediate consumption or compensation of employees are recorded as uses. Final consumption expenditure of these producers relates to the value of their output of non-market goods and services, less their receipts from the sale of non-market goods and services at prices which are not

Table 2.1.   Account II.3: Redistribution of income in kind account

Uses		Resources	
D.63	Social transfers in kind	B.6	*Disposable income*[1]
		B.63	Social transfers in kind
B.7	*Adjusted disposable income*[1]		

1 The opening and the closing balancing item of this account can be expressed in gross or in net terms.

economically significant. However, it also covers goods and services that are purchased by government or NPISHs for ultimate transfer, without transformation, to households.

2.128. The use of adjusted disposable income account (see table 2.1, Account II.4.2) records adjusted disposable income as resources and actual final consumption as uses, as well as the adjustment item referred to above, when relevant. Actual final consumption of households covers goods and services which are effectively available for individual consumption by households, regardless of whether the ultimate bearer of the expense is government, NPISHs or households themselves. Consequently, actual final consumption of government refers only to collective consumption, whereas NPISHs, whose final consumption expenditure is deemed to be in total individual, have no actual final consumption.

2.129. At the total economy level, disposable income and adjusted disposable income are equal, as are final consumption expenditure and actual final consumption. They differ only when considering the relevant sectors. For each sector, the difference between final consumption expenditure and actual final consumption is equal to social transfers in kind, provided or received. It is also equal to the difference between disposable income and adjusted disposable income.

2.130. The balancing item of the use of income account, in its two variants, is saving. The figures for saving are the same in Accounts II.4.1 and II.4.2 as income in the resources side and consumption on the uses side differ by the same amount. Saving ends the sub-sequence of current accounts, as follows:

Use of income

Use of disposable income → final consumption expenditure

                          ↘

                  saving

               ↗

Use of adjusted disposable income →actual final consumption

Accumulation accounts

2.131. Because the present accounting system is fully integrated, accumulation accounts cover all changes in assets, liabilities and net worth (the difference for any sector between its assets and liabilities).

2.132. As accumulation accounts show changes in assets, liabilities and net worth, they follow a presentation similar to balance sheets themselves. Balance sheets are conventionally presented with assets on the left side, liabilities and net worth on the right side. Consistently, in the accumulation accounts, all changes in assets, either positive or negative, are recorded on the left side; all changes in liabilities, either positive or negative, and changes in net worth, either positive or negative, are recorded on the right side. So, as already explained in section B, the left side is called "Changes in assets" and the right side "Changes in liabilities and net worth".

2.133. Saving, being the balancing item of all current transactions/accounts, is, of course, the starting element of accumulation accounts.

2.134. Accumulation accounts are structured in a way which permits various types of changes in assets, liabilities and net worth to be distinguished.

2.135. A first group of accounts covers transactions which would correspond to all changes in assets/liabilities and net worth if saving and voluntary transfers of wealth were the only sources of changes in net worth. A second group of accounts relates to changes in assets, liabilities and net worth due to other factors.

2.136. The first group of accumulation accounts contains the capital account and the financial account. These two accounts are distinguished in order to show a balancing item which is useful for economic analysis, that is, net lending/net borrowing.

a. Capital account (Account III.1)

2.137. The capital account (see table 2.1, Account III.1) records transactions linked to acquisitions of non-financial assets and capital transfers involving the redistribution of wealth. The right side includes saving, net, and capital transfers receivable and capital transfers payable (with a minus sign) in order to arrive at that part of changes in net worth due to saving and capital transfers. Account III.1 includes among uses the various types of investment in non-financial assets. Because consumption of fixed capital is a negative change in fixed assets, it is recorded, with a negative sign, on the left side of the account. Entering gross fixed capital formation (+) and consumption of fixed capital (–) on this side is equivalent to entering net fixed capital formation. The balancing item is ei-

Table 2.1.   Account II.4: Use of income account

II.4.1: Use of disposable income account

Uses		Resources	
P.3	Final consumption expenditure	B.6	*Disposable income*[1]
D.8	Adjustment for the change in net equity of households on pension funds	D.8	Adjustment for the change in net equity of households on pension funds
B.8	*Saving* [1]		

1   The opening and the closing balancing item of this account can be
expressed in gross or in net terms.

II.4.2: Use of adjusted disposable income account

Uses		Resources	
P.4	Actual final consumption	B.7	*Adjusted disposable income*[1]
D.8	Adjustment for the change in net equity of households on pension funds	D.8	Adjustment for the change in net equity of households on pension funds
B.8	*Saving*[1]		

1   The opening and the closing balancing item of this account can
be expressed in gross or in net terms.

ther net lending (+), which measures the net amount a unit or a sector finally has available to finance, directly or indirectly, other units or sectors, or net borrowing (-), which corresponds to the amount a unit or a sector finally is obliged to borrow from others.

b. Financial account (Account III.2)

2.138. The financial account (see table 2.1, Account III.2) records transactions in financial instruments for each financial instrument. These transactions in the System show net acquisition of financial assets on the left side or net incurrence of liabilities on the right side. The balancing item is again net lending (+) or net borrowing (-), which appears this time on the right side of the account.

2.139. In principle, net lending or net borrowing is measured identically whichever account is considered. In practice, achieving this identity is one of the most difficult targets of national accounts.

c. Other changes in volume assets account and revaluation account (Accounts III.3.1 and III.3.2)

2.140. The second group of accumulation accounts (see table 2.1, Account III.3.1) covers changes in assets, liabilities and net worth which are due to factors other than the accumulation transactions recorded in the previous group of accounts. Examples are discoveries or depletion of subsoil resources, destruction by political events, such as war, or by natural catastrophes, such as earthquakes. Other changes in assets

may also be linked with changes in the level and structure of prices. In the latter case, only the value of assets and liabilities is modified, not their volume. Factors such as discoveries of subsoil resources or earthquakes actually change the volume of assets, in the SNA sense. Thus the second group of accumulation accounts is subdivided between an account for other changes in volume of assets and an account for revaluation.

2.141. The other changes in volume of assets account (see table 2.1, Account III.3.1) records those exceptional events which cause not only the value but also the volume of assets and liabilities to vary. In addition to the kind of events referred to above, such as the consequences of war or earthquakes, this account also includes some adjustment elements like changes in classification and structure which may or may not have an influence on net worth (see chapter XII). The balancing item, changes in net worth due to other changes in volume of assets, is recorded on the right side.

2.142. The revaluation account (see table 2.1, Account III.3.2) records holding gains or losses. It shows first nominal holding gains/losses. This item records the full change of value due to the change in specific prices of the various assets or liabilities since the beginning of the accounting period or the time of entry and the time of exit or the end of the accounting period.

2.143. Just as transactions and other flows in assets appear on the left of the account and transactions in liabilities on the right, so nominal gains or losses on assets appear on the left side of Account III.3.2, while nominal gains/losses on financial liabilities are recorded on the right side. For a given unit or group of

Table 2.1. Account III.1: Capital account

Changes in assets		Changes in liabilities and net worth	
P.51	Gross fixed capital formation	B.8	*Saving, net*
K.1	Consumption of fixed capital(–)	D.9	Capital transfers, receivable(+)
P.52	Changes in inventories	D.9	Capital transfers, payable(–)
P.53	Acquisitions less disposals of valuables		
K.2	Acquisitions less disposals of non-produced non-financial assets		
		10.1	*Changes in net worth due to saving and capital transfers*[1] [2]
B.9	*Net lending (+)/net borrowing(-)*		

1 "Changes in net worth due to saving and capital transfers" is not a balancing item, but corresponds to the total of the right-hand side of the capital account.

2 "Changes in net worth due to saving and capital transfers" for the rest of the world refers to changes in net worth due to current external balance and capital transfers.

Table 2.1. Account III.2: Financial account

Changes in assets		Changes in liabilities and net worth	
F	Net acquisition of financial assets	F	Net incurrence of liabilities
F.1	Monetary gold and SDRs		
F.2	Currency and deposits[1]	F.2	Currency and deposits[1]
F.3	Securities other than shares	F.3	Securities other than shares
F.4	Loans[2]	F.4	Loans[2]
F.5	Shares and other equity[2]	F.5	Shares and other equity[2]
F.6	Insurance technical reserves	F.6	Insurance technical reserves
F.7	Other accounts receivable[2]	F.7	Other accounts payable[2]
		B.9	*Net lending(+)/net borrowing(–)*

1 The following memorandum items related to the elements of the category
F.2 "Currency and deposits":
    m11 denominated in national currency
    m12 denominated in foreign currency
    m21 liability of resident institutions
    m22 liability of rest of the world.
2 Memorandum item: F.m. Direct foreign investment.

units, a positive revaluation of its financial liabilities is equivalent to a nominal holding loss; a negative revaluation of its liabilities is equivalent to a nominal holding gain. The balancing item of the account is changes in net worth due to nominal holding gains/losses.

2.144. The revaluation account is then subdivided between two sub-accounts. The first sub-account (see table 2.1, Account III.3.2.1) shows the revaluation in proportion to the general price level which is obtained by applying, during the same periods of time, an index of the change in general price level to the initial value of all assets or liabilities, even to those that are

fixed in monetary terms. The results of this operation are called neutral holding gains/losses because all assets and liabilities are revalued in exactly the same proportion. The balancing item of Account III.3.2.1 is called changes in net worth due to neutral holding gains/losses.

2.145. The second sub-account (see table 2.1, Account III.3.2.2) shows the difference between the nominal holding gains/losses (see table 2.1, Account III.3.2) and the neutral holding gains/losses (see Account III.3.2.1). This difference is called real holding gains/losses. For instance, considering the left side (changes in assets) of this sub-account for a given unit

Table 2.1. Account III.3.1: Other changes in volume of assets account

Changes in assets			Changes in liabilities and net worth		
AN	Non-financial assets		AF	Liabilities	
AN.1	Produced assets		K.7	Catastrophic losses	
K.4	Economic appearance of produced assets		K.8	Uncompensated seizures	
K.7	Catastrophic losses		K.10	Other volume changes in financial assets and liabilities n.e.c.	
K.8	Uncompensated seizures		K.12	Changes in classifications and structure	
K.9	Other volume changes in non-financial assets n.e.c.				
K.12	Changes in classifications and structure				
AN.2	Non-produced assets				
K.3	Economic appearance of non-produced assets				
K.5	Natural growth of non-cultivated biological resources				
K.6	Economic disappearance of non-produced assets				
K.7	Catastrophic losses				
K.8	Uncompensated seizures				
K.9	Other volume changes in non-financial assets n.e.c.				
K.12	Changes in classifications and structure				
AF	Financial assets				
K.7	Catastrophic losses				
K.8	Uncompensated seizures				
K.10	Other volume changes in financial assets and liabilities n.e.c.				
K.12	Changes in classifications and structure				
			B.10.2	*Changes in net worth due to other changes in volume of assets*	

or group of units, if the nominal holding gains/losses are higher than the neutral holding gains/losses, there is a real holding gain, due to the fact that on average the actual prices of its assets have increased more (or decreased less) than the general price level. In other words, the relative prices of its assets have increased. Correspondingly, a decrease in relative prices of its assets leads to a real holding loss. The balancing item of Account III.3.2.2 is the total of real holding gains or losses, which is called changes in real net worth due to real holding gains/losses.

2.146. Each of the three types of holding gains or losses are subdivided according to the main groups of assets and liabilities, a decomposition which is necessary even in a simplified accounting presentation.

Balance sheets (Account IV)

2.147. The opening and closing balance sheets (see table 2.1, Accounts IV.1 and IV.3), display assets on the left side, liabilities and net worth on the right side. Assets and liabilities, as previously explained, are valued at the prices of the date a balance sheet is established. Net worth, the difference between assets and liabilities, is the balancing item of balance sheets. It is equivalent to the present value of the stock of economic value a unit or a sector holds. In more detailed presentations of balance sheets, the various types of assets and liabilities are shown using the more detailed classification of assets and liabilities.

2.148. For each group of assets and liabilities, changes between the

Table 2.1.   Account III.3.2: Revaluation account

III.3.2: Revaluation account

Changes in assets			Changes in liabilities and net worth		
K.11	Nominal holding gains(+)/losses(−)		K.11	Nominal holding gains(−)/losses(+)	
AN	Non-financial assets		AF	Liabilities	
AN.1	Produced assets				
AN.2	Non-produced assets				
AF	Financial assets				
			B.10.3	*Changes in net worth due to nominal holding gains/losses*	

III.3.2.1: Neutral holding gains/losses account

Changes in assets			Changes in liabilities and net worth		
K.11.1	Neutral holding gains(+)/losses(−)		K.11.1	Neutral holding gains(−)/losses(+)	
AN	Non-financial assets		AF	Liabilities	
AN.1	Produced assets				
AN.2	Non-produced assets				
AF	Financial assets				
			B.10.3	*Changes in net worth due to neutral holding gains/losses*	

III.3.2.2: Real holding gains/losses account

Changes in assets			Changes in liabilities and net worth		
K.11.2	Real holding gains(+)/losses(−)		K.11.2	Real holding gains(−)/losses(+)	
AN	Non-financial assets		AF	Liabilities	
AN.1	Produced assets				
AN.2	Non-produced assets				
AF	Financial assets				
			B.10.3	*Changes in net worth due to real holding gains/losses*	

opening and closing balance sheets result from the transactions and other flows recorded in the accumulation accounts, including the changes in classification of assets and liabilities. Changes in net worth are equal to changes in assets less changes in liabilities.

2.149. The changes in balance sheet account (see table 2.1, Account IV.2) recapitulates the content of the accumulation accounts, that is, the total changes in assets and liabilities and the changes in net worth by main sources: saving and capital transfers, other changes in volume of assets and nominal hold-

ing gains/losses which can be subdivided between neutral and real holding gains and losses. Saving and capital transfers, other changes in volume of assets and real holding gains/losses contribute to changes in real net worth; neutral holding gains/losses convert real net worth to nominal general purchasing power as of the end of the accounting period. Combined with the opening balance sheet (Account IV.1), Account IV.2 leads to the closing balance sheet (Account IV.3).

2.150. Account IV.2 shows the relation in the SNA between saving (net) and changes in net worth. Saving (net) is equal to changes in net worth less capital transfers, less other changes in volume of assets, less nominal holding gains/losses. Considering only changes in real net worth, saving (net) is equal to changes in real net worth less capital transfers, less other changes in volume of assets, less real holding gains/losses. This relation between saving and changes in real net worth implies that the relation between disposable income or adjusted disposable income and changes in real net worth differs from Hicks's concept of income (see chapter VIII).

2.151. Because saving is a source of changes in real net worth, it follows naturally that all current transactions, of which saving is the balancing item, make real net worth vary either positively (resources) or negatively (uses). This illustrates the definition of net worth given above as a stock of (abstract) economic value. Most transactions in assets and liabilities do not change the magnitude of net worth, but only the nature of its components. Transactions in assets and liabilities corresponding to capital transfers and other accumulation flows also change the magnitude of net worth. In general, both current and accumulation transactions and other flows deal with creation, transformation, exchange, transfer or extinction of economic value.

Transactions accounts

2.152. A transactions account shows, for a given transaction or group of transactions (for example, interest), resources and uses for each sector (or industry if relevant) engaged in this type of transaction, but it does not show direct relations between transacting sectors. In other words, the account shows relations of the "what?/from whom?" type and "what?/to whom?" type, not relations of the "what?/from whom?/to whom?" type. Transactions accounts are basically dummy accounts, or screen accounts, in the System. Totals of resources and totals of uses balance by definition (practical difficulties might be encountered, of course); there is no balancing item. A transactions account is thus a way for recapitulating what may be found for a given transaction in the accounts of the various sectors/industries. The general structure of a transactions account is shown in table 2.6 (see the appendix to this chapter for tables 2.6-2.12) using property income as an example. The type of transaction is indicated in the central column. There is a column for each institutional sector, for the total economy and for the rest of the world. The column total allows the identity between total uses and total resources in each row to be verified.

2.153. In order to make this structure workable systematically, the classification of transactions, referred to above, has been built up according to the nature of the transaction without specific reference to sector of origin or sector of destination.

2.154. In the case of transactions in goods and services (products), the transactions account, shown in table 2.2, Account 0, is particularly important. The goods and services account (Account 0) shows, for the economy as a whole or for groups of prod-

ucts, the total resources (output and imports) and uses of goods and services (intermediate consumption, final consumption, changes in inventories, gross fixed capital formation, acquisitions less disposals of valuables and exports). Taxes on products (less subsidies) are also included on the resource side of the accounts. The coverage of this item varies according to the way output is valued (see section C.3, "Valuation" above). The part (possibly the total) of taxes on products (less subsidies), that is not included in the value of output does not originate in any specific sector or industry; it is a resource of the total economy as such.

2.155. The goods and services account can show either final consumption expenditure or actual final consumption. For the economy as a whole, the data for the two items are identical. However, they differ for the sectors involved when the goods and services account is cross-classified with the classification of institutional sectors in order to show the resources and uses according to the institutional sector of origin or use.

2.156. An important feature of the goods and services account is that it is balanced globally—that is, there is a balance between all uses and all resources—not for each kind of transaction.

2.157. When looking at the goods and services account by type of products, output and intermediate consumption may be allocated by industry of origin or use, while other transactions may be shown in various ways (see the description of supply and use tables below).

2.158. Because it plays an extremely important role in the System, the goods and services account receives a special coding, Account 0. The other transactions accounts are identified, if necessary, by the code of the relevant transaction.

2.159. Another feature of the goods and services account is that uses are shown on the right side and resources on the left side. This is done in order to reflect transactions on the opposite side as compared to institutional sector accounts.

2.160. Accounts for other transactions simply follow the general model (see paragraphs 2.152 and 2.154 above). For taxes, social contributions, social benefits and a number of other transactions, the nature of the recorded transaction easily identifies the "from whom to whom?" relation or a good approximation of it. In other cases, all sectors may have resources and uses and the interrelations are not shown explicitly. For interest, dividends and transactions in financial instruments, which are the most important cases, it is very useful, in addition to the dummy account procedure, to follow a "from whom to whom?" approach for practical and analytical purposes.

Assets and liabilities accounts

2.161. Transactions in assets and liabilities and other changes in assets appear in the accounts of institutional sectors and the transactions accounts already described. Stocks of assets and liabilities at the beginning and the end of the accounting period appear in the opening and closing balance sheets, respectively.

Table 2.1.   Account IV: Balance sheets

IV.1: Opening balance sheet

Assets		Liabilities and net worth	
AN	Non-financial assets	AF	Liabilities
AN.1	Produced assets		
AN.2	Non-produced assets		
AF	Financial assets		
		B.90	*Net worth*

IV.2: Changes in balance sheet

Assets		Liabilities and net worth	
Total changes in assets		Total changes in liabilities	
AN	Non-financial assets	AF	Liabilities
AN.1	Produced assets		
AN.2	Non-produced assets		
AF	Financial assets		
		B.10	*Changes in net worth, total*
		B.10.1	*Changes in net worth due to saving and capital transfers*
		B.10.2	*Changes in net worth due to other changes in volume of assets*
		B.10.3	*Changes in net worth due to nominal holding gains/losses*

IV.3: Closing balance sheet

Assets		Liabilities and net worth	
AN	Non-financial assets	AF	Liabilities
AN.1	Produced assets		
AN.2	Non-produced assets		
AF	Financial assets		
		B.90	*Net worth*

All those data are combined in the assets and liabilities accounts.

2.162. The assets and liabilities accounts, shown in table 2.7, record for each type of asset and liability, the opening stock at the beginning of the accounting period, the various types of changes which occur during this period and the closing stock at the end of it, as illustrated below:

Opening stock
plus transactions recorded in the capital account, by type of transactions
plus transactions recorded in the financial account
plus other changes in volume of assets, by type of changes
plus nominal holding gains/losses
   of which:
   neutral holding gains/losses
   real holding gains/losses
equal
   closing stock.

Table 2.2.   Account 0: Goods and services account

Resources		Uses	
P.1	Output [1]	P.2	Intermediate consumption
P.7	Imports of goods and services	P.3/P.4	Final consumption expenditure/actual final consumption
D.21	Taxes on products [1]	P.5	Gross capital formation
D.31	Subsidies on products (–) [1]	P.51	Gross fixed capital formation
		P.52	Changes in inventories
		P.53	Acquisitions less disposals of valuables
		P.6	Exports of goods and services

1   For the valuation of output and the resulting contents of the items "Taxes on products" and "Subsidies on products", refer to chapter VI, paragraphs 6.210 to 6.227.

Of course, changes may be positive or negative. In the sequence of accounts for institutional units and sectors, this relationship between balance sheets and accumulation accounts has been presented, for sake of simplicity, only for broad types of assets (non-financial assets, distinguishing produced and non-produced ones, and financial assets) and for liabilities as a whole. However, in the structure of the System, this relationship exists for each type of asset and liability, according to the System's classification. Conceptually it exists for each elementary asset (a given dwelling or loan for example) or liability. Assets and liabilities accounts are identified by the code of the relevant asset.

Rest of the world account (external transactions account) (Account V)

2.163. The rest of the world account covers transactions between resident and non-resident institutional units and the related stocks of assets and liabilities when relevant.

2.164. As the rest of the world plays a role in the accounting structure similar to that of an institutional sector, the rest of the world account is established from the point of view of the rest of the world. A resource for the rest of the world is a use for the nation and vice versa. If a balancing item is positive, it means a surplus of the rest of the world and a deficit of the nation, and vice versa if the balancing item is negative.

2.165. The rest of the world account (see table 2.3, Account V) follows the general accounting structure, but it differs slightly in order to focus on the relevant characteristics of external transactions.

2.166. Current transactions are recorded in only two accounts. The first account, the external account of goods and services (see table 2.3, Account V.I), shows imports of goods and services as resources and exports of goods and services as uses. The balancing item is the external balance of goods and services. If positive, it is a surplus for the rest of the world and a deficit for the nation.

2.167. The second account, the external account of primary incomes and current transfers (see table 2.3, Account V.II), shows the following entries on both sides: compensation of employees; taxes, less subsidies, on production and imports; property income; current taxes on income, wealth, etc., and other current transfers, receivable and payable, respectively, by the rest of the world. The balancing item of this account is the current external balance. It plays a role in the structure of the System equivalent to saving for institutional sectors.

2.168. The accumulation accounts are relevant, although for only a limited set of flows out of financial transactions. For example, table 2.1, Account V.III.3.1, records uncompensated seizures. The external assets and liabilities account is essentially equivalent, with a reverse sign, to the part of the consolidated balance sheet of the economy which relates to financial assets and liabilities. For non-financial assets which are owned by non-residents in the economic territory, a notional institutional unit is always created. The rest of the world is deemed to have acquired a financial asset (and vice versa for assets owned in other economies by resident units).

The aggregates

2.169. The aggregates of the System—for example, value added, income, consumption and saving—are composite values which measure the result of the activity of the entire economy considered from a particular point of view. They are summary indicators and key magnitudes for purposes of macroeconomic analysis and comparisons over time and space. The SNA aims to provide a simplified but complete and detailed picture of complex economies, so the calculation of the aggregates is neither the sole nor the main purpose of national accounting. Nevertheless, summary figures are very important.

2.170. Some aggregates may be obtained directly as totals of particular transactions in the System; examples are final consumption, gross fixed capital formation and social contributions. Others may result from summing up balancing items for the institutional sectors; examples are value added, balance of primary incomes, disposable income and saving. They may need some further elaboration. Some of them are so commonly used that they deserve additional explanation at this early stage.

2.171. Gross domestic product (GDP) at market prices represents the final result of the production activity of resident producer units.

2.172. Basically, GDP is a concept of value added. It is the sum of gross value added of all resident producer units (institutional sectors or, alternatively, industries) plus that part (possibly the total) of taxes, less subsidies, on products which is not included in the valuation of output.[6] Gross value added is the difference between output and intermediate consumption.

2.173. Next, GDP is also equal to the sum of the final uses of goods and services (all uses except intermediate consumption) measured in purchasers' prices, less the value of imports of goods and services.

2.174. Finally, GDP is also equal to the sum of primary incomes distributed by resident producer units.

2.175. Net domestic product at market prices (NDP) is obtained by deducting the consumption of fixed capital from GDP.

2.176. The concept of value added should conceptually exclude the counterpart of consumption of fixed capital. The latter, in effect, is not newly created value, but a reduction in the value of previously created fixed assets when they are used up in the production process. Thus, theoretically, value added is a net concept.

2.177. This conclusion applies to domestic product as well. Theoretically, domestic product should be a net concept. However, GDP is commonly used for various reasons. The depreciation of fixed assets as calculated in business accounting does not generally meet the requirements of SNA concepts. The calculation of consumption of fixed capital requires that statisticians estimate the present value of the stock of fixed assets, the lifetime of various types of assets, patterns of depreciation, etc. Not all countries make such calculations, and when they do there may be differences in methodology (with some of them using business data even when inadequate). Consequently, gross figures are more often available, or available earlier, and they are generally considered more comparable between countries. So GDP is broadly used even if it is, on a conceptual basis, less relevant than net domestic product. However, net domestic product should also be calculated, with improved estimates of consumption of fixed capital when necessary, in order to provide a significant tool for various types of analysis.

2.178. Neither gross nor net domestic product is a measure of welfare. Domestic product is an indicator of overall production activity. As such, its interpretation relies heavily on the concept of production that is used in the System and the way the borderline between intermediate consumption and final uses

is drawn. For example, non-remunerated housekeeping services are not included within the production boundary and so are not reflected in domestic product, and in-house training activities by enterprises are considered intermediate consumption, resulting in lower domestic product than would be the case if they were treated as final uses.

2.179. On the other hand, the significance of market prices determines the meaning of the values which are measured when compiling GDP. First, no different value judgements are attached to certain goods or services in comparison with others: a given amount of tobacco consumption is equivalent to the same amount of milk consumption; the same is true for education and defence, etc. Secondly, externalities, like the nuisances in urban buildings caused by noise, are not taken into account.

2.180. In addition it should be noted that domestic product is not a concept of sustainable income to the extent that economic growth may depend on natural resources and changes in human capital and that exceptional events, such as wars or floods, are treated as directly affecting assets and net worth without influencing the measures of product and income.

2.181. Primary incomes generated in the production activity of resident producer units are distributed mostly to other resident institutional units; however, part of them may go to non-resident units. Symmetrically, some primary incomes generated in the rest of the world may go to resident units. This leads to the definition and measurement of gross national income (GNI) at market prices. GNI is equal to GDP less primary incomes payable to non-resident units plus primary incomes receivable from non-resident units. In other words, GNI is equal to GDP less taxes (less subsidies) on production and imports, compensation of employees and property income payable to the rest of the world plus the corresponding items receivable from the rest of the world. Thus GNI at market prices is the sum of gross primary incomes receivable by resident institutional units/sectors. It is worth noting that GNI at market prices was called gross national product in the 1953 SNA, and it is commonly denominated GNP. In contrast to GDP, GNI is not a concept of value added, but a concept of income (primary income).

2.182. By deducting the consumption of fixed capital from GNI, net national income (NNI) at market prices is obtained. The remarks above about the conceptual relevance of the net concept in case of product apply even more strongly to national income. The remarks about welfare or sustainability also apply.

2.183. Primary incomes receivable by resident institutional units may be used in part to make transfers to non-resident units; reciprocally, resident units may receive transfers originating out of primary incomes in the rest of the world. Gross national disposable income is equal to GNI at market prices less current transfers (other than taxes, less subsidies, on production and imports) payable to non-resident units, plus the corresponding

Table 2.3.   Account V: Rest of the world account (external transactions account)

V.I: External account of goods and services

Uses		Resources	
P.6	Exports of goods and services	P.7	Imports of goods and services
P.61	Exports of goods	P.71	Imports of goods
P.62	Exports of services	P.72	Imports of services
B.11	*External balance of goods and services*		

V.II: External account of primary incomes and current transfers

Uses		Resources	
		B.11	*External balance of goods and services*
D.1	Compensation of employees	D.1	Compensation of employees
D.2-D.3	Taxes less subsidies on production and imports	D.2-D.3	Taxes less subsidies on production and imports
D.4	Property income	D.4	Property income
D.5	Current taxes on income, wealth, etc.	D.5	Current taxes on income, wealth, etc.
D.6	Social contributions and benefits	D.6	Social contributions and benefits
D.7	Other current transfers	D.7	Other current transfers
D.8	Adjustment for the change in net equity of households on pension funds	D.8	Adjustment for the change in net equity of households on pension funds
B.12	*Current external balance*		

V.III: External accumulation accounts
V.III.1: Capital account

Changes in assets		Changes in liabilities and net worth	
K.2	Acquisitions less disposals of non-produced non-financial assets		
		B.12	*Current external balance*
		D.9	Capital transfers, receivable(+)
		D.9	Capital transfers, payable (–)
		B.10.1	*Changes in net worth due to saving and capital transfers*[1] [2]
B.9	*Net lending(+)/net borrowing(–)*		

1 "Changes in net worth due to saving and capital transfers" is not a balancing item, but corresponds to the total of the right-hand side of the capital account.
2 "Changes in net worth due to saving and capital transfers" for the rest of the world refers to changes in net worth due to current external balance and capital transfers.

transfers receivable by resident units from the rest of the world. Gross national disposable income measures the income available to the nation for final consumption and gross saving. National disposable income is the sum of disposable income of all resident institutional units/sectors.[7]

2.184. By deducting the consumption of fixed capital from gross na-tional disposal income, net national disposable income is obtained.

2.185. All the aggregates referred to above are calculated in current values. The influence of changes in prices may also be eliminated. Domestic product is calculated at constant prices in order to measure the change in volume which occurs from one period to another. This may be done because output, interme-

Table 2.3.   Account V: Rest of the world account (external transactions account) *(cont.)*

V.III.2: Financial account

Changes in assets		Changes in liabilities and net worth	
F	Net acquisition of financial assets	F	Net incurrence of liabilities
F.1	Monetary gold and SDRs		
F.2	Currency and deposits[1]	F.2	Currency and deposits[1]
F.3	Securities other than shares	F.3	Securities other than shares
F.4	Loans[2]	F.4	Loans[2]
F.5	Shares and other equity[2]	F.5	Shares and other equity[2]
F.6	Insurance technical reserves	F.6	Insurance technical reserves
F.7	Other accounts receivable[2]	F.7	Other accounts receivable[2]
		B.9	*Net lending(+)/net borrowing(−)*

1   The following memorandum items are related to the elements of the category F.2 "Currency and deposits":
      m11 denominated in national currency
      m12 denominated in foreign currency
      m21 liability of resident institutions
      m22 liability of rest of the world,
2   Memorandum item: F.m. Direct foreign investment.

V.III.3.1: Other changes in volume of assets account

Changes in assets		Changes in liabilities and net worth	
AN	Non-financial assets	AF	Liabilities
K.8	Uncompensated seizures	K.7	Catastrophic losses
K.12	Changes in classifications and structure	K.8	Uncompensated seizures
AF	Financial assets	K.10	Other volume changes in financial assets and liabilities n.e.c.
K.7	Catastrophic losses	K.12	Changes in classifications and structure
K.8	Uncompensated seizures		
K.10	Other volume changes in financial assets and liabilities n.e.c.		
K.12	Changes in classifications and structure		
		B.10.2	*Changes in net worth due to other changes in volume of assets*

(table 2.3 continues overleaf)

diate consumption and taxes, less subsidies, on products can all be calculated at constant prices. On the other hand, aggregates of income may not be expressed in volume (at constant prices) because income flows may not, strictly speaking, be broken down between a quantity and a price component. They may be calculated at constant purchasing power, or in real terms. When moving from domestic product at constant prices to national income in real terms, the effect of changes in the terms of trade between the total economy and the rest of the world is taken into account (see chapter XVI).

2.186. The analysis of net worth is an integral part of the System. Changes in real national net worth is the sum of changes in net worth of all resident institutional sectors less the neutral holding gains/losses (that is, in proportion to general price level). They are equal to the sum of saving and capital transfers, other changes in volume of assets and real holding gains or losses.

2.187. Capital formation and final consumption grouped together constitute national expenditure—gross if gross fixed capital formation is included, net if only net fixed capital formation is considered.

Table 2.3.   Account V: Rest of the world account (external transactions account) *(cont.)*

V.III.3.2: Revaluation account

Changes in assets		Changes in liabilities and net worth	
AF	Financial assets	AF	Liabilities
K.11	Nominal holding gains(+)/losses(−)	K.11	Nominal holding gains(−)/losses(+)
K.11.1	Neutral holding gains(+)/losses(−)	K.11.1	Neutral holding gains(−)/losses(+)
K.11.2	Real holding gains(+)/losses(−)	K.11.2	Real holding gains(−)/losses(+)
		B.10.3	*Changes in net worth worth due to nominal holding gains/losses*
		B.10.31	*Changes in net worth due to neutral holding gains/losses*
		B.10.32	*Changes in net worth due to real holding gains/losses*

V.IV: External assets and liabilities account
V.IV.1: Opening balance sheet

Assets		Liabilities and net worth	
AN	Non-financial assets	Af	Liabilities
AN.2	Non-produced assets		
AF	Financial assets		
		B.90	*Net worth*

V.IV.2: Changes in balance sheet

Assets		Liabilities and net worth	
Total changes in assets		Total changes in liabilities	
AN	Non-financial assets	AF	Liabilities
AN.2	Non-produced assets		
AF	Financial assets		
		B.10	*Changes in net worth, total*

V.IV.3: Closing balance sheet

Assets		Liabilities and net worth	
AN	Non-financial assets	AF	Liabilities
AN.2	Non-produced assets		
AF	Financial assets		
		B.90	*Net worth*

Integrated economic accounts: a complete view

2.188. It is now possible to put together the various elements which have been introduced in the previous sub-sections and to present in detail the integrated economic accounts.

2.189. The integrated economic accounts shown in table 2.8 give a complete picture of the accounts of the total economy, including balance sheets, in a way which permits the principal economic relations and the main aggregates to be shown. This table shows, simultaneously, the general accounting structure of the System and presents a set of data for the institutional sectors, the economy as a whole and the rest of the world.

2.190. The table takes its name from the fact that it assembles institutional sector accounts, the rest of the world accounts, transactions accounts and simplified assets and liabilities accounts. Uses, changes in assets and assets are on the left side; resources, changes in liabilities and net worth and liabilities are on the right side.

2.191. The columns refer to the institutional sectors and the rest of the world. There is also a column for the total economy and one for goods and services. As a matter of convention, a reverse order is followed on the two sides.

2.192. The rows show the transactions and other flows, assets and liabilities for balance sheets, balancing items and some important aggregates. The presentation of transactions and other flows follows the structure of the sequence of accounts for institutional sectors. With a few exceptions that are explained below, the row for a given transaction (compensation of employees or social benefits in cash, for example) shows the transactions account for this transaction.

2.193. In order to make this table simple but comprehensive, classifications of sectors, transactions and other flows, assets and liabilities are at the highest level of aggregation compatible with understanding the structure of the System. It should be understood that columns and rows can be subdivided to introduce sub-sectors or more detailed classifications of transactions and other flows, assets and liabilities.

2.194. Looking first at the institutional sectors current accounts, one can consider, for example, the columns for non-financial corporations. The production account shows output (1,753) on the right side, intermediate consumption (899) and value added (854 gross, 717 net, the difference referring to consumption of fixed capital 137) on the left side. Value added, the balancing item of the production account, appears again in the same row as a resource of the generation of income account. Then the uses of this latter account—compensation of employees (545) and other taxes, less subsidies, on production (51)[8]—are shown on the left side, the balancing item being operating surplus (258 gross, 121 net),[9] which appears again as a resource of the allocation of primary income account. After recording property income receivable on the right (86), and payable on the left (135), balance of primary incomes (209

gross, 72 net) appears as the balancing item of this account and again as a resource of the secondary distribution of income account. This latter shows current taxes on income, wealth, etc., other current transfers, when appropriate, and disposable income (185 gross, 48 net) that is undistributed income of non-financial corporations, which for this sector is then equal to saving, the balancing item of the use of income account.

2.195. The accounts for other institutional sectors may be read the same way, the relevant transactions varying according to the sector involved.

2.196. A peculiarity of the presentation of the use of income account needs to be explained. Accounts II.4.1 and II.4.2 are combined, both figures for disposable income and final consumption appearing in these accounts being shown side by side. On the right side of the use of income account, adjusted disposable income and disposable income, the balancing items, respectively, of Accounts II.2 and II.3, appear on two successive rows. On the left side, actual final consumption and final consumption expenditure are also shown on two successive rows. Disposable income, net, is 358 for general government, 40 for NPISHs and 1,164 for households. Social transfers in kind are 212 as uses by government and 16 by NPISHs. They are received (228) by households. Final consumption expenditure is 368 for government, 16 for NPISHs and 1,015 for households. Thus adjusted disposable income, net, is 146 for government (358–212), 24 for NPISHs (40–16) and 1,392 for households (1,164 + 228). Actual final consumption for government is 156 and for households is 1243. NPISHs have no actual final consumption because the goods and services composing their final consumption expenditure are transferred in total to households as social transfers in kind.

2.197. Now we may look at the rest of the world accounts. They are presented from the viewpoint of the rest of the world; a resource of the rest of the world is shown on the right side, a use on the left side. The external account of goods and services is shown at the same level as the production account for institutional sectors. Imports of goods and services (499) are a resource for the rest of the world, exports (540) are a use. The external balance of goods and services is (−41). With a positive sign, it is a surplus of the rest of the world (a deficit of the nation) and vice versa. The external account of primary incomes and current transfers covers all other current transactions. Starting with the external balance of goods and services (−41) as a resource on the right side, it shows the various kinds of taxes, compensation of employees and other current transfers when appropriate. The current external balance remains 41. Again, with a positive sign, it is a surplus of the rest of the world (a deficit of the nation) and vice versa.

2.198. As stated above, the row for a given transaction generally shows the corresponding transactions account. For example, the row for property income shows that property income was payable by non-financial corporations (135), financial corporations (167), general government (42), households (41),

NPISHs (6) and the rest of the world (68). In turn, it was receivable by non-financial corporations (86), financial corporations (141), general government (32), households (150), NPISHs (7) and the rest of the world (38). The total of payables is, of course, equal to the total of receivables (454).

2.199. The presentation of transactions on goods and services is different. In this case, as explained when presenting transactions accounts (see paragraphs 2.154 and 2.156 above), there is no balance for each type of transaction, such as exports or gross fixed capital formation, but only a global one between all uses and all resources of a good or service. Consequently, in the integrated economic accounts, the goods and services account is shown as a column, not in a row. It reflects the various transactions on goods and services which appear in the accounts of the institutional sectors. Uses of goods and services in the institutional sectors accounts are reflected on the right-hand column for goods and services; in turn, resources of goods and services in the institutional sectors accounts are reflected on the left-hand column for goods and services. On the resources side of the table, the figures appearing in the column for goods and services are the counterparts of the uses made by the various sectors and the rest of the world: exports (540), intermediate consumption (1,883), final consumption expenditure/actual final consumption (1,399), gross fixed capital formation (376), changes in inventories (28) and acquisitions less disposals of valuables (10). On the use side of the table, the figures in the column for goods and services are the counterparts of the resources of the various sectors and the rest of the world: imports (499) and output (3,604). On the same side taxes, less subsidies, on products (133) are shown directly in the column for goods and services. They are a component of the value of the supply of goods and services which has no counterpart in the value of the output of any institutional sector.[10]

2. 200. The columns for the total economy remain. Except for taxes less subsidies on products and domestic product, the figures in these columns are simply the sum of the corresponding figures for the institutional sectors. The production account for the total economy includes, as resources, output—that is, the total output of the economy—(3,604) and taxes less subsidies on products (133), the latter being the counterpart of the figure appearing on the left side in the column for goods and services. The uses side of the production account for the total economy shows intermediate consumption (1,883) and domestic product at market prices (1,854 gross, 1,632 net). The latter is the sum of value added of the various sectors and taxes less subsidies on products. Domestic product then appears on the right side as a resource of the generation of income account for the total economy. Taxes less subsidies on products are shown again on the left side in the column for total economy and on the right side as a resource of government (and the rest of the world if relevant). This double routing of taxes less subsidies

on products is made in order to get domestic product, gross and net, directly in the overall accounts, as explained above.

2.201. The other items in the columns for total economy are self-explanatory. National income at market prices (1,883 gross, 1,661 net) is shown directly as the sum of balance of primary incomes of the various sectors; national disposable income, national saving, etc. are also obtained directly.

2.202. The accumulation accounts follow the sequence of accounts for the institutional sectors.

2.203. It may be seen, for example, that saving, net of households is 160. Households receive 23 and pay 5 as capital transfers. Thus changes in their net worth due to saving and capital transfers is 178. Households have 61 as gross fixed capital formation (19 as net fixed capital formation after deduction of consumption of fixed capital), 2 as changes in inventories and 5 as acquisitions less disposals of valuables. Their acquisitions less disposals of non-produced non-financial assets (land actually) are 4. The net lending of households is 148. They incurred financial liabilities (net) of 33 and acquired financial assets (net) of 181. Other changes in volume of assets are 2. The value of the assets held by households increased by 96 due to changes in the actual prices of both non-financial assets (80) and financial assets (16); there are no nominal gains/losses on their liabilities, which means that all their liabilities are denominated in monetary terms and probably in the national currency of the economy in question.

2.204. The columns for goods and services record the counterparts of gross fixed capital formation, changes in inventories, and acquisitions less disposals of valuables on the right side. Transactions appear in the columns for the rest of the world only when it is relevant (mainly capital transfers and financial transactions).

2.205. The balance sheets also are presented. The rest of the world columns show the assets and liabilities position of the rest of the world vis-à-vis the nation (external assets and liabilities account). The row "changes in net worth due to saving and capital transfers" corresponds, for the rest of the world, to the current external balance and capital transfers.

2.206. In order to see the relations between accumulation accounts and balance sheets, general government may be taken as the example. The opening assets are 1,987 (1,591 non-financial assets and 396 financial assets) and the opening liabilities 687, net worth thus being 1,300. The total value of non-financial assets increase by 56, which results from all changes in these assets recorded in the accumulation accounts, gross fixed capital formation, 37, consumption of fixed capital, -30, acquisitions less disposals of valuables, 3, acquisitions less disposals of non-produced non-financial assets, 2, other volume changes (0 in balance) and nominal holding gains, 44. Financial assets increase by 123 (net acquisition of financial assets, 120, other volume changes, 1, nominal holding gains, 2). On the right side, liabilities increase by 176, which results again

from all changes in liabilities recorded in the accumulation accounts (net incurrence of liabilities, 170, other volume
changes, -1, revaluation of liabilities 7). So the closing assets
are 2,166 (1,647 + 519) and the closing liabilities are 863;
closing net worth, 1,302 shows an increase over the year of 2.
The sources of this change in net worth are summarized in the
right side of Account IV.2: changes in net worth due to saving
and capital transfers, -38 (see also the right side of the capital
account), to other changes in volume of assets, 2 (see also the
right side of the other changes in volume of assets account)
and to nominal holding gains/losses, 38 (see also the right side
of the revaluation account).

2.207. Taken in their entirety, the columns for the total economy
show the sequence of accounts applied to the nation as a
whole. In the table, these accounts correspond generally, in
each row, to the sum of the values for the resident institutional
sectors. This means that they are not consolidated. It is possible, outside the table itself, to show the sequence of accounts
for the total economy after consolidation of the relations between resident institutional sectors.

2.208. The integrated economic accounts provide an overview of the
economy as a whole. As already indicated, the integrated presentation contains much more than what has actually been included in the table and may be used for giving a more detailed
view if so desired. Columns might be introduced for sub-sectors. The rest of the world column could be subdivided according to various geographical zones. The column for goods and
services may show market goods and services separately. The
classification of transactions in the rows might be used at more
detailed levels (see chapter XIX) for further elaboration of
these suggestions).

2.209. However, putting more directly in this scheme at the same
time would result in a very complicated and unmanageable
table. For this reason, more detailed analysis of production
and transactions in goods and services, transactions in financial instruments, detailed balance sheets, as well as analysis by
purpose are done in other frameworks. These are presented
successively, and their links with the integrated economic accounts also explained.

3. The other parts of the accounting structure

The central supply and use table and other input-output tables

2.210. The detailed analysis of production by industries and flows of
goods and services by kind of products is an integral part of
the integrated central framework. It would be feasible to include certain details in the integrated economic accounts table.
For example, the rows for output, intermediate consumption
and value added might be subdivided by kind of economic activity; the columns for goods and services might be subdivided
by type of products. However, the System does not adopt this
solution, because the table would become cumbersome. It pro-

vides a systematic cross-classification by institutional sectors
and industries of output, intermediate consumption, and value
added and its components (see table 15.3, chapter XV).

2.211. The integrated economic accounts contain only production
and generation of income accounts by institutional sectors as
well as a global balance of transactions on goods and services.
The detailed analysis of production activities and goods and
services balances is made in the input-output tables. The
input-output framework of the System includes a number of
different approaches as regards producing units, valuation of
transactions, etc. They are presented in the relevant chapter.

2.212. The central input-output table (supply and use table) of the
System presents:

> The resources and uses of goods and services for each
> type of product

> The production and generation of income accounts for
> each industry according to kind of economic activity.

The goods and services account has already been presented
(see paragraphs 2.154 to 2.159 in section D.2 above). The
sequence of accounts for establishments and industries is
limited to the production account (Account I) and the generation of income account (Account II.1.1). These accounts,
shown in table 2.7, are identical in format to the corresponding accounts for institutional units or sectors. However, in the supply and use table, the output and
intermediate consumption of industries are broken down by
products. Data on factors of production (labour and fixed
capital) used by industries are also provided.

2.213. The supply and use table is presented fully in chapter XV, (see
table 15.1). It includes a number of specifications which are
not necessary at this stage of the presentation of the accounting
structure. Table 2.10 shows a reduced format of the supply and
use table. This reduced format is not a simplified version of the
normal one and should not be used as such. It is intended only
to introduce the overall structure of the supply and use tables.

2.214. The upper part of the table shows the origin of the resources of
goods and services. In the rows, the various types of products
are presented according to a classification which can be used
at various levels of detail. In the columns, starting from the
right side, imports are shown first. Then a matrix showing the
output of industries, according to the activity classification,
appears. This is the make matrix. It may be valued either at
basic prices or at producers' prices in the absence of a value
added tax (VAT), or at producers' prices in the presence of
VAT. The actual figures in the table are at basic prices which
is the preferred method of valuation for output. The column
for total industries records the total output of industries for
each kind of product. The output of a given industry may cover
a number of different products, the principal and the secondary ones.

2.215. Taxes, less subsidies, on products—with varying content according to the valuation of output—and trade and transport margins are recorded in two columns in order to get total supply of each type of product valued at purchasers' prices. The corresponding trade and transport services are deducted globally at the intersection between the relevant rows and the column for trade and transport margins. Thus the total of the latter is zero.

2.216. Below, uses of goods and services are recorded at purchasers' prices (i.e., including taxes, less subsidies, on products except deductible taxes) in a use or absorption matrix. The same classification of products is used in the rows. For each product, of course, total supply and total use in purchasers' prices are equal. Columns include sequentially intermediate consumption of industries, again using the same classification as in the upper part; exports; final consumption expenditure and gross capital formation. The column for total industries records total intermediate consumption of industries for each kind of product.

2.217. As the columns for final consumption record first final consumption expenditure by institutional sectors, the column for government is further subdivided between individual consumption expenditure and collective consumption expenditure, in order to allow actual final consumption for households and government to be calculated.

2.218. The lower part of table 2.10 refers to gross value added and its components: compensation of employees, taxes, less subsidies, on products, other taxes, less subsidies, on production, operating surplus/mixed income (which is shown gross and net) and consumption of fixed capital. These rows appear only in the columns for industries and the total economy.

2.219. It is easy to recognize in table 2.10 the shortened sequence of accounts for industries (production and generation of income accounts) that has been presented above. For each industry, the composition of its output by product appears in the upper part of the table; below is intermediate consumption by product, and components of value added can be seen. Data on factors of production of each industry are also shown below: labour inputs, gross fixed capital formation and stocks of fixed assets.

2.220. The total gross value added of industries differs from GDP by the amount of taxes, less subsidies, on products not included in the value added of any industry. In order to get GDP directly in the supply and use table, a column for the total economy, distinct from total industries, is added in the lowest part of the table. It records first the components of value added which already appear in the column for total industries, and then taxes, less subsidies, on products. The latter are conveyed to the lowest part of the table through the column taxes, less subsidies, on products. This can be shown in the table: total value added of industries is 1,721. It excludes all taxes, less subsidies, on products because output is valued at basic prices. GDP (1,854) appears at the intersection between the row total gross value

added/GDP and the column total economy. It is the sum of total gross value added (1,721) and taxes, less subsidies, on products (133), which appears at the intersection between the row "Taxes, less subsidies, on products" and the column "Total economy".[11]

2.221. Table 2.10 as it stands provides simple links with the integrated economic accounts. Exactly the same concepts and definitions and the same valuation are used for the central supply and use table and the institutional sector accounts. Consequently, the global figures for output, imports of goods and services, taxes, less subsidies, on products, intermediate consumption, exports of goods and services, final national expenditure, gross value added and its components and of course GDP are the same in both tables. Uses at purchasers' prices are close to the way economic units generally look at them and provide figures most current analysts require in the first instance.

2.222. The three approaches to GDP (1,854) appear in the supply and use table, as well as in the integrated economic accounts:

From the production side, GDP is equal to total output (3,604) minus total intermediate consumption (1,883) plus taxes, less subsidies, on products (133) not included in the value of output.

From the demand side, GDP is equal to final consumption expenditure (1,015 + 16 + 156 + 212) plus gross capital formation (376 + 28 + 10) plus exports (540) minus imports (499).

From the income side, GDP is equal to compensation of employees (762) plus taxes, less subsidies, on production and imports (191), plus mixed income, gross (442), plus operating surplus, gross (459).

2.223. The central supply and use table integrates various approaches which often are only followed in part on an annual basis. The lower part of table 2.10 includes the breakdown of GDP by industry of origin which is familiar to many people. The two upper parts of the table correspond to the so-called commodity-flow approach. If one does not break down the intermediate consumption by industry of use, keeping only the total by product (column for total industries), a simplified commodity flow approach may be followed. This permits the balancing of supply and disposition to be undertaken on a regular annual basis, even when intermediate consumption can not be analysed with the same frequency for each industry according to its cost structure. Additionally, if detailed complete input-output tables are established from time to time, intermediate consumption cross-classified by industry and by product may be estimated for other years as a checking procedure for the balancing of the accounts. In brief, the central supply and use table (which is in fact an input-output table) may provide means of integrating regular analysis of production by industries and flows of goods and services, in the absence of more refined input-output analysis.

2.224. In addition to what is included in the central supply and use table (see table 15.1 in chapter XV), the System allows for a number of derived and analytical input-output tables, where the use table may be valued at basic prices, or domestic and import components of uses shown separately and supply and use tables converted into symmetric tables.

The tables of financial transactions and financial assets and liabilities

2.225. The System provides for an in-depth analysis of financial transactions and financial assets and liabilities. In the integrated economic accounts, transactions in financial instruments are shown using the most aggregated level of their classification and the institutional sectors are also shown at the first level. Opening and closing financial assets and liabilities are shown only globally. This is a first overview of an integrated presentation of all financial transactions, other changes and stocks of assets and liabilities of the various institutional sectors in the context of accounts and balance sheets covering all aspects of economic life in the SNA sense. The juxtaposition of the accounts for all institutional sectors and the rest of the world allows the derivation of a balance of transactions in financial instruments for each main category of the latter. In total, the integrated economic accounts give an overall summary of the results of financial life.

2.226. However, one may want to know more about the financial transactions undertaken by a given sector. In that case, a more detailed level of the classification of financial instruments must be used. The financial account of each institutional sector showing the relevant details is presented in chapter XI. It is also necessary for financial analysis purposes to use the classification of institutional sectors at a more detailed level, especially in the case of financial corporations.

2.227. Grouping together the financial accounts for detailed sectors and sub-sectors and the detailed category of transactions in financial instruments results in a detailed table of financial transactions. In fact, this table is no more than an expansion of the financial part of the integrated economic accounts. This table (or conceivable variants) uses the full classification of transactions and more detailed levels of the sectors classification, especially for financial corporations. In addition, many of the categories of financial instruments, but particularly currency and deposits, are subdivided according to positions denominated in foreign currency and those denominated in national currency. Direct investment is recorded as a memorandum item (see chapter XI).

2.228. Tables cross-classifying financial instruments with debtor and creditor sectors, respectively, exhibit direct connections between debtors and creditors except when only one debtor sector or one creditor sector is involved. In order to show these links, which are very important for financial analysis, an additional three-dimensional approach is followed in the System. The objective is to show, first, for a given debtor sector and

each type of financial instrument, which sectors have changed their creditor position toward the given one in the period. Secondly, conversely, the objective is to show, for a given creditor sector and each type of financial instrument, which sectors have changed their debtor position toward the given one in this period. Schematically, these relations may be summarized in the reduced format of table 2.11. There is a column for each financial instrument. Then, for each debtor sector, changes in its debtor position toward each of the sectors (including itself when transactions between units composing this sector have not been consolidated) are shown successively. Of course, the symmetric information (changes in creditor position of a given sector toward the various sectors, including itself) is automatically provided for. The lower parts of the table show the totals which correspond exactly to those found in a two-dimensional table of the kind referred to previously.

2.229. In fact, the three-dimensional table of financial transactions assembles a number of matrices of the type sectors/sectors, one for each kind of financial instrument.

2.230. As such a presentation is not necessarily useful for actually presenting the data, other presentation(s) may be preferred in practice for publication. For example, a detailed classification of financial instruments combined with a sector classification may be cross-classified twice with the sector classification, in order to show, from one side, changes in the debtor positions of the debtor sectors and, from the other side, changes in the creditor positions of the creditor sectors. As compared to the presentation of the financial accounts made in the integrated economic accounts, this means, in short, introducing a sector distinction below headings of financial instruments when relevant (for a more complete explanation see chapter XI).

2.231. For financial analysis, tables showing stocks of financial assets and liabilities are very useful. As for transactions in financial instruments, these tables may show simply the assets position and the liabilities position of the various sectors without indicating which sector is the creditor or debtor of other sectors. In addition, three-dimensional tables may be elaborated showing the "from whom to whom?" links for each type of financial instrument, to permit better analysis. The presentation of such tables is exactly the same as for tables of financial transactions except that assets/liabilities are shown instead of changes in assets/liabilities and the net financial position of each sector appears instead of its net lending/-borrowing.

Complete balance sheets and assets and liabilities accounts

2.232. Balance sheets in the integrated economic accounts are presented in a very aggregated way. For each sector or sub-sector more complete balance sheets may be built up using the detailed classification of assets and liabilities when appropriate. Changes in assets and liabilities for each sector may also be analysed for each type of asset and liability and each source of change, as in table 2.12, which is an integrated presentation of balance sheet and accumulation accounts, that is, a full presentation of the assets and liabilities accounts as described in paragraph 2.162 above.

2.233. Assets, liabilities, and net worth are shown in the rows. The first column relates to the opening balance sheet (at prices as of the beginning of the period), the last one to the closing balance sheet (at prices as of the end of the period). The columns in between indicate the changes in assets, liabilities, and net worth described in the accumulation accounts. Thus this table is a cross-classification of assets/liabilities/net worth and sources of change in them, which can be done systematically if so desired.

2.234. Such tables for all institutional sectors, the total economy and the rest of the world may all be put together in a synoptic table.

Functional analysis

2.235. As explained in section B above, the purpose of a transaction is a different dimension from the ones which are dealt with in the previous tables. Some tables cross-classify, for certain sectors or sub-sectors, purposes and types of transactions when it is relevant (see chapter XVIII). As compatible but different classifications are used according to the sector concerned, these partial analyses by purpose cannot be integrated in a single table and, in most cases, no exhaustive total for the total

economy may be calculated in the central framework. The functional analysis can be further developed, outside the central framework, in satellite accounts in which significant national aggregates are calculated (see chapter XXI).

Population and labour inputs tables

2.236. A dimension is added to the usefulness of a number of national accounts figures by calculating these figures per head. For broad aggregates such as GDP, GNI or household final consumption, the denominator commonly used is the total (resident) population. When sub-sectoring the accounts or part of the accounts of the household sector, data on the number of households and the number of persons living in each sub-sector are also necessary.

2.237. In productivity studies, data on the labour inputs used by each industry in the process of production are indispensable. Total hours worked is the preferred measure of labour inputs for the System. Inferior alternatives are full-time equivalent jobs, the number of jobs or the number of persons employed.

2.238. Data on population and labour inputs must generally be adjusted in order to be consistent with the System's concepts, definitions and classifications. The resulting tables are an integral part of the SNA (see chapter XVII).

E. The integrated central framework and flexibility

1. Applying the central framework in a flexible way

2.239. The central framework presented in this chapter is coherent in terms of its concepts and its accounting structure. Links between the various elements of the integrated System have been emphasized in order to depict its structure in a simple but complete way. That presentation does not imply any order of priority or frequency (quarterly, annually, etc.) for implementing national accounts. Priorities in compiling national accounts are a matter of statistical policy; no universal recommendation can be made. (However, some indications relevant to specific circumstances are provided in the relevant handbooks.) Similarly, the accounting structure does not imply that results always have to be presented exactly as they stand in this or other chapters. A country may choose to publish mainly time series, to prepare only some accounts or aggregates, etc. However, attention needs to be drawn to the following point. Because users may find it difficult to fully understand the conceptual and practical links between the various parts of the System, it is advisable to use the kind of presentation made in table 2.8, with the appropriate adaptations to a country's circumstances and needs.

2.240. In general, the System has to be looked at in a consistent but flexible way. According to analytical requirements and data availability, emphasis put on various aspects within the central

framework may vary. In general, emphasis may be varied by using the System's classifications of institutional sectors, industries, products, transactions (including the complementary classification), sequence of accounts, etc. at various levels of detail (including additional ones); by using different methods of valuation; by using different priorities for various parts of the accounts and different frequencies; by rearranging the results; by introducing some additional elements, etc.

2.241. The household sector provides a good illustration of what may be done in order to provide an in-depth analysis of the household conditions and the functioning of the economy as a whole. The necessary detailed approach to the household sector may be undertaken, first, by deconsolidating the household sector beyond the sub-sectors included in the main classification of the System, distinguishing, for instance, the type of economic activity carried out (formal/informal), the location of the household (urban/rural) or the level of skill. Secondly, it is possible to adapt the way household activities are portrayed in the sequence of accounts. For instance, a concept of discretionary income may be used, which relates to that part of disposable income which is provided in cash and on the use of which households may take decisions, or the classification of household transactions may be complemented, for example, to isolate in-kind components or to show the industry of origin of various types of income.

2.242. The flexibility of the System is further illustrated with the public sector, whose components are systematically shown at various levels of detail in the classification of institutional sectors. The components of the public sector may be re-arranged to group the accounts of the overall public sector. These accounts may be shown before consolidation and after consolidation to describe the relations between the public sector and the private sector and between the public sector and the rest of the world (by separating out the external transactions of the public sector).

2.243. Chapter XIX provides a more detailed analysis of the above examples. It also presents illustrations of flexible uses of the central framework in the field of key sector accounting, external accounts problems and high inflation analysis. Finally, it touches briefly upon quarterly and regional accounts.

2. Introducing social accounting matrices

2.244. A social accounting matrix (SAM) is a presentation of the SNA in matrix terms that incorporates whatever degree of detail is of special interest. To date, builders of SAMs have exploited the available flexibility to highlight special interests and concerns more than compilers of regular national accounts, displaying the interconnections, disaggregating the household sector, showing the link between income generation and consumption, etc. The power of a SAM, as well as of the SNA, comes from choosing the appropriate type of disaggregation to study the topic of interest. In addition to a flexible application and the inclusion of various complements, SAMs may incorporate more extensive adjustments, which are of a satellite accounting nature, in order to serve specific analytical purposes. For further explanation of the matrix presentation and SAMs, see the annex to this chapter and chapter XX.

3. Introducing satellite accounts

2.245. In some cases, working with the central framework, even in a flexible way, is not sufficient. Even when conceptually consistent, the central framework could be overburdened with details. Moreover, some requirements may conflict with the central conceptual framework and its architecture.

2.246. In certain types of analysis, the basic intention is not to use alternative economic concepts, but simply to focus on a certain field or aspect of economic and social life in the context of national accounts. The intent is to make apparent and to describe in more depth aspects that are hidden in the accounts of the central framework or surface only in a limited number of points. Tourism is a good example. Various aspects of producing and consuming activities connected with tourism may appear in detailed classifications of activities, products and purposes. However, specific tourism transactions and purposes appear separately only in a few cases. In order to describe and measure tourism in a national accounts framework, it is necessary to make a choice between two approaches: either subdivide many elements in the accounts of the central framework to get the required figures for tourism and pay the price of overburdening and imbalancing the various components of the accounts, or elaborate a specific framework for tourism. The latter approach, the only feasible one actually, also allows adaptation of the various classifications and measurement of additional aggregates, such as national expenditure on tourism, which may cover intermediate as well as final consumption.

2.247. In other types of analysis, more emphasis is given to alternative concepts. For instance, the production boundary may be changed, generally by enlarging it. For example, the production of domestic services by members of the household for their own final consumption may be brought within the production boundary. The concept of fixed assets and the related fixed capital formation may be broadened, by covering research and development expenditures, consumer durables or human capital. It is also possible in environmental accounting to record the relations between natural assets and economic activities differently, by recording the depletion of subsoil or other natural resources and the degradation of natural assets. In these approaches, the economic process itself is depicted differently, and complementary or alternative aggregates are calculated.

2.248. The analysis of a number of important fields such as social protection, health or the environment may benefit from building a framework to accommodate elements which are included in the central accounts, explicitly or implicitly, plus complementary elements (either monetary or in physical quantities) and possibly alternative concepts and presentations. In all cases, however, the links with the central framework are made explicit, there are a number of common elements and any contradictory features are introduced, not by chance, but after explicitly considering various ways of looking at reality.

2.249. Those special constructs, which are semi-integrated with the central framework, are called satellite accounts. Chapter XXI is devoted to satellite analysis and accounts. Due to the importance of environmental concerns, a section in that chapter deals specifically with satellite accounts for environmental accounting.

Notes

1 The way producers' prices are defined means that value added type taxes are never considered in the System to be costs against production but levies on uses; producers are deemed to collect, on behalf of government, taxes which are not part of their own turnover. The use of basic prices might be interpreted as extending this scheme to all taxes on products. Business accounting practices may vary from one country to another or within a given country. The trend seems to be toward the recording of taxes on products separately from turnover.

2 However, taxes and subsidies on imports are never channelled through the accounts of producers.

3 The fact that balancing items can be expressed in gross or in net terms is not repeated in the presentation of the other accounts.

4 This balancing item is called mixed income in the case of the household sector, except for the operating surplus of the services of owner-occupied dwellings, because it covers return both to labour of self-employed and capital.

5 Adjusted disposable income is conceptually very close to the item "total income" used for a long time in the work on SNA/MPS links.

6 If basic prices are used for valuing output, GDP is equal to the sum of gross value added of all resident producer units plus all taxes on products (less subsidies on products). If producers' prices are used for valuing output, GDP is equal to the sum of gross value added of all resident producer units plus taxes and duties on imports, less import subsidies—in absence of a value added tax system—or plus taxes and duties on imports (less import subsidies) and value added type taxes—when such a taxation system does exist.

7 For the economy as a whole there is no difference between disposable income and adjusted disposable income, because current transfers in kind to or from the rest of the world are treated in the same way as transfers in cash.

8 In this table, output is valued at basic prices. Consequently, taxes less subsidies on products do not appear at all in the account of producers.

9 In order to lighten the presentation of the table, consumption of fixed capital, which always makes the difference between gross and net balancing items, has not been repeated, except when showing figures for saving.

10 Of course, if output were valued at producers' prices, the amount of taxes on products (net) recorded here would be lower.

11 If output were valued at producers' prices, figures for taxes, less subsidies, on products would appear partly in the column for these taxes, partly in the columns for industries.

Annex
Other presentations of the accounts

1. The System of National Accounts mainly uses the classical presentation of accounts in the form of balancing statements, with uses on one side and resources on the other side. Other types of presentation may be used.

A. Diagrammatic presentation

2. The diagrammatic presentation uses boxes linked together by arrows, to indicate the nature and size of the flows and stocks represented.

3. For the economy as a whole, figures corresponding to the ones which appear in the integrated economic accounts are shown in a simplified way in figure 2.4.

4. A set of equations, which are described below, corresponds to this diagram and to the integrated economic accounts.

B. Equations

5. The equalities of the System may be represented by sets of equations that are used, for example, in model building. The accounts for the total economy are shown in table 2.4 and in equation form.

6. Equations (1) and (2) cover the production and goods and services accounts. All transactions in these equations correspond to arrows going to or from the boxes "production" and "goods and services" in the diagram.

7. Equations (3) to (6) cover the distribution and use of income accounts and the corresponding box in the diagram. The aggregates are not shown directly in the latter, but they are derived easily according to the relevant equations.

8. Equations (7) to (10) and (15) cover the accumulation accounts and the box "accumulation" in the diagram.

9. Equations (11) to (17) correspond to opening and closing balance sheets and changes between balance sheets. They cover the boxes "opening stocks" and "closing stocks" and the changes between as they are shown in the diagram. Those changes are identical to the content of equations (7) to (10) and (15), the other changes in volume of assets and the revaluation being shown separately for the three types of assets and liabilities.

10. Equations (18) and (21) contain the external transactions (box "external transactions" in the diagram) and the external financial position of the nation presented from the point of view of the nation. The opening and closing positions and the changes between are shown in the diagram.

11. Thus, the diagram may be read by reading the equations, and the equations are illustrated by the diagram.

12. Similarly the various parts of the System may be presented in equation form: the full sequence of accounts for institutional sectors, the shortened sequence of accounts for industries, the transactions accounts such as the goods and services account, the rest of the world accounts, etc.

Figure 2.4. Diagram of the integrated economic accounts for the total economy

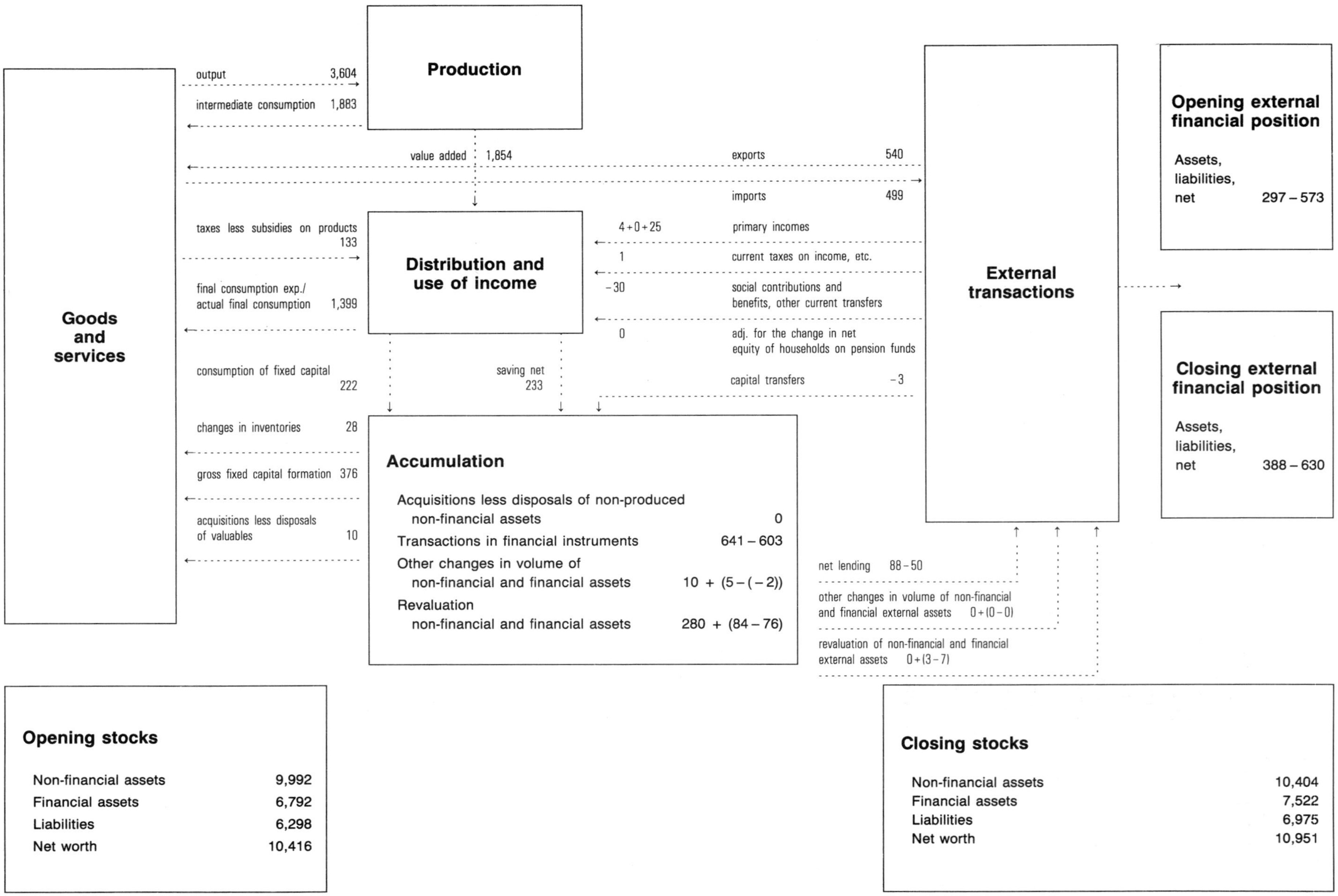

Production

output   3,604
intermediate consumption   1,883
value added   1,854

Distribution and use of income

taxes less subsidies on products   133
final consumption exp./actual final consumption   1,399
saving net   233

Accumulation

consumption of fixed capital   222
changes in inventories   28
gross fixed capital formation   376
acquisitions less disposals of valuables   10

Acquisitions less disposals of non-produced non-financial assets   0
Transactions in financial instruments   641 – 603
Other changes in volume of non-financial and financial assets   10 + (5 – (– 2))
Revaluation non-financial and financial assets   280 + (84 – 76)

Goods and services

External transactions

exports   540
imports   499
primary incomes   4 + 0 ÷ 25
current taxes on income, etc.   1
social contributions and benefits, other current transfers   – 30
adj. for the change in net equity of households on pension funds   0
capital transfers   – 3

net lending   88 – 50
other changes in volume of non-financial and financial external assets   0 + (0 – 0)
revaluation of non-financial and financial external assets   0 + (3 – 7)

Opening external financial position

Assets, liabilities, net   297 – 573

Closing external financial position

Assets, liabilities, net   388 – 630

Closing stocks

Non-financial assets   10,404
Financial assets   7,522
Liabilities   6,975
Net worth   10,951

Opening stocks

Non-financial assets   9,992
Financial assets   6,792
Liabilities   6,298
Net worth   10,416

*The illustrative data shown here are based on the "total economy" columns of table 2.6.

Table 2.4.   Equations

(1)	Gross domestic product (GDP) at market prices = Output + taxes, less subsidies, on products - intermediate consumption.	1,854 = 3,604 + 133 - 1,833
(2)	Gross domestic product (GDP) at market prices = Final consumption expenditure/actual final consumption + changes in inventories + gross fixed capital formation + acquisitions less disposals of valuables + exports of goods and services - imports of goods and services.	1,854 = 1,399 + 376 + 28 + 10 + 540 - 499
(3)	Gross national income (GNI) at market prices = GDP at market prices + taxes, less subsidies, on production and imports (net, receivable from abroad) + compensation of employees (net, receivable from abroad) + property income (net, receivable from abroad).	1,883 = 1,854 + 0 + 4 + 25
(4)	Net national income (NNI) at market prices = GNI at market prices - consumption of fixed capital.	1,661 = 1,883 - 222
(5)	Net national disposable income (NNDI) = NNI at market prices + current taxes on income, wealth, etc. (net, receivable from abroad) + social contributions and benefits and other current transfers (net, receivable from abroad).	1,632 = 1,661 + 1 + (–30)
(6)	Net national disposable income (NNDI) = Final consumption expenditure/actual final consumption + adjustment for the change in net equity of households on pension funds (net, receivable from abroad) + saving, net.	1,632 = 1,399 + 0 + 233
(7)	Saving, net + capital transfers (net, receivable from abroad) = Changes in net worth due to saving and capital transfers.	233 + (–3) = 230
(8)	Saving, net + capital transfers (net, receivable from abroad) = Gross fixed capital formation - consumption of fixed capital + changes in inventories + acquisitions less disposals of valuables + acquisitions less disposals of non-produced non-financial assets + net lending(=)/net borrowing(-).	233 + (–3) = 376 – 222 + 28 + 10 + 0 + 38
(9)	Net lending(=)/net borrowing(–) = Net acquisition of financial assets - net incurrence of liabilities.	38 = 641 - 603
(10)	Net lending (+)/net borrowing(–) = Net acquisition of financial (external) assets - net incurrence of (external) liabilities.	38 = 88 - 50
(11)	Opening assets - opening liabilities = Opening net worth.	16,714 - 6,298 = 10,416
(12)	Closing non-financial assets = Opening non-financial assets + gross fixed capital formation - consumption of fixed capital + changes in inventories + acquisitions less disposals of valuables + acquisitions less disposals of non-produced non-financial assets + other changes in volume of non-financial assets + revaluation of non-financial assets.	10,404 = 9,922 + 376 – 222 + 28 + 10 + 0 + 10 + 280

Table 2.4. **Equations** (*cont.*)

(13)	Closing financial assets = Opening financial assets + net acquisition of financial assets + other changes in volume of assets + revaluation of financial assets.	7,522 = 6,792 + 641 + 5 + 84
(14)	Closing liabilities = Opening liabilities + net incurrence of liabilities + other changes in volume of liabilities + revaluation of liabilities.	6,975 = 6,298 + 603 + (–2) + 76
(15)	Changes in net worth = Changes in net worth due to saving and capital transfers + changes in net worth due to other changes in volume of assets + changes in net worth due to nominal holding gains/losses.	535 = 230 + 17 + 288
(16)	Closing assets – closing liabilities = Closing net worth.	17,926 – 6,976 = 10,951
(17)	Closing net worth = Opening net worth + changes in net worth.	10,951 = 10,416 + 535
(18)	Exports of goods and services – imports of goods and service + taxes, less subsidies, on production and imports (net, receivable from abroad) + compensation of employees (net, receivable from abroad) + property income (net, receivable from abroad) + current taxes on income, wealth, etc. (net, receivable from abroad) + social contributions and benefits and other current transfers (net, receivable from abroad) + capital transfers (net, receivable from abroad) – acquisition less disposals of non-produced non-financial assets = Net acquisition of financial (external) assets – net incurrence of (external) liabilities.	540 – 499 + 0 + 4 + 25 + 1 + (–30) + (–3) – 0 = 88 – 50
(19)	Exports of goods and services – imports of goods and services + taxes, less subsidies, on production and imports (net, receivable from abroad) + compensation of employees (net, receivable from abroad) + property income (net, receivable from abroad) + current taxes on income, wealth, etc. (net, receivable from abroad) + social contributions and benefits and other current transfers (net, receivable from aborad) + capital transfers (net, receivable from abroad) – acquisitions less disposals of non-produced non-financial assets = Net lending(+)/net borrowing(–).	540 – 499 + 0 + 4 + 25 + 1 + (–30) + (–3) – 0 = 88 – 50
(20)	Net lending(+)/net borrowing(–) + other changes in volume of financial (external) assets + revaluation of financial (external) assets – other changes in volume of (external) liabilities – revaluation of (external) liabilities = Changes in net external financial position.	38 + 0 + 3 – 0 – 7 = 34
(21)	Net lending(+)/net borrowing(–) + other changes in volume of financial (external) assets + revaluation of financial (external) assets – other changes in volume of (external) liabilities – revaluation of (external) liabilities = Closing financial (external) assets – closing (external) liabilities – opening financial (external) assets + opening (external) liabilities.	38 + 0 + 3 – 0 – 7 = 388 – 630 – 297 + 573

C. Matrix presentation

13. A provisional matrix (table 2.5) is inserted at the back of this volume. This table demonstrates one way in which the columns for the total economy, goods and services and rest of the world from table 2.8, integrated economic accounts, can be displayed in a matrix.

14. The matrix is considered provisional because improvements are needed, particularly in the presentation of the accumulation accounts and balance sheets. The improvements will aim to make the matrix presentation less complex and easier to relate to the accounts in table 2.8.

15. The difficulty is related to the use of the main feature of the matrix presentation, i.e., that each item which is presented twice in the accounts of table 2.8—as use and resource, asset and liability—is only included once in the matrix: at the intersection of the column of the account in which it is a use or asset and the row of the account in which it is a resource or liability, or vice versa. This feature of the matrix presentation works well in the case of the current accounts and also for the capital account, as in these accounts there are always counterpart entries in the same or other accounts for each transaction. This is illustrated in the examples presented below.

16. For instance, the goods and services account (row and column 1), includes in its row and column in the same manner as in the account of table 2.8, the six major aggregates which define the main national accounts identity between supply and use. At the intersection of the column of the goods and services account and the row of production is recorded output and taxes on production and imports less subsidies (3,737) and in the same column and the row of the external account of goods and services is included the other element of supply, i.e. imports (499). In the row of the goods and services accounts are presented the four use categories, i.e., intermediate consumption (1,883), final consumption (1,399), gross capital formation (414) and exports (540).

17. Similarly the matrix items of the production account (row and column 2) correspond without any major change to those of table 2.8. Thus the account includes in the row output and taxes on production and imports less subsidies (3,737), and in the column intermediate consumption (1,883) and domestic product (1,854) which is recorded gross.

18. The next rows and columns (3 to 5) of the current account for the total economy, i.e., the primary distribution of income, secondary distribution of income and redistribution of income in kind and use of income accounts of the total economy have similar links with the items of the accounts in table 2.8 and may be read in the same manner. As consumption of fixed capital is presented as a negative item (-222) in the row of the use of income account and the column of the capital account, all main aggregates including domestic product, national income, and disposable income are recorded gross, except sav-

ing which is recorded net. One should also note that the primary distribution of income account consolidates the elements of the generation and allocation of primary income accounts and the secondary distribution of income and redistribution of income in kind accounts are combined into one account. The items of the current accounts for the rest of the world (rows and columns 13 and 14) correspond without any major changes to those presented in table 2.8.

19. The matrix presentation works less well for the other changes in volume of assets accounts and the revaluation accounts for which there are no counterpart entries. In order to incorporate the latter into the matrix presentation, several adjustments were made that affect all accumulation accounts and balance sheets. Dummy entries were introduced which cancel out in the same account. Furthermore, an additional account for net worth was incorporated to provide the link between opening and closing net worth. Finally, a different link was established between the rows and columns of the matrix and the two sides of the accounts in table 2.8. For the accounts starting with the goods and services account, production account and ending with the capital and financial accounts, the row items refer to resources and changes in liabilities and net worth and the items in the columns represent uses and changes in assets. On the other hand, in the accounts covering other changes in assets and opening balance sheets the presentation is reversed, i.e., the column items refer to liabilities, net worth and changes therein, and the row items concern assets and changes in assets; the presentation of the changes in balance sheet and the closing balance sheet is even more complex. As a consequence of these adjustments the link between the matrix presentation and the parallel accounts in table 2.8 is less obvious for the accumulation accounts and balance sheets.

20. The dummy entries in particular make the reading of the account more complex. For instance, the financial account of the total economy includes in the row two dummy items, i.e., net acquisition of financial assets and net acquisition of financial assets by rest of the world and in the column one dummy item called net incurrence of liabilities by rest of the world. These dummy items are presented twice with opposite signs and thus cancel out, and should be ignored in comparing the row and column entries with the entries in the financial account of table 2.8. Thus, the row of the financial account of the total economy opens with net lending of the total economy (38). Other transactions that correspond to items in the account of table 2.8 are in the row, transactions in financial assets between resident sectors (553) which is at the diagonal intersection between row and column of this account and net incurrence of external liabilities (50); and in the column, in addition to the diagonal element, net acquisition of external financial assets (88).

Appendix Tables 2.6-2.12

Table 2.6 Example of a transactions account: account for property income

Uses								Transactions			Resources							
Total	S.2 Rest of the world	S.1 Total economy	S.15 NPISHs	S.14 House-holds	S.13 General govern-ment	S.12 Financial corpo-rations	S.11 Non-financial corpo-rations				S.11 Non-financial corpo-rations	S.12 Financial corpo-rations	S.13 General govern-ment	S.14 House-holds	S.15 NPISHs	S.1 Total economy	S.2 Rest of the world	Total
230	13	217	6	14	35	106	56	D.41	Interest		33	106	14	49	7	209	21	230
120	36	84	0		0	36	48	D.42	Distributed income of corporations		3	25	18	57	0	103	17	120
60	0	60				36	24	D.421	Dividends		3	25	5	13	0	46	14	60
60	36	24	0		0	0	24	D.422	Withdrawals from income of quasi-corporations		0	0	13	44	0	57	3	60
14	14	0	0		0	0	0	D.43	Reinvested earnings on direct foreign investment		4	7	0	3	0	14	0	14
25		25				25		D.44	Property income attributed to insurance policy holders		5	0	0	20	0	25	0	25
65		65	0	27	7	0	31	D.45	Rent		41	3	0	21	0	65		65
454	63	391	6	41	42	167	135	D.4	*Property income, total*		86	141	32	150	7	416	38	454

Table 2.7.   Assets and liabilities accounts (example for the total economy) [1]

			Non-financial assets		Financial assets/liabilities	
			Produced assets	Non-produced assets	Financial assets	Liabilities
		Opening stocks	6 047	3 875	6 792	6 298
III.1 Capital account	P.51	Gross fixed capital formation	354	22		
	K.1	Consumption of fixed capital (−)	− 222	0		
	P.52	Changes in inventories	28	0		
	P.53	Acquisitions less disposals of valuables	10			
	K.2	Acquisitions less disposals of non-produced non-financial assets		0		
III.2 Financial account	F.1	Monetary gold and SDRs			− 1	
	F.2	Currency and deposits			119	132
	F.3	Securities other than shares			138	123
	F.4	Loans			244	217
	F.5	Shares and other equity			44	43
	F.6	Insurance technical reserves			42	42
	F.7	Other accounts receivable/payable			61	52
III.3.1 Other changes in volume of assets account	K.3	Economic appearance of non-produced assets		24		
	K.4	Economic appearance of produced assets	3			
	K.5	Natural growth of non-cultivated biological resources		4		
	K.6	Economic disappearance of non-produced assets		− 9		
	K.7	Catastrophic losses	− 9	− 2	0	0
	K.8	Uncompensated seizures	0	0	0	0
	K.9	Other volume changes in non-financial assets n.e.c.	1	0		
	K.10	Other volume changes in financial assets and liabilities n.e.c			3	− 2
	K.12	Changes in classification and structure	− 2	0	2	0
III.3.2 Revaluation account	K.11	Nominal holding gains/losses [2]	126	154	84	76
	K.11.1	Neutral holding gains/losses [2]	121	78	136	126
	K.11.2	Real holding gains/losses [2]	5	77	− 52	− 50
		Closing stocks	6 336	4 068	7 528	6 981

1   Differences between data on individual items and totals of holding
gains/losses may not be entirely consistent due to rounding errors.
2   Holding gains/losses, when:
    (+)   and applied to assets, are gains
    (−)   and applied to assets, are losses
    (+)   and applied to liabilities, are losses
    (−)   and applied to liabilities, are gains.

Table 2.8. Integrated economic accounts

Current accounts

Uses

Accounts	Total	Goods and service (res.)	Rest of the world	S.1 Total eco-nomy	S.15 NPISHs	S.14 House-holds	S.13 General govern-ment	S.12 Finan-cial corpo-rations	S.11 Non-finan-cial corpo-rations	Code	Transactions and other flows, stocks and balancing items
I. Production/ external account of goods and services	499	499								P.7	Imports of goods and services
	540		540							P.6	Exports of goods and services
	3 604	3 604								P.1	Output [1]
	1 883			1 883	9	694	252	29	899	P.2	Intermediate consumption
	133	133								D.21−D.31	Taxes less subsidies on products [1]
	1 854			1 854	31	575	188	73	854	B.1g/B.1*g	Value added, gross/Gross domestic product [2]
	222			222	3	42	30	10	137	K.1	Consumption of fixed capital
	1 632			1 632	28	533	158	63	717	B.1n/B.1*n	Value added, net/Net domestic product [2]
			−41							B.11	External balance of goods and services
II.1.1. Generation of income account	768		6	762	23	39	140	15	545	D.1	Compensation of employees
	191		0	191	0	2	2	3	51	D.2−D.3	Taxes less subsidies on production and imports
	133		0	133						D.21−D.31	Taxes less subsidies on products [1]
	58		0	58	0	2	2	3	51	D.29−D.39	Other taxes less subsidies on production
	459			459	8	92	46	55	258	B.2g	Operating surplus, gross
	442			442		442				B.3g	Mixed income, gross
	247			247	5	60	16	45	121	B.2n	Operating surplus, net
	432			432		432				B.3n	Mixed income, net
II.1.2. Allocation of primary income account	454		63	391	6	41	42	167	135	D.4	Property income
	1 883			1 883	9	1 409	227	29	209	B.5g	Balance of primary incomes, gross/National income, gross
	1 661			1 661	6	1 367	197	19	72	B.5n/B.5*n	Balance of primary incomes, net/National income, net
II.2. Secondary distribution of income account	213		1	212	0	178	0	10	24	D.5	Current taxes on income, wealth etc.
	322		0	322		322				D.61	Social contributions
	332		0	332	1	0	289	29	13	D.62	Social benefits other than social transfers in kind
	278		9	269	2	71	141	45	10	D.7	Other current transfers
	1 854			1 854	43	1 206	386	33	186	B.6g	Disposable income, gross
	1 632			1 632	40	1 164	356	23	49	B.6n	Disposable income, net
II.3. Redistribution of income in kind account	228			228	16		212			D.63	Social transfers in kind
	1 854			1 854	27	1 434	174	33	186	B.7g	Adjusted disposable income, gross
	1 632			1 632	24	1 392	144	23	49	B.7n	Adjusted disposable income, net
II.4. Use of income account										B.6g	Disposable income, gross
										B.6n	Disposable income, net
	1 399			1 399		1 243	156			P.4	Actual final consumption
	1 399			1 399	16	1 015	368			P.3	Final consumption expenditure
	11		0	11	0		0	11	0	D.8	Adjustment for the change in net equity of households on pension funds
	455			455	27	202	18	22	186	B.8g	Saving, gross
	233			233	24	160	−12	12	49	B.8n	Saving, net
	−41		−41							B.12	Current external balance

1 For the valuation of output and the resulting contents of the items "taxes on products" and "subsidies on products", refer to chapter VI, paragraphs 6.210 to 6.227.
2 For the total economy this item corresponds to gross domestic product, net domestic product respectively. It is equal to the value added of the institutional sectors plus taxes on products less subsidies.

Resources

S.11 Non-financial corporations	S.12 Financial corporations	S.13 General government	S.14 Households	S.15 NPISHs	S.1 Total economy	Rest of the world	Goods and service (uses)	Total	Accounts
						499		499	I. Production/
							540	540	external account
1 753	102	440	1 269	40	3 604			3 604	of goods and
							1 883	1 883	services
					133			133	
854	73	188	575	31	1 854			1 854	II.1.1. Generation of income account
717	63	158	533	28	1 632			1 632	
						−41			
			766		766	2		768	II.1.2. Allocation of primary
		191			191	0		191	income account
		133			133	0		133	
		58			58	0		58	
258	55	46	92	8	459			459	
			442		442			442	
121	45	16	60	5	247			247	
			432		432			432	
86	141	32	150	7	416	38		454	
209	29	227	1 409	9	1 883			1 883	II.2. Secondary distribution of income account
72	19	197	1 367	6	1 661			1 661	
		213			213	0		213	
14	39	268	0	1	322	0		322	
			332		332	0		332	
10	49	108	36	36	239	39		278	
186	33	386	1 206	43	1 854			1 854	II.3. Redistribution of income
49	23	356	1 164	40	1 632			1 632	in kind account
		228			228			228	
186	33	174	1 434	27	1 854			1 854	II.4. Use of income account
49	23	144	1 392	24	1 632			1 632	
186	33	386	1 206	43	1 854			1 854	
49	23	356	1 164	40	1 632			1 632	
							1 399	1 399	
							1 399	1 399	
		11			11	0		11	

Table 2.8. Integrated economic accounts [cont.]

Accumulation accounts

Changes in assets

Accounts	Total	Goods and service (res.)	Rest of the world	S.1 Total economy	S.15 NPISHs	S.14 Households	S.13 General government	S.12 Financial corporations	S.11 Non-financial corporations	Code	Transactions and other flows, stocks and balancing items
III.1. Capital account										B.8n	*Saving, net*
										B.12	*Current external balance*
	376			376	19	61	37	9	250	P.51	Gross fixed capital formation
	−222			−222	−3	−42	−30	−10	−137	K.1	Consumption of fixed capital (−)
	28			28	0	2	0	0	26	P.52	Changes in inventories
	10			10	0	5	3	0	2	P.53	Acquisitions less disposals of valuables
	0		0	0	1	4	2	0	−7	K.2	Acquisitions less disposals of non–produced non–financial assets
										D.9	Capital transfers, receivable
										D.9	Capital transfers, payable (−)
										B.10.1	*Changes in net worth due to saving and capital transfers [3][4]*
	0		−38	38	4	148	−52	6	−68	B.9	*Net lending (+) / net borrowing (−)*
III.2. Financial account	691		50	641	32	181	120	237	71	F	Net acquisition of financial assets\
										F	Net incurrence of liabilities
	0		1	−1			0	−1		F.1	Monetary gold and SDRs
	130		11	119	12	68	7	15	17	F.2	Currency and deposits
	143		5	138	12	29	26	53	18	F.3	Securities other than shares
	254		10	244	0	5	45	167	27	F.4	Loans
	46		2	44	0	3	36	3	2	F.5	Shares and other equity
	36		0	36	0	36	0	0	0	F.6	Insurance technical reserves
	82		21	61	8	40	6	0	7	F.7	Other accounts receivable/payable
III.3.1. Other changes in volume of assets account	15			15	0	2	1	−2	14	K.3−10 and K.12	Other volume changes, total
	24			24	0	0	0	0	24	K.3	Economic appearance of non–produced assets
	3			3	0	0	3	0	0	K.4	Economic appearance of produced assets
	4			4	0	0	4	0	0	K.5	Natural growth of non–cultivated biological resources
	−9			−9	0	0	−2	0	−7	K.6	Economic disappearance of non–produced assets
	−11		0	−11	0	0	−6	0	−5	K.7	Catastrophic losses
	0		0	0	0	0	8	−3	−5	K.8	Uncompensated seizures
	1			1	0	0	0	0	1	K.9	Other volume changes in non–financial assets n.e.c
	3		0	3	0	2	0	1	0	K.10	Other volume changes in financial assets and liabilities n.e.c
	0		0	0	0	0	−6	0	6	K.12	Changes in classifications and structure
										of which:	
	10		0	10	0	0	0	−2	12	AN	Non–financial assets
	−7			−7	0	0	−3	−2	−2	AN.1	Produced assets
	17		0	17	0	0	3	0	14	AN.2	Non–produced assets
	5		0	5	0	2	1	0	2	AF	Financial assets/Liabilities
										B.10.2	*Changes in net worth due to other changes in volume of assets*
III.3.2. Revaluation account [5]										K.11	Nominal holding gains/losses [5]
	280		0	280	8	80	44	4	144	AN	Non–financial assets
	126			126	5	35	20	2	63	AN.1	Produced assets
	154		0	154	3	45	23	2	81	AN.2	Non–produced assets
	91		7	84	1	16	2	57	8	AF	Financial assets/Liabilities
										B.10.3	*Changes in net worth due to nominal holding gains (+)/losses (−)*

3 "Changes in net worth due to saving and capital transfers" is not a balancing item, but corresponds to the total of the right-hand side of the capital account.
4 "Changes in net worth due to saving and capital transfers" for the rest of the world refers to changes in net worth due to current external balance and capital transfers.
5 Differences between data on individual items and totals of holding gains/losses may not be entirely consistent due to rounding errors.

Changes in liabilities and net worth

S.11 Non-financial corporations	S.12 Financial corporations	S.13 General government	S.14 House-holds	S.15 NPISHs	S.1 Total economy	Rest of the world	Goods and service (uses)	Total	Accounts
49	12	−12	160	24	233			233	III.1. Capital account
						−41		−41	
							376	376	
							28	28	
							10	10	
33	0	6	23	0	62	4		66	
−16	−7	−34	−5	−3	−65	−1		−66	
66	5	−40	178	21	230	−38		192	
−68	6	−52	148	4	38	−38		0	III.2. Financial account
140	232	170	33	28	603	88		691	
0	130	2	0	0	132	−2		130	
6	53	64	0	0	123	20		143	
71	0	94	28	24	217	37		254	
26	13	0		4	43	3		46	
0	36	0		0	36	0		36	
37	0	10	5	0	52	30		82	
−3	2	−1	0	0	−2	0		−2	III.3.1. Other changes in volume of assets account
0	0	0	0	0	0	0		0	
0	0	0	0	0	0	0		0	
−4	2	0	0	0	−2	0		−2	
1	0	−1	0	0	0	0		0	
−3	2	−1	0	0	−2	0		−2	
17	−4	2	2	0	17	0		17	
									III.3.2. Revaluation account
18	51	7	0	0	76	3		78	
134	10	38	96	10	288	4		292	

Table 2.8.   Integrated economic accounts [cont.]

Balance sheets

Assets

Accounts	Total	Goods and service (res.)	Rest of the world	S.1 Total eco-nomy	S.15 NPISHs	S.14 House-holds	S.13 General govern-ment	S.12 Finan-cial corpo-rations	S.11 Non-finan-cial corpo-rations	Code	Transactions and other flows, stocks and balancing items
IV.1. Opening balance sheet	9 922		0	9 922	324	2 822	1 591	144	5 041	AN	Non–financial assets
	6 047			6 047	243	1 698	1 001	104	3 001	AN.1	Produced assets
	3 875		0	3 875	81	1 124	590	40	2 040	AN.2	Non–produced assets
	7 365		573	6 792	172	1 819	396	3 508	897	AF	Financial assets/liabilities
										B.90	*Net worth*
IV.2. Changes in balance sheet [5]											Total changes in assets
	482		0	482	25	110	56	1	290	AN	Non–financial assets
	289			289	21	61	25	−1	182	AN.1	produced assets
	193		0	193	4	49	30	2	108	AN.2	non–produced assets
	787		57	730	33	199	123	294	81	AF	Financial assets/liabilities
										B.10	*Changes in net worth, total*
										B.10.1	*Saving and capital transfers*
										B.10.2	*Other changes in volume of assets*
										B.10.3	*Nominal holding gains (+)/losses (−)*
IV.3. Closing balance sheet [5]	10 404		0	10 404	349	2 932	1 647	145	5 331	AN	Non–financial assets
	6 336			6 336	264	1 759	1 026	103	3 183	AN.1	produced assets
	4 068		0	4 068	85	1 173	620	42	2 148	AN.2	non–produced assets
	8 152		630	7 522	205	2 018	519	3 802	978	AF	Financial assets/liabilities
										B.90	*Net worth*

6 Differences between data on individual items and totals of holding gains/losses may not be entirely consistent due to rounding errors.

Table 2.9.   Shortened sequence of accounts for industries

I. Production account

Uses		Resources	
P.2	Intermediate consumption	P.1	*Output [1]*
B.1g	*Value added, gross*		
K.1	Consumption of fixed capital		
B.1n	*Value added, net*		

1   For the valuation of output, refer to chapter VI, paragraphs 6.210 to 6.227.

II.1.1. Generation of income account

Uses		Resources	
D.1	Compensation of employees	B.1	*Value added [2]*
D.2	Taxes on production and imports [1]		
D.3	Subsidies (-) [1]		
B.2/B.3	*Operating surplus / mixed income [2]*		

1   For the contents of the items "taxes on production and imports and subsidies", refer to chapter VI, paragraphs 6.210 to 6.227.
2   The opening and the closing balancing item of this account can be expressed in gross or in net terms.

Liabilities

S.11 Non-finan-cial corpo-rations	S.12 Finan-cial corpo-rations	S.13 General govern-ment	S.14 House-holds	S.15 NPISHs	S.1 Total eco-nomy	Rest of the world	Goods and service (uses)	Total	Accounts
									IV.1. Opening balance sheet
1 817	3 384	687	289	121	6 298	297		6 595	
4 121	268	1 300	4 352	375	10 416	276		10 692	
									IV.2. Changes in balance sheet [6]
155	285	176	33	28	677	91		767	
216	10	2	276	31	535	−34		501	
66	5	−40	178	21	230	−38		192	
17	−4	2	2	0	17	0		17	
134	10	38	96	10	288	4		292	
									IV.3. Closing balance sheet [5]
1972	3 669	863	322	149	6 975	388		7 362	
4 337	278	1 302	4 628	406	10 951	242		11 193	

Table 2.10.   Supply and use (reduced format)

Supply of products

Resources		Total supply at purchasers' prices (1)	Trade and transport margins (2)	Taxes less subsidies on products (3)	Agriculture hunting, forestry fishing (A+B) (4)	Mining and quarrying (C) (5)	Manufacturing, electricity (D+E) (6)	Construction (F) (7)
	Goods and services (by CPC sections)							
1.	Agriculture, forestry and fishery products (0)	128	2	2	87	0	0	0
2.	Ores and minerals (1)	103	2	0	0	30	10	0
3.	Electricity, gas and water (17-18)	160	0	5	0	2	152	0
4.	Manufacturing (2-4)	2 160	74	89	2	2	1 666	11
5.	Construction work and construction, land (5)	262	0	17	0	0	7	232
6.	Trade services, restaurant and hotel services (6)	179	− 68	3	0	0	8	1
7.	Transport, storage and communication services (7)	111	− 10	5	0	0	0	0
8.	Business services (8)	590	0	8	0	1	0	0
9.	Community, social and pers. serv. excl. public admin. (9)	375	0	4	0	0	1	0
10.	Public administration (91)	168	0	0	0	0	0	0
11.	*Total*	4 236	0	133	89	35	1 844	244

Use of products, purchasers' price

Intermediate consumption in industries (by ISIC categories)

Uses		Total uses in purchasers' prices (1)	(2)	Taxes less subsidies on products (3)	Agriculture hunting, forestry fishing (A+B) (4)	Mining and quarrying (C) (5)	Manufacturing, electricity (D+E) (6)	Construction (F) (7)
	Goods and services (by CPC sections)							
1.	Agriculture, forestry and fishery products (0)	128			3	0	71	0
2.	Ores and minerals (1)	103			1	3	91	0
3.	Electricity, gas and water (17-18)	160			2	2	96	1
4.	Manufacturing (2-4)	2 160			32	7	675	80
5.	Construction work and construction, land (5)	262			1	2	7	5
6.	Trade services, restaurant and hotel services (6)	179			2	1	34	1
7.	Transport, storage and communication services (7)	111			2	1	29	3
8.	Business services (8)	590			3	1	117	23
9.	Community, social and pers. serv. exc. pub. ad. (9)	375			1	0	7	1
10.	Public administration (91)	168			0	0	0	0
11.	*Total uses in purchasers' prices*	4 236			47	17	1 127	114
12.	*Total gross value added/GDP*			133	42	18	717	130
13.	Compensation of employees				9	13	336	58
14.	Taxes less subsidies on production and imports			133	− 2	− 2	46	5
15.	Taxes less subsidies on products			133				
16.	Other taxes less subsidies on production				− 2	− 2	46	5
17.	Mixed income, net				14	0	227	35
18.	Operating surplus, net				10	4	30	21
19.	Consumption of fixed capital				11	3	78	11
20.	Mixed income, gross				17	0	228	36
21.	Operating surplus, gross				18	7	107	31
22.	*Total*				89	35	1 844	244
23.	*Labour inputs (hours worked)*				2 058	292	31 982	5 024
24.	*Gross fixed capital formation*				11	6	117	9
25.	*Stocks of fixed assets*				159	90	1 788	160

Wholesale, retail trade, repair motor vehicles and hshld goods, hotels, restaurants (G+H) (8)	Transport, storage, and communication (I) (9)	Financial intermediation, real estate, other business services (J+K) (10)	Education, health, personal services, pub. admin. and defense (M+N+O+P+L) (11)	Total industry, in basic prices (12)	(13)	Imports of goods and services (14)
0	0	0	0	87		37
1	0	0	0	41		60
0	0	0	0	154		1
16	8	7	2	1 714		283
0	5	0	0	244		1
149	7	0	0	165		79
21	75	0	0	96		20
2	3	465	98	569		13
2	2	6	355	366		5
0	0	0	168	168		0
191	100	478	623	3 604		499

								Final consumption expenditure				Gross capital formation		
Wholesale, retail trade, repair motor vehicles and hshld goods, hotels, restaurants (G+H) (8)	Transport, storage, and communication (I) (9)	Financial intermediation, real estate, other business services (J+K) (10)	Education, health, personal services, pub. admin. and defense (M+N+O+P+L) (11)	Total industry (12)	Total economy (13)	Exports of goods and services (14)	Households (14)	NPISHs individual (15)	General government individual (16)	collective (17)	Gross fixed capital formation (18)	Changes in inventories (19)	Net purchases of valuables (20)
---:	---:	---:	---:	---:	---:	---:	---:	---:	---:	---:	---:	---:	---:
3	1	5	5	88		7	28	0	0	2	2	1	
0	0	1	0	96		6	2	0	0	0		– 1	
5	3	4	10	123		1	36	0	0	0		0	
36	21	45	96	992		422	567	0	0	3	161	5	10
2	1	3	19	40		6	3	0	0	0	190	23	
9	6	4	4	61		67	51	0	0	0		0	
19	12	5	7	78		19	14	0	0	0		0	
25	15	54	71	309		8	250	0	0	0	23	0	
1	1	11	73	95		4	58	14	0	204	0	0	
0	0	0	1	1		0	6	2	156	3		0	
100	60	132	286	1 883		540	1 015	16	156	212	376	28	10
91	40	346	337	1 721	1 854								
44	16	54	232	762	762								
0	– 6	12	5	58	191								
					133								
0	– 6	12	5	58	58								
36	3	99	18	432	432								
– 4	12	127	47	247	247								
15	15	54	35	222	222								
36	7	99	19	442	442								
11	23	181	81	459	459								
191	100	478	623	3 604									
7 078	2 032	3 700	17 203	69 369									
20	39	144	30	376									
298	572	2 260	456	5 783									

Table 2.11.   Financial transactions between creditor and debtor sectors (reduced format)

Debtor sector		Creditor sector		F Total	F.1 Monetary gold and SDRs	F.2 Currency and deposits	F.3 Securities other than shares	F.4 Loans	F.5 Shares and other equity	F.6 Insurance technical reserves	F.7 Other accounts receivable/ payable
				By type of financial instrument							
				Assets of creditor sectors and liabilities of debtor sectors							
S.11	Non-financial corporations	S.11 S.12 S.13 S.14 S.15 S.2	Non-financial corporations Financial corporations General government Households NPISHs Rest of the world								
S.12	Financial corporations	S.11 S.12 S.13 S.14 S.15 S.2	Non-financial corporations Financial corporations General government Households NPISHs Rest of the world								
S.13	General government	S.11 S.12 S.13 S.14 S.15 S.2	Non-financial corporations Financial corporations General government Households NPISHs Rest of the world								
S.14	Households	S.11 S.12 S.13 S.14 S.15 S.2	Non-financial corporations Financial corporations General government Households NPISHs Rest of the world								
S.15	Non-profit institutions serving households	S.11 S.12 S.13 S.14 S.15 S.2	Non-financial corporations Financial corporations General government Households NPISHs Rest of the world								
S.2	Rest of the world	S.11 S.12 S.13 S.14 S.15 S.2	Non-financial corporations Financial corporations General government Households NPISHs Rest of the world								
				Liabilities of debtor sectors							
S.11	Non-financial corporations	All creditor sectors		140		0	6	71	26	0	37
S.12	Financial corporations			238		130	53	0	13	42	0
S.13	General government			170		2	64	94	0	0	10
S.14	Households			33		0	0	28			5
S.15	NPISHs			28		0	0	24	4	0	0
S.2	Rest of the world			88		-2	20	37	3	0	30
				Assets of creditor sectors							
All debtor sectors		S.11 S.12 S.13 S.14 S.15 S.2	Non-financial corporations Financial corporations General government Households NPISHs Rest of the world	71 237 120 187 32 50	 -1 0 1	17 15 7 68 12 11	18 53 26 29 12 5	27 167 45 5 0 10	2 3 36 3 0 2	0 0 0 42 0 0	7 0 6 40 8 21

Table 2.12. Integrated balance sheets and accumulation accounts (example for the total economy) [1]

Assets, liabilities and net worth		IV.1 Opening balance sheet	III.1/2 Capital and financial accounts	III.3.1 Other changes in volume of assets account	III.3.2 Revaluation account III.3.2.1 Nominal holding gains/ losses [2]	III.3.2.2 Neutral holding gains/ losses [2]	III.3.2.3 Real holding gains/ losses [2]	IV.3 Closing balance sheet
	Assets							
AN	Non-financial assets	9 922	192	10	280	198	81	10 404
AN.1	Produced assets	6 047	170	− 7	126	121	5	6 336
AN.11	Fixed assets	5 544	132	− 4	111	111	0	5 783
AN.111	Tangible fixed assets							
AN.1111	Dwellings							
AN.1112	Other buildings and structures							
AN.1113	Machinery and equipment							
AN.1114	Cultivated assets							
AN.112	Intangible fixed assets							
AN.1121	Mineral exploration							
AN.1122	Computer software							
AN.1123	Entertainment, literary or artistic originals							
AN.1129	Other intangible fixed assets							
AN.12	Inventories	231	28	− 1	7	5	3	265
AN.13	Valuables	272	10	− 2	8	5	2	288
AN.2	Non-produced assets	3 875	22	17	154	78	77	4 068
AN.21	Tangible non-produced assets	3 809	22	17	152	76	76	4 000
AN.211	Land							
AN.212	Subsoil assets							
AN.213	Non-cultivated biological resources							
AN.214	Water resources							
AN.22	Intangible non-produced assets	66	0	0	2	1	1	68
AF	Financial assets	6 792	641	5	84	136	− 52	7 522
AF.1	Monetary gold and SDRs	770	− 1	7	12	15	− 3	788
AF.2	Currency and deposits	1 482	119	0	0	30	− 30	1 601
AF.3	Securities other than shares	1 263	138	0	40	25	15	1 441
AF.4	Loans	1 384	244	− 4	0	28	− 28	1 624
AF.5	Shares and other equity	1 296	44	0	31	26	5	1 371
AF.6	Insurance technical reserves	370	36	2	0	7	− 7	408
AF.7	Other accounts receivable	227	61	0	0	5	− 5	288
AF	Liabilities	6 298	603	− 2	76	126	− 50	6 975
AF.2	Currency and deposits	1 471	132	0	0	29	− 29	1 603
AF.3	Securities other than shares	1 311	123	0	42	26	16	1 476
AF.4	Loans	1 437	217	− 4	0	29	− 29	1 650
AF.5	Shares and other equity	1 406	43	0	34	28	6	1 483
AF.6	Insurance technical reserves	371	36	2	0	7	− 7	409
AF.7	Other accounts payable	302	52	0	0	6	− 6	354
B.90	*Net worth*	10 416	230	17	288	208	80	10 951

1 Differences between data on individual items and totals of holding gains/losses may not be entirely consistent due to rounding errors
2 Holding gains/losses, when:
  (+) and applied to assets, are gains
  (−) and applied to assets, are losses
  (+) and applied to liabilities, are losses
  (−) and applied to liabilites, are gains.

III. Flows, stocks and accounting rules

A. Introduction

3.1. This chapter deals with the basic nature of the entries in the accounts and tables of the System. First, it defines the nature of flows and stocks. These are the two basic forms in which information about the economy can be recorded in a system of national accounts, flows referring to actions and effects of events that take place within a period of time and stocks referring to a position at a point of time. Secondly, it explains the rules of accounting that underlie the recording of flows and stocks. The discussion in this chapter is a general one; definitions of specific flows and stocks and specific applications of the accounting rules appear in later chapters.

3.2. Two general characteristics of the entries in the accounts should be emphasized. The first characteristic is that the stocks and flows are exhaustive within the boundaries defined; every flow and every stock must be reflected in the accounts. The second characteristic is the rigorousness that arises because the System is integrated and consistent. The same concepts, definitions and classifications of flows and stocks are applied to all accounts, and each flow or stock is recorded consistently for the parties involved.

3.3. To help ensure consistency, the System applies rules with respect to valuation, timing and grouping of flows and stocks in implementing the quadruple entry principle, described in the two previous chapters. These rules, which are explained in more detail later in this chapter, are summarized below to provide a context for the discussion of the nature of flows and stocks, which follows immediately:

(a) Flows and stock must be recorded consistently with respect to their valuation. Entries are at current value on the market—that is, the amount agreed upon by two parties—or at its closest equivalent. The value on the market may need to be adjusted to the coverage of the flow or stock as defined in the System and expressed appropriately given the nature of the flow or stock with respect to taxes and subsidies on products, transport costs and trade margins;

(b) Flows and stocks must be recorded consistently with respect to timing. Flows are recorded at the moment of accrual within the accounting period—that is, the moment economic value is created, transformed, exchanged, transferred or extinguished. Stocks are recorded at the moment to which the account relates, typically the beginning or end of the accounting period;

(c) Individual flow and stock entries must be recorded consistently with respect to their classification, at a minimum, according to categories in the classifications of transactions, other flows and assets and according to the categories in the classification of transactors as (sub)sectors or industries. Depending on the character of the entry, a distinction should be made between resources and uses or between assets and liabilities. In the process of grouping, netting is implicit for several items, but consolidation is not advised.

3.4. It should be noted that as a result of the application of these rules throughout the System, flows and stocks are completely integrated—that is, changes in stocks can be fully explained by recorded flows.

B. Stocks and flows

3.5. The System's accounts and tables contain information relating to the economic actions and the effects of events that take place within a given period of time and information relating to a position in assets and liabilities at the beginning and end of that period. The entries in the accounts and tables relating to actions and effects of events within a given period of time are flows and balancing items derived from them. The entries in the accounts and tables relating to assets and liabilities at a given point of time are stocks and balancing items derived from them.

3.6. Stocks appear in the balance sheets and related tables (and, for certain stocks, with the use table in an input-output context). Flows appear in all the other accounts and tables of the System. The flow accounts in the full sequence of accounts for institutional sectors consist of the current accounts, which deal with production, income and use of income, and the accumulation accounts, which show all changes between two balance sheets.

3.7. The flows and stocks are grouped according to the System's hierarchical classifications, shown in an annex at the end of the manual. The classification of transactions and other flows has four headings at the highest level, according to the nature of the flows. The classification of stocks in the balance sheets is by type of asset (liabilities being viewed as negative assets).

3.8. The flows and stocks are entered in the accounts of the insti-

tutional units involved and, accordingly, in the accounts of the sectors into which the institutional units are grouped. In general, flows and stocks are entered in the accounts of the institutional units that own or owned the goods and assets involved, in the accounts of units that deliver or take delivery of services, or in the accounts of units that provide labour and capital or use them in production. Flows relevant to establishments are entered in the accounts of the establishments involved and, accordingly, in the accounts of the industries into which establishments are grouped.

C. Flows

3.9. Economic flows reflect the creation, transformation, exchange, transfer or extinction of economic value; they involve changes in the volume, composition, or value of an institutional unit's assets and liabilities. Mirroring the diversity of the economy, economic flows have specific natures as wages, taxes, interest, capital flows, etc., that record the ways in which a unit's assets and liabilities are changed.

3.10. All entries in the accounts have to be measured in terms of money, and therefore the elements from which the entries are built up must be measured in terms of money. In some cases, the amounts entered are the actual payments that form part of flows that involve money; in other cases the amounts entered are estimated by reference to actual monetary values.

3.11. Economic flows are of two kinds. Most flows are transactions. Flows included in the System that do not meet the characteristics of transactions as described below are called "other flows". Transactions appear in all of the accounts and tables in which flows appear except two; other flows appear only in these two. The two are accumulation accounts, the other changes in the volume of assets account and the revaluation account. More meaning can be given to the definition of flows by describing the two kinds.

1. Transactions

3.12. A transaction is an economic flow that is an interaction between institutional units by mutual agreement or an action within an institutional unit that it is analytically useful to treat like a transaction, often because the unit is operating in two different capacities.

3.13. Institutional units, referred to in the definition, are the fundamental economic units of the System (see chapter IV). The following are the main attributes of institutional units that are relevant to their engaging in transactions:

(a) They are entitled to own goods or assets in their own right, and therefore are able to exchange them;

(b) They are able to take economic decisions and engage in

economic activities for which they are held to be directly responsible and accountable at law;

(c) They are able to incur liabilities on their own behalf, to take on other obligations or future commitments and to enter into contracts.

3.14. The definition of a transaction stipulates that an interaction between institutional units be by mutual agreement. When a transaction is undertaken by mutual agreement, the prior knowledge and consent of the institutional units is implied. This does not mean, however, that both units necessarily enter a transaction voluntarily, because some transactions are imposed by force of law, such as payments of taxes or other compulsory transfers. Although individual institutional units are not free to fix the amounts of taxes they pay, there is nevertheless collective recognition and acceptance by the community of the obligation to pay taxes. Thus, payments of taxes are considered transactions despite being compulsory.

3.15. Transactions take so many different forms that, even with these explanations, any general definition is inevitably rather imprecise. To give more precision, the various kinds of transactions have to be systematically described and classified. A first distinction is between monetary and non-monetary transactions. Other distinctions, such as between transactions with and without counterparts, are drawn within each of these kinds of transactions. Frequently the individual, identifiable transactions of everyday economic life are simply grouped together in the accounts; sometimes they are subdivided and rearranged in order to form the transaction categories of the System.

Monetary transactions

3.16. A monetary transaction is one in which one institutional unit makes a payment (receives a payment) or incurs a liability (receives an asset) stated in units of currency. In the System, all flows are recorded in monetary terms, but the distinguishing characteristic of a monetary transaction is that the parties to the transaction express their agreement in monetary terms. For example, a good is purchased/sold at a given number of units of currency per unit of the good, or labour is hired/provided at a given number of units of currency per hour or day.

3.17. All monetary transactions are interactions between institutional units; that is, all monetary transactions are two-party transactions. The following is a list of common monetary transactions:

   Expenditure on consumption of goods and services

   Acquisition of a security

   Wages and salaries

   Interest, dividends and rent

   Taxes

   Social assistance benefits in cash.

Transactions with and without counterparts

3.18. The expenditure on consumption of goods and services, the acquisition of a security, the wages and salaries, and the interest, dividends, and rent are two-party transactions in which one party provides a good, service, labour or asset to the other and receives a counterpart in return. This kind of transaction is sometimes called a "something for something" transaction or a transaction with a quid pro quo. Exchanges consist of such transactions.

3.19. Taxes and social assistance benefits are examples of two-party transactions in which one party provides a good, service or asset to the other but does not receive a counterpart in return. This kind of transaction, sometimes called a "something for nothing" transaction or a transaction without a quid pro quo, is called a transfer in the System.

3.20. The scope of the counterparts mentioned in describing exchanges and transfers does not cover entitlement to contingent benefits or collective services. Such benefits are generally uncertain or not quantifiable, or both. Moreover, the amount of benefit that may eventually be received by an individual unit is not proportional to the amount of the previous payment and may be very much greater or smaller than the latter. Thus, payments such as a social insurance contribution or a non-life insurance premium may entitle the unit making the payment to some contingent future benefits, and a household paying taxes may be able to consume certain collective services provided by government units, but these payments are regarded as transfers rather than exchanges.

3.21. Transfers may be either monetary or non-monetary (see the discussion below of non-monetary transfers). When transfers that are otherwise the same may be either monetary or non-monetary, as is true for social assistance benefits mentioned as an example, the two kinds are distinguished by calling the former a transfer in cash and the latter a transfer in kind. Actually, "in cash" is not fully descriptive because these transfers may provide either currency or a transferable deposit.

3.22. Another distinction is made within transfers—a distinction between current and capital. A capital transfer is one in which

the ownership of an asset is transferred or which obliges one or both parties to acquire, or dispose of, an asset. Capital transfers, which may be either in cash or in kind, redistribute saving or wealth. They include, for example, capital taxes and investment grants. Other transfers are described as current. Current transfers, which also may be either in cash or in kind, redistribute income. They include, for example, taxes on income and social benefits.

Rearrangements of transactions

3.23. Monetary transactions may not always be recorded in the accounts in the same way as they appear to the institutional units involved. The values of these actual, or observed, transactions are already available in the accounts of the units concerned, but the System rearranges certain transactions to bring out the underlying economic relationships more clearly. The three kinds of rearrangements affect the channels in which the transactions are seen as taking place, the number of transactions that are seen as taking place, or the units that are seen as being involved. The three sections below illustrate the main characteristics of these rearrangements and the kind of analytical purpose they serve.

Rerouting transactions

3.24. Rerouting records a transaction as taking place in channels that differ from the actual ones or as taking place in an economic sense when it actually does not. In the first kind of rerouting, a direct transaction between unit A and unit C is recorded as taking place indirectly through a third unit B, usually, however, with some change in the transaction category.

3.25. The recording of the payment of social security contributions is an example of the first kind of rerouting. Employees' social security contributions are recorded in the System as paid by employees out of their wages and salaries, while employers' social security contributions are recorded as constituting a part of compensation of employees. However, neither the employees' nor the employers' contributions are usually paid out to employees. Instead, they are paid directly by employers to social security funds. This arrangement is administratively convenient and efficient. However, as social security contributions are actually payable out of compensation of employees, they are shown as such in the accounts. Social security contributions are thus recorded strictly according to the general principles governing the recording of transactions in the System to bring out the economic substance behind arrangements adopted for administrative convenience. As a result of the rerouting, employer's social contributions are included as a part of labour cost.

3.26. An example of the second kind of rerouting is provided by the treatment of the retained earnings of foreign direct investment enterprises. The retention of some or all of the earnings of a foreign direct investment enterprise within that enterprise can be regarded as a deliberate investment decision by the foreign owners. Accordingly, the retained earnings are rerouted in the System by showing them as first remitted to the foreign owners as property income and then reinvested in the equity of the direct investment enterprise.

3.27. Similarly, the property income earned on the reserves of certain life insurance funds is deemed to be paid out to policyholders and then paid back again as premium supplements even though in actuality the property income is retained by the insurance enterprises. As a result, the saving of persons or households includes the amount of the rerouted property income while the saving of insurance enterprises does not. This alternative picture of saving is indeed the purpose of the rerouting.

Partitioning transactions

3.28. Partitioning records a transaction that is a single transaction from the perspective of the parties involved as two or more differently classified transactions. For example, the rental actually paid by the lessee under a financial lease is not recorded as a payment for a service; instead, it is partitioned into two transactions, a repayment of principal and a payment of interest. This partitioning of the rental payment is part of a treatment that implements an economic view of financial leasing in the System. Financial leasing is viewed as a method of financing the purchase of capital equipment, and a financial lease is shown in the System as a loan from the lessor to the lessee.

3.29. Another example is the treatment of certain financial services. For example, the System recommends partitioning interest payable and receivable by financial intermediaries into two components whenever possible. One component represents the System's notion of interest while the remainder represents the purchase of intermediation services for which the intermediaries do not charge explicitly. This partitioning to make the service item explicit affects intermediate and final consumption of particular industries and institutional sectors—indeed, that is a purpose of the reclassification—and also affects gross domestic product. However, the saving of all the units concerned, including the financial intermediaries themselves, is not affected.

3.30. The System's recording of transactions for wholesalers and retailers does not mirror the way in which those involved view them. The purchases of goods for resale by wholesalers and retailers are not recorded explicitly, and they are viewed as selling, not the goods, but the services of storing and displaying a selection of goods in convenient locations and making them easily available for customers. This partitioning implements the System's measure of output for traders, which is by the value of the margins on goods they purchase for resale.

Recognizing the principal party to a transaction

3.31. When a unit carries out a transaction on behalf of another unit, the transaction is recorded exclusively in the accounts of the principal. Some service output may be recognized with the intermediary. As a rule one should not go beyond this principle and try, for instance, to allocate taxes or subsidies to ultimate payers or ultimate beneficiaries under the adoption of assumptions.

3.32. For example, purchases a commercial agent makes under the orders of, and at the expense of, another party are directly attributed to the latter. The accounts of the agent only show the fee charged to the principal for intermediation services rendered.

3.33. A second example is the collection of taxes and the payment of subsidies, social benefits, etc., by one government unit on behalf of another. A central government may, for example, serve as an intermediary for local governments in collecting taxes. Then, if the central government lacks discretion about the amount of collection or distribution of the relevant monies, the transactions are recorded directly in the accounts of the local government. In general, tax revenues will be allocated directly to the non-collecting government when (a) it has full or partial authority over the setting of the tax, or (b) it receives automatically under the provisions of tax law a given percentage of the tax collected or arising in its territory.

Non-monetary transactions

3.34. Non-monetary transactions are transactions that are not initially stated in units of currency. The entries in the System therefore represent values that are indirectly measured or otherwise estimated. In some cases, the transaction may be an actual one, and a value has to be estimated to record it in the accounts. Barter is an obvious example. In other cases, the entire transaction must be constructed and then a value estimated for it. Consumption of fixed capital is an example. (In the past, the estimation of a value has sometimes been called imputation, but it is preferable to reserve that term for the kind of situation that involves not only estimating a value but also constructing a transaction.)

3.35. The amounts of money associated with non-monetary transactions are entries whose economic significance is different from cash payments as they do not represent freely disposable sums of money. The various methods of valuation to be employed for non-monetary transactions are dealt with in the general section on valuation.

3.36. Non-monetary transactions can be either two-party transactions or actions within an institutional unit. The two-party transactions consist of barter, remuneration in kind, payments in kind other than compensation in kind and transfers in kind. These two-party transactions will be discussed first, followed by a discussion of internal transactions.

Barter transactions

3.37. Barter transactions involve two parties, with one party providing a good, service or asset other than cash to the other in return for a good, service or asset other than cash. As mentioned above, barter is an example of an actual transaction for which a value must be estimated. Barter transactions in which goods are traded for goods have always been important. The barter of goods may be systematically organised on proper markets or, in some countries, may occur only sporadically on a small scale. Barter between nations—thus involving exports and imports—also occurs.

Remuneration in kind

3.38. Remuneration in kind occurs when an employee accepts payment in the form of goods and services instead of money. This practice is extensive in most economies for reasons ranging from the desire of employers to find captive markets for part of their output, to tax avoidance or evasion. There are various forms, and the following list includes some of the most common types of goods and services provided without charge, or at reduced prices, by employers to their employees:

> Meals and drinks
>
> Housing services or accommodation of a type that can be used by all members of the household to which the employee belongs
>
> The services of vehicles provided for the personal use of employees
>
> Goods and services produced as outputs from the employer's own processes of production, such as free coal for miners.

Also, some employees may be willing, or obliged, to accept part of their compensation in the form of financial or other assets.

Payments in kind other than remuneration in kind

3.39. Payments in kind other than remuneration in kind occur when any of a wide variety of payments are made in the form of goods and services rather than money. For example, a doctor may accept payment in wine instead of money. Or, instead of paying rent or rentals in money, the user of land or fixed capital, respectively, may pay the owner in goods or services. In agriculture, for example, the "rent" may be paid by handing over part of the crops produced to the landlord—i.e., share cropping. Tax payments, too, may be paid in kind; for example, inheritance taxes may be paid by making donations of paintings or other valuables.

Transfers in kind

3.40. Transfers in kind also are two-party transactions, but—in contrast to those just mentioned—one party provides a good, service or asset other than cash to the other without receiving a counterpart in return. Parallel to transfers in cash, these are called sometimes "something for nothing" transactions or transactions without a quid pro quo.

3.41. The System records a variety of transfers in kind, including government international cooperation, gifts, charitable contributions and social transfers in kind. The last consist of social security and social assistance benefits in kind together with goods and services provided to individual households outside any social insurance scheme by non-market producers owned by government units or non-profit institutions (NPIs). Government international cooperation, gifts, and charitable contributions are often made in kind for convenience, efficiency, or tax purposes. For example, international aid after a natural disaster may be more effective and delivered faster if made directly in the form of medicine, food, and shelter instead of money. Charitable contributions in kind sometimes avoid taxes that would be due if the item in question were sold and the money given to the charity.

3.42. For various reasons, many social security and social assistance benefits are provided in kind rather than in cash. Rather than provide a specified amount of money to be used to purchase medical and educational services, the services are often provided in kind to make sure that the need for the services is met. Sometimes the recipient purchases the service and is reimbursed by the insurance or assistance scheme. Such a transaction is still treated as being in kind because the recipient is merely acting as the agent of the insurance scheme. Social transfers in kind, other than social security or social assistance benefits, consist mostly of education, health, housing and other services provided to individual households by non-market producers owned by government units or NPIs.

3.43. Social transfers in kind involve two sets of transactions. The expenditures on the final consumption goods and services provided as social transfers in kind are recorded as being incurred by the government units (including social security schemes) or NPIs that incur the costs. These may be either monetary or non-monetary transactions depending upon whether the goods or services are purchased from market producers or produced by non-market producers owned by the government units or NPIs. The social transfers in kind, as such, are then recorded as a set of non-monetary transactions between the government units or the NPIs and the households who actually consume the goods or services, the goods and services being valued by the expenditures already incurred on them. The value of these goods and services is then added to the final consumption expenditures of households to obtain their actual consumption.

Internal transactions

3.44. The System treats as transactions certain kinds of actions within a unit to give a more analytically useful picture of final uses of output and of production. These transactions that involve only one unit are called internal, or intra-unit, transactions.

3.45. Many institutional units—households, NPIs serving households (NPISHs) and general government—operate as producers and as consumers. When an institutional unit engages in both production and final consumption, it may choose to consume some or all of the output it has produced itself. In such a case, no transaction takes place between institutional units, but it is useful to construct a transaction and estimate its value to record such output and consumption in the accounts.

3.46. For households, the principle in the System is that all goods produced by persons that are subsequently used by the same persons, or members of the same households, for purposes of final consumption are to be included in output in a manner analogous to that for goods sold on the market. This means that transactions are assumed in which the persons responsible for the production of the goods are deemed to deliver the goods to themselves, or members of their own households, and then values have to be associated with them in order to enter them in the accounts.

3.47. Establishments owned by governments or NPISHs commonly provide education, health, or other kinds of services to individual households without charge or at prices that are not economically significant. The costs of providing these services are incurred by the governments or NPISHs, and the values are recorded as internal transactions: that is, as final expenditures by governments or NPISHs on outputs produced by establishments they own themselves. (As already explained, the acquisition of these services by households is recorded separately under social transfers in kind, another form of non-monetary transactions that take place between the government units or NPISHs and the households in question.)

3.48. The System recognizes several other transactions within enterprises to give a fuller view of production. For example, when enterprises produce fixed assets for their own use, the System records deliveries by the enterprises to themselves as the subsequent users. Also, when enterprises use fixed assets—whether own-account or purchased—during production, the System charges the decline in the value of the asset during the period of production as a cost.

3.49. Further, when a single enterprise consists of two or more establishments, the System records transactions when goods or services produced in one establishment are delivered to another establishment belonging to the same enterprise for use as intermediate consumption. (On the other hand, when goods or services produced within a single establishment are fed back into intermediate consumption within the same establishment, no intra-unit transactions are recorded.)

Externalities and illegal actions

3.50. The above sections described the kinds of actions that are considered transactions in the System. This section focuses on externalities and illegal actions, explaining why externalities are not considered transactions and distinguishing among kinds of illegal actions that are and are not considered transactions.

Externalities

3.51. Certain economic actions carried out by institutional units cause changes in the condition or circumstances of other units without their consent. These are externalities: they can be regarded as unsolicited services, or disservices, delivered without the agreement of the units affected. It is an uncooperative action, usually with undesirable consequences, which is the antithesis of a market transaction. A typical example is the pollution by a producer of air or water used by other units for purposes of production or consumption. If the producer is allowed to pollute without charge or risk of being penalized, the private costs of production of the polluter will be less than the social costs to the community.

3.52. It is necessary to consider, however, whether values should be assigned to such externalities. Economic accounts have to measure economic functions such as production or consumption in the context of a particular legal and socio-economic system within which relative prices and costs are determined. Some countries, at least at certain points in their history, may choose to frame their laws so that some producers are permitted to reduce their private costs by polluting with impunity. This may be done deliberately to promote rapid industrialization, for example. The wisdom of such a policy may be highly questionable, especially in the long run, but it does not follow that it is appropriate or analytically useful for economic accounts to try to correct for presumed institutional failures of this kind by attributing costs to producers that society does not choose to recognize.

3.53. Further, there would be considerable technical difficulties involved in trying to associate economically meaningful values with externalities when they are intrinsically non-market phenomena. As externalities are not market transactions into which institutional units enter of their own accord, there is no mechanism to ensure that the positive or negative values attached to externalities by the various parties involved would be mutually consistent. Moreover, accounts including values for externalities could not be interpreted as representing equilibrium, or economically sustainable, situations. If such values were to be replaced by actual payments the economic behaviour of the units involved would change, perhaps considerably. For example, the whole purpose of trying to internalize some externalities by imposing taxes or other charges on the discharge of pollutants is to bring about a change in production methods to reduce pollution. A complete accounting for externalities also would be extremely complex as it is not sufficient merely to introduce costs into the accounts of the producers. It also would be necessary to introduce various other adjustments of questionable economic significance to balance the accounts.

Illegal actions

3.54. Illegal actions that fit the characteristics of transactions—notably the characteristic that there is mutual agreement between the parties—are treated the same way as legal actions. The production or consumption of certain goods or services, such as narcotics, may be illegal but market transactions in such goods and services have to be recorded in the accounts. If expenditures on illegal goods or services by households were to be ignored on grounds of principle, household saving would be overestimated and households presumed to obtain assets that they do not in fact acquire. Clearly, the accounts as a whole are liable to be seriously distorted if monetary transactions that in fact take place are excluded. Of course, it may be difficult, or even impossible, to obtain data about illegal transactions, but in principle they should be included in the accounts if only to reduce error in other items, including balancing items.

3.55. However, many illegal actions are crimes against persons or property that in no sense can be construed as transactions. For example, theft can scarcely be described as an action into which two units enter by mutual agreement. Conceptually, theft or violence is an extreme form of externality in which damage is inflicted on another institutional unit deliberately and not merely accidentally or casually. Thus, thefts of goods from households, for example, are not treated as transactions and estimated values are not recorded for them under household expenditures.

3.56. If thefts, or acts of violence (including war), involve significant redistributions, or destructions, of assets, it is necessary to take them into account. As explained below, they are treated as other flows, not as transactions. Less significant redistributions, such as shoplifting, may be included in change of inventories and therefore need not be recorded separately.

2. Other flows

3.57. Other flows are changes in the value of assets and liabilities that do not take place in transactions. Although these entries, which are all in the other changes in the volume of assets account and the revaluation account (which make up the other changes in assets accounts), do share the characteristic that they record changes that are not the result of transactions, they cover very different kinds of changes in assets and liabilities. The first kind consists of changes due to factors such as discoveries or depletion of subsoil resources, destruction by war or other political events or destruction by natural catastrophes, all of which actually change the volume of assets. The second kind consists of changes in the value of assets, liabilities, and net worth due to changes in the level and structure of prices, which are reflected in holding gains and losses.

Other changes in the volume of assets

3.58. Other changes in the volume of assets fall into three main categories. The reason that these flows are not transactions is linked to their not meeting one or more of the characteristics of transactions—for example, the institutional units involved may not be acting by mutual agreement, as with an uncompensated seizure of assets.

3.59. The first category relates to entrances and exits of assets and liabilities to or from the System in the normal course of events other than by transactions. Some of these may relate to naturally occurring assets, such as subsoil assets, so that the entrances and exits come about as interactions between institutional units and nature. Others relate to assets created by human activity, such as valuables. For valuables, for example, the capital account records their acquisition as newly produced goods or imports in transactions, and it records transactions in existing goods already classified as valuables. It is the recognition of a significant or special value for goods that are not already recorded in the balance sheets that is considered an economic appearance to be recorded as another—that is, non-transaction—flow. These valuables may not be in the balance sheets for any of several reasons: they antedate the accounts, or they were originally recorded as consumption goods.

3.60. The second category relates to the effects of exceptional, unanticipated events that affect the economic benefits derivable from assets (and corresponding liabilities). One such event is one institutional unit's effectively removing an asset from its owner without the owner's agreement, an action that is not considered a transaction because the element of mutual agreement is absent. These events also include those that destroy assets, such as natural disaster or war. In contrast, transactions, such as consumption of fixed capital or change in inventories, refer to normal rates of loss or damage.

3.61. The third category relates to changes in assets and liabilities that reflect changes in the classification of institutional units among sectors and in the structure of institutional units, or in the classification of assets and liabilities. For example, if an unincorporated enterprise becomes more financially distinct from its owner and takes on the characteristics of a quasi-corporation, it and the assets and liabilities it holds move from the household sector to the non-financial corporations sector; movements of the assets and liabilities are considered other flows in this category.

Holding gains and losses

3.62. Positive or negative nominal holding gains may accrue during the accounting period to the owners of financial and non-financial assets and liabilities as a result of a change in their prices. Holding gains are sometimes described as "capital gains", but "holding gain" is preferred here because it emphasizes that holding gains accrue purely as a result of holding assets over time without transforming them in any way. Holding gains include not only gains on "capital" such as fixed assets, land and financial assets but also gains on inventories of all kinds of goods held by producers, including work-in-progress, often described as "stock appreciation". Holding gains may accrue on assets held for any length of time during the accounting period, not only on assets held at the beginning or end of the period.

3.63. Nominal holding gains depend upon changes in the prices of assets and liabilities over time. The prices in question are the prices at which the assets may be sold on the market. Nominal holding gains may be further decomposed into neutral holding gains that reflect changes in the general price level and real holding gains that reflect changes in the relative prices of assets.

3. Balancing items in the flow accounts

3.64. A balancing item is an accounting construct obtained by subtracting the total value of the entries on one side of an account from the total value for the other side. It cannot be measured independently of the other entries; as a derived entry, it reflects the application of the general accounting rules to the specific entries on the two sides of the account. It does not relate to any specific set of transactions, and so it cannot be expressed in terms of its own price or quantity units.

3.65. Balancing items are not simply devices introduced to ensure that accounts balance. They encapsulate a great deal of information and include some of the most important entries in the accounts, as can be seen by the examples of balancing items for the accounts containing flows reproduced below:

> Value added/domestic product
>
> Operating surplus
>
> Disposable income
>
> Saving
>
> Net lending/net borrowing
>
> Current external balance.

D. Stocks

1. Stocks

3.66. Stocks are a position in, or holdings of, assets and liabilities at a point in time. The System records stocks in accounts, usually referred to as balance sheets, and tables at the beginning and end of the accounting period. However, stocks are connected with flows: they result from the accumulation of prior transactions and other flows, and they are changed by transactions and other flows in the period. They result in fact from a continuum of entries and withdrawals, with some changes, in volume or in value, occurring during the time a given asset or liability is held.

3.67. Values are recorded for non-financial assets, both produced and non-produced, and for financial assets and liabilities. The coverage of assets is limited to those assets used in economic activity and that are subject to ownership rights; thus for example, consumer durables and human capital, and also natural resources that are not owned, are excluded.

2. Balancing items in the balance sheets

3.68. Net worth, which is defined as the value of all the non-financial and financial assets owned by an institutional unit or sector less the value of all its outstanding liabilities, is the balancing item in the balance sheets. As is true for other balancing items in the System, net worth cannot be measured independently of the other entries, and it does not relate to any specific set of transactions.

E. Accounting rules

3.69. The valuation, time of recording and grouping by aggregation, netting and consolidation of the individual flows and stocks is explained in detail in the chapters that describe the entries in the various tables and accounts of the central framework. This section aims to set out the basic rules underlying the System.

F. Valuation

1. General rules

3.70. The power of the SNA as an analytical tool stems largely from its ability to link numerous, very varied economic phenomena by expressing them in a single accounting unit. The System does not attempt to determine the utility of the flows and stocks which come within its scope. Rather, it measures the current exchange value of the entries in the accounts in money terms, i.e., the values at which goods and other assets, services, labour or the provision of capital are in fact exchanged or else could be exchanged for cash (currency or transferable deposits).

3.71. When institutional units exchange these items with other institutional units for cash, the values required by the System are directly available. These transactions are recorded at the actual exchange value agreed upon by the two parties. Furthermore, of course, the values for all flows and stocks that concern cash holdings and liabilities are directly known.

3.72. In respect of all remaining flows and stocks, no actual exchange values are at hand, so their values must be assessed indirectly. These values should be taken from markets in which the same or similar items are traded currently in sufficient numbers and in similar circumstances against cash. The selection of the appropriate reference markets requires that attention be paid to differences between wholesale and retail markets, regional divergences, etc. Non-monetary transactions in existing goods often can be valued at the market price for similar new goods, if properly adjusted for consumption of fixed capital and other elements, such as unanticipated damage, which may have accrued to the asset since the time it was produced.

3.73. If there is no appropriate market from which the value of a particular non-monetary flow or stock item can be taken by analogy, as a second best, its valuation could be derived from prices that are established in less closely related markets. Ultimately, some goods and services can only be valued by the amount that it would cost to produce them currently. Market and own-account goods and services valued in this way should include a mark-up that reflects the net operating surplus or mixed income attributable to the producer. For non-market goods and services produced by government units or NPISHs, however, no allowance should be made for any net operating surplus.

3.74. Sometimes it is necessary to value stocks at their estimated written down current acquisition values or production costs. The write-down should then include all changes which have occurred to the item since it was purchased or produced (such as consumption of fixed capital, partial depletion, exhaustion, degradation, unforeseen obsolescence, exceptional losses and other unanticipated events). The same method could be applied to non-monetary flows of existing assets.

3.75. If none of the methods mentioned above can be applied, flows and stocks are to be recorded at the discounted present value of expected future returns. Although this method is theoretically entirely justified, it is not generally recommended since it involves many assumptions and as a consequence the outcomes are highly speculative.

3.76. Flows and stocks concerning foreign currency are converted to their value in national currency at the rate prevailing at the moment they are entered in the accounts, i.e., the moment the transaction or other flow takes place or the moment to which the balance sheet applies. The midpoint between the buying and selling rate should be used so that any service charge is excluded. In conformity with the general rule, provision of assets, services, labour or capital in exchange for foreign cash is recorded at the actual exchange value agreed upon by the two parties to the transaction. The exchange value should then be converted to national currency at the midpoint rate prevailing at the time the transaction takes place. That moment may be different from the times the payments are made; as a result, the value in national currency of the transactions in question may differ from the value in national currency of the related payments when they take place.

3.77. Business accounts, tax returns and other administrative records are main sources of data for drawing up the national accounts. One should be aware, however, that none of these necessarily satisfies the valuation requirements of the System and that accordingly adjustments may have to be made. In particular, in the interest of prudence, business accounting often adopts valuations that are not appropriate for the national accounts. Similarly, valuations for tax purposes often serve objectives that differ from those of macroeconomic analysis. For example, the depreciation methods favoured in business accounting and those prescribed by tax authorities almost invariably deviate from the concept of consumption of fixed capital employed in the System.

2. Valuation of partitioned flows

3.78. Extending the general rule in paragraph 3.71 above, where a single payment refers to more than one transaction category (such as they are defined in the System), the individual flows need to be recorded separately. For example, the System recommends dividing interest transactions with financial enterprises between two transaction categories whenever possible: one standing for pure interest and the other representing the implicit payment for financial intermediation services. Earlier in this chapter, the partitioning of financial leasing and transactions of wholesalers and retailers were discussed. Partitioning is not limited to transactions; an example is real holding gains, which are separated for analytical reasons from neutral holding gains that are simply proportionate to changes in the general price level.

3.79. In some cases partitioning is connected with deceptive behaviour. Values put on an invoice may deviate systematically or to such a large extent from the prices paid in the market for similar items that it must be presumed that the sums paid cover more than the specified transactions. An example is so-called transfer pricing: affiliated enterprises may set the prices of the transactions among themselves artificially high or low in order to effect an unspecified income payment or capital transfer. Such transactions should be made explicit if their value is considerable and would hinder a proper interpretation of the accounts.

3.80. A less obvious mingling of transactions occurs when the provision of an asset and the related money payment or payments do not take place simultaneously. When the time gap becomes unusually long and the amount of trade credit extended is very large, the conclusion may be that implicitly an interest fee has been charged. In such extreme cases, the actual payment or payments should be adjusted for accrued interest in order to arrive at the correct value of the asset transferred. Such adjustments are not recommended for normal trade credit.

3. Special valuations concerning products

3.81. Usually, the producer and the user of a given product perceive its value differently owing to the existence of taxes and subsidies on products, transport costs to be paid and the occurrence of trade margins. In order to keep as close as possible to the views of the economic transactors themselves, the System records all uses at purchasers' prices including these elements, but excludes them from the value of output of the product.

3.82. Output of products is recorded at basic prices. The basic price is defined as the amount receivable by the producer from the purchaser for a unit of good or service produced as output minus any tax payable and plus any subsidy receivable on the product as a consequence of its production or sale. It excludes any transport charges invoiced separately by the producer. If it proves impossible to obtain the required information at basic prices, output may be valued at producers' prices. The producer's price is defined as the amount receivable by the producer from the purchaser for a unit of a good or service produced as output minus any value added tax (VAT), or similar deductible tax, invoiced to the purchaser. It also excludes any transport charges invoiced separately by the producer.

3.83. Use of products is recorded at purchasers' prices. The purchaser's price is defined as the amount payable by the purchaser, excluding any deductible VAT or similar deductible tax, in order to take delivery of a unit of a good or service at the time and place required by the purchaser. The purchaser's price of a good includes any transport charges paid separately by the purchaser to take delivery at the required time and place.

3.84. The difference in value recorded for a product between when it is produced and the moment it is used for, say, final consumption expenditure can be considerable. Components of this difference may be:

(a) Taxes less subsidies on products payable by the producer;

(b) Trade and transport margins, including taxes less subsidies on products payable by wholesale and retail traders;

(c) Transport, including taxes less subsidies on products, paid separately by the consumer;

(d) Predictable quality increases producing additional output volume less current losses during storage;

(e) Holding gains while the product is with the producer and with wholesale and retail traders.

As one can see from the above, the difference between the original basic price and ultimate purchasers' price of a particular good encompasses both pure price and volume elements. In practice, of course, the estimates do not keep track of individual products but are made at a more global level for groups of products.

3.85. Imports and exports of goods are recorded in the System at border values. Total imports and exports of goods are valued free-on-board (f.o.b., that is, at the exporter's customs frontier). As it may not be possible to obtain f.o.b. values for detailed product breakdowns, the tables containing details on foreign trade show imports of goods valued at the importer's customs frontier (c.i.f. value), supplemented with global adjustments to f.o.b. C.i.f. values include the insurance and freight charges incurred between the exporter's frontier and that of the importer. The value on the commercial invoice may of course differ from both of these.

3.86. As the overall balance of imports and exports must conform to actual circumstances, border valuation of goods has consequences for the recording of freight and insurance in the System. Usually, the values of both imports and exports for these service items have to be adapted to compensate for the special conventions on goods trade with the rest of the world. Further details on this treatment are in chapters XIV and XV.

G. Time of recording

1. Introduction

3.87. When discussing timing in the System, an essential distinction should be made between stock data as recorded in balance sheets, on the one hand, and flow data as recorded in the accounts, on the other. Balance sheets, by definition, refer to specific points in time. In contrast, flows are aggregations, over some chosen accounting period, of individual transactions or other flows, which are themselves scattered over the accounting period.

3.88. Thus, the System does not show individual transactions or other flows, but there are two reasons why precise rules on their individual timing must be given. First, rules have to be formulated to say in which accounting period the discrete flows are to be recorded. Secondly, an exact timing of individual flows within the accounting period is crucial to make the distinction between changes in net worth due to transactions and those due to holding gains or losses. This distinction is particularly important in situations of high inflation.

3.89. One of the problems in pinning down the timing of transactions is that activities of institutional units often stretch over periods in which several important moments can be distinguished. For instance, many commercial sales commence with the signing of a contract between a seller and a buyer, encompass a date of delivery and a date or dates on which payments become due and are only completed as of the date the last payment is received by the seller. Each of these distinct moments in time is to some extent economically relevant.

3.90. Similarly, in analysing public spending one can distinguish the day that a budget is voted upon by the legislature, the day on which the ministry of finance authorizes a department to pay out specified funds, the day a particular commitment is entered into by the departments, the day deliveries take place and finally the days payment orders are issued and cheques are paid. With regard to taxes, for example, important moments are the day or the period in which the liability arises, the moment the tax liability is definitively assessed, the day that it becomes due for payment without penalty and the day the tax is actually paid or refunds are made.

3.91. Clearly, making entries for all successive stages discernible within the activities of institutional units, although theoretically possible, would severely overburden the System. A choice has to be made, recognizing (a) the needs of macroeconomic analysis, (b) microeconomic views, and (c) commonly available sources. Often, in this respect, a distinction is drawn between recording flows on a cash basis, due-for-payment basis and accrual basis. The System recommends recording on an accrual basis throughout.

2. Choice for recording on an accrual basis

3.92. Some systems closely related to the SNA, most notably the IMF Government Finance Statistics, recommend recording on a cash basis, at least in respect of aggregate data. Cash accounting records only cash payments and records them at the times these payments occur. This method is widely used to record government revenues and expenditures and it is also employed for certain business purposes. A practical advantage is the avoidance of problems connected with valuing non-monetary flows. Yet, cash accounting cannot be used generally for economic and national accounting as the times at which payments take place may diverge significantly from the economic activities and transactions to which they relate and it is these underlying activities and transactions that the System seeks to portray. Moreover, cash recording cannot be applied to the many non-monetary flows included in the System.

3.93. Due-for-payment recording shows flows which give rise to cash payments at the latest times they can be paid without incurring additional charges or penalties and, in addition to these, actual cash payments at the moments they occur. The period of time (if any) between the moment a payment becomes due and the moment it is actually made is bridged by recording a receivable or a payable in the financial accounts. Due-for-payment recording furnishes a more comprehensive description of monetary flows than does cash accounting. A disadvantage is, of course, that the registration is still limited to monetary flows.

3.94. Accrual accounting records flows at the time economic value is created, transformed, exchanged, transferred or extinguished. This means that flows which imply a change of ownership are entered when ownership passes, services are recorded when provided, output at the time products are created and intermediate consumption when materials and supplies are being used. The System favours accrual accounting because:

(a) The timing of accrual accounting is in full agreement with the way economic activities and other flows are defined in the System. This agreement allows one, for instance, to evaluate the profitability of productive activities correctly (i.e., without the disturbing influence of leads and lags in cash flows) and to calculate a sector's net worth correctly at any point in time;

(b) Accrual accounting can be applied to non-monetary flows.

3.95. Many transactions, such as everyday purchases of households in shops, are monetary transactions in which some asset is delivered against immediate, or nearly immediate, payment in cash. In those instances there are no differences between the three methods discussed here. Accrual accounting is particularly relevant to the timing of various internal transactions (such as output that is added to the inventories of the producer), exchanges in which the parties deliver at differing times (such as sales with deferred payments) and obligatory transfers (taxes and flows connected with social security).

3.96. Usually, accrual accounting arises naturally to the institutional units involved. Numerous transactions consist of an exchange between two enterprises of, say, goods for financial assets. In such an exchange, accounting entries will be made in the books of each enterprise, showing the same dates for the acquisition of the goods and the surrender of the financial assets, on the one hand, and for the acquisition of the financial assets and the surrender of the goods, on the other. Sometimes, however, the two parties involved in a transaction will not perceive it as occurring at the same moment. Furthermore, some transactors, in particular government units, do not keep records of purchases on an accrual basis. In these cases, the rules of consistency in the System require that efforts should be undertaken to correct basic statistics for major deviations and flaws. The application of the general rule of recording on an accrual basis to the most common circumstances is discussed below.

3. Timing of exchanges and transfers

3.97. With respect to exchanges and transfers of non-financial assets, the accrual principle usually comes down to recording at the moment when the legal ownership of those assets passes. When change of ownership is not obvious, the moment of entering in the books of the transaction partners may be a good indication and, failing that, the moment when physical possession and control is acquired. These subsidiary rules apply in particular to internal transactions or when a change of ownership is taken to occur under a financial lease or hire-purchase arrangement. Imports and exports of goods are recorded when change of ownership occurs. In the absence of sources specifying the date on which ownership changes, there is a strong presumption that the goods will cross the frontiers of the countries concerned either shortly before or soon after the change of ownership takes place and trade statistics based on customs documents reflecting the physical movement of goods across the national or customs frontier may often be used as an approximation.

3.98. Services are recorded in the System when they are provided. Some services are special in the sense that they are characteristically supplied on a continuous basis. Examples are operating leasing, insurance and housing services (including those of owner-occupied dwellings). These services are recorded as provided continuously over the whole period the contract lasts or the dwelling is available.

3.99. Following the general rule, distributive transactions are recorded at the moment the related claims arise. As a result, for example, compensation of employees, interest, rent on land, social contributions and benefits are all registered in the period during which the amounts payable are built up. Equally, entries for taxes are made at the moment on which the underlying transactions or other flows occur which give rise to the liability to pay. This implies that taxes on products and imports are recorded at the times the products in question are produced, imported or sold, depending on the basis for taxation. Current taxes on income are recorded when the income to which they pertain is earned although taxes deducted at source may have to be recorded when they are deducted. With respect to some distributive transactions, the time of accrual depends on the unit's decision when to distribute income or make a transfer. The level of dividends is not unambiguously attributable to a particular earning period, and dividends are to be recorded as of the moment they are declared payable. Other examples are withdrawals from income of quasi-corporations and various voluntary transfers, which are recorded when effected.

3.100. Transactions in financial assets (including payments of cash) are recorded in the System on a change-of-ownership basis. Some financial claims/liabilities defined in the System, in particular trade credits and advances, are the implicit result of a non-financial transaction and do not involve an explicit piece of evidence. In these cases the financial claim is deemed to arise when its non-financial counterpart occurs. The same holds for financial transactions that the System records between a quasi-corporation and its owner.

3.101. Both parties involved in a financial transaction may record it at varying dates in their own books because they acquire the documents evidencing the transaction at different times. This variation is caused by the process of clearing, the time cheques are in the mail, etc. The amounts involved in such "float" are generally substantial in the case of transferable deposits and other accounts receivable and payable. Again, reasons of consistency require that the transactions are entered on the same date for both parties. If no precise date can be fixed on which the change of ownership occurs, the date on which the transaction is fully completed (thus the date on which the creditor receives his payment) is decisive.

4. Timing of output and intermediate consumption

3.102. The principle of recording on an accrual basis implies that output is recorded over the period in which the process of production takes place. Thus, additions to work-in-progress are recorded continuously as work proceeds. When the production process is terminated, the whole of the work-in-progress accumulated up to that point is effectively transformed into a stock of finished product ready for delivery or sale.

3.103. Similarly, the intermediate consumption of a good or service is recorded at the time when the good or service enters the process of production, as distinct from the time it was acquired by the producer.

5. Timing of changes in inventories and consumption of fixed capital

3.104. Inventories may be materials and supplies held as inputs by producers, output as yet unsold, or products held by wholesale and retail traders. In all cases, additions to inventories are recorded when products are purchased, produced or otherwise acquired. Deductions from inventories are recorded when products are sold, used up as intermediate consumption or otherwise relinquished.

3.105. The timing of consumption of fixed capital is nearly inseparably linked with the question of its valuation. Consumption of fixed capital is a cost category which accrues over the whole period the fixed asset in question is available for productive purposes. The exact proportioning to accounting periods depends on the rate of depreciation which is usually assumed to be either linear or geometric (declining balance) (see chapter VI).

6. Timing of composite transactions and balancing items

3.106. Transactions which are measured as the balance of two or more other transactions follow the timing of the constituent basic flows. For example, financial intermediation services indirectly measured (FISIM) are entered according to the moments property income is earned on funds put out by financial intermediaries and interest payable by these units accrues. The same rule applies to balancing items.

3.107. In order to yield significant balancing items, the System aims at timing resources in the same period as related uses (and, in particular, at matching output with the various costs of production). However, due to the variety of transactions and other flows covered, each with its own characteristics, some thought is needed in interpreting balancing items. For instance, in analysing the balancing item "saving" of non-financial corporations, one should be aware that the time when the operating surplus arises does not necessarily tally with the timing of the other factors, such as when dividends are payable.

7. Timing of other flows

3.108. Other volume changes in assets are usually discrete events which accrue at precise moments or within fairly short periods of time. Changes in prices often have a more continuous character, particularly in respect of assets for which active markets exist. In practice, nominal holding gains or losses will be computed between two points in time:

    (*a*)   The moment at which:

        (*i*)   The accounting period begins; or

        (*ii*)   Ownership is acquired from other units (through purchase or a transaction in kind); or

        (*iii*) An asset is produced; and

    (*b*)   The moment at which:

        (*iv*) The accounting period ends; or

        (*v*)   The ownership of an assets is relinquished (through sale or a transaction in kind); or

        (*vi*) An asset is consumed in the production process.

3.109. One may wonder why nominal holding gains and losses are not calculated over a period beginning at the moment on which two units agree to a mutual exchange of assets instead of the period which starts with the moment on which the assets are acquired. After all, does not the signing of the contract fix prices, implying that the risk for any later price changes is being transferred? The System, however, regards commitments resulting from a contract as contingent until one of the parties has performed its obligation (by passing the ownership of some asset to the other party, providing a service or providing labour or capital). Also, a unit can incur holding gains and losses exclusively on the assets or liabilities it effectively holds. The combination of these two rules implies that during the period between the signing of the contract and the date on which the first party delivers, the second party cannot incur any price risks on this contract: the second party neither owns the assets to be delivered nor owns a claim on the first party to be recorded in the financial accounts.

3.110. Changes in structure and classification should be entered at the very moment when, according to the rules adopted in the System, a unit or an asset comes into a different category than it was classified previously. An integrated stock-flow system like the SNA requires that all reclassifications be recorded. Consequently, such a system does not allow reclassifications between two consecutive accounting periods.

3.111. In order to obtain statistical series which are more comparable over time, one might be tempted to stockpile major reclassifications for a number of years and enter them as one block at the end of this period. However understandable this procedure might be, it does not conform to the System's recommendations, which aim at correct estimates on levels. Keeping records of reclassifications makes it possible in principle to reconstruct time series based on the situation in any accounting period.

8. Balance sheet items

3.112. Fundamentally, balance sheets can be drawn up at any point in time. The System defines balance sheets for all sectors at the moment when one accounting period ends and a new accounting period begins. The closing balance sheet of one period is identical to the opening balance sheet of the next one, so there remain no price changes, reclassifications or other economic flows which are not duly recognized by the System.

9. The accounting period

3.113. In principle, any lapse of time may be chosen as the accounting period. Periods that are too short have the disadvantage that statistical data are influenced by incidental factors, while long periods do not adequately portray changes going on in the economy. Merely seasonal effects can be avoided by having

the accounting period cover a whole cycle of regularly recurrent economic phenomena. Most business and government accounting refers to complete years. In general, calendar years or quarters are best suited for drawing up a full set of national accounts tables.

H. Aggregation, netting, consolidation

1. Aggregation

3.114. The immense number of individual transactions, other flows and assets within the scope of the SNA have to be arranged in a manageable number of analytically useful groups. In the System, such groups are constructed by crossing two or more classifications. As a minimum, a combination of the "who" and "what" questions asked in chapter II is made, i.e., a classification of institutional sectors or industries is crossed with the classification of transactions, other accumulation entries or assets. Additionally, resources must be distinguished from uses and assets from liabilities. In order to accommodate more detailed analysis, the classes thus generated may be further subdivided: examples are specifications of "in what" (kind of product or asset), of "why" (function) and of "with whom" (transaction partners).

3.115. Since the classifications in the System contain a number of levels made explicit in the codes, corresponding levels of aggregation may be distinguished.

3.116. Although conceptually the value for each aggregate is the sum of the values for all elementary items in the relevant category, in practice other estimation methods are frequently used. First, information on elementary transactions, other flows and assets may be incomplete or even non-existent. Secondly, the data obtained from different primary sources are usually not fully consistent due to deviating definitions and varying coverage, and adjustments at aggregate level are necessary to reconcile them. The practical techniques for estimating and balancing national accounts data are to be extensively discussed in handbooks which are planned for publication by organizations of the Inter-Secretariat Working Group on National Accounts.

2. Netting

3.117. Individual units or sectors may have the same kind of transaction both as a use and as a resource (e.g., they both pay and receive interest) and the same kind of financial instrument both as an asset and as a liability. Combinations in which all elementary items are shown for their full values are called gross recordings. Combinations whereby the values of some elementary items are offset against items on the other side of the account or which have an opposite sign are called net recordings.

3.118. The System recommends gross recording apart from the degree of netting which is inherent in the classifications themselves. In fact, netting is already a feature of many of the System's recommendations. It mostly serves to highlight an economically important property which is not apparent from gross data.

3.119. Netting is implicit in various transaction categories, the most outstanding example being "changes in inventories", which underlines the analytically significant aspect of overall capital formation rather than tracking daily additions and withdrawals. Similarly, with few exceptions, the financial account and other changes in assets accounts record increases in assets and in liabilities on a net basis, bringing out the final consequences of these types of flows at the end of the accounting period. Of course, all balancing items involve netting as well. To avoid confusion, the System uses the words "gross" and "net" in a very restrictive sense. Apart from a few headings ("net premiums", "net equity of households on life insurance reserves and pension funds", "net worth and net lending/net borrowing") the System's classifications employ the word "net" exclusively to indicate the value of variables after deduction of consumption of fixed capital.

3.120. The System defines one situation in which exactly the opposite of netting should be applied. A grossing up is recommended in respect of processing to order *vis-à-vis* the rest of the world. In agreement with external trade statistics, this type of processing is not recorded "net" as a service item. Instead, the movement of goods before and after processing is registered as imports and exports for their full value as if they were purchased and subsequently sold back.

3. Consolidation

3.121. Consolidation is a special kind of cancelling out of flows and stocks which should be distinguished from other kinds of netting. It involves the elimination of those transactions or debtor/creditor relationships which occur between two transactors belonging to the same institutional sector or sub-sector. Consolidation should not be seen as a sheer loss of information; it entails an elementary specification by the transaction partner. Consolidation may be most relevant for monetary institutions and general government. For certain kinds of analysis, information on the transactions of these (sub)sectors with other sectors and the corresponding "external" financial position is more significant than overall gross figures. As a rule, however, the entries in the System are not consolidated.

3.122. The rule of non-consolidation takes a special form regarding the transaction categories "output" and "intermediate consumption". These transactions are to be recorded throughout at the level of establishments. This implies specifically that the accounts for institutional sectors and for industries should not be consolidated in respect of output delivered between establishments belonging to the same institutional unit.

IV. Institutional units and sectors

A. Introduction

4.1. This chapter is concerned with the definition and description of institutional units and the way in which they are grouped to make up the sectors and sub-sectors of the System. Economic entities that are capable of owning assets, incurring liabilities and engaging in economic activities and in transactions with other entities are described in the System as institutional units. The various sectors and sub-sectors of an economy are composed of institutional units that are resident in the economy, the total economy consisting of the entire set of resident institutional units. The definition of residence is explained later.

1. Institutional units

4.2. An institutional unit may be defined as:

> An economic entity that is capable, in its own right, of owning assets, incurring liabilities and engaging in economic activities and in transactions with other entities.

The main attributes of institutional units may be described as follows:

(a) An institutional unit is entitled to own goods or assets in its own right; it is therefore able to exchange the ownership of goods or assets in transactions with other institutional units;

(b) It is able to take economic decisions and engage in economic activities for which it is itself held to be directly responsible and accountable at law;

(c) It is able to incur liabilities on its own behalf, to take on other obligations or future commitments and to enter into contracts;

(d) Either a complete set of accounts, including a balance sheet of assets and liabilities, exists for the unit, or it would be possible and meaningful, from both an economic and legal viewpoint, to compile a complete set of accounts if they were to be required.

4.3. There are two main types of units in the real world that may qualify as institutional units, namely persons or groups of persons in the form of households, and legal or social entities whose existence is recognized by law or society independently of the persons, or other entities, that may own or control them.

4.4. The individual members of multi-person households are not treated as separate institutional units. Many assets are owned, or liabilities incurred, jointly by two or more members of the same household while some or all of the income received by individual members of the same household may be pooled for the benefit of all members. Moreover, many expenditure decisions, especially those relating to the consumption of food, or housing, may be made collectively for the household as a whole. It may be impossible, therefore, to draw up meaningful balance sheets or other accounts for members of the household on an individual basis. For these reasons, the household must be treated as the institutional unit. An unincorporated enterprise that is entirely owned by one or more members of the same household is treated as an integral part of that household and not as a separate institutional unit, except when the enterprise is treated as a quasi-corporation (see below).

4.5. The second type of institutional unit is a legal or social entity that engages in economic activities and transactions in its own right, such as a corporation, non-profit institution (NPI) or government unit. Such units are responsible and accountable for the economic decisions or actions they take, although their autonomy may be constrained to some extent by other institutional units; for example, corporations are ultimately controlled by their shareholders. Some unincorporated enterprises belonging to households or government units may behave in much the same way as corporations, and such enterprises are treated as quasi-corporations when they have complete sets of accounts.

2. Institutional sectors and sub-sectors: summary

4.6. The resident institutional units that make up the total economy are grouped into the following five mutually exclusive institutional sectors:

> The non-financial corporations sector
>
> The financial corporations sector
>
> The general government sector
>
> The non-profit institutions serving households sector

The households sector.

4.7. All resident non-financial corporations and quasi-corporations are included in the non-financial corporations sector and make up most of the sector in practice. In addition, it includes non-profit institutions (NPIs) engaged in the market production of goods and non-financial services: for example, hospitals, schools or colleges that charge fees that enable them to recover their current production costs, or trade associations financed by subscriptions from non-financial corporate or unincorporated enterprises whose role is to promote and serve the interests of those enterprises.

4.8. The financial corporations sector includes all resident corporations and quasi-corporations whose principal activity is financial intermediation or facilitating financial intermediation. In addition, it includes NPIs engaged in market production of a financial nature (e.g., insurance), including those financed by subscriptions from financial enterprises whose role is to promote and serve the interests of those enterprises.

4.9. The general government sector consists mainly of central, state and local government units together with social security funds imposed and controlled by those units. In addition, it includes NPIs engaged in non-market production that are controlled and mainly financed by government units or social security funds.

4.10. The non-profit institutions serving households sector consists of all resident NPIs, except those controlled and mainly financed by government, that provide non-market goods or services to households.

4.11. The households sector consists of all resident households. These include institutional households made up of persons staying in hospitals, retirement homes, convents, prisons, etc. for long periods of time. As already noted, an unincorporated enterprise owned by a household is treated as an integral part of the latter and not as a separate institutional unit, except when the enterprise qualifies as a quasi-corporation.

4.12. Each of the five institutional sectors listed above may be divided into sub-sectors as described in the later sections of this chapter. The division of sectors into sub-sectors depends upon the type of analysis to be undertaken, the needs of policy makers, the availability of data and the economic circumstances and institutional arrangements within a country. No single method of sub-sectoring may be optimal for all purposes or all countries, so that alternative methods of sub-sectoring are recommended below for certain sectors.

3. Relationship between sectors and types of institutional units

4.13. A cross-classification of institutional units by sector and type of unit is illustrated schematically in table 4.1. As financial corporations and quasi-corporations are essentially different kinds of institutional units from non-financial corporations and quasi-corporations, it can be seen that, with the exception

Table 4.1. Institutional units cross-classified by sector and type

Type of institutional unit	Non-financial corporations sector	Financial corporations sector	General government sector	Households sector	NPISHs sector
Corporations (including quasi-corporations)[1]	Non-financial corporations (including quasi-corporations)	Financial corporations (including quasi-corporations)			
Government units (including social security funds)			Government units (including social security funds)		
Households				Households	
Non-profit institutions (NPIs)	Non-financial market NPIs	Financial market NPIs	Non-market NPIs controlled and mainly financed by government units		Non-market NPIs serving households[2] (NPISHs)

1 All quasi-corporations, whether owned by households, government units or non-resident institutional units, are grouped with corporations for purposes of sectoring.
2 Except NPIs controlled and mainly financed by government units.

of NPIs, all institutional units of a particular type are grouped together within the same sector. Thus:

(a) All non-financial corporations and quasi-corporations are allocated to the non-financial corporations sector;

(b) All financial corporations and quasi-corporations are allocated to the financial corporations sector;

(c) All government units, including social security funds, are allocated to the general government sector;

(d) All households are allocated to the households sector.

4.14. However, NPIs may be classified as belonging to any of the five major sectors, except the households sector, depending upon the purposes they serve and the kinds of units that control and finance them. As explained below, NPIs are not necessarily non-market producers, the essential characteristic of an NPI is that it cannot be a source of income or profit to the units that control it. The way in which institutional units are grouped into sectors is, therefore, mostly self-evident except for NPIs. It is still necessary, however, to explain in more detail what are the characteristic features by which legal or social entities in the form of corporations, quasi-corporations or NPIs can be identified.

4. Residence

4.15. The total economy is defined as the entire set of resident institutional units. It is divided into sectors that consist of groups of resident institutional units. An institutional unit is resident in a country when it has a centre of economic interest in the economic territory of that country. It is said to have a centre of economic interest when there exists some location—dwelling, place of production or other premises—within the economic territory on, or from, which it engages, and intends to continue to engage, in economic activities and transactions on a significant scale either indefinitely or over a finite but long period of time. In most cases, a long period of time may be interpreted as one year or more, although this is suggested only as a guideline and not as an inflexible rule (see paragraph 14.13 of chapter XIV).

4.16. Thus, residence is not based on nationality or legal criteria (although it may be similar to the concepts of residence used for exchange control, tax or other purposes in many countries). The concept of residence is explained in detail in chapter XIV; it is identical with that used in the fifth edition of the *Balance of Payments Manual* of the International Monetary Fund (IMF). It may nevertheless be useful to elaborate here on some aspects of residence:

(a) The residence of individual persons is determined by that of the household of which they form part and not by their place of work. All members of the same household have the same residence as the household itself, even though they may cross borders to work or otherwise spend periods of time abroad. If they work and reside abroad so long that they acquire a centre of economic interest abroad, they cease to be members of their original households;

(b) Unincorporated enterprises that are not quasi-corporations are not separate institutional units from their owners and, therefore, have the same residence as their owners;

(c) Corporations and NPIs may normally be expected to have a centre of economic interest in the country in which they are legally constituted and registered. Corporations may be resident in countries different from their shareholders and subsidiary corporations may be resident in countries different from their parent corporations. When a corporation, or unincorporated enterprise, maintains a branch, office or production site in another country in order to engage in a significant amount of production over a long period of time but without creating a subsidiary corporation for the purpose, the branch, office or site is considered to be a quasi-corporation (i.e., separate institutional unit) resident in the country in which it is located (see paragraphs 14.22 to 14.28 of chapter XIV);

(d) Owners of land and buildings in the economic territory of a country are deemed always to have a centre of economic interest in that country, even if they do not engage in other economic activities or transactions in the country. All land and buildings are therefore owned by residents (see paragraph 14.14 of chapter XIV).

5. Sectoring and economic behaviour

4.17. The sectors of the System group together similar kinds of institutional units. Corporations, NPIs, government units and households are intrinsically different from each other. Their economic objectives, functions and behaviour are also different.

4.18. Corporations are institutional units created for the purpose of producing goods or services for the market. They may be a source of profit to the units that own them. They are essentially producer units and do not themselves incur expenditures on final consumption. The functions of NPIs are similar in some respects to those of corporations but they can be broader in scope. NPIs are institutional units created for the purpose of producing or distributing goods or services but not for the purpose of generating any income or profit for the units that control or finance them. In contrast to corporations, NPIs may incur final consumption expenditures in respect of final goods or services that they provide to households.

4.19. The economic objectives, functions and behaviour of government units are quite distinct. They organize and finance the provision of non-market goods and services, including both individual and collective services, to households and the community and, therefore, incur expenditures on final consumption. They may also engage in non-market production themselves. They are also concerned with distribution and redistribution of income and wealth through taxation and other transfers. Government units include social security funds.

4.20. Finally, the economic objectives, functions and behaviour of households are different again. Although primarily consumer units, they can engage in any kind of economic activity. They not only supply labour to enterprises but may operate their own producer units in the form of unincorporated enterprises.

4.21. Thus, dividing the total economy into sectors enhances the usefulness of the accounts for purposes of economic analysis by grouping together institutional units with similar objectives and types of behaviour. However, sectors and sub-sectors are also needed in order to be able to target or monitor particular groups of institutional units for policy purposes. For example, the household sector has to be divided into sub-sectors in order to be able to observe how different sections of the community are affected by, or benefit from, the process of economic development or government economic and social policy measures. Similarly, it may be important to treat corporations subject to control by non-residents as sub-sectors of the financial and non-financial corporate sectors not only because they are liable to behave differently from domestically controlled corporations but because governments may wish to be able to identify and observe those parts of the economy that are subject to influence from abroad.

B. Institutional units in the form of legal or social entities

4.22. This section is concerned with three main categories of legal or social entities that constitute institutional units, namely corporations, quasi-corporations and NPIs. Units of central, state or local government are considered in a separate section below.

1. Corporations

4.23. Corporations may be described by different names: corporations, incorporated enterprises, public limited companies, public corporations, private companies, joint-stock companies, limited liability companies, limited liability partnerships, and so on. "Corporation" is the preferred term used in the System for all these kinds of entities. A typical corporation may be described as:

> a legal entity, created for the purpose of producing goods or services for the market, that may be a source of profit or other financial gain to its owner(s); it is collectively owned by shareholders who have the authority to appoint directors responsible for its general management.

4.24. The laws governing the creation, management and operations of corporations may vary from country to country so that it is not feasible to provide a precise, legal definition of a corporation that would be universally valid. It is possible, however, to indicate in more detail the typical features of corporations that are most relevant from the point of view of the System. They may be summarized as follows:

(a) A corporation is an entity created by process of law whose existence is recognized independently of the other institutional units—i.e., households, corporations or government units—which may own shares in its equity. The existence, name and address of a corporation are usually recorded in a special register kept for this purpose. A corporation may normally be expected to have a centre of economic interest—i.e., to be resident—in the country in which it is created and registered. When it also has one or more branches engaged in significant amounts of production over long periods of time in other countries, such branches are treated as quasi-corporations that are separate institutional units resident in the countries in which they are located;

(b) A corporation is created for the purpose of producing goods or services for sale on the market at prices which are economically significant. Prices are said to be economically significant when they have a significant influence on the amounts the producers are willing to supply and on the amounts purchasers wish to buy. Any operating surplus accruing from a corporation's productive activities or holding gains or property income accruing on its assets, belong to the shareholders, but the amount of profits or income actually distributed to shareholders as dividends in any single accounting period depends on the directors of the corporation. Undistributed profits are often described as retained earnings;

(c) Ownership of a corporation is vested in the shareholders collectively. Profits are usually distributed to shareholders in proportion to the value, or amounts, of the shares or other capital participations which they own. There may be different kinds of shares in the same corporation carrying different entitlements. In the event of a corporation being wound up, or liquidated, the shareholders are similarly entitled to a share in the net worth of the corporation remaining after all assets have been sold and all liabilities paid. If a corporation is declared bankrupt because its liabilities exceed the value of its assets, the shareholders are not liable to repay the excess liabilities. The shareholders are different institutional units from the corporation itself and their liability is limited to the amounts of capital they have subscribed in shares;

(d) A corporation is fully responsible and accountable at law for its own actions, obligations and contracts, this being an essential attribute of an institutional unit in the System. A corporation is liable to pay taxes on its productive activities, income or assets;

(e) Control of a corporation is ultimately exercised by the shareholders collectively. A corporation has a board of directors that is responsible for the corporation's policy and appoints the senior management of the corporation. The board of directors is usually appointed by the collective vote of the shareholders;

(f) In practice, however, some shareholders may exert much more influence or control over the policies and operations of a corporation than others:

   (i) The voting rights of shareholders may not be equal. Some types of shares may carry no voting rights, while others may carry exceptional rights, such as the right to make specific appointments to the board of directors or the right to veto other appointments made on a majority vote. Such exceptional rights may be held by the Government when it is a shareholder in a corporation;

   (ii) Many shareholders with voting rights do not choose to exercise them. Voting usually requires attendance at general meetings of the shareholders or the nomination of another shareholder as a proxy with authority to vote on behalf of the original shareholder. In practice, many shareholders may not exercise their voting rights, so that a small, organized minority of active shareholders may be in a position to control the policy and operations of a corporation.

4.25. Two characteristics of a corporation are worth noting. The first is that a corporation cannot be a final consumer. In contrast to an NPI, it cannot incur final expenditures for the benefit of households. When a corporation provides goods or services to its employees, these must be either compensation of employees paid in kind or intermediate consumption, depending upon the reason for providing the goods and services. The second characteristic is that the whole of the profit or income accruing to a corporation ultimately benefits other institutional units, namely its shareholders. This again differentiates a corporation from an NPI, which, by definition, cannot generate an income that can be appropriated by other institutional units.

Ownership and control of corporations

4.26. The ownership of a corporation is diffused among the institutional units that own its shares in proportion to their shareholdings. It is possible for a single institutional unit, another corporation or a household or a government unit, to own all the equity or shares in a corporation but, in general, ownership is diffused among several, possibly very many, institutional units.

4.27. A single institutional unit owning more than a half of the shares, or equity, of a corporation is able to control its policy and operations by outvoting all other shareholders, if necessary. Similarly, a small, organized group of shareholders whose combined ownership of shares exceeds 50 per cent of the total is able to control the corporation by acting in concert. There may be exceptional cases in which certain shareholders enjoy privileged voting rights, such as a right of veto, but in general an individual institutional unit or group of units owning more than half the voting shares of a corporation can exercise complete control by appointing directors of its own choice. The degree of autonomy exercised by the directors and managers of a corporation is, therefore, likely to vary considerably, depending upon the extent to which the ownership of its shares is concentrated in the hands of a small number of other institutional units, whether these are other corporations, households or government units. In general, institutional units do not have to be autonomous but they do have to be responsible, and accountable, for the decisions and actions they take.

4.28. Because many shareholders do not exercise their voting rights, a single shareholder, or small number of shareholders acting together, may be able to secure control over a corporation, even though they may hold considerably less than half of the total shares. When ownership of shares is widely diffused among a large number of shareholders, control may be secured by owning 20 per cent or less of the total shares.

4.29. However, it is not possible to stipulate a minimum shareholding below 50 per cent which will guarantee control in all cases. The minimum must vary depending upon the total number of shareholders, the distribution of shares among them, and the extent to which small shareholders take an active interest, etc.

4.30. As explained later in this chapter, the sub-sectors of the System require private corporations to be separated from public corporations subject to control by government units, and also private corporations controlled by non-resident units to be separated from other private corporations. In both cases, control is defined as the ability to determine general corporate policy by appointing appropriate directors, if necessary. Owning more than half the shares of a corporation is evidently a sufficient, but not a necessary, condition for control. Nevertheless, because it may be difficult to identify those corporations in which control is exercised by a minority of shareholders, it is recommended that, in practice, corporations subject to public or foreign control should normally be confined to those in which governments or non-residents own a majority of the shares. This recommendation is intended only as a practical guideline, however, to which exceptions can be admitted if there is other evidence of control. For example, a corporation which a government is able to control as a result of special legislation should be treated as a public corporation even if the government does not own a majority of the shares.

Subsidiary, associate and holding corporations

4.31. It is common for corporations to own shares in other corporations, and certain inter-relationships between corporations need to be specified for purposes of the System.

Subsidiary corporations

4.32. Corporation B is said to be a subsidiary of corporation A when:

 (a) Either corporation A controls more than half of the shareholders' voting power in corporation B; or

 (b) Corporation A is a shareholder in corporation B with the right to appoint or remove a majority of the directors of corporation B.

4.33. Corporation A may be described as the parent corporation in this situation. As the relationship of a parent corporation to a subsidiary is defined in terms of control rather than ownership, the relationship must be transitive: that is, if C is a subsidiary of B and B is a subsidiary of A, then C must also be a subsidiary of A. If A has a majority shareholding in B while B has a majority shareholding in C, A cannot also have a majority shareholding in C. Nevertheless, A must be able to control C if it controls B. By analogy with families of persons, corporation B can be described as a first generation subsidiary of corporation A, and corporation C as a second generation subsidiary of A. Evidently, large families of corporations may be built up with any number of subsidiaries at each level or generation and also any number of generations. Very large families of corporations, described as conglomerates, are encountered in some countries. Conglomerates may include corporations resident in different countries, in which case the parent corporation is usually described as a multinational corporation.

Associate corporations

4.34. Corporation B is said to be an associate of corporation A when corporation A and its subsidiaries control between 10 per cent and 50 per cent of the shareholders' voting power in B so that A has some influence over the corporate policy and management of B.

4.35. By definition, a corporation is able to exert less influence over an associate corporation than over a subsidiary. Although some corporations may be able to exert considerable influence over their associates, this cannot be guaranteed. The relationship between associates is weaker than that between parent and subsidiary corporations, and groups of associates may not be well defined.

Groups of corporations and holding corporations

4.36. As described above, large groups of corporations, or conglomerates, may be created whereby a parent corporation controls several subsidiaries, some of which may control subsidiaries of their own, etc. Two different types of parent corporation may be distinguished. The first consists of a corporation with significant production of its own which acquires control over other corporations in order to strengthen its own position as a producer. It may, for example, acquire control of a corporation that supplies it with components, or it may acquire control of a competitor.

4.37. On the other hand, the principal function of a corporation may be to control and direct a group of subsidiaries, without having any other significant production of its own. Such a corporation is described as a "holding corporation" or "holding company".

4.38. For certain purposes, it may be desirable to have information relating to a group of corporations as a whole. However, with the exception of ancillary corporations described in the next section, each individual corporation should be treated as a separate institutional unit, whether or not it forms part of a group. Even subsidiaries which are wholly owned by other corporations are separate legal entities that are required by law and the tax authorities to produce complete sets of accounts, including balance sheets. Although the management of a subsidiary corporation may be subject to the control of another corporation, it remains responsible and accountable for the conduct of its own production activities.

4.39. Another reason for not treating groups of corporations as single institutional units is that groups are not always well defined, stable or easily identified in practice. It may be difficult to obtain data for groups whose activities are not closely integrated. Moreover, many conglomerates are much too large and heterogeneous for them to be treated as single units, and their size and composition may be continually shifting over time as a result of mergers and takeovers.

2. Ancillary corporations

4.40. An ancillary corporation may be defined as:

 a subsidiary corporation, wholly owned by a parent corporation, whose productive activities are ancillary in nature: that is, are strictly confined to providing services to the parent corporation, or other ancillary corporations owned by the same parent corporation.

4.41. As described in chapter V, a productive activity is described as ancillary when its sole function is to produce one or more common types of services for intermediate consumption within the same enterprise. The kinds of services which may be produced by ancillary activities are transportation, purchasing, sales and marketing, various kinds of financial or business services, computing and communications, security, maintenance, and cleaning. These are typically services that are likely to be needed, to some extent or other, in most enterprises, whatever the nature of their principal activities. Neither the inputs into, nor the outputs from, ancillary activities are recorded separately from others consumed or produced by the principal or secondary productive activities.

4.42. A corporation may find it advantageous for tax or other reasons to create a subsidiary corporation purely in order to perform certain ancillary activities for its own benefit. For example, it may create a subsidiary to which ownership of its land, buildings or equipment is transferred and whose sole function is to lease them back again to the parent corporation; or it may create a subsidiary to keep its accounts and records on a separate computer installation; and so on. In some cases, corporations may create "dormant" subsidiaries which are not actually engaged in any production but which may be activated at the convenience of the parent corporation.

4.43. Ancillary corporations are not treated as separate institutional units in the System. When a parent corporation has created a single ancillary corporation, the ancillary corporation should be treated as an integral part of the parent and its accounts consolidated with those of the parent. When a parent corporation has created several ancillary corporations, they should all be combined with the parent corporation to form a single institutional unit.

4.44. Ancillary corporations are not treated as separate institutional units because they can be regarded as artificial units created to avoid taxes, to minimize liabilities in the event of bankruptcy, or to secure other technical advantages under the tax or corporation legislation in force in a particular country.

3. Cooperatives, limited liability partnerships, etc.

4.45. In addition to entities calling themselves corporations or companies, there are also other legal entities created for the purpose of engaging in market production for profit but which may be described differently because they have rather specialized functions. Such entities are classified as corporations in the System.

4.46. They include, for example, cooperatives set up by producers for purposes of marketing their collective output. The profits of such cooperatives are distributed in accordance with their agreed rules and not necessarily in proportion to shares held, but effectively they operate like corporations. Similarly, partnerships whose members enjoy limited liability are separate legal entities which behave like corporations. In effect, the partners are at the same time both shareholders and managers.

4.47. In general, all entities, however they may describe themselves or whatever they may be called, which are set up for purposes of engaging in market production, which are capable of generating a profit or other financial gain for their owners and which are recognized at law as separate legal entities from their owners who enjoy limited liability, are treated as corporations in the System.

4.48. Conversely, some legal entities that are NPIs may sometimes be described "corporations". The status of an institutional unit

cannot always be inferred from its name, and it may be necessary to examine its objectives and functions.

4. Quasi-corporations

4.49. Quasi-corporations are unincorporated enterprises that functio as if they were corporations. A quasi-corporation may be:

> *either* an unincorporated enterprise owned by a resident institutional unit that is operated as if it were a separate corporation and whose de facto relationship to its owner is that of a corporation to its shareholders: such an enterprise must, of course, keep a complete set of accounts

> *or* an unincorporated enterprise owned by a non-resident institutional unit that is deemed to be a resident institutional unit because it engages in a significant amount of production in the economic territory over a long or indefinite period of time.

4.50. For purposes of sectoring and sub-sectoring, quasi-corporations are treated as if they were corporations: that is, as separate institutional units from the units to which they legally belong. Thus, quasi-corporations owned by households or government units are grouped with corporations in the non-financial or financial corporate sectors. Three main kinds of quasi-corporations are recognized in the System:

(a) Unincorporated enterprises owned by government units which are engaged in market production and which are operated in a similar way to publicly owned corporations;

(b) Unincorporated enterprises, including unincorporated partnerships, owned by households which are operated as if they were privately owned corporations;

(c) Unincorporated enterprises which belong to institutional units resident abroad: these consist of the permanent branches, or offices of foreign corporate or unincorporated enterprises, or of production units belonging to foreign enterprises which engage in significant amounts of production within the economic territory over long, or indefinite, periods of time; e.g., units engaged in the construction of bridges, dams or other large structures.

4.51. The intent behind the concept of a quasi-corporation is clear: namely, to separate from their owners those unincorporated enterprises which are sufficiently self-contained and independent that they behave in the same way as corporations. If they function like corporations, they must keep complete sets of accounts. Indeed, the existence of a complete set of accounts, including balance sheets, for the enterprise is a necessary condition for it to be treated as quasi-corporation. Otherwise, it would not be feasible from an accounting point of view to distinguish the quasi-corporation from its owner.

4.52. As a quasi-corporation is treated as a separate institutional unit from its owner, it must have its own value added, saving, assets, liabilities, etc. It must be possible to identify and record any flows of income and capital that are deemed to take place between the quasi-corporation and its owner. The amount of income withdrawn from a quasi-corporation during a given accounting period is decided by the owner, such a withdrawal being equivalent to the payment of a dividend by a corporation to its shareholder(s). Given the amount of the income withdrawn, the saving of the quasi-corporation (i.e., the amount of earnings retained within the quasi-corporation) is determined. A balance sheet is also needed for the quasi-corporation showing the values of its fixed assets—land, buildings, machinery and equipment, inventories—used in production and also the financial assets and liabilities—owned or incurred in the name of the enterprise—bank deposits, overdrafts, trade credit and debits, other receivables or payables, etc. It is assumed that the owner's net equity in a quasi-corporation is equal to the difference between the value of its assets and the value of its other liabilities so that the net worth of the quasi-corporation is always zero in practice. The owner may invest more capital in the enterprise or withdraw capital from it by disposing of some of its assets, and such flows of capital must also be identifiable in the accounts whenever they occur.

4.53. Experience has shown that countries have difficulty distinguishing quasi-corporations owned by households. However, it is not useful to introduce additional criteria, such as size, into the definition of quasi-corporations owned by households as such criteria do not help in practice if the enterprise in question is not in fact operated like a corporation and does not have a complete set of accounts of its own, however large it may be.

5. Non-profit institutions

4.54. Non-profit institutions are legal or social entities created for the purpose of producing goods and services whose status does not permit them to be a source of income, profit or other financial gain for the units that establish, control or finance them. In practice, their productive activities are bound to generate either surpluses or deficits but any surpluses they happen to make cannot be appropriated by other institutional units. The articles of association by which they are established are drawn up in such a way that the institutional units which control or manage them are not entitled to a share in any profits or other income which they receive. For this reason, they are frequently exempted from various kinds of taxes.

4.55. The motives leading other institutional units—whether persons, corporations, or government—to create NPIs are varied. For example, NPIs may be created to provide services for the benefit of the persons or corporations who control or finance them; or they may be created for charitable, philanthropic or welfare reasons to provide goods or services to other persons in need; or they may be intended to provide health or education services for a fee, but not for profit; or they may be intended

to promote the interests of pressure groups in business or politics; etc. Although they may provide services to groups of persons or institutional units, by convention they are deemed to produce only individual services and not collective services.

The characteristics of NPIs

4.56. The main features of NPIs may be summarized as follows:

(a) Most NPIs are legal entities created by process of law whose existence is recognized independently of the persons, corporations or government units that establish, finance, control or manage them. The purpose of the NPI is usually stated in the articles of association or similar document drawn up at the time of its establishment. In some countries, especially developing countries, an NPI may be an informal entity whose existence is recognized by the society but which does not have any formal legal status; such an NPI may be created for the purpose of producing non-market goods or services for the benefit of individual households or groups of households;

(b) Many NPIs are controlled by associations whose members have equal rights, including equal votes on all major decisions affecting the affairs of the NPI. Members enjoy limited liability with respect to the NPIs operations;

(c) There are no shareholders with a claim on the profits or equity of the NPI. The members are not entitled to a share in any profits, or surplus, generated by the productive activities of the NPI, such profits being retained within the NPI;

(d) The direction of an NPI is usually vested in a group of officers, executive committee or similar body elected by a simple majority vote of all the members. These officers are the counterpart of the board of directors of a corporation and are responsible for appointing any paid managers;

(e) The term "non-profit institution" derives from the fact that the members of the association controlling the NPI are not permitted to gain financially from its operations and cannot appropriate any surplus which it may make. It does not imply that an NPI cannot make an operating surplus on its production.

NPIs as market and non-market producers

4.57. As in the case of producer units owned by government units, it is important to distinguish between NPIs engaged in market and non-market production as this affects the sector of the economy to which an NPI is allocated. NPIs do not necessarily engage in non-market production.

NPIs engaged in market production

4.58. Market producers are producers that sell most or all of their output at prices that are economically significant—i.e., at prices which have a significant influence on the amounts the producers are willing to supply and on the amounts purchasers wish to buy. Schools, colleges, universities, clinics, hospitals, etc. constituted as NPIs are market producers when they charge fees which are based on their production costs and which are sufficiently high to have a significant influence on the demand for their services. Their production activities must generate an operating surplus or loss. Any surpluses they make must be retained within the institutions as their status prevents them from distributing them to others. On the other hand, because of their status as "non-profit institutions" they are also able to raise additional funds by appealing for donations from persons, corporations or government. In this way, they may be able to acquire assets which generate significant property income in addition to their revenues from fees, thereby enabling them to charge fees below average costs. However, they must continue to be treated as market producers so long as their fees are determined mainly by their costs of production and are high enough to have a significant impact on demand. Such NPIs are not charities, their real objective often being to provide educational, health or other services of a very high quality using their incomes from endowments merely to keep down somewhat the high fees they have to charge.

Market NPIs serving businesses

4.59. Most market NPIs serving businesses are created by associations of the businesses whose interests they are designed to promote. They consist of chambers of commerce, agricultural, manufacturing or trade associations, employers' organizations, research or testing laboratories or other organizations or institutes which engage in activities which are of mutual interest or benefit to the group of businesses that control and finance them. The NPIs often engage in publicity on behalf of the group, lobby politicians or provide advice or assistance to individual members in difficulty for one reason or another. The NPIs are usually financed by contributions or subscriptions from the group of businesses concerned. The subscriptions are treated not as transfers but as payments for services rendered and these NPIs are, therefore, classed as market producers. However, as explained below, when chambers of commerce or similar organizations for the benefit of businesses are controlled and mainly financed by government units, they are classified as non-market NPIs and allocated to the general government sector.

NPIs engaged in non-market production

4.60. The majority of NPIs in most countries are non-market rather than market producers. Non-market producers are producers that provide most of their output to others free or at prices which are not economically significant: that is, at prices which do not have a significant influence on the amounts the producers are willing to supply or on the amounts purchasers wish to

buy. Thus, NPIs engaged mainly in non-market production may be distinguished not only by the fact that they are incapable of providing financial gain to the units which control or manage them, but also by the fact that they must rely principally on funds other than receipts from sales to cover their costs of production or other activities. Their principal source of finance may be regular subscriptions paid by the members of the association that controls them or transfers or donations from third parties, including government.

4.61. NPIs engaged mainly in non-market production may be divided into two main groups: those NPIs controlled and mainly financed by government and those NPIs providing non-market goods and services to households financed mainly by transfers from non-governmental sources—households, corporations or non-residents. The second group are described as "NPIs serving households" (NPISHs) and constitute a separate sector in the System.

NPIs controlled and mainly financed by government

4.62. NPIs controlled and mainly financed by government must be properly constituted legal entities which exist separately from government. In this context, control is to be understood as the ability to determine the general policy or programme of the NPI by having the right to appoint the officers managing the NPI. Such NPIs may be engaged in research or development, for example, for the benefit of certain groups of producers, such as farmers. They may also be concerned with the setting or maintenance of standards in fields such as health, safety, the environment, accounting, finance, education, etc., for the benefit of both enterprises and households. Governments find it appropriate to create NPIs for this purpose, rather than using agencies of government to carry out the same functions, because NPIs concerned with public standards may need to be seen as detached and objective, and not subject to political pressures. NPIs controlled and financed by government are allocated to the general government sector, irrespectively of the types of institutional units that mainly benefit from their activities.

4.63. In some countries, certain legal entities created by government units may have the characteristics of, and behave like, NPIs controlled and mainly financed by government units and yet be formally described as "corporations". Such entities must be treated as NPIs whatever their names. In general, the status of a legal entity cannot be automatically ascertained from its name and it is necessary to take account of its functions and purpose.

NPIs serving households (NPISHs)

4.64. Non-profit institutions serving households (NPISHs) consist of NPIs which provide goods or services to households free or at prices that are not economically significant. Two main types of NPISHs may be distinguished.

4.65. The first type consists of NPISHs which are created by associations of persons to provide goods or, more often, services primarily for the benefit of the members themselves. The services are usually provided free, being financed by regular membership subscriptions or dues. They include NPISHs such as professional or learned societies, political parties, trade unions, consumers' associations, churches or religious societies, and social, cultural, recreational or sports clubs. They do not include bodies serving similar functions that are controlled and mainly financed by government units, except that churches are always treated as serving households even when mainly financed by government units. Political parties in countries with one-party political systems that are controlled and financed by government units are always included in the general government sector.

4.66. In some communities, NPISHs may be found which do not possess any legal status or formal articles of association. They should be treated as NPISHs when they perform the same kinds of functions as the societies, parties, unions, etc., de-

scribed above, even if they are not legally constituted as NPISHs. However, when groups of households collaborate on communal construction projects (such as construction of buildings, roads, bridges, ditches, dykes, etc.), they should be treated as informal partnerships engaged on own-account construction rather than NPISHs. NPISHs should normally have a continuing role to play and not be deemed to be created for single projects of limited duration.

4.67. The second type of NPISH consists of charities, relief or aid agencies that are created for philanthropic purposes and not to serve the interests of the members of the association controlling the NPISH. Such NPISHs provide goods or services on a non-market basis to households in need, including households affected by natural disasters or war. The resources of such NPISHs are provided mainly by donations in cash or in kind from the general public, corporations or governments. They may also be provided by transfers from non- residents, including similar kinds of NPISHs resident in other countries.

C. The non-financial corporations sector and its sub-sectors (S.11)

4.68. Non-financial corporations or quasi-corporations are corporations or quasi-corporations whose principal activity is the production of market goods or non-financial services. The non-financial corporations sector is composed of the following set of resident institutional units:

(a) All resident non-financial corporations, irrespectively of the residence of their shareholders;

(b) All resident non-financial quasi-corporations including the branches or agencies of foreign-owned non-financial enterprises that are engaged in significant amounts of production on the economic territory on a long-term basis;

(c) All resident NPIs that are market producers of goods or non-financial services.

4.69. Some non-financial corporations or quasi-corporations may have secondary financial activities: for example, producers or retailers of goods may provide consumer credit directly to their own customers. As explained more fully below, such corporations or quasi-corporations are nevertheless classified as belonging in their entirety to the non-financial corporate sector provided their principal activity is non-financial. Sectors are groups of institutional units, and the whole of each institutional unit must be classified to one or another sector of the System even though that unit may be engaged in more than one type of economic activity.

4.70. The non-financial corporate sector is divided into three subsectors on the basis of the types of institutional units that exercise control over the corporations, quasi-corporations or market NPIs. While control over corporations may be guaranteed by owning or controlling a majority of voting shares, it is

usually possible to secure control by owning or controlling considerably less than half the voting shares, depending upon the distribution of voting shares among shareholders as explained earlier. However, as the minimum shareholding that is sufficient to secure control may vary from corporation to corporation, it is not possible to specify a figure below 50 per cent that is guaranteed to secure control. As a practical guideline, therefore, it is recommended that control should normally be attributed to an institutional unit, or organized group of units, only when they own or control (e.g., through a subsidiary) more than 50 per cent of the voting shares of a corporation unless there is other evidence that control is exercised.

The sub-sectors of the non-financial corporations sector

4.71. Three sub-sectors are distinguished:

(a) Public non-financial corporations;

(b) National private non-financial corporations;

(c) Foreign controlled non-financial corporations.

Public non-financial corporations (S.11001)

4.72. These consist of resident non-financial corporations and quasi-corporations that are subject to control by government units, control over a corporation being defined as the ability to determine general corporate policy by choosing appropriate directors, if necessary. The government may secure control over a corporation:

(a) By owning more than half the voting shares or otherwise controlling more than half the shareholders' voting power; or

(b) As a result of special legislation, decree or regulation which empowers the government to determine corporate policy or to appoint the directors.

4.73. In order to control more than half the shareholders' voting power, a government unit need not own any of the voting shares itself. For example, a public corporation could be a subsidiary of another public corporation in which the government owns a majority of the voting shares. Public quasi-corporations are quasi-corporations owned directly by government units.

4.74. Public corporations do not include any non-market NPIs controlled and financed by government units, such NPIs being included in the general government sector.

National private non-financial corporations (S.11002)

4.75. These include all resident non-financial corporations and quasi-corporations that are not controlled by government or by non-resident institutional units. Such corporations may, or may not, be controlled by other resident institutional units. They are simply characterized by the fact that they are not subject to control by the government or from abroad. The sub-sector also includes market NPIs producing goods or non-financial services: for example, market NPIs engaged in providing education or health services on a fee—paying basis, or trade associations serving enterprises.

Foreign controlled non-financial corporations (S.11003)

4.76. These consist of all resident non-financial corporations and quasi-corporations that are controlled by non-resident institutional units. The sub-sector includes:

(a) All subsidiaries of non-resident corporations (but not associates of non-resident corporations);

(b) All corporations controlled by a non-resident institutional unit that is not itself a corporation: for example, a corporation which is controlled by a foreign government; it also includes corporations controlled by a group of non-resident units acting in concert;

(c) All branches or other unincorporated agencies of non-resident corporate or unincorporated enterprises that are engaged in significant amounts of production on the economic territory on a long-term basis and that are, therefore, treated as resident quasi-corporations.

D. The financial corporations sector and its sub-sectors (S.12)

4.77. The financial corporations sector consists of all resident corporations or quasi-corporations principally engaged in financial intermediation or in auxiliary financial activities which are closely related to financial intermediation. Because financial intermediation is inherently different from most other types of productive activity and because of the importance of financial intermediation in the economy, financial corporations are distinguished from non-financial corporations at the first level of sectoring in the System.

1. Financial intermediation

4.78. Financial intermediation may be defined as a productive activity in which an institutional unit incurs liabilities on its own account for the purpose of acquiring financial assets by engaging in financial transactions on the market. The role of financial intermediaries is to channel funds from lenders to borrowers by intermediating between them. They collect funds from lenders and transform, or repackage, them in ways which suit the requirements of borrowers. They obtain funds by incurring liabilities on their own account, not only by taking deposits but also by issuing bills, bonds or other securities. They use these funds to acquire financial assets, principally by making advances or loans to others but also by purchasing bills, bonds or other securities. A financial intermediary does not simply act as an agent for other institutional units but places itself at risk by incurring liabilities on its own account.

2. Financial enterprises

4.79. Financial enterprises are defined in the System as enterprises that are principally engaged in financial intermediation or in auxiliary financial activities which are closely related to financial intermediation. They thus include enterprises whose principal function is to facilitate financial intermediation without necessarily engaging in financial intermediation themselves. Financial enterprises consist of all those enterprises (i.e., institutional units as distinct from establishments) whose principal activity is classified under Divisions 65, 66 and 67 of the International Standard Industrial Classification of All Economic Activities (ISIC) Rev.3.

4.80. The provision of services that are auxiliary to financial intermediation may be carried out as secondary activities of financial intermediaries or they may be provided by specialist agencies or brokers. The latter consist of agencies such as securities brokers, flotation companies, loan brokers, etc. There are also other agencies whose principal function is to guarantee, by endorsement, bills or similar instruments intended for discounting or refinancing by financial enterprises and also institutions that arrange hedging instruments, such as swaps, options and futures which have evolved as a result of wide-ranging financial innovation. These enterprises provide services which border very closely on financial intermediation, but they may not constitute true financial intermediation as the enterprises may not acquire financial assets and put themselves at risk by incurring liabilities on their own account. However, it is becoming increasingly difficult to draw a clear distinction between true intermediation and certain other financial activities. The boundary between financial intermediation and many of the services which are auxiliary to financial intermediation has become rather blurred as a result of continuous evolution and innovation in financial markets.

4.81. However, this is not the only reason for classifying financial auxiliaries as financial enterprises in the System. As already mentioned, corporations whose principal function is financial intermediation also tend to provide a wide range of auxiliary services themselves as secondary activities. As a corporation as a whole has to be allocated to a sector, the auxiliary activities of financial corporations would fall within the financial corporate sector of the System anyway, even if financial auxiliaries themselves were to be excluded.

3. Unincorporated financial enterprises

4.82. Individuals or households may engage in financial activities such as money lending or buying and selling foreign currency. Unincorporated financial enterprises of this kind are included in the financial corporations sector only if they qualify as proper financial intermediaries or auxiliaries and as quasi-corporations. In particular, they must have complete sets of accounts that are separable from those of their owners in their personal capacities. As large unincorporated financial enterprises may be subject to government regulation and control, they may well be obliged to keep such accounts. However, money lenders, currency changers and similar individuals engaged in financial activities on a small scale are unlikely to qualify, in which case they cannot be treated as quasi-corporations and are not included in the financial corporations sector.

4. The sub-sectors of the financial corporations sector

4.83. Financial corporations and quasi-corporations are grouped into the following sub-sectors:

(a) The central bank;

(b) Other depository corporations, of which:

   (i)   Deposit money corporations;

   (ii) Other;

(c) Other financial intermediaries, except insurance corporations and pension funds;

(d) Financial auxiliaries;

(e) Insurance corporations and pension funds.

4.84. In addition, financial corporations and quasi-corporations may also be sub-divided according to whether they are subject to public, private or foreign control as follows:

(a) Public financial corporations;

(b) National private financial corporations;

(c) Foreign controlled financial corporations.

The criteria for determining control are exactly the same as for non-financial corporations.

4.85. The first level of sub-sectoring the financial corporations sector is the breakdown into the five categories of financial corporation listed above (central bank, other depository corporations, etc.), the division between public, private and foreign controlled corporations being made at the second level of sub-sectoring. The second breakdown is not relevant to the central bank. The corporations and quasi-corporations which make up the five sub-sectors at the first level are described below.

The central bank (S.121)

4.86. This sub-sector consists of the central bank together with any other agencies or bodies which regulate or supervise financial corporations and which are themselves separate institutional units. The central bank is the public financial corporation which is a monetary authority: that is, which issues banknotes and sometimes coins and may hold all or part of the international reserves of the country. The central bank also has liabilities in the form of demand or reserve deposits of other depository corporations and often government deposits.

4.87. In some countries, some monetary authority-type functions, such as the maintenance of the international reserves or the issue of currency, may be carried out by an agency, or agencies, of central government which remain financially integrated with central government and are directly controlled and managed by government itself as a matter of policy. Such agencies are not separate institutional units from government and must, therefore, remain in the general government sector.

Other depository corporations (S.122)

4.88. This sub-sector consists of all resident financial corporations and quasi-corporations, except the central bank, whose principal activity is financial intermediation and which have liabilities in the form of deposits or financial instruments such as short-term certificates of deposit which are close substitutes for deposits in mobilizing financial resources and which are included in measures of money broadly defined.

4.89. Traditionally, money has been interpreted as a financial instrument which may be used as a unit of account, a medium of exchange, and a store of value. A narrow concept of money is one which focuses on money as an asset which is immediately, universally and legally accepted as a means of payment. Narrow money therefore consists of currency (including coin) plus deposits which are repayable on demand and immediately transferable by cheque, standing order or other means of transferring deposits for the purpose of making payments. In the past, only deposits with certain types of financial corporations, typically called "banks", were universally acceptable for this purpose. However, two developments have led to the use of a more broadly based concept of money. The first is that, as a result of increasing competition and financial innovation, banks have been able to offer other kinds of deposits or facilities which are very close substitutes for narrow money and which can be used for payment purposes with little or no delay or financial penalty, without being technically transferable deposits payable on demand. The second is that deposits with other kinds of financial corporations (not necessarily describing themselves as "banks") which in the past may not have been repayable on demand or used as a means of payment, have become increasingly transferable, again as a result of financial innovation. They have also become increasingly close substitutes for narrow money on deposit with banks. A broad concept of money is one which embraces all these new kinds of deposits and quasi-deposit liabilities of depository corporations. The need for broader measures of money has been generally accepted for purposes of economic analysis and policy-making, as relationships previously observed to hold between narrow measures of money and levels of economic activity have tended to break down.

4.90. Given the wide variation in institutional arrangements between countries whose financial systems and markets are at different stages of development and also the continuous innovation in financial markets and instruments over time, it is not possible to provide precise, operational definitions of narrow or broad money which would be appropriate and analytically useful across a range of different countries and which would continue to be valid over any long period of time. The System does not, therefore, attempt to provide such definitions even though it recognizes the usefulness and importance of the concepts of narrow and broad money themselves.

4.91. As stated above, the sub-sector "other depository corporations" covers those corporations which have liabilities in the form of deposits or close substitutes for deposits which are included in measures of broad money. "Other depository corporations" cannot be simply described as "banks", however, because they may possibly include some corporations which may not call themselves banks, and which may not be permitted to do so in some countries, while some other corporations describing themselves as "banks" may not in fact be depository corporations as defined above. In general, there is no one-to-one correspondence between "depository corporations" and "banks".

4.92. When the financial instruments and arrangements within a country are such that it is meaningful and analytically useful to identify a sub-set of depository corporations whose deposits correspond to money in the narrow sense, it is recommended that they should be separately identified. This sub-set is described as "deposit money corporations". It may not always be feasible, however, to subdivide "other depository cor-

porations" in this way, as explained further in paragraph 4.94 below.

Deposit money corporations (S.1221)

4.93. These consist of resident depository corporations and quasi-corporations which have any liabilities in the form of deposits payable on demand, transferable by cheque or otherwise usable for making payments. Such deposits are included in the concept of money in a narrow sense. These corporations include so-called "clearing banks" which participate in a common clearing system organized to facilitate the transfer of deposits between them by cheques or other means.

Other (S.1222)

4.94. These consist of all other resident depository corporations and quasi-corporations which have liabilities in the form of deposits that may not be readily transferable or in the form of financial instruments such as short-term certificates of deposit which are close substitutes for deposits and included in measures of money broadly defined. These corporations compete for funds with deposit money corporations in financial markets even if they are unable, or unwilling, to incur liabilities in the form of transferable deposits. They may include corporations described as savings banks (including trustee savings banks and savings banks and loan associations), credit cooperatives and mortgage banks or building societies. It must be emphasized that such corporations are described in different ways in different countries and they can only be identified by examining their functions rather than their names. They may also include post office savings banks or other savings banks controlled by the government, provided these are separate institutional units from government. As a result of financial innovation, improved technology in the field of computers and communications, and also financial deregulation in many countries, some of the corporations included under this heading take deposits which, although not readily transferable by traditional methods, may increasingly be used for payments purposes and be gradually transformed into deposits which are partially or even wholly transferable without much delay, difficulty or cost. This simply underlines the difficulty of drawing a clear distinction between narrow and broad money, and the fact that the distinction between "deposit money corporations" and "other" depository corporations may be too blurred to be operational in some countries.

Other financial intermediaries except insurance corporations and pension funds (S.123)

4.95. This sub-sector consists of all resident corporations and quasi-corporations primarily engaged in financial intermediation except depository corporations, insurance corporations and pension funds. Financial corporations included under the present heading are those which raise funds on financial markets, but not in the form of deposits, and use them to acquire other kinds of financial assets. The types of corporations which may be included under this heading are those engaged in financing investment or capital formation; for example, investment corporations, corporations engaged in financial leasing, hire purchase corporations and other corporations engaged in the provision of personal finance or consumer credit.

Financial auxiliaries (S.124)

4.96. This sub-sector consists of all resident corporations and quasi-corporations engaged primarily in activities closely related to financial intermediation but which do not themselves perform an intermediation role. They consist of corporations such as securities brokers, loan brokers, flotation corporations, insurance brokers, etc. They also include corporations whose principal function is to guarantee, by endorsement, bills or similar instruments intended for discounting or refinancing by financial corporations, and also corporations which arrange hedging instruments such as swaps, options, and futures or other instruments which are continually being developed as a result of wide-ranging financial innovation.

Insurance corporations and pension funds (S.125)

4.97. This sub-sector consists of resident insurance corporations and quasi-corporations and autonomous pension funds. Insurance corporations consist of incorporated, mutual and other entities whose principal function is to provide life, accident, sickness, fire or other forms of insurance to individual institutional units or groups of units.

4.98. The pension funds included here are those which are constituted in such a way that they are separate institutional units from the units which create them. They are established for purposes of providing benefits on retirement for specific groups of employees. They have their own assets and liabilities and they engage in financial transactions in the market on their own account. These funds are organized, and directed, by individual private or government employers, or jointly by individual employers and their employees; and the employees and/or employers make regular contributions. They do not cover pension arrangements for the employees of private or government entities which do not include a separately organized fund nor an arrangement organized by a non-government employer in which the reserves of the fund are simply added to that employer's own reserves or invested in securities issued by that employer.

5. The sub-sectoring of some special cases

4.99. It is useful to specify the treatment of a number of special cases including corporations which lie close to the boundary between the financial and non-financial corporations sectors.

Holding corporations

4.100. As explained earlier in the chapter, holding corporations are corporations that control a group of subsidiary corporations and whose principal activity is owning and directing the group. Holding corporations are classified as financial if the preponderant type of activity of the group of corporations as a whole is financial. In the absence of suitable information about the relative sizes of the subsidiaries, a holding corporation may be classified as financial if a simple majority of the corporations it controls are financial. Similarly, financial holding corporations may be allocated to sub-sectors according to the type of financial activity mainly carried out by the group it controls. For example, if the group of corporations is mainly concerned with insurance, the holding corporation will itself be classified in the sub-sector, insurance corporations and pension funds. If there is no single type of financial activity which is clearly predominant within the group, the holding corporation should be classified in the sub-sector, other financial intermediaries except insurance corporations and pension funds.

Regulatory bodies

4.101. Bodies which regulate or supervise financial corporations may be classified as financial or non-financial according to their status. Such bodies which form part of government and cannot be treated as separate institutional units—i.e., cannot be treated as quasi-corporations—must remain in the general government sector and cannot be allocated to the financial corporate sector. When such bodies are separate institutional units they are to be included with the central bank.

Secondary financial activities

4.102. One form of financial innovation has been a substantial growth in activity of a kind traditionally carried out by, or through, financial corporations but which may also be done directly by non-financial enterprises themselves. For example, there is a tendency in some countries for producers or retailers of goods to provide consumer credit directly to their customers. Another example is the tendency for non-financial enterprises in some countries to raise funds themselves by selling their own obligations directly on the money or capital markets. However, provided that:

(a) A non-financial enterprise does not create a new institutional unit, such as a subsidiary corporation, to carry out the financial activity; and

(b) The financial activity remains secondary to the principal activity of the enterprise;

the enterprise as a whole must continue to be classified as non-financial.

4.103. The same principle applies to the sub-sectoring of financial corporations. For example, many central banks also engage in some commercial banking. However, as a single institutional unit, the central bank as a whole, including its commercial banking activities, is classified in the sub-sector "central banks". For the same reason, central bank or monetary authority-type functions carried out by agencies within the central government which are not separate institutional units from government are not allocated to the central bank sub-sector.

E. The general government sector and its sub-sectors

1. Introduction: governments as institutional units

4.104. Government units may be described as unique kinds of legal entities established by political processes which have legislative, judicial or executive authority over other institutional units within a given area. Viewed as institutional units, the principal functions of government are to assume responsibility for the provision of goods and services to the community or to individual households and to finance their provision out of taxation or other incomes; to redistribute income and wealth by means of transfers; and to engage in non-market production. In general terms:

(a) A government unit usually has the authority to raise funds by collecting taxes or compulsory transfers from other institutional units. In order to satisfy the basic requirements of an institutional unit in the System, a government unit—whether at the level of the nation, a region or a locality—must have funds of its own either raised by taxing other units or received as transfers from other government units and the authority to disburse some, or all, of such funds in the pursuit of its policy objectives. It must also be able to borrow funds on its own account;

(b) Government units typically make three different kinds of final outlays:

(i) The first group consists of actual or imputed expenditures on the free provision to the community of collective services such as public administration, defence, law enforcement, public health, etc. which, as a result of market failure, have to be organized collectively by government and financed out of general taxation or other income;

(ii) The second group consists of expenditures on the provision of goods or services free, or at prices that are not economically significant, to individual households. These expenditures are deliberately incurred and financed out of taxation or other income by government in the pursuit of its social or political objectives, even though individuals could be charged according to their usage;

(iii) The third group consists of transfers paid to other institutional units, mostly households, in order to redistribute income or wealth.

4.105. Within a single country there may be many separate government units when there are different levels of government—central, state or local government. In addition, social security

funds also constitute government units. These different kinds of government units are described later when the sub-sectoring of the general government sector is explained.

Government units as producers

4.106. Government units, like households, may own and operate unincorporated enterprises that are engaged in the production of goods or services. The extent to which government units decide to engage in production themselves rather than purchase the goods or services from market producers is largely a matter of political choice. The fact that governments choose to supply not only collective services but also many goods and individual services free, or at prices that are not economically significant, to households or other units does not require that they produce them themselves. Even in the case of most collective services, or so-called "public goods", for which there is market failure, governments are obliged only to assume responsibility for organizing and financing their production. They are not obliged to produce them. However, government units do usually engage in a wide range of productive activities in practice, covering not only collective services but also many other goods and individual services. Because it is largely a matter of political choice, the range of goods and services produced by government units varies greatly from one country to another. Apart from some collective services such as public administration and defence, it is therefore difficult to categorize certain types of production, such as the production of education or health services, as intrinsically governmental, even though they are often produced by government units.

4.107. When a government unit wishes to intervene in the sphere of production it has three options:

(a) It may create a public corporation whose corporate policy, including pricing and investment, it is able to control;

(b) It may create a NPI that it controls and mainly, or entirely, finances;

(c) It may produce the goods or services itself in an establishment which it owns and which does not exist as a separate legal entity from the government unit itself.

However, if a government establishment, or group of establishments engaged on the same kind of production under common management,

(a) Charges prices for its outputs that are economically significant;

(b) Is operated and managed in a similar way to a corporation; and

(c) Has a complete set of accounts that enable its operating surpluses, savings, assets and liabilities to be separately identified and measured;

it should be treated as a quasi-corporation. Such quasi-corporations are market producers that are treated as separate institutional units from the government units that own them. They are classified, sectored and sub-sectored in the same way as public corporations.

4.108. In order to be treated as a quasi-corporation the government must allow the management of the enterprise considerable discretion not only with respect to the management of the production process but also the use of funds. Government quasi-corporations must be able to maintain their own working balances and business credit and be able to finance some or all of their capital formation out of their own savings, depreciation reserves or borrowing. The ability to distinguish flows of income and capital between quasi-corporations and government implies that their operating and financing activities cannot be fully integrated with government revenue or finance statistics in practice, despite the fact that they are not separate legal entities. The net operating surplus of a government quasi-corporation is not a component of government revenue, and the accounts for government record only the actual or imputed flows of income and capital between the quasi-corporation and government.

4.109. Thus, the producer units that remain integrated with the government units that own them are those that cannot be treated as quasi-corporations. Such units remain within the general government sector. They are likely to consist largely, or entirely, of non-market producers: that is, producers most or all of whose output is supplied to other units free, or at prices that are not economically significant. In addition to providing non-market goods or services to the general public, such units may include government producers supplying non-market goods or services to other government units for purposes of intermediate consumption or gross fixed capital formation: for example, munitions factories, government printing offices, transport agencies, computer or communications agencies, etc. In principle, government units can also be market producers.

4.110. In contrast to output produced for own consumption or own gross capital formation by market producers, there are usually no suitable markets whose prices can be used to value government non-market output. By convention, therefore, such output is valued by its production costs.

2. Social security funds

4.111. Social security funds constitute special kinds of institutional units which may be found at any level of government—central, state or local. Before defining social security funds, it is

necessary to give a brief description of social insurance schemes in general. Social insurance schemes are intended to provide social benefits to members of the community, or to groups of individuals such as the employees of an enterprise and their dependants, out of funds derived mainly from social contributions. Social security schemes are social insurance schemes covering the community as a whole or large sections of the community that are imposed and controlled by government units. They generally involve compulsory contributions by employees or employers or both, and the terms on which benefits are paid to recipients are determined by government units. The schemes cover a wide variety of programmes, providing benefits in cash or in kind for old age, invalidity or death, survivors, sickness and maternity, work injury, unemployment, family allowance, health care, etc. There is usually no direct link between the amount of the contribution paid by an individual and the risk to which that individual is exposed. Social security schemes have to be distinguished from pension schemes or other social insurance schemes which are determined by mutual agreement between individual employers and their employees, the benefits being linked to contributions.

4.112. Social security funds may be distinguished by the fact that they are separately organized from the other activities of government units and hold their assets and liabilities separately from the latter. They are separate institutional units because they are autonomous funds, they have their own assets and liabilities and engage in financial transactions on their own account. However, institutional arrangements in respect of social security differ from country to country and in some countries they may become so closely integrated with the other finances of government as to bring into question whether they should be treated as a separate sub-sector. The amounts raised, and paid out, in social security contributions and benefits may be deliberately varied in order to achieve objectives of government policy that have no direct connection with the concept of social security as a scheme to provide social benefits to members of the community. They may be raised or lowered in order to influence the level of aggregate demand in the economy, for example. Nevertheless, so long as they remain separately constituted funds they must be treated as separate institutional units in the System.

3. The general government sector (S.13)

4.113. The general government sector consists of the following group of resident institutional units:

(a) All units of central, state or local government;

(b) All social security funds at each level of government;

(c) All non-market NPIs that are controlled and mainly financed by government units.

The sector does not include public corporations, even when all the equity of such corporations is owned by government units. It also does not include quasi-corporations that are owned and controlled by government units. However, unincorporated enterprises owned by government units that are not quasi-corporations remain integral parts of those units and, therefore, must be included in the general government sector.

4. Sub-sectors of the general government sector

4.114. Two alternative methods of sub-sectoring the general government sector are proposed in the System. One method is as follows:

(a)   Central government (S.1311);

(b)   State government (S.1312);

(c)   Local government (S.1313);

(d)   Social security funds (S.1314).

4.115. The alternative method is as follows:

(a)   Central government plus social security funds operating at the central government level (S.1321);

(b)   State government plus social security funds operating at the state government level (S.1322);

(c)   Local government plus social security funds operating at the local government level (S.1323).

4.116. As explained more fully later, the choice between the two methods of sub-sectoring depends mainly on the size, or importance, of social security funds within a country and on the way in which they are managed. In some countries there may not exist a proper intermediate level of government between central and local government, in which case the sub-sector "state government" is not distinguished.

Central government (S.1311)

4.117. The central government sub-sector consists of the institutional unit or units making up the central government plus those NPIs that are controlled and mainly financed by central government.

4.118. The political authority of central government extends over the entire territory of the country. Central government has therefore the authority to impose taxes on all resident and non-resident units engaged in economic activities within the country. Its political responsibilities include national defence and relations with foreign governments and it also seeks to ensure the efficient working of the social and economic system by means of appropriate legislation and regulation and also the maintenance of law and order. It is responsible for providing collective services for the benefit of the community as a whole, and for this purpose incurs expenditures on defence and public administration. In addition it may incur expenditures on the provision of services, such as education or health, primarily for the benefit of individual households. Finally, it may make

transfers to other institutional units—households, NPIs, corporations and other levels of government.

4.119. Central government is a large and complex sub-sector in most countries. It is generally composed of a central group of departments or ministries that make up a single institutional unit plus, in many countries, other institutional units. The departments may be responsible for considerable amounts of expenditure within the framework of the government's overall budget, but they are nevertheless not separate institutional units. Each department is not capable of owning assets, incurring liabilities, engaging in transactions, etc., in its own right, i.e., independently of central government as a whole. It would not be possible to compile meaningful, or analytically useful, income and accumulation accounts or balance sheets for each separate department as if it were a single legal entity. In addition, there may be agencies of central government with separate legal identity and substantial autonomy; they may have discretion over the volume and composition of their expenditures and may have a direct source of revenue such as earmarked taxes. Such agencies are often established to carry out specific functions such as road construction or the non-market production of health or education services. These should be treated as separate institutional units if they maintain full sets of accounts but are part of the central government sub-sector if they meet the criteria described in paragraph 4.104.

4.120. The departments of central government are often deliberately dispersed geographically and located in different parts of the country, but they nevertheless remain parts of a single institutional unit. Similarly, if the central government maintains branch offices or agencies in different parts of the country to meet local needs, including military bases or installations which serve national defence purposes, these must also be counted as parts of a single institutional unit for central government. However, for purposes of production accounts by type of productive activity, the establishment is used as the statistical unit, and producer units located in different regions are to be treated as different establishments, even though part of a single institutional unit.

4.121. In some countries, the central government may include units which engage in financial transactions which in other countries would be performed by central banks. In particular, units of central government may be responsible for the issue of currency, the maintenance of international reserves and the operation of exchange stabilization funds, and also transactions with the International Monetary Fund (IMF). When the units in question remain financially integrated with central government and under the direct control and supervision of central government, they cannot be treated as separate institutional units. Moreover, whatever monetary authority functions are carried out by central government are recorded in the government sector and not the corporate financial sector. However, because of the analytical importance which is attached to obtaining accounts covering the monetary authorities as a whole, and in order to provide links with other statistical systems, such as the *Balance of Payments Manual, Government Finance Statistics* and *Money and Banking Statistics* of the IMF, it is recommended that the transactions of central government agencies carrying out monetary authority and deposit-taking functions should be separately identified, so that they can be combined with those of the central bank and other depository corporations in special tabulations if desired.

4.122. Finally, it may be noted that social security funds are treated in the System as separate institutional units at each level of government, even though in some countries their finances may be partially integrated with government. Social security funds are described below. However, treating social security funds as separate institutional units does not, of course, preclude them from being included in the same sub-sector as the government units with which they are associated, and they are so included in the alternative method of sub-sectoring the general government sector.

State government (S.1312)

4.123. The state government sub-sector consists of state governments which are separate institutional units plus those NPIs that are controlled and mainly financed by state governments.

4.124. State governments are institutional units exercising some of the functions of government at a level below that of central government and above that of the governmental institutional units existing at a local level. They are institutional units whose fiscal, legislative and executive authority extends only over the individual "states" into which the country as a whole may be divided. Such "states" may be described by different terms in different countries. In some countries, especially small countries, individual states and state governments may not exist. However, in large countries, especially those which have federal constitutions, considerable powers and responsibilities may be assigned to state governments.

4.125. A state government usually has the fiscal authority to levy taxes on institutional units which are resident in, or engage in economic activities or transactions within, its area of competence (but not other areas). In any case, in order to be recognized as an institutional unit it must be able to own assets, raise funds and incur liabilities on its own account. It must also be entitled to spend or allocate some, or possibly all, of the taxes or other income that it receives according to its own policies, within the general rules of law of the country, although some of the transfers it receives from central government may be tied to certain specified purposes. It should also be able to appoint its own officers, independently of external administrative control. On the other hand, if a regional unit is entirely dependent on funds from central government, and if the central government also dictates the ways in which those funds are to be spent at the regional level, it should be treated as an agency of central government rather than as a separate institutional unit.

4.126. State governments, when they exist, are distinguished by the fact that their fiscal authority extends over the largest geographical areas into which the country as a whole may be divided for political or administrative purposes. In a few countries more than one level of government exists between the central government and the smallest governmental institutional units at a local level; in such cases, these intermediate levels of government are grouped together with the level of government, either state or local, with which they are most closely associated for purposes of sectoring in the System.

4.127. State governments may own, or control, corporations in the same way as central government. Similarly, they may have units which engage in market production, in which case the relevant producer units should be treated as quasi-corporations whenever their operations and accounting records justify this. Social security schemes may also exist at a state level and are treated as separate institutional units.

Local government (S.1313)

4.128. The local government sub-sector consists of local governments that are separate institutional units plus those NPIs which are controlled and mainly financed by local governments. In principle, local government units are institutional units whose fiscal, legislative and executive authority extends over the smallest geographical areas distinguished for administrative and political purposes. The scope of their authority is generally much less than that of central government or regional governments, and they may, or may not, be entitled to levy taxes on institutional units resident in their areas. They are often heavily dependent on grants or transfers from higher levels of government, and they may also act as agents of central or regional governments to some extent. However, in order to be treated as institutional units they must be entitled to own assets, raise funds and incur liabilities by borrowing on their own account; similarly, they must have some discretion over how such funds are spent. They should also be able to appoint their own officers, independently of external administrative control. The fact that they may also act as agents of central or state governments to some extent does not prevent them from being treated as separate institutional units provided they are also able to raise and spend some funds on their own initiative and own responsibility.

4.129. As they are the government units which are in closest contact with the institutional units resident in their localities, they typically provide a wide range of services to local residents, some of which may be financed out of transfers from higher levels of government. The same rules govern the treatment of the production of goods and services by local government units as are applied to central and state governments. Units such as municipal theatres, museums, swimming pools, etc., which supply goods or services on a market basis should be treated as quasi-corporations whenever appropriate. Units supplying services such as education or health on a non-market basis remain an integral part of the local government unit to which they belong.

Social security funds (S.1314)

4.130. The social security funds sub-sector consists of the social security funds operating at all levels of government. As explained in paragraph 111 above, social security funds are social insurance schemes covering the community as a whole or large sections of the community that are imposed and controlled by government units.

5. The alternative method of sub-sectoring

4.131. The alternative method of sub-sectoring the general government sector is to group the social security funds operating at each level of government with the corresponding government units and government controlled and financed NPIs at that level of government. The two alternative methods of sub-sectoring are designed to accommodate different analytical needs. The decision as to which method is more appropriate in a given country cannot be made a priori. It depends on how well organized and important social security funds are and on the extent to which they are managed independently of the government units with which they are associated. If the management of social security funds is so closely integrated with the short- or medium-term requirements of the government's general economic policy that contributions and benefits are deliberately adjusted in the interests of overall economic policy, it becomes difficult, at a conceptual level, to draw any clear distinction between the management of social security and the other economic functions of government. Alternatively, in some countries, social security funds may exist in only a very rudimentary form. In either of these circumstances it is difficult to justify treating social security funds as a separate sub-sector on a par with central, state and local government, and it is more appropriate to use the alternative method of sub-sectoring in which they are grouped with the corresponding government units at each level of government.

F. The households sector and its sub-sectors

1. Introduction: households as institutional units

4.132. For purposes of the System, a household may be defined as:

> a small group of persons who share the same living accommodation, who pool some, or all, of their income and wealth and who consume certain types of goods and services collectively, mainly housing and food.

4.133. In general, each member of a household should have some claim upon the collective resources of the household. At least some decisions affecting consumption or other economic activities must be taken for the household as a whole.

4.134. Households often coincide with families, but members of the same household do not necessarily have to belong to the same family so long as there is some sharing of resources and consumption. Households may be of any size and take a wide variety of different forms in different societies or cultures depending on tradition, religion, education, climate, geography, history and other socio-economic factors. The definition of a household which is adopted by survey statisticians familiar with the socio-economic conditions within a given country is likely to approximate closely to the concept of a household as defined in the System, although survey statisticians may add more precise, or operational, criteria within a particular country.

4.135. Servants or other paid domestic employees who live on the same premises as their employer do not form part of their employer's household even though they may be provided with accommodation and meals as remuneration in kind. Paid domestic employees have no claim upon the collective resources of their employers' households and the accommodation and food they consume are not included with their employer's consumption. They should therefore be treated as belonging to separate households from their employers.

4.136. Persons living permanently in an institution, or who may be expected to reside in an institution for a very long, or indefinite, period of time are treated as belonging to a single institutional household when they have little or no autonomy of action or decision in economic matters. Some examples of persons belonging to institutional households are the following:

(a) Members of religious orders living in monasteries, convents or similar institutions;

(b) Long-term patients in hospitals, including mental hospitals;

(c) Prisoners serving long sentences;

(d) Old persons living permanently in retirement homes.

4.137. On the other hand, persons who enter hospitals, clinics, convalescent homes, religious retreats, or similar institutions for short periods, who attend residential schools, colleges or universities, or who serve short prison sentences should be treated as members of the individual households to which they normally belong.

4.138. Households may engage in any kind of economic activity and not merely consumption. In this respect, their economic behaviour may be more varied than that of legal entities whose activities may be restricted to the purposes for which they are created. In particular, members of households play a major role in production either by operating their own unincorporated enterprises or by supplying labour to other unincorporated or corporate enterprises by working as employees. They lend and borrow funds, and so on. When individual members of households engage in economic activities, they are treated as acting on behalf of the households to which they belong and not as separate entities. Thus, when a member of a household owns his or her own enterprise, which is not a corporation or quasi-corporation, that enterprise forms an integral part of the household itself.

2. Households as producers

4.139. Production within the household sector takes place within enterprises that are directly owned and controlled by members of households, either individually or in partnership with others. When members of households work as employees for corporations, quasi-corporations or government, the production to which they contribute takes place outside the household sector.

4.140. Producer units within the household sector are all "unincorporated enterprises", even though this terminology is admittedly cumbersome when applied to some of the smaller, or highly specialized, producer units. Nevertheless, the term "unincorporated enterprise" emphasizes the fact that the producer unit is not incorporated as a separate legal entity from the household itself.

4.141. The fixed and other assets used in unincorporated enterprises do not belong to the enterprises but to their owners. The enterprises as such cannot engage in transactions with other economic units. They cannot enter into contractual relationships with other units nor incur liabilities on their own behalf. Their owners are personally liable, without limit, for any debts or obligations incurred in the course of production.

4.142. The owner of a household unincorporated enterprise usually has a dual role to play: first as the entrepreneur who is responsible for the creation and management of the enterprise and second as a worker who contributes labour inputs of a kind which could be provided by paid employees. The establishment of an unincorporated enterprise requires initiative, enterprise and capital equipment. Owners, in their capacity as entrepreneurs, have to raise the necessary finance at their own risk and on their own personal security; they have to find suitable premises and purchase, or lease, whatever capital equipment or materials are needed; and they may also have to engage and supervise paid employees. In some cases, the principal role of an owner is to act in this way as entrepreneur, innovator and risk-taker, in which case the surplus from production which eventually accrues to the owner represents primarily a return to entrepreneurship. In other cases, the principal function of an owner may be to provide labour, often

highly skilled professional labour, in which case most of the surplus may, in effect, represent remuneration for work done.

4.143. Thus, the surplus arising from the productive activities of a household unincorporated enterprise usually represents a mixture of two very different kinds of income, and is, therefore, described as "mixed income" instead of "operating surplus" (except for the surplus arising from the production of own-account housing services). The balance between the return to entrepreneurship and remuneration for work done may vary greatly between different kinds of household unincorporated enterprises but it can be very difficult to make a clear separation even conceptually in many cases.

Household unincorporated market enterprises

4.144. Household unincorporated market enterprises are created for the purpose of producing goods or services for sale or barter on the market. They can be engaged in virtually any kind of productive activity—agriculture, mining, manufacturing, construction, retail distribution or the production of other kinds of services. They can range from single persons working as street traders or shoe cleaners with virtually no capital or premises of their own through to large manufacturing, construction or service enterprises with many employees.

4.145. Household unincorporated market enterprises also include unincorporated partnerships that are engaged in producing goods or services for sale or barter on the market. The partners may belong to different households. The liability of the partners for the debts of the businesses must be unlimited for the partnerships to be treated as unincorporated enterprises. However, unincorporated partnerships with many partners, such as some large legal, accounting or architectural firms, are likely to behave like corporations and should be treated as quasi-corporations assuming complete sets of accounts are available for the partnerships. Partnerships whose partners enjoy limited liability are effectively separate legal entities and should be treated as corporations.

4.146. Some of the outputs of these market producers may be retained for consumption by members of the household to which the owner belongs. Such goods or services are included in the outputs of the enterprises and in the final consumption of the households, although it may be difficult to obtain the requisite data especially if taxes are being evaded in the process. Similarly, buildings or capital equipment may be used partly for production and partly for consumption. This underlines the extreme difficulty of separating unincorporated enterprises from their owners who are perfectly entitled to use such assets in any way they choose.

Household enterprises producing for own final use

4.147. These are household enterprises operated primarily for the purpose of producing goods or certain services for own final consumption or own gross fixed capital formation. The value of their output has to be imputed on the basis of the prices of similar goods or services sold on the market.

Producers of goods for own final use

4.148. Household unincorporated enterprises engaged in the production of goods for own final use may consist of:

(a) Subsistence farmers or others engaged in the production of agricultural goods for their own final consumption;

(b) Households engaged in the construction of their own dwellings or other structures for their own use, or on structural improvements or extensions to existing dwellings or structures;

(c) Households engaged in the production of other goods for their own consumption such as cloth, clothing, furniture, other household goods, foodstuffs (other than meals for immediate consumption), etc.

Such enterprises may sell any output that is surplus to their own requirements, but if they regularly sell most of their output they should be treated as market enterprises. Groups of households that engage in the communal construction of buildings, roads, bridges, etc., for their own individual or community use should be treated as informal partnerships engaged in non-market production.

Producers of services for own final use

4.149. As explained in chapter VI, section 2, only two categories of services produced by households for own final consumption are included within the production boundary of the System:

(a) Services of owner-occupied dwellings: owner-occupiers are deemed to own household unincorporated enterprises that produce housing services for their own consumption;

(b) Domestic services produced by employing paid staff: households are deemed to own household unincorporated enterprises in which they employ paid staff—servants, cooks, gardeners, etc.—to produce services for their own consumption.

4.150. The production of these services does not generate mixed income. There is no labour input into the production of the services of owner-occupied dwellings so that any surplus arising is operating surplus. There is no surplus generated by employing paid staff as, by convention, the value of the output produced is assumed to be equal to the value of the compensation of employees paid to the domestic staff, no other inputs being recognized.

3. The household sector and its sub-sectors (S.14)

4.151. The household sector consists of all resident households. Defined as institutional units, households include unincorporated enterprises owned by households, whether market producers or producing for own final use, as integral parts of those households. Only those household unincorporated market enterprises that constitute quasi-corporations are treated as separate institutional units.

4.152. The households sector may be divided into sub-sectors on the basis of the type of income that is the largest source of income for each household or, alternatively, on the basis of other criteria of an economic, socio-economic or geographical nature. Different methods of sub-sectoring may be appropriate for different economies and may be needed for different kinds of analysis and policy-making. While one method of sub-sectoring is recommended here that is considered to be useful for many purposes, statistical authorities are not necessarily expected always to choose this particular method and are advised to implement the System flexibly with respect to sub-sectoring the households sector.

4.153. Households may be grouped into sub-sectors according to the nature of their largest source of income. For this purpose, the following types of household income need to be distinguished:

(a) *Employers' mixed incomes*: these consist of the mixed incomes accruing to the owners of household unincorporated enterprises with paid employees;

(b) *Own-account workers' mixed incomes*: these consist of mixed incomes accruing to the owners of household unincorporated enterprises without paid employees;

(c) *Compensation of employees*;

(d) *Property and transfer incomes*.

Households are allocated to sub-sectors according to which of the four categories of income listed above is the largest for the household as a whole, even if it does not always account for more than half of total household income. When more than one income of a given category is received within the same household—for example, because more than one member of the household earns compensation of employees or because more than one property or transfer income is received—the classification must be based on the total household income within each category. The four sub-sectors are described as follows:

(a) Employers (S.141);

(b) Own-account workers (S.142);

(c) Employees (S.143);

(d) Recipients of property and transfer incomes (S.144).

The employers' sub-sector consists of the group of households for which employers' mixed incomes are the largest source of income for the household. Each of the other three sub-sectors is defined similarly using the income categories listed earlier. The distinction between own-account workers and employees is explained in detail in chapter VII.

4.154. The fourth sub-sector, households for which property and transfer incomes make up the largest source of income, constitutes a heterogeneous group and it is recommended that it should be divided into three further sub-sectors when possible. These sub-sectors are defined as follows:

(4.1) Recipients of property incomes (S.1441)

(4.2) Recipients of pensions (S.1442)

(4.3) Recipients of other transfer incomes (S.1443)

Pension households are households whose largest income consists of retirement or other pensions, including pensions from previous employers.

4.155. Other methods of sub-sectoring usually require a reference person to be identified for each household. The reference person is not necessarily the person that other members of the household regard as the "head of the household", as the reference person should be decided on grounds of economic importance rather than age or seniority. The reference person should normally be the person with the largest income although the reference person could also be the person who makes the major decisions with regard to the consumption of the household.

4.156. Once a reference person has been identified, it is possible to group households into sub-sectors on the basis of the reference person's characteristics. For example, sub-sectors may be defined according to:

(a) Occupation of the reference person;

(b) Industry, if any, in which the reference person works;

(c) Educational attainment of the reference person;

(d) Qualifications or skills possessed by the reference person.

Each of the criteria listed above provides its own possible scheme of sub-sectoring. It would also be possible to group households into sub-sectors according to the main income of the reference person if, for some reason, it was not possible to group on the basis of the largest income received by the household. For this purpose, the same income categories may be used as those recommended for the household's largest income.

4.157. Finally, it may be noted that households may be sub-sectored using criteria that apply to the household as a whole. For example, subsectors may be defined according to:

(a) Size of the total income of the household;

(b) Size of the household as measured by number of persons;

(c) Type of area in which the household is located.

The last criterion enables households living in agricultural, urban or metropolitan areas to be distinguished from each other, or households located in different geographical regions.

4.158. There are thus many useful ways in which the households sector may be sub-sectored and statistical agencies are advised to give due consideration to the various possibilities. More than one method may be adopted if there is a demand for different breakdowns of the households sector from different users, analysts or policy makers.

4.159. It is particularly important for many developing countries to be able to distinguish between the formal and informal sectors of the economy. The fifteenth International Conference of Labour Statisticians (Geneva, January 1993) adopted Resolution II concerning statistics of employment in the informal sector. The resolution provides, among other guidelines, an international statistical standard definition of the informal sector. The relevant paragraphs of the International Conference of Labour Statisticians' resolution are reproduced in the annex of this chapter for the benefit of those countries that wish to introduce the distinction between formal and informal sectors into their sub-sectoring of the households sector.

4.160. The System has to be applied flexibly, and not rigidly, and the adaptation of the System to countries in different circumstance is the subject of a special chapter. In order to implement any of the possible methods of sub-sectoring the households sector suggested above, individual countries are obliged to make their own decisions about what they consider to be the most relevant classification—for example, with regard to location or levels of skill—for which international guidelines may not be helpful. Thus, the fact that specific classifications may not be proposed here should not be interpreted as implying that the characteristics in question are less important for purposes of economic analysis and policy-making.

G. The non-profit institutions serving households sector (S.15)

4.161. Non-profit institutions are legal or social entities created for the purpose of producing goods or services whose status does not permit them to be a source of income, profit or other financial gain to the units that establish, control or finance them. Although they may not be a source of profit to other institutional units, NPIs may nevertheless be market producers if they provide services for which they charge prices or fees that are economically significant—that is, prices which have a significant influence both on the amounts the producers are willing to supply and on the amounts purchasers wish to buy. NPIs that are market producers are classified as belonging to one or another of the corporate sectors. Market NPIs include all NPIs serving enterprises, except those controlled and mainly financed by government units. The majority of NPIs, however, are likely to be non-market producers that provide goods or services to other institutional units either free or at prices or fees that are not economically significant.

4.162. Non-market NPIs may be divided into those controlled and mainly, or entirely, financed by government units and the remainder. The latter are described as "NPIs serving households" (NPISHs) and constitute a separate sector within the System. NPIs serving enterprises belong to the corporate or general government sectors depending upon whether they are controlled and mainly financed by government units. To summarize, therefore, the sector NPISHs is defined as the set of all resident NPIs except:

(a) NPIs that are market producers; and

(b) Non-market NPIs that are controlled and mainly financed by government units.

The NPISHs sector includes the following two main kinds of NPISHs that provide goods or services to their members or to other households without charge or at prices that are not economically significant:

(a) Trade unions, professional or learned societies, consumers' associations, political parties (except in single party states), churches or religious societies (including those financed by governments), and social, cultural, recreational and sports clubs;

(b) Charities, relief and aid organizations financed by voluntary transfers in cash or in kind from other institutional units.

H. The rest of the world (S.2)

4.163. For purposes of the System, the rest of the world consists of all non-resident institutional units that enter into transactions with resident units, or have other economic links with resident units. It is not a sector for which complete sets of accounts have to be compiled, although it is often convenient to describe the rest of the world as if it were a sector. The accounts, or tables, for the rest of the world are confined to those which record transactions between residents and non-residents or other economic relationships, such as claims by residents on non-residents, and vice versa. The rest of the world includes certain institutional units that may be physically located within the geographic boundary of a country; for example, foreign enclaves such as embassies, consulates or military bases, and also international organizations.

International organizations

4.164. Certain international organizations have all the essential attributes of institutional units. The special characteristics of an "international organization" as this term is used in the System my be summarized as follows:

(a) The members of an international organization are either national states or other international organizations whose members are national states; they thus derive their authority either directly from the national states which are their members or indirectly from them through other international organizations;

(b) They are entities established by formal political agreements between their members that have the status of international treaties; their existence is recognized by law in their member countries;

(c) Because they are established by international agreement, they are accorded sovereign status; that is, international organizations are not subject to the laws or regulations of the country, or countries, in which they are located; they are not treated as resident institutional units of the countries in which they are located;

(d) International organizations are created for various purposes including, among others, the following types of activities:

(i) The provision of non-market services of a collective nature for the benefit of their members;

(ii) Financial intermediation at an international level—that is, channelling funds between lenders and borrowers in different countries; an international organization may also act as a central bank to a group of countries.

4.165. Formal agreements concluded by all the member countries of an international organization may sometimes carry the force of law within those countries. Most international organizations are financed wholly or partly by contributions (transfers) from their member countries, but some organizations may raise funds in other ways such as borrowing on financial markets. For purposes of the System, international organizations are treated as units that are resident in the rest of the world.

Annex

Extract from the resolution of the fifteenth International Conference of Labour Statisticians, January 1993, concerning statistics of employment in the informal sector

Concept

5. (*1*) The informal sector may be broadly characterized as consisting of units engaged in the production of goods or services with the primary objective of generating employment and incomes to the persons concerned. These units typically operate at a low level of organization, with little or no division between labour and capital as factors of production and on a small scale. Labour relations—where they exist—are based mostly on casual employment, kinship or personal and social relations rather than contractual arrangements with formal guarantees.

(*2*) Production units of the informal sector have the characteristic features of household enterprises. The fixed and other assets used do not belong to the production units as such but to their owners. The units as such cannot engage in transactions or enter into contracts with other units, nor incur liabilities, on their own behalf. The owners have to raise the necessary finance at their own risk and are personally liable, without limit, for any debts or obligations incurred in the production process. Expenditure for production is often indistinguishable from household expenditure. Similarly, capital goods such as buildings or vehicles may be used indistinguishably for business and household purposes.

(*3*) Activities performed by production units of the informal sector are not necessarily performed with the deliberate intention of evading the payment of taxes or social security contributions, or infringing labour or other legislations or administrative provisions. Accordingly, the concept of informal sector activities should be distinguished from the concept of activities of the hidden or underground economy.

Operational definitions

Informal sector

6. (*1*) For statistical purposes, the informal sector is regarded as a group of production units which, according to the definitions and classifications provided in the United Nations System of National Accounts (Rev.4), form part of the household sector as household enterprises or, equivalently, unincorporated enterprises owned by households.

(*2*) Within the household sector, the informal sector comprises (i) "informal own-account enterprises" as defined in paragraph 8; and (ii) the additional component consisting of "enterprises of informal employers" as defined in paragraph 9.

(*3*) The informal sector is defined irrespective of the kind of workplace where the productive activities are carried out, the extent of fixed capital assets used, the duration of the operation of the enterprise (perennial, seasonal or casual), and its operation as a main or secondary activity of the owner.

Informal own-account enterprises

8. (*1*) Informal own-account enterprises are household enterprises (in the sense of the System of National Accounts) owned and operated by own-account workers, either alone or in partnership with members of the same or other households, which may employ contributing family workers and employees on an occasional basis, but do not employ employees on a continuous basis and which have the characteristics described in subparagraphs 5(1) and (2).

(*2*) For operational purposes, informal own-account enterprises may comprise, depending on national circumstances, either all own-account enterprises or only those which are not registered under specific forms of national legislation.

(*3*) Registration may refer to registration under factories or commercial acts, tax or social security laws, professional groups' regulatory acts, or similar acts, laws, or regulations established by national legislative bodies.

(*4*) Own-account workers, contributing family workers, employees and the employment of employees on a continuous basis are defined in accordance with the most recently adopted version of the International Classification of Status in Employment (ICSE).

Enterprises of informal employers

9. (*1*) Enterprises of informal employers are household enterprises (in the sense of the System of National Accounts) owned and operated by employers, either alone or in partnership with members of the same or other households, which employ one or more employees on a continuous basis and which have the characteristics described in subparagraphs 5(1) and (2).

(*2*) For operational purposes, enterprises of informal employers may be defined, depending on national circumstances, in terms of one or more of the following criteria:

(*i*) Size of the unit below a specified level of employment;

(*ii*) Non-registration of the enterprise or its employees.

(*3*) While the size criterion should preferably refer to the number of employees employed on a continuous basis, in practice, it may also be specified in terms of the total number of employees or the number of persons engaged during the reference period.

(*4*) The upper size limit in the definition of enterprises of informal employers may vary between countries and branches of economic activity. It may be determined on the basis of minimum size requirements as embodied in relevant national legislations, where they exist, or in terms of empirically determined norms. The choice of the upper size limit should take account of the coverage of statistical inquiries of larger units in the corresponding branches of economic activity, where they exist, in order to avoid an overlap.

(*5*) In the case of enterprises which carry out their activities in more than one establishment, the size criterion should, in principle, refer to each of the establishments separately rather than to the enterprise as a whole. Accordingly, an enterprise should be considered to satisfy the size criterion if none of its establishments exceeds the specified upper size limit.

(*6*) Registration of the enterprise may refer to registration under specific forms of national legislation as specified in subparagraph 8(3). Employees may be considered registered if they are employed on the basis of an employment or apprenticeship contract which commits the employer to pay relevant taxes and social security contributions on behalf of the employee or which makes the employment relationship subject to standard labour legislation.

(*7*) Employers, employees and the employment of employees on a continuous basis are defined in accordance with the most recently adopted version of the International Classification of Status in Employment (ICSE).

10. For particular analytical purposes, more specific definitions of the informal sector may be developed at the national level by introducing further criteria on the basis of the data collected. Such definitions may vary according to the needs of different users of the statistics.

V. Establishments and industries

A. Introduction

5.1. Institutional units were defined in chapter IV. The present chapter, which starts off with a view of institutional units in their capacity as producers, defines an institutional unit engaged in production as an enterprise. An enterprise may be a corporation (a quasi-corporate enterprise being treated as if it were a corporation in the System), a non-profit institution, or an unincorporated enterprise. Corporate enterprises and non-profit institutions are complete institutional units. An unincorporated enterprise, however, refers to an institutional unit—a household or government unit—only in its capacity as a producer of goods and services. It covers only those activities of the unit which are directed towards the production of goods or services. Many households do not contain an unincorporated enterprise.

5.2. A single enterprise, especially a large corporation, may engage simultaneously in many different kinds of productive activities, there being virtually no upper limit to the size of an enterprise. If enterprises are grouped together on the basis of their principal activities, at least some of the resulting groupings are likely to be very heterogeneous with respect to the type of production processes carried out and also the goods and services produced. Thus, for analyses of production in which the technology of production plays an important role, it is necessary to work with groups of producers who are engaged in essentially the same kind of production. This requirement means that some institutional units must be partitioned into smaller and more homogeneous units, which the System defines as establishments. Further, the System defines industries as groups of establishments. In the System, production accounts and generation of income accounts are compiled for industries as well as sectors.

5.3. This chapter first discusses productive activity and its classification in order to lay the ground for defining establishments and subsequently industries. The definitions that emerge as well as the underlying definitions of kinds of activities and of statistical units other than establishments are consistent with the definitions in the third revision of the International Standard Industrial Classification of All Economic Activities (ISIC, Rev.3), published by the United Nations. Any slight differences in wording between this chapter and the "Introduction" to the ISIC are needed to make the definitions clearer in an SNA context.

B. Productive activities

5.4. Production in the System, as will be discussed in detail in chapter VI, consists of processes or activities carried out under the control and responsibility of institutional units that use inputs of labour, capital, and goods and services to produce outputs of goods and services. Any such activity may be described, and classified, with reference to various characteristics, for example:

    Type of goods or services produced as outputs

    Type of inputs used or consumed

    Technique of production employed

    Ways in which the outputs are used.

The same goods or services may be produced using different methods of production so that there can be no one-to-one correspondence between activities and the goods or services they produce. Certain types of goods may be produced from quite different inputs; for example, sugar may be produced from sugar cane or from sugar beet, or electricity from coal, oil or nuclear power stations or from hydroelectric plants. Many production processes also produce joint products, such as meat and hides, whose uses are quite different.

1. The classification of activities in the System

5.5. The classification of productive activities used in the System is ISIC (Rev.3). The criteria used in ISIC to delineate each of its four levels—Class, Group, Division and Section (Tabulation Category)—of the classification are complex. At the Division and Group levels, substantial weight is placed on the nature of the good or service that is produced as the principal product of the activity in question. In this context, this refers to the physical composition and stage of fabrication of the item and the needs served by the item. This criterion furnishes the basis for grouping producer units according to similarities in, and links between, the raw materials consumed and the sources of demand for the items. As well, two other major criteria are considered at these levels: the uses to which the goods and services are put, and the inputs, the process and the technology of production.

5.6. While it is not necessary for purposes of this chapter to explain the concept of an activity in any detail, it is necessary to clarify the fundamental distinction between principal and secondary activities on the one hand and ancillary activities on the other.

2. Principal secondary and ancillary activities

Principal activities

5.7. The principal activity of a producer unit is the activity whose value added exceeds that of any other activity carried out within the same unit. (The producer unit may be an enterprise or an establishment as defined below.) The classification of the principal activity is determined by reference to ISIC, first at the highest level of the classification and then at more detailed levels. The output of the principal activity—its principal product and any by-products (i.e., a product necessarily produced together with principal products)—must consist of goods or services that are capable of being delivered to other units even though they may be used for own consumption or own capital formation.

Secondary activities

5.8. A secondary activity is an activity carried out within a single producer unit in addition to the principal activity and whose output, like that of the principal activity, must be suitable for delivery outside the producer unit. The value added of a secondary activity must be less than that of the principal activity, by definition of the latter. The output of the secondary activity is a secondary product. Most producer units produce at least some secondary products.

Ancillary activities

5.9. The output of an ancillary activity is not intended for use outside the enterprise. An ancillary activity is a supporting activity undertaken within an enterprise in order to create the conditions within which the principal or secondary activities can be carried out. Before trying to give more precision to the concept of an ancillary activity, it is useful to illustrate the kinds of activities that may be ancillary:

(a) Keeping records, files or accounts in written form or on computers;

(b) Communicating in written form or by telephone, telex, telefax, direct computer links, etc., or by messengers, couriers, etc.;

(c) Purchasing of materials and equipment;

(d) Hiring, training, managing and paying employees;

(e) Storing materials or equipment: warehousing;

(f) Transporting goods or persons inside or outside the producer unit;

(g) Promoting sales;

(h) Cleaning and maintenance of buildings and other structures;

(i) Repairing and servicing machinery and equipment;

(j) Providing security and surveillance.

5.10. In addition to the defining characteristic that they provide support for the principal, or secondary, activities, ancillary activities have certain common characteristics related to their output. These additional characteristics include:

(a) Ancillary activities typically produce outputs that are commonly found as inputs into almost any kind of productive activity;

(b) Ancillary activities produce services (and, as exceptions, goods provided that they do not become a physical part of the output of the principal or secondary activity) as output;

(c) The value of an individual ancillary activity's output is likely to be small compared with that of the principal or secondary activities of an enterprise.

5.11. The defining characteristic is by no means sufficient to identify an ancillary activity: there are many kinds of activities whose outputs are entirely consumed within the same enterprise but which could not possibly be considered as ancillary. The characteristic that ancillary activities tend to be found in any productive activity is related to the characteristic that ancillary activities produce services as output. Individual goods are not commonly used as inputs in the same way as services such as accounting, transportation or cleaning. For example, an enterprise may produce milk, all of which is processed into butter or cheese within the same enterprise. However, milk production cannot be considered an ancillary activity, because milk is an unusual kind of input found only in special types of productive activity. In general, goods that become embodied in the output of the principal or secondary activities cannot be outputs of ancillary activities.

5.12. Certain activities, although common, are not so common as to be considered ancillary. Many enterprises produce their own machinery and equipment, build their own structures and carry out their own research and development. These activities are not to be treated as ancillary, whether carried out centrally or not, as they are not found frequently and extensively in all kinds of enterprises, small as well as large.

5.13. By definition, an ancillary activity is not undertaken for its own sake but purely in order to provide supporting services for the principal or secondary activities with which it is associated. Therefore, both the System and ISIC treat ancillary activities as integral parts of the principal or secondary activities with which they are associated. As a result:

(a)   The output of an ancillary activity is not explicitly recognized and recorded separately in the System. It follows that the use of this output is also not recorded;

(b)   All the inputs consumed by an ancillary activity—materials, labour, consumption of fixed capital, etc.—are treated as inputs into the principal or secondary activity which it supports;

(c)   It is not possible to identify the value added of an ancillary activity because that value added is combined with the value added of the principal or secondary activity.

Thus, the production accounts of the System provide no direct information about the incidence or range of ancillary activities carried out within producer units. Their existence can only be inferred by studying the structure of the inputs consumed by producers.

Changes in ancillary activities

5.14.   In some cases an enterprise may have a choice between engaging in ancillary activities which provide supporting services for its principal or secondary activities or purchasing such services on the market from specialist service producers. In addition to the obvious difficulty of separating many ancillary activities from the associated principal and secondary activities, the choice may be restricted by the fact that, in practice,

the requisite services are often not readily available in the right quantities on local markets.

5.15.   An ancillary activity may grow to the point that it has the capacity to provide services outside the enterprise. For example, a computer processing unit may develop in-house capabilities for which there is an outside demand. When an activity starts to provide services to outsiders, that part which produces output for sale has to be treated as secondary rather than ancillary.

The role of ancillary activities in the economic system

5.16.   As the existence of ancillary activities is not explicitly recognized in the System or in production statistics generally, it is difficult to obtain information about their role in the economy. For example, it is difficult to know how much output they produce, how many persons are engaged in such activities, how many resources they consume, etc. This may be regarded as a serious disadvantage for certain purposes, such as analysing the impact of "information technology" on productivity when the processing and communication of information are typical ancillary activities. However, it would be difficult and costly to obtain detailed information about the entire range of ancillary activities undertaken within producer units. Moreover, the values of their outputs would all have to be imputed. However, for some types of analysis it may be useful and necessary to estimate and record these activities separately (see chapter XXI).

C. Partitioning enterprises into more homogeneous units

5.17.   As already stated, "enterprise" is the term used in the System to describe an institutional unit in its capacity as a producer of goods and services. An enterprise may, therefore, be any of the folowing kinds of producer units:

A corporation or quasi-corporation

An unincorporated enterprise

An NPI.

5.18.   Although it is possible to classify enterprises according to their principal activities using the ISIC and to group them into "industries", some of the resulting "industries" are likely to be very heterogeneous because some enterprises may have several secondary activities which are quite different from their principal activities. In order to obtain groups of producers whose activities are more homogeneous, enterprises have to be partitioned into smaller and more homogeneous units.

1. Kind-of-activity units

5.19.   One way to partition an enterprise is by reference to activities. A unit resulting from such a partitioning is called a kind-of-activity unit, defined as an enterprise, or a part of an enterprise,

which engages in only one kind of (non-ancillary) productive activity or in which the principal productive activity accounts for most of the value added. Each enterprise must, by definition, consist of one or more kind-of-activity units. When partitioned into two or more kind-of-activity units, the resulting units must be more homogeneous with respect to output, cost structure and technology of production than the enterprise as a whole.

2. Local units

5.20.   Enterprises often engage in productive activity at more than one location, and for some purposes it may be useful to partition them accordingly. Thus, a local unit is defined as an enterprise, or a part of an enterprise, which engages in productive activity at or from one location. The definition has only one dimension in that it does not refer to the kind of activity that is carried out. Location may be interpreted according to the purpose—narrowly, such as a specific address, or more broadly, such as within a province, state, county, etc.

3. Establishments

5.21. The establishment combines both the kind-of-activity dimension and the locality dimension. An establishment is defined as an enterprise, or part of an enterprise, that is situated in a single location and in which only a single (non-ancillary) productive activity is carried out or in which the principal productive activity accounts for most of the value added.

5.22. Although the definition of an establishment allows for the possibility that there may be one or more secondary activities carried out, they should be on a small scale compared with the principal activity. If a secondary activity within an enterprise is as important, or nearly as important, as the principal activity, then that activity should be treated as taking place within a separate establishment from that in which the principal activity takes place. The definition of an establishment does not permit an ancillary activity to constitute an establishment on its own.

5.23. Thus, establishments are designed to be units which provide data that are more suitable for analyses of production in which the technology of production plays an important role. However, it may still be necessary to transform the resulting data subsequently for purposes of input-output analysis, as explained briefly below in describing the unit of homogeneous production and in more detail in chapter XV.

5.24. In practice, an establishment may usually be identified with an individual workplace in which a particular kind of productive activity is carried out: an individual farm, mine, quarry, factory, plant, shop, store, construction site, transport depot, airport, garage, bank, office, clinic, etc. It is important to remember, however, that ancillary activities are not separately distinguished and recorded in the System so that repair shops, sales departments, accounts departments, computing departments, etc., whose activities are ancillary in nature are not treated as separate establishments.

The data for establishments

5.25. Establishments are conceptually quite distinct from institutional units. If an institutional unit contains only a single establishment, the two units coincide in the sense that the production account for the establishment is the same as that for the institutional unit. However, an establishment as such is not an institutional unit of the System, engaging in transactions on its own account, incurring liabilities, entering into contracts, and so on. For example, the purchases and sales associated with the productive activities of an establishment are actually made by the institutional unit to which it belongs and not by the establishment itself. It is not possible, therefore, to envisage a complete set of accounts, including balance sheets, being compiled for an establishment, not because of practical data difficulties but because an establishment is not an entity capable of owning goods or assets in its own right or capable of receiving or disbursing income, etc.

5.26. The only data which can meaningfully be compiled for an es-

tablishment relate to its production activities. They include the following:

(a) The items included in the production account and the generation of income account;

(b) Statistics of numbers of employees, types of employees and hours worked;

(c) Estimates of the stock of capital and land used;

(d) Estimates of changes in inventories and gross fixed capital formation undertaken.

5.27. The compilation of a production account and a generation of income account implies that it must be feasible to calculate output and intermediate consumption and thus value added and also compensation of employees, taxes on production and imports, subsidies and the operating surplus/mixed income. In principle, it must be feasible to collect at least the above kinds of statistics for an establishment, even if they may not always be available, or needed, in practice.

Application of the principles in specific situations

5.28. The application of the principles given above for partitioning an enterprise into establishments is not always straightforward. This section discusses several situations in which the organization of production is such that the application is particularly difficult.

Central ancillary activities

5.29. When the production of an enterprise takes place in two or more different establishments, certain ancillary activities may be carried out centrally for the benefit of all the establishments collectively. For example, the purchasing, sales, accounts, computing, maintenance or other departments of an enterprise may all be the responsibility of a head office which is located separately from the establishments in which the principal or secondary activities of the enterprise are carried out. In such a case the entire costs of the central ancillary activities must be distributed over the establishments which they serve, for example in proportion to the latters' outputs or costs, and added to the latters' own costs.

Establishments within integrated enterprises

5.30. A horizontally integrated enterprise is one in which several different kinds of activities which produce different kinds of goods or services for sale on the market are carried out in parallel with each other. It follows from the definition of an establishment that a separate establishment should normally be identified for each different kind of activity.

5.31. A vertically integrated enterprise is one in which different stages of production, which are usually carried out by different enterprises, are carried out in succession by different parts of the same enterprise. The output of one stage becomes an input into the next stage, only the output from the final stage being actually sold on the market. There are numerous examples of vertically integrated enterprises.

5.32. For example, an enterprise may use its own fishing fleet to catch the fish it then processes into frozen or canned food products, i.e., manufactured products. Similarly, an enterprise may have its own plantations on which it grows the tea it then processes and blends into packages of tea for sale to final consumers. A manufacturer of bricks may process clay mined from its own quarries. A striking feature of the examples just given is that the vertical integration extends beyond different stages of manufacturing by integrating fishing, agriculture, or mining with manufacturing. However, vertical integration is also very common within manufacturing, while some types of vertical integration do not involve manufacturing.

5.33. From an accounting point of view it can be difficult to partition a vertically integrated enterprise into establishments because values have to be imputed for the outputs from the earlier stages of production which are not actually sold on the market and which become intermediate inputs into later stages. Some of these enterprises may record the intra-enterprise deliveries at prices that reflect market values, but others may not. Even if adequate data are available on the costs incurred at each stage of production, it may be difficult to decide what is the appropriate way in which to allocate the operating surplus of the enterprise among the various stages. One possibility is that a uniform rate of profit could be applied to the costs incurred at each stage.

5.34. Despite the practical difficulties involved in partitioning vertically integrated enterprises into establishments, it is recommended that when a vertically integrated enterprise spans two or more headings at the first level of breakdown of the ISIC, at least one establishment must be distinguished within each heading. The first breakdown of activities in the ISIC corresponds to broad industry groups such as agriculture, fishing, mining and quarrying, manufacturing, etc.

Establishments owned by general government

5.35. Government units, especially central governments, may be particularly large and complex in terms of the kinds of activities in which they engage. The principles outlined above have to be applied consistently and systematically to government units. The procedures to be followed when dealing with the main kinds of producer units owned by government may be summarized as follows.

5.36. An unincorporated enterprise owned by government may be a market producer that sells or otherwise disposes of all or most of its output on the market at prices that are economically significant. For example, a municipal swimming pool or a government publishing office may be a market producer. Such an enterprise may be treated as a quasi-corporation if it is independently managed and if its accounts permit its income, saving and capital to be measured separately from government so that flows of income, or capital, between the unit and gov-

ernment can be identified. If it is treated as a quasi-corporation, it ceases to be part of the government sector and is treated with respect to partitioning into establishments in the same way as a publicly owned corporation. Market producers owned by government which are not quasi-corporations should be partitioned into two or more separate establishments if they are engaged in two or more different kinds of activities or if they are situated in two or more different locations.

5.37. An unincorporated enterprise owned by government may be a non-market producer that supplies output free or at prices that are not economically significant. A distinction needs to be drawn between non-market producers owned by government which deliver final goods or services to the community or to individual households and those which produce goods or services for use by other government units.

5.38. Non-market producers providing final goods or services— such as public administration, defence, health and education—should be partitioned into establishments using the activity classification given in Divisions 75, 80, 85 and 90 of the ISIC. Agencies of central government may be dispersed over the country as a whole in which case it will be necessary to distinguish different establishments for activities which are carried out in different locations.

5.39. Non-market producers which supply goods or services to other government agencies or departments should be treated as follows:

(*a*) When a government agency supplies goods to other government agencies it must be treated as a separate establishment and classified under the appropriate heading of ISIC. This applies to the production of munitions or weapons, printed documents or stationery, roads or other structures, etc. The units must always be identified as separate establishments for two reasons. First, a government which produces its own weapons to supply to its own armed forces is, in effect, a vertically integrated enterprise which spans two or more headings at the first level of ISIC. Therefore, at least one separate establishment must be distinguished in each heading. The same argument applies to a government printing office and other goods producers owned by government. Secondly, except as noted earlier with respect to goods that do not become a physical part of a principal or secondary product, production of goods is not considered ancillary activity. An activity which supplies goods to an establishment producing services should be treated as a separate establishment;

(*b*) The situation of government agencies supplying supporting services—for example, transport pools and computing departments—to other government agencies is less clear. Normally it will be appropriate to treat them as ancillary activities whose costs are to be distributed over the various establishments which they serve in proportion to the latters' own costs. However, exceptions to this general principle may be envisaged in the case of very large specialized agencies serving central government as a whole—for example, a very large computer or communications agency—which may be so large that it is appropriate to treat it as a separate establishment.

D. Industries

5.40. Industries are defined in the System in the same way as in ISIC: an industry consists of a group of establishments engaged in the same, or similar, kinds of activity. At the most detailed level of classification, an industry consists of all the establishments falling within a single Class of ISIC and which are therefore all engaged on the same activity as defined in the ISIC. At higher levels of aggregation corresponding to the Groups, Divisions and, ultimately, Sections of the ISIC, industries consist of groups of establishments engaged in similar types of activities.

1. Market, own account and other non-market producers

5.41. The term "industry" is not reserved for market producers. An industry, as defined in the ISIC and the present version of the System, consists of a group of establishments engaged in the same type of productive activity, whether the institutional units to which they belong are market producers or not. The distinction between market and other production is a different dimension of productive—and, more broadly, economic—activity. For example, the health industry in a particular country may consist of a group of establishments, some of which are market producers while others are non-market producers that provide their services free or at prices that are not economically significant. Because the distinction between market and other kinds of production is based on a different criterion from the nature of activity itself, it is possible to cross-classify establishments by type of activity and by whether they produce market, own-account or other non-market output. Thus, there is no difficulty about separating market from other production within the same industry, if desired.

2. Industries and products

5.42. As already mentioned, a one-to-one correspondence does not exist between activities and products and hence between industries and products. Certain activities produce more than one product simultaneously, while the same product may sometimes be produced by using different techniques of production.

5.43. When two or more products are produced simultaneously by a single productive activity they are "joint products". Examples of joint products are meat and hides produced by slaughtering animals or sugar and molasses produced by refining sugar canes. The by-product from one activity may also be produced by other activities, but there are examples of by-products, such as molasses, which are produced exclusively as the by-products of one particular activity.

5.44. The relationship between an activity and a product classification is exemplified by that between the ISIC and Central Product Classification (CPC) of the United Nations. The CPC is the classification of products in the System. It is a classification based on the physical characteristics of goods or on the nature of the services rendered. However, each type of good or service distinguished in the CPC is defined in such a way that it is normally produced by only one activity as defined in ISIC. Conversely, each activity of the ISIC is defined in such a way that it normally produces only one type of product as defined in the CPC (where each type of product may have a number of individual products coded under it). So far as is practically possible, an attempt is made to establish a one-to-one correspondence between the two classifications, each category of the CPC being accompanied by a reference to the ISIC class in which the good or service is mainly produced. However, such a one-to-one correspondence is not always possible. In practice, therefore, the output of an industry, no matter how narrowly defined, will tend to include more than a single product.

E. Units of homogeneous production

5.45. In most fields of statistics the choice of statistical unit, and methodology used, are strongly influenced by the purposes for which the resulting statistics are to be used. A unit which is defined in such a way that it would be optimal for a particular type of analysis is described as an "analytical unit".

5.46. For purposes of input-output analysis, the optimal situation would be one in which each producer unit were engaged in only a single productive activity so that an industry could be formed by grouping together all the units engaged in a particular type of productive activity without the intrusion of any secondary activities. The appropriate analytical unit for purposes of input-output analysis is, therefore, a "unit of homogeneous production", which may be defined as a producer unit in which only a single (non-ancillary) productive activity is carried out. If a producer unit carries out a principal activity and also one or more secondary activities, it will be partitioned into the same number of units of homogeneous production. If it is desired to compile production accounts and input-output tables by region, it is necessary to treat units of homogeneous production located in different places as separate units even though they may be engaged in the same activity and belong to the same institutional unit.

5.47. Although the unit of homogeneous production may be the optimal unit for purposes of certain kinds of analysis, particularly input-output analysis, it may not always be feasible to partition establishments or even establishments with one or more secondary productive activities into a series of mutually exclusive units of homogeneous production. In situations of this kind, it will not be possible to collect directly from the enterprise or establishment the accounting data corresponding to units of homogeneous production. Such data may have to be estimated subsequently by transforming the data supplied by enterprises on the basis of various assumptions or hypotheses. These are discussed in chapter XV.

VI. The production account

A. Introduction

6.1. The production account is the first in the sequence of accounts compiled for institutional units, sectors and the total economy. The incomes generated by production are carried forward into subsequent accounts so that the way in which the production account is compiled can exert a considerable influence on the System. In any case, information about production is extremely important in its own right. It is therefore necessary to spell out in some detail exactly how production is measured in the System.

6.2. Production accounts are compiled for establishments and industries as well as for institutional units and sectors. Basic concepts such as output or intermediate consumption have, therefore, to be defined and measured in the same way whether they appear in the production account for industries or sectors. Overall numerical consistency requires that the output of an institutional unit engaged in production—that is, an enterprise—should be equal to the sum of the outputs of the individual establishments of which it is composed. As these outputs include deliveries of goods or services to other establishments belonging to the same enterprise, such inter-establishment deliveries are counted as part of the output of the enterprise as a whole even though they do not leave the enterprise.

6.3. The production account for institutional units and sectors is illustrated in table 6.1. It contains only three items apart from the balancing item. The output from production is recorded under resources on the right-hand side of the account. This item may, of course, be disaggregated to distinguish different kinds of output. For example, non-market output should be shown separately from market output in the sector accounts, when possible. The inputs recorded under uses on the left-hand side of the account consist of intermediate consumption and consumption of fixed capital. Both of these may also be disaggregated.

6.4. Most of this chapter is concerned with defining and describing the three basic elements—output, intermediate consumption and consumption of fixed capital—that enter into the production account. The balancing item in the production account is value added. It can be measured either gross or net: that is, before or after deducting consumption of fixed capital:

(a) Gross value added is defined as the value of output less the value of intermediate consumption;

(b) Net value added is defined as the value of output less the values of both intermediate consumption and consumption of fixed capital.

6.5. As value added is intended to measure the additional value created by a process of production, it ought to be measured net, since the consumption of fixed capital is a cost of production. However, as explained later, consumption of fixed capital can be difficult to measure in practice and it may not always be possible to make a satisfactory estimate of its value and hence of net value added. Provision has therefore to be made for value added to be measured gross as well as net. It follows that provision has also to be made for the balancing items in subsequent accounts of the System that depend upon value added—operating surplus, mixed income, balance of primary incomes, etc.—to be measured gross or net of the consumption of fixed capital.

B. Production

1. Production as an economic activity

6.6. Production can be described in general terms as an activity in which an enterprise uses inputs to produce outputs. However, it is necessary to specify what is meant by "input" and "output" to make such a description more operational. The economic analysis of production is mainly concerned with activities that produce outputs of a kind that can be delivered or provided to other institutional units. Unless outputs are produced that can be supplied to other units, either individually or collectively, there can be no division of labour, no specialization of production and no gains from trading. There are two main kinds of output, namely goods and services, and it is necessary to examine their characteristics in order to be able to de-

Table 6.1. Account I: Production account

Uses: Total	Uses: Corresponding entries of the Goods and service account	Uses: Corresponding entries of the Rest of the world account	Uses: S.1 Total economy	Uses: S.15 NPISHs	Uses: S.14 Households	Uses: S.13 General government	Uses: S.12 Financial corporations	Uses: S.11 Non-financial corporations	Transactions and balancing items		Resources: S.11 Non-financial corporations	Resources: S.12 Financial corporations	Resources: S.13 General government	Resources: S.14 Households	Resources: S.15 NPISHs	Resources: S.1 Total economy	Resources: Corresponding entries of the Rest of the world account	Resources: Corresponding entries of the Goods and service account	Resources: Total
3 604	3 604								P.1	Output [1]	1 753	102	440	1 269	40	3 604			3 604
3 057	3 057								P.11	Market output	1 722	102	80	1 129	24	3 057			3 057
171	171								P.12	Output for own final use	31	0	0	140	0	171			171
376	376								P.13	Other non-market output			360		16	376			376
1 883			1 883	9	694	252	29	899	P.2	Intermediate consumption								1 883	1 883
133	133								D.21-D.31	Taxes less subsidies on products [1]						133			133
1 854			1 854	31	575	188	73	854	B.1g/B.1*g	Value added, gross/ gross domestic product [2]									
222			222	3	42	30	10	137	K.1	Consumption of fixed capital									
1 632			1 632	28	533	158	63	717	B.1n/B.1*n	*Value added, net/ net domestic product* [2]									

1 For the valuation of output and the resulting contents of the items "Taxes on products" and "Subsidies on products", refer to chapter VI, paragraphs 6.210 to 6.227.
2 For the total economy this item corresponds to gross domestic product, net domestic product respectively. It is equal to the value added of the institutional sectors plus taxes less subsidies on products.

lineate activities that are productive in an economic sense from other activities.

Goods and services

Goods

6.7. Goods are physical objects for which a demand exists, over which ownership rights can be established and whose ownership can be transferred from one institutional unit to another by engaging in transactions on markets. They are in demand because they may be used to satisfy the needs or wants of households or the community or used to produce other goods or services. The production and exchange of goods are quite separate activities. Some goods may never be exchanged while others may be bought and sold numerous times. The separation of the production of a good from its subsequent sale or resale is an economically significant characteristic of a good that is not shared by a service.

Services

6.8. Services are not separate entities over which ownership rights can be established. They cannot be traded separately from their production. Services are heterogeneous outputs produced to order and typically consist of changes in the conditions of the consuming units realized by the activities of producers at the demand of the consumers. By the time their production is completed they must have been provided to the consumers.

6.9. The production of services must be confined to activities that are capable of being carried out by one unit for the benefit of another. Otherwise, service industries could not develop and there could be no markets for services. It is also possible for a unit to produce a service for its own consumption provided that the type of activity is such that it could have been carried out by another unit.

6.10. The changes that consumers of services engage the producers to bring about can take a variety of different forms—in particular:

(a) Changes in the condition of the consumer's goods: the producer works directly on goods owned by the consumer by transporting, cleaning, repairing or otherwise transforming them;

(b) Changes in the physical condition of persons: the producer transports the persons, provides them with accommodation, provides them with medical or surgical treatments, improves their appearance, etc.;

(c) Changes in the mental condition of persons: the producer provides education, information, advice, entertainment or similar services;

(d) Changes in the general economic state of the institu-

tional unit itself: the producer provides insurance, financial intermediation, protection, guarantees, etc.

6.11. The changes may be temporary or permanent. For example, medical or education services may result in permanent changes in the condition of the consumers from which benefits may be derived over many years. In general, the changes may be presumed to be improvements, as services are produced at the demand of the consumers. The improvements usually become embodied in the persons of the consumers or the goods they own and are not separate entities that belong to the producer. Such improvements cannot be held in inventory by the producer or traded separately from their production.

6.12. A single process of production may provide services to a group of persons, or units, simultaneously. For example, groups of persons or goods belonging to different institutional units may be transported together in the same plane, ship, train or other vehicle. People may be instructed or entertained in groups by attending the same class, lecture or performance. Certain services are provided collectively to the community as a whole, or large sections of the community: for example, the maintenance of law and order, and defence.

6.13. There is a group of industries generally classified as service industries that produce outputs that have many of the characteristics of goods, i.e., those industries concerned with the provision, storage, communication and dissemination of information, advice and entertainment in the broadest sense of those terms—the production of general or specialized information, news, consultancy reports, computer programs, movies, music, etc. The outputs of these industries, over which ownership rights may be established, are often stored on physical objects—paper, tapes, disks, etc.—that can be traded like ordinary goods. Whether characterized as goods or services, these products possess the essential common characteristic that they can be produced by one unit and supplied to another, thus making possible division of labour and the emergence of markets.

2. The production boundary

6.14. Given the general characteristics of the goods and services produced as outputs, it becomes possible to define production. A general definition of production is given first, followed by the rather more restricted definition that is used in the System.

The general production boundary

6.15. Economic production may be defined as an activity carried out under the control and responsibility of an institutional unit that uses inputs of labour, capital, and goods and services to produce outputs of goods or services. There must be an institutional unit that assumes responsibility for the process and owns any goods produced as outputs or is entitled to be paid, or otherwise compensated, for the services provided. A purely natural process without any human involvement or direction

System of National Accounts 1993   124

is not production in an economic sense. For example, the un-
managed growth of fish stocks in international waters is not
production, whereas the activity of fish farming is production.

6.16. While production processes that produce goods can be identified without difficulty, it is not always so easy to distinguish
the production of services from other activities that may be
both important and beneficial. Activities that are not productive in an economic sense include basic human activities such
as eating, drinking, sleeping, taking exercise, etc., that it is impossible for one person to obtain another person to perform instead. Paying someone else to take exercise is no way to keep
fit. On the other hand, activities such as washing, preparing
meals, caring for children, the sick or aged are all activities that
can be provided by other units and, therefore, fall within the
general production boundary. Many households employ paid
domestic staff to carry out these activities for them.

The production boundary in the System

6.17. The production boundary in the System is more restricted than
the general production boundary. For reasons explained
below, production accounts are not compiled for household
activities that produce domestic or personal services for own
final consumption within the same household, except for services produced by employing paid domestic staff. Otherwise,
the production boundary in the System is the same as the more
general one given in the previous section.

6.18. Activities that fall within the production boundary of the System may, therefore, be summarized as follows:

(a) The production of all individual or collective goods or
services that are supplied to units other than their producers, or intended to be so supplied, including the production of goods or services used up in the process of
producing such goods or services;

(b) The own-account production of all goods that are retained by their producers for their own final consumption or gross capital formation;

(c) The own-account production of housing services by
owner-occupiers and of domestic and personal services
produced by employing paid domestic staff.

*Domestic and personal services produced for own final
consumption within households*

6.19. The own-account production of domestic and personal services by members of the household for their own final consumption has traditionally been excluded from measured
production in national accounts and it is worth explaining
briefly why this is so.

6.20. First, it is useful to list those domestic and personal services
for which no entries are recorded in the accounts when they
are produced and consumed within the same household:

(a) The cleaning, decoration and maintenance of the dwell-

ing occupied by the household, including small repairs of a kind usually carried out by tenants as well
as owners;

(b) The cleaning, servicing and repair of household durables or other goods, including vehicles used for household purposes;

(c) The preparation and serving of meals;

(d) The care, training and instruction of children;

(e) The care of sick, infirm or old people;

(f) The transportation of members of the household or their
goods.

6.21. In most countries a considerable amount of labour is devoted
to the production of these domestic and personal services,
while their consumption makes an important contribution to
economic welfare. However, national accounts serve a variety
of analytical and policy purposes and are not compiled simply
to produce indicators of welfare. The reasons for not imputing
values for unpaid domestic or personal services produced and
consumed within households may be summarized as follows:

(a) The own-account production of services within households is a self-contained activity with limited repercussions on the rest of the economy. The decision to
produce a household service entails a simultaneous decision to consume that service. This is not true for goods.
For example, if a household engages in the production
of agricultural goods, it does not follow that it intends to
consume them all. Once the crop has been harvested, the
producer has a choice about how much to consume, how
much to store for future consumption or production, and
how much to offer for sale or barter on the market. Indeed, although it is customary to refer to the own-account production of goods, it is not possible to
determine at the time the production takes place how
much of it will eventually be consumed. For example, if
an agricultural crop turns out to be better than expected,
the household may dispose of some of it on the market
even though it may have been originally intended all for
own consumption. This kind of possibility is non-existent for services;

(b) As the vast majority of household domestic and personal services are not produced for the market, there are
typically no suitable market prices that can be used to
value such services. It is therefore extremely difficult to
estimate values not only for the outputs of the services
but also for the associated incomes and expenditures
which can be meaningfully added to the values of the
monetary transactions on which most of the entries in
the accounts are based;

(c) Imputed values have a different economic significance
from monetary values. The imputed incomes generated

by the imputed production would be difficult to tax in practice. They would have to be shown as being all spent on the same services. However, if the incomes were to be available in cash, the resulting expenditures might be quite different. For example, if a household member were offered the choice between producing services for own consumption and producing the same services for another household in return for remuneration in cash, the paid employment would likely be preferred because of the greater range of consumption possibilities it affords. Thus, imputing values for the own-account production of services would not only be very difficult, but would yield values which would not be equivalent to monetary values for analytic or policy purposes.

6.22. Thus, the reluctance of national accountants to impute values for the outputs, incomes and expenditures associated with the production and consumption of domestic and personal services within households is explained by a combination of factors, namely the relative isolation and independence of these activities from markets, the extreme difficulty of making economically meaningful estimates of their values, and the adverse effects it would have on the usefulness of the accounts for policy purposes and the analysis of markets and market disequilibria—the analysis of inflation, unemployment, etc. It could also have unacceptable consequences for labour force and employment statistics. According to International Labour Organisation (ILO) guidelines, economically active persons are persons engaged in production included within the boundary of production of the System. If that boundary were to be extended to include the production of own-account household services, virtually the whole adult population would be economically active and unemployment eliminated. In practice, it would be necessary to revert to the existing boundary of production in the System, if only to obtain meaningful employment statistics.

The production boundary within households

6.23. Although personal and domestic services produced for own consumption within households fall outside the boundary of production used in the System, it is nevertheless useful to give further guidance with respect to the treatment of certain kinds of household activities which may be particularly important in some developing countries.

Own-account production of goods

6.24. The System includes the production of all goods within the production boundary. At the time the production takes place it may not even be known whether, or in what proportions, the goods produced are destined for the market or for own use. The following types of production by households are, therefore, included whether intended for own final consumption or not:

(a) The production of agricultural products and their subse-

quent storage; the gathering of berries or other uncultivated crops; forestry; wood-cutting and the collection of firewood; hunting and fishing;

(b) The production of other primary products such as mining salt, cutting peat, the supply of water, etc.;

(c) The processing of agricultural products; the production of grain by threshing; the production of flour by milling; the curing of skins and the production of leather; the production and preservation of meat and fish products; the preservation of fruit by drying, bottling, etc.; the production of dairy products such as butter or cheese; the production of beer, wine, or spirits; the production of baskets or mats; etc.;

(d) Other kinds of processing such as weaving cloth; dress making and tailoring; the production of footwear; the production of pottery, utensils or durables; making furniture or furnishings; etc.

The storage of agricultural goods produced by households is included within the production boundary as an extension of the goods-producing process. The supply of water is also considered a goods-producing activity in this context. In principle, supplying water is a similar kind of activity to extracting and piping crude oil.

6.25. It is not feasible to draw up a complete, exhaustive list of all possible productive activities but the above list covers the most common types. When the amount of a good produced within households is believed to be quantitatively important in relation to the total supply of that good in a country, its production should be recorded. Otherwise, it is not worthwhile trying to estimate it in practice.

"Do-it-yourself" decoration, maintenance and small repairs

6.26. "Do-it-yourself" repairs and maintenance to consumer durables and dwellings carried out by members of the household constitute the own-account production of services and are, therefore, excluded from the production boundary of the System. The materials purchased are treated as final consumption expenditure.

6.27. In the case of dwellings, "do-it-yourself" activities cover decoration, maintenance and small repairs, including repairs to fittings, of types which are commonly carried out by tenants as well as by owners. On the other hand, more substantial repairs, such as replastering walls or repairing roofs, carried out by owners, are essentially intermediate inputs into the production of housing services. However, the production of such repairs by an owner-occupier is only a secondary activity of the owner in his capacity as a producer of housing services. The production accounts for the two activities may be consolidated so that, in practice, the purchases of materials for repairs become intermediate expenditures incurred in the production of housing services. Major renovations or extensions to dwellings are fixed capital formation and recorded separately.

The use of consumption goods

6.28. In general, the use of goods within the household for the direct satisfaction of human needs or wants cannot be treated as production. This applies not only to materials or equipment purchased for use in leisure or recreational activities but also to foodstuffs purchased for the preparation of meals. The preparation of a meal for immediate consumption is a service type activity and is treated as such in the System and in International Standard Industrial Classification (ISIC). It therefore falls outside the production boundary when the meal is prepared for own consumption within the household. The use of a durable good, such as a vehicle, by persons or households for their own personal benefit or satisfaction is intrinsically a consumption activity and should not be treated as if it were an extension, or continuation, of production.

Services of owner-occupied dwellings

6.29. The production of housing services for their own final consumption by owner-occupiers has always been included within the production boundary in national accounts, although it constitutes an exception to the general exclusion of own-account service production. The ratio of owner-occupied to rented dwellings can vary significantly between countries and even over short periods of time within a single country, so that both international and intertemporal comparisons of the production and consumption of housing services could be distorted if no imputation were made for the value of own-account housing services. The imputed value of the income generated by such production is taxed in some countries.

Illegal production

6.30. Despite the obvious practical difficulties in obtaining data on illegal production, it is included within the production boundary of the System. There are two kinds of illegal production:

(a)   The production of goods or services whose sale, distribution or possession is forbidden by law;

(b)   Production activities which are usually legal but which become illegal when carried out by unauthorized producers; e.g., unlicensed medical practitioners.

6.31. Both kinds of production are included within the production boundary of the System provided they are genuine production processes whose outputs consist of goods or services for which there is an effective market demand. The units who purchase such outputs may not be involved in any kind of illegal activities other than the illegal transactions themselves. Transactions in which illegal goods or services are bought and sold need to be recorded not simply to obtain comprehensive measures of production and consumption but also to prevent errors appearing elsewhere in the accounts if the funds exchanged in illegal transactions are presumed to be used for other pur-

poses. The incomes generated by illegal production may be disposed of quite legally, while conversely, expenditures on illegal goods and services may be made out of funds obtained quite legally. The failure to record illegal transactions may lead to significant errors in the financial account and also the external account of some countries.

6.32. Examples of activities which may be illegal but productive in an economic sense include the manufacture and distribution of narcotics, illegal transportation in the form of smuggling (often a form of own-account illegal production) and services such as prostitution.

6.33. Illegal production does not refer to the generation of externalities such as the discharge of pollutants. Externalities may result from production processes which are themselves quite legal. Externalities are created without the consent of the units affected, and no values are imputed for them in the System. Illegal production also does not refer to stolen output. The theft of legally produced output by employees or others needs to be clearly distinguished from illegally produced output which is sold to willing buyers on the market.

Concealed production and the underground economy

6.34. Certain activities may be both productive in an economic sense and also quite legal (provided certain standards or regulations are complied with) but deliberately concealed from public authorities for the following kinds of reasons:

(a)   To avoid the payment of income, value added or other taxes;

(b)   To avoid the payment of social security contributions;

(c)   To avoid having to meet certain legal standards such as minimum wages, maximum hours, safety or health standards, etc.;

(d)   To avoid complying with certain administrative procedures, such as completing statistical questionnaires or other administrative forms.

All such activities clearly fall within the production boundary of the System provided that they are genuine processes of production. Producers engaged in this type of production may be described as belonging to the "underground economy". The underground economy may account for a substantial proportion of the total output of certain industries—for example, construction or certain service industries where small enterprises predominate.

6.35. There may be no clear borderline between the underground economy and illegal production. For example, production which does not comply with certain safety, health or other standards could be described as illegal. Similarly, the evasion of taxes is itself usually a criminal offence. However, it is not necessary for the purposes of the System to try to fix the precise borderline between underground and illegal production as both are included within the production boundary in any case. It follows that transactions on unofficial markets which exist in parallel with official markets (e.g., for foreign exchange or goods subject to official price controls) must also be included in the accounts, whether or not such markets are actually legal or illegal.

6.36. Because certain kinds of producers try to conceal their activities from public authorities, it does not follow that they are not included in national accounts in practice. Many countries have had considerable success in compiling estimates of production which cover the underground economy as well as the ordinary economy. In some industries, such as agriculture or construction, it may be possible by using various kinds of surveys and the commodity flow method to make satisfactory estimates of the total output of industry without being able to identify or measure that part of it which is underground (or indeed illegal). Because the underground economy may account for a significant part of the total economy of some countries, it is particularly important to try to make estimates of total production which include it, even if it cannot always be separately identified as such.

C. The measurement of production

1. Introduction

6.37. In the System, the intermediate inputs are recorded and valued at the time they enter the production process, while outputs are recorded and valued as they emerge from the process. Intermediate inputs are normally valued at purchasers' prices and outputs at basic prices, or alternatively at producers' prices if basic prices are not available. The increase between the value of the intermediate inputs and the value of the outputs is the gross value added against which must be charged the consumption of fixed capital, taxes on production (less subsidies) and compensation of employees. The positive or negative balance remaining is the net operating surplus or mixed income. The definition, measurement and valuation of outputs and inputs is, therefore, fundamental to the System and is described in detail in the following sections.

2. Output (P.1)

6.38. Certain goods and services produced by processes of production, including services produced by ancillary activities, are used up within the same accounting period by other processes carried out within the same establishment. Such goods and services do not leave the establishment and are therefore not counted as part of the establishment's output. Thus, output is a concept that applies to a producer unit—an establishment or enterprise—rather than a process of production. Output has to be defined in the context of a production account, and production accounts are compiled for establishments or enterprises, and not for processes of production. Output therefore consists only of those goods or services that are produced within an establishment that become available for use outside that establishment. When an enterprise contains more than one establishment, the output of the enterprise is the sum of the outputs of its component establishments.

6.39. For simplicity, the output of most goods or services is usually recorded when their production is completed. However, when it takes a long time to produce a unit of output, it becomes necessary to recognize that output is being produced continuously and to record it as "work-in-progress". For example, the production of certain agricultural goods or large durable goods such as ships or buildings may take months or years to complete. In such cases, it would distort economic reality to treat the output as if it were all produced at the moment of time when the process of production happens to terminate. In any case, whenever a process of production, however long or short, extends over two or more accounting periods, it is necessary to calculate the work-in-progress completed within each of the periods in order to be able to measure how much output is produced in each period.

6.40. Output in the form of finished goods or services is ready to be supplied or provided to other institutional units. However, work-in-progress consists of output which, by definition, is not complete and, therefore, is not yet in a state in which it is normally marketed. In due course, however, the work-in-progress is transformed into a finished product that is marketable.

6.41. Goods or services produced as outputs may be used in several different ways and by listing these uses it is possible to obtain a clearer indication of the coverage of output. Apart from certain service producers, such as financial intermediaries and wholesale and retail traders whose outputs have special characteristics, goods or services produced as outputs must be disposed of by their owners in one or more of the following ways during the period in which they are produced:

(a) They may be sold: (only goods or services sold at economically significant prices are included here);

(b) They may be bartered in exchange for other goods, services or assets, provided to their employees as compensation in kind, or used for other payments in kind;

(c) They may enter the producer's inventories prior to their eventual sale, barter or other use: incomplete outputs enter the producer's inventories in the form of additions to work-in-progress;

(d) They may be supplied to another establishment belonging to the same enterprise for use as intermediate inputs into the latter's production;

(e) They may be retained by their owners for own final consumption or own gross fixed capital formation;

(f) They may be supplied free, or sold at prices that are not economically significant, to other institutional units, either individually or collectively.

6.42. The entire output of an establishment or enterprise must be used in one or other of the above ways. For example, some of the crop produced by a farmer may be sold or bartered; some may be used for final consumption by members of the farmer's household; while the remainder may be put into inventory for future sale or use.

6.43. In practice, some of the goods sold or otherwise used within any given accounting period may have been withdrawn from inventories of goods produced in previous periods. Thus, in the normal situation in which the available accounting data on sales or other uses refer to the total sales or other uses in that period, it is necessary to deduct the value of such withdrawals from the value of total sales or uses to obtain the output of the period in question. It is therefore necessary to record the value of changes in inventories, i.e., entries less withdrawals, and not simply additions to inventories. This leads to the well-known accounting identity:

> the value of output = the value of total sales or other uses of goods or services produced as outputs + the value of changes in the inventories of goods produced as outputs.

Market output, output produced for own final use and other non-market output

6.44. A fundamental distinction is drawn between market output, output produced for own final use and other non-market output.

Market output (P.11)

6.45. Market output is output that is sold at prices that are economically significant or otherwise disposed of on the market, or intended for sale or disposal on the market. Prices are said to be economically significant when they have a significant influence on the amounts the producers are willing to supply and on the amounts purchasers wish to buy. Apart from certain service industries for which special conventions are adopted, the value of the market output of a producer is given by the sum of the values of the following items for the period in question:

(a) The total value of goods and services sold (at economically significant prices);

(b) The total value of goods or services bartered;

(c) The total value of goods or services used for payments in kind, including compensation in kind;

(d) The total value of goods or services supplied by one establishment to another belonging to the same market enterprise to be used as intermediate inputs;

(e) The total value of changes in inventories of finished goods and work-in-progress intended for one or other of the above uses.

Items (a) to (d) refer to values of all goods and services sold or otherwise disposed of, whether produced in the current period or previous periods.

Output produced for own final use (P.12)

6.46. This type of output consists of goods or services that are retained for their own final use by the owners of the enterprises in which they are produced. As corporations have no final consumption, output for own final consumption is produced only by unincorporated enterprises: for example, agricultural goods produced and consumed by members of the same household. The output of domestic and personal services produced for own consumption within households is not included, however, for reasons already given, although housing services produced for own consumption by owner-occupiers and services produced on own account by employing paid domestic staff are included under this heading.

6.47. Goods or services used for own gross fixed capital formation can be produced by any kind of enterprise, whether corporate or unincorporated. They include, for example, the special machine tools produced for their own use by engineering enterprises, or dwellings, or extensions to dwellings, produced by households. A wide range of construction activities may be undertaken for the purpose of own gross fixed capital formation in rural areas in some countries, including communal construction activities undertaken by groups of households.

6.48. The value of output produced for own final use is given by the sum of the values of the following items for the period in question:

(a) The total value of goods and services produced by household enterprises and consumed by the same households;

(b) The total value of the fixed assets produced by an establishment that are retained within the same enterprise for use in future production (own-account gross fixed capital formation);

(c) The total value of changes in inventories of finished goods and work-in-progress intended for one or another of the above uses.

Additions to work-in-progress on structures intended for own use are treated as acquisitions of fixed assets by their producers. They are therefore recorded under (b) instead of (c) above. Goods or services produced for own final use are valued at the basic prices of similar products sold on the market or by their costs of production if no suitable basic prices are available.

Other non-market output (P.13)

6.49. This consists of goods and individual or collective services produced by non-profit institutions serving households (NPISHs) or government that are supplied free, or at prices that are not economically significant, to other institutional units or the community as a whole. Such output may be produced for two reasons:

(a) It may be technically impossible to make individuals pay for collective services because their consumption cannot be monitored or controlled. The pricing mechanism cannot be used when transactions costs are too high and there is market failure. The production of such services has to be organized collectively by government units and financed out of funds other than receipts from sales, namely taxation or other government incomes;

(b) Government units and NPISHs may also produce and supply goods or services to individual households for which they could charge but choose not to do so as a matter of social or economic policy. The most common examples are the provision of education or health services, free or at prices that are not economically significant, although other kinds of goods and services may also be supplied.

6.50. A price is said to be not economically significant when it has little or no influence on how much the producer is prepared to supply and is expected to have only a marginal influence on the quantities demanded. It is thus a price that is not quantitatively significant from the point of view of either supply or demand. Such prices are likely to be charged in order to raise some revenue or achieve some reduction in the excess demand that may occur when services are provided completely free, but they are not intended to eliminate such excess demand. Once a decision has been taken on administrative, social or political grounds about the total amount of a particular non-market good or service to be supplied, its price is deliberately fixed well below the equilibrium price that would clear the market. The difference between a price that is not economically significant and a zero price is, therefore, a matter of degree. The price merely deters those units whose demands are the least pressing without greatly reducing the total level of demand.

6.51. The value of the non-market output of a producer (other than output produced for own final use) is given by the sum of the values of the following items for the period in question:

(a) The total value of goods and services supplied free, or at prices that are not economically significant, to other institutional units, either individually or collectively;

(b) The total value of goods or services supplied by one establishment to another belonging to the same non-market producer to be used as intermediate inputs;

(c) The total value of changes in inventories of finished goods and work-in-progress intended for one or another of the above uses.

As prices that are not economically significant may reflect neither relative production costs nor relative consumer preferences, they do not provide a suitable basis for valuing the outputs of goods or services concerned. The non-market output of goods or services sold at these prices is, therefore, valued in the same way as goods or services provided free, i.e., by their costs of production. Part of this output is purchased by households, the remainder constituting final consumption expenditures by government units or NPISHs.

Market, own account and other non-market producers

6.52. A market producer is an establishment or enterprise all or most of whose output is marketed. It is perfectly possible for market producers, both small unincorporated enterprises and large corporations, to have some non-market output in the form of production for own final consumption or gross fixed capital formation. Own-account producers consist of establishments engaged in gross fixed capital formation for the enterprises of which they form part or unincorporated enterprises owned by households all or most of whose output is intended for final consumption or gross fixed capital formation by those households: for example, owner-occupiers or subsistence farmers who sell none, or only a small fraction, of their output. Other non-market producers consist of establishments owned by government units or NPISHs that supply goods or services free, or at prices that are not economically significant, to households or the community as a whole. These producers may also have some sales of secondary market output whose prices are intended to cover their costs or earn a surplus: for example, sales of reproductions by non-market museums.

D. The measurement of market output

6.53. Five uses of market output were distinguished in paragraph 6.45 above. The ways in which these uses should be recorded are described in the following sections.

1. Recording of sales

6.54. The times at which sales are to be recorded are when the receivables and payables are created: that is, when the ownership of the goods passes from the producer to the purchaser or when the services are provided to the purchaser. The goods or services are valued at the basic prices at which they are sold. If valuation at basic prices is not feasible, they may be valued at producers' prices instead. The values of sales are determined by the amounts receivable and payable by the producers and purchasers, which do not always coincide with the amounts actually received and paid. When payments are made in advance or in arrears, the values of sales should not include any interest or other charges incurred by the producer or purchaser. Such charges are recorded as separate transactions.

2. Recording of barter

6.55. Barter occurs when goods and services are exchanged for other goods, services or assets. The value of goods or services bartered should be recorded when the ownership of the goods is transferred or the services are provided: they should be valued at the basic prices that would have been received if they had been sold.

3. Recording of compensation in kind or other payments in kind

6.56. Goods or services provided to employees as compensation in kind, or used for other payments in kind, should be recorded when the ownership of the goods is transferred or the services are provided. They should be valued at the basic prices that would have been received if they had been sold.

4. Changes in inventories of outputs

Introduction

6.57. The treatment of inventories of finished goods is considered first, followed by the treatment of work-in-progress. The principles governing the recording of changes in inventories and work-in-progress are the same for both market and non-market output.

6.58. The basic principle underlying the measurement of changes in inventories is that output should be recorded at the time it is produced and valued at the same price whether it is immediately sold or otherwise used or entered into inventories for sale or use later. No output is recorded when goods produced previously are withdrawn from inventories and sold or otherwise used. It follows that entries into inventories must be valued at the basic prices prevailing at the time of entry, while withdrawals must be valued at the prices at which they are then sold. In this way, the value of the sales or other uses of goods produced previously is cancelled out by the (negative) value for withdrawals from inventories. This method of valuing changing inventories, which may be described as the "perpetual inventory method" or PIM, is not always easy to implement in practice, however, and it sometimes leads to results which may be counter intuitive.

6.59. When prices are stable, the measurement of changes in inventories is relatively simple. However, when there is inflation, significant price increases may occur while goods are held in inventory. Holding gains accruing on goods held in inventory after they have been produced must not be included in the value of output. The perpetual inventory method ensures their exclusion by valuing goods withdrawn from inventory at the prices prevailing at the time they are withdrawn and not at the prices at which they are entered, or their "historic costs". This method of valuation can lead to much lower figures for both output and profits in times of inflation than those obtained by business accounting methods based on historic costs.

Output, sales and changes in inventories

6.60. It follows from the general principles outlined in the previous section that:

(a) Goods entering inventory are valued at the basic prices prevailing at that time: that is, at the prices at which they could have been sold when first produced;

(b) Goods withdrawn from inventory are valued at the basic prices prevailing at that time: that is, at the prices at which they can then be sold.

6.61. The total value of the changes in inventories of finished goods recorded within a specified accounting period is then given by:

the sum of the values of all goods entering inventory

less the sum of the values of all goods withdrawn from inventory

less the value of any recurrent losses of goods held in inventory.

6.62. Goods held in inventory are subject to deterioration through the passage of time and are at risk from theft or accidental damage. Recurrent losses due to normal rates of wastage, theft and accidental damage reduce the value of the total change in inventories, and hence output.

6.63. It follows from the valuation method used that, when prices are changing, goods entering and leaving inventory at different times are valued at different prices, even within the same accounting period (as also are goods sold at different times). This requires all entries to, and withdrawals from, inventories to be recorded continuously as they occur, and helps explain the complexity of the perpetual inventory method. Assuming that sales and other uses are also appropriately recorded at the prices at which they actually occur and there are no changes in work-in-progress, the following identity must hold for goods or services produced for sale or other use:

the value of output = the value of sales + other uses + the value of changes in inventories

This identity holds whether the goods are all sold or otherwise used within the same accounting period in which they are produced, or whether some goods are sold or used in different periods.

Storage services

6.64. For simplicity, the above presentation of the recording of changes in inventories has ignored the fact that inventories of goods have to be physically stored somewhere. Many goods have to be stored in a properly controlled environment and the activity of storage can become an important process of production in its own right whereby goods are "transported" from one point of time to another. In economics, it is generally recognized that the same goods available at different times, or locations, may be qualitatively different from each other and command different prices for this reason.

6.65. When goods are first produced, they may be held in store for a time in the expectation that they may be sold, exchanged or used more advantageously in the future. In these circumstances, storage can be regarded as an extension of the production process over time. The storage services become incorporated in the goods, thereby increasing their value while being held in store. Thus, in principle, the values of additions to inventories should include not only the values of the goods at the time they are stored but also the value of the additional output produced while the goods are held in store. The measurement of storage is considered in more detail in a later section.

Approximate measures of changes in inventories

6.66. As the PIM requires entries to, and withdrawals from, inventories to be recorded and valued continuously, it may be very difficult to obtain the requisite data, although it may become easier in the course of time as the increased use of microcomputers leads to improved methods of inventory management and control. In many countries, however, data on changes in inventories are among the least reliable information available and it is necessary to consider whether satisfactory approximations can be used which require less data.

6.67. One special case of some interest occurs when output prices remain constant over time. In this case, all entries to and withdrawals from inventories are valued at the same prices, so that the cumulative value of entries less withdrawals simplifies to the difference between the values of the inventories recorded in the opening and closing balance sheets. In this case, information on actual inventory movements between the beginning and end of the accounting period becomes superfluous.

6.68. This suggests that even when prices are changing a good approximation to the PIM may be obtained by taking the difference between the quantities of goods held in inventory at the beginning and the end of the accounting period and valuing this difference at the average prices prevailing within the period. This method, which may be described as the "quantity" measure, is widely used in practice and is sometimes mistakenly considered to be the theoretically appropriate measure under all circumstances. The quantity measure will be the same, or virtually the same, as the perpetual inventory method measure not only when prices are constant but also when the quantities of goods held in inventory rise or fall at a steady pace throughout the period. Conversely, the conditions under which the quantity measure may provide only a poor approximation to the PIM are when prices are rising or falling and

when inventory levels fluctuate within the accounting period. Unfortunately, there are several important industries, including agriculture, in which inventories normally fluctuate because of seasonal variations either in the sequence of outputs produced or in the pattern of demand. Approximate measures of PIM inventory changes may be subject to considerable margins of error in such cases.

Changes in inventories in business accounts

6.69. The value of output in business accounts is also usually derived by adding the value of changes in inventories of outputs to the value of the sales. However, the normal practice in business accounting is to value goods held in (and withdrawn from) inventory at the price at which they were recorded as entering (i.e., "at historic cost") if this price is lower than the current price. The intention is to value inventories prudently for balance sheet purposes, but it may lead to measures of profit which are by no means prudent in inflationary conditions. Under historic cost accounting, a good withdrawn from inventory is liable to be valued at a lower price than that at which it is sold so that the value of output includes the value of the holding gain which accrues between the time of production and time of sale. As a result, the holding gain is not separated from the operating surplus on production under historic cost accounting. Composite measures of profit that combine holding gains with the operating surplus may be useful for certain purposes provided that the composite profit measure is not presented, or interpreted, as if it referred to the operating surplus only, i.e., the profit arising out of production. Unfortunately, the distinction between these two different components of historic cost profits is frequently neither made nor appreciated, and may even be deliberately blurred in order to make the production activities of an enterprise appear more profitable than they are. In periods of high inflation, profit as recorded in business accounts is likely to exceed the operating surplus recorded in economic accounts by a considerable margin.

6.70. Although it is not proposed to go into great detail about business accounting practices in the present context, it is useful to add some further points for clarification. When goods withdrawn from inventory are valued at historic costs in business accounts, it is necessary to know, or assume, the order in which the goods are withdrawn. The most common assumption is FIFO, or first-in-first-out, which implies goods are withdrawn in the same order as they entered. For example, if goods are held in inventory for three months on average, the combination of FIFO with historic cost accounting during inflation implies that the price of each unit sold will include a three months holding gain. As business accountants recognize that this may be undesirable for many purposes, an alternative assumption which has found increasing favour is LIFO, or last-in-first-out, which implies that a good withdrawn from inventory is the last one which entered. This implies that withdrawals are valued at current prices as in the SNA, provided that the level of inventory is not depleted. The proviso is important because, under LIFO, the goods which remain in inventory are those which are assumed to have been there for the longest periods of time. If inventories are eventually run down, those assumed to have been there for a very long time start to be withdrawn and may be valued at very low prices indeed when historic costs are used. Thus, even under LIFO substantial holding gains may be recorded if inventories are greatly diminished. Another method used in business accounting is to value goods withdrawn from inventory at the weighted average of the prices at which they entered. This method values withdrawals at prices between those used for FIFO and LIFO. Finally, in situations of very high inflation, the use of NIFO has been proposed, namely, next-in-first-out. This implies valuing goods withdrawn from inventory at the prices expected to prevail at some point in the near future.

6.71. Other, and more sophisticated, ways of valuing changes in inventories are, of course, also used in business accounts, especially in accounts drawn up for purposes of internal management as distinct from financial reporting. The methods used for management accounting are often very similar to, and possibly identical with, the PIM used in the SNA. Because so many different methods are liable to be used in business accounts, it is impossible to suggest algorithms, or rules of thumb, which would be generally applicable for purposes of transforming data on inventory changes in business accounts to the data required by the System. Each case has to be treated individually, depending upon the precise way in which the business accounts have been drawn up.

Work-in-progress

6.72. When the process of production takes a long time to complete, output must be recognized as being produced continuously as work-in-progress. As the process of production continues, intermediate inputs are continually being consumed so that it is necessary to record some corresponding output to avoid obtaining meaningless figures for value added by recording the inputs and outputs as if they took place at different times, or even in different accounting periods. Work-in-progress is essentially incomplete output that is not yet marketable: that is, output that is not sufficiently processed to be in a state in which it can easily be supplied or sold to other institutional units. It is essential to record such output whenever the process of production is not completed within a single accounting period so that work-in-progress is carried forward from one period to the next. In this case, the current value of the work-in-progress completed up to the end of the first period is recorded in the closing balance sheet that also serves as the opening balance sheet for the next period.

6.73. Work-in-progress may need to be recorded in any industry, including service industries such as the production of movies, depending upon the length of time it takes to produce a unit of output. It is particularly important in industries with long ges-

tation periods, such as certain types of agricultural production or durable producers' goods production, where the period of production may extend over several years.

6.74. Work-in-progress is treated in the System as one component of inventories of outputs held by producers. However, the borderline between inventories of partially completed structures and gross fixed capital formation may not always be clear. Gross fixed capital formation is undertaken by users of fixed assets so that gross fixed capital formation cannot be recorded until the ownership of the assets is transferred from their producers to their users. This transfer does not usually occur until the process of production is completed. However, in the case of buildings or structures for which a contract of sale has been concluded in advance, the transfer of ownership may be deemed to occur in stages as value is put in place. Such transfer of ownership may actually take place legally. In such cases, stage payments made by the purchaser can often be used to approximate the value of the gross fixed capital formation although stage payments may sometimes be made in advance or in arrears of the completion of the stage, in which case short-term credits are also extended from the purchaser to the producer, or vice versa. In the absence of a contract of sale, the output produced must be treated as additions to the producer's inventories, i.e., as work-in-progress, however large the partially completed structure may be.

6.75. Additions to, and withdrawals from, work-in-progress are treated in the accounts in the same way as entries to, and withdrawals from, inventories of finished goods. They must be recorded at the times they take place and at the basic prices prevailing at those times. However, further explanation is needed of the time of recording and valuation in view of the special characteristics of work-in-progress.

Time of recording of work-in-progress

6.76. Additions to work-in-progress take place continuously as work proceeds. Within any given accounting period, such as a year or a quarter, it is therefore necessary to record the cumulative amount of work-in-progress produced within that period. Until a sale is ultimately recorded, the addition to work-in-progress is the only component of output recorded each period. When the production process is terminated, the whole of the work-in-progress accumulated up to that point is effectively transformed into an inventory of finished product ready for delivery or sale. When a sale takes place, the value of the sale must be cancelled out by a withdrawal from inventory of equal value so that only the additions to work-in-progress recorded while production was taking place remain as measures of output. In this way, the output is distributed over the entire period of production.

Valuation of work-in-progress

6.77. Assuming the basic price of the finished product remains unchanged over the periods during which it is being produced, the value of the addition to work-in-progress in a given period is obtained by multiplying the basic price by the share of the total production costs incurred during that period. In other words, the value of the final output is distributed over the various periods during which production takes place in proportion to the costs incurred.

6.78. It may be necessary to estimate the value of additions to work-in-progress in successive periods in advance of knowing what basic price will eventually be realized. In this situation, provisional estimates of the value of additions to work-in-progress should be made on the basis of the total production costs incurred each period plus a mark-up for expected operating surplus or estimated mixed income. Such estimates can be revised subsequently when the actual sale price, and hence actual operating surplus or mixed income, become known.

6.79. The situation is more complicated when the expected sales price is itself continually increasing during the process of production as a result of general inflation. In this case, each addition to work-in-progress should be valued using the expected sale price at that point in time. This implies that during inflation additions to work-in-progress in successive accounting periods may have to be calculated on the basis of progressively higher expected sales prices. Despite the practical difficulties, this procedure has to be followed in order to match the values of inputs and output each period to obtain economically meaningful measures of value added. It is merely an application of the general rule that additions to inventories must always be valued at the basic prices (actual or estimated) prevailing at the times they occur.

5. Deliveries between establishments belonging to the same enterprise

6.80. As explained in chapter V, an establishment is an enterprise, or part of an enterprise, that is situated in a single location and in which only a single (non-ancillary) productive activity is carried out or in which the principal productive activity ac-

counts for most of the value added. It may coincide with an enterprise, or be part of an enterprise, in which case it may be producing goods or services for the use of other establishments belonging to the same enterprise.

6.81. Goods or services produced and consumed within the same accounting period and within the same establishment are not separately identified and, therefore, not recorded as part of the output or intermediate consumption of that establishment. On the other hand, goods which are produced by an establishment and remain in inventory at the end of the period in which they are produced must be included in output, whatever their subsequent use. If they are intended to be used within the establishment subsequently, they should be recorded as work-in-progress: this implies that they are not recorded as intermediate consumption in the period in which they are withdrawn from inventories.

6.82. Goods and services that one establishment provides to a different establishment belonging to the same enterprise are counted as part of the output of the producing establishment. Such goods and services may be used for intermediate consumption by the receiving establishment, but they could also be used for gross fixed capital formation. The goods and services should be valued by the producing establishment at current basic prices; the receiving establishment should value them at the same prices plus any additional transportation costs paid to third parties. The use of artificial transfer prices employed for internal accounting purposes within the enterprise should be avoided, if possible.

6.83. The accounts and tables of the System include production accounts for groups of enterprises and groups of establishments, i.e., for both sectors and industries. In order to ensure that the total output and total intermediate inputs of an enterprise are the same as the corresponding totals for the establishments which make up that enterprise, the enterprise totals must include any inter-establishment deliveries of goods and services.

E. Measurement of output produced for own final use

6.84. Goods and services produced for own final use are included within the production boundary of the System except for domestic and personal services produced by members of households for consumption by themselves or other members of the same household. Goods and services produced for own use should be recorded as their production takes place.

6.85. The goods and services should be valued at the basic prices at which they could be sold if offered for sale on the market. In order to value them in this way, goods or services of the same kind must actually be bought and sold in sufficient quantities on the market to enable reliable market prices to be calculated which can be used for valuation purposes. When reliable mar-

ket prices cannot be obtained, a second best procedure must be used in which the value of the output of the goods or services produced for own use is deemed to be equal to the sum of their costs of production: that is, as the sum of:

Intermediate consumption

Compensation of employees

Consumption of fixed capital

Other taxes (less subsidies) on production.

6.86. It will usually be necessary to value the output of own-account construction on the basis of costs as it is likely to be difficult to make a direct valuation of an individual and specific construction project that is not offered for sale. When the construction is undertaken for itself by a business enterprise, the requisite information on costs may be easily ascertained, but not in the case of the construction of dwellings by households or communal construction for the benefit of the community undertaken by informal associations or groups of households. Most of the inputs into communal construction projects, including labour inputs, are likely to be provided free so that even the valuation of the inputs may pose problems. As unpaid labour may account for a large part of the inputs it is important to make some estimate of its value using wage rates paid for similar kinds of work on local labour markets. While it may be difficult to find an appropriate rate, it is likely to be less difficult than trying to make a direct valuation of a specific construction project itself.

Output of services for own consumption

6.87. In practice, the recording of the production of services for own consumption is less common than for goods. Most of the services produced for own consumption by an enterprise (e.g., transportation, storage, maintenance, etc.) are produced by ancillary activities and are thus not separately identified or recorded either under the output or the intermediate consumption of the establishment or the enterprise to which it belongs. Domestic or personal services produced by members of households for each other are, by convention, treated as falling outside the production boundary of the System. There are, however, two specific categories of services produced for own final consumption whose output must be valued and recorded.

Services produced by employing paid domestic staff

6.88. Paid domestic servants, cooks, gardeners, chauffeurs, etc. are formally treated as employees of an unincorporated enterprise that is owned and managed by the head of the household. The services produced are therefore consumed by the same unit which produces them and they constitute a form of own-account production. By convention, any intermediate costs and consumption of fixed capital incurred in the production of the domestic services are ignored and the value of the output produced is deemed to be equal to the compensation of employees paid, including any compensation in kind such as food or accommodation. The same value is, therefore, recorded under the household's final consumption expenditures.

Services of owner-occupied dwellings

6.89. Heads of household who own the dwellings which the households occupy are formally treated as owners of unincorporated enterprises that produce housing services consumed by those same households. As well-organized markets for rented housing exist in most countries, the output of own-account housing services can be valued using the prices of the same kinds of services sold on the market in line with the general valuation rules adopted for goods or services produced on own account. In other words, the output of the housing services produced by owner-occupiers is valued at the estimated rental that a tenant would pay for the same accommodation, taking into account factors such as location, neighbourhood amenities, etc. as well as the size and quality of the dwelling itself. The same figure is recorded under household final consumption expenditures.

F. Measurement of other non-market output

6.90. As explained above, government units or NPISHs may engage in non-market production because of market failure or as a matter of deliberate economic or social policy. Such output is recorded at the time it is produced, which is also the time of delivery in the case of non-market services. In general, however, it cannot be valued in the same way as goods or services produced for own final consumption or own capital formation that are also produced in large quantities for sale on the market. There are no markets for collective services such as public administration and defence, but even in the case of non-market education, health or other services provided to individual households, suitable prices may not be available. It is not uncommon for similar kinds of services to be produced on a market basis and sold alongside the non-market services but there are usually important differences between the types and quality of services provided. In most cases it is not possible to find enough market services that are sufficiently similar to the corresponding non-market services to enable their prices to be used to value the latter, especially when the non-market services are produced in very large quantities.

6.91. For these reasons, and also to ensure that the various non-market services produced by government units and NPISHs are valued consistently with each other, they are all valued in the System by the sum of the costs incurred in their production: that is, as the sum of:

Intermediate consumption

Compensation of employees

Consumption of fixed capital

Other taxes, less subsidies, on production.

The net operating surplus on the production of non-market goods or services produced by government units and NPISHs is assumed always to be zero.

Valuation of the total output of other non-market producers

6.92. Government units and NPISHs may be engaged in both market and non-market production. Whenever possible, separate establishments should be distinguished for these two types of activities, but this may not always be feasible. Thus, a non-market establishment may have some receipts from sales of market output produced by a secondary activity: for example, sales of reproductions by a non-market museum. However, even though a non-market establishment may have sales receipts, its total output covering both its market and its non-market output, is still valued by the production costs. The

value of its market output is given by its receipts from sales of market products, the value of its non-market output being obtained residually as the difference between the values of its total output and its market output. The value of its receipts from the sale of non-market goods or services at prices that are not economically significant remain as part of the value of its non-market output.

G. The output of particular industries

1. Introduction

6.93. The general rules governing the recording and valuation of output are not sufficient to determine the way in which the output of certain kinds of industries, mostly service industries, such as wholesale and retail trade and financial intermediaries, are measured. The following sections therefore provide further information about the measurement of the output of a number of specific industries. For convenience, the industries concerned are given in the same order as they appear in the ISIC.

2. Agriculture, forestry and fishing

6.94. First, it should be noted that the growth of crops, trees, livestock or fish which is organized, managed and controlled by institutional units constitutes a process of production in an economic sense. Growth is not to be construed as a purely natural process which lies outside the production boundary. Most processes of production merely exploit natural forces for economic purposes: for example, hydroelectric plants exploit rainfall and gravity to produce electricity.

6.95. The measurement of the output of agriculture, forestry and fishing is complicated by the fact that the process of production may extend over many months, or even years. Growing crops, standing timber, and stocks of fish or livestock reared for purposes of food have to be treated as work-in-progress—that is, as output which is not yet sufficiently processed to be in a form which is ready to be marketed. When the crops are harvested, the trees felled, or the livestock slaughtered, the process of production is completed and the work-in-progress is transformed into inventories of finished products ready for sale or other use. Conceptually, therefore, output in agriculture, forestry and fishing can be measured in exactly the same way as other types of production which take a long time to complete, i.e., by the value of sales plus other uses plus changes in inventories including additions to work-in-progress. Output should be recorded as being produced continuously over the entire period of production and not simply at the moment of time when the process is completed, i.e., when the crops are harvested or animals slaughtered.

6.96. Assume the process of production takes several periods (months, quarters, or years, as the case may be) to complete.

The value of the output produced in each period can then be measured as work-in-progress by distributing the value of the finished agricultural products (harvested crops, slaughtered animals, etc.) in proportion to the costs incurred each period. For this purpose, farms that are corporate enterprises need to be distinguished from those that are unincorporated (presumably the great majority of farms in most countries). The output of corporate farms can be distributed in proportion to the actual costs incurred each period, including compensation of employees. However, in the case of unincorporated farms, unpaid labour inputs provided by the owner(s) may account for much of the real costs incurred. The allocation of the finished output of these farms may be accomplished as follows. First, actual costs (expenditures on seed, fuels, etc.) are allocated to the periods in which they were incurred. Secondly, the remaining part of the value of the finished output, i.e., the realized mixed income—is distributed in proportion to the unpaid hours worked by the owner(s). For this purpose, rough indicators of the relative amounts of work done in different periods may be sufficient. The value of the finished products is given by the sum of the values of the following three items:

(a)   Finished products sold or bartered valued at current basic prices;

(b)   Entries of finished products into inventories, less withdrawals, valued at current basic prices;

(c)   Finished products used by their producer for final consumption, valued at current basic prices.

6.97. When the value of the finished products is distributed as work-in-progress it is essential also to record the reduction in work-in-progress which takes place at the moment when the production is completed and the work-in-progress is transformed into finished agricultural products. Otherwise, output would be recorded twice: first as additions to work-in-progress and then as sales, barter or additions to inventories of finished products. The negative figure for the reduction in work-in-progress cancels out the value of the finished products sold, bartered or entered into inventories so that no output is recorded at the moment when the production process is terminated, all of it having been previously recorded as additions to work-in-progress during the period of production.

6.98. If the entire production process is completed within a single accounting period, such as a year, it may be unnecessary to distribute the output as work-in-progress in the way described above. However, if the accounting period ends before the process is completed, or if accounts have to be compiled for sub-periods such as quarters, the total value of the finished products has to be distributed as work-in-progress. It must be remembered that the corresponding inputs into the same production process are in fact distributed over time and recorded in the different periods or sub-periods. Thus, if outputs are not similarly distributed as work-in-progress, inputs are recorded without outputs, in which case economically meaningless figures are liable to be recorded for value added, operating surplus or mixed income and balance of primary incomes. Moreover, it may be necessary to record work-in-progress, even when the production process is completed within a single accounting period, in order to obtain an appropriate match between the values of inputs and outputs when the general price level is rising strongly within the accounting period.

The estimation of work-in-progress in advance

6.99. In agriculture, as in other industries, it may sometimes be necessary to estimate the value of work-in-progress in advance of the production process being completed and the value of the finished products being known, although most accounts are compiled long after the production processes to which they relate are finished. It is recommended therefore that work-in-progress be calculated provisionally on the basis of the actual costs incurred, plus a mark-up for the estimated operating surplus or mixed income. An estimate of mixed income may be made by distributing the expected mixed income in proportion to the volume of unpaid labour. As soon as the actual value of the finished products becomes known, the provisional estimates should be replaced by those obtained by distributing the actual value of the finished products in the ways described earlier. If a growing crop, i.e., work-in-progress, is badly damaged or destroyed prior to the harvest, the earlier provisional estimates of the value of the work-in-progress obviously may have to be revised downwards, to zero if necessary, even before the production is completed.

6.100. There may be circumstances in which the uncertainties attached to the estimation of the value of work-in-progress in advance of the harvest are so great that no useful analytic or policy purpose is served by compiling such estimates. However, this does not prevent useful estimates from being compiled in many other situations in which the margin of uncertainty is much less. In any case it is necessary to specify the appropriate way in which the output of agricultural products is to be recorded and valued when complete information is available. Accounts are essentially *ex post facto* records, even though initial estimates made in advance are inevitably subject to error.

3. Machinery, equipment and construction

6.101. The production of large durable goods such as ships, heavy machinery, buildings and other structures may take several months or years to complete. The output from such production must, therefore, usually be measured by work-in-progress and cannot be recorded simply at the moment in time when the process of production is completed. The way in which work-in-progress is to be recorded and valued has been explained in earlier sections of this chapter, including the preceding section on agricultural output.

6.102. It is worth noting, however, that when a contract of sale is agreed in advance for the construction of a building or other structure extending over several accounting periods, the output produced each period is treated as being sold to the purchaser at the end of the period: i.e., as a sale rather than work-in-progress. In effect, the output produced by the construction contractor is treated as being sold to the purchaser in stages as the latter takes legal possession of the output. It is therefore recorded as gross fixed capital formation by the purchaser and not as work-in-progress by the producer. When the contract calls for stage payments, the value of the output may often be approximated by the value of stage payments made each period. In the absence of a contract of sale, however, the incomplete output produced each period must be recorded as work-in-progress.

4. Transportation and storage

Transportation

6.103. The output of transportation is measured by the value of the amounts receivable for transporting goods or persons. In economics a good in one location is recognized as being a different quality from the same good in another location, so that transporting from one location to another is a process of production in which an economically significant transformation takes place even if the good remains otherwise unchanged. The volume of transport services may be measured by indicators such as ton-kilometres or passenger-kilometres, which combine both the quantities of goods, or numbers of persons, and the distances over which they are transported. Factors such as speed, frequency or comfort also affect the quality of services provided. Transportation is a typical service activity in that the output produced consists of transformations of persons or goods that do not themselves form part of the output of the service producers. While the services performed are easily identified and quantified, they are not separate entities from the goods or persons in which they are incorporated. The production of transportation for own use within enterprises is an ancillary activity that is not separately identified and recorded.

Storage

6.104. Although the production of storage for the market may not be very extensive, the activity of storage is important in the economy as a whole as it is carried out in many enterprises. A good available at a later point in time may need to be treated as a different quality of good from the same good available at an earlier point in time if its supply and demand conditions change in the meanwhile. Thus, storing a good can be a process of production in which an economically significant transformation may take place even if the good remains physically unchanged otherwise. Storage can be viewed as transportation over time rather than space. Of course, if the good, such as wine, also matures while in store—i.e., its physical properties are improved by the passage of time—the amount of production which takes place is correspondingly greater. The volume of storage services produced can be measured by indicators such as space-days which combine the volume of storage space provided with the length of time over which the goods are stored, taking account of other relevant factors such as the environment in which the goods are stored which affect the quality of service provided.

Storage and the measurement of changes in inventories

6.105. The price of a good may change while it is being stored for at least three reasons:

(a)   The physical qualities of the good may improve or deteriorate with the passage of time;

(b)   There may be seasonal factors affecting the supply or the demand for the good that lead to regular, predictable variations in its price over the year, even though its physical qualities may not otherwise change;

(c)   There may be general inflation or other general factors that lead to a change in the price of the good in question even though its physical or economic characteristics are not changed over time.

6.106. In the absence of general inflation, the difference between the prices at which goods enter and are withdrawn from storage in the first two cases should reflect the value of additional output produced while the goods are being stored. General inflation, however, leads to price changes that generate nominal or real holding gains. In practice, however, it may be difficult to disentangle the effects of the different factors at work.

6.107. Suppose that there is no general price inflation. Consider the case of a good whose quality improves while being stored (e.g., wine). Conceptually, the good entering storage can be regarded as work-in-progress if its production continues while it is being stored. The increase in its value while being stored must be treated as an addition to work-in-progress; i.e., as additional output, and not as a price increase. By assumption, the good leaving storage is not the same as the one that entered. The accounting rules for the recording of changes in the value of inventories must be applied in such a way that the entries to inventories include not only the value of the good (work-in-progress) when it entered but also the value of the addition to work-in-progress that took place while it was being stored. In

effect, the output produced while in storage is valued by the price of the good when it is withdrawn less the value of the (immature) good that was entered into storage.

6.108. Goods subject to seasonal fluctuations in price due to changing demand or supply conditions over time must be treated in a similar way. Suppose an annual crop is harvested at one point in time, put into storage and then gradually sold off, or used, over the remaining 12 months. Suppose further that the price gradually rises to reflect the increased scarcity of the good until the next harvest. In the absence of general price changes, the increase in the price of the good while being stored must be interpreted as measuring the value of an addition to work-in-progress, as in the previous example. The goods withdrawn from storage some months after the crop is harvested are economically different from those that entered because of the changing supply conditions over time. A similar argument may be used for goods that are produced throughout the year and entered into storage because they are sold at only one time of the year, such as Christmas: in this case the demand conditions change over time.

6.109. However, most manufactured goods are produced and sold continuously throughout the year and are not subject to regular changes in supply or demand conditions. Nor do they "mature" while being stored. Changes in the prices of such goods while in inventories cannot therefore be treated as additions to work-in-progress.

5. Wholesale and retail distribution

6.110. Although wholesalers and retailers actually buy and sell goods, the goods purchased are not treated as part of their intermediate consumption when they are resold with only minimal processing such as grading, cleaning, packaging, etc. Wholesalers and retailers are treated as supplying services rather than goods to their customers by storing and displaying a selection of goods in convenient locations and making them easily available for customers to buy. Their output is measured by the total value of the trade margins realized on the goods they purchase for resale. A trade margin is defined as the difference between the actual or imputed price realized on a good purchased for resale and the price that would have to be paid by the distributor to replace the good at the time it is sold or otherwise disposed of. The margins realized on some goods may be negative if their prices have to be marked down. They must be negative on goods that are never sold because they go to waste or are stolen.

6.111. The standard formula for measuring output has to be modified for wholesalers or retailers by deducting from the value of the goods sold or otherwise used the value of the goods that would need to be purchased to replace them. The latter include the additional goods needed to make good recurrent losses due to normal wastage, theft or accidental damage. In practice, the output of a wholesaler or retailer is given by the following identity:

the value of output =the value of sales, including sales at reduced prices

plus the value of other uses of goods purchased for resale

minus the value of goods purchased for resale

plus the value of additions to inventories of goods for resale

minus the value of goods withdrawn from inventories of goods for resale

minus the value of recurrent losses due to normal rates of wastage, theft or accidental damage.

6.112. The following points should be noted:

(a) Goods sold are valued at the prices at which they are actually sold, even if the trader has to mark their prices down to get rid of surpluses or avoid wastage;

(b) Goods provided to employees as remuneration in kind should be valued at the current purchasers' prices payable by the traders to replace them; that is, the realized margins are zero. Similarly, goods withdrawn by the owners of unincorporated enterprises for their own final consumption should be valued at the current purchasers' prices payable by the traders to replace them;

(c) Goods purchased for resale should be valued excluding any transport charges invoiced separately by the suppliers or paid to third parties by wholesalers or retailers: these transport services form part of the intermediate consumption of the wholesalers or retailers;

(d) Additions to inventories of goods for resale should be valued at the prices prevailing at the time of entry;

(e) Goods withdrawn from inventory of goods for resale should be valued at the prices prevailing at the time they are withdrawn (as distinct from the prices at which they were originally purchased and entered inventories). Goods withdrawn from inventory include recurrent losses due to normal rates of wastage, theft or accidental damage; goods lost are valued in the same way as goods withdrawn for sale.

6.113. The margins realized on goods purchased for resale thus vary according to their eventual use. The margins realized on goods sold at the full prices intended by the traders could be described as the normal margins. In fixing these margins, traders take account not only of their ordinary costs such as intermediate consumption and compensation of employees but also of the fact that some goods may ultimately have to be sold off at reduced prices while others may go to waste or be stolen. The margins realized on goods whose prices have to be marked down are obviously less than the normal margins and could be negative. The margins on goods used to pay employees as compensation in kind or withdrawn for final consumption by

owners are zero because of the way these goods are valued. Finally, the margins on goods wasted or stolen are negative and equal to the current purchasers' prices of replacements for them.

6.114. The average margin realized on goods purchased for resale may thus be expected to be less then the normal margin—possibly significantly less for certain types of goods such as fashion goods or perishable goods. Finally, it should be noted that margins are defined to exclude holding gains or losses on goods for resale while they are being held in inventory by wholesalers or retailers. As in the case of other types of production, holding gains and losses are excluded from output by valuing all entries to, or withdrawals from, inventories at the prices prevailing at the times the entries or withdrawals take place.

6. Operating leasing

6.115. The activity of renting out machinery or equipment for specified periods of time which are shorter than the total expected service lives of the machinery or equipment is termed operating leasing. It is a form of production in which the owner, or lessor, provides a service to the user, or lessee, the output of which is valued by the rental which the lessee pays to the lessor. Operating leasing has to be clearly distinguished from financial leasing, which is not itself a process of production but a method of financing the acquisition of fixed assets.

6.116. Operating leasing can be identified by the following characteristics:

(a) The lessor, or owner of the equipment, normally maintains a stock of equipment in good working order which can be hired on demand, or at short notice, by users;

(b) The equipment may be rented out for varying periods of time. The lessee may renew the rental when the period expires and the user may hire the same piece of equipment on several occasions. However, the user does not undertake to rent the equipment over the whole of the expected service life of the equipment;

(c) The lessor is frequently responsible for the maintenance and repair of the equipment as part of the service which he provides to the lessee. The lessor must normally be a specialist in the operation of the equipment, a factor that may be important in the case of highly complicated equipment, such as computers, where the lessee and his employees, may not have the necessary expertise or facilities to service the equipment properly themselves. The lessor may also undertake to replace the equipment in the event of a serious or prolonged breakdown.

6.117. Thus, the service provided by the lessor goes beyond the mere provision of a piece of equipment. It includes other elements such as convenience and security which can be important from the user's point of view. Operating leasing developed originally to meet the needs of users who require certain types of equipment only intermittently. However, with the evolution of increasingly complicated types of machinery, especially in the electronics field, the servicing and back-up facilities provided by a lessor are important factors which may influence a user to rent. Other factors which may persuade users to rent over long periods rather than purchase are the consequences for the enterprise's balance sheet, cash flow or tax liability.

Financial leasing

6.118. In contrast to operating leasing, financial leasing is not itself a process of production. It is an alternative to lending as a method of financing the acquisition of machinery and equipment. A financial lease is a contract between a lessor and a lessee whereby the lessor purchases machinery or equipment that is put at the disposal of the lessee and the lessee contracts to pay rentals which enable the lessor, over the period of the contract, to recover all, or virtually all, of his costs including interest. Financial leases may be distinguished by the fact that all the risks and rewards of ownership are, de facto, transferred from the legal owner of the good, the lessor, to the user of the good, the lessee. In order to capture the economic reality of such arrangements, a change of ownership from the lessor to the lessee is deemed to take place, even though legally the leased good remains the property of the lessor, at least until the termination of the lease when the legal ownership is usually transferred to the lessee. The lessor is treated as making a loan to the lessee which enables the latter to finance the acquisition of the equipment. The rentals are then treated as covering repayments of the loan and interest payments.

6.119. Thus, operating leasing and financial leasing are treated as totally different kinds of activity, one being a process of production while the other is a method by which funds are channelled from a lender to a borrower. Of course, some incidental services are provided by the lessor in the process of arranging the lease, but the value of these services is very small compared with the total rentals paid. It is therefore essential to distinguish between the two types of leasing, even though financial arrangements may be devised which are hybrids of the two and which are consequently difficult to classify.

7. Financial intermediaries except insurance corporations and pension funds

Introduction

6.120. This section is concerned with financial intermediaries except insurance corporations and pension funds, which are dealt with in the following sections.

6.121. Financial intermediaries incur liabilities on their own account on financial markets by borrowing funds which they lend on different terms and conditions to other institutional units. As explained in chapter IV, they intermediate between lenders and borrowers by channelling funds from one to the other, put-

ting themselves at risk in the process. They include almost all institutions describing themselves as "banks". They also include unincorporated enterprises engaged on financial intermediation on a small scale; these may be important in some developing countries.

6.122. Some financial intermediaries raise most of their funds by taking deposits; others do so by issuing bills, bonds or other securities. They lend funds by making loans or advances, or by purchasing bills, bonds or other securities. The pattern of their financial assets is different from that of their liabilities and in this way they transform the funds they receive in ways more suited to the requirements of borrowers. The rates of return they receive on the funds they lend are generally higher than the rates they pay on the funds they borrow, and they obtain most of the funds to defray their expenses and provide an operating surplus in this way. Many financial intermediaries do not charge explicitly for the intermediation services which they provide to their customers so that there may be no receipts from sales which can be used to value these services, although there may be an increasing tendency to make charges.

6.123. Financial intermediaries are also increasingly tending to provide various kinds of auxiliary financial services, or business services, as secondary activities: for example, currency exchange, or advice about investments, the purchase of real estate, or taxation. The output of such services is valued on the basis of the fees or commissions charged, in the same way as other services. The measurement of the production and consumption of these services poses no special conceptual or practical problems. The question to be resolved here is how to value the output of financial intermediation for which no explicit charges are made and for which there are no sales receipts. Such output has to be valued indirectly and the way in which this is done is explained in the following section.

The output of financial intermediation services indirectly measured

6.124. Some financial intermediaries are able to provide services for which they do not charge explicitly by paying or charging different rates of interest to borrowers and lenders (and to different categories of borrowers and lenders). They pay lower rates of interest than would otherwise be the case to those who lend them money and charge higher rates of interest to those who borrow from them. The resulting net receipts of interest are used to defray their expenses and provide an operating surplus. This scheme of interest rates avoids the need to charge their customers individually for services provided and leads to the pattern of interest rates observed in practice. However, in this situation, the System must use an indirect measure, financial intermediation services indirectly measured (FISIM), of the value of the services for which the intermediaries do not charge explicitly.

6.125. The total value of FISIM is measured in the System as the total property income receivable by financial intermediaries minus their total interest payable, excluding the value of any property income receivable from the investment of their own funds, as such income does not arise from financial intermediation. Whenever the production of output is recorded in the System the use of that output must be explicitly accounted for elsewhere in the System. Hence, FISIM must be recorded as being disposed of in one or more of the following ways—as intermediate consumption by enterprises, as final consumption by households, or as exports to non-residents.

6.126. In principle, the total output should, therefore, be allocated among the various recipients or users of the services for which no explicit charges are made. In practice, however, it may be difficult to find a method of allocating the total output among different users in a way which is conceptually satisfactory from an economic viewpoint and for which the requisite data are also available. Some flexibility has therefore to be accepted in the way in which the output is allocated. Some countries may prefer to continue to use the convention proposed in the 1968 version of the SNA whereby the whole of the output is recorded as the intermediate consumption of a nominal industry. This convention makes total GDP for the economy as a whole invariant to the size of the estimated output.

6.127. When the output is allocated among different users, one possible way of proceeding is to base the allocation on the difference between the actual rates of interest payable and receivable and a "reference" rate of interest. When the requisite information is available, estimates of the following may be calculated and used to allocate the total output:

(a) For those to whom the intermediaries lend funds, both resident and non-resident, the difference between the interest actually charged on loans, etc. and the amount that would be paid if a reference rate were used;

(b) For those from whom the intermediaries borrow funds, both resident and non-resident, the difference between the interest they would receive if a reference rate were used and the interest they actually receive.

6.128. The reference rate to be used represents the pure cost of borrowing funds—that is, a rate from which the risk premium has been eliminated to the greatest extent possible and which does not include any intermediation services. The type of rate chosen as the reference rate may differ from country to country but the inter-bank lending rate would be a suitable choice when available; alternatively, the central bank lending rate could be used.

6.129. If this type of information is not available or not appropriate, the total value of FISIM could be allocated using different indicators. For example, it could be allocated in proportion to the total financial assets and liabilities that exist between financial intermediaries and various groups of users, or in proportion to other relevant financial variables.

6.130. For the System as a whole, the allocation of FISIM among different categories of users is equivalent to reclassifying certain parts of interest payments as payments for services. This reclassification has important consequences for the values of certain aggregate flows of goods and services—output, intermediate and final consumption, imports and exports—which affect the values added of particular industries and sectors, and also total gross domestic product (GDP). There are also implications for the flows of interest recorded in the primary distribution of income accounts. However, the saving of all the units concerned, including the financial intermediaries themselves, are not affected. Nor is the financial account affected.

6.131. Because of these effects, it is desirable for compilers to provide additional information to give some indication to users of the accounts of the consequences of alternative treatments. When FISIM is actually allocated among users, the resulting values should be identified and shown separately. Conversely, when the whole of the value of FISIM is, by convention, allocated to the intermediate consumption of a nominal industry, it is recommended that compilers should provide supplementary estimates, even if only approximate and very aggregative, of the allocation of FISIM between intermediate consumption and the main categories of final demand and of the effects that such an allocation would have on GDP, GNI and other relevant aggregates. The treatment of FISIM is explained in greater detail in annex III on this subject at the end of this manual.

Central banks

6.132. The services of financial intermediation provided by central banks should be measured in the same way as those of other financial intermediaries. Because of the unique functions which may be performed by central banks, the value of their output may sometimes appear exceptionally large in relation to the resources employed. Services other than financial intermediation which may be carried out by central banks should be valued by the fees or commissions charged, in the same way as for other financial enterprise.

Unincorporated financial intermediaries and money lenders

6.133. The output of unincorporated financial intermediaries, including those whose activities are not monitored and subject to regulation by central banks or other authorities, is measured in the same way as for financial corporations. Money lenders who incur liabilities on their own account in order to mobilize funds which they lend to others are clearly engaged in financial intermediation. Their output must be measured by the difference between the property income they receive from the lending of borrowed funds and the interest paid on the borrowed funds. As in the case of large corporations, the income they receive from the investment of their own funds is excluded from this calculation.

6.134. Some money lenders lend only their own funds. The activity of such small-scale money lenders, including many village money lenders, is not financial intermediation as they do not channel funds from one group of institutional units to another. Lending as such is not a process of production and the interest received from the lending of own funds cannot be identified with the value of any services produced.

8. Insurance

6.135. The activity of insurance is intended to provide individual institutional units exposed to certain risks with financial protection against the consequences of the occurrence of specified events. It is also a form of financial intermediation in which funds are collected from policyholders and invested in financial or other assets which are held as technical reserves to meet future claims arising from the occurrence of the events specified in the insurance policies. Although insurance involves transfers in which funds are redistributed among institutional units, insurance enterprises also produce services that are paid for, directly or indirectly, by their policyholders. It is not easy to disentangle the different elements involved in the transactions between insurance enterprises and their policyholders and to record them appropriately in the System. Accordingly, a comprehensive explanation of insurance and pensions and the ways in which the various elements interact is given in annex IV at the end of this manual. The purpose of the present section is to explain how the output of the services produced by insurance enterprises is calculated and valued in the System.

6.136. Typically, insurance enterprises do not make a separate charge for the service of arranging the financial protection or security which insurance is intended to provide. Whenever insurance enterprises do make explicit charges to their policyholders or others, these are treated as payments for services rendered in the normal way. For those services for which no explicit charges are made the value of the services they provide has to be estimated indirectly, however, from the total receivables and payables of insurance enterprises, including the income accruing from the investment of their reserves.

6.137. Insurance enterprises build up technical reserves for several reasons. One is that insurance premiums are payable in advance at the start of each period covered by the policy so that insurance enterprises typically hold funds for a period of time before an eventuality giving rise to a payment occurs. This applies to non-life insurance as well as to life insurance. Another reason is that there is sometimes an important time-lag between the eventuality occurring and the payment of the subsequent claim taking place. In addition, insurance enterprises must hold considerable reserves in the form of actuarial reserves, including reserves on "with-profits" life policies, in respect of life insurance. The technical reserves built up for those reasons are invested in financial or non-financial assets, including real estate. The income generated by these investments in the form of the property income or net operating surpluses earned by renting residential or non-residential buildings has a considerable influence on the level of premiums insurance enterprises need to charge. The management of its investment portfolio is an integral part of the business of insurance which has a considerable bearing on the profitability and competitiveness of the enterprise.

6.138. The value of the total output of insurance services is obtained residually from an accounting relationship in which the following elements are involved:

(a) Actual premiums earned: these refer to those parts of the premiums payable in the current or previous periods which cover the risks incurred during the accounting period in question. They are not equal to the premiums actually payable during the accounting period, as only part of the period covered by an individual premium may fall within the accounting period in which it is payable. The prepayments of premiums, which refer to those parts of the premiums which cover risks in the subsequent accounting period or periods, form part of the technical reserves. Thus, total premiums earned are equal to premiums receivable less the value of the changes in the reserves due to prepayments of premiums;

(b) Income from investment of the insurance technical reserves, as described above. Although the reserves are held and managed by the insurance enterprises, they are treated in the System as assets of the policyholders. The income earned on the investment of the reserves is, therefore, attributed to the policyholders for whose benefit the reserves are held. The income is recorded as receivable by the policyholders who pay it all back again to the insurance enterprises as premium supplements. These premium supplements must therefore always be equal in value to the corresponding income from the investment of the technical reserves;

(c) Claims which become due for payment during the accounting period: claims become due when the eventuality takes place which gives rise to a valid claim; they are equal to claims actually payable within the accounting period plus changes in the reserves against outstanding claims;

(d) Changes in the actuarial reserves and reserves for with-profits insurance: these changes consist of allocations to the actuarial reserves and reserves for with-profits insurance policies to build up the capital sums guaranteed under these policies. Most of these reserves relate to life insurance but they may be needed in the case of non-life insurance when claims are paid out as annuities instead of lump sums.

All changes in insurance technical reserves referred to in (a), (c) and (d) are measured excluding any nominal holding gains or losses.

6.139. Items (a) and (b), i.e.:

Actual premiums earned; and

Premium supplements (= income from investments)

determine the total resources of an insurance enterprise arising from its insurance activities. Items (c) and (d), i.e.:

Claims due; and

Changes in actuarial reserves and reserves for with-profits insurance

determine the total technical charges to be met out of these resources. The difference between the total resources and total technical charges represents the amount available to an insurance enterprise to cover its costs and provide for an operating surplus. It is therefore taken as measuring the value of the output of services produced by the enterprise. Insurance enterprises take all the items (b) to (d) into consideration when fixing the levels of the premiums they charge in order to ensure that the excess of total resources over total charges provides sufficient remuneration for their own services.

6.140. Thus, the basic accounting used to estimate the value of the output of insurance services is as follows:

Total claims due

plus Changes in actuarial and reserves for with-profits insurance

plus Total actual premiums earned

plus Total premium supplements

= Value of the output of insurance services

The value of the output of insurance services is determined residually as the item that balances both sides of the above account. The outputs of both life and non-life insurance services are estimated by means of this identity.

9. Autonomous pension funds

6.141. Autonomous pension funds are separate funds (i.e., separate institutional units) established for purposes of providing incomes on retirement for specific groups of employees which are organized, and directed, by private or public employers or jointly by the employers and their employees. These funds engage in financial transactions on their own account on financial markets and make investments by acquiring financial and non-financial assets. They do not include social security schemes organized for large sections of the community which are imposed, controlled or financed by general government. The output produced by pension funds is measured in the same way as that of insurance enterprises, as described above, except that in the case of pension funds, "premiums" are generally described as "contributions", while "claims" are generally described as "benefits".

10. Research and development

6.142. Research and development by a market producer is an activity undertaken for the purpose of discovering or developing new products, including improved versions or qualities of existing products, or discovering or developing new or more efficient processes of production. Research and development is not an ancillary activity, and a separate establishment should be distinguished for it, when possible. The research and development undertaken by market producers on their own behalf should, in principle, be valued on the basis of the estimated basic prices that would be paid if the research were sub-contracted commercially, but is likely to have to be valued on the basis of the total production costs, in practice. Research and development undertaken by specialized commercial research laboratories or institutes is valued by receipts from sales, contracts, commissions, fees, etc. in the usual way. Research and development undertaken by government units, universities, non-profit research institutes, etc. is non-market production and is valued on the basis of the total costs incurred. The activity of research and development is different from teaching and is classified separately in ISIC. In principle, the two activities ought to be distinguished from each other when undertaken within a university or other institute of higher education, although there may be considerable practical difficulties when the same staff divide their time between both activities. There may also be interaction between teaching and research which makes it difficult to separate them, even conceptually, in some cases.

11. The production of originals and copies

6.143. The production of books, recordings, films, software, tapes, disks, etc. is a two-stage process of which the first stage is the production of the original and the second stage the production and use of copies of the original. The output of the first stage is the original itself over which legal or de facto ownership can be established by copyright, patent or secrecy. The value of the original depends on the actual or expected receipts from the sale or use of copies at the second stage, which have to cover the costs of the original as well as costs incurred at the second stage.

6.144. The output of the first stage is an intangible fixed asset that belongs to the producer of the original (author, film company, program writer, etc.). It may be produced for sale or for own-account gross fixed capital formation by the original producer. As the asset may be sold to another institutional unit the owner of the asset at any given time need not be the original producer, although they are often one and the same unit. If the original is sold when it has been produced, the value of the output of the original producer is given by the price paid. If it is not sold, its value could be estimated on the basis of its production costs with a mark-up. However, the size of any mark-up must depend on the discounted value of the future receipts expected from using it in production, so that it is effectively this discounted value, however uncertain, that determines its value.

6.145. The owner of the asset may use it directly or to produce copies in subsequent periods. Consumption of fixed capital is recorded in respect of the use of the asset in the same way as for any other fixed asset used in production.

6.146. The owner may also license other producers to make use of the original in production. The latter may produce and sell copies, or use copies in other ways; for example, for film or music performances. In these cases, the owner is treated as providing services to the licensees that are recorded as part of their intermediate consumption. The payments made by the licenses may be described in various ways, such as fees, commissions or royalties, but however they are described they are treated as payments for services rendered by the owner. The use of the asset is then recorded as consumption of fixed capital in the production of services by the owner. These services are valued by the fees, commissions, royalties, etc. received from the licensees.

H. Intermediate consumption (P.2)

1. Introduction

6.147. Intermediate consumption consists of the value of the goods and services consumed as inputs by a process of production, excluding fixed assets whose consumption is recorded as consumption of fixed capital. The goods or services may be either transformed or used up by the production process. Some inputs re-emerge after having been transformed and incorporated into the outputs; for example, grain may be transformed into flour which in turn may be transformed into bread. Other inputs are completely consumed or used up; for example, electricity and most services.

6.148. Intermediate consumption does not include expenditures by enterprises on valuables consisting of works of art, precious metals and stones and articles of jewellery fashioned out of them. Valuables are assets acquired as stores of value: they are not used up in production and do not deteriorate physically over time. Expenditures on valuables are recorded in the capital account. Intermediate consumption also does not include costs incurred by the gradual using up of fixed assets owned by the enterprise: the decline in their value during the accounting period is recorded as consumption of fixed capital. However, intermediate consumption does include the rentals paid on the use of fixed assets, whether equipment or buildings, that are leased from other institutional units, and also fees, commissions, royalties, etc., payable under licensing arrangements, as explained above.

6.149. Intermediate consumption includes the value of all the goods or services used as inputs into ancillary activities such as purchasing, sales, marketing, accounting, data processing, transportation, storage, maintenance, security, etc. The goods and services consumed by these ancillary activities are not distinguished from those consumed by the principal (or secondary) activities of a producing establishment even though the levels at which ancillary activities are carried out do not usually vary proportionately with the level of the principal activity.

2. The timing and valuation of intermediate consumption

6.150. The intermediate consumption of a good or service is recorded at the time when the good or service enters the process of production, as distinct from the time it was acquired by the producer. In practice, the two times coincide for inputs of services, but not for goods, which may be acquired some time in advance of their use in production. A good or service consumed as an intermediate input is normally valued at the purchaser's price prevailing at the time it enters the process of production; that is, at the price the producer would have to pay to replace it at the time it is used. As explained in more detail in paragraphs 6.215 to 6.217, the purchaser's price, at least in the case of certain goods, can be regarded as being composed of three elements:

(a) The basic price received by the producer of the good or service;

(b) Any transportation costs paid separately by the purchaser in taking delivery of a good at the required time and location plus the cumulative trade margin on a good which passes through the chain of wholesale or retail distribution;

(c) Any non-deductible tax (less subsidy) on the product payable on the good or service when it was produced or while in transit to the purchaser.

For purposes of the System's input-output tables, it may be necessary to distinguish all three elements but not in the accounts for institutional sectors or the central supply and use table.

6.151. In practice, establishments do not usually record the actual use of goods in production directly. Instead, they keep records of purchases of materials and supplies intended to be used as inputs and also of any changes in the amounts of such goods held in inventory. An estimate of intermediate consumption during a given accounting period can then be derived by subtracting the value of changes in inventories of materials and supplies from the value of purchases made. Changes in inventories of materials and supplies are equal to entries less withdrawals and recurrent losses on goods held in inventory. Thus, by reducing the value of changes in inventories recurrent losses increase intermediate consumption. Goods entering and leaving inventory are valued at the purchasers' prices prevailing at the times the entries, withdrawals or recurrent losses take place. This is exactly the same method as that used to value changes in inventories of goods produced as outputs from the production process. Thus, the earlier discussion of the properties and behaviour of the PIM applies, *mutatis mutandis*, to inventories of inputs.

6.152. When goods or services produced within the same establishment are fed back as inputs into the production within the same establishment, they are not recorded as part of the intermediate consumption or the output of that establishment. On the other hand, deliveries of goods and services between different establishments belonging to the same enterprise are recorded as outputs by the producing establishments and must, therefore, be recorded as intermediate inputs by the receiving establishments.

3. The boundary between intermediate consumption and compensation of employees

6.153. Certain goods and services used by enterprises do not enter directly into the process of production itself but are consumed by employees working on that process. In such cases it is necessary to decide whether the goods and services are intermediate consumption or, alternatively, remuneration in kind to employees. In general, when the goods or services are used by employees in their own time and at their own discretion for the direct satisfaction of their needs or wants, they constitute remuneration in kind. However, when employees are obliged to use the goods or services in order to enable them to carry out their work, they constitute intermediate consumption.

6.154. It is immaterial to the employer whether they are treated as intermediate consumption or compensation of employees—they are both costs from the employer's viewpoint—and the net operating surplus is the same. However, reclassifying such goods and services from remuneration in kind to intermediate consumption, or vice versa, changes value added and balance of primary incomes, and hence GDP as a whole.

6.155. The following types of goods and services provided to employees must be treated as part of intermediate consumption.

 (a) Tools or equipment used exclusively, or mainly, at work;

 (b) Clothing or footwear of a kind which ordinary consumers do not choose to purchase or wear and which are worn exclusively, or mainly, at work; e.g., protective clothing, overalls or uniforms. However, uniforms or other special clothing which employees choose to wear extensively off-duty instead of ordinary clothing should be treated as remuneration in kind;

 (c) Accommodation services at the place of work of a kind which cannot be used by the households to which the employees belong—barracks, cabins, dormitories, huts, etc.;

 (d) Special meals or drinks necessitated by exceptional working conditions, or meals or drinks provided to servicemen or others while on active duty;

 (e) Transportation and hotel services provided while the employee is travelling on business;

 (f) Changing facilities, washrooms, showers, baths, etc. necessitated by the nature of the work;

 (g) First aid facilities, medical examinations or other health checks required because of the nature of the work.

Employees may sometimes be responsible for purchasing the kinds of goods or services listed above and be subsequently reimbursed in cash by the employer. Such cash reimbursements must be treated as intermediate expenditures by the employer and not as part of the employee's wages and salaries.

6.156. The provision of other kinds of goods and services, such as meals, ordinary housing services, the services of vehicles or other durable consumer goods used extensively away from work, transportation to and from work, etc. should be treated as remuneration in kind, as explained more fully in chapter VII.

4. The boundary between intermediate consumption and gross fixed capital formation

6.157. Intermediate consumption measures the value of goods and services that are transformed or entirely used up in the course of production during the accounting period. It does not cover the costs of using fixed assets owned by the enterprise nor expenditures on the acquisition of fixed assets. The boundary between these kinds of expenditures and intermediate consumption is explained in more detail below.

Small tools

6.158. Expenditures on durable producer goods which are small, inexpensive and used to perform relatively simple operations may be treated as intermediate consumption when such expenditures are made regularly and are very small compared with expenditures on machinery and equipment. Examples of such goods are hand tools such as saws, spades, knives, axes, hammers, screwdrivers, spanners and so on. However, in countries where such tools account for a significant part of the stock of producers' durable goods, they may be treated as fixed assets.

Maintenance and repairs

6.159. The distinction between maintenance and repairs and gross fixed capital formation is not clear-cut. The ordinary, regular maintenance and repair of a fixed asset used in production constitutes intermediate consumption. Ordinary maintenance and repair, including the replacement of defective parts, are typical ancillary activities but such services may also be provided by a separate establishment within the same enterprise or purchased from other enterprises.

6.160. The practical problem is to distinguish ordinary maintenance and repairs from major renovations, reconstructions or enlargements which go considerably beyond what is required simply to keep the fixed assets in good working order. Major renovations, reconstructions, or enlargements of existing fixed assets may enhance their efficiency or capacity or prolong their expected working lives. They must be treated as gross fixed capital formation as they add to the stock of fixed assets in existence.

6.161. Ordinary maintenance and repairs are distinguished by two features:

(a) They are activities that owners or users of fixed assets are obliged to undertake periodically in order to be able to utilize such assets over their expected service lives. They are current costs that cannot be avoided if the fixed assets are to continue to be used. The owner or user cannot afford to neglect maintenance and repairs as the expected service life may be drastically shortened otherwise;

(b) Maintenance and repairs do not change the fixed asset or its performance, but simply maintain it in good working order or restore it to its previous condition in the event of a breakdown. Defective parts are replaced by new parts of the same kind without changing the basic nature of the fixed asset.

6.162. On the other hand, major renovations or enlargements to fixed assets are distinguished by the following features:

(a) The decision to renovate, reconstruct or enlarge a fixed asset is a deliberate investment decision which may be undertaken at any time and is not dictated by the condition of the asset. Major renovations of ships, buildings or other structures are frequently undertaken well before the end of their normal service lives;

(b) Major renovations or enlargements increase the performance or capacity of existing fixed assets or significantly extend their previously expected service lives. Enlarging or extending an existing building or structure obviously constitutes a major change in this sense, but a complete refitting or restructuring of the interior of a building, or ship, also qualifies.

Research and development

6.163. Research and development are undertaken with the objective of improving efficiency or productivity or deriving other future benefits so that they are inherently investment—rather than consumption—type activities. However, other activities, such as staff training, market research or environmental protection, may have similar characteristics. In order to classify such activities as investment type it would be necessary to have clear criteria for delineating them from other activities, to be able to identify and classify the assets produced, to be able to value such assets in an economically meaningful way and to know the rate at which they depreciate over time. In

practice it is difficult to meet all these requirements. By convention, therefore, all the outputs produced by research and development, staff training, market research and similar activities are treated as being consumed as intermediate inputs even though some of them may bring future benefits.

6.164. As already noted, research and development is not an ancillary activity like purchasing, book-keeping, storage and maintenance which tend to be found frequently in all kinds of establishments. When research and development is carried out on a significant scale within an enterprise, it would be desirable to identify a separate establishment for it so that the relevant inputs and outputs could be distinguished for analytical purposes. Because of the difficulty of obtaining price data, the output will usually have to be valued by total costs of production, as in the case of most other own-account production. The output produced has then to be treated as being delivered to the establishment, or establishments, which make up the rest of the enterprise and included in their intermediate consumption. When there are several other establishments, the amounts of research and development delivered can be distributed in proportion to their total costs or other indicator, in much the same way that the output of head offices or other central facilities has to be allocated.

6.165. When an enterprise contracts an outside agency to undertake research and development, staff training, market research or similar activities on its behalf, the expenditures incurred by the enterprise are treated as purchases of services used for purposes of intermediate consumption.

Mineral exploration

6.166. Expenditures on mineral exploration are not treated as intermediate consumption. Whether successful or not, they are needed to acquire new reserves and are, therefore, all classified as gross fixed capital formation.

Military equipment

6.167. In the past, it has been conventional in national accounts to treat all goods except dwellings acquired by governmental establishments engaged in the production of defence services, that is Class 7522 of the ISIC, as intermediate inputs whether the goods are non-durable or durable. Thus, ships, aircraft, vehicles and other equipment acquired by military establishments, and the construction of buildings, roads, airfields, docks, etc. for use by military establishments have always been treated as intermediate consumption rather than capital formation. This implies that the output from Class 7522 is produced without any inputs of capital although the rationale for this has never been clear. It has sometimes been suggested that it is impossible to estimate service lives for the assets concerned, but this is not true for most of them.

6.168. In order to be treated as capital, a good must not only be durable but used repeatedly or be continuously in production over a number of accounting periods. However, if military weapons such as rockets, missiles and their warheads, are actually used in combat, they are used to destroy and not to produce. Thus, the actual use of destructive weapons can scarcely be treated as an input into an economic process of production.

6.169.   The provision of defence, however, can certainly be construed as a form of production from which people benefit and for which they are prepared to pay, individually or collectively. Moreover, the provision of defence, like any other productive activity, does require the repeated or continuous usage of certain durable goods over a number of accounting periods. Thus, a distinction can be drawn between those durable goods that are actually used in much the same way as in any other type of production, and those which either are never used or, if they are used, do not constitute inputs into a productive process. This suggests a distinction between ordinary producers' durable goods of a kind used throughout the economy and destructive military weapons designed for combat.

6.170.   On this line of reasoning, rockets, missiles and their warheads are not to be treated as fixed assets. By extension, missile silos, warships, submarines, fighter aircraft and bombers, and tanks whose sole function is to release such weapons should also not be treated as fixed assets. On the other hand, the airfields, docks or other facilities used as bases by these same ships, submarines or aircraft can be used with little or no modification for quite different purposes of a non-military nature. Very often such facilities are shared between military and civilian use. Moreover, the manner in which the facilities are utilized is essentially the same whether they are used by military personnel or others.

6.171.   For these reasons, only expenditures by the military on weapons of destruction and the equipment needed to deliver them should be classified as intermediate consumption. Conversely, the construction of buildings for use by military personnel, including hospitals and schools, and also of roads, bridges, airfields, docks, etc. for use by military establishments should be treated as gross fixed capital formation. In addition, machinery and equipment of the same type as that used by civil establishments for non-military purposes should also be treated as fixed capital formation; for example, vehicles, ships or aircraft used for the transport of persons or goods; computers and office machinery and equipment; etc.

6.172.   Light weapons and armoured vehicles are also acquired by non-military establishments engaged in internal security or policing activities, including establishments owned by market security services. Weapons or armoured vehicles acquired by police and security services are treated as fixed assets, even though expenditures on the same kind of equipment by military establishments would be treated as intermediate.

5. Collective services

6.173.   Collective services provided by government units are not included in the intermediate consumption of enterprises, even though enterprises benefit from the provision of transport facilities, security, etc. It would be impossible to identify those collective services that benefit enterprises rather than households and to allocate such services between individual enterprises. Some individual non-market goods or services may also be provided to market producers, such as free veterinary services to farmers. By convention they are not included in their intermediate consumption and they are not separated from collective services.

6. Social transfers

6.174.   Expenditures by government or NPISHs on goods or services produced by market producers that are provided directly to households, individually or collectively without any further processing constitute final consumption expenditures by government or NPISHs and not intermediate consumption. The goods and services in question are one form of social transfers and enter into the actual consumption of households.

7. Services of business associations

6.175.   Non-profit institutions in the form of business associations that exist to protect the interests of their members and are financed by them are market producers. The subscriptions paid by the businesses constitute payments for services rendered. These services are consumed as intermediate inputs by the members of the association and are valued by the amounts paid in subscriptions, contributions or dues.

8. The boundary between intermediate consumption and value added

6.176.   The boundary between intermediate consumption and value added is not a rigid one fixed purely by the technology of production. It is also influenced by the way in which the production is organized and distributed between different establishments or enterprises.

6.177.   The types of services produced by ancillary activities can either be produced for own use within the same establishment or obtained from outside, i.e., from specialist market enterprises. If an establishment obtains the services from outside instead of from ancillary activities, its value added is reduced and intermediate consumption increased, even though its principal activity remains completely unchanged. As ancillary activities themselves have intermediate inputs, however, the increase in intermediate consumption is likely to be less than the value of the additional services purchased. Nevertheless, the distribution of value added between establishments and enterprises is bound to be influenced by the extent to which the services of ancillary activities are produced in-house or obtained from outside. Similarly, observed input-output ratios may vary significantly for the same reason, even between equally efficient establishments utilizing the same technology for their principal activity.

6.178. The decision to rent, rather than purchase buildings, machinery or equipment, can also have a major impact on the ratio of intermediate consumption to value added and the distribution of value added between producers. Rentals paid on buildings or on machinery or equipment under an operating lease constitute purchases of services that are recorded as intermediate consumption. However, if an enterprise owns its buildings, machinery and equipment, most of the costs associated with their use are not recorded under intermediate consumption. The capital consumption on the fixed assets forms part of gross value added while interest costs, both actual and implicit, have to be met out of the net operating surplus. Only the costs of the materials needed for maintenance and repairs appear under intermediate consumption. Decisions to rent rather than purchase may be influenced by factors quite unrelated to the technology of production, such as taxation, the availability of finance, or the consequences for the balance sheet.

I. Consumption of fixed capital (K.1)

1. Introduction

6.179. Consumption of fixed capital is a cost of production. It may be defined in general terms as the decline, during the course of the accounting period, in the current value of the stock of fixed assets owned and used by a producer as a result of physical deterioration, normal obsolescence or normal accidental damage. It excludes the value of fixed assets destroyed by acts of war or exceptional events such as major natural disasters which occur very infrequently. Such losses are recorded in the System in the account for "Other changes in the volume of assets". Consumption of fixed capital is defined in the System in a way that is intended to be theoretically appropriate and relevant for purposes of economic analysis. Its value may deviate considerably from depreciation as recorded in business accounts or as allowed for taxation purposes, especially when there is inflation.

6.180. Fixed assets may have been purchased in the past at times when both relative prices and the general price level were very different from prices in the current period. In order to be consistent with the other entries in the same production account, consumption of fixed capital must be valued with reference to the same overall set of current prices as that used to value output and intermediate consumption. Consumption of fixed capital should reflect underlying resource costs and relative demands at the time the production takes place. It should therefore be calculated using the actual or estimated prices and rentals of fixed assets prevailing at that time and not at the times the goods were originally acquired. The "historic costs" of fixed assets, i.e., the prices originally paid for them, may become quite irrelevant for the calculation of consumption of fixed capital if prices change sufficiently over time.

2. Consumption of fixed capital and rentals on fixed assets

6.181. The rental is the amount payable by the user of a fixed asset to its owner, under an operating lease or similar contract, for the right to use that asset in production for a specified period of time. The rental needs to be large enough to cover not only the reduction in the value of the asset over that period—i.e., the consumption of fixed capital—but also the interest costs on the value of the asset at the start of the period and any other costs incurred by the owner. The interest costs may consist either of actual interest paid on borrowed funds or the loss of interest incurred as a result of investing own funds in the purchase of the fixed asset instead of a financial asset. Whether owned or rented, the full cost of using the fixed asset in production is measured by the actual or imputed rental on the asset and not by consumption of fixed capital alone. When the asset is actually rented under an operating lease or similar contract, the rental is recorded under intermediate consumption as the purchase of a service produced by the lessor. When the user and the owner are one and the same unit, consumption of fixed capital represents only part of the cost of using the asset.

6.182. The value of a fixed asset to its owner at any point of time is determined by the present value of the future rentals (i.e., the sum of the discounted values of the stream of future rentals) that can be expected over its remaining service life. Consumption of fixed capital is therefore measured by the decrease, between the beginning and the end of the current accounting period, in the present value of the remaining sequence of rentals. The extent of the decrease will be influenced not only by the amount by which the efficiency of the asset may have declined during the current period but also by the shortening of its service life and the rate at which its economic efficiency declines over its remaining service life. The flow of future rentals which determine the present values used to derive consumption of fixed capital must, of course, be valued at current prices or rentals.

6.183. The calculation of consumption of fixed capital is a forward-looking measure that is determined by future, and not past, events. The future rentals on which its value depend themselves depend upon the benefits which institutional units expect to derive in the future from using the asset in production over the remainder of its service life. Unlike depreciation as usually calculated in business accounts, consumption of fixed capital is not, at least in principle, a method of allocating the costs of past expenditures on fixed assets over subsequent accounting periods. The value of a fixed asset at a given moment in time depends only on the remaining benefits to be derived from its use, and consumption of fixed capital must be based on values calculated in this way.

3. The calculation of consumption of fixed capital

6.184. Depreciation as recorded in business accounts may not provide the right kind of information for the calculation of consumption of fixed capital, for the reasons given above. If data on depreciation are used, they must, at the very least, be adjusted from historic costs to current prices. However, depreciation allowances for tax purposes have often been grossly manipulated in quite arbitrary ways to try to influence rates of investment and are best ignored altogether in many cases. It is therefore recommended that independent estimates of consumption of fixed capital should be compiled in conjunction with estimates of the capital stock. These can be built up from data on gross fixed capital formation in the past combined with estimates of the rates at which the efficiency of fixed assets decline over their service lives. As a result of market forces, the purchaser's price of a new fixed asset should provide a good initial estimate of the present value of the future rentals which can be derived from it. Subsequent changes in its value can then be deduced analytically from information or assumptions about the rate at which its efficiency in production declines over time. This method of building up estimates of the capital stock and changes in the capital stock over time is known as the perpetual inventory method, or PIM. Estimates of consumption of fixed capital are obtained as a by-product of the PIM.

4. The coverage of consumption of fixed capital

6.185. Capital consumption is calculated for all fixed assets—that is, tangible and intangible fixed assets—owned by producers, but not for valuables (precious metals, precious stones, etc.) that are acquired precisely because their value, in real terms, is not expected to decline over time. Fixed assets must themselves have been produced as outputs from processes of production as defined in the System. Consumption of fixed capital does not, therefore, cover the depletion or degradation of non-produced assets such as land, mineral or other deposits, or coal, oil, or natural gas.

6.186. Capital consumption must, however, be calculated in respect of fixed assets which are constructed to improve land, such as drainage systems, dykes, or breakwaters or on assets which are constructed on or through land—roads, railway tracks, tunnels, dams, etc. Although some structures such as roads or railway tracks may appear to have infinite lives if properly maintained, it must be remembered that the value of assets may decline not merely because they deteriorate physically but because of a decrease in the demand for their services as a result of technical progress and the appearance of new substitutes for them. In practice, many structures, including roads and railway tracks, are scrapped or demolished because they

have become obsolete. Even though the estimated service lives may be very long for some structures, such as roads, bridges, dams, etc., they cannot be assumed to be infinite. Thus, capital consumption needs to be calculated for all types of structures, including those owned and maintained by government units, as well as machinery and equipment.

6.187. Losses of fixed assets due to normal accidental damage are also included under consumption of fixed capital; that is, damage caused to assets used in production resulting from their exposure to the risk of fires, storms, accidents due to human errors, etc. When these kinds of accidents occur with predictable regularity they are taken into account in calculating the average service lives of the goods in question. At the level of the economy as a whole, the actual normal accidental damage within a given accounting period may be expected to be equal, or close, to the average. However, for an individual unit, or group of units, any difference between the average and the actual normal accidental damage within a given period is recorded in the other changes in volume of assets account. On the other hand, losses due to war or to major natural disasters which occur very infrequently—major earthquakes, volcanic eruptions, tidal waves, exceptionally severe hurricanes, etc.— are not included under consumption of fixed capital. There is no reason for such losses to be charged in the production account as costs of production. The values of the assets lost in these ways are recorded in the other changes in volume of assets account. Similarly, although consumption of fixed capital includes reductions in the value of fixed assets resulting from normal, expected rates of obsolescence, it should not include losses due to unexpected technological developments that may significantly shorten the service lives of a group of existing fixed assets. Such losses are treated in the same way as losses due to above average rates of normal accidental damage. In practice, however, it may be difficult to measure such losses.

5. The perpetual inventory method

6.188. A brief explanation of how consumption of fixed capital may be calculated as a by-product of the perpetual inventory method of calculating the capital stock is given in this section.

Calculation of the gross capital stock at current prices

6.189. The perpetual inventory method requires an estimate to be made of the stock of fixed assets in existence and in the hands of producers. This is done by estimating how many of the fixed assets installed as a result of gross fixed capital formation undertaken in previous years have survived to the current period. Average service lives, or survival functions, based on observations or technical studies may be applied to past investments for this purpose. Fixed assets purchased at different prices in the past have then to be revalued at the prices of the current period. This may be done by utilizing appropriate price indices for fixed assets. The construction of suitable price indices covering long periods of time raises difficult conceptual and practical problems, but these technical problems of price measurement are not peculiar to the PIM method and will not be pursued further in the present context. The stock of fixed assets surviving from past investment and revalued at the purchasers' prices of the current period is described as the gross capital stock. The gross capital stock can also be measured at the prices of some base year if it is desired to have annual time series for the gross capital stock at constant prices.

Relative efficiencies and rentals

6.190. The inputs into production obtained from the use of a given fixed asset tend to diminish over time. The rate at which the efficiency declines may vary from one type of asset to another. Various profiles are possible; for example:

(a)   Constant efficiency until the asset disintegrates; for example, an electric light bulb;

(b)   A linear decline in efficiency; the service life ends when efficiency declines to zero;

(c)   A constant geometric, or exponential, decline in efficiency.

In each of these cases, it is sufficient to know one parameter, the length of the service life or the rate of geometric decline, in order to have full information about the pattern of relative efficiency over time.

6.191. Another plausible profile is a combination of cases (a) and (b) above; i.e., a linear rate of decline with the asset disintegrating before efficiency has fallen to zero. This mixed case will be referred to later.

6.192. The amounts of rentals which users are prepared to pay will be proportional to the relative efficiencies of the assets. If one is twice as efficient as another for the user's purposes, the user will be prepared to pay a rental which is also twice as great. Thus, the efficiency profiles of fixed assets determine the profiles of the rentals which they command over their service lives (assuming that prices remain, or are held, constant). Once the profiles of the rentals over the service lives of the fixed asset have been determined, it becomes possible to calculate the consumption of fixed capital, period by period.

Rates of capital consumption

6.193. Consumption of fixed capital is proportional to the reduction in the present value of the remaining rentals, as explained earlier. This reduction, and the rate at which it takes place over time, must be clearly distinguished from the decline in the efficiency of the capital assets themselves. The distinction is most obvious in the first case listed in paragraph 6.190. Although the efficiency, and hence the rental, of an asset may remain constant from period to period until it disintegrates, the capital consumption is not constant. It can easily be shown in this case that the decline in the present value of the remaining

rentals from period to period is considerably lower earlier in the life of the asset than when the asset is approaching the end of its life. Capital consumption tends to increase as the asset gets older even though the efficiency and rental remain constant to the end. However, the gradual increase in capital consumption could be eliminated if the efficiency and rentals were tending to decrease over time even before the asset disintegrates. This is the mixed case referred to above obtained by combining profiles (a) and (b) so that the rentals fall at a linear rate to a cut-off point before they reach zero. It can easily be demonstrated that this kind of profile is capable of generating a constant rate of capital consumption over the life of the asset. In other words, it can lead to constant or "straight-line depreciation" as it is commonly described.

6.194. One major advantage of straight-line depreciation is its simplicity. It can be estimated merely by dividing the purchaser's price of a new fixed asset by the number of years of service life, assuming that the purchaser's price of a new asset approximates the present value of the future rentals. From a theoretical point of view, the validity of straight-line depreciation depends upon whether it is reasonable to assume some combination of profiles (a) and (b) for the rentals. Because of its simplicity, straight-line depreciation is widely used in business accounting. In principle, it is also acceptable for purposes of calculating consumption of fixed capital in the System, provided that the implied profile for the rentals is believed to be not unrealistic.

6.195. On the other hand, when the efficiency and rentals on a fixed asset decline at a constant geometric rate from period to period it can easily be shown that capital consumption also declines at the same rate. The coincidence between the two rates is extremely convenient analytically and this case figures prominently in the theoretical literature. It is also easy to calculate. In theory the life of an asset is infinite under geometric depreciation. However, when an asset has an observed average service life of n years, a good approximation to geometric depreciation can be obtained by calculating the rate of depreciation as a constant fraction, $2/n$, of the written down value of the good at the start of each year. This is the so-called double declining balance method.

6.196. The rate of depreciation using the double-declining balance method is obviously twice that of linear depreciation in the first year. However, the absolute value of capital consumption declines from year to year under any geometric, or declining balance, formula, so that at some point it must fall below the corresponding figure that would be obtained using straight-line depreciation. In other words, the double-declining balance method leads to a much more "accelerated" pattern of capital consumption. This profile is considered to be more realistic by many economists, and observations on the prices of many existing tangible fixed assets tend to support it. Many business accountants also prefer an accelerated depreciation method as being more "prudent" because it tends to lead to lower values for assets in the balance sheet.

6.197. Both the linear and the geometric, or declining-balance, methods are easy to apply. The choice between them depends upon knowledge, or assumptions, about the implied profiles of rentals which underlie them. It is not possible on a priori grounds to recommend the use of one in preference to the other in all circumstances. It is possible, for example, that linear depreciation may be realistic in the case of structures, while geometric depreciation is more realistic in the case of machinery or equipment. In practice, the choice of formula seems to rest between one or the other of these two methods, and there seems little justification for the use of more complex formulae.

Values of consumption of fixed capital

6.198. The value of the capital consumption on a fixed asset may be estimated by applying either the linear or geometric depreciation formula to the actual or estimated current purchaser's price of a new asset of the same type. In the case of geometric depreciation, the absolute value of the consumption of fixed capital depends on the age of the asset in question, but not, of course, in the case of linear depreciation. Consumption of fixed capital has to be calculated in this way for all the fixed assets which make up the gross capital stock valued at current prices. The consumption of fixed capital for a particular sector or industry is then obtained as the sum of the estimates for all the fixed assets owned by the units in that sector or industry.

Gross and net capital stocks

6.199. The value at current prices of the gross capital stock is obtained by making use of price indices for fixed assets to value all fixed assets still in use at the actual or estimated current purchasers' prices for new assets of the same type, irrespective of the age of the assets. The net, or written-down value of a fixed asset is equal to the actual or estimated current purchaser's price of a new asset of the same type less the cumulative value of the consumption of fixed capital accrued up to that point in time. The values in earlier periods must, of course, all be calculated with reference to the current purchaser's price of a new asset for this purpose. The sum of the written-down values of all the fixed assets still in use is described as the net capital stock.

6.200. Fixed assets figure prominently in the balance sheets of their

owners. The values to be recorded in the balance sheets of the System are the net, or written-down values just described. To be precise, the value of a fixed asset shown in the balance sheet is the actual or estimated purchaser's price of a new asset of that type at the time the balance sheet is drawn up less the cumulative consumption of fixed capital incurred up to that time calculated with reference to the same purchaser's price.

6. "Gross" and "net" recording

6.201. The consumption of fixed capital is one of the most important elements in the System. In most cases, when a distinction is drawn between "gross" and "net" recording "gross" means without deducting consumption of fixed capital while recording "net" means after deducting consumption of fixed capital. In particular, all the major balancing items in the accounts from value added through to saving may be recorded gross or net: i.e., before or after deducting consumption of fixed capital. It should also be noted that consumption of fixed capital is typically quite large compared with most of the net balancing items. It may account for 10 per cent or more of total GDP.

6.202. It is clear from the previous sections that the consumption of fixed capital is one of the most difficult items in the accounts to measure and estimate. The depreciation figures recorded in business accounts, or allowed for tax purposes, may be very difficult to adjust to bring them into line with consumption of fixed capital as understood in economic theory and defined in the System, while it may not be possible to estimate consumption of fixed capital using the perpetual inventory method if long time series of gross fixed capital formation are not available in some detail. Moreover, consumption of fixed capital does not represent the aggregate value of a set of transactions. It is an imputed value whose economic significance is different from entries in the accounts based mainly on market transactions.

6.203. For these reasons, the major balancing items in national accounts have always tended to be recorded both gross and net of consumption of fixed capital. This tradition is continued in the System where provision is also made for balancing items from value added through to saving to be recorded both ways. In general, the gross figure is obviously the easier to estimate and may, therefore, be more reliable, but the net figure is usually the one that is conceptually more appropriate and relevant for analytical purposes.

J. Basic, producers' and purchasers' prices

1. Introduction

6.204. More than one set of prices may be used to value outputs and inputs depending upon how taxes and subsidies on products, and also transport charges, are recorded. Moreover, value

added taxes, (VAT), and similar deductible taxes may also be recorded in more than one way. The methods of valuation used in the System are explained in this section.

2. Basic and producers' prices

6.205. The System utilizes two kinds of output prices, namely, basic prices and producers' prices:

(a) The *basic price* is the amount receivable by the producer from the purchaser for a unit of a good or service produced as output minus any tax payable, and plus any subsidy receivable, on that unit as a consequence of its production or sale. It excludes any transport charges invoiced separately by the producer;

(b) The *producer's price* is the amount receivable by the producer from the purchaser for a unit of a good or service produced as output minus any VAT, or similar deductible tax, invoiced to the purchaser. It excludes any transport charges invoiced separately by the producer.

The amounts charged by non-market producers when they sell output at prices that are not economically significant do not constitute basic or producers' prices as just defined. Prices that are not economically significant are not used to value the output sold at such prices: instead, such output is valued by its costs of production (see paragraph 6.220). Neither the producer's nor the basic price includes any amounts receivable in respect of VAT, or similar deductible tax, invoiced on the output sold. The difference between the two is that to obtain the basic price any other tax payable per unit of output is deducted from the producer's price while any subsidy receivable per unit of output is added. Both producers' and basic prices are actual transaction prices which can be directly observed and recorded. Basic prices are often reported in statistical inquiries and some official "producer price" indices actually refer to basic prices rather than to producers' prices as defined here. When output produced for own final consumption, or own gross fixed capital formation, is valued at basic prices, it is valued at the estimated basic prices that would be receivable by the producer if the output were to be sold on the market.

6.206. When output is recorded at basic prices, any tax on the product actually payable on the output is treated as if it were paid by the purchaser directly to the government instead of being an integral part of the price paid to the producer. Conversely, any subsidy on the product is treated as if it were received directly by the purchaser and not the producer. The basic price measures the amount retained by the producer and is, therefore, the price most relevant for the producer's decision-taking. It is becoming increasingly common in many countries for producers to itemize taxes separately on their invoices so that purchasers are informed about how much they are paying to the producer and how much as taxes to the government.

VAT and similar deductible taxes

6.207. Many countries have adopted some form of VAT. VAT is a wide-ranging tax usually designed to cover most or all goods and services. In some countries, VAT may replace most other forms of taxes on products, but VAT may also be levied in addition to some other taxes on products, such as excise duties on tobacco, alcoholic drink or fuel oils.

6.208. VAT is a tax on products collected in stages by enterprises. There exist in some countries taxes that are narrower in scope than VAT but may also be deductible by producers. They are treated in the System in the same way as VAT. Producers are required to charge certain percentage rates of VAT on the goods or services they sell. The VAT is shown separately on the sellers' invoices so that purchasers know the amounts they have paid. However, producers are not required to pay to the government the full amounts of the VAT invoiced to their customers because they are usually permitted to deduct the VAT that they themselves have paid on goods and services purchased for their own intermediate consumption or gross fixed capital formation. Producers are obliged to pay only the difference between the VAT on their sales and the VAT on their purchases for intermediate consumption or capital formation—hence the expression value added tax. VAT is not usually charged on sales to non-residents—i.e., exports. The percentage rate of VAT is also liable to vary between different categories of goods and services and also according to the type of purchaser.

6.209. The following terminology needs to be defined:

(a) *Invoiced VAT*: this is the VAT payable on the sales of a producer; it is shown separately on the invoice which the producer presents to the purchaser;

(b) *Deductible VAT*: this is the VAT payable on purchases of goods or services intended for intermediate consumption, gross fixed capital formation or for resale which a producer is permitted to deduct from his own VAT liability to the government in respect of VAT invoiced to his customers;

(c) *Non-deductible VAT*: this is VAT payable by a purchaser which is not deductible from his own VAT liability, if any.

Thus, a market producer is able to recover the costs of any deductible VAT payable on his own purchases by reducing the amount of his own VAT liability in respect of the VAT invoiced to his own customers. On the other hand, the VAT paid by households for purposes of final consumption or fixed capital formation in dwellings is not deductible. The VAT payable by non-market producers owned by government units or NPIs may also not be deductible.

Gross and net recording of VAT

6.210. There are two alternative systems that may be used to record VAT, i.e., the "gross" or "net" systems. Under the gross system all transactions are recorded including the amounts of any invoiced VAT. Thus, the purchaser and the seller record the same price, irrespective of whether or not the purchaser is able to deduct the VAT subsequently.

6.211. While the gross system of recording seems to accord with the traditional notion of recording at "market" prices, it presents some difficulties. First, practical experience with the operation of VAT over many years in a number of countries has shown it may be difficult, if not impossible, to utilize the gross system because of the way in which business accounts are computed and records are kept. Sales are normally reported excluding invoiced VAT in most industrial inquiries and business surveys. Conversely, purchases of goods and services by producers are usually recorded excluding deductible VAT. Although the gross system has been tried in some countries, it has had to be abandoned for these reasons. Secondly, it can be argued that the gross system distorts economic reality to the extent that it does not reflect the amounts of VAT actually paid by businesses. Large amounts of invoiced VAT are deductible and thus represent only notional or putative tax liabilities.

6.212. The System therefore requires that the net system of recording VAT should be followed. In the net system:

(a) Outputs of goods and services are valued excluding invoiced VAT: imports are similarly valued excluding invoiced VAT;

(b) Purchases of goods and services are recorded including non-deductible VAT.

Under the net system, VAT is recorded as being payable by purchasers, not sellers, and then only by those purchasers who are not able to deduct it. Almost all VAT is therefore recorded in the System as being paid on final uses—mainly on household consumption. Small amounts of VAT may, however, be paid by businesses in respect of certain kinds of purchases on which VAT may not be deductible.

6.213. The disadvantage of the net system is that different prices must be recorded for the two parties to the same transaction when the VAT is not deductible. The price recorded for the producer does not include invoiced VAT whereas the price recorded for the purchaser does include the invoiced VAT whenever it is not deductible. Thus, on aggregate, the total value of the expenditures recorded for purchasers must exceed the total value of the corresponding sales receipts recorded for producers by the total amount raised in non-deductible VAT.

6.214. The traditional concept of the "market" price becomes somewhat blurred under a system of VAT or similar deductible taxes because there may be two different prices for a single transaction: one from the seller's point of view and another from the purchaser's, depending upon whether or not the tax is deductible. Moreover, it is difficult to interpret the producer's price defined to exclude invoiced VAT—i.e., a tax on a product—as a "market" price in the traditional sense of that term. The producer's price thus defined is a hybrid which excludes some, but not all, taxes on products. The basic price, which does not include any taxes on the output (but includes subsidies on the output) becomes a clearer concept in these circumstances and, partly for this reason, is the preferred method for valuing the output of producers.

3. Purchasers' prices

6.215. The purchaser's price is the amount paid by the purchaser, excluding any deductible VAT or similar deductible tax, in order to take delivery of a unit of a good or service at the time and place required by the purchaser. The purchaser's price of a good includes any transport charges paid separately by the purchaser to take delivery at the required time and place.

6.216. When comparing the purchaser's price with the producer's or basic price, it is important to specify whether they refer to the same transaction or two different transactions. For certain purposes, including input-output analysis, it may be convenient to compare the price paid by the final purchaser of a good after it has passed through the wholesale and retail distribution chains with the producer's price received by its original producer. In this case the prices refer to two different transactions taking place at quite different times and locations: they must differ at least by the amount of the wholesale and retail trade margins.

6.217. When the prices refer to the same transaction, that is, the purchaser buys directly from the producer, the purchaser's price may exceed the producer's price by:

(a) The value of any non-deductible VAT, payable by the purchaser; and

(b) The value of any transport charges on a good paid separately by the purchaser and not included in the producer's price.

It follows that the purchaser's price may exceed the basic price by the amount of the two items just listed plus the value of any taxes less subsidies on the product (other than VAT).

K. Valuation of outputs and inputs

1. Output

6.218. Goods and services produced for sale on the market at economically significant prices may be valued either at basic prices or at producer's prices. The preferred method of valuation is at basic prices, especially when a system of VAT, or similar deductible tax, is in operation, although producer's prices may be used when valuation at basic prices is not feasible.

6.219. Output produced for own final use should be valued at the average basic prices of the same goods or services sold on the market, provided they are sold in sufficient quantities to enable reliable estimates to be made of those average prices. If not, such non-market output should be valued by the total production costs incurred, including consumption of fixed capital and any taxes (less subsidies) on production other than taxes or subsidies on products. The non-market output produced by government units and NPIs and supplied free, or at prices that are not economically significant, to other institutional units or the community as a whole is valued by total production costs, including consumption of fixed capital and taxes (less subsidies) on production other than taxes or subsidies on products.

2. Intermediate consumption

6.220. Expenditures by enterprises on goods or services intended to be used for intermediate consumption should be valued at purchasers' prices. Intermediate inputs obtained from other establishments belonging to the same enterprise should be valued at the same prices as were used to value them as outputs of those establishments plus any additional transport charges not included in the output values.

6.221. In the absence of VAT or similar deductible taxes, the total value of the intermediate consumption of an enterprise is the same whether valued at purchasers' prices or at producers' or ex-customs prices, (see chapter XV for the definition of ex-customs prices). The use of producers' or ex-custom prices implies that purchasers are treated as purchasing the services of wholesalers and retailers separately from the goods which pass through wholesale and retail distribution: they are also treated as purchasing goods and transportation services separately when they are invoiced or purchased separately. While the use of producers' prices leads to a different allocation of expenditures from the use of purchasers' prices, it does not change the total value of the expenditures. However, when a system of VAT or similar taxes is in operation, expenditures by enterprises on goods or services intended for intermediate use may include small amounts of non-deductible VAT which are excluded from the producers' prices.

L. Gross and net value added (B.1)

1. Introduction

6.222. Value added is the balancing item in the production account for an institutional unit or sector, or establishment or industry. It measures the value created by production and may be calculated either before or after deducting the consumption of fixed capital on the fixed assets used. As stated above:

(a) *Gross value added* is defined as the value of output less the value of intermediate consumption;

(b) *Net value added* is defined as the value of output less the values of both intermediate consumption and consumption of fixed capital.

To avoid repetition, only gross value added will be cited in the following sections when the corresponding conclusions for net value added are obvious.

6.223. Gross value added is an unduplicated measure of output in which the values of the goods and services used as intermediate inputs are eliminated from the value of output. The production process itself can be described by a vector of the quantities of goods and services consumed or produced in which inputs carry a negative sign. By associating a price vector with this quantity vector, gross value added is obtained as the inner product of the two vectors.

Let q = the vector of quantities consumed or produced

p = the vector of prices

Then

gross value added = $p'q$

Alternative measures of gross value added may be obtained by combining different price vectors with a single quantity vector. For example, gross value added may be measured using the prices of some other time period or some other country. However, the price and quantity vectors are not independent of each other. The technology used—i.e., the particular production process selected—is itself influenced by the relative input and output prices confronting the producer. The quantities therefore depend on the prices. A process which is economically efficient and profitable at one set of prices may cease to be so at another and would, therefore, not be used at those prices. For this reason, figures of gross value added obtained by revaluing the quantities at very different sets of relative prices may have little economic significance and may even become negative.

6.224. From an accounting point of view, gross value added is essentially a balancing item. As such, it is not an independent entity. It is defined in the context of a production account, being a function of all the other entries in the account. There is no actual set of goods or services that can be identified with the gross value added of an individual producer, sector or industry. Gross value added is not measured as the sum of any specific set of transactions. As a balancing item it lacks dimensions in the sense that it has no quantity units of its own in which it can be measured, and hence also no prices of its own.

2. Alternative measures of value added

6.225. As indicated above, alternative measures of gross value added may be obtained by associating different price vectors with a given vector of input and output quantities. The various measures which may be derived using the different sets of prices recognized in the System are considered below.

Gross value added at basic prices

6.226. Gross value added at basic prices is defined as output valued at basic prices less intermediate consumption valued at purchasers' prices. Although the outputs and inputs are valued using different sets of prices, for brevity the value added is described by the prices used to value the outputs. From the point of view of the producer, purchasers' prices for inputs and basic prices for outputs represent the prices actually paid and received. Their use leads to a measure of gross value added which is particularly relevant for the producer. The resulting measure has also some convenient properties for aggregation purposes as explained later, although there is no named aggregate in the System which corresponds to the sum of the gross values added of all enterprises measured at basic prices.

Gross value added at producers' prices

6.227. Gross value added at producers' prices is defined as output valued at producers' prices less intermediate consumption valued at purchasers' prices. As already explained, in the absence of VAT, the total value of the intermediate inputs consumed is the same whether they are valued at producers' or at purchasers' prices, in which case this measure of gross value added is the same as one which uses producers' prices to value both inputs and outputs. It is an economically meaningful measure that is equivalent to the traditional measure of gross value added at market prices. However, in the presence of VAT, the producer's price excludes invoiced VAT, and it would be inappropriate to describe this measure as being at "market" prices.

6.228. Both this measure of gross value added and that described in the previous section use purchasers' prices to value intermediate inputs. The difference between the two measures is entirely attributable to their differing treatments of taxes or subsidies on products payable on outputs (other than invoiced VAT). By definition, the value of output at producers' prices exceeds that at basic prices by the amount, if any, of the taxes, less subsidies, on the output so that the two associated measures of gross value added must differ by the same amount.

Gross value added at factor cost

6.229. Gross value added at factor cost is not a concept used explicitly in the System. Nevertheless, it can easily be derived from either of the measures of gross value added presented above by subtracting the value of any taxes, less subsidies, on production payable out of gross value added as defined. For example, the only taxes on production remaining to be paid out of gross value added at basic prices consist of "other taxes on production". These consist mostly of current taxes (or subsidies) on the labour or capital employed in the enterprise, such as payroll taxes or current taxes on vehicles or buildings. Gross value added at factor cost can, therefore, be derived from gross value added at basic prices by subtracting "other taxes, less subsidies, on production".

6.230. The conceptual difficulty with gross value added at factor cost is that there is no observable vector of prices such that gross value added at factor cost is obtained directly by multiplying the price vector by the vector of quantities of inputs and outputs that defines the production process. By definition, "other taxes or subsidies on production" are not taxes or subsidies on products that can be eliminated from the input and output prices. Thus, despite its traditional name, gross value added at factor cost is not strictly a measure of value added.

6.231. Gross value added at factor cost is essentially a measure of income and not output. It represents the amount remaining for distribution out of gross value added, however defined, after the payment of all taxes on production and the receipt of all subsidies on production. It makes no difference which measure of gross value added is used because the measures considered above differ only in respect of the amounts of the taxes or subsidies on production which remain payable out of gross value added.

6.232. Claims on gross value added, other than payments of taxes, less subsidies, to government used to be described as "factor incomes". While the concept of factor income is no longer used in the System, gross value added at factor cost could be interpreted as measuring the value of the fund out of which so-called "factor incomes" can be paid: it follows that it is equal to the total value of the "factor" incomes generated by production.

M. The main aggregates associated with value added

1. Introduction

6.233. The underlying rationale behind the concept of gross domestic product (GDP) for the economy as a whole is that it should measure the total gross values added produced by all institutional units resident in the economy. However, while the concept of GDP is based on this principle, GDP as defined in the System may include not only the sum of the gross values added of all resident producers but also various taxes on products, depending upon the precise ways in which outputs, inputs and imports are valued.

6.234. Assume initially that there is no VAT and that production accounts are compiled at "market prices", i.e., with outputs valued at producers' prices and intermediate inputs at purchasers' prices. Suppose further that the production accounts for all resident producers are aggregated and consolidated, thereby eliminating intermediate sales and purchases. It follows that the sum of the gross values added must be identical with the sum of final expenditures on consumption, gross capital formation and exports less imports. This is, of course, the basic identity of national accounting. The identity must hold provided final expenditures and imports are valued consistently with the inputs and outputs in the production accounts. The identity makes it possible to calculate GDP directly from data on final expenditures and imports without utilizing production (or income) data. Total GDP can therefore be estimated from production accounts—the production approach—or quite independently from final expenditures and imports—the expenditure approach.

6.235. In the System, however, GDP at market prices is defined from the expenditure side as total final expenditures at purchasers' prices less total imports valued free on board (f.o.b.) (and not at purchasers' prices including taxes less subsidies on imports). Thus, although imports valued f.o.b. are valued in the same way as exports, they are not valued consistently with other final expenditures nor with the entries in the production account, so that the identity between GDP from the expenditure side and GDP from the production side breaks down. As import taxes are not deducted along with total imports f.o.b. when calculating GDP from the expenditure side, it follows that import taxes must be added to GDP from the production side in order to restore the identity. Thus, GDP at market prices as defined in the System is the sum of the gross values added of all resident producers at market prices plus taxes less subsidies on imports.

6.236. The situation is more complicated when a system of VAT, or similar deductible taxes, is in operation. As explained above, the net system of recording VAT is used in the System: i.e., the sales of producers are recorded excluding invoiced VAT while purchases are recorded including VAT which is not deductible by the purchaser. In consequence, the total value of purchases throughout the economy exceeds the value of the corresponding sales by the amount of non-deductible VAT. It follows that not only import taxes but all non-deductible VAT (or similar taxes) must be added to the sum of the gross values added of all resident producers in order to arrive at GDP as defined from the expenditure side.

2. A résumé of the main identities

6.237. Given the general explanations of the previous section, the main identities connecting the aggregates of the System are summarized in this section. GDP at market prices is defined from the expenditure side as:

> Household final consumption expenditure at purchasers' prices
> + NPI final consumption expenditure at purchasers' prices
> + Government final consumption expenditure at purchasers' prices
> + Gross fixed capital formation at purchasers' prices
> + Acquisition less disposals of valuables at purchasers' prices
> + Changes in inventories
> + Exports at purchasers' prices at the frontier (f.o.b.)
> - Imports valued f.o.b.

Given this definition of GDP, the following identities hold when the summations are taken over all resident producers:

(a) GDP =
the sum of the gross values added at producers' prices
+ taxes, less subsidies, on imports
+ non-deductible VAT;

(b) GDP = ·
the sum of the gross values added at basic prices
+ all taxes, less subsidies, on products;

(c) GDP =
the sum of the gross values added at factor cost
+ all taxes, less subsidies, on products
+ all other taxes, less subsidies, on production.

In cases (b) and (c) the item taxes, less subsidies, on products includes taxes and subsidies on imports as well as on outputs.

3. Domestic production

6.238. GDP is intended to be a measure of the value created by the productive activity of resident institutional units. Although for the kinds of technical reasons just given, it may not be identical with the sum of the gross values added of resident producers it nevertheless consists mainly of the latter.

6.239. It should be noted, however, that GDP is not intended to measure the production taking place within the geographical boundary of the economic territory. Some of the production of a resident producer may take place abroad, while some of the production taking place within the geographical boundary of the economy may be carried out by non-resident producer units. For example, a resident producer may have teams of employees working abroad temporarily on the installation, repair or servicing of equipment. This output is an export of a resident producer and the productive activity does not contribute to the GDP of the country in which it takes place. Thus, the distinction between resident and non-resident institutional units is crucial to the definition and coverage of GDP. In practice, of course, most of the productive activity of resident producers takes place within the country in which they are resident. However, producers in service industries which typically have to deliver their outputs directly to their clients wherever they are located are increasingly tending to engage in production in more than one country, a practice which is encouraged by rapid transportation and instantaneous communication facilities. Geographical boundaries between adjacent countries are becoming less significant for mobile service producers, especially in small countries bordered by several other countries.

VII. The primary distribution of income account

A. Introduction

7.1. The primary distribution of income account consists of two consecutive accounts: the generation of income account and the allocation of primary income account (see tables 7.1 and 7.2). When appropriate, the latter may be divided into two further sub-accounts: the entrepreneurial income account and the allocation of other primary income account (see table 7.3).

7.2. The general purpose of the primary distribution of income account is to show how primary incomes are distributed among institutional units and sectors. Primary incomes are incomes that accrue to institutional units as a consequence of their involvement in processes of production or ownership of assets that may be needed for purposes of production. They are payable out of the value added created by production. The primary incomes that accrue by lending or renting financial or tangible non-produced assets, including land, to other units for use in production are described as property incomes. Receipts from taxes on production and imports are treated as primary incomes of governments even though not all of them may be recorded as payable out of the value added of enterprises. Primary incomes do not include social contributions and benefits, current taxes on income, wealth, etc. and other current transfers, such current transfers being recorded in the secondary distribution of income account.

1. The generation of income account

7.3. The generation of income account is compiled for resident enterprises or groups of resident enterprises, i.e., for resident institutional units in their capacities as producers of goods and services. It represents a further extension or elaboration of the production account in which the primary incomes accruing to government units and to the units participating directly in production are recorded. Like the production account, it may be compiled for establishments and industries as well as for institutional units and sectors. The generation of income account shows the sectors, sub-sectors or industries in which the primary incomes originate, as distinct from the sectors or subsectors destined to receive such incomes. For example, the compensation of employees recorded in the generation of income account for the household sector consists of the total compensation of employees payable by unincorporated enterprises owned by households. This item is very different from the total compensation of employees receivable by the household sector that is recorded in the account below, the allocation of primary income account.

7.4. The resources, listed on the right side of the generation of income account, consist of only a single item, value added, the balancing item carried forward from the production account. As stated in chapter VI, gross value added is defined as the value of output minus the value of intermediate consumption. Value added may also be measured net: i.e., after deducting the consumption of fixed capital on the fixed assets used in the production process. Consumption of fixed capital is a cost of production that should preferably be deducted from output along with intermediate consumption whenever possible. However, the data available do not always permit satisfactory estimates to be made of consumption of fixed capital, so that provision has to be made in the accounts of the System for value added to be measured gross as well as net. Provision must therefore also be made throughout the remaining accounts of the System for the relevant balancing items to be measured gross or net of consumption of fixed capital. The concept and measurement of consumption of fixed capital has already been explained in detail in chapter VI. For simplicity, it will be assumed that value added is measured net, except when the context requires gross value added to be referred to explicitly.

7.5. The left side of the generation of income account records the uses of value added. As property incomes payable by enterprises are recorded in the following account, there are only two main types of charges that producers have to meet out of value added: compensation of employees payable to workers employed in the production process and any taxes, less subsidies, on production payable or receivable as a result of engaging in production. The latter consist of taxes payable or subsidies receivable on goods or services produced as outputs and other taxes or subsidies on production, such as those payable on the labour, machinery, buildings or other assets used in production. Taxes on production do not include any income taxes payable by the recipients of incomes accruing from production, whether employers or employees. Both compensation of employees and taxes on production may be payable by resident producers to non-residents.

Table 7.1.   Account II.1.1: Generation of income account

Uses Total	Uses: Goods & service acct	Uses: Rest of world acct	Uses S.1 Total economy	Uses S.15 NPISHs	Uses S.14 Households	Uses S.13 General government	Uses S.12 Financial corporations	Uses S.11 Non-financial corporations	Code	Transactions and balancing items	Res S.11 Non-financial corporations	Res S.12 Financial corporations	Res S.13 General government	Res S.14 Households	Res S.15 NPISHs	Res S.1 Total economy	Res: Rest of world acct	Res: Goods & service acct	Res Total
									B.1g/B.1*g	Value added, gross/ gross domestic product [1]	854	73	188	575	31	1 854			1 854
									B.1n/B.1*n	*Value added, net/ net domestic product* [1]	717	63	158	533	28	1 632			1 632
762			762	23	39	140	15	545	D.1	Compensation of employees									
569			569	12	39	87	10	421	D.11	Wages and salaries									
193			193	11	0	53	5	124	D.12	Employers' social contributions									
174			174	10	0	48	4	112	D.121	Employers' actual social contributions									
19			19	1	0	5	1	12	D.122	Employers' imputed social contributions									
235			235	0	3	2	3	86	D.2	Taxes on production and imports									
141			141						D.21	Taxes on products [2]									
121			121						D.211	Value added type taxes (VAT)									
17			17						D.212	Taxes and duties on imports excluding VAT									
17			17						D.2121	Import duties									
0			0						D.2122	Taxes on imports excluding VAT and duties									
1			1						D.213	Export taxes									
2			2						D.214	Taxes on products except VAT, import and export taxes									
94			94	0	3	2	3	86	D.29	Other taxes on production									
-44			-44	0	-1	0	0	-35	D.3	Subsidies									
-8			-8						D.31	Subsidies on products [2]									
0			0						D.311	Import subsidies									
0			0						D.312	Export subsidies									
-8			-8						D.319	Other subsidies on products									
-36			-36	0	-1	0	0	-35	D.39	Other subsidies on production									
459			459	8	92	46	55	258	B.2g	Operating surplus, gross									
442			442		442				B.3g	Mixed income, gross									
247			247	5	60	16	45	121	B.2n	*Operating surplus, net*									
432			432		432				B.3n	*Mixed income, net*									

1   For the total economy this item corresponds to gross domestic product, net domestic product respectively. It is equal to the value added of the institutional sectors plus taxes less subsidies on products.

2   For the valuation of output and the resulting contents of the items "Taxes on products" and "Subsidies on products", refer to chapter VI, paragraphs 6.210 to 6.227.

Table 7.2. Account II.1.2: Allocation of primary income account

Uses Total	Uses Goods and service account	Uses Rest of the world account	Uses S.1 Total economy	Uses S.15 NPISHs	Uses S.14 Households	Uses S.13 General government	Uses S.12 Financial corporations	Uses S.11 Non-financial corporations	Transactions and balancing items	Resources S.11 Non-financial corporations	Resources S.12 Financial corporations	Resources S.13 General government	Resources S.14 Households	Resources S.15 NPISHs	Resources S.1 Total economy	Resources Rest of the world account	Resources Goods and service account	Resources Total
									B.2g Operating surplus, gross	258	55	46	92	8	459			459
									B.3g Mixed income, gross				442		442			442
									B.2n Operating surplus, net	121	45	16	60	5	247			247
									B.3n Mixed income, net				432		432			432
6		6							D.1 Compensation of employees				766		766	2		768
6		6							D.11 Wages and salaries				573		573	2		575
									D.12 Employers' social contributions				193		193	0		193
									D.121 Employers' actual social contributions				174		174	0		174
									D.122 Employers' imputed social contributions				19		19	0		19
									D.2 Taxes on production and imports			235			235	0		235
									D.21 Taxes on products			141			141	0		141
									D.211 Value added type taxes (VAT)			121			121	0		121
									D.212 Taxes and duties on imports excluding VAT			17			17	0		17
									D.2121 Import duties			17			17	0		17
									D.2122 Taxes on imports excluding VAT and duties									
									D.213 Export taxes			0			0	0		0
									D.214 Taxes on products except VAT, import and export taxes			1			1	0		1
									D.29 Other taxes on production			94			94	0		94
									D.3 Subsidies			−44			−44	0		−44
									D.31 Subsidies on products			−8			−8	0		−8
									D.311 Import subsidies			0			0	0		0
									D.312 Export subsidies			0			0	0		0
									D.319 Other subsidies on products			−8			−8	0		−8
									D.39 Other subsidies on production			−36			−36	0		−36
454		63	391	6	41	42	167	135	D.4 Property income	86	141	32	150	7	416	38		454
230		13	217	6	14	35	106	56	D.41 Interest	33	106	14	49	7	209	21		230
120		36	84	0		0	36	48	D.42 Distributed income of corporations	3	25	18	57	0	103	17		120
60		0	60				36	24	D.421 Dividends	3	25	5	13	0	46	14		60
									D.422 Withdrawals from income of quasi-corporations									
14		14	0	0	0	0	0	0	D.43 Reinvested earnings on direct foreign investment	4	7	0	3	0	14	0		14
25		0	25				25		D.44 Property income attributed to insurance policy holders	5	0	0	20	0	25	0		25
65		0	65		27	7	0	31	D.45 Rent	41	3	0	21	0	65			65
1 883			1 883	9	1 409	227	29	209	B.5g/B.5*g Balance of primary incomes, gross/National income, gross									
1 661			1 661	6	1 367	197	19	72	B.5n/B.5*n *Balance of primary incomes, net/National income, net*									

Table 7.3. Primary distribution of income — identification of entrepreneurial income

Uses

Accounts	Total	Corresponding entries of the Goods and service account	Rest of the world account	S.1 Total economy	S.15 NPISHs	S.14 Households	S.13 General government	S.12 Financial corporations	S.11 Non-financial corporations	Transactions and balancing items	
II.1.2.1. Entrepreneurial income										B.2g	Operating surplus, gross
										B.3g	Mixed income, gross
										B.2n	*Operating surplus, net*
										B.3n	*Mixed income, net*
	260		24	236	2	7	9	131	87	D.4	Property income [1]
	176		10	166	2	0	2	106	56	D.41	Interest
										D.42	Distributed income of corporations
										D.421	Dividends
										D.422	Withdrawals from income of quasi-corporations
	14		14							D.43	Reinvested earnings on direct foreign investment
	25			25				25		D.44	Property income attributed to insurance policyholders
	45			45	0	7	7	0	31	D.45	Rent
	901			901	6	532	41	65	257	B.4g	Entrepreneurial income, gross
	679			679	3	490	11	55	120	B.4n	*Entrepreneurial income, net*
II.1.2.2. Allocation of other primary income										B.4g	Entrepreneurial income, gross
										B.4n	*Entrepreneurial income, net*
	6		6							D.1	Compensation of employees
	6		6							D.11	Wages and salaries
										D.12	Employers' social contributions
										D.121	Employers' actual social contributions
										D.122	Employers' imputed social contributions
	0		0							D.2	Taxes on production and imports
	0		0							D.21	Taxes on products
	0		0							D.211	Value added type taxes (VAT)
	0		0							D.212	Taxes and duties on imports excluding VAT
	0		0							D.2121	Import duties
	0		0							D.2122	Taxes on imports excluding VAT and duties
	0		0							D.213	Export taxes
	0		0							D.214	Taxes on products except VAT, import and export taxes
	0		0							D.29	Other taxes on production
	0		0							D.3	Subsidies
	0		0							D.31	Subsidies on products
	0		0							D.311	Import subsidies
	0		0							D.312	Export subsidies
	0		0							D.319	Other subsidies on products
	0		0							D.39	Other subsidies on production
	194		39	155	4	34	33	36	48	D.4	Property income [1]
	54		3	51	4	14	33			D.41	Interest
	120		36	84				36	48	D.42	Distributed income of corporations
	60		0	60				36	24	D.421	Dividends
	60		36	24				0	24	D.422	Withdrawals from income of quasi-corporations
	0			0				0	0	D.43	Reinvested earnings on direct foreign investment
										D.44	Property income attributed to insurance policyholders
	20			20	0	20				D.45	Rent
	1 883			1 883	9	1 409	227	29	209	B.5g/B.5*g	Balance of primary incomes, gross/National income, gross
	1 661			1 661	6	1 367	197	19	72	B.5n/B.5*n	*Balance of primary incomes, net/National income, net*

1 For the distribution of property income between the two sub-accounts II.1.2.1. and II.1.2.2. refer to chapter VII, paragraphs 7.17 to 7.19.

Resources

| S.11 | S.12 | S.13 | S.14 | S.15 | S.1 | Corresponding entries of the | | Total | Accounts |
| | | | | | | Rest of the world account | Goods and service account | | |
Non-financial corporations	Financial corporations	General government	House-holds	NPISHs	Total economy				
258	55	46	92	8	459			459	II.1.2.1.
			442		442			442	Entrepre-
121	45	16	60	5	247			247	neurial
			432		432			432	income
86	141	4	5	0	236	20		256	
33	106	0	0	0	139	15		154	
3	25	4	5	0	37	5		42	
3	25	4	5	0	37	5		42	
0	0	0	0	0	0	0		0	
4	7	0			11			11	
5	0	0	0		5			5	
41	3	0			44			44	
257	65	41	532	6	901			901	II.1.2.2.
120	55	11	490	3	679			679	Allocation
			766		766	2		768	of other
			573		573	2		575	primary
			193		193	0		193	income
			174		174	0		174	
			19		19	0		19	
		235			235	0		235	
		141			141	0		141	
		121			121	0		121	
		17			17	0		17	
		17			17	0		17	
		0			0	0		0	
		1			1	0		1	
		2			2	0		2	
		94			94	0		94	
		− 44			− 44	0		− 44	
		− 8			− 8	0		− 8	
		0			0	0		0	
		0			0	0		0	
		− 8			− 8	0		− 8	
		− 36			− 36	0		− 36	
		28	145	7	180	18		198	
		14	49	7	70	6		76	
		14	52	0	66	12		78	
		1	8	0	9	9		18	
		13	44	0	57	3		60	
			3	0	3			3	
			20	0	20			20	
			21	0	21			21	

7.6. The content of the item taxes, less subsidies, on production payable out of value added varies according to the way in which output is valued. Value added tax (VAT), or other similar deductible tax, invoiced on output is never treated as part of the price receivable by the producer from the purchaser. Invoiced VAT is therefore always omitted from value of output, whether output is valued at producers' or basic prices. Hence, invoiced VAT is not a charge against value added and is not recorded as a payable in the producer's generation of income account. However, when output is valued at producers' prices any other tax on product payable on the output is treated as an integral part of the price receivable by the producer from the purchaser. The tax is therefore recorded as being payable by the producer out of value added at producers' prices in the generation of income account—that is, as a component of the item "taxes less subsidies on production". Similarly, any subsidy on product on the output is recorded as being receivable by the producer from government in the generation of income account as a supplement to value added at producers' prices. In practice, however, it is not recorded under resources but as a component of "taxes less subsidies on production" as if it were a negative tax on output.

7.7. As explained in chapter VI, the basic price is obtained from the producer's price by deducting any tax on product payable on a unit of output (other than invoiced VAT already omitted from the producer's price) and adding any subsidy on product receivable on a unit of output. In consequence, no product taxes or subsidies on outputs are to be recorded as payables or receivables in the producer's generation of income account when value added is measured at basic prices. It follows that the item "taxes less subsidies on production" refers only to other taxes or subsidies on production.

7.8. After deducting compensation of employees and taxes, less subsidies, on production from value added, the balancing item of the generation of income account is obtained, described either as the operating surplus or mixed income depending upon the nature of the enterprise. This balancing item is also shown on the left side of the account under uses, regardless of whether output and value added are measured at basic prices or at producers' prices. It measures the surplus or deficit accruing from production before taking account of any interest, rent or similar charges payable on financial or tangible non-produced assets borrowed or rented by the enterprise, or any interest, rent or similar receipts receivable on financial or tangible non-produced assets owned by the enterprise. The balancing item is described as the operating surplus except for unincorporated enterprises owned by households in which the owner(s) or members of the same household may contribute unpaid labour inputs of a similar kind to those that could be provided by paid employees. In the latter case, the balancing item is described as mixed income because it implicitly contains an element of remuneration for work done by the owner,

or other members of the household, that cannot be separately identified from the return to the owner as entrepreneur.

7.9. When the enterprise is a non-market producer owned by a government unit or a non-profit institution (NPI), the output that it provides to other units cannot be valued on the basis of actual or estimated market prices. By convention, such output is valued by its costs of production—intermediate consumption, consumption of fixed capital, compensation of employees plus taxes, less subsidies, on production other than taxes or subsidies or products. No net operating surplus is generated when output is valued in this way by the sum of the values of the inputs.

7.10. All the inputs into, and outputs from, processes of production are valued at the times they are used, or produced, as distinct from the times they were acquired or disposed of (see chapter VI). In consequence, output, intermediate consumption and consumption of fixed capital are all defined and valued in such a way as to exclude holding gains on the inventories and fixed assets employed in production. The operating surplus, or mixed income, is therefore a measure of profit that also excludes holding gains. On the other hand, profits as reported in business accounts based on historic costs usually do not separate holding gains on inventories and fixed assets from the operating surplus and may therefore be much larger than the operating surplus on its own when there is inflation.

7.11. As noted in chapter VI, gross domestic product (GDP) at market prices for the total economy is equal to the sum of the gross values added of all resident enterprises plus those taxes, less subsidies, on products that are not payable on the values of the outputs of those enterprises, i.e., taxes or subsidies on imports plus non-deductible VAT when output is valued at producers' prices, and all taxes or subsidies on products when output is valued at basic prices. Taxes and subsidies on imports and VAT must therefore also be recorded under uses of GDP in the generation of income account for the total economy, even though they do not appear in the generation of income account for individual institutional units or sectors.

2. The allocation of primary income account

7.12. The allocation of primary income account focuses on resident institutional units or sectors in their capacity as recipients of primary incomes rather than as producers whose activities generate primary incomes. It includes the amounts of property incomes receivable and payable by institutional units or sectors. As already noted, the generation of income account, being related to production activities, can be compiled for establishments and industries as well as for institutional units and sectors. However, the allocation of primary income account has no such direct link with production and can only be compiled for institutional units and sectors.

7.13. There are two kinds of income listed under resources on the right side of the allocation of primary income account. The first consists of primary incomes already recorded in the generation of income account that are receivable by resident institutional units, these consist of:

(a) Compensation of employees receivable by households;

(b) Taxes (less subsidies) on production or imports receivable (or payable) by government units;

(c) Operating surplus, or mixed income, of enterprises carried forward from the generation of income account.

The second kind consists of property incomes receivable from the ownership of financial or tangible non-produced assets (mainly land or sub-soil assets):

(d) Interest, dividends and similar incomes receivable by the owners of financial assets;

(e) Rents receivable by owners of land or sub-soil assets leased to other units.

The incomes receivable under the above items (a), (b) and (d) include incomes receivable from non-resident institutional units.

7.14. The uses, listed on the left side of the allocation of primary income account, consist only of the property incomes payable by institutional units or sectors to creditors, shareholders, landowners, etc. Except for rents on land and sub-soil assets, these may be payable to non-residents as well as residents. The remaining item recorded under uses is the balancing item, the balance of primary incomes, defined as the total value of the primary incomes receivable by an institutional unit or sector less the total of the primary incomes payable. At the level of the total economy it is described as national income.

7.15. The composition of the balance of primary incomes varies considerably from one sector to another as certain types of primary incomes are receivable by certain sectors only or by non-residents. In particular, taxes are received only by the general government sector and non-residents while compensation of employees is received only by the household sector and non-residents. These balances consist of:

(a) The balance of primary incomes of the non-financial and financial corporate sectors consists only of operating surplus plus property income receivable less property income payable;

(b) The balance of primary incomes of the general government sector consists of taxes, less subsidies, receivable or payable on production and on imports, plus property income receivable less property income payable. It may also include a small amount of operating surplus from government-owned unincorporated enterprises;

(c) The balance of primary incomes of the household sector consists of compensation of employees and mixed incomes accruing to households, plus property income re-

ceivable less property income payable. It also includes the operating surplus from housing services produced for own consumption by owner-occupiers;

(d) The balance of primary incomes of the non-profit institutions (NPIs) serving household sectors consists almost entirely of property income receivable less property income payable.

Primary incomes in the form of compensation of employees, taxes or subsidies on production or imports, and property incomes (except rents on land) may all be receivable by residents from non-residents and payable to non-residents. The difference between the total values of the primary incomes receivable from, and payable to, non-residents is often described as "net income from abroad".

Gross national income and net national income

7.16. The aggregate value of the net balances of primary incomes summed over all sectors is described as net national income (NNI). Similarly, the aggregate value of the gross balances of primary incomes for all sectors is defined as gross national income (GNI). The latter is identical with gross national product (GNP), as hitherto understood in national accounts generally. However, conceptually, both NNI and GNI are measures of income and not product.

7.17. Gross value added is strictly a production measure defined only in terms of output and intermediate consumption. It follows that GDP at market prices is also essentially a production measure as it is obtained by summing the gross values added of all resident institutional units, in their capacities as producers, and adding the values of any taxes, less subsidies, on production or imports not already included in the values of the outputs, and values added, of resident producers. GNI is obtained by summing the balance of primary incomes of the same resident institutional units. It follows that the difference between the numerical values of GNI and GDP is equal to the difference between the total primary incomes receivable by residents from non-residents and the total primary incomes payable by residents to non-residents (i.e., net income from abroad). However, as both GDP and GNI are obtained by summing over the *same set* of resident institutional units, there is no justification for labelling one as "domestic" and the other as "national". Both aggregates refer to the total economy defined as the complete set of resident institutional units or sectors. The difference between them is not one of coverage but the fact that one measures output while the other measures income. Both have an equal claim to be described as domestic or as national. However, as the terms "domestic" and "national" are deeply embedded in economic usage, it is not proposed to change them but to emphasize the fact that GNP is actually an income concept by renaming it GNI.

3. The entrepreneurial income account

7.18. The allocation of primary income account may be partitioned into two sub-accounts: the entrepreneurial income account and the allocation of other primary income account. The purpose is to identify an additional balancing item, entrepreneurial income, that may be useful for market producers. Like the operating surplus and mixed income, it is a balancing item that is only relevant to producers, but one that can only be calculated for institutional units and sectors and not for establishments and industries. The entrepreneurial income for a corporation, quasi-corporation, or institutional unit owning an unincorporated enterprise engaged in market production is defined as its

> operating surplus or mixed income,

plus property income receivable on the financial or other assets owned by the enterprise,

minus interest payable on the liabilities of the enterprise and rents payable on land or other tangible non-produced assets rented by the enterprise.

Entrepreneurial income may also be calculable in respect of the production of housing services for own final consumption. It should be noted that, in the case of the non-financial and financial corporations sectors, the only difference between entrepreneurial income and the balance of primary incomes is that entrepreneurial income is measured before the payment of dividends and withdrawals of income from quasi-corporations. It is an income concept that is close to the concept of profit and loss as understood in business accounting (at least when there is no inflation) because it is calculated after deducting from the operating surplus any interest and rents payable and adding property incomes receivable. On the other hand, it should be remembered that when profits are calculated at historic costs in business accounts, they also include nominal holding gains on the inventories and other assets owned by the enterprise that may be quite substantial during inflationary conditions.

7.19. The entrepreneurial income of a corporation can be readily identified in its accounts. However, in the case of an institutional unit that owns an unincorporated enterprise, it is necessary to separate the assets and liabilities of the enterprise from those of its owner, typically a household or a government unit. In practice, it may be difficult to make this separation, bearing in mind that the owner of an unincorporated enterprise is, by definition, legally indistinguishable from the enterprise itself and therefore responsible for all liabilities incurred by the enterprise. When an unincorporated enterprise is treated as a quasi-corporation, it must be possible to identify the entrepreneurial income out of which income may be withdrawn by the owner(s), as the availability of the necessary accounting information is a prerequisite for being able to treat the enterprise as a quasi-corporation. For a household that owns an ordinary unincorporated enterprise, however, it may not be feasible to divide the property incomes payable and receivable into those attributable to the enterprise and those attributable to the owner(s) in a personal capacity. In such cases it is not possible to estimate entrepreneurial income.

7.20. When the entrepreneurial income account is compiled for an institutional unit or sector, it is followed by the allocation of other primary income account in order to arrive at the balance of primary incomes. In the allocation of other primary income account the first item listed under resources is entrepreneurial income, the balancing item carried forward from the entrepreneurial income account instead of operating surplus or mixed income carried forward from the generation of income account. The remaining primary incomes listed under resources in the allocation of other primary income account, therefore, consist of the following items:

(*a*)   Compensation of employees receivable by households;

(*b*)   Taxes, less subsidies, on production and imports receivable or payable by government units;

(*c*)   Property incomes receivable on assets owned *except* those receivable by enterprises and included in entrepreneurial income.

Under uses, the only items recorded are property incomes payable, except the interest or rents payable by enterprises. The balancing item of the allocation of other primary income account is identical with the balancing item of the allocation of primary income account.

B. Compensation of employees (D.1)

Introduction

7.21. Compensation of employees is recorded under uses in the generation of income account and under resources in the allocation of primary income account. Compensation of employees is defined as:

> the total remuneration, in cash or in kind, payable by an enterprise to an employee in return for work done by the latter during the accounting period.

Compensation of employees is recorded on an accrual basis; i.e., it is measured by the value of the remuneration in cash or in kind which an employee becomes entitled to receive from an employer in respect of work done during the relevant period, whether paid in advance, simultaneously or in arrears of the work itself. No compensation of employees is payable in respect of unpaid work undertaken voluntarily, including the work done by members of a household within an unincorporated enterprise owned by the same household. Compensation of employees does not include any taxes payable by the employer on the wage and salary bill—for example, a payroll tax. Such taxes are treated as taxes on production in the same way as taxes on buildings, land or other assets used in production.

7.22. It is not always self-evident whether a worker is an employee or self-employed: for example, some workers paid by results may be employees while others may be self-employed. It is necessary, therefore, to clarify the nature of the employment relationship in order to fix the boundary between compensation of employees and other kinds of receipts. The boundary also affects the sub-sectoring of the household sector.

The employment relationship

7.23. In order to be classified as occupied—i.e., employed or self-employed—the person must be engaged in an activity that falls within the production boundary of the System. Unoccupied persons consist of the unemployed and persons not in the labour force. The relationship of employer to employee exists when there is an agreement, which may be formal or informal, between an enterprise and a person, normally entered into voluntarily by both parties, whereby the person works for the enterprise in return for remuneration in cash or in kind. The remuneration is normally based on either the time spent at work or some other objective indicator of the amount of work done.

7.24. Self-employed workers, on the other hand, are persons who are the sole owners, or joint owners, of the unincorporated enterprises in which they work, excluding those unincorporated enterprises that are classified as quasi-corporations. The self-employed are persons who work for themselves, when the enterprises they own are neither distinguished as separate legal entities nor separate institutional units in the System. Self-employed persons receive mixed incomes and not compensation of employees. It is useful to clarify the status of certain categories for whom it may not always be obvious as to whether they are employees, self-employed or unoccupied.

(a) Workers engaged in production undertaken entirely for their own final consumption or own capital formation, either individually or collectively, are self-employed. Although a value may be imputed for the output of own-account production based on costs, including estimated labour costs, no imputation is made for the wages of workers engaged in such production, even in the case of collective, or communal, projects undertaken by groups of persons working together. The surplus of the imputed value of the output over any monetary costs or taxes on production explicitly incurred is treated as gross mixed income;

(b) Unpaid family workers, including those working in unincorporated enterprises engaged wholly or partly in market production, are also treated as self-employed;

(c) The whole of the equity of a corporation may be owned by a single shareholder or small group of shareholders. When those shareholders also work for the corporation and receive paid remuneration other than dividends, they are treated as employees of the corporation. The owners of quasi-corporations are also treated as employees when they work in those quasi-corporations;

(d) Outworkers may be either employees or self-employed depending on their exact status and circumstances. The treatment of outworkers is specified in more detail below;

(e) Students in their capacity as consumers of educational or training services are not employees. However, if students also have a formal commitment whereby they contribute some of their own labour as an input into the enterprise's process of production— for example, as apprentices or similar kinds of worker trainees, articled clerks, student nurses, research or teaching assistants, hospital interns, etc.—they are treated as employees, whether or not they receive any remuneration in cash for the work which they do.

Employers and own-account workers

7.25. Self-employed persons may be divided into two groups: those with and those without paid employees of their own. Those with paid employees are described as employers and those without paid employees are described as own-account workers. The distinction is used for purposes of sub-sectoring the household sector. Own-account workers may be further subdivided into outworkers who are under some kind of formal or informal contract to supply goods or services to a particular enterprise, and ordinary own-account workers who may be engaged in either market production or production for own final consumption or own capital formation.

Outworkers

7.26. An outworker is a person who agrees to work for a particular enterprise or to supply a certain quantity of goods or services to a particular enterprise, by prior arrangement or contract with that enterprise, but whose place of work is not within any of the establishments which make up that enterprise. The enterprise does not control the time spent at work by an outworker and does not assume responsibility for the conditions in which that work is carried out, although it may carry out checks on the quality of work. Most outworkers work at home but may use other premises of their own choice. Some outworkers are provided by an enterprise with the equipment or materials, or both, on which they work, but other outworkers may purchase their own equipment or materials, or both. In any case, outworkers have to meet some production costs themselves: for example, the actual or imputed rent on the buildings in which they work; heating, lighting and power; storage or transportation; etc.

7.27. Outworkers have some of the characteristics of employees and some of the characteristics of self-employed workers. The way in which they are to be classified is determined primarily by the basis on which they are remunerated. A distinction can be drawn between two cases which, in principle, are quite different from one another:

(a) The person is remunerated directly, or indirectly, on the basis of the amount of work done—i.e., by the amount of labour that is contributed as an input into some process of production, irrespective of the value of the output produced or the profitability of the production process. This kind of remuneration implies that the worker is an employee; or

(b) The income received by the person is a function of the value of the outputs from some process of production for which that person is responsible, however much or little work was put in. This kind of remuneration implies that the worker is self-employed.

7.28. In practice it may not always be so easy to distinguish between employees and self-employed on the basis of these criteria. Outworkers who employ and pay others to do the same kind of work must be treated as the self-employed owners of unincorporated enterprises: i.e., as employers. The issue, therefore, is to distinguish own-account workers from employees.

7.29. An outworker is considered an employee when there exists an employment relationship between the enterprise and the outworker of the kind described in paragraph 7.22 above. This implies the existence of an implicit or explicit contract or agreement whereby it is agreed that the outworker is remunerated on the basis of the work done. Conversely, an outworker is considered to be an own-account worker when there is no such implicit or explicit contract or agreement and the income earned by the outworker depends on the value of the goods or services supplied to the enterprise. This suggests that decisions on markets, scale of operations and finance are likely to be in the hands of outworkers who are also likely to own, or rent, the machinery or equipment on which they work.

7.30. The status of an outworker has important implications for the accounts. When the outworker is an own-account worker, the payment from the enterprise to the outworker constitutes a purchase of intermediate goods or services. When the outworker is an employee, the payment constitutes compensation of employees and is therefore paid out of the value added of the enterprise. Thus, the outworker's status affects the distribution of value added between enterprises as well as the distribution of incomes between compensation of employees and net mixed income.

The components of compensation of employees

7.31. Compensation of employees has two main components:

(a) Wages and salaries payable in cash or in kind;

(b) The value of the social contributions payable by employers: these may be actual social contributions payable by employers to Social Security schemes or to private funded social insurance schemes to secure social benefits for their employees; or imputed social contributions by employers providing unfunded social benefits.

Wages and salaries (D.11)

7.32. Wages and salaries include the values of any social contributions, income taxes, etc., payable by the employee even if they are actually withheld by the employer for administrative convenience or other reasons and paid directly to social insurance schemes, tax authorities, etc., on behalf of the employee. Wages and salaries may be paid in various ways, including goods or services provided to employees as remuneration in kind instead of, or in addition to, remuneration in cash.

Wages and salaries in cash

7.33. Wages and salaries in cash include the following kinds of remuneration:

(a) Wages or salaries payable at regular weekly, monthly or other intervals, including payments by results and piecework payments; enhanced payments or special allowances for working overtime, at nights, at weekends or other unsocial hours; allowances for working away from home or in disagreeable or hazardous circumstances; expatriation allowances for working abroad; etc.;

(b) Supplementary allowances payable regularly, such as housing allowances or allowances to cover the costs of travel to and from work, but excluding social benefits (see below);

(c) Wages or salaries payable to employees away from work for short periods, e.g., on holiday or as a result of a temporary halt to production, except during absences due to sickness, injury, etc. (see below);

(d) Ad hoc bonuses or other exceptional payments linked to the overall performance of the enterprise made under incentive schemes;

(e) Commissions, gratuities and tips received by employees: these should be treated as payments for services rendered by the enterprise employing the worker, and should therefore also be included in the output and gross value added of the employing enterprise when they are paid directly to the employee by a third party.

7.34. Wages and salaries in cash do *not* include the reimbursement by employers of expenditures made by employees in order to enable them to take up their jobs or to carry out their work. For example:

(a) The reimbursement of travel, removal or related expenses made by employees when they take up new jobs or are required by their employers to move their homes to different parts of the country or to another country;

(b) The reimbursement of expenditures by employees on tools, equipment, special clothing or other items that are needed exclusively, or primarily, to enable them to carry out their work.

The amounts reimbursed are treated as intermediate consumption by employers. To the extent that employees who are required by their contract of employment to purchase tools, equipment, special clothing, etc., are not fully reimbursed, the remaining expenses they incur should be deducted from the amounts they receive in wages and salaries and the employers' intermediate consumption increased accordingly. Expenditures on items needed exclusively, or primarily, for work do not form part of household final consumption expenditures, whether reimbursed or not.

7.35. Wages and salaries in cash also do *not* include unfunded employee social benefits (see chapter VIII, paragraph 8.80) paid by employers in the form of:

(a) Children's, spouse's, family, education or other allowances in respect of dependants;

(b) Payments made at full, or reduced, wage or salary rates to workers absent from work because of illness, accidental injury, maternity leave, etc.;

(c) Severance payments to workers or their survivors who lose their jobs because of redundancy, incapacity, accidental death, etc.

In practice, it may be difficult to separate payments of wages or salaries during short periods of absence due to sickness, accidents, etc., from other payments of wages and salaries, in which case they have to be grouped with the latter.

7.36. Unfunded employee social benefits are not a form of remuneration because they are paid selectively to individual employees when certain events occur, or certain conditions exist, that are unrelated to the amount of work done by the employee. However, as explained below, an amount equal to the value of the additional contingent liabilities that employers incur by undertaking to provide such benefits to their employees out of their own resources, should the need arise, must be treated as a form of compensation made collectively to their employees.

Wages and salaries in kind

7.37. Employers may remunerate their employees in kind for various reasons. For example:

(a) There may be tax advantages for the employer, the employee, or both by avoiding payments in cash;

(b) The employer may wish to dispose of outputs which are periodically in excess supply;

(c) The nature of the work may require frequent, or pro-

longed, absence from home so that the employee has to be provided with accommodation, travel, etc.

7.38. Income in kind may bring less satisfaction than income in cash because employees are not free to choose how to spend it. Some of the goods or services provided to employees may be of a type or quality which the employee would not normally buy. Nevertheless, they must be valued consistently with other goods and services. When the goods or services have been purchased by the employer, they should be valued at purchasers' prices. When produced by the employer, they should be valued at producers' prices. When provided free, the value of the wages and salaries in kind is given by the full value of the goods and services in question. When provided at reduced prices, the value of the wages and salaries in kind is given by the difference between the full value of the goods and services and the amount paid by the employees.

7.39. Goods or services that employers are obliged to provide to their employees in order for them to be able to carry out their work are treated as intermediate consumption by the employer: for example, special protective clothing. A list of such items is given in paragraph 6.162 of chapter VI. Remuneration in kind, on the other hand, consists of goods and services that are not necessary for work and can be used by employees in their own time, and at their own discretion, for the satisfaction of their own needs or wants or those of other members of their households.

7.40. Almost any kind of consumption good or service may be provided as remuneration in kind. The following includes some of the most common types of goods and services provided without charge, or at reduced prices, by employers to their employees:

(a) Meals and drinks, including those consumed when travelling on business;

(b) Housing services or accommodation of a type that can be used by all members of the household to which the employee belongs;

(c) Uniforms or other forms of special clothing which employees choose to wear frequently outside of the workplace as well as at work;

(d) The services of vehicles or other durables provided for the personal use of employees;

(e) Goods and services produced as outputs from the employer's own processes of production, such as free travel for the employees of railways or airlines, or free coal for miners;

(f) Sports, recreation or holiday facilities for employees and their families;

(g) Transportation to and from work, car parking;

(h) Crèches for the children of employees.

7.41. Some of the services provided by employers, such as transportation to and from work, car parking and crèches have some of the characteristics of intermediate consumption. However, employers are obliged to provide these facilities to attract and retain labour, and not because of the nature of the production process or the physical conditions under which employees have to work. On balance, they are more like other forms of compensation of employees than intermediate consumption. Many workers have to pay for transportation to and from work, car parking and crèches out of their own incomes, the relevant expenditures being recorded as final consumption expenditures.

7.42. Remuneration in kind may also include the value of the interest foregone by employers when they provide loans to employees at reduced, or even zero rates of interest for purposes of buying houses, furniture or other goods or services. Its value may be estimated as the amount the employee would have to pay if average mortgage, or consumer loan, interest rates were charged *less* the amount of interest actually paid. The sums involved could be large when nominal interest rates are very high because of inflation but otherwise they may be too small and too uncertain to be worth estimating.

Employers' social contributions (D.12)

7.43. An amount equal to the value of the social contributions incurred by employers in order to obtain social benefits for their employees needs to be recorded as compensation of employees. Employers' social contributions may be either actual or imputed. They are intended to secure for their employees the entitlement to social benefits should certain events occur, or certain circumstances exist, that may adversely affect their employees' income or welfare—sickness, accidents, redundancy, retirement, etc. Social benefits are described in chapter VIII, and also in annex IV at the end of this manual.

Employers' actual social contributions (D.121)

7.44. These consist of social contributions payable by employers for the benefit of their employees to social security funds, insurance enterprises or other institutional units responsible for the administration and management of social insurance schemes. Although they are paid by the employer directly to the Social Security fund or other scheme, the payments are made for the benefit of the employees. Accordingly, employees should be treated as being remunerated by an amount equal to the value of the social contributions payable. This imputed remuneration is recorded in the generation of income account as a component of compensation of employees. Employees are then recorded as paying social contributions of equal value as current transfers to Social Security funds, other schemes, etc., in the secondary distribution of income account.

Employers' imputed social contributions (D.122)

7.45. Some employers provide social benefits themselves directly to their employees, former employees or dependants out of their own resources without involving an insurance enterprise or autonomous pension fund, and without creating a special fund or segregated reserve for the purpose. In this situation, existing employees may be considered as being protected against various specified needs or circumstances, even though no payments are being made to cover them. Remuneration should therefore be imputed for such employees equal in value to the amount of social contributions that would be needed to secure the de facto entitlements to the social benefits they accumulate. These amounts depend not only on the levels of the benefits currently payable but also on the ways in which employers' liabilities under such schemes are likely to evolve in the future as a result of factors such as expected changes in the numbers, age distribution and life expectancies of their present and previous employees. Thus, the values that should be imputed for the contributions ought, in principle, to be based on the same kind of actuarial considerations that determine the levels of premiums charged by insurance enterprises.

7.46. In practice, however, it may be difficult to decide how large such imputed contributions should be. The enterprise may make estimates itself, perhaps on the basis of the contributions paid into similar funded schemes, in order to calculate its likely liabilities in the future, and such estimates may be used when available. Otherwise, the only practical alternative may be to use the unfunded social benefits payable by the enterprise during the same accounting period as an estimate of the imputed remuneration that would be needed to cover the imputed contributions. While there are obviously many reasons why the value of the imputed contributions that would be needed may diverge from the unfunded social benefits actually paid in the same period, such as the changing composition and age structure of the enterprise's labour force, the benefits actually paid in the current period may nevertheless provide the best available estimates of the contributions and associated imputed remuneration.

7.47. The two steps involved may be summarized as follows:

(*a*) Employers are recorded, in the generation of income account, as paying to their existing employees as a component of their compensation an amount, described as imputed social contributions, equal in value to the estimated social contributions that would be needed to provide for the unfunded social benefits to which they become entitled;

(*b*) Employees are recorded, in the secondary distribution of income account, as paying back to their employers the same amount of imputed social contributions (as current transfers) as if they were paying them to a separate social insurance scheme.

C. Taxes on production and on imports (D.2)

1. Introduction

7.48. Taxes are compulsory, unrequited payments, in cash or in kind, made by institutional units to government units. They are described as unrequited because the government provides nothing in return to the individual unit making the payment, although governments may use the funds raised in taxes to provide goods or services to other units, either individually or collectively, or to the community as a whole.

7.49. Taxes on production and imports consist of:

> taxes on products payable on goods and services when they are produced, delivered, sold, transferred or otherwise disposed of by their producers; they include taxes and duties on imports that become payable when goods enter the economic territory by crossing the frontier or when services are delivered to resident units by non-resident units; when outputs are valued at basic prices, taxes on domestically produced products are not recorded in the accounts of the System as being payable by their producers

plus

> other taxes on production, consisting mainly of taxes on the ownership or use of land, buildings or other assets used in production or on the labour employed, or compensation of employees paid.

Taxes on the personal use of vehicles, etc., by households are recorded under current taxes on income, wealth, etc.

7.50. At the level of an individual enterprise, taxes on production are recorded as being payable out of its value added. Similarly, in business accounting, taxes on production, except invoiced VAT, are usually regarded as costs of production that may be charged against sales or other receipts when calculating profits for tax or other purposes. They correspond *grosso modo* to "indirect taxes" as traditionally understood, indirect taxes being taxes that supposedly can be passed on, in whole or in part, to other institutional units by increasing the prices of the goods or services sold. However, it is extremely difficult, if not impossible, to determine the real incidence of different kinds of taxes, and the use of the terms "direct" and "indirect" taxes has fallen out of favour in economics and is no longer used in the System.

The recording of taxes on production
and imports in the accounts

7.51. Taxes on production and imports are recorded under uses in the generation of income account and under resources in the allocation of primary income account.

7.52. In the generation of income account, taxes on imports are recorded only at the level of the total economy as they are not payable out of the values added of domestic producers. Moreover, at the level of an individual institutional unit or sector, only those taxes on products that have not been deducted from the value of the output of that unit or sector need to be recorded under uses in its generation of income account. These vary depending upon the way in which output is valued. When output is valued at basic prices, all taxes (subsidies) on products payable (receivable) on the goods or services produced as outputs are deducted from (added to) the value of that output at producers' prices. They do not, therefore, have to be recorded under uses in the generation of income account of the units or sectors concerned, being recorded only at the level of the total economy, in the same way as taxes on imports. When output is valued at producers' prices, all taxes or subsidies on products payable or receivable on outputs have to be recorded under uses in the generation of income account of the units or sectors concerned, except invoiced VAT or similar deductible taxes as invoiced VAT is never included in the value of output. Non-deductible VAT and similar taxes are recorded under uses only at the level of the total economy, like taxes on imports.

7.53. Other taxes or subsidies on production—i.e., taxes payable on the land, assets, labour, etc., employed in production—are not taxes payable per unit of output and cannot be deducted from the producer's price. They are recorded as being payable out of the values added of the individual producers or sectors concerned.

7.54. In the allocation of primary income account, taxes on production and imports appear under resources only for the general government sector and the total economy, apart from any such taxes payable to non-residents.

Taxes versus fees

7.55. One of the regulatory functions of governments is to forbid the ownership or use of certain goods or the pursuit of certain activities, unless specific permission is granted by issuing a licence or other certificate for which a fee is demanded. If the issue of such licences involves little or no work on the part of government, the licences being granted automatically on payment of the amounts due, it is likely that they are simply a device to raise taxes, even though the government may provide some kind of certificate, or authorization, in return. However, if the government uses the issue of licences to exercise some proper regulatory function—for example, checking the competence, or qualifications, of the person concerned, checking the efficient and safe functioning of the equipment in question, or carrying out some other form of control which it would otherwise not be obliged to do—the payments made should be treated as purchases of services from government rather than payments of taxes, unless the payments are clearly out of all proportion to the costs of providing the services. The borderline between taxes and payments of fees for services rendered is not always clear cut in practice, however.

Links with the IMF and OECD tax classifications

7.56. The coverage of taxes in the SNA coincides with that of "tax revenue" as defined in the *Manual on Government Finance Statistics, 1986*, or GFS, of the International Monetary Fund (IMF), and also with "taxes" as defined in the Organisation for Economic Co-operation and Development's (OECD) annual publication *Revenue Statistics of OECD Member Countries*, except that the SNA includes imputed taxes or subsidies resulting from the operation of official multiple exchange rates and does not classify Social Security Contributions under the heading of taxes. Chapter IV of the GFS contains a detailed listing and classification of taxes according to the nature of the tax. This classification is also reprinted as annex IV in the *Handbook of National Accounting: Public Sector Accounts* (United Nations, 1988). Part II of *Revenue Statistics* contains an almost identical classification.

7.57. The categories of tax distinguished in the System depend on the following interaction of three factors, of which the nature of tax is only one:

    (*a*)   The nature of the tax, as specified in the GFS/OECD classification;

    (*b*)   The type of institutional unit paying the tax;

    (*c*)   The circumstances in which the tax is payable.

7.58. Thus, payments of exactly the same tax may be recorded under two different headings in the SNA. For example, payment of an excise duty may appear under "taxes on imports, except VAT and duties" or under "taxes on products, except VAT, import and export taxes", depending upon whether the excise duty is paid on an imported or on a domestically produced good. Similarly, payment of an annual tax on automobiles may be recorded under "taxes on production" or under "current taxes on income, wealth, etc.", depending upon whether the tax is paid by an enterprise or by a household. For this reason it is not possible to arrive at the SNA categories simply by regrouping the IMF/OECD classifications. However, in order to take advantage of the existence of these detailed classifications, each category of tax listed below contains a cross-reference to the corresponding IMF and OECD classifications.

The accrual basis of recording

7.59. In contrast to the GFS and similar systems that require taxes to be recorded when they are actually paid, all taxes should be recorded on an accrual basis in the SNA, i.e., when the activities, transactions or other events occur which create the liabilities to pay taxes. However, some economic activities, transactions or events, which under tax legislation ought to impose on the units concerned the obligation to pay taxes, permanently escape the attention of the tax authorities. It would be unrealistic to assume that such activities, transactions or events give rise to financial assets or liabilities in the form of

payables and receivables. For this reason the amounts of taxes to be recorded in the System are determined by the amounts due for payment only when evidenced by tax assessments, declarations or other instruments such as sales invoices or customs declarations, which create liabilities in the form of clear obligations to pay on the part of taxpayers. Nevertheless, in accordance with the accrual principle, the times at which the taxes should be recorded are the times at which the tax liabilities arise. For example, a tax on the sale, transfer or use of output should be recorded when that sale, transfer or use took place, which is not necessarily the same time as that at which the tax authorities were notified, at which a tax demand was issued, at which the tax was due to be paid or the payment was actually made.

7.60. In some countries, and for some taxes, the amounts of taxes eventually paid may diverge substantially and systematically from the amounts due to be paid to the extent that not all of the latter can be effectively construed as constituting financial liabilities as these are understood within the System. In such cases, it may be preferable for analytic and policy purposes to ignore unpaid tax liabilities and confine the measurement of taxes within the System to those actually paid. Nevertheless, the taxes actually paid should still be recorded on an accrual basis at the times at which the events took place which gave rise to the liabilities.

Interest, fines or other penalties

7.61. In principle, interest charged on overdue taxes or fines, or penalties imposed for the attempted evasion of taxes, should be recorded separately and not as taxes. However, it may not be possible to separate payments of interest, fines or other penalties from the taxes to which they relate, so that they are usually grouped with taxes in practice.

2. Taxes on products (D.21)

7.62. A tax on a product is a tax that is payable per unit of some good or service. The tax may be a specific amount of money per unit of quantity of a good or service (the quantity units being measured either in terms of discrete units or continuous physical variables such as volume, weight, strength, distance, time, etc.), or it may be calculated *ad valorem* as a specified percentage of the price per unit or value of the goods or services transacted. A tax on a product usually becomes payable when it is produced, sold or imported, but it may also become payable in other circumstances, such as when a good is exported, leased, transferred, delivered, or used for own consumption or own capital formation. An enterprise may or may not itemize the amount of a tax on a product separately on the invoice or bill which they charge their customers.

Value added type taxes (D.211)

7.63. A value added type tax (VAT) is a tax on goods or services collected in stages by enterprises but which is ultimately charged in full to the final purchasers. It has already been described in chapter VI, paragraphs 6.213 to 6.220. It is described as a "deductible" tax because producers are not usually required to pay to the government the full amount of the tax they invoice to their customers, being permitted to deduct the amount of tax they have been invoiced on their own purchases of goods or services intended for intermediate consumption or fixed capital formation. VAT is usually calculated on the price of the good or service including any other tax on the product. VAT is also payable on imports of goods or services in addition to any import duties or other taxes on the imports.

Taxes and duties on imports, excluding VAT (D.212)

7.64. Taxes on imports consist of taxes on goods and services that become payable at the moment when those goods cross the national or customs frontiers of the economic territory or when those services are delivered by non-resident producers to resident institutional units.

7.65. Imported goods on which all the required taxes on imports have been paid when they enter the economic territory may subsequently become subject to a further tax, or taxes, as they circulate within the economy. For example, excise duties or sales taxes may become due on goods as they pass through the chain of wholesale or retail distribution, such taxes being levied on all goods at the same point, whether those goods have been produced by resident enterprises or imported. Taxes payable subsequently on goods which have been already imported are not taxes on imports, being recorded under taxes on products, excluding VAT, import and export taxes.

Import duties (D.2121)

7.66. These consist of customs duties, or other import charges, which are payable on goods of a particular type when they enter the economic territory. The duties are specified under customs tariff schedules. They may be intended as a means of raising revenue or discouraging imports in order to protect resident goods producers (GFS, 6.1; OECD, 5123).

Taxes on imports, excluding VAT and duties (D.2122)

7.67. These consist of all taxes except VAT and import duties as defined in the GFS/OECD classifications that become payable when goods enter the economic territory or services are delivered by non-residents to residents. They include the following:

(a) *General sales taxes*: these consist of general sales taxes (excluding VAT) that are payable on imports of goods and services when the goods enter the economic territory or the services are delivered to residents (GFS, 5.1; OECD, 5110-5113);

(b) *Excise duties*: excise duties are taxes levied on specific kinds of goods, typically alcoholic beverages, tobacco and fuels; they may be payable in addition to import duties when the goods enter the economic territory (GFS, 5.2; OECD, 5121);

(c) *Taxes on specific services*: these may be payable when non-resident enterprises provide services to resident units within the economic territory (GFS, 5.4; OECD, 5126);

(d) *Profits of import monopolies*: these consist of the profits transferred to governments of import marketing boards, or other public enterprises exercising a monopoly over the imports of some good or service. The justification for treating these profits as implicit taxes on products is the same as that shown in paragraph 7.69 below for fiscal monopolies (GFS, 6.3; OECD, 5127);

(e) *Taxes resulting from multiple exchange rates*: these consist of implicit taxes resulting from the operation of multiple exchange rates by the central bank or other official agency. These implicit taxes are not recorded in the same way as other taxes (see chapters XIV and XIX, for an explanation of the treatment of multiple exchange rates in the System as a whole).

Export taxes (D.213)

7.68. Export taxes consist of taxes on goods or services that become payable when the goods leave the economic territory or when the services are delivered to non-residents. They include the following:

(a) *Export duties*: general or specific taxes or duties on exports (GFS, 6.2; OECD, 5124);

(b) *Profits of export monopolies*: these consist of the profits transferred to governments of export marketing boards, or other public enterprises exercising a monopoly over the exports of some good or service. The justification for treating these profits as implicit taxes on products is the same as that shown in paragraph 7.69 below for fiscal monopolies (GFS, 6.3; OECD, 5124);

(c) *Taxes resulting from multiple exchange rates*: these consist of implicit taxes on exports resulting from the operation of an official system of multiple exchange rates (see chapters XIV and XIX).

Taxes on products, excluding VAT, import and export taxes (D.214)

7.69. Taxes on products, excluding VAT, import and export taxes, consist of taxes on goods and services that become payable as a result of the production, sale, transfer, leasing or delivery of those goods or services, or as a result of their use for own consumption or own capital formation. They include the following commonly occurring taxes:

(a) *General sales or turnover taxes*: these include manufacturers', wholesale and retail sales taxes, purchase taxes, turnover taxes, and so on, but excluding VAT (GFS, 5.1; OECD, 5110-5113);

(b) *Excise duties*: these consist of taxes levied on specific kinds of goods, typically alcoholic beverages, tobacco and fuels (GFS, 5.2; OECD, 5121);

(c) *Taxes on specific services*: these include taxes on transportation, communications, insurance, advertising, housing services, hotels or lodging, restaurants, entertainments, gambling and lotteries, sporting events, etc. (GFS, 5.4; OECD, 5126);

(d) *Taxes on financial and capital transactions*: these consist of taxes payable on the purchase or sale of non-financial and financial assets including foreign exchange. They become payable when the ownership of land or other assets changes, except as a result of capital transfers (mainly inheritances and gifts) (GFS, 4.4; OECD, 4400). They are treated as taxes on the services of intermediaries;

(e) *Profits of fiscal monopolies*: these consist of the profits of fiscal monopolies that are transferred to government. Fiscal monopolies are public corporations, public quasi-corporations, or government-owned unincorporated enterprises that have been granted a legal monopoly over the production or distribution of a particular kind of good or service in order to raise revenue and not in order to further the interests of public economic or social policy. Such monopolies are typically engaged in the production of goods or services which may be heavily taxed in other countries, for example, alcoholic beverages, tobacco, matches, petroleum products, salt, playing cards, etc. The exercise of monopoly powers is simply an alternative way for the government to raise revenue instead of the more overt procedure of taxing the private production of such products. In such cases the sales prices of the monopolies are deemed to include implicit taxes on the products sold. While in principle only the excess of the monopoly profits over some notional "normal" profits should be treated as taxes, it is difficult to estimate this amount, and, in practice, the value of the taxes should be taken as equal to the amount of the profits actually transferred from fiscal monopolies to government (GFS, 5.3; OECD, 5122). When a public enterprise is granted monopoly powers as a matter of deliberate economic or social policy because of the special nature of the good or service or the technology of production—for example, public utilities, post offices and telecommunications, railways, etc.—it should not be treated as a fiscal monopoly. As a general rule, fiscal monopolies tend to be confined to the production of consumer goods or fuels. As the profits of a fiscal monopoly are calculated for the enterprise as a whole, it is not possible to estimate the average amount of the tax per unit of good or service sold when the enterprise has more than one good or service as output without introducing an assumption about the rates of tax on the different

products. Unless there is good reason otherwise, it should be assumed that the same *ad valorem* rate of tax is applied to all products, this rate being given by the ratio of the total value of the implicit taxes to the value of total sales less the total value of the implicit taxes. It is necessary to establish this rate in order to be able to calculate the basic prices of the products concerned.

3. Other taxes on production (D.29)

7.70. These consist of all taxes except taxes on products that enterprises incur as a result of engaging in production. Such taxes do not include any taxes on the profits or other income received by the enterprise and are payable irrespective of the profitability of the production. They may be payable on the land, fixed assets or labour employed in the production process or on certain activities or transactions. Other taxes on production include the following:

(a) *Taxes on payroll or work force*: these consist of taxes payable by enterprises assessed either as a proportion of the wages and salaries paid or as a fixed amount per person employed. They do not include compulsory social security contributions paid by employers or any taxes paid by the employees themselves out of their wages or salaries (GFS, 3; OECD, 3000);

(b) *Recurrent taxes on land, buildings or other structures*: these consist of taxes payable regularly, usually each year, in respect of the use or ownership of land, buildings or other structures utilized by enterprises in production, whether the enterprises own or rent such assets (GFS, 4.1; OECD, 4100);

(c) *Business and professional licences*: these consist of taxes paid by enterprises in order to obtain a licence to carry on a particular kind of business or profession. However, if the government carries out checks on the suitability, or safety of the business premises, on the reliability, or safety, of the equipment employed, on the professional competence of the staff employed, or on the quality or standard of goods or services produced, as a condition for granting such a licence, the payments are not unrequited and should be treated as payments for services rendered, unless the amounts charged for the licences are out of all proportion to the costs of the checks carried out by governments (GFS, 5.5.1; OECD, 5210). (See also paragraph 8.54 (c) of chapter VIII for the treatment of licences obtained by households for their own personal use.);

(d) *Taxes on the use of fixed assets or other activities*: these include taxes levied periodically on the use of vehicles, ships, aircraft or other machinery or equipment used by enterprises for purposes of production, whether such assets are owned or rented. These taxes are often described as licences, and are usually fixed amounts which do not depend on the actual rate of usage (GFS, 5.5.2 and 5.5.3; OECD, 5200);

(e) *Stamp taxes*: these consist of stamp taxes which do not fall on particular classes of transactions already identified, for example, stamps on legal documents or cheques. These are treated as taxes on the production of business or financial services. However, stamp taxes on the sale of specific products, such as alcoholic beverages or tobacco, are treated as taxes on products (GFS, 7.2; OECD, 6200);

(f) *Taxes on pollution*: these consist of taxes levied on the emission or discharge into the environment of noxious gases, liquids or other harmful substances. They do not include payments made for the collection and disposal of waste or noxious substances by public authorities, which constitute intermediate consumption of enterprises (GFS, 7.3; OECD, 5200);

(g) *Taxes on international transactions*: these consist of taxes on travel abroad, foreign remittances or similar transactions with non-residents (GFS, 6.5 and 6.6; OECD, 5127).

D. Subsidies (D.3)

7.71. Subsidies are current unrequited payments that government units, including non-resident government units, make to enterprises on the basis of the levels of their production activities or the quantities or values of the goods or services which they produce, sell or import. They are receivable by resident producers or importers. In the case of resident producers they may be designed to influence their levels of production, the prices at which their outputs are sold or the remuneration of the institutional units engaged in production. Subsidies are equivalent to negative taxes on production in so far as their impact on the operating surplus is in the opposite direction to that of taxes on production.

7.72. Subsidies are not payable to final consumers, and current transfers that governments make directly to households as consumers are treated as social benefits. Subsidies also do not include grants that governments may make to enterprises in order to finance their capital formation, or compensate them for damage to their capital assets, such grants being treated as capital transfers.

1. Subsidies on products (D.31)

7.73. A subsidy on a product is a subsidy payable per unit of a good or service. The subsidy may be a specific amount of money per unit of quantity of a good or service, or it may be calculated *ad valorem* as a specified percentage of the price per unit. A subsidy may also be calculated as the difference between a specified target price and the market price actually paid by a buyer. A subsidy on a product usually becomes payable when the good or service is produced, sold or imported, but it may also be payable in other circumstances such as when a good is transferred, leased, delivered or used for own consumption or own capital formation.

Import subsidies (D.311)

7.74. Import subsidies consist of subsidies on goods and services that become payable when the goods cross the frontier of the economic territory or when the services are delivered to resident institutional units. They include implicit subsidies resulting from the operation of a system of official multiple exchange rates (see chapters XIV and XIX). They may also include losses incurred as a matter of deliberate government policy by government trading organizations whose function is to purchase products from non-residents and then sell them at lower prices to residents (see also export subsidies in paragraph 7.76 below.)

7.75. As in the case of taxes on products, subsidies on imported goods do not include any subsidies that may become payable subsequently on such goods after they have crossed the frontier and entered into free circulation within the economic territory of the country.

Export subsidies (D.312)

7.76. Export subsidies consist of all subsidies on goods and services that become payable when the goods leave the economic territory or when the services are delivered to non-resident units. They include the following:

(a) *Direct subsidies* on exports payable directly to resident producers when the goods leave the economic territory or the services are delivered to non-residents;

(b) *Losses of government trading organizations*: these consist of losses incurred as a matter of deliberate government policy by government trading organizations whose function is to buy the products of resident enterprises and then sell them at lower prices to non-residents. The difference between the buying and selling prices is an export subsidy (see also paragraph 7.78 (b) below);

(c) *Subsidies resulting from multiple exchange rates*: these consist of implicit subsidies resulting from the operation of an official system of multiple exchange rates (see chapters XIV and XIX).

Exclusions from export subsidies

7.77. Export subsidies do not include the repayment at the customs frontier of taxes on products previously paid on goods or services while they were inside the economic territory. They also exclude the waiving of the taxes that would be due if the goods were to be sold or used inside the economic territory instead of being exported. General taxes on products such as sales or purchase taxes, VAT, excise taxes or other taxes on products are usually not payable on exports.

Other subsidies on products (D.319)

7.78. Other subsidies on products consist of subsidies on goods or services produced as the outputs of resident enterprises that become payable as a result of the production, sale, transfer, leasing or delivery of those goods or services, or as a result of their use for own consumption or own capital formation. The most common types are the following:

(a)   *Subsidies on products used domestically*: these consist of subsidies payable to resident enterprises in respect of their outputs which are used or consumed within the economic territory;

(b)   *Losses of government trading organizations*: these consist of the losses incurred by government trading organizations whose function is to buy and sell the products of resident enterprises. When such organizations incur losses as a matter of deliberate government economic or social policy by selling at lower prices than those at which they purchased the goods, the difference between the purchase and the selling prices should be treated as a subsidy. Entries to the inventories of goods held by such organizations are valued at the purchasers' prices

paid by the trading organizations and the subsidies recorded at the time the goods are sold;

(c)   *Subsidies to public corporations and quasi-corporations:* these consist of regular transfers paid to public corporations and quasi-corporations which are intended to compensate for persistent losses—i.e., negative operating surpluses—which they incur on their productive activities as a result of charging prices which are lower than their average costs of production as a matter of deliberate government economic and social policy. In order to calculate the basic prices of the outputs of such enterprises, it will usually be necessary to assume a uniform ad valorem implicit rate of subsidy on those outputs determined by the size of the subsidy as a percentage of the value of sales plus subsidy.

2. Other subsidies on production

7.79. These consist of subsidies except subsidies on products which resident enterprises may receive as a consequence of engaging in production. Examples of such subsidies are the following:

(a)   *Subsidies on payroll or workforce*: these consist of subsidies payable on the total wage or salary bill, or total workforce, or on the employment of particular types of persons such as physically handicapped persons or persons who have been unemployed for long periods. The subsidies may also be intended to cover some or all of the costs of training schemes organized or financed by enterprises;

(b)   *Subsidies to reduce pollution:* these consist of subsidies intended to cover some or all of the costs of additional processing undertaken to reduce or eliminate the discharge of pollutants into the environment.

E. Operating surplus or mixed income (B.2/B.3)

7.80. Operating surplus and mixed income are two alternative names for the same balancing item used for different types of enterprises. Operating surplus or mixed income is the balancing item in the generation of income account it is defined as:

value added

minus compensation of employees payable

minus taxes on production payable

plus subsidies receivable.

As already noted, value added should be measured net—after deducting consumption of fixed capital—but provision has to be made in the accounts of the system for value added, and hence all subsequent balancing items that depend on value added, to be measured gross or net of consumption of fixed capital because of the practical difficulty of measuring the lat-

ter. Value added may be assumed to be measured net, unless stated to the contrary.

7.81. *Mixed income* is the term reserved for the balancing item of the generation of income account of unincorporated enterprises owned by members of households, either individually or in partnership with others, in which the owners, or other members of their households, may work without receiving any wage or salary. In practice, all unincorporated enterprises owned by households that are not quasi-corporations are deemed to fall in this category, except owner-occupiers in their capacity as producers of housing services for own final consumption and households employing paid domestic staff, an activity that generates no surplus.

7.82. Operating surplus/mixed income is a measure of the surplus accruing from processes of production before deducting any explicit or implicit interest charges, rents or other property incomes payable on the financial assets, land or other tangible non-produced assets required to carry on the production. It is, therefore, invariant as to whether:

(*a*) The land or other tangible non-produced assets used in production are owned or rented by the enterprise; and

(*b*) The inventories, fixed assets, land or other non-produced assets owned by the enterprise and used in production are financed out of own funds (or equity capital) or out of borrowed funds (or loan capital).

Although the operating surplus/mixed income is invariant to the extent to which land is owned or assets in general are financed, it needs to be sufficient to cover both any explicit, or implicit, rents on land and the explicit, or implicit interest charges on the value of all the assets owned by the enterprise in order to justify their continued use in production. The implicit interest costs of using the enterprise's own funds to purchase inventories, fixed assets or other assets are the opportunity costs of using the funds in this way rather than to acquire financial assets on which actual interest could be earned. The amounts of rents and interest actually payable on rented land and borrowed funds are recorded in the allocation of primary income account, and the entrepreneurial income account, but the implicit rents on land owned by the enterprise and the implicit interest chargeable on the use of the enterprise's own funds are not recorded in the accounts of the System.

7.83. The operating surplus/mixed income is not invariant, however, to the extent to which the fixed assets used in production are owned or rented. When buildings, other structures, machinery or equipment are rented by an enterprise, the payments of rentals under an operating lease or similar lease are recorded as purchases of services. These services form part of intermediate consumption. Thus, as explained in chapter VI, paragraphs 6.181 to 6.183, the payment of the rental on a fixed asset tends to reduce gross value added below what it would be if the producer owned the asset. The impact on net value added, however, is mitigated by the fact that a tenant, or lessee, incurs no consumption of fixed capital whereas an owner would. In general, however, even net value added will tend to be lower when a fixed asset is rented as the rental has to cover the lessor's operating and interest costs as well as the consumption of fixed capital. Thus, the net operating surplus/mixed income is not invariant to the extent to which fixed assets are rented rather than purchased. At the level of the total economy, however, the lower surpluses accruing to tenants or lessees will tend to be counterbalanced by the operating surpluses earned by the lessors.

7.84. It should also be noted that enterprises may invest surplus funds in financial assets or even land, especially in times of uncertainty and high interest rates. Considerable property income may be received from such investments. The property income paid out by a corporation will be influenced by the amount of property income received as well as by its operating surplus. Thus, it is not appropriate to record all the property income paid out by an enterprise as if it were chargeable against the operating surplus. Some interest costs, especially implicit costs, may be attributable to assets other than those used in production. For this reason, the explicit and implicit interest costs payable by an enterprise ought not to be recorded in the generation of income account in which the resources consist only of value added accruing from production. They are recorded in the allocation of income account after taking account of any property income receivable as well as the operating surplus.

Mixed income

7.85. "Mixed income" has already been used to describe the balancing item in the generation of income account for a sub-set of enterprises, i.e., unincorporated enterprises owned by members of households either individually or in partnership with others in which the owners, or other members of their households, may work without receiving a wage or salary. Owners of such enterprises must be self-employed: those with paid employees are employers, while those without paid employees are own-account workers. In a few cases it may be possible to estimate the wage or salary element implicitly included within mixed income, but there is usually not enough information available about the number of hours worked or appropriate rates of remuneration for values to be imputed systematically. Thus, mixed income contains an unknown element of remuneration for work done by the owner of the enterprise, or other members of the same household, as well as the surplus accruing from production. The element of remuneration could be predominant in some cases.

7.86. A further difficulty with unincorporated enterprises is that it is often not possible to draw a clear distinction between the assets, including financial assets and liabilities, of an unincorporated enterprise and those of the owner in a personal capacity. Many fixed assets, such as buildings and vehicles, may be used partly for business purposes and partly for purposes of household final consumption. In addition, some goods ostensibly purchased for intermediate consumption may in fact be consumed by members of the household. Owners of enterprises may have an incentive to portray durable or non-durable goods used for final consumption as being used by the enterprise in order to reduce profits as reported to tax authorities. Even when there is no such incentive, owners may have genuine difficulty in separating their business expenditures or liabilities from their personal expenditures or liabilities. Thus, mixed incomes may be less reliable than the operating surpluses reported by corporations or government enterprises, and it may be useful to separate them for this reason also.

F. Property incomes (D.4)

1. Introduction

7.87. Property incomes are received by the owners of financial assets and tangible non-produced assets, mainly land and subsoil assets. Property incomes accrue when the owners of such assets put them at the disposal of other institutional units. Institutional units with funds to invest do so by lending them to other units. As a result, financial assets are created whose owners are entitled to receive property incomes in the form of interest, dividends, etc. Owners of land and subsoil assets may put them at the disposal of other units by arranging contracts or leases under which the tenants, or users of the assets, agree to pay the owners property incomes in the form of rents. The regular payments made by the lessees of subsoil assets are often described as royalties, but they are treated as rents in the System. The term "rent" is reserved in this manual for rents on land and subsoil assets, payments under operating leases being described as "rentals".

7.88. Property income may therefore be defined as:

> the income receivable by the owner of a financial asset or a tangible non-produced asset in return for providing funds to, or putting the tangible non-produced asset at the disposal of, another institutional unit.

The terms governing the payment of property incomes are usually specified in the financial instrument created when the funds are transferred from the creditor to the debtor or in the contract or lease signed when the right to exploit the land or subsoil assets is transferred from the owner to the tenant or lessee. Such arrangements are typically made only for a limited period of time, after which the funds must be repaid or the right to exploit the land or subsoil assets reverts to the owner. The period of time may be several months or several years, and such arrangements may of course be renewed.

7.89. Property incomes are classified in the following way in the System:

> Interest
> Distributed income of corporations
> > Dividends
> > Withdrawals from income of quasi-
> > corporations
> Reinvested earnings on direct foreign investment
> Property income attributed to insurance policy holders
> Rent.

Each of these items is described in more detail below. The income that the owners of quasi-corporations withdraw from them is analogous to the income withdrawn from corporations by paying out dividends to their shareholders. It is therefore treated as property income accruing to the owners of quasi-corporations.

2. Property incomes distinguished from rentals

7.90. The distinction between property incomes and the rentals receivable and payable under operating leases is fundamental to the System as rentals are treated as sales or purchases of services. The nature of operating leasing has already been described in chapter VI. In the present context, it is sufficient to emphasize the following differences between operating leasing and the renting of land and subsoil assets:

(a) Under an operating lease, the items leased consist of fixed assets such as buildings, ships, aircraft, vehicles, etc., that are all produced assets;

(b) The lessors of produced assets are typically engaged in processes of production whereby they provide services to the lessees by purchasing and maintaining inventories of fixed assets that they are able to lease out at short notice and for varying lengths of time for the convenience of their clients;

(c) The lessors engage in gross fixed capital formation in order to acquire the assets and incur consumption of fixed capital in respect of the assets they lease.

7.91. The rentals payable by lessees to lessors are therefore treated as purchases of services produced by the latter. They may be recorded under the intermediate consumption of enterprises or under the final consumption of households or government. On the other hand, the owners of funds, land or subsoil assets who merely place these assets at the disposal of other units are not considered to be themselves engaged in productive activity. The assets loaned, rented or leased have not been produced and no capital consumption is incurred in respect of their use. The property incomes payable by enterprises that borrow funds or rent land or subsoil assets do not affect the calculation of their value added or operating surpluses.

7.92. The renting of buildings, including dwellings, is not usually described as operating leasing, but the rentals paid by tenants under a building lease are treated in the same way as the rentals paid by lessees of other fixed assets. The rentals paid by tenants are treated as payments for the provision of building or housing services. Similarly, permitting other units to make use of intangible fixed assets is treated in the same way as operating leasing. Although the payments made by units using processes or producing products covered by patents are usually described as "royalties", they are treated as purchases of services produced by the owners of the patents.

3. Interest (D.41)

Introduction

7.93. Interest is a form of property income that is receivable by the owners of certain kinds of financial assets, namely:

Deposits

Securities other than shares

Loans

Other accounts receivable.

These financial assets are all claims of creditors over debtors. Creditors lend funds to debtors that lead to creation of one or other of the financial instruments listed above. The amount of the debtor's liability to the creditor at any point of time may be described as the principal outstanding. It is the amount that the debtor must repay to discharge the liability and thereby extinguish the creditor's claim over the debtor.

Interest may be defined as follows:

> Under the terms of the financial instrument agreed between them interest is the amount that the debtor becomes liable to pay to the creditor over a given period of time without reducing the amount of principal outstanding.

However, the interest may not necessarily be due for payment until a later date and sometimes not until the loan, or other financial instrument matures. Interest may be a predetermined sum of money or percentage of the principal outstanding. If some or all of the interest accruing to the creditor is not paid during the period in question, it may be added to the amount of the principal outstanding or it may constitute an additional, separate liability incurred by the debtor. As explained in chapter XI, there are many different kinds of financial instruments and new instruments are continually being evolved. Interest may therefore be paid in various different ways, not always explicitly described as interest.

The accrual basis of recording

7.94. Interest is recorded on an accrual basis, i.e., interest is recorded as accruing continuously over time to the creditor on the amount of principal outstanding. The interest accruing is the amount receivable by the creditor and payable by the debtor. It may differ not only from the amount of interest actually paid during a given period but also the amount due to be paid within the period. Some financial instruments are drawn up in such a way that the debtor is obliged to make regular interest payments, period by period, as the interest accrues but in other cases there may be no such requirement.

7.95. Certain financial instruments, for example, bills and zero coupon bonds, are such that the debtor is under no obligation to make any payments to the creditor until the asset matures. In effect, no interest becomes due for payment until the end of the asset's life at which point the debtor's liability is discharged by a single payment covering both the amount of the funds originally provided by the creditor and the interest accumulated over the entire life of the asset. However, in the System, the interest accruing in each accounting period must be recorded whether or not it is actually paid or added to the principal outstanding. When it is not paid, the increase in the principal must also be recorded in the financial account as a

further acquisition of that kind of financial asset by the creditor and an equal incurrence of a liability by the debtor.

Interest on deposits, loans and accounts receivable and payable

7.96. The nature of financial assets and liabilities in the form of deposits, loans and accounts receivable and payable is explained in chapter XI. In general, the interest receivable and payable on these financial assets and liabilities is determined simply by applying the relevant rate of interest to the principal outstanding at each point of time throughout the accounting period.

Interest on securities

Interest on bills and similar instruments

7.97. As explained in chapter XI, bills are short-term securities that give the holder (creditor) the unconditional right to receive a stated fixed sum on a specified date. They are issued and traded in organized markets at a discount that depends on current market short-term interest rates and the time to maturity. Most bills mature after a period ranging from one month to one year.

7.98. Let the price paid for a bill at its time of issue be L: this represents the amount of funds that the purchaser (creditor) provides to the issuer (debtor) and measures the value of the initial liability incurred by the issuer. Let the face value of the bill be F: this represents the sum paid to the holder of the bill (the creditor) when it matures. The difference, F-L, or discount on the bill, measures the interest payable over the life of the bill.

7.99. Bills are traded on money markets at values which gradually rise to reflect the interest accruing on the bills as they approach maturity. The increase in the value of a bill due to the accumulation of accrued interest does not constitute a holding gain because it is due to an increase in the principal outstanding and not a change in the price of the asset.

Interest on bonds and debentures

7.100. Bonds and debentures are long-term securities that give the holder the unconditional right to:

(*a*)   A fixed or contractually determined variable money income in the form of coupon payments;

or

(*b*)   A stated fixed sum on a specified date or dates when the security is redeemed;

or

(*c*)   Both (a) and (b). Most bonds fall into this category.

The amounts of the fixed or variable money incomes or coupon payments due for payment within the accounting period are treated as interest receivable and payable by the creditor and debtor respectively. In addition, when a bond is issued at a discount, the difference between the face value, or redemption price, and the issue price constitutes interest that accrues over the life of the bond, in the same way as for a bill. However, as accounts are compiled for time periods that are typically much shorter than the life of the bond, the interest must be distributed over those periods. They way in which this may be done is explained below.

Zero-coupon bonds

7.101. Zero-coupon bonds are long-term securities that are similar to bills. They do not entitle their holders to any fixed or variable money income but only to receive a stated fixed sum as repayment of principal and accrued interest on a specified date or dates. When they are issued they are usually sold at a price that is substantially lower than the price at which they are redeemed on maturity. Let L equal the issue price and F the redemption price, F-L is the value of the interest receivable and payable over the life of the bond. This interest has to be distributed over the years to its maturity. One possible method is to assume interest is credited at the end of each year at an annual rate that is constant over the life of the bond, in which case the rate is given by the following expression:

$$r = (F/L)^{1/n} - 1$$

where n is the number of years from the time of issue to maturity. The interest accruing during the course of year t is then given by

$$rL(1 + r)^{t-1}$$

where $t = 1$ at the end of the first year.

7.102. The interest accruing each year is effectively reinvested in the bond by its holder. Thus, counterpart entries equal to the value of the accrued interest must be recorded in the financial account as the acquisition of more bond by the holder and as a further issue of more bond by the issuer or debtor.

Other bonds, including deep-discounted bonds

7.103. Most bonds pay a fixed or variable money income and may also be issued at a discount or, possibly, a premium. In such cases, the interest receivable by the holders of the bonds has two components:

(*a*) The amount of the money income receivable from coupon payments each period;

    plus

(b) The amount of interest accruing each period attributable to the difference between the redemption price and the issue price.

The second component is calculated in the same way as for zero-coupon bonds, as described above. In the case of deep-discounted bonds, the amounts of money income payable each period are relatively small and most of the interest accruing is attributable to the difference between the redemption price and the issue price. At the other extreme, some bonds offer an income stream in perpetuity and are never redeemed.

Index linked securities

7.104. Index linked securities are financial instruments for which the amounts of the coupon payments (interest) and/or the principal outstanding are linked to a general price index, a specific price index or an exchange rate index. When the coupon payments are index linked, the full amounts of such payments are treated as interest receivable and payable, in the same way as the interest receivable and payable on any other security paying a contractually agreed variable income. When the value of the principal is index linked, the difference between the eventual redemption price and the issue price is treated as interest accruing over the life of the asset in the same way as for a security whose redemption price is fixed in advance. In practice, the change in the value of the principal outstanding between the beginning and end of a particular accounting period due to the movement in the relevant index may be treated as interest accruing in that period, in addition to any interest due for payment in that period. The interest accruing as a result of the indexation is effectively reinvested in the security and this additional investment must be recorded in the financial accounts of the holder and issuer.

Interest rate swaps and forward rate agreements

7.105. Swaps are contractual arrangements between two institutional units who agree to exchange streams of payables on the same amount of indebtedness over time. Common varieties of swaps are interest rate swaps and currency swaps. Interest rate swaps consist of the exchange of interest payments of different character, for example:

    Fixed rate payments for floating or variable rate payments

    One kind of floating rate payments for another

    Fixed rate payments in one currency for floating rate payments in another currency

and so on. The streams of interest payments resulting from swap arrangements should be recorded net of the payments between the two parties to the swap. Neither of the parties is treated as providing a service to the other, but any payments made to third parties, such as specialized brokers, for arranging the swaps are recorded as purchases of services.

7.106. The same principle is applied to transactions under forward rate agreements (FRAs). These are arrangements in which two parties, in order to protect themselves against interest rate changes, agree on an interest rate to be paid on a specified settlement date on a nominal amount of principal that is never exchanged. The only payment that takes place relates to the difference between the agreed FRA rate and the prevailing market rate on the settlement date. The buyer of the FRA receives payment from the seller if the prevailing rate exceeds the agreed rate, while the seller receives payment if the latter exceeds the former. These payments are recorded as interest receivable and payable.

Interest on financial leases

7.107. Financial leases may be distinguished from other leases by the fact that all the risks and rewards of ownership are, de facto, transferred from the legal owner of the fixed asset, the lessor, to the user of the asset, the lessee. In order to capture the economic reality of such arrangements the fixed asset is treated in the System as if it were purchased by the lessee, instead of the lessor, out of funds provided by the latter. The lessor is treated as making a loan to the lessee equal to the value of the purchaser's price paid for the asset, this loan being gradually paid off in full over the period of the lease. The rental paid each period by the lessee is therefore treated as having two components: the first consists of a repayment of principal, the remainder being treated as a payment of interest. The rate of interest on the imputed loan is implicitly determined by the total amount paid in rentals over the life of the lease in relationship to the purchaser's price of the asset. It is easily calculated using standard formulas. Assuming that the rental remains constant from period to period, the share of the rental that represents interest gradually declines over the life of the lease as the principal is repaid. The initial loan by the lessee, together with the subsequent repayments of principal, are recorded in the Financial Accounts of the lessor or lessee. The interest payments are recorded under interest in their respective Primary Distribution of Income Accounts.

Interest payable and receivable by financial intermediaries

7.108. As explained in chapter VI, the amounts of interest payable to and receivable by financial intermediaries are set in order to provide a margin that is used to defray the costs of providing certain services to their customers, both depositors and borrowers, for which they do not charge explicitly. When the value of the services provided by financial intermediaries is allocated among different customers the actual payments or receipts of interest to or from financial intermediaries need to be adjusted to eliminate the margins that represent the implicit charges made by financial intermediaries. The amounts of interest paid by borrowers to financial intermediaries must be reduced by the estimated values of the charges payable, while the amounts of interest receivable by depositors must be similarly increased. The values of the charges must, of course, be treated as payments for services rendered by financial intermediaries to their customers and not as payments of interest. They are recorded as sales of services in the production accounts of financial intermediaries and as uses in the accounts of their customers. However, when the whole output of financial intermediaries is, by convention, allocated as the intermediate consumption of a nominal industry, no such adjustments to interest payments and receipts are called for, although an

adjustment item is needed in the allocation of income account of financial intermediaries and of the nominal industry.

Nominal and real interest

7.109. When a debtor is able to discharge his liability to the creditor by repaying principal equal in money value to the funds borrowed the associated interest payments are described as "nominal". Such interest payments do not represent the "real" return to the creditor when, as a result of inflation, the purchasing power of the funds repaid is less than that of the funds borrowed. In situations of chronic inflation the nominal interest payments demanded by creditors typically rise in order to compensate them for the losses of purchasing power that they expect when their funds are eventually repaid.

7.110. In inflationary situations it is possible to view an actual payment of nominal interest as consisting of two elements:

(a) A payment equal to the loss of purchasing power on the monetary value of the principal during the accounting period;

(b) The balance remaining that represents the real interest accruing to the creditor.

The first element may be calculated by multiplying the value of the principal by the change in some general price index. It may be regarded as a payment made by the debtor to compensate the creditor for the real holding loss on the principal outstanding. The remainder of the nominal interest payment, which could be positive or negative, constitutes real interest.

7.111. In practice, the interest recorded in the allocation of primary income account is not partitioned in this way. The interest recorded is always the amount of nominal interest receivable or payable (plus or minus the charges for services of financial intermediaries for which no explicit charges are made, when relevant). However, the information needed to calculate real interest is provided within the System as a whole as the real holding losses incurred by creditors should be recorded in the revaluation account. A further discussion of the treatment of interest under inflation is given in chapter XIX. Annex B to chapter XIX proposes a parallel treatment of interest under significant inflation.

4. Distributed income of corporations (D.42)

Dividends (D.421)

7.112. Corporations obtain funds by issuing shares in their equity which entitle the holders to shares both of distributed profits and the residual value of the assets of the corporation in the event of its liquidation. Shareholders are the collective owners of a corporation.

7.113. Dividends are a form of property income to which shareholders become entitled as a result of placing funds at the disposal of corporations. Raising equity capital through the issue of shares is an alternative way of raising funds to borrowing. In contrast to loan capital, however, equity capital does not give rise to a liability that is fixed in monetary terms and it does not entitle the holders of shares of a corporation to a fixed or predetermined income.

7.114. Just as corporations are understood in the System to cover a set of institutional units engaged in production which may be described by different names—private or public corporations, private or public companies, cooperatives, limited liability partnerships, etc.—dividends must also be understood to cover all distributions of profits by corporations to their shareholders or owners, by whatever name they are called. Dividends may occasionally take the form of an issue of shares, but issues of bonus shares which represent the capitalization of own funds in the form of reserves and undistributed profits are not included.

Withdrawals from income of quasi-corporations (D.422)

7.115. Although a quasi-corporation is treated as if it were a corporation, it cannot distribute income by paying dividends to its owner. Nevertheless, the owner, or owners, of a quasi-corporation may choose to withdraw some or all of the entrepreneurial income of the enterprise. Conceptually, the withdrawal of such income is equivalent to the distribution of corporate income through dividends and is treated as if it were a type of dividend. It needs to be identified in order to be able to distinguish the income of the quasi-corporation from that of its owner.

7.116. In order for an unincorporated enterprise to be treated as a quasi-corporation it must have a complete set of accounts of its own. It follows that any income withdrawn from a quasi-corporation should be explicitly identifiable in its accounts, where it is likely to be recorded as a payment, or transfer, to an account of the owner kept separately from the accounts relating to the activities of the quasi-corporation itself.

7.117. The amount of income which the owner of a quasi-corporation chooses to withdraw will depend largely on the size of its entrepreneurial income, i.e., its operating surplus *plus* property income receivable on any assets owned by the enterprise *minus* any interest or rents payable on its liabilities, land or other tangible non-produced assets. When deciding exactly how much to withdraw, the owner has to take into account the size of its entrepreneurial income in much the same way as the board of directors of a corporation in deciding how much to pay out in dividends. Conceptually, the income withdrawn is a form of property income accruing to the owner of a quasi-corporation in respect of funds invested in the enterprise.

7.118. Withdrawals of income from a quasi-corporation do not, of course, include withdrawals of funds realized by the sale or disposal of the quasi-corporation's assets: for example, the sale of inventories, fixed assets or land or other non-produced assets. Such sales would be recorded as disposals in the capital

account of the quasi-corporation and the transfer of the resulting funds would be recorded as a withdrawal from the equity of quasi-corporations in the financial accounts of the quasi-corporation and its owner(s). Similarly, funds withdrawn by liquidating large amounts of accumulated retained savings or other reserves of the quasi-corporation, including those built up out of provisions for consumption of fixed capital, are treated as withdrawals from equity. Conversely, any funds provided by the owner(s) of a quasi-corporation for the purpose of acquiring assets or reducing its liabilities should be treated as additions to its equity. Just as there cannot be a negative distribution from the entrepreneurial income of corporations in the form of negative dividends, it is not possible to have a negative distribution from the entrepreneurial income of quasi-corporations in the form of negative withdrawals. However, if the quasi-corporation is owned by government, and if it runs a persistent operating deficit as a matter of deliberate government economic and social policy, any regular transfers of funds into the enterprise made by government to cover its losses should be treated as subsidies, as explained in paragraph 7.78 (c) above.

5. Reinvested earnings on direct foreign investment (D.43)

7.119. As explained in chapter XIV, a direct foreign investment enterprise is a corporate or unincorporated enterprise in which a foreign investor has made a direct foreign investment. A direct foreign investment enterprise may be either:

(a) The (unincorporated) branch of a non-resident corporate or unincorporated enterprise: this is treated as a quasi-corporation; or

(b) A corporation in which at least one foreign investor (which may, or may not, be another corporation) owns sufficient shares to have an effective voice in its management.

7.120. Actual distributions may be made out of the entrepreneurial income of direct foreign investment enterprises in the form of dividends or withdrawals of income from quasi-corporations. The payments made in these ways to foreign direct investors are recorded in the accounts of the SNA and in the balance of payments statistics of the IMF as international flows of property income. However, both systems also require the saving or retained earnings of a direct foreign investment enterprise to be treated as if they were distributed and remitted to foreign direct investors in proportion to their ownership of the equity of the enterprise and then reinvested by them. In other words, two additional entries are required in the accounts of the enterprises and their foreign owners, one of which is the imputed remittance of retained earnings, while the other is the imputed reinvestment of those earnings. The imputed remittance of these retained earnings is classified in the System as a form of distributed income that is separate from, and additional to, any actual payments of dividends or withdrawals of income from quasi-corporations.

7.121. The rationale behind this treatment is that, since a direct foreign investment enterprise is, by definition, subject to control, or influence, by a foreign direct investor or investors, the decision to retain some of its earnings within the enterprise must represent a conscious deliberate investment decision on the part of the foreign direct investor(s). In practice, the great majority of direct investment enterprises are subsidiaries of foreign corporations or the unincorporated branches of foreign enterprises, i.e., quasi-corporations, that are completely controlled by their parent corporations or owners.

7.122. The retained earnings in question are equal to:

the operating surplus of the direct foreign investment enterprise

plus any property incomes or current transfers receivable

minus any property incomes or current transfers payable, including actual remittances to foreign direct investors and any current taxes payable on the income, wealth, etc., of the direct foreign investment enterprise.

Thus, the retained earnings are equal to the entrepreneurial income of the foreign direct investment enterprise, plus or minus any current transfers receivable or payable, including any current taxes on income, wealth, etc. payable. If the direct enterprise is wholly owned by a single foreign direct investor (for example, a branch of a foreign enterprise) the whole of the retained earnings are deemed to be remitted to that investor and then reinvested, in which case the saving of the enterprise must be zero. When a foreign direct investor owns only part of the equity of the direct investment enterprise, the amount which is deemed to be remitted to, and reinvested by, the foreign investor is proportional to the share of the equity owned.

6. Property income attributed to insurance policyholders (D.44)

7.123. The technical reserves held by insurance enterprises consist of the actuarial reserves against outstanding risks in respect of life insurance policies, including reserves for with-profit policies which add to the value on maturity of with-profit endowments or similar policies, prepayments of premiums and reserves against outstanding claims. Although held and managed by insurance enterprises, the technical reserves are held in trust for the benefit of policyholders, or beneficiaries in the case of reserves against outstanding claims. The reserves are, therefore, considered to be assets of the policyholders or beneficiaries and liabilities of the insurance enterprises. In the financial accounts, the claims of holders of both life and non-life insurance policies over the insurance enterprises are described as the net equity of households on life insurance reserves and on pension funds and prepayments of insurance premiums and reserves for outstanding claims.

7.124. Insurance technical reserves are invested by insurance enterprises in various ways. They are commonly used to purchase financial assets, land or buildings. The insurance enterprises receive property income from the financial assets and land, and earn net operating surpluses from the renting or leasing of residential and other buildings. The total of the primary incomes received in this way from the investment of insurance technical reserves is described as *investment income*. It does not, of course, include any income received from the investment of insurance enterprises' own assets. However, as the technical reserves are assets of the insurance policyholders, the investment income receivable by insurance enterprises must be shown in the accounts as being paid by the insurance enterprises to the policyholders. The income payable by insurance enterprises to policyholders in this way is described as property income attributed to insurance policyholders. However, this income is retained by the insurance enterprises in practice. It is therefore treated as being paid back to the insurance enterprises in the form of premium supplements that are additional to actual premiums payable under the terms of the insurance policies. These premium supplements on non-life insurance policies and on life insurance policies taken out under social insurance schemes are recorded together with the actual premiums in the secondary distribution of income accounts of the units concerned. The premium supplements on individual life insurance policies not taken out under social insurance schemes, like the actual premiums, are not current transfers and are therefore not recorded in the secondary distribution of income accounts. They are used directly to acquire financial claims over the life insurance reserves and are included as one of the elements contributing to the change in the net equity of households on life insurance reserves and pension funds recorded in the financial accounts of the units concerned.

7.125. Receipts of income by insurance enterprises from the investment of the technical reserves are recorded in the primary distribution of income account of insurance enterprises in the normal way. Net operating surpluses earned from the activity of renting buildings are recorded in the generation of income account while property incomes receivable from investment in financial assets or land are shown in the allocation of primary income account. An amount equal to the total value of this investment income is then shown under uses in the allocation of primary income account as being payable to policyholders as property income attributed to insurance policyholders. Thus, the balance of primary incomes and the disposable incomes of insurance enterprises are not influenced by the amounts of income received from the investment of technical reserves.

7.126. The total value of the investment income of an insurance enterprise is allocated among policyholders in proportion to the actual premiums paid. The amounts receivable by individual policyholders as property income attributed to insurance policyholders are shown under resources in the allocation of primary income accounts of the institutional units and sectors concerned.

7.127. Pension funds consist of the reserves held by autonomous funds established by employers and/or employees to provide pensions for employees after retirement. The reserves, and the income received by investing the reserves in financial assets, land or buildings, are treated in the same way as technical reserves and investment income associated with life insurance taken out under a social insurance scheme. The pension funds are assets of the households entitled to receive pensions in the present or future periods and constitute liabilities of the institutional units administering the funds. The investment income receivable by the pension funds is therefore recorded as being payable by the pension funds to the entitled households in the primary income accounts of the pension funds and the households under the heading property income attributed to insurance policyholders. Households are then treated as paying an equal amount back again to the funds as premium or contribution supplements in the secondary distribution of income accounts.

7. Rents (D.45)

Rents on land

7.128. The rent received by a landowner from a tenant constitutes a form of property income. Rent is recorded on an accrual basis, i.e., rent is treated as accruing continuously to the landowner throughout the period of the contract agreed between the landowner and the tenant. The rent recorded for a particular accounting period is, therefore, equal to the value of the accumulated rent payable over that period of time, as distinct from the amount of rent due to be paid during that period or the rent actually paid.

7.129. Rent may be paid in cash or in kind. Under share-cropping or similar schemes, the value of the rent payable is not fixed in advance in monetary terms and is measured by the value at basic prices of the crops that the tenants are obliged to provide to the landowner under the contract between them. Rents on land also include the rents payable to the owners of inland waters and rivers for the right to exploit such waters for recreational or other purposes, including fishing.

7.130. A landowner may be liable to pay land taxes or incur certain maintenance expenses solely as a consequence of owning the land. By convention, such taxes or expenses are treated as payable by the tenant who is deemed to deduct them from the rent that he would otherwise be obliged to pay to the landowner. Rent reduced in this way by taxes or other expenses for which the landowner is liable is described as "net rent". By adopting the convention that the tenant pays only the net rent, the taxes or expenses are recorded in the production or generation of income accounts of the tenant. This treatment does not change the income of the tenant. The convention avoids the necessity to create a notional enterprise for the landowner if the landowner is not already engaged in some other kind of productive activity.

7.131. As already noted, the rentals payable on buildings or other structures are treated as purchases of services. In practice, however, a single payment may cover both rent and rentals when an institutional unit rents land and any buildings situated on it in a single contract, or lease, in which the two kinds of payments are not differentiated from each other. For example, a farmer may rent a farmhouse, farm buildings and farmland in a contract in which only a single payment is required to cover all three. If there is no objective basis on which to split the payment between rent on land and rental on the buildings, it is recommended to treat the whole amount as rent when the value of the land is believed to exceed the value of the buildings on it, and as a rental otherwise.

Rents on subsoil assets

7.132. The ownership of subsoil assets in the form of deposits of minerals or fossil fuels—coal, oil or natural gas—depends upon the way in which property rights are defined by law and also on international agreements in the case of deposits below international waters. In some cases the assets may be owned by the owner of the ground below which the deposits are located but in other cases they may be owned by a local or central government unit.

7.133. The owners of the assets, whether private or government units, may grant leases to other institutional units permitting them to extract such deposits over a specified period of time in return for the payment of rents. These payments are often described as royalties, but they are essentially rents that accrue to owners of the assets in return for putting them at the disposal of other institutional units for specified periods of time and are treated as such in the System. The rents may take the form of periodic payments of fixed amounts, irrespective of the rate of extraction or, more likely, they may be a function of the quantity or volume of the asset extracted. Enterprises engaged in exploration may make payments to the owners of surface land in exchange for the right to make test drillings or investigate by other means the existence and location of subsoil assets. Such payments are also to be treated as rents even though no extraction may take place.

VIII. The secondary distribution of income account

A. Introduction

8.1. The secondary distribution of income account (see table 8.1), shows how the balance of primary incomes of an institutional unit or sector is transformed into its disposable income by the receipt and payment of current transfers excluding social transfers in kind. This redistribution represents the second stage in the process of income distribution as shown in the accounts of the System.

8.2. The redistribution of income in kind account (see table 8.2), takes the process of income redistribution one stage further. It shows how the disposable income of households, non-profit institutions serving households (NPISHs) and government units are transformed into their adjusted disposable income by the receipt and payment of social transfers in kind. Non-financial and financial corporations are not involved in this process.

1. The secondary distribution of income account

8.3. Apart from disposable income and balance of primary incomes, the balancing item carried forward from the primary distribution of income accounts, all the entries in the secondary distribution of income account consist of current transfers. A transfer is a transaction in which one institutional unit provides a good, service or asset to another unit without receiving from the latter any good, service or asset in return as counterpart. A capital transfer is one in which the ownership of an asset is transferred or which obliges one or both parties to acquire, or dispose of an asset. Other transfers are described as current. The concept of a transfer is explained in more detail in section B below. Three main kinds of current transfers are distinguished in the account:

> Current taxes on income, wealth, etc.
>
> Social contributions and benefits
>
> Other current transfers.

8.4. The transfers payable by an institutional unit or sector are recorded on the left-hand side of the account under uses. For example, in table 8.1, taxes on income payable by the household sector are recorded at the intersection of the row for this item and the uses column for the household sector. The transfers receivable by an institutional unit or sector are recorded on the right-hand side of the account under resources. For example, the social security benefits in cash receivable by the household

sector are recorded at the intersection of the row for this item and the resources column for the household sector. In accordance with the general accounting rules of the System, the entries in the account, apart from the balancing items, refer to amounts payable and receivable. These may not necessarily coincide with the amounts actually paid or received in the same accounting period. Current transfers may take place between resident and non-resident units as well as between resident institutional units.

8.5. Much of this chapter is concerned with the detailed definition, description and classification of the various types of current transfers recorded in the secondary distribution of income and redistribution of income in kind accounts. Their general nature and the purposes they serve are summarized in the following paragraphs.

Current taxes on income, wealth, etc. (D.5)

8.6. Most of these taxes consist of taxes on the incomes of households or profits of corporations and of taxes on wealth that are payable regularly every tax period (as distinct from capital taxes levied infrequently). In table 8.1, current taxes receivable appear under resources for the general government sector while taxes payable appear under uses for the household and non-financial and financial corporation sectors, and possibly for the non-profit institutions serving households (NPISHs) sector.

Social contributions and benefits (D.6)

8.7. Social benefits are current transfers received by households intended to provide for the needs that arise from certain events or circumstances, for example, sickness, unemployment, retirement, housing, education or family circumstances. There are two kinds of social benefits: social insurance benefits and social assistance benefits. To qualify as social insurance benefits the transfers must be provided under organized social insurance schemes. Social insurance benefits may be provided under general social security schemes, under private funded social insurance schemes or by unfunded schemes managed by employers for the benefit of their existing or former employees without involving third parties in the form of insurance enterprises or pension funds. Payments by insurance

Table 8.1. Account II.2: Secondary distribution of income account

Column groups — Left block = **Uses**; Right block = **Resources**. "Corresponding entries of the" columns are the Goods and service account (G&S) and the Rest of the world account (RoW).

Uses Total	Uses G&S acct	Uses RoW acct	Uses S.1 Total economy	Uses S.15 NPISHs	Uses S.14 Households	Uses S.13 General government	Uses S.12 Financial corporations	Uses S.11 Non-financial corporations	Code	Transactions and balancing items	Res S.11 Non-financial corporations	Res S.12 Financial corporations	Res S.13 General government	Res S.14 Households	Res S.15 NPISHs	Res S.1 Total economy	Res RoW acct	Res G&S acct	Res Total
									B.5g / B.5*g	Balance of primary incomes, gross/National income, gross	209	29	227	1 409	9	1 883			1 883
									B.5n / B.5*n	*Balance of primary incomes, net/National income, net*	72	19	197	1 367	6	1 661			1 661
213		1	212		178		10	24	D.5	Current taxes on income, wealth, etc.			213			213			213
204		1	203		176		7	20	D.51	Taxes on income			204			204			204
9			9		2		3	4	D.59	Other current taxes			9			9			9
322			322		322				D.61	Social contributions	14	39	268		1	322			322
303			303		303				D.611	Actual social contributions	2	38	263			303			303
174			174		174				D.6111	Employers' actual social contributions	1	18	155			174			174
160			160		160				D.61111	Compulsory employers' actual social contributions	1	15	144			160			160
14			14		14				D.61112	Voluntary employers' actual social contributions		3	11			14			14
97			97		97				D.6112	Employees' social contributions	1	20	76			97			97
85			85		85				D.61121	Compulsory employees' social contributions	1	15	69			85			85
12			12		12				D.61122	Voluntary employees' social contributions		5	7			12			12
32			32		32				D.6113	Social contributions by self- and non-employed persons			32			32			32
22			22		22				D.61131	Compulsory social contributions by self- and non-employed persons			22			22			22
10			10		10				D.61132	Voluntary social contributions by self- and non-employed persons			10			10			10
19			19		19				D.612	Imputed social contributions	12	1	5		1	19			19
332			332	1		289	29	13	D.62	Social benefits other than social transfers in kind				332		332			332
232			232			232			D.621	Social security benefits in cash				232		232			232
29			29				28	1	D.622	Private funded social benefits				29		29			29
19			19	1		5	1	12	D.623	Unfunded employee social benefits				19		19			19
52			52			52			D.624	Social assistance benefits in cash				52		52			52
278		9	269	2	71	139	46	11	D.7	Other current transfers	10	49	108	36	36	239	39		278
45		2	43		31	4		8	D.71	Net non-life insurance premiums		45				45			45
45			45				45		D.72	Non-life insurance claims	6		1	35		42	3		45
100		4	96			96			D.73	Current transfers within general government			96			96	4		100
32		1	31			31			D.74	Current international cooperation			1			1	31		32
56		2	54	2	40	8	1	3	D.75	Miscellaneous current transfers	4	4	10	1	36	55	1		56
1 854			1 854	43	1 206	388	32	185	B.6g	Disposable income, gross									
1 632			1 632	40	1 164	358	22	48	B.6n	*Disposable income, net*									

Table 8.2. Account II.3: Redistribution of income in kind account

Uses									Transactions and balancing items		Resources								
Total	Corresponding entries of the Goods and service account	Rest of the world account	S.1 Total economy	S.15 NPISHs	S.14 Households	S.13 General government	S.12 Financial corporations	S.11 Non-financial corporations			S.11 Non-financial corporations	S.12 Financial corporations	S.13 General government	S.14 Households	S.15 NPISHs	S.1 Total economy	Rest of the world account	Goods and service account	Total
									B.6g	Disposable income, gross	185	32	388	1 206	43	1 854			1 854
									B.6n	*Disposable income, net*	48	22	358	1 164	40	1 632			1 632
228			228	16		212			D.63	Social transfers in kind				228		228			228
162			162	0		162			D.631	Social benefits in kind				162		162			162
78			78			78			D.6311	Social security benefits, reimbursements				78		78			78
65			65			65			D.6312	Other social security benefits in kind				65		65			65
19			19			19			D.6313	Social assistance benefits in kind				19		19			19
66			66	16		50			D.632	Transfers of individual non-market goods and services				66		66			66
1 854			1 854	27	1 434	176	32	185	B.7g	Adjusted disposable income, gross									
1 632			1 632	24	1 392	146	22	48	B.7n	*Adjusted disposable income, net*									

enterprises under policies arranged individually and on the individual's own initiative and not under an organized social insurance scheme are excluded even when the same risks and conditions are concerned. Social assistance benefits are intended to meet the same kinds of needs as social insurance benefits but are provided outside of an organized social insurance scheme and are not conditional on previous payments of contributions. Social insurance benefits in kind provided under private funded social insurance schemes or unfunded schemes are treated as if they were paid in cash and included in the secondary distribution of income account. However, social insurance benefits in kind provided under general social security schemes and all social assistance benefits in kind constitute social transfers in kind and are therefore included in the redistribution of income in kind account. Thus, in table 8.1 social benefits, except social transfers in kind, are recorded under resources for the household sector and may, in principle, be recorded under uses for any sector as any institutional unit in its capacity as an employer may operate an unfunded scheme in which it receives imputed contributions and pays benefits.

8.8. Social contributions are actual or imputed payments to social insurance schemes to make provision for social insurance benefits to be paid. They may be made by employers on behalf of their employees or by employees, self-employed or non-employed persons on their own behalf. Social contributions may, in principle, be recorded under resources for any sector. Most contributions, however, are likely to be recorded under resources for the general government sector, including social security funds, and for insurance corporations and pension funds in the financial corporate sector. Social contributions are recorded under uses only for households, either resident or non-resident.

Other current transfers (D.7)

8.9. Several kinds of transfers serving quite different purposes are included under this heading. For example, one important group consists of net premiums and claims for non-life insurance. The net non-life insurance premiums receivable by insurance corporations (the actual premiums plus premium supplements reduced by the associated service charges) are recorded under resources for the insurance corporations subsector, while the net premiums payable may be recorded under uses for any sector. Conversely, the claims payable by insurance corporations are recorded as uses for the financial corporate sector, while the claims receivable may be recorded under resources for any sector.

8.10. Another group consists of current transfers between different kinds of government units, usually at different levels of government, and also between general government and foreign governments. This heading also includes other current transfers such as between different households.

2. Disposable income (B.6)

8.11. Disposable income is the balancing item in the secondary distribution of income account. It is derived from the balance of primary incomes of an institutional unit or sector by:

(a) Adding all current transfers, except social transfers in kind, receivable by that unit or sector; and

(b) Subtracting all current transfers, except social transfers in kind, payable by that unit or sector.

8.12. Disposable income, like the balance of primary incomes, may be recorded gross or net of consumption of fixed capital. It may be necessary to record it gross because of the difficulty of measuring consumption of fixed capital even though consumption of fixed capital is a cost of production and not a component of income. The following discussion refers to the *net* concept of disposable income.

8.13. Disposable income is not all available in cash. The inclusion in the accounts of non-monetary transactions associated with production for own consumption or barter, or with remuneration in kind, means that households have no choice but to consume certain kinds of goods and services for which the values of the corresponding expenditures out of disposable income are imputed. Although social transfers in kind from government units or NPIs to households are recorded separately in the redistribution of income in kind account, other transfers in kind are recorded in the secondary distribution of income account together with transfers in cash. They may include international transfers of food, clothing, medicines, etc., to relieve the effects of famine or other hardships caused by natural disasters or wars. The recipients of transfers in kind, other than social transfers in kind, are, by convention, recorded as making imputed consumption expenditures on the goods or services in question as if the transfers were received in cash.

8.14. Households also receive several kinds of property income that is not made available in cash. These include the income accruing from the investment of insurance and pension reserves that is attributed to the households that have taken out insurance policies or have pension entitlements. This income is recorded as being received by the appropriate households in the allocation of primary income account but is automatically repayable as premium supplements to the insurance enterprises or pension funds and cannot be used for purposes of consumption expenditures. Another example is provided by the interest accruing on a zero-coupon bond which is automatically reinvested in the bond.

Links with economic theoretic concepts of income

8.15. Disposable income as measured in the System can be compared with the concept of income as it is generally understood in economics. From a theoretical point of view, income is often defined as the maximum amount that a household, or other unit, can consume without reducing its real net worth.

However, the real net worth of a unit may be changed as a result of the receipt or payment of capital transfers and as a result of real holding gains or losses that accrue on its assets or liabilities. It may also be changed by events such as natural disasters that change the volume of assets. Capital transfers, real holding gains or losses and other changes in the volume of assets due to the effect of events such as natural disasters are specifically excluded from disposable income as measured here. Capital transfers are recorded in the capital account of the System, while other changes in the volume of assets and real holding gains or losses are recorded in the other changes in assets account. According to the concept of disposable income used in the System, the net worth that needs to be maintained intact is that at the beginning of the accounting period adjusted for the value of any capital transfers received or paid, for other changes in the volume of assets and for any real holding gains or losses accruing during the accounting period. Disposable income is better interpreted in a narrower sense as the maximum amount that a household or other unit can afford to spend on consumption goods or services during the accounting period without having to finance its expenditures by reducing its cash, by disposing of other financial or non-financial assets or by increasing its liabilities. This concept is equivalent to the economic theoretic concept only when the net worth at the beginning of the period is not changed by capital transfers, other changes in the volume of assets or real holding gains or losses.

National disposable income

8.16. Most current transfers, whether in cash or in kind, can take place between resident and non-resident institutional units as well as between resident units. However, it should be noted that all social transfers made to or received from non-residents are treated as if they were in cash. It follows that gross or net national disposable income may be derived from gross or net national income by:

(a) Adding all current transfers in cash or in kind receivable by resident institutional units from non-resident units; and

(b) Subtracting all current transfers in cash or in kind payable by resident institutional units to non-resident units.

8.17. Among the more important current transfers taking place between residents and non-residents are the following:

Current international cooperation: i.e., current transfers between different governments, such as transfers under aid programmes intended to sustain the consumption levels of populations affected by war or natural disasters such as droughts, floods or earthquakes

Social contributions and/or benefits

Insurance premiums and claims

Payments of current taxes on income or wealth

Remittances between resident and non-resident households.

8.18. The net disposable income of a country is a better measure than its net national income (NNI) for purposes of analysing its consumption possibilities.

3. The redistribution of income in kind account

8.19. Apart from the balancing items, disposable income and adjusted disposable income, all the entries in the redistribution of income in kind account consist of social transfers in kind. Social transfers in kind consist only of social benefits in kind and transfers of individual non-market goods and services provided to resident households by government units, including social security funds, and NPISHs.

8.20. The most common types of individual non-market goods and services are education and health services provided free, or at prices that are not economically significant, to individual households by non-market producers owned by government units or NPISHs. They are described in chapter IX. As social transfers in kind only take place between government units, NPISHs and households, the redistribution of income in kind account is not needed for the non-financial and financial corporate sectors.

8.21. The social transfers in kind payable by government units or NPISHs are recorded on the left-hand side of their redistribution of income in kind accounts under uses. For example, in table 8.2, the value of individual non-market goods or services provided free, or at prices that are not economically significant, by government units, is recorded at the intersection of the row for this item and the uses column for the general government sector. (These goods and services are valued by their costs of production.) The social transfers receivable by the household sector are recorded on the right-hand side of their account under resources. For example, the value of social security benefits in kind receivable by the household sector is recorded at the intersection of the row for this item and the resources column for the household sector. As only the household sector receives social transfers in kind, the resources columns for the other four sectors are empty.

8.22. There are only four main categories of social transfers in kind, i.e, social benefits in kind, divided into:

Social security benefits, reimbursements

Other social security benefits in kind

Social assistance benefits in kind

Transfers of individual non-market goods and services.

Each of these categories is described in more detail below.

8.23. Most of the non-market services produced by NPISHs are individual in nature, although some have some of the characteristics of collective services. For simplicity, all the non-market services of NPISHs are treated as individual and are, therefore, recorded under social transfers in kind.

4. Adjusted disposable income (B.7)

8.24. Adjusted disposable income is the balancing item in the redistribution of income in kind account. It is derived from the disposable income of an institutional unit or sector by:

(a) Adding the value of the social transfers in kind receivable by that unit or sector; and

(b) Subtracting the value of the social transfers in kind payable by that unit or sector.

8.25. Adjusted disposable income, like disposable income, may be recorded gross or net of consumption of fixed capital. Because social transfers in kind are payable only by government units and NPISHs to households, it follows that the adjusted disposable incomes of the general government and NPISHs sectors are lower than their disposable incomes, while the adjusted disposable income of the household sector exceeds its disposable income by the total value of social transfers in kind. The adjusted disposable income for the total economy is the same as its disposable income. In practice, the concept of adjusted disposable income is mainly relevant to government units and households, the distinction between adjusted disposable income and disposable income being irrelevant at the level of the economy as a whole.

8.26. The adjusted disposable income of a household can be interpreted as measuring the maximum value of the final consumption goods or services that it can afford to consume—the use for the satisfaction of the needs or wants of its members—in the current period without having to reduce its cash, dispose of other assets or increase its liabilities for the purpose. Its consumption possibilities are determined not only by the maximum amount it can afford to spend on consumption goods and services (its disposable income), but also by the value of the consumption goods and services it receives from government units or NPISHs as social transfers in kind. Conversely, the adjusted disposable income of general government can be interpreted as measuring the maximum value of the collective services that it can afford to provide to the community without having to reduce its cash, dispose of other assets or increase its liabilities for the purpose.

B. Transfers

1. Introduction

8.27. A transfer is defined as a transaction in which one institutional unit provides a good, service or asset to another unit without receiving from the latter any good, service or asset in return as counterpart. A cash transfer consists of the payment of currency or transferable deposit by one unit to another without any counterpart. A transfer in kind consists either of the transfer of ownership of a good or asset, other than cash, or the provision of a service, again without any counterpart.

8.28. A unit making a transfer receives no specific quantifiable benefit in return that can be recorded as part of the same transaction. Nevertheless, the payment of a social insurance contribution or non-life insurance premium may entitle the unit making the payment to some contingent future benefits. For example, a household may be entitled to receive some social benefits should certain events occur or certain conditions prevail. Alternatively, a household paying taxes may be able to consume certain collective services provided by government units. Such benefits, however, are generally uncertain or not quantifiable, or both. Moreover, the amount of benefit that may eventually be received by an individual unit may bear no relation to the amount of the transfers previously paid. The entitlement to contingent benefits or collective services cannot be treated as if it were itself some kind of asset that could be valued and recorded in the accounts. Hence, items such as non-life insurance premiums, social insurance contributions and taxes are treated in the accounts as transfers.

8.29. However, payments of premiums on individual life insurance policies taken out by members of households on their own initiative outside any social insurance scheme are not transfers. Similarly, the benefits received when the policies mature are not transfers. Holders of such life insurance policies themselves own the life insurance reserves administered by insurance enterprises into which the premiums are paid and out of which benefits are paid. Payments of premiums and premium supplements (less associated service charges) and the sums received on maturity are, therefore, not transfers between different institutional units. They constitute the acquisition and disposal of financial assets and are recorded as such in the financial accounts of the System as components of the change in the net equity of households in life insurance reserves and pension funds.

8.30. Households participating in funded pension schemes also own the pension reserves so that, in principle, pension contributions and benefits should also be treated in the same way as life insurance premiums and benefits. However, because the payment of pension contributions and the receipt of pensions are widely perceived by the households concerned and others as being transfers, and to avoid treating them differently from state pensions received under social security schemes, they are recorded in the secondary distribution of income accounts as if they were current transfers. In consequence, it is necessary to introduce an adjustment item in the use of income account (see Introduction to chapter IX) in order to ensure overall consistency between the income accounts and the financial accounts of the System.

2. The distinction between current and capital transfers

8.31. Transfers may be either current or capital. In order to distinguish one from the other, it is preferable to focus on the special characteristics of capital transfers. First, a transfer in kind is capital when it consists of the transfer of ownership of an asset, other than inventories. Secondly, a transfer of cash is capital when it is linked to, or conditional on, the acquisition or disposal of an asset (other than inventories) by one or both parties to the transaction, for example, an investment grant. Institutional units must be capable of distinguishing capital from current transfers and must be presumed to treat capital transferred during the course of the accounting period in the same way as capital held throughout the period. For example, a prudent household will not treat a capital transfer that happens to be received during a particular period as being wholly available for final consumption within the same accounting period. Conversely, a household making a capital transfer (e.g., the payment of an inheritance tax) will not plan to reduce its final consumption by the whole amount of the transfer. Unless institutional units are capable of distinguishing capital from current transfers and react differently to them, it becomes impossible to measure income, both in theory and in practice.

8.32. Current transfers consist of all transfers that are not transfers of capital. They directly affect the level of disposable income and should influence the consumption of goods or services. In practice, capital transfers tend to be large, infrequent and irregular, whereas current transfers tend to be comparatively small and are often made frequently and regularly. However, while size, frequency and regularity help to distinguish current from capital transfers they do not provide satisfactory criteria for defining the two types of transfer. For example, Social Security benefits in the form of maternity or death benefits are essentially current grants designed to cover the increased consumption expenditures occasioned by births or deaths, even though the events themselves are obviously very infrequent.

8.33. It is possible that some cash transfers may be regarded as capital by one party to the transaction and as current by the other. For example, the payment of an inheritance tax may be regarded as a capital transfer by the household but as a current transfer by government. Similarly, a large country that regularly makes investment grants to a number of smaller countries may regard the outlays as current, even though they may be specifically intended to finance the acquisition of assets. In an integrated system of accounts such as the SNA, however, it is not feasible to have the same transaction classified differently in different parts of the System. Accordingly, a transfer should be classified as capital for both parties if it clearly involves a transfer of an asset for one of the parties.

3. The recording of transfers

8.34. Although no good, service or asset is received in return as counterpart, the recording of a transfer nevertheless must give rise to four entries in the accounts. The ways in which transfers in cash, ordinary transfers in kind and social transfers in kind are recorded are shown below in the following paragraphs.

Transfers in cash

8.35. Below is an example of a current transfer in cash, such as the payment of a social security benefit in cash. The following entries are needed:

Household	*Social security fund*
Transfer received (secondary distribution of income account)	Transfer made (secondary distribution of income account)
Increase in currency, transferable deposits or other credit (financial account)	Decrease in currency, transferable deposits or other credit (financial account)

The transfer increases the disposable income of the household and reduces that of the social security fund. The eventual use of the cash by the household is recorded subsequently as a separate transaction. If the transfer were a capital transfer, it would be recorded in the capital account instead of the secondary distribution of income account.

Transfers in kind, except social transfers in kind

8.36. Below is an example of an enterprise producing medicines that donates some of its output free of charge to a charity (NPISH). The following entries are needed:

NPISH	*Enterprise*
Transfer received (secondary distribution of income account)	Transfer made (secondary distribution of income account)
Imputed expenditure on medicine (use of disposable income account)	Output (imputed sales) of medicine (production account)

Although the transfer is in kind rather than cash, the recording of the transfer has the same impact on the disposable incomes of the NPISH and the enterprise as a transfer in cash. The acquisition of the medicine by the NPISH has to be recorded in the use of disposable income account as an imputed expenditure out of disposable income, in the same way as the acquisition of a good or service received as remuneration in kind.

8.37. A more complex variant involving two interrelated transactions occurs if enterprise A purchases the medicine from enterprise B and then gives it to an NPISH. Although A actually purchases the goods from B, they do not form part of A's intermediate consumption or capital formation. Nor can they be recorded as final consumption by A, since it is an enterprise. In this case, the following entries are needed:

NPISH	Enterprise A	Enterprise B
Transfer received (under resources in secondary distribution of income account)	Transfer made (under uses in secondary distribution of income account)	
Imputed expenditure on medicine (use of disposable income account)		Output (sale) (production account)
	Decrease in currency, transferable deposits or other credit (financial account)	Increase in currency, transferable deposits or other credit (financial account)

As in the previous case, the disposable income of the NPISH receiving the transfer in kind is increased by the transfer, an imputed expenditure of equal value being recorded in the use of disposable income account.

Social transfers in kind

8.38. In the System, final consumption expenditure is incurred only by general government, NPISHs and households. All of households' consumption expenditure is incurred on their own behalf. Consumption expenditure by general government, on the other hand, is either for the benefit of the community at large (collective consumption) or for the benefit of individual households. By convention, all consumption expenditure by NPISHs is treated as being for the benefit of individual households. This distinction between collective and individual consumption expenditure is of considerable importance in the System and is discussed in detail in chapter IX. Consumption expenditures by general government and NPISHs on behalf of households (their individual consumption expenditures) are undertaken for the purpose of making social transfers in kind. They cover the non-market output of both general government and NPISHs delivered to households free, or at prices that are not economically significant, as well as goods and services bought from market producers and provided to households free or at prices that are not economically significant. Social transfers in kind are recorded differently from other transfers in kind.

8.39. Below is an example of an education service provided to a household by a non-market producer owned by a government unit. The provision of the service is actually recorded twice in the accounts of the System. First, it is recorded in the traditional way in national accounting as production for own final consumption expenditure by government. As this is recorded as an internal transaction within government, it leads to only two, not four entries, in the accounts, both being recorded under general government:

Imputed consumption expenditure on education services (use of disposable income account)	Non-market output of education services (production account)

This method of recording ignores, and obscures, the fact that in the real economy the education service is actually provided to a household as a transfer in kind paid for by government. A second method of recording is, therefore, also now adopted in the System that recognizes this fact. The following four entries are needed in this second method:

Household	Government
Social transfer received (under resources in redistribution of income in kind account)	Social transfer made (under uses in redistribution of income in kind account)
Actual consumption of education services (use of adjusted disposable income account)	Non-market output of educational services (production account)

In this case the consumption of the education service must be recorded as actual consumption (i.e., the acquisition of the service) and not as imputed consumption expenditure because the expenditure has already been attributed to the government in the use of disposable income account. The distinction between actual consumption and consumption expenditure for households, general government and NPISHs is further elaborated in chapter IX. However, this distinction is not recognized in the System for other current transfers in kind for which the acquisition of the good or service is always recorded as involving both the receipt of a transfer and an imputed expenditure by the recipient. In consequence, current transfers in kind, except social transfers, received by households or other institutional units such as NPISHs are recorded in the secondary distribution of income account and therefore affect disposable income.

8.40. Finally, the more complex case involving two interrelated transactions in which a government unit, or NPISH, purchases a good or service, such as a medicine, from a market producer and then provides it free to a household, may be illustrated. The following six entries are needed:

	NPISH or	
Household	*government*	*Market producer*
Social transfer received (under resources in redistribution of income in kind account)	Social transfer made (under uses in redistribution of income in kind account)	
Actual consumption of medicine (use of adjusted disposable income account)		Output (sale) (production account)
	Decrease in currency, transferable deposits or other credit (financial account)	Increase in currency, transferable deposits or other credit (financial account)

This example also covers the case in which the household purchases the medicine directly from a pharmacist and is then reimbursed by a social security fund or other government unit or NPISH. In this case, the household is not recorded as actually incurring any expenditure, the expenditure being attributed to social security fund or other unit that ultimately bears the cost.

4. The treatment of transfers in kind: summary

8.41. Two separate accounts exist in the System to allow for the special recording of social transfers in kind. The transfers as such are recorded in the redistribution of income in kind account under resources for households and under uses for the government unit or NPISH making the transfer. The consumption of the goods and services transferred is recorded in the use of adjusted disposable income account.

8.42. All other transfers in kind are recorded in the secondary distribution of income account along with those taking place in cash. The goods and services transferred are recorded as consumption expenditures by the recipients in the use of disposable income account.

C. Current taxes on income, wealth, etc. (D.5)

1. Introduction

8.43. Taxes are compulsory, unrequited payments, in cash or in kind, made by institutional units to government units. They are transfers because the government provides nothing in return to the individual unit paying the tax, although governments do provide goods or services to the community as a whole or to other individual units, or groups of units, depending on their general economic and social policy. Current taxes on income, wealth, etc., consist mainly of taxes levied on the incomes of households and corporations. They constitute charges against income and are recorded under uses for the households and corporate sectors in the secondary distribution of income account. The taxes may also be payable by non-residents or possibly by government units or non-profit institutions. Current taxes on income, wealth, etc. would have been described as "direct taxes" in the past, but the terms "direct" and "indirect" are no longer used in the System, as explained in chapter VII. The taxes cannot be described simply as "current taxes on income and wealth" because they include some periodic taxes on households which are assessed neither on the income nor the wealth of the household or its members, for example, poll taxes.

8.44. The general nature of taxes and the accounting rules governing their recording in the System were described in paragraphs 7.56 to 7.62 of chapter VII. For convenience, these paragraphs are repeated below.

Taxes versus fees

8.45. One of the regulatory functions of governments is to forbid the ownership or use of certain goods or the pursuit of certain activities, unless specific permission is granted by issuing a licence or other certificate for which a fee is demanded. If the issue of such licences involves little or no work on the part of government, the licences being granted automatically on payment of the amounts due, it is likely that they are simply a device to raise taxes, even though the government may provide some kind of certificate, or authorization, in return. However, if the government uses the issue of licences to exercise some proper regulatory function—for example, checking the competence, or qualifications, of the person concerned, checking the efficient and safe functioning of the equipment in question, or carrying out some other form of control which it would otherwise not be obliged to do—the payments made should be treated as purchases of services from government rather than payments of taxes, unless the payments are clearly out of all proportion to the costs of providing the services. The borderline between taxes and payments of fees for services rendered is not always clear-cut in practice (see paragraph 8.54 (c) below for a further explanation of this matter in the case of households).

Links with the IMF and OECD tax classifications

8.46. The coverage of taxes in the SNA coincides with that of "tax revenue" as defined in the *Manual on Government Finance Statistics, 1986* (GFS), of the International Monetary Fund (IMF), and also with "taxes" as defined in the Organisation for Economic Co-operation and Development's (OECD) annual publication *Revenue Statistics of OECD Member Countries*, except that the SNA includes imputed taxes or subsidies resulting from the operation of official multiple exchange rates and does not classify Social Security contributions under the heading of taxes. Chapter IV of the GFS contains a detailed listing and classification of taxes according to the nature of the tax. This classification is also reprinted as annex IV in the *Handbook of National Accounting: Public Sector Accounts* (United Nations, 1988). Part II of *Revenue Statistics* contains an almost identical classification.

8.47. The categories of tax distinguished in the System depend on the interaction of the following three factors, of which the nature of tax is only one:

(a) The nature of the tax, as specified in the GFS/OECD classification;

(b) The type of institutional unit paying the tax;

(c) The circumstances in which the tax is payable.

8.48. Thus, payments of exactly the same tax may be recorded under two different headings in the SNA. For example, payment of an excise duty may appear under "taxes on imports, except value added taxes (VAT) and duties" or under "taxes on products, except VAT, import and export taxes" depending upon whether the excise duty is paid on an imported or domestically produced good. Similarly, payments of an annual tax on automobiles may be recorded under "taxes on production" or under "current taxes on income, wealth, etc." depending upon whether the tax is paid by an enterprise or by a household. For this reason, it is not possible to arrive at the SNA categories simply by regrouping the IMF/OECD classifications. However, in order to take advantage of the existence of these detailed classifications, each category of tax listed below contains a cross-reference to the corresponding IMF and OECD classifications.

The accrual basis of recording

8.49. In contrast to the GFS and similar systems that require taxes to be recorded when they are actually paid, all taxes should be recorded on an accrual basis in the SNA, i.e., when the activities, transactions or other events occur which create the liabil-

ities to pay taxes. However, some economic activities, transactions or events, which under tax legislation ought to impose on the units concerned the obligation to pay taxes, permanently escape the attention of the tax authorities. It would be unrealistic to assume that such activities, transactions or events give rise to financial assets or liabilities in the form of payables and receivables. For this reason the amounts of taxes to be recorded in the System are determined by the amounts due for payment only when evidenced by tax assessments, declarations or other instruments, such as sales invoices or customs declarations, which create liabilities in the form of clear obligations to pay on the part of taxpayers. Nevertheless, in accordance with the accrual principle, the times at which the taxes should be recorded are the times at which the tax liabilities arise. For example, a tax on the sale, transfer or use of output should be recorded when that sale, transfer or use took place, which is not necessarily the same time as that at which the tax authorities were notified, at which a tax demand was issued, at which the tax was due to be paid or the payment was actually made. Some flexibility is permitted, however, as regards the time of recording of income taxes deducted at source (see paragraph 8.52 below).

8.50. In some countries, and for some taxes, the amounts of taxes eventually paid may diverge substantially and systematically from the amounts due to be paid to the extent that not all of the latter can be effectively construed as constituting financial liabilities as these are understood within the System. In such cases, it may be preferable for analytic and policy purposes to ignore unpaid tax liabilities and confine the measurement of taxes within the System to those actually paid. Nevertheless, the taxes actually paid should still be recorded on an accrual basis at the times at which the events took place that gave rise to the liabilities.

Interest, fines or other penalties

8.51. In principle, interest charged on overdue taxes or fines, or penalties imposed for the attempted evasion of taxes, should be recorded separately and not as taxes. However, it may not be possible to separate payments of interest, fines or other penalties from the taxes to which they relate, so that they are usually grouped with taxes in practice.

2. Taxes on income (D.51)

8.52. These consist of taxes on incomes, profits and capital gains. They are assessed on the actual or presumed incomes of individuals, households, NPIs or corporations. They include taxes assessed on holdings of property, land or real estate when these holdings are used as a basis for estimating the income of their owners. In some cases the liability to pay income taxes can only be determined in a later accounting period than that in which the income accrues. Some flexibility is therefore needed in the time at which such taxes are recorded. Income taxes deducted at source, such as pay-as-you-earn taxes, and regular prepayments of income taxes, may be recorded in the periods in which they are paid and any final tax liability on income can be recorded in the period in which the liability is determined. Taxes on income include the following types of taxes:

(a) *Taxes on individual or household income*: These consist of personal income taxes, including those deducted by employers (pay-as-you-earn taxes), and surtaxes. Such taxes are usually levied on the total declared or presumed income from all sources of the person concerned: compensation of employees, property income, pensions, etc.—after deducting certain agreed allowances. Taxes on the income of owners of unincorporated enterprises are included here (GFS, 1.1; OECD, 1110);

(b) *Taxes on the income of corporations*: These consist of corporate income taxes, corporate profits taxes, corporate surtaxes, etc. Such taxes are usually assessed on the total incomes of corporations from all sources and not simply profits generated by production (GFS, 1.2; OECD, 1210);

(c) *Taxes on capital gains*: These consist of taxes on the capital gains (described as holding gains in the System's terminology) of persons or corporations which become due for payment during the current accounting period, irrespective of the periods over which the gains have accrued. They are usually payable on nominal, rather than real, capital gains and on realized, rather than unrealized, capital gains (GFS, 1.1, 1.2; OECD, 1120, 1220);

(d) *Taxes on winnings from lotteries or gambling*: These are taxes payable on the amounts received by winners as distinct from taxes on the turnover of producers that organize gambling or lotteries which are treated as taxes on products (GFS, 1.3; OECD, 1130).

3. Other current taxes (D.59)

Current taxes on capital

8.53. Current taxes on capital consist of taxes that are payable periodically, usually annually, on the property or net wealth of institutional units, excluding taxes on land or other assets owned or rented by enterprises and used by them for production, such taxes being treated as other taxes on production. They also exclude taxes on property or wealth levied infrequently and at irregular intervals, or in exceptional circumstances (e.g., death duties), such taxes being treated as capital taxes. They also exclude income taxes assessed on the basis of the value of the property owned by institutional units when their incomes cannot be estimated satisfactorily, such taxes being recorded under the previous heading, taxes on income. Current taxes on capital include the following:

(a) *Current taxes on land and buildings*: These consist of

taxes payable periodically, in most cases annually, on the use or ownership of land or buildings by owners (including owner-occupiers of dwellings), tenants or both, excluding taxes on land or buildings rented or owned by enterprises and used by them in production (GFS, 4.1; OECD, 4100);

(b) *Current taxes on net wealth*: These consist of taxes payable periodically, in most cases annually, on the value of land or fixed assets less any debt incurred on those assets, excluding taxes on assets owned by enterprises and used by them in production (GFS, 4.2; OECD, 4200);

(c) *Current taxes on other assets*: These include taxes payable periodically, usually annually, on assets such as jewellery or other external signs of wealth (GFS, 4.6; OECD, 4600).

Miscellaneous current taxes

8.54. These consist of various different kinds of taxes payable periodically, usually annually, of which the most common are the following:

(a) *Poll taxes*: These are taxes levied as specific amounts of money per adult person, or per household, independently of actual or presumed income or wealth. The amounts levied may vary, however, according to the circumstances of the person or household (GFS, 7.1; OECD, 6000);

(b) *Expenditure taxes*: These are taxes payable on the total expenditures of persons or households instead of on their incomes. Expenditure taxes are alternatives to income taxes and may be levied at progressively higher rates in the same way as personal income taxes, depending upon the total level of expenditure. They are uncommon in practice (GFS, 7.3; OECD, 6000);

(c) *Payments by households to obtain certain licences*: Payments by persons or households for licences to own or use vehicles, boats or aircraft and for licences to hunt, shoot or fish are treated as current taxes. Payments for all other kinds of licences (e.g., driving or pilot's licences, television or radio licences, firearm licences, etc.) or fees to government (e.g., payments for passports, airport fees, court fees, etc.) are treated as purchases of services rendered by governments. The boundary between taxes and purchases of services is based on the practices actually followed in the majority of countries in their own accounts (GFS, 5.5.2 and 5.5.3; OECD, 5200);

(d) *Taxes on international transactions*: These consist of taxes on travel abroad, foreign remittances, foreign investments, etc., except those payable by producers (GFS, 6.5 and 6.6; OECD, 5127).

D. Social insurance schemes

1. Introduction

8.55. Social insurance schemes are schemes in which social contributions are paid by employees or others, or by employers on behalf of their employees, in order to secure entitlement to social insurance benefits, in the current or subsequent periods, for the employees or other contributors, their dependants or survivors. They may be organized privately or by government units. Social insurance benefits may be provided in cash or in kind. They become payable when certain events occur, or certain circumstances exist, that may adversely affect the welfare of the households concerned either by imposing additional demands on their resources or reducing their incomes. The contingencies covered are liable to vary from scheme to scheme. However, the identification of certain receivables as social insurance benefits depends not just on the contingencies covered but also the way in which coverage is provided.

2. Circumstances covered by social insurance schemes

8.56. Six kinds of circumstances illustrate when social insurance benefits may be payable as follows:

(a) The beneficiaries, or their dependants, require medical, dental or other treatments, or hospital, convalescent or long-term care, as a result of sickness, injuries, maternity needs, chronic invalidity, old age, etc. The social insurance benefits are usually provided in kind in the form of treatment or care provided free or at prices which are not economically significant, or by reimbursing expenditures made by households. Social insurance benefits in cash may also be payable to beneficiaries needing health care;

(b) The beneficiaries have to support dependants of various kinds—spouses, children, elderly relatives, invalids, etc. The social insurance benefits are usually paid in cash in the form of regular dependants' or family allowances;

(c) The beneficiaries suffer a reduction in income as a result of not being able to work, or not being able to work full-time. The social insurance benefits are usually paid regularly in cash for the duration of the condition. In some instances a lump sum may be provided additionally or instead of the regular payment. People may be prevented from working for various different reasons, in particular:

(i) Voluntary or compulsory retirement;

(ii) Involuntary unemployment, including temporary lay-offs and short-time working;

(iii) Sickness, accidental injury, the birth of a child, etc. that prevents a person from working, or from working full-time;

(d) The beneficiaries suffer a reduction in income because of the death of the main income earner. The social insurance benefits are usually paid in cash in the form of regular allowances or, in some instances, a lump sum;

(e) The beneficiaries are provided with housing either free or at prices which are not economically significant or by reimbursing expenditure made by households;

(f) The beneficiaries are provided with allowances to cover education expenses incurred on behalf of themselves or their dependants; education services may occasionally be provided in kind.

8.57. The above are typical circumstances in which social insurance benefits are payable. However, the list is illustrative rather than exhaustive. It is possible, for example, that under some schemes other benefits may be payable. Conversely, by no means all schemes provide benefits in all the circumstances listed above. In practice, the scope of social insurance schemes is liable to vary significantly from country to country, or from scheme to scheme within the same country.

3. The organization of social insurance schemes

8.58. The schemes themselves are intended to cover beneficiaries and their dependants during their working lives and usually also into retirement, whether they are employees, employers, own-account workers, or persons temporarily without employment. Eligibility for social insurance benefits requires social contributions to have been paid by, or on behalf of, the beneficiaries or their dependants in the current or previous accounting periods. As already noted, the social contributions may be payable not only by the participants themselves but also by employers on behalf of their employees.

8.59. Social insurance schemes must be organized collectively for groups of workers or be available by law to all workers or designated categories of workers, possibly including non-employed persons as well as employees. They may range from private schemes arranged for selected groups of workers employed by a single employer to social security schemes covering the entire labour force of a country. Participation in such schemes may be voluntary for the workers concerned, but it is more common for it to be obligatory. For example, participation in schemes organized by individual employers may be required by the terms and conditions of employment collectively agreed between employers and their employees. Participation in nationwide Social Security schemes organized by government units may be compulsory by law for the entire labour force, except perhaps for persons who are already covered by private schemes.

8.60. Many social insurance schemes are organized collectively for groups of workers so that those participating do not have to take out individual insurance policies in their own names. In such cases, there is no difficulty about distinguishing social insurance from private insurance. However, some social insurance schemes may permit, or even require, participants to take out policies in their own names. In order for an individual policy to be treated as part of a social insurance scheme the eventualities or circumstances against which the participants are insured must be of the kind listed in paragraph 8.56 above, and in addition, one or more of the following conditions must be satisfied:

(a) Participation in the scheme is obligatory either by law for a specified category of worker, whether employer or non-employed, or under the terms and conditions of employment of an employee, or group of employees;

(b) The scheme is a collective one operated for the benefit of a designated group of workers, whether employees or non-employed, participation being restricted to members of that group;

(c) An employer makes a contribution (actual or imputed) to the scheme on behalf of an employee, whether or not the employee also makes a contribution.

The premiums payable, and claims receivable, under individual policies taken out under a social insurance scheme are recorded as social contributions and social insurance benefits.

8.61. Thus, social insurance schemes are essentially schemes in which workers are obliged, or encouraged, by their employers or by general government to take out insurance against certain eventualities or circumstances that may adversely affect their welfare or that of their dependants. When individuals take out insurance policies in their own names, on their own initiative and independently of their employers or government, the premiums payable and claims receivable are not treated as social contributions and social insurance benefits, even though the policies may be taken out against the same kinds of eventualities or situations as are covered by social insurance schemes—accident, ill health, retirement, etc. The premiums payable and claims receivable under such individual insurance policies are recorded as current transfers in the secondary distribution of income account in the case of non-life insurance, while the premiums payable and claims receivable under individual life insurance policies are recorded as acquisitions and disposals of financial assets in the financial account.

8.62. As can be seen from the consideration of individual insurance policies, the nature of the benefit is by no means sufficient to identify the social nature of the transactions. For example, the receipt of free medical services does not always constitute a social benefit. If the medical services received by one household are paid for by another, they are not social benefits but transfers in kind between households. First aid rendered to employees at work is not a social benefit, the costs involved being recorded as intermediate consumption of the employer. In general, social benefits cannot be provided by one household to another except in the relatively rare case in which an unincorporated enterprise owned by a household operates an unfunded scheme for the benefit of its employees.

8.63. Three main types of social insurance schemes may be distinguished:

(a) The first consists of social security schemes covering the entire community, or large sections of the community, that are imposed, controlled and financed by government units;

(b) The second type consists of private funded schemes. There are two categories of private funded schemes. The first consists of schemes in which the social contributions are paid to insurance enterprises or autonomous pension funds that are separate institutional units from both the employers and the employees. The insurance enterprises and autonomous pension funds are responsible for managing the resulting funds and paying the social benefits. The second consists of schemes in which employers maintain special reserves which are segregated from their other reserves even though such funds do not constitute separate institutional units from the employers. These are referred to as non-autonomous pension funds. The reserves are treated in the System as assets that belong to the beneficiaries and not to the employers;

(c) The third type consists of unfunded schemes in which employers pay social benefits to their employees, former employees or their dependants out of their own resources without creating special reserves for the purpose.

Social insurance schemes organized by government units for their own employees, as opposed to the working population at large, are classified as private funded schemes or unfunded schemes as appropriate and are not classified as social security schemes.

Social security schemes

8.64. In many countries, social security schemes are by far the most important category of social insurance schemes and it is worth summarizing their main characteristics. Social security schemes are schemes imposed and controlled by government units for the purpose of providing social benefits to members of the community as a whole, or of particular sections of the community. The social security funds established for this purpose are separate institutional units organized and managed separately from other government funds. Their receipts consist mainly of contributions paid by individuals and by employers on behalf of their employees, but they may also include transfers from other government funds. The payment of social security contributions by, or on behalf of, certain specified individuals, such as employees, may be compulsory by law, but some other individuals may choose to pay voluntarily in order to qualify for the receipt of social security benefits. The benefits paid to individuals, or households, are not necessarily determined by the amounts previously paid in contributions, while the levels of the benefits paid out to the community as a whole may be varied in accordance with the requirements of the government's overall economic policy.

Private funded social insurance schemes

8.65. In the case of private funded social insurance schemes that are arranged by employers, via insurance enterprises and autonomous pension funds, the premiums paid by employees to obtain social benefits include a service charge. This service charge is recorded as final consumption expenditure by households. In the case of non-autonomous pension funds, however, no service charge is deducted from contributions paid by the employees. As such funds do not constitute separate institutional units from the employers, the costs of managing and administering the funds are assimilated with the employers' general production costs.

4. Different types of social contributions and benefits

8.66. Social contributions and social benefits have various characteristics that affect their classification:

(a) Social benefits may be divided into those paid as social insurance benefits under a social insurance scheme and those paid as social assistance benefits outside any such scheme;

(b) Social insurance schemes may be classified according to the type of scheme—social security, private funded or unfunded;

(c) Social contributions may be divided into actual contributions payable under social security and private funded schemes and imputed contributions recorded for unfunded schemes;

(d) Social contributions may be divided into those paid by employers on behalf of their employees and those paid by employees, self-employed or non-employed persons on their own behalf;

(e) Social contributions may be divided into those that are compulsory by law and those that are not;

(f) Social benefits may be divided into those paid in cash and those in kind.

These various characteristics are built into the classification of social contributions and benefits utilized in the secondary distribution of income account and in the redistribution of income in kind account. Sections *E* and *F* below describe the social contributions or benefits included under each heading of the classification in the secondary distribution of income account. The final section of this chapter (see section *H*) describes the social benefits included under each heading in the redistribution of income in kind account.

E. Social contributions (D.61)

1. Employers' actual social contributions (D.6111)

8.67. These are social contributions paid by employers to social security funds, insurance enterprises, or autonomous pension funds, administering social insurance schemes to secure social benefits for their employees. As employers' actual social contributions are made for the benefit of their employees their value is recorded as one of the components of compensation of employees together with wages and salaries in cash and in kind. The social contributions are then recorded as being paid by the employees as current transfers to the social security funds, insurance enterprises or autonomous pension funds. Although it is administratively more efficient for employers to pay the contributions on behalf of their employees, this must not be allowed to obscure the underlying economic reality. The payment made by the employer to the social security fund, insurance enterprise or autonomous pension fund is not, in fact, a current transfer by the employer. The transfer takes place between the employee and the social security fund, insurance enterprise or autonomous pension fund out of remuneration provided by the employer. The situation is parallel to one in which income taxes payable by employees are deducted by employers from the wages or salaries and paid directly to the tax authorities. In this case, it is evident that the taxes are not current transfers payable by the employers. It is customary to describe the employers' social contributions as being rerouted in the accounts via the employees' primary and secondary distribution of income accounts. However, the accounts depict the various payables and receivables correctly. The direct payment of social contributions, or income taxes, by employers to social security funds, insurers or tax authorities is merely a short cut taken on grounds of administrative convenience and efficiency.

8.68. An amount equal in value to employers' social contributions is first recorded in the generation of income account as one of the components of compensation of employees and then recorded in the secondary distribution of income account as being transferred by households to social security funds, insurance enterprises, or autonomous or non-autonomous pension funds as the case may be. The transactions are recorded simultaneously in both accounts at the times when the work is carried out that gives rise to the liability to pay the contributions. The contributions paid to social security funds may be fixed amounts per employee or may vary with the levels of wages or salaries paid. The amounts paid under privately organized schemes depend on the arrangements agreed between employers and employees. When social security schemes exist the relevant employers' social security contributions are usually compulsory, but not necessarily so. A distinction is made in the System's classification between those employers' actual social contributions that are compulsory by law and those that are not.

2. Employees' social contributions (D.6112)

8.69. These are social contributions payable by employees to social security funds and private funded social insurance schemes. They are recorded at the times when the work is carried out that gives rise to the liability to pay the contributions. Employees' social contributions consist of the actual contributions payable each period plus, in the case of private funded schemes, the contribution supplements payable out of the property income attributed to insurance policyholders received by employees participating in the schemes less the service charges, when appropriate. The property income accrues on the investment of reserves built up out of both employers' and employees' contributions in the past, but the reserves belong only to the employees, not to the employers. The whole of the property income from the investment of the reserves is, therefore, attributed to the participating employees who are then treated as paying it back into schemes as contribution supplements. The employees' social contributions payable into private funded schemes are recorded after deducting the associated services charges, except for contributions to non-autonomous pension funds where there are no service charges. All the service charges are treated as charges against the employees' contributions and not the employers'. The contributions to social security funds, when these exist, are usually compulsory, although voluntary contributions may sometimes also be made by employees. A distinction is made between those employees' actual social contributions that are compulsory by law and those that are not.

3. Social contributions by self-employed and non-employed persons (D.6113)

8.70. These are social contributions payable for their own benefit by persons who are not employees—i.e., self-employed persons (employers or own-account workers), or non-employed persons. They are recorded when the liabilities to pay are created. Some may consist of compulsory social security contributions, while others consist of voluntary contributions to social security or to other social insurance schemes. They also include the value of the contribution supplements payable out of the property income attributed to insurance policyholders received by participating individuals that they are recorded as paying back to the insurance enterprises in addition to their

other contributions. The contributions payable to private insurance enterprises are equal to the total contributions payable less the service charges. Again, a distinction is made in the classification between contributions that are compulsory by law and others.

4. Imputed social contributions (D.612)

8.71. An entry is needed in the secondary distribution of income account for the imputed social contributions payable by employees when employers operate unfunded social insurance schemes. For convenience, the discussion of the corresponding item in chapter VII, paragraphs 7.45 to 7.47 is repeated here.

8.72. Some employers provide social benefits themselves directly to their employees, former employees or dependants out of their own resources without involving an insurance enterprise or autonomous pension fund, and without creating a special fund or segregated reserve for the purpose. In this situation, existing employees may be considered as being protected against various specified needs, or circumstances, even though no payments are being made to cover them. Remuneration should therefore be imputed for such employees equal in value to the amount of social contributions that would be needed to secure the de facto entitlements to the social benefits they accumulate. These amounts depend not only on the levels of the benefits currently payable but also on the ways in which employers' liabilities under such schemes are likely to evolve in the future as a result of factors such as expected changes in the numbers, age distribution and life expectancies of their present and previous employees. Thus, the values that should be imputed for the contribution ought, in principle, to be based on the same kind of actuarial considerations that determine the levels of premiums charged by insurance enterprises.

8.73. In practice, however, it may be difficult to decide how large such imputed contributions should be. The enterprise may make estimates itself, perhaps on the basis of the contributions paid into similar funded schemes, in order to calculate its likely liabilities in the future, and such estimates may be used when available. Otherwise, the only practical alternative may be to use the unfunded social benefits payable by the enterprise during the same accounting period as an estimate of the imputed remuneration that would be needed to cover the imputed contributions. While there are obviously many reasons why the value of the imputed contributions that would be needed may diverge from the unfunded social benefits actually paid in the same period, such as the changing composition and age structure of the enterprise's labour force, the benefits actually paid in the current period may nevertheless provide the best available estimates of the contributions and associated imputed remuneration.

8.74. The two steps involved may be summarized as follows:

   (a)   Employers are recorded, in the generation of income account, as paying to their existing employees as a component of their compensation an amount, described as imputed social contributions, equal in value to the estimated social contributions that would be needed to provide for the unfunded social benefits to which they become entitled;

F. Social benefits

1. Introduction

8.75. As already noted, there are two kinds of social benefits, i.e., social insurance benefits and social assistance benefits. The latter consist of transfers made by government units or NPIs to households to meet the same kinds of needs as social insurance benefits but outside of any social insurance scheme. The kinds of events or circumstances that may occasion the payment of social insurance benefits are described in paragraph 8.56 above. Social benefits may be paid in cash or in kind. For example, institutional units administering social insurance schemes may maintain their own clinics, convalescent or retirement homes for the treatment and care of the beneficiaries or their dependants.

8.76. When employers provide unfunded social benefits to their own employees it may not always be easy to distinguish them from the payment of wages or salaries in cash. For example, the continued payment of wages and salaries to employees during absence from work as a result of sickness, accident, maternity needs, etc. is a social benefit but it may be difficult to separate such payments from ordinary wages and salaries, except perhaps in the case of prolonged absences of several months or more. However, when the value of the imputed social contributions is estimated to be equal to the payment of such benefits in the same period, the total compensation of employees of the group of workers in question is not affected.

2. Social benefits other than social transfers in kind (D.62)

8.77. These consist of all social benefits except social transfers in kind. They therefore consist of:

(a) All social benefits in cash—both social insurance and social assistance benefits—provided by government units, including social security funds, and NPISHs; and

(b) All social insurance benefits provided under private funded and unfunded social insurance schemes, whether in cash or in kind.

In the classification used in the System, social benefits in cash provided by government units and NPISHs, category (a) above, are divided into:

    Social security benefits in cash
    Social assistance benefits in cash.

(b) Employees are recorded, in the secondary distribution of income account, as paying back to their employers the same amount of imputed social contributions (as current transfers) as if they were paying them to a separate social insurance scheme.

Social insurance benefits in category (b) above are divided into:

    Private funded social insurance benefits

    Unfunded employee social insurance benefits.

Social benefits in kind provided by general government and NPISHs are not recorded in the secondary distribution of income account. They form part of social transfers in kind and are recorded in the redistribution of income in kind account.

Social security benefits in cash (D.621)

8.78. These are social insurance benefits payable in cash to households by social security funds. They may take the form of:

    Sickness and invalidity benefits

    Maternity allowances

    Childrens' or family allowances, other dependants' allowances

    Unemployment benefits

    Retirement and survivors' pensions

    Death benefits

    Other allowances or benefits.

The list is intended to be illustrative only as the coverage and range of benefits provided under social security schemes may vary from country to country.

Private funded social insurance benefits (D.622)

8.79. These are social insurance benefits payable to households by insurance enterprises or other institutional units administering private funded social insurance schemes. The kinds of benefits provided are similar to those listed above for social security funds. Unlike social security benefits, however, no distinction is made between benefits in cash and in kind as private funded benefits cannot be social transfers in kind. Both types of benefit are recorded in the secondary distribution of income account.

Unfunded employee social insurance benefits (D.623)

8.80. These are social benefits payable to their employees, their dependants or survivors by employers administering unfunded social insurance schemes. All unfunded benefits are recorded in the secondary distribution of income account whether in cash or in kind. They typically include:

(a)   The continued payment of normal or reduced wages during periods of absence from work as a result of ill health, accidents, maternity needs, etc.;

(b)   The payment of family, education or other allowances in respect of dependants;

(c)   The payment of retirement or survivors' pensions to former employees or their survivors, and the payment of severance allowances to workers or their survivors in the event of redundancy, incapacity, accidental death, etc.;

(d)   General medical services not related to the employee's work;

(e)   Convalescent and retirement homes.

Social assistance benefits in cash (D.624)

8.81.   Social assistance benefits are current transfers payable to households by government units or NPISHs to meet the same needs as social insurance benefits but which are not made under a social insurance scheme incorporating social contributions and social insurance benefits. They therefore exclude all benefits paid by social security funds. They may be payable in cash and in kind. Those in kind are part of social transfers in kind, entered in the redistribution of income in kind account.

8.82.   Social assistance benefits may be payable in the following circumstances:

(a)   No social insurance scheme exists to cover the circumstances in question;

(b)   Although a social insurance scheme, or schemes, may exist, the households in question do not participate and are not eligible for social insurance benefits;

(c)   Social insurance benefits are deemed to be inadequate to cover the needs in question, the social assistance benefits being paid in addition.

8.83.   Social assistance benefits do not include current transfers paid in response to events or circumstances that are not normally covered by social insurance schemes. Thus, social assistance benefits do not cover transfers in cash or in kind made in response to natural disasters such as drought, floods or earthquakes. Such transfers are recorded separately under other current transfers.

G. Other current transfers (D.7)

1. Introduction

8.84.   Other current transfers consist of all current transfers between resident institutional units, or between residents and non-residents, except those already described in previous sections of this chapter, except for current taxes on income, wealth, etc., and social contributions and benefits. Other current transfers include a number of different kinds of transfers serving quite different purposes. The most important categories are described below.

2. Net non-life insurance premiums (D.71)

8.85.   Non-life insurance premiums included under this heading refer to those payable under policies taken out by enterprises or individual households. The policies taken out by individual households are those taken out on their own initiative and for their own benefit, independently of their employers or government and outside any social insurance scheme.

8.86.   Non-life insurance premiums, as stated earlier, comprise both the actual premiums payable by policyholders to obtain insurance cover during the accounting period (premiums earned) and the premium supplements payable out of the property income attributed to insurance policyholders. The total of the non-life insurance premiums payable in this way has to cover payments of service charges to the insurance enterprises for arranging the insurance and payments for the insurance itself. The way in which the service charges are calculated was explained in chapter VI, paragraphs 6.138 to 6.140. After deducting the service charges from total non-life insurance premiums, the remainder is described as net non-life insurance premiums. These are the amounts available to provide cover against various events or accidents resulting in damage to goods or property or harm to persons as a result of natural or human causes—fires, floods, crashes, collisions, sinkings, theft, violence, accidents, sickness, etc.—or against financial losses resulting from events such as sickness, unemployment, accidents, etc. Only the net non-life insurance premiums constitute current transfers and are recorded in the secondary distribution of income account. The service charges constitute purchases of services by the policyholders and are recorded as intermediate or final consumption, as appropriate.

3. Non-life insurance claims (D.72)

8.87.   Non-life insurance claims do not include payments to households in the form of social insurance benefits. They are the amounts payable in settlement of claims that become due during the current accounting period. Claims become due at the moment when the eventuality occurs which gives rise to a valid claim accepted by the insurance enterprise. As the service charges on non-life insurance are calculated by subtracting claims due from the combined value of the premiums earned and premium supplements, it follows that the total claims due for an insurance enterprise must equal the net non-life premiums receivable by that enterprise during the same accounting period. This emphasizes the fact that the essential function of non-life insurance is to redistribute resources.

8.88. The settlement of a non-life insurance claim is treated as a transfer to the claimant. Such payments are always treated as current transfers, even when large sums may be involved as a result of the accidental destruction of a fixed asset or serious personal injury to an individual. The amounts received by claimants are usually not committed for any particular purpose and goods or assets which have been damaged or destroyed need not necessarily be repaired or replaced.

8.89. Some claims arise because of damages or injuries that the policyholders cause to the property or persons of third parties, for example, the damages or injuries that insured drivers of vehicles may cause to other vehicles or persons. In these cases, valid claims are recorded as being payable directly by the insurance enterprise to the injured parties and not indirectly via the policyholder.

4. Current transfers within general government (D.73)

8.90. These consist of current transfers between different government units or different sub-sectors of general government. They include current transfers between different levels of government, such as frequently occur between central and state or local government units, and between government units and social security funds. They do not include transfers of funds committed to finance gross fixed capital formation, such transfers being treated as capital transfers.

8.91. One government unit may act as an agent on behalf of a second government unit by, for example, collecting taxes which are due to the second unit, at the same time as it collects its own taxes. Taxes collected on behalf of the second unit in this way are to be recorded as accruing directly to the second unit and are not to be treated as a current transfer from the first to the second unit. Delays in remitting the taxes from the first to the second government unit give rise to entries under "other accounts receivable/payable" in the financial account.

5. Current international cooperation (D.74)

8.92. Current international cooperation consists of current transfers in cash or in kind between the governments of different countries or between governments and international organizations. This includes:

(a) Transfers between governments that are used by the recipients to finance current expenditures, including emergency aid after natural disasters; they include transfers in kind in the form of food, clothing, blankets, medicines, etc.;

(b) Annual or other regular contributions paid by member governments to international organizations (excluding taxes payable to supra-national organizations);

(c) Payments by governments or international organizations to other governments to cover the salaries of those technical assistance staff who are deemed to be resident in the country in which they are working.

Current international cooperation does not cover transfers intended for purposes of capital formation, such transfers being recorded as capital transfers.

6. Miscellaneous current transfers (D.75)

8.93. These consist of various different kinds of current transfers that may take place between resident institutional units or between resident and non-resident units. Some of the more important are shown below.

Current transfers to NPISHs

8.94. Most current transfers to NPISHs consist of cash transfers received from other resident or non-resident institutional units in the form of membership dues, subscriptions, voluntary donations, etc. whether made on a regular or occasional basis. Such transfers are intended to cover the costs of the non-market production of NPISHs or to provide the funds out of which current transfers may be made to resident or non-resident households in the form of social assistance benefits. This heading also cover transfers in kind in the form of gifts of food, clothing, blankets, medicines, etc. to charities for distribution to resident or non-resident households. However, payments of membership dues or subscriptions to market NPIs serving businesses, such as chambers of commerce or trade associations, are treated as payments for services rendered and are therefore not transfers (see chapter VI, paragraph 6.59).

Current transfers between households

8.95. These consist of all current transfers in cash or in kind made, or received, by resident households to or from other resident or non-resident households. They include regular remittances between members of the same family resident in different parts of the same country or in different countries, usually from a member of a family working in a foreign country for a period of a year or longer. Earnings remitted by seasonal workers to their families are not international transfers as the workers remain resident in their country of origin, i.e., members of their original households, when they work abroad for short periods of less than a year.

Fines and penalties

8.96. Fines and penalties imposed on institutional units by courts of law or quasi-judicial bodies are treated as compulsory current transfers. However, fines or other penalties imposed by tax authorities for the evasion or late payment of taxes cannot usually be distinguished from the taxes themselves and are, therefore, grouped with the latter in practice and not recorded under this heading; nor are payments of fees to obtain licences, such payments being either taxes or payments for services rendered by government units (see paragraph 8.45).

Lotteries and gambling

8.97. The amounts paid for lottery tickets or placed in bets consist of two elements: the payment of a service charge to the unit organizing the lottery or gambling and a residual current transfer that is paid out to the winners. The service charge may be quite substantial and may have to cover taxes on the production of gambling services. The transfers are regarded in the System as taking place directly between those participating in the lottery or gambling, that is, between households. When

non-resident households take part there may be significant net transfers between the household sector and the rest of the world.

Payments of compensation

8.98. These consist of current transfers paid by institutional units to other institutional units in compensation for injury to persons or damage to property caused by the former excluding payments of non-life insurance claims. Payments of compensation could be either compulsory payments awarded by courts of law, or *ex gratia* payments agreed out of court. This heading covers only compensation for injuries or damages caused by other institutional units. It also covers *ex gratia* payments made by government units or NPISHs in compensation for injuries or damages caused by natural disasters.

H. Social transfers in kind (D.63)

1. Introduction

8.99. The only items other than balancing items recorded in the redistribution of income in kind account are social transfers in kind. These consist of individual goods and services provided as transfers in kind to individual households by government units (including social security funds) and NPISHs, whether purchased on the market or produced as non-market output by government units or NPISHs. They may be financed out of taxation, other government income or social security contributions, or out of donations and property income in the case of NPISHs. If it is not possible to segregate the accounts of social security funds from those of other sub-sectors of government, it may not be possible to divide social benefits into those provided by social security and other. Social security benefits in kind are subdivided into two types: those where beneficiary households actually purchase the goods or services themselves and are then reimbursed, and those where the relevant services are provided directly to the beneficiaries.

8.100. The number and type of social transfers in kind provided to households by government units reflects their general economic and social policy concerns. Whereas the recipients of current cash transfers may dispose of them as they wish, the recipients of social transfers in kind have little or no choice. The attraction of transfers in kind over transfers in cash to policy makers is that the resources transferred can be targeted towards meeting specific needs, such as health or education, and must be consumed in the ways that their providers intend.

2. Social security benefits, reimbursements (D.6311)

8.101. The reimbursement by social security funds of approved expenditures made by households on specified goods or services is a form of social benefit in kind. Examples of expenditures that may be reimbursable are expenditures on

medicines, medical or dental treatments, hospital bills, optometrists' bills, etc.

8.102. When a household purchases a good or service for which it is subsequently reimbursed, in part or in whole, by a social security fund, the household can be regarded as if it were an agent acting on behalf of the social security fund. In effect, the household provides a short-term credit to the social security fund that is liquidated as soon as the household is reimbursed. The amount of the expenditure reimbursed is recorded as being incurred directly by the social security fund at the time the household makes the purchase, while the only expenditure recorded for the household is the difference, if any, between the purchaser's price paid and the amount reimbursed. Thus, the amount of the expenditure reimbursed is not treated as a current transfer in cash from the Social Security fund to households.

3. Other social security benefits in kind (D.6312)

8.103. These consist of social transfers in kind, except reimbursements, made by Social Security funds to households. Most are likely to consist of medical or dental treatments, surgery, hospital accommodation, spectacles or contact lenses, medical appliances or equipment, and similar goods or services associated with the provision of health care. The services may be provided by market or non-market producers and should be valued accordingly. In both cases any nominal payments made by the householders themselves should be deducted. The transfers should be recorded at the times the goods are transferred or services provided.

4. Social assistance benefits in kind (D.6313)

8.104. These consist of transfers in kind provided to households by government units or NPISHs that are similar in nature to social security benefits in kind but are not provided in the context of a social insurance scheme. Like social assistance benefits in cash, they tend to be provided under the following circumstances:

(a)   No social insurance scheme exists to cover the circumstances in question;

(b)   Although a social insurance scheme, or schemes, may exist, the households in question do not participate and are not eligible for its social benefits;

(c)   Social insurance benefits are deemed to be inadequate to cover the needs in question, the social assistance benefits being paid in addition.

5. Transfers of individual non-market goods or services (D.632)

8.105. These consist of goods or services provided to individual households free, or at prices which are not economically significant, by non-market producers of government units or NPISHs. Although some of the non-market services produced by NPISHs have some of the characteristics of collective services, all the non-market services produced by NPISHs are, for simplicity and by convention, treated as individual in nature. Non-market producers are described in more detail in chapter VI. Services provided free, or at prices that are not economically significant, to households are described as individual services to distinguish them from collective services provided to the community as a whole, or large sections of the community. Individual services consist mainly of education and health services, although other kinds of services such as housing services, cultural and recreational services are also frequently provided. They may be provided either by market or non-market producers and are valued accordingly. They are described in more detail in chapter IX.

8.106. The services provided as social transfers in kind to households are recorded at the times they are provided. These are the times at which they are produced. Any goods provided directly to households by non-market producers should be recorded at the times the change of ownership takes place.

IX. The use of income account

A. Introduction

9.1. The purpose of the use of income account is to show how households, government units and non-profit institutions serving households (NPISHs) allocate their disposable income between final consumption and saving. There are two versions of the use of income account that correspond to two concepts of disposable income and consumption. In the first version, shown in table 9.1, attention is focused on disposable income and the expenditure on consumption goods and services that can be met out of that income. In the second version, shown in table 9.2, attention is focused on the consumption goods and services acquired and used by institutional units, especially households, whether acquired by expenditure or by social transfers in kind.

9.2. In the first version of the use of income account, final consumption expenditure is subtracted from gross, or net, disposable income to obtain gross, or net, saving as the balancing item. In the second version, actual final consumption is subtracted from gross, or net, adjusted disposable income to obtain the same balancing item. In both accounts, in addition, there is an adjustment item that is needed in order to reconcile saving with the change in net equity of households in pension funds recorded in the financial account.

9.3. As explained in chapter VIII, the adjusted disposable income of households is derived from their disposable income by adding the value of social transfers in kind receivable, while that for government units and NPISHs is derived by subtracting the value of social transfers in kind payable. Similarly, the actual final consumption of households is derived from their final consumption expenditure by adding the value of social transfers in kind receivable, while the actual final consumption of government units and NPISHs is derived by subtracting the value of social transfers in kind payable. It follows that saving is the same whether it is defined as disposable income less final consumption expenditure or as adjusted disposable income less actual final consumption. Saving, like disposable and adjusted disposable income, may have to be recorded gross of consumption of fixed capital because of the difficulty of measuring the latter. However, consumption of fixed capital is a cost of production and should be excluded, if possible.

9.4. Corporations do not make final consumption expenditures. They may purchase the same kinds of goods or services as households use for final consumption—e.g., electricity or food—but such goods or services are either used for intermediate consumption or provided to employees as remuneration in kind. It is assumed in the System that corporations do not make transfers of consumption goods or services to households (see chapter XIX for the treatment of expenditures by enterprises on behalf of employees that is recommended for countries in transition to market-oriented economies). As corporations neither make nor receive social transfers in kind, it is also not possible to draw a meaningful distinction between their disposable and adjusted disposable incomes. It follows that both the use of disposable income account and the use of adjusted disposable income account for corporations are only dummy accounts that contain no entries for final consumption expenditure or actual final consumption. Apart from the adjustment item for pension funds referred to below, the gross or net saving of corporations must be equal to their gross or net disposable, or adjusted disposable, incomes. In other contexts, the saving of corporations is often described as the "retained earnings" or "undistributed incomes" of corporations.

1. The use of disposable income account

9.5. Apart from the balancing item, saving, this account contains only three entries. Disposable income, the balancing item carried forward from the secondary distribution of income account, is recorded on the right-hand side of the account under resources, while final consumption expenditure is recorded on the left-hand side under uses. As just noted, the account is relevant mainly for the three sectors that make final consumption expenditures, namely the general government, NPISHs and household sectors, and, of course, for the total economy.

9.6. The balancing item for the account is saving. Before the balance is struck, however, the adjustment item referred to earlier and explained in more detail in paragraphs 9.14 to 9.16 below is entered in order to reallocate a certain amount of saving between sectors. This item, adjustment for the change in net equity of households in pension funds, is needed because of the way in which pension contributions and benefits are recorded in the secondary distribution of income accounts. The adjustment is shown on the right-hand side under resources for households and on the left-hand side under uses for financial

Table 9.1.   Account II.4.1: Use of disposable income account

Uses: Total	Uses: Goods and service account	Uses: Rest of the world account	Uses: S.1 Total economy	Uses: S.15 NPISHs	Uses: S.14 Households	Uses: S.13 General government	Uses: S.12 Financial corporations	Uses: S.11 Non-financial corporations	Transactions and balancing items	Res: S.11 Non-financial corporations	Res: S.12 Financial corporations	Res: S.13 General government	Res: S.14 Households	Res: S.15 NPISHs	Res: S.1 Total economy	Res: Rest of the world account	Res: Goods and service account	Res: Total
									B.6g Disposable income, gross	185	32	388	1 206	43	1 854			1 854
									B.6n Disposable income, net	48	22	358	1 164	40	1 632			1 632
1 399			1 399	16	1 015	368			P.3 Final consumption expenditure								1 399	1 399
1 243			1 243	16	1 015	212			P.31 Individual consumption expenditure								1 243	1 243
156			156			156			P.32 Collective consumption expenditure								156	156
11		0	11	0		0	11	0	D.8 Adjustment for the change in net equity of households on pension funds				11		11	0		11
455			455	27	202	20	21	185	B.8g Saving, gross									
233			233	24	160	−10	11	48	B.8n Saving, net									
−41		−41							B.12 Current external balance									

Table 9.2.   Account II.4.2: Use of adjusted disposable income account

Uses: Total	Uses: Goods and service account	Uses: Rest of the world account	Uses: S.1 Total economy	Uses: S.15 NPISHs	Uses: S.14 Households	Uses: S.13 General government	Uses: S.12 Financial corporations	Uses: S.11 Non-financial corporations	Transactions and balancing items	Res: S.11 Non-financial corporations	Res: S.12 Financial corporations	Res: S.13 General government	Res: S.14 Households	Res: S.15 NPISHs	Res: S.1 Total economy	Res: Rest of the world account	Res: Goods and service account	Res: Total
									B.7g Adjusted disposable income, gross	185	32	176	1 434	27	1 854			1 854
									B.7n Adjusted disposable income, net	48	22	146	1 392	24	1 632			1 632
1 399			1 399		1 243	156			P.4 Actual final consumption								1 399	1 399
1 243			1 243		1 243				P.41 Actual individual consumption								1 243	1 243
156			156			156			P.42 Actual collective consumption								156	156
11		0	11	0		0	11	0	D.8 Adjustment for the change in net equity of households in pension funds				11		11	0		11
455			455	27	202	20	21	185	B.8g Saving, gross									
233			233	24	160	−10	11	48	B.8n Saving, net									
−41		−41							B.12 Current external balance									

corporations or employers operating non-autonomous funded pension schemes.

9.7.   Final consumption expenditure is shown as a single figure in table 9.1 above, with individual consumption and collective consumption expenditure shown separately to bring out accounting interrelationships described below. However, it is usually desirable to break down final consumption expenditure using a classification of expenditure by purpose or by type of good or service. Disaggregated expenditure data may be needed for various analytical or policy purposes. Most users will expect at least some degree of disaggregation, for example, between expenditures on goods or services or between expenditures on durable and non-durable goods.

9.8.   As explained in later sections of this chapter, expenditures are attributed to the institutional units that bear the costs even if they are not the units to whom the goods or services are delivered. Thus, expenditures that government units or NPISHs make on individual goods and services that they provide to households as social transfers in kind must be recorded as final expenditure incurred by government units or NPISHs. Although they do not physically consume the goods and services provided as social transfers in kind, government units or NPISHs are the units that pay for them and take the decisions about the amounts to be provided. Information about their expenditure on such goods and services must, therefore, be recorded in the accounts of the System in conjunction with their disposable income. However, merely to record the expenditure is not sufficient when the goods and services are consumed by different units from those that control and finance the expenditure. In order to identify the units that benefit from their consumption it is necessary to recognize that the goods and services are in fact transferred to households. Actual final consumption must be recorded as well as final consumption expenditure.

2. The use of adjusted disposable income account

9.9.   Apart from the balancing item, saving, this account also contains only two other entries (and the adjustment item, which hereafter will not be mentioned in order to simplify the discussion). Adjusted disposable income, the balancing item brought forward from the redistribution of income in kind account, is recorded under resources, while actual final consumption is recorded under uses. The account is relevant only to government units, NPISHs and households.

9.10. As already noted, the actual final consumption of households is obtained by augmenting their final consumption expenditure by the value of social transfers in kind receivable, while that for government units and NPISHs is obtained by subtracting from their final consumption expenditure social transfers in kind payable. Assuming that social transfers in kind take place only between resident units, the total value of the transfers in kind receivable by resident households must equal the

total value of those payable by government units and NPISHs, so that the value of actual final consumption for the total economy must be equal to that of total final consumption expenditure.

9.11. The actual final consumption of households is intended to measure the value of the consumption goods acquired by households, whether by purchase or by transfer from government units or NPISHs, and used by them for the satisfaction of their needs and wants. It is therefore a better indicator of their living standards than their final expenditure alone. In some countries, the value of the individual non-market goods and services provided to households as social transfers in kind may be quite large, depending upon the kinds of economic and social policies pursued by their governments, so that the value of the actual final consumption of households may exceed that of their expenditure by a significant margin. For these reasons, the actual final consumption of households has sometimes been described as their "enlarged" consumption or their "total" consumption, although these terms are not used in the System. The actual final consumption of the general government sector may, of course, be considerably smaller than government final consumption expenditure.

3. The relationship between the two versions of the use of income account

9.12. The two versions of the use of income account are not sequential or hierarchical. They are parallel accounts that serve different analytical or policy purposes. The values of the goods and services involved in social transfers in kind are recorded in two different ways in the System, both of which represent uses of resources by government units or NPISHs:

(a)   As final consumption expenditure, payable by government units or NPISHs; and

(b)   As current transfers in kind, payable by government units or NPISHs.

9.13. Although the difference between disposable and adjusted disposable income is attributable to social transfers in kind, disposable income should not be interpreted as if it were a measure of income available in cash. Its several non-cash elements, such as those associated with production for own consumption or remuneration in kind, were pointed out in paragraphs 8.13 and 8.14 of chapter VIII on the secondary distribution of income account.

4. Adjustment for the change in the net equity of households in pension funds (D.8)

9.14. The reserves of private funded pension schemes are treated in the System as being collectively owned by the households with claims on the funds. The payments of pension contributions into the funds and the receipts of pensions by pensioners are, therefore, not transfers between different institutional units. They constitute the acquisition and disposal of financial assets. However, this may not accord with the perception of the households concerned, especially pensioners' households, who tend to regard the pensions they receive as income in the form of current transfers. Moreover, pensions received under social security schemes are in fact treated as current transfers in the System.

9.15. In order to present income information that may be more useful for analysing the behaviour of the households concerned, the payments of pension contributions under private funded and unfunded social insurance schemes and the receipts of pensions by pensioners' households under such schemes are recorded in the secondary distribution of income account as social contributions and social insurance benefits, respectively. They are therefore recorded as determinants of the disposable incomes of households.

9.16. However, in order to reconcile this treatment with the fact that households are treated in the financial accounts and balance sheets of the System as owning the reserves of private funded pension schemes, both autonomous and non-autonomous, it is necessary to introduce an adjustment item to ensure that the balance of pension contributions over pension receipts (i.e., of "transfers" payable over "transfers" receivable) does not enter into household saving. In order to achieve this, it is necessary to add back pension contributions to, and subtract pension receipts from, the disposable income, or adjusted disposable income, of households recorded in the secondary distribution of income accounts in order to get back to a figure for the saving of households that is the same as what it would have been if pension contributions and pension receipts had not been recorded as current transfers in the secondary distribution of income account. The necessary adjustment item is therefore equal to:

the total value of the actual social contributions payable into private funded pension schemes

plus the total value of contribution supplements payable out of the property income attributed to insurance policy holders (i.e., holders of pension rights)

minus the value of the associated service charges

minus the total value of the pensions paid out as social insurance benefits by private funded pension schemes.

This adjustment item is equal to the change in the net equity of households in pension funds described in paragraphs 11.93 to 11.96 of chapter XI. It must be added to the disposable in-

come, or adjusted disposable income, of households before calculating saving in order to reconcile the saving of households with the change in their net equity in life insurance reserves and pension funds recorded in the financial account of the System. Opposite adjustments are, of course, needed in the use of income accounts of the insurance enterprises, autonomous pension funds or employers maintaining non-autonomous pension funds. These adjustments can affect non-resident institutional units, both households and pension funds.

5. Saving (B.8)

9.17. Saving is the balancing item in the two versions of the use of income account. Its value is the same whether it is derived as disposable income less final consumption expenditure or as adjusted disposable income less actual final consumption (in both cases, after adding to income the adjustment item for pension funds just described).

9.18. As already noted, non-financial and financial corporations have no final consumption expenditure or actual final consumption. Their net saving is equal to their net disposable, or adjusted disposable, income (apart from the adjustment item for pension funds).

9.19. Saving represents that part of disposable income that is not spent on final consumption goods and services. It may be positive or negative depending on whether disposable income exceeds final consumption expenditure, or vice versa. Assuming that saving is positive, the unspent income must be used to acquire assets or reduce liabilities. In so far as unspent income is not used deliberately to acquire various financial or non-financial assets, or to reduce liabilities, it must materialize as an increase in cash, itself a financial asset. If saving is negative, some financial or non-financial assets must have been liquidated, cash balances run down or some liabilities increased. Thus, saving provides the link between the current accounts of the System and the subsequent accumulation accounts.

9.20. If saving is zero, i.e., if final consumption expenditure equals disposable income, the institutional unit is not obliged to liquidate any assets or change any of its liabilities. As already indicated in chapter VIII, disposable income can, therefore, be interpreted as the maximum amount that an institutional unit can afford to spend on final consumption goods and services in the accounting period without having to reduce its cash, liquidate other assets or increase its liabilities.

B. Expenditures, acquisitions and uses

9.21. The distinction between final consumption expenditure and actual final consumption depends on the general distinction between expenditures on, and acquisitions of, goods and services, a distinction that applies to other types of activities, such

as production and capital formation, as well as consumption. The purpose of this section is to explain not only how expenditure differs from acquisition but also how both of them differ from the actual or physical use of goods and services. The explanation concentrates on consumption, but is also relevant to other types of activities.

1. Expenditures

9.22. Expenditures are defined as the values of the amounts that buyers pay, or agree to pay, to sellers in exchange for goods or services that sellers provide to them or to other institutional units designated by the buyers. The buyer incurring the liability to pay need not be the same unit that takes possession of the good or service. As already noted, it is common for government units or NPISHs to pay for goods or services that the sellers provide to households. Moreover, as explained below, the liability incurred by the buyer does not necessarily have to be settled by a payment of cash.

The incidence of expenditures

9.23. In the System, expenditures are attributed to the units which ultimately bear the costs as distinct from the units that may make payments to the sellers. The unit making the payment is usually also the one that bears the cost, but this is not always the case. For example, one unit may pay a seller acting as the agent of another unit to whom the ownership of the good is transferred. In this case, the agent provides a short-term credit to the buyer that is extinguished when the agent is reimbursed. Another example is that of a household which purchases a good or service that it retains itself but is subsequently reimbursed out of social security funds for some or all of the amount spent. In this case, the amount reimbursed is treated as expenditure incurred by the social security fund.

The timing of expenditures

9.24. Expenditures on goods or services occur at the times when buyers incur liabilities to sellers. These are usually the times when:

(a) The ownership of the good is transferred from the seller to the new owner; or

(b) The delivery of a service by the producer is completed to the satisfaction of the consumer.

9.25. The times at which sellers are actually paid for the goods or services they deliver are not necessarily the times at which the expenditures occur. As explained in chapter III, payments may either precede, or lag behind the actual deliveries of the goods or services sold. For this reason, the values of expenditures are measured by the values of the amounts receivable and payable at the times the expenditures are incurred. When payments are advanced or deferred there must be consequential changes in the financial assets or liabilities (other than cash) of the two units concerned at the time the change of ownership takes place or the service is delivered.

9.26. The precise moment at which the ownership of a good is transferred, or delivery of service completed to the satisfaction of

the consumer, may not be easy to determine in practice in some cases. It may be perceived differently, or even disputed, by the two parties concerned.

Imputed expenditures

9.27. By mutual agreement between the buyer and the seller, the liability incurred by the buyer may be discharged by providing a good, service or asset other than cash in exchange. For example, goods or services may be exchanged for each other in barter transactions, or employees may provide labour in exchange for goods or services received as remuneration in kind.

9.28. Since the buyers do not pay cash, or expect to pay cash, values have to be imputed for the expenditures using the appropriate prices of similar goods or services sold for cash on the market. For example, workers receiving remuneration in kind are treated as making expenditures equal to the market value of the goods or services received (at producers' prices if produced by the employer or at purchasers' prices if bought by the employer), the costs of the expenditures being met out of the income they receive as remuneration in kind. In barter, both parties to a transaction must be recorded as making expenditures. As the market values of the goods or services bartered may not be the same, the values imputed for the expenditures should be a simple average of the estimated values of the goods or services exchanged, so that equal expenditures are recorded for both parties.

9.29. When institutional units retain goods or services produced by themselves for their own consumption or gross fixed capital formation, they clearly bear the costs themselves. They are, therefore, recorded as incurring expenditures whose values have to be imputed using the basic prices of similar goods or services sold on the market or their costs of production in the absence of suitable basic prices.

9.30. In the interests of brevity, an expenditure for which a value has to be imputed may be described as an "imputed expenditure". Strictly speaking, however, the imputation refers to the value of goods or services involved and not to the expenditure itself.

Sales of existing goods as negative expenditures

9.31. An existing good is a good which has already been disposed of to a user by the unit that produced or imported it, either in the current or a previous period. Most existing goods are used structures and machinery and equipment or second-hand consumer durables (see paragraph 9.38 below), but they may include some unused goods. When an existing good is resold, the amount received from its sale is recorded as negative expenditure on the part of the seller. Durable goods may have to be reclassified as a result of being resold; for example, the sale to a household of an automobile previously used by an enterprise for business purposes is recorded as negative gross capital formation and positive household final consumption expenditure.

2. Acquisitions

9.32. Goods and services are acquired by institutional units when they become the new owners of the goods or when the delivery of services to them is completed. The value of the goods or services acquired by an institutional unit or sector consists of the value the goods or services acquired through its expenditure plus the value of goods or services received through transfers in kind less the value of goods or services transferred to other units. Transfers in kind made to other units are recorded as negative acquisitions. This statement needs to be qualified to the extent that several categories of current transfers—i.e., current transfers within general government, current international cooperation, and miscellaneous current transfers—may include some transfers in kind. These transfers in kind are treated as if they were transfers in cash. Accordingly, the values of the goods or services received are actually recorded as expenditures by the institutional units or sectors that acquire them.

9.33. As described above, acquisition can refer to goods and services of any kind. Producers may, for example, acquire structures and machinery and equipment by their own expenditure (including imputed expenditure for own-account capital formation) and by capital transfers in kind. The System gives special recognition to the importance of acquisition for purposes of final consumption; it defines the total value of goods and services acquired for purposes of final consumption as actual consumption.

9.34. The times at which goods and services are acquired are when the change of ownership occurs or the delivery of the services is completed. Acquisitions are valued at the prices paid by the units that incur the expenditures.

3. Uses

9.35. Goods and services are used when institutional units make use of them in a process of production or for the direct satisfaction of human needs or wants.

9.36. In the case of goods, the distinction between acquisition and use is clear. Producers acquire goods which they may hold for varying periods of time before physically using them up in processes of production. Households may hold consumption goods before using them for the satisfaction of their needs or wants. Few goods are so perishable that they have to be used immediately. For example, most foodstuffs need not be eaten until some time after they have been acquired.

9.37. In the case of services, however, the distinction between acquisition and use may not be relevant in a practical sense. The situations of units to whom services are delivered are automatically affected by those services and no further action may be needed in order to benefit from them.

Durable versus non-durable goods

9.38. In the case of goods, the distinction between acquisition and use is analytically important. It underlies the distinction between durable and non-durable goods extensively used in economic analysis. In fact, the distinction between durable and non-durable goods is not based on physical durability as such. Instead, the distinction is based on whether the goods can be used once only for purposes of production or consumption or whether they can be used repeatedly, or continuously. For example, coal is a highly durable good in a physical sense, but it can be burnt only once. A durable good is therefore defined as one which may be used repeatedly or continuously over a period of more than a year, assuming a normal or average rate of physical usage. A consumer durable is a good that may be used for purposes of consumption repeatedly or continuously over a period of a year or more.

Consumption as an activity

9.39. The activity of consumption consists of the use of goods and services for the satisfaction of individual or collective human needs or wants. A consumption function that expresses utility as a function of the quantities of goods and services consumed describes the use of those goods and services rather than expenditures or acquisitions. In order to measure consumption as an activity, it would be necessary to adopt accounting procedures similar to those used in a production account, where a clear distinction is drawn between purchases of goods to be used in production and their subsequent use as inputs.

9.40. In practice, the System measures household consumption only by expenditures and acquisitions. This means that the only way in which the repeated use of durables by households could be recognized would be to extend the production boundary by postulating that the durables are gradually used up in hypothetical production processes whose outputs consist of services. These services could then be recorded as being acquired by households over a succession of time periods. However, durables are not treated in this way in the System.

C. Consumption goods and services

9.41. A consumption good or service is defined as a good or service that is used (without further transformation in production as defined in the System) by households, NPISHs or government units for the direct satisfaction of individual needs or wants or the collective needs of members of the community.

9.42. An individual consumption good or service is one that is acquired by a household and used to satisfy the needs and wants of members of that household. Individual goods and services can always be bought and sold on the market, although they may also be provided free, or at prices that are not economically significant, as transfers in kind. In practice, all goods and most services are individual.

9.43. A collective consumption service is a service provided simultaneously to all members of the community or to all members of a particular section of the community, such as all households living in a particular region. Collective services are automatically acquired and consumed by all members of the community, or group of households in question, without any action on their part. Typical examples are public administration and the provision of security, either at a national or local level. Collective services are the "public goods" of economic theory. By their nature, collective services cannot be sold to individuals on the market, and they are financed by government units out of taxation or other incomes. The differences between individual and collective consumption goods or services are elaborated further in paragraphs 9.80 to 9.89 below.

9.44. Some of the services provided by NPISHs to the members of the associations that own them have some of the characteristics of collective services; for example, some research carried out by NPISHs may benefit all members of the community. However, most of the services provided by NPISHs are individual in nature and, for simplicity, all the services provided by NPIs are treated by convention as individual.

D. Household final consumption expenditure (P.3)

1. Introduction

9.45. Household final consumption expenditure consists of expenditure incurred by resident households on consumption goods or services. Final consumption expenditure excludes expenditure on fixed assets in the form of dwellings or on valuables. Dwellings are goods used by their owners to produce housing services. Expenditure on dwellings by households, therefore, constitutes gross fixed capital formation. When dwellings are rented by their owners, rentals are recorded as output of housing services by owners and final consumption expenditure by tenants. When dwellings are occupied by their owners, the imputed value of the housing services enters into both the output and final consumption expenditure of the owners. Valuables are expensive durable goods that do not deteriorate over time, are not used up in consumption or production, and are acquired primarily as stores of value. They consist mainly of works of art, precious stones and metals and jewellery fashioned out of such stones and metals. Valuables are held in the expectation that their prices, relative to those of other goods and services, will tend to increase over time, or at least not decline. Although the owners of valuables may derive satisfaction from possessing them, they are not used up in the way that household consumption goods, including consumer durables, are used up over time.

9.46. The treatment of expenditure in some specific situations and on certain specific types of goods and services is outlined in the following sections.

2. Expenditures by households owning unincorporated enterprises

9.47. When a household includes one or more persons who own an unincorporated enterprise, it is necessary to ensure that only expenditure for the direct satisfaction of human needs and wants is included in household final consumption expenditure; all expenditure incurred for business purposes is excluded from household consumption expenditure. This may not be easy in practice when the same good or service (for example, electricity or other fuels) may be used equally well for business purposes or for final consumption. Business expenditures cannot therefore be identified purely on the basis of the type of good or service purchased. Particular care needs to be exercised in the case of farms, including subsistence farms, where goods that have been purchased, or produced on own account, may be used either for household final consumption or for intermediate consumption; for example, corn or potatoes may be consumed by members of the households, fed to animals or used as seeds for future crops.

9.48. Care is also needed with purchases of consumer durables such as vehicles, furniture, or electrical equipment which are to be classified as gross fixed capital formation by the household enterprise when purchased for business purposes but as final consumption expenditure when purchased for the personal use of household members. While the nature of the distinction may be clear in principle, it is often blurred in practice, especially when the owner of the business uses a durable good, such as a vehicle, partly for business purposes and partly for personal benefit. In such cases, the expenditure on the purchase of the durable should be split between gross fixed capital formation by the enterprise and household final consumption expenditure in proportion to its usage for business and personal purposes. When durables are purchased wholly or partly for business purposes, the decline in their value attributable to their use within the business should be recorded under the consumption of fixed capital of the unincorporated enterprise.

3. Barter transactions

9.49. The values of the goods or services acquired in barter transactions constitute imputed expenditures. Values have to be imputed for goods or services exchanged in barter transactions equal to their market values, or their average market values, if the market values of the goods or services exchanged are not the same. Thus, when the goods or services obtained through barter are used for household consumption their imputed values must be recorded as household final consumption expenditure. When a good offered for barter is an existing good and not newly produced output, negative imputed expenditure must be recorded for the unit offering the good, in the same way that sales of existing goods are recorded as negative expenditures.

4. Expenditures on goods and services received as income in kind

9.50. Income in kind received by employees is measured by the value of the goods and services provided by employers to their employees in remuneration for work done. This income is simultaneously spent by the employees on the goods and services in question. Thus, the values of the goods and services must be recorded as final consumption expenditure incurred by households as well as income in kind.

9.51. A distinction has to be made between goods or services provided to employees as remuneration in kind and goods or services provided because they are needed at work, the latter constituting intermediate consumption by the enterprise. In principle, the distinction is clear. Goods or services that employers are obliged to provide to their employees to enable them to carry out their work, such as tools, equipment, special clothing, etc., constitute intermediate consumption. On the other hand, goods or services that employees are able to use in their own time for the direct satisfaction of their needs or wants, or those of their families, constitute remuneration in kind. In practice, there are inevitably borderline cases, such as uniforms that must be worn at work but are also worn extensively by employees away from work. A detailed listing of the kinds of goods and services that are included in remuneration in kind is given in the section on compensation of employees in chapter VII.

5. Expenditures on goods and services produced on own account

9.52. Household final consumption expenditure includes the imputed values of goods or services produced as outputs of unincorporated enterprises owned by households that are retained for consumption by members of the household. The production of services for own consumption within the same household falls outside the production boundary of the System, except for housing services produced by owner-occupiers and services produced by employing paid domestic staff. As the costs of producing goods or services for own consumption are borne by the households themselves, it is clear that the expenditures on them are also incurred by households, even though their values must be imputed. The main types of goods

and services produced and consumed within the same household are as follows:

(a)   Food or other agricultural goods produced for own final consumption by farmers, including subsistence farmers, or others for whom agricultural production is only a secondary, or even leisure, activity;

(b)   Other kinds of goods produced by unincorporated enterprises owned by households that are consumed by members of the same households;

(c)   Housing services produced for own final consumption by owner-occupiers (discussed further below);

(d)   Domestic or other services produced for own final consumption by households that employ paid staff for this purpose—servants, cooks, gardeners, chauffeurs, etc.

Values are imputed for these goods or services on the basis of the estimated current basic prices of similar goods or services sold on the market, or by costs of production when suitable prices are not available, except for the services of paid staff; services of paid staff, by convention, are valued simply by the compensation of employees paid, in cash and in kind.

6. Expenditures on particular types of goods and services

Expenditures on financial intermediation services

9.53. When appropriate, values must be imputed for the expenditures which households incur on services provided by financial intermediaries for which no explicit charges are made. Expenditures on services for which financial intermediaries do make charges are recorded in the usual way.

Financial intermediation services, except insurance and pension fund services

9.54. Financial intermediaries, except insurance corporations and pension funds, which include all corporations engaged in banking, may not charge households (or their other clients) explicitly for some of the services they provide. Instead, the nominal rates of interest they charge households on advances, overdrafts, mortgages or other loans are higher than they themselves pay on the deposits that households hold with them. The differences between the various rates of interest charged and paid constitute an indirect method of charging customers for services. As already explained in chapter VI, the total value of these services is estimated as the difference between the property income received by these financial intermediaries (excluding income from the investment of their own funds) less the interest they pay to creditors. This total value, may, or may not, be allocated to the household and other sectors, depending upon the procedures adopted in the country in question.

9.55. When the value of the services is actually allocated among sectors using one or another of the methods suggested in chapter VI, the imputed values of the services are recorded as expenditures on the services of financial intermediaries in the use of income account for households. The interest recorded in the primary distribution of income account for households as being received from financial intermediaries is equal to the amount actually received plus the imputed value the service charge paid on household lending. The amount of interest recorded as paid to financial intermediaries is equal to the amount actually paid less the imputed value of the service charge on household borrowing. Household saving is the same, whether the service charge is allocated or not.

Insurance and pension fund services

9.56. The way in which the value of the services produced by insurance enterprises is calculated in the System has been explained in chapter VI. The same method is used to calculate the output of autonomous pension funds.

9.57. The values of the insurance services consumed by different sectors, sub-sectors or institutional units are estimated by allocating the total value of the services produced by an insurance enterprise or autonomous pension fund in proportion to the actual premiums or pension contributions paid. The amounts paid by households are recorded as final consumption expenditure (except for the insurance services purchased by unincorporated enterprises owned by households).

Services of dwellings, repairs and improvements

Services of owner-occupied dwellings

9.58. Persons who own the dwellings in which they live are treated as owning unincorporated enterprises that produce housing services that are consumed by the household to which the owner belongs. The housing services produced are deemed to be equal in value to the rentals that would be paid on the market for accommodation of the same size, quality and type. The imputed values of the housing services are recorded as final consumption expenditures of the owners.

Decoration, maintenance and repair

9.59. As already noted in chapter VI, expenditures that an owner-occupier incurs on the decoration, maintenance and repair of the dwelling should not be treated as household final consumption expenditure but as intermediate expenditure incurred in the production of housing services. These expenditures may consist either of payments for services provided by professional builders or decorators or purchases of materials for "do-it-yourself" repairs and decoration. In the latter case, simple, routine repairs and interior decoration of a kind carried out by tenants as well as owners may be treated as falling outside the production boundary. Purchases of materials used for such repairs or decoration should therefore be treated as final consumption expenditure.

Major improvements

9.60. Expenditures on major improvements—that is, reconstructions, renovations or enlargements—to dwellings are not classed as repairs and maintenance. They are excluded from household consumption expenditure and are treated as gross fixed capital formation on the part of the owners of those dwellings.

The repair and maintenance of durables

9.61. Expenditures on the repair and maintenance of consumer durables, including vehicles, are treated in the same way as simple repairs to dwellings. They constitute final consumption expenditure whether the repairs and maintenance are carried out by specialist producers or by members of the household as "do-it-yourself" activities. In the latter case, only the values of the materials purchased should be included in household consumption expenditure.

Licences and fees

9.62. Households make payments to government units to obtain various kinds of licences, permits, certificates, passports, etc., and in some cases it is not clear whether the government units actually provide services in return, such as testing or inspection, or whether the payments are de facto taxes. As explained in chapter VIII, paragraph 8.54 (c), the treatment of certain controversial borderline cases has been decided by the following convention, based on the practices followed in the majority of countries: payments by households for licences to own or use vehicles, boats or aircraft and also licences to hunt, shoot or fish are treated as taxes, while payments for all other kinds of licences, permits, certificates, passports, etc., are treated as purchases of services and included in household consumption expenditure.

7. Classification of household final consumption expenditure

9.63. Household final consumption expenditure is typically a large aggregate covering a wide range of goods and services. It is thus usually desirable to break down the figure. The Central Product Classification (CPC) may be used for a breakdown by type of good or service. The Classification of Individual Consumption by Purpose may be used for a breakdown by purpose or function, e.g., food, health and education services. Chapter XVIII briefly describes this classification and how its inclusion in the System facilitates several kinds of analyses.

8. Timing and valuation of household final consumption expenditure

Timing

9.64. In accordance with the general principles adopted in the System, expenditures should be recorded when the payables are created, that is, when the purchaser incurs a liability to the seller. This implies that expenditure on a good is to be recorded at the time its ownership changes while expenditure on a service is recorded when the delivery of the service is completed.

9.65. Expenditures on a good under a hire purchase or similar credit agreement (and also under a financial lease) should be recorded at the time the good is delivered even though there is no legal change of ownership at this point. De facto, the purchaser exercises the rights and responsibilities of ownership from the time the good is delivered under a hire purchase agreement, financial lease or similar method of financing. A change of ownership is therefore imputed at the time of delivery. The purchaser must also be shown in the financial accounts as incurring a liability to the hire purchase or finance corporation.

Valuation

9.66. Household expenditure is recorded at the purchasers' prices paid by households including any taxes on products which may be payable at the time of purchase. As defined in chapter VI, paragraphs 6.216 to 6.218, the purchaser's price of a good is the amount payable to take delivery of a unit of the good at the time and place required by the purchaser. It includes any transport charges incurred by the purchaser not already included in the seller's invoice price.

9.67. Different households may pay different prices for identical products because of market imperfections. Price differences may persist because households may not be aware of them, or they may have imperfect information because the costs of searching for the retail outlets selling at the lowest prices may be too great. Even when households are aware of the price differences, it may be too inconvenient or costly to visit the outlets selling at the lowest prices. Another reason for the persistence of price differences is that many service producers deliberately practice price discrimination by charging different households different prices for identical services—e.g., by charging lower prices or fees to pensioners or people with low incomes. As services cannot be retraded, price discrimination is extremely common, or even prevalent, among service producers. Household expenditures are nevertheless recorded at the prices actually paid, even though this may mean that goods and services may not be valued uniformly.

9.68. Apparent price differences between the same goods or services are often not genuine price differences as they may be due to differences in quality, including differences in the terms or conditions of sale. For example, lower prices are often charged for bulk purchases of goods or off-peak purchases of services. Such expenditures must, of course, be recorded at the prices actually paid; that is, after deducting from the standard or list prices or charges any discounts for bulk or off-peak purchases.

Valuation of purchases on credit

9.69. The purchaser's price does not include any interest or service charges that may be added when the seller arranges for credit to be provided to the purchaser. Similarly, the purchaser's price does not include any extra charges which may be incurred as a result of failing to pay within the period stated at the time the purchases were made, such charges being effectively interest payments on the credit extended by the seller.

Expenditures by resident and non-resident households

9.70. Resident households make expenditures while travelling abroad, while non-resident households may make expenditures inside the economic territory of a country. Household final consumption expenditure in the System refers to the expenditure incurred by resident households, whether that expenditure is incurred within the economic territory or abroad.

9.71. In order to calculate total household final consumption expenditure it may be convenient to calculate the total expenditure made by all households, whether resident or not, within the economic territory and to adjust this figure by adding expenditures by residents abroad and subtracting expenditures by non-residents within the economy territory. Expenditures by residents abroad constitute imports, while expenditures by non-residents are exports. However, while the total expenditures by all households within the economic territory may be used for calculation in this way, it is not an aggregate recognized within the System.

E. Household actual final consumption (P.4)

9.72. Household actual final consumption consists of the consumption goods or services acquired by individual households by expenditures or through social transfers in kind received from government units or non-profit institutions serving households NPISHs. The value of household actual final consumption is given by the sum of three components:

(a) The value of households' expenditures on consumption goods or services including expenditures on non-market goods or services sold at prices that are not economically significant;

(b) The value of the expenditures incurred by government units on individual consumption goods or services provided to households as social transfers in kind;

(c) The value of the expenditures incurred by NPISHs on individual consumption goods or services provided to households as social transfers in kind.

9.73. The values of expenditures on social transfers incurred by government units or NPISHs are equal to imputed values of the goods or services supplied to households less the amounts of any expenditures incurred by households when prices are charged that are not economically significant.

9.74. The term "consumption" on its own can be ambiguous and misleading. Sometimes it is used by economists to refer to consumption expenditures, sometimes to acquisitions of consumption goods and services and sometimes to the physical use of the goods and services for the direct satisfaction of human needs or wants. By distinguishing between consumption expenditure and actual final consumption, such ambiguity can be avoided. When consumption is recorded on an expenditure basis, the purpose is to identify the institutional units that incur the expenditures and hence control and finance the amounts of such expenditures. When consumption is recorded on an acquisitions basis, the purpose is to identify the units that actually acquire the goods and services and benefit from their use, either immediately or subsequently. The value of total final consumption is the same, however, whichever basis is used.

F. Consumption expenditures incurred by general government and NPISHs (P.3)

9.75. The treatment of consumption expenditures incurred by general government and NPISHs serving households is the same so that it is convenient to describe them together. Expenditures on a wide range of consumption goods and services are incurred by general government or by NPISHs, either on collective services or on selected individual goods or services. The government expenditures are financed principally out of taxation or other government revenues while those of the NPISHs are financed principally out of subscriptions, contributions or donations or property income.

9.76. The consumption expenditures of general government and NPISHs can be classified in several ways. In particular, they may be classified:

   (a) According to whether the goods or services have been produced by market or non-market producers;

   (b) According to whether the expenditures are on collective services or individual goods or services;

   (c) By function or purpose according to the classification of the functions of government (COFOG);

   (d) By type of good or service according to the CPC.

1. Expenditures on the outputs of market and non-market producers

9.77. Expenditures on the outputs of non-market producers that are provided free, or at prices that are not economically significant, to individual households or the community account for most of the final consumption expenditure by governments and NPISHs. It is therefore appropriate to take them first.

Expenditures on the outputs of non-market producers

9.78. It is important to distinguish between expenditures made by general government or NPISHs on the outputs of non-market producers—i.e., the goods, individual or collective services they actually produce—and the intermediate expenditures and other costs incurred by non-market producers owned by general government or NPISHs in the course of producing those goods or services. The distinction between the inputs to, and outputs from, non-market processes of production needs to be emphasized because the final consumption expenditure made by general government or NPISHs must be incurred on the outputs. The values of these expenditures are equal to the imputed values of the non-market outputs less the values of any receipts from sales. These receipts may be derived from sales of some goods or services at prices that are not economically significant or from sales of a few goods or services at prices that are economically significant (sales of secondary market output).

Expenditures on consumption goods or services produced by market producers

9.79. Government units and NPISHs also purchase consumption goods and services produced by market producers that are supplied directly to households. The role of the government unit or NPISH is confined to paying for the goods or services and ensuring that they are distributed to households as social transfers in kind. The government unit or NPISH does not engage in any further processing of such goods or services and their expenditures are treated as final and not intermediate. The values of the goods or services distributed in this way are also recorded under social benefits in kind, including social assistance benefits in kind.

2. Expenditures on individual and collective goods and services (P.31/P.32)

9.80. The consumption expenditures incurred by government units and NPISHs have to be divided into those incurred for the benefit of individual households and those incurred for the benefit of the community as a whole, or large sections of the community.

Individual goods or services

9.81. Individual goods and services are essentially "private", as distinct from "public" goods. They have the following characteristics:

(a) It must be possible to observe and record the acquisition of the good or service by an individual household or member thereof and also the time at which it took place;

(b) The household must have agreed to the provision of the good or service and take whatever action is necessary to make it possible—for example, by attending a school or clinic;

(c) The good or service must be such that its acquisition by one household or person, or possibly by a small, restricted group of persons, precludes its acquisition by other households or persons.

The reference to a small, restricted group of persons is needed because certain services are provided to small groups of people simultaneously; for example, several persons may travel in the same bus, train, ship or plane or attend the same class, lecture, concert or live theatre performance. However, these are still essentially individual services if there is a restriction on the number of individuals who can consume them. Other members of the community are excluded and derive no benefit from them.

9.82. From a welfare point of view, the important characteristic of an individual good or service is that its acquisition by one household, person or group of persons brings no (or very little) benefit to the rest of the community. While the provision of certain individual health or education services (for example, vaccination or immunization) may bring some external benefits to the rest of the community, in general the individuals concerned derive the main benefit. Thus, when a government unit or NPISH incurs expenditures on the provision of individual goods or services, it must decide not only how much to spend in total but how to allocate, or distribute, the goods or services among individual members of the community. From the point of view of economic and social policy, the way in which they are distributed may be as important as the total amount spent.

Collective services

9.83. Most goods can be privately owned and are individual in the sense used here. On the other hand, certain kinds of services can be provided collectively to the community as a whole. The characteristics of these collective services may be summarized as follows:

(a) Collective services can be delivered simultaneously to every member of the community or of particular sections of the community, such as those in a particular region of a locality;

(b) The use of such services is usually passive and does not require the explicit agreement or active participation of all the individuals concerned;

(c) The provision of a collective service to one individual does not reduce the amount available to others in the same community or section of the community. There is no rivalry in acquisition.

9.84. The collective services provided by government consist mostly of the provision of security and defence, the maintenance of law and order, legislation and regulation, the maintenance of public health, the protection of the environment, research and development, etc. All members of the community can benefit from such services. As the individual usage of collective services cannot be recorded, individuals cannot be charged according to their usage or the benefits they derive. There is market failure and collective services that must be financed out of taxation or other government revenues.

9.85. The services provided by NPISHs are often confined to the members of the associations that control them, although they may also provide individual goods or services to third parties. Many NPISHs are only concerned with protecting the interests or welfare of their members or providing recreational, sporting or cultural facilities which households or persons cannot otherwise easily obtain for themselves acting individually. Although NPISHs may provide services to their members in groups, the services are essentially individual rather than collective. In general, persons other than their members are excluded and derive no benefit from the services provided. Therefore, as already noted, all the services provided by NPISHs are by convention treated as individual.

The borderline between individual and collective services

9.86. Expenditures incurred by governments at a national level in connection with individual services such as health and education are to be treated as collective when they are concerned with the formulation and administration of government policy, the setting and enforcement of public standards, the regulation, licensing or supervision of producers, etc. For example, the expenditures incurred by Ministries of Health or Education at a national level are to be included in collective consumption expenditures as they are concerned with general matters of policy, standards and regulation. On the other hand, any overhead expenses connected with the administration or functioning of a group of hospitals, schools, colleges or similar institutions are to be included in individual expenditures. For example, if a group of private hospitals has a central unit which provides certain common services such as purchasing, laboratories, ambulances, or other facilities, the costs of these common services would be taken into account in the prices charged to patients. The same principle must be followed when the hospitals are non-market producers: all the costs which are associated with the provision of services to particular individuals, including those of any central units providing common services, should be included in the value of expenditures on individual services.

The classification of individual and
collective government expenditures

9.87. The classification of the functions of government is a classification of transactions designed to apply to general government and its subsectors. This classification, which is described briefly in chapter XVIII, is used to help distinguish between expenditure by government on individual services and collective services. By convention, all government final consumption expenditures under each of the following headings should be treated as expenditures on individual services except for expenditures on general administration, regulation, research, etc.:

04   Education

05   Health

06   Social Security and Welfare

08.01   Sport and recreation

08.02   Culture.

In addition, expenditures under the following sub-headings should also be treated as individual when they are important:

07.11   part of the provision of housing

07.31   part of the collection of household refuse

12.12   part of the operation of transport system.

Non-market services to enterprises

9.88. Many government expenditures benefit enterprises as much as households; expenditures on the cleaning, maintenance and repair of public roads, bridges, tunnels, etc. including the provision of street lighting are examples. These are individual services whose consumption can be monitored and for this reason they are frequently provided on a market basis by charging tolls on road usage. However, it would be difficult to separate the services provided free to households from those provided free to enterprises and, by convention, all these expenditures are treated as collective final expenditure.

9.89. Enterprises also benefit from a number of genuinely collective services such as the research and development undertaken by non-market producers, the provision of security by the police, fire services, etc. The usage of such collective services by individual enterprises cannot be recorded, so that expenditures on such services have to be treated as government final expenditure.

G. Actual final consumption of general government (P.4)

9.90. As noted above, all the services provided by NPISHs are treated as individual even though some are partly collective in nature. All the goods and services covered by the final expenditures of NPISHs are, therefore, assumed to be provided to individual households as social transfers in kind. It follows that NPISHs have no actual final consumption, so that their adjusted disposable income is equal to their saving.

9.91. The value of the actual final consumption of government units is taken to be equal to the value of the expenditures they incur on collective services. Although collective services benefit the community, or certain sections of the community, rather than the government, the actual consumption of these services cannot be distributed among individual households, or even among groups of households such as subsectors of the household sector. It is therefore attributed to the same government units that incur the corresponding expenditures. As government final consumption expenditure must be either individual or collective, the value of the actual final consumption of general government is equal to the value of its total final consumption expenditure less its expenditure on individual goods or services provided as social transfers in kind to households.

9.92. The identification and measurement of government actual

final consumption serves two main analytical or policy purposes:

(a)   Collective services can be identified with "public goods" as defined in public finance and economic theory. While it may be technically possible to charge individual consumers of certain collective services according to their usage or benefits they derive, the transactions costs of so doing would be prohibitively high, leading to market failure. This provides an economic, rather than political, rationale for government involvement as the provision of such services has to be financed collectively out of taxation or other government revenues;

(b)   Collective services do not provide a mechanism for redistributing resources among individual households. As redistribution may be one of the main economic objectives of government policy, it is useful to separate the collective services which do not serve this purpose from the individual goods and services which are ultimately channelled to individual households, even though paid for by government.

H. Final consumption expenditure and actual final consumption: summary

9.93. The purpose of this section is to summarize the conceptual interrelationship between the main consumption aggregates for the three sectors in which final consumption takes place, namely, the household sector, the NPISH sector and the general government sector. On a practical level, it may be noted that each of the aggregates, whether referring to consumption expenditure or actual final consumption, has to be derived from data on expenditures.

1. The expenditure aggregates

9.94. (a) Household final consumption expenditure: This consists of the expenditure, including imputed expenditure, incurred by resident households on individual consumption goods and services, including those sold at prices that are not economically significant;

(b) Final consumption expenditure of NPISHs: This consists of the expenditure, including imputed expenditure, incurred by resident NPISHs on individual consumption goods and services;

(c) Government final consumption expenditure: This consists of expenditure, including imputed expenditure, incurred by general government on both individual consumption goods and services and collective consumption services. This expenditure may be divided into:

   (i) Government expenditure on individual consumption goods and services;

   (ii) Government expenditure on collective consumption services.

2. Actual final consumption

9.95. NPISHs have no actual final consumption, as explained above. Thus, actual final consumption is confined to households and general government.

Actual final consumption of households (P.41)

9.96. This is measured by the value of all the individual consumption goods and services acquired by resident households. There are three sets of goods and services entering into household actual final consumption:

(a) Those acquired through expenditure by households themselves: their value is given by item (a) in paragraph 9.94 above;

(b) Those acquired as social transfers in kind from NPISHs: their value is given by item (b) in paragraph 9.94 above;

(c) Those acquired as social transfers in kind from general government: their value is given by item (i) in paragraph 9.94 above.

Actual final consumption of general government (P.41/P.42)

9.97. This is measured by the value of the collective consumption services provided to the community, or large sections of the community, by general government. Its value is given by item (c) in paragraph 9.94 above.

3. Total final consumption in the economy

9.98. Total final consumption in the economy may be viewed from two angles. It may be defined from the expenditure side as the total value of all expenditures on individual and collective consumption goods and services incurred by resident households, resident NPISHs serving households and general government units. Or, it may be defined in terms of actual final consumption as the value of all the individual goods and services acquired by resident households plus the value of the collective services provided by general government to the community or large sections of the community.

9.99. The coverage of the goods and services is the same in both cases. In order to ensure that the values of the two aggregates are the same, the goods and services acquired by resident households through transfers in kind must always be valued at the same prices at which they are valued in the expenditure aggregates and the time of recording the good and services acquired by transfers in kind must be the same as the time of recording in the expenditure aggregates.

X. The capital account

General introduction to the accumulation accounts and balance sheets

1. Introduction

10.1. The balance sheets and accumulation accounts form a group of accounts that are concerned with the values of the assets owned by institutional units or sectors, and their liabilities, at particular points in time and with the evolution of those values over time. Balance sheets measure the values of stocks of assets or liabilities and are typically compiled at the beginning and end of the accounting period. The total value of the assets owned by an institutional unit or sector minus the total value of its liabilities is described as its net worth. It is a measure of the wealth of a unit or sector at a point in time. The accumulation accounts record the changes in the values of the assets, liabilities and net worth that take place during the accounting period. They are flow accounts, whose entries depend on the amounts of economic or other activities that take place within a given period of time and on transactions and other flows associated with them.

2. Assets

10.2. The assets recorded in the balance sheets of the System are economic assets. These are defined as entities:

(*a*) Over which ownership rights are enforced by institutional units, individually or collectively; and

(*b*) From which economic benefits may be derived by their owners by holding them, or using them, over a period of time.

10.3. Every economic asset must function as a store of value that depends upon the amounts of the economic benefits that its owner can derive by holding it or using it. However, this value does not usually remain constant as the benefits remaining often diminish with the passage of time. Different kinds of benefits may be derived from different kinds of assets, as follows:

(*a*) Some benefits are derived by using assets such as buildings or machinery in production;

(*b*) Some benefits consist of property incomes: for example, interest, dividends, rents, etc., received by the owners of financial assets and land;

(*c*) Finally, assets act as stores of value that may be realized by disposing of them or terminating them. While some assets may be held until the benefits derivable from them are exhausted, others may be disposed of before that point in order to realize the capitalized values of the benefits still remaining. Some assets may be held purely as stores of values (precious metals or stones, etc.) without any other benefits being derived from them.

Financial assets

10.4. Most financial assets are financial claims. Financial claims and obligations arise out of contractual relationships entered into when one institutional unit provides funds to the other. A financial claim may be defined as:

> An asset that entitles its owner, the creditor, to receive a payment, or series of payments, from the other unit, the debtor, in certain circumstances specified in the contract between them.

The claim is extinguished when the liability is discharged by the debtor paying a sum agreed in the contract. In addition, the creditor may receive a series of interest payments: i.e., property income. Financial claims include not only claims on financial intermediaries in the form of cash and deposits but also loans, advances and other credits and securities such as bills and bonds.

10.5. Financial assets may now be defined as assets in the form of financial claims, monetary gold, Special Drawing Rights (SDRs) allocated by the International Monetary Fund (IMF), shares in corporations, and certain of the instruments called derivatives. Monetary gold and SDRs are treated as financial assets even though their holders do not have claims over other designated units. Shares, even though their holders do not have a fixed or predetermined monetary claim on the corporation, and certain derivatives, are treated as financial assets by convention. For convenience, the term "financial asset" may be used to cover both financial assets and liabilities, except when the context requires liabilities to be referred to explicitly.

Non-financial assets

10.6. Two different categories of non-financial assets need to be distinguished from each other: produced and non-produced assets.

Produced assets are defined as non-financial assets that have come into existence as outputs from processes that fall within the production boundary of the System as defined in chapter VI.

Non-produced assets are defined as non-financial assets that have come into existence in ways other than through processes of production.

Produced assets

10.7. There are three main types of produced assets: fixed assets, inventories and valuables. Both fixed assets and inventories are assets that are held only by producers for purposes of production.

Fixed assets are defined as produced assets that are themselves used repeatedly, or continuously, in processes of production for more than one year.

The distinguishing feature of a fixed asset is not that it is durable in some physical sense, but that it may be used repeatedly or continuously in production over a long period of time that is taken to be more than one year. Some goods, such as coal, may be highly durable physically but cannot be fixed assets because they can be used once only. Fixed assets include not only structures, machinery and equipment but also cultivated assets such as trees or animals that are used repeatedly or continuously to produce other products such as fruit or dairy products. They also include intangible assets such as software or artistic originals used in production.

Inventories consist of:

(a) Stocks of outputs that are still held by the units that produced them prior to their being further processed, sold, delivered to other units or used in other ways; and

(b) Stocks of products acquired from other units that are intended to be used for intermediate consumption or for resale without further processing.

Valuables are defined as goods of considerable value that are not used primarily for purposes of production or consumption but are held as stores of value over time.

The economic benefits that valuables bring are that their values are not expected to decline relatively to the general price level. They consist of precious metals and stones, jewellery, works of art, etc.

Non-produced assets

10.8. Non-produced assets consist of assets that are needed for production but have not themselves been produced. They include naturally occurring assets such as land and certain uncultivated forests and deposits of minerals. They also include certain intangible assets such as patented entities.

10.9. Not all environmental assets qualify as economic assets. It is

useful, therefore, to delineate those naturally occurring assets that fall within the asset boundary of the System from those that do not.

The asset boundary

10.10. First, it must be noted that the System's accounts and balance sheets are compiled for institutional units or groups of units and can only refer to the values of assets that belong to the units in question. Only those naturally occurring assets over which ownership rights have been established and are effectively enforced can therefore qualify as economic assets and be recorded in balance sheets. They do not necessarily have to be owned by individual units, and may be owned collectively by groups of units or by governments on behalf of entire communities. Certain naturally occurring assets, however, may be such that it is not feasible to establish ownership over them: for example, air, or the oceans. In addition, there may be others that cannot be treated as economic assets because they do not actually belong to any particular units. These include not only those whose existence is unknown but also those, including uncultivated forests, that may be known to exist but remain so remote or inaccessible that, in practice, they are not under the effective control of any units.

10.11. Secondly, in order to comply with the general definition of an economic asset, natural assets must not only be owned but capable of bringing economic benefits to their owners, given the technology, scientific knowledge, economic infrastructure, available resources and set of relative prices prevailing on the dates to which the balance sheet relates or expected in the near future. Thus, known deposits of minerals that are not commercially exploitable in the foreseeable future are not included in the balance sheets of the System, even though they may possibly become commercially exploitable at a later date as a result of major, unforeseen advances in technology or major changes in relative prices such as those resulting from the oil shocks of the 1970s and 1980s.

10.12. Naturally occurring assets in the form of biota—trees, vegetation, animals, birds, fish, etc.—are renewable. The growth of trees, crops or other vegetation or the rearing of animals, birds, fish, etc., may take place under the direct control, responsibility and management of institutional units. In this situation, the assets are cultivated, and the activity is treated as falling within the production boundary of the System. The resulting assets are obviously produced assets that fall within the asset boundary of the System. However, some renewable assets in the form of biota may also be classified under the heading of non-produced assets: namely, forests and the wildlife inhabiting them that are actually owned by institutional units but whose renewal is not under the direct control, responsibility and management of those units. The growth of animals, birds, fish, etc., living in the wild, or growth of uncultivated vegetation in forests, is not an economic process of production so that the resulting assets cannot be produced assets. Nevertheless, when the forests and/or the animals, birds, fish, etc. are actually owned by institutional units and are a source of benefit to their owners, they constitute economic assets. Finally, when wild animals, birds, fish, etc. live in locations such that no institutional units are able to exercise effective ownership rights over them—for example, in the oceans or quite inaccessible regions—they fall outside the asset boundary. Similarly, the forests or other vegetation growing in such regions are not counted as economic assets.

Valuation

10.13. To ensure consistency between the accumulation accounts and the balance sheets, assets recorded in balance sheets should be valued as if they were being acquired on the date to which the balance sheet relates. For example, if fixed assets were to be acquired on the balance sheet date they would be recorded at their current purchasers' prices, including any costs of ownership transfer, or at their current basic prices if produced on own account. The valuation of fixed assets that were acquired some time before the balance sheet date is more problematic. In general, they are valued by writing-down the current purchasers' or basic prices of new assets by the accumulated consumption of fixed capital on the assets. With good information and efficient markets, the written-down values of the assets should equal, or at least approximate, both the present, or discounted, values of the remaining future benefits to be derived from them and their market values when active secondhand markets exist. In practice, these values may differ from each other because of lack of information or other imperfections. As already stated, the written-down value of the asset is generally the most practical and also the preferred method of valuing an existing fixed asset, bearing in mind that the calculation of consumption of fixed capital should take into account the observed values of secondhand assets when they are actively traded.

10.14 Most financial assets consist of financial claims. A financial claim is usually valued by the amount of the principal outstanding: i.e., by the amount that a debtor must pay to the creditor to extinguish the claim. When financial assets are traded on markets, this value is equal to the market price of the security in question as the debtor, or issuer of the security, can extinguish the claim by buying back the security at the current market price.

3. Balance sheets and the sequence of accumulation accounts

10.15. The basic accounting identity linking the opening and the closing balance sheet values for a single type of asset can be summarized as follows:

(a)   The value of the stock of a specific type of asset in the opening balance sheet;

plus

(b)   The total value of the assets acquired, less the total value of those disposed of, in transactions that take place within the accounting period: transactions in non-financial assets are recorded in the capital account and transactions in financial assets in the financial account;

plus

(c)   The value of other positive or negative changes in the volume of the assets held (for example, as a result of the discovery of a subsoil asset or the destruction of assets as a result of war or a natural disaster): these changes are recorded in the other changes in the volume of assets account;

plus

(d)   The value of the positive or negative nominal holding gains accruing during the period resulting from a change in the price of the asset: these are recorded in the revaluation account where they may be further decomposed into neutral holding gains that reflect changes in the general price level and real holding gains that reflect a change in the relative price of the asset;

is *identical* with

(e)   The value of the stock of the asset in the closing balance sheet.

10.16. This identity requires transactions or other changes in the amounts of the asset held to be valued at the prices prevailing at the times they occur and the stocks of the asset recorded in the opening and closing balance sheets to be valued at the prices prevailing on the dates to which the balance sheets relate. The identity is valid even in the case of assets that are held only temporarily within the accounting period and that do not appear in either the opening or the closing balance sheets.

10.17. Each of the five elements involved in the above identity can be measured directly without the others. However, it follows from the identity that if any four of the elements are known, the fifth can be determined residually. Nevertheless, none of the elements is defined residually.

10.18. As the above identity applies to each individual type of asset and liability recorded in the balance sheets, it must be possible to decompose the change in the net worth of an institutional unit or sector between the beginning and end of the accounting period into that part due to transactions, that part due to other changes in the volume of assets held and that part due to holding gains or losses. The accumulation accounts record these various components of changes in net worth. Moreover, as nominal holding gains are decomposed into neutral and real holding gains, it is also possible to measure not only the change in real net worth over the period but also to identify the components of that change.

Table 10.1 Account III.1: Capital account

Changes in assets

Total	Corresponding entries of the — Rest of the world account	Corresponding entries of the — Goods and service account	S.1 Total economy	S.15 NPISHs	S.14 Households	S.13 General government	S.12 Financial corporations	S.11 Non-financial corporations	Code	Transactions and balancing items
									B.8n	Saving, net
									B.12	Current external balance
376			376	19	61	37	9	250	P.51	Gross fixed capital formation
303			303	14	49	23	8	209	P.511	Acquisitions less disposals of tangible fixed assets
305			305	13	50	24	7	211	P.5111	Acquisitions of new tangible fixed assets
11			11	1	4	1	1	4	P.5112	Acquisitions of existing tangible fixed assets
−13			−13		−5	−2		−6	P.5113	Disposals of existing tangible fixed assets
51			51	5	12	12	1	21	P.512	Acquisitions less disposals of intangible fixed assets
53			53	10	9	12	1	21	P.5121	Acquisitions of new intangible fixed assets
6			6		3	2		1	P.5122	Acquisitions of existing intangible fixed assets
−8			−8	−5		−2		−1	P.5123	Disposals of existing intangible fixed assets
22			22			2		20	P.513	Additions to the value of non-produced non-financial assets
5			5			2		3	P.5131	Major improvements to non-produced non-financial assets
17			17					17	P.5132	Costs of ownership transfer on non-produced non-financial assets
−222			−222	−3	−42	−30	−10	−137	K.1	Consumption of fixed capital
28			28		2			26	P.52	Changes in inventories
10			10		5	3		2	P.53	Acquisitions less disposals of valuables
				1	4	2		−7	K.2	Acquisitions less disposals of non-produced non-financial assets
				1	3	2		−6	K.21	Acquisitions less disposals of land and other tangible non-produced assets
					1			−1	K.22	Acquisitions less disposals of intangible non-produced assets
									D.9	Capital transfers, receivable
									D.91	Capital taxes
									D.92	Investment grants
									D.99	Other capital transfers
									D.9	Capital transfers, payable
									D.91	Capital taxes, payable
									D.92	Investment grants, payable
									D.99	Other capital transfers, payable
−38	−38		38	4	148	−50	5	−69	B.9	Net lending (+) / net borrowing (−)
									B.10.1	Changes in net worth due to saving and capital transfers [1][2]

Changes in liabilities and net worth

Code	Transactions and balancing items	S.11 Non-financial corporations	S.12 Financial corporations	S.13 General government	S.14 Households	S.15 NPISHs	S.1 Total economy	Corresponding entries of the — Rest of the world account	Corresponding entries of the — Goods and service account	Total
B.8n	Saving, net	48	11	−10	160	24	233			233
B.12	Current external balance							−41		−41
P.51	Gross fixed capital formation								376	376
P.511	Acquisitions less disposals of tangible fixed assets								303	303
P.5111	Acquisitions of new tangible fixed assets								305	305
P.5112	Acquisitions of existing tangible fixed assets								11	11
P.5113	Disposals of existing tangible fixed assets								−13	−13
P.512	Acquisitions less disposals of intangible fixed assets								51	51
P.5121	Acquisitions of new intangible fixed assets								53	53
P.5122	Acquisitions of existing intangible fixed assets								6	6
P.5123	Disposals of existing intangible fixed assets								−8	−8
P.513	Additions to the value of non-produced non-financial assets								22	22
P.5131	Major improvements to non-produced non-financial assets								5	5
P.5132	Costs of ownership transfer on non-produced non-financial assets								17	17
K.1	Consumption of fixed capital									
P.52	Changes in inventories								28	28
P.53	Acquisitions less disposals of valuables								10	10
K.2	Acquisitions less disposals of non-produced non-financial assets									
K.21	Acquisitions less disposals of land and other tangible non-produced assets									
K.22	Acquisitions less disposals of intangible non-produced assets									
D.9	Capital transfers, receivable	33		6	23		62	4		66
D.91	Capital taxes			2			2			2
D.92	Investment grants	23					23	4		27
D.99	Other capital transfers	10		4	23		37			37
D.9	Capital transfers, payable	−16	−7	−34	−5	−3	−65	−1		−66
D.91	Capital taxes, payable				−2		−2			−2
D.92	Investment grants, payable			−27			−27			−27
D.99	Other capital transfers, payable	−16	−7	−7	−3	−3	−36	−1		−37
B.9	Net lending (+) / net borrowing (−)									
B.10.1	Changes in net worth due to saving and capital transfers [1][2]	65	4	−38	178	21	230	−38		192

1 "Changes in net worth due to saving and capital transfers" is not a balancing item but corresponds to the total of the right hand side of the capital account.

2 "Changes in net worth due to saving and capital transfers" for the rest of the world refers to changes in net worth due to current external balance and capital transfers.

10.19. The accounting links between balance sheets and the accumulation accounts are further described in chapter XIII. The remainder of this chapter is concerned with transactions in the capital account.

Capital account

A. Introduction

10.20. The purpose of the capital account, shown in table 10.1, is to record the values of the non-financial assets that are acquired, or disposed of, by resident institutional units by engaging in transactions and to show the change in net worth due to saving and capital transfers. The transactions may be either with other institutional units, both resident and non-resident, or internal transactions in which units retain for their own use assets that they have produced themselves. The account does not, however, cover changes in the volume of non-financial assets owned by units that do not result from transactions, these being recorded in the other changes in volume of assets account described below in chapter XII.

10.21. As already explained in the general introduction to the accumulation accounts and balance sheets, the capital account is the first of four accounts dealing with changes in the values of assets held by institutional units. These four accounts enable the change in the net worth of an institutional unit or sector between the beginning and end of the accounting period to be decomposed into its constituent elements by recording all changes in the prices and volumes of assets held, whether resulting from transactions or not.

10.22. When compiling balance sheets, it is customary to record assets on the left side and liabilities and net worth on the right. The same convention is followed in the accumulation accounts, where changes in assets are recorded on the left and other items on the right. As in the current accounts, the balancing item of the capital account, i.e., net lending or borrowing, is recorded on the left side. Consumption of fixed capital is also recorded on the left side of the capital account.

10.23. The right side of the capital account records the resources available for the accumulation of assets. These consist of net saving, the balancing item carried forward from the use of income account, and capital transfers. Capital transfers payable are recorded with a negative sign.

1. Changes in non-financial assets

10.24. The left side of the capital account records the values of the non-financial assets acquired, or disposed of, in transactions of various kinds. The assets may be bought or sold, or acquired or disposed of as a result of capital transfers in kind, barter or production for own use. Values must be estimated for assets that are not bought or sold.

10.25. Five categories of changes in assets are distinguished in the capital account:

(a)   Gross fixed capital formation;

(b)   Consumption of fixed capital;

(c)   Changes in inventories;

(d)   Acquisitions less disposals of valuables;

(e)   Acquisitions less disposals of non-produced non-financial assets.

The treatment given to each of these categories of changes in assets is described in later sections of this chapter. The annex to chapter XIII defines and describes the assets.

10.26. The gross fixed capital formation of an institutional unit or sector is measured largely by the value of its acquisitions less disposals of new or existing fixed assets. Disposals do not include consumption of fixed capital. Fixed assets consist of tangible or intangible assets that have come into existence as outputs from processes of production and that are themselves used repeatedly or continuously in other processes of production over periods of time of more than one year. Changes in assets may be either positive or negative, and it is possible for the gross fixed capital formation of an individual institutional unit or sector to be negative if it sells off, or transfers, enough of its existing fixed assets to other units or sectors.

10.27. Consumption of fixed capital is also recorded as a change in assets on the left side of the capital account. This implies that the saving figure carried forward from the use of income account and recorded on the right side of the account should be net saving. Consumption of fixed capital represents the reduction in the value of the fixed assets used in production during the accounting period resulting from physical deterioration, normal obsolescence or normal accidental damage. It may be deducted from gross fixed capital formation to obtain net fixed capital formation, although net fixed capital formation is not shown as a separate item in the capital account. If it is not feasible to measure consumption of fixed capital because of lack of data, the saving figure carried forward from the use of income account has to be gross, while fixed capital formation can also only be recorded gross. If consumption of fixed capital has to be omitted from both sides of the account for this reason, the balancing item of the account is not affected, of course; net lending or borrowing can be derived residually whether or not consumption of fixed capital can be estimated. However, if consumption of fixed capital is not estimated, the accumulation accounts do not record all changes between two successive balance sheets.

10.28. The remaining items on the left side of the capital account refer to inventories, valuables and non-produced non-financial assets. Changes in inventories, including work-in-progress, are measured by the value of the entries into inventories less the value of withdrawals and the value of any recurrent losses of goods held in inventories. Products entering and leaving inventories are implicitly treated as if they were sold to, or purchased from, inventories and are valued at the same prices as actual sales or purchases taking place at the same time. The total value of the changes in inventories for an institutional unit or sector may equally well be positive or negative. The total value of the changes—acquisitions less disposals—in the other two items, valuables and non-produced non-financial assets, may also, of course, be positive or negative.

2. Saving and capital transfers

10.29. The items recorded on the right side of the capital account consist of net saving and capital transfers receivable and payable, capital transfers payable being recorded with a negative sign. Capital transfers are transactions in which the ownership of an asset (other than cash and inventories) is transferred from one institutional unit to another, in which cash is transferred to enable the recipient to acquire another asset or in which the funds realised by the disposal of another asset are transferred. The total of the resources, on the right side of the account, is explicitly shown and described as changes in net worth due to saving and net capital transfers. It is not a balancing item. It represents the positive or negative amount available to the unit or sector for the acquisition of non-financial and financial assets.

3. Net lending or borrowing (B.9)

10.30. The balancing item of the capital account, described as net lending or borrowing, is defined as follows:

(a)   Net saving plus capital transfers receivable minus capital transfers payable;

minus

(b)   The value of acquisitions less disposals of non-financial assets, less consumption of fixed capital.

When positive, net saving represents that part of disposable income that is not spent on consumption goods and services and must, therefore, be used to acquire non-financial or financial assets of one kind or another, including cash, or to repay liabilities. When negative, net saving measures the amount by which final consumption expenditure exceeds disposable income: the excess must be financed by disposing of assets or incurring new liabilities (in both cases, the adjustment for the change in the net equity of households on pension funds has to be added to disposable income before calculating net saving in order to ensure that pension contributions and receipts are treated as acquisitions and disposals of financial assets: see the introduction to chapter IX). Similarly, capital transfers receivable, whether in cash or kind, are intended to enable the recipient to acquire assets or repay liabilities, while capital transfers payable imply that assets are disposed of. Thus, the balancing item in the capital account, being the difference between changes in net worth due to saving and capital transfers and net acquisitions of non-financial assets, shows the amount of the resources remaining for purposes of lending or that need to be borrowed.

10.31. The identity between the balancing items of the capital account and the financial account is an important feature of the set of the accounts as a whole. This feature stems mainly from the fact that monetary transactions require simultaneous entries in the financial accounts of the two units concerned and in one or other of their current and capital accounts. The conceptual identity between the balancing items provides a check on the numerical consistency of the set of accounts as a whole, although the two balancing items are likely to diverge significantly in practice because of errors of measurement.

B. Gross capital formation (P.5)

10.32. Gross capital formation is measured by the total value of the gross fixed capital formation, changes in inventories and acquisitions less disposals of valuables.

1. Gross fixed capital formation (P.51)

10.33. Gross fixed capital formation is measured by the total value of a producer's acquisitions, less disposals, of fixed assets during the accounting period plus certain additions to the value of non-produced assets realised by the productive activity of in-

stitutional units. Fixed assets are tangible or intangible assets produced as outputs from processes of production that are themselves used repeatedly or continuously in other processes of production for more than one year.

10.34. There is substantial diversity in the different types of gross fixed capital formation that may take place. The following main types may be distinguished:

(a)   Acquisitions, less disposals, of new or existing tangible fixed assets, subdivided by type of asset into:

(i)   Dwellings;

(ii)   Other buildings and structures;

(iii)   Machinery and equipment;

(iv)   Cultivated assets—trees and livestock—that are used repeatedly or continuously to produce products such as fruit, rubber, milk, etc.;

(b)   Acquisitions, less disposals, of new and existing intangible fixed assets, sub-divided by type of asset into:

(i)   Mineral exploration;

(ii)   Computer software;

(iii)   Entertainment, literary or artistic originals;

(iv)   Other intangible fixed assets;

(c)   Major improvements to tangible non-produced assets, including land;

(d)   Costs associated with the transfers of ownership of non-produced assets.

10.35. The various components of acquisitions and disposals of fixed assets, as referred to in categories (a) and (b) above, are listed below:

(a)   Value of fixed assets purchased;

(b)   Value of fixed assets acquired through barter;

(c)   Value of fixed assets received as capital transfers in kind;

(d)   Value of fixed assets retained by their producers for their own use, including the value of any fixed assets being produced on own account that are not yet completed or fully mature;

less

(e)   Value of existing fixed assets sold;

(f)   Value of existing fixed assets surrendered in barter;

(g)   Value of existing fixed assets surrendered as capital transfers in kind.

The value of the acquisitions less disposals of fixed assets of a producer is given by the sum of (a) to (d) less the sum of (e) to (g). The components of acquisitions each may refer to new or existing fixed assets, the latter being defined in paragraph 10.39 in the next section below. Acquisition of new assets covers not only complete assets but also any renovations, reconstruction or enlargements that significantly increase the productive capacity or extend the service life of an existing asset. In recognition of the newly increased capacity or newly extended service life, these improvements are treated as part of acquisitions of new assets even though physically they function as part of the existing asset (see paragraphs 10.45 to 10.54 below for a discussion of major improvements). Items

(e), (f) and (g) above include disposals of assets that may cease to be used as fixed assets by their new owners: for example, vehicles sold by businesses to households for their personal use or assets that are scrapped or demolished by their new owners.

10.36. The general principles governing the time of recording and valuation of acquisitions less disposals of fixed assets may be summarized as follows. The time at which gross fixed capital formation is recorded is when the ownership of the fixed assets is transferred to the institutional unit that intends to use them in production. Except for assets produced on own account, this time is not generally the same as the time at which the fixed assets are produced. Nor is it necessarily the time at which they are put to use in the production of other goods or services.

10.37. New fixed assets acquired by purchase are valued at purchasers' prices: that is, including not only all transport and installation charges but also all costs incurred in the transfer of ownership in the form of fees paid to surveyors, engineers, architects, lawyers, estate agents, etc., and any taxes payable on the transfer. New fixed assets acquired through barter or transfers in kind are valued similarly at their estimated basic prices plus taxes, transport, installation and other costs of ownership transfer. Fixed assets produced for own gross fixed capital are valued at their estimated basic prices, or by their costs of production when satisfactory estimates of their basic prices cannot be made. Purchases of existing fixed assets are valued including all transport, installation and other costs of ownership transfer incurred by the purchaser while sales of existing fixed assets are valued after deducting any costs of ownership transfer incurred by the seller.

10.38. Not all gross fixed capital formation consists of acquisitions less disposals of fixed assets. Before describing gross fixed capital formation by type of fixed asset it is, therefore, convenient to describe the other components of gross fixed capital formation—i.e., major improvements and costs of ownership transfer—as these may involve any type of asset. It is also useful to define at the outset the term "existing assets" and to describe the treatment of these assets and also the treatment of fixed tangible assets under financial leases.

Existing assets

10.39. Because assets have service lives that may range up to 50 years or more for dwellings or other structures, their ownership may change several times before they are eventually scrapped, demolished or abandoned. A good becomes an existing good as soon as its ownership passes from its original producer or importer, to a resident unit that uses it, or intends to use it. Thus, an existing fixed asset is one that has already been acquired by at least one user, or produced on own account, and whose value has, therefore, already been included in the gross fixed capital formation of at least one user at some earlier point in time in the current or some previous accounting period. In many countries, well-organized markets exist to facilitate the buying and selling of many kinds of existing fixed assets, notably automobiles, ships, aircraft, dwellings and other structures. Indeed, the number of existing dwellings bought and sold within a given time period may considerably exceed the number of new dwellings. In practice, most existing fixed assets will have been used in production by their current owners, but an existing capital good might be sold by its owner before it has actually been used.

10.40. In general, sales or other disposals of existing goods, whether fixed assets or not, are recorded as negative expenditures or negative acquisitions. Thus, when the ownership of an existing fixed asset is transferred from one resident producer to another, the value of the asset sold, bartered or transferred is recorded as negative gross fixed capital formation by the former and as positive gross fixed capital formation by the latter. The value of the positive gross fixed capital formation recorded for the purchaser exceeds the value of the negative gross fixed capital formation recorded for the seller by the total value of the costs of ownership transfer incurred by both parties to the transaction. The treatment of these costs is explained in more detail in a later section.

10.41. When the sale takes place between two resident producers, the positive and negative values recorded for gross fixed capital formation cancel out for the economy as a whole except for the costs of ownership transfer. Similarly, if an existing immovable fixed asset, such as a building, is sold to a non-resident, by convention the latter is treated as purchasing a financial asset that is the equity of a notional resident unit while the notional resident unit is deemed to purchase the asset, so that the sale and purchase of the asset takes place between residents. However, if an existing movable fixed asset, such as a ship or aircraft, is exported, no positive gross fixed capital formation is recorded elsewhere in the economy to offset the seller's negative gross fixed capital formation.

10.42. Some durable goods, such as vehicles, may be classified as fixed assets or as consumer durables depending upon the owner and the purpose for which they are used. If, therefore, the ownership of such a good were transferred from an enterprise to a household to be used for final consumption, negative gross fixed capital formation is recorded for the enterprise and positive consumption expenditure by the household. If a vehicle owned by a household were to be acquired by an enterprise, it would be recorded as an acquisition of a "new" fixed asset even though it is an existing good. A similar treatment is applied to imports of used assets acquired by resident producers.

10.43. Thus, it is perfectly possible for the gross fixed capital formation of individual institutional units to be negative as a result of the sale or disposal of existing fixed assets, although aggregate gross fixed capital formation is unlikely to be negative for large groups of units—subsectors, sectors or the economy as a whole.

Tangible fixed assets under financial leases

10.44. A financial lease is a contract between lessor and lessee whereby the lessor purchases the good and the lessee pays rentals which enable the lessor, over the period of the contract, to cover all, or virtually all, costs including interest. Financial leases may be distinguished by the fact that all the risks and rewards of ownership are, de facto, transferred from the legal owner of the good, the lessor, to the user of the good, the lessee. In order to capture the economic reality of such arrangements, the goods under a financial lease are treated in the System as if they were purchased by the user, that is, as if a change in ownership had occurred. For tangible fixed assets—in practice, mostly machinery and equipment—the purchase appears in the capital account of the user/owner.

Major improvements to existing assets

10.45. Gross fixed capital formation may take the form of improvements to existing fixed assets, such as buildings or computer software, or tangible non-produced assets, such as land, that increase their productive capacity, extend their service lives, or both. By definition, such gross fixed capital formation does not lead to the creation of new assets that can be separately identified and valued.

Improvements to fixed assets

10.46. The distinction between ordinary maintenance and repairs and improvements to existing fixed assets is not clear cut. Ordinary maintenance and repairs constitute intermediate consumption.

10.47. As explained in paragraphs 6.166 to 6.169 of chapter VI, ordinary maintenance and repairs are distinguished by two features:

(a) They are activities that must be undertaken regularly in order to maintain a fixed asset in working order over its expected service life. The owner or user of the asset has no choice about whether or not to undertake ordinary maintenance and repairs if the asset in question is to continue to be used in production;

(b) Ordinary maintenance and repairs do not change the fixed asset's performance, capacity or expected service life. They simply maintain it in good working order, if necessary by replacing defective parts by new parts of the same kind.

10.48. On the other hand, improvements to existing fixed assets that constitute gross fixed formation must go well beyond the requirements of ordinary maintenance and repairs. They must bring about significant changes in some of the characteristics of existing fixed assets. They may be distinguished by the following features:

(a) The decision to renovate, reconstruct or enlarge a fixed asset is a deliberate investment decision that may be taken any time, even when the good in question is in good working order and not in need of repair. Major renovations of ships, buildings or other structures are frequently undertaken well before the end of their normal service lives;

(b) Major renovations, reconstructions or enlargements increase the performance or productive capacity of existing fixed assets or significantly extend their previously expected service lives, or both. Enlarging or extending an existing building or structure constitutes a major change in this sense, as does the refitting or restructuring of the interior of a building or ship or a major extension to or enhancement of an existing software system.

10.49. It is difficult to provide simple objective criteria that enable improvements to be distinguished from repairs because any repair may be said to improve the performance or extend the working life of the unrepaired asset. For example, machines may cease to function at all because of the failure of one small part, especially equipment with electric circuits. The replacement of such a part does not, however, constitute gross fixed capital formation. Thus, improvements have to be identified either by the magnitude of the changes in the characteristics of the fixed assets—that is, by major changes in their size, shape, performance, capacity, or expected service lives—or by the fact that improvements are not the kinds of changes that are observed to take place routinely in other fixed assets of the same kind, as part of ordinary maintenance and repair programmes.

10.50. Gross fixed capital formation in the form of improvements to existing fixed assets is to be classified with acquisitions of new fixed assets of the same kind. Accordingly, it is the improved asset that is henceforth relevant to the System and on which consumption of fixed capital must be calculated subsequently. However, it may also be useful for some analytical purposes to record improvements separately so that they may also be grouped with the improvements considered in the following section, if needed.

Improvements to tangible non-produced assets

10.51. In practice, these consist of improvements to land. Acquisitions that lead to major improvements in the quantity, quality or productivity of land, or prevent its deterioration, are treated as gross fixed capital formation. They consist of acquisitions related to the following kinds of activities:

(a) Reclamation of land from the sea by the construction of dykes, sea walls or dams for this purpose;

(b) Clearance of forests, rocks, etc. to enable land to be used in production for the first time;

(c) Draining of marshes or the irrigation of deserts by the construction of dykes, ditches or irrigation channels;

(d) Prevention of flooding or erosion by the sea or rivers by the construction of breakwaters, sea walls or flood barriers.

10.52. These activities may lead to the creation of substantial new structures such as sea walls, flood barriers, dams, etc., but these are not themselves used directly to produce other goods and services in the way that most structures are. Their construction is undertaken to obtain more or better land, and it is the land, a non-produced asset, that is needed for production. For example, a dam built to produce electricity serves quite a different purpose from a dam built to keep out the sea, and it is useful to classify them separately.

10.53. Acquisitions of tunnels and other structures associated with the mining of mineral deposits, etc., are classified as gross fixed capital formation in structures and not as improvements to land. These activities lead to the creation of assets that are used separately from the land through which they are drilled or bored. Site clearance and preparation for purposes of construction—i.e., the clearance of land previously used in production—is also not classified as improvements to land but treated as an integral part of the gross fixed capital formation in buildings or other structures.

10.54. Acquisitions or disposals of land itself are recorded as purchases or sales of non-produced assets and not as gross fixed capital formation. Thus, improvements to land must be shown on their own in a classification of gross fixed capital formation. The decline, between the beginning and the end of the accounting period, in the value of the improvement to land is shown, by convention, in consumption of fixed capital. This treatment is a convention in that, as noted above, an improvement does not lead to the creation of a new fixed asset that can be separately identified and valued, but it is consistent with the need to write down the value of all gross fixed capital formation over time as a result of consumption of fixed capital.

Costs of ownership transfer

Fixed assets

10.55. Acquisitions of new assets are valued at actual or estimated purchasers' prices plus the associated costs of ownership transfer incurred by units acquiring the assets. Similarly, acquisitions of existing assets are valued at the actual or estimated prices payable to their previous owners plus the associated costs of ownership transfer incurred by the units acquiring the assets. The costs of ownership transfer consist of the following kinds of items:

(a) All professional charges or commissions incurred by the unit acquiring the asset—fees paid to lawyers, architects, surveyors, engineers, valuers, etc., and commissions paid to estate agents, auctioneers, etc.;

(b) All taxes payable by the unit acquiring the asset on the transfer of ownership of the asset.

Costs of ownership transfer incurred by the unit acquiring the asset are treated as an integral part of the value of that unit's gross fixed capital formation. The value at which the asset enters the balance sheet of its new owner therefore includes the costs of ownership transfer.

10.56. Consistently with this method of valuation, disposals of existing fixed assets are valued at the prices payable by the units acquiring the assets to the units disposing of the assets minus any associated costs of ownership transfer incurred by the latter. Such costs are similar to those listed above, for example, lawyers' fees, estate agents' fees or commissions, auctioneers' commissions, taxes, etc. Taxes on ownership transfer do not, however, include capital gains taxes payable by the units disposing of the assets.

10.57. When a fixed asset is produced and sold for the first time, the costs of ownership transfer incurred by the first owner are included as an integral part of the value of the gross fixed capital formation recorded at the time. They are therefore gradually written off as part of the consumption of fixed capital charged on the use of the asset over its service life. If an asset is sold, however, before the end of its service life, this process is interrupted and a second set of costs of ownership transfer are incurred by both the first and the second owner. The value of the positive gross fixed capital formation recorded for the second owner is equal to the price paid by the second owner to the first owner plus the transfer costs incurred by the second owner. On the other hand, the value of the negative gross fixed capital formation recorded for the first owner is equal to the price paid by the second owner to the first owner minus the transfer costs incurred by the first owner. The positive gross fixed capital formation undertaken by the second owner must, therefore, exceed the negative gross fixed capital formation recorded for the second owner by the value of the costs of ownership transfer incurred by both units. This amount measures the total value of the gross fixed capital formation undertaken by the two units together.

10.58. Because of costs of ownership transfer, the value at which the disposal of an asset is recorded for the first owner may be less than the value of the asset in the opening balance sheet or at which it entered the balance sheet if acquired within the same period. In this case, a nominal holding loss equal to the difference between the two values is recorded for the first owner. Holding losses are incurred when owners of existing assets are unable to recover the costs of ownership transfer incurred on both the initial purchase and subsequent sale of an asset, although it may be difficult to separate such losses from other holding gains or losses when the prices of existing assets are changing for other reasons. The treatment of costs of ownership transfer is explained in more detail in the annex to this chapter where it is shown that, other things being equal, that part of the transfer costs incurred by the first owner on the initial acquisition of the asset that have not already been written off as consumption of fixed capital by the time it is sold plus

the transfer costs incurred on the subsequent sale result in a holding loss for the first owner.

Land

10.59. The costs of ownership transfer incurred on purchases and sales of land affect the values recorded in the same way as the costs of ownership transfer on fixed assets described above. However, as land is not a produced asset, it is not possible to have gross fixed capital formation in land itself. The value of the costs of ownership transfer associated with purchases and sales of land must therefore be separated from the purchases and sales themselves. They are recorded under a separate heading in the classification of gross fixed capital formation. Consumption of fixed capital may then be charged using suitably long service lives. However, as land that has been sold disappears from the balance sheet of the seller, any acquisition costs previously incurred by the seller that have not already been written off as consumption of fixed capital together with the selling costs result in a holding loss for the seller.

10.60. All owners and purchasers of land within the economic territory are deemed to have a centre of economic interest in the economy. If an owner or purchaser would not otherwise qualify as a resident unit, a notional resident unit is created for this purpose. The notional resident unit is deemed to purchase the land while the non-resident is deemed to purchase the equity of the notional unit—i.e., to acquire a financial instead of a non-financial asset. Thus, all purchases and sales of land take place between resident units except when the boundaries of the economic territory itself are changed as a result of the purchase or sale—for example, when a foreign government, or international organization, purchases or sells land that is added to, or taken away from, the enclave in which its embassy or offices are located. Moreover, as purchases and sales of land between residents are also recorded excluding costs of ownership transfer for both buyers and sellers, the total value of the purchases and sales of land between residents must be equal to each other at the level of the total economy, although not at the level of individual sectors or subsectors.

Other non-produced assets

10.61. The costs of ownership transfer incurred on purchases and sales of these assets, which include, for example, mineral deposits that are used in production, are treated in the same way as land, being recorded under the same heading of the classification of gross fixed capital formation.

Acquisitions less disposals of tangible fixed assets (P.511)

10.62. Acquisitions less disposals of tangible fixed assets usually constitute by far the largest component of gross fixed capital formation, at least at the level of the total economy. The tangible fixed assets included under the general headings of structures, machinery and equipment and cultivated assets are defined and described in the annex to chapter XIII, so that there is no need to repeat such a description here. Also, the fact that the major improvements to tangible fixed assets are classified with acquisitions of new assets is not repeated for each of the various kinds of fixed assets. The purpose of the present section is different, namely to describe the treatment of certain less well-documented cases, including cultivated assets, borderline cases or exceptions.

Producers' durables excluded from gross fixed capital formation

10.63. As already mentioned in chapter VI, when describing intermediate consumption, there are two kinds of durable goods used by producers that are excluded from gross fixed capital formation, i.e., small tools and some kinds of military equipment.

Small tools

10.64. Some goods may be used repeatedly, or continuously, in production over many years but may nevertheless be small, inexpensive and used to perform relatively simply operations. Hand tools such as saws, spades, knives, axes, hammers, screwdrivers and spanners or wrenches are examples. If expenditures on such tools take place at a fairly steady rate and if their value is small compared with expenditures on more complex machinery and equipment, it may be appropriate to treat the tools as materials or supplies used for intermediate consumption. Some flexibility is needed, however, depending on the relative importance of such tools. In countries in which they account for a significant part of the value of the total stock of an industry's durable producers' goods, they may be treated as fixed assets and their acquisition and disposal by producers recorded under gross fixed capital formation.

Military equipment

10.65. Destructive weapons such as missiles, rockets, bombs, etc., cannot be treated as fixed assets, because they are not in fact used repeatedly or continuously in production. Although durable, they are single-use goods. Moreover, the actual use of such weapons in combat to destroy lives or property cannot be construed as the production of goods or services. By extension, vehicles and equipment such as warships, submarines, military aircraft, tanks, missile carriers and launchers, etc., whose function is to release such weapons should also not be treated as fixed assets.

10.66. On the other hand, most of the structures used by military establishments—such as airfields, docks, roads and hospitals—are not only used continuously and repeatedly in production, but are used in much the same way as similar structures utilized by civilian producers. Such structures are often switched from military to civilian use, or vice versa. There is no justification for not treating them as fixed assets.

10.67. Thus, whereas structures such as military hospitals, and the equipment contained therein, are fixed assets, weapons and their supporting systems are not. It may sometimes be difficult to determine where to draw the line between the two kinds of

goods, and it is also necessary to recognize that it may not always be possible to obtain the necessary data to distinguish different categories of military expenditures. By convention, therefore, all expenditures on durable goods by the military are treated as gross fixed capital formation except for expenditures on weapons and on equipment that can only be used to support and deliver such weapons: warships, submarines, bombers, fighter aircraft, tanks, missile carriers, etc. In practice, almost all structures are likely to be fixed assets and certain types of equipment that have alternative non-military uses—such as transport equipment, computers and communications equipment and hospital equipment—are also treated as fixed assets. If it is not feasible to separate expenditures on such equipment from expenditures on weapons and their support systems, all expenditures on equipment for the military have by default to be treated as intermediate consumption.

10.68. Light weapons and armoured vehicles are also used by non-military establishments engaged in internal security or policing activities. The producers concerned may be either market or non-market, as there are enterprises that provide various kinds of security services commercially in addition to government controlled security or police forces. All the durable producers' goods used by such services or forces are treated as fixed assets and all their expenditures on fixed assets are counted as gross fixed capital formation notwithstanding the fact that such expenditures might be treated as intermediate consumption if intended for the armed forces. As already noted, many types of durable goods cannot be automatically classified as fixed assets purely on the basis of their physical characteristics.

Dwellings and other buildings and structures

10.69. Gross fixed capital formation in buildings, including dwellings, and other structures by producers consists of the value of their acquisitions of new and existing buildings and other structures less the value of their disposals of their existing buildings and structures. All buildings and other structures within the economic territory are deemed, by convention, to be owned by residents. If an owner or purchaser would not otherwise qualify as a resident unit, a notional resident unit is created for the purpose. The notional resident unit is deemed to purchase the building or other structure and the non-resident is deemed to purchase the equity of the notional unit (i.e., acquire a financial asset).

10.70. All dwellings, including houseboats, barges, mobile homes and caravans used as principal residences of households and any associated structures such as garages are fixed assets. Owner-occupiers are treated as the owners of enterprises engaged in the production of housing services for their own final consumption so that dwellings are not consumer durables.

10.71. The construction of new historic monuments constitutes gross fixed capital formation and similarly, major improvements to existing historic monuments are also included in gross fixed capital formation. Historic monuments are identifiable because of particular historic, national, regional, local, religious or symbolic significance. They are usually accessible to the general public, and visitors are often charged for admission to the monuments or their vicinity. Their owners, who may be government units, non-profit institutions (NPIs), corporations or households, typically use historic monuments to produce cultural or entertainment-type services. In principle, the gross fixed capital formation in historic monuments should be included in dwellings, non-residential buildings, and other structures as appropriate; in practice, it may be desirable to classify them with other structures. Consumption of fixed capital on new monuments, or on major improvements to existing monuments, should be calculated on the assumption of appropriately long service lives.

Consumption of fixed capital on buildings and other structures

10.72. All buildings and other structures are assumed to have finite service lives, even when properly maintained, so that consumption of fixed capital is calculated for all such fixed assets, including railways, roads, bridges, tunnels, airports, harbours, pipe-lines, dams, etc. Service lives are not determined purely by physical durability, and many buildings and structures are eventually scrapped because they have become obsolete. However, the service lives for some structures such as certain roads, bridges, dams, etc., may be very long—perhaps a century or more.

Time of recording and valuation except for own-account construction

10.73. Many construction projects take a long time to complete. Until such time as the ownership of at least some of the output produced is transferred to the eventual user of the structure, no gross fixed capital formation can take place. Output that is not so transferred and continues to belong to the builder or construction enterprise must be recorded as either work-in-progress or as an addition to inventories of finished goods, depending on whether the construction is finished or not.

10.74. When the construction takes place under a contract of sale agreed in advance, the ownership of the structure is effectively transferred in stages as the work proceeds. The value of the output transferred at each stage under such a contract is recorded as gross fixed capital formation by the purchaser.

10.75. When there is no contract of sale agreed in advance, the output produced by the construction enterprise must be recorded as work-in-progress or as additions to the producers' inventories of finished goods, depending on whether the construction is completed. For example, finished dwellings built speculatively remain as additions to producers' inventories of finished goods until they are sold or otherwise acquired by users.

10.76. Acquisitions of new buildings and structures are valued at

their actual or estimated purchasers' prices plus the associated costs of ownership transfer incurred by units acquiring the assets. Similarly, acquisitions of existing buildings and structures are valued at the actual or estimated prices payable to their previous owners plus the associated costs of ownership incurred by the units acquiring the assets. Disposals of existing buildings and structures are valued at the prices payable by the units acquiring the assets to the units disposing of the assets minus the costs of ownership transfer incurred by the latter. For buildings and structures acquired in an incomplete state, a value is estimated based on costs to date, including a mark-up for operating surplus. Stage or progress payments are usually required under a contract of sale agreed in advance, and the amounts paid may often be used to approximate the values of the gross fixed capital formation undertaken by the purchaser at each stage. (If the stage payments are made in advance, or in arrears, of the completion of the relevant work, short-term credits are effectively extended by the purchaser to the construction enterprise, or vice versa, and these credits must be adjusted for in approximating the value of the gross fixed capital formation.) It should be noted that the costs of clearing and preparing the site for construction are part of the costs and are therefore included in the value of the acquisition.

Time of recording and valuation of own-account construction

10.77. When construction is carried out for own use, the producer and the eventual user of the structure are one and the same institutional unit, by definition. No formal transfer of ownership takes place and the unit in its capacity as user of the structure effectively takes possession as the construction proceeds. Thus, the whole of the output of own-account construction during a given accounting period should be recorded as gross fixed capital formation, even if the structure is not finished.

10.78. In principle, the finished structure should be valued at its estimated basic price. If the structure is not completed within a single accounting period, the value of the output and corresponding gross fixed capital formation should be estimated by applying the fraction of the total costs of production incurred during the relevant period to the estimated current basic price. If it is not possible to estimate the basic price of the finished structure, it must be valued by its total costs of production, with a mark-up for operating surplus. If some or all of the labour is provided free, as may happen with communal construction by households, an estimate of what the cost of paid labour would be must be included in the estimated total production costs using wage rates for similar kinds of labour in the vicinity or region. Otherwise, the value of the finished structure will be seriously underestimated.

10.79. Certain structures may be produced for own communal use by groups of households: for example, buildings, roads, bridges, etc. After they are finished, the ownership of such structures may then be transferred to some government unit that assumes responsibility for their maintenance. When the transfer occurs, the gross fixed capital formation on own account originally attributed to the group of households is cancelled by their negative gross fixed capital formation resulting from the capital transfer in kind they make to the government unit. The final gross fixed capital formation remaining is that of the government unit resulting from its acquisition of the asset through the capital transfer in kind.

Machinery and equipment

10.80. Gross fixed capital formation in machinery and equipment by producers consists of the value of their acquisitions of new and existing machinery and equipment less the value of their disposals of their existing machinery and equipment. It covers transport equipment and other machinery and equipment, including office equipment, furniture, etc. As explained above, machinery and equipment under financial lease is treated as acquired by the user (lessee) (rather than as acquired by the lessor).

10.81. Gross fixed capital formation is not recorded until the ownership of the fixed assets is transferred to the unit that intends to use them in production. Thus, new machinery and equipment that has not yet been sold forms part of additions to inventories of finished goods held by the producers of the assets. Similarly, imported machinery and equipment is not recorded as gross fixed capital formation until it is acquired by the unit that intends to use it.

10.82. Machinery and equipment such as vehicles, furniture, kitchen equipment, computers, communications equipment, etc. that are acquired by households for purposes of final consumption are not fixed assets and their acquisition is not treated as gross fixed capital formation. However, houseboats, barges, mobile homes and caravans that are used as the principal residences of households are treated as dwellings, so that their acquisition by households is included in gross fixed capital formation.

Cultivated assets

10.83. Cultivated assets consist of livestock or trees that are used repeatedly or continuously over periods of time of more than one year to produce other goods or services. Thus, livestock that continue to be used in production year after year are fixed assets. They include, for example, breeding stock, dairy cattle, sheep reared for wool and draught animals. On the other hand, animals raised for slaughter, including poultry, are not fixed assets. Similarly, trees (including shrubs) that are cultivated in plantations for the products they yield year after year—such as fruit trees, vines, rubber trees, palm trees, etc.—are fixed assets. On the other hand, trees grown for timber that yield a finished product once only when they are ultimately felled are not fixed assets, just as cereals or vegetables that produce only a single crop when they are harvested cannot be fixed assets.

10.84. In general, when the production of fixed assets takes a long time to complete, those assets whose production is not yet completed at the end of the accounting period are recorded as work-in-progress. However, when the assets are produced on own account they are treated as being acquired by their users at the same time as they are produced and cannot therefore be recorded under the inventories, i.e., work-in-progress. Uncompleted assets produced on own account are therefore recorded as being acquired by their users, i.e., as gross fixed capital formation. These general principles must be applied to the production of cultivated assets such as animals or trees that may take a long time to reach maturity. Two cases need to be distinguished from each other: the production of natural assets by specialized producers, such as breeders or tree nurseries, and the own-account production of cultivated assets by their users.

10.85. In the case of the specialist producers, animals or trees whose production is not yet complete and are not ready for sale or delivery must be recorded as work-in-progress. Examples are one-year-old horses bred for sale as two-year-old race horses, or young fruit trees that need further growth before being marketable. Such work-in-progress is recorded and valued in exactly the same way as that originating in any other kind of production.

10.86. However, when animals or trees intended to be used as fixed assets are produced on own account by farmers or others, uncompleted assets in the form of immature animals, trees, etc. that are not ready to be used in production are not treated as work-in-progress but as gross fixed capital formation by the producing unit in its capacity as eventual user. The value of an uncompleted asset produced and acquired within a given period is obtained by multiplying the actual and estimated current basic price of the finished asset by the share of the production costs incurred in that period. If it is not feasible to estimate in this way, the value of the output and corresponding gross fixed capital formation may be approximated by the actual production costs incurred in the period.

Livestock

10.87. Gross fixed capital formation in livestock that are cultivated for the products they yield year after year (dairy cattle, draught animals, etc.) is measured by the value of acquisitions less disposals, taking account of the treatment just described of immature livestock produced on own account. It is therefore equal to the total value of all mature animals and immature animals produced on own account acquired by users of the livestock less the value of their disposals. Disposals consist of animals sold or otherwise disposed of, including those sold for slaughter, plus those animals slaughtered by their owners. Exceptional losses of animals due to major outbreaks of disease, contamination, drought, famine, or other natural disasters are recorded in the other changes in the volume of assets account and not as disposals. Incidental losses of animals due to occasional deaths from natural causes form part of consumption of

System of National Accounts 1993

230

fixed capital. Consumption of fixed capital on an individual animal is measured by the decline in its value as it gets older.

Plantations, orchards, etc.

10.88. Gross fixed capital formation in plantations, orchards, etc., consists of the value of the acquisitions less disposals of mature trees, shrubs, etc., including acquisitions of immature trees, shrubs, etc., produced on own account. As explained above, the value of the latter may be approximated, if necessary, by the value of costs incurred in their production during the period: for example, the costs of preparing the ground, planting, staking, protection from weather or disease, pruning, training, etc., until the tree reaches maturity and starts to yield a product. Disposals consist of trees, shrubs, etc., sold or otherwise transferred to other units plus those cut down before the end of their service lives. Disposals do not include exceptional losses of trees due to drought or other natural disasters such as gales or hurricanes, these being recorded in the other changes in the volume of assets account.

Acquisitions less disposals of intangible fixed assets (P.512)

10.89. Acquisitions less disposals of intangible fixed assets constitute the remaining component of gross fixed capital formation to be discussed. Intangible assets are defined and described in the annex to chapter XIII. They share with tangible fixed assets the characteristics that they are both produced as outputs from processes of production and are themselves used repeatedly or continuously in other processes of production. Intangible fixed assets include, for example, computer software or artistic originals whose use in production is restricted to the units that have established ownership rights over them or to other units licensed by the latter. Major improvements to these assets count as acquisitions; for example, the enhancement and extension of existing software systems.

Mineral exploration

10.90. Mineral exploration is undertaken in order to discover new deposits of minerals or fuels that may be exploited commercially. Such exploration may be undertaken on own account by enterprises engaged in mining or the extraction of fuels. Alternatively, specialized enterprises may carry out exploration either for their purposes or for fees. The information obtained from exploration influences the production activities of those who obtain it over a number of years. The expenditures incurred on exploration within a given accounting period, whether undertaken on own account or not, are therefore treated as expenditures on the acquisition of an intangible fixed asset and included in the enterprise's gross fixed capital formation.

10.91. The expenditures included in gross fixed capital formation include not only the costs of actual test drillings and borings, but also the costs incurred to make it possible to carry out tests, for example, the costs of aerial or other surveys, transportation costs, etc. The value of the resulting asset is not measured by the value of new deposits discovered by the exploration but by the value of the resources allocated to exploration during the accounting period. Consumption of fixed capital may be calculated for such assets by using average service lives similar to those used by mining or oil corporations in their own accounts.

Computer software

10.92. Computer software that an enterprise expects to use in production for more than one year is treated as an intangible fixed asset. Such software may be purchased on the market or produced for own use. Acquisitions of such software are therefore treated as gross fixed capital formation. Software purchases on the market is valued at purchasers' prices, while software developed in-house is valued at its estimated basic price, or at its costs of production if it is not possible to estimate the basic price.

10.93. Gross fixed capital formation in software also includes the purchase or development of large databases that the enterprise expects to use in production over a period of time of more than one year. These databases are valued in the same way as software, described above.

Entertainment, literary or artistic originals

10.94. Originals consist of the original films, sound recordings, manuscripts, tapes, models, etc., on which drama performances, radio and television programming, musical performances, sporting events, literary and artistic output, etc., are recorded or embodied.

10.95. The acquisition of an original constitutes gross fixed capital formation. The original is often retained by its producer, but it may also be sold after it has been produced in order to be exploited by another unit. When it is sold the gross fixed capital formation is measured by the price paid by the purchaser to acquire the asset. If it is not sold, its valuation may be difficult because it depends on the future benefits that the owner expects to derive. These benefits may be very difficult to estimate in advance. In the absence of other information it may be necessary to value the original by its costs of production, as in the case of many other kinds of output produced for own gross fixed capital formation.

2. Changes in inventories (P.52)

10.96. Transactions involving inventories are treated in the same way as transactions involving any other asset, whether non-financial or financial. Thus, the value of changes in inventories recorded in the capital account is equal to the value of the inventories acquired by an enterprise less the value of the inventories disposed of during the accounting period. Some of these acquisitions and disposals are attributable to actual purchases or sales, but others reflect transactions that are internal to the enterprise.

10.97. In this context it is useful to distinguish between two functions performed by an enterprise: its function as a producer of goods and services and its function as an owner of assets. When a good is entered into inventories it is acquired as an asset by the owner either by purchase (or barter) or by an internal transaction with the producer. Conversely, a good leaving inventories represents the disposal of an asset by the owner either by sale or other use, by an internal transfer to the producer or possibly as a result of recurrent losses (recurrent wastage, accidental damage or pilfering). Inventory movements that are not attributable to actual purchases or sales of the goods concerned are valued as if the goods were being bought or sold at that time. Thus, changes in inventories are recorded as acquisitions and disposals by the enterprise and valued the same general way as changes in other assets.

10.98. The enterprise in its capacity as a producer may obtain goods or services for intermediate consumption either by purchasing them on the market for immediate use as intermediate inputs or by internal transfers from the owner out of inventories. In order to ensure that all the goods and services used for intermediate consumption are consistently valued at current prices, the goods transferred out of inventories are valued at current purchasers' prices. Similarly, the output produced by the producer may either be sold or otherwise disposed of or be transferred to inventories as finished products or work-in-progress. In order to ensure that output is consistently valued, finished goods transferred into inventories are valued as if they were sold at that time, while additions to work-in-progress are valued in proportion to the estimated current basic price of the finished product.

Materials and supplies

10.99. Materials and supplies consist of all goods that an enterprise holds in stock with the intention of using them as intermediate inputs into production. Not all necessarily get used in this way, however, as some may be lost as a result of physical deterioration, or recurrent accidental damage or pilfering. Such losses of materials and supplies are recorded and valued in the same way as materials and supplies actually withdrawn to be used up in production.

10.100. Materials and supplies consist of the kinds of goods that are entirely used up when they are fed into the production process. They do not, therefore, include stocks of newly acquired fixed assets, such as vehicles or microcomputers, although they may include small tools when these are not treated as fixed assets. Enterprises may hold a variety of quite different kinds of goods under the heading of materials and supplies, the most common types being fuels, industrial raw materials, agricultural materials, semi-processed goods, components for assembly, packaging materials, foodstuffs, office supplies, etc. Every enterprise, including non-market producers owned by government units, may be ex-

pected to hold some inventories of materials and supplies, if only inventories of office supplies.

10.101. Materials and supplies do not include works of art or stocks of precious metals or stones acquired by enterprises as valuables. By definition, valuables are assets held as stores of value and they are not intended to be used as intermediate inputs into production. On the other hand, there are some producers that do use gold, diamonds, etc. as intermediate inputs into the production of other goods or services—for example, manufacturers of jewellery or dentists. Stocks of gold, diamonds, etc., intended for industrial use or other production in this way are, of course, recorded under materials and supplies.

Work-in-progress

10.102. **Work-in-progress** consists of output produced by an enterprise that is not yet finished, i.e., not yet sufficiently processed to be in a state in which it is normally supplied to other institutional units. Work-in-progress occurs in all industries, but is especially important in those in which some time is needed to produce a unit of finished output—for example, in agriculture, or in industries producing complex fixed assets such as ships, dwellings, computers, software or films. Work-in-progress can therefore take a wide variety of different forms ranging from growing crops to partially completed film productions or computer programs. Although work-in-progress is output that has not reached the state in which it is normally supplied to others, its ownership is nevertheless transferable, if necessary. For example, it may be sold under exceptional circumstances such as the liquidation of the enterprise.

10.103. As explained in chapter VI also, work-in-progress must be recorded for any production process that is not finished at the end of the accounting period. The shorter the accounting period, the more important work-in-progress is likely to be relatively to finished output. In particular, it is likely to be more significant for quarterly accounts than annual accounts, if only because the production of many agricultural crops is completed within a year but not within a quarter. Assuming that prices and costs remain stable during the period of production, the value of the additions to work-in-progress within a given accounting period is obtained by calculating the fraction of the total production costs incurred in that period and applying that fraction to the basic price realized by the finished product. Thus, the value of the output of the finished product is distributed over the accounting periods in which it was produced in proportion to the costs incurred in each period. If the average levels of prices and costs change from period to period, the output should be allocated initially using the prices and costs at the time the production is finished, and then the values of the work-in-progress thus calculated for earlier periods should be revalued in proportion to the change in average cost levels from period to period.

10.104. If the accounts have to be compiled before the production process is finished and it is not feasible to make a satisfactory estimate of the basic price, additions to work-in-progress may be provisionally estimated by the value of the production costs incurred in the period with some mark-up for net operating surplus or mixed income. Provisional estimates of this kind may be subsequently revised, if necessary, when the relevant basic prices become known.

10.105. Reductions in work-in-progress take place when the production process is completed. At that point, all work-in-progress is transformed into a finished product. Thus, the entire stock of work-in-progress carried forward from earlier accounting periods is recorded as being withdrawn from stock when the production process is finished. If prices and costs have risen, work-in-progress carried forward from previous periods must be revalued using the prices and costs of the period in which the production is finished. Current losses from work-in-progress resulting from physical deterioration or recurrent accidental damage or pilfering should be deducted from the additions to work-in-progress accruing as a result of the production carried out in the same period.

Work-in-progress on cultivated assets

10.106. The natural growth of plants, trees and livestock, including farmed fish, is included within the production boundary when it is carried out under the direct control, responsibility and management of an institutional unit. In the present context it is necessary to distinguish single-use plants, trees and livestock that produce an output once only (when the plants or trees are cut down or uprooted or the livestock slaughtered) from trees (including vines and shrubs) and livestock that are used repeatedly or continuously for more than one year to produce outputs such as fruit, nuts, rubber, milk, wool, power, transportation and entertainment. Work-in-progress may need to be recorded for both types of crops or livestock.

10.107. In the case of single-use plants or livestock, any such crops or livestock that have not yet been harvested or slaughtered at the end of the accounting period constitute work-in-progress, as follows:

(a)   When accounts are compiled quarterly, the value of the finished output of an annual crop—i.e., the value of the grain or other crop actually harvested—may be distributed over the quarters in which production has been taking place in proportion to the costs incurred each quarter. The value of the output produced in the quarter in which the crop is harvested is then equal to the value of the harvested crop less the value of the additions to work-in-progress produced in the previous quarters;

(b)   If the accounts are compiled annually and if the crop year is contained within the accounting year, it will be unnecessary to calculate work-in-progress, except possibly under conditions of high inflation;

(c)   If the accounts are compiled annually and if the accounting year ends in the middle of the crop year, it becomes

necessary to calculate both additions to, and reductions of, work-in-progress during the accounting year. This does not imply, however, that the value of the additions to work-in-progress for the latest year covered must be estimated in advance of knowing the value of the harvested crop, as any annual crop sown in year t is likely to have been harvested by the time the annual accounts for year t are compiled and published. In any case, provisional estimates of additions to work-in-progress can always be calculated on the basis of costs plus a mark-up and revised when the value of the harvested crop becomes known.

10.108. Changes in work-in-progress for livestock reared for slaughter, including poultry, may be approximated by changes in the numbers of such livestock between the beginning and the end of the accounting period multiplied by the average price of the animals or poultry concerned.

10.109. In the case of trees and livestock that are intended for repeated or continuous use in production and are treated as fixed assets when they reach maturity, work-in-progress may have to be calculated in the case of specialist producers of such assets: for example, breeders of race horses or other special animals. However, when they are being cultivated or reared for own use—i.e., produced on own account—the output produced is classified as gross fixed capital formation (see paragraphs 10.85 and 10.86 above).

Work-in-progress on other fixed assets

10.110. Structures and some other fixed assets, such as ships, typically take a long time to complete and frequently span two or more accounting periods. However, the output produced each period is classified as work-in-progress only when the producer, and not the eventual user, is the owner of the output produced. Uncompleted fixed assets that are being produced on own account by their eventual users, and also structures that are being produced under a contract of sale agreed in advance, are treated as being acquired by their users and cannot, therefore, be recorded as work-in-progress of the producers.

Finished goods

10.111. Finished goods consist of goods produced as outputs that their producer does not intend to process further before supplying them to other institutional units. A good is finished when its producer has finished with it, even though it may subsequently be used as an intermediate input into other processes of production. Thus, inventories of coal produced by a mining enterprise are classified as finished products, although inventories of coal held by a power station are classified under materials and supplies. Inventories of batteries produced by a manufacturer of batteries are finished goods, although inventories of the same batteries held by manufacturers of vehicles and aircraft are classified under materials and supplies.

10.112. Inventories of finished goods may be held only by the enterprises that produce them. Finished goods entering or leaving inventories are valued at the basic prices of those goods at the times the entries or withdrawals take place. Current losses of finished goods resulting from physical deterioration or recurrent accidental damage or pilfering should be treated in the same way as withdrawals.

Goods for resale

10.113. Goods for resale are goods acquired by enterprises, such as wholesalers or retailers, for the purpose of reselling them to their customers. Goods for resale are not processed further by the enterprises that purchase them, except for presenting them for resale in ways that are attractive to their customers. Thus, goods for resale may be transported, stored, graded, sorted, washed, packaged, etc. by their owners but are not otherwise transformed.

10.114. Goods for resale entering the inventories of the enterprises are valued at their actual or estimated purchasers' prices. These prices include any additional transportation charges paid to enterprises other than the suppliers of the goods, but not the costs of any transport services produced on own account by the enterprise taking delivery. Goods acquired by barter are valued at their estimated purchasers' prices at the time of acquisition.

10.115. Goods for resale withdrawn from inventories are valued at the purchasers' prices at which they can be replaced at the time they are withdrawn as distinct from the purchasers' prices that may have been paid for them when they were acquired. Reductions in inventories are valued in this way whether the goods withdrawn are sold at a profit or at a loss, or even not sold at all as a result of physical deterioration or recurrent accidental damage or pilfering.

3. Acquisitions less disposals of valuables (P.53)

10.116. Valuables are assets that are not used primarily for production

or consumption, that do not deteriorate over time under normal conditions and that are acquired and held primarily as stores of value. They are held in the expectation that their prices, relative to other goods and services, will not decline over time and possibly increase. In other words, valuables are expected to hold their value in real terms in the long run, even though there may be some periods of time when their real value declines. Valuables consist of:

(a)   Precious stones and metals such as diamonds, non-monetary gold, platinum, silver, etc., held by any units including enterprises provided that they are not intended to be used as intermediate inputs into processes of production;

(b)   Paintings, sculptures, etc., recognized as works of art and antiques;

(c)   Other valuables, such as jewellery fashioned out of precious stones and metals and collections.

10.117. Acquisitions and disposals of new or existing assets in the form of valuables are recorded in the capital account. Acquisitions are valued at the actual or estimated prices payable by the units acquiring the assets to the units disposing of the assets plus any associated costs of ownership transfer incurred by the units acquiring the assets such as fees payable to expert valuers, agents, auctioneers, etc. The prices of valuables payable to dealers include their margins, of course. Disposals are valued at the prices payable by the units acquiring the assets to the units disposing of the assets minus any associated costs of ownership transfer incurred by the latter. On aggregation, therefore, acquisitions less disposals of valuables include dealers' margins and the costs of ownership transfer on new and existing valuables, whether the transactions consist of purchases and sales, barter or capital transfers in kind.

C. Consumption of fixed capital

10.118. Consumption of fixed capital constitutes a negative change in the value of the fixed assets used for production. It covers both tangible fixed assets and intangible fixed assets, such as mineral exploration costs and software. Consumption of fixed capital must be measured with reference to a given set of prices, i.e., the average prices of the period. It may then be defined as the decline, between the beginning and the end of the accounting period, in the value of the fixed assets owned by an enterprise, as a result of their physical deterioration and normal rates of obsolescence and accidental damage. The value of a fixed asset depends upon the benefits that can be expected from using it in production over the remainder of its service life. This value is given by the present discounted value, calculated at the average prices of the period, of the

stream of rentals that the owner of a fixed asset could expect if it were rented out to producers over the remainder of its service life. Consumption of fixed capital is then measured by the proportionate decline in this value between the beginning and end of the accounting period.

10.119. Consumption of fixed capital thus measures the decline in the usefulness of a fixed asset for purposes of production. It is a measure that depends on the productive potential of an asset over its normal service life. The value of a fixed asset at any point in time inevitably involves expectations about the future, but this is true of virtually all assets including financial assets and valuables. It is possible to derive reasonable estimates of the consumption of fixed capital on the basis of the average service lives of assets and simple assumptions about the rates of decline of their efficiency in production over time. Despite elements of uncertainty, producers and users of fixed assets have to take views about their values in practice, and markets in which new and existing fixed assets are actively traded provide information that should be taken into account in calculating consumption of fixed capital. Consumption of fixed capital has also to be calculated in respect of major improvements to non-produced assets and costs of ownership transfer associated with non-produced assets as these add to the value of such assets and are a component of gross fixed capital formation. The concept and measurement of the consumption of fixed capital has been explained in chapter VI, and it is not necessary to go into further detail at this point.

D. Acquisitions less disposals of non-produced non-financial assets (P.513)

10.120. Non-produced non-financial assets consist of land, other tangible assets that may be used in the production of goods and services, and intangible assets. Changes in the value of these assets owned by institutional units resulting from transactions with other institutional units are recorded in the capital account. These assets may be acquired or disposed of by purchase or sale, barter or capital transfer in kind. The changes recorded in the capital account consist of the total values of the assets acquired during the accounting period less the total value of the assets disposed of.

1. Acquisitions less disposals of land

10.121. Land is defined in the System as the ground itself, including:

    (*a*)   The soil covering;

    (*b*)   Associated surface water;

but *excluding*:

    (*a*)   Buildings or other structures constructed on the land or through it—roads, office buildings, tunnels, etc.;

    (*b*)   Vineyards, orchards, or other plantations of trees and any growing crops, etc.;

    (*c*)   Subsoil assets;

    (*d*)   Non-cultivated biological resources;

    (*e*)   Water resources below the ground.

The associated surface water includes any inland waters—reservoirs, lakes, rivers, etc.—over which ownership rights can be exercised and which can, therefore, be the subject of transactions between institutional units.

10.122. The total stock of land is not fixed. For example, it may be marginally increased or decreased by reclaiming land from the sea or by erosion by the sea. Its quality may also be improved by clearing forests or rocks and by building dykes, irrigation channels, or windbreaks, etc. Similarly, its quality may be damaged by inappropriate agricultural use, pollution, natural disasters, etc. Activities that lead to major improvements in the quantity, quality or productivity of land or prevent its deterioration are treated as gross fixed capital formation and shown separately in the classification. These activities represent productive activity of institutional units that add to the value of land.

10.123. By convention, all owners or purchasers of land located within the economic territory are resident institutional units. If an institutional unit owning land has no centre of economic interest in the territory, a notional resident institutional unit has to be created that is deemed to own the land, while the non-resident unit is deemed to own the notional unit. All transactions whereby land is acquired or disposed of, therefore, take place between resident units (except when the boundary of the economic territory is itself changed by the purchase or sale of land: e.g., the purchase of land by a foreign government that increases the size of its enclave).

10.124. As explained in paragraphs 10.59 and 10.60 above, the costs involved in the transfer of ownership of land are not included in the value of land. The fees payable by the purchaser to surveyors, valuers, estate agents, lawyers, etc., together with any taxes payable on the transfer of land, are treated as expenditures on gross fixed capital formation by the purchaser. The corresponding fees or taxes payable by the seller also contribute to gross fixed capital formation as they reduce the value of the seller's negative gross fixed capital formation. In consequence, acquisitions and disposals of land are recorded at the same value for both the purchaser and the seller. If the ownership of land is transferred by barter or by a capital transfer in kind, the same value must be imputed for both parties to the transaction based on the current market value of the type of land in question. Assuming that both parties to the transaction are residents, it follows that, for the economy as a whole, the aggregate value of total purchases of land must equal the aggregate value of total sales, although this is not generally true at lower levels of aggregation, such as individual sectors or sub-sectors. The value of acquisitions less disposals of land is thus zero for the economy as a whole (excluding transactions that change the boundary of the economic territory itself, as noted above).

10.125. Buildings, or other structures, and plantations are often purchased or sold together with the land on which they are situated, without separate valuations being placed on the structures and the land. Even if it is not feasible to obtain separate valuations, as may be the case for existing structures, it may be possible to determine which out of the land or the structure accounts for most of their combined value and to classify the transaction as the purchase of land or of a structure depending upon which has the greater value. If it is not possible to determine whether the land or the structure is the more valuable, by convention, the transaction should be classified as the purchase of a structure, that is, as gross fixed capital formation. A similar principle holds for plantations.

2. Acquisitions less disposals of other tangible non-produced assets

10.126. In practice, these consist of acquisitions less disposals of subsoil assets. Subsoil assets consist of known deposits of coal, oil, gas or other fuels and metallic ores, and non-metallic minerals, etc., that are located below or on the earth's surface, including deposits under the sea. The transactions recorded in the capital account refer, of course, only to those subsoil assets over which ownership rights have been established. In most cases, subsoil assets may be owned separately from land below which they are located, but in other cases the law may stipulate that the ownership of the subsoil assets is inseparably linked to that of the land.

10.127. The transactions in subsoil assets recorded in the capital account refer to acquisitions or disposals of deposits of subsoil assets by purchases or sales, barter or transfers in kind; in other words, they consist of transactions in which the ownership of such assets passes from one institutional unit to another. Reductions in the value of known reserves of subsoil assets resulting from their depletion as a result of extracting the assets for purposes of production are not recorded in the capital account. However, depletion should be taken into account when valuing the reserves shown in the opening and closing balance sheets in which case it is recorded in the other changes in the volume of assets account.

10.128. Acquisitions and disposals of subsoil assets are recorded and valued in the same way as transactions in land. By convention, all owners are resident institutional units, and therefore all transactions whereby subsoil assets are acquired or disposed of take place between resident units. The acquisitions and disposals exclude the associated costs of ownership transfer.

These costs are grouped with those for land and classified as gross fixed capital formation.

10.129. The owner of subsoil assets, who is often a government unit, may grant a concession or lease to another institutional unit entitling the latter to extract the asset over a specified period of time in return for a series of payments (usually described as royalties). This arrangement is similar to a landowner conceding to a tenant the right to exploit the land in return for the payment of rents, except that subsoil assets are exhaustible. The payments are property incomes and recorded as rent in the primary distribution of income account. However, the holder of the concession or lease may be entitled, or permitted by the owner, to sell the concession or lease to a third party. Such a sale is recorded in the capital account, but as the sale of an intangible non-produced asset. It is therefore recorded under a separate heading in the account. Sales of leases on land or buildings are treated similarly.

3. Acquisitions less disposals of intangible non-produced assets

10.130. Intangible non-produced assets consist of patented entities, leases or other transferable contracts, purchased goodwill and other intangible non-produced assets. Such leases are on land, subsoil assets and residential and non-residential buildings. The value of the acquisitions or disposals of leases or other transferable contract recorded in the capital account consists of payments made to the original or subsequent tenants or lessees when the leases or concessions are sold or transferred to other institutional units. The value of acquisitions of intangible non-produced assets include the associated costs of ownership transfer incurred by the purchaser while disposals are valued after deducting the costs of ownership transfer incurred by the seller. The costs of ownership transfer are a component of gross fixed capital formation.

E. Capital transfers (D.9)

1. Introduction

10.131. Capital transfers receivable and payable are recorded on the right side of the capital account. A transfer is defined as a transaction in which one institutional unit provides a good, service or asset to another unit without receiving in return from the latter any counterpart in the form of a good, asset or service (see chapter VIII). Transfers may be made in cash or in kind as follows:

(a) A cash transfer consists of the payment of money by one unit to another without any counterpart;

(b) A transfer in kind consists of the transfer of ownership of a good or asset (other than cash), the cancellation of

a liability or the provision of a service without any counterpart.

10.132. Transfers in cash and in kind may both be divided into current and capital transfers as follows:

(a) A capital transfer in kind consists of the transfer of ownership of an asset (other than inventories and cash) or the cancellation of a liability by a creditor, without any counterpart being received in return;

(b) A capital transfer in cash consists of the transfer of cash that the first party has raised by disposing of an asset, or assets (other than inventories), or that the second party is expected, or required, to use for the acquisition of an asset, or assets (other than inventories). The second party, the recipient, is often obliged to use the cash to acquire an asset, or assets, as a condition on which the transfer is made.

Thus, whether the transfer is made in cash or in kind, it should result in a commensurate change in the financial, or non-financial, assets shown in the balance sheets of one or both parties to the transaction. A capital transfer in cash serves a similar purpose to the actual transfer of an asset in so far as it should lead either to a decrease in the first party's assets or an increase in the second party's assets, or both. Capital transfers may also be distinguished by the fact that they tend to be large and infrequent, but they cannot be defined in terms of size or frequency. Their essential characteristic is that they should involve the disposal or acquisition of assets by one or both parties to the transaction.

10.133. A current transfer reduces the income and consumption possibilities of the first party and increases the income and consumption possibilities of the second party. Current transfers are therefore not linked to, or conditional, on the acquisition or disposal of a tangible fixed asset or assets by one or both parties to the transaction. Some cash transfers may be regarded as capital by one party to the transfer but as current by the other. For example, the payment of an inheritance tax may be regarded as the transfer of capital by the taxpayer but be regarded as a current receipt by government because it receives many such transfers. Similarly, a large country that makes investment grants to a number of smaller countries may regard the grants as current transfers even though they are specifically intended to finance the acquisition of capital assets. In an integrated system of accounts, such as the SNA, it is not feasible, however, to classify the same transaction differently in different parts of the system. Accordingly, a transfer should be classified as capital for both parties even if it involves the acquisition or disposal of an asset, or assets, by only one of the parties.

10.134. There may be cases in which it is difficult to decide on the evidence available whether to classify a cash transfer as current or capital. When there is serious doubt, the transfer should be classified as current rather than capital. It should be noted, however, that the decision as to which way to classify a transfer has important consequences for the allocation of saving between sectors and subsectors, and possibly between the economy as a whole and the rest of the world. Other things being equal, a current transfer increases the saving of the recipient and reduces that of the donor, whereas a capital transfer does not affect the saving of either party. If, therefore, cash transfers are incorrectly classified between current and capital, the saving behaviour recorded for the units or subsectors involved may be misleading for purposes of economic analysis and policymaking.

10.135. A capital transfer in kind is recorded when the ownership of the asset is transferred or the liability cancelled by the creditor.

A capital transfer in cash is recorded when the payment is due to be made. The transfer of a non-financial asset is valued by the estimated price at which the asset, whether new or used, could be sold on the market plus any transport, installation or other costs of ownership transfer incurred by the donor but excluding any such charges incurred by the recipient. Transfers of financial assets, including the cancellation of debts, are valued in the same way as other acquisitions or disposals of financial assets or liabilities.

2. Capital taxes (D.91)

10.136. Capital taxes consist of taxes levied at irregular and very infrequent intervals on the values of the assets or net worth owned by institutional units or on the values of assets transferred between institutional units as a result of legacies, gifts *inter vivos* or other transfers. They include the following taxes:

(a) *Capital levies*: These consist of taxes on the values of the assets or net worth owned by institutional units levied at irregular, and very infrequent, intervals of time. Capital levies are treated as exceptional both by units concerned and by the government. They may be payable by households or enterprises. They include betterment levies: i.e., taxes on the increase in the value of agricultural land due to planning permission being given by government units to develop the land for commercial or residential purposes (Government Finance Statistics (GFS): 4.5);

(b) *Taxes on capital transfers*: These consist of taxes on the values of assets transferred between institutional units. They consist mainly of inheritance taxes, or death duties, and gift taxes, including gifts *inter vivos* made between members of the same family to avoid, or minimize, the payment of inheritance taxes. They do not include taxes on sales of assets as these are not transfers (GFS: 4.3).

3. Investment grants (D.92)

10.137. Investment grants consist of capital transfers in cash or in kind made by governments to other resident or non-resident institutional units to finance all or part of the costs of their acquiring fixed assets. The recipients are obliged to use investment grants received in cash for purposes of gross fixed capital formation, and the grants are often tied to specific investment projects, such as large construction projects. If the investment project continues over a long period of time, an investment grant in cash may be paid in instalments. Payments of instalments continue to be classified as capital transfers even though they may be recorded in a succession of different accounting periods.

10.138. Investment grants in kind consist of transfers of transport equipment, machinery and other equipment by governments to other resident or non-resident units and also the direct provision of buildings or other structures for resident or non-resident units. These may be constructed by enterprises owned by the donor government or by other enterprises that are paid directly by the donor government. Investment grants do not include transfers of military equipment in the form of weapons or equipment whose sole function is to fire such weapons, as these are not classified as fixed assets.

4. Other capital transfers (D.99)

10.139. Other capital transfers consist of all capital transfers except capital taxes and investment grants. One notable category included here is the cancellation of debt by mutual agreement between the creditor and the debtor. Such a cancellation is treated as a capital transfer from the creditor to the debtor equal to the value of the outstanding debt at the time of cancellation. It includes the cancellation of debt owned by non-residents to residents, and vice versa.

10.140. However, the writing off of debt is not a transaction between institutional units and therefore does not appear either in the capital account or the financial account of the System. If the creditor accepts such a write off or default, it should be recorded in the other changes in the volume of assets account of the creditor and the debtor. Provisions for bad debt are treated as book-keeping entries that are internal to the enterprise and do not appear anywhere in the System. The unilateral repudiation of debt by a debtor is also not a transaction and is not recognized in the System.

10.141. Capital transfer may take various other forms, of which some examples are given below:

(a) Major payments in compensation for extensive damages or serious injuries not covered by insurance policies. The payments may be awarded by courts of law or settled out of court. They may be made to resident or non-resident units. They include payments of compensation for damages caused by major explosions, oil spillages, the side effects of drugs, etc;

(b) Transfers from government units to publicly or privately owned enterprises to cover large operating deficits accumulated over two or more years;

(c) Transfers from central government to units at lower levels of government to cover some, or all, of the costs of gross fixed capital formation or large expenditure deficits accumulated over two or more years;

(d) Legacies or large gifts *inter vivos*, including legacies to NPIs;

(e) Exceptionally large donations by households or enterprises to NPIs to finance gross fixed capital formation: for example, gifts to universities to cover the costs of building new residential colleges, libraries, laboratories, etc.

Annex

Gross fixed capital formation and costs of ownership transfer

1. Consider first the simple example of a newly produced fixed asset that is purchased by a resident producer and then immediately sold to another resident producer in the same condition and at the same price, excluding costs of ownership transfer, as that at which it was bought. Assume the prices and costs involved are as follows:

Initial purchase

Price paid by the first owner to the producer of the asset	=	1,000
Costs of ownership transfer incurred by the first owner	=	200
First owner's acquisition value	=	1,000 + 200 = 1,200

Resale of the asset

Price paid by the second owner to the first owner	=	1,000
Costs of ownership transfer incurred by the first owner (seller)	=	100
First owner's disposal value	= 1,000–100 = 900	
Costs of ownership transfer incurred by the second owner (buyer)	=	150
Second owner's acquisition value	=	1,000 + 150 = 1,150

The gross fixed capital formation undertaken by the first owner during the period as a whole is equal to the value of the acquisition minus the value of the disposal: i.e., 1,200—900 = 300. The gross fixed capital formation of the second owner is equal to the value of the acquisition: i.e., 1,150. The total gross fixed capital formation for the two units together is therefore 1,450. This is equal to the price of the asset (1,000) plus the total costs of ownership transfer incurred by both units on both the initial purchase (200) and subsequent resale (250).

2. Assuming the second owner continues to own the asset to the end of the accounting period, and assuming that no price changes occur, the value of the asset recorded in the closing balance sheet of the second owner should equal 1,150, the acquisition value, less any consumption of fixed capital accruing between the time of acquisition and the end of the period. In effect, the value of the asset is transferred from the balance sheet of the first owner to that of second owner adjusted for

any differences there may happen to be between the costs of ownership transfer they incur when acquiring the asset.

3. Although the first owner is recorded as undertaking gross fixed capital formation of 300 during the accounting period, no asset is held at the end of the period. In order to reconcile this gross fixed capital formation with the zero value recorded in the closing balance sheet, it is necessary to record a holding loss of 300 in the revaluation account. This figure is equal to the value obtained by the first owner on disposing of the asset minus the value previously recorded for the acquisition of the asset. This holding loss is equal to the combined value of the acquisition and selling costs incurred by the first owner. In practice, no economic benefit or return is received from the first owner's gross fixed capital formation and it has to be written off as a holding loss.

4. Before leaving this example, it is worth noting that if the second owner were to be a non-resident unit, both the purchase of a movable asset and the associated costs of ownership transfer would, of course, be recorded as exports and not as gross fixed capital formation.

5. Consider next the general case in which an existing fixed asset is purchased by a resident producer and then sold to a second resident producer in a later accounting period. It may also be illustrated by a numerical example. The example, effectively an adaptation of the previous example, assumes a quarter of the initial balance sheet value of the asset has been written off as consumption of fixed capital by the time the asset is sold:

Written down value of the asset in the first owner's balance sheet,	900

of which:

written down value of the first owner's acquisition costs	150

Resale of the asset

Price paid by the second owner to the first owner	750
Costs of ownership transfer incurred by the first owner (seller)	80
First owner's disposal value	670
Costs of ownership transfer incurred by the second owner (buyer)	130
Second owner's acquisition value	880

The example assumes, for simplicity, that levels of prices and costs remain constant over time and that the value of the existing asset in the first owner's balance sheet is equal to price at which it can be sold plus the written down value of the original acquisition costs.

6. In this example, the gross fixed capital formation of the first owner is –670, the disposal value, while that of the second owner is 880, the acquisition value. The value of the total gross fixed capital formation for the two units together is, therefore, equal to 210 even though no new asset has been created nor improvement made. This is equal to the value of the costs of ownership transfer incurred by the two units together on the resale of the asset. The asset enters the second owner's balance sheet at a value of 880. In effect, the written-down value of the asset is transferred from the balance sheet of the first owner to that of the second owner, adjusted for any differences between the transfer costs incurred by the second owner and the written-down value of the first owner's previous acquisition costs.

No asset remains in the balance sheet of the first owner who incurs a holding loss, thus:

Opening balance sheet	900
Gross fixed capital formation	–670
Holding loss	–230
Closing balance sheet	0

The value of the holding loss is equal to that part of the value of the original transfer costs of the first owner not already written off, namely 150, plus the value of the first owner's selling costs, namely 80. As in the previous example, the gross fixed capital formation attributable to these costs of ownership transfer does not yield any economic benefit or return and results in a holding loss recorded in the revaluation account. In practice, it may be difficult to separate holding losses of this kind from other holding gains or losses due to changes in the prices of assets over time.

XI. The financial account

A. Introduction

11.1. The financial account records transactions that involve financial assets and liabilities and that take place between institutional units and between institutional units and the rest of the world.[1] The left side of the account (table 11.1. Account III.2) records acquisitions less disposals of financial assets, while the right side records incurrence of liabilities less their repayment. Net incurrence of liabilities less net acquisition of financial assets is equal in value, with the opposite sign, to net lending/borrowing, the balancing item in the capital account. In the SNA, financial assets are classified under seven major categories (the full classification is presented in table 11.2):

F.1   Monetary gold and special drawing rights (SDRs)

F.2   Currency and deposits

F.3   Securities other than shares

F.4   Loans

F.5   Shares and other equity

F.6   Insurance technical reserves

F.7   Other accounts receivable/payable.

Depending upon whether they are assets or liabilities of the unit or sector in question, these categories are listed on both sides of the financial account.

11.2. This chapter addresses five issues: (a) the role of the financial account within the SNA; (b) the nature of financial transactions and special cases; (c) the accounting rules for financial transactions; (d) the classification of financial transactions; and (e) detailed flow-of-funds tables.

B. The role of the financial account

11.3. The financial account is the second of the accounts that deal with accumulation. From the opening of the accounting period to the close, all balance sheet changes involving financial assets and liabilities must be accounted for by financial transactions (described in this chapter) and by other changes in the volume of financial assets and revaluations covered in chapter XII. The financial account is also the final account, in the full sequence of accounts, that records transactions between institutional units. The financial account does not have a balancing item that is carried forward to another account, as has been the case with all accounts previously discussed. Rather, the net balance of the financial account is equal in magnitude, but with the opposite sign, to the balancing item of the capital account.

11.4. Net saving is the balancing item of the use of income account, and net saving plus net capital transfers receivable/payable can be used to accumulate non-financial assets. If they are not exhausted in this way, the resulting surplus is called net lending. Alternatively, if net saving and capital transfers are not sufficient to cover the net accumulation of non-financial assets, the resulting deficit is called net borrowing. This surplus or deficit, net lending or net borrowing, is the balancing item

that is carried forward from the capital account into the financial account.

11.5. Some sectors or subsectors are net lenders while others are net borrowers. When institutional units engage in financial transactions with each other, the surplus resources of one sector can be made available, by the units concerned, for the use of other sectors. The financial account indicates how deficit, or net borrowing, sectors obtain the necessary financial resources by incurring liabilities or reducing assets and how the net lending sectors allocate their surpluses by acquiring financial assets or reducing liabilities. The account also shows the relative contributions of various categories of financial assets to these transactions.

11.6. The evolution of net lending/borrowing can be seen clearly in table 10.2, Account III.1. Capital account. In this example, general government and financial and non-financial corporations have a deficit or net borrowing requirement, while households and non-profit institutions have surpluses or net lending capacity. In table 11.1, Account III.2. Financial account, non-financial corporations are shown to have a net borrowing requirement of 69. This requirement is financed by incurring liabilities of 140 and acquiring financial assets of 71;

Table 11.1.   Account III.2: Financial account

Left block: **Changes in assets** — Corresponding entries of the: Goods and service account, Rest of the world account; S.1 Total economy; S.15 NPISHs; S.14 Households; S.13 General government; S.12 Financial corporations; S.11 Non-financial corporations.

Right block: **Changes in liabilities and net worth** — S.11 Non-financial corporations; S.12 Financial corporations; S.13 General government; S.14 Households; S.15 NPISHs; S.1 Total economy; Corresponding entries of the: Rest of the world account, Goods and service account; Total.

Total	G&S acct	RoW acct	S.1	S.15	S.14	S.13	S.12	S.11	Transactions and balancing items	S.11	S.12	S.13	S.14	S.15	S.1	RoW acct	G&S acct	Total
									B.9 Net lending (+)/net borrowing (–)	-69	5	-50	148	4	38	-38		0
691		50	641	32	181	120	237	71	F Net acquisition of financial assets/									
									F Net incurrence of liabilities	140	232	170	33	28	603	88		691
		1	-1				-1		F.1 Monetary gold and SDRs									
130		11	119	12	68	7	15	17	F.2 Currency and deposits [1]		130	2			132	-2		130
37		3	34	2	10	2	15	5	F.21 Currency		35				35	2		37
64		2	62	7	41	4		10	F.22 Transferable deposits		63	2			65	-1		64
29		6	23	3	17	1		2	F.29 Other deposits		32				32	-3		29
143		5	138	12	29	26	53	18	F.3 Securities other than shares	6	53	64			123	20		143
56		2	54	2	22	11	4	15	F.31 Short-term	2	34	15			51	5		56
87		3	84	10	7	15	49	3	F.32 Long-term	4	19	49			72	15		87
254		10	244		5	45	167	27	F.4 Loans [2]	71		94	28	24	217	37		254
86		3	83		3	1	63	16	F.41 Short-term	16		32	11	17	76	10		86
168		7	161		2	44	104	11	F.42 Long-term	55		62	17	7	141	27		168
46		2	44		3	36	3	2	F.5 Shares and other equity [2]	26	13			4	43	3		46
36			36		36				F.6 Insurance technical reserves		36				36			36
33			33		33				F.61 Net equity of households on life insurance reserves and in pension funds		33				33			33
22			22		22				F.611 Net equity of households in life insurance reserves		22				22			22
11			11		11				F.612 Net equity of households in pension funds		11				11			11
3			3		3				F.62 Prepayment of premiums and reserves against outstanding claims		3				3			3
82		21	61	8	40	6		7	F.7 Other accounts receivable/payable [2]	37		10	5		52	30		82
36		18	18		11	1		6	F.71 Trade credits and advances	8		6	4		18	18		36
46		3	43	8	29	5		1	F.79 Other accounts receivable/payable except trade credits and advances	29		4	1		34	12		46

1 The following memorandum items related to the elements of the category F.2 "Currency and deposits":
    m11   denominated in national currency
    m12   denominated in foreign currency
    m21   liability of resident institutions
    m22   liability of rest of the world.
2 Memorandum item: F.m. Direct foreign investment.

the difference between the two equals net borrowing. Similarly, the household sector, which has a net lending balance of 148, achieves this result by acquiring financial assets of 181 and incurring liabilities of 33. The financial corporations sector has a net borrowing balance of 5, which is financed by incurring liabilities of 232 and acquiring financial assets of 237. In comparison with other sectors, financial corporations will generally have small amounts of net lending/borrowing.

Table 11.2. Classification of transactions in financial assets and liabilities

F.1.	Monetary gold and SDRs	
F.2.	Currency and deposits	
F.21		Currency
F.22		Transferable deposits
F.29		Other deposits
F.3.	Securities other than shares	
F.31		Short-term
F.32		Long-term
F.4.	Loans	
F.41		Short-term
F.42		Long-term
F.5.	Shares and other equity	
F.6.	Insurance technical reserves	
F.61		Net equity of households in life insurance reserves and in pension funds
F.611		Net equity of households in life insurance reserves
F.612		Net equity of households in pension funds
F.62		Prepayments of premiums and reserves against outstanding claims
F.7.	Other accounts receivable/payable	
F.71		Trade credit and advances
F.79		Other
Memorandum item:		
Direct foreign investment		
		Equity
		Loans
		Other

Notes—The recommended breakdown of items F.2, F.3, and F.4 into (a), (b), or (c) is optional. F.3 may also optionally be subdivided between securities other than shares, excluding financial derivatives, and financial derivatives.

This provides the classification for both transactions in financial assets and liabilities and holdings of financial assets and liabilities in balance sheets.

However, their transactions in financial assets and liabilities will be comparatively large as a reflection of their primary role of intermediating between other borrowers and lenders by incurring liabilities and acquiring financial assets. Net borrowers can transact directly with net lenders. For example, governments can issue securities in the market; these securities can be purchased by households, non-financial corporations, and the rest of the world. In many other cases, financial intermediaries have as their special function the creation of a financial market that indirectly links lenders and borrowers by incurring liabilities to net lenders through taking deposits or issuing securities and providing the financial resources thus mobilized to borrowers. An examination of the financial transactions of the subsectors of the financial corporations sector, in addition to the those of the consolidated financial sector, is often useful.

11.7. It is important to note that, for each institutional sector, the financial account indicates the types of financial assets utilized by that sector to incur liabilities and acquire financial assets. The financial account does not, however, indicate to which sectors the liabilities are incurred and on which sectors the assets indicate financial claims. A more detailed and complex analysis of financial flows between sectors is discussed in the final section of this chapter. This analysis illustrates debtor/creditor relationships by type of financial asset.

11.8. In the hypothetical case of a closed economy in which resident institutional units do not engage in transactions with non-residents, the total net lending and total net borrowing of the various sectors would have to be equal since the net borrowing requirements of deficit sectors would be met by net lending of surplus sectors. For the economy as a whole, net lending or borrowing would have to be zero. This equality reflects the symmetric nature of financial assets and liabilities described in paragraph 11.59 below. When residents engage in transactions with non-residents, the sum of the net lending and net borrowing of each of the sectors making up the total economy must equal the economy's net lending to, or borrowing from, the rest of the world. In table 11.1 the total economy has acquired financial assets of 641 and incurred liabilities of 603. Net borrowing for the total economy to the rest of the world is therefore 38.

Counterparts of financial transactions

11.9. While some entries in the financial account have counterparts in other accounts of the SNA, other entries take place entirely within the financial account. In the SNA, most transactions involving the transfer of ownership of a good or non-financial asset, or the provision of a service or labour, entail a counterpart entry in the financial account. This most often takes the form of the exchange of goods, assets, and services for means of payment or claims on future means of payment. As the SNA records transactions on an accrual basis, any transaction expected to lead to eventual payment, either in financial assets or in kind, has a counterpart in the financial account. Even transactions in kind, such as barter sales and transfers in kind, lead to entries in the financial account when all elements of the in-kind transaction are not completed simultaneously.

11.10. The sale of a good, service, or asset may have as its counterpart a change in currency or transferable deposit. Alternatively, the counterpart may be reflected in the financial account in a trade credit or other account receivable/payable. In certain cases, a transaction may have its counterpart in other types of financial assets, such as the provision of fixed assets for long-term indebtedness, and the liability may be evidenced by a loan or security. Thus, counterparts involving changes in financial assets are recorded in the financial account for most transactions recorded in other SNA accounts.

11.11. However, in the SNA, many transactions take place entirely within the financial account. Transactions limited to the financial account occur whenever one financial asset is exchanged for another or when a liability is repaid with an asset. For example, trade credits are extinguished by exchanging means of payment. The claim represented by the trade credit no longer exists when the debtor provides means of payment to the creditor. The resulting four entries in the financial account are (a) the creditor reduces his holdings of trade credits and increases his means of payment (currency or transferable deposits); and (b) the debtor reduces his liabilities (in the form of trade cred-

its) and reduces his financial assets (in the form of means of payment).

11.12. When existing financial assets are exchanged for other financial assets, all entries take place in the financial account and only affect assets. For example, if an existing bond is sold by one institutional unit to another on the secondary market, in his financial account, the seller reduces his holdings of securities and increases equally his holdings of means of payment. The purchaser makes the opposite entries in his financial account. When a new financial asset is created through the incurrence of a liability by an institutional unit, all related entries may also be made in the financial account. For example, a corporation may issue short-term securities in exchange for means of payment. The financial account of the corporate sector accordingly shows an increase in liabilities in the form of securities and an increase in financial assets in the form of means of payment; the financial account of the purchasing sector shows a recomposition of financial assets—reduction in means of payment and an increase in securities. Transactions that are wholly within the financial account involve the exchange of one asset for another or the simultaneous creation or reduction of both assets and liabilities. These transactions change the distribution of the portfolio of financial assets and liabilities and may change the totals of both assets and liabilities, but they do not change the difference between total financial assets and liabilities.

C. Financial transactions

1. The nature of financial transactions and special cases

11.13. All financial transactions between institutional units and between institutional units and the rest of the world are recorded in the financial account. Financial transactions between institutional units and between institutional units and the rest of the world cover all transactions involving change of ownership of financial assets, including the creation and liquidation of financial claims. As noted above in section B of this chapter, the creation or other change in ownership of a financial asset may have its counterpart in other accounts of the SNA, or transactions in the financial account may involve exchanges of financial assets or incurrence of new liabilities for other financial assets; in these latter cases, all counterparts are recorded within the financial account.

11.14. Identifying financial transactions requires:

(a)   Distinguishing financial assets from non-financial assets (non-financial assets are covered in detail in chapters X and XII);

(b)   Distinguishing financial transactions from other changes that affect the existence, volume, and value of financial assets covered in this chapter and chapter XII; and

(c)   Distinguishing transactions in financial assets from financial operations involving contingent rather than actual financial assets.

The remaining paragraphs of this section deal with a number of these distinctions, as well as with some special cases involving financial assets.

11.15. The identification of financial transactions has also become more difficult because of financial innovation that has led to the development and proliferation of new and often complex financial assets and other financial instruments to meet the needs of investors with respect to maturity, yield, avoidance of risk, and other factors. Some of these instruments are tied to prices of commodities, so the distinction between financial and non-financial transactions may be blurred. The identification issue is further complicated by variations in characteristics of financial instruments across countries and variations in national practices on accounting and classification of instruments. These factors tend to limit the scope for firm recommendations with respect to the treatment of certain transactions within the SNA. A substantial degree of flexibility in presentation is therefore appropriate to meet national needs and to reflect national practices.

Financial assets

11.16. As explained in the general introduction to the accumulation accounts and balance sheets in chapter X, economic assets are entities over which ownership rights are enforced and from which economic benefits may be derived by their owners by holding them, or using them, over a period of time. At a minimum, all financial assets fulfil this definition in that they are stores of value; some financial assets generate property income and/or possibilities of holding gains. Currency and transferable deposits are assets because they can be used directly to acquire goods, services, or other assets. Securities and shares are assets because benefits may be derived in the form of property income and holding gains. Most loans generate property income, and trade credits represent a claim on other financial assets, usually means of payment such as transferable deposits. Most financial assets differ from other assets in the SNA in that there are counterpart liabilities on the parts of another institutional units, i.e., financial assets consist of claims on other institutional units. However, financial assets also include monetary gold, International Monetary Fund (IMF) Special Drawing Rights (SDR), shares in corporations (which their holders treat much the same as financial claims), and certain kinds of derivatives. There are no liabilities outstanding in respect of monetary gold and SDR, while the SNA treats both shares and these derivatives as liabilities by convention.

Financial claims and obligations

11.17. Many types of financial arrangements between transactors are possible. Financial claims and obligations arise out of contractual relationships between pairs of institutional units. Many of these will result in a creditor/debtor relationship between the two parties. In most cases, the relationship between the creditor and debtor will be unconditional on the part of both parties. Clearly, in such standard financial assets as deposits, securities, and loans, the creditor has an unconditional legal contract to receive property income and repayment of principal, and the debtor has a symmetric unconditional liability. This unconditional relationship does not hold, however, for shares and certain derivative instruments (see paragraphs 11.34 to 11.35 and 11.85 below which otherwise behave as financial assets and are treated as such in the SNA. In these cases, liabilities are introduced by convention, even though the "debtor" does not have an unconditional liability. A financial claim:

(a) Entitles a creditor to receive a payment, or payments, from a debtor in circumstances specified in a contract between them; or

(b) Specifies between the two parties certain rights or obligations, the nature of which requires them to be treated as financial.

11.18. When a debtor accepts an obligation to make future payment to a creditor, a claim is created. Usually, the amount that the debtor must pay to extinguish the liability, and the circumstances under which payment may be required, are also fixed at the time the claim is created. Claims may also be created by force of law; in particular, obligations to pay taxes or to make other compulsory payments will give rise to entries in the financial account when the tax is accrued. The criteria that determine the amounts of interest to be paid have also to be specified in the contract. Interest is property income, and payments of interest do not reduce the amount that the debtor is obliged to pay to extinguish the claim.

11.19. The variety of forms taken by financial claims is manifested in a variety of financial assets. Different types of financial assets are devised to meet the differing requirements and financial circumstances of both creditors and debtors. These assets and their classification are described in some detail in section E of this chapter.

Other changes in volume and value
of financial assets and liabilities

11.20. Other changes in the volume and value of financial assets take place during an accounting period without involving transactions between institutional units. All of these other changes are excluded from the financial account, but they must be recorded, either in the other changes in volume of assets account or in the revaluation account. Some of these changes are discussed in the following sections.

Monetary gold and SDRs

11.21. The creation or disappearance of monetary gold (referred to as monetization or demonetization of gold) is—unlike transactions in already existing monetary gold—recorded in the other changes in volume account. Similarly, transactions in SDRs appear in the financial account, but the process (called allocation/cancellation) by which SDRs are created or destroyed is recorded in the other changes in volume of assets account (see paragraphs 11.65 and 11.67 below of this chapter and chapter XII).

Valuation

11.22. Changes in the value of financial assets that result from price changes or exchange rate changes are recorded in the revaluation account. When there is a change in ownership and an asset acquired at one price is disposed of at another price, the transactions are recorded at their respective values in the financial account; the disposal value includes the realized holding gain or loss (see chapter XII).

Debt operations

11.23. There are a number of circumstances that may lead to reduction or cancellation, by other than normal repayment, of liabilities. These are treated in various ways in the SNA. A debtor and creditor may become parties to a bilateral agreement (often referred to as "debt forgiveness") that a financial claim no longer exists. Such an agreement gives rise in the SNA to the recording of a capital transfer payable/receivable (recorded in the capital account at the time the debt forgiveness occurs) and the simultaneous extinction of the claim (recorded in the financial account). Changes in claims resulting from debt assumption or rescheduling should be reflected in the financial account when the terms of the debt contract (maturity, interest rate, etc.) change, or when the institutional sector of the creditor or debtor changes, as these are considered new contractual arrangements. However, all other changes in claims resulting from write-offs and write-downs are excluded from the financial account. Specifically, a creditor may recognize that a financial claim can no longer be collected because of bankruptcy or other factors and he may remove the claim from his balance sheet. This recognition (by the creditor) should be accounted for in the other changes in volume account. (The corresponding liability must also be removed from the balance sheet of the debtor to maintain balance in the accounts of the total economy.) Unilateral cancellation of a financial claim by a debtor (debt repudiation) is not recognized in the SNA. Write-downs that reflect the actual market values of financial assets should be accounted for in the revaluation account. However, write-downs or write-offs that are imposed solely to meet regulatory or supervisory requirements and do not reflect the actual market values of those financial assets should not be recorded in the SNA.

11.24. Another debt related operation that is allowed by generally accepted accounting principles in many countries and that raises questions as to how they should be recorded in the SNA relates to debt defeasance. Debt defeasance allows a debtor (whose debts are in the form generally of securities other that shares and loans) to remove certain liabilities from the balance sheet by pairing irrevocably assets of equal value to the liabilities. Subsequent to the defeasance, neither the assets nor the liabilities are included in the balance sheet of the debtor, nor, frequently, need they be reported for statistical purposes. Defeasance may be carried out (a) by placing the paired assets and liabilities in a trust account within the institutional unit concerned, or (b) they may be transferred to another statistical unit. In the former case, the SNA will not record any transactions with respect to defeasance and the assets and liabilities will not be excluded from the balance sheet of the unit. In the latter case, the transactions by which the assets and liabilities are moved to the second statistical unit are recorded in the financial account of the units concerned and reported in the balance sheet of the unit that holds the assets and liabilities. Therefore, in the SNA, debt defeasance as such never results in liabilities being removed from the System, although it sometimes leads to a change in the institutional unit that reports those liabilities.

Contingent assets

11.25. Many types of contractual financial arrangements between institutional units do not give rise to unconditional requirements either to make payments or to provide other objects of value; often the arrangements themselves do not have transferable economic value. These arrangements, which are often referred to as contingencies, are not actual current financial assets and should not be recorded in the SNA. The principal characteristic of contingencies is that one or more conditions must be fulfilled before a financial transaction takes place. Guarantees of payment by third parties are contingencies since payment is only required if the principal debtor defaults. Lines of credit provide a guarantee that funds will be made available but no financial asset exists until funds are actually advanced. Letters of credit are promises to make payment only when certain documents specified by contract are presented. Underwritten note issuance facilities (NIFs) provide a guarantee that a potential debtor will be able to sell short-term securities (notes) that he issues and that the bank or banks issuing the facility will take up any notes not sold in the market or will provide equivalent advances. The facility itself is contingent, and the creation of the facility gives rise to no entry in the financial account. Only if the underwriting institution is requested to make funds available will it acquire an actual asset, which is recorded in the financial account.

11.26. For the purposes of the SNA, the treatment of contingencies is clear. Any payments of fees related to the establishment of contingent arrangements are treated as payments for services. Transactions are recorded in the financial account only when an actual financial asset is created or changes ownership. However, by conferring certain rights or obligations that may affect future decisions, contingent arrangements obviously produce an economic impact on the parties involved. Collectively, such contingencies may be important for financial programming, policy, and analysis. Therefore, where contingent positions are important for policy and analysis, it is recommended that supplementary information be collected and presented as supplementary data in the SNA.

11.27. Country practices vary in determining which instruments are considered contingent and which are considered actual assets to be recorded in the balance sheet. An example, which is quantitatively important in trade financing, is the bankers' acceptance. A banker's acceptance involves the acceptance by financial institutions of drafts or bills of exchange and the unconditional promise to pay a specific amount at a specified date. The banker's acceptance represents an unconditional claim on the part of the holder and an unconditional liability on the part of the accepting bank; the bank's counterpart asset is a claim on its customer. For this reason, the SNA recommends that the banker's acceptance be treated as an actual financial asset even though no funds may have been exchanged. Flexibility in the application of this recommendation will be required to take national practices and variations in the nature of these instruments into account.

11.28. In a number of financial arrangements, the contract is conditional on the part of one or both parties, but the arrangement itself has value because it is tradable. When transactions in such arrangements occur, the transactions should be recorded in the financial account. These are discussed further in paragraphs 11.34 to 11.43 below.

2. Exceptions to general rules

11.29. Conventions of the SNA or analytical requirements create a number of exceptions to the general rules described thus far in this chapter. These exceptions are discussed in the following sections.

11.30. The conventions adopted in the SNA result in the ownership of some non-financial assets being construed as the ownership of financial assets. Specific cases include:

   (a) Immovable assets, such as land and structures, are construed as being owned by residents of the economy where they are located, except when those structures are owned by foreign government entities and are thus located out of the economic territory of the country. When the owner of such assets is a non-resident, therefore, he is considered to have a financial claim on a notional resident unit that is construed to be the owner;

   (b) An unincorporated enterprise that operates in a different economy from the one in which its owner resides is considered to be a quasi-corporation. That entity is a resident of the economy where it operates, rather than a resident of the economy of its owner. The owner of the enterprise is deemed to own foreign financial assets equal in value to all the assets, non-financial as well as financial, belonging to the quasi-corporation.

11.31. When goods are acquired under a financial lease, a change of ownership from the lessor to the lessee is deemed to take place, even though legally the leased good remains the property of the lessor, at least until the termination of the lease when the legal ownership is usually transferred to the lessee. The lessee contracts to pay rentals which enable the lessor, over the period of the contract, to recover all, or virtually all, of his costs including interest. Financial leases may be distinguished by the fact that all the risks and rewards of ownership are, de facto, transferred from the legal owner of the good, the lessor, to the user of the good, the lessee. This de facto change in ownership is financed by a financial claim, which is the asset of the lessor and the liability of the lessee. At the time this change in ownership occurs, the market value of the good is recorded and counterpart entries, as assets/liabilities, are made by the institutional units in the financial account. In subsequent periods, the actual rental payment must be divided into interest, which is recorded as property income payable/receivable, and debt repayment, which is recorded in the financial account and which reduces the value of the asset of the lessor and the liability of the lessee. The financial asset should be classified as a loan (see paragraph 11.82 below).

11.32. Repurchase agreements are arrangements whereby an institutional unit sells securities at a specified price to another unit. The sale is made under a commitment to repurchase the same or similar securities at a fixed price on a specified future date (usually very short-term, e.g., overnight or one day) or at a date subject to the discretion of the purchaser. The arrangement appears to involve two separate transactions in financial assets. However, its economic nature is similar to that of a collateralized loan in that the purchaser of the securities is providing to the seller advances backed by the securities for the period of the agreement and is receiving a return from the fixed price when the repurchase agreement is reversed. In most cases, the securities do not change hands and the buyer does not have the right to sell them, so it is unclear even in a legal sense whether a change of ownership has taken place. Therefore, in the SNA, a repurchase agreement is treated as a newly created financial asset that is not related to the underlying securities. Repurchase agreements are to be classified under loans unless they involve bank liabilities and are classified in national measures of broad money; in the latter case, repurchase agreements are classified under other deposits (see paragraphs 11.56 and 11.57 below for a discussion of the relationship of money measures to the SNA).

11.33. Foreign exchange and gold swaps (not to be confused with interest rate or currency swaps discussed in paragraph 11.37 below) are a form of repurchase agreement commonly undertaken between central banks or between a central bank and banking institutions in a country. Central bank to central bank swaps involve an exchange of deposits and, for each of the two parties, the acquisition of a financial asset (the deposit at the foreign central bank) and the incurrence of a liability (the deposit by the foreign central bank). Central bank to central bank swaps should be recorded as transactions in the financial account. When a central bank acquires foreign exchange from a domestic bank in return for a deposit at the central bank and there is a commitment to reverse the transaction at a later date, this transaction should be treated as a new financial instrument (a loan from the central bank) and recorded as such in the financial account.

3. Financial derivatives

11.34. Many of the recently created financial instruments are linked to a specific financial instrument or indicator (foreign currencies, government bonds, share price indices, interest rates, etc.) or to a particular commodity (gold, coffee, sugar, etc.). The new instruments are therefore often referred to as derivative or secondary instruments. Since risk avoidance is frequently a motivation for the creation of these instruments, they are also often referred to as hedging instruments. Some of these give rise to contingent assets and liabilities and thus are not included in the balance sheets or financial account transactions. Others give rise to property income flows but, as there is no underlying transaction in a financial asset, there are no entries in the financial account. A third class of derivatives may involve conditional rights similar to other contingent instruments, but these derivatives have market value and are tradable; transactions in these derivatives give rise to entries in the financial account. An exhaustive treatment of derivatives is not possible here, and market innovations would render such a treatment incomplete or obsolete within a short period. Nevertheless, some general guidelines can be given on the basis of existing derivatives, and specific treatment in the SNA can be recommended for several broad classes of derivatives.

11.35. The SNA recommends that derivatives should be treated as financial assets and that transactions in them should, in general, be treated as separate (mainly financial) transactions, rather than as integral parts of the value of underlying transactions to which they may be linked as hedges. This is because a different institutional unit will be the party to the derivative transaction than is the case for the underlying transaction that is being hedged. Moreover, the two parties to the derivatives may have different motives for entering into the transaction. One may be hedging, while the other may be dealing in derivative instruments or acquiring the derivative as an investment. Even if both parties are hedging, they may be hedging transactions or risks that involve different financial assets or even transactions in different accounts of the SNA. Therefore, if derivative transactions were treated as integral parts of other transactions, such treatment would lead to asymmetries of measurement in different parts of the accounts or to asymmetries of measurement between institutional sectors.

11.36. Any explicit commissions paid to or received from brokers or other intermediaries for arranging options, futures, swaps, and other derivatives contracts are treated as payments for services in the appropriate accounts. Adjustment payments between parties to interest rate swaps are treated, in the SNA, as payments of interest and classified accordingly. Most commodity-related derivatives contracts are closed out before maturity, and a cash payment is made between the two parties; this payment does not include an element of service payment and thus should be recorded within the financial account. For those commodity-related contracts that do proceed to delivery, the ensuing transactions should be recorded in the usual way as a purchase/sale of commodities. All other transactions associated with derivatives are treated in the SNA as financial transactions that are entered in the financial account. These financial transactions in derivatives will include changes in margin deposit accounts, purchases and sales of traded options, warrants and covered warrants, premiums on over-the-counter (OTC) options, payments and receipts of various margins on traded futures and options, and all other payments and receipts relating to investment in derivatives and payments made or received during the life of a derivatives contract, except those specified before as relating to other accounts of the SNA.

11.37. Swaps are contractual arrangements between two parties who agree to exchange, according to predetermined rules, streams of payment on the same amount of indebtedness over time. The two most prevalent varieties are interest rate swaps and currency swaps. Interest rate swaps involve an exchange of interest payments of different character, such as fixed rate for floating rate, two different floating rates, fixed rate in one currency and floating rate in another, etc. Currency swaps involve an exchange of specified amounts of two different currencies with subsequent repayments, which include both interest and repayment flows, over time according to predetermined rules. Streams of interest payments resulting from swap arrangements are to be recorded as property income and repayments of principal are to be recorded in the financial account. Within the SNA, the parties to a swap are not considered to be providing a service to each other, but any payment to a third party for arranging the swap should be treated as payment for a service.

11.38. Options are contracts that give the purchaser of the option the right, but not the obligation, to buy (a "call" option) or to sell (a "put" option) a particular financial instrument or commodity at a predetermined price (the "strike" price) within a given time span (American option) or on a given date (European option). Many options contracts, if exercised, are settled by a cash payment rather than by delivery of the underlying assets or commodities to which the contract relates.

11.39. There are two basic types of options—traded options and OTC options. Options are sold or "written" on many types of underlying bases such as equities, interest rates, foreign currencies, commodities, and specified indexes. The buyer of the option pays a premium (the option price) to the seller for the latter's commitment to sell or purchase the specified amount of the underlying instrument or commodity on demand of the buyer. By convention, that commitment is treated as a liability of the seller and represents the current cost to the seller of buying out his contingent liability. While the premium paid to the seller of the option can conceptually be considered to include a service charge, in practice, it is usually not possible to distinguish the service element. Therefore, it is recommended in the SNA that the full price be recorded as acquisition of a financial asset by the buyer and as incurrence of a liability by the seller.

11.40. The timing of premium payments on options varies. With some types of options, premiums are paid when the contracts begin, when the options are exercised, or when the options expire. With other types of options, particularly traded options, parts of the premiums are paid on the days of purchase (the purchase price) and the remainders are paid if the market prices of the option decline through the variation margins. Subsequent purchases and sales of options are also to be recorded in the financial account. If an option based on a financial asset is exercised or if a commodity based option proceeds to delivery, the transactions are to be recorded in the SNA according to the nature of the transaction. Whenever initial margin payments and increases or decreases in margin payments are repayable, they should be recorded, as both assets and liabilities, under deposits in the financial account. Changes in the balances on variation margin accounts should be recorded under deposits. Payments into and withdrawals from these accounts will also be reflected in transactions in the traded options or futures contracts to which the variation margin accounts relate, and these payments and withdrawals should be recorded under transactions in securities other than shares.

11.41. Warrants are tradable instruments giving the holder the right to buy, under specified terms for a specified period of time, from the issuer of the warrant (usually a corporation) a certain number of shares or bonds. There are also currency warrants based on the amount of one currency required to buy another and cross-currency warrants tied to third currencies. Thus, warrants are a form of options. They can be traded apart from the underlying securities to which they are linked and therefore have a market value. In the financial account, the treatment of warrants is the same as that for options, and the issuer of the warrant is considered by convention to have incurred a liability, which is the counterpart of the asset held by the purchaser and represents the current cost of buying out the issuer's contingent liability.

D. Accounting rules for financial transactions

1. Valuation

11.44. Transactions in financial assets are recorded at the prices at which the assets are acquired or disposed of. These prices should exclude service charges, fees, commissions, and similar payments for services provided in carrying out the transactions; these should be recorded as payments for services. Taxes on financial transactions should also be excluded from the values recorded in the financial account and treated as taxes on services within taxes on products. In these respects, care should be taken that the same entry be recorded for both parties to the transaction. When a financial transaction involves a new issue of liabilities, the transaction should be recorded by both creditor and debtor at the amount of the liability incurred, i.e., exclusive of any fees, commissions, etc., and also exclusive of any prepaid interest that may be included in the price. Similarly, when a liability is reduced or extinguished, the entries in the financial account for both creditor and debtor must correspond to the reduction of the liability. When a security is issued at a discount, the proceeds to the issuer at the time of sale, and not the face value, are recorded in the financial account. The difference between the issue price and the face value is treated as interest that is accrued over the life of the instrument.

11.45. Financial transactions with respect to proprietors' net additions to the accumulation of quasi-corporate enterprises and changes in households' claims on insurance enterprises and pension funds raise complex issues of valuation that are

11.42. Transactions with respect to traded financial futures, including those for equities, interest rates, foreign currencies, commodities, etc., are to be recorded in the financial account in a manner similar to options because the former also have transaction value. Non-traded financial futures, which have no market value, are not to be recorded in the SNA as they are contingent positions.

11.43. Forward rate agreements (FRA) are arrangements in which two parties, in order to protect themselves against interest rate changes, agree on an interest rate to be paid, at a specified settlement date, on a notional amount of principal that is never exchanged. The only payment that takes place is related to the difference between the agreed forward rate agreement rate and the prevailing market rate at the time of settlement. The buyer of the forward rate agreement receives payment from the seller if the prevailing rate exceeds the agreed rate; the seller receives payment if the prevailing rate is lower than the agreed rate. These payments are recorded as property income in the SNA; as there is no underlying actual asset but only a notional one, there are no entries with respect to forward rate agreement in the financial account.

treated in the relevant item under classification of these categories (paragraphs 11.86 and 11.89 to 11.95 below, respectively).

11.46. When securities are marketed by issuers through underwriters or other intermediaries and then sold at higher prices to final investors, the assets and liabilities should be recorded at the values paid by the investors. The differences between the amounts paid by the investors and those received by the issuers should be treated as service payments paid by the issuers to the underwriters.

2. Time of recording

11.47. In principle, the two parties to a financial transaction should record the transaction at the same point in time. When the counterpart to an entry in the financial account is non-financial, the time of recording of financial claims is to be aligned with the time of recording, in the other accounts of the SNA, the transactions that gave rise to the financial claim. For example, when sales of goods or services give rise to a trade credit, the entries in the financial accounts should take place when the entries are made in the relevant non-financial account, i.e., when ownership of the goods is transferred or when the service is provided. Similarly, when accounts receivable/payable arise from transactions related to taxes, compensation of employees, and other distributive transactions, the entries in the financial account should take place when the entries are made in the relevant non-financial account.

11.48. When all entries relating to a transaction pertain only to the financial account, they should be recorded when the ownership of the asset is transferred. This point in time is usually clear when the transaction involves the sale of existing financial assets. When the transaction involves the incurrence or redemption of a liability, both parties should record the transaction when the liability is incurred or redeemed. In most cases, this will occur when money or some other financial asset is paid by the creditor to the debtor or repaid by the debtor to the creditor.

11.49. In practice, the two parties of a financial transaction may perceive the transaction as being completed at different points in time. This is especially true when trade credits or other accounts payable/receivable are extinguished by final payments and there is a lag (float) between the point in time when payments are made and received. There are several stages at which creditors and debtors could record a transaction. The debtor could record the liability as being extinguished when the check or other means of payment is issued to the creditor. A substantial period of time may elapse before the creditor receives the means of payment and records the payment in his accounts. There may then be further time-lags between presentation of a cheque to a bank, cheque clearance, and final settlement of the transaction. Asymmetries in time of recording of this transaction are, therefore, likely to emerge unless the debtor records his transaction on a "cheques cleared" basis, a fairly uncommon accounting procedure. A financial claim exists up to the point that the payment is cleared and the creditor has control of the funds; this would be the optimal point in time for recording the transaction. The float, in practice, may be very large and may affect, in particular, transferable deposits, trade credits, and other accounts receivable; this effect is especially pronounced in countries where the postal system and bank clearing procedures are weak. When the float is significant and accounts for large discrepancies in reporting, it will be necessary to develop estimates of the size of the float in order to adjust the accounts.

3. Basis of recording—netting and consolidation

11.50. The degree of netting at which transactions in financial assets and liabilities should be recorded depends to a great extent on the analysis for which the data are to be used. In practice, the degree of netting will depend on how data can be reported, and reporting may vary substantially for different classes of institutional units. If detailed information on financial transactions is maintained and reported, gross presentations are possible; if transactions must be inferred from balance sheet data, a certain level of netting is inevitable. A number of degrees of netting can be identified:

(a) No netting or fully gross reporting in which purchases and sales of assets are separately recorded, as are incurrences and repayments of liabilities;

(b) Netting within a given specific asset, such as subtracting sales of bonds from acquisition of bonds and redemption of bonds from new incurrences of liabilities in the form of bonds;

(c) Netting within a given category of assets, such as subtracting all sales of securities other than shares from all purchases of such assets;

(d) Netting transactions in liabilities against transactions in assets in the same asset category; and

(e) Netting transactions in groups of liability categories against transactions in assets in the same groups.

11.51. In the SNA, transactions are recorded in the financial account as net acquisition of assets and net incurrence of liabilities. As the financial account is broken down by main categories of financial assets, the desirable degree of netting would correspond to paragraph 11.50 (c) above, netting within a given category of assets. However, it is clear that, when data are collected on as gross a basis as possible, they can be netted to whatever degree is necessary for a particular use; when data are collected net, they cannot be grossed up. In general, netting beyond the level described in paragraph 11.50 (c) above would hinder the usefulness of the financial accounts for tracing how the economy mobilizes resources from institutional units with positive net lending and transmits them to net borrowers. For detailed flow of funds analysis, gross reporting or netting at level paragraph 11.50 (b) above would be desirable, particularly for analysis of securities, but netting at level paragraph 11.50 (c) above would still provide useful information on financial flows.

11.52. Consolidation in the financial account refers to the process of offsetting transactions in assets for a given grouping of institutional units against the counterpart transactions in liabilities for the same group of institutional units. Consolidation can be performed at the level of the total economy, institutional sectors, and subsectors. Different levels of consolidation will be appropriate for different types of analysis. For example, consolidation of the financial accounts for the total economy emphasizes the economy's financial position with the rest of the world since all domestic financial positions are netted on consolidation. Consolidation for sectors permits the tracing of overall financial movements between sectors with positive net lending and those with net borrowing and the identification of financial intermediation. Consolidation only at the subsector level for financial corporations can provide much more detail on intermediation and allow, for example, the identification of the central bank's operations with other financial intermediaries.

E. Classification of financial transactions

1. Classification criteria

11.53. The SNA classification of transactions in financial assets and liabilities is presented in table 11.2 above. The same classification is used in the balance sheets for stocks of financial assets and liabilities. This classification scheme is based primarily on two kinds of criteria: the liquidity of the asset and the legal characteristics that describe the form of the underlying creditor/debtor relationship. The concept of liquidity embraces other more specific characteristics—such as negotiability, transferability, marketability or convertibility—and these characteristics play a major role in determining the categories, although they are not separately identified in a systematic way. This classification is designed to facilitate the analysis of transactions of institutional units and is a framework for assessing the sources and uses of financing and degree of liquidity for these units.

11.54. The classification requires reporting of asset categories at the one digit level except for insurance technical reserves (F.6), which must be divided between net equity of households in life insurance reserves and in pension funds (F.61) and prepayments of premiums and reserves against outstanding claims (F.62) and other accounts receivable/payable (F.7), which must be divided between trade credits and advances (F.71) and other (F.79). In the case of currency and deposits, the category can be subdivided between currency, transferable deposits, and other deposits when these subdivisions are useful for analysis. Securities other than shares (F.3) and loans (F.4) may be divided between short- and long-term when such a maturity distinction is useful.

11.55. The detail in which the classification is employed depends on the institutional sector to be analysed. The types of financial assets in which households transact are more limited than those for other sectors, and sources of information are generally more limited than those for other sectors. Financial corporations, on the other hand, transact in the full range of instruments, and information on their operations is often the most detailed and timely for any institutional units. Consequently, a detailed breakdown may be developed for financial corporations. It should be noted that the SNA classification scheme is considered to be generally applicable as a framework for classifying financial assets and liabilities and provides a useful basis for international comparison of national data. Presentation of data for individual countries, however, must be tailored to meet their analytical needs and to reflect national practices that include differing institutional arrangements, variety in the extent and nature of national financial markets, varying degrees of complexity of financial assets available, and varying degrees of regulation and other financial control exercised. In all cases, the SNA recommends compiling and presenting data at the first-digit level for asset categories 1 through 5 and at the two-digit level for categories

6 and 7 (see table 11.2). A substantial amount of flexibility, particularly with regard to further breakdowns, is therefore required to match the classification scheme to national capabilities, resources, and needs. In particular, further breakdowns of these categories are desirable for many countries to distinguish important types of assets within categories (such as derivatives within securities and deposits and short-term securities included in measures of money).

Money

11.56 In the SNA, there is no concept or measure of money within the classification of financial assets. Money is very important as a financial variable, but the wide range of ways in which money is defined in different countries precludes a simple definition within the SNA. Even measures of narrow money, which generally include currency and transferable deposits, may be difficult to define as the boundary between transferable and non-transferable deposits may not be stable in many countries. For example, certain financial institutions may start to provide partial or full checking facilities or to issue bank or credit cards, for deposit accounts that were previously not transferable. As a result of financial innovation, technological progress in computers and communications, and the force of competition, the distinction between transferable and non-transferable deposits and between the financial institutions that accept these deposits has become both blurred and unstable. In addition, few countries find that a stable relationship exists between narrowly defined money and other target variables. For these reasons, it may be difficult and not very useful analytically, at least in some countries, to try to draw a clear distinction between transferable and non-transferable deposits. Therefore, the SNA does not build this distinction into the classification at the first level. When the financial market is such that a clear distinction can be drawn, the SNA recommends that the distinction should be made, although it comes in at the second level of the classification.

11.57. The composition of broad money aggregates varies even more widely among countries and encompasses many classes of deposits and certain categories of short-term securities, particularly negotiable certificates of deposit. In addition, many countries compile a range of money measures, as well as broader liquidity measures, that include short-term liabilities of non-financial sectors. Even within a single country, innovation, deregulation or technical progress cause definitions of narrow or broad money to shift over time in response to changes in financial instruments and the organization of money markets. It follows that there can be no single concept of money supply implicit in the SNA. However, this does not preclude countries from organizing, either as the primary classification scheme or as a supplementary scheme, their financial classification and accounts around a specific money measure or measures. Such an approach would be very useful in integrating national accounts and monetary analysis.

Maturity

11.58. The classification de-emphasizes maturity as a basic classification criterion. Innovations in financial markets and more aggressive approaches to management of assets and liabilities—rollovers of short-term instruments, borrowing through short-term instruments under long-term facilities such as NIFs, adjustable rates on long-term assets that effectively make them a series of short-term arrangements, and early redemption of callable liabilities—have diminished the usefulness of a simple short-term/long-term distinction. In addition, when maturity analysis is important, such as for analysis of interest rates and asset yields, a breakdown of a range of maturities may be required. For these reasons, maturity distinction is recognized as a secondary classification criterion when relevant and national compilers should determine whether maturity breakdown is necessary. Short-term is defined for the classification as one year or less, with a maximum of two years to accommodate national practices, while long-term is defined as more than one year, or more than two years to accommodate national practices.

Asset/liability symmetry

11.59. All financial claims and the associated liabilities constitute financial assets and liabilities. However, financial assets also include certain assets that cannot properly be described as claims over other designated institutional units when there are no matching liabilities. There are four such types of asset:

(a) Monetary gold, i.e., gold owned by monetary authorities and others subject to the authorities' effective control and held as a financial asset and as a component of foreign reserves;

(b) SDRs, reserve assets issued by the IMF and not considered a liability of the IMF (IMF members, to whom SDRs are allocated, do not have an actual, i.e., unconditional, liability to repay their SDR allocations);

(c) Shares, other corporate equity securities, and capital participation (shares are close substitutes for other financial assets from the point of view of the investor. The SNA treats shares as liabilities by convention. However, these liabilities do not represent fixed redemption values, as is the case for many other assets, but claims on the net worth of the corporation);

(d) Certain financial derivatives for which liabilities are attributed by convention to the issuer.

Functional categories

11.60. The classification does not contain functional categories, such as direct investment, portfolio investment, and international reserves, that are basic classification criteria for the balance of payments capital account. In view of the importance of these transactions, the classification does provide for a memorandum item for financial account transactions related to direct foreign investment relationships. This topic is treated in greater detail in annex II at the end of this manual.

Reserve assets

11.61. Reserve assets consist of those external assets that are readily available to and controlled by a country's authorities for direct financing of international payments imbalances, for indirect regulation of the magnitude of such imbalances through intervention in foreign exchange markets to affect their currency's exchange rate, and for other purposes. Reserve assets comprise monetary gold, SDRs, reserve position in the IMF, foreign exchange assets (consisting of currency, deposits, and securities), and other claims, such as non-marketable claims arising from arrangements between central banks or governments. Reserves must be claims on non-residents but they may be denominated in the currency of the creditor or debtor. Only the central bank and central government can hold reserves. However, not all financial claims held by the authorities on non-residents are reserves, as reserves must be readily available, i.e., highly liquid.

2. Summary descriptions of transactions in financial assets and liabilities

11.62. Seven main categories of financial assets are distinguished in the SNA and are listed in table 11.2. The contents of each category are described in detail in later sections.

Monetary gold and SDRs (F.1)

11.63. Monetary gold and SDRs issued by the IMF are assets for which there are no outstanding financial liabilities.

11.64. Transactions in monetary gold consist of sales and purchases of gold among monetary authorities. Monetary gold is owned by monetary authorities or others subject to their effective control.[2] Only gold that is held as a financial asset and as a component of foreign reserves is classified as monetary gold. Therefore, except in limited institutional circumstances, gold can be a financial asset only for the central bank or central government. Purchases (sales) of monetary gold are recorded in the financial account of the domestic monetary authority as increases (decreases) in assets, and the counterparts are recorded as decreases (increases) in assets of the rest of the world. Transactions of other sectors in gold (including non-reserve gold held by the authorities and all gold held by financial institutions other than the central bank) are treated as acquisitions less disposals of valuables (if the sole purpose is to provide a store of wealth) and otherwise as final or intermediate consumption, and/or change in inventories. However, deposits, loans, and securities denominated in gold are treated as financial assets (not as gold) and are classified along with similar assets denominated in foreign currencies in the appropriate category.

11.65. If authorities add to their holdings of monetary gold by acquiring commodity gold, i.e., newly mined gold or existing gold offered on the private market, or release monetary gold from their holdings for non-monetary purposes, i.e., for sale to private holders or users, they are deemed to have monetized or demonetized gold, respectively. When the authorities acquire gold, the transaction is recorded in the capital account as a positive entry under acquisition less disposals of valuables or change in inventories, and counterpart entries are recorded in the accounts of the institutional units or the rest of the world supplying the gold. When non-monetary gold is acquired from abroad, the entry is recorded under imports. Monetization or demonetization itself does not give rise to entries in the financial accounts; instead, the change in balance sheet positions is accounted for by entries in the other changes in volume of assets account as a reclassification, i.e., the reclassification of gold in inventories or gold as valuables to monetary gold. Demonetization is recorded symmetrically. If monetary gold is pledged by the authorities or otherwise used as collateral, no transaction is deemed to have taken place, nor has the gold been demonetized simply by the pledging. However, as pledging may affect the gold's usability as a reserve asset, supplementary information, such as that for contingencies, should be collected. With respect to the treatment of gold swaps, national practices vary. Some favour treating them as actual transfers of ownership while others favour treating such swaps as the creation of a new financial asset, as is recommended for other repurchase agreements. In the SNA, they should be treated as new financial assets and classified as loans.

11.66. Monetary gold normally takes the form of coins, ingots, or bars with a purity of at least 995/1,000; it is usually traded on organized markets or through bilateral arrangements between central banks. Therefore, valuation of transactions is usually not a problem.

11.67. SDRs are international reserve assets created by the IMF and allocated to its members to supplement existing reserve assets. Transactions in SDRs are recorded in the financial accounts of the monetary authorities and the rest of the world, respectively. They are not considered liabilities of the IMF, and IMF members to whom SDRs are allocated do not have an actual (unconditional) liability to repay their SDRs allocations. SDRs are held exclusively by official holders, which are normally central banks, and are transferable among participants in the IMF's Special Drawing Rights Department and other holders designated by the IMF (central banks and certain other international agencies). SDRs represent each holder's assured and unconditional right to obtain other reserve assets, especially foreign exchange. The value of the SDR is determined daily on the basis of a basket of currencies. The basket and the weights are revised from time to time. Valuation of transac-

tions in SDRs raises no difficulties since they are used only in official transactions with a determined daily exchange rate.

11.68. The mechanism by which SDRs are created (referred to as allocations of SDRs) and extinguished (cancellations of SDRs) is not treated as one that gives rise to transactions in the SNA but rather to entries in the other changes in volume of assets account.

Currency and deposits (F.2)

11.69. The total of currency, transferable deposits, and other deposits should always be calculated. If separate data are considered useful for individual countries, they should be compiled for each component.

Currency (F.21)

11.70. Currency comprises those notes and coins in circulation that are commonly used to make payments. (Commemorative coins that are not actually in circulation should be excluded.) Distinctions should be drawn between national currency and foreign currencies, i.e., currency that is the liability of resident units, such as central banks, other banks and central government, and currencies that are liabilities of non-resident units, such as foreign central banks, other banks and governments. All sectors may hold currency as assets, but only financial corporations and government may issue currency.

Transferable deposits (F.22)

11.71 Transferable deposits comprise all deposits that are:

(a) Exchangeable on demand at par, without penalty or restriction;

(b) Freely transferable by check or giro-order; and

(c) Otherwise commonly used to make payments.

Transferable deposits should be cross-classified according to (a) whether they are denominated in national currency or in foreign currencies, and (b) whether they are liabilities of resident institutions or the rest of the world.

Other deposits (F.29)

11.72. Other deposits include all claims, other than transferable deposits, on the central bank, other depository institutions, government units, and, in some cases, other institutional units that are represented by evidence of deposit. Typical forms of deposits that should be included under this classification are non-transferable savings deposits, term deposits, and non-transferable deposits denominated in foreign currencies. The category also covers shares or similar evidence of deposit issued by savings and loan associations, building societies, credit unions, and the like; these shares or deposits are legally, or in practice, redeemable on demand or at relatively short notice. Claims on the IMF that are components of international reserves and are not evidenced by loans should be recorded in other deposits. (Claims on the IMF evidenced by loans should be included in loans (F.4.) Margin payments related to options or futures contracts are included in other deposits, as are overnight and very short-term repurchase agreements if they are considered part of national broad money definitions. Other repurchase agreements should be classified under loans. It will often be useful to cross-classify the other deposits category according to: (a) whether the deposits are denominated in national currency or in foreign currencies, and (b) whether they are liabilities of resident institutions or the rest of the world.

11.73. Transferable and other deposits may be held by all sectors. Deposits are most often accepted as liabilities by financial corporations and general government, but institutional arrangements in some countries permit non-financial corporations and households to accept deposits.

Securities other than shares (F.3)

11.74. The category of securities other than shares includes bills, bonds, certificates of deposit, commercial paper, debentures, tradable financial derivatives, and similar instruments normally traded in the financial markets. Bills are defined as securities that give the holders the unconditional rights to receive stated fixed sums on a specified date; bills are issued and traded in organized markets at discounts that depend on the rate of interest and the time to maturity. Examples of short-term securities are Treasury bills, negotiable certificate of deposit, banker's acceptances, and commercial paper. Bonds and debentures are securities that give the holders the unconditional right to fixed money incomes or contractually determined variable money incomes, i.e., payment of interest is not dependent on earnings of the debtors. With the exception of perpetual bonds, bonds and debentures also give holders the unconditional rights to fixed sums as repayments of principal on a specified date or dates.

11.75. New negotiable securities are often issued backed by existing assets such as loans, mortgages, credit card debt, or other assets (including accounts receivable). This repackaging of assets is often referred to as securitization. The creation of the new assets gives rise to entries in the financial account and the new assets should be classified as securities other than shares. The previously existing assets will continue to be reported on the balance sheet of the institutional units that hold them. Loans which have become negotiable de facto should also be classified under securities other than shares. Preferred stocks or shares that pay a fixed income but do not provide for participation in the distribution of the residual value of an incorporated enterprise on dissolution are included. Bonds that are convertible into shares should be classified in this category. The conversion option may be viewed as an asset separate from the underlying security and considered a tradable derivative. Splitting the value of the transaction between the bond and the value of the option can be accomplished by reference to transactions in similar bonds traded without the option.

Mortgages are not classified as bonds; they are included under loans.

11.76. Questions concerning the treatment in the accounts of zero-coupon (and other deep-discounted) bonds and indexed securities may be raised.

11.77. Zero-coupon bonds are long-term securities that do not involve periodic interest payments during the life of the bond; instead, they are sold at a discount from par value and the full return is paid at maturity. Deep-discount bonds pay some interest during the life of the instrument but the amount is substantially below market interest. For both of these assets, the difference between the discounted issue price and the price at maturity is substantial. In the SNA that difference is treated as interest and is recorded as accruing over the life of the bond rather than when due for payment. This treatment requires that the difference between issue price and the price at maturity be converted into a series of payments (quarterly or annual) recorded as interest (property income). The counterpart of this interest flow is entered in the financial account, under securities other than shares, and the effect is that the interest is reinvested. This treatment allows the costs of providing the capital to be matched to the periods for which the capital is provided.

11.78. Index-linked securities are instruments for which either the coupon payments (interest) or the principal are linked to a price index, the price of a commodity, or to an exchange rate index; the objective is to conserve purchasing power or wealth during a period of inflation in addition to earning interest income. When the coupon payments are index-linked they are treated entirely as interest income, as is the case with any variable interest rate financial asset. When the value of the principal is indexed, the issue price of the security is recorded as the principal and the index payment paid periodically and at maturity is treated as interest. The payment owing to indexation should be recorded as interest (property income) over the life of the security, and the counterpart should be recorded under securities other than shares in the financial account.

11.79. An optional subclassification of securities other than shares by maturity into short-term and long-term should be based on the following criteria:

Short-term (F.31)

11.80. Short-term securities other than shares include those securities that have an original maturity of one year or less; however, to accommodate variations in practice between countries, short-term may be defined to include an original maturity of two years or less. Securities with a maturity of one year or less should be classified as short-term even if they are issued under long-term facilities such as NIFs.

Long-term (F.32)

11.81. Long-term securities other than shares include those securities that have an original maturity of more than one year; however, to accommodate variations in practice between countries, long-term may be defined to include an original maturity in excess of two years. Claims with optional maturity dates, the latest of which is more than one year away, and claims with indefinite maturity dates should be classified as long-term.

11.82. An additional optional subclassification of securities other than shares may be used where financial derivatives are important from the point of view of analysis and policy. The total category "securities other than shares" may be subdivided between "securities other than shares excluding financial derivatives" and "financial derivatives".

Loans (F.4)

11.83. Loans include all financial assets that:

(a) Are created when creditors lend funds directly to debtors;

(b) Are evidenced by non-negotiable documents; or

(c) For which the lender receives no security evidencing the transaction.

This category includes all loans and advances (apart from trade credit and advances receivable or payable, see F.71) extended to business, government, and households, etc., by banks, finance companies, and others. The category includes instalment loans, hire-purchase credit, and loans to finance trade credit. Claims on the IMF that are evidenced by loans should be included in this category. Repurchase agreements not included in national broad money definitions, as well as financial leases and similar arrangements, should also be classified as loans. It is useful to subdivide the category of loans according to the resident sectors and the rest of the world for debtors and creditors, respectively. All sectors may acquire assets and incur liabilities in the form of loans.

Short-term (F.41)

11.84. Short-term loans comprise loans that normally have an original maturity of one year or less; however, to accommodate variations in practice between countries, short-term may be defined to include an original maturity of two years or less. All loans repayable on demand should be classified as short-term even when these loans are expected to be outstanding for more than one year.

Long-term (F.42)

11.85. Long-term loans comprise loans that normally have an original maturity of more than one year, except that, to accommodate variations in practice between countries, long-term may be defined to require an original maturity in excess of two years. It may also be useful to distinguish loans secured by mortgages from other long-term loans.

Shares and other equity (F.5)

11.86. Shares and other equities comprise all instruments and records acknowledging, after the claims of all creditors have been met, claims to the residual value of corporations. Equity securities do not provide the right to a pre-determined income or to a fixed sum on dissolution of the corporations. Ownership of equity is usually evidenced by shares, stocks, participation, or similar documents. Preferred stocks or shares, which also provide for participation in the distribution of the residual value on dissolution of an incorporated enterprise, are included. It is often useful to compile data separately for shares that are and are not quoted on an exchange.

11.87. Shares and other equity includes proprietors' net equity in quasi-corporations, as well as shares and equities in corporations. In the SNA, incorporated enterprises may have their own net worth in addition to the owners' equity in the corporations; for quasi-corporations, all net worth is assumed to be held by the owners. Proprietors' net additions to the equity of quasi-corporate enterprises are the net additions that owners of such enterprises make to the funds and other resources of these enterprises. The owners make these additions for purposes of the capital investment of the quasi-corporate enterprise. This category is not separately identified under "shares and other equity". Included under proprietors' net additions are the net results of actual additions to, and withdrawals from, the capital of quasi-corporations. The capital consists of funds for use by the enterprise in purchasing fixed assets, accumulating inventories, acquiring financial assets or redeeming liabilities. Transfers by owners of fixed and other assets to the quasi-corporation are also included. Withdrawals may take the form of proceeds from sales of fixed or other assets, transfers of fixed and other assets from the quasi-corporation to the owner, and funds taken from accumulated retained savings and reserves for the consumption of fixed capital. This category excludes current withdrawals from and contributions to the income of quasi-corporations.

11.88. Financial transactions related to immovable assets and unincorporated enterprises owned by non residents (see paragraph 11.30 above) are classified under shares and other equity. In the case of a quasi-corporation that is a direct investment enterprise wholly owned by non-residents (typically the foreign branch of a corporate or unincorporated enterprise), it is assumed that all of the quasi-corporation's retained earnings are remitted to the parent enterprise(s) and then reinvested as an addition to the net equity of the quasi-corporation. It is, of course, up to the proprietor(s) to make additional investments in the equity of direct investment enterprises over and above the amount of the retained earnings or, alternatively, to withdraw capital. For a direct investment quasi-corporation partly owned by non-residents, only that portion of the retained earnings proportional to the degree of ownership is imputed to be paid and reinvested. The same assumptions are made for incorporated enterprises, i.e., retained earnings are assumed to be remitted in proportion to the percentage of the equity owned by foreigners and the reinvestment is recorded in this category.

Insurance technical reserves (F.6)

11.89 Insurance technical reserves are subdivided between net equity of households in life insurance and pension funds (F.61) and prepayments of premiums and reserves against outstanding claims (F.62). The former category comprises reserves against outstanding risks and reserves for with-profit insurance and pension funds; it is subdivided between net equity of households in life insurance reserves (F.611) and net equity of households in pension funds (F.612). F.62 comprises prepayment of premiums and reserves held by insurance enterprises (including automobile, health, term life, accident/injury, income maintenance, and other forms of non-life insurance) against claims. Reserves against outstanding risks, reserves for with-profits insurance, and prepayments of premiums are considered to be assets of policyholders, while reserves against outstanding claims are assets of the beneficiaries. Insurance technical reserves may be liabilities, not only of life or non-life insurance enterprises (whether mutual or incorporated) but also of autonomous pension funds, which are included in the insurance enterprise sub-sector, and non-autonomous pension funds which are included in the institutional sector that manages the funds.

Net equity of households in life insurance reserves and pension funds (F.61)

This category is divided between households' claims on life insurance reserves and on pension funds.

Net equity of households in life insurance reserves (F.611)

11.90. Life insurance reserves consist of reserves against outstanding risks and reserves for with-profit insurance that add to the value on maturity of with-profit endowments or similar policies. Although held and managed by insurance enterprises, life insurance reserves are considered assets of the insured persons or households and not part of the net worth of the insurance enterprises. Life insurance reserves are collectively described as the net equity of households in life insurance reserves. The financial account of the SNA records changes in the net equity of households in life insurance reserves. Such changes, which result from transactions in which insurance enterprises or households engage, consist of additions less reductions.

11.91 Additions to the equity of households in life insurance funds consist of:

(a) The total value of the actual premiums earned during the current accounting period;

(b) The total value of the premium supplements (equal to

the income from the investment of the reserves which is attributed to policy holding households);

(c) Less the service charges for life insurance.

11.92 Reductions in the equity of households in life insurance funds consist of:

(a) The amounts due to holders of endowment and similar insurance policies when they mature, including the bonuses or profits earned on such policies;

(b) The amounts, including bonuses or profits due to beneficiaries, from deaths of insured persons;

(c) Payments due on policies that are surrendered before maturity.

Changes in the net equity of households that occur between the beginning and end of the accounting period and that result from nominal holding gains or losses on the reserves invested by insurance enterprises are recorded in the revaluation account.

Net equity of households in pension funds (F.612)

11.93 Pension funds consist of the reserves held by funds established by employers and/or employees to provide pensions for employees after retirement. These reserves, like reserves against life insurance, are considered to be assets of households—not assets of the institutional units that manage them. Therefore, these reserves are referred to as the net equity of households in pension funds. The financial account of the SNA records change in the net equity of households in pension funds. Such changes, which result from transactions in which the funds or the households may be involved, consist of additions less reductions.

11.94 Additions to the equity in pension funds consist of:

(a) The total value of the actual contributions into pension funds payable by employees, employers, or other institutional units on behalf of individuals or households with claims on the funds;

(b) The total value of the contribution supplements (equal to the income earned from the investment of the reserves of the pension funds which is attributed to participating households);

(c) Less the service charges for managing the funds.

11.95 Reductions in the equity in pension funds consist of:

(a) The total value of the amounts payable to retired persons or their dependants in the form of regular payments each week, month, or other period;

(b) The total value of any lump sums payable to persons when they retire.

11.96 Changes in the net equity of households that occur between the beginning and the end of the accounting period and that result from nominal holding gains or losses on the invested reserves of pension funds are recorded in the revaluation account and are not included in the financial account.

*Prepayments of insurance premiums and reserves
for outstanding claims (F.62)*

11.97 Prepayments of premiums result from the fact that, in general, insurance premiums are paid in advance. Insurance premiums are due to be paid at the start of the period covered by the insurance, and this period does not normally coincide with the accounting period itself. Therefore, at the end of the accounting period when the balance sheet is drawn up, parts of the insurance premiums payable during the accounting period are intended to cover risks in the subsequent period. These prepayments of premiums are assets of the policyholders and form part of the insurance technical reserves. The amounts of premiums recorded in the accounts as transactions between policyholders and insurance enterprises consist of the premiums earned—those parts of the premiums that are paid in the current period or the preceding period and that are intended to cover risks outstanding during the current period.

11.98 Reserves against outstanding claims are reserves that insurance enterprises hold in order to cover the amounts they expect to pay out in respect of claims that are not yet settled or claims that may be disputed. Valid claims accepted by insurance enterprises are considered due for payment when the eventuality or accident that gives rise to the claim occurs—however long it takes to settle disputed claims. Reserves against outstanding claims are therefore considered to be assets of the beneficiaries and liabilities of the insurance enterprises.

11.99 The financial account of the SNA records changes in prepayments of premiums and reserves for outstanding claims that result from transactions between policyholders and insurance enterprises under the general heading of changes in insurance technical reserves. Changes in these reserves resulting from holding gains or losses are recorded in the revaluation account and not in the financial account.

Other accounts receivable/payable (F.7)

Trade credit and advances (F.71)

11.100 This category comprises:

(a) Trade credit for goods and services extended directly to corporations, government, NPIs, households, and the rest of the world; and

(b) Advances for work that is in progress (if classified as such under inventories) or is to be undertaken.

Trade credits and advances do not include loans to finance trade credit, which are classified under category 4 in table 11.2. It may also be valuable to separate short-term trade credits and advances from long-term trade credit and advances by employing the same criteria used to distinguish between other short- and long-term financial assets.

Other (F.79)

11.101 This category includes accounts receivable and payable, other than those described previously (e.g., in respect of taxes, dividends, purchases and sales of securities, rent, wages and salaries, and social contributions). Interest that is accruing on financial assets may be recorded under various categories in the classification. In general, interest accruing on securities other than shares should be recorded as increasing the value of the security. With respect to interest accruing on deposits and loans, the recording of interest may have to follow national practices as to whether the interest is capitalized in the underlying asset. If such interest is not capitalized, it may be classified in this category. When accrued interest is not paid when due on any financial asset, this gives rise to interest arrears. As accrued interest is already recorded in the accounts under the appropriate asset or under this category, no separate entry for such arrears is required. When they are important it may be useful to group all arrears of interest and repayment under a memorandum item. This category does not include statistical discrepancies.

Memorandum item: direct foreign investment

11.102 Transactions in financial assets and liabilities arising from the provision of, or receipt of, direct foreign investment are to be recorded under the appropriate categories listed above in table 11.2, i.e., shares and other equity (category 5), loans (category 4), and other accounts receivable/payable (category 7). However, the amounts of direct foreign investment included within each of those categories should also be recorded separately as memorandum items.

F. Detailed flow of funds accounts

11.103 The financial account, as presented in table 11.2, records the net acquisition of financial assets and net incurrence of liabilities for all institutional sectors by type of financial asset. For each sector, the financial account shows the financial liabilities that the sector incurs to mobilize financial resources and the financial assets that the sector acquires. The financial account thus presents a two-dimensional view of financial transactions—the financial asset or liability involved in the transaction and whether the transaction involves an asset or a liability. This information is very valuable in identifying the financial assets that net borrowing sectors use to finance their deficits and the assets that net lending sectors use to allocate their surpluses. Although the movement of financial flows can be mapped at this level of recording, the question of who is fi-

Table 11.3a. Detailed flow of funds (financial assets)

Financial assets of:

					Financial corporations							
						Other deposit institutions						
The rest of the world (12)	Households (11)	NPISHs (10)	General government (9)	Non-financial corporations (8)	Central bank (7)	Deposit money institutions (6)	Other deposit accepting (5)	Other financial intermediaries (4)	Financial auxiliaries (3)	Insurance corporations and pension funds (2)	Total (1)	Type of claim and debtor
												1. Monetary gold and SDRs
												2. Currency and deposits
												a. Currency
												i. National
												- Residents
												- Non-residents
												ii. Foreign
												- Residents
												b. Transferable deposits
												i. In national currency
												- Residents
												- Non-residents
												ii. Foreign currency
												- Residents
												- Non-residents
												c. Other deposits
												i. In national currency
												- Residents
												- Non-residents
												ii. Foreign currency
												- Residents
												- Non-residents
												3. Securities other than shares
												a. Short-term
												i. Non-financial corporations
												ii. Financial corporations
												iii. Central government
												iv. State and local government
												v. Other resident sectors
												vi. The rest of the world
												b. Long-term
												i. Non-financial corporations
												ii. Financial corporations
												iii. Central government
												iv. State and local government
												v. Other resident sectors
												vi. The rest of the world
												4. Loans
												a. Short-term
												i. Non-financial corporations
												ii. Financial corporations
												iii. Central government
												iv. State and local government
												v. Other resident sectors
												vi. The rest of the world
												b. Long-term
												i. Non-financial corporations
												ii. Financial corporations
												iii. Central government
												iv. State and local government
												v. Other resident sectors
												vi. The rest of the world
												5. Shares and other equity
												a. Resident enterprises
												i. Quoted
												ii. Not quoted
												b. Non-resident enterprises
												i. Quoted
												ii. Not quoted
												6. Insurance technical reserves
												6.1 Net equity of households on life insurance reserves and on pension funds
												6.2 Prepayments of premiums and reserves against outstanding claims
												7. Other accounts receivable and payable
												7.1 Trade credit and advances
												a. Non-financial corporations
												b. Households
												c. Central government
												d. State and local government
												e. Other resident sectors
												f. The rest of the world
												7.2 Other
												a. Resident sectors
												b. The rest of the world
												Memorandum items:
												Direct investment
												Equity
												Loans
												Other

Table 11.3b.   Detailed flow of funds (financial liabilities)

Financial liabilities of:

The rest of the world (12)	House-holds (11)	NPISHs (10)	General govern-ment (9)	Non-financial corpor-ations (8)	Central bank (7)	Financial corporations		Other financial inter-mediaries (4)	Financial auxi-liaries (3)	Insurance corpora-tions and pension funds (2)	Total (1)	Type of claim and creditor
						Other deposit institutions						
						Deposit money institutions (6)	Other deposit accepting (5)					

2. Currency and deposits
   a. Currency
      i. National
         - Residents
         - Non-residents
      ii. Foreign
         - Residents
   b. Transferable deposits
      i. In national currency
         - Residents
         - Non-residents
      ii. Foreign currency
         - Residents
         - Non-residents
   c. Other deposits
      i. In national currency
         - Residents
         - Non-residents
      ii. Foreign currency
         - Residents
         - Non-residents

3. Securities other than shares
   a. Short-term
      i. Non-financial corporations
      ii. Financial corporations
      iii. Central government
      iv. State and local government
      v. Other resident sectors
      vi. The rest of the world
   b. Long-term
      i. Non-financial corporations
      ii. Financial corporations
      iii. Central government
      iv. State and local government
      v. Other resident sectors
      vi. The rest of the world

4. Loans
   a. Short-term
      i. Non-financial corporations
      ii. Financial corporations
      iii. Central government
      iv. State and local government
      v. Other resident sectors
      vi. The rest of the world
   b. Long-term
      i. Non-financial corporations
      ii. Financial corporations
      iii. Central government
      iv. State and local government
      v. Other resident sectors
      vi. The rest of the world

5. Shares and other equity
   a. Resident enterprises
      i. Quoted
      ii. Not quoted
   b. Non-resident enterprises
      i. Quoted
      ii. Not quoted

6. Insurance technical reserves
   6.1 Net equity of households on life insurance reserves and on pension funds
   6.2 Prepayments of premiums and reserves against outstanding claims

7. Other accounts receivable and payable
   7.1 Trade credit and advances
      a. Non-financial corporations
      b. Households
      c. Central government
      d. State and local government
      e. Other resident sectors
      f. The rest of the world
   7.2 Other
      a. Resident sectors
      b. The rest of the world
   Memorandum items:
      Direct investment
         Equity
         Loans
         Other

nancing whom is not answered. In table 11.1, it is clear that non-financial corporations incurred liabilities of 140 predominantly in the form of loans (71) and shares and other equities (69). Financial corporations incurred net liabilities of 232 by using the full range of financial instruments. While the instrument by which the liabilities are incurred is clearly presented in this account, it is not possible to identify the sector that is providing the funds. Similarly, the net acquisition of financial assets can be tracked. Households acquired a net of 181 spread across a range of assets, while financial corporations acquired net financial assets of 237, mostly in the form of loans and securities. However, it cannot be determined from this level of recording to which sectors the financing is being provided.

11.104 For a full understanding of financial flows and the role they play in the economy, it is often important to know more detailed financial relationships between sectors and the financial assets by which these relationships are carried out. For example, it is often important for the government to know not just what types of liabilities it is using to finance its deficit but also which sectors (or the rest of the world) are providing the financing. For financial corporations (and those supervising them), it is important to know not only the composition of financial assets (loans and securities) that they have acquired but also which sectors these are claims upon. In addition, it is often necessary to analyse financial flows between subsectors within a sector (central government financial transactions with local governments or central bank financial transactions with depository institutions) and across sector boundaries (changes in depository institutions' claims on public non-financial corporations). Such detailed information is necessary to understand how financing is being carried out and how it is changing over time.

11.105 This more detailed approach is particularly important in spelling out the role that financial intermediaries play in financial transactions. As was previously noted, financial corporations often have very small net lending or borrowing balances in comparison with their volume of transactions in both financial assets and liabilities. This reflects the basic role of financial intermediation of mobilizing financial resources through certain financial transactions and making these financial resources available to other sectors in forms suitable to these sectors through maturity/asset transformation. Thus, financial corporations play a critical role in directing financing flows from net lending sectors to net borrowing sectors and allow lenders to choose their asset instruments and borrowers their forms of indebtedness.

11.106 To facilitate the more detailed financial analysis just described, the SNA contains two tables, tables 11.3a and 11.3b. Table 11.3a records transactions in assets cross-classified by type of asset and by the debtor sector. The sectors transacting in assets are shown horizontally across the top of the table while the type of asset, disaggregated by sector of debtor, is arrayed vertically. Table 11.3b records transactions in liabili-

ties cross-classified by type of liability and by the creditor sector. Since all financial assets other than monetary gold and SDRs have an asset/liability symmetry, it would be conceptually possible to present all debtor/creditor relationships in a single table but this would require a table of very many cells, many of which would be blank. The tables, as presented, are merely examples of the type of detail that a country may wish to develop. They identify the full sectors for households, non-profit institutions, general government, and non-financial corporations. Subsectors are shown for the financial corporations to emphasize the special role these units play in financial transactions. For particular analysis or policy purposes, it may be useful to break down the other sectors into subsectors as well. In many circumstances, it will be necessary, for example, to identify financial transactions of central government or of non-financial public corporations. The sector breakdown under each type of financial asset is suggestive rather than prescriptive. For securities and loans, it is suggested to identify the debtor sectors (in table 11.3a) as follows: non-financial corporations, financial corporations, central government, state and local government, other resident sectors, and the rest of the world. Alternative breakdowns are illustrated for other types of assets.

11.107 These more detailed flow of funds tables can be used in at least three important areas related to economic policy. Data from these tables can be used in economic analysis and description of activity and trends in current periods. They can be used as an aid to projections in the context of the production of economic plans or to assess the effect of current economic policies, or changes in them, on the future path of the economy. They can also be used in projects that undertake modelling of the economy to study economic behaviour as an aid to the formulation of economic policy. Such studies, of course, would be complementary to similar work on data from other accounts in the SNA. In particular it is useful, when using the flow of funds accounts to facilitate the operation of the financial system in the economy, to relate these transactions to the behaviour of the non-financial economy. The capital and financial accounts provide these links between the "real" economy and financial activity. Similarly, the flow of funds accounts facilitate study of the saving/investment process, by tracing the channels by which saving reaches ultimate borrowing, after passing through various financial institutions and assets.

11.108 In the policy area, a few examples will illustrate the usefulness of these tables. Common policy problems faced by many nations include questions such as: Will foreign exchange reserves be adequate? How will the central government's deficit be financed? How will the major non-financial public corporations be financed and by whom? In each of these examples, the provision of answers to the questions requires an impact analysis on various sectors and types of transaction. The articulation of the accounts within the flow of funds table facilitates the analysis and provides a framework in which to assess the answers.

11.109 In the area of financial projects, the use of time-series from relevant parts of the flow of funds tables enables an examination of the implications of parts of an economic plan, including testing for consistency of a number of separately prepared sector or market forecasts, and the implications for future financial transactions of a particular set of assumptions about future events (e.g., interest rates, exchange rates, growth, sector surpluses/deficits).

11.110 Other policy areas where these projections and studies can be of assistance are in considering the long-term development of financial markets and institutions in the economy and assessments of the need for new types of assets to satisfy the potential demand of savers and investors requiring access to reliable liquid assets.

11.111 Tables 11.3a and 11.3b above should be interpreted as a general model, and substantial flexibility should be allowed in specific country circumstances. In many countries, the dimensions of the tables will be severely constrained by data availability. It should also be noted that these tables are extensions of the basic financial account and that adding the third dimension to the analysis can be done on a selective basis by identifying particular assets or sector (or subsector) relationships for which this level of detail would be useful.

Notes

1 Except when the context requires, the term "financial assets" should be read to include liabilities. The terms "financial assets" and "liabilities" are used to designate those financial instruments for which there are transactions in the financial account; the term "financial instrument" is broader in coverage than "financial asset" as it includes various financial contracts and other arrangements, such as contingencies, that are not actual assets.

2 Monetary gold will normally consist of the gold to which the central bank and the central government actually hold title. In some circumstances, other institutional units such as financial corporations may hold title to gold that can only be sold with the specific consent of the monetary authorities. In such restricted circumstances, the concept of effective control can be applied to the gold holdings of other units. The same criterion of eccective control can also be applied to other components of reserves.

XII. Other changes in assets account

12.1. This chapter is concerned with the recording of changes in the values of assets, liabilities, and net worth between opening and closing balance sheets that result from other flows—i.e., flows that are not transactions, the transactions being recorded in the capital account and financial account of the System.

12.2. Although the entries in the other changes in assets accounts do share the characteristic that they record changes that are not the result of transactions, the entries cover very different kinds of changes in assets, liabilities, and net worth. The first kind consists of changes that are due to factors such as discoveries or depletion of subsoil resources, destruction by war or other political events or destruction by natural catastrophes, all of which actually change the volume of assets. The second kind consists of changes in the values of assets, liabilities, and net worth due to changes in the level and structure of prices, which are reflected in holding gains and losses. Thus, the other changes in assets accounts are subdivided into the other changes in the volume of assets account and the revaluation account.

12.3. The chapter discusses the two accounts separately, beginning in each case with an introduction that explains the structure of the account.

A. Other changes in the volume of assets account

1. Introduction

12.4. The other changes in the volume of assets account records the changes in assets, liabilities, and net worth between opening and closing balance sheets that are due neither to transactions between institutional units, as recorded in the capital and financial accounts, nor to holding gains and losses. The structure of the other changes in the volume of assets account, shown in table 12.1, is similar to that of the other accumulation accounts. The entries for changes in assets are on the left, where non-financial assets, both produced and non-produced, and financial assets are all shown separately. The entries for changes in liabilities and the balancing item, change in net worth due to other changes in volume of assets, are on the right. The balancing item in the account is the sum of the entries for the various categories of changes recorded in the account.

Functions of the other changes in
the volume of assets account

12.5. In the capital account, produced assets enter and leave the System through acquisition less disposal of fixed assets, consumption of fixed capital and inventory additions, withdrawals and recurrent losses. In the financial account, most financial assets—claims on other institutional units—enter the System when the debtor acquires something of value and accepts the obligation to make payment, or payments, to the creditor, and they are extinguished when the debtor has fulfilled the obligation under the terms of the agreement. Both the capital and financial accounts also record transactions in existing assets among the institutional sectors, but, aside from associated costs of ownership transfer on assets, these acquisitions and disposals merely change the ownership of the assets without changing the total for the economy as a whole except where the transactions are between residents and the rest of the world.

12.6. One important function of the other changes in the volume of assets account, therefore, is to allow certain assets to enter and leave the System in the normal course of events. These entrances and exits may relate to naturally occurring assets, such as subsoil assets. Such entrances and exits come about as interactions between institutional units and nature, thus contrasting with entrances and exits that come about as a result of transactions, which typically are interactions by mutual agreement between institutional units. These entrances and exits may also relate to assets created by human activity, such as valuables and purchased goodwill or financial assets for which there is neither an actual nor a notional liability.

12.7. A second function of the account is to record the effects of exceptional, unanticipated events that affect the economic benefits derivable from assets (and corresponding liabilities). These events include one institutional unit's effectively removing an asset from its owner without the owner's agreement, an action that is not considered a transaction because the element of mutual agreement is absent. These events also include those that destroy assets, such as natural disaster or war. In contrast, transactions, such as consumption of fixed capital

Table 12.1. Account III.3.1: Other changes in volume of assets account

Changes in assets

Total	Corresponding entries of the Goods and service account	Rest of the world account	S.1 Total economy	S.15 NPISHs	S.14 House-holds	S.13 General government	S.12 Financial corporations	S.11 Non-financial corporations	Transactions and balancing items	
10			10				−2	12	AN	Non-financial assets
−7			−7			−3	−2	−2	AN.1	Produced assets
3			3			3			K.4	Economic appearance of produced assets
−9			−9			−4		−5	K.7	Catastrophic losses
						1		−1	K.8	Uncompensated seizures
1			1					1	K.9	Other volume changes in non-financial assets n.e.c.
−2			−2			−3	−2	3	K.12	Changes in classifications and structure
						−3		3	K.12.1	Changes in sector classification and structure
−2			−2				−2		K.12.2	Changes in classification of assets and liabilities
−2			−2				−2		K.12.21	Monetization/demonetization of gold
									K.12.22	Changes in classification of assets or liabilities other than monetization/demonetization of gold
									of which:	
−4			−4			−3		−1	AN.11	Fixed assets
−1			−1					−1	AN.12	Inventories
−2			−2				−2		AN.13	Valuables
17			17			3		14	AN.2	Non-produced assets
24			24					24	K.3	Economic appearance of non-produced assets
4			4			4			K.5	Natural growth of non-cultivated biological resources
−9			−9			−2		−7	K.6	Economic disappearance of non-produced assets
−8			−8			−2		−6	K.61	Depletion of natural assets
−1			−1					−1	K.62	Other economic disappearance of non-produced assets
−2			−2			−2			K.7	Catastrophic losses
						4		−4	K.8	Uncompensated seizures
									K.9	Other volume changes in non-financial assets n.e.c.
						−1		1	K.12	Changes in classifications and structure
						−1		1	K.12.1	Changes in sector classification and structure
									K.12.2	Changes in classification of assets and liabilities
									K.12.22	Changes in classification of assets or liabilities other than monetization/demonetization of gold
									of which:	
17			17			3		14	AN.21	Tangible non-produced assets
									AN.22	Intangible non-produced assets
5			5		2	1		2	AF	Financial assets/liabilities
									K.7	Catastrophic losses
						3	−3		K.8	Uncompensated seizures
3			3		2	1			K.10	Other volume changes in financial assets and liabilities n.e.c.
2			2			−2	2	2	K.12	Changes in classifications and structure
						−2		2	K.12.1	Changes in sector classification and structure
2			2				2		K.12.2	Changes in classification of assets and liabilities
2			2				2		K.12.21	Monetization/demonetization of gold
									K.12.22	Changes in classification of assets or liabilities other than monetization/demonetization of gold
									of which:	
7			7					7	AF.1	Monetary gold and SDRs
									AF.2	Currency and deposits
						3	−3		AF.3	Securities other than shares
−4			−4				−4		AF.4	Loans
						−2		2	AF.5	Shares and other equity
2			2		2				AF.6	Insurance technical reserves
									AF.7	Other accounts receivable/payable
									B.10.2	*Changes in net worth due to other changes in volume of assets*

Changes in liabilities and net worth

S.11 Non-financial corporations	S.12 Financial corporations	S.13 General government	S.14 Households	S.15 NPISHs	S.1 Total economy	Corresponding entries of the Rest of the world account	Goods and service account	Total
− 3	2	− 1			− 2			
− 4	2				− 2			
1		− 1						
1		− 1						
− 3		− 1			− 4			
	2				2			
17	− 4	2	2		17			

or change in inventories, allow for normal rates of loss or destruction.

12.8. A third function of the account is to record changes in classifications of institutional units and assets and in the structure of institutional units.

12.9. It may be noted that the other changes in the volume of assets account provide a link to the emerging environmental satellite accounts. All of the tangible non-produced assets are natural assets, and recording their economic appearance and disappearance is accomplished here. Moreover, this account provides a place for recording environmental degradation to fixed assets that is not allowed for in consumption of fixed capital. These features of the System that facilitate its use as a starting point for environmental accounting are discussed in chapter XXI.

Categories of changes in assets/liabilities and their valuation

12.10. The other changes in the volume of assets account shows changes in assets/liabilities in nine categories:

K.3 Economic appearance of non-produced assets

K.4 Economic appearance of produced assets

K.5 Natural growth of non-cultivated biological resources

K.6 Economic disappearance of non-produced assets

K.7 Catastrophic losses

K.8 Uncompensated seizures

K.9 Other volume changes in non-financial assets n.e.c.

K.10 Other volume changes in financial assets and liabilities n.e.c., and

K.12 Changes in classifications and structure.

12.11. Most of these entries are specific to produced assets, to non-produced assets, or to financial assets/liabilities, as table 12.1 indicates. (For convenience, the term "financial asset" will be used to cover both financial assets and liabilities, except when the context requires liabilities to be referred to explicitly.) Three entries—catastrophic losses, uncompensated seizures and changes in classifications and structure—may in principle apply to any asset. The annex to chapter XIII may be referenced to see, at the level of detail of the classification of assets and liabilities, all possible entries provided by the System.

12.12. Many of the entries in the other changes in the volume of assets account are closely linked to entries in the other accumulation accounts. Several of the entries are associated with transactions in the capital account, for example, when an economic appearance is evidenced by a transaction; a number of others reflect changes in assets already on the balance sheet, for example, when a fixed asset is retired prematurely. The application of the general principle of valuation applied to transactions—at the prices observed on the market—is discussed in vari-

oussectionsofchapter X; the general principle of valuation applied to stocks—valued as if they were being acquired on the market on the date to which the balance sheet relates—is discussed in chapter XIII, paragraphs 13.25 to 13.35. That chapter discusses the use of observed prices on the market, the present, or discounted, value of expected future benefits, and current written down values. Some generalizations about the relevance of these valuation principles to the categories of flows in the account are indicated below:

(a) Economic appearance—that is, when something is deemed to move inside the asset boundary to appear on the balance sheet—in some cases is associated with a transaction on the market, and that transaction can be used to estimate a value. This situation occurs, for example, for purchased goodwill, valuables and historic monuments. In a number of other cases the appearance will probably have to be valued, as will the asset in the balance sheet, at the present or discounted value of the stream of expected future benefits from the asset. This approach must be used, for example, for economic appearance of subsoil assets and of intangible non-produced non-financial assets other than purchased goodwill;

(b) Economic disappearance of non-produced assets, catastrophic losses and uncompensated seizures refer to the effects of exceptional, unanticipated events on assets already within the asset boundary. Thus, the valuation of the entry in the other changes in the volume of assets account would be the amount recorded for the asset in the last balance sheet (updated as needed for price changes) if the disappearance was total or some percentage of it if less than total.

12.13. Each of the categories of the account will be explained below, with numerical examples drawn from the entries in table 12.1 as illustrations. The subheadings included in the text are for convenience only; they are not subheadings of the classification. The definition of the assets and liabilities are provided only to the extent needed to provide the context for discussing the volume change; for definitions at the level of detail of the classification, reference can be made to the annex to chapter XIII. Valuation is mentioned when category-specific guidance is appropriate. When a category's valuation is clearly tied to a transaction or to an entry in the balance sheet, reference should be made to the appropriate section in the other chapters.

2. Economic appearance of non-produced assets (K.3)

12.14. By definition, non-financial non-produced assets are not created by processes of production. Thus, they are not among the assets that result from gross capital formation, as recorded in the capital account. Some of these assets occur in nature, and others come into existence in ways other than through processes of production as what may be referred to as constructs devised by society. The cases below represent the additions to the volume of these kinds of assets. The term "appearance" is used to contrast with additions that are the result of processes of production as defined in the System. Table 12.1, Account III 3.1 shows an entry for economic appearance of non-produced assets on the left side of the account for non-financial corporations, an addition of 24 to the stock of tangible non-produced assets. Examples of such economic appearance include changes in proven reserves of subsoil assets and bringing natural assets under the direct control, responsibility and management of institutional units.

Gross additions to the level of exploitable subsoil resources

12.15. In the System, subsoil assets are defined as those proven subsoil reserves of coal, oil and natural gas, of metallic minerals or of non-metallic minerals that are economically exploitable, given current technology and relative prices. The capital account records acquisitions and disposals among sectors of the reserves that exist under those conditions. The other changes in the volume of assets account, in contrast, records increases and decreases that change the total volume for the economy as a whole.

12.16. One way in which the reserves may increase is by the discovery of new exploitable deposits, whether as a result of systematic scientific explorations or surveys or by chance. The definition of subsoil assets points to the other way in which economic appearance may occur—by change of the conditions. That is, reserves may be increased by the inclusion of deposits for which exploitation may have been previously uneconomic but becomes economic as a result of technological progress or relative price changes.

Transfers of other natural assets to economic activity

12.17. The definition of subsoil assets just referred to follows from application of the guidelines for identifying economic assets in the System. As explained in the general introduction to the accumulation accounts and balance sheets in chapter X, economic assets are entities over which ownership rights are enforced by institutional units and from which economic benefits may be derived by their owners. Naturally occurring entities that qualify as economic assets are those that are under the direct control, responsibility and management of institutional units (see especially chapter X, paragraphs 10.10 to 10.12). Economic appearance is the move to this status.

12.18. Not all land included in the geographic surface area of a country is necessarily within the System's asset boundary. Land makes its appearance in the System, therefore, when it is transferred from a wild or waste state to one in which ownership may be established and the land can be put to economic use.

In addition, the stock of land may be marginally increased by reclaiming land from the sea by the construction of dykes, as described in chapter X. Increases in the stock of land of this kind are recorded in the other changes in the volume of assets account.

12.19. For other natural assets, the first substantial market appearance, generally involving commercial exploitation, is the reference point for recording in this account. For virgin forests, gathering firewood is not commercial exploitation, but large-scale harvesting of a virgin forest for timber is, and brings the forest into the asset boundary. Similarly, drawing water from a natural spring does not bring an aquifer into the asset boundary of the System, but a significant diversion of groundwater does.

Quality changes in non-produced assets
due to changes in economic uses

12.20. The System, in general, treats differences in quality as differences in volume. As explained with respect to goods and services in chapter XVI, different qualities reflect different use values (and in the case of goods and services, different resource costs). Different qualities are, therefore, economically different from each other. The same principle applies to assets. The quality changes recorded here occur as the counterpart of the changes in economic use that are shown as changes in classification, as described below—for example, from cultivated land to land underlying buildings. In this case, the asset is already within the asset boundary, and it is the change in quality of the asset due to changes in its economic use that is regarded as the appearance of additional amounts of the asset.

Appearance of intangible non-produced assets

12.21. Non-financial intangible non-produced assets are constructs devised by society evidenced by legal or accounting actions. They make their appearance in the System when entities are patented, transferable contracts are written, or enterprises are sold at prices that exceed the net worth of the enterprise in question, etc. The patenting consists of the entity being granted legal protection by law or judicial decision. The writing of transferable contracts consists of the coming into force of a binding agreement that provides some economic benefit that can be passed on to a third party independently of the provider of that benefit.

12.22. When an enterprise is sold at a price that exceeds its net worth, this excess of purchase price over net worth is the asset "purchased goodwill." Goodwill that is not evidenced by a sale/purchase is not considered an economic asset: the only way that goodwill enters the System is for such a purchase to occur. Two cases must be distinguished. For the sale/purchase of an unincorporated enterprise not treated as a quasi-corporation, the purchased goodwill represents the excess of the purchase price of this enterprise over its net worth (derived from its separately identified and valued assets and liabilities). Conceptually, the entries are as follows. Prior to the sale, the excess of the purchase price of an enterprise over its net worth enters the balance sheet of the seller, via the other changes in the volume of assets account, as an economic appearance of a non-produced asset so that the enterprise can be sold at its purchase price; this excess is then disposed of by the seller as "disposals of intangible non-produced assets" in the capital account and acquired by the purchaser as "acquisitions of intangible non-produced assets" in the capital account. The purchased goodwill is then recorded in the closing balance sheet of the purchaser. For the sale/purchase of a corporation or quasi-corporation, the purchased goodwill represents the excess of the purchase price of its shares and other equity over their value just prior to the sale/purchase. This excess enters the balance sheet of the seller of shares and other equity prior to the sale as a revaluation of a financial asset so that the shares and other equity can be sold at their purchase price. At the same time, the purchased goodwill enters the other changes in the volume of assets account as an economic appearance of an intangible non-produced asset and is recorded as such in the closing balance sheet of this corporation or quasi-corporation. The sales and purchases of the shares and other equity are recorded in the financial accounts of the seller and the purchaser.

3. Economic appearance of produced assets (K.4)

12.23. The produced assets whose appearance is recorded in the other changes in the volume of assets account are valuables and historic monuments, the latter included with dwellings and with other buildings and structures in the classification of assets. As was described in chapter X, they are objects, structures or sites of significant or special value. The capital account records the acquisition of valuables and historic monuments as newly produced goods or as imports, and it records transactions in existing goods already classified as valuables and historical monuments. In the case of goods that are not already recorded in the balance sheets, it is the recognition of a significant or special value—whether evidenced by a transaction or by the formal appraisal of a good that remains in its owner's possession—that is considered an economic appearance to be recorded in the other changes in the volume of assets account. These valuables and historic monuments have not already been recorded in the balance sheets for any of several reasons: they antedate the accounts, they were originally recorded as consumption goods, or if structures, they have already been written off. An entry for economic appearance of produced assets is shown in table 12.1 on the left side of the account for general government, when the government's stock of fixed assets increases by 3, reflecting the recognition of the historic significance of a monument.

12.24. For valuables, such as precious stones, antiques and other art objects, when the high value or artistic significance of an object not already recorded in the balance sheet is first recog-

nized, it is classified as an economic appearance. Hitherto, the object may have been of little value and not considered an asset. For example, a piece of jewellery might have been considered an ordinary good whose purchase would be included in household final consumption expenditure were it not to make its appearance as a valuable because it was made of precious metals or stones. Such an appearance would be recorded for the valuable in the other changes in the volume of assets account, even though it is immediately the subject of a transaction recorded in the capital account.

12.25. For historic monuments, when the special archaeological, historical, or cultural significance of a structure or site not already recorded in the balance sheet is first recognized, it is classified as an economic appearance and recorded in the other changes in the volume of assets account. For example, such recognition might be accorded an existing structure or site that is fully written off and thus no longer recorded in the balance sheet. Such recognition would also refer to quality changes in structures and sites that are already within the asset boundary because they are new or only partially written off; the counterpart entry in changes in classification may not be observable, however, at the level of detail in the classification of assets. The structure or site is immediately the subject of a transaction recorded in the capital account.

4. Natural growth of non-cultivated biological resources (K.5)

12.26. The natural growth of non-cultivated biological resources—natural forests, fishstocks, etc.—may take various forms: a stand of natural timber may grow taller, or fish in the estuaries may become more numerous. Although these resources are economic assets, growth of this kind is not under the direct control, responsibility and management of an institutional unit and thus is not production. The increment in the asset must then be regarded as an economic appearance, and it is recorded in the other changes in the volume of assets account. Table 12.1 shows an entry for natural growth of non-cultivated biological resources on the left side of the account for general government, reflecting growth of 4 in, for example, natural forests owned by government.

12.27. In principle, natural growth should be recorded gross, and the depletion of these resources should be recorded as an economic disappearance, as described below. This recording would be consistent with the separate recording of acquisitions and disposals described, for example, in the capital account. In practice, however, many countries will record natural growth net because the physical measures that are likely to be the only basis available for the recording are, in effect, net measures. These measures may be used in conjunction with a market price for a unit of the asset to estimate the value of the volume change to be recorded.

5. Economic disappearance of non-produced assets (K.6)

12.28. The capital and financial accounts provide three ways in which an asset can leave the System: through consumption of fixed capital, through withdrawals and recurrent losses of inventories, and through extinguishing financial claims under the terms of the contractual agreements that created them. None of these apply to non-financial non-produced assets. The other changes in the volume of assets account records the departures of these assets in another way—economic disappearance. One form of economic disappearance is depletion. In table 12.1, entries for depletion of natural economic assets are shown on the left side of the accounts for non-financial corporations and general government, reflecting depletion of mineral reserves or other natural assets owned by non-financial corporations (-6) and by general government (-2). Economic disappearance can take other forms as well, for example, reductions in the level of proven reserves that reflect changes in technology and relative prices or degradation of land and wildlife from improper agricultural practices. In table 12.1, other economic disappearance of non-produced assets is illustrated by an entry of -1 on the left side of the account for non-financial corporations, reflecting such events as revisions in estimated proven reserves.

Depletion of natural economic assets (K.61)

12.29. The depletion of natural deposits covers the reduction in the value of deposits of subsoil assets as a result of the physical removal and using up of the assets.

12.30. In principle, the depletion of natural forests, fishstocks in the open seas and other non-cultivated biological resources included in the asset boundary as a result of harvesting, forest clearance, or other use should be included here, as should the depletion of water resources.

Other economic disappearance of non-produced assets (K.62)

Other reductions in the level of exploitable subsoil resources

12.31. The changes recorded here are the negative counterparts of gross additions to the level of exploitable subsoil resources that result from reassessments of exploitability because of changes in technology or relative prices. In practice, only net additions may be available, and these will be recorded under economic appearance of non-produced assets.

Quality change in non-produced assets due to changes in economic uses

12.32. The changes recorded here are, for example, decreases in the value of land that are the counterpart of the changes in land use—for example, from cultivated land to communal grazing land—recorded as changes in classification, as described below. This is symmetrical with the quality changes recorded under economic appearance of non-produced assets, as described above.

Degradation of non-produced assets due to economic activity

12.33. All degradation of land, water resources and other natural assets from economic activity is recorded in the other changes in the volume of assets account. The degradation may be either ordinary, recurring—and, therefore, anticipated—deterioration resulting from economic activity or less predictable erosion and other damage to land from deforestation or improper agricultural practices, the harmful effects on fishstocks of acid rain or excess nutrients from agricultural run-off, etc.

Write-off and cancellation of purchased goodwill, transferable contracts, etc., and exhaustion of patent protection

12.34. Just as the appearance of intangible non-produced assets is recorded in the other change in the volume of assets account, so is their write-off, termination, or exhaustion. For purchased goodwill, amortization should be recorded over a period of time after the purchase of an enterprise, following country accounting standards; the exhaustion of patent protection should be recorded over the duration of the patent.

6. Catastrophic losses (K.7)

12.35. Consumption of fixed capital, recorded in the capital account, is intended to cover normal accidental damage to the various categories of fixed assets, including cultivated assets. Changes in inventories include recurrent losses on goods held in inventory. Elsewhere in the other changes in the volume of assets account, depletion of non-produced natural assets covers normal rates of extraction, harvesting, etc., and degradation of non-produced assets covers damage due to economic activity. The volume changes recorded as catastrophic losses in the other changes in the volume of assets account, however, are the result of large scale, discrete, and recognizable events that may destroy assets within any of the categories of assets. Table 12.1 shows entries for catastrophic losses on the left side of the accounts for general government and non-financial corporations, reflecting damage resulting from a major earthquake, for example. These catastrophic losses are shown for produced assets—fixed assets (-4) and inventories (-1) — held by non-financial corporations (-5 in all), to fixed produced assets held by general government (-1), and to tangible non-produced assets, such as natural forests, held by general government (-2).

12.36. Such events will generally be easy to identify. They include major earthquakes, volcanic eruptions, tidal waves, exceptionally severe hurricanes, drought and other natural disasters; acts of war, riots and other political events; and technological accidents such as major toxic spills or release of radioactive particles into the air.

12.37. Included here are such major losses as deterioration in the quality of land caused by abnormal flooding or wind damage;

destruction of cultivated assets by drought or outbreaks of disease; destruction of buildings, equipment or valuables in forest fires or earthquakes; and the accidental destruction of currency or bearer securities as a result of natural catastrophe or political events.

7. Uncompensated seizures (K.8)

12.38. Governments or other institutional units may take possession of the assets of other institutional units, including non-resident units, without full compensation for reasons other than the payment of taxes, fines, or similar levies. The seizures of assets by governments or other institutional units may contravene national, or international, law. Such seizures are not capital transfers recorded in the capital account.

12.39. If the compensation falls substantially short of the market or related values of the assets as shown in the balance sheet, the difference should be recorded in the entry for uncompensated seizures of assets, as an increase in assets for the institutional unit doing the seizing and a decrease in assets for the institutional unit losing the asset. Table 12.1 illustrates the recording of such uncompensated seizures, when government seizes assets from corporations. The left side of the account for general government records increases in holdings of produced fixed assets (1), tangible non-produced assets (4) and securities other than shares (3). The left side of the account for non-financial corporations records decreases in holdings of produced fixed assets (-1) and tangible non-produced assets (-4), and the left side of the account for financial corporations records decreases in holdings of securities other than shares (-3).

12.40. It should be noted that foreclosures and repossessions of goods by creditors are not treated as uncompensated seizures. They are treated as transactions—disposals by debtors and acquisitions by creditors—because, explicitly or by general understanding, the agreement between debtor and creditor provided this avenue of recourse.

8. Other volume changes in non-financial assets n.e.c. (K.9)

12.41. The other changes in the volume of assets account also systematically records the effects of unexpected events on the economic benefits derivable from assets, especially the effect of events not anticipated when allowances were specified for the consumption of fixed capital—which reflects normal rates of physical deterioration, obsolescence and accidental damage—or for normal rates of inventory shrinkage. These events include untimely retirements of fixed assets because of unforseen obsolescence, fragility, etc., and exceptional losses in inventories. In practice it may be difficult to distinguish among the categories shown below.

12.42. Although most of the examples given above of items to be re-

corded here are decreases in assets, the illustration of other volume changes in non-financial assets n.e.c. given in table 12.1 is the entry of 1 on the left side of the account for non-financial corporations, which represents an increase in holdings of fixed assets. Such an increase could come about, for example, to restore to the System an asset that remains in productive use even though it has been fully written off through consumption of fixed capital, as explained in more detail in paragraph 12.48 below.

Unforeseen obsolescence

12.43. Consumption of fixed capital does not cover unforeseen obsolescence in these assets, and the amount included for their normally expected obsolescence may fall short of the actual obsolescence. Entries must, therefore, be made in the other changes in the volume of assets account for the decline in the value of the fixed assets—whether a complete or partial write-off—resulting from the introduction of improved technology. The improvement may take the form of improved models of the asset or of a new production process that no longer requires the asset.

Differences between allowances included in consumption of fixed capital for normal damage and actual losses

12.44. Consumption of fixed capital does not cover unforeseen damage, and the amount included for their normally expected damage may fall short of (or exceed) the actual damage. For the economy as a whole, this difference should normally be small; for individual units this difference is normally significant and may fluctuate in sign. Adjustments must therefore be made in the other changes in the volume of assets account for the decline (or increase) in the value of the fixed assets due to these events. These losses are larger than normal, but are not on a scale sufficiently large to be considered catastrophic.

Degradation of fixed assets not accounted for in consumption of fixed capital

12.45. Consumption of fixed capital does not cover unforeseen environmental degradation in these assets. Entries must, therefore, be made in the other changes in the volume of assets account for the decline in the value of the fixed assets from, for example, the effects of acidity in air and rain on building surfaces or vehicle bodies.

Abandonment of production facilities before completion or being brought into economic use

12.46. Production facilities with long construction periods may cease to have an economic rationale before they are complete or are put into service. For example, some nuclear power plants and industrial sites, especially in formerly centrally planned economies or developing countries, may never be put into service. When the decision to abandon is made, the value of the fixed asset (or in some case, work-in-progress inventories, as explained in chapter X), as recorded in the balance sheet should be written off in the other changes in the volume of assets account.

Exceptional losses in inventories

12.47. Exceptional losses from fire damage, from robberies, from insect infestation of grain stores, etc., should be recorded here. In this context, exceptional losses tend to be less regular and larger in value than the recurrent losses mentioned in the descriptions of inventory change in chapter X.

Other volume changes in non-financial assets, n.e.c.

12.48. Any changes in non-financial assets that are not transactions in the capital account, that should not be attributed to holding gains or losses, and that do not fall into one of the categories already enumerated above are to be recorded here. For example, assets may last longer than expected either economically or physically. An entry in the other changes in the volume of assets account permits the restoration to the System of an asset that has been fully written off but is still productive because its anticipated replacement never materialized or because it was much more durable than anticipated. Increases (or decreases) in value resulting from conversions of dwellings to commercial use (or vice versa) also are recorded here as counterparts to changes in classification.

9. Other volume changes in financial assets and liabilities n.e.c. (K.10)

12.49. Most financial assets—claims on other institutional units—are created when the debtor accepts the obligation to make a payment, or payments, to the creditor in the future; they are extinguished when the debtor has fulfilled the obligation under the terms of the agreement. Those assets for which not even a notional liability exists, however, cannot be created and extinguished in this way; hence, they enter and leave the System through the other changes in the volume of assets account. Also recorded here are the effects of events not anticipated when the terms of financial claims were set.

Allocations and cancellations of SDRs

12.50. Special Drawing Rights (SDRs) are international reserve assets created by the International Monetary Fund (IMF) and allocated to its members to supplement existing reserve assets. As explained in paragraph 11.67 of chapter XI, transactions in SDRs are recorded in the financial accounts of the monetary authorities and the rest of the world. However, a new allocation of SDRs by the IMF is recorded in the other changes in the volume of assets account, as is the cancellation of SDRs by the IMF. The first increases assets for the monetary authorities, the second decreases their assets. There is no IMF liability for these assets. The flows can be valued by reference to the value of SDRs as determined daily by the IMF on the basis of a basket of currencies. Table 12.1 shows on the left side of the

account for financial corporations an entry for other volume changes in financial assets and liabilities n.e.c. that increases holdings of monetary gold and SDRs by 5; there is no corresponding change in liabilities.

Writing-off bad debts by creditors

12.51. Recognition by a creditor that a financial claim can no longer be collected, due to bankruptcy or other factors, and the consequent removal of that claim from the balance sheet of the creditor should be accounted for here, along with removal of the liability of the debtor. Table 12.1 illustrates this type of other volume changes in financial assets and liabilities n.e.c. On the left side of the account for financial corporations there is an entry of -4 for loan assets, which is matched by an entry of -4 for loan liabilities on the right side of the account for non-financial corporations.

12.52. Cancellation of debt by mutual agreement between debtor and creditor is not included here; it is treated as a capital transfer from the creditor to the debtor in the capital account with a simultaneous extinction of a claim in the financial account, as explained in paragraph 11.23 of chapter XI.

Counterpart of "other accounts receivable/payable" for defined benefit pension funds

12.53. Defined benefit pension plans are those in which the level of pension benefits promised to participating employees is guaranteed. Benefits are related by some formula to participants' length of service and salary and are not totally dependent on the assets in the fund. For defined benefit plans, an entry in the other changes in the volume of assets account captures changes in the actuarially determined liability that result from changes in benefits structure, which are to be distinguished from changes in the age and service composition of the beneficiary pool. Examples of changes in benefit structure include changes in the formula, reductions in the pensionable age, or funding for an annual increase (usually defined as constant x per cent per year) in future pensions or in all pensions in the course of payment. Such a change is illustrated in table 12.1 by entries for other volume changes in financial assets and liabilities n.e.c. on the right side of the account for financial corporations, where liabilities in the form of insurance technical reserves increase by 2, and on the left side of the account for households, where assets in the form of insurance technical reserves also increase by 2.

Miscellaneous other volume changes in financial assets

12.54. Any changes in financial assets and liabilities that are not transactions in the financial account, that should not be attributed to holding gains or losses, that are not changes in classification and that do not fall into one of the enumerated categories above are to be recorded here.

10. Changes in classifications and structure (K.12)

12.55. The other changes in the volume of assets account records changes in assets and liabilities that reflect nothing more than changes in the classification of institutional units among sectors, changes in the structure of institutional units and changes in the classification of assets and liabilities.

Changes in sector classification and structure (K.12.1)

12.56. Reclassifying an institutional unit from one sector to another transfers its entire balance sheet. For example, if an unincorporated enterprise becomes more financially distinct from its owner and takes on the characteristics of a quasi-corporation, it and its balance sheet move from the household sector to the non-financial corporations sector; or if a financial corporation is newly authorized to take deposits, it may be reclassified from "other financial intermediaries" to "other depository corporations".

12.57. Table 12.1 shows an example of such a change in sector classification, for example, when an unincorporated government enterprise becomes a public non-financial quasi-corporation and moves from general government to non-financial corporations. The entries for changes in sector classification and structure are shown on the left side of the account for general government as decreases in holdings of produced fixed assets (-3), tangible non-produced assets (-1), and shares and other equity (-2); on the right side of the account for general government there is a decrease in loan liabilities (-1). Corresponding entries are shown on the left side of the account for non-financial corporations as increases in holdings produced fixed assets (3), tangible non-produced assets (1), and shares and other equity (2); on the right side of the account for non-financial corporations is an increase in loan liabilities (1).

12.58. Changes in structure are also recorded here. The financial account does not cover the disappearance or appearance of certain financial assets and liabilities because of corporate restructuring. When a corporation disappears as an independent legal entity—and thus as an institutional unit in the System—because it is absorbed by one or more other corporations, all claims/liabilities, including shares and other equity that existed between that corporation and those that absorbed it, are eliminated. The disappearance of these financial instruments is recorded under changes in sector classification and structure.

12.59. Symmetrically, when a corporation is legally split up into two or more institutional units, new claims and liabilities, including shares and other equity, may appear between the new institutional units. The appearance of these financial instruments is recorded in this category also.

Changes in classification of assets and liabilities (K.12.2)

12.60. The capital account and the financial account may record transactions in which an asset is classified differently from the category in which it was held in the opening balance sheet. This is the case when the purpose for which an asset is used changes, such as for example, non-monetary gold becoming monetary gold or pasture becoming building lots. The change in classification is recorded here with the same value for both entries—the value of the asset before its use changed. If the change in the use of a non-produced non-financial asset means a change in its value, this change in value is treated as a change in quality—i.e., a volume change—and recorded under economic appearance or economic disappearance of non-produced assets, as described above.

Monetization/demonetization of gold (K.12.21)

12.61. As explained in paragraph 11.65 of chapter XI, monetization and demonetization of gold are accomplished by entries for changes in the classification of gold held by the monetary authorities, as counterparts to entries in the capital account. In the capital account, the monetary authorities purchase gold from inventories or valuables held by institutional units or the rest of the world. Monetization occurs when the monetary authorities reclassify the gold from a produced asset to the reserve assets held by the monetary authorities. Similarly, demonetization occurs when the monetary authorities transfer gold from reserve assets to inventories or valuables, which are subsequently sold to institutional units or the rest of the world, with these transactions being recorded in the capital account. The flows can usually be valued by reference to the price on organized markets or in bilateral arrangements through central banks. Table 12.1 illustrates monetization of gold on the left side of the account for financial corporations, with a decrease in holdings of valuables (-2) and an increase holdings of monetary gold and SDRs (2) by financial corporations.

Changes in classification of assets or liabilities other than monetization/demonetization of gold (K.12.22)

12.62. Changes in land use for a particular parcel of land are recorded here, with the same absolute value used for both entries — a negative entry for the old category, a positive one for the new category. The change in land value resulting from this change in use — the counterpart flow — is recorded in economic appearance and disappearance of non-produced assets as a change in quality, which is considered a change in volume, as discussed above. An economic appearance records an increase in quality, and an economic disappearance records a decrease in quality. Other changes that might be recorded here are conversions of dwellings to commercial use or vice versa.

B. The revaluation account

1. Introduction

12.63. The revaluation account, shown in table 12.2, records the positive or negative holding gains accruing during the accounting period to the owners of financial and non-financial assets and liabilities. Holding gains on assets, whether positive or negative, are recorded on the left side of the account and those on liabilities on the right side. The revaluation account shows the nominal holding gains accruing on assets and liabilities. These are then decomposed into neutral holding gains and real holding gains, shown in two sub-accounts. The nominal holding gain on a given quantity of an asset is defined as the value of the benefit accruing to the owner of that asset as a result of a change in its price or, more generally, its monetary value over time. The value of the holding gain on a liability is equal to the change in the price, or monetary value, of that liability but with the sign reversed. A positive holding gain, whether due to an increase in the value of a given asset or a reduction in the value of a given liability, increases the net worth of the unit in question. Conversely, a negative holding gain—i.e., a holding loss—whether due to a reduction in the value of a given asset or an increase in the value of a given liability, reduces the net worth of the unit in question.

12.64. A neutral holding gain is defined as the value of the holding gain that would accrue *if* the price of the asset changed in the same proportion as the general price level—i.e, merely kept pace with the general rate of inflation or deflation. It is the value of the holding gain needed to preserve the real value of the asset in question intact over time. A real holding gain is defined as the value of the additional command over real resources accruing to the holding of an asset as a result of a change in its price relatively to the prices of goods and services in general in the economy. Nominal, neutral and real holding gains, and the interrelationships between them are explained more fully in the following sections.

12.65. The balancing item in the revaluation account is described as changes in net worth due to nominal holding gains/losses. It is defined as the algebraic sum of the positive or negative nominal holding gains on all the assets and liabilities of an institutional unit. As the revaluation account is decomposed into two separate accounts for neutral and real holding gains, its balancing item may similarly be decomposed into two further balancing items: changes in net worth due to neutral holding gains/losses and those due to real holding gains/losses. The latter shows how much of the change in the real net worth of an institutional unit is attributable to real holding gains. It is therefore an item of considerable analytic interest.

12.66. In order to simplify the terminology and exposition, holding losses will not usually be referred to explicitly unless the context requires it. The term "holding gains" is used to cover both holding gains and losses on the clear understanding that holding gains may be negative as well as positive. Similarly, the term "assets" may be used collectively to cover both assets and liabilities, unless the context requires liabilities to be referred to specifically.

12.67. Holding gains are sometimes described as "capital gains". The term "holding gain" is widely used in business accounting and is preferred here because it emphasizes the fact that holding gains accrue purely as a result of holding assets over time without transforming them in any way. Holding gains include not only gains on "capital" such as fixed assets, land and financial assets but also gains on inventories of all kinds of goods held by producers, including work-in-progress, often described as "stock appreciation".

Nominal holding gains (K.11)

12.68. Nominal holding gains depend upon changes in the prices or, more generally, the monetary values, of assets and liabilities over time. The relevant prices or values for assets that are exchanged in transactions between institutional units are those recorded in the accumulation accounts of the System. In order to be consistent with the accumulation accounts, assets in the opening and closing balance sheets are valued at their acquisition values at the times the balance sheets are drawn up: i.e., including the costs of ownership transfer that would be incurred by the purchaser in the case of non-financial assets. These are the values at which assets enter the balance sheets of their owners. In the case of non-transferable financial assets and liabilities such as loans, the monetary value is the amount of principal outstanding. Not all assets and liabilities have market prices in the ordinary sense of the term "price". In particular, assets and liabilities denominated in purely monetary terms—such as cash and deposits—do not have physical units with which prices can be associated. In such cases, the relevant "quantity" unit is effectively a unit of currency itself—e.g., one dollar—so that the price per unit is always unity. By definition, therefore, the market prices of such assets and their corresponding liabilities cannot change over time. On the other hand, the relevant quantity unit for an asset such as a bill, bond or share is the security itself, the market price of which may change over time. The term "price" has therefore to be used in a broad sense to cover the unitary prices of assets such as cash, deposits, loans, etc., and the corresponding liabilities as well as conventional market prices.

12.69. Nominal holding gains may accrue on assets held for any length of time during the accounting period and not merely on assets that appear in the opening or closing balance sheets. Nominal holding gains may refer to any period of time and must be defined accordingly. The nominal holding gain accruing to the owner of a particular asset, or given quantity of a specific type of asset, between two points of time is defined as:

Table 12.2.   Account III.3.2: Revaluation account

Changes in assets

Accounts	Total	Corresponding entries of the Goods and service account	Rest of the world account	S.1 Total economy	S.15 NPISHs	S.14 House-holds	S.13 General government	S.12 Financial corporations	S.11 Non-financial corporations	Other flows and balancing items	
III.3.2.										K.11	Nominal holding gains / losses [1][2]
Revaluation account	280			280	8	80	44	4	144	AN	Non-financial assets
	126			126	5	35	20	2	63	AN.1	Produced assets
	111			111	5	28	18	2	58	AN.11	Fixed assets
	7			7		2	1		4	AN.12	Inventories
	8			8		5	1		1	AN.13	Valuables
	154			154	3	45	23	2	81	AN.2	Non-produced assets
	152			152	3	45	23	1	80	AN.21	Tangible non-produced assets
	2			2					1	AN.22	Intangible non-produced assets
	91		7	84	1	16	2	57	8	AF	Financial assets/liabilities
	12			12			1	11		AF.1	Monetary gold and SDRs
										AF.2	Currency and deposits
	44		4	40	1	6		30	3	AF.3	Securities other than shares
										AF.4	Loans
	34		3	31	1	10		16	5	AF.5	Shares and other equity
										AF.6	Insurance technical reserves
										AF.7	Other accounts receivable/payable
										B.10.3	*Changes in net worth due to nominal holding gains/losses*
III.3.2.1.										K.11.1	Neutral holding gains / losses [1][2]
Neutral holding gains account	198			198	6	56	32	3	101	AN	Non-financial assets
	121			121	5	34	20	2	60	AN.1	Produced assets
	111			111	5	28	18	2	58	AN.11	Fixed assets
	5			5		2	1		2	AN.12	Inventories
	5			5		4	1		1	AN.13	Valuables
	78			78	2	22	12	1	41	AN.2	Non-produced assets
	76			76	2	22	12	1	40	AN.21	Tangible non-produced assets
	1			1					1	AN.22	Intangible non-produced assets
	147		11	136	3	36	8	70	18	AF	Financial assets/liabilities
	15			15			2	14		AF.1	Monetary gold and SDRs
	32		2	30	2	17	3		8	AF.2	Currency and deposits
	28		3	25	1	4		19	2	AF.3	Securities other than shares
	29		1	28			2	24	1	AF.4	Loans
	28		2	26		8		13	4	AF.5	Shares and other equity
	8		1	7		6		1	1	AF.6	Insurance technical reserves
	7		3	5		1			3	AF.7	Other accounts receivable/payable
										B.10.31	*Changes in net worth due to neutral holding gains/losses*
III.3.2.2.										K.11.2	Real holding gains / losses [1][2]
Real holding gains account	81			81	2	24	12	1	43	AN	Non-financial assets
	5			5					3	AN.1	Produced assets
										AN.11	Fixed assets
	3			3					3	AN.12	Inventories
	2			2		1				AN.13	Valuables
	77			77	2	22	12	1	40	AN.2	Non-produced assets
	76			76	2	22	12	1	40	AN.21	Tangible non-produced assets
	1			1						AN.22	Intangible non-produced assets
	− 57		− 5	− 52	− 2	− 20	− 6	− 13	− 10	AF	Financial assets/liabilities
	− 3			− 3				− 3		AF.1	Monetary gold and SDRs
	− 32		− 2	− 30	− 2	− 17	− 3		− 8	AF.2	Currency and deposits
	17		1	15		2		11	1	AF.3	Securities other than shares
	− 29		− 1	− 28			− 2	− 24	− 1	AF.4	Loans
	6			5		2		3	1	AF.5	Shares and other equity
	− 8		− 1	− 7		− 6		− 1	− 1	AF.6	Insurance technical reserves
	− 7		− 3	− 5		− 1			− 3	AF.7	Other accounts receivable/payable
										B.10.32	*Changes in net worth due to real holding gains/losses*

1 Differences between data on individual items and totals of holding gains/losses may not be entirely consistent due to rounding errors.
2 Holding gains/losses, when:
   (+) and applied to assets, are gains

(−) and applied to assets, are losses
(+) and applied to liabilities, are losses
(−) and applied to liabilities, are gains.

Changes in liabilities and net worth

S.11 Non-finan-cial corpo-rations	S.12 Finan-cial corpo-rations	S.13 General govern-ment	S.14 House-holds	S.15 NPISHs	S.1 Total eco-nomy	Corresponding entries of the		Total	Accounts
						Rest of the world account	Goods and service account		
									III.3.2. Revaluation account
18	51	7			76	3		78	
1	34	7			42	2		44	
16	17				34			34	
134	10	38	96	10	288	4		292	
									III.3.2.1. Neutral holding gains account
36	68	14	6	2	126	6		132	
1	26	2		1	29	2		32	
1	21	4			26	2		28	
18		7	3	1	29			29	
14	14				28			28	
	7				7	1		8	
3			2	1	6	1		7	
82	5	26	87	8	208	6		214	
									III.3.2.2. Real holding gains account
− 18	− 17	− 7	− 6	− 2	− 50	− 3		− 54	
− 1	− 26	− 2		− 1	− 29	− 2		− 32	
1	13	3			16	1		17	
− 18		− 7	− 3	− 1	− 29			− 29	
3	3				6			6	
	− 7				− 7	− 1		− 8	
− 3			− 2	− 1	− 6	− 1		− 7	
51	5	12	9	2	80	− 1		78	

the monetary value of that asset at the later point in time

minus

the monetary value of that asset at the earlier point in time

assuming that the asset itself does not change, qualitatively or quantitatively, in the meanwhile. The nominal holding gain G accruing on a given quantity q of some asset between times o and t can be simply expressed as follows:

$$G = (p_t - p_o) q \tag{1}$$

where p_o and p_t are the prices of the asset at times o and t respectively. For monetary assets and liabilities for which both p_o and p_t are unity by definition, nominal holding gains are always zero. However, the neutral holding gains on monetary assets and liabilities are not zero when the general price level is changing, in which case the real holding gains are also not zero.

12.70. Nominal holding gains are calculated with reference to assets or liabilities that themselves remain qualitatively and quantitatively unchanged during the period over which the holding gain is measured. Thus, changes in the value of physical assets such as structures, equipment or inventories held by producers that are attributable to some physical or economic transformation of those assets over time, whether improvement or deterioration, are not counted as holding gains. In particular, the decline in the value of the fixed assets owned by producers due to their physical deterioration or normal rates of obsolescence or accidental damage is recorded as consumption of fixed capital and not as a negative holding gain. Similarly, as explained in chapter VI, paragraphs 6.64 and 6.65, when the storage of goods whose supply or demand is subject to seasonal influences is essentially an extension of the process of production, the increase in the value of the goods that is due to this production is not to be counted as a nominal holding gain.

12.71. The characteristics of financial assets and liabilities may also change over time, in particular the proximity to maturity of securities with fixed redemption dates. For example, most or all of the increase in the market value of a bill or a bond issued at a discount as it approaches its redemption date may be attributable to the accumulation of unpaid interest accruing to its holder. The increase in the market value of a bill or bond due to the accumulation of accrued interest in this way represents a growth in the asset itself and is not a price increase. It does not generate a holding gain.

12.72. The nominal holding gains recorded in the revaluation account are those accruing on assets or liabilities, whether realized or not. A holding gain is said to be realized when the asset in question is sold, redeemed, used or otherwise disposed of, or the liability repaid. An unrealized gain is therefore one accruing on an asset that is still owned or a liability that is still outstanding at the end of the accounting period. A realized gain is usually understood as the gain realized over the entire period over which the asset is owned or liability outstanding

whether this period coincides with the accounting period or not. However, as holding gains are recorded on an accruals basis in the System, the distinction between realized and unrealized gains, although useful for some purposes, is not so important in the System and does not appear in the classifications and accounts.

12.73. For purposes of calculating nominal holding gains, acquisitions and disposals of assets must be valued in the same way as in the capital and financial accounts in order to ensure consistency within the System as a whole. In the case of fixed assets, therefore, the value of an acquisition is the amount paid by the purchaser to the producer, or seller, plus the associated costs of ownership transfer incurred by the purchaser, while the value at which the disposal of an existing fixed asset is recorded is the amount received by the seller from the purchaser minus the costs of ownership transfer incurred by the seller. It is useful to distinguish four different situations giving rise to nominal gains and the methods of valuation to be employed in each case:

(a) An asset held throughout the accounting period: the nominal holding gain accruing during the accounting period is equal to the closing balance sheet value minus the opening balance sheet value. These values are the estimated values of the assets if they were to be acquired at the times the balance sheets are drawn up. The nominal gain is unrealized;

(b) An asset held at the beginning of the period that is sold during the period: the nominal holding gain accruing is equal to the actual or estimated disposal value minus the opening balance sheet value. The nominal gain is realized;

(c) An asset acquired during the period and still held at the end of the period: the nominal holding gain accruing is equal to the closing balance sheet value minus the actual, or estimated, acquisition value of the asset. The nominal gain is unrealized;

(d) An asset acquired and disposed of during the accounting period: the nominal holding gain accruing is equal to the actual, or estimated, disposal value minus the actual, or estimated, acquisition value. The nominal gain is realized.

As already noted in chapter X, it follows that if an non-financial asset is purchased and subsequently resold at the same price, excluding costs of ownership transfer, the unit involved incurs a nominal holding loss equal to the value of the costs of ownership transfer incurred on both the initial purchase and subsequent resale of the asset.

Neutral holding gains (K.11.1)

12.74. Nominal holding gains are partitioned into neutral holding gains and real holding gains. Neutral holding gains can be regarded as analytical constructs designed to facilitate the derivation of real holding gains. A neutral holding gain is defined as the value of the holding gain that would accrue if the price of the asset changed over time in the same proportion as the general price level. If the price of the asset changes by the same proportion as other prices, on average, its real value—i.e., the volume of other goods and services for which it can be exchanged—is neither increased nor decreased, whatever the general rate of inflation. In other words, a neutral holding gain is the value of the nominal holding gain needed to preserve the real value of the asset intact.

12.75. In order to calculate the neutral holding gain on an asset, it would be desirable to select a comprehensive price index covering as wide a range of goods, services and assets as possible. In practice, the price index for final expenditures would be an acceptable choice for most countries, although other comprehensive indices could be used depending upon the availability of data. A comprehensive index of this kind, however, may be available only once a year, or at best quarterly, and after a significant lapse of time. As holding gains may accrue on assets held for only short periods of time, it may also be necessary to make use of an index that measures changes in prices monthly and which becomes available without too much delay. The consumer price index (CPI) usually meets these requirements and an acceptable procedure would be to use the CPI to interpolate and extrapolate movements in a more broadly based index in order to calculate neutral holding gains.

12.76. Let the general price index be denoted by r. The neutral holding gain NG on a given quantity q of an asset between times o and t is then given by the following expression:

$$NG = p_o q \ (r_t/r_o - 1) \qquad (2)$$

where $(p_o q)$ is the monetary value of the asset at time o. The same term r_t/r_o is applied to all assets and liabilities. Thus, the proportionate movements in neutral holding gains are the same for all assets and liabilities, both financial and non-financial.

Real holding gains (K.11.2)

12.77. The real holding gain on an asset can be expressed as the difference between the nominal and the neutral holding gain on that asset. Subtracting expression (2) from (1) above, the real holding gain RG on a given quantity q of an asset between times o and t is given by

$$RG = G - NG$$

$$= (p_t/p_o - r_t/r_o)p_o q \qquad (3)$$

The values of the real holding gains on assets thus depend on the movements of their prices over the period in question, relatively to movements of other prices, on average, as measured by the general price index. An increase in the relative price of an asset leads to a positive real holding gain and a decrease in the relative price of an asset leads to a negative real gain,

whether the general price level, as measured by r, is rising, falling or stationary.

12.78. When the relative price of an asset rises over a given period of time, the asset can be exchanged for a greater volume of the goods, services and assets covered by the general price index at the end of the period than at the beginning. The holding gain is described as "real" because it measures the value of the additional (positive or negative) goods, services and assets that may be acquired by the owner of the asset by disposing of it at the end of the period instead of at the beginning.

12.79. As already noted, the nominal holding gains on financial assets and liabilities whose values are fixed in monetary terms are always zero. During inflation, the neutral gains on such assets and liabilities must be positive, and hence the real holding gains must be negative and equal in absolute value to the neutral gains. In other words, the real value of an asset/liability of fixed monetary value declines both for the creditor and the debtor as a result of inflation. Of course, from the point of view of the debtor a reduction in the real value of a liability represents an increase in real net worth. In effect, there is implicit transfer of real purchasing power from the creditor to the debtor equal in value to the negative real holding gain on the asset/liability. When such transfers are anticipated by creditors, correspondingly higher nominal rates of interest may be demanded on loans to compensate for the expected transfers or loans with fixed monetary values may be replaced by indexed loans.

12.80. As changes in relative prices may be either positive or negative, the owners of some assets benefit from real holding gains while the owners of other assets experience real holding losses. It cannot be assumed that such real gains and losses cancel each other out, even in a closed economy, as it is possible that asset owners benefit at the expense of units that do not own any or vice versa. Whether or not they cancel out, it is clear that real holding gains may lead to a significant redistribution of real net worth among institutional units, sectors and even countries, the extent of which depends on the amount of variation in the relative price changes taking place. While such variation may occur even when there is no general inflation, there are systematic effects that are associated with the general rate of inflation as a result of the decline in the real values of monetary assets and liabilities when the general price level is rising.

12.81. As real holding gains increase or decrease the purchasing power of the owners of assets, they must exert an influence on their economic behaviour. Real holding gains are important economic variables in their own right that need to be taken into account as well as income for purposes of analysing consumption or capital formation. It can be argued that real holding gains ought to be assimilated with income as defined in the System to obtain a more comprehensive measure of income, but there is no consensus on this. Apart from the practical difficulty of estimating real holding gains and losses, it is likely that their impact on economic behaviour is not the same as that of income received in cash or in kind. Nevertheless, it is clear that information on real holding gains needs to be made available to users, analysts and policy makers.

2. The measurement of holding gains

12.82. In order to obtain precise definitions of holding gains over periods of time during which the quantities of assets held may be varying from day to day, it is necessary to utilize algebraic expressions involving prices and quantities similar to those used to define index numbers. In order to simplify the main text, the derivation of the algebraic expressions that define nominal, neutral and real holding gains is given in an annex to this chapter. The main conclusions of the annex are summarized in this section.

Nominal holding gains

12.83. As explained above, the total nominal holding gains accruing on a particular category of asset over a given period of time include those accruing on assets acquired or disposed of during the accounting period as well as on assets that figure in the opening or closing balance sheets. It follows that it is not possible to calculate total holding gains from balance sheet data on their own, except in certain special cases or on certain assumptions. In order to calculate total holding gains directly, therefore, it is necessary to keep records of all the assets acquired and disposed during the accounting period and the prices at which they were acquired and disposed of, as well as the price and quantities of assets held at the beginning and end of the period. In practice, however, the requisite data are unlikely to be available, although the increasing use of microcomputers for both management and accounting purposes by businesses may make the direct calculation of total nominal holding gains using the kinds of formulas given in the annex increasingly feasible.

12.84. However, if records are kept of the values of all transactions and other volume changes in assets, without necessarily recording the prices at which those transactions or changes occur, it is shown in the annex that the value of the total nominal gains may be derived residually by subtracting the total value of all transactions and other volume changes from the difference between the values of the asset recorded in the closing and opening balance sheets. This indirect method of calculating total nominal holding gains is only valid when appropriate valuation methods are used both for balance sheets and for transactions and other changes. Quantities of the asset held at the beginning and end of the period must be valued in the opening and closing balance sheets at the prices that would have to be paid to acquire them at the times to which the balance sheets relate, and all actual or imputed transactions or other volume changes must be valued at the prices prevailing at the times they take place.

12.85. The basic identity linking balance sheets, transactions, other

volume changes and nominal holding gains may be expressed as follows:

> the value of the stock of the asset in the opening balance sheet

plus

> the value of quantities of the asset acquired, or disposed of, in transactions

plus

> the value of other volume changes in the asset

plus

> the value of the nominal holding gains on the asset

equals

> the value of the stock of the asset in the closing balance sheet.

The identity follows from the ways in which the various items are defined and valued. Each of the five elements that make up the identity can be calculated directly and independently of the other four elements. Thus, each element has the same status, none of them being defined residually as a balancing item. The identity is similar in this respect to the identity between the values of the total supplies and total uses of some good or service.

12.86. Nevertheless, it follows that if any four out of the five elements are calculated directly, the fifth can be estimated residually. For this reason, the identity can be exploited to estimate nominal holding gains from the other four elements, but without this implying that nominal holding gains are a balancing item in the System.

12.87. There may be situations in which the only information available about certain kinds of assets consists of their values in the opening and closing balance sheets. This may happen in the case of certain financial assets, for example, or inventories. It can be seen from the above identity that it is not possible to infer from balance sheet data alone either the total value of the transactions and other volume changes taking place within the accounting or the total value of the holding gains, but only their combined value. However, in certain special cases it may be possible to isolate one or the other. For example, if the price of the asset remains constant throughout the accounting period, the difference between the opening and closing balance sheet values must be entirely attributable to transactions and other volume changes. This condition is satisfied for monetary assets, for example, but not for financial assets such as bills or bonds whose market prices may change during the accounting period. Similarly, it is not possible to infer the value of changes in inventories from balance sheet data alone unless the price of the good in question happens to remain constant throughout the period. In general, goods entering or leaving inventories must be valued at the prices prevailing at the times the changes occur as if they were actually being bought or sold on the market.

12.88. Nominal holding gains may accrue on an asset that does not appear in either the opening or closing balance sheet if there have been transactions or other changes in the asset during the accounting period. Suppose a financial asset, such as a share, is purchased speculatively and sold again within the same accounting period. If the sale price is not equal to the purchase price, neither the total value of the transactions nor nominal holding gains can be zero. Indeed, the nominal holding gain must be equal to the total value of the transactions (the sale less purchase) but with the opposite sign. Unless the nominal holding gain is recorded, the value of the transactions cannot be reconciled with the zero values in the balance sheets. Another example is provided by producers who build up inventories and run them down again, all within a single accounting period. If the price of the good rises while held in inventory, the value of the withdrawals exceeds that of the entries, so that the total value of the changes in inventories is negative. The value of the nominal holding gains is equal to the value of the change in inventories, but with the opposite sign.

Neutral holding gains

12.89. Neutral holding gains have to be subtracted from nominal holding gains to obtain real holding gains. As already explained, the neutral holding gain on an asset over a given period of time is equal to the value of the asset at the beginning of the period multiplied by the proportionate change in some comprehensive price index selected to measure the change in the general price level. Neutral holding gains can therefore easily be calculated for assets held throughout the accounting period that appear in both the opening and closing balance sheets. It is more difficult, however, to keep track of the neutral holding gains on assets that are acquired or disposed of during the accounting period as it is necessary to know the times at which the various acquisitions and disposals took place—information that is unlikely to be available in practice. For this reason it will usually be difficult, and sometimes impossible, to obtain accurate, precise estimates of neutral, and hence real, holding gains.

12.90. A possible method of estimation suggested in the annex to this chapter is to use the same information, and a similar methodology, as that used to calculate nominal holding gains. The method of estimating neutral holding gains has three steps:

(a) The closing balance sheet value is revalued to what it would have been if the price of the asset had changed at the same rate as the general price index over the period;

(b) The total value of the transactions and other volume changes is revalued to eliminate the effect of any change in the relative price of the asset during the period;

(c) The adjusted value for total transactions and other volume changes is subtracted from the difference between the adjusted closing balance sheet value and the opening balance sheet value.

12.91. It is worth noting that there is no simple method that can be used in all circumstances to divide, or partition, the absolute values of nominal holding gains into neutral and real holding gains given that holding gains—whether nominal, neutral or real—can be negative as well as positive. For example, the nominal holding gains on monetary assets are zero, but there can nevertheless be substantial positive neutral gains and negative real gains, depending upon the general rate of inflation.

Real holding gains

12.92. As real holding gains may be obtained residually by subtracting neutral from nominal holding gains, the feasibility of calculating real holding gains depends on the feasibility of calculating neutral and nominal gains. There is nothing further to add so far as their estimation is concerned.

3. Estimates of holding gains from balance sheet data

12.93. As noted above, there may be situations in which the only information available about certain kinds of assets consists of balance sheet data. This situation is quite common in the case of inventories, for example, or certain types of financial assets. It should be noted that in the case of inventories, estimates of both the transactions and the nominal holding gains have to be made in order to be able to compile the production account and hence other accounts of the System.

12.94. Although it is not possible to obtain reliable, accurate estimates of transactions and holding gains from balance sheet data alone, it becomes possible to deduce the values of both the transactions and other changes and the nominal holding gains if assumptions are made about the paths followed by both the prices and the quantities of an asset between the beginning and the end of the accounting period.

12.95. The simplest and most convenient assumptions to make are that both the prices and quantities of the asset change at constant linear rates between the beginning and end of the accounting period; i.e., that the sequences of prices and quantities linking the opening and closing levels are simple arithmetic progressions. Given these assumptions it is easy to show that:

$$\text{the value of the transactions and other volume changes} = \bar{p}(q_n - q_o) \qquad (4)$$

$$\text{the value of the nominal holding gains} = \bar{q}(p_n - p_o) \qquad (5)$$

$$\text{where} \quad \bar{p} = \tfrac{1}{2}(p_o + p_n)$$

$$\text{and} \quad \bar{q} = \tfrac{1}{2}(q_o + q_n)$$

12.96. It is also easily verified that (4) and (5) sum identically to equal the value of the difference between the values recorded in closing and opening balance sheets, $(p_n q_n - p_o q_o)$. If $q_n/q_o > p_n/p_o$, the value of the transactions given by (4) exceeds the value of the holding gains given by (5). If the two ratios are equal, the difference between the values of the opening and closing stocks is divided equally between transactions and holding gains. Equation (4) is often used to estimate the value of changes in inventories, although it is equally applicable to other assets, including financial assets.

12.97. The nominal holding gains given by (5) may be further decomposed into neutral and real holding gains, given the additional information on the change in the general price index over the accounting period. Let r_n equal the value of the general price index on day n based on $r_o = 1$. It can easily be shown that:

the value of the neutral holding
gains $\qquad = (r_n - 1)p_o \bar{q}$ (6)

the value of the real holding
gains $\qquad = (p_n/p_o - r_n)p_o \bar{q}$ (7)

The real holding gains are, of course, zero if the change in the price of the asset p_n/p_o is equal to the change in the general price index r_n.

12.98. The quality of the approximate measures given in expressions (4) and (5) depends on the realism of the underlying assumptions about the movements of prices and quantities. While the assumption that the price of the asset increases at a constant rate during the accounting period may be not unreasonable, the assumption that the quantity of the asset changes at a constant rate may be questionable in many cases. In particular, if there are fluctuations in the quantity of the asset held, estimates based on expressions (4) to (7) may diverge significantly from the true figures. Fluctuations in inventories are likely to occur in industries in which the supply or the demand for the product is subject to strong seasonal influences. The use of expressions (4) to (7) may give poor estimates in such situations.

12.99. Expressions (4) and (5), which differ only in so far as the p's and q's are interchanged, display clearly the duality between the values of transactions and other changes in assets and the values of the nominal holding gains on those assets. Approximate estimates of this kind may also serve as a useful check on the value of nominal holding gains derived residually from data on transactions and other changes and the difference between the closing and opening balance sheet values. In many situations, there may be no good reason for expecting the approximate measure of the value of nominal holding gains given by (5) to diverge markedly from the true measure. In such cases, a major discrepancy between a measure of nominal holding gains obtained residually from transactions and balance sheet data and the approximate measure may bring into question the reliability and consistency of the entire data set, including the transactions data, and signal the need for revisions.

4. Holding gains by type of asset

12.100. This section examines the ways in which holding gains may be measured for different types of assets.

Non-financial assets

Fixed assets

12.101. Nominal holding gains on fixed assets may be obtained by subtracting the total value of transactions, including consumption of fixed capital, and other volume changes from the difference between values of the assets recorded in the closing and opening balance sheets. For this purpose, the stocks of assets recorded in the balance sheets must be measured net of the accumulated consumption of fixed capital and must be valued at the purchasers' prices prevailing on the date to which the balance sheet relates.

12.102. In this context, it is convenient to make use of the concept of net fixed capital formation even though this aggregate is not shown explicitly in the accounts of the System. Net fixed capital formation is defined as:

gross fixed capital formation

minus

consumption of fixed capital.

The basic identity linking transactions, other volume changes, nominal holding gains and balance sheet values is then written as follows for fixed assets:

(*a*) The value of the net stock of the fixed asset at the beginning of the period;

plus

(*b*) The value of net fixed capital formation in the asset (i.e., the net value of all transactions);

plus

(*c*) The value of other volume changes in the asset;

plus

(*d*) The value of nominal holding gains on the asset;

equals

(*e*) The value of the net stock of the fixed asset at the end of the period.

It is worth noting that, even in the absence of other volume changes, the difference between the net (or gross) values of the opening and closing stock of an asset valued at current prices is not equal to net (or gross) fixed capital formation at current prices, unless the price of the asset remains constant throughout the period. Apart from any other volume changes, the difference between the net values of the opening and closing stocks of fixed assets, valued at the beginning and end of period prices, respectively, must include nominal holding gains as well as net fixed capital formation. Such gains could be relatively large when the price of the asset is rising strongly within the period. In effect, the transactions taking place within the period are valued at the average prices of the period, which may be expected to lie between the opening and closing prices. For this reason, it is important to base the calculation of the consumption of fixed capital on the average prices of the period, as recommended in chapter VI, and not on the opening and closing prices.

12.103. Nominal holding gains may occur on existing fixed assets either because of general inflation or because the relative price of the asset changes over time. When assets of the same kind are still being produced and sold on the market, an existing asset should be valued in the opening or closing balance sheet at the current purchasers' price of a newly produced asset less the accumulated consumption of fixed capital up to that time also calculated on the basis of the prices prevailing at the time the balance sheet is drawn up. Changes in the prices of new assets between the beginning and end of the accounting period will, therefore, lead to nominal holding gains on existing assets of the same type. When new assets of the same type are no longer being produced, the valuation of existing assets may pose difficult conceptual and practical problems. If broadly similar kinds of assets are still being produced, even though their characteristics may differ significantly from those of existing assets (for example, new models of vehicles or aircraft), it may be reasonable to assume that, if the existing assets were still being produced, their prices would have moved in the same way as those of new assets. However, such an assumption becomes questionable when the characteristics of new assets are much improved by technical progress.

Inventories

12.104. The estimation of nominal holding gains on inventories may be difficult because of lack of data on transactions or other volume changes in inventories. As explained in chapter VI, transactions in inventories may not be adequately recorded because they are internal transactions. Goods entering inventories can be regarded as being acquired by the owner of an enterprise from itself as producer, while goods leaving inventories can be regarded as being disposed of by the owner to the producer for use in production or for sale. These internal transactions should be valued at the prices prevailing at the times they take place in the same way as transactions in any other kind of asset. When the transactions are properly valued in this way, nominal holding gains on inventories are given as follows:

(*a*)   The value of the closing inventories at end-of-the-period prices;

minus

(*b*)   The value of the opening inventories at beginning-of-the-period prices;

minus

(*c*)   The value of entries minus the value of withdrawals and recurrent losses, valued at the prices prevailing at the times the entries and withdrawals take place;

minus

(*d*)   The value of other volume changes.

Other volume changes are likely to consist of inventories of goods destroyed as a result of exceptional events such as natural disasters (floods, earthquakes, etc.) or major fires. Current losses of goods from inventories—for example, losses due to regular wastage or pilfering—are grouped with withdrawals. Both exceptional and current losses on inventories obviously reduce the magnitude of any nominal holding gains on inventories.

12.105. Unless records are kept of the quantities of goods entering and leaving inventories and their prices at those times, it is not possible to measure the value of changes in inventories directly. As such records may not be available, it becomes necessary to try to deduce the value of changes in inventories from the value and quantities of the opening and closing inventories using methods such as those illustrated in equations (4) and (5) above that attempt to partition the difference between the values of the opening and closing stocks of assets into transactions and nominal holding gains. Such methods are only as good as the assumptions on which they are based. The difficulty of estimating the value of changes in inventories from balance sheet data alone obviously increases as the rate of inflation increases. It should also be noted that this is not only a problem for the accumulation accounts as the values of changes in inventories of inputs and outputs are needed in order to measure intermediate consumption, output and value added and hence all the balancing items of the System.

12.106. Work-in-progress is a stock of outputs that are not yet in a form in which they are ready for sale, use or transfer to other institutional units. Additions to work-in-progress are recorded as they occur and valued at the prices at those times. The prices are estimated by multiplying the actual or estimated basic price of the finished product at the time the addition to the work-in-progress takes place by the fraction of the total production costs incurred in producing the addition. Work-in-progress carried forward from the previous period is valued in the opening balance sheet using the price of the finished product at the date to which the balance sheet relates. Similarly, the total amount of work-in-progress recorded in the closing balance sheet is valued using the price of the finished product at the end of the period. Withdrawals from work-in-progress take place when the production is completed, the total work-in-progress completed during the entire production process being then transformed into a finished product. Nominal holding gains on work-in-progress may then be obtained residually by subtracting the value of the additions minus withdrawals from work-in-progress during the period from the difference between the opening and closing balance sheet values. Because some production processes may take years to complete, the whole of the output from some production process during a given period may be entered into inventories as additions to work-in-progress. Even when there is only modest inflation there may be substantial nominal holding gains on the work-in-progress.

Financial assets

Assets and liabilities with fixed monetary values

12.107. The monetary values of some assets and liabilities—cash, deposits, loans, advances, credits, etc.—remain constant over time. As already noted, the "price" of such an asset is always unity while the quantity is given by the number of units of the currency in which they are denominated. The nominal holding gains on such assets are always zero. For this reason the difference between the values of the opening and closing stocks of such assets is entirely accounted for by the values of the transactions in the assets, this being one case in which it is possible to deduce the latter from the balance sheet figures.

12.108. In order to calculate the neutral and real holding gains on assets of fixed monetary value, however, data on the times and values of transactions are needed as well as the opening and closing balance sheet values. In principle, the exact expression for neutral holding gains given in the annex to this chapter should be used. Suppose, for example, a loan is made and repaid within the accounting period while the general price level is rising. The neutral gain on the loan is positive and the real gain negative, the amount depending upon the length of time the loan is outstanding and the rate of inflation. It is impossible to record such real losses without data on the value of the loans made and repaid during the accounting period and the times at which they are made and repaid. In general, it may be inferred that if the total absolute value of the positive and negative transactions is large in relation to the opening and closing balance sheet levels, approximate estimates of the neutral and real holding gains on monetary assets and liabilities derived from balance sheet data alone may not be very satisfactory. Even recording the values of financial transactions on a gross basis—i.e., recording loans made and repaid separately as distinct from the total value of loans minus repayments—may not be sufficient without information on the timing of the loans.

Bonds

12.109. A bond is a security that gives the holder the unconditional right to a fixed money income or contractually determined variable money income over a specified period of time and also the right to a fixed sum as repayment of principal on a specified date or dates, except in the case of perpetual bonds. Bonds are usually traded on markets and the holder of a bond may change several times during the life of the bond. The issuer of such a bond may, therefore, repay the principal outstanding at any time by purchasing it back in advance of the date on which it matures.

12.110. As explained in chapter VII, when bonds are issued at a discount, including deep discounted and zero coupon bonds, the difference between its issue price and its face or redemption value when it matures measures interest that the issuer is obliged to pay over the life of the bond. Such interest is recorded as property income payable by the issuer of the bond and receivable by the holder of the bond in addition to any coupon interest actually paid by the issuer at specified intervals over the life of the bond. In principle, the interest accruing is treated as being simultaneously reinvested in the bond by the holder of the bond. It is, therefore, recorded in the financial account as the acquisition of an asset which is added to the existing asset. Thus the gradual increase in the market price of a bond that is attributable to the accumulation of accrued, reinvested interest reflects a growth in the principal outstanding—i.e., in the size of the asset. It is essentially a quantum or volume increase and not a price increase. It does not generate any holding gain for the holder of the bond or holding loss for the issuer of the bond. The situation is analogous to that of a good, such as wine, that matures while it is being stored. Any increase in the price of the wine that is attributable to an improvement in its quality reflects an increase in volume and not price. Bonds change qualitatively over time as they approach maturity and it is essential to recognize that increases in their values due to the accumulation of accrued interest are not price changes and do not generate holding gains.

12.111. The prices of marketable bonds also change, however, when the market rates of interest change, the prices varying inversely with the interest rate movements. The impact of a given interest rate change on the price of an individual bond is less, the closer the bond is to maturity. Changes in bond prices that are attributable to changes in market rates of interest constitute price and not quantum changes. They therefore generate nominal holding gains or losses for both the issuers and the holders of the bonds. An increase in interest rates generates a nominal holding gain for the issuer of the bond and an equal nominal holding loss for the holder of the bond, and vice versa in the case of fall in interest rates.

12.112. Nominal holding gains or losses may accrue on bills in the same way as for bonds. However, as bills are short-term securities with much shorter times to maturity, the holding gains generated by interest rate changes are generally much smaller than on bonds with the same face values.

5. Foreign assets

12.113. Foreign assets consist mainly of financial claims over non-resident institutional units. All immovable assets such as land and buildings within an economic territory are treated in the System as owned by resident units, including those legally owned by foreigners. When foreigners own land or buildings, their ownership is deemed to be delegated to notional resident units. The equity of such a notional unit is then owned by the foreign unit.

12.114. The value of a foreign asset is measured by its current value in foreign currency converted into the currency of the country in which its owner is resident at the exchange rate. Nominal holding gains may therefore occur not only because the price of the asset in local currency changes but also because the exchange rate changes. The total value of the nominal holding gains accruing over the period may be calculated in the usual way by subtracting the value of transactions from the difference between the opening and closing balance sheet values. For this purpose, transactions in the foreign assets must be converted into the national currency using the exchange rates at the times the transactions occur, while the opening and closing balance sheet values must be converted using the exchange rates prevailing at the dates to which the balance sheets relate. This implies that the total value of the transactions—acquisitions less disposals—expressed in the foreign currency is, in effect, converted by a weighted average exchange rate in which the weights are given the values of transactions conducted on different dates.

12.115. Neutral holding gains are calculated in the same way as for any other type of asset by calculating what the holding gains would have been if the prices of the assets, expressed in national currency, had moved in the same way as the general internal price level. Real holding gains, again expressed in national currency, can then be derived residually by subtracting the neutral from the nominal gains. The real holding gains (losses) of creditors in one country need not be equal to the real holding losses (gains) of debtors on the same assets in another country when the general rates of inflation are not the same in the two countries.

Annex

The definition and measurement of holding gains

A. The measurement of nominal holding gains

1. Nominal holding gains must be calculated not only for assets held throughout the accounting period but also for assets acquired or disposed of during the course of the period. Otherwise, as explained below, it is not possible to reconcile data on transactions or other changes in assets with the opening and closing balance sheet figures. The first requirement, therefore, is to obtain a measure of the total nominal holding gains on the stock of some asset, given that the quantity held and its price may vary at any time throughout the accounting period. The asset may be of any kind—a financial asset, a fixed asset or a stock of some material, work-in-progress, or a finished product held by a producer.

2. The accounting period must be divided into a large number n of short sub-periods, say days. The price of the asset may vary from day to day and transactions or other changes may take place each day.

   Let q_t=the quantity of the asset held at the end of day t;

         p_t=the price of a unit of the asset during day t;

   and $d_t=q_t-q_{t-1}$

       $t=0, 1, 2 \ldots n.$

   The change in the quantity of an asset from one day to another, d_t, has two distinct components: one is due to the deliberate acquisition or disposal of an asset in transactions with other institutional units; the other is due to other volume changes such as the destruction of a physical asset by a natural disaster. Thus, $p_t d_t$ represents the combined value of the transactions and other volume changes in the asset taking place on day t. Balance sheets are compiled at the ends of day o and day n but not in between. Note that, by definition,

   $$= q_n - q_o = \sum_1^n d_t \qquad (1)$$

   and $\Sigma p_t d_t$ denotes the value of all the transactions or other volume changes in the asset taking place during the accounting period and recorded in the capital, financial and other changes in the volume of assets accounts of the System.

3. Suppose, initially, that the opening stock of the asset is held throughout the accounting period. The nominal holding gain on that stock would be $(p_n-p_o)q_o$.

4. Suppose, next, a single change in the quantity occurs on day t as a result of a purchase, sale or other factor. The total nominal holding gain over the period as a whole, denoted by G, is then given by

   $$G=(p_n-p_o)q_o + (p_n-p_t)d_t \qquad (2)$$

   If d_t is positive, the second term in (2) measures the holding gain on the additional quantity of the asset between time t when it is acquired and the end of the accounting period. If d_t is negative, the second term measures the amount that needs to be deducted from $(p_n-p_o)q_o$ because of the quantity disposed of on day t. Equation (2) can be generalized to cover any number of changes within the accounting period, as follows:

   $$G = (p_n-p_o)q_o + \sum_1^n (p_n - p_t)d_t \qquad (3)$$

   This expression gives the total nominal holding gain accruing to the holder of an asset over the period as a whole, however many changes occur in the quantity of the asset held. The expression is valid in all circumstances, covering situations in which either or both of q_o and q_n are zero.

5. Expression (3) provides a direct definition of the value of the total nominal holding gains on asset over a given period of time and shows how they may be calculated independently of the other accounts of the System. It follows that neutral and real holding gains may similarly be calculated directly and independently of the rest of the System. It can also be seen that holding gains are the duals of the values of transactions and other quantity changes in the sense that the values of transactions and other quantity changes are obtained by applying prices to changes in quantities whereas the values of holding gains are obtained by applying quantities to changes in prices.

6. In practice, however, business accounting records are usually not kept in such a way as to make it possible to calculate holding gains directly, except in certain special cases or on certain assumptions, as explained below. In order to calculate holding gains directly, it would be necessary to keep records of the times and prices at which all assets are acquired and the times and prices of which they are subsequently disposed of whether

by sale, use or transfer. Such information is not readily available in practice.

7. However, because of the duality between transactions or other quantity changes and holding gains, it is possible to derive the value of holding gains indirectly from balance sheet data and the values of transactions and other changes. This may be shown as follows. It follows from (1) above that

$$p_n (q_n - q_o) = p_n \sum_{1}^{n} d_t \qquad (4)$$

Substituting for $p_n \Sigma d_t$ in (3) and rearranging, we obtain the following identity:

$$G = (p_n q_n - p_o q_o) - \Sigma p_t d_t. \qquad (5)$$

In this identity, $p_o q_o$ and $p_n q_n$ are the opening and closing balance sheet values while $\Sigma p_t d_t$ is the total value of the transactions and other changes taking place within the accounting period.

8. Expression (5) is one form of the basic identity that closes the entire System of accounts including the balance sheets. It also provides a practical method of calculating nominal holding gains by subtracting the value of all transactions or other changes from the difference between the values of the stock of the asset recorded in the opening and closing balance sheets. For the identity to hold, it is of course necessary that the System's general valuation rules are respected: all transactions or other changes in assets have to be recorded at the prices prevailing at the times they take place and the assets recorded in the balance sheets must be valued at the prices prevailing at the dates to which the balance sheets relate. For example, goods entering or leaving inventories must be valued at the prices prevailing at the times they enter or leave as distinct from the prices at which the goods may have been originally acquired.

9. The basic identity given in (5) can be expressed verbally as follows:

(a) The difference between the values of the stock of a given type of asset in the closing and opening balance sheets;

must be equal to

(b) The total value of all transactions and other volume changes in the asset occurring during the accounting period;

plus

(c) The total value of all the nominal holding gains accruing within the accounting period.

The identity follows from the ways in which the various elements are defined, valued and recorded. Given the identity, it is unnecessary to estimate all three components directly; the value of any one component can be estimated residually from the other two components.

10. It is important to note that, although nominal holding gains may be estimated residually by subtracting the value of transactions and other volume changes in assets from the difference between the closing and opening balance sheet values, they are not defined residually. Nominal holding gains are not a balancing item like value added, operating surplus, etc. As already noted, nominal holding gains can be measured directly and independently of all other items in the accounts. In principle, either of the other two components in the above identity could equally well be derived residually from information on the other two. For example, the difference between the opening and closing balance sheet values (but not their absolute levels) can be deduced from complete information on transactions, other changes in assets and nominal holding gains.

B. The measurement of neutral and real holding gains

1. Neutral holding gains

11. A neutral holding gain has been defined as the holding gain that would accrue if the price of the asset moved over time in exactly the same way as some specified general price index. In order to calculate it, therefore, it is necessary to value the quantity of the asset held at each point of time in the accounting period by its price at the beginning of the period multiplied by the general price index based on the beginning of the period. Let r_t be the selected general price index based on day o so that $r_o = 1$. If the price of the asset moved in proportion to this index, the value of the stock of the asset held at the end of the accounting period, that is, on day n, would be $r_n p_o q_n$ instead of $p_n q_n$. The value of the transactions or other volume changes taking place during the period would be

$$\sum_{1}^{n} r_t p_o d_t.$$

The value of the neutral holding gains, NG, is therefore given by

$$NG = (r_n p_o q_n - p_o q_o) - \Sigma r_t p_o d_t. \qquad (6)$$

This expression is the equivalent of that for nominal holding gains given in (5).

12. While it is possible to calculate $r_n p_o q_n$, it is likely to be impossible to calculate $\Sigma r_t p_o d_t$ exactly as it requires data on the values of the transactions on individual days and not simply their aggregate for the accounting period as a whole. In practice, therefore, it may be necessary to estimate the value of $\Sigma r_t p_o d_t$ by adjusting the known value of $\Sigma p_t d_t$, the total value of all transactions and other volume changes. For this purpose, it is convenient to make use of the ratio of the change in the general price index to the change in the price of the asset over the period as a whole. Define:

$$k = \frac{r_n / r_o}{p_n / p_o} = \frac{r_n p_o}{p_n} \tag{7}$$

when $r_o = 1$. k is a measure of the change in the relative price of the asset over the period as a whole and must be known if there is to be any possibility of calculating neutral and real holding gains. The corresponding ratio at the middle of the period can be estimated to be $k^{1/2}$ and this term can be applied to $\Sigma p_t d_t$ to obtain an estimate of what the total value of the transactions and other changes would have been if the price of the asset had increased over the period as a whole by the same proportion as the general price index. Replacing $\Sigma r_t p_o d_t$ by $k^{1/2} \Sigma p_t d_t$ and $r_n p_o q_n$ by $k p_n q_n$ gives the following estimate of neutral holding gains

$$NG = (k p_n q_n - p_o q_o) - k^{1/2} \Sigma p_t d_t \tag{8}$$

This expression is computable. It requires the same information as that used to calculate nominal holding gains plus information on the change in the relative price of the asset over the period as a whole.

2. Real holding gains

13. Real holding gains are obtained by subtracting the value of the neutral holding gains from the nominal holding gains. Subtracting (6), the exact expression for neutral holding gains, from (5), we obtain:

$$RG = (1-k) p_n q_n - \Sigma (p_t - r_t p_o) d_t. \tag{9}$$

Alternatively, subtracting (8), the estimate of neutral holding gains, from (7), we obtain:

$$RG = (1-k) p_n q_n - (1 - k^{1/2}) \Sigma p_t d_t. \tag{10}$$

14. The feasibility of calculating (10) is, of course, determined by the feasibility of calculating (8). Once the value of the neutral holding gains have been calculated, the real holding gains are obtained simply by subtracting the neutral gains from the corresponding nominal gains. It can be seen from (10) that the estimated real holding gains must be zero if $k=1$: that is, if the relative price of the asset is unchanged over the period as a whole. It may also be noted that if there are no transactions or other volume changes taking place in the accounting period, both expressions (9) and (10) reduce to the following:

$$(1-k) p_n q_n = (p_n / p_o - r_n) p_o q_o \tag{11}$$

This is the same as the original expression (3) in the main text used to define the real holding gain on a given quantity of an asset.

XIII. The balance sheet

A. Introduction

13.1. A balance sheet is a statement, drawn up at a particular point in time, of the values of assets owned and of the financial claims—liabilities—against the owner of those assets. A balance sheet may be drawn up for institutional units, institutional sectors and the total economy.

13.2. For an institutional unit or sector, the balance sheet provides an indicator of economic status—i.e., the financial and non-financial resources at its disposal that are summarized in the balancing item net worth. For the economy as a whole, the balance sheet shows what is often referred to as national wealth—the sum of non-financial assets and net claims on the rest of the world.

13.3. The balance sheet completes the sequence of accounts, showing the ultimate result of the entries in the production, distribution and use of income, and accumulation accounts. As explained in the general introduction to the accumulation accounts and balance sheets in chapter X, the accumulation accounts record the changes in the value of assets, liabilities and net worth that take place during the accounting period. A basic accounting identity links the opening balance sheet and the closing balance sheet for a given asset:

(a) The value of the stock of a specific type of asset in the opening balance sheet;

plus

(b) The total value of the assets acquired, less the total value of those disposed of, in transactions that take place within the accounting period: transactions in non-financial assets are recorded in the capital account and transactions in financial assets in the financial account;

plus

(c) The value of other positive or negative changes in the volume of the assets held for example, as a result of the discovery of a subsoil asset or the destruction of an asset (as a result of war or a natural disaster): these changes are recorded in the other changes in the volume of assets account;

plus

(d) The value of the positive or negative nominal holding gains accruing during the period resulting from a change in the price of the asset: these are recorded in the revaluation account where they may be further decomposed into neutral holding gains that reflect changes in the general price level and real holding gains that reflect changes in the relative price of the asset;

is identical with

(e) The value of the stock of the asset in the closing balance sheet.

13.4. The existence of a set of balance sheets integrated with the flow accounts encourages analysts to look more broadly in monitoring and assessing economic and financial conditions and behaviour. Balance sheets provide information necessary for analysing a number of topics. For example, in studies of the factors determining household behaviour, consumption and saving functions have often included wealth variables to capture the effects of such factors as price fluctuations in corporate securities or the deterioration and obsolescence of stocks of durable consumer goods on households' purchasing patterns. Further, household balance sheets are needed in order to assess the distribution of wealth and liquidity.

13.5. For corporations, balance sheets permit the computation of widely used ratios that involve data on the level of the item. Banks and other financial institutions, for example, observe specific reserve ratios. Non-financial corporations also pay heed to certain ratios—for instance, current assets in relation to current liabilities and the market value of corporate shares in relation to the adjusted book value. Data on the stocks of fixed assets owned by corporations, as well as by other institutional units, are useful also in studies of their investment behaviour and needs for financing.

13.6. Balance sheet data on the mineral deposits, land and similar natural resources owned by the institutional units in the economy are of interest for monitoring the availability and exploitation of these resources and for formulating environmental policies. Balance sheet data on the level and the composition of tangible and financial assets also are of considerable interest as indicators of the economic resources of a nation and for assessing the external debtor or creditor position of a country.

Table 13.1. Account IV: Balance sheets

Assets

Accounts	Total	Corresponding entries of the Goods and service account	Rest of the world account	S.1 Total economy	S.15 NPISHs	S.14 Households	S.13 General government	S.12 Financial corporations	S.11 Non-financial corporations		Transactions, other flows, stocks and balancing items
IV.1.	9 922			9 922	324	2 822	1 591	144	5 041	AN	Non-financial assets
Opening	6 047			6 047	243	1 698	1 001	104	3 001	AN.1	Produced assets
balance	5 544			5 544	231	1 423	913	99	2 878	AN.11	Fixed assets
sheet	231			231	2	97	47		85	AN.12	Inventories
	272			272	10	178	41	5	38	AN.13	Valuables
	3 875			3 875	81	1 124	590	40	2 040	AN.2	Non-produced assets
	3 809			3 809	81	1 124	578	37	1 989	AN.21	Tangible non-produced assets
	66			66			12	3	51	AN.22	Intangible non-produced assets
	7 365		573	6 792	172	1 819	396	3 508	897	AF	Financial assets/liabilities
	770			770			80	690		AF.1	Monetary gold and SDRs
	1 587		105	1 482	110	840	150		382	AF.2	Currency and deposits
	1 388		125	1 263	25	198		950	90	AF.3	Securities other than shares
	1 454		70	1 384	8	24	115	1 187	50	AF.4	Loans
	1 409		113	1 296	22	411	12	651	200	AF.5	Shares and other equity
	396		26	370	4	291	20	30	25	AF.6	Insurance technical reserves
	361		134	227	3	55	19		150	AF.7	Other accounts receivable/payable
										B.90	*Net worth*
IV.2.											Total changes in assets/liabilities:
Changes	482			482	25	110	56	1	290	AN	Non-financial assets
in	289			289	21	61	25	− 1	182	AN.1	Produced assets
balance	239			239	21	47	20	1	150	AN.11	Fixed assets
sheet [1]	34			34		4	1		29	AN.12	Inventories
	16			16		10	4	− 2	3	AN.13	Valuables
	193			193	4	49	30	2	108	AN.2	Non-produced assets
	191			191	4	48	30	1	108	AN.21	Tangible non-produced assets
	2			2		1				AN.22	Intangible non-produced assets
	787		57	730	33	199	123	294	81	AF	Financial assets/liabilities
	19		1	18			1	17		AF.1	Monetary gold and SDRs
	130		11	119	12	68	7	15	17	AF.2	Currency and deposits
	187		9	178	13	35	29	80	21	AF.3	Securities other than shares
	250		10	240		5	45	163	27	AF.4	Loans
	80		5	75	1	13	34	19	9	AF.5	Shares and other equity
	38			38		38				AF.6	Insurance technical reserves
	82		21	61	8	40	6		7	AF.7	Other accounts receivable/payable
										B.10	*Changes in net worth, total due to:*
										B.10.1	*Saving and capital transfers*
										B.10.2	*Other changes in volume of assets*
										B.10.3	*Nominal holding gains/losses*
										B.10.31	*Neutral holding gains/losses*
										B.10.32	*Real holding gains/losses*
IV.3.	10 404			10 404	349	2 932	1 647	145	5 331	AN	Non-financial assets
Closing	6 336			6 336	264	1 759	1 026	103	3 183	AN.1	Produced assets
balance	5 783			5 783	252	1 470	933	100	3 028	AN.11	Fixed assets
sheet [1]	265			265	2	101	48		114	AN.12	Inventories
	288			288	10	188	45	3	41	AN.13	Valuables
	4 068			4 068	85	1 173	620	42	2 148	AN.2	Non-produced assets
	4 000			4 000	85	1 172	608	38	2 097	AN.21	Tangible non-produced assets
	68			68		1	12	3	51	AN.22	Intangible non-produced assets
	8 152		630	7 522	205	2 018	519	3 802	978	AF	Financial assets/liabilities
	788			788			81	707		AF.1	Monetary gold and SDRs
	1 717		116	1 601	122	908	157	15	399	AF.2	Currency and deposits
	1 575		134	1 441	38	233	29	1 030	111	AF.3	Securities other than shares
	1 704		80	1 624	8	29	160	1 350	77	AF.4	Loans
	1 489		118	1 371	23	424	46	670	209	AF.5	Shares and other equity
	434		26	408	4	329	20	30	25	AF.6	Insurance technical reserves
	443		155	288	11	95	25		157	AF.7	Other accounts receivable/payable
										B.90	*Net worth*

1 Differences between data on individual items and totals of holding gains/losses may not be entirely consistent due to rounding errors.

Liabilities and net worth

S.11 Non-financial corporations	S.12 Financial corporations	S.13 General government	S.14 Households	S.15 NPISHs	S.1 Total economy	Corresponding entries of the Rest of the world account	Goods and service account	Total	Accounts
									IV.1. Opening balance sheet
1 817	3 384	687	289	121	6 298	297		6 595	
40	1 281	102	10	38	1 471	116		1 587	
44	1 053	212	2		1 311	77		1 388	
897		328	169	43	1 437	17		1 454	
687	715	4			1 406	3		1 409	
12	335	19		5	371	25		396	
137		22	108	35	302	59		361	
4 121	268	1 300	4 352	375	10 416	276		10 692	
									IV.2. Changes in balance sheet [1]
155	285	176	33	28	677	91		767	
	130	2			132	−2		130	
7	87	71			165	22		187	
68		93	28	24	213	37		250	
42	30			4	77	3		80	
	38				38			38	
37		10	5		52	30		82	
216	10	2	276	31	535	− 34		501	
65	4	− 38	178	21	230	− 38		192	
17	− 4	2	2		17			17	
134	10	38	96	10	288	4		292	
82	5	26	87	8	208	6		214	
51	5	12	9	2	80	− 1		78	
									IV.3. Closing balance sheet [1]
1 972	3 669	863	322	149	6 975	388		7 362	
40	1 411	104	10	38	1 603	114		1 717	
51	1 140	283	2		1 476	99		1 575	
965		421	197	67	1 650	54		1 704	
729	745	4		4	1 483	6		1 489	
12	373	19		5	409	25		434	
174		32	113	35	354	89		443	
4 337	278	1 302	4 628	406	10 951	242		11 193	

13.7. Information on stocks of fixed assets are used in the analysis of production and productivity. For this purpose, however, data are needed for industries, rather than for sectors. The System provides for data on stocks of fixed assets and inventories by industry, as described in chapter XV, as part of the use table.

1. Structure of the account

13.8. The balance sheet records assets on the left and liabilities and net worth on the right, as do the accumulation accounts for changes in these items. In table 13.1, Account IV, two categories of non-financial assets are distinguished: produced assets, which have come into existence as outputs from production processes, and non-produced assets, which either are naturally occurring or are devised by man outside the production boundary. A more detailed balance sheet can be derived using the full detail of the classification of assets, which is given in the annex to this chapter.

13.9. In addition to non-financial assets, the balance sheet also includes financial assets and liabilities. Most financial assets are matched by a liability; they come into existence by the establishment of a claim on another institutional unit. However, financial assets also include monetary gold, Special drawing rights (SDR) of the International Monetary Fund (IMF), shares in corporations (which their holders treat much the same as financial claims) and certain financial derivatives; there are no liabilities outstanding with respect to monetary gold and SDRs, while the System treats both shares and these derivatives as liabilities by convention.

13.10. The balancing item in the balance sheet is net worth, which is defined as the value of all the assets owned by an institutional unit or sector less the value of all its outstanding liabilities. Changes in net worth can thus be explained fully only by examining the changes in all the other items that make up the balance sheet.

13.11. A balance sheet relates to the values of assets and liabilities at a particular moment of time. The System provides for balance sheets to be compiled at the beginning of the accounting period (the same as the end of the preceding period) and at its end. The System then provides for a complete recording of the changes in the values of the various items in the balance sheet between the beginning and end of the accounting period—i.e., over the same time period as that to which the flow accounts of the System relate. The recording of these changes in the changes in balance sheets account is discussed in section C below.

2. Main categories of assets: their scope and characteristics

13.12. An economic asset, as described in the general introduction to the accumulation accounts and balance sheets paragraph 10.2 of chapter X, is an entity functioning as a store of value:

(a) Over which ownership rights are enforced by institutional units, individually or collectively; and

(b) From which economic benefits may be derived by its owner by holding it, or using it, over a period of time.

The economic benefits consist of primary incomes derived from the use of the asset and the value, including possible holding gains/losses, that could be realized by disposing of the asset or terminating it.

13.13. The coverage of each asset category is set out in the annex to this chapter. The discussion that follows here only sketches the content of the categories of assets and liabilities in the balance sheet.

Non-financial produced assets (AN.1)

13.14. Produced assets are non-financial assets that have come into existence as outputs from production processes.

13.15. The classification of produced assets is designed to distinguish among assets on the basis of their role in production. It consists of fixed assets, inventories and valuables. Fixed assets—buildings and other structures, machinery and equipment, cultivated assets and certain intangible assets—are used repeatedly or continuously in production. Inventories are used up in production as intermediate consumption, sold or otherwise disposed of. Valuables are not used primarily for production or consumption, but are instead acquired and held primarily as stores of value.

13.16. As explained in chapter X, paragraphs 10.69 to 10.74, two kinds of durable goods used by producers—namely, small tools and certain kinds of military equipment—are excluded from gross fixed capital formation so that there are no corresponding fixed assets. In addition, transport equipment and other machinery and equipment acquired by households for final consumption are not considered fixed assets, although they are included in the memorandum item "consumer durables" in the balance sheet.

Non-financial non-produced assets (AN.2)

13.17. By definition, non-produced assets come into existence other than through processes of production. The classification is designed to distinguish assets on the basis of the way they come into existence. Some of these assets occur in nature; others, which may be referred to as constructs devised by society, come into existence by legal or accounting actions.

13.18. Tangible non-produced assets are natural assets—land, subsoil assets, non-cultivated biological resources and water resources—over which ownership may be established and transferred. The natural asset boundary in the System is determined, in compliance with the general definition of an economic asset, by whether the assets are subject to effective ownership and are capable of bringing economic benefits to their owners, given the existing technology, knowledge, economic opportunities, available resources, and set of relative prices. Environmental assets over which ownership rights have not, or cannot, be established, such as open seas or air, are excluded.

13.19. Intangible non-produced assets include patented entities, transferable contracts, purchased goodwill, etc. Entities not evidenced by legal or accounting actions—i.e., such actions as the granting of a patent or the conveyance of some economic benefit to a third party—are excluded.

Financial assets and liabilities (AF.)

13.20. Financial assets are entities meeting the general criteria for economic assets—i.e., they are entities over which ownership rights are enforced by institutional units, individually or collectively, and from which economic benefits may be derived by their owners by holding them, or using them over a period of time—that differ, except for monetary gold and SDRs, from other assets in the System in that there is a counterpart liability on the part of another institutional unit.

13.21. The classification of financial assets and liabilities is designed to distinguish types of instruments according to the liquidity of the instrument and the legal characteristics of the instrument that describe the form of the underlying creditor/debtor relationship. On this basis it distinguishes monetary gold and SDR, currency and deposits, securities other than shares, loans, shares and other equity, insurance technical reserves and other accounts receivable/payable. A more detailed level of classification is recommended in the case of instruments for which information about the class of debtor or creditor is of particular importance analytically and is feasible to gather, such as liabilities to, and claims on, non-residents.

13.22. Two major exclusions should be noted. First, contingent assets or liabilities are treated as financial assets and liabilities only if the claim or liability is unconditional to both parties and/or the arrangement has an observable value because it is tradable. Otherwise, contingent assets or liabilities are not treated as financial assets or liabilities in the System, as discussed in chapter XI. Secondly, sums set aside in business accounting to provide for transactors' future liabilities, either certain or contingent, or for transactors' future expenditures generally are not recognized in the System. (The only "provision" recognized in the System is accumulated consumption of fixed capital.) Only actual current liabilities to another party or parties are explicitly included. When the anticipated liability becomes actual—for example, a tax lien—it is included.

3. Financial leasing

13.23. A financial lease is a contract between lessor and lessee whereby the lessor purchases a good that is put at the disposal of the lessee and the lessee pays rentals that enable the lessor, over the period of the contract, to cover all, or virtually all, costs, including interest. Financial leases may be distin-

guished by the fact that all the risks and rewards of ownership are, de facto, transferred from the legal owner of the good (the lessor) to the user of the good (the lessee.) The System's treatment of financial leasing is designed to move away from the legal arrangements to capture the economic reality of such arrangements, by treating goods under a financial lease as if they were purchased by the user. The transactions involved were described in chapter X, paragraph 10.44, and in chapter XI, paragraphs 11.31 and 11.82.

13.24. In the System, goods under a financial lease—in practice, almost exclusively machinery and equipment—are treated as if purchased and owned by the user. The acquisition of a fixed asset by the lessee is treated as being financed by a financial claim, classified as a loan. For example, if a bank leases a railway car to a railroad, at the time the railroad is deemed to take ownership of the railway car, the market value of the railway car is recorded as an asset and the loan is recorded as a liability in the balance sheet of the railroad. The loan also appears as an asset in the balance sheet of the bank. Subsequent balance sheets reflect the value of the railway car less the accumulated consumption of fixed capital and the amount of the loan less the accumulated part of the rental that is considered a repayment, in instalments, of the loan.

4. General principles of valuation

13.25. For the balance sheets to be consistent with the accumulation accounts of the System, a particular item in the balance sheet should be valued as if it were being acquired on the date to which the balance sheet relates, including any associated costs of ownership transfer in the case of non-financial assets. This implies that assets and liabilities (and thus net worth) are to be valued using a set of prices that are current on the date to which the balance sheet relates and that refer to specific assets.

13.26. Ideally, these prices should be observable prices on markets whenever such prices are available for the assets and liabilities in question. Prices at which assets may be bought or sold on markets are the basis of decisions by investors, producers, consumers and other economic agents. For example, investors in financial assets (such as securities) and tangible assets (such as land) make decisions in respect of acquisitions and disposals of these assets in the light of their values in the market. Producers make decisions about how much of a particular commodity to produce and about where to sell their output by reference to prices on markets. For a given asset, the price is the same for purchaser and seller, and, in the case of financial assets, for creditor and debtor.

13.27. When there are no observable prices because the items in question have not been purchased/sold on the market in the recent past, an attempt has to be made to estimate what the prices would be were the assets to be acquired on the market on the date to which the balance sheet relates. In estimating the current market price for balance sheet valuation, a price averaged over all transactions in a market can be used if the market is one on which the items in question are regularly, actively and freely traded.

13.28. In addition to prices observed in markets or estimated from observed prices, current prices may be approximated for balance sheet valuation in two other ways. In some cases, prices may be approximated by accumulating and revaluing acquisitions less disposals of the asset in question over its lifetime; this generally is the most practical and also the preferred method for fixed assets, but it can be applied to other assets as well. In other cases, market prices may be approximated by the present, or discounted, value of future economic benefits expected from a given asset; this is the case for a number of financial assets, natural assets and intangible assets. With good information and efficient markets, the values of the assets obtained by accumulating and revaluing transactions should equal, or at least approximate, both the present, or discounted, values of the remaining future benefits to be derived from them and their market values when active secondhand markets exist. These three price bases are discussed below in general terms.

Value observed in markets

13.29. The ideal source of price observations for valuing balance sheet items is a market, like the stock exchange, in which each asset traded is completely homogeneous, is often traded in considerable volume and has its market price listed at regular intervals. Such markets yield data on prices that can be multiplied by indicators of quantity in order to compute the total market value of different classes of assets held by sectors and of different classes of their liabilities. These prices are available for nearly all financial claims, existing real estate (i.e., existing buildings and other structures plus the underlying land), existing transportation equipment, crops, and livestock as well as for newly produced fixed assets and inventories.

13.30. For securities quoted on a stock exchange, for example, it is feasible to gather the prices of individual assets and of broad classes of assets and, in addition, to determine the global valuation of all the existing securities of a given type. In some countries, another example of a market in which assets may be traded in sufficient numbers to provide useful price information is the market for existing dwellings.

13.31. In addition to providing direct observations on the prices of assets actually traded there, information from such markets may also be used to price similar assets that are not traded. For example, information from the stock exchange also may be used to price unquoted securities by analogy with similar, quoted securities, making some allowance for the inferior marketability of the unquoted securities. Similarly, appraisals of tangible

assets for insurance or other purposes generally are based on observed prices for items that are close substitutes, although not identical, and this approach can be used for balance sheet valuation. For a discussion of the special valuation problems associated with direct investment enterprises, see chapter XIV, paragraphs 14.49 and 14.159.

Values obtained by accumulating and revaluing transactions

13.32. For some assets, initial acquisition costs (appropriately revalued) are written off—amortized—over the asset's expected life. For this method, a pattern of decline must be chosen, and reference may be made to tax laws, accounting conventions, etc. The value of such an asset at a given point in its life is given by its current acquisition price less the accumulated value of these write-offs. This valuation is typically used for non-produced intangible assets, such as purchased goodwill and patented entities.

13.33. In addition, most fixed assets are recorded in the balance sheets at current written-down value—i.e., at current purchasers' or basic prices written-down for the accumulated consumption of fixed capital, a valuation frequently referred to as "written-down replacement cost". When fixed assets are valued in this way, the balance sheet values are consistent with the measures of consumption of fixed capital elsewhere in the System.

Present value of future returns

13.34. In the case of assets for which the returns either are delayed (as with timber) or are spread over a lengthy period (as with subsoil assets), although normal prices are used to value the ultimate output, a rate of discount must, in addition, be used to compute the present value of the expected future returns. It is thus necessary to derive a capitalization factor—a factor that works back from the present value of the expected future return to the value of the asset—from information about the market. The rate of discount and the capitalization factors should be derived from information based on transactions in the particular type of assets under consideration—forest lands, mines and quarries—rather than using a general rate of interest, such as one derived from the yield on government bonds.

Assets in foreign currencies

13.35. Assets and liabilities denominated in foreign currencies should be converted into the national currency at the market exchange rate prevailing on the date to which the balance sheet relates. This rate should be the mid-point between the buying and selling spot rates for currency transactions. Valuation when a multiple exchange rate system is in operation is discussed in chapters XIV and XIX.

B. The entries in the balance sheet

13.36. Definitions of the assets in the balance sheet at the most detailed level of the classification of assets are in the annex to this chapter. Definitions are repeated in this section only to the extent needed to provide the context for information on valuation specific to particular assets and other specialized topics.

1. Produced assets (AN.1)

Fixed assets (AN.11)

Tangible fixed assets (AN.111)

13.37. Tangible fixed assets include buildings and other structures (including historic monuments); transportation equipment and other machinery and equipment; and cultivated assets in the form of livestock and plantations of trees yielding repeat products, orchards, vineyards, etc.

13.38. In general, tangible fixed assets have to be recorded at current written-down values—i.e., at the current purchasers' prices (or basic prices in the case of own-account production) of new assets written down by the accumulated consumption of fixed capital on the assets. Purchasers' costs of ownership transfer associated with these assets, appropriately written down, are included in the balance sheet values (see chapter X for a numerical example). The common method of making these estimates is the perpetual inventory method (PIM), which is described in chapter VI. When the PIM is used, the value of the stock of fixed assets on a given date is based on estimates of fixed capital formation, classified by type of asset and year of acquisition, that have been accumulated (after deduction of the accumulated consumption of fixed capital) and revalued over a long enough period to cover the acquisition of all fixed assets in the stock in question. Where there exists an active market for a particular existing asset, the PIM calculation of consumption of fixed capital should take into account the observed prices on markets for these assets when they are actively traded (see chapter X).

13.39. Because dwellings are traded in the normal course of events, prices observed in the real estate market may also be used to supplement the valuation at written-down replacement cost. Markets for existing automobiles, aircraft, and other transportation equipment also may be sufficiently representative to yield useful price observations to supplement the valuation at written-down replacement cost. For assets for which prices exist on markets, a valuation at these prices may be shown as a memorandum item in addition to the current written-down value in order to preserve the record of these prices.

13.40. In the case of existing industrial plant and equipment, however, observed prices on markets may not be suitable for determining values for use in the balance sheets, however,

because many of the transactions involve assets that for some reason are not typical—i.e., they embody specialized characteristics, they are obsolete or they are being disposed of under financial duress.

13.41. Historic monuments are included in the balance sheets only when their significance has been recognized by someone other than the owner, as evidenced by a sale or by a formal appraisal. They should be valued at the most recent sale price, updated, if need be, by a general price index.

13.42. For Balance Sheet purposes, livestock (including fish) that continue to be used in production year after year should be valued on the basis of the current purchasers' prices (or basic prices in the case of own-account) for animals of a given age. Such information is less likely to be available for trees (including shrubs) cultivated for products they yield year after year; they should then be recorded at the current written-down value of the cumulative capital formation.

Intangible fixed assets (AN.112)

13.43. Mineral exploration should be valued either on the basis of the amounts paid under contracts awarded to other institutional units for the purpose or on the basis of the costs incurred for exploration undertaken on own account. That part of exploration undertaken in the past that has not yet been fully written off should be revalued at the prices and costs of the current period.

13.44. Computer software should be valued on the basis of the purchasers' price paid for the software or, in the absence of such prices, on the basis of costs of production when produced in-house. Software acquired in previous years and not yet fully written down should be revalued at current prices or costs (which may be less than the original price or cost).

13.45. Entertainment, literary or artistic originals and other intangible fixed assets should be valued at the acquisition price when these intangible assets are actually traded on markets. In the case of intangible assets that have been produced on own-account, it may be necessary to value them on the basis of their costs of production, appropriately revalued at prices of the current period and written down. Otherwise, it may be necessary to use estimates of the present value of the expected future receipts to be received by the owners of such assets.

Inventories (AN.12)

13.46. Inventories are stocks of goods and services held by producers that are intended for sale, use in production or other use at a later date.

13.47. With respect to the time of recording, it should be emphasized that inventories produced as outputs or intended for intermediate consumption in production should be valued at the prices prevailing on the date to which the balance sheet relates, and not at the prices at which the products were valued when they entered inventory. In the balance sheets, figures for inventories frequently have to be estimated by adjusting figures of book values of inventories in business accounts, as described in chapter VI.

13.48. As is the case elsewhere in the System, inventories of materials and supplies are valued at purchasers' prices, and inventories of finished goods and work-in-progress are valued at basic prices. Inventories of goods intended for resale without further processing by wholesalers and retailers are valued at prices paid for them, excluding any transportation costs incurred by the wholesalers or retailers. For work-in-progress inventories, the value for the closing balance sheet can be calculated by applying the fraction of the total production cost incurred by the end of the period to the basic price realized by the finished product on the date to which the balance sheet relates. If the basic price of the finished product is not available, it can be estimated by the value of production cost with a mark-up for expected net operating surplus or estimated net mixed income, as explained in chapter X, paragraphs 10.108 to 10.115. This approach can be used, for example, for partially completed structures, machinery and equipment, software and architectural and design services with long production periods, which are included in work-in-progress inventories to the extent that no transfer of ownership to the intended user is deemed to have taken place. (Own-account production of buildings and structures produced under a contract of sale/purchase agreed in advance are treated as gross fixed capital formation because the transfer of ownership to the intended user is deemed to have taken place.)

13.49. Growing single-use crops (including timber) cultivated by human activity and livestock being raised for slaughter are also counted as work-in-progress inventories. The conventional way of valuing standing timber is to discount the future proceeds of selling the timber at current prices after deducting the expenses of bringing the timber to maturity, felling, etc. For the most part, other crops and livestock can be valued by reference to the prices of such products on markets.

Valuables (AN.13)

13.50. Valuables are items that are not used primarily for production or consumption, that are of significant value, that are expected to appreciate or at least not to decline in real value, that do not deteriorate over time in normal conditions, and that are acquired and held primarily as stores of value.

13.51. Given their primary role, it is especially important to value works of art, antiques, jewellery, precious stones and metals at current prices. To the extent that well-organized markets exist for these items, they should be valued at the actual or estimated prices that would be paid for them were they purchased on the market, including any agents' fees or commissions, on the date to which the balance sheet relates.

13.52. An approach in the absence of organized markets is to value these items using data on the values at which they are insured against fire, theft, etc., to the extent information is available.

2. Non-produced assets (AN.2)

Tangible non-produced assets (AN.21)

13.53. Tangible non-produced assets are assets that occur in nature and over which ownership rights have been established. Environmental assets over which ownership rights have not, or cannot, be established, such as the high seas or air, are excluded because they do not qualify as economic assets.

Land (AN.211)

13.54. Land is defined in the System as the ground itself, including the covering soil and any associated surface waters over which ownership rights are enforced. Excluded are any buildings or other man-made structures situated on it or running through it; cultivated crops, trees and animals; subsoil assets; non-cultivated biological resources and water resources.

13.55. The value of land includes the value of the stock of major improvements that cannot be physically separated from the land itself. Thus, although expenditures on land improvements are treated as gross fixed capital formation in the System, they do not lead to tangible assets that can be shown in the balance sheets separately from the land itself. Land is valued at its current price paid by a new owner, including written-down costs of ownership transfer.

13.56. Because the current market value of land can vary enormously according to its location and the uses for which it is suitable or sanctioned, it is essential to identify the location and use of a specific piece or tract of land and to price it accordingly. In a number of instances it may be difficult, if not impracticable, to separate the value of land from that of the buildings erected on it, because in the market for real estate, as well as in the accounting records of transactors, distinctions are often not made between the buildings and the land on which they stand.

13.57. For land underlying buildings, the market will, in some instances, furnish data directly on the value of the land. More typically, however, such data are not available and a more usual method is to calculate ratios of the value of the site to the value of the structure from valuation appraisals and to deduce the value of land from the replacement cost of the buildings or from the value on the market of the combined land and buildings. When the value of land cannot be separated from the building, structure, or plantation, vineyard, etc. above it, the composite asset should be classified in the category representing the greater part of its value.

13.58. It is usually much easier to make a division between land and buildings for the total economy than for individual sectors or sub-sectors. Separate figures are needed for studies of national wealth and environmental problems. Fortunately, combined figures are often suitable for purposes of analysing the behaviour of institutional units and sectors.

Subsoil assets (AN.212)

13.59. Subsoil assets are proven reserves of mineral deposits located on or below the earth's surface that are economically exploitable given current technology and relative prices. Mine shafts, wells and other extraction sites are included with structures rather than with the subsoil asset.

13.60. The value of the reserves is usually determined by the present value of the expected net returns resulting from the commercial exploitation of those assets, although such valuations are subject to uncertainty and revision. As the ownership of subsoil assets does not change frequently on markets, it may be difficult to obtain appropriate prices which can be used for valuation purposes. In practice, it may be necessary to use the valuations which the owners of the assets place on them in their own accounts.

Other natural assets (AN.213 and AN.214)

13.61. Non-cultivated biological resources and water resources are included in the balance sheet to the extent that they have been recognized as having economic value that is not included in the value of the associated land. As observed prices are not likely to be available, they are usually valued by the present value of the future returns expected from them.

Intangible non-produced assets (AN.22)

13.62. Intangible non-produced assets entitle their owners to engage in certain specific activities or to produce certain specific goods or service and to exclude other institutional units from doing so except with the permission of the owner. The owners of the assets may be able to earn monopoly profits by restricting the use of the assets to themselves. Included are patented entities, leases and other transferable contracts, and purchased goodwill.

13.63. Whenever possible, intangible assets should be valued at current prices when they are actually traded on markets. Otherwise, it may be necessary to use estimates of the present value of the expected future returns to be received by the owners of such assets. For purchased goodwill, valuation should be at acquisition cost less accumulated amortization (appropriately revalued).

3. Financial assets/liabilities (AF.)

13.64. In line with the general valuation principles described above, financial assets and liabilities should be valued at current prices whenever they are regularly traded on organized financial markets, and they should also be assigned the same value in the balance sheets whether they appear as assets or liabili-

ties. The prices should exclude service charges, fees, commissions and similar payments for services provided in carrying out the transactions. Financial claims that are not traded on organized financial markets should be valued by the amount that a debtor must pay to the creditor to extinguish the claim.

Monetary gold and SDRs (AF.1)

13.65. Monetary gold is to be valued at the price established in organized markets or in bilateral arrangements between central banks. The value of the SDR is determined daily by the IMF on the basis of a basket of currencies, and rates against domestic currencies are obtainable from the prices in foreign exchange markets; both basket and weights are revised from time to time.

Currency and deposits (AF.2)

13.66. For currency, the valuation is the nominal or face value of the currency. For deposits, the values to be recorded in the balance sheets of both creditors and debtors are the amounts of principal that the debtors are contractually obliged to repay the creditors under the terms of the deposits when the deposits are liquidated. Any margin payments related to options or futures contracts are included in other deposits.

Securities other than shares (AF.3)

13.67. In principle, short-term securities, and the corresponding liabilities, are to be valued at their current market values. Such a valuation is particularly important under conditions of high inflation or high nominal interest rates. If market values are not available, short-term bonds issued at par should be valued at the face value plus accrued interest not due for payment or not paid, and discounted bonds should be valued at the issue price plus accrued interest. The longer the original maturity of a security issued at a discount, however, the less acceptable it becomes to value such a security at its face or par value. It is recommended, therefore, that the use of par values should be restricted to bills issued at a discount whose original maturities do not exceed three months and to short-term bills or bonds issued at par that carry a stated rate of interest.

13.68. As a general principle, long-term securities, and the corresponding liabilities, are to be valued at the current prices of the securities on financial markets when they are regularly traded.

13.69. Long-term securities should always be valued at their current prices on markets, whether they are bonds on which regular payments of interest are paid or deep-discounted or zero-coupon bonds on which little or no interest is paid. Although the nominal liability of the issuer of a long-term security may be fixed in money terms, the market prices at which fixed interest securities are traded may vary considerably in response to variations in general market rates of interest. As the issuer of a long-term security usually has the opportunity to refinance the debt by repurchasing the security on the market, valuation at market prices is generally appropriate for both issuers and holders of long-term securities, especially financial transactors who actively manage their assets or liabilities. Deep-discounted and zero-coupon bonds should always be valued in the balance sheets at their current market values. When general market rates of interest fluctuate, the market value of such bonds may diverge significantly from their face or par values reduced by the remaining actual and/or imputed interest payments which are still due to be paid on them.

13.70. The treatment of derivatives is discussed in chapter XI. Traded financial options, traded financial futures and warrants should be included in the balance sheets at market value. Depending on how margin systems operate, it may be appropriate to enter zero for the value of the option, as any profits (losses) will have been received (paid) daily by the holder. The counterpart of these asset entries should be entered as a liability.

13.71. Other financial options should be valued in the balance sheets as either the current value of the option, if this is available, or the amount of the premium paid. A liability should be entered in the sector of the writer of the option to represent, by convention, either the current value of buying out the rights of the option holder or the accrual of a holding gain.

Loans (AF.4)

13.72. The values to be recorded in the balance sheets of both creditors and debtors are the amounts of principal that the debtors are contractually obliged to repay the creditors when the loans mature.

Shares and other equity (AF.5)

13.73. Shares and other equities should be valued in the balance sheets at their current prices when they are regularly traded on stock exchanges or other organized financial markets. The value of shares in corporations that are not quoted on stock exchanges or otherwise traded regularly should be estimated using the prices of quoted shares that are comparable in earnings and dividend history and prospects, adjusting downward, if necessary, to allow for the inferior marketability or liquidity of unquoted shares. Equity in quasi-corporations should be valued as equal to the value of the quasi-corporations' assets less the value of their liabilities.

13.74. As noted in the discussion of net worth paragraph 13.83 below, shares and other equities are liabilities of corporations, and even though a corporation is wholly owned by its shareholders collectively, it is seen to have a net worth—derived in the same way as for all other institutional units—in addition to the value of the shareholders' equity. By convention, reinvested earnings of direct investment enterprises are considered to be distributed in property income and subsequently reinvested, and the net worth of those resident direct investment enterprises that are branches of non-resident enterprises, which are treated as quasi-corporations in the System, is zero. Direct investment enterprises may receive or pay capital transfers, incur holding gains/losses, etc., so that their actual

change in net worth is not the same as the change in shares and other equity recorded in the financial account.

Insurance technical reserves (AF.6)

13.75. Insurance technical reserves consist of net equity of households in life insurance reserves and in pension funds, prepayment of premiums and reserves against outstanding claims. These reserves are invested in various other kinds of assets such as land, buildings, financial assets, valuables, etc. The assets of which the reserves are composed are valued in the balance sheet at their actual or estimated current prices.

13.76. In the case of net equity of households in life insurance, the covered individuals have claims to the future payment of a capital sum on the occurrence of death, and it is possible to ascertain the present value of the individuals' actuarially determined claims to the payment of capital or income. This value is the liability of life insurance enterprises for reserves against outstanding risks and reserves for with-profit insurance that add to the value on maturity of with-profit endowments or similar policies; this amount is counterbalanced by an equivalent amount of assets. In the case of with-profit insurance, the reserves include various types of gains distributed to the insured as deferred profits. The usual accounting practice of mutual insurance enterprises—i.e., where the policyholders are the owners—is to transfer realized and perhaps unrealized holding gains to policyholders' reserves when they become large and are considered to be permanent.

13.77. In the case of net equity of households in pension funds, the covered individuals have claims to the future payment of income on the attainment of a specified age and/or period of coverage. The nature of liability of the funds—and asset of households—depends on the kind of pension plan.

13.78. Defined benefit pension plans are those in which the level of pension benefits promised to participating employees is guaranteed. Benefits are related by some formula to participants' length of service and salary and are not totally dependent on the assets in the fund. A case can be made that a defined benefit pension fund can have a net worth, positive or negative, if assets of the fund exceed or fall short of the fund's liability for the guaranteed benefits. Whether assets of the fund exceed the fund's liability for the guaranteed benefits—i.e., if the plan is over-funded—or fall short the fund's liability—i.e., if the plan is under-funded—there is some expectation that the situation will be temporary, typically by adjusting contributions. Further, national law, especially with respect to over-funding, varies with respect to the question to whom, employers or households, a surplus or shortfall is to be attributed. The System, in this situation, allows a defined benefit pension plan to have a net worth. The liability of a defined benefit pension plan is equal to the present value of the promised benefits.

13.79. Money purchase plans are those for which the level of contributions to the fund is guaranteed, but benefits are directly dependent on the assets of the fund. The liability of a money purchase plan is the current market value of the funds' assets.

13.80. The value of the prepaid premiums component of insurance technical reserves is determined on the basis of the proportion of the risks involved in relation to time for the time remaining on the contract—in other words, premiums payable less premiums earned, which are recorded as a transaction in the financial account. Reserves against outstanding claims are the present value of the amounts expected to be paid out in settlement of claims, including disputed claims.

Other accounts receivable/payable (AF.7)

13.81. Trade credit and advances and other items due to be received or paid (such as taxes, dividends, rent, wages and salaries, and social contributions) should be valued for both creditors and debtors at the amount of principal the debtors are contractually obliged to pay the creditors when the obligation is extinguished. Interest accrued on securities other than shares is recorded as increasing the value of the underlying asset, but interest accruing on deposits and loans may have to follow national practices and be classified here if it is not capitalized in the underlying asset. As discussed in chapter XI, paragraph 11.102, no separate entry is needed for interest in arrears because it is already recorded under the appropriate asset or under this category.

4. Net worth (B.90)

13.82. Net worth is the difference between the value of all assets—produced, non-produced, and financial—and all liabilities at a particular moment in time. For this calculation, each asset and each liability is to be identified and valued separately. As the balancing item, net worth is calculated for institutional units and sectors and for the total economy.

13.83. Shares and other equities are liabilities of corporations, and by valuing them at current market prices it is possible to arrive at the net worth of a corporation in the same way as for all other institutional units by subtracting the total value of all its liabilities—including equities—from the total value of its assets. Thus, even though a corporation is wholly owned by its shareholders collectively, it is seen to have a net worth (which could be positive or negative) in addition to the value of the shareholders' equity. In the case of quasi-corporations, net worth is zero, because the value of the owners' equity is assumed to be equal to its assets less its liabilities. In the case of financial corporations, the net worth of pension funds includes an amount that is positive or negative if the assets of defined benefit pension funds exceed or fall short of the funds' liability for the guaranteed benefits—i.e., the plans are over- or underfunded. Some defined benefit pension funds (unsegregated funds) are not autonomous financial corporations; in this case it is the net worth of the employer that is increased or decreased if the plan is over- or underfunded.

5. Memorandum items

13.84. The System allows for two memorandum items to the balance sheets in order to show items not separately identified as assets in the central framework that are of more specialized analytic interest for particular institutional sectors. These two—consumer durables and direct foreign investment—are discussed below, along with two other items that may be usefully included as memorandum items in some cases.

Consumer durables (AN.m)

13.85. Consumer durables—i.e., durable goods used by households for final consumption—are to be included in the balance sheets only as memorandum items. As explained in chapter IX, their inclusion in the balance sheet would be appropriate if the System postulated that the durables were gradually used up in production processes whose outputs consist of services. The System does not treat consumer durables in this way. The stocks of consumer durables held by households—transport equipment and other machinery and equipment—are to be valued at current prices, both gross and net of accumulated charges equivalent to consumption of fixed capital. The figures shown as memorandum items in the balance sheet should be net of these accumulated charges.

13.86. Durable goods owned by owners of unincorporated enterprises may be used partly by the enterprise for production and partly by members of the household for final consumption. The values shown in the balance sheet for the enterprise should reflect the proportion of the use that is attributable to the enterprise, but this may not always be known in practice.

Direct foreign investment (AF.m)

13.87. Financial assets and liabilities that constitute direct investment are to be recorded under the appropriate categories listed in the classification of assets, i.e., shares and other equity, loans, and other accounts receivable and payable. However, the amounts of direct investment included within each of those categories should also be recorded separately as a memorandum item.

Net equity of households in unfunded pension schemes

13.88. Unfunded occupational pension schemes, which include some classified as social security funds, are by definition defined benefit schemes. There is no pool of assets accumulated from which to pay benefits, however. It is recommended that the present value to households of promises by these schemes to pay future pension benefits be shown as a memorandum item in the balance sheets as assets of households. Liabilities of equivalent amount may also be shown as memorandum items for the employer sectors liable to pay these benefits.

Alternative valuations for long-term debt and corporate equity

13.89. Alternatives to current market values in valuing long-term bonds and corporate equity securities may be shown as memorandum items in the balance sheets for corporations. Examples of alternative valuation include nominal (face) value for long-term bonds and revalued paid-in and equivalent value for

C. The changes in balance sheets account

13.90. In both opening and closing balance sheets, assets and liabilities, as previously explained, are valued at the prices prevailing on the date to which the balance sheet relates. Net worth, the difference between assets and liabilities, is the balancing item. It is equivalent to the present value of the stock of economic claims a unit or a sector holds. In more detailed presentations of balance sheets, the various types of assets and liabilities are shown using the detailed classification of assets and liabilities.

13.91. For each element or group of assets and liabilities, changes between the opening and closing balance sheets result from the entries recorded in the accumulation accounts, including changes in classification of assets and liabilities. Changes in net worth are equal to changes in assets less changes in liabilities. The changes in balance sheets account shown in table 13.1 summarizes these entries both by major groups of assets and liabilities and by the summary element in each of the accumulation accounts.

13.92. The change in the value of any individual item between the opening and closing balance sheets may be decomposed into the following elements:

  (a)   Changes due to transactions in the item in question—acquisitions or disposals of non-financial assets; consumption of fixed capital; the creation, transfer, or extinction of financial claims, etc.;

  (b)   Changes in the volume of assets that are not due to transactions—discoveries of assets or recognition of their value; the unanticipated destruction or disappearance of assets; changes in classification; etc.;

  (c)   Nominal holding gains/losses on assets due to changes in their prices, which may be decomposed into

      (i)   "Neutral" holding gains/losses, which are due to changes in the general price level; and

      (ii) "Real" holding gains/losses, which are due to changes in the price of the asset relative to the prices of other goods, services, or assets.

13.93. The changes in balance sheets account recapitulates the total changes in assets by major group and in total liabilities and then recapitulates the changes in net worth in terms of saving and capital transfers, other changes in volume of assets and nominal holding gains/losses (subdivided between neutral and real holding gains/losses). Saving, capital transfers, other

corporate equity. These valuations refer to the same date for each issue of a security and would be meaningful in the analysis of both liabilities and financial assets.

changes in volume of assets, and real holding gains/losses contribute to changes in real net worth.

13.94. The changes in balance sheets account shows the relation in the System between saving (net) and changes in net worth. Because saving is a source of changes in real net worth, it follows that all current transactions, of which saving is the final balancing item, make real net worth vary either positively (resources) or negatively (uses). Saving (net) is equal to changes in net worth less net capital transfers received, less other changes in volume of assets, less nominal holding gains/losses. Considering only changes in real net worth, saving (net) is equal to changes in real net worth less net capital transfers received, less other changes in volume of assets, and less real holding gains/losses.

13.95. The accounting link between the opening and closing balance sheets via the sequence of accumulation accounts holds at the level of an individual asset or liability or at any higher level of aggregation. The links are displayed schematically in table 13.2.

13.96. Each row of table 13.2 refers to individual assets or groups of assets following the classification of assets and liabilities used in the System. The full classification is given in the annex to this chapter, in which the characteristics of the various assets or liabilities are described in more detail. (The basis of this classification is type of asset; the basis of the classifications used in the accumulation accounts, however, is type of transaction, volume change, or holding gain/loss.) The last row of table 13.2 shows the components of net worth or changes in net worth.

13.97. Each column of table 13.2 refers to a particular balance sheet or account, arranged in sequence to follow the basic accounting identity described earlier.

13.98. The codes recorded in the various cells of table 13.2 are the standard classification codes used in the System to identify particular kinds of transactions or other entries. They therefore indicate which kinds of transactions or other entries in the accounts may appear for the various assets and liabilities.

13.99. Consider, for example, the row for dwellings. The entry in the column for the capital account should record the value of gross fixed capital formation less consumption of fixed capital in dwellings, the other items in the capital account being irrelevant to this type of asset. The cell at the intersection of the row for dwellings and the column for the financial account must be empty. The cell at the intersection with the column for the other changes in the volume of assets account might also be empty, but might well record the consequences of some happening such as an earthquake or other natural disaster. The entries at the intersection with the columns for the revaluation account should record the value of any neutral and real holding gains/losses on dwellings due to changes in prices during the accounting period.

13.100. Subsoil assets provide a less familiar example. The entry in the column for the capital account should record the value of acquisitions and disposals, which redistribute the ownership of these assets among sectors but balance for the total economy. The cell for the financial account is again empty. The cell for the other changes in the volume of assets account would record depletion of subsoil deposits and new discoveries of proven reserves, among other possible entries. The cell for the revaluation account should record the value of any neutral and real holding gains/losses due to changes in the prices of the assets.

13.101. The accounting for the change in the value of other non-produced assets between opening and closing balance sheets is worth detailing. For land, for example, the following elements my be involved:

(a) Gross fixed capital formation in the form of land improvements and costs of ownership transfer; consumption of fixed capital on those land improvements and costs of ownership transfer; and acquisitions less disposals of land, which transfer land among domestic residents and may, as well, change the boundary of the economic territory if the transactions involving non-res-

idents affect the size of territorial enclaves—all of which are recorded in the capital account;

(b) Economic appearance of land (for example, reclaiming land from the sea), economic disappearance (degradation and other negative quality changes resulting from economic activity), catastrophic losses, uncompensated seizures, volume changes in non-financial assets not elsewhere classified, and changes in classification and structure—all recorded in the other changes in the volume of assets account;

(c) Neutral holding gains/losses and real holding gains/losses, recorded in the revaluation account.

For an intangible non-produced asset, such as a patented entity, the following elements may be involved:

(a) Acquisitions less disposals of patented entities, which transfer these assets among sectors and the rest of the world and are recorded in the capital account;

(b) Creation (economic appearance) of patented entities, economic disappearance—i.e., the exhaustion of patent protection, catastrophic losses, uncompensated seizures, volume changes in non-financial assets not elsewhere classified, and changes in classification and structure—all recorded in the other changes in the volume of assets account;

(c) Neutral holding gains/losses and real holding gains/losses, recorded in the revaluation account.

D. Stocks of financial assets and liabilities analysed by sector of debtor and creditor

13.102. The balance sheet, as presented in table 13.1, records the financial assets and liabilities for all institutional sectors by type of financial instrument. For each sector, the balance sheet shows the financial liabilities that the sector has incurred to mobilize financial resources and the financial assets that the sector has acquired. The balance sheet, like the financial account, thus presents a two-dimensional view of a sector's financial instruments and whether the sector is a creditor or a debtor. This information is valuable in identifying the financial assets that net borrowing sectors use to finance their deficits and the assets that net lending sectors use to allocate their surpluses, but the question of who is financing whom is not answered.

13.103. For a full understanding, it is often important to know in more detail the financial relationships between sectors and the financial assets by which these relationships are carried out. For example, it is often important for the government to know not just what types of liabilities it has built up in financing its deficit but also which sectors (or the rest of the world) have provided the financing. For financial corporations (and those

supervising them), it is important to know not only the composition of financial assets (loans and securities) that they have acquired, but also which sectors these are claims upon. In addition, it is often necessary to analyse debtor/creditor relationships between sub-sectors within a sector (central government financial transactions with local governments or central bank financial transactions with depository institutions) and across sector boundaries (changes in depository institutions' claims on public non-financial corporations). Such detailed information is necessary to understand how financing has been carried out and how it has changed over time.

13.104. This more detailed approach is particularly important in spelling out the role that financial intermediaries play in mobilizing financial resources through certain financial transactions and making these financial resources available to other sectors in forms suitable to these sectors through maturity/asset transformation. Thus, financial corporations play a critical role in directing financial flows from net lending sectors to net borrowing sectors, allowing lenders to choose their asset instruments and borrowers their forms of indebtedness.

Table 13.2. Balance sheets and accumulation accounts
(a map of entries from opening balance sheet to closing balance sheet)

Classifications of assets, liabilities and net worth	IV.1 Opening balance sheet	III.1 Capital account	III.2 Financial account	III.3.1 Other changes in the volume of assets account	III.3.2 Revaluation account III.3.2.1 Neutral holding gains and losses	III.3.2.2 Real holding gains and losses	IV.3 Closing balance sheet
Non-financial assets	AN	P.5, K.1, K.2	...	K.3, K.4, K.5, K.6, K.7, K.8, K.9, K.12.1, K.12.22	K.11.1	K.11.2	AN
Produced assets	AN.1	P.5, K.1	...	K.4, K.7, K.8, K.9, K.12.1, K.12.22	K.11.1	K.11.2	AN.1
Fixed assets [1]	AN.11	P.51, K.1	...	K.4, K.7, K.8, K.9, K.12.1, K.12.22	K.11.1	K.11.2	AN.11
Tangible fixed assets	AN.111	P.511, K.1	...	K.4, K.7, K.8, K.9, K.12.1, K.12.22	K.11.1	K.11.2	AN.111
Dwellings	AN.1111	P.511, K.1	...	K.4, K.7, K.8, K.9, K.12.1, K.12.22	K.11.1	K.11.2	AN.1111
Other buildings and structures	AN.1112	P.511, K.1	...	K.4, K.7, K.8, K.9, K.12.1, K.12.22	K.11.1	K.11.2	AN.1112
Machinery and equipment	AN.1113	P.511, K.1	...	K.7, K.8, K.9, K.12.1, K.12.22	K.11.1	K.11.2	AN.1113
Cultivated assets	AN.1114	P.511, K.1	...	K.7, K.8, K.9, K.12.1, K.12.22	K.11.1	K.11.2	AN.1114
Intangible fixed assets	AN.112	P.512, K.1	...	K.7, K.8, K.9, K.12.1, K.12.22	K.11.1	K.11.2	AN.112
Inventories	AN.12	P.52	...	K.7, K.8, K.9, K.12.1, K.12.22	K.11.1	K.11.2	AN.12
Valuables	AN.13	P.53	...	K.4, K.7, K.8, K.9, K.12.1, K.12.22	K.11.1	K.11.2	AN.13
Non-produced assets	AN.2	K.2, P.513, K.1	...	K.3, K.5, K.61, K.62, K.7, K.8, K.9, K.12.1, K.12.22	K.11.1	K.11.2	AN.2
Tangible non-produced assets	AN.21	K.21, P.513, K.1	...	K.3, K.5, K.61, K.62, K.7, K.8, K.9, K.12.1, K.12.22	K.11.1	K.11.2	AN.21
Land	AN.211	K.21, P.513, K.1	...	K.3, K.62, K.7 K.8, K.9, K.12.1, K.12.22	K.11.1	K.11.2	AN.211
Subsoil assets	AN.212	K.21, P.513,	...	K.3, K.61, K.62, K.7, K.8, K.9, K.12.1, K.12.22	K.11.1	K.11.2	AN.212
Non-cultivated biological resources	AN.213	K.21, P.513,	...	K.3, K.5, K.61, K.62, K.7, K.8, K.9, K.12.1, K.12.22	K.11.1	K.11.2	AN.213
Water resources	AN.214	K.21, P.513,		K.3, K.61, K.62, K.7, K.8, K.9, K.12.1, K.12.22	K.11.1	K.11.2	AN.214
Intangible non-produced assets	AN.22	K.22, P.513,		K.3, K.62, K.7 K.8, K.9, K.12.1, K.12.22	K.11.1	K.11.2	AN.22
Financial assets/liabilities [2]	AF	...	F	K.7, K.8, K.10, K.12.1, K.12.21, K.12.22	K.11.1	K.11.2	AF

Table 13.2. **Balance sheets and accumulation accounts**
(a map of entries from opening balance sheet to closing balance sheet) [cont.]

Classifications of assets, liabilities and net worth	IV.1 Opening balance sheet	III.1 Capital account	III.2 Financial account	III.3.1 Other changes in the volume of assets account	III.3.2 Revaluation account III.3.2.1 Neutral holding gains and losses	III.3.2.2 Real holding gains and losses	IV.3 Closing balance sheet
Monetary gold and SDRs (ass (assets only)	AF.1	...	F.1	K.7, K.8, K.10, K.12.1, K.12.21, K.12.22	K.11.1	K.11.2	AF.1
Currency and deposits ³	AF.2	...	F.2	K.7, K.8, K.10, K.12.1, K.12.22	K.11.1	K.11.2	AF.2
Securities other than shares	AF.3	...	F.3	K.7, K.8, K.10, K.12.1, K.12.22	K.11.1	K.11.2	AF.3
Loans	AF.4	...	F.4	K.7, K.8, K.10, K.12.1, K.12.22	K.11.1	K.11.2	AF.4
Shares and other equity	AF.5	...	F.5	K.7, K.8, K.10, K.12.1, K.12.22	K.11.1	K.11.2	AF.5
Insurance technical reserves	AF.6	...	F.6	K.7, K.8, K.10, K.12.1, K.12.22	K.11.1	K.11.2	AF.6
Other accounts receivable/payable	AF.7	...	F.7	K.7, K.8, K.10, K.12.1, K.12.22	K.11.1	K.11.2	AF.7
Net worth	B.90	B.10.1	B.10.1	B.10.2	B.10.31	B.10.32	B.90

1 Memorandum item: AN.m. Consumer durables.
2 Memorandum item: AF.m. Direct foreign investment.
3 Memorandum items:
  m11 Denominated in national currency
  m12 Denominated in foreign currency
  m21 Liability of resident institutions
  m22 Liability of the rest of the world.

AN ..., AF ... are from classification of assets.

Balancing items
B.10.1 Changes in net worth due to saving and net capital transfers
B.10.2 Changes in net worth due to other changes in volume of assets
B.10.3.1 Changes in net worth due to neutral holding gains/losses
B.10.3.2 Changes in net worth due to real holding gains/losses
B.90 Net worth

Transactions in financial instruments
F Transactions in financial instruments
F.1 Monetary gold and SDRs
F.2 Currency and deposits
F.3 Securities other than shares
F.4 Loans
F.5 Shares and other equity
F.6 Insurance technical reserves
F.7 Other accounts receivable/payable

Transactions in goods and services
P.5 Gross capital formation
P.51 Gross fixed capital formation
P.511 Acquisitions less disposals of tangible fixed assets
P.512 Acquisitions less disposals of intangible fixed assets
P.513 Additions to the value of non-produced non-financial assets

P.52 Changes in inventories
P.53 Acquisitions less disposals of valuables

Other accumulation entries
K.1 Consumption of fixed capital
K.2 Acquisitions less disposals of non-produced non-financial assets
K.21 Acquisitions less disposals of land and other tangible non-produced assets
K.22 Acquisitions less disposals of intangible non-produced assets
K.3 Economic appearance of non-produced assets
K.4 Economic appearance of produced assets
K.5 Natural growth of non-cultivated biological resources
K.61 Depletion of natural assets
K.62 Other economic disappearance of non-produced assets
K.7 Catastrophic losses
K.8 Uncompensated seizures
K.9 Other volume changes in non-financial assets n.e.c.
K.10 Other volume changes in financial assets and liabilities n.e.c.
K.11 Nominal holding gains/losses
K.11.1 Neutral holding gains/losses
K.11.2 Real holding gains/losses
K.12 Changes in classifications and structure
K.12.1 Changes in sector classification and structure
K.12.21 Monetization/demonetization of gold
K.12.22 Changes other than monetization/demonetization of gold in classifications of assets or liabilities

Table 13.3a. Stocks of financial assets analysed by sector of debtor and creditor

Financial assets of:

The rest of the world (12)	House-holds (11)	NPISHs (10)	General govern-ment (9)	Non-financial corpo-rations (8)	Financial corporations			Other financial inter-mediaries (4)	Financial auxi-liaries (3)	Insurance corpora-tions and pension funds (2)	Total (1)	Type of claim and debtor
					Central bank (7)	Other deposit institutions						
						Deposit money institutions (6)	Other deposit accepting (5)					

Type of claim and debtor

1. Monetary gold and SDRs

2. Currency and deposits
    a. Currency
        i. National
            - Residents
            - Non-residents
        ii. Foreign
            - Residents
    b. Transferable deposits
        i. In national currency
            - Residents
            - Non-residents
        ii. Foreign currency
            - Residents
            - Non-residents
    c. Other deposits
        i. In national currency
            - Residents
            - Non-residents
        ii. Foreign currency
            - Residents
            - Non-residents

3. Securities other than shares
    a. Short-term
        i. Non-financial corporations
        ii. Financial corporations
        iii. Central government
        iv. State and local government
        v. Other resident sectors
        vi. The rest of the world
    b. Long-term
        i. Non-financial corporations
        ii. Financial corporations
        iii. Central government
        iv. State and local government
        v. Other resident sectors
        vi. The rest of the world

4. Loans
    a. Short-term
        i. Non-financial corporations
        ii. Financial corporations
        iii. Central government
        iv. State and local government
        v. Other resident sectors
        vi. The rest of the world
    b. Long-term
        i. Non-financial corporations
        ii. Financial corporations
        iii. Central government
        iv. State and local government
        v. Other resident sectors
        vi. The rest of the world

5. Shares and other equity
    a. Resident enterprises
        i. Quoted
        ii. Not quoted
    b. Non-resident enterprises
        i. Quoted
        ii. Not quoted

6. Insurance technical reserves
    6.1 Net equity of households on life insurance reserves and on pension funds
    6.2 Prepayments of premiums and reserves against outstanding claims

7. Other accounts receivable and payable
    7.1 Trade credit and advances
        a. Non-financial corporations
        b. Households
        c. Central government
        d. State and local government
        e. Other resident sectors
        f. The rest of the world
    7.2 Other
        a. Resident sectors
        b. The rest of the world
    Memorandum items:
        Direct investment
            Equity
            Loans
            Other

Table 13.3b. Stocks of financial liabilities analysed by sector of debtor and creditor

Financial liabilities of:

The rest of the world (12)	House-holds (11)	NPISHs (10)	General govern-ment (9)	Non-financial corpo-rations (8)	Central bank (7)	Deposit money institutions (6)	Other deposit accepting (5)	Other financial inter-mediaries (4)	Financial auxi-liaries (3)	Insurance corpora-tions and pension funds (2)	Total (1)	Type of claim and creditor

In the header, columns (6) and (5) are grouped under "Other deposit institutions", and columns (7), (6), (5), (4), (3), (2) are grouped under "Financial corporations".

												Type of claim and creditor
												2. Currency and deposits
												a. Currency
												i. National
												- Residents
												- Non-residents
												ii. Foreign
												- Residents
												b. Transferable deposits
												i. In national currency
												- Residents
												- Non-residents
												ii. Foreign currency
												- Residents
												- Non-residents
												c. Other deposits
												i. In national currency
												- Residents
												- Non-residents
												ii. Foreign currency
												- Residents
												- Non-residents
												3. Securities other than shares
												a. Short-term
												i. Non-financial corporations
												ii. Financial corporations
												iii. Central government
												iv. State and local government
												v. Other resident sectors
												vi. The rest of the world
												b. Long-term
												i. Non-financial corporations
												ii. Financial corporations
												iii. Central government
												iv. State and local government
												v. Other resident sectors
												vi. The rest of the world
												4. Loans
												a. Short-term
												i. Non-financial corporations
												ii. Financial corporations
												iii. Central government
												iv. State and local government
												v. Other resident sectors
												vi. The rest of the world
												b. Long-term
												i. Non-financial corporations
												ii. Financial corporations
												iii. Central government
												iv. State and local government
												v. Other resident sectors
												vi. The rest of the world
												5. Shares and other equity
												a. Resident enterprises
												i. Quoted
												ii. Not quoted
												b. Non-resident enterprises
												i. Quoted
												ii. Not quoted
												6. Insurance technical reserves
												6.1 Net equity of households on life insurance reserves and on pension funds
												6.2 Prepayments of premiums and reserves against outstanding claims
												7. Other accounts receivable and payable
												7.1 Trade credit and advances
												a. Non-financial corporations
												b. Households
												c. Central government
												d. State and local government
												e. Other resident sectors
												f. The rest of the world
												7.2 Other
												a. Resident sectors
												b. The rest of the world
												Memorandum items:
												Direct investment
												Equity
												Loans
												Other

13.105. To facilitate the more detailed financial analysis just described, the System contains two tables, tables 13.3a and 13.3b. These are the balance sheet, or stocks versions of tables 11.3a and 11.3b. Table 13.3a records assets cross-classified by type of asset and by the debtor sector. The sectors holding assets are shown horizontally across the top of the table, and the type of asset, disaggregated by sector of debtor, is arrayed vertically. Table 13.3b records liabilities cross-classified by type of liability and by the creditor sector. The tables, as presented, identify the full sectors for households, non-profit institutions serving households, general government, and non-financial corporations. Sub-sectors are shown for the financial corporations to emphasize the special role these units play. For particular analysis or policy purposes, it may be useful to break down the other sectors into sub-sectors as well—for example, to identify financial positions of central government or of non-financial public corporations. The sector breakdown under each type of financial asset is suggestive rather than prescriptive. For securities and loans, it is suggested to identify the debtor sectors as follows: non-financial corporations, financial corporations, central government, state and local government, other resident sectors, and the rest of the world. Alternative breakdowns are illustrated for other types of assets.

13.106. These tables can be used in at least three important areas related to economic policy, corresponding to the uses of their counterpart flow tables in chapter XI: in economic analysis and description of activity and trends in current periods, as an aid to projections in the context of economic plans or to assess the effect of economic policies on the future path of the economy and in projects that undertake modelling of the economy to study economic behaviour as an aid to the formulation of economic policy. Such studies, of course, would be complementary to similar work on data from other accounts in the System.

13.107. Like their counterparts in chapter XI, tables 13.3a and 13.3b should be interpreted as a general model, and substantial flexibility should be allowed in specific country circumstances. In many countries, the dimensions of the tables will be severely constrained by data availability. It should also be noted that these tables are extensions of the basic balance sheet and that adding the third dimension to the analysis can be done on a selective basis by identifying particular assets or sector (or sub-sector) relationships for which this level of detail would be useful.

Annex
Definitions of assets

Classification of assets[a]	Definitions
Non-financial assets	**(AN)** Entities, over which ownership rights are enforced by institutional units, individually or collectively, and from which economic benefits may be derived by their owners by holding them, or using them over a period of time, that consist of tangible assets, both produced and non-produced, and most intangible assets for which no corresponding liabilities are recorded.
Produced assets	**(AN.1)** Non-financial assets that have come into existence as outputs from production processes. Produced assets consist of fixed assets, inventories and valuables, as defined below.
Fixed assets	**(AN.11)** Produced assets that are used repeatedly or continuously in production processes for more than one year. Fixed assets consist of tangible and intangible fixed assets, as defined below.
Tangible fixed assets	**(AN.111)** Fixed assets that consist of dwellings; other buildings and structures; machinery and equipment and cultivated assets, as defined below.
Dwellings	**(AN.1111)** Buildings that are used entirely or primarily as residences, including any associated structures, such as garages, and all permanent fixtures customarily installed in residences. Houseboats, barges, mobile homes and caravans used as principal residences of households are also included, as are historic monuments identified primarily as dwellings. Costs of site clearance and preparation are also included. Examples include products included in Central Product Classification (CPC)[a] class 5211, residential buildings and CPC group 387, prefabricated buildings, such as one- and two-dwelling buildings and other residential buildings intended for non-transient occupancy. Uncompleted dwellings are included to the extent that the ultimate user is deemed to have taken ownership, either because the construction is on own-account or as evidenced by the existence of a contract of sale/purchase. Dwellings acquired for military personnel are included because they are used, as are dwellings acquired by civilian units, for the production of housing services.
Other buildings and structures	**(AN.1112)** Non-residential buildings and other structures, as defined below.

---

[a] *Provisional Central Product Classification* (United Nations publication, Sales No. E.91.XVII.7).

Classification of assets[a]	Definitions

Uncompleted buildings and structures are included to the extent that the ultimate user is deemed to have taken ownership, either because the construction is for own use or as evidenced by the existence of a contract of sale/purchase. Buildings and structures acquired for military purposes are included to the extent that they resemble civilian buildings acquired for purposes of production and are used in the same way.

Non-residential buildings
(AN.11121)
Buildings other than dwellings, including fixtures, facilities and equipment that are integral parts of the structures and costs of site clearance and preparation. Historic monuments identified primarily as non-residential buildings are also included.

Examples include products included in CPC class 5212, non-residential buildings, such as warehouse and industrial buildings, commercial buildings, buildings for public entertainment, hotels, restaurants, educational buildings, health buildings, etc.

Other structures
(AN.11122)
Structures other than buildings, including the cost of the streets, sewers and site clearance and preparation other than for residential or non- residential buildings. Also included are historic monuments for which identification as dwellings or non-residential buildings is not possible and shafts, tunnels and other structures associated with mining subsoil assets. (Major improvements to land, such as dams and dykes for flood control, are included in the value of land.)

Examples include products included in CPC group 522, civil engineering works, such as highways, streets, roads, railways and airfield runways; bridges, elevated highways, tunnels and subways; waterways, harbours, dams and other waterworks; long-distance pipelines, communication and power lines; local pipelines and cables, ancillary works; constructions for mining and manufacture; and constructions for sport and recreation.

Machinery and equipment

(AN.1113)
Transport equipment and other machinery and equipment, as defined below other than that acquired by households for final consumption. Tools that are relatively inexpensive and purchased at a relatively steady rate, such as hand tools, may be excluded. Also excluded are machinery and equipment integral to buildings that are included in dwellings and non-residential buildings.

Uncompleted machinery and equipment are excluded, unless produced for own use, because the ultimate user is deemed to take ownership only on delivery of the asset. Machinery and equipment acquired for military purposes are included to the extent that they resemble goods acquired by civilian units for purposes of production and that the military uses in the same way.

Machinery and equipment acquired by households for final consumption are not treated as an asset. They are instead included in the memorandum item "consumer durables" in the balance sheet for households. Houseboats, barges, mobile homes and caravans used by households as principal residences are included in dwellings.

Transport equipment
(AN.11131)
Equipment for moving people and objects. Examples include products other than parts included in CPC division 49, transport equipment, such as motor vehicles, trailers and semitrailers; ships; railway and tramway locomotives and rolling stock; aircraft and spacecraft; and motorcycles, bicycles, etc.

Classification of assets[a]	Definitions

Other machinery and equipment
(AN.11132)
Machinery and equipment not elsewhere classified. Examples include products other than parts included in CPC divisions 43, general purpose machinery; 44, special purpose machinery; 45, office, accounting and computing equipment; 46, electrical machinery and apparatus; 47, radio, television and communication equipment and apparatus; and 48, medical appliances, precision and optical instruments, watches and clocks. Other examples are products other than parts included in CPC groups 337, fuel elements (cartridges) for nuclear reactors; 381, furniture; 383, musical instruments; 384, sports goods; and 423, steam generators except central heating boilers.

Cultivated assets

(AN.1114)
Livestock for breeding, dairy, draught, etc. and vineyards, orchards and other plantations of trees yielding repeat products that are under the direct control, responsibility and management of institutional units, as defined below.

Immature cultivated assets are excluded unless produced for own use.

Livestock for breeding, dairy, draught, etc.
(AN.11141)
Livestock that are cultivated for the products they provide year after year. They include breeding stocks (including fish and poultry), dairy cattle, draft animals, sheep or other animals used for wool production and animals used for transportation, racing or entertainment.

Vineyards, orchards and other plantations of trees yielding repeat products
(AN.11142)
Trees (including vines and shrubs) cultivated for products they yield year after year, including those cultivated for fruits and nuts, for sap and resin and for bark and leaf products.

Intangible fixed assets

(AN.112)
Fixed assets that consist of mineral exploration, computer software, entertainment, literary or artistic originals and other intangible fixed assets, as defined below, intended to be used for more than one year.

Mineral exploration

(AN.1121)
The value of expenditures on exploration for petroleum and natural gas and for non-petroleum deposits. These expenditures include prelicence costs, licence and acquisition costs, appraisal costs and the costs of actual test drilling and boring, as well as the costs of aerial and other surveys, transportation costs, etc., incurred to make it possible to carry out the tests.

Computer software

(AN.1122)
Computer programs, program descriptions and supporting materials for both systems and applications software. Included are purchased software and software developed on own account, if the expenditure is large. Large expenditures on the purchase, development or extension of computer databases that are expected to be used for more than one year, whether marketed or not, are also included.

Entertainment, literary or artistic originals

(AN.1123)
Original films, sound recordings, manuscripts, tapes, models, etc., on which drama performances, radio and television programming, musical performances, sporting events, literary and artistic output, etc., are recorded or embodied. Included are works produced on own account. In some cases, such as films, there may be multiple originals.

Classification of assets[a]	Definitions
Other intangible fixed assets	(AN.1129) New information, specialized knowledge, etc., not elsewhere classified, whose use in production is restricted to the units that have established ownership rights over them or to other units licensed by the latter.
Inventories	(AN.12) Produced assets that consist of goods and services that came into existence in the current period or in an earlier period held for sale, use in production or other use at a later date. They consist of materials and supplies, work-in-progress, finished goods and goods for resale, as defined below. Included are all inventories held by government, including, but not limited to, inventories of strategic materials, grains and other commodities of special importance to the nation.
Materials and supplies	(AN.121) Goods that their owners intend to use as intermediate inputs in their own production processes, not to resell.
Work-in-progress	(AN.122) Goods and services that are partially completed but that are not usually turned over to other units without further processing or that are not mature and whose production process will be continued in a subsequent period by the same producer. Excluded are partially completed structures for which the ultimate owner is deemed to have taken ownership, either because the production is for own use or as evidenced by the existence of a contract of sale/purchase. They consist of work-in-progress on cultivated assets and other work-in-progress, as defined below.
Work-in-progress on cultivated assets	(AN.1221) Livestock raised for products yielded only on slaughter, such as fowl and fish raised commercially, trees and other vegetation yielding once-only products on destruction and immature cultivated assets yielding repeat products.
Other work-in-progress	(AN.1222) Goods other than cultivated assets and services that have been partially processed, fabricated or assembled by the producer but that are not usually sold, shipped or turned over to others without further processing.
Finished goods	(AN.123) Goods that are ready for sale or shipment by the producer.
Goods for resale	(AN.124) Goods acquired by enterprises, such as wholesalers and retailers, for the purpose of reselling them without further processing (that is, not transformed other than by presenting them in ways that are attractive to the customer).
Valuables	(AN.13) Produced assets that are not used primarily for production or consumption, that are expected to appreciate or at least not to decline in real value, that do not deteriorate over time under normal conditions and that are acquired and held primarily as stores of value. Valuables consist of precious metals and stones, antiques and other art objects and other valuables, as defined below.
Precious metals and stones	(AN.131) Precious metals and stones that are not held by enterprises for use as inputs into processes of production.

Classification of assets[a]	Definitions
Antiques and other art objects	(AN.132) Paintings, sculptures, etc., recognized as works of art and antiques.
Other valuables	(AN.139) Valuables not elsewhere classified, such as collections and jewellery of significant value fashioned out of precious stones and metals.
Non-produced assets	(AN.2) Non-financial assets that come into existence other than through processes of production. Non-produced assets consist of tangible assets and intangible assets, as defined below. Also included are costs of ownership transfer on and major improvements to these assets.
Tangible non-produced assets	(AN.21) Non-produced assets that occur in nature and over which ownership may be enforced and transferred. Environmental assets over which ownership rights have not, or cannot, be enforced, such as open seas or air, are excluded. Tangible non-produced assets consist of land, subsoil assets, non-cultivated biological resources and water resources, as defined below.
Land	(AN.211) The ground, including the soil covering and any associated surface waters, over which ownership rights are enforced. Also included are major improvements that cannot be physically separated from the land itself. Excluded are any buildings or other structures situated on it or running through it; cultivated crops, trees and animals; subsoil assets; non-cultivated biological resources and water resources below the ground. Land consists of land underlying buildings and structures, land under cultivation, recreational land and associated surface water and other land and associated surface water, as defined below.
Land underlying buildings and structures	(AN.2111) Land on which dwellings, non-residential buildings and structures are constructed or into which their foundations are dug, including yards and gardens deemed an integral part of farm and non-farm dwellings and access roads to farms.
Land under cultivation	(AN.2112) Land on which agricultural or horticultural production is carried on for commercial or subsistence purposes, including, in principle, land under plantations, orchards and vineyards.
Recreational land and associated surface water	(AN.2113) Land that is used as privately owned amenity land, parklands and pleasure grounds and publicly owned parks and recreational areas, together with associated surface water.
Other land and associated surface water	(AN.2119) Land not elsewhere classified, including private gardens and plots not cultivated for subsistence or commercial purposes, communal grazing land, land surrounding dwellings in excess of those yards and gardens deemed an integral part of farm and non-farm dwellings and associated surface water.
Subsoil assets	(AN.212) Proven reserves of mineral deposits located on or below the earth's surface that are economically exploitable, given current technology and relative prices. Ownership rights to the subsoil assets are usually separable from those to the land itself. Subsoil assets consist of coal, oil and natural gas reserves, metallic mineral reserves and non-metallic mineral reserves, as defined below.

Classification of assets[a]	Definitions
Coal, oil and natural gas reserves	(AN.2121) Anthracite, bituminous and brown coal deposits; petroleum and natural gas reserves and fields.
Metallic mineral reserves	(AN.2122) Ferrous, non-ferrous and precious metal ore deposits.
Non-metallic mineral reserves	(AN.2123) Stone quarries and clay and sand pits; chemical and fertilizer mineral deposits; salt deposits; deposits of quartz, gypsum, natural gem stones, asphalt and bitumen, peat and other non-metallic minerals other than coal and petroleum.
Non-cultivated biological resources	(AN.213) Animals and plants that yield both once-only and repeat products over which ownership rights are enforced but for which natural growth and/or regeneration is not under the direct control, responsibility and management of institutional units. Examples are virgin forests and fisheries within the territory of the country. Only those resources that are currently, or are likely soon to be exploitable for economic purposes should be included.
Water resources	(AN.214) Aquifers and other groundwater resources to the extent that their scarcity leads to the enforcement of ownership and/or use rights, market valuation and some measure of economic control.
Intangible non-produced assets	(AN.22) Non-produced assets that are constructs of society. They are evidenced by legal or accounting actions, such as the granting of a patent or the conveyance of some economic benefit to a third party. Some entitle their owners to engage in certain specific activities and to exclude other institutional units from doing so except with the permission of the owner. Intangible non-produced assets consist of patented entities, leases and other transferable contracts, purchased goodwill and other intangible non-produced assets.
Patented entities	(AN.221) Inventions in categories of technical novelty that, by law or by judicial decision, can be afforded patent protection. Examples include constitutions of matter, processes, mechanisms, electrical and electronic circuits and devices, pharmaceutical formulations and new varieties of living things produced by artifice.
Leases and other transferable contracts	(AN.222) Leases or contracts where the lessee has the right to convey the lease to a third party independently of the lessor. Examples include leases of land and buildings and other structures, concessions or exclusive rights to exploit mineral deposits or fishing grounds, transferable contracts with athletes and authors and options to buy tangible assets not yet produced. Leases on the rental of machinery are excluded from non-financial intangible assets.
Purchased goodwill	(AN.223) The difference between the value paid for an enterprise as a going concern and the sum of its assets less the sum of its liabilities, each item of which has been separately identified and valued. The value of goodwill, therefore, includes anything of long-term benefit to the business that has not been separately identified as an asset, as well as the value of the fact that the group of assets is used jointly and is not simply a collection of separable assets.

Classification of assets[a]	Definitions
Other intangible non-produced assets	(AN.229) Intangible non-produced assets not elsewhere classified.

Financial assets

(AF)
Entities, over which ownership rights are enforced by institutional units, individually or collectively, and from which economic benefits may be derived by their owners by holding them, or using them over a period of time, differing, except for monetary gold and Special Drawing Rights, from other assets in the System in that there is a counterpart liability on the part of another institutional unit.

Except when the context requires, the term "financial assets" should be read to include liabilities.

Monetary gold and SDRs

(AF.1)
Financial assets for which there is no corresponding financial liability. These are monetary gold and Special Drawing Rights issued by the International Monetary Fund, as defined below.

Monetary gold: Gold owned by the monetary authorities or others subject to their effective control that is held as a financial asset and as a component of foreign reserves. Other gold held by any entity (including non-reserve gold held by the monetary authorities and all gold held by financial institutions other than the central bank) is treated as a commodity, either inventories or valuables.

Special Drawing Rights: International reserve assets created by the International Monetary Fund and allocated to its members to supplement existing reserve assets. They are held exclusively by official holders, which are normally central banks.

Currency and deposits

(AF.2)
Financial assets that are used to make payments or that may be included in money, broadly defined, consisting of currency, transferable deposits and other deposits, as defined below.

Distinctions may be drawn, for currency and for deposits, according to whether they are denominated in national currency or in foreign currencies, and, for deposits, according to whether they are liabilities of resident institutions or the rest of the world.

Currency

(AF.21)
Notes and coin in circulation that are commonly used to make payments. (Commemorative coins that are not actually in circulation should be excluded.)

Transferable deposits

(AF.22)
Deposits that are (A) exchangeable on demand at par, without penalty or restriction; (B) freely transferable by cheque or giroorder and (C) otherwise commonly used to make payments.

Other deposits

(AF.29)
Claims, other than transferable deposits, on the central bank, other depository institutions, government units and, in some cases, other institutional units that are represented by evidence of deposit. Examples include non-transferable savings deposits, term deposits and non-transferable deposits denominated in foreign currencies. Also included are shares or similar evidence of deposit issued by savings and loan associations, building societies, credit unions and the like; claims on the International Monetary Fund that are components of international reserves, other than those evidenced by loans; margin payments related to options or futures contracts and overnight and very short-term repurchase agreements that are considered part of national broad money definitions.

Classification of assets[a]	Definitions
Securities other than shares	**(AF.3)** Financial assets that are normally traded in the financial markets and that give the holders the unconditional right to receive stated fixed sums on a specified date (such as bills) or the unconditional right to fixed money incomes or contractually determined variable money incomes (bonds and debentures). With the exception of perpetual bonds, bonds and debentures also give holders the unconditional right to fixed sums as repayments of principal on a specified date or dates. Examples include securities such as bills, bonds, debentures, tradable financial derivatives, negotiable certificates of deposit, bankers' acceptances, commercial paper, negotiable securities backed by loans or other assets, preferred stocks or shares that pay a fixed income but do not provide for participation in the residual earnings or value of a corporation and bonds that are convertible into shares. Securities other than shares may be subdivided between short-term and long-term, as defined below.
Short-term	**(AF.31)** Securities other than shares that have an original maturity of one year or less but with a maximum of two years or less to accommodate variations in practice between countries. Securities with a maturity of one year or less should be classified as short-term even if they are issued under long-term facilities such as note issuance facilities.
Long-term	**(AF.32)** Securities other than shares that have an original maturity of more than one year; however, to accommodate variations in practice between countries, long-term may be defined to include an original maturity in excess of two years. Claims with optional maturity dates, the latest of which is more than one year away, and claims with indefinite maturity dates should be classified as long-term.
Loans	**(AF.4)** Financial assets that are created when creditors lend funds directly to debtors, that are evidenced by non-negotiable documents, or for which the lender receives no security evidencing the transaction. Included are instalment loans, hire-purchase credit, loans to finance trade credit, claims on the International Monetary Fund evidenced by loans, repurchase agreements not included in national broad money definitions and financial leases and similar arrangements. Loans may be subdivided between short-term and long-term, as defined below.
Short-term	**(AF.41)** Loans that have an original maturity normally of one year or less, but with a maximum of two years or less to accommodate variations in practice between countries. All loans repayable on demand should be classified as short-term even when these loans are expected to be outstanding for more than one year.
Long-term	**(AF.42)** Loans that have an original maturity normally of more than one year, except that, to accommodate variations in practice between countries, long-term may be defined to require an original maturity in excess of two years. It may also be useful to distinguish loans secured by mortgages from other long-term loans.

Classification of assets[a]	Definitions
Shares and other equity	(AF.5) Financial assets that are instruments and records acknowledging, after the claims of all creditors have been met, claims to the residual value of incorporated enterprises. Equity securities do not provide the right to a pre-determined income or to a fixed sum on dissolution of the incorporated enterprise. Ownership of equity is usually evidenced by shares, stocks, participation, or similar documents. Preferred stocks or shares, which also provide for participation in the distribution of the residual value on dissolution of an incorporated enterprise, are included. Proprietors' net equity in quasi-corporate enterprises is one of the components of shares and other equity, although it is not distinguished as a separate category in the classification.
Insurance technical reserves	(AF.6) Financial assets that are reserves against outstanding risks, reserves for with-profit insurance, prepayments of premiums and reserves against outstanding claims. Insurance technical reserves may be liabilities not only of life or non-life insurance enterprises (whether mutual or incorporated) but also of autonomous pension funds, which are included in the insurance enterprise sub-sector, and certain non-autonomous pension funds that are included in the institutional sector that manages the funds. Insurance technical reserves are subdivided between net equity of households on life insurance reserves and on pension funds and prepayments of premiums and reserves against outstanding claims, as defined below.
Net equity of households on life insurance reserves and on pension funds	(AF.61) Reserves held against life insurance and annuity policies by insurance enterprises, whether mutual or incorporated, and by pension funds. These reserves are considered to be assets of the policyholders and not of the institutional units that manage them. Life insurance and pension fund reserves consist of reserves against outstanding risks and reserves for with-profits insurance that add to the value on maturity of with-profit endowment or similar policy.
Prepayment of premiums and reserves against outstanding claims	(AF.62) Reserves in the form of prepayments of premiums result from the fact that, in general, insurance premiums are paid in advance. Such reserves are assets of the policyholders. Reserves against outstanding claims are reserves that insurance enterprises hold in order to cover the amounts they expect to pay out in respect of claims that are not yet settled or claims that may be disputed. Reserves against outstanding claims are considered to be assets of the beneficiaries.
Other accounts receivable/payable	(AF.7) Financial assets consisting of trade credit and advances and other items due to be received or paid, as defined below.
Trade credits and advances	(AF.71) Trade credit for goods and services extended directly to corporations, to government, to non-profit institutions, to households and to the rest of the world and also advances for work that is in progress (if classified as such under inventories) or is to be undertaken.
Other	(AF.79) Accounts receivable and payable, other than those described previously (e.g., in respect of taxes, dividends, purchases and sales of securities, rent, wages and salaries and social contributions). Interest accruing that is not capitalized in the underlying asset may be included.

Classification of assets[a]	Definitions
Memorandum items	The System calls for several memorandum items to show assets not separately identified in the central framework that are of more specialized analytic interest.
Consumer durables	(AN.m) Durable goods acquired by households for final consumption (i.e., those that are not used by households as stores of value or by unincorporated enterprises owned by households for purposes of production).
Direct foreign investment	(AF.m) Financial assets and liabilities arising from the provision of, or receipt of, direct foreign investment are to be recorded under the appropriate categories listed above, i.e., shares and other equity, loans and other accounts receivable and payable. However, the amounts of direct foreign investment included within each of those categories should also be recorded separately as memorandum items.

XIV. The rest of the world account (external transactions account)

A. Introduction

14.1. In the System, the accounts relating to the resident institutional sectors portray various facets of economic activity, i.e., production, the generation, distribution and redistribution of income, consumption and accumulation. The relevant accounts capture both transactions taking place between the resident institutional sectors of the total economy and transactions with non-resident units that make up the rest of the world. In an analogous fashion, the balance sheets of the System cover the stocks of assets and of liabilities of resident institutional sectors *vis-à-vis* each other as well as *vis-à-vis* the rest of the world.

14.2. The System is closed in the sense that both ends of every transaction are recorded; i.e., each transaction is shown as a "use" or outgoing from one part of the System and a "resource" or incoming into another part. The stocks of assets during an accounting period vary as a result of these transactions, together with other flows, i.e., other changes in volume, such as uncompensated seizures or catastrophic losses of assets, and holding gains or losses.

14.3. The transactors and holders of assets and liabilities in the System are the resident institutional units of a given economy. In order for the System to be closed, a segment must be provided to capture those flows that are not reflected as "uses" or "resources" for two resident units but rather only for one. That segment is known in the System as "the rest of the world". The rest of the world account, following the general accounting structure with only minor variation, comprises those categories of accounts necessary to capture the full range of transactions that take place between the total economy and the rest of the world see table 4.1. Specifically, they are:

(a)   The external account of goods and services;

(b)   The external account of primary incomes and current transfers;

(c)   The external accumulation accounts, consisting of:

   (i)   The capital account, covering transactions involving capital transfers and acquisitions less disposals of non-produced non-financial assets;

   (ii)   The financial account, covering transactions in financial assets and liabilities;

   (iii)   Other changes in volume of assets account, covering uncompensated seizures, etc.; and

   (iv)   Revaluation account, covering nominal holding gains and losses (accounts (iii) and (iv) reflect those changes (flows) in external assets and liabilities that are not attributable to transactions); and

(d)   The external assets and liabilities account, which presents the opening and closing balance sheets and the changes in the value of those assets and liabilities between the opening and closing balance sheets.

14.4. The full coverage of the items enumerated in each of the above accounts, together with the relevant balancing items, appears in subsequent sections of this chapter. It should be noted that the rest of the world account is presented from the point of view of the rest of the world so that a resource for the rest of the world is a use for the total economy and vice versa. If a balancing item is positive, it signifies a surplus of the rest of the world and a deficit for the total economy, and vice versa if the balancing item is negative.

14.5. In one sense, the rest of the world account has a unique character because it is not linked to any specific type of economic activity such as production, consumption, capital formation, etc. Instead, all transactions between resident institutional units and non-resident units in respect of all kinds of economic activity are captured under the broad label of the rest of the world account.

14.6. The flows relating to property income in the primary distribution of income accounts for the resident institutional sectors contain elements of property incomes receivable (payable) from (to) the rest of the world that are reflected in the external account of primary incomes and current transfers. In the generation of income account for resident sectors, the item "compensation of employees" includes compensation payable to non-resident employees, which also is recorded in the external account of primary incomes and current transfers on the re-

Table 14.1. Account V: Rest of the world account (external transactions account)

V.I: External account of goods and services

Uses		Resources	
P.6	Exports of goods and services	P.7	Imports of goods and services
P.61	Exports of goods	P.71	Imports of goods
P.62	Exports of services	P.72	Imports of services
B.11	*External balance of goods and services*		

V.II: External account of primary income and current transfers

Uses		Resources	
		B.11	*External balance of goods and services*
D.1	Compensation of employees	D.1	Compensation of employees
D.2-D.3	Taxes less subsidies on production and imports	D.2-D.3	Taxes less subsidies on production and imports
D.4	Property income	D.4	Property income
D.5	Current taxes on income, wealth, etc.	D.5	Current taxes on income, wealth, etc.
D.6	Social contributions and benefits	D.6	Social contributions and benefits
D.7	Other current transfers	D.7	Other current transfers
D.8	Adjustment for the change in net equity of households on pension funds	D.8	Adjustment for the change in net equity of households on pension funds
B.12	*Current external balance*		

V.III: External accumulation accounts

V.III.1: Capital account

Changes in assets		Changes in liabilities and net worth	
K.2	Acquisitions less disposals of non-produced non-financial assets	B.12	*Current external balance*
		D.9	Capital transfers, receivable(+)
		D.9	Capital transfers, payable (–)
		B.10.1	*Changes in net worth due to saving and capital transfers* [1] [2]
B.9	*Net lending(+)/net borrowing(–)*		

1 "Changes in net worth due to saving and capital transfers" is not a balancing item but corresponds to the total of the right-hand side of the capital account.
2 "Changes in net worth due to saving and capital transfers" for the rest of the world refers to changes in net worth due to current external balance and capital transfers.

Table 14.1. Account V: Rest of the world account (external transactions account) [cont.]

V.III.2: Financial account

Changes in assets		Changes in liabilities and net worth	
F	Net acquisition of financial assets	F	Net incurrence of liabilities
F.1	Monetary gold and SDRs		
F.2	Currency and deposits [1]	F.2	Currency and deposits [1]
F.3	Securities other than shares	F.3	Securities other than shares
F.4	Loans [2]	F.4	Loans [2]
F.5	Shares and other equity [2]	F.5	Shares and other equity [2]
F.6	Insurance technical reserves	F.6	Insurance technical reserves
F.7	Other accounts receivable [2]	F.7	Other accounts receivable [2]
		B.9	*Net lending(+)/net borrowing(–)*

1   The following memorandum items are related to the elements of the category F.2 "Currency and deposits":
    m11   denominated in national currency
    m12   denominated in foreign currency
    m21   liability of resident institutions
    m22   liability of rest of the world.
2   Memorandum item: F.m. Direct foreign investment.

V.III.3.1: Other changes in volume of assets account

Changes in assets		Changes in liabilities and net worth	
AN	Non-financial assets	AF	Liabilities
K.8	Uncompensated seizures	K.7	Catastrophic losses
K.12	Changes in classifications and structure	K.8	Uncompensated seizures
		K.10	Other volume changes in financial assets and liabilities n.e.c.
AF	Financial assets	K.12	Changes in classifications and structure
K.7	Catastrophic losses		
K.8	Uncompensated seizures		
K.10	Other volume changes in financial assets and liabilities n.e.c.		
K.12	Changes in classifications and structure		
		B.10.2	*Changes in net worth due to other changes in volume of assets*

V.III.3.2: Revaluation account

Changes in assets		Changes in liabilities and net worth	
AF	Financial assets	AF	Liabilities
K.11	Nominal holding gains(+)/losses(–)	K.11	Nominal holding gains(–)/losses(+)
K.11.1	Neutral holding gains(+)/losses(–)	K.11.1	Neutral holding gains(–)/losses(+)
K.11.2	Real holding gains(+)/losses(–)	K.11.2	Real holding gains(–)/losses(+)
		B.10.3	*Changes in net worth due to nominal holding gains/losses*
		B.10.31	*Changes in net worth due to neutral holding gains/losses*
		B.10.32	*Changes in net worth due to real holding gains/losses*

Table 14.1.   Account V: Rest of the world account (external transactions account) [cont.]

V.IV: External assets and liabilities account

V.IV.1: Opening balance sheet

Assets			Liabilities and net worth		
AN	Non-financial assets		AF	Liabilities	
AN.2	Non-produced assets				
AF	Financial assets				
			B.90	*Net worth*	

V.IV.2: Changes in balance sheet

Assets			Liabilities and net worth		
	Total changes in assets			Total changes in liabilities	
AN	Non-financial assets		AF	Liabilities	
AN.2	Non-produced assets				
AF	Financial assets				
			B.10	*Changes in net worth, total*	

V.IV.3: Closing balance sheet

Assets			Liabilities and net worth		
AN	Non-financial assets		AF	Liabilities	
AN.2	Non-produced assets				
AF	Financial assets				
			B.90	*Net worth*	

sources side. In an analogous fashion, transactions in the financial account for resident sectors contain transactions in financial instruments *vis-à-vis* non-residents that have their counterpart entries in the financial account component of the

external accumulation accounts. Viewed from this perspective, the various components of the rest of the world account are indeed complementary to the sequence of accounts for resident institutional sectors.

B. Residence

14.7. The sectors and sub-sectors of an economy are composed of two main types of institutional units which are resident in the economy—(a) households covering individuals who make up a household, and (b) legal and social entities, such as corporations and quasi-corporations (e.g., branches of foreign direct investors), non-profit institutions (NPIs), and the government of that economy. Residence is an important attribute of an institutional unit, particularly in respect of the rest of the world account, which records transactions between residents and non-residents. The residency status of producers determines the limits of domestic production and affects the measurement of gross domestic product (GDP) and many important flows in the System. The concept and coverage of residence here are identical to those in the *Balance of Payments Manual* of the International Monetary Fund (IMF).

14.8. The concept of residence used here is not based on nationality or legal criteria (although it may be similar to concepts of residence which are used for exchange control, tax or other purposes in many countries). Moreover, the boundaries of a country which may be recognized for political purposes may not always be appropriate for economic purposes and it is necessary to introduce the concept of the "economic territory" of a country as the relevant geographical area to which the concept of residence is applied. An institutional unit is then said to be a resident unit when it has a centre of economic interest in the economic territory of the country in question. The following explains what is meant by "economic territory" and "centre of economic interest".

1. The economic territory of a country

14.9. The economic territory of a country consists of the geographic territory administered by a government within which persons, goods, and capital circulate freely. In the case of maritime countries, it includes any islands belonging to that country which are subject to exactly the same fiscal and monetary authorities as the mainland, so that goods and persons may move freely to and from such islands without any kind of customs or immigration formalities. The economic territory of a country includes: (a) the airspace, territorial waters, and continental shelf lying in international waters over which the country enjoys exclusive rights or over which it has, or claims to have, jurisdiction in respect of the right to fish or to exploit fuels or minerals below the sea bed; (b) territorial enclaves in the rest of the world (clearly demarcated areas of land which are located in other countries and which are used by the government

which owns or rents them for diplomatic, military, scientific or other purposes—embassies, consulates, military bases, scientific stations, information or immigration offices, aid agencies, etc.—with the formal political agreement of the government of the country in which they are physically located). Goods or persons may move freely between a country and its territorial enclaves abroad, but become subject to control by the government of the country in which they are located if they move out of the enclave; and (c) any free zones, or bonded warehouses or factories operated by offshore enterprises under customs control (these form part of the economic territory of the country in which they are physically located).

14.10. The economic territory of an international organization (see chapter IV), consists of the territorial enclave, or enclaves, over which it has jurisdiction; these consist of clearly demarcated areas of land or structures which the international organization owns or rents and which it uses for the purposes for which the organization was created by formal agreement with the country, or countries, in which the enclave or enclaves are physically located.

14.11. It follows that the economic territory of a country does not include the territorial enclaves used by foreign governments or international organizations which are physically located within the geographical boundaries of that country.

2. Centre of economic interest

14.12. An institutional unit is said to have a centre of economic interest within a country when there exists some location—dwelling, place of production, or other premises—within the economic territory of the country on, or from, which it engages, and intends to continue to engage, in economic activities and transactions on a significant scale, either indefinitely or over a finite but long period of time. The location need not be fixed so long as it remains within the economic territory.

14.13. In most cases, it is reasonable to assume that an institutional unit has a centre of economic interest in a country if it has already engaged in economic activities and transactions on a significant scale in the country for one year or more, or it intends to do so. The conduct of economic activities and transactions over a period of one year normally implies a centre of interest, but the choice of any specific period of time is somewhat arbitrary and it must be emphasized that one year is suggested only as a guideline and not as an inflexible rule.

14.14. The ownership of land and structures within the economic territory of a country is deemed to be sufficient in itself for the owner to have a centre of economic interest in that country. Land and buildings can obviously only be used for purposes of production in the country in which they are located and their owners, in their capacity as owners, are subject to the laws and regulations of that country. It may happen, however, that an owner is resident in another country and does not have any economic interest in the country in which he owns the land or buildings other than the land or buildings themselves. In that case, the owner is treated as if he transferred his ownership to a notional institutional unit which is actually resident in the country. The notional unit is itself treated as being entirely owned and controlled by the non-resident actual owner, in much the same way as a quasi-corporation is owned and controlled by its owner. In this way, the rents and rentals paid by the tenants of the land or buildings are deemed to be paid to the notional resident unit which in turn makes a transfer of property income to the actual non-resident owner.

3. The residence of households and individuals

14.15. A household has a centre of economic interest when it maintains a dwelling, or succession of dwellings, within the country which members of the household treat, and use, as their principal residence. All individuals who belong to the same household must be resident in the same country. If a member of an existing household were to be considered no longer resident in the country in which that household is resident, that individual would cease to be a member of that household.

14.16. A member of a resident household who leaves the economic territory to return to that same household after a limited period of time (i.e., less than one year) continues to be a resident even if that individual makes frequent journeys outside the economic territory. The individual's centre of economic interest remains in the economy in which the household is resident. The following categories of such individuals are treated as residents:

(a) Travellers or visitors: i.e., individuals who leave the economic territory for less than one year for recreation, business, health, education (see paragraph 14.20 below), religious, or other purposes;

(b) Individuals who work some, or all of the time in a different economic territory from that in which the household to which they belong is resident;

(i) Workers who work for part of the year in another country, in some cases in response to the varying seasonal demand for labour, and then return to their households;

(ii) Border workers who regularly cross the frontier each day or somewhat less regularly (e.g., each week) to work in a neighbouring country;

(iii) The staff of international organizations who work in the enclave of those organizations;

(iv) The locally recruited staff of foreign embassies, consulates, military bases, etc.;

(v) The crews of ships, aircraft, or other mobile equipment operating partly, or wholly, outside the economic territory.

14.17. The circumstances in which an individual is likely to cease to be a resident are when that individual lives or works continuously for one year or more in a foreign country. If the individual rejoins his or her original household only very infrequently for short visits and sets up a new household or joins a household in the country of work, the individual can no longer be treated as a member of the original household. Most of the individual's consumption takes place in the country in which he lives or works, and the individual clearly has a centre of economic interest there.

14.18. Even if an individual continues to be legally employed and paid by an enterprise which is resident in his home country, that individual should be treated as resident in the host country if the individual works continuously in that country for one year or more. As explained below, in these circumstances the person has to be treated as being employed either by a quasi-corporation which is owned by the enterprise and which is resident in the country in which the work takes place, or, alternatively, as being employed by a foreign agent. The latter case is intended to cover technical assistance personnel working in a foreign country on contracts or assignments of one year or more. Technical assistance personnel on long-term assignments should be treated as residents of the country in which they work and deemed to be employed by their host government on behalf of the government, or international organization, which is actually financing their work. A transfer of funds should then be imputed from the government or international organization which actually employs them to the host government to cover the cost of their salaries and allowances.

14.19. The situation of military personnel and civil servants, including diplomats, whom a government employs in its own enclaves abroad, is different. Those enclaves—military bases, embassies and the like—form part of the economic territory of the employing government and the personnel often live as well as work in the enclaves. Therefore, the employees whom a government transfers to work in such enclaves continue to have a centre of economic interest in their home country however long they work in the enclaves. They continue to be resident in their home country even if they live in dwellings outside the enclaves.

14.20. Students should be treated as residents of their country of origin however long they study abroad, provided they continue to form part of a household in that country. In these circumstances, their centre of economic interest remains in their country of origin rather than the country in which they study. Medical patients abroad also are treated as residents of their country of origin even if their stay is one year or more, provided they continue to form part of a household in their country of origin.

14.21. As to the treatment of individuals who have several international residences, where they may remain for short periods of time during a given year (for instance, three months in each of four countries), the centre of economic interest for such individuals often is "international", not a specific economy. Considerations should be given to such factors as tax status, citizenship (can be dual), etc., but the System does not recommend a specific treatment. The latter is left to the discretion of the economies concerned; the treatment should be coordinated, if possible, to foster international comparability.

4. The residence of corporations and quasi-corporations

14.22. Corporations and quasi-corporations are said to have a centre of economic interest and to be resident units of a country (economic territory) when they are engaged in a significant amount of production of goods or services there, or own land or buildings located there. They must maintain at least one production establishment there which they plan to operate indefinitely or over a long period of time—a guideline of one year or more is suggested, to be applied flexibly—together with other considerations covered in paragraph 14.23. (For a detailed description of corporations, quasi-corporations and other institutional units, see chapter IV.)

Attribution of production

14.23. Production undertaken by the personnel (and plant and equipment) of a resident unit outside its economic territory is to be treated as part of the production of the host country and the unit treated as a resident unit (branch or subsidiary) of that country if it meets the conditions noted above (see paragraph 14.22 above). Such a unit usually maintains a complete and separate set of accounts of local activities (i.e., income statement, balance sheet, transactions with the parent enterprise), pays income taxes to the host country, has a substantial physical presence, receives funds for its work for its own account, etc. The above considerations also apply to the particular case of construction activity carried out abroad by a resident producer. If they are not present, the activity should be classified as an export of services by the resident enterprise. Production can generate such an export only if the production is classified as domestic production (undertaken by a resident even though the physical process takes place outside the economic territory). Construction involved with major specific projects—bridges, dams, power stations, etc.—that often takes several years to complete, and is carried out and managed by non-resident units through an unincorporated site office in an economy warrants special mention. In most instances, such a site office will meet the criteria that require its production to be

treated as a resident unit and to be part of the production of the host economy (as would that of a branch or affiliate), rather than as an export of services to that economy (for further discussion and treatment of installation projects, see paragraphs 14.101 to 14.103 below).

14.24. "Offshore" units engaged in manufacturing processes (including assembly of components manufactured elsewhere) are residents of the economy in which they are located. This statement applies regardless of location in special "zones" of exemption from customs or other regulations or concessions, and also applies to non-manufacturing operations (i.e., trading and financial enterprises), including so-called special purpose units.

Units operating mobile equipment

14.25. The principles concerning the determination of resident units are likewise applicable to units using mobile equipment, such as ships, aircraft, drilling rigs and platforms, railway rolling stock, etc., that operate outside the economic territory in which the units are resident—either in (a) international waters or airspace, or (b) in other economies. In the first case (a), these activities should be attributed to the economy of residence of the operator (the same applies if the activity takes place in more than one economy during the course of, but for less than a year). In the second case (b), the unit is a resident of the economy in which the activity (production) occurs, if accounted for separately by the operator and is so recognized by the tax and licensing authorities there. Otherwise, the activity may be attributed to the country of residence of the original operator. If operations are carried out by a unit on a regular and continuing basis in two or more countries—such as the operation of a railway network—the unit is deemed to have a centre of economic interest in each country and thus separate resident units in each, subject to the qualifications for (b) above. In cases involving the leasing of mobile equipment to one unit by another for a long or indefinite period, the lessee unit is deemed to be the operator and activities are attributed to the country in which the lessee is resident.

14.26. In the particular case of ships flying flags of convenience, it is often difficult to determine the residence of the operating unit, because of complex arrangements involving the ownership, mode of operation and chartering of such ships, and the fact that the country of registry in most instances is different than the country of residence of the operator (or owner). Nonetheless, in principle, the shipping activity is to be attributed to the country of residence of the operating unit. If that unit establishes a branch (direct investment) in another country to manage the operation, for tax or other considerations, the operation is to be attributed to the resident (branch) of that country.

14.27. There are certain exceptional cases in which it may be difficult to determine the residence of a unit which operates mobile equipment because it consists of a corporation which is established by special legislation by two or more governments acting jointly and which is registered in each of the countries concerned. There are two possible ways of treating such units. One is to allocate all of the transactions to each of the countries concerned in proportion to the amounts of financial capital which they have contributed, or in proportion to their shares in the equity of the corporation. Another possibility would be to treat the corporation as resident in the country in which its headquarters are located and to treat the premises of the corporation in the other countries as foreign branches (direct investment enterprises (see paragraph 14.152 below), which are resident in the country in which they are located. On balance, the first method is preferable, but both ways of treating such corporations are consistent with the general principles of both the System and the *Balance of Payments Manual* and the choice between them may be made on the basis of statistical convenience, with reference to consistent treatment by partner countries.

14.28. In the case of agents, a transaction should be attributed to the economy of the principal on whose behalf a transaction is undertaken and not to the economy of the agent representing or acting on behalf of that principal. However, the services rendered by the agent to the principal represented should be attributed to the economy of which the agent is a resident.

5. The residence of non-profit institutions

14.29. An NPI is resident in the country or economic territory in which it has a centre of economic interest, in most instances coinciding with the country under whose laws and regulations it was created and in which its existence as a legal or social entity is officially recognized and recorded. In practice, the residence of the vast majority of NPIs may be determined without ambiguity. However, when an NPI is engaged in charity or relief work on an international scale, it is necessary to specify the residence of any branches it may maintain in individual countries in dispensing relief. If an NPI maintains a branch or unit for one year or more in a particular country, that branch or unit should be considered as a resident NPI of that country, financed largely or entirely by transfers from abroad.

6. General government

14.30. The general government agencies that are residents of an economy include all departments, establishments, and bodies of its central, state, and local governments located in its territory and the embassies, consulates, military establishments, and other entities of its general government located elsewhere. (For a detailed description of general government, see paragraphs 4.113 to 4.130 of chapter IV.)

14.31. Embassies, consulates, military establishments, and other entities of a foreign general government are to be considered as extraterritorial by the economy in which they are physically located. The construction of embassies, structures, and other works in extraterritorial enclaves by resident producers of the economy in which the enclaves are located is part of the production and exports of that economy. Wages and salaries paid to locally recruited staff of foreign diplomatic, military, and other establishments are payments to residents of the economy in which the households to which those staff belong are located.

14.32. International organizations (see paragraphs 4.163 and 4.164 of chapter IV), are not considered residents of any national economy, including that in which they are located or conduct their affairs. They are treated as extraterritorial by that economy. (However, pension funds operated by these bodies are treated as residents of the economy in which the organization is located.) The employees of these bodies are, nevertheless, residents of a national economy, specifically, of the economy in which they are expected to have their abode for one year or more. In most cases that economy will be the one in which the given international unit is located or in which the employees are engaged in technical assistance or other activities on behalf of the international organization. It follows that the wages and salaries paid by the international organizations to their own employees are payments to residents of the economy in which those employees are stationed for one year or more. (For details concerning technical assistance personnel, see paragraph 14.18 above.)

14.33. In contrast, corporations or quasi-corporations that are owned jointly by two or more governments are not treated as international bodies but are, like other corporations, considered to be residents of the economies on whose territories they operate.

7. Regional central banks

14.34. A regional central bank is an international financial institution which acts as a common central bank for a group of member countries. Such a bank has its headquarters in one country and maintains national offices in each of the member countries. Each national office acts as the central bank for that country and must be treated as a separate institutional unit from the institution's headquarters. Each national office is a resident unit of the country in which it is located. The financial assets and liabilities of a regional central bank should be allocated among the national offices in proportion to the claims which they have over its collective assets.

C. General accounting rules

1. Valuation

14.35. Current prices on markets are the basis of valuation in the rest of the world account for both transactions in (flows of) goods and services, in income distribution and redistribution, and in financial assets and liabilities, and for stocks of assets and liabilities (see paragraphs 3.70 to 3.72 of chapter III). Thus, transactions are to be valued at the actual prices agreed upon by transactors, while stocks of assets and liabilities are to be valued at current prices at the time to which the balance sheet relates. (For instances where application of the rule may be difficult to implement, see below).

Goods

14.36. Exports and imports of goods should be recorded at the market value of the goods at the point of uniform valuation, (the customs frontier of the economy from which they are exported), i.e., the goods are valued free on board (f.o.b.) at that frontier. The value includes that of the goods and of the related distributive services up to that point, including the cost of loading on to a carrier for onward transportation, where appropriate.

14.37. Conceptually, the f.o.b. price can be regarded as the purchaser's price that would be paid by an importer taking delivery of the goods after it has been loaded on to his own carrier, or other carrier, at the exporter's frontier after payment of any export taxes or the receipt of any tax rebates. This method of valuation implicitly determines the boundary between exports of goods and exports of services in the System and in balance-of-payments statistics. The costs of transporting exported goods up to the frontier are treated in the same way as other production costs and hence are an integral part of the costs of delivering the goods at the required location. In general, the purchaser's price for a good is an inclusive measure of the value of a good at a particular location which treats the costs of transportation no differently from other production costs. If, therefore, the transportation up to the frontier were actually carried out by a resident other than the producer or manufacturer, the transportation costs have to be added to the price received by the producer and included in the value of the goods exported. In principle, the transportation should be treated as an intermediate input into the complete process of production which terminates when the exported goods are delivered at the required location. Even if the transportation up to the frontier of the exporting country were actually carried out by the importer or other non-resident, the costs should nevertheless still be included in the value of the goods exported. Although the importer may be transporting his own goods and hence not engaging in transactions with foreigners in respect of this activity, it is necessary to recognize the transportation costs by imputing the purchase of transportation services by the exporter and increasing the price actually received by the exporter accordingly. In this way, the imputed f.o.b. price recorded for the goods minus the imputed import of transport services will equal the actual price received by the exporter, so that the balance between exports and imports of goods and services is the same whether or not the imputation is made. In general, however, it is desirable that the f.o.b. price should not be affected by the way in which transportation up to the frontier of the exporting country is organized or paid for.

14.38. Imports as well as exports of goods are to be valued f.o.b. in the System: in other words, imports are also to be valued at the customs frontier of the exporting country. Valuing exports and imports in the same way promotes consistency in the recording of trade flows at a world level and enables trade balances in goods to be shown correctly. The use of f.o.b. values for imports implies that the costs of transporting imports of goods after they have left the frontier of the exporting country have to be treated as imports of services when the transport is provided by non-resident carriers. When the goods are transported from the frontier by resident carriers there are no service imports as there are no transactions with non-residents.

14.39. In practice, importers may take delivery of the goods which they import at any convenient location which will not always coincide with the point at which they are valued for purposes of recording exports and imports in the accounts of the System. Importers need not take delivery at a frontier: they may take delivery inside their own country or possibly inside the exporting country or even in a third country. Moreover, the costs of transportation, together with the costs for storage, loading and insurance, as well as the movement of the goods, may initially be incurred wholly or partly by the exporter, wholly or partly by the importer, or by some third party. Thus, there are many different ways in which international trade in goods may be organized, so that the transactions which actually take place between residents and non-residents may sometimes require re-arrangement or manipulation to get them into the format required by the System.

14.40. In the case of most exports, it should be possible to derive the f.o.b. price with reasonable accuracy from the prices or values recorded in customs documentation submitted at the frontier, or similar documentation submitted to other administrative agencies. In the case of imports, however, the customs documentation or other administrative records often provide information on the costs, insurance, freight (c.i.f.) price rather than the f.o.b. price. Conceptually, the c.i.f. price can be regarded as the purchaser's price that would be paid by an importer taking delivery of the good at his own frontier, before paying any import duty or other tax levied at the frontier. The difference between the c.i.f. and the f.o.b. price represents the costs of transportation, together with insurance charges, between the customs frontier of the exporting country and that of the importing country. This difference varies according to the country of origin of the exports and may be quite substantial when the exporting and importing countries are at some distance from each other. In practice it is usually difficult to convert from recorded c.i.f. prices to estimated f.o.b. prices for individual imports or categories of imports, so that adjustments can often be made only globally for large groups of imports or even total imports. Estimates of transport and insurance costs (see services below) between the frontiers of the exporting and importing countries can be made from a knowledge of average freight charges, insurance rates, average distances travelled, etc. for large groups of exports. Sample surveys of trade invoices also provide information on c.i.f./f.o.b. ratios which may be used to estimate the global adjustment needed to the c.i.f. value of imports (see *Balance of Payments Compilation Guide*, IMF).

14.41. Thus, while total imports of goods must be recorded f.o.b. in the System, the extent to which it may be feasible to disaggregate imports valued f.o.b. by type of good or country of origin is uncertain in practice. It may be much easier for some countries than others, but many countries find it difficult, if not impossible, to provide detailed figures of imports valued f.o.b. For this reason it is sufficient for purposes of the System to record total imports f.o.b., together with the value of associated transportation costs, included under services.

14.42. In the input-output tables of the System, including the tables which display the supply and use of goods and services at a detailed level, it may only be feasible to show detailed figures of imports c.i.f. In such tables, however, there may be analytical advantages to be derived from valuing imports c.i.f. The input-output and supply and use tables also contain the information on transportation and insurance costs needed to make the transition from the sum of detailed imports of goods valued c.i.f. to total imports of goods valued f.o.b. A global c.i.f./f.o.b. adjustment for imports is made in these tables.

14.43. There are circumstances under which it may be difficult to determine appropriate prices for imports and exports of goods, such as a barter exchange of goods, transactions between affiliated enterprises (which often involve "transfer pricing"), or goods transferred under a financial lease arrangement where a legal change of ownership does not actually occur. Under such circumstances, it may be necessary to develop proxies, or substitute measures. For example, a barter exchange of commodities between two parties should be valued at the basic prices that would have been received if they had been sold. However, such an approach must be limited to those transactions to which it is readily applicable. Likewise, the substitution of an imputed or notional market value for an actual transfer value in the case of goods transactions between affiliated enterprises should be the exception rather than the

rule because of both conceptual and practical difficulties involved. In any event, if it is determined that certain transfer prices are so divorced from those of similar transactions that they significantly distort measurement, they should, if possible, be replaced by market equivalents or, if not, be separately identified for analytical purposes (see *Balance of Payments Manual*).

Services

14.44. Exports and imports of services are to be valued at the actual prices agreed upon, subject to the above-mentioned limitations. Two specific service components warrant special mention as to valuation: insurance services and financial services. International insurance services are valued by the amount of service charges and not by the total premiums earned. Also, by convention because of data constraints, estimates of the insurance service charge in the external account of goods and services are calculated ignoring investment income on technical reserves. As for international financial services, in addition to explicit commissions and fees, there are "financial intermediation services indirectly measured", derived from and valued according to the difference between the property income received from loans or debt securities and the interest paid on deposits (see exports and imports of goods and services below).

Primary incomes

14.45. Primary income payments and receipts are valued at the current price on the market. For investment income, holding gains and losses are excluded in that they are not considered to be part of the income on investment but rather to be part of the value of investments included under revaluations in the other changes in assets accounts. Any income in kind included in compensation of employees is valued at purchasers' prices when the goods and services involved are purchased by the employer, and at basic prices when produced by the employer.

Transfers

14.46. One type of transaction that, by definition, is non-commercial and thus has no market price, is the provision of economic values as transfers. For resources transferred by government, NPIs, or individuals of an economy to non-residents without a quid pro quo, the same values must be reflected in the external transactions accounts of both the recipient and the donor. Such resources should be valued at the basic prices that would have been received if they had been sold. Such imputations may not always approximate the desired basis of valuation, often because the values of these transactions as they appear to the donor may be quite different from those that the recipient would be inclined to impute. Thus, it is suggested that, as a rule of thumb, the values assigned by the donor be used as a basis for recording.

Financial items (see also chapter XI)

14.47. Changes in financial assets should be recorded in the external financial account at the prices at which the assets are acquired or disposed of. For financial items that are traded in an organized market, with the buyer and seller dealing with each other through an agent, the price established in the market—which will probably be the one that is recorded in the statistics in any case—will be appropriate for purposes of the rest of the world Account. For financial items not traded in the market, however, the relevant price may not be so apparent. In fact, cash items, i.e., currency and transferable deposits that can be redeemed on demand, at their nominal value, have only one value which could be assigned for any purpose, so that this value could be regarded as the actual market price. The price that is to be attributed to non-marketable financial items, which are primarily loans in one form or another, is their nominal value. However, if a secondary market in such items is created, and they become marketable—often, as in the case of loans to some heavily debt-burdened countries, at substantial discounts from nominal value—that market price should be recorded for transactions in such loans. Valuation of financial items in the external financial account should exclude any service charges, fees, commissions, or income, which should be recorded in the appropriate component of the external account of goods and services.

Stocks of assets and liabilities (see also chapter XIII and section G.2 of this chapter)

14.48. In principle, all stocks of external assets and liabilities that comprise a country's external balance sheet or international investment position should be measured at current market values, as of the date involved, i.e., the beginning or end of the reference period. This concept assumes that such stocks are continuously (regularly) revalued at current prices—e.g., by reference to actual market prices for financial assets such as shares and bonds, or by reference to enterprise balance sheets in the case of direct investment.

14.49. For those financial items (e.g., shares and other equity securities other than shares, etc.) included in the category of direct investment (see paragraphs 151 to 153 in the *Balance of Payments Manual*), it is recognized that, in practice, book values from the balance sheets of direct investment enterprises (or of direct investors) generally are utilized to determine the value of the stock of direct investment. These balance sheet values, if on a current market value basis, would be in accordance with the principle. If based on historical cost or on an interim but not current revaluation, they would not conform to the principle, and thus market prices may have to be estimated or approximated (see paragraph 14.158 below). However, because balance sheet values of enterprises often represent the only basis of valuation available in most countries, the *Balance of Payments Manual* recommends that they may be utilized to determine the value of the stock of direct investment both for individual economies and for international comparisons, and that it would be desirable to have such data collected and available on a current market value basis. In instances where the

shares of direct investment enterprises are listed on stock exchanges, the listed prices should be used as the market value of shares in those enterprises.

14.50. Investment in other equity securities, debt securities, and financial derivatives is to be recorded at current market values at the appropriate reference date (for details, see chapter XIII).

14.51. Those financial items that are not readily transferable among transactors—e.g., loans, deposits, miscellaneous accounts receivable and payable—are to be recorded at nominal value (as is the case for currency). In recent years, loans to a number of heavily indebted countries often have been subject to significant discounts quoted in secondary markets that emerged for the trading of such debt, bringing into question the valuation of these loans. The secondary market quotations should, in principle, be the basis of valuation of both transactions and stocks of assets and liabilities. However, the basis of valuation of the latter on the debtor side is nominal value, i.e., the amount of principal that the debtor is contractually obliged to repay the creditor when the loan matures, representing a departure from the market price principle. In this particular case, the departure is associated with the contractual restrictions usually applicable to such loans that prohibit the debtor from buying back the loans in secondary markets, unless the restrictions are waived (these limitations usually do not apply to bonds or other securities). The use of market value on the creditor side and nominal value on the debtor side results in an asymmetry between debtor and creditor positions. In order to deal with that asymmetry, if feasible, creditors should provide supplementary data on nominal values of discounted loans, and debtors should provide such data on market value, as follows:

(a) An exchange of such loans for equity (i.e., debt/equity swap), in which case two transactions are recorded in the financial accounts, one in loans and one in shares and other equity, valued at the (lesser) value of the equity obtained, with the difference between the nominal value of the loan and the (lesser) value of the equity obtained treated as a holding gain/loss;

(b) Forgiveness of the loans, where a capital transfer offsets the reduction of the debtor's liability and the position is reduced on the liability side;

(c) Rescheduling of the loan, so that a new arrangement in effect replaces the old loan, with the new loan's nominal value to be the basis of valuation and a holding gain/loss recorded if the new nominal value is less than the old value; or

(d) Unilateral cancellation of the loan by the creditor, to be recorded in the other changes in volume of assets account.

14.52. Monetary gold and Special Drawing Rights (SDRs) issued by the IMF are financial assets for which there are no outstanding financial liabilities. Monetary gold is to be valued at its prevailing price on the market, and SDRs are to be valued at market rates calculated by the IMF.

2. Time of recording

14.53. The general principle governing the time of recording transactions in the System (including the rest of the world) is that of accrual accounting, i.e., the time when economic value is created, transformed, exchanged, transferred, or extinguished. Claims and liabilities are deemed to arise when there is a change in ownership, either a legal change or one involving a change in control or possession (physical or economic change), e.g., goods shipped under financial lease arrangements and certain transactions between parent enterprises and their branches or affiliates. An exchange of resources involving a change in ownership entails the recording of the two sides of the transaction in the rest of the world account. In accordance with the double-entry system, in principle there should be simultaneous recording of the two sides—first, the provision of one resource accompanied by the acquisition of a financial claim on the recipient of the resource, and subsequently, the extinguishment of the claim by the provision of another resource.

14.54. The time of change of ownership may not coincide with the various stages of the transactions process—i.e., the time of contract or commitment (contract date), the time of provision of goods or services and acquisition of a claim for payment (transfer date), or the time of settlement of that claim (payment date). In practice, when a change in ownership may not be obvious, it is considered to occur at (or is proxied by) the time the parties to the transaction record it in their books or accounts. However, simultaneous recording of the two sides to the transaction may not be achieved, because the entries may be derived independently from different sources and accounting records, and conventions for time of recording for participants in the transaction may differ (see below).

Goods

14.55. In line with the general principles adopted in the System, the exports and imports of goods should be recorded at the time at which ownership of the goods in question passes from a resident to a non-resident, or vice versa. This principle is sufficient to determine the coverage of international trade in goods, but in practice certain exceptions, which are specified below, are made to the principle, at least when ownership is interpreted in a strict legal sense. In any case it is useful to indicate how the coverage of international trade in goods between resident and non-resident units relates to international trade in the sense of actual movements of goods between countries. When the ownership of a good is exchanged between a resident and non-resident, there is a strong presumption that the good will cross the frontiers of the countries concerned either shortly before, or soon after, the change of ownership takes place, but

not all exports and imports do so. Conversely, many goods cross frontiers without any change in ownership taking place, so that they are not to be counted as exports or imports. It is therefore useful to specify the different coverage of the flows in some detail.

14.56. Statistics of international trade in goods in most countries rely heavily on customs documentation submitted at the time goods are cleared at the frontier. This constitutes a further reason for clarifying the differences between the coverage of exports and imports as defined in the System and the actual physical movements of goods between countries. However, it should also be noted that when countries belong to a free trade area, customs union or common market, most goods may cross the frontiers between different member countries without any kind of customs clearance or documentation at the frontier and quite different methods of recording exports and imports may be required. Some kind of documentation may still be needed for customs or tax purposes, especially when a VAT system is in operation, but it may be submitted to a central office within a country instead of being cleared at the frontier. Alternatively, or in addition, direct inquiries may be made to exporters or importers or records of foreign exchange transactions may be utilized. It should not be assumed, therefore, that documentation submitted at a frontier invariably constitutes the principal source of data on exports or imports.

Exceptions to the change of ownership principle

14.57. Before indicating the differences between exports and imports as recorded in the accounts and the physical movements of goods across frontiers, it is necessary to specify the exceptions which the System itself makes to the change of ownership principle when the latter is interpreted in a strict legal sense. There are four main types of exception.

14.58. The first exception concerns goods which are the subject of a financial lease. The System imputes a change of ownership from lessor to lessee when a financial lease is arranged even though legally the leased good remains the property of the lessor, at least until the termination of the lease when legal ownership of the good is usually transferred to the lessee. The rationale for imputing a change of ownership is that the lessee assumes all the rights, risks and responsibilities of ownership in practice, so that from an economic point of view the lessee can be regarded as the de facto owner. The financial lease is essentially a method of financing the imputed purchase of the good by the lessee which can be used instead of taking out a loan for this purpose. The System therefore imputes a change of ownership at the start of the lease and this treatment is adopted throughout the System and not merely for international leasing. When a good is exported (imported) under a financial lease, the amount recorded as an export or import should be based on the purchaser's price paid for the good by the lessor and not on the cumulative value of the rental payments. The transaction should be recorded when the lessee takes possession of the good, (the time of commencement of the lease), although the time at which the good crosses the frontier may be used as a proxy for this if necessary. This treatment requires that a loan from the lessor to the lessee should also be recorded in the financial account.

14.59. The second exception to the change in ownership principally concerns goods shipped by an enterprise to a branch or subsidiary which it owns in a foreign country or to a foreign affiliate which belongs to the same group of enterprises as the exporter. Legally, the ownership of the goods may remain unchanged in such circumstances, but a de facto change of ownership is imputed between the exporting enterprise and the foreign branch or subsidiary whenever goods are shipped between affiliated enterprises. The rationale for this treatment is similar to that for financial leasing, namely that from an economic point of view ownership rights and responsibilities are effectively exercised by the enterprise which receives the goods. The time of recording is when entries are made in the books or accounts of the enterprise concerned.

14.60. The third exception is one in which a change of ownership may occur but is ignored in the accounts. The exception relates to merchants or commodity dealers who buy commodities or other goods from non-residents and then sell them again to non-residents within the same accounting period without the commodities actually entering the economy in which the merchants are resident. The difference between the receipts and the sales of such dealers is treated as measuring the value of the services they provide and recorded under exports or imports of services. If, however, the goods are not resold within the same accounting period, the purchases have to be recorded as imports of goods which are temporarily held in inventory; when they are sold abroad in a later period they should be treated as negative imports.

14.61. The fourth and final exception to the change in ownership principle relates to goods which are sent for processing abroad. In general, the principle adopted in the System is that goods sent abroad temporarily without change of ownership between resident and non-resident units are not to be counted as exports or imports. Goods sent abroad temporarily are to be understood as goods which return in more or less the same condition as they left, apart possibly from any maintenance, servicing or routine repairs carried out on them. However, these conditions are not satisfied when an enterprise engages or contracts with another enterprise to carry out certain manufacturing processes on the goods while abroad. In this case the enterprise may ship materials or semi-processed goods abroad, which become inputs into the foreign manufacturer's production processes, and then receive back the outputs from these processes, paying the manufacturer a fee for the production carried out. In these circumstances the goods originally sent abroad lose their identity by being transformed or incorporated into other goods. Similarly, the goods received back are essentially new goods produced abroad. The goods re-

ceived back may well be classified quite differently, by customs authorities and in international trade statistics, from those which were sent. In these circumstances the System requires that the goods sent abroad be recorded as exports, even though they may not be sold to a non-resident, while the goods received back are recorded as imports, even though they were not purchased from a non-resident.

14.62. Essentially, the treatment of processing involves two issues—whether to record certain flows on a gross or a net basis, and whether to classify those flows as goods or services. If the goods are excluded from exports and imports on the grounds that there has been no change of ownership, then it becomes necessary to identify and record separately as the import of a service the payment which the enterprise makes to the foreign producer for the value added by his processing. If, on the other hand, the flows are recorded gross, as the System requires, the difference between the value of the imports and the value of the exports should be equal to the payment made for the service provided by the foreign processor. The balance between total exports and imports of goods and services is the same in either case, the difference being whether the balance appears as a net import of goods or a net import of services.

14.63. When goods are sent abroad temporarily to return in the same form as they left without change of ownership, their leaving the economy has no impact on the domestic economy and can, therefore, be ignored in the accounts. However, when the goods which return are different in form from those which left, the supply and disposition of goods or resources within the economy which sent the goods abroad for processing are changed and for this reason the export and import of the goods concerned cannot be ignored. Another relevant consideration is that it is often difficult to separate goods sent out for processing, and those returned after processing, from other movements of goods in records of international trade flows, so that the gross treatment required by the System is usually easier to implement in practice. However, when it is actually feasible to identify in the trade statistics goods intended for processing abroad and returned after processing, it is recommended that they should be shown separately in both exports and imports in the external account for goods and services in the System. When goods sent abroad for processing in one accounting period are not re-imported until a later accounting period, it is necessary to enter a counterpart financial claim (liability) in the financial accounts of the countries concerned.

14.64. When goods are returned after only a very small amount of processing abroad, such as storage or packaging, it can be argued that the net treatment should be adopted on the grounds that the processing is insignificant, so that it is preferable to record the small amount of value added abroad as an import of a service. It is difficult, however, to provide objective criteria as to what constitutes a significant amount of processing which would make it possible to delineate certain kinds of processes from others. It is suggested, therefore, that goods should be treated as being processed when the goods from abroad have to be classified in a different group (3 digit level) of the Central Product Classification (CPC) from the goods sent abroad out of which they have been processed. On the other hand, when the goods returned fall in the same group of the CPC as the goods sent abroad, they should not be included in exports and imports of goods, the processing being treated as a service activity.

Timing in relation to physical movements of goods

14.65.   For various reasons the flows of goods which leave and enter a country within a given accounting period are not identical with the exports and imports which need to be recorded in the accounts. One reason why they may differ is simply that the time at which the ownership of a good changes, or is deemed to change, from a resident to a non-resident or vice versa, is often not the same as the time at which the good is transported from one country to the other. Transportation may precede, or lag behind, the change of ownership by varying lengths of time. Moreover, because time elapses between a good leaving one country and arriving at the other country, it is impossible for the change in ownership to coincide with both the time of departure and the time of arrival. If the time at which a good crosses a frontier is used as a proxy for the time at which ownership changes, discrepancies are likely to be created between the values of exports and imports and other items in the national accounts such as sales, purchases and changes in inventories as reported by producers. Such discrepancies are unavoidable if statistics on physical movement of goods across frontiers are the principal source of data for estimating exports and imports. Discrepancies of this kind which are due to differences in timing tend to become relatively more important the shorter the accounting period, and they may be a significant source of error in quarterly accounts, especially for countries whose foreign trade is large in relation to domestic production. When the estimates of exports and imports are based on direct inquiries to producers, the incidence of such discrepancies may be less.

14.66.   A further problem is that exporters and importers of goods may not perceive the change of ownership as taking place at the same moment of time. When there is a firm sales contract, the exporter may record the change of ownership in his accounts as occurring when the goods are dispatched, whereas the importer may not acknowledge change of ownership until signing and accepting the relevant import documents (generally at the time the importer takes possession of the goods). While such differences may not introduce any discrepancies between the recording of different items within the domestic accounts of each of the countries concerned, they may introduce asymmetries into the recording of international trade flows at a world level.

14.67.   A probable need for a timing adjustment to trade statistics arises from a failure of the statistics themselves to reflect phys-

ical movements correctly in all cases, although some systematic defects of that sort would not create noticeable errors unless the value of trade changed sharply from period to period. Such a need, for example, arises when compilers of trade accounts cut off each month's statistics before all customs declarations have been tabulated, leaving a residue to fall into the next month. When practices of this sort lead to distortions, the amounts should be estimated and timing adjustments applied.

14.68.   The change of ownership of goods can occur at times widely different from the recording of those goods in trade statistics when a lengthy voyage forms part of the process of importing or exporting. If the volume or unit value of trade changes substantially from the beginning to the end of the reporting period, the possible difference of one or two months between the shipment or receipt of goods, on the one hand, and the change of ownership, on the other hand, can be a source of error in the statement for a given country and of asymmetries between partner countries. No empirical basis has been established for presuming that ownership normally changes either at the beginning or the end of a voyage; inquiries, perhaps on a sample basis, are required to ascertain specific practice, and timing adjustments should in principle be applied to correct the trade statistics for those classes of goods that are found to change ownership at a time other than that at which they are recorded in the trade statistics.

14.69.   Goods on consignment, i.e., goods intended for sale that have not actually been sold at the time they cross the frontier, should in principle be included in merchandise only at the time ownership changes. Such goods are often recorded instead at the time that they cross the frontier, on the assumption that a change of ownership has occurred or in the expectation that a change will shortly occur. If that treatment is followed but there is no change of ownership, the goods will subsequently have to be recorded again as a deduction from exports and imports.

Services

14.70.   The time at which the export or import of a service is to be recorded is the time at which it is rendered (delivered or received), which mostly coincides with the time at which the service is produced. In some instances (e.g., freight and insurance, port services, etc.), as may be the case with trade in goods, there may be pre-payments or post-payments for such services. Entries in the appropriate accounts should then be made as explained in paragraph 14.75 below. For processing and repairs excluded from goods, the value added is to be recorded as services at the time performed.

Primary incomes

14.71.   Income in the form of interest is to be recorded on an accrual basis, i.e., as accruing continuously over time on the amount of principal outstanding (see chapter VII, paragraphs. 7.94 to 7.104 for discussion). If the interest is not actually paid, an entry is required in the external account of primary incomes and current transfers, together with an offsetting entry in the financial account for the claim associated with non-payment, i.e., an increase in liabilities.

14.72. Dividends are to be recorded as of the moment they are payable. Reinvested earnings on direct foreign investment are to be recorded in the period when they are earned. Distributed (remitted) earnings of branches and other unincorporated enterprises, i.e., withdrawals from income of quasi-corporations, are to be recorded as of the time that they are transferred. In explanation of this difference in time of recording between earnings that are formally distributed and other earnings, it should be noted that reinvested earnings represent the net income accruing during a given period. In contrast, remitted earnings of branches are discretionary distributions that can be made at any time—even in a period when a net loss is sustained—and therefore are not attributable to the earnings of a particular period. To determine the period in which those reinvested earnings are earned or other investment income becomes payable, reference to balance sheets, annual reports, and similar documents of the direct investor or the enterprise may be helpful.

Transfers

14.73. Various taxes, fines, etc., and other components of transfers that are imposed by one party on another are to be recorded at the moment at which the underlying transactions or other flows occur which give rise to the liability to pay. In some instances, taxes on income may be recorded in a subsequent period. Other transfers are to be recorded at the time that the resources (e.g., goods, services, financial items) to which they are offsets change ownership.

Financial transactions

14.74. The time at which external transactions in financial items is considered to take place is when both the creditor and debtor enter the claim and liability, respectively, on their books (see chapter XI). A date (the "value date") may actually be specified for the very purpose of ensuring that the timing agrees in the books for both parties. If no precise date can be fixed, the date on which the creditor receives payment (or some other financial claim) is decisive. Loan drawings are to be entered in the accounts when actual disbursements are made; loan repayments are to be entered when due for payment. In the case of overdue repayments, entries are to be recorded for the repayment of the contractual obligation involved as if it were made and (a) its replacement by a new liability that is short-term (for immediate payment), or (b) if under rescheduling or other special financing arrangements associated with balance of payments difficulties of an economy, replacement by a new loan.

14.75. Recording trade in goods and other current external transactions on a change of ownership basis requires that timing differences between the flow of goods, services and income, and the corresponding flow of payments should give rise to corresponding claims and liabilities, i.e., payments made in advance of change of ownership (pre- or progress-payments) represent a claim on the payee; payments made subsequent to the change of ownership (post-payments) represent the extinguishing of a liability incurred at the time of change of ownership. In other words, when the counterpart to an entry in the financial account is non-financial, the time of recording of financial claims is to be aligned with the time of recording, in the other accounts of the SNA, the transactions that generate the financial claim. For example, when exports of goods or services give rise to a trade credit, an entry in the financial account should be made at the time when the entry is made in the relevant component of the external account of goods and services.

14.76. The time of recording stocks of external financial assets and liabilities (the international investment position) is at the moment to which the account relates, typically the beginning or the end of the accounting period.

3. Conversion and the unit of account

14.77. The compilation of the rest of the world account is complicated by the fact that the values of transactions in resources and financial items and of the components of the stocks of external financial assets and liabilities may be expressed initially in a variety of currencies or in other standards of value, such as SDRs or European currency units (ECUs). The conversion of these values into a reference unit of account (usually the national currency of the compiler) is a requisite for the construction of consistent and analytically meaningful national statements.

14.78. In concordance with the principles of time of recording and of valuation both in the System and in the *Balance of Payments Manual*, the appropriate exchange rate to be used for conversion from a transactions currency into a unit of account is the market rate prevailing on the transaction date, or if that is not available, the average rate for the shortest period applicable. The midpoint between buying and selling rates should be used so that any service charge—the spread between the midpoint and those rates—is excluded.

14.79. For conversion of data on stocks of external financial assets and liabilities, the market exchange rate prevailing on the date to which the balance sheet relates is to be used, i.e., the midpoint between the buying and selling spot rate.

Multiple official exchange rates

14.80. Under an official multiple exchange rate regime, i.e., when two or more exchange rates are applicable to different categories of transactions, favouring some and discouraging others, those rates incorporate elements similar to those of taxes or subsidies. Thus, because the multiple rates influence the undertaking of and values of transactions that are expressed in national currency, the net proceeds implicitly accruing to the authorities as a result of these transactions are to be calculated as implicit taxes and subsidies in the System. The amount of the implicit tax or subsidy can be calculated for each transaction as the difference between the value of the transaction converted into national currency at the actual exchange rate applicable and the value of the transaction converted at a "unitary rate", the latter calculated as a weighted average of all official rates used for external transactions. The System records external transactions using the actual rate applicable to specific transactions. However, implicit taxes/subsidies appear as global adjustments in the rest of the world account with counterpart entries under current and capital transfers in the central bank or government accounts. (For a detailed explanation of multiple exchange rates, including the complete accounting treatment in the System, see Chapter XIX, annex A.)

14.81. The "unitary rate" approximates a single official rate that would exist in the absence of multiple rates. However, because this single calculated rate may not approximate any sort of equilibrium or market rate, the calculated implicit taxes/subsidies/transfers may not fully reflect the impact of a multiple rate system.

14.82. As to conversion of stocks of external financial assets and liabilities in an official multiple rate system, the actual exchange rate applicable to specific assets or liabilities is to be used.

Black or parallel market rates

14.83. Until this point in the discussion of multiple exchange rates, no mention has been made of (unofficial) parallel or black market rates. The latter rates cannot be ignored in the context of a multiple rate regime and can be treated in different ways.

For instance, if there is one official rate and a parallel market rate, the two should be handled separately, with transactions converted at the exchange rate for each. If there are multiple official rates together with a parallel rate, the two should be treated as distinct markets in any calculation of a unitary rate. That is, the multiple official rates—which involve implicit official taxes and subsidies—should be used to calculate a weighted average rate that can serve as the basis for estimating the tax or subsidy component of the various official rates. Transactions effected at the parallel rate usually should be converted at that rate separately. No implicit taxes/subsidies are involved in parallel markets which are not part of the official exchange rate regime. However, in some instances, parallel markets may be considered to be effectively integrated with the official exchange rate regime. Such is the case when most or all transactions in the parallel market are sanctioned by the authorities and/or when the authorities actively intervene in the market to affect the parallel rate. In this instance the calculation of the unitary rate should include both the official and parallel market rates. If only limited transactions in the parallel market are sanctioned by the authorities, the parallel rate should not be included in the calculation of the unitary rate.

14.84. The midpoint between buying and selling rates in the parallel market should be calculated (separately from official rates) for conversion, as is recommended for official rates, so that any service charge is excluded. (Revenues obtained from trading currencies between official and parallel markets are to be treated as holding gains, except when revenues accrue to the monetary authorities as a result of such transactions between authorized parallel and official markets (see paragraph 35, chapter XIX, annex A).

D. The external accounts of goods and services and of primary incomes and current transfers

14.85. The external account for goods and services has on the resources side the flows "imports of goods" and "imports of services", which collectively represent the goods and services acquired by the total economy and conversely, on the uses side, the goods and services supplied by the total economy (represented by the flows "exports of goods" and "exports of services") to the rest of the world. These flows also have their counterpart entries in the goods and services account. The external account of goods and services has a balancing item called "external balance of goods and services". If the balance is positive, it represents a surplus on transactions in goods and services for the rest of the world and conversely a deficit for the total economy, and vice versa if the balance is negative.

14.86. The external account of primary incomes and current transfers covers, on the resources side, as receivables by the rest of the world (payables by the total economy), and, on the uses side, as payables by the rest of the world (receivables by the total economy): (a) compensation of employees, (b) property in-

come (including reinvested earnings on foreign direct investment), (c) taxes minus subsidies on production and imports, (d) current taxes on income, wealth, etc., (e) social contributions and benefits, and (f) other current transfers. Items (a) through (c) are reflected in the primary distribution of income account and items (d) through (f) are reflected in the secondary distribution of income account in respect of the resident sectors, as well as the accounts for the total economy.

14.87. Together with the external balance of goods and services, the transactions in items (a) through (f) yield a balancing item "current external balance". When this balance is positive, it signifies a surplus of the rest of the world on current transactions with the total economy (a deficit of the total economy), while a negative balance denotes a deficit of the rest of the world on current transactions (a surplus of the total economy). As items (a) through (f) feature in the primary and secondary distribution of income accounts of the various institutional sectors and the nation as a whole, they affect, respectively, the resultant measures of primary income and national income and of sector and national disposable income and saving.

1. The external account of goods and services

14.88. Exports of goods and services consist of sales, barter, or gifts or grants, of goods and services from resident to non-residents, while imports consist of purchases, barter, or receipts of gifts or grants, of goods and services by resident from non-residents. The treatment of exports and imports in the System is generally identical with that in the balance of payments accounts as described in the *Balance of Payments Manual*, to which reference may be made for further elaboration on the points made here.

14.89. International transactions in services differ in many respects from those in goods. As explained in chapter VI, the production and the delivery of a service is usually a single operation carried out by mutual agreement between producer and consumer, which requires some kind of prior contact between them. As a result, the organization of international trade in services is quite different from trade in goods. Goods are typically produced in advance of any contract of sale and may be transported over considerable distances from their original place of production to be sold long after they have been produced, whereas services are typically delivered directly from producer to user when they are produced. Thus, international trade in services is not only different in character from trade in goods but may have different implications for economic analysis and policy-making. For this reason, and also because of the growing importance of international trade in services, exports and imports of goods and services are considered and classified separately from each other.

14.90. However, the boundary between them is not always clear-cut in practice, as a single transaction may sometimes cover elements of both. For example, in the external account of goods and services of the system, exports and imports of goods are valued f.o.b.—i.e., including the costs of transportation and insurance up to the border of the exporting country—even though in other contexts, such as input-output tables, the costs of transportation and insurance may be shown separately from the producer's or basic price of a good as it leaves the premises of its producer. Conversely, other transactions involving a mixture of goods and services, such as expenditures by foreign travellers in the domestic market, may all have to be recorded under services in the rest of the world account.

Goods

14.91. Apart from discrepancies due to the fact that the physical movements of goods across frontiers may not coincide with the times at which changes of ownership occur, as mentioned above, there are also differences in coverage between exports and imports of goods as recorded in the System and the flows of goods across frontiers.

Examples of goods which may be sold as exports or purchased as imports without crossing the country's frontier

(a) Transportation equipment or other movable equipment not tied to a fixed location which, therefore, need not necessarily cross the frontiers of either the exporting or the importing country as a result of being sold (purchased) by a resident to (from) a non-resident;

(b) Goods produced by resident units operating in international waters—oil, natural gas, fishery products, maritime salvage, etc.—which are sold directly to non-residents in foreign countries;

(c) Goods consumed in resident-owned offshore installations, ships or aircraft operating in international waters or airspace which are purchased from non-residents in foreign countries;

(d) Goods which are lost or destroyed after changing ownership but before they have crossed the frontier of the exporting country or the importing country.

Examples of goods which may cross frontiers but are excluded from exports or imports

(a) Goods in transit through a country;

(b) Transportation equipment and other movable kinds of equipment which leave or enter a country without change of ownership; for example, construction equipment used for installation or construction purposes abroad;

(c) Equipment and other goods which are sent abroad for minor processing, maintenance, servicing, or repair (goods processed and transformed into different goods are included in exports or imports (see paragraphs 14.61 to 14.64 above), as is the value of repairs on fixed assets, such as ships, which are sent abroad for extensive repair, renovation or refitting);

(d) Other goods which leave, or enter, a country temporarily, being generally returned in their original state and without change of ownership; various examples may be cited: goods sent abroad for exhibition purposes only; equipment for orchestras, stage performances, etc., while on tour abroad; goods on consignment which are returned because an expected sale does not materialize; goods shipped under an operating lease; animals sent abroad for racing, shows, other forms of entertainment, or breeding purposes;

(e) Goods shipped to or from a country's own embassies, military bases, or other enclaves which are geographically situated inside the national frontiers of another country;

(f) Goods on consignment lost or destroyed after crossing a frontier but before change of ownership occurs.

14.92. Sometimes the classification of certain physical items as goods is questioned, most often because they may be accorded exceptional treatment under customs regulations or in the trade returns. The following examples are listed as items of this kind which should be included in goods: commodity gold (i.e., non-monetary gold), silver bullion, diamonds and other precious metals and stones; paper money and coin not in current circulation and unissued securities, all of which should be valued as commodities rather than at their face value; electricity, gas, and water; livestock driven across frontiers; parcel post; government exports and imports (other than those to and from the government's own agencies and personnel), including goods financed by grants and loans; goods transferred to or from the ownership of a buffer stock organization; migrants' effects; smuggled goods, whether or not detected by customs; and other unrecorded shipments, such as gifts and those of less than a stated minimum value.

14.93. There are certain physical items which are regarded as financial items that should not be included in goods, among which are the following examples:

(a) Evidence of financial claims, even though they have a material form and are movable, are treated as financial items. Examples of such goods are paper money and coin that are in current circulation and securities that have been issued;

(b) Monetary gold is treated as a financial asset, so that transfers of monetary gold between the authorities of different countries are reflected in the financial account;

(c) Non-financial assets belonging to an enterprise, including land, structures, equipment, and inventories, are considered to be financial assets for the owner of that enterprise, when the owner is not a resident of the economy where the enterprise operates. A change of ownership of these assets resulting from the acquisition of an existing enterprise is thus treated as a financial transaction and is not included in goods, except to the extent that such a change of ownership is actually accompanied by a physical movement of goods.

Services

14.94. The export or import of a service requires some kind of contact between a resident producer and a non-resident consumer at the time production actually takes place. In the case of transportation, the contact between producer and consumer is made possible by the mobility of the transport equipment itself. For other types of services, including information services, the contact may be established by means of telecommunications links of one kind or other. However, the production of most services, both producer services and consumer services, requires the producer and consumer to come together in some manner and in a convenient location: this is the case for a wide range of services such as most business and financial services,

health, education, recreation, entertainment, etc. At an international level the producer may have to travel to the country of the consumer, or vice versa. The mobility of service producers has been greatly enhanced by fast and frequent air travel, while telecommunication links enable staff abroad to continue to draw on the resources of expertise of staff in head offices.

14.95. For example, it is common for producers of business services, such as consultancy or other advisory services, to send teams of staff to work abroad on assignments resulting from specific contracts negotiated with non-residents. As explained in paragraphs 14.22 and 14.23 above, such production units operating abroad are considered to be integral parts of the parent corporation to which they belong, provided that the volume of production which they carry out abroad does not become so large and the length of time over which that production takes place so long that the unit cannot reasonably be treated as not having a centre of economic interest in the country concerned. When a production unit operating abroad establishes a substantial physical presence in a foreign country by purchasing or renting business premises, acquiring capital equipment, recruiting local staff, etc., with the intention of engaging in production over a long period of time (a guideline is one year or more, applied flexibly), the production unit in question must be treated as a foreign branch—i.e., as a quasi-corporation which is resident in the country in which it is operating. In these circumstances, the output of the branch counts as part of the GDP of the country in which it is located so that it cannot be treated as an export of a service from the parent which owns and controls it.

14.96. The criterion of residence outlined above, that was described in detail earlier in this chapter (see paragraph 14.23 above) applies equally to all corporations, whether engaged in the production of goods or services. However, the issue is particularly relevant to services producers because establishing a foreign branch (or subsidiary) which supplies services directly to the residents of a foreign country may be the only means by which a unit engaged in service production can expand its sales to non-residents. A corporation which creates a foreign branch for this purpose may regard itself as continuing to "export" services, even when the branch is established on an indefinite, or permanent, basis. However, such a branch is classified in the System as a quasi-corporation which is resident in the country in which it operates, so that there may be an important difference between the way in which exports and imports of services are recorded in the System—and in the balance of payments—and the way in which some corporations themselves may perceive them. Corporations may not recognize any threshold beyond which the production is classified as contributing to the GDP of the country in which the branch is located instead of contributing to the GDP of the country in which the parent is located.

14.97. From a national accounts viewpoint, the central issue is not so much the exact definition, or coverage, of exports or imports as the definition and coverage of GDP itself. When a branch office is producing services on a permanent basis inside a country, the value added must be considered part of the GDP of that country, not of the country of residence of the parent corporation.

14.98. The services which enter into exports and imports of services must have been produced as outputs from processes of production. They do not include incomes which are sometimes described as payments for "services" rendered in the course of production. Payments of compensation of employees from residents to non-residents, or vice versa, are international flows of primary incomes. Such payments occur, for example, in the case of seasonal or border workers who work in a different country from that in which they are resident. Similarly, flows of property income, such as interest and dividends, between residents and non-residents are excluded from international trade in services.

14.99. The coverage of exports and imports of services corresponds broadly to the types of services which are described in sections 6 to 9 of the CPC. However, whereas the CPC treats all repairs and processing as service activities, the System does not, as already noted. As the CPC provides a comprehensive listing of the other kinds of services which may enter into international trade, and the *Balance of Payments Manual* describes a list of standard components of such services, it is not necessary to give all such details here. Nevertheless, it is useful to indicate how some of the more important types of trade in services are treated in the System.

Construction

14.100. The treatment of international construction raises the same issues as those discussed in paragraphs 14.95 to 14.98 above with reference to business consultancy or other services. Contracts for the construction of major projects such as bridges, power stations, or dams are frequently awarded to non-resident corporations. When a construction corporation in country A is awarded a contract in country B, the corporation is obliged to create a site office in country B from which the construction is managed and carried out, in much the same way that a corporation exporting services may have to open a branch office abroad. Although the site office may have no separate legal identity, it may nevertheless be treated as a quasi-corporation for this purpose. The main argument against this treatment is that the site office is created for the duration of a specific project and is dismantled when the project terminates. Thus, it cannot be interpreted as evidence of a lasting economic interest in country B by the corporation.

14.101. If a site office is not treated as a quasi-corporation, the consequences are that the construction site has to be treated as an enclave of country A inside of country B which is similar to that of an embassy or military base maintained by country A. The value added inside the enclave can then be treated as part of the GDP of country A and the value of the final output pro-

duced, i.e., the dam or bridge itself, is treated as an export from country A to country B. In line with the general principles applied to the measurement of the output of construction, the dam or bridge can be treated as being completed and delivered to the client in stages. While this solution has some merit, it has the serious disadvantage that the value added generated by a major construction project, such as the construction of a dam or bridge which may last several years, is not attributed to the country in which the activity actually takes place. This seems particularly anomalous when most of the labour and materials employed on the project are likely to be supplied locally, while the project itself is likely to have an important impact on incomes and expenditures in the locality. For this reason the System recommends that quasi-corporations should be created for major construction projects which last for a year or more (subject to the considerations noted in paragraph 14.23 above), even though there may be no lasting economic interest in the country by the construction unit.

14.102. The consequence of creating a quasi-corporation unit for a construction project undertaken in country B in the above example is that the only exports which are recorded from country A to country B are the goods and services supplied from country A which are incorporated into the final structure: for example, surveyors' plans prepared in country A or turbines or other hydroelectric equipment manufactured in country A which are installed in the dam in country B. Although there may be no change of legal ownership when the parent construction corporation in country A ships equipment to its own construction site located in country B, the system imputes a change of ownership for deliveries of goods to branches or subsidiaries abroad which are not returned. The project may also generate important international flows of income, including compensation of employees, as well as profits and financial flows, but these are not exports or imports of goods and services.

Installation

14.103. The installation of equipment is an activity which has much in common with construction. However, as the installation of a specific amount of equipment abroad is clearly a project of limited duration which, in itself, does not signal any lasting economic interest in the country in which it takes place, it is not appropriate to create a quasi-corporation in respect of that activity, even if it happens to take more than a year to complete. Thus, the installation of equipment abroad is always treated as an export of a service in the System and in the *Balance of Payments Manual*. In practice, the value of the installation costs, like transportation costs, if included in the global value of the equipment exported, may not always be separately recorded.

Transportation

14.104. Transportation services encompass all modes of transportation—sea, air, and other, including land, internal waterway, space and pipeline—performed by residents of one economy for those of another, that are involved with either the movement of goods (freight), or the carriage of passengers, together with related supporting and auxiliary services. Most transportation services often are provided by corporations through their operation of carriers and similar equipment. Questions arise as to the residence of such units or operators, because the carrier may operate outside the economic territory in which the corporation is resident, either in international waters, in airspace, or in one or more other economies. (The residence of corporations is discussed in section B.4, where paragraphs 14.25 to 14.27 above are particularly relevant in this context.)

Goods transportation

14.105. As stated above, by valuing both exports and imports f.o.b. at the frontier of the exporting country, the boundary between trade in goods and trade in services in the System is implicitly fixed (see paragraphs 14.36 to 14.40 above). This method of valuation also determines the treatment of goods transportation. It is necessary to distinguish transportation within the exporting country up to its frontier, i.e., the point at which goods are valued f.o.b., from transportation beyond that point, which covers both transportation between the frontier of the exporting country and the frontier of the importing country and transportation within the importing country to the final destination of the goods.

14.106. Transportation costs up to the customs frontier of the exporting country should be incorporated into the f.o.b. price of the goods at that point. The transportation services must not be counted twice, however, so that when they are provided by the exporter or other resident of the exporting country they should not also be recorded as exports of services. However, when the importer (or other resident of the importer's country) is responsible for the transportation of the goods from the factory of the foreign producer up to the frontier of the exporter's country, these transportation costs must be added to the price received by the foreign producer to arrive at the f.o.b. price. This procedure requires an offsetting imputation to be made whereby the foreign producer is deemed to purchase these services from the importer or other resident of the importer's country: Otherwise, the foreign earnings of the exporter would be overstated.

14.107. Transportation beyond the customs frontier of the exporting country, whether outside or inside the importing country, should be recorded as imports of services when the transportation is provided by a carrier who is not a resident of the importing country. When the imports of goods are initially recorded c.i.f. instead of f.o.b. the transport costs between the customs frontiers of the exporting and importing countries should first be deducted from the c.i.f. price to arrive at the f.o.b. price. These transportation services should then be recorded as imports of services when they are provided by a non-resident, as stated above.

14.108. The transportation by resident carriers of goods owned by non-residents which do not enter the resident carrier's country as imports are recorded as exports of services. Conversely, the transportation within a country by non-resident carriers of goods owned by residents which do not leave that country as exports are recorded as imports of services.

Passenger transportation

14.109. Exports cover the international transportation of non-residents by resident carriers, while imports cover the international transportation of residents by non-resident carriers. These services also include the transportation of residents within their own country by non-resident carriers. Services provided by resident carriers within their own country to non-residents are not recorded under transportation services but are shown under the global headings of "direct purchases in the domestic market by non-residents" and "direct purchases abroad by residents" in the supply and use tables, as adjustment items. Passenger transportation includes the food, drink or other goods supplied to passengers while travelling when passenger fares cover the cost of these items which are provided without additional charge. Any additional services provided to passengers, such as the transport of excess baggage or vehicles or other effects belonging to passengers which are transported with them on the same train, ship, aircraft, etc., are also included under passenger transportation.

Tourism[1]

14.110. The item "tourism" does not refer to a particular type of service as such, and hence for this reason is not identified in the CPC. Exports of tourism (receipts) cover purchases of all types of goods and services made by non-residents visiting an economy for business or personal purposes, for less than one year. An exception to the one-year rule applies to students and medical patients who are treated as non-residents even if their stay is for a longer period. Expenditures on health and education should be separately recorded when feasible. Imports of tourism (payments) cover all purchases of goods and services made by residents while travelling abroad for business or personal purposes (see reference in paragraph 14.109 above to adjustment in the supply and use tables).

14.111. Expenditures on tourism, and also passenger services, must be subdivided to distinguish those expenditures made by business travellers, which are paid for, or reimbursed by, their employers from those expenditures made by households. Expenditures by business travellers are part of the intermediate consumption of producers, whereas expenditures by other travellers on personal trips are part of household final consumption expenditures. In order to calculate final consumption expenditure of resident households from the expenditure made by all households, both resident and non-resident, within the domestic market, it is necessary to add direct purchases abroad by residents and to subtract direct purchases in the domestic market by non-residents (see chapter XV).

Insurance

14.112. Exports of insurance services cover the provision of insurance to non-residents by resident insurance enterprises, while imports cover the provision of insurance to residents by non-resident insurance enterprises. The treatment of the cost of insurance on goods which are in the process of being exported and imported has to be consistent with the valuation principles adopted for exports and imports of goods and the same conventions must be followed as for goods transportation in these circumstances. These conventions may be summarized as follows: insurance on internationally traded goods from the exporter's factory, or warehouse, up to the frontier of the exporter's country is to be included in the f.o.b. value of the goods exported. If this insurance is paid for by the importer using an enterprise resident in the importer's country, the exporter is deemed to purchase the insurance and simultaneously recover its cost out of the f.o.b. price recorded in the accounts. Insurance services on goods after they have passed the frontier of the exporting country are recorded as imports of insurance services by the importer when the insurance is provided by a non-resident of the importing country. If the insurance is provided by an enterprise resident in the importer's country, it should not be recorded in the external account of goods and services, bearing in mind that imports, as well as exports, are recorded f.o.b. and not c.i.f.

14.113. International insurance services are to be estimated or valued by the amount of service charge included in total premiums earned, not by the total premiums themselves. In principle, the measurement of transactions in international insurance services is consistent with that of insurance services for resident sectors. However, in practice, both the System and the *Balance of Payments Manual* allow resident/non-resident flows associated with investment income on technical reserves to be ignored because of problems of estimation, particularly for imports. Thus, for goods, the insurance service charge for resident issuers providing insurance services to non-residents (export) is the difference between premiums earned and claims payable on goods lost or destroyed in transit. The service charge for non-resident issuers providing services to residents (import) can be estimated by applying the ratio of estimated service charges to total premiums for exports of insurance services to total premiums paid to non-resident issuers. The ratio should be based on a medium- to long-term period. In respect to other types of direct insurance, the service charge for nonresident insurers providing services to residents can be estimated by applying the ratio of estimated service charges to total premiums for resident insurers. Again, the ratio should be based on a medium- to long-term period. For non-life insurance, total premiums minus the estimated service charge and claims payable should be recorded under current transfers. For life insurance, premiums minus the service charge and claims payable are to be recorded in the financial account, under insurance technical reserves. For reinsurance,

exports of services are, in principle, estimated as the balance of all flows occurring between resident reinsurers and non-resident insurers. Imports are, in principle, estimated as the balance of all flows occurring between resident insurers and non-resident reinsurers.

Licence fees

14.114. Licence fees cover receipts (exports) and payments (imports) of residents and non-residents associated with the authorized use of intangible non-produced non-financial assets and proprietary rights, such as patents, copyrights, trademarks, industrial processes, franchises, etc., and with the use through licensing agreements, of produced originals or prototypes, such as manuscripts, films, etc.

Financial services

14.115. Financial services are financial intermediary and auxiliary services (except those of insurance corporations and pension funds) conducted between residents and non-residents. Included are fees for intermediaries' services, such as those associated with letters of credit, bankers acceptances, lines of credit, financial leasing, foreign exchange transactions, etc.; commissions and other fees related to transactions in securities—brokerage, placements of issues, underwritings, redemptions, arrangements of swaps, options, and other hedging instruments, etc.; commissions of commodity futures traders; and services related to asset management, administration of stock and other financial market exchanges, etc. Service charges on purchases of IMF resources are included among an economy's financial services payments, as are charges (similar to a commitment fee) associated with undrawn balances under stand-by or extended arrangements with the IMF. In addition to the above explicit commissions and fees, there are financial intermediation services indirectly measured (FISIM), reflecting services that are not explicitly charged but whose values are estimated from the difference between the property incomes received by financial intermediaries from the investment of borrowed funds, and the interest they themselves pay on such funds (see chapter VI). FISIM may, or may not be allocated between different users of these services, including non-residents as well as residents, depending upon country practices. The way in which imports and exports of FISIM may be treated in the accounts when these services are actually allocated among different users is explained in annex III at the end of this manual.

2. The external account for primary incomes and current transfers

14.116. As noted in paragraph 14.86 above, on the resources side, this account covers as receivables by the rest of the world (payables by the total economy), and on the uses side payables by the rest of the world (receivables by the total economy): (a) compensation of employees; (b) property income (including reinvested earnings on foreign direct investment); (c) taxes minus subsidies on production and imports; (d) current taxes on income, wealth, etc.; (e) social contributions and benefits; and (f) other current transfers. Items (a) through (c) make up the external component of the primary distribution of income account, while items (d) through (f) (all current transfers), make up the external component of the secondary distribution of income account. Excluded from primary incomes are receipts derived from the renting of tangible and intangible assets, which are classified as rentals, under services. Financial leasing arrangements are taken as evidence that a de facto change of ownership has occurred, and part of the lease payments is construed as interest on a financial asset.

Compensation of employees

14.117. A full discussion of compensation of employees appears in chapter VII. In the external account of primary incomes and current transfers, compensation of employees comprises wages, salaries, and other remuneration, in cash or in kind, earned by individuals in an economy other than the one in which they are resident for work performed for (and paid by) a resident of that economy. Included are contributions paid by employers on behalf of employees to Social Security schemes or to private insurance schemes or pension funds—including imputed contributions to unfunded pension schemes—to secure benefits for employees. Employees in this context include seasonal or other short-term workers (less than one year) and border workers (with a centre of economic interest in their own economies). In the case of local (host country) staff of embassies, consulates, bases, etc., because these are extraterritorial enclaves, the compensation received by local staff is that of a resident from a non-resident.

14.118. Compensation paid to employees by international organizations (also extraterritorial enclaves) represent payments to residents from a non-resident, (a) if the employees are residents of the economy of location, or (b) if the employees are from other economies but are employed for one year or more and thus are treated as residents of the economy of location. In the case of employees from other economies who are employed for less than one year, there is no payment to a resident involved. (For the treatment of technical assistance personnel working on assignments of one year or more, see paragraph 14.18 above.)

14.119. Personal expenditures by non-resident workers in the economy where employed, including those on installation projects, are to be recorded under direct purchases in the domestic market by non-residents, and taxes paid, contributions to social insurance schemes, etc., in that economy are to be recorded as current transfer payments. Gross recording of compensation and expenditures is recommended, although, this may not always be possible in practice.

14.120. The distinction between those individuals whose earnings are to be classified as "compensation of employees" (persons who

are not residents of the economy where they work) and migrants (persons who have become residents of that economy by virtue of being expected to live there for a year or more) is often hard to draw in practice. The transactions of the compiling economy with the rest of the world as the result of an individual's activities will be in balance whether that individual is regarded as a resident or a non-resident. An effort should nonetheless be made to observe the distinction between foreign workers and migrants if possible, as lack of uniformity in the statistical treatment of the same individuals by the two compiling economies concerned can create problems of comparability between the external transactions accounts or balance of payments statements for those economies.

Taxes minus subsidies on production and imports

14.121. A discussion of the various types of taxes on production and imports and subsidies appears in chapter VII, including links with the IMF and the Organisation for Economic Co-operation and Development (OECD) tax classifications and references to taxes and subsidies resulting from multiple exchange rates. (A more detailed discussion of the latter, together with the guidelines for conversion, appears in section C.3. of this chapter.)

Property income

14.122. Property income covers income derived from a resident entity's ownership of foreign financial assets. The most common types of such income are interest and dividends. (Property income is fully discussed in chapter VII.) Interest, including discounts in lieu of interest, comprises income on loans and debt securities, i.e., such financial claims as bank deposits, bills, bonds, notes, and trade advances. Net interest flows arising from interest rate swaps are also included. Dividends, including stock dividends, are the distribution of earnings in respect of the shares and other forms of participation in the equity of public and private corporations.

14.123. Among other types of property income are the earnings of branches and other unincorporated direct foreign investment enterprises (see paragraphs 14.152 to 14.154 below), and the direct investor's portion of the earnings of incorporated direct foreign investment enterprises that are not formally distributed, i.e., earnings other than dividends or withdrawals from income of quasi-corporations. The part of those reinvested earnings that is attributed to the direct investor is proportionate to his participation in the equity of the enterprise. Another type of property income is that attributed to insurance policyholders, as described in chapter VII, paragraphs 7.126 and 7.127.

Current transfers

14.124. Three main types of current transfers are distinguished in the external account of primary incomes and current transfers, as in the secondary distribution of income account: (a) current taxes on income and wealth, etc.; (b) social contributions and benefits; and (c) other current transfers. (A full discussion of these transfers appears in chapter VIII.) It is sufficient to note here that many of the taxes included in (a) above are payable regularly every tax period (as distinct from capital taxes levied infrequently), while others include taxes on international transactions such as on foreign exchange purchases or sales, travel, etc.; that (b) consists of current transfers in the form of contributions made under social insurance schemes organized by government units (Social Security schemes) or by public or private employers, and of transfers in the form of social benefits, e.g., pensions; and that (c) consists of various other cur-

rent transfers between general government and foreign governments, etc. Before the current external balance can be calculated, an adjustment item for the change in net equity of households in pension funds must be recorded (see chapter IX, paragraphs 9.14 to 9.16). The adjustment reflects the net result of both the change in net equity held by resident households in non-resident pension funds (liability of the rest of the world) on the uses side, and the change in net equity held by non-resident households in resident pension funds (financial asset of the rest of the world) on the resources side.

E. External accumulation accounts

14.125. There are two pairs of external accumulation accounts: first, the capital account and the financial account, which together comprise the "capital and financial account" of the balance of payments as set forth in the *Balance of Payments Manual*, and secondly, the other changes in assets accounts, comprising two types of changes in assets, liabilities, and net worth (the other changes in assets accounts are covered in detail for the System as a whole in chapter XII) between opening and closing balance sheets that do not reflect transactions as recorded in the capital account and financial account. The first type, reflected in the other changes in volume of assets account, covers changes that result from factors which change the volume of assets held abroad by residents, e.g., uncompensated seizures, recognition by a creditor that a loan to a non-resident is not collectible, etc. The second type, reflected in the revaluation account, covers holding gains and losses on foreign financial assets resulting from changes in prices and exchange rates.

1. Capital account

14.126. The capital account covers, on the changes in liabilities side, capital transfers receivable and payable, and on the change in assets side, acquisitions less disposals of non-produced, non-financial assets, between non-residents (the rest of the world) and residents (the total economy). Acquisitions and disposals of producers' durables such as machinery and equipment, whether new or used, are recorded under imports and exports of goods. Thus, there are no entries in the external capital account corresponding to the acquisitions and disposals of fixed assets recorded in the capital accounts of resident units or sectors. Capital transfers are discussed fully in chapter X. It is sufficient to note here that such transfers may be in kind or in cash. The former consists of the transfer of ownership of a tangible or intangible fixed asset, or the cancellation of a financial claim by mutual agreement between a creditor and a debtor (debt forgiveness); the latter requires (or expects) the recipient to use the cash transferred for the acquisition of an asset or assets. Thus, the essential characteristic of a capital transfer is that it involves the disposal or acquisition of assets by one or

both of the parties to the transaction and that it results in changes in net worth of one or both parties. In the System, a transfer should be classified as a capital transfer by both parties even if it involves the acquisition or disposal of an asset, or assets, by only one of the parties. (The time of recording and valuation aspects of capital transfers, along with a description of specific examples, such as capital taxes, investment grants, debt forgiveness, etc., appear in chapter X.)

14.127. Acquisitions less disposals of non-produced, non-financial assets appear on the changes in assets side of the account, recording changes in the value of these assets resulting from transactions of non-residents with residents. The acquisitions less disposals recorded in the capital account comprise the total value of such assets acquired by the rest of the world during the accounting period less the total value of such assets disposed of. In the external capital account, this item does not cover land in a given economic territory because, by convention, all owners or purchasers of land must be resident institutional units. If a non-resident owns or purchases land, a notional resident unit is created and deemed to own the land, and the non-resident is deemed to have acquired a financial claim on the notional resident unit. Thus, all transactions in land within a given economic territory are deemed to occur between resident units. However, there may be uncommon cases in which land shifts from one economic territory to another, e.g., the purchase of land by a foreign embassy. That land then is located in the economic territory of the country of that embassy, and is no longer part of the economic territory of the country of location. The same holds true in the case of a foreign embassy selling land. In these instances, a transaction in land between residents and non-residents is to be recorded. In addition, acquisitions less disposals of intangible non-financial assets are recorded here, including patented entities, leases or other transferable contracts and purchased goodwill (see chapter X for discussion and definitions).

2. Changes in net worth and net lending or borrowing

14.128. The total of the right-hand side of the capital account reflects the changes in net worth (of the rest of the world) due to the current external balance and capital transfers. It represents the positive or negative resources available for the accumulation of assets by the rest of the world *vis-à-vis* the economy. When combined with acquisitions less disposals of non-produced non-financial assets on the left side, the result is a balancing item labelled net lending (if a surplus) or net borrowing (if a deficit) of the rest of the world.

3. Financial account

14.129. The financial account is the second account in the external accumulation accounts, following the capital account in the accounting structure. It records all transactions in financial assets between the rest of the world and resident units. On the asset side of the account, acquisitions less disposals of financial assets by non-residents from residents are recorded; on the liability side, incurrence of liabilities less repayments by non-residents to residents are recorded. The balancing item of the financial account, net lending/net borrowing, i.e., net acquisition of financial assets minus net incurrence of liabilities, is equal to the balancing item in the capital account (for a full discussion of the financial account in the System, see chapter XI).

14.130. All external transactions, with the exception of transfers in kind, involve an entry in the financial account, whether they are current account transactions or are associated only with an exchange of financial assets or the creation of assets and offsetting liabilities. All these transactions involve a legal or effective change of ownership.

Financial assets

14.131. Although an extensive discussion of financial assets appears in chapter XI, and is fully applicable to the external financial account, those items of particular importance to the external account will be elaborated upon here. In particular it is appropriate to note that although monetary gold and IMF SDRs are included among foreign financial assets, they have no counterpart liabilities in that they do not represent claims on other units. Also, for corporate equity shares, the liability does not represent a fixed redemption value. In addition, for certain financial derivatives, such as options, liabilities are attributed by convention to the issuer.

14.132. In the determination of which financial assets constitute claims on or liabilities to non-residents, the creditor and debtor (or transactors) must be residents of different economies. The unit in which the claim or liability is denominated—whether the national currency, a foreign currency, or a unit like the SDR—is not relevant. Furthermore, assets must represent actual claims that are legally in existence. The authorization, commitment, or extension of an unutilized line of credit or the incurrence of a contingent obligation does not establish such a claim, and the pledging or setting aside of an asset (as in a sinking fund) does not settle a claim or alter the ownership of the asset. Although contingent assets and liabilities are ex-

cluded from financial items, as noted above, options and related derivatives are included among financial assets and transactions when they are tradable and have a current market value (see chapter XI).

14.133. By convention, the ownership of some non-financial assets is transformed into the ownership of financial assets, i.e., claims. Three specific cases may be noted:

(a) Immovable assets, such as land and structures (except when the land and structures are owned by foreign government entities and thus are not part of the economic territory), are construed as always being owned by residents of the economic territory where they are located. When the owner of such assets is a non-resident, therefore, that entity is considered to have a financial claim on a resident entity that is construed as being the owner;

(b) An unincorporated enterprise that operates in a different economy from the one in which its owner resides is considered to be a separate entity; that entity is a resident of the economy where it operates rather than of the economy of its owner. All assets, non-financial as well as financial, attributed to such an enterprise are to be regarded as foreign financial assets for the owner of the enterprise;

(c) Any goods transferred under a financial leasing arrangement are presumed to have changed ownership. This change in ownership is financed by a financial claim, i.e., an asset of the lessor and a liability of the lessee. The financial asset should be classified as a loan.

Selected transactions in financial assets

14.134. Transactions in monetary gold between residents and non-residents, i.e., transactions between the authorities and their counterparts in other economies, or with international monetary organizations, are recorded on the left (changes in assets) side of the financial account. A purchase by the rest of the world is recorded as a positive entry, a sale by the rest of the world as a negative entry. (Transactions in non-monetary gold between residents and non-residents are recorded as exports or imports of goods.) Monetary gold, like SDRs, (see paragraph 14.135 below), is an asset for which there is no outstanding financial liability.

14.135. Transactions in SDRs, international reserve assets created by the IMF to supplement other reserve assets of official holders, also are recorded on the left (changes in assets) side of the financial account. Changes in the authorities' holdings of SDRs can arise through: (a) transactions involving SDR payments to or receipts from the IMF, other participants in the SDR department of the IMF, or other IMF-designated holders, or (b) allocation or cancellation. Transactions such as those enumerated under (a) above are included in the financial account, while allocations/cancellations are not entered in the financial account but rather are included in the other changes in volume of assets account.

14.136. Trade credits are a sub-item of "other accounts receivable/payable" and reflect trade credit for goods and services extended directly (not loans to finance trade credit, which are classified under "loans") and advances for work-in-progress. Such credits from suppliers may be measured by the difference between the entries for the underlying goods and services recorded as of the date of change of ownership and the entries for payments related to these transactions.

14.137. Use of IMF credit and loans from the IMF is a component of "loans", and comprises the compiling country's drawings on the Fund (except from the "reserve tranche", i.e., a reserve deposit in the Fund). Included are purchases and borrowings under stand-by, extended and various structural adjustment arrangements, together with Trust Fund loans. A reduction in the Fund's holdings of the compiling country's currency that are in excess of the country's quota in the Fund minus its reserve tranche position reflects a repayment of the use of Fund credit. Claims on the IMF that are a component of international reserves and that are not evidenced by loans are to be recorded under "other deposits".

14.138. Direct foreign investment-related transactions in financial assets and liabilities, for both inward and outward investment, are to be recorded under the appropriate classifications, i.e., equity capital under "shares and other equity", loans and other intercompany transactions under "other accounts receivable/payable". The above transactions also are to be recorded separately as a memorandum item.

14.139. Reinvested earnings of direct foreign investment enterprises (see paragraph 14.152 below for definition of the latter), wholly or partly owned by non-residents (unincorporated branches, subsidiaries and, when so decided, associates as defined) are recorded in the external account of primary incomes and current transfers as property income paid to the parent or direct investor, and in the financial account as reinvested in the enterprise, thus adding to the net equity of that enterprise.

4. Other changes in assets accounts

14.140. This pair of accounts was described in paragraph 14.125 above. The following paragraphs refer to the two individual accounts covered.

Other changes in volume of assets account

14.141. The left side of the account records those changes in assets of the rest of the world, the right side those changes in liabilities that are not due transactions between residents and non-residents as recorded in the preceding external account. One type of entry on the left side relates to non-financial assets. There may be instances of uncompensated seizures, e.g., for intangible non-financial assets, the seizure of patents, software, or other originals owned by non-residents. For tangible assets,

there may be uncompensated seizures associated with territorial annexations. For financial assets, there may be entries for a variety of uncompensated seizures, other volume changes in financial assets and liabilities n.e.c. (e.g., writing off bad debts), and for changes in classification and structure. A possible example of the latter might be changes resulting from the merger of a non-resident corporation, in which a resident owns shares and on which he has claims (loans), with another non-resident corporation, i.e., the resident receives shares in the new corporation equal to the shares in, plus loans to, the original corporation. On the right side of the accounts (changes in liabilities), there are entries for uncompensated seizures, for other volume changes in financial assets and liabilities n.e.c. (e.g., the counterpart to the writing off of bad debt by the creditor on the left side), and for changes in classification and structure (see example above).

14.142. The above-noted types of changes in the volume of assets as shown on the left side (changes in assets of the rest of the world) and right side (changes in liabilities of the rest of the world) of the account, result in the balancing item "changes in net worth due to other changes in volume of assets".

Revaluation account

14.143. The revaluation account, for the System as a whole, is described in chapter XII. It is sufficient here to summarize the aspects of the account that pertain particularly to external financial assets and liabilities. While the revaluation account in the System records the holding gains/losses accruing to the owners of financial and non-financial assets and liabilities during the accounting period involved, the external revaluation account applies only to financial assets and liabilities.

14.144. The account first shows nominal holding gains/losses, with a subsequent breakdown into two components—neutral holding gains/losses and real holding gains/losses. (The term "capital gains" is sometimes used elsewhere, rather than holding gains, but the latter is used in the System.) The nominal holding gain/loss is that value accruing to the non-resident creditors and debtors as a result of a change in their assets'/liabilities' monetary value, during the time that they are held, from the beginning to the end of the accounting period. The change in the monetary value of the asset may reflect a change in its price (in national currency) and/or a change in the relevant exchange rate. As to the latter, the value of the nominal holding gains accruing from a period may be calculated by the difference between the opening and closing balance sheet values minus the value of transactions or other volume changes for the period. For this calculation, transactions in foreign assets are to be converted into national currency using the exchange rate prevailing at the time of transaction, i.e., the midpoint between buying and selling rates, while the opening and closing balance sheet values are to be converted using the exchange rates prevailing at the respective dates the balance sheets are drawn up.

14.145. The neutral holding gain component is defined as the value of the holding gain that would be required to maintain the purchasing power of the asset—expressed in national currency—over the time period involved, i.e., the holding gain needed to keep pace with the overall change in the general price level. The real holding gain/loss component is that value—expressed in national currency—of the asset resulting from the difference between the nominal and the neutral gain/loss. The real holding gains (losses) of creditors in one economy may not be equal to the real holding losses (gains) of debtors in another economy, in regard to the same asset, if the rate of change in the general price level in the two economies differs.

14.146. The balancing item in the external revaluation account is "changes in net worth due to nominal holding gains/losses", representing the difference between the sum of holding gains/losses on the financial assets owned by non-residents and the sum of holding gains/losses on their liabilities. (A holding gain (loss) may reflect a positive (negative) revaluation of an asset or a negative (positive) revaluation of a liability.) The balancing item is subdivided into two components, neutral holding gains/losses, reflecting changes in net worth due to changes in the general price level, and real holding gains/losses due to changes in relative prices (including the effects of exchange rate changes on conversions into national currency).

F. Relationship between the current external transactions and accumulation accounts and the balance of payments accounts

14.147. Although a detailed reconciliation between the balance of payments accounts as reflected in the *Balance of Payments Manual* and the external transactions and accumulation accounts in the System is presented in annex III at the end of this manual, a brief summary of the relationship between the two is appropriate at this point. First, it should be noted that the integration of the balance of payments accounts with the System is reinforced by the fact that in almost all countries, balance of payments data are compiled first, and subsequently incorporated into the national accounts. There is virtually complete concordance between balance of payments concepts as delineated in the *Balance of Payments Manual* and in the System's rest of the world account in respect of definitions of residence, valuation and time of recording of transactions, currency conversion procedures, coverage of international transactions in goods, services, primary incomes, and current transfers, coverage of capital transfers and coverage of transactions in external financial assets and liabilities.

14.148. In the balance of payments accounts, the current account contains the flows reflected in the External Account of Goods and Services plus the external account of primary incomes and current transfers in the System. The capital account in the balance of payments is identical with that account in the System's external accumulation accounts, and the financial account in both systems essentially has the same coverage (see paragraphs 14.126 to 14.133 above). There are differences only in the degree of detail (reflected in annex III of this manual), in the treatment of one specific item, and in the classification of financial items.

14.149. As to the specific item mentioned above, financial intermediation services indirectly measured (FISIM) is included in the external account of goods and services, reflecting services that are not explicitly charged, but is not shown under imports and exports of services in the balance of payments accounts. How-ever, it is included indistinguishably under "investment income, interest" in those accounts.

14.150. As to the classification of financial items, whereas in the System the primary basis for classification of financial assets is by type of instrument, as reflected in the seven major categories, in the balance of payments accounts the primary basis for classification is by function, i.e., direct (foreign) investment, portfolio investment, other capital and reserve assets. Within those functional areas, the next level of breakdown is by type of instrument, that breakdown encompassing the seven major categories of transactions in financial assets and liabilities classified in the System. However, "securities other than shares" in the System is subdivided in the balance of payments accounts into bonds and notes, money-market instruments and financial derivatives. Also, the two components of insurance technical reserves in the System—net equity of households in life insurance reserves and pension funds, and prepayments of premiums and reserves against outstanding claims—are included indistinguishably in the balance of payments accounts under "other investment", other assets.

14.151. "Direct foreign investment" appears as a memorandum item in the classification of transactions in financial assets and liabilities in chapter XI. However, as noted above, direct investment is a major functional category in the balance of payments accounts, as is "portfolio investment". The *Balance of Payments Manual* concept of direct investment (consistent with that of the OECD *Detailed Benchmark Definition of Foreign Direct Investment*, second edition), reflects the objective of a resident institutional unit (direct investor) obtaining a lasting interest in an enterprise in another economy, together with a significant influence as evidenced by an effective voice in management of the (direct investment) enterprise.

14.152. A direct investment enterprise is defined as an incorporated or unincorporated enterprise in which an investor resident in another economy owns 10 per cent or more of the ordinary shares or voting power (for an incorporated enterprise) or the equivalent (for an unincorporated enterprise). Direct investment enterprises comprise those entities that are identified as subsidiaries (investor owns more than 50 per cent), associates (investor owns 50 per cent or less) and branches (wholly or jointly owned unincorporated enterprises), either directly or indirectly owned by the investor. Foreign-controlled enterprises in the System include direct investment subsidiaries and branches, but associates may be included or excluded by individual countries according to their qualitative assessment of foreign control (most direct investment enterprises, in fact, either are branches or are subsidiaries that are wholly or majority-owned by non-residents or in which a clear majority of the voting stock is held by a single direct investor or group). It warrants noting that in some instances, a public enterprise may be a direct investment enterprise, but not a foreign-controlled enterprise.

14.153. The benefits that direct investors expect to derive from their voice in management are different from those anticipated by portfolio investors having no significant influence over the operations of the enterprises. From the viewpoint of the direct investors, enterprises often represent units in a multinational operation, the overall profitability of which depends on the advantages to be gained by deploying the various resources available to the investors in units located in different economies. Direct investors are thereby in a position to derive benefits in addition to the property income that may accrue on the capital that they invest, e.g., the opportunity to earn management fees or other sorts of income. Such extra benefits are likely to be derived from the investors' association with the enterprises over a considerable period of time. In contrast, portfolio investors are primarily concerned about the safety of their capital, the likelihood of an appreciation in its value, and the return that it generates. They will evaluate the prospects separately with respect to each independent unit in which they might invest and may often shift their capital with changes in these prospects, which may be affected by short-term developments in financial markets.

14.154. The System's concept of foreign-controlled resident corporations is linked to the balance of payments concept of direct foreign investment enterprises in that the former is a component of the latter (see paragraph 14.152 above for definitions). While the primary distinguishing feature of direct investment in the balance of payments is significant influence or effective voice in management, the feature for foreign-controlled enterprises in the System is control.

14.155. The functional category "reserve assets" in the balance of payments accounts is an important analytical element in that system, as noted in the *Balance of Payments Manual*, although it has no counterpart as such in the System. Reserve assets consist of those external assets that are readily available to, and controlled by, the authorities for direct financing of payments imbalances and for indirect regulation of the magnitude of such imbalances through various actions (e.g., exchange market intervention). Transactions in the components of reserve assets—monetary gold, SDRs, reserve position in the IMF, foreign exchange assets (currency, deposits, and securities) and other claims—are indistinguishably included under transactions in those financial assets in the System.

G. External assets and liabilities account

14.156. This account completes the sequence of the external accounts, reflecting the level and composition of the stock of external financial assets and liabilities of the economy that result from the external transactions accounts and accumulation accounts. In contrast to the balance sheets of resident institutional units and sectors which include non-financial assets, the external assets and liabilities account consists entirely of financial assets and liabilities. The opening and closing balance sheets are equivalent to the international investment position, as delineated in the *Balance of Payments Manual*,[2] at the respective dates, while the changes in the balance sheet are equivalent to changes in the position. It warrants noting that the external assets and liabilities account should include, on the asset side, the cumulative net result of all transactions in monetary gold (sales/purchases) and SDRs. Also, it should be noted that the net result, or figures on the asset side (point of view of the rest of the world) may be negative if the balance of accumulated transactions reflects net sales by the rest of the world. An economy's net claims on the rest of the world, or net international investment position, when summed with the economy's stock of non-financial assets, comprise the total economy's net worth.

1. Structure of the account

14.157. The financial assets and liabilities included in the account are the same as those in the financial account. The values of the financial assets and liabilities in the balance sheet are as of a particular point in time. The System requires balance sheets to be drawn up at both the beginning and end of the accounting period, which usually covers one year, and requires a full accounting of the changes in value of the financial assets and liabilities between the opening and closing balance sheets. Those changes in value may be due to transactions, to changes in the volume of assets and/or to nominal holding gains and losses, as previously discussed. The net result of the changes in value is changes in net worth, i.e., changes in assets less changes in liabilities, which is reflected in the net worth balancing item in the closing balance sheet.

2. Valuation

14.158. In principle, all external financial assets and liabilities should be recorded at their current market values at the time to which the balance sheet relates. Market values may have to be estimated or approximated, in some instances.[3] The basis of valuation of financial assets/liabilities in the balance sheet is covered in detail in paragraphs 14.48 to 14.52 above in section C.1 of this chapter and in chapter XIII. It warrants repetition here that assets and liabilities denominated in foreign currencies are to be converted into national currency at the market exchange rate prevailing at the date for which the balance sheet is drawn up, using the midpoint between the buying and selling spot rate. Conversion under a multiple rate system is discussed in section C.3 in this chapter.

3. Direct foreign investment

14.159. Financial assets and liabilities that are associated with direct foreign investment—both outward and inward—are to be recorded under the appropriate financial assets listed in the classification, i.e., shares and other equity (including reinvested earnings), loans, and other accounts receivable and payable. These direct investment-related entries are also to be recorded separately as a memorandum item.

4. External debt and the balance sheet

14.160. The net financial claims of an economy on the rest of the world, i.e., external financial assets less financial liabilities, often are the basis for characterizing an economy as a "net creditor" or "net debtor". Such a label is not accurate as a depiction of the net external position of the economy. Rather, it is more relevant to view only the non-equity components of the external balance sheet as debt, i.e., all recorded liabilities other than shares and other equity. This view is in general concordance with the "core" definition of external debt[4] in *External Debt: Definition, Statistical Coverage, and Methodology* (1988), a joint study by the IMF, World Bank, OECD, and the Bank for International Settlements.

14.161. Particularly for countries experiencing external debt problems, identifying debtor and creditor sectors for the rest of the world and counterpart domestic sectors is of analytical importance. The three-dimensional tables provided in the System show the links between debtor and creditor sectors, such as foreign sources of financing, etc., and can be supplemented or rearranged to identify such items as debt reorganization, arrears of interest and amortization, etc. In this respect, the *Balance of Payments Manual* covers specific recording procedures for the above and other "exceptional financing" entries in the international accounts.

Notes

1 This item is "travel" in the *Balance of Payments Manual*.

2 It should be noted that the international investment position (as are the balance of payments accounts) is presented from the point of view of the total economy (residents), while the external assets and liabilities account in the System is presented from the point of view of the rest of the world (non-residents). As a result, credit and debit entries in the investment position are reversed in the external assets and liabilities account.

3 For example, for quasi-corporations such as direct investment branches, the market value of proprietor's net equity is approximated as the market value of the enterprises' assets minus the market value of any liabilities to third parties (including the value of shares held by portfolio investors), and non-equity liabilities to shareholders.

4 "Gross external debt is the amount, at any given time, of disbursed and outstanding contractual liabilities of residents of a country to non-residents to repay principal, with or without interest, or to pay interest, with or without principal".

XV. Supply and use tables and input-output

A. Input-output in the System

1. Introduction

15.1. The System includes an integrated set of supply and use tables, or matrices, as well as symmetric input-output tables, or matrices. They provide a detailed analysis of the process of production and the use of goods and services (products) and the income generated in that production. The concepts and definitions in the input-output tables of the SNA are the same as in the rest of the System.

15.2. The integration of "input-output" in the overall system of national accounts is an important feature of the SNA. Its role in the System is primarily related to the goods and services accounts and to the shortened sequence of accounts for industries. In complement to the full sequence of accounts for institutional sectors, which cover all kinds of accounts in the System, the supply and use tables, and subsequently the symmetric tables, serve to provide a more detailed basis for analysing industries and products in the System through a breakdown of the production account and the generation of income account in the System, and the goods and services account leading to the symmetric input-output table. "Symmetric" means there are the same classifications or units (i.e., same groups of products) which are used in both rows and columns. In the supply and use table, when the number of rows of products and columns of industries happens to be equal, we shall refer to a square (not symmetric) supply and use table. However, supply and use tables are most often rectangular (having more products than industries).

15.3. The input-output tables and in particular the supply and use tables serve two purposes: statistical and analytical. They provide a framework for checking the consistency of statistics on flows of goods and services obtained from quite different kinds of statistical sources—industrial surveys, household expenditure inquiries, investment surveys, foreign trade statistics etc. The System, and the input-output tables in particular, serves as a coordinating framework for economic statistics, both conceptually for ensuring the consistency of the definitions and classifications used and as an accounting framework for ensuring the numerical consistency of data drawn from different sources. The input-output framework is also appropriate for calculating much of the economic data contained in the national accounts and detecting weaknesses. This is particularly important for the decomposition of values of flows of goods and services into prices and volumes for the calculation of an integrated set of price and volume measures. As an analytical tool, input-output data are conveniently integrated into macroeconomic models in order to analyse the link between final demand and industrial output levels. Input-output analysis also serves a number of other analytical purposes or uses.

15.4. This chapter has three main parts or stages:

  (a)   Goods and services accounts;

  (b)   Supply and use tables;

  (c)   Analytical input-output tables.

15.5. A fundamental and extremely important role is played in the System by the goods and services account. In fact, this is the basis from which the supply and use balances are derived. It shows for the economy as a whole and for groups of products the total resources in terms of output and imports, and the uses of goods and services in terms of intermediate consumption, final consumption, gross capital formation and exports. By then incorporating also the production and generation of income accounts of the System, an overall accounting framework is obtained for depicting the production sphere by the construction of integrated supply and use tables.

15.6. The symmetric input-output tables are also part of the System, serving as a well-established tool for various analytical purposes related to production. Many analyses require adjustments to the supply and use table, in particular with respect to valuation, treatment of imported products and common classification for rows and columns.

15.7. While supply and use tables are data-oriented in nature, the symmetric tables are always constructed from having made certain analytical assumptions, usually from existing supply and use tables. The System recommends that the statistical supply and use tables should serve as the foundation from which the analytical input-output tables are constructed. This explains the importance given to the description of supply and use tables in this chapter, while the more technical description of constructing symmetric input-output tables will mainly be shown in the planned *Handbook on National Accounting: Input-Output Tables*, which is being prepared by the Statistical Division of the United Nations Secretariat.

2. The input-output context

15.8. In national accounting and economic analysis two kinds of input-output tables (or matrices) are referred to:

(a)   Supply and use tables;

(b)   Symmetric input-output tables.

15.9. The supply and use tables are sometimes referred to as rectangular input-output tables, make and use tables, supply and disposition of commodities, etc. In the System, we shall use the term supply and use tables. The symmetric input-output tables are also often termed square (input-output) tables or matrices, Leontief-type input-output tables (matrices), etc. The square symmetrical tables are either product-product or industry-industry (producer-producer). In this chapter we shall be referring to tables rather than matrices, and to product-by-product tables and industry-by-industry tables.

15.10. The concepts and definitions in the supply and use tables are the same as elsewhere in the System. This applies in particular to transaction categories defined in a number of chapters. Most of the contents of chapter VI have direct relevance to this chapter. The same is true for the generation of income account with uses of value added (chapter VII), chapter IX describing final consumption expenditure and actual final consumption, chapter X on gross capital formation, and chapter XIV on exports and imports flows.

15.11. The supply and use and input-output tables also adopt the accounting rules of the System, i.e., the general rules of treatment for transactions and transactors apply to the input-output framework as part of the System. Chapter III contains a number of issues that become crucial in the input-output framework, in particular valuation, and which therefore need further elaboration.

15.12. Other issues of great importance to the input-output framework, dealt with in other chapters as well, include in particular:

(a)   Statistical units (chapter V), in particular establishments grouped in industries serve as a common basis for the production accounts and the supply and use tables, while using institutional units is not recommended for input-output compilation;

(b)   Principal, secondary and ancillary activities (chapter V), the distinction between which plays a key role in the compilation of the symmetric tables;

(c)   Constant-price estimation (chapter XVI), for which an entire set of price and volume measures, including for balancing items defined in the System (value added, gross domestic product (GDP), might be derived by using the supply and use tables as a framework;

(d)   Chapter XX, in which the supply and use table is re-garded as one social accounting matrix (SAM) building-block;

(e)   Employment measures (chapter XVII), the use of which is important to productivity studies.

3. Statistical units for input-output

15.13. Institutional units may engage in several different kinds of productive activities simultaneously. For the detailed analysis of production, the System, therefore, recommends that they should be partitioned into separate establishments each of which engages in only a single kind of productive activity at a single location. Industries are then defined as groups of establishments engaged in the same kind of productive activities. Ideally, the industries in the System would be composed of establishments that are homogeneous production units.

15.14. A unit of homogeneous production is defined as a producer unit in which only a single (non-ancillary) productive activity is carried out. However, the unit of hemogeneous production is not normally observable and is more an abstract or conceptual unit underlying the symmetric (product-by-product) input-output tables.

15.15. To be operational for statistics the establishment needs to be sufficiently distinct as a production unit to supply meaningful information. For the supply and use tables, the System needs a unit which can be observed and for which data can be collected. Furthermore, the choice of units is often dictated by the units being carried forward from the basic statistics.

15.16. When an establishment engages in more than one kind of activity, by reference to a given classification of activities, it is necessary to observe the fundamental distinction between principal and secondary activities on the one hand and ancillary activities on the other:

(a)   The principal activity of an establishment is the activity whose gross value added exceeds that of any other activity carried out within the same unit;

(b)   A secondary activity is an activity carried out within a single establishment in addition to the principal activity;

(c)   An ancillary activity is a supporting activity which is undertaken in order to create the conditions within which the activities of an enterprise can be carried out.

15.17. The establishment unit used for the sequence of accounts for industries may include principal as well as secondary productive activities within it, although secondary activities should be separated as far as practically possible. The further treatment of secondary production is one of the central issues met in the construction of symmetric input-output tables.

15.18. Ancillary activities typically produce outputs of services which are used as inputs into almost all kinds of productive activities, and their values are likely to be small compared with that of the principal and secondary activities of the enterprise.

Consequently, they are treated as integral parts of the principal or secondary activities with which they are associated. In a production account and input-output context, ancillary activities are treated as follows:

(a)   Outputs of ancillary activities are not explicitly recognized and recorded in the System;

(b)   Inputs into ancillary activities are treated as inputs into the principal and secondary activities which they support;

(c)   Value added is not identified separately as it is combined with that of the principal and secondary activi-

ties. However, satellite analysis might try to identify inside the producing units some ancillary activities and their output.

15.19.   In addition, output of an industry may include more than a single product when two or more products are produced simultaneously by a single productive activity as "joint products" (e.g., molasses linked to the production of sugar, natural gas linked to crude oil). Joint products may be distinguished as the principal product (by largest proportion) and the by-product (or by-products). In practice, by-products are often treated in the same way as secondary products in the input-output framework.

B. Disaggregation of goods and services account

1. Goods and services account

15.20.   The goods and services account shows, both for groups of products and for the total economy, how the total amount of a product available (supply) is equal to the total amount used. Before additional terms necessary for valuation are introduced, the main items of this basic equation (balance) are as follows:

Output + imports (= total resources)

= intermediate consumption + exports + final consumption + gross capital formation (= total uses).

15.21.   Goods and services are traced through the economy from their original producers (either resident producers or producers abroad) to their users (either resident users or users abroad).

15.22.   Compiling detailed flows is traditionally referred to as the commodity-flow method, utilizing basic statistics on goods and services (products) with the additional items required for the proper valuation. The full power of the commodity-flow method is reached when independent estimates could be made for each of the use items, i.e., when specific information establishes the basis of the distribution of the supply of products to the various kinds of uses. Reconciliation of the supply and use side of the equation is necessary. In some cases, the commodity-flow method is necessarily less sophisticated, when one of the uses (e.g., changes in inventories, gross fixed capital formation or even final consumption) has to be derived residually, or the distribution to users—fully or partly—has to be made in fixed proportions without enough direct information on or from users.

15.23.   The product groups constitute the rows of the disaggregated supply and use table. The product classification scheme recommended for classifying data on goods and services is the Central Product Classification (CPC). It should be applied at a detailed level; the more detailed, the cleaner the view (and the less product mix). The CPC contains more than 1,800 products at its 5-digit level. For application in the national accounts countries lacking the full benefit from the commodity-

flow approach might use the intermediate 3-digit level of the CPC, counting some 300 products. Furthermore, in input-output work it may be necessary to group products according to the activity to which they relate.

15.24.   In order to keep the tables presented in the SNA within a manageable format, the breakdown of product groups as they appear in the supply and use table mainly refers to the 1-digit CPC classification. Of course, these aggregated product groups are illustrative only.

2. Valuation and appropriate treatment of taxes and margins

Valuation concepts and their interrelationships

15.25.   Before moving into the format of the supply and use table, the basic valuation concepts of the System and their interrelationships need to be spelt out.

15.26.   The components of the price paid by the purchaser of a product that are recognized in the System are the following:

Basic price of the product as output

Taxes on the product

Less subsidies on the product

Trade and transport margins in delivering the product to the purchaser.

15.27.   Some of these four components could be subdivided, for example to treat trade and transport margins in a more decomposed way, including to split the margins into separate wholesale and retail components, or to specify the value added tax (VAT) as a separate component. However, the input-output framework of the System needs as a minimum the specification of the four components. Two clarifications should be made:

(a)   Trade and transport margins also bear taxes less subsidies on the product linked to the trade and transport margins;

(b) Trade and transport margins are also services which have a basic price.

15.28. The three central price concepts of the System—the purchaser's price, the producer's price and the basic price—have been defined in chapter VI, but are repeated here for the sake of convenience in the development of the chapter:

(a) The purchaser's price is the amount paid by the purchaser, excluding any deductible VAT or similar deductible tax, in order to take delivery of a unit of a good or service at the time and place required by the purchaser. The purchaser's price of a good includes any transport charges paid separately by the purchaser to take delivery at the required time and place;

(b) The producer's price is the amount receivable by the producer from the purchaser for a unit of a good or service produced as output minus any VAT, or similar deductible tax, invoiced to the purchaser. It excludes any transport charges invoiced separately by the producer;

(c) The basic price is the amount receivable by the producer from the purchaser for a unit of a good or service produced as output minus any tax payable, and plus any subsidy receivable, on that unit as a consequence of its production or sale. It excludes any transport charges invoiced separately by the producer.

15.29. There are definitional relationships between these three price concepts which have a central role in the input-output framework:

(a) Purchaser's price (which includes non-deductible VAT)—trade and transport margins (including taxes other than invoiced VAT less subsidies on product payable/receivable by wholesalers and retailers)—non-deductible VAT-type taxes = producer's price (which excludes non-deductible VAT);

(b) Producer's price—taxes (other than VAT) less subsidies on products payable/receivable by their producers = basic price.

15.30. Higher price after storage might be due to additional output volume during storage (e.g., improvement in quality) or to holding gains (for further discussion, see chapter VI).

15.31. Producers' and purchasers' prices must in general—apart from any non-deductible VAT—coincide for services, as services are supplied directly from the producer to the user. If, in fact, retailers exist in the services' area (like travel agencies in tourism), the price equality still holds, since the System by convention treats these retailers as producing services other than trade services. When goods are purchased directly from their original producers, the two prices will also tend to coincide in many cases, but there could be cases of transport margins as well. At any rate, the distinction between the purchaser's price and the producer's price is mainly relevant for goods which pass through the chains of wholesale and retail distribution.

Valuation of product flows

15.32. Chapter VI includes a comprehensive description of the valuation and the measurement of output, so it is sufficient here to refer to the main points that are very important in the input-output framework. The System recognizes two kinds of prices for output, both defined to exclude any VAT or similar deductible tax invoiced on the output sold:

Basic prices

Producers' prices.

15.33. The preferred method of valuation is at basic prices. Producers' prices may be used when valuation at basic prices is not feasible. The preference for basic prices over producers' prices is based on several considerations, of which the following may be emphasized:

(a) Basic prices provide the most homogeneous valuation along the rows;

(b) Basic prices are found most useful when a system of VAT or similar deductible tax is in operation;

(c) Basic prices record the amounts available to the producer.

15.34. Uses of goods and services—both intermediate consumption and final uses—are recorded at purchasers' prices (i.e., including the margins and taxes less subsidies on products except deductible taxes).

15.35. For exports and imports, the System adopts analogous price concepts: the free on board (f.o.b.) price for exports and total imports and the cost, insurance and freight (c.i.f.) price for detailed imports. The difference between the f.o.b. price and the c.i.f. price represents the costs of transportation and insurance between the frontier of the exporting country and the frontier of the importing country. The definition of the c.i.f. price is as follows:

The c.i.f. price is the price of a good delivered at the frontier of the importing country, or the price of a service delivered to a resident, before the payment of any import duties or other taxes on imports or trade and transport margins within the country.

15.36. The f.o.b. price is considered to be a special purchaser's price applied to flows of exports. As explained in chapter XIV, the f.o.b. price can be regarded as the purchaser's price that would be paid by an importer taking delivery of the goods at the exporter's frontier after loading on to a carrier and after payment of any export taxes or the receipt of any tax rebates. The c.i.f. price is considered to be a basic price applied to flows of imports, equivalent to the basic price of a good or service produced by resident producers. The valuation of an imported good or service which is equivalent to the producer's price of a good or service produced by resident producers is the total of the c.i.f. price and any import duty and excise duty or special tax payable on the import at the frontier (sometimes referred to as the ex-customs price). This equivalence holds as well between producer's price excluding invoiced VAT and the c.i.f. price plus taxes and duties on imports, excluding VAT.

15.37. The implicit valuation of value added depends on the valuation of the two flows from which it is derived, output and intermediate consumption. While intermediate consumption is always valued at purchasers' prices (in total, excluding deductible VAT), two alternative valuations are used for output leading to two alternative measures of gross value added:

    (a)   Gross value added at basic prices defined as output valued at basic prices less intermediate consumption valued at purchasers' prices;

    (b)   Gross value added at producers' prices defined as output valued at producers' prices less intermediate consumption valued at purchasers' prices.

15.38. The measure recommended throughout the System and reflected in the supply and use table, is gross value added at basic prices. In order to arrive at GDP at market prices, taxes less subsidies on products—not being allocated to industries—must be added to total gross value added at basic prices. If output and thus value added were at producers' prices, non-allocated VAT and taxes less subsidies on imports must be added to arrive at GDP at market prices (see chapter VI, paragraph 6.235 and 6.236).

15.39. Gross value added at factor cost is not a concept used explicitly in the System. Nevertheless, it could be derived from gross value added at basic prices by subtracting other taxes less subsidies on production. However, this item is not recommended as a measure of value added in the System, since there are no observable prices such that output minus intermediate consumption equals gross value added directly in this case. Other taxes less subsidies on production, by definition, are in fact taxes or subsidies that cannot be eliminated from the prices of outputs and inputs. Therefore, gross value added at factor cost is essentially a measure of income and not output. In the input-output framework, it means that neither the output entries in the supply table nor the values added in the use table are given at factor cost.

Trade and transport margins

15.40. As explained in chapter VI paragraph 6.110 and 6.111, the output of wholesale and retail trade is measured by the value of the trade and transport margins realized on the goods they sell. Goods resold are not included either in the output or the inputs of wholesale and retail trade. The trade and transport margins include trade margins plus any transport charges paid separately by the purchaser in taking delivery at the required time and place.

15.41. As indicated in chapter VI, input-output analysis—and the commodity flow method—may find it convenient to compare the price paid by the final purchaser of a good after it has passed through the wholesale and retail distribution chains with the price received by its original producer. Differences between price concepts were explained in paragraphs 15.25 to 15.31 above. The trade margins may be defined at basic as well as producers' prices, as the first, or the first and second, of the following components:

    (a)   The basic trade margins on the product; i.e., the cumulative wholesale and retail trade margins before taxes are added and subsidies subtracted;

    (b)   Taxes (except invoiced VAT) less subsidies on the product payable by wholesale and retail traders.

15.42. The full cost of transporting a good from the place where it is manufactured to the place where the purchaser takes delivery of it may be included in a number of items. If the producer transports the good, or arranges for it to be transported without extra cost to the purchaser, these transportation costs will be included in the basic price. If the producer transports the goods himself this represents an ancillary activity and the individual costs will be included but not identifiable as transportation costs. If the producer pays a third party to transport the goods then transportation will appear as one of the intermediate costs to the producer. Similarly, wholesale and retail traders may arrange for goods to be moved from where they take delivery of them to where another purchaser takes delivery. As in the case of producers, these costs will be included in the trade margin if no separate charge is made for transportation to the purchaser. Again, as with producers, these costs may represent ancillary activity of wholesale and retail traders or the purchase of an intermediate service, thus entering trade margins. Finally, when transport is arranged in such a way that the purchaser has to pay for the transport costs even when done by the producer or the wholesale or retail trader, these are separately identified as transport margins. The full component of transport services in the trade and transport margins—composed of the transport margins themselves and the transport services included in the trade margins—may be analysed separately in a more analytical version of the supply and use table.

15.43. In order to fit in with the input-output framework, data on margins should have the format of products by uses as in table 15.2. These data might have been originally compiled at some industry level of wholesale and retail trade, from which the conversion to the appropriate format has to be made. Trade margins by products are obtained by adding across the various use categories of the product rows of the supporting table.

15.44. In the supply table, output of goods is at basic prices; output of the associated trade services and transport services are given at basic prices in their respective columns and rows. This means that taxes (except invoiced VAT) on the product payable by wholesalers and retailers are pooled with the other taxes (except invoiced VAT) on products and total non-deductible VAT to form the additional column of taxes on products in the supply table, and correspondingly the additional column of subsidies on products. Trade and transport margins are additionally distributed by products in the additional column of trade and transport margins of the supply table. In that column, negative entries appear on the rows for trade and transport services in order to have the total of that column equal to zero. In purchasers' prices, total supply of trade services does not include trade margins, nor does total supply of transport services include transport margins; both of these having been allocated to the goods to which they relate.

Taxes and subsidies on products

15.45. Different valuation concepts in the input-output framework are to a large extent consequences of treatments of taxes and subsidies. As already seen above, taxes less subsidies on products make up part of the difference between the purchaser's price and the basic price.

15.46. The taxes that appear in the input-output framework are all taxes on production and imports. These are taxes levied on goods and services at the time they are produced, sold or imported, or possibly on other occasions, together with taxes which become due as a consequence of engaging in production. Taxes on production and imports are subdivided into two min groups (see chapter VII, paragraph 7.49):

    (a)   Taxes on products;

    (b)   Other taxes on production.

15.47. The separation of taxes on products from other taxes on production is very important in varying valuations of product flows. Taxes on products are defined as follows (with the four constituent sub-categories):

> A tax on a product is a tax that is payable per unit of some good or service, either as a specified amount of money per unit of quantity or as a specified percentage of the price per unit or value of the good or service transacted.

    (a)   A value added type tax is a tax on goods or services collected in stages by enterprises;

    (b)   Taxes and duties on imports, excluding VAT, consist of taxes on goods and services that become payable at the moment when the goods cross the national or customs frontiers of the economic territory or when the services are delivered by non-resident producers to resident institutional units;

    (c)   Export taxes consist of taxes on goods and services that become payable when the goods leave the economic territory or when the services are delivered to non-residents;

    (d)   Taxes on products, excluding VAT, and import and export taxes consist of taxes on goods and services that become payable as a result of the production, sale, transfer, leasing or delivery of those goods and services, or as a result of their use for own consumption or own capital formation.

15.48. Value added type taxes in the System include VAT proper and taxes which are deductible in a way similar to VAT and are treated in the same way as VAT. They are defined and described as follows (see also chapter VI):

> VAT is a tax on products collected in stages by enterprises. There exist in some countries taxes that are narrower in scope than VAT but may also be deductible by producers. They are treated in the System in the same way as VAT. Producers are required to charge certain percentage rates of VAT on the goods or services they sell. The VAT is shown separately on the sellers' invoices so that purchasers know the amounts they have paid. However, producers are not required to pay to the government the full amounts of the VAT invoiced to their customers because they are usually permitted to deduct the VAT that they themselves have paid on goods and services purchased for their own intermediate consumption or gross fixed capital formation. Producers are obliged to pay only the difference between the VAT on their sales and the VAT on their purchases for intermediate consumption or capital formation — hence the expression value added tax. VAT is not usually charged on sales to non-residents—i.e., exports. The percentage rate of VAT is also liable to vary between different categories of goods and services and also according to the type of purchaser.

15.49. The System recommends the use of the so-called net system of recording VAT. In this net treatment, output even at producers' prices is valued excluding VAT invoiced by the producer; imports also are valued excluding invoiced VAT. For intermediate and final uses the purchases of goods and services are recorded including non-deductible VAT only.

15.50. VAT may be deductible, non-deductible or just not applicable as follows:

Deductible VAT:

> Most of intermediate consumption
>
> Most of gross fixed capital formation
>
> Part of changes in inventories.

> Non-deductible VAT:

> Final consumption expenditure
>
> Part of gross fixed capital formation
>
> Part of changes in inventories

Part of intermediate consumption.

VAT not applicable:

Exports

Any goods or services subject to a zero rate of VAT regardless of their use

Any producers exempted from VAT registration (small businesses or the like).

15.51. Depending on the tax regimes in countries, the contents of the tax column in the supply table would be as follows:

Absence of VAT:

When output is at basic prices, the taxes column will contain all taxes on products (i.e. taxes and duties on imports, export taxes, and taxes on products excluding import and export taxes).

When output is at producers' prices, it will include just taxes and duties on imports.

Presence of VAT (net treatment):

When output is at basic prices, the taxes column will contain total non-deductible VAT on products, taxes and duties on imports excluding VAT, export taxes, and taxes on products excluding VAT and import and export taxes.

When output is at producers' prices, the taxes column will include taxes and duties on imports (excluding VAT), plus total non-deductible VAT on those products.

15.52. Subsidies are treated as if they were negative taxes on products or negative taxes on production. In the System, subsidies are current unrequited payments that government units make to enterprises on the basis of the levels of their production activities or the quantities or values of goods and services which they produce, sell or import. They are classified in the same way as taxes:

(a)   Subsidies on products;

(b)   Other subsidies on production.

15.53. The separation of subsidies on products from other subsidies on production, as in the case of taxes, is fundamental to the valuation of product flows. Subsidies on products are defined as follows:

A subsidy on a product is a subsidy payable per unit of a good or service produced, either as a specific amount of money per unit of quantity of a good or service or as a specified percentage of the price per unit. It may also be calculated as the difference between a specified target price and the market price actually paid by a buyer.

C. Supply and use table

1. Format of the supply and use tables

15.54. The recommended supply and use tables of the System are presented in table 15.1. An early reference is given to the supply and use tables in chapter II, using a reduced format in order to introduce the overall structure of the supply and use tables. It is not a simplified version of the latter.

15.55. As emphasized already, the level of details in the rows and columns of the supply and use and input-output tables should be reasonably disaggregated; the tables presented in this chapter are very aggregated merely in order to keep to a manageable format. That applies to the breakdown of products, of industries, of final uses as well as uses of value added. In this sense, the tables of the chapter are both recommended tables and illustrative tables.

15.56. The supply and use tables show the following information.

(a)   Table 15.1 S shows the supply of products;

(b)   Table 15.1 U shows:

(i)   The use of products along the rows; and

(ii)   The production and generation of income accounts of industries down the columns.

15.57. The main part of the supply table is at basic prices, but there are columns added so as to arrive at total supply at purchasers' prices in order to balance with the use table at purchasers' prices. In general, when preparing supply and use tables and making the proper balancing between the two sides, there is always a choice of emphasis between two opposite lines of adjusting statistical data:

(a)   Supply of each product at basic prices could be adjusted to a purchasers' prices valuation to allow balancing with uses at purchasers' prices;

(b)   Each of the uses at purchasers' prices could be adjusted to a basic prices' valuation to match with supply at basic prices.

15.58. In practice, both types of balances may be needed in the process of building up a supply and use table. Both alternatives deal with or require similar kinds of adjustments, i.e., for taxes less subsidies on products and trade and transport margins by products. In fact, the first alternative is not possible without the second, since it is usually not possible to know the columns of taxes on products, subsidies on products and trade and transport margins broken down by products in the supply table unless the distribution among uses of the individual products are known from table 15.2.

Table 15.1.   Supply of products at basic prices and use of products at purchasers' prices

Supply of products		Total supply at purchasers' prices (1)	Trade and transport margins (2)	Taxes on products (3)	Subsidies on products (−) (4)	Total supply (basic prices) (5)	Agric., hunting, forestry, fishing (A+B) (6)	Mining and quarrying (C) (7)	Manufacturing, electricity (D+E) (8)
	Goods and services (by CPC sections)								
1.	Agriculture, forestry and fishery products (0)	128	2	5	−3	124	78	0	0
2.	Ores and minerals (1)	103	2	0	0	101	0	30	10
3.	Electricity, gas and water (17−18)	160	0	5	0	155	0	2	152
4.	Manufacturing (2−4)	2 160	74	94	−5	1 997	0	2	1 666
5.	Construction work and construction, land (5)	262	0	17	0	245	0	0	7
6.	Trade services, restaurant and hotel services (6)	136[7]	−68	3	0	201	0	0	8
7.	Transport, storage and communication services (7)	111[8]	−10	5	0	116	0	0	0
8.	Business services (8)	590[9]	0	8	0	582	0	1	0
9.	Community, social and pers. serv. exc. pub. ad. (9)	375	0	4	0	371	0	0	1
10.	Public administration (91)	168	0	0	0	168	0	0	0
	Adjustments:								
11.	C.i.f./f.o.b. adjustment on imports	0				0			
12.	Direct purchases abroad by residents	43				43			
13.	*Total*	4 236	0	141	−8	4 103	78	35	1 844
	of which								
14.	*Market*	3 689		141	−8	3 556	75	35	1 824
15.	*Own final use*	171		0		171	3	0	20
16.	*Other non−market*	376		0		376			

Use of products		Total supply at purchasers' prices (1)	(2)	Taxes on products (3)	Subsidies on products (4)	(5)	Agric., hunting, forestry, fishing (A+B) (6)	Mining and quarrying (C) (7)	Manufacturing, electricity (D+E) (8)
	Goods and services, (by CPC section)								
	Total uses								
1.	Agriculture, forestry and fishery products (0)	128					2	0	71
2.	Ores and minerals (1)	103					1	3	91
3.	Electricity, gas and water (17−18)	160					2	2	96
4.	Manufacturing (2−4)	2 160					27	7	675
5.	Construction work and construction, land (5)	262					1	2	7
6.	Trade services, restaurant and hotel services (6)	136[7]					2	1	34
7.	Transport, storage and communication services (7)	111					2	1	29
8.	Business services (8)	590					3	1	117
9.	Community, social and pers. serv. exc. pub. ad. (9)	375					1	0	7
10.	Public administration (91)	168					0	0	0
	Adjustments:								
11.	Direct purchases abroad by residents	43							
12.	Dir. purchases in domestic market by non−residents	0							
13.	*Total uses in purchasers' prices*	4 236					41	17	1 127
	of which								
14.	*Market*	3 689					41	17	1 127
15.	*Own final use*	171							
16.	*Other non−market*	376					0	0	0
17.	*Total gross value added/GDP*			141	−8		37	18	717
18.	Compensation of employees						9	13	336
19.	Taxes less subsidies on production and imports			141	−8		−2	−2	46
20.	Taxes on products			141					
21.	Subsidies on products				−8				
22.	Other taxes less subsidies on production						−2	−2	46
23.	Mixed income, net						14	0	227
24.	Operating surplus, net						7	4	30
25.	Consumption of fixed capital						9	3	78
26.	Mixed income, gross						15	0	228
27.	Operating surplus, gross						15	7	107
28.	*Total output*						78	35	1 844
29.	*Labour inputs (hours worked)*						1 840	292	31 982
30.	*Gross fixed capital formation*						10	6	117
31.	*Closing stacks of fixed assets*						142	90	1 788

Top table

Construction (F) (9)	Wholesale, retail trade, repair motor vehicles, household goods, hotels and restaurants (G+H) (10)	Transport, storage, communication (I) (11)	Financial intermediation, real estate, other business services (J+K) (12)	Education, health, social services (M+N+O) (13)	Sub-total market (14)	Own final use: Agric., hunting, forestry, fishing (A+B) (15)	Construction (F) (16)	Real estate, private household services (K+P) (17)	Sub-total own final use (18)	Other non-market: Education, health, social services (M+N+O) (19)	Public admin., defence, compulsory soc. security, other public services (L) (20)	Sub-total other non-market (21)	Total industry (22)	Total economy (23)	C.i.f./f.o.b. adjustements on imports (24)	Imports Goods (25)	Imports Services (26)
0	0	0	0	0	78	9	0	0	9	0	0	0	87			37	
0	1	0	0	0	41	0	0	0	0	0	0	0	41			60	
0	0	0	0	0	154	0	0	0	0	0	0	0	154			1	
6	16	8	7	2	1 707	2	5	0	7	0	0	0	1 714			283	
201	0	5	0	0	213	0	31	0	31	0	0	0	244			1	
1	149	7	0	0	165	0	0	0	0	0	0	0	165				36
0	21	75	0	0	96	0	0	0	0	0	0	0	96	−6[1]			26[4]
0	2	3	370	98	474	0	0	95	95	0	0	0	569	−4[2]			17[5]
0	2	2	1	143	149	0	0	5	5	212	0	212	366				5
0	0	0	0	0	0	0	0	0	0	0	168	168	168				0
															10[3]	−10	
																20	23
208	191	100	378	243	3 077	11	36	100	147	212	168	380	3 604		0	392[6]	107
205	191	100	378	243	3 051	2	0	0	2	3	1	4	3 057			392	107
3					26	9	36	100	145				171				
										209	167	376	376				0

Bottom table (by ISIC categories)

Construction (F) (9)	Wholesale, retail trade, repair motor vehicles, household goods, hotels and restaurants (G+H) (10)	Transport, storage, communication (I) (11)	Financial intermediation, real estate, other business services (J+K) (12)	Education, health, social services (M+N+O) (13)	Sub-total market (14)	Own final use: Agric., hunting, forestry, fishing (A+B) (15)	Construction (F) (16)	Real estate, private household services (K+P) (17)	Total own final use (18)	Other non-market: Education, health, social services (M+N+O) (19)	Public admin., defence, compulsory soc. security, other public services (L) (20)	Sub-total for other non-market (21)	Total industry (22)	Total economy (23)	Exports Goods (24)	Exports Services (25)	Sub-total final consumption expenditure (26)	Households (27)	NPISHs Individual (28)	General government Sub-total (29)	Collective (30)	Individual (31)	Sub-total gross capital formation (32)	Gross fixed capital formation[10] (33)	Changes in inventories (34)	Acquisition less disposals of valuables (35)
0	3	1	5	0	82	1	0	0	1	3	2	5	88		7		30	28	0	2	0	2	3	2	1	
0	0	0	1	0	96	0	0	0	0	0	0	0	96		6		2	2	0	0	0	0	−1		−1	
1	5	3	4	1	114	0	0	0	0	5	4	9	123		1		36	36	0	0	0	0	0			
63	36	21	35	16	880	5	17	10	32	42	38	80	992		422		570	567	0	3	0	3	176	161	5	10
5	2	1	3	1	22	0	0	0	0	11	7	18	40		6		3	3	0	0	0	0	213	190	23	
1	9	6	4	0	57	0	0	0	0	2	2	4	61			38	37	37	0	0	0	0	0			
3	19	12	5	0	71	0	0	0	0	3	4	7	78			19	14	14	0	0	0	0	0			
16	25	15	44	6	227	0	7	10	17	33	32	65	309			8	250	250	0	0	0	0	23	23	0	
1	1	1	11	23	45	0	0	0	0	21	29	50	95			4	276	58	14	204	0	204	0			
0	0	0	0	0	0	0	0	0	0	1	0	1	1			0	167	6	2	159	156	3	0			
															20	9	43	43								
																	−29	−29								
90	100	60	112	47	1 594	6	24	20	50	121	118	239	1 883		462	78	1 399	1 015	16	368	156	212	414	376	28	10
90	100	60	112	47	1 594	6	24	20	50	121	118	239	1 883		462	78	913	898	0	15	2	13	353	318	25	10
																	110	110					61	58	3	
0	0	0	0	0	0	0	0	0	0				0		0		376	7	16	353	154	199				

Lower block (total supply rows)

(9)	(10)	(11)	(12)	(13)	(14)	(15)	(16)	(17)	(18)	(19)	(20)	(21)	(22) Total industry	(23) Total economy
118	91	40	266	196	1 483	5	12	80	97	91	50	141	1 721	1 854
46	44	16	54	123	641	0	12	0	12	70	39	109	762	762
5	0	−6	12	3	56	0	0	0	0	1	1	2	58	191
														141
														−8
5	0	−6	12	3	56	0	0	0	0	1	1	2	58	58
35	36	3	99	18	432	0	0	0	0				432	432
21	−4	12	67	47	184	3	0	60	63				247	247
11	15	15	34	5	170	2	0	20	22	20	10	30	222	222
36	36	7	99	19	440	2	0	0	2				442	442
31	11	23	101	51	346	3	0	80	83	20	10	30	459	459
208	191	100	378	243	3 077	11	36	100	147	212	168	380	3 604	
4 244	7 078	2 032	3 700	1 904	53 072	218	780	0	998	7 299	8 000	15 299	69 369	
8	20	39	20	5	225	1	1	124	126	13	12	25	376	
143	298	572	409	86	3 528	17	17	1 851	1 885	201	169	370	5 783	

1 Transport services on imports rendered by residents and non–residents.
2 Insurance services on imports rendered by residents and non–residents.
3 Transport and insurance services on imports rendered by residents and non–residents.
4 Including transport services on imports rendered by non–residents.
5 Including insurance services on imports rendered by non–residents.
6 Imports of individual goods are valued c.i.f. With global f.o.b/c.i.f adjustments, total value of imports of goods is valued f.o.b.
7 Total supply of trade services (136) does not include trade margins (68). Trade margins which are included in output of wholesale and retail trade in basic prices are allocated by products in column 2.
8 Total supply of transport services does not include transport margins (10). Transport margins which are included in output of transport in basic prices are allocated by products in column 2. Total supply of transport services also excludes transport services on imports (6) rendered by residents and non–residents which are included in imports by products values c.i.f.
9 Total supply of business services including insurance services does not cover insurance services on imports (4) rendered by residents and non–residents which are included in imports by products valued c.i.f.
10 This column may be broken down into gross fixed capital formation by institutional sectors or industries.

15.59. Thus, three tables are involved in the balancing between supply and use of products:

(a)   Table 15.1: the supply and use table, showing the final results of balancing totals of supply and totals of use by products at purchasers' prices;

(b)   Table 15.2: a supporting table in the same format as the intermediate use and final use quadrants of the use table;

(c)   Table 15.3: an alternative use table at basic prices, in which the elements of the supporting table just mentioned are deducted and reorganized from the elements of the initial use table (for presentation, see section D.2 below).

2. The supply table

Introduction

15.60. The supply table of the System (table 15.1 S) gives information about the resources of goods and services. For pedagogical reasons, its layout is arranged in the same way as in the use table (15.1 U), i.e., showing products in rows and industries in columns. In the rows, the various types of products are presented according to CPC classification groups. Additional rows for two adjustment items are required, one for the c.i.f./f.o.b. adjustment on imports and one for direct purchases abroad by residents. In the columns, three different sets of information are set out:

(a)   Output, by industries according to the activity classification in International Standard Industrial Classification (ISIC), Rev.3, and broken down to distinguish between market output, output produced for own final use and other non-market output and showing the product breakdown of industries' output by CPC sections, also showing the same three-way split for total product of each industry;

(b)   Imports, broken down into goods and services respectively;

(c)   Adjustment items, i.e., one additional column for trade and transport margins and one each for taxes and subsidies on products, plus one additional column for the c.i.f./f.o.b. adjustment.

15.61. The supply table cannot be compiled independently, since table 15.2 has to be prepared before completing table 15.1 S. Before adding in additional columns for trade and transport margins and taxes and subsidies on products, total supply is shown at basic prices. When including the additional columns—which have to be calculated from the use format as given by table 15.2—total supply is shown at purchasers' prices.

Output of market, own account and other non-market producers

15.62. The format of the table, industries by products, is usually (but not necessarily) rectangular, with more rows (products) than columns (industries).

15.63. The level of industry detail should also be reasonably disaggregated. The ISIC Rev.3 is recommended, while the degree of detail for the industry breakdown is up to the countries to decide. One possibility might be an intermediate level of ISIC Rev.3 (for example the 2-digit level).

15.64. A distinction is made in the System between market output, output produced for own final use and other non-market output, which also is carried over into the supply and use table.

15.65. Outputs from own-account producers and other non-market producers are broken down by products in the same way as for outputs of market producers, thereby making possible an integrated exposition of product data in the System. For instance, it makes it possible to add together outputs of health services or education services from both market and other non-market producers to arrive at output totals for these groups of services.

15.66. The valuation of other non-market goods and services is special, as there are either no prices, or no economically significant prices, for the non-market output of government and non-profit institutions serving households (NPISHs). By convention, the value which is assigned to the output from non-market production of government units and NPISHs is equal to the sum of costs incurred in producing that output:

> Intermediate consumption
>
> Compensation of employees
>
> Consumption of fixed capital
>
> Other taxes less subsidies on production.

15.67. For output produced for own final consumption or own gross fixed capital formation, the valuation in terms of total costs should not apply in principle, though it might be a second best procedure in practice. When produced for own final use, the goods and services should be valued at the basic prices at which they could be sold if offered for sale on the market, and it is only when reliable market prices cannot be obtained that the procedure of valuing output equal to the sum of the costs of production might apply. Services of owner-occupied dwellings should also be valued using the prices of the same kinds of services sold on the market. On the other hand, most often the valuation of output of own-account construction has to be based on costs. For services produced when households employ paid domestic staff, output is valued by the compensation of employees paid.

Imports recorded c.i.f. and f.o.b.

15.68. In the System, total imports are valued f.o.b. However, data on detailed flows of imports from foreign trade statistics are most usually valued at c.i.f. prices. To reconcile the different valuation used for total imports and the product components of imports, a global c.i.f./f.o.b. adjustment on imports is added.

15.69. The recording in the supply table of imports and the c.i.f./f.o.b. adjustment item is as follows:

(a)   Imports of goods detailed by products are valued c.i.f.;

(b)   All transport and insurance services on imports, provided by both resident and non-resident producers, which are included in the c.i.f. value of imports by products, are globally deducted (see column for imports of goods and row for the c.i.f./f.o.b. adjustment on imports). Thus, the total of imports of goods in the System is always recorded f.o.b. in the table;

(c)   Those transport and insurance services on imports that are provided by non-resident producers, are recorded under imports of services (part of the entries on rows for transport services and business services in the imports of services column);

(d)   Those transport and insurance services on imports that are provided by resident producers, are included in the output of transport and insurance services for the relevant industries (part of the entries on rows for transport services and business services in the output columns of the respective industries);

(e)   The supply by resident producers and imported supply of transport and insurance services on imports—i.e., (c) and (d) above—is not conveyed to users as transport and insurance services because the value of these services on imports is already included in the c.i.f. value of imports of goods and, therefore, not to be included in total supply of transport and insurance services. Thus, transport and insurance services on imports provided by resident and non-resident producers must be deducted from the total supply of such services in the supply table (in the column of the c.i.f./f.o.b. adjustment on imports on the rows for transport services and business services);

(f)   These services are recorded on the c.i.f./f.o.b. adjustment row, making row and column totals of the adjustment item equal to zero.

15.70. The parallel treatment to producers' prices would be to record details of imports at c.i.f. prices plus taxes and duties on imports, excluding VAT. These prices—referred to as ex-customs prices—may be useful for certain types of analysis. The System does, however, not recommend such parallel treatment at ex-customs prices, not even in the circumstance of recording flows of output of resident producers at producers' prices.

3. The use table

Introduction

15.71. The use table of the System (table 15.1 U) gives information on the uses of goods and services, and also on cost structures of the industries. It is convenient to refer separately to three quadrants of the use table (the fourth "quadrant" in this presentation being empty):

(a)   The intermediate use quadrant (I);

(b)   The final use quadrant (II);

(c)   The uses of value added quadrant (III).

15.72. The intermediate use quadrant shows intermediate consumption at purchasers' prices by industries in the columns and by products on the rows. The total row shows intermediate consumption by industries at purchasers' prices. No separate entries of trade and transport margins, taxes or subsidies on products would be needed in this quadrant due to the valuation of products at purchasers' prices in which they are embodied. As explained elsewhere, the purchasers' prices are net of deductible VAT, but may include some non-deductible VAT. Non-deductible VAT is included in each of the elements (where applicable) in the intermediate use quadrant. As regards the format (number of industries and products) of the intermediate use quadrant, it is identical to other formats within the supply and use table:

To the format of the output part of the supply table in terms of products and industries

To the format of quadrant II in terms of products

To the format of quadrant III in terms of industries.

15.73. The final use quadrant shows exports, final consumption expenditure and gross capital formation at purchasers' prices—with some further subdivision of final uses in the columns—each classified by products on the rows. The total row shows final use by use categories at purchasers' prices, including non-deductible VAT. Non-deductible VAT is included in each of the elements (where applicable) in the final use quadrant. The purchasers' prices are the observable market prices for the entries of the final use quadrant. Exports f.o.b. are considered equivalent to purchasers' prices.

15.74. The uses of value added quadrant shows those production costs of producers other than intermediate consumption, which is shown in quadrant I. The main uses of value added are the following:

(a)   Compensation of employees;

(b)   Taxes less subsidies on production and imports broken down into taxes on products, subsidies on products and other taxes less subsidies on production;

(c)   Consumption of fixed capital;

(d)   Net mixed income and net operating surplus.

15.75. The sequence of accounts for industries is readily recognized. For each industry its output (by products) appears in the supply table; then intermediate consumption (by products), and finally, gross value added and the uses of value added can be seen in the use table. The column for the total economy records the corresponding information at that aggregate level. In this column, rows for taxes and subsidies on products also bring together the non-allocated part from the respective columns of taxes and subsidies on products. Thus, it is possible to find GDP directly in the use table, as the entry on the row for total gross value added/GDP in the column for total economy.

15.76. Consumption of fixed capital may be difficult to calculate by industry. The value added quadrant therefore shows, as an alternative, gross operating surplus and gross mixed income.

15.77. Appended to the uses of value added quadrant—not considered part of it, but rather as conveniently located there—three rows provide additional information on industries' inputs:

> Gross fixed capital formation
>
> Stocks of fixed assets
>
> Labour inputs (usually hours worked).

Breakdown of uses

15.78. Intermediate consumption is broken down by the same industries as for output (see paragraph 15.60 above).

15.79. In the final use quadrant, some breakdowns of the main headings have already been introduced (while further breakdowns can of course readily be introduced if required):

(a) Two sub-groups—goods and services—for exports (as for imports);

(b) Two sub-groups of government final consumption expenditure: collective consumption expenditure and individual consumption expenditure;

(c) Three sub-groups of gross capital formation: gross fixed capital formation, changes in inventories and acquisitions less disposals of valuables.

15.80. For exports (and imports) the countries may establish reasonably detailed sub-classifications (in columns). As in the supply table, for direct purchases abroad adjustment rows are added to the product details in the final use quadrant (although a breakdown by products might be provided if data were to be available):

(a) Direct purchases abroad by residents added in total in the column for final consumption expenditure by households;

(b) Direct purchases in the domestic market by non-residents added in exports of goods and exports of services and deducted from final consumption expenditure by households.

15.81. Final consumption expenditure is attributed to the sectors that bear the costs: households, NPISHs, government. Government final consumption expenditure is further subdivided between expenditure incurred by general government on individual consumption goods and services and on collective consumption services.

15.82. Actual final consumption is the other basic consumption concept in the System, defined in terms of acquisitions rather than expenditures. Actual final consumption of general government is simply equal to its collective consumption expenditure. Actual final consumption of households is not shown explicitly in the final use quadrant, but can be derived simply by adding together three columns presented there:

(a) Households' final consumption expenditures (including any expenditures by households on goods and services from government and NPISHs supplied at prices that are not economically significant);

(b) The final consumption expenditures incurred by NPISHs (all considered individual);

(c) The individual consumption expenditure of government.

15.83. Final consumption expenditures by general government and NPISHs include not only government and NPISH non-market output (valued by costs and deducting values of any receipts from sales), but also direct purchases of goods and services by government and NPISHs that are not channelled through intermediate consumption because they are distributed to the population without any processing. The latter are goods and services which are produced by market producers and delivered directly to households but paid for by government or NPISHs.

15.84. There are three main kinds of gross capital formation in the System and input-output framework:

> Gross fixed capital formation
>
> Changes in inventories
>
> Acquisitions less disposals of valuables.

15.85. The main description of these items is given in chapter X. In the input-output framework, these items are separate use categories appearing in different columns and classified by products. Included in the column of gross fixed capital formation are acquisitions less disposals of both tangible and intangible fixed assets, such as mineral exploration, computer software or originals—and improvements to non-produced assets (e.g., improvements to land). Included in the column of changes in inventories are changes in inventories of materials and supplies, of finished goods, of goods for resale, and work-in-progress. The third category, valuables, consists of precious stones and metals (gold, diamonds, etc.), jewellery fashioned out of precious stones and metals, and paintings, sculptures etc., recognized as works of art, that are acquired as "stores of value" and not for production or consumption.

Table 15.2. Supply and use: trade and transport margins, taxes and subsidies on intermediate and final use of products

Uses of products	Total uses (1)	Intermediate consumption of industries (by ISIC categories) Market									Own final use			
		Agric., hunting, forestry, fishing (A+B) (6)	Mining and quarrying (C) (7)	Manufac-turing, electricity (D+E) (8)	Construc-tion (F) (9)	Wholesale, retail trade, repair motor vehicles, hotels and restaurants (G+H) (10)	Transport, storage, communi-cation (I) (11)	Financial interme-diation, real estate, business services (J+K) (12)	Education, health, social services (M+N+O) (13)	Sub-total market (14)	Agric., hunting, forestry, fishing (A+B) (15)	Construc-tion (16)	Real estate, house-hold services (K+P) (17)
Goods and services, (by CPC sections)													
Total uses													
1. Agriculture, forestry and fishery products													
Trade margins	2	0	0	1	0	0	0	0	0	1	0	0	0
Taxes on products	5	0	0	0	0	0	0	0	0	0	0	0	0
Subsidies on products	− 3	0	0	0	0	0	0	0	0	0	0	0	0
2. Ores and minerals													
Trade margins	2	0	0	2	0	0	0	0	0	2	0	0	0
Taxes on products	0	0	0	0	0	0	0	0	0	0	0	0	0
3. Electricity, gas and water													
Trade margins	0	0	0	0	0	0	0	0	0	0	0	0	0
Taxes on products	5	0		4	0		0	0	0	4			0
4. Manufacturing													
Trade margins	64	1	0	20	3	0	2	0	0	26	0	0	0
Transport margins	10	0	0	5	0	0	0	0	0	5	0	0	0
Taxes on products	94	1	0	26	4	0	0	0	0	31	0	0	0
Subsidies on products	− 5	0	0	0	0	0	0	0	0	0	0	0	0
5. Construction work and construction, land													
Taxes on products	17	0	0	0	0	0	0	0	0	0	0	0	0
6. Trade services, restaurant and hotel services													
Taxes on products	3	0	0	1	0	0	0	0	0	1	0	0	0
7. Transport, storage and communication services													
Taxes on products	5	0	0	2	0	2	0	0	0	4	0	0	0
8. Business services													
Taxes on products	8	0	0	5	0	0	0	0	0	5	0	0	0
9. Community, social and pers. serv. exc. pub. adm.													
Taxes on products	4	0	0	0	0	0	0	0	0	0	0	0	0
10. Public administration													
Taxes on products	0	0	0	0	0	0	0	0	0	0	0	0	0
Adjustments:													
11. Direct purchases abroad by residents													
12. Dir. purchases in domestic market by non-residents													
13. *Total trade margins*	68	1	0	23	3	0	2	0	0	29	0	0	0
14. *Total transport margins*	10	0	0	5	0	0	0	0	0	5	0	0	0
15. *Total taxes on products*	141	1	0	38	4	2	0	0	0	45	0	0	0
16. *Total subsidies on products*	− 8	0	0	0	0	0	0	0	0	0	0	0	0

Other non-market

Education, health, social services (M+N+O) (19)	Public admin., defence, soc. security, other public services (L) (20)	Sub-total other non-market (21)	Total industry (22)	Exports Goods (23)	Services (24)	Final consumption expenditure			General government			Gross capital formation			Acquisition less disposals of valuables (34)
						Sub-total (25)	Households (26)	NPISHs Individual (27)	Sub-total (28)	Collective (29)	Individual (30)	Sub-total (31)	Gross fixed capital formation (32)	Changes in inventories (33)	
0	0	0	1	0		1	1	0	0	0	0	0	0	0	
0	0	0	0	0		5	5	0	0	0	0	0	0	0	
0	0	0	0	0		−3	−3								
0	0	0	2	0		0	0	0	0	0	0	0		0	
0	0	0	0	0		0	0	0	0	0	0	0		0	
0	0	0	0	0		0	0	0	0	0	0	0		0	
0	0	0	4	0		1	1	0	0	0	0	0		0	
0	4	4	30	14		17	17	0	0	0	0	3	3	0	0
0	0	0	5	2		3	3	0	0	0	0	0	0	0	0
0	1	1	32	10		48	48	0	0	0	0	4	4	0	0
0	0	0	0	0		−5	−5								
0	0	0	0	0		0	0	0	0	0	0	17	17	0	
0	0	0	1	0		2	2	0	0	0	0	0		0	
0	0	0	4		0	1	1	0	0	0	0	0		0	
0	0	0	5		1	2	2	0	0	0	0	0	0	0	
0	0	0	0		0	4	4	0	0	0	0	0	0	0	
0	0	0	0		0	0	0	0	0	0	0	0		0	
0	4	4	33	14	0	18	18	0	0	0	0	3	3	0	0
0	0	0	5	2	0	3	3	0	0	0	0	0	0	0	0
0	1	1	46	10	1	63	63	0	0	0	0	21	21	0	0
0	0	0	0	0	0	−8	−8	0	0	0	0	0	0	0	0

15.86. All three categories of gross capital formation are measured by acquisitions less disposals:

> Gross fixed capital formation measured by the value of acquisitions less disposals of new or existing fixed assets
>
> Changes in inventories by the value of entries to inventories less the value of goods leaving inventories during the accounting period including the value of any recurrent losses of goods held in inventories
>
> Acquisitions less disposals of valuables.

15.87. Fixed assets—most important of the three—consist of tangible or intangible assets that have been produced as outputs and are themselves used repeatedly or continuously in other processes of production over long periods of time exceeding at least one year. The time at which gross fixed capital formation is recorded is when the ownership of the fixed assets is transferred to the units that intend to use them in production. This time is generally later than the time when they are produced, and not necessarily the time at which they are actually put to use.

15.88. When fixed assets are purchased in instalments or under a financial lease, legal ownership may not change until some time after the goods have actually been used in production, but in the System the user is treated as acquiring the rights of ownership at the time he takes physical possession of the goods. Gross fixed capital formation is therefore recorded at this point. This treatment leads to a more homogeneous registration of the use of fixed capital and localization of value added in the input-output framework.

15.89. An existing fixed asset can be sold and its ownership passes from its original owner to an other. The value of an existing fixed asset has already been included in gross fixed capital formation—or in final consumption expenditure in some instances—of at least one user at some earlier point of time. When ownership of an existing fixed asset is transferred, it is recorded as a positive acquisition for the new owner and as a negative acquisition (a disposal) for the previous owner. Two movements should be distinguished in the supply and use tables:

a) Along the row of that type of capital asset (product) in the final use quadrant:

   (i)   From gross fixed capital formation of one producer to gross fixed capital formation of another producer the two transactions cancel out;

   (ii) From gross fixed capital formation of a producer to final consumption of a consumer;

   (iii) From gross fixed capital formation of a resident-producer to a non-resident as exports;

   (iv) From final consumption of a consumer to gross-

fixed capital formation of a producer (less likely,-e.g., car);

(b) Along the row for gross fixed capital formation by owner (industry) below the uses of value added quadrant (see paragraph 15.77 above):

   (i)   Gross fixed capital formation from one producer to another, i.e., recorded as negative gross fixed capital formation by the former and positive gross fixed capital formation by the latter.

15.90. There are often transfer costs associated with the acquisition and disposal of fixed assets. A full description of these transfer costs is given in the annex to chapter X. In the supply and use table, the value of the asset without the transfer costs is shown under gross fixed capital formation on the product row appropriate to that asset, while the transfer costs are shown under gross fixed capital formation on the row of business services.

Uses of value added

15.91. The supply and use table adds to the balance between the supply and use of products a quadrant which contain the industry breakdown of the balancing item of the production account (gross value added/GDP) and the industry breakdown of the items in the generation of income account (the uses of value added). Some further breakdown of the standard transaction categories might be useful.

15.92. Compensation of employees could be subdivided into:

> Wages and salaries
>
> Employers' social contributions, with a breakdown between actual contributions and imputed contributions.

15.93. Taxes less subsidies might further distinguish value added type taxes, taxes and duties on imports (excluding VAT) and import subsidies, export taxes and export subsidies, and taxes on products, excluding VAT, import and export taxes, and other subsidies on products. Since taxes and subsidies on products are non-allocated items when output is valued at basic prices, a breakdown by industries would only be needed for other taxes less subsidies on production. This latter item might also be split into one part for taxes and another for subsidies.

15.94. Consumption of fixed capital might be classified by type of fixed assets as for gross fixed capital formation.

15.95. Mixed income and operating surplus, however, are balancing items which do not call for further breakdown. Mixed income is the term reserved for the balancing item of the generation of income account in respect of production by the household sector (unincorporated enterprises) other than owner-occupiers as producers of housing services.

Industry breakdown of gross fixed capital formation, stocks of fixed assets and labour inputs

15.96. The production account, the generation of income account and the supply and use tables include the sequence of accounts for industries from output down to net mixed income/net operating surplus. In addition, the industry breakdown is particularly of interest for gross fixed capital formation, stocks of fixed assets and labour inputs, since these data would provide a basis for productivity studies and other kinds of analysis at the industry level.

15.97. In the input-output framework, two sets of entries for gross fixed capital formation are introduced:

(a) Column of gross fixed capital formation in the final use quadrant of the use table broken down by products (several columns if total is also broken down by type of fixed assets);

(b) Row of gross fixed capital formation appended to the uses of value added quadrant broken down by industries of ownership.

15.98. As to the chosen format of this industry breakdown, two kinds of clarifications should be made:

(a) The appended row for gross fixed capital formation by industry (and the other two rows) are not part of the uses of value added quadrant of the use table. It is an additional table that—as a matter of convenience—has been aligned to the other rows of the supply and use tables which give an industry breakdown;

(b) Alternatively—as stated in a footnote to the supply and use table—the column of gross fixed capital formation by product might be broken down by industries (or also by institutional sectors).

15.99. Below the row for gross fixed capital formation by industry is another row of the use table showing stocks of fixed assets by industries.

15.100. The categories of fixed assets to be included are the following:

(a) Tangible fixed assets: dwellings, other buildings and structures, machinery and equipment, and cultivated fixed assets (livestock for breeding, dairy, draught, etc., and vineyards, orchards and other plantations of trees yielding repeat products);

(b) Intangible fixed assets: mineral exploration, computer software, entertainment, literary or artistic originals, and other intangible fixed assets.

15.101. The so-called "perpetual inventory method" is usually employed to obtain estimates of the current values of the gross and net stocks needed for the analysis of production and productivity growth and for balance sheet purposes. In the central framework of national accounts, the stock data should be valued by writing down the current market prices of these assets by the cumulative consumption of fixed capital valued at current replacement costs which has occurred since the time they were acquired for purposes of production. The net basis (i.e.,

stocks of fixed assets, net) would be consistent with the concepts used in the balance sheet of the institutional sectors. However, in order to obtain productivity measures—to match similar data on labour inputs—data on gross stocks of fixed assets by industries are useful as well.

15.102. Chapter XVII deals with labour input data, which are required in order to analyse productivity. Several concepts of employment are introduced, in particular the following three measures:

(a) Jobs, which are contracts (explicit or implicit) between a person and an institutional unit to perform work in return for compensation (or mixed income) for a defined period or until further notice;

(b) Total hours worked, which are the aggregate number of hours actually worked during the period in employee and self-employment jobs;

(c) Full-time equivalent jobs, which are total hours worked divided by average annual hours worked in full-time jobs.

15.103. The choice of labour concept for the input-output framework should be the one that best reflects labour input for the purpose of productivity. Total hours worked is therefore the preferred measure of labour inputs in the System. The concept of full-time equivalent jobs may treat part-time work inadequately.

15.104. Not all countries may be able to implement the concept of total hours worked in the national accounts context. In view of this, the following recommendations are made:

(a) For countries providing data on total hours worked: a row broken down by industries for total hours worked in jobs, with a breakdown between employee jobs and self-employed jobs;

(b) For countries not providing data on total hours worked: a row broken down by industries for the number of jobs, with a breakdown between employee jobs and self-employed jobs.

15.105. If even (b) is impossible to work out, an average number of persons employed might be considered as a second-best proxy, based on as many head counts as possible during the period under consideration, with a breakdown between numbers of employees and self-employed.

Cross-classification of uses of value added
by institutional sectors and industries

15.106. Both the production account and the generation of income account are provided for in the System by sector and by industry. The definitions and valuations of the aggregates are the same.

15.107. As an establishment always belongs to an institutional unit it is possible to link the production activities of industries and institutional sectors. Output of an institutional unit is equal to

Table 15.3.   Cross classification of production account items by industries and institutional sectors

Sectors, output intermediate consumption value added components	Market									Own final use				Other non-market			Total industr (22)
	Agric., hunting, forestry, fishing (A+B) (6)	Mining and quarrying (C) (7)	Manufacturing, electricity (D+E) (8)	Construction (F) (9)	Wholesale, retail trade, repair motor vehicles, hotels and restaurants (G+H) (10)	Transport, storage, communication (I) (11)	Financial intermediation, real est., other bus. services (J+K) (12)	Education health, social services (M+N+O) (13)	Sub-total market (14)	Agric., hunting, forestry, fishing (A+B) (15)	Construction (F) (16)	Real estate, household services (K+P) (17)	Sub-total own use (18)	Education health, social services (M+N+O) (19)	Public admin., defence, soc. sec., other public services (L) (20)	Sub-total other non-market (21)	
1. Non-financial corporations																	
Output	21	35	1 120	123	123	68	137	93	1 720	7	26	0	33				1 753
Market	21	35	1 120	123	123	68	137	93	1 720	2	0	0	2				1 722
Own final use	0	0	0	0	0	0	0	0	0	5	26	0	31				31
Other non-market																	
Intermediate consumption	3	17	641	52	68	40	43	15	879	4	16	0	20				899
Value added gross	18	18	479	71	55	28	94	78	841	3	10	0	13				854
Compensation of employees	7	13	336	36	44	11	39	49	535	0	10	0	10				545
Other taxes less subsidies on production	-2	-2	46	4	0	-6	9	2	51	0	0	0	0				51
Operating surplus, net	7	4	30	21	-4	12	22	26	118	3	0	0	3				121
Consumption of fixed capital	6	3	67	10	15	11	24	1	137	0	0	0	0				137
Operating surplus, gross	13	7	97	31	11	23	46	27	255	3	0	0	3				258
2. Financial corporations																	
Output	0	0	0	0	0	0	102	0	102	0	0	0	0				102
Market	0	0	0	0	0	0	102	0	102	0	0	0	0				102
Own final use	0	0	0	0	0	0	0	0	0	0	0	0	0				0
Other non-market																	
Intermediate consumption	0	0	0	0	0	0	29	0	29	0	0	0	0				29
Value added gross	0	0	0	0	0	0	73	0	73	0	0	0	0				73
Compensation of employees	0	0	0	0	0	0	15	0	15	0	0	0	0				15
Other taxes less subsidies on production	0	0	0	0	0	0	3	0	3	0	0	0	0				3
Operating surplus, net	0	0	0	0	0	0	45	0	45	0	0	0	0				45
Consumption of fixed capital	0	0	0	0	0	0	10	0	10	0	0	0	0				10
Operating surplus, gross	0	0	0	0	0	0	55	0	55	0	0	0	0				55
3. General government																	
Output	0	0	0	0	0	0	0	76	76	0	0	0	0	196	168	364	440
Market	0	0	0	0	0	0	0	76	76	0	0	0	0	3	1	4	80
Own final use	0	0	0	0	0	0	0	0	0	0	0	0	0	0	0	0	0
Other non-market	0	0	0	0	0	0	0	0	0	0	0	0	0	193	167	360	360
Intermediate consumption	0	0	0	0	0	0	0	18	18	0	0	0	0	116	118	234	252
Value added gross	0	0	0	0	0	0	0	58	58	0	0	0	0	80	50	130	188
Compensation of employees	0	0	0	0	0	0	0	40	40	0	0	0	0	61	39	100	140
Other taxes less subsidies on production	0	0	0	0	0	0	0	0	0	0	0	0	0	1	1	2	2
Operating surplus, net	0	0	0	0	0	0	0	16	16	0	0	0	0	0	0	0	16
Consumption of fixed capital	0	0	0	0	0	0	0	2	2	0	0	0	0	18	10	28	30
Operating surplus, gross	0	0	0	0	0	0	0	18	18	0	0	0	0	18	10	28	46

Table 15.3.   Cross classification of production account items by industries and institutional sectors [cont.]

Industries (by ISIC categories)

Sectors, output intermediate consumption value added components	Market Agric., hunting, forestry, fishing (A+B) (6)	Mining and quarrying (C) (7)	Manufacturing, electricity (D+E) (8)	Construction (F) (9)	Wholesale, retail trade, repair motor vehicles, hotels and restaurants (G+H) (10)	Transport, storage, communication (I) (11)	Financial intermediation, real est., other bus. services (J+K) (12)	Education health, social services (M+N+O) (13)	Sub-total market (14)	Own final use Agric., hunting, forestry, fishing (A+B) (15)	Construction (F) (16)	Real estate, household services (K+P) (17)	Sub-total own use (18)	Other non-market Education health, social services (M+N+O) (19)	Public admin., defence, soc. sec., other public services (L) (20)	Sub-total other non-market (21)	Total industr (22)
4. Non-profit institutions serving households																	
Output	0	0	0	0	0	0	0	24	24	0	0	0	0	16	0	16	40
Market	0	0	0	0	0	0	0	24	24	0	0	0	0	0	0	0	24
Own final use	0	0	0	0	0	0	0	0	0	0	0	0	0	0	0	0	0
Other non-market	0	0	0	0	0	0	0	0	0	0	0	0	0	16	0	16	16
Intermediate consumption	0	0	0	0	0	0	0	4	4	0	0	0	0	5	0	5	9
Value added gross	0	0	0	0	0	0	0	20	20	0	0	0	0	11	0	11	31
Compensation of employees	0	0	0	0	0	0	0	14	14	0	0	0	0	9	0	9	23
Other taxes less subsidies on production	0	0	0	0	0	0	0	0	0	0	0	0	0	0	0	0	0
Operating surplus, net	0	0	0	0	0	0	0	5	5	0	0	0	0	0	0	0	5
Consumption of fixed capital	0	0	0	0	0	0	0	1	1	0	0	0	0	2	0	2	3
Operating surplus, gross	0	0	0	0	0	0	0	6	6	0	0	0	0	2	0	2	8
5. Households																	
Output	57	0	724	85	68	32	139	50	1 155	4	10	100	114	0	0	0	1 269
Market	54	0	704	82	68	32	139	50	1 129	0	0	0	0	0	0	0	1 129
Own final use	3	0	20	3	0	0	0	0	26	4	10	100	114	0	0	0	140
Other non-market	0	0	0	0	0	0	0	0	0	0	0	0	0	0	0	0	0
Intermediate consumption	38	0	486	38	32	20	40	10	664	2	8	20	30	0	0	0	694
Value added gross	19	0	238	47	36	12	99	40	491	2	2	80	84	0	0	0	575
Compensation of employees	2	0	0	10	0	5	0	20	37	0	2	0	2	0	0	0	39
Other taxes less subsidies on production	0	0	0	1	0	0	0	1	2	0	0	0	0	0	0	0	2
Mixed income, net	14	0	227	35	36	3	99	18	432	0	0	0	0	0	0	0	432
Operating surplus, net	0	0	0	0	0	0	0	0	0	0	0	60	60	0	0	0	60
Consumption of fixed capital	3	0	11	1	0	4	0	1	20	2	0	20	22	0	0	0	42
Mixed income, gross	15	0	228	36	36	7	99	19	440	2	0	0	2	0	0	0	442
Operating surplus, gross	2	0	10	0	0	0	0	0	12	0	0	80	80	0	0	0	92
6. Total economy																	
Output	78	35	1 844	208	191	100	378	243	3 077	11	36	100	147	212	168	380	3 604
Market	75	35	1 824	205	191	100	378	243	3 051	2	0	0	2	3	1	4	3 057
Own final use	3	0	20	3	0	0	0	0	26	9	36	100	145	0	0	0	171
Other non-market	0	0	0	0	0	0	0	0	0	0	0	0	0	209	167	376	376
Intermediate consumption	41	17	1 127	90	100	60	112	47	1 594	6	24	20	50	121	118	239	1 883
Value added gross/GDP	37	18	717	118	91	40	266	196	1 483	5	12	80	97	91	50	141	1 721
Compensation of employees	9	13	336	46	44	16	54	123	641	0	12	0	12	70	39	109	762
Other taxes less subsidies on production	-2	-2	46	5	0	-6	12	3	56	0	0	0	0	1	1	2	58
Mixed income, net	14	0	227	35	36	3	99	18	432	0	0	0	0	0	0	0	432
Operating surplus, net	7	4	30	21	-4	12	67	47	184	3	0	60	63	0	0	0	247
Consumption of fixed capital	9	3	78	11	15	15	34	5	170	2	0	20	22	20	10	30	222
Mixed income, gross	15	0	228	36	36	7	99	19	440	2	0	0	2	0	0	0	442
Operating surplus, gross	15	7	107	31	11	23	101	51	346	3	0	80	83	20	10	30	459

the sum of the outputs of the individual establishments of which the institutional unit is composed, thus including deliveries between establishments within the institutional unit (i.e., inter-establishment flows). To clarify relationships and contents of industries and sectors, the System calls for the cross-classification of value added and its uses (and if possible also for output and intermediate consumption) by both industry and sector.

15.108. The table of value added and its uses cross-classified by industries and sectors is essentially the uses of value added quadrant of the use table broken down also by sectors to become a three-dimensional table.

15.109. The illustrated figures in table 15.3 indicate which are the entries of the three dimensions that usually or mostly appear together. The chapter has already dealt with the correlation between uses of value added and industries and for some uses also the institutional sectors involved. The most interesting correlation at this point is however that between sector and industry:

(a) Non-financial corporations: market industries (most ISIC sections);

(b) Financial corporations: market industries of financial intermediation including insurance and pension funds and activities auxiliary to financial intermediation;

(c) General government: non-market industries of public administration and defence, compulsory Social Security, education, health and social work, real estate activities, other community and social service activities, etc.; market industries might also occur;

(d) NPISHs: non-market industries of education, health and social work, other community and social service activities, etc.;

(e) Households: market industries (various ISIC sections) and own use industries (private households with employed persons, services of owner-occupied dwellings, subsistence production of agriculture etc.).

15.110. In order to implement the three-dimensional table, it would be a great advantage to have good register capabilities. Furthermore, it might be necessary to make the similar cross-classifications for output and intermediate consumption as well, especially for countries which in general follow the production approach in estimating the GDP.

4. Illustrations of the supply and use table

15.111. The tables of the input-output framework are all presented with figures for illustration to facilitate the comprehension of their contents. This sub-section of illustrations is meant as a guide to readers who want to make direct references to row and column numbers of the supply and use table.

15.112. The notations used are the following:

$X.i.j$ = Entry of row no. i and column no. j

$R.i.(j1+ +jN)$ = Row no. i, sum of columns 1 to N

$C.(i1+ +iM).j$ = Column no. j, sum of rows 1 to M

15.113. For example, total output at basic prices is defined in the supply table as:

$$X.13.22 = R.13.(14+18+21) = C.(1+ +10).22 \quad = 3,604$$

which means that the intersection of row 13 and column 22 will give total output at basic prices equal to 3,604, alternatively arrived at by taking the sum of columns 14, 18 and 21 on row 13, or the sum of rows 1 through 10 in column 22.

15.114. To illustrate the contents of the supply table 15.1 S, the following aggregates might be defined from the table as shown:

Total output, market industries =
$$X.13.14 = R.13.(6+ +13) = C.(1+ +10).14 \quad = 3,077$$

Total output, own use industries =
$$X.13.18 = R.13.(15+ +17) = C.(1+ +10).18 \quad = \quad 147$$

Total output, other non-market industries =
$$X.13.21 = R.13.(19+20) = C.(1+ +10).21 \quad = \quad 380$$

Total output, basic prices =
$$X.13.22 = R.13.(14+18+21) = C.(1+ +10).22 \quad = 3,604$$

Total imports of goods and services =
$$R.13.(25+26) \quad = \quad 499$$

Total supply, basic prices =
$$X.13.5 \quad = R.13.(22+25+26) = C.(1+ +12).5 \quad = 4,103$$

Total supply, purchasers' price =
$$X.13.1 \quad = R.13.(3+4+5) = C.(1+ +12).1 \quad = 4,236$$

15.115. Likewise, to illustrate the contents of the use table 15.1 U, the following aggregates might be defined from the table as shown:

Total intermediate consumption, market industries =
$$X.13.14 = R.13.(6+ +13) = C.(1+ +10).14 \quad = 1,594$$

Total intermediate consumption, own use industries =
$$X.13.18 = R.13.(15+ +17) = C.(1+ +10).18 \quad = \quad 50$$

Total intermediate consumption, other non-market industries =
$$X.13.21 = R.13.(19+20) = C.(1+ +10).21 \quad = \quad 239$$

Total intermediate consumption, total industry =
$$X.13.22 = R.13.(14+18+21) = C.(1+ +10).22 \quad = 1,883$$

Total exports of goods and services =
$$R.13.(24+25) \quad = \quad 540$$

Total final consumption expenditure, total economy =
$$X.13.26 = R.13.(27+28+29) = C.(1+ +12).26 \quad = 1,399$$

Total gross capital formation, total economy =
$$X.13.32 = R.13.(33+34+35) = C.(1+ +10).32 \quad = \quad 414$$

Total national final uses, total economy =
$$R.13.(26+32) \quad = 1,813$$

Total final uses, total economy =
$$R.13.(24+25+26+32) \quad = 2,353$$

Total uses, total economy =

X.13.1 = R.13.(22+24+25+26+32) = C.(1+ +12).1 = 4,236

15.116. The illustration of industry flows involves both the supply table 15.1 S and the use table 15.1 U. Since the aggregates of output and intermediate consumption already have been illustrated, emphasis is here on value added and GDP, and the uses of value added, to illustrate the industry flows (when both tables are referred to, S indicates the supply table and U the use table):

Total gross value added, market industries =

X.17.14 = R.17.(6+ +13) = C.(S13 – U13).14 = 1,483

Total gross value added, own use industries =

X.17.18 = R.17.(15+ +17) = C.(S13 – U13).18 = 97

Total gross value added, other non-market industries =

X.17.21 = R.17.(19+20) = C.(S13 – U13).21 = 141

Total gross value added, industries, basic prices =

X.17.22 = R.17.(14+18+21) = C.(S13 – U13).22 = 1,721

Gross domestic product (GDP) (production approach) =

X.17.23 = R.S13.(3+4+22) – R.U13.22 = 1,854

Gross domestic product (GDP) (income approach) =

X.17.23 = C.(18+19+23+24+25).23 = 1,854

15.117. For GDP, in addition to the two illustrations above on the production approach and the income approach, the GDP

using the expenditure approach could also be illustrated from table entries:

Gross domestic product (GDP) (expenditure approach) =

X.17.23 = R.U13.(24+25+26+32) – R.S13.(25+26) = 1,854

15.118. For each product and for the total economy there is the constraint that total supply equals total use. This is shown in table 15.1 (S and U) at purchasers' prices:

Total supply, total economy =

R.13.(3+4+22+25+26) = 141–8+3,613+392+107 = 4,236

Total uses, total economy =

R.13.(22+24+25+26+32) = 1,902+462+78+1,391+412 = 4,236

15.119. This sets out the basic equation (or balance) of national accounts aggregates reflected in the goods and services account:

Output (3,604)

+ Imports of goods and services (392+107)

+ Taxes, less subsidies, on products (141 – 8)

= Intermediate consumption (1,883)

+ Exports of goods and services (462+78)

+ Final consumption expenditure/actual final consumption (1,399)

+ Gross capital formation (414)

D. Derived and analytical input-output tables

1. Introduction

15.120. The remaining part of this chapter relates to making the input-output data even more useful for analysis. While some users might find that in many instances the supply and use table could serve analytical as well as statistical purposes, others traditionally may want to prepare more analytical tables to meet their needs.

15.121. Supply and use tables certainly can provide the framework for input-output analysis, including the construction of economic models needed for economic analysis. Indeed, analysts increasingly find that there are advantages in starting off directly from the rectangular input-output tables instead of basing the analysis on symmetric input-output tables (see also discussion of framework in chapter XX).

15.122. It should also be noted that the supply and use tables—sometimes referred to as statistical supply and use tables—in fact represent an intermediate stage between the basic statistics and the symmetric tables. Although the supply and use tables may have strong ties to data observations and various basic statistics, it is also the case that a series of imputations, reconciliations and other national accounts requirements in fact usually entail considerable and varied compilation work on basic data to complete and balance the supply and use tables.

15.123. The following considerations might be taken into account—starting from supply and use tables—in order to arrive at useful analytical input-output tables:

(a) Decompose purchasers' prices of uses into basic price, taxes, subsidies, and trade and transport margins, and separately analyse these components;

(b) Distinguish use of imported products from use of products from resident producers;

(c) Express rows and columns in the same classification, i.e., direct links (products-to-products or industries-to-industries) rather than indirect (products-to-industries).

15.124. In order to respond to these requirements, the System recommends the following set of input-output tables to complement the basic supply and use table (table 15.1) and its supporting table on trade and transport margins and taxes and subsidies on products (table 15.2):

Table 15.4a and 15.4b

Table 15.6

Table 15.6

Table 15.7.

15.125. Two important assumptions underlie the static input-output analysis, i.e., the notions of:

Table 15.4a. Supply and use: final and intermediate uses at basic prices, market/non-market distinction and ISIC breakdown

Uses of products		Total uses at basic prices (1)	Trade and transport margins (2)	Taxes less subsidies on products (3)..	Agric., hunting, forestry, fishing (A+B) (6)	Mining and quarrying (C) (7)	Manufacturing, electricity (D+E) (8)	Construction (F) (9)	Wholesale, retail trade, repair motor vehicles, hotels and restaurants (G+H) (10)	Transport, storage, communication (I) (11)	Financial intermediation, real est., other business services (J+K) (12)	Educ., health, social services (M+N+O) (13)	Sub-total market (14)
	Goods and services, (by CPC sections)												
	Total uses												
1.	Agriculture, forestry and fishery products (0)	124			2	0	70	0	3	1	5	0	81
2.	Ores and minerals (1)	101			1	3	89	0	0	0	1	0	94
3.	Electricity, gas and water (17-18)	155			2	2	92	1	5	3	4	1	110
4.	Manufacturing (2-4)	1 997			25	7	624	56	36	19	35	16	818
5.	Construction work and construction, land (5)	245			1	2	7	5	2	1	3	1	22
6.	Trade services, restaurant and hotel services (6)	201			3	1	56	4	9	8	4	0	85
7.	Transport, storage and communication services (7)	116			2	1	32	3	17	12	5	0	72
8.	Business services (8)	582			3	1	112	16	25	15	44	6	222
9.	Community, social and pers. serv. exc. pub. adm. (9)	371			1	0	7	1	1	1	11	23	45
10.	Public administration (91)	168			0	0	0	0	0	0	0	0	0
	Adjustments:												
11.	Direct purchases abroad by residents	43											
12.	Dir. purchases in domestic market by non-residents	0											
13.	*Total uses at basic prices*	4 103			40	17	1 089	86	98	60	112	47	1 549
14.	*Taxes less subsidies on products*	133			1	0	38	4	2	0	0	0	45
16.	*Total uses at purchasers' prices*	4 236			41	17	1 127	90	100	60	112	47	1 594
17.	*Total gross value added/GDP*			133	37	18	717	118	91	40	266	196	1 483
18.	Compensation of employees				9	13	336	46	44	16	54	123	641
19.	Taxes less subsidies on production and imports			133	− 2	− 2	46	5	0	− 6	12	3	56
20.	Taxes on products			141									
21.	Subsidies on products			− 8									
22.	Other taxes less subsidies on production				− 2	− 2	46	5	0	− 6	12	3	56
23.	Mixed income, net				14	0	227	35	36	3	99	18	432
24.	Operating surplus, net				7	4	30	21	− 4	12	67	47	184
25.	Consumption of fixed capital				9	3	78	11	15	15	34	5	170
26.	Mixed income, gross				15	0	228	36	36	7	99	19	440
27.	Operating surplus, gross				15	7	107	31	11	23	101	51	346
28.	*Total output*				78	35	1 844	208	191	100	378	243	3 077

Intermediate consumption of industries (by ISIC categories) — Market

Own final use				Other non-market					Exports		Final consumption expenditure			General government			Gross capital formation			
Agric., hunting, forestry, fishing (A+B) (15)	Construction (F) (16)	Real estate, household services (K+P) (17)	Sub-total (18)	Educ., health, social services (M+N+O) (19)	Public admin., defence, soc. sec., other public services (L) (20)	Sub-total non-market (21)	Total industry (22)	Total economy (23)	Goods (24)	Services (25)	Sub-total (26)	Households (27)	NPISHs Individual (28)	Sub-total (29)	Collective (30)	Individual (31)	Sub-total (32)	Gross fixed capital formation (33)	Changes in inventories (34)	Acquisition less disposals of valuables (35)
1	0	0	1	3	2	5	87		7		27	25	0	2	0	2	3	2	1	
0	0	0	0	0	0	0	94		6		2	2	0	0	0	0	− 1		− 1	
0	0	0	0	5	4	9	119		1		35	35	0	0	0	0	0		0	
5	17	10	32	42	33	75	925		396		507	504	0	3	0	3	169	154	5	10
0	0	0	0	11	7	18	40		6		3	3	0	0	0	0	196	173	23	
0	0	0	0	2	6	8	93		14	38	53	53	0	0	0	0	3	3	0	0
0	0	0	0	3	4	7	79		2	19	16	16	0	0	0	0	0	0	0	0
0	7	10	17	33	32	65	304			7	248	248	0	0	0	0	23	23	0	
0	0	0	0	21	29	50	95			4	272	54	14	204	0	204	0	0	0	
0	0	0	0	1	0	1	1			0	167	6	2	159	156	3	0		0	
											43	43								
									20	9	− 29	− 29								
6	24	20	50	121	117	238	1 837		452	77	1 344	960	16	368	156	212	393	355	28	10
0	0	0	0	0	1	1	46		10	1	55	55	0	0	0	0	21	21	0	0
6	24	20	50	121	118	239	1 883		462	78	1 399	1 015	16	368	156	212	414	376	28	10
5	12	80	97	91	50	141	1 721	1 854												
0	12	0	12	70	39	109	762	762												
0	0	0	0	1	1	2	58	191												
								141												
								− 8												
0	0	0	0	1	1	2	58	58												
0	0	0	0	0	0	0	432	432												
3	0	60	63	0	0	0	247	247												
2	0	20	22	20	10	30	222	222												
2	0	0	2	0	0	0	442	442												
3	0	80	83	20	10	30	459	459												
11	36	100	147	212	168	380	3 604													

System of National Accounts 1993

Table 15.4b.   Supply and use: final and intermediate uses at basic prices, ISIC breakdown

Uses of products		Total uses at basic prices (1)	Trade and transport margins (2)	Taxes less subsidies on products (3)..	Agric., hunting, forestry, fishing (A+B) (6)	Mining and quarrying (C) (7)	Manufacturing, electricity (D+E) (8)	Construction (F) (9)	Wholesale, retail trade, repair motor vehicles, hotels and restaurants (G+H) (10)	Transport, storage, communication (I) (11)	Financial intermediation, real est., other business services (J+K) (12)	Educ., health, social, pers. services (M+N+O+P) (13)	Public admin. defence soc. se other public service (L) (14)
	Goods and services, (by CPC sections)												
	Total uses												
1.	Agriculture, forestry and fishery products (0)	124			3	0	70	0	3	1	5	3	
2.	Ores and minerals (1)	101			1	3	89	0	0	0	1	0	
3.	Electricity, gas and water (17-18)	155			2	2	92	1	5	3	4	6	
4.	Manufacturing (2-4)	1 997			30	7	624	73	36	19	45	58	
5.	Construction work and construction, land (5)	245			1	2	7	5	2	1	3	12	
6.	Trade services, restaurant and hotel services (6)	201			3	1	56	4	9	8	4	2	
7.	Transport, storage and communication services (7)	116			2	1	32	3	17	12	5	3	
8.	Business services (8)	582			3	1	112	23	25	15	54	39	
9.	Community, social and pers. serv. exc. pub. adm. (9)	371			1	0	7	1	1	1	11	44	
10.	Public administration (91)	168			0	0	0	0	0	0	0	1	
	Adjustments:												
11.	Direct purchases abroad by residents	43											
12.	Dir. purchases in domestic market by non-residents	0											
13.	*Total uses at basic prices*	4 103			46	17	1 089	110	98	60	132	168	
14.	*Taxes less subsidies on products*	133			1	0	38	4	2	0	0	0	
16.	*Total uses at purchasers' prices*	4 236			47	17	1 127	114	100	60	132	168	
17.	*Total gross value added/GDP*			133	42	18	717	130	91	40	346	287	
18.	Compensation of employees				9	13	336	58	44	16	54	193	
19.	Taxes less subsidies on production and imports			133	−2	−2	46	5	0	−6	12	4	
20.	Taxes on products			141									
21.	Subsidies on products			−8									
22.	Other taxes less subsidies on production				−2	−2	46	5	0	−6	12	4	
23.	Mixed income, net				14	0	227	35	36	3	99	18	
24.	Operating surplus, net				10	4	30	21	−4	12	127	47	
25.	Consumption of fixed capital				11	3	78	11	15	15	54	25	
26.	Mixed income, gross				17	0	228	36	36	7	99	19	
27.	Operating surplus, gross				18	7	107	31	11	23	181	71	
	Total output				89	35	1 844	244	191	100	478	455	

Total industry (15)	Total economy (16)	Exports Goods (17)	Services (18)	Final consumption expenditure Sub-total (19)	House-holds (20)	NPISHs Individual (21)	General government Sub-total (22)	Collec-tive (23)	Indivi-dual (24)	Gross capital formation Sub-total (25)	Gross fixed capital forma-tion (26)	Changes in inven-tories (27)	Acqui-sition less dispo-sals of valu-ables (28)
87		7		27	25	0	2	0	2	3	2	1	
94		6		2	2	0	0	0	0	– 1		– 1	
119		1		35	35	0	0	0	0	0		0	
925		396		507	504	0	3	0	3	169	154	5	10
40		6		3	3	0	0	0	0	196	173	23	
93		14	38	53	53	0	0	0	0	3	3	0	0
79		2	19	16	16	0	0	0	0	0	0	0	0
304			7	248	248	0	0	0	0	23	23	0	
95			4	272	54	14	204	0	204	0	0	0	
1			0	167	6	2	159	156	3	0		0	
				43	43								
		20	9	– 29	– 29								
1 837		452	77	1 344	960	16	368	156	212	393	355	28	10
46		10	1	55	55	0	0	0	0	21	21	0	0
1 883		462	78	1 399	1 015	16	368	156	212	414	376	28	10
1 721	1 854												
762	762												
58	191												
	141												
	– 8												
58	58												
432	432												
247	247												
222	222												
442	442												
459	459												
3 604													

A single technique of production for each product

A linear fixed-coefficient production function.

15.126. In a modern economy with millions of products and techniques, the first assumption would seem highly abstract as one is rather unlikely to find an aggregation of these to properly represent techniques of production.

15.127. Most analysis requires that transactions between producers and users must be valued as homogeneously as possible. Consequently, the System recommends the use of basic prices in the valuation of both inputs and outputs for input-output analysis. Also valuing final uses at basic prices means that the impact of various uses on the level of output valued at basic prices can be estimated. Thereby, for example, differences between various classes of buyers in the rates of taxation are also avoided.

15.128. The original use tables contain the elements for alternative valuations, i.e., the alternative use table at basic prices can be derived by combining the use table (table 15.1 U) and the supporting table on trade and transport margins and taxes and subsidies on products (table 15.2)—a table showing entries of margins and taxes and subsidies on products embodied in the purchasers' prices of the intermediate use and final use quadrants.

2. The use table at basic prices

15.129. The use table at basic prices is both an alternative statistical use table and a step towards the conversion to analytical input-output table. Against the first interpretation, it may be noted that intermediate and final uses calculated at basic prices are one step further removed from basic statistics.

15.130. Table 15.4a presents the use table at basic prices. In a supply and use table at basic prices, the columns on taxes on products and subsidies on products, as well as the column on trade and transport margins as it is presented in the supply table (table 15.1 S), become irrelevant. However, (non-deductible) taxes less subsidies on products form an additional row in quadrants I and II for intermediate use and final uses, as the total uses continue to be valued at purchasers' prices.

3. Distinction between use of products from resident producers and of imported products

15.131. In the supply and use tables presented so far, imports are shown by products in the supply table, while not distinguished among uses in the use table. In this recording, no information is required on the origin (resident or foreign) of products used by each category of demand. The principal disadvantage of this simple method is that in most analyses the impacts of a certain level of final demand on production of resident producers and on imports need to be assessed separately.

15.132. There are several ways to treat imports in the input-output framework:

(a) Classified by purchasers;

(b) Classified into complementary and competitive imports;

(c) A separate input-output table for imported products.

15.133. The most comprehensive method is to prepare separate input-output tables for imported products and products from resident producers. The statistical requirements are demanding, but the results allow considerable flexibility in the treatment of imports and permit a very clear analysis of the impact of demand on supplies from resident producers and foreign supplies. When it is useful for analytical and economic policy purposes, such an import table may be established even if an analytical symmetric input-output table is not prepared.

15.134. In the System it is recommended in the analytical input-output tables to make a separate input-output table for imported products. Table 15.5 illustrates this method. This table is given in the same format as the subsequent symmetric product-by-product tables, particularly because of its orientation towards products rather than industries. It may be added that the method also permits the separation of technical coefficients into resident and imported components when applied for modelling work.

15.135. The column totals of table 15.5 classify imports by purchasers with no classification of imports by products. Imports are instead shown in a single row entering into each category of demand. The disadvantage of this method is that imports are explicitly shown only as a margin of the input-output framework which conceals the nature of the imports. It is very likely that this method will require more statistical information than it actually reveals.

15.136. Classifying imports only by purchaser might be refined by dividing imports into the two categories of complementary imports and competitive imports. In this case, the effects on production of resident producers and imports can be more accurately assessed. The decisions on classification may however be arbitrary in some cases and may need revision over time if production by resident producers ceases or commences. In practice, actual compilation is usually more complicated than the definitions of the two categories suggest:

(a) Complementary products are those for which no resident industry exists and are available only from imports;

(b) Competitive products are those for which there is a resident industry and which may therefore be produced either by resident producers or imported.

4. Conversion of the supply and use tables into symmetric tables

Kind of amendments to the supply and use table

15.137. There is a change in format to be made when converting the supply and use tables into symmetric tables. The description that follows refers to the product-by-product table, in which the columns of the table refer to inputs into the production of a CPC group. The conversion, or transformation, can be divided into three steps or amendments to the supply and use table:

(a) Allocation of all products in the supply table to the productive activity in which they are principally (characteristically) produced;

(b) Rearranging the columns of the use table from inputs into industries to inputs into homogeneous activities (without aggregation of the rows);

(c) Aggregation of the detailed products (rows) of the new use table to the homogeneous activities recognized in the columns, if appropriate.

15.138. Step (a), in fact, involves transfers of outputs in the form of secondary products in the supply table. Since secondary products appear as ("off-diagonal") entries in the supply table, this kind of transfer would be a comparatively simple matter (merely rearrange products in sequences and "move" to diagonal). These secondary products are treated as additions into the activities for which they are principal and removed from the activities in which they were produced.

15.139. Step (b) is more complicated as the basic data on inputs relate to industries and not to particular products produced in those industries. The kind of conversion to be made here entails the transfer of inputs associated with secondary outputs from the industry in which that secondary output actually takes place to the activity to which they principally (characteristically) belong. In making this transfer, two different approaches might be taken:

By means of supplementary statistical information

By means of mechanical methods.

15.140. Supplementary statistical information should be utilized as much as possible, i.e., specific information on inputs required to produce certain kinds of output, in order to separate out inputs relating to a secondary product. Information of this kind is usually incomplete, however. Ultimately it will be necessary to resort to simple mathematical means for making the transfers. Mathematical methods are briefly described in the next section and will be elaborated in the *Handbook on Input-Output Tables*.

15.141. Step (c) involves the aggregation of the products of the new use table to the activities that generate them according to step (a) and this results in a symmetric input-output table with di-

mensions product-by-product. While these amendments start from data based on establishment units, the resulting entries are brought to conform to those of units of homogeneous production.

15.142. The transfer of secondary products may also include the transfer of by-products. When the product produced as a by-product is the principal product of another activity, it may be transferred to that activity, with the inputs assumed to be attributable to the production of the by-product. Splitting off the production of by-products in this way may not be merely difficult, but also rather artificial if they cannot be separated technologically from the process of production in which they are actually produced.

15.143. In summary, the conversion might be seen as moving from an accounting tool designed primarily to provide a framework within which statistics can be assembled, organized and collated, to an analytical tool which is intended primarily for economic analysis. The two kinds of tool are, however, not so very different from each other; supply and use tables can also be used themselves for various analytical purposes—and they already involve a lot of adjustments and analytical work—while the symmetric tables impose even stronger accounting constraints on the data, since row and column totals of the input-output table in the same classification have to be identical for each product.

Adding analytical assumptions to basic data

15.144. The mathematical methods used when transferring outputs and associated inputs hinge on two types of technology assumptions:

(a) Industry (producer) technology, assuming that all products produced by an industry are produced with the same input structure;

(b) Product (commodity) technology, assuming that a product has the same input structure in whichever industry it is produced.

15.145. The importance of the role played by the assumptions depends on the extent of secondary production, which depends not only on how production is organized in the economy, but also on the statistical units and the industry breakdown in the tables. More secondary production will appear with institutional units than with establishments, and more secondary production will inevitably be found in more detailed tables.

15.146. On theoretical grounds, which are spelt out in more detail in the forthcoming *Handbook on National Accounting: Input-Output tables*, which is being prepared by the Statistical Division of the United Nations Secretariat, by referring to certain axioms of desirable properties one may come somewhat closer to a choice between these two technology assumptions. On this basis, the industry technology assumption performs rather poorly, as being:

Table 15.5. Import matrix, basic prices (c.i.f.)

Uses of products		Intermediate consumption Homogeneous units of production										Total industry (11)
		Agric., fishery, forestry products (0) (1)	Ores and minerals (1) (2)	Elec., gas, water (17-18) (3)	Manufac-turing (2-4) (4)	Construc-tion work, construc-tion, land (5) (5)	Trade services, restaurants, hotels (6) (6)	Transport, storage, communi-cation services (7) (7)	Business services (8) (8)	Community, social, personal services (9) (9)	Public admin., defence, other public services (91) (10)	
		Goods and services, (by CPC sections)										
		Total uses										
1.	Agriculture, forestry and fishery products (0)	0	0	0	27	0	0	0	0	0	0	27
2.	Ores and minerals (1)	0	0	0	60	0	0	0	0	0	0	60
3.	Electricity, gas and water (17-18)	0	0	0	1	0	0	0	0	0	0	1
4.	Manufacturing (2-4)	0	0	10	85	5	0	0	0	0	0	100
5.	Construction work and construction, land (5)	0	0	0	0	0	0	0	0	0	0	0
6.	Trade services, restaurant and hotel services (6)	0	0	0	15	0	3	3	0	0	0	21
7.	Transport, storage and communication services (7)	0	0	0	10	0	5	0	1	0	0	16
8.	Business services (8)	0	0	0	5	5	2	0	5	0	0	17
9.	Community, social and pers. serv. exc. pub. adm. (9)	0	0	0	0	0	0	0	0	0	0	0
10.	Public administration (91)	0	0	0	0	0	0	0	0	0	0	0
	Adjustments:											
11.	Direct purchases abroad by residents											
12.	C.i.f./f.o.b. adjustment											
13.	*Total imports*	0	0	10	203	10	10	3	6	0	0	242

| | Final consumption expenditure | | | | | Gross capital formation | | | | | | |
| | | | | General government | | | | | | | | Imports | |
Sub-total (12)	House-holds (13)	NPISHs Individual (14)	Sub-total (15)	Collec-tive (16)	Indivi-dual (17)	Sub-total (18)	Gross fixed capital forma-tion (19)	Changes in inven-tories (20)	Acquisition less disposals of valuables (21)	C.i.f./ f.o.b. adjust-ment (22)	Goods (23)	Services (24)
10	10	0	0	0	0	0	0	0			37	
0	0	0	0	0	0	0		0			60	
0	0	0	0	0	0	0		0			1	
100	100	0	0	0	0	83	73	0	10		283	
0	0	0	0	0	0	1	1	0			1	
15	15	0	0	0	0	0	0	0	0			36
10	10	0	0	0	0	0	0	0	0			26
0	0	0	0	0	0	0	0	0				17
5	5	0	0	0	0	0	0	0				5
0	0	0	0	0	0	0		0				0
43	43										20	23
										− 10	− 10	
183	183	0	0	0	0	84	74	0	10	− 10	392	107

(a) Highly implausible;

(b) Not price invariant, which means that values at current prices are affected;

(c) Not scale invariant, due to its fixed market share property, which means that the coefficients that follow may vary without change in technique;

(d) Not maintaining financial balance, which means that the axiom of revenue being equal to cost plus value added for each commodity is not met;

(e) The Leontief material balance (total output = input-output coefficients * total output + final demand) is however met.

15.147. From the same theoretical point of view, the product (commodity) technology model seems to meet the most desirable properties, i.e., the axioms of material balance, financial balance, scale invariance and price invariance. It also appeals to common sense and is found a priori more plausible than the industry technology assumption. While the product technology assumption thus is favoured from a theoretical and a common sense viewpoint, it may need some kind of adjustment in practice. The automatic application of this method has often shown results that are unacceptable, insofar as input-output coefficients sometimes appear as extremely improbable or even impossible. There are even numerous examples of the method leading to negative coefficients which are clearly nonsensical from an economic point of view. Improbable coefficients may partly be due to errors in measurement and partly to heterogeneity (product-mix) in the industry of which the transferred product is the principal product. Heterogeneity results from working on aggregated data with a high occurrence of non-characteristic products. This might be overcome by making adjustments based on supplementary information or exploiting informed judgement to the fullest extent possible.

15.148. Further improvement of the input-output tables can be made in the following ways:

(a) Make proper adjustments to the basic data so as to obtain a supply and use table of good quality, since this will in fact mean more to the quality of the symmetric tables than the choice of technology assumption;

(b) Introduce other models like mixed technology models whenever modifications of the basic input-output model are to be made, however complicated to implement.

15.149. Finally, it must be said that the question of technology assumption should be viewed against the background of the kind of aggregated data dealt with in the input-output framework. Since input-output tables contain only highly aggregated macro data, it is in fact difficult to relate them to micro assumptions of a certain production technology.

5. Symmetric input-output tables

Format of the recommended tables

15.150. Symmetric means having the same dimensions, either product-by-product or industry-by-industry. The product-by-product table shows which products are used in the production of which other products; the industry-by-industry table shows which industry uses the output of which other industry. Since the product-by-product table will often prove most useful, only this table is actually described in detail in this manual. It is shown in two versions:

(a) Product-by-product input-output table, i.e., table 15.6;

(b) Product-by-product input-output table separating out the part of the product flows produced by resident producers from the part imported, i.e., table 15.7.

15.151. The format of the product-by-product table is the familiar one consisting of three quadrants:

(a) The upper-left part, quadrant I on intermediate use, gives the name to the table, as it is shown in the form of product-by-product (i.e., rows were products already, while columns change, actually referring to homogeneous activities);

(b) The upper-right part, quadrant II on final use, has a format close to the corresponding use table, except for imports (see below);

(c) The lower-left part, quadrant III on uses of value added, also has a format close to that of the use table in that the rows are the same, but the columns reflect homogeneous activities, while the appended rows of the use table have been deleted.

15.152. The symmetric tables 15.6 and 15.7, on their rows of quadrants I and II, have kept the same items as of the supply and use table 15.1, i.e., an illustrative product breakdown of 10 groups, plus the three adjustment row items presented before. By the nature of the table, the same 10 product groups now appear as columns in quadrant I. The separation of market products from other products in intermediate use is, however, not introduced. The columns of exports, final consumption expenditure and gross capital formation in the use table and in the product-by-product table all have more or less the same format. The rows of uses of value added are almost identical with the use table. Taxes and subsidies on products are not considered uses of value added of homogeneous activities (in columns), but are instead introduced as a single entry in order to get GDP at market prices.

15.153. The GDP can be seen as follows:

(a) GDP from the production approach = the sum of gross value added by products (homogeneous activities) at basic prices + single item of taxes less subsidies on products, all on row for total gross value added;

(b)   GDP from the expenditure approach = the sum of the final uses categories at purchasers' prices (imports counted as negative), on the row for total uses;

(c)   GDP from the income approach = the sum of the uses of gross value added, in the column for the total economy.

15.154. In the first version (table 15.6), imports are deducted in the final use quadrant as negative elements by products (at c.i.f. prices and with a c.i.f./f.o.b. adjustment item to arrive at imports f.o.b.). Product output is thus the grand total for each row and column.

15.155. In the second version (table 15.7), the import table (table 15.5) has been deducted from the intermediate use and final use quadrants of table 15.6, so that they now show only uses of output of resident producers (by product). The imported component is shown as a separate row at the bottom of that part of the table. This allows studies of the impact of economic events on production of resident producers and on imports separately. In fact, the imports table 15.5, actually makes it possible to show every cell in quadrants I and II separated into output of resident producers and imported products, rather than just treating imports globally for each activity and final use category on a separate row.

Illustrations of the product-by-product table

15.156. To illustrate the contents of the product-by-product tables the same method of illustration is used as for the supply and use tables earlier in the chapter. In this case, first, entries of the composite manufacturing product as an example of individual product flows and then some of the aggregates are illustrated, for each of the two tables.

15.157. Illustrations of table 15.6:

Total product output, basic prices =
$X.28.11 = R.28.(1+ +10) = C.(16+17).11$ = 3,604

Manufacturing product output, basic prices =
$X.4.27 = X.28.4$ = 1,714

Total imports =
$- X.14.(24 + 25)$ = 499

Imported manufacturing product =
$- X.4.24$ = 283

Total resources, basic prices =
$R.14.(- 24 - 25+27)$ = 4,103

Supply of manufacturing product =
$R.4.(- 24 - 25+27)$ = 1,997

Total resources, purchasers' prices =
$R.16.(- 24 - 25+27)$ = 4,236

Total intermediate consumption, basic prices =
$X.14.11 = R.14.(1+ +10)$ = 1,837

Manufacturing product for intermediate consumption, basic prices =

$R.4.11 =$ 925

Total intermediate consumption, purchasers' prices =
$X.16.11 = R.16.(1+ +10) = C.(14+15).11$ = 1,883

Intermediate consumption, manufacturing, purchasers' prices =
$X.16.4 =$ 1,043

Total gross value added, basic prices =
$X.17.11 = R.17.(1+ +10) = C.(18+ +25).11$ = 1,721

Gross value added, manufacturing =
$X.17.4 =$ 671

Gross domestic product =
$X.17.29 = R.17.(11+28) = C.(18+ +25).29$ = 1,854

Total national final uses, basic prices =
$R.14.(12+18)$ = 1,737

Total final uses, basic prices =
$R.14.(12+18+22+23)$ = 2,266

Manufacturing product for final use, basic prices =
$R.4.(12+18+22)$ = 1,072

Total uses, basic prices =
$R.14.(11+12+18+22+23)$ = 4,103

Manufacturing product for total use, basic prices =
$R.4.(11+12+18+22)$ = 1,997

Total national final uses, purchasers' prices =
$R.16.(12+18)$ = 1,813

Total final uses, purchasers' prices =
$R.16.(12+18+22+23)$ = 2,353

Total uses, purchasers' prices =
$R.16.(11+12+18+22+23)$ = 4,236

15.158. Illustrations of table 15.7 (not repeating items which are similar in both tables):

Total resources, basic prices =
$X.13.27 = C.(1+ +12).27$ = 4,103

Total resources, purchasers' prices =
$X.15.27 = C.(13+14).27$ = 4,236

Output of manufacturing product by resident producers for intermediate consumption, basic prices =
$R.4.11 =$ 825

Output of manufacturing product by resident producers for final use =
$R.4.(12+18+22)$ = 889

Total uses, basic prices =
$X.13.27 = R.13.(11+12+18+22+23)$ = 4,103

Output of manufacturing product by resident producers for total use =
$R.4.(11+12+18+22)$ = 1,714

Total uses, purchasers' prices =
$X.15.27 = R.15.(11+12+18+22+23)$ = 4,236

Table 15.6. Input-output symmetric table, basic prices—product by product

Uses of products		Intermediate consumption / Homogeneous units of production										
		Agric., fishery, forestry products (0) (1)	Ores and minerals (1) (2)	Elec., gas, water (17-18) (3)	Manufac-turing (2-4) (4)	Construc-tion work, construc-tion, land (5) (5)	Trade services, restaurants, hotels (6) (6)	Transport, storage, communi-cation services (7) (7)	Business services (8) (8)	Comm., social, personal services (9) (9)	Public admin., defence, other public services (91) (10)	Total industry (11)
		Goods and services, (by CPC sections)										
		Total uses										
1.	Agriculture, forestry and fishery products (0)	3	0	6	64	0	3	1	6	2	2	87
2.	Ores and minerals (1)	1	3	8	81	0	0	0	1	0	0	94
3.	Electricity, gas and water (17-18)	2	2	8	84	1	5	3	5	5	4	119
4.	Manufacturing (2-4)	28	10	51	574	73	32	18	59	47	33	925
5.	Construction work and construction, land (5)	1	2	0	7	5	2	1	6	9	7	40
6.	Trade services, restaurant and hotel services (6)	3	1	5	52	4	8	7	5	2	6	93
7.	Transport, storage and communication services (7)	2	1	2	32	4	14	11	6	3	4	79
8.	Business services (8)	3	2	9	107	23	21	14	57	31	32	299
9.	Community, social and pers. serv. exc. pub. adm. (9)	1	0	1	7	1	1	1	20	39	29	100
10.	Public administration (91)	0	0	0	0	0	0	0	0	1	0	1
		Adjustments:										
11.	Direct purchases abroad by residents											
12.	Dir. purchases in domestic market by non-residents											
13.	C.i.f./f.o.b. adjustment											
14.	*Total uses at basic prices*	44	21	90	1 008	111	86	56	165	139	117	1 837
15.	Taxes less subsidies on products	1	0	3	35	4	2	0	0	0	1	46
16.	*Total uses at purchasers' prices*	45	21	93	1 043	115	88	56	165	139	118	1 883
17.	*Total gross value added/GDP*	42	20	61	671	129	77	40	404	227	50	1 721
18.	Compensation of employees	9	14	37	305	57	37	17	95	152	39	762
19.	Taxes less subsidies on production and imports	- 2	- 1	4	40	5	0	- 4	12	3	1	58
20.	Taxes on products	0	0	0	0	0	0	0	0	0	0	0
21.	Susidies on products	0	0	0	0	0	0	0	0	0	0	0
22.	Other taxes less subsidies on production	- 2	- 1	4	40	5	0	- 4	12	3	1	58
23.	Mixed income, net	14	0	4	226	35	29	6	103	15	0	432
24.	Operating surplus, net	10	4	9	25	20	- 2	9	135	37	0	247
25.	Consumption of fixed capital	11	3	7	75	12	13	12	59	20	10	222
26.	Mixed income, gross	15	0	4	229	36	32	8	103	15	0	442
27.	Operating surplus, gross	20	7	16	97	31	8	19	194	57	10	459
28.	*Output of products at basic prices*	87	41	154	1 714	244	165	96	569	366	168	3 604

	Final consumption expenditure			General government			Gross capital formation				Exports f.o.b.		Imports		C.i.f./f.o.b. adjust-ment	Output of products	Taxes less subsidies on products	Total economy
	Sub-total (12)	House-holds (13)	NPISHs Individual (14)	Sub-total (15)	Collec-tive (16)	Indivi-dual (17)	Sub-total (18)	Gross fixed capital forma-tion (19)	Changes in inven-tories (20)	Acquisition less disposals of valuables (21)	Goods (22)	Services (23)	Goods (24)	Services (25)	(26)	(27)	(28)	(29)
	27	25	0	2	0	2	3	2	1		7		− 37			87		87
	2	2	0	0	0	0	− 1		− 1		6		− 60			41		41
	35	35	0	0	0	0	0		0		1		− 1			154		154
	507	504	0	3	0	3	169	154	5	10	396		− 283			1 714		1 714
	3	3	0	0	0	0	196	173	23		6		− 1			244		244
	53	53	0	0	0	0	3	3	0	0	14	38		− 36		165		165
	16	16	0	0	0	0	0	0	0	0	2	19		− 26	6	96		96
	253	253	0	0	0	0	23	23	0			7		− 17	4	569		569
	267	49	14	204	0	204	0	0	0			4		− 5		366		366
	167	6	2	159	156	3	0		0			0		0		168		168
	43	43											− 20	− 23		0		0
	− 29	− 29									20	9				0		0
													10		− 10	0		0
	1 344	960	16	368	156	212	393	355	28	10	452	77	− 392	− 107	0	3 604		4 103
	55	55		0	0	0	21	21	0	0	10	1			0	133		133
	1 399	1015	16	368	156	212	414	376	28	10	462	78	− 392	− 107		3 737		4 236
																	133	1 854
																		762
																		191
																	141	141
																	− 8	− 8
																		58
																		432
																		247
																		222
																		442
																		459

E. Some aspects of input-output compilation

1. Input-output strategy

15.159. The supply and use table is both a framework for basic statistics and the foundation from which the analytical input-output tables are constructed. This sets an ambitious target including the following elements:

(a) Supply and use table as working basis, possibly every year and at least from time to time in great detail;

(b) Compilation of at least "commodity flows" data (goods and services account by products) annually and fully consistent with national accounts, providing a powerful tool for the calculation and verification of the national accounts;

(c) Flexibility for analytical needs, responsiveness to aggregation, more details and rearrangements of flows.

15.160. If this ideal approach is not possible, mathematical techniques can be used to link benchmark year estimates to partial data for intervening years to generate at least aggregated annual series.

2. Constant-price estimation

15.161. Chapter XVI contains a comprehensive description of the decomposition of flows of goods and services into prices and volumes. In fact, the supply and use tables are the most complete consistent framework for constant price estimation and provide:

(a) Interdependent measures of prices and volumes;

(b) An important check on the numerical consistency and reliability of the entire set of such measures, interlinking values at constant and current prices, value and volume indices and deflators.

15.162. Constant price measures for gross value added are possible in the input-output framework by using the double deflation method, as the difference between:

(a) The value of output deflated by a price index of output;

(b) The value of intermediate consumption deflated by a price index for these inputs.

15.163. In most cases, volumes or volume indices might be derived indirectly, but not without carrying out certain plausibility checks. The price component can usually (except when inflation is high) be estimated more reliably than the volume component, since price indices (deflators) tend to be less variable or volatile than the corresponding quantity relatives.

15.164. The deflation process may be best carried out within the framework of the supply and use table. One possible approach might be to adopt direct deflators for output of resident producers, imports and exports of each product, while the deflator for "use of residents" of each product is derived residually.

15.165. Consumer price indices (CPI) might have a role to play in checking the resulting flows of household consumption expenditure at purchasers' prices. This provides a close link between the national accounts deflator of household consumption expenditure and the CPI.

15.166. Constant-price estimates also involve other general issues that become particularly important in an input-output (supply and use) context, such as change of base year and use of chain indices. These are dealt with in chapter XVI. Depending upon circumstances and which data are found most suitable for the various purposes, a choice has to be made between:

(a) A fixed base of Laspeyres type volume measures;

(b) More frequent rebasing, in particular annual chaining, which may especially appeal to countries experiencing a high degree of inflation or "structural change" in their economy.

15.167. Symmetric input-output tables should also be prepared at constant prices, both because of their wide use and because most of the traditional input-output assumptions are related to such tables. They are obtained in the same way as the input-output tables at current prices, i.e., from the supply and use tables at constant prices.

F. Purposes and uses of input-output data

1. Input-output as a framework

15.168. In addition to their use for analytical purposes, input-output tables and the concept of input-output serve various statistical needs:

(a) Framework for basic data compilation;

(b) Framework for weighting and calculation of index numbers;

(c) Framework for assessing quality and completeness;

(d) Framework for developing interrelated price and volume measures;

(e) Framework for consistency checking.

15.169. Input-output as a framework for basic data compilation is important in terms of identifying gaps and inconsistencies in basic data to be collected. The integration of input-output with other parts of national accounts is equally important; compilation of input-output tables should be closely linked to economic statistics and national accounts in general.

15.170. Input-output as a framework for weighting and compilation of index numbers must be viewed from the central role input-output has in the production account and goods and services account of the national accounting framework. As a consequence, it becomes an invaluable frame for various purposes such as:

(a) Determining the weights in the base-year and the current year of the system of index numbers;

(b) Selecting interrelated samples for collecting integrated series of quantity, price and value indicators;

(c) Selecting samples and weights in the various types of inquiries;

(d) Compiling linked and consistent series of index numbers of price, volume and value.

15.171. Input-output as a framework for assessing quality and completeness is particularly enhanced in national accounting work when basing its compilation on supply and use tables. The needs of national accounts should count heavily when collecting new data or altering the design of existing basic statistics. Improvements in basic statistics will inevitably lead to improvements in the reliability of national accounts data.

15.172. Input-output as a framework for price and volume measures is considered a most complete environment for accurate constant-price calculation. Input-output tables at constant prices form part of the whole statistical system of price and quantity index numbers.

15.173. Input-output as a framework for consistency checking has been stressed various times throughout this chapter and applies as well to estimation at constant prices. The fact of decomposing into price and volume provides yet more checks on plausibility. Price statistics that are available should be applied to the relevant product flows in the accounting framework. This might mean a more sophisticated use of price deflators or extrapolators in the balancing of products.

2. Input-output for analysis

15.174. Input-output tables are a powerful analytical tool. Running from supply and use tables through symmetric input-output tables to the inverse tables (see below) they are put to use in various kinds of economic analysis. Some of the most important areas in which the input-output framework is used for analytical purposes, are listed below and described briefly:

Analysis of production

Analysis of structure of demand, export ratios, etc.

Analysis of employment

Analysis of prices and costs

Analysis of imports required

Analysis of investment and capital

Analysis of exports

Analysis of energy

Analysis of environment

Sensitivity analysis.

15.175. In describing these points briefly, the inverse table and the notion of direct and indirect requirements should first be introduced. The input structure in the columns of the input-output table shows what is required of intermediate and other inputs to produce the corresponding output. Any increase in output of a product starts a long chain of production, since the new inputs also need to be produced, in turn requiring inputs of their own. The Leontief input-output model defines output of each product in terms of the amounts used by other producers and the amounts sold to final uses. This defines a set of structural equations which express the input-output relations in terms of the entries in the table or matrix. It is very useful for analysis to express these relations in terms of coefficients. A coefficient table records the amount of each product used as input per unit of output of the various products. By solving the basic equations, one arrives at the so-called Leontief inverse table which shows the full impact of a given demand for outputs on all the other producers. Thus, the columns of the inverse table show the total input requirements, both direct and indirect, generated by one unit of output.

15.176. Turning back to the applications, the basic role of input-output analysis is to analyse the link between final demand and industrial output levels. The inverse table could be used to assess the effects on the productive system of a given level of final demand. Employment implications are equally important in this respect. Input-output tables can also be used for analysing changes in prices stemming from changes in costs or from changes in taxes or subsidies. The determination of the level of imports is often a vital part of an input-output exercise, particularly in economies where the balance of payments imposes a constraint on their economic policies. There are both the question of direct demand for imports, and secondly, indirect demand for imported inputs from all industries involved directly or indirectly. The input-output framework might be extended to also cover demands for fixed assets, by relating the investment table to output. One of the standard input-output applications is the analysis between exports and the necessary direct and indirect inputs, some of which may be imported.

15.177. There has been an increased use of input-output for more structural analysis. Two prominent areas might be mentioned: energy and environment. It is possible to calculate the energy content of the different products in intermediate and final demand, and thereby direct and indirect energy needs from energy matrices, either in physical or value terms. The input-output approach is an essential component in environmental analysis, as it enables the determination of direct and

Table 15.7. Input-output symmetric table, basic prices—product by product with imported products separated from domestic products

		Intermediate consumption of industries Homogeneous units of production										
Uses of products		Agric., fishery, forestry products (0) (1)	Ores and minerals (1) (2)	Elec., gas, water (17-18) (3)	Manufac-turing (2-4) (4)	Construc-tion work, construc-tion, land (5) (5)	Trade services, restaurants, hotels (6) (6)	Transport, storage, communi-cation services (7) (7)	Business services (8) (8)	Comm., social, personal services (9) (9)	Public admin., defence, other public services (91) (10)	Total industry (11)
	Goods and services, (by CPC sections) *Total uses*											
1.	Agriculture, forestry and fishery products (0)	3	0	6	37	0	3	1	6	2	2	60
2.	Ores and minerals (1)	1	3	8	21	0	0	0	1	0		34
3.	Electricity, gas and water (17-18)	2	2	8	83	1	5	3	5	5	4	118
4.	Manufacturing (2-4)	28	10	41	489	68	32	18	59	47	33	825
5.	Construction work and construction, land (5)	1	2	0	7	5	2	1	6	9	7	40
6.	Trade services, restaurant and hotel services (6)	3	1	5	37	4	5	4	5	2	6	72
7.	Transport, storage and communication services (7)	2	1	2	22	4	9	11	5	3	4	63
8.	Business services (8)	3	2	9	102	18	19	14	52	31	32	282
9.	Community, social and pers. serv. exc. pub. adm. (9)	1	0	1	7	1	1	1	20	39	29	100
10.	Public administration (91)	0	0	0	0	0	0	0	0	1		1
	Adjustments:											
11.	Direct purchases in domestic market by non-residents											
12.	Imports	0	0	10	203	10	10	3	6	0	0	242
13.	*Total uses at basic prices*	44	21	90	1 008	111	86	56	165	139	117	1 837
14.	Taxes less subsidies on products	1	0	3	35	4	2	0	0	0	1	46
15.	*Total uses at purchasers' prices*	45	21	93	1 043	115	88	56	165	139	118	1 883
16.	*Total gross value added/GDP*	42	20	61	671	129	77	40	404	227	50	1721
17.	Compensation of employees	9	14	37	305	57	37	17	95	152	39	762
18.	Taxes subsidies on production and imports	− 2	− 1	4	40	5	0	− 4	12	3	1	58
19.	Taxes on products	0	0	0	0	0	0	0	0	0	0	0
20.	Subsidies on products	0	0	0	0	0	0	0	0	0	0	0
21.	Other taxes less subsidies linked to production	− 2	− 1	4	40	5	0	− 4	12	3	1	58
22.	Mixed income, net	14	0	4	226	35	29	6	103	15	0	432
23.	Operating surplus, net	10	4	9	25	20	− 2	9	135	37	0	247
24.	Consumption of fixed capital	11	3	7	75	12	13	12	59	20	10	222
25.	Mixed income, gross	15	0	4	229	36	32	8	103	15	0	442
26.	Operating surplus, gross	20	7	16	97	31	8	19	194	57	10	459
27.	*Output of products at basic prices*	87	41	154	1714	244	165	96	569	366	168	3 604

| | Final consumption expenditure | | | | | | Gross capital formation | | | | Exports | | | | | |
| | Sub-total (12) | House-holds (13) | NPISHs Individual (14) | General government | | | Sub-total (18) | Gross fixed capital forma-tion (19) | Changes in inven-tories (20) | Acquisition less disposals of valuables (21) | Goods (22) | Services (23) | C.i.f./ f.o.b. adjust-ment (24) | Output of products (25) | Taxes less subsidies on products (26) | Total economy (27) |
				Sub-total (15)	Collec-tive (16)	Indivi-dual (17)										
	17	15	0	2	0	2	3	2	1		7			87		87
	2	2	0	0	0	0	− 1		− 1		6			41		41
	35	35	0	0	0	0	0		0		1			154		154
	407	404	0	3	0	3	86	81	5	0	396			1 714		1714
	3	3	0	0	0	0	195	172	23		6			244		244
	38	38	0	0	0	0	3	3	0	0	14	38		165		165
	6	6	0	0	0	0	0	0	0	0	2	19	6	96		96
	253	253	0	0	0	0	23	23	0			7	4	569		569
	262	44	14	204	0	204	0	0	0			4		366		366
	167	6	2	159	156	3	0		0			0		168		168
	− 29	− 29									20	9		0		
	183	183	0	0	0	0	84	74	0	10			− 10	499		499
	1 344	960	16	368	156	212	393	355	28	10	452	77	0	3 604		4 103
	55	55	0	0	0	0	21	21	0	0	10	1		133		133
	1 399	1 015	16	368	156	212	414	376	28	10	462	78	0	3 737		4 236
															133	1 854
																762
																58
															141	141
															− 8	− 8
																58
																432
																247
																222
																442
																459

indirect sources of pollution by linking data on emissions in physical terms to the input-output tables. The "pollution" content of final demand can then be calculated. Input-output tables with environment-related extensions are a major component of the basic framework for satellite accounting of the environment (chapter XXI).

15.178. Finally, input-output could also be used for various kinds of sensitivity analysis. This analysis reveals the effects if some variables in the output model are changed. Increased attention has also been devoted to dynamic input-output models. The essential distinction of a dynamic model is that it traces the path of the economy from the base year to the target year, and it may be applied to calculate the requirements of a given final output not only in the current year, but also through direct and indirect capital requirements in all preceding years. Dynamic models look at the future growth path of the economy year by year, and while data and computational limitations presently hinder their practical application, this may be somewhat less of a problem in the future.

XVI. Price and volume measures

A. Introduction

16.1. The System provides a framework within which an integrated set of price and volume measures can be compiled which are conceptually consistent and analytically useful. The primary objective is not simply to provide comprehensive measures of changes in prices and volumes for the main aggregates of the System but to assemble a set of interdependent measures which make it possible to carry out systematic and detailed analyses of inflation and economic growth and fluctuations.

16.2. Changes over time in the values of flows of goods and services can be directly factored into two components reflecting changes in the prices of the goods and services concerned and changes in their volumes. Similarly, changes in the values of stocks of many kinds of assets can usually also be decomposed into their own price and volume components. However, many flows in the System, such as cash transfers, do not have price and quantity dimensions of their own and cannot, therefore, be decomposed in their way. Such flows cannot be measured at constant prices but can nevertheless be measured "in real terms" by deflating their values by price indices in order to measure their real purchasing power over some selected basket of goods and services that serves as numeraire. However, there may be more than one way to do this. There may be no obvious choice of numeraire in which to measure the purchasing power and it may well be appropriate to choose different numeraires for the units paying and receiving the same transfers when these are different kinds of units—e.g., government units and households. Moreover, a flow such as wages and salaries can be treated in two quite different ways. For purposes of analysing production and productivity in which wages and salaries constitute costs of production, it may be necessary to measure inputs of labour at constant input prices—i.e., at constant wage and salary rates—whereas when wages and salaries are recorded as receivables in the primary distribution of income account they may need to be measured in terms of their purchasing power over some basket of final household consumption goods and services.

16.3. As the impact of changes in prices may need to be treated differently for the two parties to the same transaction it is not possible to compile a single, consistent multi-purpose set of accounts in real terms embracing all entries in the accounts that would be useful for all types of economic analysis. On the other hand, it is feasible to compile a consistent and integrated set of price and volume measures covering all flows of goods and services, as recorded in the supply and use tables, for example, and this chapter is mainly concerned with the methods that may be used for this purpose. In the final section of the chapter, however, the measurement of real income, as distinct from real product, is examined at the level of the total economy.

16.4. One major advantage of compiling price and volume measures within an accounting framework, such as that provided by the supply and use tables, is that a check is provided on the numerical consistency and reliability of the set of measures as a whole. This is particularly important when every flow of goods and services in the economy has to be covered, including non-market goods and services whose valuation is difficult at current as well as constant prices. Free standing indices, such as consumer price indices or industrial production indices, present far fewer problems because they are much more restricted in their coverage.

16.5. Another advantage of compiling price and volume measures within an accounting framework is that price or volume measures can be derived for certain important balancing items. In particular, gross value added can be measured at constant prices by subtracting intermediate consumption at constant prices from output at constant prices, the so-called "double deflation" method. Double deflation may be used at the level of an individual enterprise, industry or sector, or for the total economy as a whole by subtracting imports at constant prices from total final expenditures at constant prices.

16.6. Although most price and volume index numbers were developed to measure changes in prices and volumes over time, they can also be adapted to compare levels of prices and volumes between different regions or countries in the same period of time. Such comparisons are needed in order to be able to compare standards of living, levels of economic development or levels of productivity in different countries and also to compare the price levels in different countries when prices are converted at exchange rates. Such comparisons are important both for purposes of economic analysis and policy-making. The additional methodological questions raised by international comparisons are dealt with in a separate section below.

16.7. The contents of this chapter may be summarized as follows:

(a) The first group of sections is concerned with inter-temporal price and volume index numbers: i.e., with the choice of an appropriate methodology for compiling intertemporal price and volume measures for flows of goods and services in a national accounting context. The construction of a set of suitable price and volume indices for the flows of goods and services in the System is the essential first step, even if it is intended to go on to utilize the resulting price indices to compile measures of real income at a later stage;

(b) Another section examines the methodology for compiling international price and volume measures for purposes of comparing living standards or productivity levels in different countries in the same period of time;

(c) Another section deals with the consequences of price variation and price discrimination: that is, how to treat goods or services that are sold to different purchasers at different prices on the same market in the same period of time. Such differences need to be clearly distinguished from price differences attributable to differences in qualities;

(d) Another section is concerned with the treatment of changes in quality over time, including the appearance of new products and the disappearance of old products, and also with differences in the quality of products found in different countries. This can be most difficult, and the most serious practical problem encountered in the construction of both intertemporal and international price and volume indices. This section includes a brief description of the use of the hedonic hypothesis to adjust for changes in quality over time, or differences in quality between countries, especially for high technology products and fixed assets;

(e) The final section considers the differences between real product and real income at the level of the total economy. These differences may be quite substantial over certain periods of time for open economies that experience substantial changes in their terms of trade with other countries.

B. Values, prices and quantities

16.8. For each individual type of good or service it is necessary to specify an appropriate quantity unit in which that good or service can be measured. Goods or services may be supplied in units that are either discrete or continuously variable:

(a) Automobiles, aircraft, microcomputers, haircuts, appendectomies, etc., are examples of goods or services provided in discrete or integral units, described by generic terms such as "automobile". The quantities of such goods and services are obtained simply by counting the number of units;

(b) Oil, electricity, sugar, transportation, etc., are examples of goods or services provided in units that vary continuously in respect of characteristics such as weight, volume, power, duration, distance, etc. The choice of physical unit is therefore a matter of convenience: for example, it may be one pound, one kilo or one ton; one gallon or one litre; one minute or one hour; etc. The price of such a good or service is quoted in relation to the particular physical unit selected. Its absolute value is therefore quite arbitrary: for example, if the price is quoted per ton it is one thousand times greater than if it is quoted per kilo.

16.9. Value (v) at the level of a single, homogeneous good or service is equal to the price per unit of quantity (p) multiplied by the number of quantity units (q): that is,

$$v = pq$$

In contrast to price, value is independent of the choice of quantity unit. Values have quite different dimensions from prices and the terms "value" and "price" cannot be used interchangeably for each other. Certain important properties of quantities, prices and values may be briefly noted:

(a) Quantities are additive only for a single homogeneous product. Quantities of different products are not commensurate and not additive even when measured in the same kinds of physical units. For example, it is not economically meaningful to add 10 tons of coal to 20 tons of sugar, even though their combined weight of 30 tons may provide relevant information for other purposes, such as loading ships or vehicles. Less obviously, the addition of 10 automobiles of one type to 20 automobiles of another type may also not be economically meaningful (see below);

(b) The price of a good or service is defined as the value of one unit of that good or service. It varies directly with the size of the unit of quantity selected and can therefore be made to vary arbitrarily in many cases by choosing to measure in tons, for example, instead of in kilos. Prices, like quantities, are not additive across different goods or services. An average of the prices of different goods or services has no economic significance and cannot be used to measure price changes over time;

(c) Values are expressed in terms of a common unit of currency and are commensurate and additive across different products. As already noted, values are invariant to the choice of quantity unit.

16.10. The aggregation of the values of different goods and services is justified by the fact that, in a market system, the relative prices of different goods and services should reflect both their relative costs of production and their relative utilities to purchasers, whether the latter intend to use them for production or consumption. Relative costs and relative utilities influence the rates at which sellers and buyers are prepared to exchange goods and services on markets.

Volumes

16.11. A volume index is an average of the proportionate changes in the quantities of a specified set of goods or services between two periods of time. The quantities compared must be homogeneous, while the changes for different goods and services must be weighted by their economic importance as measured by their values in one or other, or both, periods. The concept of a volume index may be illustrated by a simple example. Consider an industry that produces two different models of automobile, one selling for twice the price of the other. From an economic point of view these are two quite different products even though described by the same generic term "automobile". Suppose that between two periods of time:

(a)   The price of each model remains constant;

(b)   The total number of automobiles produced remains constant;

(c)   The proportion of higher priced models produced increases from 50 per cent to 80 per cent.

It follows that the total value of the output produced increases by 20 per cent because of the increase in the proportion of higher-priced models. This constitutes a volume increase of 20 per cent. As each higher-priced automobile constitutes twice as much output as each lower-priced automobile, a switch in production from low- to high-priced models increases the volume of output even though the total number of automobiles produced remains unchanged. The fact that the value increase is entirely attributable to an increase in volume also follows from the fact that no price change occurs for either model. The price index must remain constant in these circumstances.

16.12. The term "volume increase" is used in preference to "quantity increase" because there is a possible ambiguity about the use

of the term "quantity increase". It is sometimes argued that the situation described in the example is one in which the quantities remain unchanged (because the total number of automobiles remain unchanged), whereas the average quality of the automobiles produced increases (because of the increase in the proportion of higher-priced models). However, such an interpretation is based on a semantic confusion due to the fact that the same generic term, "automobile", is applied to two products that are actually quite different from an economic point of view. It is not legitimate to add together quantities that are not identical with each other, even though they may be measured in the same kind of physical units. Adding together quite different models of "automobiles" is no more meaningful than adding together tons of different kinds of "foods"— for example, adding tons of rice to tons of apples or beef. In general, it is not possible to decompose a volume change into a quantity change and a change in average quality. The so-called "quantity index" has no meaning from an economic point of view if it involves adding quantities that are not commensurate. For quite different purposes, however, such as loading aircraft, ships or vehicles, adding quantities may provide useful information. Similarly, for purposes of traffic control or pollution, it may be useful to know the increase in the total numbers of vehicles produced or imported, irrespective of their price. However, such measures are not volume measures in an economic sense.

Quantity and unit value indices

16.13. Unfortunately, it may sometimes happen, especially in the field of foreign trade statistics, that as a result of lack of information the data on which price and volume indices have to be calculated are not adequate for the purpose. For example, the basic information available may be limited to the total numbers of units of some group of products imported or exported, or their total weight: for example, the total numbers of pairs of shoes, or total weight of equipment of certain type. Indices built up from information of this kind are not volume indices when the numbers, or weights, cover different items selling at different prices. They are sometimes described as "quantity indices" for this reason. The "price" indices associated with such indices are usually described as average or "unit value" indices as they measure the change in the average value of units that are not homogeneous and may therefore be affected by changes in the mix of items as well as by changes in their prices. Unit value indices cannot therefore be expected to provide good measures of average price changes over time.

C. Intertemporal index numbers of prices and volumes

1. Introduction

16.14. A price index is an average of the proportionate changes in the prices of a specified set of goods and services between two periods of time. Similarly, a volume index is an average of pro-

portionate changes in the quantities of a specified set of goods and services. As already emphasized, the price and quantity changes refer to individual goods or services as distinct from groups of similar products. Different qualities of the same kind of product must be treated as separate goods or services in this context.

16.15. In line with normal conventions, the period that serves as the reference point will be designated as period o and the period which is compared with it designated as period t. The two periods may be consecutive or be separated by intervening periods. The ratio of the price, or quantity, of a specific product in period t to the price, or quantity, of the same product in period o, is described as a price relative, or quantity relative: namely, p_t/p_o or q_t/q_o. Price and quantity relatives are pure numbers that are independent of the units in which the quantities are measured and the prices are quoted. Most index numbers can be expressed as, or derived from, weighted averages of these price or quantity relatives, the various formulas differing from each other mainly in the weights which they attach to the individual price or quantity relatives and the particular form of averages used—arithmetic, geometric, harmonic, etc.

2. Laspeyres and Paasche indices

16.16. The two most commonly used indices are the Laspeyres and Paasche indices. Both may be defined as weighted averages of price or quantity relatives, the weights being the values of the individual goods or services in one or other of the two periods being compared.

Let $v_{ij} = p_{ij} q_{ij}$: the value of the ith product in period j

The Laspeyres price index (Lp) is defined as a weighted arithmetic average of the price relatives using the values of the earlier period o as weights:

$$Lp = \sum_i \frac{v_{io} \cdot p_{it}/p_{io}}{\sum_i V_{io}} \qquad (1)$$

where the summation takes place over different goods and services. The Laspeyres volume index (Lq) is a similar weighted average of the quantity relatives, that is:

$$Lq = \sum_i \frac{v_{io} \cdot q_{it}/q_{io}}{\sum_i V_{io}} \qquad (2)$$

The period that provides the weights for an index is described as the "base" period. It usually (but not always) coincides with the reference period to which the comparisons relate. As the summation always takes place over the same set of goods and services it is possible to dispense with the subscript i in expressions such as (1) and (2). As v_j is equal to $p_j q_j$ by definition, it is also possible to substitute for v_j in (1) and (2) to obtain:

$$Lp = \frac{\Sigma p_t q_o}{\Sigma p_o q_o} \qquad (3)$$

and

$$Lq = \frac{\Sigma p_o q_t}{\Sigma p_o q_o} \qquad (4)$$

Expressions (1) and (3) are algebraically identical with each other, as are (2) and (4).

16.17. Paasche price and volume indices are defined reciprocally to Laspeyres indices by using the values of the later period t as weights and a harmonic average of the relatives instead of an arithmetic average. A Paasche index (P_p or P_q) is defined as follows:

$$P_p = \frac{\Sigma v_t}{\Sigma v_t \cdot p_o/p_t} = \frac{\Sigma p_t q_t}{\Sigma p_o q_t} \qquad (5)$$

and

$$P_q = \frac{\Sigma v_t}{\Sigma v_t \cdot q_o/q_t} = \frac{\Sigma p_t q_t}{\Sigma p_t q_o} \qquad (6)$$

When a time series of Paasche indices is compiled, the weights therefore vary from one period to the next.

16.18. The Paasche index may also be interpreted as the reciprocal of a "backward looking" Laspeyres: that is, the reciprocal of a "Laspeyres" index for period o that uses period t as the base period. Because of this reciprocity between Laspeyres and Paasche indices there are important symmetries between them. In particular, the product of a Laspeyres price (volume) index and the corresponding Paasche volume (price) index is identical with the proportionate change in the total value of the flow of goods or services in question, that is:

$$Lp \cdot P_q = \frac{\Sigma p_t q_o}{\Sigma p_o q_o} \frac{\Sigma p_t q_t}{\Sigma p_t q_o} = \frac{\Sigma v_t}{\Sigma v_o} \qquad (7)$$

and

$$Lq \cdot P_p = \frac{\Sigma p_o q_t}{\Sigma p_o q_o} \frac{\Sigma p_t q_t}{\Sigma p_o q_t} = \frac{\Sigma v_t}{\Sigma v_o} \qquad (8)$$

This relationship can be exploited whenever the total values for both periods are known. When both Σv_t and Σv_o are known, one or the other out of a complementary pair of Laspeyres and Paasche indices can be derived indirectly. For example,

$$Lq = \frac{\Sigma v_t/\Sigma v_o}{P_p} \qquad (9)$$

and

$$P_q = \frac{\Sigma v_t/\Sigma v_o}{Lp} \qquad (10)$$

Thus, the Laspeyres volume index can be derived indirectly by dividing the proportionate change in values by the Paasche price index, a procedure described as price deflation. As it is usually easier, and less costly, to calculate direct price than direct volume indices, it is common to obtain volume measures indirectly both in national accounts and economic statistics generally.

Values at constant prices

16.19. Consider a time series of Laspeyres volume indices, namely:

$$\frac{\Sigma p_0 q_0}{\Sigma p_0 q_0}, \frac{\Sigma p_0 q_1}{\Sigma p_0 q_0} \dots \frac{\Sigma p_0 q_t}{\Sigma p_0 q_0} \qquad (11)$$

Multiplying through the series by the common denominator $\Sigma p_0 q_0$ yields the constant price series:

$$\Sigma p_0 q_0, \Sigma p_0 q_1 \dots \Sigma p_0 q_t \qquad (12)$$

The relative movements from period to period for this series are identical with those of the associated Laspeyres volume indices given by (11), the two series differing only by a scalar. Constant price series of the kind illustrated by (12) are easy to understand and used extensively in national accounts. The term volume "measure" is used to cover both time series of monetary values at constant prices and the corresponding series of volume index numbers.

3. The relationship between Laspeyres and Paasche indices

16.20. Before considering other possible formulas, it is necessary to establish the behaviour of Laspeyres and Paasche indices *vis-à-vis* each other. In general, a Laspeyres index tends to register a larger increase over time than a Paasche index:

that is, in general

$$\text{both } L_p > P_p \text{ and } L_q > P_q \qquad (13)$$

It can be shown that relationship (13) holds whenever the price and quantity relatives (weighted by values) are negatively correlated. Such negative correlation is to be expected for price takers who react to changes in relative prices by substituting goods and services that have become relatively less expensive for those that have become relatively more expensive. In the vast majority of situations covered by index numbers, the price and quantity relatives turn out to be negatively correlated so that Laspeyres indices tend systematically to record greater increases than Paasche with the gap between them tending to widen with the passage of time.

The economic theoretic approach to index numbers

16.21. From the point of view of economic theory, the observed quantities may be assumed to be functions of the prices, as specified in some utility or production function. Assuming that a consumer's expenditures are related to an underlying utility function, a cost of living index may then be defined as the ratio of the minimum expenditures required to enable a consumer to attain the same level of utility under the two sets of prices. It is equal to the amount by which the money income of a consumer needs to be changed in order to leave the consumer as well off as before the price changes occurred. This amount depends not only on the consumer's preferences, or indifference map, but also on the initial level of income and expenditures of the consumer. The value of the theoretic index is not the same for different consumers with a different set of preferences, nor even for the same consumer starting from different income levels.

16.22. The following conclusions may be drawn about the relationships between Laspeyres, Paasche and the underlying theoretic cost of living indices:

(a) The Laspeyres index provides an upper bound to the theoretic index. Suppose the consumer's income were to be increased by the same proportion as the Laspeyres index. It follows that the consumer must be able to purchase the same quantities as in the base period and must therefore be at least as well off as before. However, by substituting products that have become relatively less expensive for ones that have become relatively more expensive the consumer should be able to obtain a higher level of utility. This substitution will set up a negative correlation between the price and quantity relatives. As the consumer can thereby attain a higher level of utility, the Laspeyres price index must exceed the theoretic index;

(b) Similarly, the Paasche index can be shown to provide a lower bound to the theoretic index based on the later period. The reasoning behind this runs along the same lines as that just used for the Laspeyres index.

16.23. While these conclusions show that the Laspeyres and Paasche indices provide upper and lower bounds to the corresponding theoretic indices, it must be noted that two theoretic indices are involved and not one. The theoretic index depends upon the situation in the base period and income level which are not the same in the two periods. However, if it can be assumed that the preferences of the consumer are homothetic—i.e., if each indifference curve is a uniform enlargement, or contraction, of each other—the two theoretic indices coincide. In this case, the Laspeyres and Paasche indices provide upper and lower bounds to the same underlying theoretic index. This is still not sufficient to identify the latter. In order to do this it is necessary to go one step further by specifying the precise functional form of the indifference curves. As early as 1925 it was proved that if the utility function can be represented by a homogeneous quadratic function (which is homothetic) Fisher's Ideal Index (F) is equal to the underlying theoretic index. Although a special case, this result has had a considerable influence on attitudes towards index numbers.

16.24. Fisher's Ideal Index (F) is defined as the geometric mean of the Laspeyres and Paasche indices, that is:

$$F_p = \left(L_p \cdot P_p\right)^{1/2} \qquad (14)$$

and

$$F_q = \left(L_q \cdot P_q\right)^{1/2} \qquad (15)$$

Fisher described this index as "ideal" because it satisfies various tests that he considered important, such as the "time reversal" and "factor reversal" tests. The time reversal test requires that the index for t based on o should be the reciprocal of that for o based on t. The factor reversal test requires that the product of the price index and the volume index should be equal to the proportionate change in the current values, $\Sigma v_t / \Sigma v_o$. Laspeyres and Paasche indices on their own do not pass either of these tests. On the contrary, assuming the relationships given in (13) hold, it follows from (7), (8) and (13) that:

$$L_p \cdot L_q > \Sigma v_t / \Sigma v_o \qquad (16)$$

while

$$P_p \cdot P_q < \Sigma v_t / \Sigma v_o \qquad (17)$$

so that neither index passes the factor reversal test.

16.25. The Fisher index therefore has a number of attractions that have led it to be extensively used in general economic statistics. However, it is worth noting that it also has some disadvantages, some practical, some conceptual:

(a) The Fisher index is demanding in its data requirements as both the Laspeyres and the Paasche indices have to be calculated, thereby not only increasing costs but also possibly leading to delays in calculation and publication;

(b) The Fisher index is not so easy to understand as Laspeyres or Paasche indices which can be interpreted simply as measuring the change in the value of a specified basket of goods and services;

(c) The particular preference function for which Fisher provides the exact measure of the underlying theoretic index is only a special case;

(d) The Fisher index is not additively consistent. As explained below, it cannot be used to create an additive set of "constant price" data.

16.26. Although the underlying theoretic index may be unknown, the Fisher index seems likely to provide a much closer approxi-

mation to it than either the Laspeyres or Paasche indices on their own. However, the Fisher index is not alone in this respect. It has been shown that any symmetric mean of the Laspeyres and Paasche indices is likely to approximate the theoretic index quite closely, the Fisher index being only one example of such a symmetric mean.

16.27. The notion of symmetry can be extended to describe any index that attaches equal weight or importance to the two situations being compared. Another important example of a symmetric index is the Tornqvist, or translog, index (T) the volume version of which is defined as follows:

$$T_p = \prod \left\{ (q_t / q_o)^{1/2(s_0 + s_t)} \right\} \qquad (18)$$

where s_o and s_t denote the share of the total values ($v / \Sigma v$) accounted for by each product in the two periods. The Tornqvist index is a weighted geometric average of the quantity relatives using arithmetic averages of the value shares in the two periods as weights. The Tornqvist price index is obtained by replacing the quantity relatives (q_t / q_o) in (18) by price relatives (p_t / p_o).

16.28. The Tornqvist index is commonly used to measure volumes changes for purposes of productivity measurement. When the production possibilities being analysed can be represented by a homogeneous translog production function, it can be shown that the Tornqvist index provides an exact measure of the underlying theoretic volume index. Thus, the Tornqvist index, like the Fisher index, provides an exact measure under certain very specific circumstances. Both indices are examples of "superlative indices": i.e., indices that provide exact measures for some underlying functional form that is "flexible", the homogeneous quadratic and homogeneous translog functions being particular examples of such flexible functional forms.

16.29. The Tornqvist index, like the Fisher, utilizes information on the values in both periods for weighting purposes and attaches equal importance to the values in both periods. For this reason, its value may be expected to be close to that of an average of the Laspeyres and Paasche indices, such as the Fisher, especially if the index number spread between them is not very large. The difference between the numerical values of the Tornqvist and Fisher indices is likely to be small compared with the difference between either of them and the Laspeyres or Paasche indices.

16.30. Thus, economic theory suggests that, in general, a symmetric index that assigns equal weight to the two situations being compared is to be preferred to either the Laspeyres or Paasche indices on their own. The precise choice of symmetric index—whether Fisher, Tornqvist or other superlative index—may be of only secondary importance as all the symmetric indices are likely to approximate each other, and the underlying theoretic index, fairly closely, at least when the index number spread between the Laspeyres and Paasche is not very great.

D. Chain indices

1. The rebasing and linking of indices

16.31. It is convenient to start by considering the example of a time series of Laspeyres volume indices on a fixed base period and its associated series of values at constant prices. In the course of time, the pattern of relative prices in the base period tends to become progressively less relevant to the economic situations of later periods to the point at which it becomes unacceptable to continue using them to measure volume measures from one period to the next. It may then be necessary to update the base period and to link the old series to the series on the new base period.

16.32. For a single index taken in isolation linking is a simple arithmetic operation. However, within an accounting framework it is not possible to preserve the accounting relationships between an aggregate and its components while at the same time linking the aggregate and its components separately. The difficulties involved are best explained by referring to the numerical example given in table 16.1.

16.33. Part I of the table presents the underlying price, quantity and value data for two products, A and B, and the aggregate (A+B). It is assumed that constant price series are calculated for periods 0 to 10 using period 0 prices, with a change of base year in period 10. Constant price data for periods 10 onwards are calculated at period 10 prices. The resulting constant price data, and the Laspeyres volume indices for the aggregate, are shown in part II of the table. The question to be addressed is the best way to link these two *sets* of data as a whole.

16.34. Assuming it is desired to present a continuous run of "constant price" data from period 0 to period 15, there are several ways in which such data could be compiled. One possibility is to scale down the constant price data from periods 10 to 15 (calculated at period 10 prices) to the general level of prices in period 0 by multiplying through by a constant equal to $\Sigma p_0 q_{10} / \Sigma p_{10} q_{10}$. This ensures that there is no break in continuity for the aggregate when the weights are switched from period 0 prices to period 10 prices. It yields a set of data which, from period 10 onwards, is expressed at the general price level of period 0 but at the relative prices of period 10. This solution is illustrated in part III of the table.

16.35. The difficulty with this solution is apparent from the table. In period 10 in which the link occurs two different sets of relative prices have to be used. As a result, discontinuities are introduced into the "constant price" series for A and B at the point at which the switch is made from one set of relative prices to the other. For this reason, the linked measures for A and B do not reflect the underlying volume movements. For example, the ratio of the "constant price" figure for A in period 15 to the corresponding value in period 0, namely 71.9/30 = 2.40, is very different from the actual change in the quantity of A, namely 15/5 = 3.

16.36. The same difficulties would arise if the series before the link were to be scaled up to the general price level of period 10. As illustrated in part IV of table 16.1 the constant price data valued at the prices of period 0 can be scaled up to the prices of period 10 by multiplying by the constant $\Sigma p_0 q_{10} / \Sigma p_0 q_0$. Discontinuities are again created for A and B at the point at which the switch is made from one set of relative prices to the other. The ratio of the "constant price" for A in period 15 to that in period 0 is 135/56.4 = 2.39 which again is very different from the actual quantity change, 3.

16.37. In order to preserve the volume movements at each level of aggregation, components have to be linked as well as the aggregates. This procedure is followed in parts V and VI of table 16.1. In part V the linked values are at the constant prices of period 0 while in part VI they are at the constant prices of period 10. The linked volume movements for A and B reflect the underlying quantity changes, while the linked volume movements for the aggregate A + B take account of the change in weights in period 10. The problem that emerges with this method is that the constant price values for the components do not add up to the constant price values of the aggregates after the series have been linked. This can be seen in part V for the linked values of period 15 at prices of 0 and in part VI for the linked values of period 0 at prices of 15. In other words when every series at each level of aggregation is individually linked, the resulting constant price data are not additively consistent after the linking has taken place.

16.38. When data are not additively consistent, as in the last column of part V and the first column of part VI, there is a discrepancy between the sum of the components and the corresponding aggregate at each individual level of aggregation. One way of eliminating the discrepancy would be to distribute it in proportion to the components. For example, the figures of 45 and 80 in the first column could be scaled down 42.9 and 74.6 to make them add to 116.5, the required total. However, this would automatically distort the volume comparisons for both A and B in period 0 as compared with periods 10 and 15. Alternatively, the total for (A+B) could be adjusted to make it equal to the sum of the components, i.e., 125 instead of 116.5. By distorting the volume comparisons at the aggregate level, however, this would defeat the main purpose of the exercise.

16.39. A choice has to be made between the two different methods illustrated in the table. The first approach, using the scalar adjustment as illustrated in parts III and IV of the table, preserves additive consistency at the expense of distorting the linked comparisons at a detailed level. The second approach, illustrated in parts V and VI, preserves the validity of the linked comparisons at each level of aggregation at the cost of destroying additive consistency. The volume movements for the overall aggregate are the same in both cases. On balance,

Table 16.1. The rebasing and linking of volume indices and series at constant prices: a numerical example

I. The basic data

Product	Period 0			Period 10			Period 15		
	p_0	q_0	v_0	p_{10}	q_{10}	v_{10}	p_{15}	q_{15}	v_{15}
A	6	5	30	9	12	108	11	15	165
B	4	8	32	10	11	110	14	11	154
A+B	–	–	62			218			319

II. Laspeyres

Product	Base year 0		Base year 10	
	Period 0	Period 10	Period 10	Period 15
	p_0q_0	p_0q_{10}	$p_{10}q_{10}$	$p_{10}q_{15}$
A	30	72	108	135
B	32	44	110	110
A+B	62	116	218	245
Index	100	187.1	100	112.4
Linked index (0)	100	187.1	187.1	210.3
Linked index (10)	53.4	100	100	112.4

III. Linking by scaling down values from periods 10 to 15 by ratio $\Sigma p_0 q_{10}/\Sigma p_{10} q_{10} = 116/218$

Product	Actual values		Scaled down to 0 price level	
	p_0q_0	p_0q_{10}	$p_{10}q_{10}$	$p_{10}q_{15}$
A	30	72	57.5	71.9
B	32	44	58.5	58.5
A+B	62	116	116	130.4
Linked index	100	187.1	187.1	210.3

IV. Linking by scaling up values from periods 0 to 10 by ratio $\Sigma p_{10} q_{10}/\Sigma p_0 q_{10} = 218/116$

Product	Scaled up to 10 price level		Actual values	
	p_0q_0	p_0q_{10}	$p_{10}q_{10}$	$p_{10}q_{15}$
A	56.4	135.3	108	135
B	60.1	82.7	110	110
A+B	116.5	218	218	245
Linked index	53.4	100	100	112.4

Table 16.1   The rebasing and linking of volume indices and series at constant prices: a numerical example (*cont.*)

V.   Linking individual series at prices of period 0

Product	$p_0 q_0$	$p_0 q_{10}$	$p_0 q_{15}$ (linked)
A	30	72	90
B	32	44	44
A+B	62	116	130.4
Linked index	100	187.1	210.3

VI.   Linking individual series at prices of period 10

Product	$p_{10} q_0$ (linked)	$p_{10} q_{10}$	$p_{10} q_{15}$
A	45	108	135
B	80	110	110
A+B	116.5	218	245
Linked index	53.4	100	112.4

the second method seems preferable, given that the main purpose is to obtain good price and volume measures.

16.40. When the base year is updated for constant price series in national accounts, the problem is how to present data for years prior to the new base year. In practice, the method illustrated in part VI of the table is usually followed which preserves the integrity of the volume movements at each level of aggregation at the cost of destroying additivity for years prior to the new base year. The question of how to deal with the resulting discrepancies is considered further below.

2. Rebasing and linking each period

Introduction

16.41. If the objective is to measure the actual movements of prices and volumes from period to period indices should be compiled only between consecutive time periods. Changes in prices and volumes between periods that are separated in time are then obtained by cumulating the short-term movements: i.e., by linking the indices between consecutive periods together to form "chain indices". Such chain indices have a number of practical as well as theoretical advantages. For example, it is possible to obtain a much better match between products in consecutive time periods than between periods that are far apart, given that products are continually disappearing from markets to be replaced by new products, or new qualities. Chain indices are also being increasingly demanded by economists and others for analytical purposes and are being in-

creasingly used for special purpose indices, such as consumer price indices, in order to have indices whose weighting structures are as up-to-date and relevant as possible.

Chain Laspeyres and Paasche indices

16.42. In order to understand the properties and behaviour of chain indices in general, it is necessary to establish first how chain Laspeyres and Paasche indices behave in comparison with fixed base indices. A chain Laspeyres volume index connecting periods 0 and n is an index of the following form:

$$L_q^c = \frac{\Sigma p_o q_1}{\Sigma p_o q_o} \cdot \frac{\Sigma p_1 q_2}{\Sigma p_1 q_1} \cdot \ldots \cdot \frac{\Sigma p_{t-1} q_t}{\Sigma p_{t-1} q_{t-1}} \cdot \ldots \cdot \frac{\Sigma p_{n-1} q_n}{\Sigma p_{n-1} q_{n-1}} \quad (19)$$

A chain Paasche volume index P_q^c is obtained by adding 1 to each of the price subscripts in (19). Laspeyres and Paasche price indices are obtained by interchanging the *p*'s and *q*'s in the expressions for the volume indices.

16.43. In general, Laspeyres indices, whether volume or price, tend to increase more (or decrease less) than Paasche indices, but if fixed base indices are replaced by chain indices, the index number spread between Laspeyres and Paasche is likely to be greatly reduced. The relationship between a fixed base index and the corresponding chain index is not always the same, however, as it must depend upon the paths followed by individual prices and quantities over time.

16.44. If individual prices and quantities tend to increase or decrease monotonically over time it can be shown that the chain Laspeyres will tend to increase less than the fixed weight

Laspeyres while the chain Paasche will tend to increase more than the fixed Paasche. In these circumstances, therefore, chaining will reduce the index number spread, possibly almost eliminating it.

16.45. On the other hand, if individual prices and quantities fluctuate so that the relative price and quantity changes occurring in earlier periods are reversed in later periods, it can be shown that the chain Laspeyres may increase faster than the fixed base Laspeyres, while the chain Paasche may increase less than the fixed Paasche. In this case, the index number spread is increased by chaining, thereby accentuating the problem of choice of formula. It is possible to give a simple demonstration of this effect.

16.46. Suppose that the changes in prices and quantities that occur between the base period 0 and some intervening period t are subsequently reversed so that by the time the final period n is reached all the individual prices and quantities have returned to their initial levels in period 0. As the prices and quantities for period n are identical with those in period 0, it would be reasonable to require the price and volume indices for period n based on period 0 to be unity. The direct Laspeyres and Paasche for period n based on period 0 would clearly both be unity in these circumstances. However, a chain Laspeyres (or Paasche) that used the intervening period t as a link would not be unity. The chain volume index is given the following expression:

$$\frac{\Sigma p_0 q_t}{\Sigma p_0 q_0} \cdot \frac{\Sigma p_t q_n}{\Sigma p_t q_t}$$

If $q_n = q_0$ by assumption for every product, then the chain index can be written as:

$$\frac{\Sigma p_0 q_t}{\Sigma p_0 q_0} \cdot \frac{\Sigma p_t q_0}{\Sigma p_t q_t} = L_q / P_q$$

where L_q and P_q are the Laspeyres and Paasche volume indices for period t based on period 0. As L_q may be expected to be greater than P_q, it follows that the chain Laspeyres is greater than unity (and therefore greater than the direct Laspeyres for period n on period 0). This reflects the fact that a Laspeyres index does not satisfy Fisher's "time reversal" test. The more the prices and quantities in period t diverge from those in periods 0 and n (i.e., the more the prices and quantities fluctuate), the greater the difference between L_q and P_q, and hence the more the chained Laspeyres volume index exceeds unity in this example.

16.47. If the whole process is repeated again and again, the chain Laspeyres volume index linking successive rounds together will drift further and further away from unity, even though the prices and quantities keep returning to their initial values by assumption. Such drifting is a signal that the circumstances are not appropriate for a chain index. When the sets of relative

prices and quantities in two time periods are similar to each other they should be compared directly and not indirectly via another period whose relative prices and quantities are very different. A chain Laspeyres, or Paasche, index should not be used if the chaining involves an economic detour; i.e., linking through a period, or periods, in which the sets of relative prices and quantities differ more from those in both the first and the last period than the latter do from each other.

16.48. Conversely, a chain index should be used when the relative prices in the first and last periods are very different from each other and chaining involves linking through intervening periods in which the relative prices and quantities are intermediate between those in the first and last periods. Relative prices and quantities are described as intermediate when they may be approximated by some average of those in the first and last periods. This will happen when the opening prices and quantities are transformed into those of the final period by the gradual accumulation of successive changes which tend to be in the same direction. In this case, the individual links in the chain are strong as they involve comparisons between situations that are very similar to each other.

16.49. On balance, situations favourable to the use of chain Laspeyres and Paasche indices over time seem more likely than those that are unfavourable. The underlying economic forces that are responsible for the observed long-term changes in relative prices and quantities, such as technological progress and increasing incomes, do not often go into reverse. However, when data are collected more frequently than once per year, regular fluctuations occur in certain monthly or quarterly data as a result of seasonal factors affecting the supply or demand for individual goods or services. Applying the conclusions reached above suggests that if it is desired to measure the change in prices or volumes between a given month, or quarter, and the same month, or quarter, in the following year, the change should be measured directly and not through a chain index linking the data over all the intervening months, or quarters. As noted above, even if the prices and quantities for a particular month, or quarter, were to be identical with those in the previous year, a chained Laspeyres volume index could not be expected to return to its previous level. Chaining seasonal data that are not adjusted for seasonal fluctuations is not desirable and fixed weight indices would be preferable. This does not preclude the use of chain indices to measure year to year changes in the corresponding annual data.

Chain Fisher or Tornqvist indices

16.50. As explained in the previous section, the index number spread between Laspeyres and Paasche indices may be greatly reduced by chaining when prices and quantities move smoothly over time, even if the cumulative changes in the relative prices and quantities are quite large in the long run leading to a wide spread between the direct Laspeyres and Paasche. Indeed, in the limit, as the time paths of prices and quantities converge on steady exponential rates of increase or decline, the chain Laspeyres and Paasche converge on a single chain index.

16.51. When the index number spread can be reduced by chaining, the choice of index number formula assumes less significance as all relevant index numbers lie within the upper and lower bounds of the Laspeyres and Paasche indices. Nevertheless, there may still be some advantages to be gained by choosing an index such as the Fisher or Tornqvist that treats both periods being compared symmetrically.

16.52. Such indices are likely to more closely approximate the theoretic indices based on underlying utility or production functions even though chaining may reduce the extent of their advantages over their Laspeyres or Paasche counterparts in this respect. A chained symmetric index, such as Fisher or Tornqvist, is also likely to perform better when there are fluctuations in prices and quantities. The example given in the previous section showed that if all the price and quantity changes that occur between period 0 and t are subsequently reversed between t and n, the chain Laspeyres linking 0 to n through t does not return to unity. In other words, Laspeyres indices do not satisfy Fisher's time reversal test. However, the Fisher index does satisfy this test and returns to unity in the circumstances postulated. It may be conjectured that, in general, chain Fisher indices are likely to yield results that are more acceptable in the presence of fluctuations. While it remains desirable to avoid economic detours when compiling chain indices (i.e., linking through periods with very different economic structures) chain Fisher indices are likely to be much less sensitive to such detours than chain Laspeyres or Paasche indices.

Chaining and data coverage

16.53. One major practical problem in the construction of index numbers is the fact that products are continually disappearing from markets to be replaced by new products as a result of technological progress, new discoveries, changes in tastes and fashions, catastrophes of one kind or another, etc. Thus, it is not possible to compile price and quantity relatives for every product available in one or another period. In such situations the best that can be done is to compile price or quantity relatives for as many products as possible and then to assume that either the price or the volume changes for the remaining products, which include products available in only one of the two periods, are the same as for some similar product, or group of products, for which price or quantity relatives can be calculated. In general, it would be more reasonable to assume equality of price than volume changes, given that some quantities are zero in one or other period.

16.54. In a time series context, the overlap between the products available in the two periods is almost bound to be greatest for consecutive time periods (except for sub-annual data subject to seasonal fluctuations). The amount of price and quantity information that can be utilized directly for the construction of

the price or volume indices is, therefore, likely to be maximized by compiling chain indices linking adjacent time periods. Conversely, the further apart the two time periods are, the smaller the overlap between the ranges of products available in the two periods is likely to be, and the more necessary it becomes to resort to indirect methods of price comparisons based on assumptions. Thus, the difficulties created by the large spread between the direct Laspeyres and Paasche indices for time periods that are far apart are compounded by the practical difficulties created by the poor overlap between the sets of products available in the two periods.

Additivity and chaining

16.55. Additivity is a property pertaining to a set of interdependent index numbers related by definition or by accounting constraints. An aggregate is defined as the sum of its components. Additivity requires this identity to be preserved when the values of both an aggregate and its components in some reference period are extrapolated over time using a set of volume index numbers. Although desirable from an accounting viewpoint, additivity is actually a very restrictive property. As already noted, Laspeyres volume indices are additive because extrapolating the base period values by Laspeyres volume indices is equivalent to revaluing quantities in later periods by the same set of base period prices. Additivity implies that, at each level of aggregation, the volume index for an aggregate takes the form of a weighted arithmetic average of the volume indices for its components that uses their base period values as weights. This requirement virtually defines the Laspeyres index. Other volume indices in common use are therefore not additive.

16.56. As already shown, a single link is sufficient to destroy additivity in the linked data expressed in value terms even when additive indices such as Laspeyres volume indices, are linked together. If, therefore, chain volume indices are converted into time series of values by using the indices to extrapolate the values of the base period, components fail to add to aggregates in later periods. For this reason it is common to publish the data only in the form of index numbers. However, this procedure cannot be recommended in general because it may merely conceal the problem from users who may be unaware of the breakdown in additivity and its consequences. Even if they are aware of the non-additivity, they are not able to assess its seriousness for the kinds of analysis on which they may be engaged if the data are published only in index number form. Users may be confused when the index for an aggregate is patently not a weighted arithmetic average of those for its components and may wrongly conclude that there must be errors in the data.

16.57. A perverse form of non-additivity occurs when the chain index for the aggregate lies outside the range spanned by the chain indices for its components, a result that may be regarded as intuitively unacceptable by many users. This case cannot be dismissed as very improbable. In fact, it may easily occur when the range spanned by the components is very narrow and it has been observed on various occasions. In any case, publishing data only in the form of index numbers and not as values means abandoning any attempt to construct accounts at constant prices.

16.58. When base year values are extrapolated by chain volume indices there are effectively three ways of dealing with the ensuing non-additivity. The first is simply to publish the non-additive "constant price" data as they stand without any adjustment. This method is transparent and indicates to users the extent of the problem. Users may, or may not choose to eliminate the discrepancies for analytical purposes, choosing whatever method they consider most appropriate for their purposes. Some countries prefer to publish unadjusted non-additive data for these reasons. The second possibility is to distribute the discrepancies over the components at each level of aggregation. This is equivalent to methods V and VI in the table. As already explained, this procedure is not without its cost as the volume movements for the components are distorted as a result. For certain types of analysis such distortion could be a serious disadvantage. On balance, it would seem preferable to let users decide whether or not to eliminate the discrepancies so that users mainly interested in volume

changes for particular components are not disadvantaged. A third possibility would be to eliminate the discrepancies by building up the values of the aggregates as the sum of the values of the components at each level of aggregation. This procedure cannot be recommended in general. Not only would it introduce distortions into the volume movements of the aggregates but it would also make the results for the aggregates depend quite arbitrarily on the level of disaggregation distinguished within the accounts. By distorting the volume movements for the aggregates this method would appear to defeat the whole objective of trying to obtain improved volume measures at an aggregate level through chaining.

16.59. Similar considerations have to be taken into account when time series of fixed base Laspeyres volume indices and their accompanying constant price series have to be rebased. As noted above, assuming the rebasing is not carried backwards, the linked data for series prior to the new base year will not be additive. For reasons just given, the transparent procedure is simply to publish the non-additive data without adjustment leaving it to users to decide whether, or how to deal with the resulting discrepancies. This does not preclude the possibility that there may be circumstances in which compilers may judge it preferable to eliminate the discrepancies in order to improve the overall reliability of the data.

E. Volume measures for gross value added and GDP

16.60. The gross value added of an establishment, enterprise, industry or sector is measured by the amount by which the value of the outputs produced by that establishment, enterprise, industry or sector exceeds the value of the intermediate inputs consumed, the goods and services produced and consumed being valued using the same vector of prices: i.e., by:

$$\Sigma pQ - \Sigma pq$$

where the Q's refer to outputs and the q's to intermediate inputs. Value added in year t at current prices is given by:

$$\Sigma p_t Q_t - \Sigma p_t q_t$$

while value added in year t at the prices of the base year is given by:

$$\Sigma p_o Q_t - \Sigma p_o q_t$$

This measure of value added is generally described as being obtained by "double deflation" as it can be obtained by deflating the current value of output by an appropriate (Paasche type) price index and by similarly deflating the current value of intermediate consumption.

16.61. Within an integrated set of price and volume measures such as those relating to the flows of goods and services in the use ma-

trix or an input-output table, gross value added has to be measured by double deflation method. Otherwise, it will not be possible to balance uses and resources identically. However, the measurement of gross value added in year t at the prices of some base year is liable to throw into sharp relief some underlying index number problems. Vectors of prices and quantities are not independent of each other. In practice, relative quantities produced or consumed are functions of the relative prices at the time. If relative prices change, relative quantities will be adjusted in response. A process of production which is efficient at one set of prices may not be very efficient at another set of relative prices. If the other set of prices is very different the inefficiency of the process may reveal itself in a very conspicuous form, namely negative gross value added. Even if the revalued gross value added is not actually negative, the gross operating surplus may change from positive to negative, thereby signalling the fact that the production process would not be used at those prices.

16.62. Thus, the measurement of value added using a vector of prices that is very different from that prevailing at the time the production process is carried out may lead to results that are not very acceptable for analytical purposes. In a time series context, this implies that the relative prices of the base year must not be too divergent from those of the current year, so that base years may have to be updated frequently and some form of chaining used. Chain indices for value added are considered in the next section.

1. Chain indices for value added and GDP

16.63. In order to derive balancing items such as gross value added residually the various elements involved must be additive. Consider the following example:

Let

O_o = the value of output in period o;

I_o = the value of intermediate consumption in period o;

C_t = the chain volume index for output in period t;

B_t = the chain volume index for intermediate consumption in period t.

One possibility would be to measure the change in the volume of value added between periods O and t by extrapolating the base period values of both output and intermediate input by the relevant chain indices, as follows:

$$\frac{O_o C_t - I_o B_t}{O_o - I_o} \qquad (20)$$

However, an index such as (20) would have no clear meaning because the chain indices C_t and B_t are not additive. In addition, its behaviour could be unpredictable and erratic, especially if the difference between O_o and I_o is small compared with their absolute levels. This method must be rejected on both conceptual and practical grounds.

16.64. When chain indices are used for output and intermediate consumption, an additional chain index must be compiled for value added itself. Suppose chain Laspeyres type volume indices are calculated for output and intermediate consumption. A Laspeyres type chain volume index for value added can then be calculated, each link in the chain being defined as follows:

$$L_q^{VA} = \frac{\Sigma p_{t-1} Q_t - \Sigma p_{t-1} q_t}{\Sigma p_{t-1} Q_{t-1} - \Sigma p_{t-1} q_{t-1}} \qquad (21)$$

where the capital letters refer to outputs and the small letters to intermediate inputs. The denominator in (21) is value added in period t-1 while the numerator is obtained by revaluing the outputs and inputs in period t at t-1 prices. Expression (21) can be interpreted as measuring the change in value added between t-1 and t at the prices of t-1. As constant prices are used, the resulting measures are additively consistent.

16.65. A chain volume index for value added can be compiled in this way using Laspeyres type volume indices for each link in the chain. However, in common with all chain indices, it should be noted that the three indices involved—the output index, the input index and the value added index—are not additively consistent among themselves. This can produce counter intuitive and unacceptable results in the long run. For example, for each individual link in the chain it is impossible for the output

index to lie outside the range spanned by the intermediate consumption and value added indices. However, because chain indices are not additively consistent, in the long run the chain index for output may drift outside the range spanned by the other two chain indices. Such cases have been observed and documented.

16.66. It is equally possible, of course, to compile a chain volume index for value added using Paasche type volume indices linking successive periods, each link being defined as follows:

$$P_q^{VA} = \frac{\Sigma p_t Q_t - \Sigma p_t q_t}{\Sigma p_t Q_{t-1} - \Sigma p_t q_{t-1}} \qquad (22)$$

Each link provides an economically meaningful measure of the volume change in value added by using the prices of period t to value output and intermediate consumption in both periods.

16.67. A third possibility is to compile a chain volume index for value added that uses a Fisher volume index for each link—i.e., the geometric mean of the Laspeyres and Paasche indices given by (21) and (22). Such an index may provide the best volume measure of value added from a theoretical point of view. However, the chain Laspeyres index should provide a very close approximation to the chain Fisher in situations in which it is too difficult or time consuming to calculate the Fisher.

2. Single indicators

16.68. As value added at constant prices is equal to the difference between output at constant prices and intermediate consumption at constant prices it is affected by errors of measurement in both series. Assuming that such errors are at least partly random, the errors will tend to be cumulative, making value added extremely sensitive to error, especially in industries or sectors where value added accounts for only a relatively small proportion of the value of the total output. In some cases, it may be better to abandon the attempt to measure value added as the difference between two series subject to error and to try to estimate the volume movements of value added directly using only one time series—i.e., a "single indicator" instead of double deflation. Although single indicators may be biased, they are much less sensitive to error. Over the short run the potential bias involved in using single indicators may be negligible compared with the potential errors in the double deflation estimates.

16.69. If there are good data on gross value added at current prices, one alternative to double deflation is to deflate current value added directly by a price index for gross output. This procedure can be described as single deflation. It is likely to yield a close approximation to the change in value added at constant prices, at least in the short run. Another possible procedure is to extrapolate value added in the base year by a volume index for output. This method is likely to yield similar results to the first method and can be used when data are not available for value added at current prices. The volume index used to extrapolate base year value added can itself be calculated either directly from quantity data or by deflating the current value of output by an appropriate price index. If the data on output at current prices are comprehensive and reliable, the latter method is likely to yield the better estimates.

16.70. The estimation of changes in value added at constant prices by deflating current value added by an output price index or extrapolating base year value added by an output volume index is an acceptable second-best solution when the data available are not sufficiently reliable and robust to permit the use of double deflation. Unfortunately, however, it is sometimes not even possible to obtain satisfactory estimates of price or volume changes for output—for example, in certain market and non-market service industries such as finance, business services, education or defence. In these cases it may be necessary to resort to third-best solutions by estimating movements of value added at constant prices on the basis of the estimated volume changes of the inputs into the industries. The inputs may be total inputs, labour inputs on their own or intermediate inputs on their own. For example, it is not uncommon to find the movement of value added at constant prices estimated by means of changes in compensation of employees at constant wage rates, or even simply by changes in numbers employed, in both market and non-market service industries. Compilers of data may be forced to adopt such expedients, even when there is no good reason to assume that labour productivity remains unchanged in the short- or long-term. Sometimes, volume changes for intermediate inputs may be used: for example, short-term movements of value added at constant prices for the construction industry may be estimated from changes in the volume of building materials consumed—cement, bricks, timber, etc. The use of indicators of this kind may be the only way in which to estimate short-term movements in output or value added, but they are not acceptable over long time periods.

3. GDP volume

16.71. Movements in the volume of GDP are always calculated by recalculating the values of the various components of GDP at the constant prices either of the previous year or of some fixed base year. Thus, the volume measure of GDP is frequently referred to as "GDP at constant prices". When time series are constructed by multiplying the values of the base year by fixed base Laspeyres volume indices, it is appropriate to describe the resulting series as being at the constant prices of the base year. However, when the values of the base year are extrapolated by multiplying them by annual chain volume indices it is no longer strictly correct to describe them in this way. This is reflected by the non-additivity of the resulting data. Nevertheless, the series of values are expressed at the general price level of the base year and it is convenient to continue to de-

scribe them as being "at constant prices". It is preferable to avoid the term "real GDP" as this may suggest the deflation of GDP by some general price not necessarily that of GDP itself.

16.72. Changes in the volume of GDP for the total economy may be calculated from the expenditure side from data on final expenditures and imports. The double deflation method used to measure gross value added at the level of an industry or sector may be applied at the level of the total economy by replacing output and intermediate consumption by final expenditures and imports.

16.73. The conclusions reached above with regard to the measurement of real value added by industry or sector apply equally at the level of the total economy and may be summarized as follows:

(a) The preferred measure of year to year movements of GDP volume is a Fisher volume index; changes over longer periods being obtained by chaining: i.e., by cumulating the year to year movements;

(b) The preferred measure of year to year inflation for GDP is, therefore, a Fisher price index; price changes over long periods being obtained by chaining the year to year price movements: the measurement of inflation is accorded equal priority with the volume movements;

(c) Chain indices that use Laspeyres volume indices to measure year to year movements in the volume of GDP and Paasche price indices to measure year to year inflation provide acceptable alternatives to Fisher indices;

(d) The chain indices for total final expenditures, imports and GDP cannot be additively consistent whichever formula is used, but this need not prevent time series of values being compiled by extrapolating base year values by the appropriate chain indices;

(e) Chain indices should only be used to measure year-to-year movements and not quarter to quarter movements.

16.74. Two further advantages of using chain indices for GDP may be noted. The quality of the inflation measures is greatly improved compared with the year-to-year movements in the implicit Paasche type deflators calculated on a reference period. A second advantage is that chaining avoids introducing apparent changes in growth or inflation as a result of changing the base year. When the base year for a time series of fixed weight Laspeyres type volume indices is brought forward, the underlying trend rate of growth may appear to slow down if the previous base has become very out of date. This slowing down is difficult to explain to users and may bring the credibility of the measures into question.

4. The publication of alternative volume and price series

16.75. Although the preferred measure of real growth and inflation for GDP is a chain Fisher index, or alternatively a chain

Laspeyres or Paasche index, it must be recognized that the lack of additive consistency can be a serious disadvantage for many types of analysis in which the interrelationships between various flows in the economy are the main focus of interest. Most macroeconometric models fall into this category. It is therefore recommended that disaggregated constant price data should be compiled and published in addition to the chain indices for the main aggregates. The need to publish two sets of data that may appear to conflict with each other should be readily appreciated by analysts engaged in macroeconometric modelling and forecasting. Users whose interests are confined to a few global measures of real growth and inflation can be advised to utilize the chain indices and ignore the more detailed constant price estimates.

16.76. Constant price series have nevertheless to be rebased in the course of time. In general, constant price series should not be allowed to run for more than five, or at the most, ten years without rebasing. It is therefore recommended that disaggre-gated constant price data should be published for as many of the flows of goods and services in the System as possible, with a change of base year about every five years. When the base year is changed it is customary to link the data on the old base to the data on the new base rather than to carry the rebasing backwards.

16.77. In effect, the underlying issue is not whether to chain or not but how often to rebase. Sooner or later the base year for fixed weight Laspeyres volume indices and their associated constant price series has to be updated because the prices of the base year become increasingly irrelevant. When the base year is updated, series on the old base have to be linked to those on the new base. Thus, sooner or later additivity is lost as a result of linking (assuming the rebasing is not carried backwards). Long runs of data, therefore, almost inevitably involve some form of chain indices. Annual chaining is simply the limiting case in which rebasing is carried out each year instead of every five or ten years.

F. International price and volume indices

16.78. It is possible to compare prices and volumes between countries using the same general methodology as for intertemporal comparisons within a single country. International volume indices are needed in order to compare levels of productivity or standards of living in different countries, while comparisons of prices can be used to measure purchasing power parities between different currencies.

16.79. However, the theory of index numbers developed in a time series context cannot be applied mechanically to international comparisons simply by replacing the term "period" by the term "country". International comparisons differ in a number of respects:

(a) In time series, it is customary to compare two time periods of the same duration, such as a year. In international comparisons, however, it is not customary to compare areas or regions of equal size. On the contrary, comparisons may be made between economies that are of entirely different orders of magnitude, one perhaps being 10 or 100 times greater than the other. It is as though a volume comparison were to be made between a complete decade and a single year. It is difficult to interpret such data as if they were different points on the same underlying production function. It is also less obvious that two economies of very different sizes should be treated symmetrically;

(b) Countries are also modifiable units. They can be disaggregated into smaller units, such as regions, or aggregated into larger blocks such as free trade areas or economic communities. Price and volume measures are needed for blocks as well as individual countries. In these circumstances, the weight attached to the eco-nomic activities in a country ought to be invariant to whether the country is considered as a group of regions, a unit in itself or as part of a larger international block;

(c) In time series there is continuity between the prices and quantities in successive time periods as the prices and quantities move over time. There is no such continuity between prices and quantities in different countries. In consequence there is no obvious, objective way in which countries can be ordered for purposes of compiling chain indices. Chain indices cannot be expected to play the same role in international comparisons as in intertemporal price and volume measurement.

1. Binary comparisons

16.80. Price and volume indices may be compiled between pairs of countries using the same kinds of index numbers as those used to measure changes between time periods. A Laspeyres type volume index for country B based on country A may be defined as follows:

$$
{}_a^q L_b = \frac{\Sigma v_a \cdot q_b / q_a}{\Sigma v_a} = \frac{\Sigma p_a q_b}{\Sigma p_a q_a} \tag{23}
$$

The fact that the prices in the two countries may be expressed in different currency units is immaterial as only the prices and values in country A are used. The exchange rate between the two countries is irrelevant and plays no part in the comparison. Volume indices such as (23) may be calculated for any flow of goods and services but in practice they have been calculated mainly for total final domestic expenditure and its components—household final consumption expenditure, government final consumption expenditure, and gross fixed capital formation. It is, of course, equally possible to utilize the prices and values in country B as weights by defining a Paasche type volume index for B based on A as follows:

$$\underset{a}{\overset{q}{P}}\underset{b}{} = \frac{\Sigma v_b}{\Sigma v_b \cdot q_a/q_b} = \frac{\Sigma p_b q_b}{\Sigma p_b q_a} \qquad (24)$$

16.81. Given the complementary relationships between Laspeyres and Paasche price and volume indices noted earlier, it follows that the Laspeyres volume index for B based on A can be derived indirectly by deflating the ratio of the values in B and A, each expressed in their own currencies, by the Paasche price index for B based on A. This Paasche index is defined as follows:

$$\underset{a}{\overset{p}{P}}\underset{b}{} = \frac{\Sigma v_b}{\Sigma v_b \cdot p_a/p_b} = \frac{\Sigma p_b q_b}{\Sigma p_a q_b} \qquad (25)$$

The individual price relatives, p_a/p_b, that enter into the calculation of (25) are ratios of the prices of the same products in the two countries. It is much less easy to ensure that the same product is being priced in different countries than to collect prices for the same product in different time periods within the same country. By careful specification and identification of products, however, price relatives can be calculated directly from information collected in price surveys in different countries, but there is little doubt that it is more difficult to compile reliable international than intertemporal price relatives.

Purchasing power parities

16.82. In an international index such as (25), the prices in each country are quoted in its own currency units. Each of the individual price relatives p_b/p_a can, therefore, be interpreted as measuring the number of units of B's currency that are needed in B to purchase the same quantity of an individual good or service as 1 unit of A's currency will purchase in A. This ratio is usually described as the purchasing power parity (PPP) between the two currencies for the particular good or service in question. Thus, a weighted harmonic average of the individual PPPs such as (25) is better described as a Paasche type PPP index than a price index. It is, of course, equally possible to calculate the Laspeyres type PPP index for B based on A using the expenditures in country A as weights.

16.83. In practice, PPP indices are mainly used to derive international volume indices by using them to deflate ratios of values in national currencies. They also have considerable intrinsic interest in themselves. They have the same dimensions as exchange rates and may be directly compared with the latter. Dividing a PPP index by the corresponding exchange rate yields a price index that is similar to an intertemporal price index. Such an index shows the average percentage by which

the prices of goods and services in country B, when converted into A's currency at the current exchange rate, exceed, or fall below, the prices of the same goods and services in country A. Such information is useful for individuals or institutional units moving from one country to another or engaged in economic activities within both countries. As the PPPs typically relate to domestic final expenditures, they are not designed for the analysis of international flows of goods and services but may still be of considerable interest for the analysis of foreign trade.

16.84. There is a systematic tendency, observed in many empirical investigations, for the domestic price level to be positively correlated with the volume of per capita GDP. As price levels may vary considerably between countries, comparisons of per capita GDP in a common currency using exchange rates must not be interpreted as measuring volume differences only. Such differences in per capita GDP are likely to reflect differences in domestic price levels as well as difference in volumes. Thus, differences in per capita GDP based on exchange rates tend to exceed the differences in the volumes of per capita GDP, especially when comparisons are made between developed and developing countries with very different standards of living.

The spread between Laspeyres and Paasche indices

16.85. Intertemporal price and volume comparisons tend to be confined either to adjacent time periods or to periods that are not very far apart. The differences between the patterns of relative prices and quantities for two different time periods for the same country tend, therefore, to be relatively small compared with those found between different countries, especially between countries with different standards of living, cultures and climates. International price and quantity relatives also tend to be negatively correlated. Institutional units in a country tend to purchase relatively more of goods and services that are relatively cheap in that country compared with other countries. This negative correlation, when combined with substantial differences in the patterns of relative prices, is capable of generating a large spread between the Laspeyres and Paasche indices, both for prices and volumes. For example, the Laspeyres volume index for country B based on country A using A's prices has been observed to be more than twice as large as the corresponding Paasche index using B's prices. Direct quantitative comparisons between economic situations that have little in common with each other are inherently difficult, not only in terms of finding sufficient common data on which to base a meaningful comparison, but also from a conceptual and theoretical viewpoint. Indeed, there may come a point at which it ceases to be useful to attempt such comparisons, although some analysts and policy makers nevertheless may insist on trying to make them.

16.86. Given the existence of such large index number spreads between the Laspeyres and Paasche indices, it is inevitable that some average of the two, such as Fisher's index, should be widely used for international comparisons. Fisher indices appeal particularly to third parties, such as international or supra-national organizations, that do not assign priority to the prices or expenditure patterns in either of the two countries.

2. Multilateral comparisons

16.87. The need for multilateral international comparisons may arise for various reasons: for example, when an international organization needs to know the relative sizes of the GDPs of all of its member countries or when aggregates for blocks of countries are needed. Such aggregates can also serve as norms by which the situations of individual member countries can be appraised. In these cases the block constitutes an entity in its own right with its own characteristics. Unique, objective rankings of the volumes of GDP, or per capita GDP, for all the countries in the block require multilateral measures.

Transitivity

16.88. Consider a group of n countries A, B, C, D, etc. As binary comparisons of volumes and prices may be made between any pair of countries, the total number of possible binary comparisons is equal to $n(n-1)/2$. Let the price, or volume, index number for country j based on country i be written as $_iI_j$. A set of indices is said to be transitive when the following condition holds for every pair of indices in the set:

$$_iI_j \cdot {_jI_k} = {_iI_k} \qquad (26)$$

This condition implies that the direct (binary) index for country k based on country i is equal to the indirect index obtained by multiplying the direct (binary) index for country j based on country i by the direct (binary) index for country k based on country j. The indirect index is, in fact, the chain index connecting k and i using j as the link country. If the entire set of indices is transitive, the indirect indices connecting pairs of countries are always equal to the corresponding direct indices. In practice, none of the standard indices in common use—such as Laspeyres, Paasche or Fisher—is transitive.

16.89. Transitivity is not important in a time series context because time periods form an ordered sequence. For this reason, there is little interest in direct comparisons between all possible pairs of time periods. Direct comparisons tend to be confined either to comparisons with a selected base period, typically the first period in the sequence (leading to fixed base Laspeyres or Paasche indices) or to comparisons between consecutive time periods (leading to chain indices). Comparisons between other possible pairs of periods are not usually needed or undertaken.

16.90. However, no one country in a group of countries has the same status as the first period in a time series. There is usually no good economic reason why one particular country should be singled out to assume the role of base country. Moreover, the choice of base can be much more critical in an international

context as patterns of relative prices and quantities are capable of differing much more between countries than between successive time periods within the same country. In general, the use of a single country as base country is not likely to be acceptable to users when the results are so sensitive to the subjective choice of the country to act as base.

16.91. The objective is to find a multilateral method that generates a transitive set of price and volume measures while at the same time assigning equal weight either to all countries or to all economic activities wherever they take place. There are two quite different approaches that may be used. The first achieves transitivity by using the average prices within the block to calculate the multilateral volume indices. The second starts from the binary comparisons between all possible pairs of countries and transforms them in such a way as to impose transitivity.

The block approach

16.92. The block approach assigns priority to the economic characteristics of the block as a whole. The most widely used method in this category is one in which the average prices of the block are used to revalue quantities in all countries in the block. This automatically ensures transitivity. The volume index for country B relative to country A is therefore defined as:

$$_a\mathrm{GK}_b = \frac{\Sigma \bar{p} q_b}{\Sigma \bar{p} q_a} \qquad (27)$$

The average price $\bar{p}$ for each individual good or service is defined in the normal way as its total value in the block, expressed in some common currency, divided by its total quantity:

$$\bar{p} = \frac{\sum\limits_j c_j p_j q_j}{\sum\limits_j q_j} \qquad (28)$$

where the summation is over the different countries in the block. The term c_j in expression (28) is a currency convertor, that could be either a market exchange rate or a PPP, that is used to convert each $p_j q_j$ into the common currency. In the limit, the block consists of all countries in the world. The use of average world prices has certain attractions, including simplicity and transparency, both from an economic and a statistical viewpoint. The use of world prices ensures that volume comparisons are not affected by the way in which blocks of countries are defined, by the subsequent inclusion or exclusion of countries from a particular block, or by the way in which countries may be grouped hierarchically to form regional blocks. It facilitates the aggregation of data for different countries that make up regional blocks and comparisons between the aggregate data for such blocks.

16.93. The most common block method is the Geary Khamis (GK) method in which the currency convertors used in (28) are the

PPPs implied by the volume indices defined by (27). In this method, the average prices and PPPs are interdependent being defined by an underlying set of simultaneous equations. In practice, they can be derived iteratively. The first step is to use exchange rates as currency convertors to calculate an initial set of average prices and then to use the resulting volume indices to derive the implied set of PPPs. The latter are then used to calculate a second set of average prices, volume indices and PPPs, etc. This iterative process converges quickly. Alternatively, the PPPs and average prices can be obtained directly by solving the underlying set of simultaneous equations.

16.94. The average prices defined by (28) play the same role in international comparisons as the constant prices of the base period play in a time series of Laspeyres volume indices on a fixed base. The use of constant prices ensures that the resulting volume indices between all pairs of countries must be transitive: clearly,

$$\frac{\Sigma \bar{p} q_k}{\Sigma \bar{p} q_i} = \frac{\Sigma \bar{p} q_j}{\Sigma \bar{p} q_i} \cdot \frac{\Sigma \bar{p} q_k}{\Sigma \bar{p} q_j} \qquad (29)$$

whatever average prices are used.

16.95. A block method such as the GK method has the following advantages:

(a) The block of countries is recognized as an entity in itself with its own vector of relative prices that is used for volume measurements within the block;

(b) The use of a single vector of prices ensures that the resulting volume measures, and associated implicit PPPs, are all transitive;

(c) The volume measures are additively consistent and can be presented in value terms using the average prices of the block expressed in the common currency in a user friendly way;

(d) Because the same vector of prices is used for all countries, it is possible to compare the relative amounts of resources allocated for different purposes in different countries, such as the shares of GDP devoted to gross fixed capital formation, or to expenditures on health, education or research and development.

16.96. On the other hand it can be argued that the volume comparisons for individual aggregates are not all optimal. The difficulty is that relative prices and quantities in some countries are bound to diverge more than others from the averages for the block as a whole. Suppose country A's relative prices are close to the average for the block while country B's diverge because B is atypical. Country B might, for example, be relatively rich or relatively poor compared with the rest of the block. When the average prices for the block are used, the volume index for B on A is likely to be close to a Laspeyres index based on A and, therefore, greater than a symmetric binary index, such as

Fisher's index. This may be considered a disadvantage for the two countries considered in isolation although it cannot be assumed that symmetric binary measures are optimal in a multilateral context. The fact that symmetric binary measures are intransitive shows that they are mutually inconsistent from the point of view of the block as a whole.

The binary approach

16.97. An alternative approach to the calculation of a set of multilateral volume measures and PPPs is a start from the binary comparisons between all possible $n(n-1)/2$ pairs of countries. If each binary comparison is considered in isolation, the preferred measure is likely to be a Fisher.

16.98. Fisher indices are not transitive but it is possible to derive from them a set of n-1 transitive indices that resemble the original Fisher indices as closely as possible, using the traditional criterion of least squares for this purpose. Minimizing the deviations between the original Fisher indices and the desired transitive indices leads to the so-called EKS formula proposed independently by Eltetes, Kovecs and Sculz.

16.99. The EKS index utilizes all the indirect indices linking country i and country k as well as the direct index between them. The indirect volume index between i and k via country j is a chain index that uses country j as the link country: that is, if $_iF_j$ is the Fisher volume index between countries i and j, the indirect index between i and k that uses j as the link is then the index $_iF_j \cdot _jF_k$. The EKS index between countries i and k is the geometric average of the direct index between i and k and every possible indirect index connecting countries i and k, in which the direct index is given twice the weight of each indirect index. Transitivity is achieved by involving every other country in the block in the EKS index for any given pair of countries.

16.100. The EKS index is not additively consistent. The consequences are similar to those for chain indices in a time series context. It is not possible to convert the EKS volume indices for an aggregate and its components into a set of values, expressed in a common currency, in such a way that the values of the components of some aggregate add up to the value of that aggregate. Thus, in contrast to the GK method, it is not possible to present the results for a group of countries in the form of a table with countries in the columns and the various final expenditure components in the rows, in which the values add up in the columns as well as across the rows.

16.101. As in the analogous time series case, the discrepancies between the values of the aggregates and the sums of their components could be eliminated in mechanical ways either by distributing the discrepancies over the various components or by defining aggregates as the sums of their components. However, as already explained, such methods distort the comparisons between pairs of countries either for the components or for the aggregates, whichever method is adopted.

The publication of alternative volume and price measures

16.102. The GK and the EKS methods have the same kind of advantages and disadvantages as fixed price volume indices and chain volume indices in a time series context. The EKS index may provide the best possible transitive measure for a single aggregate between a pair of countries, in much the same way as a chain Fisher index may provide the best possible measure of the movement of a single aggregate over time. However, lack of additive consistency is a disadvantage when comparing interrelated aggregates for several countries within an accounting framework: for example, analyses that require information on the relative shares of resources devoted to particular purposes in different countries or analyses that involve differences in relative prices. The GK method is better suited to structural analyses of this kind. It enables individual types of expenditures to be summed across all the countries to obtain aggregates for the block exactly as if the different countries were simply different regions within a country. The GK method recognizes the block as an entity in itself and utilizes its characteristics for measurements within the block. On the other hand, the EKS method adopts an atomistic approach by treating the countries themselves as independent entities whose relative sizes are first determined by comparing each country with each other country and then seeks to disturb these measures as little as possible when transforming them into a set of transitive measures.

16.103. In general, the methods used to compile statistics must be influenced by the purposes for which they are to be used. As in the case of time series of national accounts, it is therefore suggested that two sets of data should be compiled and published:

(a) EKS indices should be compiled for GDP and the main expenditure aggregates—household final consumption expenditures, government final consumption expenditures and gross capital formation. These would consist of both volume and PPP indices. The EKS indices are most useful for purposes of comparing individual aggregates taken in isolation, such as GDP or total household consumption;

(b) GK results should also be published in the form of values at the average prices of the block of countries expressed in some common currency such as the US dollar. As these data are additively consistent, they can be published in full detail for the benefit of users interested in interrelationships between components and aggregates. Such data are needed for structural analyses involving ratios and shares.

16.104. These conclusions are similar to those reached for intertemporal comparisons. In both cases, the best measures for individual aggregates, such as GDP, taken in isolation are provided by indices that are not additive—chain indices in a time series context and EKS indices in an international context. As sets of additive data are also needed for modelling and analytical work, it is also necessary to provide data in the form of values at constant prices—either at the prices of some base period or at the average prices of a block of countries.

G. The treatment of differences and changes in quality

1. Quality differences, price variation and price discrimination

16.105. In general, most types of goods or services, whether simple food products such as potatoes or high technology products such as computers, are available on the market in many different qualities whose physical characteristics differ from each other. For example, potatoes may be old or new, red or white, washed or unwashed, loose or prepacked, graded or ungraded, etc. Unwashed, loose, old red potatoes are clearly different qualities of potatoes from washed, prepacked, new white potatoes. Consumers recognize and appreciate the differences and are prepared to pay different prices.

16.106. The expression "different qualities" is used to cover sets of goods or services whose characteristics are sufficiently different to make them distinguishable from each other from an economic point of view but which are sufficiently similar to each other to be described by the same generic term, such as potato, computer or transportation. Different prices are charged for different qualities of the same kinds of goods or services in much the same way that different prices are charged for goods or services which are generically different from each other and described by different names. Different qualities have to be treated in exactly the same way as different kinds of goods or services.

16.107. Differences in quality that are attributable to differences in the physical characteristics of the goods or services concerned are easily recognized, but not all differences in quality are of this kind. There are other factors which can give rise to differences in quality. For example, goods or services delivered in different locations, or at different times, must be treated as different qualities even if they are otherwise physically identical. These differences stem from the fact that the marginal utility of a particular kind of good or service for purchasers or consumers situated in one location may be very different from that for purchasers in other locations, while the costs of delivering goods or services in different locations also vary. Transporting a good to a location in which it is in greater demand is a process of production in its own right in which the good is transformed into a higher quality good.

16.108. Similarly, goods or services provided at different times of the day or at different periods of the year must be treated as different qualities even if they are otherwise identical. For example, electricity or transport provided at peak times must be treated as being of higher quality than the same amount of electricity or transport provided at off-peak times. The fact that peaks exist shows that purchasers or users attach greater utility to the services at these times, while the marginal costs of production are usually higher at peak times. The different prices or rates charged at peak and off-peak times provide measures of these differences in quality. Similarly, fruit and vegetables supplied out of season must be treated as higher qualities than the same fruit and vegetables in season which are cheaper to produce and of which consumers may be satiated.

16.109. Apart from differences in location or timing there are other factors which may contribute to quality differences. For example, the conditions of sale, or circumstances or environment in which the goods or services are supplied or delivered can make an important contribution to differences in quality. A restaurant meal provided with more attentive service in more luxurious or pleasant surroundings is a higher quality meal than exactly the same food and drink provided with less service in a less pleasant environment. A durable good sold with a guarantee, or free after-sales service, is higher quality than the same good sold without guarantee or service. Thus, the same goods or services sold by different kinds of retailers, such as local shops, specialist shops, department stores or supermarkets may have to be treated as different qualities for these kinds of reasons. Alternatively, the goods may be envisaged as being parts of different composite products which incorporate different amounts, or kinds, of retail services. Purchasers in large supermarkets may have to find, select and transport their own purchases to check-outs, but they are also offered the advantage of greater choice and the opportunity to reduce the amount of time spent shopping by making purchases in bulk. All these kinds of factors introduce qualitative differences.

16.110. In general, therefore, it is necessary to pay attention to differences in the situation, or conditions, in which goods and services are supplied, as prima facie these may all be expected to introduce qualitative differences into the goods or services supplied. In economic theory it is generally assumed that whenever a difference in price is found between two goods and services which appear to be physically identical there must be some other factor, such as location, timing, conditions of sale, etc., which is introducing a difference in quality. Otherwise, it can be argued that the difference could not persist, as rational purchasers would always buy lower priced items and no sales would take place at higher prices. In most cases, therefore, differences in prices at the same moment of time must be taken as prima facie evidence that the goods or services concerned represent different qualities of the same general kind of good or service. As explained in the first section of this chapter, this implies that if there is a switch towards

higher priced—i.e., higher quality—goods or services, this will be recorded as an increase in volume and not price.

16.111. Nevertheless, it must be questioned whether the existence of observed price differences always implies corresponding differences in quality. There are strong assumptions underlying the standard argument which are seldom made explicit and are often not satisfied in practice: for example, that purchasers are well informed and that they are free to choose between goods and services offered at different prices.

16.112. First, purchasers may not be properly informed about existing price differences and may therefore inadvertently buy at higher prices. While they may be expected to search out for the lowest prices, costs are incurred in the process. Given the uncertainty and lack of information, the potential costs incurred by searching for outlets in which there is only a possibility that the same goods and services may be sold at lower prices may be greater than the potential savings on expenditures, so that a rational purchaser may be prepared to accept the risk that he or she may not be buying at the lowest price. Situations in which the individual buyers or sellers negotiate, or bargain over prices, provide further examples in which purchasers may inadvertently buy at a higher price than may be found elsewhere. On the other hand, the difference between the average price of a good purchased in a market or bazaar in which individual purchasers bargain over the price and the price of the same good sold in a different type of retail outlet, such as a department store, should normally be treated as reflecting differences in quality attributable to the differing conditions under which the goods are sold.

16.113. Secondly, purchasers may not be free to choose the price at which they purchase because the seller may be in a position to charge different prices to different categories of purchasers for identical goods and services sold under exactly the same circumstances—in other words, to practise price discrimination. Economic theory shows that sellers have an incentive to practise price discrimination as it enables them to increase their revenues and profits. However, it is difficult to discriminate when purchasers can retrade amongst themselves; i.e., when purchasers buying at the lowest prices can resell the goods to other purchasers. While most goods can be retraded, it is usually impossible to retrade services, and for this reason price discrimination is extensively practised in industries such as transportation, finance, business services, health, education, etc., in most countries. Lower prices are typically charged to purchasers with low incomes, or low average incomes, such as pensioners or students. When governments practise or encourage the practice of price discrimination it is usually justified on welfare grounds, but market producers also have reasons to discriminate in favour of households with low incomes as this may enable them to increase their profits. Thus, when different prices are charged to different consumers it is essential to establish whether or not there are in fact any quality differences associated with the lower prices. For example, if senior citizens, students or schoolchildren are charged lower fares for travelling on planes, trains or buses, at whatever time they choose to travel, this must be treated as pure price discrimination. However, if they are charged lower fares on condition that they travel only at certain times, typically off-peak times, they are being offered lower quality transportation.

16.114. Thirdly, buyers may be unable to buy as much as they would like at a lower price because there is insufficient supply available at that price. This situation typically occurs when there are two parallel markets. There may be a primary, or official, market in which the quantities sold, and the prices at which they are sold are subject to government or official control, while there may be a secondary market—a free market or unofficial market—whose existence may or may not be recognized officially. If the quantities available at the price set in the official market are limited there may be excess demand so that supplies have to be allocated by rationing or some form of queuing. As a result, the price on the secondary or unofficial market will tend to be higher. It is also possible, but less likely, that lower prices are charged on the secondary or unofficial market, perhaps because the payment of taxes on products can be evaded in such a market.

16.115. For the three reasons just given, i.e., lack of information, price discrimination or the existence of parallel markets, identical goods or services may sometimes be sold to different purchasers at different prices. Thus, the existence of different prices does not always reflect corresponding differences in the qualities of the goods or services sold.

16.116. When there is price variation for the same quality of good or service, the price relatives used for index number calculation should be defined as the ratio of the weighted average price of that good or service in the two periods, the weights being the relative quantities sold at each price. Suppose, for example, that a certain quantity of a particular good or service is sold at a lower price to a particular category of purchaser without any difference whatsoever in the nature of the good or service offered, location, timing or conditions of sale, or other factors. A subsequent decrease in the proportion sold at the lower price raises the average price paid by purchasers for quantities of a good or service whose quality is the same and remains unchanged, by assumption. It also raises the average price received by the seller without any change in quality. This must be recorded as a price and not a volume increase.

16.117. It may be difficult to distinguish genuine price discrimination from situations in which the different prices reflect differences in quality. Nevertheless, there may be situations in which large producers—especially large service producers in fields such as transportation, education or health—are able to make the distinction and provide the necessary information. If there is doubt as to whether the price differences constitute price discrimination, it seems preferable to assume that they reflect quality differences, as they have always been assumed to do so in the past.

2. Changes in quality over time

16.118. Goods and services, and the conditions under which they are marketed, are continually changing over time, with some goods or services disappearing from the market and new qualities or new goods or services replacing them. In principle, the price relatives that enter into the calculation of intertemporal price indices should measure pure price changes by comparing the prices of identical goods and services in different time periods. If the qualities of goods or services being compared are not identical, there are effectively four options:

(a)   To ignore the change in quality and compile a price relative as if no difference in quality existed;

(b)   To omit the items in question and not compile a price relative for them;

(c)   To adjust the observed price of the new quality for the change in quality which has taken place;

(d)   To treat the two qualities as if they were two separate goods and to estimate their prices in the periods in which they are not sold.

16.119. The first option should be avoided. Ignoring changes in quality is likely to introduce serious biases of unknown size, or even direction, into the measured price or volume indices. The second option is also not to be recommended. It will also tend to introduce bias. If goods or services are omitted from the calculation of price indices that are intended to be comprehensive in coverage, their omission is equivalent to assuming that their rate of price change is the same as the average for the items covered by the indices. However, items subject to quality change tend to be atypical and unrepresentative, so that assuming that their prices change at the same rate as for goods or services whose characteristics do not change is highly questionable.

16.120. The third and fourth options are clearly to be preferred although they are not always easy to implement in practice. Some methods that may be employed are explained in the following paragraphs.

16.121. The adjustment for quality change may be based on the relative prices of the two qualities on the market when there is at least one period when both qualities are on sale on the market at the same time. Suppose, for example, that one quality is replaced by another as follows:

Period	Old quality	New quality
0	p_0	
t	p_t	p_t^*
n		p_n^*

In period 0, only the old quality is available while in period n only the new quality is available. If both are available simultaneously in some intervening period t, the ratio of their relative prices in period t, namely p_t/p_t^*, may be used as a measure of the relative volumes of the old and the new qualities. Thus, the price relative connecting the new quality in period n with the old quality in period 0, after adjusting for the difference in their qualities, is given by:

$$P_n*(p_t/p_t*)/p_0$$

This is equivalent to constructing a price relative connecting p_n* with p_0 by splicing the price change for the new quality to the price change for the old quality, using period t as the link period: that is,

$$(p_n*/p_t*)(p_t/p_0)$$

16.122. This procedure may be used to deal with quality changes in all those cases in which the new and the old qualities overlap on the market for a significant amount of time. If the relative prices of the two qualities do not remain constant during this time, some kind of average of their relative prices may be used to estimate their relative qualities.

16.123. When the two qualities are not produced and sold on the market at the same time it becomes necessary to resort to indirect methods of quantifying the change in quality between the old and new qualities. Producers of many kinds of durable goods, such as automobiles, deliberately stop producing the old model when the new model is introduced on the market. Such producers typically vary the characteristics of their product—size, performance, style, etc.—in order to stimulate demand without changing the general nature of the product or the purposes for which it is used. In such cases it is necessary to estimate what would be the relative prices of the old and new models, or qualities, if they were produced and sold on the market at the same time and to use the estimated relative prices as measures of the relative qualities.

16.124. One possibility is to use the estimated relative costs of production as estimates of their relative prices and hence their relative qualities. It may often be feasible for producers to provide such estimates, The observed change in price between the old and the new qualities may then be adjusted as follows. Suppose the price of the new quality or model is x per cent higher than the price of the old, while it is estimated that the new quality would cost y per cent more to produce than the old, then the price relative connecting the old and new qualities, adjusted for the change in their qualities, is equal to

$$\frac{100+x}{100+y}$$

16.125. The characteristics of buildings and other structures are so variable that it may be almost impossible to find identical buildings and structures being produced in successive periods of time. In these circumstances, instead of trying to compare the prices of actual buildings or structures in one period with those of other, possibly not very similar, buildings or struc-

tures in another period, it may be better to specify a small number of hypothetical and relatively simple standard buildings and structures and to estimate what their prices would be in each of the periods. The specifications of these standard buildings or structures are chosen on the advice of construction experts who are also asked to estimate what their prices would be in each of the periods. Alternatively, the experts can be asked to estimate the costs of construction in both periods, the price relatives being assumed to be equal to the ratios of the construction costs. Construction experts are frequently asked to make such estimates in practice. This method has been used successfully to make international comparisons of the prices of buildings and structures as well as for estimating price changes over time.

The use of the hedonic hypothesis

16.126. A more general and powerful method of dealing with changes in quality is to make use of the so-called "hedonic" hypothesis to estimate the prices of qualities or models that are not available on the market in particular periods, but whose prices in those periods are needed in order to be able to construct price relatives. The hedonic hypothesis assumes that the prices of different models on sale on the market at the same time are functions of certain measurable characteristics such as size, weight, power, speed, etc. Provided there are enough observations—i.e., provided enough different models are on sale at the same time—regression methods can be used to estimate by how much price varies in relation to each of the characteristics. The resulting regression coefficients can be used to predict the prices of models with different mixes of characteristics that are not actually on sale in the period in question.

16.127. Suppose, for purposes of argument, that the price of a model is a function of only one characteristic such as size. Suppose further, that the following sizes are on sale in two different periods of time:

Period 0	Period t
s_1	
s_2	
	s_3
s_4	
	s_5
	s_6

By calculating the regression of price on size in each period, it should be possible to obtain a reliable estimate of the price of s_3 in period 0 and s_4 in period t, thus enabling at least two price relatives to be calculated connecting periods 0 and t. Furthermore, if it is deemed legitimate to make estimates outside the range spanned by the observations in each of the periods, it may be possible to estimate prices for sizes s_5 and s_6 in period o, and for sizes s_1 and s_2 in period t, thereby enabling price relatives to be calculated for all six sizes. The validity of making estimates outside the range of observations cannot be settled a priori: it depends on the nature of the data and the form of the relationship. If the underlying functional form is the same in both periods it may be possible to pool the two sets of observations to obtain improved estimates of the price coefficient, using a dummy variable to distinguish observations in one period from those in the other. Similarly, the choice of functional form—linear, log-linear, log-log, etc.—must be settled empirically, case by case. In general, the choice of appropriate statistical technique has to depend on the nature of the data set in each case.

16.128. The hedonic hypothesis has been used with some success to deal with changes in the quality of computers over time. The quality of a computer depends mainly on two basic characteristics: its capacity and its speed of operation. Regressions of prices on those two characteristics have made it possible to estimate the prices of models in periods in which they were not actually on sale. For example, new models are continually being produced with much greater capacities and speeds than were available in earlier periods. By using regression methods, however, it becomes possible to estimate what their prices would have been if they had been produced in earlier periods, thereby enabling price relatives to be estimated that refer to the same kinds of models in different time periods. By using such methods, it has been shown that the price of a computer of unchanged quality—i.e., with a given capacity and speed—tended to fall dramatically during the 1970s and 1980s.

16.129. The hedonic hypothesis may be used for any goods or services whose prices depend mainly on a few basic characteristics and for which sufficient numbers of different models, or qualities, are on sale on the market at the same time. In addition to computers it may be used for other high technology goods whose characteristics are both measurable and varying significantly over time. It has also been used for housing by regressing house prices (or rents) on characteristics such as area of floor space, number of rooms, location, etc. The method has been used not only for intertemporal price measurements but also international comparisons.

H. Choice between direct and indirect measurement of prices and volumes

16.130. When independent, reliable and comprehensive data are available at current prices it is not necessary to calculate both the price and the volume measures as one can be derived indirectly from the other as explained above. In most cases it is better to calculate the price index directly and to derive the volume index indirectly.

16.131. There are two reasons for this: first, it is usually necessary to estimate the average price or volume change from a selection, or sample, of goods and services, and price relatives tend to have a smaller variance than the corresponding quantity relatives. Thus, the sampling error for a price index tends to be smaller than for a volume index. Secondly, the volume changes associated with new and disappearing products are properly reflected when current values are deflated by price indices. Suppose, for example, that there are some new products which are sold in the later period but not the base period; their quantities are known in both periods (being zero in the base period), whereas their prices are known for only one period, the later period. This quantity information is incorporated in the current value series and is also automatically incorporated in the volume series when the latter is obtained by deflating the current value series. This may be illustrated by a simple numerical example:

Good	P_0	Q_0	P_t	Q_t
1	4	10	6	12
2	–	–	5	2
Current value		40		82

Good 2 is a new good not on the market in period 0. The price and quantity relatives for good 1 are 150 and 120 respectively, while for good 2, the price relative is unknown whereas the quantity relative is plus infinity. This information must be utilized. The best estimate of the price index for both goods is 150, based on good 1 alone. If this is used to deflate the value index covering both goods the derived volume index is

$$\frac{82/40}{1.5} = 1.367$$

This volume index exceeds the quantity relative for good 1 alone because the increase in the quantity of good 2 incorporated in the current value series has been taken into account.

16.132. The above argument rests on the tacit assumption that the values at current prices are obtained from different sources from the price and quantity data and are reliable and comprehensive. However, it may happen that the movements of the series at current prices have been estimated by multiplying together the estimated price and volume movements. Alternatively, estimates of the current values—for example, values of agricultural output—may be made by multiplying estimates of the quantities by estimates of their prices, and not by collecting separate information on the values of goods produced. In such

cases the deflation of current values merely leads back to the original quantity estimates.

I. Non-market goods and services

16.133. The value of the output of non-market goods and services produced by government units or non-profit institutions is estimated on the basis of the total costs incurred in their production, as explained in chapter VI. This output consists of individual goods and services delivered to households as social transfers in-kind or collective services provided to the community as a whole. The fact that such output is valued on the basis of the value of the inputs needed to produce them does not mean that it cannot be physically distinguished from the inputs used to produce it. Nor does it imply that changes in such output over time cannot be distinguished from changes in the inputs. Changes in productivity may occur in all fields of production, including the production of non-market services.

16.134. In principle, volume indices may always be compiled directly by calculating a weighted average of the quantity relatives for the various goods or services produced as outputs using the values of these goods and services as weights. Exactly the same method may be applied even when the output values have been estimated on the basis of their costs of production.

16.135. Of course, the calculation of quantity relatives for the outputs of many kinds of non-market services, especially collective services, presents problems. In the case of health and education services provided as social transfers to individual households, however, the problems are much less, both conceptually and in practice, than for collective services such as public administration or defence. The objective is to measure the quantities of services actually delivered to households. These should not be confused with the benefits or utility derived from those services. For example, individual health services consist of various kinds of consultations and treatments provided to patients, which can be described and documented in considerable detail. Detailed records of such services frequently exist for administrative purposes.

16.136. The output of health services needs to be clearly distinguished from the health of the community. Indeed, one reason for trying to measure the output of health services may be to see the effect of an increase in the volume of health services on the health of the community. This obviously requires a measure of the volume of health services that is different from health itself. It is well-known that there are many other factors such as sanitation, housing, nutrition, education, consumption of tobacco, alcohol and drugs, pollution, etc., whose collective impact on the health of the community may be far greater than that of the provision of health services.

16.137. Similarly, the output of education services is quite different from the level of knowledge or skills possessed by members of the community. Education services consist principally of teaching provided by producers of education services—schools, colleges, universities—to the pupils and students who consume such services. The level of knowledge or skills in the community depends in addition on other factors, such as the amount of study or effort made by consumers of education services and their attitudes and motivation. As in the case of other types of output, when compiling indicators of the output of educational services it is important to distinguish as many different kinds of education service as possible as their relative costs, or qualities, may vary considerably. Moreover, the quality of education services provided may vary over time in the same way as other goods and services. The quality of education services is likely to depend on the amount of resources provided per pupil or student: for example, the numbers of teachers or amount of capital equipment in the form of laboratories, libraries, computers, etc.

16.138. There is no mystique about non-market health or education services which make changes in their volume more difficult to measure than volume changes for other types of output, such as financial or business services or fixed tangible assets. Moreover, changes in their volume are also needed in order to be able to measure volume changes for the actual consumption of households. The same principles apply to the measurement of consumption as to production.

16.139. Measuring changes in the volume of collective services is distinctly more difficult, however, as it is not possible to observe and record the delivery of such services. Many collective services are preventive in nature: protecting households or other institutional units from acts of violence including acts of war, or protecting them from other hazards, such as road accidents, pollution, fire, theft or avoidable diseases. It is difficult to measure the output of preventive services, and this is an area in which further research is needed. In practice, it may not be feasible to avoid using changes in the volumes of inputs into such services as proxies for changes in volumes of outputs, just as it may sometimes be necessary to use changes in inputs as proxies for changes in outputs in certain market industries, such as agriculture or construction.

16.140. When it is not possible to avoid using an input measure as a proxy for an output measure, the input measure should be a comprehensive one and not confined to labour inputs. As explained below, the volume of labour inputs can be measured by compensation of employees valued at the wage and salary rates of the previous year or some fixed base year, the remuneration of each individual type of worker being revalued at the appropriate rate. The volumes of intermediate consumption, consumption of fixed capital and any taxes on production measured at the prices or rates of the previous year or the fixed base year should be added to obtain a comprehensive volume measure covering all inputs. These volume measures can, of course, also be derived by deflating the current values by suitably weighted wage rate, price or tax rate indices.

16.141. A possible alternative method when input measures are used as proxies for outputs is to use a volume measure for labour alone combined with an explicit assumption about changes in labour productivity; for example, that labour productivity grows at 1 per cent per year in the production of the non-market service in question. An assumption of zero productivity growth is the most common one in practice because it is felt to be more neutral, even though it is inevitably somewhat arbitrary. The attention of users should always be drawn to any built-in assumption about the rate of growth of labour productivity which should be stated explicitly, even when it is zero.

J. Scope of price of volume measures in the System

16.142. The price and volume measures considered up to this point relate mainly to flows of goods and services produced as outputs from processes of production. However, it is possible to decompose a few other flows directly into their own price and volume components, the most important of which is compensation of employees.

1. Compensation of employees

16.143. The quantity unit for compensation of employees may be considered to be an hour's work of a given type and level of skill. As with goods and services, different qualities of work must be recognized and quantity relatives calculated for each separate type of work. The price associated with each type of work is the compensation paid per hour which may vary considerably, of course, between different types of work. A volume measure of work done may be calculated as a weighted average of the quantity relatives for different kinds of work weighted by the values of compensation of employees in the previous year or fixed base year. Alternatively, a "price" index may be calculated for work by calculating a weighted average of the proportionate changes in hourly rates of compensation for different types of work, again using compensation of employees as weights. If a Laspeyres type volume index is calculated indirectly by deflating the changes in compensation of employees at current values by an index of the average change in hourly rates of compensation, the latter should be a Paasche type index.

2. Consumption of fixed capital

16.144. Another cost of production and charge against gross value added, namely consumption of fixed capital, may also be measured at the prices of the previous year or some fixed base year. Indeed, when estimates of the gross and net capital stocks are compiled using the perpetual inventory method, an estimate of consumption of fixed capital at the constant prices of some base year is already built into such calculations.

3. Taxes and subsidies on products

16.145. It is also possible to factor taxes or subsidies on products into their own price and volume components because the quantity units on the basis of which such taxes or subsidies are payable can also be used as quantity units to define "tax prices". A tax price is the amount of tax payable per unit of good or service, whether the tax is payable per unit of quantity or *ad valorem*. The tax prices can be used to construct tax price relatives which can then be averaged to obtain "tax price indices" using the values of the amounts paid in tax as weights. A "tax volume index" can be derived indirectly by deflating changes in the total amounts of taxes paid by the appropriate version of the tax price index. A tax volume index is essentially a volume index for a flow of goods and services in which the relative importance of the goods and services is measured not by their relative market prices but the relative amounts of tax paid per product. It shows by how much the receipts from taxes on products change purely in response to changes in the volumes of goods and services subject to tax. Factoring tax receipts into price and volume components may be useful for purposes of fiscal analysis and may also be useful in the context of the input-output table.

4. Net operating surplus

16.146. The net operating surplus is an accounting residual which does not possess quantity and price dimensions of its own. It may also be negative, of course. It is not possible, therefore, to decompose the net operating surplus into its own price and volume components. It is therefore also not possible to calculate the average volume change for all the uses of gross value added shown in the generation of income account.

16.147. Thus, the limit to a set of integrated price and volume measures within the accounting framework of the System is effectively reached with the net operating surplus. It is conceptually impossible to factor all the flows in the income accounts of the System, including current transfers, into their own price and volume components. Of course, any income flow can be deflated by a price index for a numeraire set of goods and services to measure the increase or decrease of the purchasing power of the income over the numeraire, but as explained at the beginning of this chapter, this is quite different from decomposing a flow into its own price and volume components.

K. Measures of real income for the total economy

1. Introduction

16.148. It is possible to deflate any income flow in the accounts, and even a balancing item such as saving, by a price index in order to measure the purchasing power of the item in question over a designated numeraire set of goods and services. By comparing the deflated value of the income with the actual value of the income in the base year, it is possible to determine by how much the real purchasing power of the income has increased or decreased. Income deflated in this way is generally described as "real income".

16.149. In interpreting real incomes two points need to be borne in mind:

(a)   Real incomes are measured with reference to the price level in some selected reference year. Real values cannot exist in isolation: they vary depending upon the choice of reference year;

(b)   Real incomes measure changes in purchasing power over some selected numeraire; they thus also depend upon the choice of numeraire.

16.150. As there may often be no obvious, or uncontroversial choice of numeraire there has always been some reluctance to show real incomes in national accounts on the grounds that the choice of numeraire should be left to the user of the statistics and not the compiler. However, when major changes in prices occur, it can be argued that compilers of statistics are under an obligation to present at least some measures of real income. Not all users of the accounts have the opportunity, inclination or expertise to calculate the real incomes which may be most suited to their needs. Moreover, there is a demand from many users for multi-purpose measures of real income, at least at the level of the economy as a whole and the purpose of this section is to indicate how such measures may be compiled.

2. Trading gains and losses from changes in the terms of trade

16.151. Before considering the various different real income aggregates which may be defined for the total economy, it is necessary to explain the fundamental difference between gross domestic product at constant prices, and real gross domestic income, or real GDI. GDP at constant prices is essentially an output volume measure. It may be calculated at the level of the total economy by a form of double deflation in which imports valued at the basic prices of the previous year, or some fixed base year, are subtracted from total final expenditures valued at the purchasers' prices of the previous year, or the fixed base year. A measure of this kind is essentially a volume measure of the output from domestic production, even though it includes taxes on imports and possibly some other taxes on products that are excluded from the gross values added of resident producers.

16.152. However, the total real income which residents derive from domestic production depends also on the rate at which exports may be traded against imports from the rest of the world. If the prices of a country's exports rise faster (or fall more slowly) than the prices of its imports—i.e., if its terms of trade improve—less exports are needed to pay for a given volume of imports so that at a given level of domestic production goods and services can be reallocated from exports to consumption or capital formation. Thus, an improvement in the terms of trade makes it possible for an increased volume of goods and services to be purchased by residents out of the incomes generated by a given level of domestic production. Real GDI measures the purchasing power of the total incomes generated by domestic production so that when the terms of trade change there may be a significant divergence between the movements of GDP at constant prices and real GDI. The difference between the change in GDP at constant prices and real GDI is generally described as the "trading gain" (or loss). The differences between movements in GDP at constant prices and real GDI are not always small. If imports and exports are large relative to GDP, and if the commodity composition of the goods and services which make up imports and exports are very different, the scope for potential trading gains and losses may be large. This may happen, for example, when the exports of a country consist mainly of a small number of primary products, such as cocoa, sugar or oil, while its imports consist mainly of manufactured products. It can easily be shown that trading gains or losses, T, are measured by the following expression:

$$T = \frac{X - M}{P} - \left(\frac{X}{P_x} - \frac{M}{P_m} \right) \qquad (30)$$

where

X = exports at current prices

M = imports at current prices

P_x = the price index for exports

P_m = the price index for imports

P = a price index based on some selected numeraire.

P_x, P_m and P all equal to 1 in the base year. It can be seen that the term in brackets measures the trade balance calculated at the export and import prices of the reference year whereas the first term measures the actual current trade balance deflated by the numeraire price index. It is perfectly possible for one to have a different sign from the other.

16.153. There is one important choice to be made in the measurement of trading gains or losses, i.e., the selection of the price index P with which to deflate the current trade balance. There is a large but inconclusive literature on this topic, but one point on which there is general agreement is that the choice of P can sometimes make a substantial difference to the results. Thus, the measurement of real GDI can sometimes be sensitive to the choice of P and this has prevented a consensus being reached on this issue.

16.154. It is not necessary to try to summarize here all the various arguments in favour of one deflator rather than another, but it is useful to indicate what are the main alternatives which have been advocated for P. They can be grouped into three classes, as follows:

(a) One possibility is to deflate the current balance, $X-M$, either by the import price index (which has been strongly advocated) or by the export price index, with some authorities arguing that the choice between P_m and P_x should depend on whether the current trade balance is negative or positive;

(b) The second possibility is to deflate the current balance by an average of P_m and P_x: various different kinds of averages have been suggested—simple arithmetic or harmonic averages, or more complex trade weighted averages;

(c) The third possibility is to deflate the current balance by some general price index not derived from foreign trade: for example, the price index for gross domestic final expenditure, or the consumer price index.

16.155. The failure to agree on a single deflator reflects the fact that no one deflator is optimal in all circumstances. The choice of deflator may depend on factors such as whether the current balance of trade is in surplus or deficit, the size of imports and exports in relation to GDP, etc. On the other hand, there is general agreement that it is highly desirable, and for some countries vitally important, to calculate the trading gains and losses resulting from changes in the terms of trade. In order to resolve this deadlock it is recommended to proceed as follows:

(a) Trading gains or losses, as defined in equation (30) above, should be treated as an integral part of the System;

(b) The choice of appropriate deflator for the current trade balances should be left to the statistical authorities in a country, taking account of the particular circumstances of that country;

(c) If the statistical authorities within a country are uncertain what is the most appropriate general deflator P to be used, some average of the import and export price indices should be used, the simplest and most transparent average being an unweighted arithmetic average of the import and export price indices. (This is referred to in the specialist literature on the subject as the Geary method.)

16.156. These proposals are intended to ensure that the failure to agree on a common deflator does not prevent aggregate real income

measures from being calculated. Some measure of the trading gain should always be calculated even if the same type of deflator is not employed by all countries. In those circumstances in which there is uncertainty about the choice of deflator an average of the import and the export price indices is likely to provide a suitable deflator.

3. The interrelationship between volume measures and real income aggregates

16.157. Assuming that measures of trading gains or losses are available, various different real income aggregates may be identified within the System. The links between them are displayed in the following list:

(a) *Gross domestic product at constant prices*: i.e., GDP in the current year valued at the prices, or price level, of the base year obtained by extrapolating (i.e., multiplying) the value of GDP in the base year by the volume index for GDP, whether a fixed weight or a chain index;

plus the trading gain or loss resulting from changes in the terms of trade:

(b) equals: *real gross domestic income*;

plus real primary incomes receivable from abroad

minus real primary incomes payable abroad;

(c) equals: *real gross national income;*

plus real current transfers receivable from abroad

minus real current transfers payable abroad;

(d) equals: *real gross national disposable income* ;

minus consumption of fixed capital at constant prices;

(e) equals: *real net national disposable income.*

16.158. In the above accounting scheme, each aggregate is derived sequentially starting from gross domestic product at constant prices, the volume measure of GDP. The transition from (a) to (b) above has been explained in the previous section. The steps needed in order to move from (b) to (d) above involve the deflation of flows between resident and non-resident institutional units, namely, primary incomes and current transfers received from abroad and paid to abroad. There may be no automatic choice of price deflator, but it is recommended that the purchasing power of these flows should be expressed in terms of a broadly based numeraire, namely the set of goods and services that make up gross domestic final expenditure. In other words, primary incomes and current transfers should both be deflated by a price index for gross domestic final expenditures. This price index should, of course, be defined consistently with the volume and price indices for GDP.

16.159. A possible alternative which could be considered is to use the following accounting framework:

(a)   *Gross domestic product at constant prices* as defined above

plus   imports at constant prices

minus exports at constant prices;

(b)   equals: *gross domestic final expenditures at constant prices,* i.e., final consumption expenditure plus gross capital formation at constant prices

     less consumption of fixed capital at constant prices;

(c)   equals: *net domestic final expenditures at constant prices*

plus   net current receipts from abroad measured in real terms (i.e., deflated by the price index for net domestic final expenditure), namely:

    (i)   Deflated value of the current trade balance (exports *minus* imports);

plus (ii)   Deflated values of primary incomes receivable *minus* primary incomes payable abroad;

plus (iii)   Deflated value of current transfers receivable *minus* current transfers payable abroad;

(d)   equals: *real net national disposable income.*

16.160.   In this framework, all current flows to and from abroad are deflated by a single deflator, that for item (c), i.e., net domestic final expenditures. In effect, this index acts as a general price deflator for all items from row (c) onwards. If there are no satisfactory estimates available for consumption of fixed capital at constant prices so that all expenditure measures have to remain gross, the price index for gross domestic final expenditures may be used instead.

16.161.   This alternative framework has the advantage that the various components of real income are all measured with reference to a single numeraire, the set of goods making up net domestic final expenditures. It is easier, therefore, to grasp the significance of real net national disposable income as its deflator is explicit. The alternative framework measures the trading gain or loss by using the deflator for net domestic final expenditures as the general deflator P, whereas it can be argued that P ought always to be based on flows which enter into foreign trade. There is, for example, a possibility that the implicit trading gain may be negative when there is a positive change in the terms of trade, or vice versa, and this may be considered a serious disadvantage. On balance, therefore, the original framework presented above is to be preferred. However, the guidelines laid down by the System need to be somewhat more tolerant in the domain of real income measurement than elsewhere, and the use of alternative deflators, for what may be considered to be good statistical or economic reasons, is by no means incompatible with the basic philosophy underlying the System, which in certain other fields also (e.g., sub-sectoring the households sector) needs to be implemented flexibly and not rigidly.

XVII. Population and labour inputs

A. Introduction

17.1. The SNA requires a definition of population to express gross domestic product and consumption aggregates in per capita terms. It also requires labour input variables in order to examine productivity.

17.2. Many of the complications in the concepts described here stem from the existence of national boundaries. To facilitate exposition, consideration of these has been postponed to part C of this chapter, which thus starts off without any reference to them, as if a country without any cross-border movement of persons and with no cross-border ownership of enterprises were being considered.

B. Population and labour concepts without national boundaries

17.3. Figure 17.1 summarizes the first part of the chapter. Those concepts which are part of the SNA are in heavy boxes. The formal definitions of these concepts are set out in part C of this chapter.

1. Population and employment

17.4. Population is, in principle, an annual average of frequent head counts, each of which relates to a point in time. (Censuses usually ascertain the number of people present on a specified night.) Thus population is the annual average number of people present. It includes the institutional population, though this is not covered by most labour force surveys.

17.5. The division of the number enumerated at a point in time into three categories, i.e., "employed", "unemployed" and "not in the labour force" depends upon each person's activity (or lack of it) during a reference period (usually a week) ending with the point in time to which the count relates. Employment has been defined by the International Labour Organisation (ILO) in the "Resolution concerning statistics of the economically active population, employment, unemployment and under-employment", adopted by the thirteenth International Conference of Labour Statisticians. No definition is required here, but, as figure 1 indicates, provided that the definitions of employment and of jobs match one another, the average annual number of jobs exceeds the annual average number of persons employed by the average annual number of second, third, etc., jobs. Note that the second, third, etc., jobs of a person may either successively follow one another in a reference week or, as when someone has an evening job as well as a daytime job, run in parallel.

17.6. Employed persons who have more than one job during a reference week can only be classified by industry and by status in employment through the application of some essentially arbitrary convention as to which of their jobs is the most important one. On the practical plane, while household surveys can provide data about either or both of employment and jobs, establishment surveys only provide data about jobs, so data on jobs tend to be more plentiful than data on persons employed.

17.7. Employment does not enter into the System, but jobs do; a job is like a transaction, while an employed person is not.

2. Jobs

17.8. In daily speech, a job is used in two senses: first, as a filled post in an institutional unit, e.g., "B has a job as truck driver with XYZ Company", and, second, to signify the occupation or nature of the activity, e.g., "B's job is driving an XYZ truck". The first of these is relevant here. Thus a job is defined as an explicit or implicit contract between a person and an institutional unit to perform work in return for compensation for a defined period or until further notice. The institutional unit may be the proprietor of an unincorporated enterprise; in this case the person is described as being self-employed and earns a mixed income.

17.9. There are a number of points here which require expansion:

(a) Both employee jobs and self-employment jobs are covered. The distinction between employee and compensation of employees on the one hand, and self-employment and mixed income on the other hand, is set out in chapter VII. Figure 17.2 summarizes part of that discussion;

Figure 17.1. Population and labour concepts

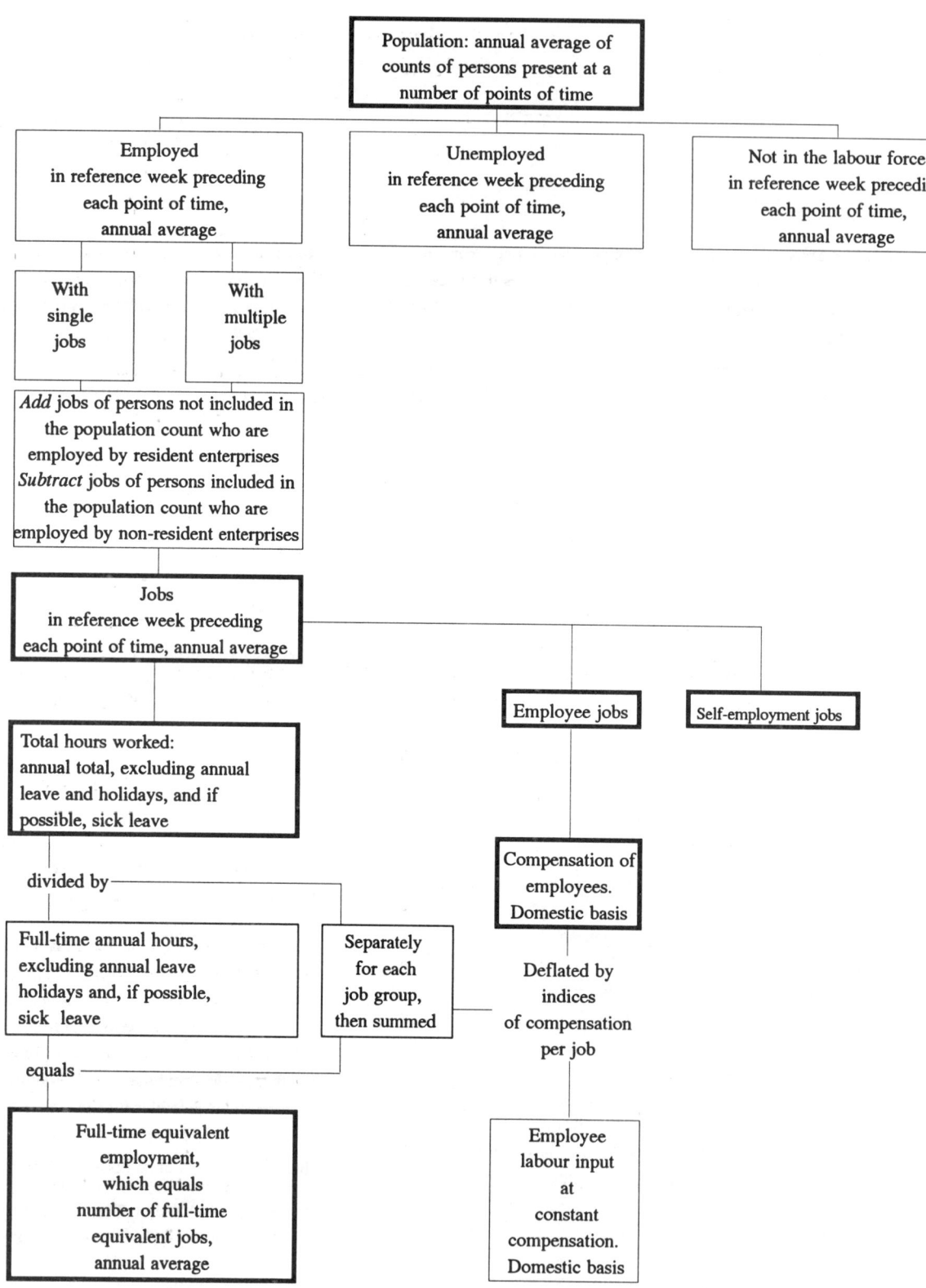

Note: Those concepts which are part of the SNA are in heavy boxes.

Figure 17.2.   Distinguishing between employment as employee and in self-employment

Is B's job with an enterprise an employee or a self-employment job?

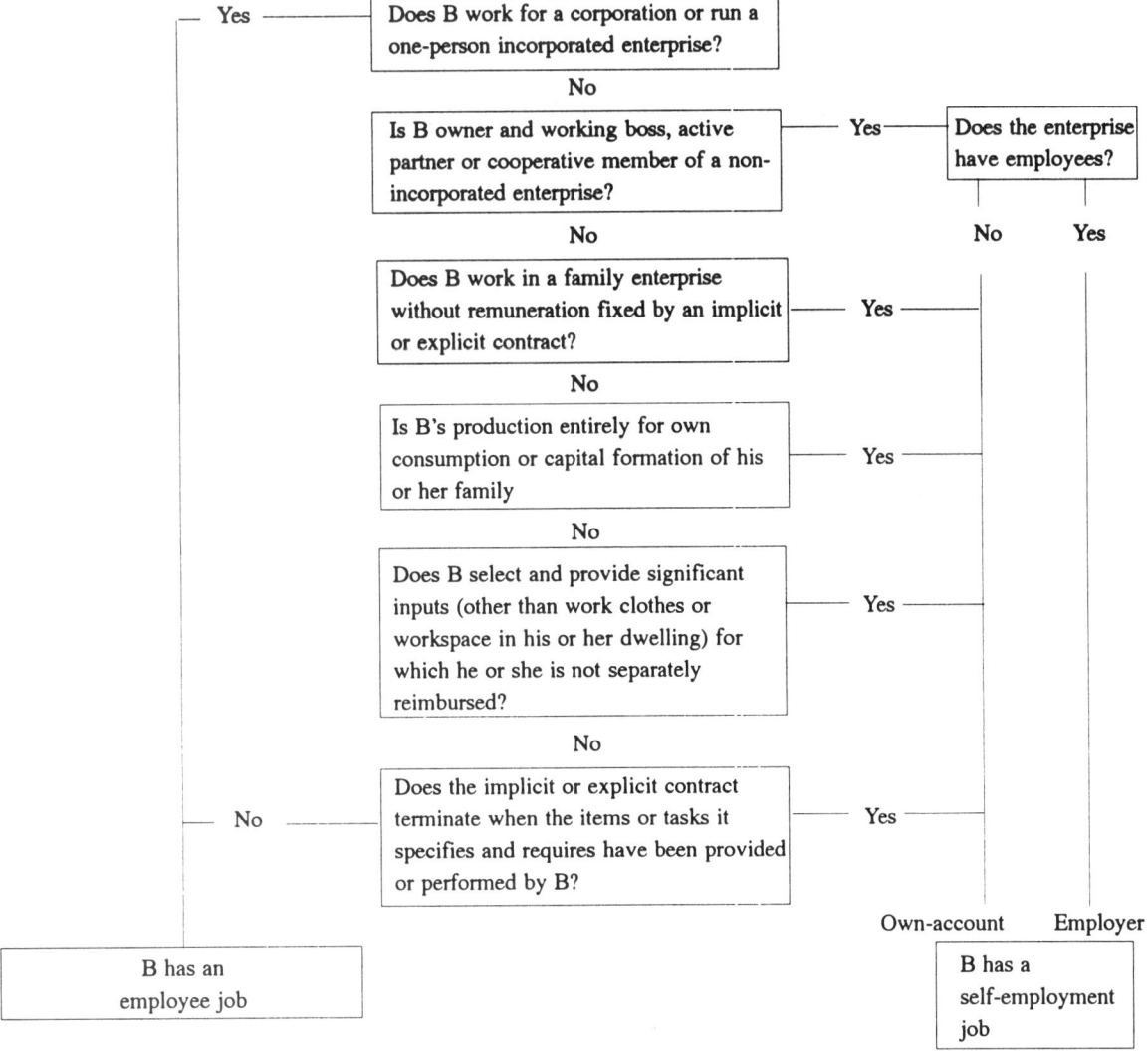

(b)   Work means any activity which contributes to the production of goods or services within the production boundary as defined in chapter VI. The legality of the work and the age of the worker are, in principle, irrelevant;

(c)   Mixed income and the compensation of employees are defined in chapter VII. Compensation differs from labour cost, as defined by the ILO "Resolution concerning statistics of labour cost", adopted by the eleventh International Conference of Labour Statisticians, only in including imputed employer contributions to unfunded social insurance schemes, and in excluding any taxes regarded as labour cost, together with the costs of training, welfare, recruitment and the provision of work clothing;

(d)   The explicit or implicit contract relates to the provision of labour input, not to supplying output of a good or service, which is why it is described as for a defined period or until further notice. A bricklaying job, paid by time or according to the number of bricks laid, is an employee job, while a contract to lay a certain number of bricks for a given payment is not a job; the job is the bricklayer's notional self-employment contract. Similarly, a self-employment job of window-cleaning is regarded as an implicit contract by a person to hire himself or herself to do cleaning work. Quite separately, the person has contracts with customers to provide the service of window-cleaning;

(e)   There is one minor difference between a job as defined here and the category of persons "with a job but not at work" who are considered as employed in the ILO resolution adopted by the thirteenth International Conference of Labour Statisticians, referred to above. This is that, on the ILO definition, the employed may include persons who are not being paid but have a "formal attachment to their job" in the form of "an assurance of return to work ... or an agreement as to the date of return". Such an understanding between an employer and a person on layoff or away on training is not counted as a job in the System.

17.10. Jobs may be classified not only as employee or self-employment, but also according to the standard activity classification.

3. Total hours worked

17.11. Output per job would be an excessively crude measure of productivity and total hours worked is the preferred measure of labour inputs for the System. The ILO "Resolution concerning statistics of hours of work", adopted by the tenth International Conference of Labour Statisticians, defines hours worked as follows:

Statistics of hours worked should include:

(a) Hours actually worked during normal periods of work;

(b) Time worked in addition to hours worked during normal periods of work, and generally paid at higher rates than normal rate (overtime);

(c) Time spent at the place of work on work such as the preparation of the workplace, repairs and maintenance, preparation and cleaning of tools, and the preparation of receipts, time sheets and reports;

(d) Time spent at the place of work waiting or standing-by for such reasons as lack of supply of work, breakdown of machinery, or accidents, or time spent at the place of work during which no work is done but for which payment is made under a guaranteed employment contract;

(e) Time corresponding to short periods of rest at the workplace, including tea and coffee breaks.

Statistics of hours actually worked should exclude:

(a) Hours paid for but not worked, such as paid annual leave, paid public holidays, paid sick leave;

(b) Meal breaks;

(c) Time spent on travel from home to work and vice versa.

17.12. Total hours worked is the aggregate number of hours actually worked during the year in employee and self-employment jobs.

17.13. The truism, for employee jobs, that hours worked equal hours paid less hours paid but not worked, plus hours worked but not paid, is a useful one, since many establishment surveys record

hours paid, not hours worked, so that hours worked have to be estimated for each job group, using whatever information is available about paid leave, etc.

4. Full-time equivalence

17.14. An inferior alternative to expressing labour input in terms of total hours worked is to measure it in terms of full-time equivalent work years. Full-time equivalent employment is the number of full-time equivalent jobs, defined as total hours worked divided by average annual hours worked in full-time jobs.

17.15. The definition does not necessarily describes how the concept is estimated. The method sometimes used, of simply counting all part-time jobs as half a full-time job, is the crudest possible way of making an estimate. Since the length of a full-time job has changed through time and differs between industries, more sophisticated methods which establish the average proportion and average hours of less than full-week full-time jobs in each job group separately are preferable.

17.16. Even if the data are good enough to permit an estimation of total hours worked, full-time equivalent employment should nevertheless also appear in the national accounts. One reason is that this facilitates international comparisons with countries which can only estimate full-time equivalent employment. The other reason is that, since the full-time annual hours of a job group vary through time, the two concepts carry a partially different message. If, for example, more sickness or annual leave is taken, both shortening average annual full-time hours and, *ceteris paribus*, reducing total hours worked, full-time equivalent employment will scarcely change, while total hours worked will fall. So if the former rather than the latter is used as the denominator in calculating productivity changes, productivity will rise less or fall more. A similar point applies to international comparisons. If, however, full-time annual hours did not exclude paid sick leave, but total hours worked continued to do so, more sickness would cause full-time equivalent employment to rise more or fall less than would an equal increase in annual leave, so that productivity would rise less or fall more. This would make good sense—sickness undesirably interferes with production, while annual leave is a desirable alternative to it. But if information on absence from work through sickness is not available for estimating full-time annual hours, it will not be available either for estimating total hours worked.

17.17. In practice, total hours worked and average annual full-time hours may have to be estimated. In many countries, especially for monthly paid employee jobs, only normal or usual hours, any paid overtime, and annual and holiday leave entitlements can be ascertained, and it may be impossible to estimate the subtraction to be made for average sickness leave from either total hours worked or annual full-time hours. This error will not affect full-time equivalent employment if sickness rates in part-time jobs are the same as in full-time jobs, so can be tolerated if it is unavoidable.

17.18. If the reference weeks used in the surveys that provide the data are not fully representative, the best available information on variations throughout the year should be used in estimating data for the year as a whole.

5. Employee labour input at constant compensation

17.19. Total hours worked and full-time equivalent employment are both physical measures of labour input. Output too can usually be measured in physical terms, such as tons or cubic metres, but this is not done in the national accounts, because the basic value per ton or cubic metre varies so much between products that these physical measures lack general economic significance. But compensation per hour or per full-time year of work varies enormously too, so that the physical measures of labour input also lack general economic significance. Their usefulness thus rests either upon the assumption that the mix of different kinds of labour is much the same in the different countries or at the different times examined, or upon their application in a social or political context, where interest centres upon personal welfare rather than upon the economics of production and income generation.

17.20. When output is measured both at current and at constant prices, it is natural to do the same with labour inputs as well as with intermediate inputs. However, mixed income, which is the return to self-employment, cannot be unambiguously divided between the return to labour and the returns to capital and entrepreneurship. For this reason, only the value of employee labour input (and not self-employed labour input) forms part of the System. Note that the measurement of employee labour inputs at current and constant prices is symmetrical with the measurement of output:

(a) Market prices and market compensation are assumed to measure the relative economic importance of different goods, services and jobs; the advantages and disadvantages of this assumption are the same for inputs as for outputs;

(b) Though the constant price and constant compensation concepts are defined as revaluations of quantities at base period prices or compensation levels, they can be estimated in practice as the sum, over all groups, of values at current price or compensation levels, each divided by an appropriate index;

(c) These group indices are estimates, calculated for a representative sample of jobs or of goods or services, with weights reflecting the relative importance of each of the sub-groups represented by a selected and specified job, or by a selected and specified good or service. In other words, a compensation index is constructed like a price index.

17.21. While the value of employee labour input at constant compensation can be estimated by deflation of current values, as mentioned above, the data may also permit the direct approach of multiplying the current number of jobs in each job group by the base-period average annual compensation for jobs in that job group.

C. National boundaries

17.22. The complications that arise from the existence of national boundaries must now be examined. (Similar complications arise for regional accounts from regional boundaries.) Conceptual clarity requires that the everyday concept of a person or firm in a country be replaced by the precise notion of an institutional unit being resident in an economic territory. Residence and economic territory are discussed at length and defined in chapter XIV, in a way which fits together with the concept of gross domestic product.

17.23. Without reproducing these definitions in their entirety, certain major features deserve to be stressed:

(a) A country's military bases and diplomatic premises abroad are part of its economic territory;

(b) The residence of an institutional unit is determined according to the location of its "centre of economic interest" which, for an enterprise is an establishment where it produces over a long period of time and, for a household, its principal residence;

(c) This means that an enterprise producing for one year or more in another economic territory is treated as having a centre of economic interest there. A quasi-corporation is deemed to exist and be resident in that other economic territory;

(d) It also means that persons living and working for one year or more in another economic territory are treated as resident there.

1. Population

17.24. Population is the annual average number of persons present in the economic territory of a country. In this and other definitions, the fact that, by convention, economic territory includes embassies, military bases and ships and aircraft abroad should not be forgotten.

2. Jobs

17.25. Jobs, too, could be looked at in terms of the residence of the employee or self-employed person. For measuring labour input, however, only the residence of the employing or self-employing institutional unit is relevant, because resident producers alone contribute to gross domestic product. Thus the compensation of a person who lives in country C but works in country D is part of the value added of country D although it is part of the national income of country C.

17.26. The principles thus determining the location of jobs apply equally to the territorial scope of total hours worked, of compensation of employees and mixed income, of full-time equivalent employment and of the value of employee labour input at constant compensation. Since these principles are different from those determining the territorial scope of the population, it should be remembered that full-time equivalent employment cannot be compared with population. The jobs held by persons resident in the country's economic territory, which can be looked at in relation to population, are not quite the same as the jobs with employers in the country's economic territory which are those that correspond to labour inputs into domestic production.

Note in particular that:

(*a*) The jobs carried out within a country's economic territory that are not counted are the jobs performed for institutional units resident in other countries which have not already engaged in transactions for a year or more. Thus the work of foreign short-term consultants and repairmen are not counted;

(*b*) Jobs carried out wholly or partly in another economic territory for a domestic institutional unit are included in the domestic count, unless the nature and duration of that employing institutional unit's activity in the other territory are such as to warrant treating it as owning a quasi-corporation located there;

(*c*) The jobs of the staff of international organizations and of local staff of foreign embassies are excluded, since these employing units are not resident. Thus their compensation is not in the gross domestic product, though it is part of national income.

A job in the economic territory of country X is an explicit or implicit contract between a person (who may be resident in another economic territory than that of X) and an institutional unit (which may be itself acting as self-employer) resident in the economic territory of X to perform work in return for compensation (or to earn a mixed income) for a defined period or until further notice.

3. Total hours worked

17.27. Total hours worked in country X is the aggregate number of hours actually worked during the registration period in employee and self-employment jobs within its economic territory,

including

work outside that economic territory for domestic employer institutional units who have no centre of economic interest there,

excluding

work for foreign employer institutional units who have no centre of economic interest within the economic territory of country X.

Hours actually worked are to be interpreted as set out in the ILO definition quoted above.

4. Full-time equivalent employment

17.28. Full-time equivalent employment in country X, which equals the number of full-time equivalent jobs, is its total hours worked divided by average annual hours worked in full-time jobs within its economic territory. Average annual hours are defined in the same way as hours worked.

5. Employee labour input at constant compensation

17.29. Employee labour input at constant compensation of country X is what the current annual compensation of employee jobs would be if it were calculated using the levels of compensation ruling during a selected base period. Division of employee labour input at constant compensation into compensation of employees will yield an implicit compensation deflator comparable with the implicit expenditure deflators of the national accounts.

D. Classifications

17.30. Labour inputs should be classified in the same way that value-added and compensation of employees are classified. The International Standard Classification of All Industrial Activities (ISIC) is the basic classification for these variables in the System and the ISIC is widely used for studies of employment and labour productivity. Labour inputs should, therefore, be classified according to the ISIC. However, the System also provides other classifications that may be useful for particular types of analysis.

17.31. Figure 20.1 in chapter XX suggests the following breakdown:

Rural

Self-employed

    Agricultural

        Small farmers

        Medium farmers

        Large farmers

    Non-agricultural

 Informal, own-account
 Informal, employers
 Formal, own-account
 Informal, employers

Employees

 Agricultural

 Non-agricultural
 Unskilled
 Skilled
 Highly skilled

Urban

Self-employed

 Informal

 Formal

Employees

 Unskilled

 Skilled

 Highly skilled

For some purposes, it may also be useful to classify employees according to the sectors or subsectors in which they are employed—such as households and non-profit institutions serving households (NPISH); public corporations and government; national private corporations; and foreign corporations.

17.32. Table 20.6 in chapter XX provides an alternative classification for employees. This is by sex and four occupational groups—agricultural workers; manual workers; clerical, sales and service workers; professional, managerial; etc.

XVIII. Functional classifications

A. Introduction

18.1. "Functional" classifications are proposed in the System for classifying certain transactions of producers and of three institutional sectors—namely households, general government and non-profit institutions serving households. They are described as "functional" classifications because they identify the "functions"—in the sense of "purposes" or "objectives"—for which these groups of transactors engage in certain transactions. The classifications concerned are:

Classification of individual consumption by purpose

Classification of the functions of government

Classification of the purposes of non-profit institutions serving households

Classification of outlays of producers by purpose.

18.2. The functional classifications serve three purposes. The first is quite specific; as noted in chapter IX, the classification of the functions of government is used to distinguish between collective services and individual consumption goods and services provided by Government. Individual goods and services are treated as social transfers in kind and they are deducted from total consumption expenditure of government to obtain actual collective consumption of government. They are also added to individual consumption expenditure of households to obtain actual individual consumption of households. Social transfers in kind identified by the classification of functions of government code-numbers are shown in table 18.1.

18.3. The second purpose is to provide statistics which experience has shown to be of general interest for a wide variety of analytic uses. For example, classification of individual consumption by purpose shows household expenditure on food, health and education services all of which are important indicators of national welfare; classification of the functions of government shows government expenditure on "merit goods" such as health and education services as well as on "bads" such as defence and prison services; classification of outlays of producers by purpose may provide information on the "externalization" of business services, i.e., on the increasing tendency for producers to buy-in catering, cleaning, transport, auditing and other services which were previously carried out as ancillary activities within the enterprise.

18.4. The third purpose of these functional classifications is to pro-

vide users with the means to recast key aggregates of the System for particular kinds of analyses, some of which are described in chapter XXI. For example:

(a) It can be argued that for several analytic purposes, the SNA definition of gross capital formation is too narrow. In studies of labour productivity, researchers often need a measure of "human capital" which is normally derived from information on past expenditures on education. The four functional classifications therefore identify expenditures on education incurred by households, government, non-profit institutions and producers;

(b) In studying the process of economic growth, researchers sometimes prefer to treat some or all research and development (R and D) expenditures as capital formation rather than as consumption expenditure. Both classification of outlays of producers by purpose and classification of the purposes of non-profit insititutions serving households report R and D separately; classification of the functions of government does not presently identify all R and D undertaken by government but it may be possible to do so in a revised version of this classification;

(c) In studies of household expenditure and saving, some researchers have found it more useful to consider expenditures on consumer durables as capital rather than current expenses. For this reason, classification of individual consumption by purpose provides for the separate identification of expenditures on durable goods;

(d) In studies of the impact of economic growth on the environment, researchers often need information on expenditures undertaken to repair or prevent damage to the environment. "Outlays on pollution abatement and control" is a major heading in classification of outlays of producers by purpose, and classification of the functions of government identifies "Sanitary affairs and services, including pollution abatement and control". It should be noted, however, that certain industry-specific expenditure on pollution control and abatement are included elsewhere in classification of the functions of government without being separately identified.

Table 18.1. Classification of individual consumption by purpose (COICOP)

Categories of COICOP		Individual consumption expenditure P.31	Social transfers in kind (categ. COFOG) D.63	Actual individual consumption P.41
1.	Food, beverages and tobacco			
	1.1 Food			
	1.2 Beverages			
	1.3 Tobacco			
2.	Clothing and footwear			
	2.1 Clothing			
	2.2 Footwear			
3.	Housing, water, electricity, gas and other fuels		* (7.11)	
	3.1 Gross rents			
	3.2 Regular maintenance and repair of dwelling			
	3.3 Other services relating to the dwelling		* (7.31)	
	3.4 Electricity, gas and other fuels			
4.	Furnishings, household equipment and routine maintenance of the house			
	4.1 Furniture, furnishings and decorations, carpets and other floor coverings, and repairs			
	4.2 Household textiles			
	4.3 Heating and cooking appliances, refrigerators, washing machines and similar major household appliances, including fittings and repairs			
	4.4 Glassware, tableware and household utensils			
	4.5 Tools and equipment for the house and garden			
	4.6 Goods and services for routine household			
5.	Health		(05)	
	5.1 Medical and pharmaceutical products and therapeutic appliances and equipment			
	5.2 Non-hospital medical and paramedical			
	5.3 Hospital services			
	5.4 Sickness and accident insurance services			
6.	Transport			
	6.1 Purchase of vehicles			
	6.2 Operation of personal transport equipment			
	6.3 Transport services		* (12.12)	
7.	Leisure, entertainment and culture			
	7.1 Equipment and accessories, including repairs			
	7.3 Newspapers, books and stationery			
8.	Education		(04)	
	8.1 Educational services			
	8.2 Educational materials			
	8.3 Ancillary educational services			
9.	Hotels, cafes and restaurants			
	9.1 Catering			
	9.2 Accomodation services			
10.	Miscellaneous goods and services			
	10.1 Personal care			
	10.2 Personal effects n.e.c.			
	10.3 Communications			
	10.4 Social services		(06)	
	10.5 Financial services n.e.c.			
	10.6 Other services n.e.c.			

* Only part of COFOG category is included.

Table 18.2. Classification of total outlays of government by function (COFOG)

Categories of COFOG	Final consumption expenditure		Gross capital formation P.5	Subsidies D.3	Property income D.4	Other current transfers D.7	Capital transfers D.9	Securities other than shares F.3	Loans F.4	Shares and other equity F.5	Total outlays
	Total P.3	of which: compensation of employees D.1									
1. General public services											
2. Defence affairs and services											
3. Public order and safety affairs											
4. Education affairs and services											
5. Health affairs and services											
6. Social security and welfare affairs and services											
7. Housing and community amenity affairs and services											
8. Recreational, cultural and religious affairs services											
9. Fuel and energy affairs and services											
10. Agriculture, forestry, fishing and hunting affairs and services											
11. Mining and mineral resource affairs and services, other than fuels; manufacturing affairs and services; and construction affairs and services											
12. Transportation and communication affairs and services											
13. Other economic affairs and services											
14. Expenditures not classified by major group											

Table 18.3. Classification of total outlays of non-profit institutions serving households by purpose (COPNI)

Categories of COPNI	Final consumption expenditure		Gross capital formation P.5	Subsidies D.3	Property income D.4	Other current transfers D.7	Capital transfers D.9	Securities other than shares F.3	Loans F.4	Shares and other equity F.5	Total outlays
	Total P.3	of which: compensation of employees D.1									
1. Research and scientific services											
2. Education services											
3. Health services											
4. Welfare services											
5. Recreational, cultural and related services											
6. Religious services											
7. Services of professional and labour organizations and civic associations											
8. Miscellaneous services not elsewhere classified											

Table 18.4. Classification of selected outlays of producers by purpose (COPP)

Categories of COPP	Intermediate consumption P.2	Compensation of employees D.1	Other taxes less subsidies on production D.29 - D.39	Consumption of fixed capital K.1	Gross fixed capital formation P.51
1. Outlays on current production programs					
2. Outlays on repair and maintenance					
3. Outlays on engineering and related technological work					
4. Outlay on research and development					
5. Outlays on pollution abatement and control					
6. Outlays on sales promotion					
7. Outlays on external transportation					
8. Outlays on employee training, welfare and morale					
9. Outlays on general administration					

18.5. Tables 18.1 through 18.4 give the main headings of the four classifications. The classification of individual consumption by purpose and the classification of outlays of producers by purpose are provisional and classification of outlays of producers by purpose in particular may be substantially revised before it can be published. The classification of the purposes of non-profit institutions serving households is unchanged from the 1968 version of the SNA. The classification of the functions of government is described in a publication of the United Nations Statistical Office (Series M, No. 70, New York 1980). The classification of the functions of government needs modifying both to identify more precisely social transfers in kind and to identify more fully functions that are of increasing policy concern such as relief of poverty, preventive health care and repair and prevention of environmental damage.

B. Applying the classifications

18.6. In principle, the unit of classification for these four classifications is a transaction or group of transactions; what are being classified are actual or imputed expenditures made in connection with particular functions or to achieve particular purposes. In practice, it will not always be possible to work at such a detailed level.

18.7. Classification of individual consumption by purpose is used to classify both individual consumption expenditure and actual individual consumption. The latter is derived from the former by adding social transfers in kind as shown in table 18.1.

18.8. Some countries base their estimates of individual consumption expenditure on households budget surveys which frequently collect data according to functional groups of the kind used in classification of individual consumption by purpose. In these cases, estimates will be directly available of individual consumption expenditure by purpose, although data from such surveys usually need to be adjusted for various kinds of systematic errors and omissions. In many cases, however, estimates of consumption expenditure are built up either from statistics on retail sales or by a "commodity-flow" method in which the total supply of goods and services from domestic production and imports is allocated to intermediate and final uses. In such cases the starting point for applying classification of individual consumption by purpose will be a breakdown of goods and services for household consumption according to type of product or by kind of activity as an approximation to type of product. Several goods and services are multi-purpose—for example, fabrics may be used for clothing or furnishing, diesel fuel can be used for passenger vehicles or for home-heating and insurance services may be for risks relating to housing, transport or health. Some approximation is inevitably involved in conversion to classification of individual consumption by purpose from a product classification and, a fortiori, from a kind of activity classification.

18.9. Classification of the functions of government is designed for classifying current transactions (such as consumption expenditure, subsidies and current transfers), capital outlays (capital formation and capital transfers) and acquisition of financial assets by general government and its subsectors. The full list of transactions is given in table 18.2.

18.10. For current and capital transfers and for net acquisition of certain financial assets it will usually be feasible to classify transactions by assigning a classification of the functions of government code directly to them. For most other outlays it may not be possible to classify transactions and, as an approximation, the units of classification may have to be agencies, offices, bureaus or project units within government departments. All outlays by the selected classification unit will be assigned a single classification of the functions of government code. It may happen of course that the smallest units that can be identified still perform two or more classification of the functions of government functions; in such cases it will usually be best to make an approximate division of the unit's outlays among the different functions performed rather than to allocate them all to that which is judged the largest.

18.11. Property income payable by government consists almost entirely of interest on the public debt. Although table 18.2 shows property income as an item to be classified by function, it is usually not possible to link interest payments with the function or purpose for which the debt was originally incurred. Probably all, or most, property income will have to be allocated to function 14—"Expenditures not classified by major group."

18.12. The classification of the purposes of non-profit insititutions serving households covers the same range of transactions as classification of the functions of government, i.e., current transactions, capital outlays and the acquisition of certain financial assets. Most countries find it difficult to collect detailed information on the activities of non-profit institutions serving households and it is likely that, in general, institutions will have to be assigned in their entirety to one of the eight purposes. Of course, if an institution is known to be multi-purpose—a religious mission that provides education as well as religious services, for example—attempts should be made to divide their outlays between the different purposes served even if this can only be done very approximately. The classification is given in table 18.3.

18.13. The classification of outlays of producers by purpose is used to classify certain expenditures by producers—i.e., intermediate consumption, compensation of employees, other taxes less subsidies on production, consumption of fixed capital and gross fixed capital formation. The classification is given in table 18.4.

18.14. In principle, the classification of outlays of producers by purpose applies to all producers, whether market or non-market, although not all the classification of outlays of producers by purpose categories are of equal interest for both kinds of producers; for example, "Outlays on sales promotion" will not usually apply to non-market producers. It is probable that, in practice, classification of outlays of producers by purpose will mainly be of interest for classifying transactions of market-producers. There is currently very little experience with classifications of this kind. Although the classifications units should be transactions, it seems likely that in practice they will often have to be "cost-centres" or other units mainly serving a particular purpose, such as sales promotion, book-keeping, employee training, etc.

XIX. Application of the integrated framework to various circumstances and needs

A. Introduction

19.1. The central framework of the SNA pursues at least two objectives. First, it tries to help the development of a country's own system of national accounts by providing guidance to the national accountants of that country so that they are spared the trouble of searching and experimenting with approaches already tried by others. Secondly, it aims at facilitating international comparability between the national accounts of various countries in order to facilitate economic and social analysis in the worldwide economy. As such it is a set of integrated international standards.

19.2. These two objectives may appear to be in conflict in so far as many differences exist among countries with respect to their stage of development, economic and social structure, legal organization, economic and social policy, etc. The conflict may indeed exist to a certain extent, especially when looking at countries in very different situations. However, the premise is that the accounting structure is general enough to suit most cases. This does not mean, of course, that all countries' distinctive features are reflected in the SNA standards; that would be impracticable. It does mean that such features may normally be accommodated within the margins of flexibility provided by the System, especially when designing classifications of transactions and transactors and determining the related definitions. Even the most detailed levels of the System's classifications remain general in character and are not a priori relevant for any economy. Some items may not exist in some countries, like value added tax or import subsidies, and consequently they will not be retained in their national classifications. Alternatively, a country could find it useful to show more details at a given level of a classification or to introduce additional levels. The national accountants of any country are encouraged to do this, bearing in mind the objective of international comparability.

19.3. The intent behind the SNA is that countries should find it possible to implement the integrated framework without conflict with their own requirements. Conversely, countries should find it possible to innovate when elaborating their own national accounts so that they do not depart from the main international standards.

19.4. In general, in response to analytical requirements and data availability, the emphasis put on various aspects may vary within the context of the integrated System. This may be achieved by using the System's classifications of institutional sectors, industries, products, transactions, accounts, etc. at various levels or including additional ones; by applying alternative methods of valuation; by giving different priorities for various parts of the accounts and different frequencies; by rearranging the results for publication; etc. The elements of complementary classifications of transactions and other flows were especially designed for additional presentations and analysis. It is also possible to re-order the institutional subsectors in order to give more importance to the criterion of control which, in the hierarchic classification, does not appear at the first or even second level. Moreover, one may introduce additional criteria which, while not being included in the basic classifications of the SNA, do not conflict with the logic of the System. For example, these additional criteria might be size of employment for enterprises, size of income for households or the distinction between rural and urban segments of the economy.

19.5. The flexibility of the SNA such as just described deserves special emphasis because in the past the narrow perception had developed that the SNA was a limited set of accounts that did not display all the interconnections of the economy and lacked flexibility for application to different conditions in different countries. Solutions to these drawbacks had sometimes been sought through the building of social accounting matrices (SAMs), which displayed the interconnections, disaggregated the household sector, showed the link between income generation and consumption, etc. Further, sometimes the incorrect impression had been given that a SAM is an alternative to the SNA. A SAM is not an alternative to the SNA. A SAM is the SNA—in matrix terms and incorporating whatever degree of detail is of special interest. (For further explanation of the matrix presentation and SAMs, see chapter XX.) To date, builders of SAMs have exploited their flexibility to highlight special interests and concerns more than compilers of regular national accounts. The power of a SAM, as well as of the SNA, comes from choosing the appropriate type of disaggregation to study the topic of interest. It is an aim of the System to show the advantages of applying such flexibility as a regular part of compiling some or all aspects of the accounts, whether the presentation is a full set of accounts or an equivalent matrix.

19.6. The purpose of this chapter is not to elaborate in detail how a country may design its system following the SNA, but to show how, by using it in a flexible way, a country may adapt the central framework to special circumstances or types of analysis. The chapter provides a number of examples of such adaptations. In order to avoid misunderstanding it must be clear that these adaptations are not outside the central framework, but rather they are ways and means of building up a central framework with specific features according to national circumstances and needs.

B. Detailed analysis of the household sector

19.7. For in-depth analysis of economic and social conditions of the population, great importance has to be given to the analysis of the household sector. In the SNA as much importance is attached to the accounts of the household sector as to the accounts of other sectors. The household sector is a complex one. It covers first, the domestic transactions of households, i.e., transactions relating to the households' role as final consumers. Secondly, it covers activities households carry out and transactions they realize in connection with production activities which are not organized on a corporate or quasi-corporate enterprise basis. For those households which are engaged in production activities, the household institutional unit realizes both kinds of transactions and holds assets and liabilities belonging to and incurred by the household in question. There is only one figure for this unit's saving and one for its net worth. In effect there is no way of observing, after entrepreneurial income has been calculated, how this income is distributed partly to the household as consumer, and partly retained in the enterprise, because no such distribution actually takes place. Although some assets and liabilities may be identified as being of an enterprise type or a domestic type, others may not, but in any case it is the household as such which is the owner of all assets and is responsible for all liabilities.

19.8. Most households include several individuals who differ not only in physical characteristics, like sex and age, but also as to whether they are employed or not, and if employed, in the kind of productive activities in which they engage. So the economic characteristics of a given household may be rather heterogeneous. However, the socio-economic status of a household is a useful way to characterize the household as a group of individuals because all its members live together and because they are linked by family or similar relationships and share many common features both from a social and economic point of view.

1. Sub-sectoring the household sector

19.9. As the household sector as a whole is very heterogeneous economically and socially, it is necessary to separate more homogeneous groups within the sector. The System includes a classification of sub-sectors of households. Households are allocated to these sub-sectors according to their largest source of income (see chapter IV). Countries may want to introduce more detail or use a different method, such as the socio-economic characteristics of a reference person—who normally provides the main source of income, or more than one method of sub-sectoring. Various criteria might be used.

19.10. For employers and own-account workers, the kind of economic activity in which they are engaged, such as agriculture, mining, manufacturing or construction, or services, is obviously meaningful. However, inside these broad categories, the type and size of the business and consequently income and wealth may differ considerably. Countries may therefore want to introduce additional criteria, which may vary from one activity to the other, relative to the size and type of the enterprise owned by a household. The size can generally be defined in terms of number of employees and family workers, except in agriculture and trade. In agriculture, the area, the number of cattle, etc., have to be taken into account; in trade, the amount of sales is more significant. The type of enterprise refers to the way it is organized and operated, taking into consideration the legal status or its absence, the existence of accounts or their absence, the stability of the activity or its absence, etc. A distinction commonly referred to is the one between formal and informal activities, which relies upon these kinds of criteria. Although a certain degree of informal activity may exist in developed countries, the distinction is particularly relevant for developing countries. In many of them it is crucial due to the number of people involved (street traders, shoe cleaners, etc.) who are generally own-account workers, but may be employers too. The distinction between formal and informal activities/enterprises is recommended in the System, when relevant. The distinction can be used for further sub-sectoring employers and own-account workers.

19.11. For employees, various levels of skills may be distinguished. Other criteria, like the broad categories of activities or type of enterprise in which people work, may also be used.

19.12. The rural/urban distinction may be essential in certain circumstances. The only feasible way to introduce it in the overall accounting structure is based on household survey data, adjusted in order to take account of production surveys and administrative data. Also, a distinction between ethnic groups may be relevant in certain countries.

19.13. Table 19.1 summarizes these alternatives.

Table 19.1. Sub-sectoring of households

Socio-economic status	Economic activity	Type and/or size of enterprise	Skill	Location
Employers	Agriculture Mining, manufacturing and construction services	Formal Informal Size		Urban Rural
Own-account workers	Agriculture Mining, manufacturing and construction services	Formal Informal		Urban Rural
Employees	Agriculture Mining, manufacturing and construction services		High Medium Low	Urban Rural
Recipients of property and transfer income Property Pensions Other transfers				Urban Rural

2. Applying the sequence of accounts to sub-sectors

19.14. The full sequence of accounts is relevant for all sub-sectors. However, the production and generation of income accounts are important mainly for the employers'[1] and own-account workers' sub-sectors. In many cases, building up these accounts, even roughly, is the only way to get an approximation of the mixed income accruing to those households. Production and generation of income accounts in the case of the other sub-sectors cover services of owner-occupied dwellings, services produced by employing paid domestic staff, incidental production activities and other unincorporated enterprises that constitute only a secondary source of income.

19.15. The accounting structure of the System is designed in order to describe the three main stages of income distribution and redistribution:

(a) Primary incomes (which in the case of the household sector cover operating surplus, mixed income, compensation of employees, net property income received);

(b) Disposable income, measured after allowing for current taxes on income, wealth, etc. and other current transfers, excluding social transfers in kind; and

(c) Adjusted disposable income, measured after allowing for social transfers in kind.

The magnitudes of these three concepts of income may differ widely at the level of the overall household sector. The differences between them are even greater for some types of households, which means that in principle it is necessary to take all of them into account to give a correct picture of income redistribution. In addition, distinguishing the three concepts leads to the measurement of actual final consumption and saving. Actual final consumption gives the best approximation of the total of consumer goods and services actually acquired by the various groups of households, which is necessary for assessing their living standards. On the other hand, saving approximates the change in assets available for the future, at least when destruction of assets by natural catastrophes or political events and holding gains/losses due to inflation are not very important.

19.16. Paragraph 19.15 above shows the importance of depicting the complete process of income redistribution, including a thorough study of transfers (see paragraph 19.25 below). Conversely, for purposes more closely linked to short-term analysis of purchasers' behaviour, a concept of income relating to that part of income over whose use households can actually take decisions may be required. Such a concept might be called discretionary disposable income. It differs from disposable income by the amount of the in-kind components which are included in the latter. See chapter VIII, paragraphs 8.13 and 8.14, for a presentation of the components in kind included in disposable income.

19.17. Income distribution is commonly studied according to size of income. Various statistical units are used in such studies—households, individuals or the tax cluster, depending on the data source and the kind of income in question. For analysing the distribution of compensation of employees or more narrowly wages and salaries, individuals are used because they are the wage earners. In this case the type of income and source of data lead to the same choice of statistical unit. For operating surplus and mixed income, the relevant statistical unit may be either the enterprise or the household, because in most circumstances more than one member of the household is working in this producing unit. For global concepts of income (primary, discretionary, disposable, adjusted disposable income), the household is the appropriate statistical unit. The tax cluster may have to be used if administrative data organized that way are the only sources of income data, especially the only regular ones. Household surveys may be designed in order to best approximate the concept of the household as the statistical unit but they have to be supplemented by other sources of data if the picture is to be complete. When using statistical units which do not relate to individuals, it is necessary to make calculations of income by head (or by a statistical standard like consumption units) in order to avoid misinterpretation.

19.18. One could think of subdividing the household sector, in the context of national accounts, by income size and of trying to establish a full set of accounts for each income bracket. This might be thought of as an alternative to the breakdown by socio-economic groups or as a complementary subdivision inside each such group or sub-group. While this approach presents no conceptual difficulty (except in choosing the most relevant income concept), it is improbable that available data permit it in practice. However, the size of income criterion might be used for decomposing certain items, such as discretionary income or disposable income and at least some of their main components.

19.19. Apart from the capital account, the other accumulation accounts and the balance sheets may be very difficult to establish for disaggregated kinds of households, due to data problems. Studying wealth inequalities is, however, an essential part of economic and social analysis. Various statistical tools may be used, mainly saving and wealth surveys, records on capital taxes, data on stocks of buildings and on financial assets and liabilities. Even in countries where their integration in a national account framework is a long-term objective, partial analysis, depending on various circumstances and needs, may be feasible and very useful for complementing figures from the current accounts and the capital account. For example, estimates of real holding gains and losses on monetary assets and liabilities are important for assessing the effects of inflation on households. In a country where floods, earthquakes or wars destroy an important part of household assets, even a rough estimate of such destruction is highly desirable.

3. Introducing complementary details in transactions and balancing items

19.20. So far this section dealt with the disaggregation of the household sector in terms of the corresponding column in the integrated economic accounts, commenting on the sequence of accounts and the redistribution and accumulation process. We now look at the rows of those accounts, i.e., at the transactions and some balancing items. A number of features of the System's classifications and relevant complements are introduced. They are examined in the order of the sequence of accounts and the classifications of transactions.

19.21. Similar purposes may be pursued either by subdividing the column for the household sector or by distinguishing various components of certain transactions or balancing items in the rows. When the first approach is not feasible in practice, an approximation might be available by analysing only some important items, such as compensation of employees or mixed income, in the rows. For example, the rural/urban distinction mentioned in the previous section might be very useful for at least certain income concepts even if it cannot be implemented fully. Of course, combining both approaches would permit the richest analysis, when necessary data are available or valid approximations derivable.

19.22. Output may distinguish between components which are sold, bartered or destined for own-account uses, such as own-account final consumption and own-account fixed capital formation, or added to inventories (the net variation of which may be positive or negative).

19.23. Compensation of employees (and the corresponding figures on employment) lends itself to an analysis by kind of labour (for example, level of education, skill—based on a classification of occupations—and sex), industry of employment or location (as in the rural/urban distinction). Compensation of employees in cash and in kind may also be separated. As explained above, the distribution of compensation of employees or, if not feasible, wages and salaries by income brackets is an important element of economic and social analysis.

19.24. Mixed income and entrepreneurial income may be broken down in various ways (in the case of households, operating surplus refers only to the services of owner-occupied dwellings). Here again, various criteria may be used. Industry of origin, formal or informal segments of the economy or location have been referred to previously. In addition, the distinction between modern and traditional activities used in production (which is not synonymous with the distinction between formal and informal activities[2]) or, as an approximation, between capital intensive and labour intensive activities, may be introduced. If the subsistence economy represents a significant share of a country's economy, it is recommended that this should be separated from the other informal traditional activities.

19.25. The analysis of transfers is an important part of the study of income redistribution. Data on transfers may come from household surveys and administrative records. The System's multi-level classification may be complemented in various ways. For example, social benefits might be broken down according to the type of risk covered (unemployment, sickness, old age, etc.). Or, in a country where the responsibility for redistributing income is still found at the level of the family, transfers between resident households and remittances from members of the family living abroad might be isolated by subdividing the miscellaneous current transfers of the classification, while using the remaining part of the latter at a more aggregated level.

19.26. Final consumption expenditure covers components already met above when considering output. Own-account consumption at least should be distinguished from other consumption elements. If barter transactions are important in a country or a region, they might also be isolated. Another possibility is to distinguish more systematically monetary components from in-kind elements. The latter will also include the counterparts of compensation of employees in kind and transfers in kind from the rest of the world and corporations, if any. Further, the various components of non-monetary consumption transactions may be identified.

19.27. Transfers in kind by government or non-profit institutions serving households (NPISHs) have to be taken into account in order to go from consumption expenditure to actual consumption. They are of course non-monetary by definition.

19.28. The need for separating monetary and non-monetary transactions leads to the isolation in the capital account of own-account capital formation.

19.29. Table 19.2 presents the sequence of accounts for the household sector with the classification of transactions and balancing items complemented by additional subdivisions. A number of the subdivisions are elements of complementary classifications.

C. Expenditures by enterprises in transition economies on behalf of employees

19.30. One of the reasons for separating institutional units into sectors has to do with the basic objectives of the units (see chapter IV). Non-financial and financial corporations produce goods and services with the intention of selling them on the market at prices that cover their costs and making a profit. Government units and NPISHs produce or purchase goods and services in order to provide them free, or at prices which are not economically significant, to individual households or to the community as a whole. The individual goods and services provided mainly concern health and education. Even in a market economy, some enterprises may also provide schools and hospitals for their employees. For example, mining companies operating in remote areas may do so. However, this provision of services is not solely, or even primarily, a concern with social policy; rather it is dictated by the demands of the market place. If schools and hospitals are not available close to the mines, people would not be willing to work there. In these circumstances, the provision of the education and health services is seen as being part of the remuneration package offered to employees, and the value of these services is treated in the System as wages and salaries in kind.

19.31. Under a planned economy, enterprises frequently provided health, education and recreational services for their employees (and sometimes the general population), not primarily to attract employees but as an extension of a government policy of providing these services throughout the economy. Since the enterprises were state controlled, the state could use them as "agents" to ensure that the services were provided in specific regions or to particular groups of workers. The costs of the services were taken into account, at least implicitly, when calculating the transfers to be paid from the enterprise to government (taxes) or from government to the enterprise (subsidies). Within the system of statistical balances of the national economy, the expenditures were recorded as part of total consumption of the population (equivalent to actual final consumption of households in the SNA).

19.32. As countries make the transition from planned to market economy, and from using the system of material product balances (MPS) to using the SNA, there is a question about how to record these expenditures by enterprises on behalf of their employees. The SNA does not recognize a concept of final consumption expenditure of enterprises because, as mentioned above, the concept of enterprise is based on considerations of matching supply and demand through the market place.

19.33. One possibility would be to treat the expenditures as wages and salaries in kind, as in the case of the mining company quoted above. The treatment of wages and salaries in kind in the System is such that the output of health and other social services by the enterprise would then be recorded as purchased by the employees using these in-kind wages and salaries as the matching resources. This would balance supply and demand and show the correct level of household consumption of the services in question. However they would appear as part of household final consumption expenditure and not as social transfers in kind. The rationale for introducing the difference between consumption expenditure and actual consumption into the System is precisely to be able to see the difference between who finances the consumption and who benefits from it. Not recognizing these expenditures as a form of social transfer in kind would seriously distort the analysis of who pays and who consumes just at the moment when monitoring the emerging patterns of market behaviour is of most importance.

19.34. To resolve the problem for the duration of the transition, it is suggested that, for countries in transition, enterprises undertaking significant amounts of social expenditure on behalf of their employees should be treated as two institutional units.

Table 19.2. Integrated economic accounts for the household sector

Account	Total	Employers	Own-acct. workers	Employees	Prop. inc.	Pensions	Other transf.	Code	Transactions and balancing items	Other transf.	Pensions	Prop. inc.	Employees	Own-acct. workers	Employers	Total	Account
I. Production								P.1	Output								I. Production
								P.2	Intermediate consumption								
								B.1g	Value added, gross [1]								II.1.1 Generation of income
								K.1	Consumption of fixed capital								
								B.1n	Value added, net								
II.1.1. Generation of income								D.1	Compensation of employees								II.1.2. Allocation of primary income
								D.11	** Wages and salaries								
								D.12	Employers' social contribution								
								D.121	Employers' actual social contributions								
								D.122	Employers' imputed social contributions								
									* by industry of origin								
									* by kind of labour (skill,educ.,sex,age)								
								D.2-D.3	Taxes less subsidies on production and imports								
								D.21-D.31	Taxes less subsidies on products								
								D.29-D.39	Other taxes less subsidies on production								
								B.2g	Operating surplus, gross								
								B.3g	Mixed income, gross								
								B.2n	Operating surplus, net								
								B.3n	Mixed income, net								
									* by industry of origin								
									* formal/informal								
									* modern/traditional								
II.1.2. Allocation of primary income								D.4	Property income								
								D.41	Interest								
								D.42	Distributed income of corporations								
								D.421	Dividends								
								D.422	Withdrawals from income of quasi-corporations								
								D.43	Reinvested earnings of direct foreign foreign investment								
								D.44	Property income attributed to insurance policy holders								
								D.45	Rent								
								B.5g	Balance of primary incomes, gross								II.2. Secondary distribution of income
								B.5n	Balance of primary incomes, net								
II.2. Secondary distribution of income								D.5	Current taxes on income, wealth etc.								
								D.61	Social contributions								
								D.611	Actual social contributions								
								D.6111	Employers'actual social contributions								
								D.6112	Employees' social contributions								
								D.6113	Social contributions by self- and non-employed persons								
								D.612	Imputed social contributions								
								D.62	Social benefits other than social transfers in kind								
								D.621	** Social security benefits in cash								
								D.622	Private funded social benefits								
								D.623	Unfunded employee social benefits								
								D.624	Social assistance benefits in cash								
									* by type of risk covered								
								D.7	Other current transfers								
								D.71	Non-life insurance premiums less service charges								
								D.72	Non-life insurance claims								
								D.75	Miscellaneous current transfers								
									Transfers between households								
									Remittances from family members living abroad								
								B.6g	Disposable income, gross								II.3. Redistribution of income in kind
								B.6n	Disposable income, net								
									Discretionary disposable income								
									Disposable income in kind								

Table 19.2.   Integrated economic accounts for the household sector [cont.]

Account	To-tal	Em-plo-yers	Own-acct. wor-kers	Em-plo-yees	Prop. inc.	Pen-sions	Other transf.	Transactions and balancing items	Other transf.	Pen-sions	Prop. inc.	Em-plo-yees	Own-acct. wor-kers	Em-plo-yers	To-tal	Account
.3. edistri- ution of ncome kind								**D.63** Social transfers in kind								
								D.631 Social benefits in kind								
								D.6311 * * Social security benefits, reimbursements								
								D.6312 Other social security benefits in kind								
								D.6313 Social assistance benefits in kind * by type of risk covered Transfers of Individual non-market goods and services (not incl. in soc. benefits)								
								B.7g Adjusted disposable income, gross								II.4. Use of income
								B.7n *Adjusted disposable income, net* Discretionary disposable income Disposable income in kind Social transfers in kind from gov./NPI								
.4. se of ncome								**B.6g** Disposable income, gross								
								B.6n *Disposable income, net*								
								P.4 Actual final consumption								
								P.3 Final consumption expenditure purchases (net) Bartered consumption goods and services in kind Own-account final consumption subsistence economy services of owner-occupied dwellings domestic services other Compensation of employees in kind Transfers in kind from non-govern-ment/ NPI origin Insurance service charge Implicit serv. charge for fin. intermed.								
								D.8 Adjustment for the change in net equity of households on pension funds								
								B.8g Saving, gross								III.1. Capital
								K.1 Consumption of fixed capital								
I.1. apital								**B.8n** *Saving, net*								
								P.5 Gross capital formation								
								P.51 Gross fixed capital formation Purchases (less sales of existing fixed assets) Own gross fixed capital formation Capital transfers in kind (net)								
								P.52 Changes in inventories of which: changes in invent. of finished goods and work in progress								
								P.53 Acquisitions less disposals of valuables								
								K.1 Consumption of fixed capital (–)								
								K.2 Acquisition less disposals of non-produced assets								
								D.9 Capital transfers, receivable								
								D.92 Investment grants								
								D.99 Other capital transfers								
								D.9 Capital transfers, payable (–)								
								D.91 Capital taxes								
								D.99 Other capital transfers								
								B.10.1 *Changes in net worth due to saving and capital transfers* ²								
I.2. nancial								**B.9** *Net lending (+) / borrowing (–)* Acquisition of financial assets Incurrence of financial liabilities								III.2. Financial

Table 19.2. Integrated economic accounts for the household sector [cont.]

Account	To-tal	Em-plo-yers	Own-acct. wor-kers	Em-plo-yees	Prop. inc.	Pen-sions	Other transf.	Transactions and balancing items	Other transf.	Pen-sions	Prop. inc.	Em-plo-yees	Own-acct. wor-kers	Em-plo-yers	To-tal	Account
								F.2 Currency and deposits								
								of which: denominated in national currency								
								denominated in foreign currency								
								of which liability of:								
								resident units								
								rest of the world								
								F.3 Securities other than shares								
								F.4 Loans								
								F.5 Shares and other equity								
								F.6 Insurance technical reserves								
								F.7 Other accounts receivable/payable								
III.3.1. Other changes in volume of assets								**K.3** Economic appearance of non-produced assets								**III.3.1.** Other changes in volume of assets
								K.4 Economic appearance of produced assets								
								K.5 Natural growth of non-cultivated biological resources								
								K.6 Economic disappearance of non-produced assets								
								K.7 Catastrophic losses								
								K.8 Uncompensated seizures								
								K.9 Other volume changes in non-financial assets n.e.c.								
								K.10 Other volume changes in financial assets and liabilities n.e.c.								
								K.12 Changes in classifications and structure								
								B.10.2 *Changes in net worth due to other changes in volume of assets*								
III.3.2. Re-valuation								**K.11** Nominal holding gains /losses								**III.3.2.** Re-valuation
								AN. Non-financial assets								
								AN.1 Produced assets								
								AN.2 Non-produced assets								
								AF. Financial assets								
								AF. Liabilities								
								B.10.3 *Changes in net worth due to nominal holding gains/losses*								
IV.1. Opening balance sheet								**AN.** Non-financial assets								**IV.1.** Opening balance sheet
								AN.1 Produced assets								
								AN.2 Non-produced assets								
								AF. Financial assets								
								AF. Liabilities								
								B.90 *Net worth*								
IV.2. Changes in balance sheet								Total changes in assets								**IV.2.** Changes in balance sheet
								AN. Non-financial assets								
								AN.1 Produced assets								
								AN.2 Non-produced assets								
								AF. Financial assets								
								AF. Total changes in liabilities								
								B.10 *Changes in net worth due to:*								
								B.10.1 *Saving and capital transfers*								
								B.10.2 *Other changes in volume of assets*								
								B.10.3 *Nominal holding gains/losses*								
								B.10.31 Neutral holding gains/losses								
								B.10.32 Real holding gains /losses								
IV.3. Closing balance sheet								**AN.** Non-financial assets								**IV.3.** Closing balance sheet
								AN.1 Produced assets								
								AN.2 Non-produced assets								
								AF. Financial assets								
								AF. Liabilities								
								B.90 *Net worth*								

** Indicates the first item of the breakdown in the full sequence of accounts for the household sector.

* Indicates a possible alternative breakdown.

1 All balancing items can be measured gross or net of consumption of fixed capital. The code for gross balancing item is the code for the item plus the letter "g". Similarly, the letter "n" attached to a code indicates net values.

2 "Changes in net worth due to saving and capital transfers" is not a balancing item in the structure of the System. It is the total of the right-hand side of the capital account. However, as a significant component of changes in net worth, it is coded with the other components of the latter.

That part of their activity concerned with producing goods and services for sale on the market should be treated as a financial or non-financial enterprise as appropriate. That part of the activity concerned with the provision of social services to their employees should be treated as an NPISH, even if there is not a complete set of accounts, including a balance sheet, relating to these activities alone. Given the book-keeping practices in countries in transition, it is likely that in many cases complete accounts will be available and treating these as relating to an NPISH would in fact simply be the direct implementation of SNA principles. In cases where less complete records exist, a "quasi-NPISH" should be established using whatever information is available. This may consist of data relating to a production account only, in which case the output will be recorded as produced by the quasi-NPISH. Alternatively, it may not be possible to separate production costs. In this case the total production of the financial or non-financial enterprise will include the production of the social services, which will appear as being sold to the quasi-NPISH.

19.35. In all three cases, individual consumption expenditure will be recorded by the NPISH or quasi-NPISH, financed by a transfer of the same amount by the parent enterprises. These will form part of social transfers in kind and thus enter households' actual final consumption but not their consumption expenditure. Because of their importance, all these NPISHs should be grouped together in a special sub-sector of NPISHs called enterprise NPISHs so that their changing role during the transition process can be monitored. When the sub-sector is no longer significant, any remaining expenditure of this type by enterprises should be treated as wages and salaries in kind and the quasi-units merged back with their parent enterprises.

D. Public, national private and foreign controlled sectors

19.36. The classification of institutional sectors systematically includes the distinction between public, national private and foreign controlled corporations. For non-financial corporations, it appears at the second level of the classification; in the case of financial corporations, the distinction is made only at the third or fourth level. The existence of these distinctions permits their rearrangement for analytical purposes according to need and circumstance.

1. The public sector

19.37. The elements composing the public sector are present in the main classifications of the System and can be rearranged in order to show the accounts of the overall public sector. This is done by putting together the sub-sectors of general government and the public sub-sectors of non-financial and financial corporations. The accounts of the public sector portray the role of the public authorities in supplying goods and services to the economy and the demands made on the resources for production by the public authorities. The accounts also delineate the means of financing production, consumption and capital formation used by the public sector, its contribution to inflationary or deflationary pressures and to the external surplus or deficit and external debt. The role of the public sector in the redistribution of income already appears in the general government accounts.

19.38. The full sequence of accounts lends itself to the analysis of the public sector (though it may be difficult to obtain the data in some cases even if they normally exist for all units composing the public sector). At a minimum, the production and generation of income accounts have to be studied to identify the principal activities carried out by public non-financial corporations. In addition, it is advisable to establish, whenever feasible, a complete set of accounts for sub-sectors of public non-financial corporations according to their main economic activity.

19.39. The public sector accounts may be presented in a framework similar to the integrated economic accounts but with columns shown first for the various components of the public sector, then for the rest of the economy (the private sector). As analysts are interested in the relation of the public sector as a whole with the rest of the economy, consolidated accounts are necessary. However, in order to preserve an understanding of the System, it seems preferable to present the accounts of the public sector before consolidation, than after consolidation. (As explained in paragraph 2.82 of chapter II, transactions appearing in different accounts are never consolidated in order not to change the balancing items.)

19.40. These rearrangements of sectors might be shown in a presentation similar to the integrated economic accounts. They are shown in the five columns labelled "Public sector" in table 19.3.[3]

19.41. If a country is facing balance of payments problems, it would be extremely useful to record separately the external transactions of the public sector, if feasible (the main difficulty refers to exports and imports which necessitate a special analysis). This would allow the external balance of goods and services, the current external balance and the net lending of the rest of the world to be measured separately for the public sector and the private sector. The necessary breakdown of the rest of the world columns is shown in table 19.3.

19.42. For certain analyses, narrower concepts of the public sector are useful when dealing with capital and financial accounts. They refer to the non-financial public sector (i.e., general government plus public non-financial corporations) and the non-monetary public sector (i.e., the non-financial public sector plus public financial corporations except the central bank and

Table 19.3. Integrated economic accounts with public sector details and national/foreign distinction

Uses

Accounts	Total	Rest of the world — Goods and services (res.)	Rest of the world — Private sector external transactions	Rest of the world — Public sector external transactions	Total economy	National private sector	Foreign controlled sector	Public sector — Total after consolidation	Public sector — Total before consolidation	Public sector — General government	Public sector — Financial corporations	Public sector — Non-financial corporations	Transactions and balancing items
I. Production/ external account of goods and services													Imports of goods and services
													Exports of goods and services
													Output
													Intermediate consumption
													Taxes on products (net)
													Value added, gross/GDP
													Consumption of fixed capital
													Value added, net/NDP,
													ext. bal. of goods and
													services
....													....
....													....
IV.3. Closing balance sheet													Non-financial assets
													Produced assets
													Non-produced assets
													Financial assets
													Liabilities
													Net worth

Resources

Public sector								Rest of the world				
Non-financial corpo-rations	Finan-cial corpo-rations	General govern-ment	Total before consoli-dation	Total after consoli-dation	Foreign controlled sector	National private sector	Total economy	Public sector external transactions	Private sector external transactions	Goods and services (uses)	Total	Accounts
												I. Production/external account of goods and services
												II.1.1. Generation of income
												.... ..
												IV.3. Closing balance sheet

other depository corporations). Consolidated capital and financial accounts for these alternative definitions are recommended.

2. The national private and foreign controlled sectors

19.43. Accounting for the public sector implies interest in the accounts of the private sector. The latter covers private corporations, households and NPISHs. However, private corporations in turn include foreign controlled and national ones. Foreign controlled non-financial and financial corporations may be grouped in order to show their transactions separately from those of the national private sector (which covers national private non-financial and financial corporations, households and NPISHs).[4] For foreign controlled units from one side, and for national private units from the other, there is no obvious need for consolidation.

19.44. Table 19.3 shows an arrangement in which the private sector is the sum of the foreign controlled sector and the national private sector. Of course, the components of foreign controlled (non-financial and financial corporations) and national private sectors (non-financial, financial corporations, households and NPISHs) may be shown in such a presentation if so desired.

19.45. The analysis of the public sector, the national private and the foreign controlled sector and the moving of units from one

sector to another due to privatization and the sale of previously state-owned entities is a major issue in various parts of the world. It is a special concern in the case of countries in transition toward a market economy and has many implications for the national accounts of these countries.

19.46. It would also be analytically useful in certain circumstances to show separately, if feasible, the external transactions of the foreign controlled and the national private sector, respectively.

3. Restatement of purpose

19.47. The intention of the above paragraphs is not to propose a choice between the presentation of sub-sectors described and the standard one (incorporated, for example in the integrated economic accounts shown in chapter II), where the hierarchic classification is directly used. Both types of analysis and presentation are parts of the central framework and may be used together if relevant for a country.

19.48. Accounting for the public, foreign controlled and national private segments of the economy gives important structural information, such as their respective shares in value added, various income concepts and saving. Data on employment in these various parts of the economy are also very useful. Above all, such accounts allow the economic behaviour and results of those sectors to be analysed in a consistent way.

E. Key sector and other special sector accounts

19.49. The System permits an integrated analysis of economic activities within each institutional sector. For example, accounts for sub-sectors of non-financial corporations may be established by grouping corporations or, if more meaningful, sub-groups of corporations according to their principal economic activity. The analysis may cover the full economic process, from production to accumulation. This may be done systematically at a given level, probably fairly aggregated, of the International Standard Industrial Classification (ISIC) or for a number of selected industries which are of special interest in a given country. Similar analysis can be made for household production activities, at least up to the point where entrepreneurial income is calculated.

19.50. In certain cases it is very useful for economic analysis to put special emphasis on activities that play a predominant role in the economy's external transactions and equilibrium in general. These key activities may include the petroleum sector, mining activities or crops (coffee, for example), which account for an important part of exports, foreign exchange assets and, very often, government resources. In certain economies, banking itself is a key activity. The System does not try to provide specific and precise criteria for the definition of what a key sector or activity is. It is a matter of judgement in a given

country, based on economic analysis and economic and social policy requirements. For instance, even a small industry at an infant stage might deserve to be treated as a key activity.

19.51. First, these key activities and their corresponding products have to be defined. For this, items shown in distinct places of ISIC or the national classification may need to be grouped together. For example, accounting for oil and natural gas may cover extraction of crude petroleum and natural gas (ISIC division 11), manufacture of refined petroleum products (ISIC class 2320), transport via pipelines (ISIC class 6030), wholesale of solid, liquid and gaseous fuels and related products (class 5141) and retail sale of automobile fuel (class 5050). The extension of the key sector(s) depends on the circumstances. For example, the oil sector may have to cover petrochemical processing.

19.52. A goods and services account for the key products is established showing the resources and uses of these products. A production account and a generation of income account for the key industries are built up. For both activities and products, detailed classifications have to be used to fully understand the economic process and the related valuation procedures in this field. There generally exists a combination of market and administered prices, a complex system of taxes and subsidies, etc.

19.53. The key products and key industries accounts may be analysed in the context of a supply and use table (see table 19.4). Key industries are shown in detail in columns, and other industries may be aggregated. In the rows, key products are similarly shown in detail, and other products aggregated. Of course, all or some other industries or products may be shown in detail depending on the purpose of the table. At the bottom of the supply and use table, rows show labour inputs, gross fixed capital formation and stocks of fixed assets; the relevant figures for key industries appear at the intersection between these rows and the columns for industries. In the use part of the table, columns for gross fixed capital formation and changes in inventories respectively may be broken down between key sector(s) or industry(ies) and other sectors or industries. In a country where the key activity is carried out by very heterogeneous types of producers, such as small farmers and big plantations owned and operated by corporations, the two groups of producers can be distinguished, as they have wholly different cost structures and behave differently.

19.54. Then, a set of accounts, as complete as feasible, is compiled for the key sector, which has to be delimited. In the case of oil and mining activities, the key sector generally consists of a limited number of big corporations. All transactions of the latter are covered, even when they carry out secondary activities, giving rise to secondary products. It is useful to know the nature of these secondary products, but not necessarily their destination. The distinction between public, foreign controlled or private corporations is of course fundamental when dealing with a key sector. The business accounts themselves have to be carefully studied for each big corporation involved to carry out an integrated analysis, a task that is neither straightforward nor easy. Part of mining activities may be carried out by small corporations or even unincorporated enterprises. These units must be included in the key sector, even if it is necessary to rely on partial information coming from statistical surveys or administrative data.

19.55. When the key activity is an agricultural one, like coffee in certain countries, the situation is more complex. Most producers are probably unincorporated enterprises that do not qualify as quasi-corporations. Ideally, the key sector accounts would include a complete set of accounts for the households that carry out these productive activities. Because this may be difficult to do in practice, it may be necessary to limit oneself to showing only the accounts and transactions which are most closely linked with the key activity. These may include production, generation of income and entrepreneurial income accounts from one side and main transactions of the capital and financial accounts from the other.

19.56. In many cases, government plays an important role in connection with key activities, either via taxes and property income receipts, regulatory activity and/or subsidies. Accordingly, the

detailed study of transactions between the key sector and general government is very important. The classification of transactions may be extended to identify those flows connected with the key activity, including the relevant taxes on products. These flows may be received, in addition to the general budget itself, by various government agencies, such as ministries for special purposes, universities, funds and special accounts, etc. Similarly, it is very useful for economic analysis to indicate what uses are made by government of these resources, especially, of course, in the case of oil when they do not go into the general budget. This calls for a specific analysis by purpose of this part of government expenditure.

19.57. When the key activities are based on natural non-renewable resources, like subsoil resources, the key sector accounts have to record carefully the changes in these resources (new discoveries and depletion) in the other changes in volume of assets account and holding gains/losses on them in the revaluation account. These data are crucial for assessing correctly the economic performance of the economy in question. More broadly, the key sector accounts may be extended in the direction of environmental accounting (see chapter XXI).

19.58. The key sector accounts may be presented in the framework of integrated economic accounts. Table 19.5 is an example. A column or group of columns is introduced for key sector(s) and some other columns are renamed when relevant, like "other non-financial corporations" and/or "other households". Doing so makes it possible to see at a glance the respective shares of the key sector and other sectors in transactions and balancing items. Of course, the precise format of such a table depends on the circumstances and the objectives pursued. In the example given in table 19.5, the key sector is supposed to include institutional units which are either foreign controlled, public or national private ones.

19.59. One more step may consist in showing in additional tables the "from whom to whom?" relationship between the key sector and each other sector and the rest of the world. In any case, the external transactions of the key sector(s) are essential for economic analysis and may be shown in the integrated economic accounts framework by subdividing the column for the rest of the world accordingly, as shown in table 19.5.

19.60. Tourism as a special sector raises specific problems because tourism is not always easily identifiable directly as a set of activities, products and producing units. Consequently, tourism accounts are dealt with in the context of satellite accounts. Of course it is possible to define more narrowly a key sector made out of institutional units which are mainly engaged in certain industries, obviously tourist in nature and to treat it directly in the central framework. This may be especially workable and meaningful in a country where tourist services are rendered mainly to non-residents, mostly in specific establishments.

19.61. On the model of key sector accounts, similar accounts may be built up for other special sectors which are not key sectors in

Table 19.4.   Supply and use table with key activities and products details

Resources

Resources	Total supply in purchasers' prices	Trade and transport margin	Taxes on products — Key products	Taxes on products — Other	Subsidies on products — Key products	Subsidies on products — Other	Key industries — Ind. 1 (Output)	Ind. 2	...	Ind. n	Other industries	Total economy	Imports of goods and service
Goods and services supply:													
Key products													
1.													
2.													
...													
n.													
Other products													
Total													

Uses

Uses	Total uses in purchasers' prices	Key industries — Ind. 1 (Intermediate consumption)	Ind. 2	...	Ind. n	Other industries	Total economy	Exports of goods and service	Final consumption expenditure — House-holds	NPISHs Individual	Government Collective	Government Individual	Gross capital formation — Gross fixed capital formation	Changes in inventories	Acquisitions less disposals of valuables
Goods and services uses:															
Key products															
1.															
2.															
...															
n.															
Other products															
Total															
Total gross value added/GDP															
Compensation of employees															
Taxes on products															
Other taxes on production															
Subsidies on products (−)															
Other subsidies on production (−)															
Operating surplus, net															
Mixed income, net															
Consumption of fixed capital															
Operating surplus, gross															
Mixed income, gross															
Total															
Labour inputs															
Gross fixed capital form.															
Stock of fixed assets, net															

the sense of paragraph 19.50 above, but deserve special consideration from the point of view of economic and social policy. Agriculture is often a good example in developed countries because it generates surpluses and necessitates an important amount of subsidies.

F. External accounts problems

19.62. The rest of the world accounts provide an overall view of a country's external transactions. This view is elaborated for imports and exports in the supply and use table where they are broken down by products and for external assets and liabilities and financial transactions in the three-dimensional tables where relations between creditor and debtor sectors are shown.

19.63. Countries which experience difficulties in their external equilibrium may want to incorporate further details in their national accounts in order to provide a basis for more refined analysis. The measurement and analysis of the external transactions of the public/private sectors and of the key sectors and of the foreign controlled sector, both referred to above, may be of special relevance.

19.64. On the other hand, it is also possible to subdivide the rest of the world account according to various groupings of countries that are relevant in light of a country's external relations. For example, such groupings may distinguish countries that are members of a regional pact, like the European Economic Community or the Andean Pact, countries that have similar economic conditions, like OPEC countries or the main exporting developed economies, etc. The SNA does not make any specific recommendation in this respect, because the relevant subdivision depends on countries themselves or regional agreements.

19.65. The analysis of imports by products and the elasticity of imports in relation to the rate of growth of gross domestic product (GDP) or changes in the rate of foreign exchange may be usefully supplemented by the study of the import content of intermediate and final consumption and capital formation. This may be done by using a variant of the supply and use table which distinguishes imported products from domestically produced goods and services in the various uses of goods and services (see chapter XV).

19.66. The System recommends the calculation of the global amounts of implicit taxes and subsidies or other transfers involved in multiple exchange rates if they exist in a country (see annex A to this chapter). This procedure allows a better and more consistent analysis of external accounts both in national and foreign currency. However, the System uses the actual exchange rates applied in the various transactions to convert their value in foreign currency to the one in the national currency, in order not to depart from the actual rates which have influenced the behaviour of the economic agents. In addition to this, a country may find it analytically useful to calculate each transaction in national currency by using the average exchange rate. The difference, for each transaction, between the latter value and the one previously obtained when using the actual exchange rate represents the implicit taxes and subsidies or other transfers attached to the specific transaction. These figures are of interest when analysing the distortions a system of multiple exchange rate implies. A country with a unique exchange rate artificially stated may find it useful to do the same exercise. The additional difficulty in this case is the determination of the exchange rate of reference since it cannot be calculated as a weighted average exchange rate in such a situation.

19.67. Emphasis must be put on debt stocks and transactions when external debt problems are important. As recalled at the beginning of this section, the System provides for three-dimensional tables where transactions in financial instruments and stocks of such assets/liabilities are recorded according to creditor and debtor sectors. Even if a country does not find it feasible to elaborate these tables completely, they are worth doing at least for the rest of the world and the counterpart sectors. Such tables may be supplemented or arranged in order to show arrears and debt reorganization, if any. The servicing of external debt covers interest, which appears directly in the rest of the world accounts, and reimbursement of the principal of the debt. The latter does not appear explicitly in the financial account of the rest of the world because only net incurrence of liabilities by the nation is included. In such circumstances it is necessary to record separately incurrence of new debt and reimbursement.

G. High inflation

19.68. Establishing meaningful national accounts in a country where high inflation prevails is indeed a challenge for national accounting. This challenge does not arise because those conditions create totally new national accounting problems. In fact, the same problems also exist conceptually in the very common situation of creeping inflation, with low rates of changes in the general level of prices. However, high rates of inflation exacerbate the problems. A method of measurement which gives acceptable approximate measures in more or less normal conditions may no longer be acceptable with significant inflation.

Table 19.5.　Integrated economic accounts with key sector details

Uses

Accounts	Total	Goods and services (res.)	Rest of the world		Total eco-nomy	NPISHs	(Other) house-holds	General govern-ment	(Other) financial corpo-rations	(Other) non-financial corpo-rations	Key sector			Transactions and balancing items
			Other external transact.	Key sector external transact.							Public control	Private control	Foreign control	
I. Production/ external account of goods and services						⋮ ⋮	⋮ ⋮	⋮ ⋮	⋮ ⋮	⋮ ⋮	⋮ ⋮	⋮ ⋮	⋮ ⋮	Imports of goods and services
														Exports of goods and services
														Output
														Intermediate consumption
														Taxes on products (net)
														Value added, gross/GDP
														Consumption of fixed capital
														Value added, net/NDP, ext. bal. of goods and services
⋮														⋮
⋮														⋮
IV.3. Closing balance sheet														Non-financial assets
														Produced assets
														Non-produced assets
														Financial assets
														Liabilities
														Net worth

Resources

Key sector			(Other) non-financial corpo-rations	(Other) finan-cial corpo-rations	General govern-ment	(Other) house-holds	NPISHs	Total eco-nomy	Rest of the world		Goods and services (uses)	Total	Accounts
Foreign control	Private control	Public control							Key sector external transact.	Other external transact.			
...			...	...	...	...	...	...					I. Production/external account of goods and services
...			...	...	...	...	...	...					
													II.1.1. Generation of income
													.....
													.....
													IV.3. Closing balance sheet

19.69. Basically, under high inflation the three classic roles of the currency are disrupted. The disruption in the currency's role as instrument of payment is minor; most transactions continue to be cleared in the national currency even though—sometimes legally, more often illegally—foreign currencies may be used for some domestic payments. The main difficulties are encountered in the currency's role of reserve of value. This aspect is well-known. When the annual rate of inflation is 500 per cent, for example, it is not advisable to keep any saving in the form of monetary assets, unless a mechanism of compensation against inflation is established explicitly through indexation or implicitly through high market rates of interest. Perhaps less obvious is the crisis of the currency's role as unit of account even for short periods of time. This aspect is, of course, connected with the previous one. Even within a period of one year, the value (i.e., the purchasing power) of the currency diminishes sharply when inflation is high, with the result that the sum of the values of transactions which take place at different times of the year is not at all easy to interpret. If all transactions were evenly distributed and inflation regular during the year, it could be said that the unit of account is the mid-year value of the currency. However, this condition is not fulfilled in practice. This means that under high inflation flows as conventionally measured give a distorted picture of the economic structure.

19.70. On certain aspects the SNA provide rules which, rigorously applied, are capable of providing correct measures. For example, rules related to time of recording transactions are essential: transactions have to be recorded at the same point in time in the various accounts in question for both transactors. Differences in the time of recording by transactors have much more serious distorting effects when inflation is high.

19.71. A particular and very important aspect concerns transactions and balancing items that are measured by the difference between flows. This is the case, for example, for trade margins measured as the difference between sales and the purchase value of the goods which are sold (the method followed in practice being very often: sales less purchases plus changes in inventories). The correct measurement of trade margins at any point in time supposes that the purchase value of the goods sold is the price prevailing at the time the goods are sold, not at the time the purchase was actually made. In other words it means that changes in inventories have to reflect adequately the difference in value between entries to and withdrawals from inventories valued at prices at the time of entry and withdrawal, respectively (see chapter VI).

19.72. The measurement of value added is a very important case in point when the process of production extends over a long period of time (under high inflation "long" is usually much shorter than when inflation is low) and there is a significant lag between intermediate consumption and the recording of output. (In agriculture, for example, harvesting may even take place in a different calendar year). In principle, the System

provides the solution for correct measurement. It relies upo careful recording of work in progress. In effect, if intermedia consumption takes place mainly, for example, in the first pa of the year and output (harvests or, in other cases, deliverie taken as a measure of output) is recorded mostly in the secon part of the year, under high inflation value added will be ove estimated. Since compensation of employees is recorde when due or paid, the figure for operating surplus is heavi distorted. Of course, for agriculture if harvests occur main in the first half of the year and intermediate consumption in th second, the distortion is inverted.

19.73. The solution in such cases, in principle, is to record output pr gressively as work-in-progress. Then at the end of the proce of production, the previously recorded work-in-progress withdrawn from inventories after due revaluation, while fro the other side the output of finished products is entered in i ventories at the prices prevailing at this time. This solutic shows that, basically, the right rule of recording output and i ventories is the perpetual inventory method, careful attentic being paid to the recording of work-in-progress. This is tru for business accounts and national accounts as well. Depa tures from this ideal treatment cause more significant bias when inflation is high. In practice, the right solution may difficult to apply, especially if business accounts do not pr vide adequate data. However, it should be approximated as f as possible, in order to minimize distortions.

19.74. Applying the System's solutions referred to in the previo paragraphs is a means of trying to get correct measures as f as it is feasible. However, they do not solve the difficulty r lated to the loss of meaning of the unit of account under hig inflation. Rigorously, a unit of the currency at the beginni of the year is not additive with a unit of the currency in the la months of the same year. Strictly speaking, this holds eve time the purchasing power of the currency changes, eve when the rate of inflation is low. However, under normal co ditions (low inflation) it is assumed that over a short period time (one year) the loss of significance of the currency as a ur of account is limited. For longer periods, this assumption is n acceptable, and comparisons are made either at constant pric (for goods and services) or in real terms (constant purchasi power of the currency). A short period of hyper-inflation i volves the same measurement problems as a much longer p riod of low inflation.

19.75. As explained above, because transactions are not evenly di tributed and inflation is not regular during the year, it may n be assumed that the implicit unit of account is the mid-ye currency. Consequently, the economic relations are distorte Phenomena occurring mainly in the first part of the year ha their shares understated; conversely, those occurring main in the last part of the year have their shares overstated.

19.76. In order to avoid such distortions, it would be possible to u the currency at a certain point or during a short period of tim (one month, for example) as the unit of account. All transa tions would then be revalued at the (constant purchasing power of the) currency at the chosen point or period by applying to current values an indicator of the change in the general price level. Applying such a procedure systematically might, of course, be burdensome, but it might be appropriate to implement it for certain flows or certain aggregates only, possibly using simplified methods of calculation.

19.77. Because of the difficulties in interpreting national accounts in current values, one could conclude that it is useless to establish these accounts. However, they remain necessary for use in conjunction with monetary and financial variables. Further, under such circumstances more emphasis should be given to accounts covering shorter time periods. As monthly accounts are obviously impracticable, except for some items, quarterly accounts covering more than just GDP and its uses would be of great value for analysis. The use of the currency as a unit of account on a quarterly basis, while subject to the general criticism in principle, provides results which are easier to interpret than annual data, at least if hyper-inflation is avoided. In addition, quarterly accounts might provide a short-cut method for determining annual accounts, using the average value of the currency in a given quarter as the unit of account.

19.78. Constant price estimates, which play an important role in national accounting in general, are given even more emphasis for flows of goods and services and the production account when inflation is high. As far as possible it is probably appropriate to attempt to estimate volume increases directly rather than rely on deflation methods applied to current prices. In effect, the degree of approximation in the measurement of price changes may well be of the order of magnitude of the volume changes. The danger is increased when the base period for price increases is very out of date.

19.79. In general, frequent rebasing of national accounts in constant prices is advisable when changes in relative prices are important. The choice of the base period, which is always a delicate one, may be especially complex under high inflation due to the fact that price adjustments are irregularly timed. Studying how relative prices move in the short, medium and long term in periods of high inflation, as compared with other periods, is of particular importance.

19.80. To assess the effects of inflation it is not sufficient to measure only flows in the current accounts and in the capital and financial accounts of the System. This is so because inflation may redistribute wealth and because changes in real wealth due to

inflation may amplify or counterbalance changes in these flows. The revaluation account of the System, which shows real holding gains and losses incurred by institutional sectors and the rest of the world according to the types of assets and liabilities they hold, is of special importance in this context.

19.81. Calculating these gains and losses supposes, of course, that a country has previously established sector balance sheets. Establishing sector balance sheets for financial assets and liabilities is of prime importance because the dramatic changes in the purchasing power of the currency when inflation is high undermine its role as a reserve of value. The face value of monetary assets covers a vanishing real value of these assets. For interest-bearing monetary assets and liabilities (non-interest bearing monetary assets may hardly exist when inflation is high, except at the minimum level necessary for current payments), the decrease in their real value is generally compensated, at least in part, by explicit indexation or inclusion of an element compensating for inflation in the rate of interest. This means that nominal interest, under these circumstances, can include a component which may be viewed as an anticipated reimbursement/refund of the real value of the principal of the financial liability/asset. The higher the rate of inflation, the quicker is this process of reimbursement/refund.

19.82. The element of compensation for inflation should not be considered as a return to capital by the lender and a current cost by the borrower. The System treats these components of explicit or implicit indexation as interest received and paid in the current accounts, and this treatment does not create great difficulties when inflation is low. However, the measurement of these components is essential when inflation is high if one wants to interpret correctly figures such as government disposable income or saving (or government deficit) and the corresponding figures for creditor sectors, etc. For this reason, the System recommends showing real holding gains and losses on monetary assets as memorandum items to the current accounts. Countries with high inflation would benefit greatly from following this procedure and, in addition, giving great emphasis to a careful scrutiny of holding gains and losses in the revaluation account.

19.83. Going one step further, countries experiencing significant inflation may want to apply a parallel treatment of interest that gives a more meaningful picture of the economy under such circumstances. A possible such treatment is described in annex B to this chapter.

H. Quarterly accounts

19.84. When using the System for short-term analysis, annual accounts are not sufficient because they do not generally permit the various short-term movements to be followed as closely as necessary. On the other hand, relying only on the analysis of short-term indicators is not an adequate alternative for various

reasons. These indicators are very often incomplete in terms of coverage, and economic interrelationships are not always easily understandable through them. Further, changes in annual national accounts figures and in the corresponding statistical indicators may differ. National accounts try to be exhaustive, and they result from a process of trade-off and adjustment between basic data which are not fully consistent. Consequently, quarterly accounts tend to be broadly used in conjunction with short-term indicators, either current statistics or subjective business surveys. They are increasingly implemented in developing countries as well as in developed ones.

19.85. No country establishes the complete System, including balance sheets, for every quarter. The coverage of quarterly accounts varies considerably from country to country. It consists in many cases of a calculation of GDP only, using a value added approach by broad economic categories, or a balance between GDP and its uses. At the other extreme, some countries try to cover most of current accounts and capital and financial accounts. As indicated above, quarterly accounts which are as complete as feasible may help overcome the difficulties of interpretation encountered with annual accounts in high inflation. Quarterly accounts for general government may facilitate the transition from fiscal year to calendar year when they are different.

19.86. Quarterly accounts are based on intensive use of short-term statistical indicators. Some data used for annual accounts—for example, accounting data—are not available more frequently. When they are, they may not be fully available in time for early estimates. However, short-term indicators should be used with caution. Combinations of these indicators may differ from the corresponding annual national accounts figures.

For instance, the annual changes of industrial output measured through monthly or quarterly surveys may differ from the results of annual surveys, where establishments and products are generally better covered, and both may differ from national accounts, which have to make estimates for the missing items, to use additional data and to check the overall consistency of the accounts. Because short-term statistics must be adjusted when used for quarterly accounts purposes, the most specific contribution of quarterly accounts work to national accounting is the study, generally using econometric methods, of the relationship between annual accounts figures and corresponding short-term indicators.[5]

19.87. Apart from deciding which parts of the System and what level of detail to use, quarterly accounts do not in general need adaptation of the conceptual framework. However, the correct definition and measurement of quarterly output requires much attention to be paid to the analysis of changes in inventories in general and work in progress in particular. The latter may have greater implications for the allocation of output between different quarters than between different years (for which it is nevertheless non-negligible). This is especially important for industries in which the process of production extends over a long period of time. In many cases output may not be correctly approximated by recording goods and services when they are finished. Agriculture is of course a good case in point. See paragraphs 19.72 and 19.73 above which already refer to this problem in connection with the problems of high inflation.

I. Regional accounts

19.88. Regional accounts are of special importance when there are important gaps between the economic and social development of the various regions of a country.

19.89. A full system of accounts at the regional level implies treating each region as a different economic entity. In this context, transactions with other regions become a kind of external transactions. External transactions of the region have, of course, to distinguish between transactions with other regions of the country and transactions with the rest of the world.

19.90. Three types of institutional units have to be considered in the context of regional accounts. First, there are regional units, the centre of interest of which is in one region and most of their activities take place in this region. Among regional units are households, corporations whose establishments are all located in the region, local and state governments, at least part of social security and many NPISHs. Secondly, there are multi-regional units, the centre of interest of which is in more than one region but does not relate to the country overall. Many corporations and a number of NPISHs are in this situation. Finally, a small number of units are national units, which means that their centre of interest is really not located geographically even in the sense of multi-regional location. This is the case of

central government and may be the case for a small number of corporations (probably public), generally in a monopolistic or quasi-monopolistic situation, like the national railway corporation or the national electricity corporation.

19.91. Locating transactions of the regional institutional units does not raise any conceptual problem. These units are clearly regional resident units. Allocating the transactions of multi-regional units between various regions raises more difficulties. Even when these transactions are physically locatable, like output, it is necessary to actually value intra-corporate flows between establishments located in different regions. The System recommends including inter-establishments deliveries in the definition of output and this is especially important for regional accounts. A further consideration is that part of the transactions of multi-regional units is not, strictly speaking, regionalizable, in concept. This is the case for most property income and transactions in financial instruments. Consequently, balancing items of multi-regional units may not be unambiguously defined at the regional level for multi-regional units except value added and operating surplus. This means that, by definition, multi-regional institutional units may not be broken down in a number of regional institutional units.

19.92. One could argue that the measurement problems for multi-regional corporations are very similar to those of multinational corporations. There is obviously some similarity between these two kinds of enterprises. However, in the case of multinational corporations, national legislation and other considerations generally lead to establishing different legal entities in different countries. Even if these legal entities are not fully independent and the valuation of their external transactions within the same multinational corporation are not based on true market values, these units fulfil the conditions necessary to be treated as institutional units in the System. Only foreign branches which are not established as separate legal entities are in more or less the same situation as establishments belonging to multi-regional corporations. However, in the accounts of the nation as a whole, they are few in number and play a marginal role. Conventions of measurement in their case do not have an important impact on national accounts results. Moreover they are generally obliged to submit certain data. In regional accounts, on the contrary, these units are very common.

19.93. The location of national institutional units raises more complex issues. In their case, breaking down their centre of interest between all the regions is conceptually dubious. Those units do not seem properly regionalizable. Of course, this does not mean that many transactions they carry out cannot be located in the regions, like sales of electricity and railway services or compensation of employees paid by central government. But it is not conceptually possible to regionalize their accounts totally. For instance, interest on the public debt payable by central government may not be geographically located (even when this interest is locatable when receivable by other units). The same is true for interest on their debt payable by national corporations. This probably leads to considering the introduction, in addition to the regions, of a kind of national sector, not allocated as such between the regions or constituting an extra

region. This national sector would have establishments located in the regions.

19.94. One may think of allocating all transactions of multi-regional units or even national units between regions according to some rules of thumb. However, this should not be considered simply as a practical approximation. It implies a conceptual adaptation of the System. The reasons which prevent including a full sequence of accounts for establishments/industries in the central framework also forbid, in principle, completely distributing all institutional units and their accounts between regions, which means, in principle, building up a full set of accounts for establishments.

19.95. These conceptual difficulties partly explain why no country establishes the complete System for every region. In most cases regional accounts are limited to recording production activities (with conceptual problems arising for locating some of them, like transportation and communication) by industry and more complete accounts for institutional sectors composed of regional units, like households and local and state government. Establishing accounts for goods and services and input-output tables by region does not raise unsolvable conceptual issues, deliveries to and from other regions being, of course, treated as exports and imports. However, the practical difficulties are very important in the absence of a sophisticated system of transport statistics.

19.96. Nonetheless regional accounts, even with the limitations mentioned above, are a very useful tool for economic policy. Partial regional accounts may be inserted in a set of regional statistical indicators on labour participation, unemployment, poverty, etc. The greater the contrast between the regions in a country, the more useful is such a system of regional indicators, including GDP per capita according to broad economic categories, household disposable income and household consumption per capita. It is up to the countries themselves to devise their own regional accounts and statistical indicators, taking into consideration their specific circumstances, data system and resources which might be devoted to this work.

Notes

1 Note that a household whose reference person is the owner of a quasi-corporation will be classified in the sub-sector for employers. However, the production and generation of income accounts of this enterprise are recorded in the sector non-financial corporations, not in the household sector. The owner receives an income called "withdrawal from income of quasi-corporations".

2 Formal activities in agriculture may be modern or traditional, even in the same country, for example, intensive poultry breeding or extensive cattle farming.

3 The sub-sectors of general government may be shown separately.

4 In certain countries, transactions of foreign controlled non-profit institutions serving households may be significant and should be added to the foreign controlled sector and deducted from the national private sector.

5 However, preliminary estimates of annual accounts, especially when incomplete data are available, must benefit from quarterly accounts methodology.

Annex A

The treatment of official multiple exchange rate systems

A. Introduction

1. A number of countries in the world have experienced or currently experience situations in which there exist more than one exchange rate. This is always linked to the introduction by the monetary authorities of an official exchange rate regime. An official exchange rate regime may consist of one single exchange rate, with a control of foreign exchange imposing a certain kind of rationing on the purchases of foreign currencies. If this rationing is respected or actually enforced, a very questionable assumption, of course, in most situations, no parallel market exists and the exchange rate is unique. This unique exchange rate does not correspond, except perhaps by chance, to an equilibrium rate. However, the System uses the actual official single rate for the conversion of external flows or stocks from foreign to national currency.

2. Usually, official exchange rate regimes introduce two or more exchange rates that are applicable to different categories of transactions, favouring some or discouraging others. Those rates incorporate elements which are similar to taxes or subsidies. This means that a system of official multiple exchange rates is equivalent to a regime with a single official exchange rate combined with a set of taxes and subsidies on different categories of sales and purchases of foreign currencies. The equivalent single rate is the "unitary rate" calculated as a weighted average of all official rates used for external transactions. The amount of the implicit taxes or subsidies involved in the different official rates can be calculated for each transaction as the difference between the value of the transaction converted into national currency at the actual exchange rate applicable and the value of this transaction converted at the "unitary rate". For instance, let us suppose that the "unitary rate" between the U.S. dollar and the national currency is 10

and that, in order to discourage certain imports, the official rate applicable to these imports is 11; every time one dollar of goods of this type is imported, an implicit tax of 1 unit of national currency is levied. Let us suppose also that in order to encourage certain exports, the official rate applicable to these exports is 10.5; every time one dollar of goods of this type is exported, an implicit subsidy of 0.5 unit of national currency is attributed to exporters.

3. When an official multiple exchange rates regime exists, the System records external transactions using the actual rate applicable to specific transactions. This means that the System always uses the actual applicable exchange rate, whatever the exchange rate regime is. The reason for doing this is that the behaviour of economic agents is influenced by the actual rate(s) applicable to their transactions, which determines the value of these transactions in national currency. However, when imports and exports, or certain types of imports or exports, or other transactions, are converted into national currency using different exchange rates, the relationships between the values of given flows in foreign currency and the values of the same flows in national currency are different. This means, as far as flows of goods and services are concerned—the underlying physical quantities being the same—the relative prices of certain imports or exports, and/or of total imports and exports are not the same when they are calculated from values in foreign or national currency. In other words, the prices of international trade being generally considered truer market prices because they result from more competition, the price relationships based on flows in national currency are considered under such circumstances to be distorted.

B. A simple example

4. The distortions referred to in the paragraph above have consequences on the balancing items of the accounts of the rest of the world (external transactions accounts). The magnitudes of balancing items may be changed in relation to the underlying external transactions. The sign of certain balancing items may even become different. Let us illustrate this possibility with a simple example. Suppose the external transactions of a country are only imports, exports, dividends and the corresponding flows of foreign currency. The figures in foreign currency are: exports 1,000, imports 950 and dividends receivable by the rest of the world 50. All flows are paid during the same period in which they are due. The rest of the world accounts are presented from the point of view of the rest of the world. The external balance of goods and services is thus–50, which means

a surplus of the nation. The current external balance is then zero, as are net lending/net borrowing and net changes in liabilities (rest of the world)/assets (the total economy) of currency and deposits in foreign currency. Suppose now an official system of multiple exchange rates is run by the central bank of the country in question. The central bank buys all foreign currency from exporters, at a rate of 10 (units of national currency for one unit of foreign currency), and sells foreign currency to importers at a rate of 11 and to corporations paying dividends to non-residents at a rate of 12. Let us remember that, in this annex, all exchange rates referred to are rates prevailing at the transaction dates and they exclude any service charge. Let us convert external transactions in national currency using the specific applicable exchange rates. We get exports 10,000 (1,000 x 10), imports 10,450 (950 x 11) and dividends 600 (50 x 12). The external balance of goods and services is now, from the point of view of the rest of the world, +450. Its sign is different because imports are greater than exports in national currency, whereas they are lower than exports in foreign currency. Thus a surplus of the nation has been turned into a deficit. Look now at the current external balance. We get +450 + 600, that is +1,050, a positive balance of the rest of the world, when the accounts are simply equilibrated in foreign currency. These changes are due to the distortions introduced by the system of official multiple exchange rates between flows in foreign currency and flows in national currency. Under such circumstances, the structural relationships of external relations are biased when the analysis is based on flows converted in national currency using the specific exchange rates that are actually applicable to various types of transactions.

5. What should be done if we want both to convert external transactions using the specific applicable exchange rates and to avoid distorting the structural pattern of external relations in national currency? The System recommends recording in the central framework global adjustment items corresponding to the implicit taxes/subsidies or other types of transfers which are implied by a system of official multiple exchange rates. These implicit taxes/subsidies or transfers are calculated as indicated in paragraph 2 above. Let us continue the same simple example. The unitary exchange rate is in this case 10.525, that is, the sum of 10,000 + 10,450 + 600 (21,050), divided by 2,000. As the central bank buys foreign currency at a rate (10) which is lower than the "unitary rate" and sells foreign currency at rates (11 and 12) which are higher than the "unitary rate", only implicit taxes are at stake here. Their amounts are 525 on exports (1,000 x 10.525, that is, 10,525 minus 1,000 x 10, that is -10,000), 451.25 on imports (950 x 11, that is 10,450, minus 950 x 10.525, that is 9,978.75) and 78.75 on dividends (50 x 12, that is 600, minus 50 x 10.525, that is -526.25). We now get:

> External balance of goods and services = [imports of goods and services (10,450) - implicit taxes on imports (451.25)] - [exports of goods and services (10,000) + implicit taxes on exports (525)] = -526.25

> Current external balance = external balance of goods and services (-526.25) + dividends (600) - implicit taxes on dividends (73.75) = 0.

The sign of the external balance of goods and services is now the same in national as in foreign currency (-526.25, -50). It may be seen that this balance is implicitly converted now by using the "unitary rate" (-526.25 = -50 x 10.525).[a] The current external balance is now zero as in foreign currency. We may also notice that the figure for current external balance which appeared before recording the implicit taxes (1,050) is equal to the total of the implicit taxes themselves (525 + 451.25 + 73.75). It is also equal, by construction, to the difference between total sales (10,450 + 600, that is 11,050) and total purchases (10,000) of foreign currency by the central bank.

C. A full-scale case and the complete accounting treatment in the System

6. The principle followed by the System in the treatment of official multiple exchange rates is the one which has been illustrated in section B of this annex on the basis of the analysis of a simple case. An adjustment item is associated with each type of transaction converted in national currency using the specific exchange rate applicable to it. This adjustment item measures the implicit transfers (taxes or subsidies or other transfers) which result from the difference between the value of a flow converted at the exchange rate actually applicable to it and the value which this flow would have had if it had been converted using a single weighted exchange rate (a unitary rate) applied to all flows. Recording both the flows at the actual applicable exchange rate and the associated implicit transfers is equivalent to recording all flows at the unitary rate. In order to get balancing items in the rest of the world accounts that have the same interpretation in national and in foreign currency the implicit transfers must be entered in the same account where the corresponding transactions are recorded. As the balancing items of the rest of the world accounts have implications for the measurement of the main aggregates of the economy in question, the correct recording of the implicit transfers also bears consequences on the measurement of these aggregates. Additionally, the management of an official regime of multiple exchange rates may result in a surplus or deficit for the monetary authorities managing the System. The way the accounts of the central bank and general government are influenced must thus be taken into account.

7. This section is devoted to the presentation of the complete recording of an official system of multiple exchange rates. In

Table 19.6.   Account V.I: External account of goods and services

P.6	Exports of goods and services	9,570		P.7	Imports of goods and services	9,800
	Implicit taxes on exports resulting from multiple exchange rates[1]	630			Implicit taxes on imports resulting from multiple exchange rates[3]	–1,100
	Implicit subsidies on exports resulting from multiple exchange rates[2]	–200			Implicit subsidies on imports resulting from multiple exchange rates[4]	800
B.11	External balance of goods and services	–500				

1   Sub-heading of D213, Taxes on exports.
2   Sub-heading of D312, Export subsidies.
3   Sub-heading of D122, Taxes on imports excluding VAT and duties.
4   Sub-heading of D311, Imports subsidies.

Table 19.7.   Account V.II: External account of primary incomes and current transfers

...				B.11	External balance of goods and services	–500
D.29	Other taxes on production			D.4	Property income	
D ...	Implicit taxes on primary incomes resulting from multiple exchange rates			D.41	Interest	2,000
				D.421	Dividends	450
D.39	Other subsidies on production					
D ...	Implicit subsidies on primary incomes resulting from multiple exchange rates	–50				
...						
D.59	Other current taxes					
D ...	Implicit other current taxes resulting from multiple exchange rates					
...						
D.75	Miscellaneous current transfers					
D ...	Remittances from family members living abroad	825				
D ...	Implicit other current transfers resulting from multiple exchange rates	–75				
B.12	Current external balance	1,250				

Table 19.8.   Account V.III.1: Capital account

...		B.12	Current external balance	1,250
		D.9	Capital transfers receivable (+)	
		...		
		D.99	Other capital transfers	
		D. ...	Implicit other capital transfers resulting from multiple exchange rates	25
		D.9	Capital transfers payable (-)	
		D.91	Capital taxes	
		D ...	Implicit capital taxes resulting from multiple exchange rates	
B.9 Net lending (+)/ Net borrowing (-)	1,000	D.92	Investment grants	-275
		...		

Table 19.9.   Account V.III.2:   Financial account

...		F.2	Currency and deposits	0
F.4 Loans	4,000	...		
	-4,000	...		
F.5 Shares and other equity	1,100	B.9	Net lending (+)/ Net borrowing (-)	1,000
		D.99	Other capital transfers	
		D. ...	Implicit other capital transfers, resulting from multiple exchange rates	100
		D.91	Capital taxes	
		D. ...	Implicit capital taxes resulting from multiple exchange rates (-)	-0

that such a system is fully respected, that is to say the constraints imposed by the government are totally followed. No parallel exchange market exists. At the end of this section (see paragraph 27 below), the existence of those parallel exchange markets that may be considered as effectively integrated in the official exchange policy is introduced. Later on, in section D below, the existence of other parallel markets is taken into account. The treatment followed in the SNA is illustrated by way of a full-scale numerical example which permits the implications throughout the accounts to be seen. As always in the System, exchange rates exclude any service charge. It is also assumed in the example, for the sake of simplification, that the exchange rates are

not changed during the period under review. Thus no holding gains/losses have to be taken into consideration.

8. The data in foreign currency concerning the external relations of the economy are as follows: imports of goods and services 950, exports of goods and services 1,000, interest receivable by the rest of the world 200, dividends receivable 50, miscellaneous current transfers (remittances from workers resident abroad) payable by the rest of the world 75, capital transfers payable 25, new loans granted by the rest of the world to non-financial corporations 400, reimbursements of previous loans by non-financial corporations 400, shares and other equity acquired by the rest of the world 100, changes in liabilities (rest

of the world)/assets (the economy) in foreign currency and deposits 0. In foreign currency, the external balance of goods and service is thus –50 from the point of view of the rest of the world, the current external balance is 125 and net lending 100.

9. The central bank runs the system of official multiple exchange rates, as is usually the case. The purchases of foreign currency by the central bank are as follows:

Exports	100	at the rate of 12	1,200
	900	at the rate of 9.3	8,370
Miscellaneous current transfers	75	at the rate of 11	825
Capital transfers	25	at the rate of 11	275
Shares and other equity	100	at the rate of 11	1,100
New loans	400	at the rate of 10	4,000

that is, in total, 1,600 for an amount of 15,770 in national currency. The sales of foreign currency by the central bank are as follows:

Imports	400	at the rate of 8	3,200
	550	at the rate of 12	6,600
Interest	200	at the rate of 10	2,000
Dividends	50	at the rate of 9	450
Loans repayable	400	at the rate of 10	4,000

that is, in total, 1,600 for an amount of 16,250 in national currency. Thus the unitary rate is approximately 10 which is used for sake of convenience. The management of the system leaves a surplus of 480, that is, 16,250 – 15,770. An interpretation of this hypothetical situation is, for instance, that certain exporting activities are encouraged, as are transfers from abroad and acquisition of shares by and the payment of dividends to foreign investors; certain imports are favoured, whereas others are discouraged. The rates applicable to flows connected with the external debt are neutral. Most exporters receive a rate which is lower than the unitary rate, in order not to discourage exports but to give a margin of flexibility on other rates.

10. The implicit taxes are 1,100 on imports (6,600 – 5,500) and 630 on exports (9,000 – 8,370). The implicit subsidies or other transfers are 800 on imports (4,000 – 3,200), 200 on exports (1,200 – 1,000), 75 on miscellaneous current transfers (825 – 750), 25 on capital transfers (275 – 250), 100 on shares and other equity (1,100 – 1,000) and 50 on dividends (500 – 450). Implicit taxes as a whole are 1,730 and implicit subsidies or other transfers 1,250, the surplus being of course 480.

11. Let us build up the accounts of the rest of the world in national currency (see tables 19.6, 19.7, 19.8 and 19.9). For the sake of simplicity, only the transactions existing in the above example are shown.

12. Some words of explanation are useful. In the external account of goods and services, implicit taxes and implicit subsidies on imports are recorded on the same side as imports. Implicit taxes are shown with a negative sign. In effect, in the absence of such taxes, the amount of imports of goods and services in national currency would be lower. Implicit subsidies are shown with a positive sign. Symmetrically, in the absence of such subsidies, the amount of imports of goods and services in national currency would be higher. The right-hand side of this account thus shows, as a total, what would have been the value of imports if they had been converted using the unitary rate (9,800 – 1,100 + 800 = 950 x 10). On the left-hand side of the account, implicit taxes on exports are recorded with a positive sign and implicit subsidies with a negative sign. In the absence of such taxes (subsidies), the amount of exports in national currency would have been higher (lower). Again combining the first three rows shows what would have been the value of exports if they had been converted using the unitary rate (9,570 + 630 – 200 = 1,000 x 10) It may be seen easily from this account that, if the implicit taxes/subsidies were not recorded, the external balance of goods and services would seem to be +230, a surplus for the rest of the world (a deficit of the nation), when in foreign currency it is –50. Recording the implicit taxes/subsidies gives a more consistent figure (–500, that is –50 x 10).

13. The adjustment items to be entered in the external account of primary incomes and current transfers are a bit more complex. Implicit taxes/subsidies or other transfers on transactions consisting of primary incomes (compensation of employees, taxes minus subsidies on production and imports and property income) must be recorded separately from implicit taxes/transfers on current transfers (current taxes on income, wealth, etc..., social contributions and benefits, other current transfers). The reason is that the former influence the measurement of national income, when going from domestic product to national income, whereas the latter influence the measurement of national disposable income, when going from national income to national disposal income (see below, paragraphs 17 and 26). Implicit taxes/subsidies on primary incomes resulting from multiple exchange rates are entered as sub-headings under other taxes on production or other subsidies on production. For the sake of simplification they are recorded only on the left-hand side of the accounts, positively for implicit taxes, negatively for implicit subsidies. In the numerical example there is only an implicit subsidy related to the payment of dividends to the rest of the world (in the absence of such subsidy, the dividends receivable by the rest of the world would be equivalent to 500 in national currency, that is 50 x 10, or 450 + 50). More generally, there is an implicit tax when primary incomes receivable by the rest of the world are converted at a specific rate(s) that is (are) higher than the unitary rate or when primary incomes payable by the rest of the world are converted at a specific rate(s) that is (are) lower than the unitary rate. Symmetrically, there is an implicit subsidy when primary incomes receivable by the rest of the world are converted at a specific rate(s) that is (are) lower than the uni-

Table 19.10. Account V.IV: Goods and services account

Resources			Uses		
P.1	Output	89,000	P.2	Intermediate consumption	45,000
P.7	Imports of goods and services	9,000	P.3/P.4	Final consumption expenditure/actual final consumption	40,000
	Implicit taxes on imports resulting from multiple exchange rates	−1,100	P.5	Gross capital formation	18,000
			P.6	Exports of goods and services	9,570
	Implicit subsidies on imports resulting from multiple exchange rates	+800		Implicit taxes on exports resulting from multiple exchange rates	630
D.21	Taxes on products	17,710		Implicit subsidies on exports resulting from multiple exchange rates	−200
D.31	Subsidies on products (−)	−3,210			
		113,000			113,000

Table 19.11. Account V.V: Supply of products

	Taxes on products (3)	Subsidies on products (4)		Implicit taxes /subsidies on imports resulting from multiple exchange rates (22b)	Imports (23) (24)
Goods and services					
. . .					
12b. Implicit taxes resulting from multiple exchange rates	1,730			−1,100	
12c. Implicit subsidies resulting from multiple exchange rates		−1,000		800	
13. Total	17,710	−3,210		−300	9,800

tary rate or when primary incomes payable by the rest of the world are converted at a specific rate(s) that is (are) higher than the unitary rate. A parallel reasoning is made concerning implicit taxes/transfers related to flows of current transfers. Implicit taxes on current transfers are entered as a sub-heading under other current taxes. Implicit transfers are entered as a sub-heading under miscellaneous current transfers. If implicit taxes/subsidies or other transfers were not recorded, the current external balance would seem to be 1,855 (+230 + 2,000 + 450 − 825) instead of 1,250, which is equivalent to 125 x 10.

14. Implicit capital taxes/transfers related to transactions recorded

in the capital account are entered in the right-hand side of the capital account as they influence net worth. Implicit capital taxes resulting from multiple exchange rates are a sub-heading of capital taxes. Implicit other capital transfers are a sub-heading of other capital transfers. If implicit taxes/subsidies or other transfers were not recorded, the net lending of the rest of the world would seem to be 1,580 in the capital account (1,855 − 275). There would be a discrepancy between net lending measured in the capital account (1,580) and net lending measured from the financial account (1,100), this discrepancy being equal to the surplus accruing to the monetary authorities

Table 19.12. Account V.VI: Use of products

				Implicit taxes /subsidies on exports resulting from multiple exchange rates (21b)	Exports (22) (23)
Goods and services					
. . .					
12b. Implicit taxes resulting from multiple exchange rates				630	
12c. Implicit subsidies resulting from multiple exchange rates				-200	
13. Total uses in purchasers' prices				430	9,570
. . .					

from the management of the official multiple exchange rates system (480). Recording the implicit taxes/subsidies or other transfers gives a consistent figure for net lending in both the capital and the financial accounts (1,000, that is, 100 in foreign currency x 10).

15. Implicit capital taxes/transfers related to financial transactions are recorded in the financial account, also on the right-hand side of the account as they influence net worth. They are shown below net lending/net borrowing. They should not be interpreted as financial transactions; they are adjustment items. Combining the value of transactions in shares and other equity, using the actual rate applied to them, and the related implicit transfers shows what would have been the value of transactions in shares and other equity if they had been converted using the unitary rate (1,100 - 100 = 100 x 10).

16. The recording of implicit taxes/subsidies in the external account of goods and services has parallel implications for the goods and services account of the economy. The numerical example is completed with hypothetical figures for other transactions in goods and services (see table 19.10).

17. The total of taxes on products (17,710) includes the implicit taxes on imports and exports. Similarly, the total of subsidies on products (3,210) includes the implicit subsidies on imports and exports. Gross domestic product measured from the production side is equal to output (89,000) minus intermediate consumption (-45,000) plus taxes on products (17,710) minus subsidies on products (-3,210), that is, 58,500. Without re-

cording the implicit taxes/subsidies, the measure of GDP from the production side would have been 57,770 (89,000 - 45,000 + [17,710 - 1,730] - [3,210 - 1,000]). GDP measured from the expenditure side is equal to final consumption (40,000), plus gross capital formation (18,000), plus exports of goods and services (9,570), plus implicit taxes less subsidies on exports (630 - 200), less imports of goods and services (-9,800), plus implicit taxes less subsidies on imports (+ 1,100 - 800), that is, 58,500. In other words, GDP from the expenditure side is calculated as if exports and imports were converted using the same unitary rate. Without recording the implicit taxes/subsidies, the measure of GDP from the expenditure side would have been 57,770 (40,000 + 18,000 + 9,570 - 9,800). The difference between the two measures of GDP (730) is equal to the implicit taxes (1,100 + 630) less the implicit subsidies (- 800 - 200) on imports and exports.

18. The implicit taxes/subsidies are also shown as global adjustments in the supply and use table in accordance with their recording in the goods and services account. On the supply side, a column is added close to the column for imports: "Implicit taxes/subsidies on imports resulting from multiple exchange rates" Two rows are also added for implicit taxes and implicit subsidies. On the use side, a column is added close to the column for exports: "Implicit taxes/subsidies on exports resulting from multiple exchange rates". Two rows are also added for implicit taxes and implicit subsidies. These additions are shown in tables 19.11 and 19.12.

19. As far as the accounts of institutional sectors are concerned, the System records the influence of the implicit taxes/subsidies or other transfers only in the accounts of general government and the central bank or other monetary authority managing the system of official multiple exchange rates. The accounts of other institutional sectors are not influenced. Their transactions with the rest of the world are converted, following the general rule, at the actual exchange rate(s) applicable. The global adjustments related to implicit taxes and subsidies or other transfers inserted in the accounts of the rest of the world all have their counterparts in the accounts of general government, either directly or through the goods and services account. These counterparts are not recorded directly in the accounts of the central bank because, among resident sectors, only general government is allowed to receive taxes in the System.

20. Following the numerical example used in this section, general government thus receives:

1,730	under taxes on products
–1,000	under subsidies on products
–50	under other subsidies on production
–75	under miscellaneous current transfers
–125	under other capital transfers

i.e., in total it receives 480.

21. According to the assumption made in this section that the central banks managing the official system of multiple exchange rates, an amount equivalent to implicit current taxes less subsidies or other current transfers, i.e., 605, is then transferred to the central bank by general government under miscellaneous current transfers. Also an amount equivalent (–125) is transferred to the central bank by general government under other capital transfers partly in the capital account (–25), partly in the financial account (–100).

22. The entries in the accounts of general government related to multiple exchange rates are shown in table 19.13. Implicit taxes and subsidies on imports, exports and primary incomes are recorded in the allocation of primary income account. As a result the balance of primary incomes of general government (actually central government) is altered by the difference between implicit taxes and implicit subsidies (+680 according to the numerical example). Implicit other current taxes and implicit other current transfers resulting from multiple exchange rates are recorded in the secondary distribution of income account. Then an amount equivalent to the balance between all current taxes and subsidies or other current transfers (680 – 75, that is, 605) is transferred to the Central Bank under "Implicit current transfers between monetary authorities in relation to multiple exchange rates". As a consequence, the disposable income of general government is not altered and nor is adjusted disposable income or saving. Implicit capital transfers (taxes or other transfers) related to transactions recorded in the capital account are entered in the capital account (–25 according to the numerical example). Then an amount equivalent to

the balance between implicit capital transfers receivable and payable (–25) is transferred to the Central Bank under "Implicit capital transfers between monetary authorities in relation to multiple exchange rates": – (–25). Consequently, the net lending/net borrowing of general government is not influenced.

23. The entries in the accounts of financial corporations (actually the Central Bank) related to multiple exchange rates are shown in table 19.14. The secondary distribution of income account records the implicit current transfers from general government under "Implicit current transfers between monetary authorities in relation to multiple exchange rates" (605). As a consequence, the disposable income of financial corporations is influenced by the same amount, as is their saving. Then an implicit capital transfer is received from government in the capital account: + (–25). The net lending of financial corporations is thus influenced by 580. In the financial account, again an implicit capital transfer is received from general government: + (–100). The surplus resulting from the management of the official system of multiple exchange rates is 480 [580 + (–100)], as already calculated in paragraph 9 of this annex. On the left-hand side, the changes in assets of currency and deposits in foreign currency are recorded at the unitary rate (+16,000 – 16,000). The surplus from the management of the system results in the first instance in an increase in assets of currency and deposits in national currency (480).

24. According to the accounts presented in paragraphs 22 and 23 of this annex, the existence of the system of multiple exchange rates and its management by the Central Bank alter the balance of primary income of general government but not, in the first instance, its disposable income, saving and net lending/net borrowing. Conversely, the disposable income, saving and net lending of financial corporations are, in the first instance, altered. In practice, depending on the institutional arrangements between the government and the central bank, surpluses yielded by multiple exchange rates may contribute to transfers from the Central Bank to the government (or deficits may reduce such transfers) which may take a number of different forms. In the SNA, the actual transfers are recorded according to the nature of the actual transactions that take place between the Central Bank and the government, possibly including all or part of surpluses or deficits generated by multiple exchange rates. Thus, ultimately, disposable income, saving and net lending/net borrowing of general government may be altered indirectly by the system of multiple exchange rates, and the effect on the corresponding balancing items for financial corporations may be reduced accordingly.

25. It remains to be seen how the recording of a system of official multiple exchange rates affects the integrated economic accounts. The only changes in presentation are the addition of two rows in the upper part of the integrated economic accounts, where the external account of goods and services and

Table 19.13.   Accounts for general government

Account II.1.2:   Allocation of primary income account

D.2	Taxes on production and imports	
...		
	Implicit taxes on imports resulting from multiple exchange rates	1,100
...		
	Implicit taxes on exports resulting from multiple exchange rates	630
...		
	Implicit taxes on primary incomes resulting from multiple exchange rates	
D.3	Subsidies (–)	
...		
	Implicit subsidies on imports resulting from multiple exchange rates	–800
...		
	Implicit subsidies on exports resulting from multiple exchange rates	–200
...		

B.5	Balance of primary incomes	680	Implicit subsidies on primary incomes resulting from multiple exchange rates	–50

Account II.2:   Secondary distribution of income account

...			B.5	Balance of primary income	680
D.7	Other current transfers		D.5	Current taxes on income, wealth, etc.	
...			...		
	Implicit other current transfers resulting from multiple exchange rates	75		Implicit other current taxes resulting from multiple exchange rates	0
	Implicit current transfers between monetary authorities in relation to multiple exchange rates	605	...		
...					
B.6	Disposal income	0			

Table 19.13   Accounts for general government (*cont.*)

Account III.1:   Capital account

	B.8	Saving, net	0
	D.9	Capital transfers receivable (+)	
	. . .		
	.	Implicit capital taxes resulting from multiple exchange rates	0
	D.9	Capital transfers payable (–)	
		Implicit other capital transfers resulting from multiple exchange rates	–25
B.9 Net lending (+)/ Net borrowing (–)	0	Implicit capital transfers between monetary authorities in relation to multiple exchange rates	(–25)

Account III.2:   Financial account

	. . .		
	. . .		
	B.9	Net lending (+)/Net borrowing (–)	0
	D.9	Capital transfers receivable (+)	
	. . .		
		Implicit capital taxes resulting from multiple exchange rates	0
	D.9	Capital transfers payable (–)	
		Implicit other capital transfers resulting from multiple exchange rates	–100
		Implicit capital transfers between monetary authorities in relation to multiple exchange rates	–(–100)

the goods and services account are shown, and the inclusion of three rows in the financial account, if relevant, below net lending/net borrowing. The first two rows are introduced below the row P.6 Exports goods and services. They cover respectively implicit taxes and implicit subsidies resulting from multiple exchange rates. This presentation is shown in table 19.15.

26. Then the implicit taxes/subsidies or other transfers, and the transfers between general government and the Central Bank

are included mostly as sub-headings under the relevant transactions: taxes less subsidies on products, other taxes less subsidies on production, current taxes on income, wealth, etc., other current transfers, etc. When relevant three rows are added in the financial account, on the right-hand side, below net lending/net borrowing, for "Implicit other capital transfers resulting from multiple exchange rates", "Implicit capital taxes resulting from multiple exchange rates", and "Implicit capital transfers between monetary authorities in relation to

Table 19.14.   Accounts for financial corporations

Account II.2: Secondary distribution of income account

			B.5	Balance of primary incomes	0
			. . .		
			D.7	Other current transfers	
				Implicit current transfers between monetary authorities in relation to multiple exchange rates	605
B.6	Disposable income	605	. . .		

Account III.1:   Capital account

			B.8	Saving, net	605
			. . .		
			D.9	Capital transfers receivable (+)	
B.9	Net lending (+)/ Net borrowing (–)	580		Implicit capital transfers between monetary authorities in relation to multiple exchange rates	+(–25)

Account III.2:   Financial account

. . .			. . .		
F.2	Currency and deposits		. . .		
	m11: denominated in national currency	480	B.9	Net lending (+)/ Net borrowing (–)	580
	m12: denominated in foreign currency	+16,000	D.9	Capital transfers receivable (+)	
		–16,000		Implicit capital transfers between monetary authorities in relation to multiple exchange rates	+ (–100)
. . .					

multiple exchange rates". GDP, following the numerical example, has already been calculated (see paragraph 17 above of this annex). It is 58,500. Gross national income (GNI) is equal to GDP (58,500), minus interest (–2,000), minus dividends (–450), plus implicit taxes (0), minus implicit subsidies (–50) on primary incomes resulting from multiple exchange rates. GNI is thus 56,000. Without recording implicit taxes/subsidies,

GNI would have been calculated as 55,320 (57,770 – 2,000 – 450). Gross national disposable income (GNDI) is equal to GNI (56,000) plus remittances from family members living abroad (825) plus implicit other current taxes (0) less implicit other current transfers resulting from multiple exchange rates (–75). GNDI is thus 56,750. Without recording implicit taxes/subsidies or other transfers, GNDI would have been cal-

Table 19.15. Account V.VII: Integrated economic accounts

	Uses			Transactions and balancing items		Resources		
	Goods and services (resources)	Rest of the world					Rest of the world	Goods and services (uses)
Production/ external account of goods and services								
	9,800			P.7 Imports of goods and services			9,800	
		9,570		P.6 Exports of goods and services				9,570
	−1,100	630		Implicit taxes resulting from multiple exchange rates			−1,100	630
	800	−200		Implicit subsidies resulting from multiple exchange rates			800	−200

culated as 56,145 (55,320 + 825). Saving is affected to the same extent (+ 605). The figures for net lending of the rest of the world (net borrowing of the economy) have already been commented upon (see paragraph 14 above of this annex).

27. Until this point, only pure official systems of multiple exchange rates directly operated by the monetary authorities have been dealt with. However, in certain circumstances, some parallel exchange markets may be considered as effectively integrated in the official exchange rate policy. When parallel markets are clearly part of the official exchange rate policy, the treatment described in this section applies to the total of the official regime and the parallel market, for which total a single unitary rate is calculated. It is difficult to specify exact criteria for determining when a parallel market is effectively integrated in the exchange rate regime. This will usually be the case when most or all transactions in the parallel market are sanctioned by the authorities and/or when the authorities actively intervene in the market by buying and selling foreign exchange to affect the parallel rate. When only limited transactions in the parallel market, such as transactions of non-resident tourists, are sanctioned by the authorities, neither these transactions nor the parallel market as a whole should be taken into consideration in calculating the unitary rate. Of course, practical difficulties are greater in such situations because, even if the exchange rate in the parallel authorized market is generally well-known every day, the associated quantities of foreign currency that are exchanged and the type of external transactions with which they are connected are more difficult to estimate. Nevertheless, it should be stressed that estimating these flows is necessary in order to assess correctly the external relations and main aggregates of economies experiencing this type of situation.

28. Finally, it should be stressed again that implicit taxes/subsidies or other transfers are recorded in the system as global adjustments. They are neither allocated by products nor by industry/institutional sectors (except for their influence on government and central bank accounts). More detailed analysis may be useful in order to assess the implications of multiple exchange rate systems. This is not done in the central framework of the SNA and requires complementary work.

D. Taking into account the existence of parallel exchange markets which are not part of the official exchange policy

29. Unauthorized parallel exchange markets (black markets) often tend to develop beyond the official exchange policy. Data concerning black markets are very scarce, apart from indications on the exchange rate itself. However, when transac-

tions in black markets are important, it is recommended that extra estimates be made, in complementary analyses outside the central framework.

30. Conceptually, the existence of a black market in addition to official and authorized parallel multiple exchange rates has similar implications for the conversion to national currency of external flows measured in foreign currency, as the situations previously analysed. The structural relationships and the measurement of balancing items may be influenced in a similar way. In fact, if all external flows both official, authorized and illegal are known in foreign currency, as well as the corresponding actual exchange rates, a weighted general unitary rate can be calculated and enlarged implicit transfers estimated. These enlarged implicit transfers are calculated for each transaction as the difference between the value of the transaction converted in national currency at the actual exchange rate applicable and the value of this transaction converted at the generalized unitary rate. By deducting from these enlarged implicit transfers the taxes and subsidies/or other transfers calculated following the treatment described in section C above, in this annex, one could estimate the global "private" implicit transfers involved in the kind of situation referred to in this paragraph. The interpretation of the enlarged implicit transfers is straightforward. The economic units selling foreign currency in the black market at a rate which is higher than the general unitary rate and the economic units buying currency in the official system or the authorized parallel market at a rate which is lower than the general unitary rate benefit from positive implicit transfers. Symmetrically, the economic units selling foreign currency in the official system or the authorized parallel market at a rate which is lower than the general unitary rate and the economic units purchasing foreign currency in the black market at a rate which is higher than the general unitary rate incur negative implicit transfers.

31. For exchange transactions realized through the official exchange policy, the "private" implicit transfers are that part of the enlarged implicit transfers which is not accounted for by the taxes/subsidies or other transfers directly resulting from the official exchange policy. It is easy to see that for each transaction, the implicit "private" transfers are equal to the value of the corresponding flow in foreign currency multiplied by the difference between the generalized unitary rate and the unitary rate corresponding to the official exchange policy. They are positive for purchasers of foreign currency and negative for sellers of foreign currency (under the assumption that the generalized unitary rate is always higher than the "official" unitary rate, because the black market rate is higher than the latter). For exchange transactions realized through the black market, "private implicit transfers" are the same as "enlarged

implicit transfers". For each transaction they are equal to the value of the corresponding flow in foreign currency multiplied by the difference between the actual exchange rate and the generalized unitary rate. They are positive for sellers of foreign currency and negative for purchasers of foreign currency.

32. It is to be noted that no "private" implicit transfers, as defined above, occur between transactors of foreign currency in the black market. As a matter of fact, there is no price discrimination between various types of transactors or transactions in the black market. "Private" implicit transfers result from the coexistence of the official or authorized exchange system and the black market. They are transfers between transactors of foreign currency in the official or authorized exchange system and transactors of foreign currency in the black market.

33. Whenever calculated, "private" implicit transfers are recorded as global adjustment items in the rest of the world accounts and the goods and services accounts. For the sake of simplicity, their counterparts are recorded in the first instance in a dummy sector which forms part of the total economy. As already indicated (see paragraph 28 of this annex), in more detailed analysis one may try to allocate them by products and by industry/institutional sectors in order to assess more completely the incidence of multiple exchange rates.

34. The unitary exchange rates referred to in this annex are only weighted averages of actual exchange rates. They are not equilibrium rates. The purpose of the treatment recommended in this annex is not to calculate the hidden transfers which may result from the gap between these empirical unitary rates and any equilibrium rate possibly estimated using a theoretical model.

35. Some economic units may trade foreign currencies purchased at a favourable official rate for certain purposes which they do not actually fulfil illegally in parallel markets. Revenues obtained from such transactions are to be treated as holding gains. Note however that, when the monetary authorities sell currencies which they have purchased in the official system in the parallel authorized market, the proceeds accruing to the authorities as a result of these transactions are part of the implicit taxes generated by the official exchange policy (see paragraph 27 of this annex).

Note

a Combining imports at their actual exchange rate and implicit taxes on imports is equivalent to recording imports at the "unitary rate". Similarly, combining exports at their actual ecxchange rate and implicit taxes on exports is equivalent to recording exports at the "unitary rate". It is thus not surprising that the external balance of goods and services is also recorded at the "unitary rate".

Annex B
A parallel treatment of interest under significant inflation

A. Introduction: two ways of adjusting nominal interest in the context of significant inflation

1. Countries experiencing significant inflation may want to adjust nominal interest in order to get more meaningful measures of primary incomes, disposable income and saving of the various institutional sectors and possibly the total economy. Two main approaches may be followed:

    (*a*) Deduct from nominal interest (leaving aside here the possible service charge component in case of interest receivable/payable by financial intermediaries except insurance corporations and pension funds) the amount which has been or would have been necessary in order to keep the purchasing power of the capital intact (the capital being the principal of the financial asset/liability to which the interest refers); or

    (*b*) Deduct from nominal interest the component of protection against inflation of the principal of the asset which is actually included in nominal interest.

2. The first approach is usually referred to as the calculation of "real interest". Real interest is the excess of nominal interest on monetary assets over the amount which has been or would have been necessary in order to fully protect the creditor against inflation. The latter amount is calculated using an index representative of the change in the general purchasing power of the currency. When nominal interest is higher than the amount necessary to keep capital intact, real interest is positive. When nominal interest is lower than the amount necessary to keep capital intact, real interest is negative.

3. Real interest is derived from nominal interest by taking account of real holding gains/losses on the underlying assets/liabilities. For this reason, however, real interest may not be introduced in the central framework of the System since it is a basic principle of the System that holding gains or losses should not be recorded in the current accounts of the central framework, but only in the revaluation account. This is true for nominal holding gains/losses (and *a fortiori* real holding gains/losses) on all types of assets/liabilities. Thus real interest as well as other adjustments of current incomes for real holding gains/losses may only be introduced in a satellite construct (see for instance paragraphs 21.19 to 21.28 of chapter XXI).

4. In the second approach, the component of protection of the principal of the asset against inflation which is actually included in nominal interest is deducted. Clearly the component of protection against inflation can not, by definition, be greater than nominal interest itself; it can only be lower than or equal to nominal interest (continuing to leave aside the service charge issue). In order to avoid any confusion with real interest from one side, and interest as currently defined in the central framework from the other side, let us call the excess of nominal interest over the component of protection against inflation of the principal of the asset actually included in nominal interest "interest prime". By definition, "interest prime" may be positive or zero, but never negative.

5. Real interest and interest prime serve different purposes. Interest prime takes into account the actual influence of inflation on nominal interest, by deducting from the latter the actual component of protection against inflation of the principal of the asset which it includes. Real interest takes into account the impact of inflation on the purchasing power of the underlying assets, by deducting from the nominal interest the amount which has been or would have been necessary in order to keep the purchasing power of the asset intact.

6. Reflecting their different purposes, real interest and interest prime have different roles and places in the SNA. Real interest is a very useful analytical tool; as already stated in paragraph 3 above of this annex, it may be calculated as a satellite construct, something which the System strongly recommends. Although it does not go so far as real interest, interest prime allows for a possible adjustment of nominal interest in the SNA central framework itself in the context of significant inflation. In the case of other property income, such as dividends, the protection against inflation of the value of the underlying asset is sought through the change in the market prices of the underlying assets, such as shares, recorded in the revaluation account. This element is not included in dividends in current terms. Thus, in terms of economic significance, the meaning of "interest prime" resembles the meaning of dividends. Both "interest prime" and dividends may then be adjusted for real holding gains/losses, outside the central framework, in order to get real interest or real dividends (not to be confused with interest in real terms or dividends in real terms). In terms of economic significance, the sum of dividends and holding gains/losses on shares can be interpreted as

parallel to nominal interest. This shows that "interest prime" actually provides a concept whose definition is closer to the definition and measure of other property income than nominal interest.

7. Real interest and interest prime only coincide when the component of protection against inflation actually included in

nominal interest is strictly equal to the amount necessary in order to give the creditor full protection against inflation. In other cases, real holding gains or losses are still experienced by debtors and creditors. They may be combined with interest prime, outside the central framework, in order to derive real interest.

B. Parallel treatment of interest under significant inflation within the central framework

8. The rest of this annex presents a parallel treatment of interest under significant inflation consisting of the recording of interest prime in the central framework.

9. In the SNA central framework, because holding gains/losses are never recorded in the current accounts, both an income and a possible real holding gain or loss on the corresponding asset may exist at the same time. In terms of contracts between transactors, this may be interpreted as implying two different contracts: the first one concerns current income—i.e., the agreement on the amount required by an institutional unit for putting an asset at the disposal of another unit; the second one is the agreement on a price adjustment mechanism applicable to the value of the asset itself. In a number of cases, the price adjustment mechanism is explicit. It is the market price of the asset in question when it exists (shares, land); it is the rate of exchange for financial assets/liabilities denominated in foreign currency; it may be the price of another asset, good or service, or a price index, general or specific, used in index-linking. In other cases, when only nominal interest exists and there is no index-linking of the principal of a financial asset/liability, the price adjustment mechanism is implicit, which of course complicates the picture. Whether explicit or implicit, the price adjustment mechanism of the principal of the asset/liability determines the component of protection against inflation actually included in nominal interest.

10. The issue of the service charge component of interest is left aside in this annex, except briefly at the end, although, it has to be taken into account in practice.

11. The case of financial instruments denominated in foreign currency is simple. The central framework follows a treatment which is consistent with the method applied in this annex. The price adjustment mechanism applicable to the value of the assets/liabilities in question is the change in the relevant rate of exchange. Interest prime thus coincides with interest in the accounts of the rest of the world. Incidentally this shows that interest in the relationship with the rest of the world is different in nature from nominal interest recorded on assets denominated in national currency.

12. The identification of the component of protection against inflation of the principal of monetary assets denominated in national currency and of interest prime is straightforward in the case of index-linked financial instruments. In this case the two

elements are explicitly distinguished in practice (they are combined afterwards by the SNA central framework as nominal interest). The amount which results from the revaluation of the principal of the financial assets/liabilities in question through the existing explicit index-linking mechanism is the actual element of protection of the creditor against inflation. Under such circumstances, interest prime is, therefore, equivalent to what is referred to as interest under such arrangements. The index-linking of interest must be distinguished from the index-linking of the principal and the interest includes the amount corresponding to the index-linking of interest itself, if such a mechanism exists.

13. The identification of these two components of nominal interest is less simple when there is no explicit price adjustment mechanism applicable to the principal of the financial assets/liabilities in question. In such a case, only nominal interest is observable. A breakdown between the component of protection against inflation and a possible interest prime may only be approximate. Two main types of situation may be encountered:

(a) In the first situation, non-index-linked financial instruments coexist with index-linked ones. In such a case it is possible to apply to the first instruments the same rate of interest prime, or the same price adjustment mechanism—i.e., the same index—or the same proportion between the two components as for index-linked instruments;

(b) In the second situation, only non-index-linked financial instruments exist. In such a case the simplest procedure seems to be to take the ex-post rate of inflation as approximating the implicit price adjustment mechanism and derive the component of protection against inflation of the principal of the asset actually included in nominal interest, accordingly. Interest prime is then determined as the excess of nominal interest over this component, unless the component for protection against inflation exceeds nominal interest in which case interest prime is set at zero (see paragraph 4 above of this annex).

14. The existence of a margin of uncertainty in the cases covered in the previous paragraph should not be cause for alarm. When inflation is significant, this margin of uncertainty is much less

important than the error made when recording nominal interest in the current accounts.

C. The accounting treatment in detail

15. Supposing now that interest prime is known or has been estimated, the full accounting treatment must be described. This is done first by explaining the accounting entries as such; then numerical examples are provided.

16. In the primary distribution of income accounts, interest prime is recorded in place of nominal interest.

17. In the revaluation account, the amount which corresponds to the revaluation of the principal of the financial assets/liabilities in question, through the explicit or implicit price adjustment mechanism, is recorded as nominal holding gains/losses. The explicit mechanism if there is index-linking of the principal, or the approximation of it in the case of nominal interest, is equivalent to a change in the specific price of the financial instrument in question. The amount entered as nominal holding gains/losses is the following, for the three types of financial instruments which have been distinguished:

    (a) For financial instruments denominated in foreign currency, it is the change in value of the stock of assets and liabilities which results from the change of the exchange rate;

    (b) For index-linked financial instruments denominated in national currency it is straightforwardly the amount which results from the application of the index-linking mechanism;

    (c) For non-index-linked financial instruments (denominated in national currency), it is the difference between the amount of nominal interest and the amount of interest prime which has been estimated and recorded in the primary distribution of income accounts.

18. The financial assets/liabilities are then recorded in the balance sheets at a value which includes these nominal holding gains or losses (in principle on a perpetual inventory basis).

19. The financial account records the part of the principal of the assets/liabilities which is repaid in a given period, including the revaluation component, as a change in assets and a change in liabilities of the creditor and the debtor, respectively. It is important to interpret correctly the repayment of the element which originates in the revaluation mechanism. Two cases must be considered:

    (a) In the first case, the revaluation element which is repaid in a given period corresponds to the accumulated revaluation of that fraction of the nominal value of the principal which is repayable during this period. The total repayment (the initial nominal and the revaluation ele-

ment) thus represents an equivalent fraction of the approximate initial purchasing power of the principal;

    (b) In the second case, the revaluation element which is repaid in a given period corresponds to the full value of the revaluation that occurred during this period. It is actually payable. This procedure is to be analysed as an accelerated repayment of a part of the initial purchasing power of the principal of the financial asset/liability in question. This case corresponds both to certain index-linked financial instruments denominated in national currency, depending on the contractual arrangements, and to all non-index-linked financial instruments (denominated in national currency) bearing only nominal interest.

20. The changes in assets and liabilities recorded in the financial account are then balanced by equivalent decreases in the value of the stocks of financial assets/liabilities in the balance sheets.

21. With respect to the revaluation account, the real holding gains or losses must be calculated by subtracting the neutral holding gains/losses from the nominal holding gains or losses (see paragraph 17 of this annex). Again the various types of financial instruments previously distinguished may be considered separately:

    (a) For financial instruments denominated in foreign currency, a country incurs real holding gains, as a creditor, if the rate of exchange (number of units of the national currency per unit of the foreign currency) increases more than the general price level, or as a debtor, if the rate of exchange increases less than the general price level. Conversely, a country incurs real holding losses, as a creditor, if the rate of exchange increases less than the general price level, or as a debtor, if the rate of exchange increases more than the general price level;

    (b) For index-linked financial instruments denominated in national currency, there is a real holding loss for the creditors and a real holding gain for the debtors if the index used for index-linking increases less than the general price level. Conversely, there is a real holding gain for the creditor and a real holding loss for the debtor if the index used for index-linking increases more than the general price level;

    (c) For non-index-linked financial instruments (denominated in national currency), the two types of situation encountered in paragraph 13 above of this annex must be distinguished again. In the first one (these instruments are treated by reference to coexisting index-linked instruments), the analysis is the same as that in (b) above. In the second type of situation (only non-index-linked instruments exist), real holding gains for the debtors/losses for the creditors appear when the rate of ex-post inflation is higher than the nominal rate of interest.

22. The numerical examples below may help to illustrate what is explained above:

(a) Financial instruments denominated in foreign currency: a non-financial corporation borrows from a foreign bank, on 1 January, 100 units of foreign currency, the exchange rate being 10 at that time, at an interest rate of 12 per cent. Interest is payable at the end of the year, and the principal is also repaid at that time. The general price index is 300 at the end of the year (against 100 at the beginning) and the exchange rate is 27. The entries in the accounts are the following, in national currency:

The primary distribution of income accounts record 324[a] (12 x 27) as interest payable by non-financial corporations to the rest of the world.

The financial account records:

+ 1,000 (100 x 10) as a change in liabilities of non-financial corporations (a change in assets of the rest of the world) under loans;

– 2,700 (100 x 27) as a change in liabilities of non-financial corporations (a change in assets of the rest of the world) under loans.

The corresponding entries under currency and deposits, assuming the payments are made simultaneously, are the following:

+ 1,000 – 2,700 – 324 as changes in assets for non-financial corporations;

+ 1,000 – 2,700 – 324 as changes in liabilities for the rest of the world.

The revaluation account records:

1,700 (2,700 – 1,000) as a nominal holding loss for non-financial corporations (revaluation of a liability) and as a nominal holding gain for the rest of the world (revaluation of an asset);

1,700 as a nominal holding loss for the rest of the world (revaluation of the initial 1,000 additional liability under currency and deposits); these 1,700 are counterbalanced somewhere by an equivalent holding gain of the resident unit(s) holding the 100 units of foreign currency during the year (of course the story may be a bit more complex).

The balance sheets record the corresponding changes:

for non-financial corporations:

  financial assets: + 1,000 – 2,700 – 324[b]
  liabilities: + 1,000 + 1,700 – 2,700

for the rest of the world:

  financial assets: + 1,000 + 1,700 – 2,700
  liabilities: + 1,000 + 1,700 – 2,700 – 324
for some other resident unit(s)
  financial assets: + 1,700

The real holding gains or losses are obtained by subtracting 2,000, the amount of the neutral holding gains/losses (1000 x 2), from the nominal holding gains/losses (1,700); they are +300 (gain) on liabilities, –300 (loss) on assets;

(b) Index-linked financial instruments denominated in national currency: A non-financial corporation borrows 2,000 for two years from a resident bank, on 1 January, at an interest rate of 15 per cent; interest is payable at the end of the year, and the principal is repaid half at the end of the first year and half at the end of the second year. The principal is indexed on the internal wholesale price index, which is 300 at the end of the first year, against 100 at the beginning. Only the entries during the first year are described here; they are as follows:

The primary distribution of income account records 300 as interest payable/receivable.

The financial account records:

+ 2,000 as a change in liabilities of the corporation, a change in assets of the bank, under loans;

– 3,000 (1,000 + 2,000) as a change in liabilities of the corporation, a change in assets of the bank.

The corresponding entries, under currency and deposits, assuming the payments are made simultaneously through the account of the corporation in the same bank, are as follows:

+ 2,000 – 3,000 – 300 as changes in assets of the non-financial corporation;

+ 2000 – 3000 – 300 as changes in liabilities of the bank.

The revaluation account records 4,000 (2,000 x 2) as a nominal holding loss for the non-financial corporation (revaluation of a liability) and a nominal holding gain for the bank (revaluation of an asset). It must be noted that 2,000 nominal holding gain or loss corresponds to the part of the loan which is repayable at the end of the first year, whereas the other 2,000 refers to the rest of the loan.

The balance sheets record the corresponding changes:

for the non-financial corporation:

  financial asset: + 2,000 – 3,000 – 300[c]
  liabilities: + 2,000 – 3,000 + 4,000

for the bank:

  financial assets: + 2,000 – 3,000 + 4,000
  liabilities: + 2,000 – 3,000 – 300

Real holding gains/losses: If the change in the general price level is 300, the same as the wholesale price index used for index-linking, there are no real holding gains/losses, because the neutral holding gains/losses are equal to the nominal ones. If the change in the general price level is higher, for instance 310, the real holding gains are 200 for the debtor, and the creditor incurs a real holding loss of 200 (the neutral holding gains/losses are 4,200 in this case). If the change in the general price level is lower, for instance 295, the debtor incurs a real holding loss of 100 and the creditor has a real holding gain of 100 (the neutral holding gains/losses are 3,900 in this case).

Notes

(*i*)   The amount which is repaid at the end of the first year represents approximately half of the initial purchasing power of the amount borrowed/lent: 3,000 (1,000 + 2,000) corresponding more or less to the initial value of 1,000 in real terms (see paragraph 19 (*a*) above of this annex);

(*ii*)   The rest of the loan existing in balance sheets at the end of the first year is also 3,000 (1,000 + 2,000); it also corresponds to approximately half of the initial purchasing power of the loan;

(*iii*) Corresponding to the apparent rate of interest (15 per cent) there is actually a much lower rate, under the assumptions made, of 5 per cent (300 – 200/2,000) because the 300 paid at the end of the year is worth only 100 in terms of the initial purchasing power of the currency comparable with the amount borrowed/lent (2,000). It is interesting to note that when the revaluation of the principal is treated as interest and recorded in the current accounts, the apparent rate of interest is 215 per cent (3,000 + 4,000/2,000), instead of 15 per cent, and the corresponding lower rate in terms of the initial purchasing power of the currency is 71.6 per cent;

(*c*) Index-linked financial instruments denominated in national currency, with the full value of the revaluation of the principal payable during the period in which this revaluation occurs (see paragraph 19 (b) above): keeping the same assumption as in paragraph 22 (b) except the one above, the entries during the first year are as follows:

The primary distribution of income account records 300 as interest payable/receivable.

The financial account records:

+ 2,000 as a change in liabilities of the corporation, a change in assets of the bank, under loans;

–5,000 (1,000 + 4,000) as a change in liabilities of the corporation, a change in assets of the bank (loans);

+ 2,000 – 5,000 - 300 as changes in assets of the non-financial corporation;

+ 2,000 – 5,000 - 300 as changes in liabilities of the bank.

The revaluation account records 4,000 as a nominal holding loss/gain for the non-financial corporation and the bank, respectively.

The changes in balance sheets are:

for the non-financial corporation:

    financial assets: + 2,000 – 5,000 – 300

    liabilities: + 2,000 + 4,000 – 5,000

for the bank:

    financial assets: + 2,000 + 4,000 – 5,000

    liabilities: + 2,000 – 5,000 – 300

real holding gains/losses: no difference with case (b).

Notes

(*i*)   The amount (5,000) which is repaid at the end of the first year corresponds to half of the principal falling due at that time, that is, 3,000 (1,000 + 2,000), plus 2,000 which results from the revaluation of the rest of the principal. This payment of 2,000 represents an accelerated repayment of approximately two thirds of the initial purchasing power of that part of the principal which remains in the balance sheets at the end of the first year;

(*ii*)   The nominal value of the part of the loan which remains in the balance sheet at the end of the first year is 1,000 (note the difference with case (b)). It is easy to verify that it corresponds to approximately one third of its initial purchasing power;

(*d*) Non-index-linked financial instruments (which are in national currency): the same example is used except that there is a nominal rate of interest of 215 per cent. Interest prime is calculated using the ex-post index of inflation, which is supposed to be 300 (against 100 at the beginning of the year). The nominal interest (4,300) is thus broken down between a revaluation component (4,000) and a component of interest prime (300). The entries are then the same as that in case (c) above and the same comments are relevant in general. Under the assumptions of this example, there would be no real holding gain or loss. In addition, it should be noted that if the index of general price level were 325 instead of 300, interest prime would be zero, the nominal holding gains/losses would be 4,300 (corresponding in this situation to the total amount of nominal interest) and a real holding gain/loss of 200 would be recorded, as the neutral holding gain/loss is 4,500 (2,000 x 2.25).

D. A link with the calculation of the output of financial intermediaries

23. When interest prime is calculated, it should normally be used for calculating the financial intermediation services indirectly measured (FISIM). However, as the last example above shows, interest prime may be zero. This may happen when there is no explicit index-linking of the principal of financial instruments in a country, which is not an uncommon situation. Under such circumstances, the value of the output of financial intermediaries indirectly measured continues to be calculated as the "global interest margin" (property income receivable except on own funds, less interest payable), using nominal interest (the case of the Central Banks, for which no interest is payable on a significant share of their liabilities, necessitates a specific analysis). It is this "global interest margin" that corresponds to the financing of the costs of production and operating surplus of financial intermediaries. This follows from the assumption that nominal interest charged to debtors of the intermediaries should cover as a priority the implicit service charges and that, similarly, the fraction of interest not included in the nominal interest payable to creditors of the intermediaries covers, as is obvious, the implicit service payment charged to these creditors. It follows that, in such a situation, interest prime receivable by creditors of financial intermediaries is calculated as nominal interest receivable less implicit revaluation of the principal of their claims (not higher than the nominal interest itself) plus service charges payable by creditors which may be viewed equivalently as interest prime received in kind. Interest prime payable by debtors of financial intermediaries is calculated as nominal interest payable less service charges included in nominal interest less implicit revaluation of the principal of their liabilities (not higher than the previous difference).

Notes

a It may be noted that the expost rate of interest, assuming a regular adjustment of the rate of exchange is 17.5 per cent.

b These entries refer only to the transactions directly linked to the foreign loan. In addition, the non-financial corporation in question may have acquired domestic assets using the 1,000 borrowed at the beginning of the year and nominal holding gains are to be recorded on these assets, an increased operating surplus may have been obtained, etc.

c See note (iii)

XX. Social accounting matrices

A. Introduction

20.1. Previous chapters which focus on accounts for institutional sectors have adopted a sequence of T accounts as the basic method of presentation. At the same time it has been illustrated that the concepts and definitions of the System allow other methods of presentation. These serve to provide additional insights and to enable different types of analysis.

20.2. The presentation of national accounts in a matrix has a long and distinguished tradition. In the 1968 SNA the accounting structure was explained on the basis of an illustrative matrix covering the full System (table 2.1 of the 1968 publication) and in addition much emphasis was given to the System as a basis for input-output analysis. By now, the input-output table is a widely used matrix framework to supply detailed and coherently arranged information on the flow of goods and services and on the structure of production costs. This matrix contains more information than T accounts for goods and services, production and the generation of income; for example, final consumption expenditure is shown by product or industry of origin and intermediate consumption is shown both by product or industry of origin and by product or industry of destination. Disaggregated linkages between these accounts are further developed in the SNA's supply and use table, through a specification of output of categories of goods and services by industry—see table 2.5 in chapter II, appendix, and table 15.1 in chapter XV. However, those matrices do not incorporate the interrelationships between value added and final expenditures. By extending a supply and use table, or an input-output table, to show the entire circular flow of income at a meso-level, one captures an essential feature of a social accounting matrix (SAM).

20.3. Chapter II has demonstrated that the full sequence of accounts and balancing items for institutional sectors can also be presented in a matrix format—see the annex to chapter II. In those tables, all transactions are presented for institutional sectors, whereby the supply and use table, which uses a cross-classification by categories of goods and services and by industries, is not incorporated. In fact, the supply and use table opts for a classification of rows and columns which is most suitable to describe the economic processes under consideration, i.e., the processes of production and use of products. This principle of flexible classification can also be applied to a matrix presentation of a wider set of accounts, to arrive at a SAM.

20.4. A SAM is defined here as the presentation of SNA accounts in a matrix which elaborates the linkages between a supply and use table and institutional sector accounts. In many instances SAMs have been applied to an analysis of interrelationships between structural features of an economy and the distribution of income and expenditure among household groups. Evidently, SAMs are closely related to national accounts whereby their typical focus on the role of people in the economy may be reflected by, among other things, extra breakdowns of the household sector and a disaggregated representation of labour markets (i.e., distinguishing various categories of employed persons). On the other hand, SAMs usually encompass a somewhat less detailed supply and use table or input-output table. Since the design and construction method of SAMs are not standardized, their presentation in this chapter also has an illustrative character.

20.5. Before an attempt is made to sketch a few possible SAMs, it seems appropriate to provide an elementary explanation of accounting matrices and their properties. To this end, section B of this chapter builds on the reduced format matrix in chapter II and highlights the advantages of using a matrix presentation which includes both input-output and sector accounts. Section C explains how SAMs, supplemented with some (non-monetary) satellite tables, can provide a flexible and yet consistent framework for socio-economic analyses. Section D then introduces and explains the structure of an illustrative SAM. Section E provides some guidelines to the design of classifications. These are commonly based on the standard classifications but further developed to reflect national circumstances and needs. In order to illustrate this, section E also contains a somewhat elaborated SAM and a full-fledged value-added submatrix. Section F then lists some variants and sketches a SAM, including balance sheets. Finally, section G discusses the use of SAMs as a tool of statistical integration and as a framework for modelling and policy analysis.

Table 20.1. Consolidated version of the reduced SNA matrix (chapter II, annex)

Account	Codes	Goods and services 1	Production 2	Distribution of income 3 & 4 & 5	Use of income 6	Capital 7	Rest of the world, current and capital 10 & 11	Total
0. Goods and services	1		Intermediate consumption 1 883		Final consumption expenditure 1 399	Gross capital formation 414	Exports of goods and services 540	4 236
I. Production	2	Output and taxes on products less subsidies 3 737						3 737
II.1 and II.2 Distribution of income	3 4 5		Net domestic product 1 632	Property income and current taxes on income, wealth, etc. and current transfers 1 488			Compensation of employees and property income and current taxes and current transfers from ROW [1] 79	3 199
II.4. Use of income	6			Net disposable income 1 632	Adjustment for the change in net equity of households on pension funds 11		Adjustment for the change in net equity of households on pension funds from ROW 0	1 643
III.1. Capital	7		Consumption of fixed capital 222		Net saving 233	Capital transfers and acquisitions less disposals of non-produced assets 61	Capital transfers receivable (+) /payable (–) and acquisitions less disposals of non-produced assets by ROW –3	513
V.I, V.II and V.III.1. Rest of the world, current and capital	10 11	Imports of goods and services 499		Compensation of employees and property income and current taxes and current transfers to ROW [1] 222	Adjustment for the change in net equity of households on pension funds to ROW 79	Net lending (+)/ Net borrowing (–) of the total economy 38		616
Total		4 236	3 737	3 199	1 643	513	616	

1 Including taxes on production and imports from (cell 3&4&5, 10&11) and to (cell 10&11 and 3&4&5) the rest of the world (ROW).

B. A matrix presentation of SNA accounts

20.6. This section elaborates on the general purposes that can be served by an accounting matrix, which is defined here as a presentation of SNA accounts in matrix format. A crucial feature is the wide range of possibilities for expanding or condensing such a matrix in accordance with specific circumstances and needs.

1. A matrix presentation of several accounts for the total economy

20.7. Table 20.1 presents a number of important transactions of the System, aggregated for the total economy. Five types of (consolidated) accounts are distinguished: supply and use of goods and services, production, distribution of income, use of income, and capital transactions. In the last account, all these transactions with the rest of the world have been combined. The code numbers behind and below each account heading serve to facilitate the linkage of all tables in this chapter. This table is a consolidated version of the matrix in the annex to chapter II (cf. the account numbers), except that a breakdown of value added payable by producers into various categories of value added payable by them, as recorded in the generation of income account, is not incorporated in this matrix of transactions. The main reason is that in SAM-type analyses a different type of unit and classification thereof are typically used in the generation of income account (see section D.2 below).

20.8. The figures which are presented in the tables of this chapter exactly correspond to the numerical example worked out in the other chapters of this manual. In all matrices the boxes containing a balancing item have been framed with bold lines.

20.9. As already stated in the annex to chapter II, a matrix presentation permits each transaction to be represented by a single entry and the nature of the transaction to be inferred from its position. Each account is represented by a row and column pair and the convention is followed that incomings are shown in the rows and outgoings are shown in the columns. For instance, net domestic product (NDP) (1632) is payable by the economy's producers and received on the distribution of income account. Table 20.1 shows this in cell (3&4&5,2), that is, in row 3&4&5 and column 2. Since this table distinguishes transactions with the rest of the world in a separate account, its diagonal items, that is, cells (3&4&5,3&4&5) and (7,7), only contain transactions among national institutional units.

20.10. The row and column totals have not been named. In effect, some of these totals are not economically meaningful. Their main function in matrix accounting is to ensure that all accounts indeed represent complete balances, in the sense that total incomings (row sums) equal total outgoings (column sums). In turn, meaningful balancing items, which connect successive accounts, can only be derived if this condition is fulfilled.

20.11. Table 20.1 can be expanded to arrive at the reduced format matrix (see the matrix in the annex to chapter II). This implies the following:

(a) Break down the distribution of income account into a primary distribution of income account and a secondary distribution of income account;

(b) Incorporate on the diagonal of the primary distribution of income account, the categories of value added distinguished in the generation of income account;

(c) Add a financial account, an other changes in assets account, a changes between balance sheets account, a net worth account and opening and closing balance sheets;

(d) Break down the rest of the world account, current and capital into an account for external trade, an account for other current external transactions and a capital account for the rest of the world; and

(e) Add for the rest of the world: a financial account, an other changes in assets account, a changes between balance sheets account, a net worth account and opening and closing balance sheets.

In the next section of this chapter, the method to (re-)locate each set of transactions in an expanded matrix will be briefly discussed and illustrated (see table 20.2 below).

20.12. This reduced format matrix can be disaggregated to show the full sequence of accounts including details for transactors and transaction categories, to arrive at an extended SNA-matrix table. Naturally, it is also possible to distinguish both institutional sectors and transaction categories in a more consolidated accounting matrix, such as table 20.1. A concise example of showing an account both by institutional sector and by transaction category is presented in the next section of this chapter (see table 20.3 below).

2. Possibilities for expanding or contracting an accounting matrix

20.13. Each entry in an aggregate matrix such as table 20.1 can be considered as the grand total of a submatrix in which categories of transactors involved at either end of the set of transactions under consideration are presented. A very useful option in a matrix presentation of accounts is that different types of transactors and groupings thereof can be selected in each account, without giving up the coherence and the integration of the complete accounting system. This means that one may apply "multiple actoring and multiple sectoring", by choosing in each account a unit and a classification of units which are most relevant to the set of economic flows under consideration. In the illustrative SAM worked out below, four types of units are included: products, establishments, primary input

Table 20.2. Consolidated SNA matrix with sub-accounts

Account	Codes	Goods and services 1	Production 2	Primary distribution of income 3 & 4	Secondary distribution of income 5	Use of income 6	Capital 7	Rest of the world, current and capital 10 & 11	Total
0. Goods and services	1		Intermediate consumption 1 883			Final consumption expenditure 1 399	Gross capital formation 414	Exports of goods and services 540	4 236
I. Production	2	Output and taxes on products less subsidies 3 737							3 737
II.1. Primary distribution of income	3 4		Net domestic product 1 632	Property income 353				Compensation of employees and property income from ROW[1] 69	2 054
II.2. Secondary distribution of income	5			Net national income 1 661	Current tax on income, wealth etc. and current transfers 1 096			Current taxes on income, wealth etc. and current transfers from ROW 10	2 767
II.4. Use of income	6				Net disposable income 1 632	Adjustment for the change in net equity of households on pension funds 11		Adjustment for the change in net equity of households on pension funds from ROW 0	1 643
III.1. Capital	7		Consumption of fixed capital 222			Net saving 233	Capital transfers and acquisitions less disposals of non-produced assets 61	Capital transfers receivable (+)/payable (−) and acquisitions less disposals of non-produced assets by ROW −3	513
V.I, V.II and V.III.1. Rest of the world, current and capital	10 11	Imports of goods and services 499		Compensation of employees and property income to ROW[1] 40	Current tax on income, wealth etc. and current transfers to ROW 39	Adjustment for the change in net equity of households on pension funds to ROW 0	Net lending (+)/ Net borrowing (−) of the total economy 38		616
Total		4 236	3 737	2 054	2 767	1 643	513	616	

1 Including taxes on production and imports from (cell 3&4, 10&11) and to (cell 10&11 and 3&4) ROW.

units (employed persons, cultivated hectares of agricultural land, etc.) and institutional units. Naturally, the application of different units in a single table ("multiple actoring") entails that the classifications differ as well ("multiple sectoring"). In addition, it is sometimes desirable to use several classifications of the same unit in a single table; for instance, if a detailed taxonomy is only relevant in part of the accounts, or if for one or more accounts only aggregate information is available.

20.14. In principle, each account can be broken down in two rather different ways:

    (a)   By subdividing the total economy into groups of units; and

    (b)   By assigning the categories of transactions shown in an account to various sub-accounts.

It is discussed next how these two options are applied when developing the aggregate accounts in table 20.1 into a matrix presentation of the System's central framework, including both a supply and use table and sector accounts.

20.15. First, a subdivision of the total economy in each of the accounts could run as follows:

    (a)   Distinguish products in the goods and services account and classify these by categories of the Central Product Classification (CPC) (see chapter XV);

    (b)   Distinguish establishments in the production account and classify these by categories of the International Standard Industrial Classification (ISIC) (see chapter XV);

    (c)   Distinguish institutional units in the distribution of income account and classify these by institutional sectors, including a breakdown by sub-sector for non-financial corporations, general government and households;

    (d)   Distinguish institutional units in the use of income account and classify these by institutional sectors, including a breakdown by sub-sector for general government and households;

    (e)   Distinguish institutional units in the capital account and classify these by institutional sectors, including a breakdown by sub-sector for non-financial corporations, financial corporations and households; and

    (f)   If desired, introduce a geographical breakdown in the rest of the world account.

20.16. These subdivisions have two major consequences. First, for all categories of transactions distinguished in a single cell of table 20.1 it becomes clear which group of paying units has exchanged what with which group of receiving units. Secondly, the interrelationships among various economic flows are revealed through detailed cross-classifications: mappings of one classification to another. For instance, in the example

given above, a simple circular flow of income is presented, at a meso-level, through the following mappings:

    (a)   Submatrix (3&4&5,2) shows which institutional sub-sector receives the total of all net value added components from which industries;

    (b)   Submatrix (6,3&4&5) shows net disposable income allocated from the institutional sub-sectors in the distribution of income account to the institutional sub-sectors in the use of income account (naturally, if an identical classification is applied in the distribution of income account and in the use of income account, this is a one-to-one mapping, reflected by a diagonal submatrix);

    (c)   Submatrix (1,6) shows which category of goods and services is consumed by which institutional sub-sectors; and

    (d)   Submatrix (2,1) shows which categories of goods and services are produced by which industry.

In this enumeration, the submatrices are identified by means of their location (row and column number, respectively) in table 20.1. The above sequence represents a closed loop because all account numbers appear just as frequently in the rows as in the columns. This demonstrates the circularity of the flows described.

20.17. The second option for expanding table 20.1 refers to a distinction of subaccounts. For example, table 20.2 presents a breakdown of the distribution of income account into a primary distribution of income account and a secondary distribution of income account. This means that the diagonal item (3&4&5,3&4&5) in table 20.1 is split into property income flows on one hand (cell 3&4,3&4), and flows of current taxes on income, wealth, etc. plus all current transfers on the other (cell 5,5). Analogously, compensation of employees, property income and taxes on production and imports from and to the rest of the world are separated from current taxes on income, wealth, etc., and current transfers from and to the rest of the world. As a consequence, a new balancing item, net national income (NNI), is introduced in order to close the first subaccount (primary distribution of income). The balancing item of the last subaccount (secondary distribution of income) is typically the same as the balancing item of the aggregate account.

20.18. It goes without saying that accounts need not always be broken down but that a further consolidation is also possible. For instance, the distribution and use of income accounts in table 20.1 could have been combined. As a result, the balancing item net disposable income would have disappeared.

20.19. The processes of subdivision (or aggregation) of categories of units and (de)consolidation of accounts are closely linked. In practice, a subaccount for one or a few transaction categories

Table 20.3.   Consolidated SNA matrix with dummy accounts

Account	Codes	Goods and services 1	Production 2	Primary distribution of income 3 & 4	Secondary distribution of income — Current transfers, excl. misc. current transfers 5A — Corp.	Govt.	Househ.	NPISHs	Miscellaneous current transfers 5B	Use of income 6	Capital 7	Rest of the world, current and capital 10 & 11	Total
0. Goods and services	1		Intermediate consumption 1 883							Final consumption expenditure 1 399	Gross capital formation 414	Exports of goods and services 540	4 236
I. Production	2	Output and taxes on products less subsidies 3 737											3 737
II.1. Primary distribution of income	3 / 4		Net domestic product 1 632	Property income 353								Compensation of employees and property income from ROW[1] 69	2 054
II.2. Secondary distribution of income — Corp.	5A			Net national income 91	14	4	84	0	8			Curr. taxes on income, wealth, etc. and curr. transfers from ROW excl. misc. curr. transf. 2	203
— Govt.				197	35	92	446	0	10			6	786
— Household				1 367	77	289	0	1	1			0	1 735
— NPISHs				6	0	0	1	0	36			0	43
Miscellaneous current transfers	5B				4	8	40	2				Miscellaneous current transfers from ROW 2	56
II.4. Use of income	6				Net disposable income 70	358	1 164	40		Adjustment for the change in net equity of households on pension funds 11		Adjustment for the change in net equity of households on pension funds from ROW 0	1 643
III.1. Capital	7		Consumption of fixed capital 222							Net saving 233	Capital transfers and acquisitions less disposals of non-produced assets 61	Capital transfers receivable (+) /payable (−) and acquisitions less disposals of non-produced assets by ROW −3	513
V.I, V.II and V.III.1. Rest of the world, current and capital	10 / 11	Imports of goods and services 499		Compensation of employees and property income to ROW[1] 40	Current taxes on income, wealth etc. and transfers to ROW, excl. misc. current transfers 3	35	0	0	Miscellaneous current transfers to ROW 1	Adjustment for the change in net equity of households on pension funds to ROW 0	Net lending (+)/Net borrowing (−) of the total economy 38	0	616
Total		4 236	3 737	2 054	203	786	1 735	43	56	1 643	513	616	

1   Including taxes on production and imports from (cell 3&4, 10&11) and to (cell 10&11 and 3&4) ROW.

466

is inserted either because a separate classification is required for these categories, or because groups of receiving and paying units should be presented separately for the transactions in these categories. Naturally, an important criterion for maintaining or introducing a separate account is also that it yields a relevant balancing item.

20.20. When compiling such a matrix it is convenient to start with designing an accounting structure which is relevant to the applications envisaged. Subsequently, in each account the most appropriate units and classifications of units are selected. However, in practice it will be an interactive process. Suppose, for instance, that there is a transaction category for which only total receipts and payments of transactors (the row and column totals of a submatrix) are known, and not who paid whom (the interior structure of the submatrix). Unless this problem applies to many or all transaction categories (see paragraph 20.23 (e) below), it can be solved by the insertion of one or a few undivided, dummy accounts.

20.21. To illustrate this, let us try to complete the secondary distribution of income account in a detailed version of table 20.2, assuming that sufficient data are available on the groups of transactors at either end of the current taxes and current transfer flows, except for miscellaneous current transfer flows. In this case, a single, aggregated account for the latter flows should be inserted. This is shown in table 20.3. The row of the additional account contains total miscellaneous transfer flows payable by each sector (outgoings of the secondary distribution of income account) and by the rest of the world, and the column shows such transfer flows receivable by each sector (incomings of the secondary distribution of income account) and by the rest of the world. Obviously, the items in submatrix (5A,5A) no longer contain national, intersector miscellaneous transfer flows, and analogously miscellaneous transfer flows are eliminated from the vectors (5A,10&11) and (10&11,5A). Apart from this, the accounting matrix does not change, while the meaning of each balancing item is not affected at all.

20.22. The matrix which results from such manipulations presents a detailed and fully integrated picture of the economic situation, taking into account the data limitations that exist in the field of miscellaneous current transfer flows. In other words, if detailed information is not available on all transaction categories, this can be solved with the help of additional accounts. Conversely, if on some transaction category abundant information is available and considered relevant for the purposes of the matrix, then a separate account for this category can also be introduced, showing not less but more details (section F.1 below). Finally, if, for instance, the capital account can only be compiled for three major sectors, this does not imply that the other accounts must also be limited to that number. Instead, in a single matrix any combination of classifications considered relevant and feasible can be presented.

3. Properties of accounting matrices

20.23. At this stage, some general properties of a matrix presentation of accounts can be listed:

(a) An aggregate matrix (such as table 20.2) can present a bird's eye view of an economy as a whole; i.e., one page is sufficient to show the interrelationships between main transaction categories leading to a set of domestic and national balancing items. For a set of accounts giving a breakdown of transactions by paying and receiving units, a matrix presentation is more concise than other methods of presentation; the payment of one unit and the receipt of another unit involved in each transaction are represented by a single entry;

(b) A detailed matrix presentation is very general, in view of the possibility to apply multiple actoring and multiple sectoring in a matrix (see paragraph 20.13 above). This is particularly useful when integrating a detailed supply and use table and sectoral data. It does not imply, however, that in all cases information is most efficiently presented in a matrix format (see (e) below);

(c) A detailed matrix presentation is suitable for mathematical treatment using matrix algebra; this can be of help in analytical applications and also when balancing the accounts;

(d) A detailed matrix presents a simultaneous breakdown of interrelated transactions by paying and receiving units; as a consequence, it is an appropriate format to reveal, at a meso-level, interrelationships among economic flows; this includes those flows which involve two different types of units (e.g., final consumption expenditures of various categories of goods and services by a number of household sub-sectors);

(e) A matrix is not the most efficient format for presenting a set of accounts if, on one hand, the same unit and grouping of units are used in each account (including e.g., the production account) and, on the other hand, transactions are not broken down by paying and receiving units (refer to e.g., table 2.6 in the appendix to chapter II). In addition, a matrix format is suboptimal if one wants to portray for institutional sectors full details of the classification of transactions, without specifying who exchanged what with whom; and

(f) A detailed matrix is quite suited to experiments with alternative representations of transactions in non-adjacent accounts; in principle, transactions can be paid from one account and received by any other account without upsetting the transparency of the system. However, this reshuffle generally leads to different balancing items (see paragraph 20.130 below).

20.24. An aggregate matrix for the total economy can serve as a ref-

erence table for subsequent, more detailed tables. As soon as
the reader is then introduced to a detailed presentation of parts
of the System (supply and use table, sector accounts, etc.), the
relationship of the detailed submatrices to the aggregate matrix should be clear through a system of codes. The matrix format is particularly advantageous if it is not possible or
desirable to show an equally detailed classification in all accounts of the System. The 1968 SNA expressed this as follows: "By following a concise, economical notation, a good

notation as mathematicians would say, we can see the wood
and at the same time retain the trees" (paragraph 1.24).

20.25. The matrix presentation is a suitable tool to explore the flexibility of the System. For instance, one may further elaborate
on the interrelationships between the social and economic aspects of the System to arrive at a SAM. The SAM-approach is
set out and illustrated in the following sections of this chapter.

C. The SAM approach

1. Social accounting

20.26. A SAM applies the properties of a matrix format to incorporate
specific details on various economic flows. Traditionally, it
has been applied to specific types of analysis, focusing on
causes and consequences of various aspects of inequality
among household groups. For that purpose it is crucial to show
the detailed linkages which exist between the supply and use
table on one hand, and the accounts for the institutional sectors on the other.

20.27. A SAM provides a framework and consistent (base-year) data
for economy-wide models with detailed classifications of ac-
tors, such as industries, categories of employed persons and
institutional sub-sectors, including various socio-economic
household groups. The application of SAMs to model building will be elaborated in the final section of this chapter.

20.28. An important social concern is the level and composition of
(un)employment. SAMs have often provided additional information on this issue, via a subdivision of compensation of employees by type of person employed. This subdivision applies
to both the use of labour by industry, as shown in the supply
and use table, and the supply of labour by socio-economic subgroup, as shown in the allocation of primary income account
for households. It implies that the matrix presents not only the
supply and use of various products, but also the supply and use
of various categories of labour services.

20.29. In many cases, it is expedient to reconcile the SAM-figures
and related data which are available from all kinds of dispersed sources. This leads to an integrated set of satellite tables, showing:

(a) Various stocks underlying the SAM-flows, such as size
and composition of the population by household group
(including the potential labour force), production capacity by industry and the possession of assets (e.g., agricultural land, consumer durables and financial assets)
and liabilities (e.g., external debts) by sub-sector;

(b) A decomposition of (changes in) values into (changes
in) volumes and prices; this refers not only to products
but also to various categories of labour services, and to

fixed capital formation by industry (paragraph 20.63
below);

(c) Related non-monetary socio-economic indicators, such
as life expectancy, infant mortality, adult literacy, nutri-
ent intake, access to (public) health and education facilities, and housing situation by household group (see the
United Nations publication *Towards a System of Social
and Demographic Statistics*);

(d) Some re-routings (e.g., final consumption by household
group paid for by government and non-profit institutions serving households (NPISHs).

Such an extended set of tables (i.e., a "core" SAM and its various satellite tables) may be called: a system of economic and
social accounting matrices and extensions.

20.30. In particular, confronting (a) labour incomes of all employed
persons as shown in the SAM, (b) a decomposition of these
incomes into full-time equivalent employment and average
wage rates, and (c) the potential labour force by type of person
and household group (expressed in "full-time" equivalents),
yields detailed information on the composition of unemployment and an aggregate indicator ("full-time equivalent unemployment") which is consistent, both conceptually and
numerically, with the other macroeconomic indicators; these
can also be derived from the SAM-framework. Moreover, jux-
taposing the head-count of a subset of the employed persons
and the potential labour force in this data set agrees with unemployment as it is conventionally defined (paragraphs
20.50, 20.53, 20.77, 20.89 and 20.102 below).

20.31. A system of economic and social accounting matrices and extensions as outlined above becomes all the more important if
one wants to obtain a more general insight into the state of
human development without giving up a system's approach.
Bringing together dispersed pieces of monetary and non-monetary information into a system of economic and social accounting matrices and extensions opens up possibilities for:

(a) Rigorous theorizing based on microeconomic insights;

(b) Formal modelling, including feed-backs from non-
monetary to monetary variables;

(c) Monitoring and forecasting the impact of government policies or external influences on non-monetary variables.

20.32. Key features in such a system are integration and multiple classifications; in other words, a conceptual and numerical linkage of all kinds of related monetary and non-monetary phenomena, which are expressed in different measurement units. If, for instance, employed persons are classified by education obtained, including a group which is supposedly illiterate (i.e., completed less than three years of primary school), and the same is done for the non-employed potential labour force by socio-economic subgroup, a SAM plus concomitant population and employment matrices would reveal, for example:

Adult literacy by socio-economic subgroup

Labour force participation rates of literate and illiterate citizens, by socio-economic subgroup

Employment, average wage rate and labour income by socio-economic background and by education obtained of the employed persons, the illiterate being a separate category

Employment, average wage rate and labour income by education obtained (including the illiterate as a separate subgroup) and by industry in which these employed persons are engaged

National aggregates for these variables which are consistent with the more detailed data.

Such a data system would encompass more than a simple calculation of the literacy rate: it would enable analyses into the causes and consequences of this phenomenon and into the macroeconomic trade-offs of policies which aim at improving the situation.

20.33. A system of economic and social accounting matrices and extensions registers for all variables both the national total value and its distribution among socio-economic household groups, categories of employed persons, etc. As a next step, a whole range of summary indicators can be derived from such a data set, including one or more indices which cover distributional aspects. Whatever set of aggregates is preferred, they would all share one crucial feature: every indicator is computed from the same, fully consistent statistical system. The advantages in terms of relevance and reliability are self-evident. This approach could equally well be followed when dealing with environmental issues (see the discussion of the SAM-approach in integrated satellite accounts for environmental accounting in chapter XXI).

2. SAMs as an illustration of the SNA's flexibility

20.34. In general, elements of the SNA framework can be applied in a flexible way. In a SAM it is often even desirable that concepts, accounting structure and classifications are tailored to the economy described, to the specific purposes for which the SAM is constructed, and to the availability of data, skilled statisticians, computer capacity, etc. in the construction process. It should be stressed however, that this reflects a choice in practice and not in principle: it is very well possible to construct a SAM and adhere to all the concepts developed in the central framework of the System.

20.35. Several features of a regular SAM are also incorporated elsewhere in this manual. The specific purpose of a SAM is to render a complete account of the interlinkages which exist at the meso-level, through cross-classifications of transactions involving different units or groupings of units. An example may illustrate this point. Assume that the government would like to analyse the impact of two different scenarios for cutting back on its expenditures: one in which the federal civil service is trimmed, and another in which various investment projects in rural infrastructure are shelved. Quite apart from the divergence in long-term impact, the immediate burden of both policy actions is likely to be borne by very different population groups. Suppose that in the second option many rural construction workers are laid off. In turn, the consumption patterns of their households and those of metropolitan civil servants may not be congruent; in case of an unequal share of imports in the respective consumption expenditures even the external account may be affected differently. With a SAM, these linkages can be traced *ex post*. Besides, the effects can be simulated *ex ante* with the help of a SAM-based model, whereby various options exist as to the complexity of such a model.

20.36. In addition to a flexible application of the central framework of the System, some SAMs may incorporate adjustments which go beyond this, in order to serve specific analytical purposes. This concerns, for instance, recording the payment of taxes on products to the government on the goods and services account and not on the allocation of primary income account; concomitantly, NDP then excludes product taxes less subsidies. Or the use of concepts which are slightly different and tuned to a description of the behaviour of households (concerning the registration of interest on life insurance and of pension fund premiums and claims, the valuation of non-market output, etc.). In the SNA terminology, this means that one then enters into the realm of satellite accounting. Obviously, such SAMs must still represent a coherent and integrated accounting structure; wherever they deviate from the central framework, this should be incorporated consistently throughout the accounts. In many practical applications of SAMs, however, the concepts adopted are generally the same as those in the central framework.

20.37. At this stage, it is perhaps useful to work out an illustrative SAM. This is done below.

Table 20.4. Schematic presentation of a SAM

Account (classification)	Codes	Goods and services (products) 1	I. Production (industries) 2	II.1.1. Generation of income (value added categories) 3	II.1.2. Allocation of primary income (institutional sectors) 4	II.2. Secondary distribution of income (institutional sectors) 5	II.4. Use of income (institutional sectors) 6	III.1. Capital (institutional sectors) 7	Fixed capital formation (industries) 8	III.2. Financial (financial assets) 9	V. Rest of the world — II. Current 10	III.1. Capital 11	Total
Goods and services (products)	1	Trade and transport margins 0	Intermediate consumption 1 883				Final consumption expenditure 1 399	Changes in inventories [1] 38	Gross fixed capital formation 376		Exports of goods and services 540		4 236
Production (industries)	2	Output 3 604											3 604
Generation of income (value added categories)	3		*Net value added, at basic prices* 1 499								Compensation of employees from ROW 6		1 505
Allocation of primary income (institutional sectors)	4	Taxes on products less subsidies 133		*Net generated income, at basic prices* 1 503	Property income 353						Property income and taxes less subsidies on prod. and imports from ROW 63		2 052
Secondary distribution of income (institutional sectors)	5				*Net national income* 1 661	Current taxes on inc., wealth, etc. and curr. transfers 1 096					Current taxes on income, etc. and current transfers from ROW 10		2 767
Use of income (institutional sectors)	6					*Net disposable income* 1 632	Adj. for change in net equity househ. on pension funds 11				Adj. for change in net equity hh. on pension funds from ROW 0		1 643
Capital (institutional sectors)	7						*Net saving* 233	Capital transfers [2] 61		Borrowing 603		Capital transfers from ROW [2] 1	898
Fixed capital formation (industries)	8		Consumption of fixed capital 222					Net fixed capital formation 154					376
Financial (financial assets)	9							Lending 641				*Net lending of ROW* −38	603
Rest of the world, current	10	Imports of goods and services 499	Compensation of employees to ROW 2		Prop. income and taxes less subsid. on prod. and imp. to ROW 38	Current taxes on income, etc. and curr. transf. to ROW 39	Adj. for change in net equity hh. on pension funds to ROW 0						578
Rest of the world, capital	11							Capital transfers to ROW [2] 4			*Current external balance* −41		−37
Total		4 236	3 604	1 505	2 052	2 767	1 643	898	376	603	578	−37	

1 Including acquisition less disposals of valuables.
2 Including acquisitions less disposals of non-produced non-financial assets.

D. Schematic presentation of a social accounting matrix

20.38. Table 20.4 exemplifies the design of a SAM which records all transactions distinguished in the System (i.e., all flows excluding "other changes in assets"). It can be seen as a framework that results from a trade-off between analytic usefulness and commonly available data. In order to maintain a close linkage with the previous chapters, the concepts applied here are generally the same as those in the central framework. The most important deviation refers to a different meaning which is attached to the generation of income account, in order to facilitate a linkage of detailed labour market analyses and the national accounts. This and some other novelties are elaborated below.

20.39. This table reflects an extension and a slight rearrangement of table 20.2. A generation of income account, a fixed capital formation account and a financial account have been added, while for the rest of the world separate current and capital accounts have been distinguished. As discussed above, the addition of one or more accounts entails that some flows are recorded on another account. The numbering of accounts in this matrix exactly corresponds to that in the preceding tables of this chapter.

20.40. The aggregate SAM shown here is meant as a summary table, to which subsequent, more detailed tables can refer. Possible types of classifications in each account are indicated in parentheses in the row and column headings.

20.41. The sequence of accounts in this table is the same as in the reduced format matrix presentation of the full sequence of accounts and balancing items (see the matrix in the annex to chapter II). Turning that matrix into the aggregate SAM presented here implies:

(a) Deleting the other changes in assets account, the opening balance sheet, the changes between balance sheets account, the closing balance sheet and the net worth account, both for the total economy and for the rest of the world;

(b) De-consolidating the capital account so that a separate fixed capital formation account for industries is distinguished;

(c) Combining the external trade account and the other current external transactions account;

(d) Recording a few transaction categories in a slightly different way, in order to enable specific SAM-type analyses.

20.42. An example may illustrate the last item on this list. In this SAM, taxes on products minus subsidies have been channelled directly from the goods and services account to the allocation of primary income account (cell (4,1) of this table). Therefore, in cell (3,2) the term net value added, at basic prices replaces NDP, which is valued at market prices. As taxes on

products relate to goods and services, and not to industries or sectors, the way they are recorded here is appropriate to an analysis of interrelations between economic flows at the meso-level. This applies in particular to import duties and value added tax (VAT). Naturally, the sum of total net value added at basic prices (1,499 in the SNA numerical example) and total taxes minus subsidies on products (133) equals NDP, at market prices (1,632), see table 20.2, cell (3,2). This treatment is in conformity with the sequence of accounts in the central framework.

20.43. Another example concerns the consumption of fixed capital. As this can be seen as a cost of production (see paragraph 6.5 of chapter VI), and that means it is not income, it is booked here as an outgoing from the production account and an incoming of the fixed capital formation account (cell 8,2). As a consequence, all balancing items are recorded net of depreciation in this table. This is similar to the presentation in the integrated economic accounts (table 2.6); albeit that this item is there shown as an incoming of the capital account.

1. The supply and use table as a SAM building-block

20.44. The first two rows and columns of table 20.4 contain an aggregated version of the supply and use table, here explicitly linked up with the other accounts of the System. Note that rows and columns of the makematrix have been transposed.

20.45. Column 1 presents the supply of goods and services. Although trade and transport margins do not need to be added to output at an aggregate level, they are registered in the top left-hand corner of this table because they are non-zero in a more detailed SAM (e.g., table 20.5 below), and because the structure of the aggregate matrix and the more detailed tables should be the same, to facilitate cross-references. Output at basic prices (3,604) is shown in row 2. As explained above, taxes on products less subsidies (133) are not included in the output value, but directly booked on the allocation of primary income account for the government (row 4). Imports (499) originate from the current account for the rest of the world (row 10).

20.46. The elements in column 1 add up to total supply of goods and services, at purchasers' prices (4,236). Row 1 shows the uses of goods and services, at purchasers' prices (also totalling 4,236, of course): intermediate consumption (1,883) in column 2, final consumption expenditure (1,399) in column 6, changes in inventories (38) in column 7, gross fixed capital formation (376) in column 8 and exports, free on board (f.o.b.) (540) in column 10.

20.47. Row 2 shows output, at basic prices. Because of this valuation, the sum of row 2 (3,604), and the concomitant sum of column 2, are exclusive of taxes minus subsidies on products. In turn, this means that this amount is not included in total net value added (1,499) either, see cell (3,2). Consumption of fixed cap-

Table 20.5. Example of a more detailed SAM

Account (classification)	Table 20.4 / 20.5 codes	Goods and services (CPC): 1a Agriculture, etc. (0)	1b Manufacturing, etc. (1-5)	1c Services (6-9)	Production (ISIC): 2a Agriculture, etc. (A,B)	2b Manufacturing, etc. (C-F)	2c Services (H-O)	Generation of income — Compensation of employees: 3a Domestic resident male	3b resident female	3c non-resident	3d Residents abroad	3e Mixed income, gross	3f Operating surplus, gross	3g Other taxes less subsidies	Allocation of primary income: 4a Households, employees	4b Households, other	4c Corporations and NPISHs	4d Government
Goods and services (CPC) Agriculture, forestry and fishing (0)	1a				3	71	14											
Mining, manufact., electr., construction (1-5)	1b				36	969	246											
Services (6-9)	1c	2	76	-78	8	218	318											
Production (ISIC) Agriculture, forestry and fishing (A+B)	2a	87	2	0														
Mining, manufact., electr., constr. (C+D+E+F)	2b	0	2 112	11														
Services (G+H+I+J+K+M+N+O)	2c	0	39	1 353														
Generation of income Compensation of employees — Domestic — Resident male	3a				8	311	153											
Resident female	3b				1	95	192											
Non-residents	3c				0	1	1											
Residents abroad	3d																	
Mixed income, gross	3e				17	264	161											
Operating surplus, gross	3f				18	145	296											
Other taxes less subsidies on production	3g				-2	49	11											
Allocation of primary income Households, employees	4a							452	278		6	17	0		0	0	18	11
Households, other	4b							20	10		0	425	92		0	0	65	24
Corporations and NPISHs	4c												321		3	26	193	7
Government	4d	2	111	20									46	58	0	0	25	0
Secondary distribution of income Households, employees	5a														775			
Households, other	5b															634		
Corporations and NPISHs	5c																247	
Government	5d																	227
Use of (adjusted) disposable income Households, employees	6a																	
Households, other	6b																	
Corporations and NPISHs	6c																	
Government	6d																	
Capital Households, employees	7a																	
Households, other	7b																	
Corporations and NPISHs	7c																	
Government	7d																	
Gross fixed capital formation (ISIC) Agriculture, forestry and fishing (A+B)	8a																	
Mining, manufact., electr., constr. (C+D+E+F)	8b																	
Services (G+H+I+J+K+M+N+O)	8c																	
Financial Currency and deposits	9a																	
Loans	9b																	
Other financial assets	9c																	
Rest of the world Current	10	37	345	117						2					4	8	26	0
Capital	11																	
Total		128	2 685	1 423	89	2 123	1 392	472	288	2	6	442	459	58	782	668	574	269

Column groups and sub-classifications (codes):

- **Secondary distribution of income** — 5a Households, employees; 5b Households, other; 5c Corporations, NPISHs; 5d Government
- **Use of (adjusted) disposable income** — 6a Households, employees; 6b Households, other; 6c Corporations, NPISHs; 6d Government
- **Capital** — 7a Households, employees; 7b Households, other; 7c Corporations, NPISHs; 7d Government
- **Gross fixed capital form. (ISIC)** — 8a Agriculture, etc. (A,B); 8b Manufacturing, etc. (C–F); 8c Services (H–O)
- **Financial** — 9a Currency and deposits; 9b Loans; 9c Other financial assets
- **Rest of the world** — 10 Current; 11 Capital

Account (classification)	Codes	5a	5b	5c	5d	6a	6b	6c	6d	7a	7b	7c	7d	8a	8b	8c	9a	9b	9c	10	11	Total
Goods and services (CPC)	1a					16	12	0	2	2	5	28	7	2	0	0				7		128
	1b					339	269	0	3					9	109	233				435		2 685
	1c					211	168	16	363					0	23	0				98		1 423
Production (ISIC)	2a																					89
	2b																					2 123
	2c																					1 392
Generation of income	3a																					472
	3b																					288
	3c																					2
	3d																			6		6
	3e																					442
	3f																					459
	3g																					58
Allocation of primary income	4a																			0		782
	4b																			32		668
	4c																			24		574
	4d																			7		269
Secondary distribution of income	5a	0	0	56	197															0		1 028
	5b	0	0	23	92															0		749
	5c	58	59	16	12															4		396
	5d	320	134	37	92															35		816
Use of (adjusted) disposable income	6a	650						2														652
	6b		556					9														565
	6c			260																		260
	6d				388																	388
Capital	7a					86													1			87
	7b						116					16	7					28	4			171
	7c							233			4	4	25				130	95	175			666
	7d								20	1	4						2	94	74		1	196
Gross fixed capital formation (ISIC)	8a									1	7	3	0									11
	8b									1	38	93	0									132
	8c									0	14	182	37									233
Financial	9a									56	12	44	7								11	130
	9b									0	5	194	45								10	254
	9c									26	82	102	68								29	307
Rest of the world	10			4	35												−2	37	53	−41		578
	11																					51
Total		1 028	749	396	816	652	565	260	388	87	171	666	196	11	132	233	130	254	307	578	51	

ital (222) is put directly on the fixed capital formation account (row 8 and column 2).

2. Focus on income generation

20.48. The third account records the generation of income and plays an important role. It is classified by (net) primary input category: (a) compensation of employees, (b) net mixed income, (c) net operating surplus, and (d) other taxes and subsidies on production.

20.49. In the central framework this is an intermediate account which mainly serves to derive operating surplus/mixed income as a balancing item for example, (see tables 2.1 in chapter II or 7.1 in chapter VII). Except for the payment of compensation of employees to non-residents, it does not record both ends of a transaction. Instead, it breaks down value added payable by the producers into various components of value added payable by them (see paragraph 7.3 of chapter VII). The breakdown is into primary input categories like those mentioned in the previous paragraph. It is only in the next account (on the allocation of primary income), that these incomes are received, namely by households and other institutional units.

20.50. Here, the meaning of this account is changed a bit, in order to accommodate transactions between two different types of units. In particular, this refers to compensation of employees, which is recorded as a transaction (work in return for compensation) between an institutional unit (employer) and a person (employee). In this SAM, employed persons are considered as separate units who receive compensation of employees in the generation of income account and distribute this income to their household in the allocation of primary income account. These units are subsequently classified into groups of (self-) employed persons (see paragraphs 20.52, 20.76 and 20.77 below) and these groups are then a subset of the primary input categories distinguished in this account. This representation serves to integrate labour market analyses (distinguishing categories of employed persons) and the national accounts (distinguishing industries and institutional sectors).

20.51. The central framework of the System does not distinguish the employed person as a separate entity (i.e., as a separate unit). In this sense, the SAM discussed here falls under "satellite accounting". However, separating employed persons from the households to which they belong, is an operation which does not fundamentally differ from separating establishments from the institutional units (enterprises) to which they belong. In both cases, the smaller unit is more homogeneous and also fairly autonomous with respect to the economic process in which it is involved (income generation and production, respectively). These units thus serve to obtain a more accurate description of a specific economic process. It may be noted that an employed person as a unit can receive a compensation from more than one job (refer also to chapter XVII).

20.52. The (residual) mixed income and operating surplus remain

with the producing unit, but the classification of producing units need not be the same as in the production account. In effect, some classification by institutional sub-sector is particularly relevant to operating surplus and mixed income. This implies a cross-classification of these value added components by industry and institutional sub-sector in the SAM (analogous to the content of a similar table in chapter XV).

20.53. If one wants to record domestic net value added as a balancing item in cell (3,2), the primary input categories must encompass all persons employed in resident enterprises. In column 3, compensation of non-resident persons employed in resident enterprises is then handed over to the rest of the world. This implies that a meaningful, national balancing item is only obtained in account 3 if compensation of resident persons employed in non-resident enterprises is added first. This is done in row 3 and for this purpose a separate category, resident persons employed in non-resident enterprises, may be created. An additional advantage of inserting this category is that it facilitates the estimation of employment as it is conventionally defined (see paragraph 20.77 below).

20.54. Analogous to compensation of employees from abroad, other value added received from and paid to abroad should be registered in this table, in cell (3,10) and cell (10,3) respectively. For example, mixed income of a resident market-vendor in a neighbouring country where he sets up his stall one day a week. Notice, however, that cell (3,10) only contains value added generated abroad by resident institutional units. This implies that value added created in any substantial amount of production in another country over long, or indefinite, periods of time is excluded; for that leads to the creation of a (quasi-corporate) unit in that country (see chapter IV). Only in a satellite approach could the border-line between resident and non-resident units be changed somewhat, so that, for instance, direct investment income from abroad would be registered in the generation of income account, while other investment income from abroad would remain to be registered in the allocation of primary income account.

20.55. The result of all this is that the generation of income account is closed with a new balancing item (1,503), in between total net value added and NNI. This balancing item, named, total net generated income, at basic prices, gives total income earned by resident institutional units as a result of being engaged in production.

3. Distribution and use of income

20.56. The allocation of primary income account of a detailed SAM presents household labour income(s) as a contribution by one or more (self-)employed household members. Among other things, this will indicate to what extent each household group depends on multiple sources of labour income. Apart from this, the transaction categories shown in the distribution and use of income accounts of a SAM are typically about the same as in the central framework.

20.57. In the row of the allocation of primary income account (account 4), net generated income is augmented with taxes less subsidies on products, and with property income from the rest of the world (63). The latter item is recorded in cell (4,10), which also includes taxes on production and imports less subsidies collected abroad and then handed over to the national government. National, intersector property income flows (353) are recorded on the diagonal (row 4 and column 4), for they change only the distribution, not the total of national income. To get NNI, this diagonal item, as well as property income including taxes on production and imports less subsidies paid to the rest of the world (38), must be subtracted from the total of column 4, which is derived from the identical total of row 4.

20.58. NNI (1,661) appears on the credit side of the secondary distribution of income account (account 5). Current taxes on income, wealth, etc. and all current transfers from abroad (10) are also shown here. National, intersector current taxes on income, wealth, etc., social contributions and benefits and other current transfers (1,096) are recorded on the diagonal (row 5 and column 5). Current transfers and the like to the rest of the world (39) are recorded on the debit side as is the balancing item, net disposable income (1,632), which is put on the use of income account.

20.59. In table 20.4, the use of income account (account 6) records spending of net disposable income: final consumption expenditure on goods and services and net saving (233), which is put on the capital account. This SAM does not include an account for the redistribution of income in kind and account 6 thus describes the use of disposable income and not the use of adjusted disposable income (see paragraph 20.106 below).

4. Capital and financial flows

20.60. In the design of this SAM, the capital and financial accounts have been interlaced, with the financial account classified not by institutional sector but by type of financial asset. As a consequence, a disaggregation of this SAM would show, by institutional sub-sector, both acquisitions less disposals of various financial assets, see cell (9,7), and incurrence less repayment of various liabilities, see cell (7,9). Here, these two categories of transactions have been combined as far as the rest of the world is involved. This serves to include the aggregate balancing item net lending in table 20.4, though with a reverse sign when viewed from the standpoint of the total economy, see cell (9,11).

20.61. Row 7 presents the availability of funds to the total economy: net saving, borrowing (603), capital transfers receivable from the rest of the world (1), including acquisitions less disposals of non-produced assets, by the rest of the world (0), and the diagonal item, national intersector capital transfers receivable

(61) plus intersector sales of land and other non-produced assets (7). If only net purchases of these assets are known, this may be shown in an extra dummy row which then adds up to zero (so that no extra column is required). Column 7 records how these funds have been allocated: changes in inventories, national intersector capital transfers payable, net fixed capital formation (154), lending (641) and capital transfers payable to the rest of the world (4). Obviously, the balancing item net lending of the nation (38) can also be derived from this account, i.e., by subtracting borrowing (603) from lending (641).

20.62. The main part of total volume changes in net worth probably consists of increases in fixed assets. If one is particularly interested in the dynamics of an economy, it is important to show in which industries production capacity has been expanded. This is the aim of the fixed capital formation account (account 8) inserted in this SAM. A more detailed table would then present:

(a)   Who invests where in the rows of this account—cell (8,7);

(b)   Where does one invest in what in the columns—cell (1,8).

In this case, the who refers to an institutional sub-sector, the where refers to an industry, and the what refers to a category of products. Note that through this fixed capital formation account the SAM shows at a meso-level the linkages which exist between fixed capital formation by institutional sector, as presented in the capital account, and fixed capital formation by category of goods and services, as contained in the supply and use table.

20.63. Often, estimates of gross fixed capital formation, in column 8, and of the consumption of fixed capital, in row 8, are already available. As a consequence, the residual, net capital formation, shown in row 8 and column 7, should be found. In a supplementary table, net capital formation by industry could be decomposed into a "volume-effect", i.e., the increase in capacity of an industry expressed in terms of its maximum output volume(s), and a "price-effect", i.e., the price per volume unit of capital formation. As a result the capacity effects of investment would be conceptually integrated in a national accounts framework. In practice, however, production capacity figures may be hard to find.

20.64. In the financial account (account 9), lending is presented row-wise, and borrowing column-wise. The balancing item is given in row 9, and not in column 9, because it is at the same time the balancing item of the capital account for the rest of the world. It equals net lending of the rest of the world (-38).

5. External transactions

20.65. The elements in the current and capital account for the rest of the world (accounts 10 and 11) have all been discussed above, except the current external balance (-41) shown in row 11 and column 10. If one wants to consider this balance from the per-

spective of the total economy, it should be put in row 10 and column 11 and the sign reversed.

E. A more detailed SAM

1. Criteria for classifications

20.66. Typically, SAMs for different countries have selected a common type of classification in each account, while the actual (detailed) classifications have been based on local conditions. Defining these taxonomies is a vital phase in the construction of a SAM, as its uses depend very much on the categories distinguished.

20.67. When it comes to the design of classifications, a broad, and perhaps slightly artificial, distinction could be made between two types of SAMs:

(a)   SAMs principally used for monitoring;

(b)   SAMs principally used for analysis.

The taxonomies in the first type of SAMs should be determined by what one wants to monitor, or by the taxonomies in the object of comparison (e.g., a SAM for an earlier period or another economy). For the rest, not many general remarks can be made. The remaining part of this section will thus focus on classifications in an "analytical" SAM.

20.68. As transactions in a SAM are shown simultaneously as a receipt of one (sub)account and an outlay of another, they are usually cross-classified. The usefulness and feasibility of such cross-classifications should thus be considered when designing the taxonomies for each account. In an "analytical" SAM this implies that a well-balanced number of categories is distinguished in each ("endogenous") account. For example, in an analysis of the circular flow of income on the basis of 200 products, 50 industries, 2 labour categories and 3 household groups, a bottleneck appears in between the primary income and final expenditure flows. In other words, such an analysis requires that the number of labour and household categories is not much smaller than the number of products and industries.

20.69. The following considerations may serve to guide in defining a classification:

(a)   The homogeneity of the categories distinguished, regarding the transactions recorded in the account under consideration; ideally, all units in a single category operate on the same markets, both on the supply (input) and on the use (output) side;

(b)   The recognizability of the subgroups and their relevance to economic analyses and to policy preparation and monitoring (including e.g., key industries, regional aspects, and identifiable target groups);

(c)   The stability and measurability of the characteristic(s)

on which the classification is based, and how few survey questions are needed to establish the classification;

(d)   The degree to which the (cross-)classification(s) can be derived from (a combination of) existing data sources.

20.70. For many purposes of a SAM, the classification of households is particularly crucial. Conclusions regarding (changes in) inequality, and perhaps even poverty, may have to be based on subgroup averages, and thus depend very much on how the population has been subdivided. On one hand, any feasible number of household groups may lead to categories containing over a million people, for instance, and this must imply that average figures conceal considerable within-group disparities. On the other hand, integrating distributional statistics into a SAM considerably increases their reliability as well as their relevance. Summarizing, this heterogeneity should not be a problem if a proper classification is selected, i.e., if the shapes of the underlying within-subgroup distributions are fairly similar, or if the spread mainly concerns incidental or less relevant differences (e.g., life-cycle effects).

20.71. In the light of the considerations in the above two paragraphs, main income source seems a more adequate criterion than income size when it comes to classifying households in an "analytical" SAM. This means that, in addition to the criteria determining the standard SNA sub-sectors, location (urban/rural or distinguishing several regions), possession of assets (e.g., agricultural land) and size and composition (with/without children) of the household may be considered relevant. A further breakdown could then be based on main economic activity of the household and main sub-sector of employment, occupation, educational attainment, etc. of the reference person. In a "monitoring" SAM, classifying households by income size or expenditure bracket cannot be ruled out, although the problem remains that income and expenditure are neither easily measurable nor stable and that they require a lot of survey questions—so that the information contained in, e.g., household and population surveys which do not ask these questions, cannot be linked up with such a SAM.

20.72. Obviously, in practice only a few classification criteria can be applied simultaneously. It is therefore most workable to start from an inverted tree-structure. Figure 20.1 exemplifies this process of successive subdivisions. All in all, this yields 43 subgroups (23 in rural areas, 19 in urban areas and a separate subgroup for institutional households). This taxonomy may be considered as an example of the flexible allocation of households to sub-sectors which is advocated in section G.3 of chapter IV. If one wanted to derive all standard SNA sub-sectors through an aggregation of the subgroups distinguished here, a further subdivision of the (three) categories of farmers into own-account workers and employers would be required. Obviously, this example serves merely to illustrate, if only because it has been constructed with a particular type of country in mind; other types of countries require a different classification-tree. When using this classification to (re-)process surveys, it is advisable to add an "unclassified" subgroup by way of safety net.

20.73. The classification of households need not be the same in each type of account. For instance, a breakdown of the category of other transfer income recipients may be more useful in the secondary distribution of income account than in the allocation of primary income account. Moreover, in some cases it may be necessary to define a "collective household sub-sector" for a few categories of transactions, such as final consumption expenditures of pension fund administration services

20.74. The classifications of other institutional units typically resemble those in the central framework (see annex V at the end of this manual). Again, it is possible to introduce in the SAM proper a specific classification or a specific level of detail in each account. For instance, it stands to reason to show a more detailed taxonomy of financial corporations in the capital account than in the secondary distribution of income account. Or a grouping of government expenditures according to function (see chapter XVII), may be appropriate in the use of income account but less so in the other accounts. Conversely, if for a certain transaction category only fairly aggregate data are available, this necessitates the use of a limited breakdown in some accounts, but not in all of them.

20.75. Some or all accounts for the rest of the world may be geographically subdivided, especially if the SAM-economy (country or region) belongs to a larger community where special (trade) regulations apply, or if its functioning is closely linked to a particular part of the outside world (e.g., through a tied currency).

20.76. The classification of (self-)employed persons may be based on a combination of background and (main) job characteristics, like sex, schooling, age, ethnicity and place of residence on one hand, and occupation, type of job contract (full-time/part-time, permanent/ temporary) and region and sub-sector of employment on the other. Another consideration should be that within-group variations in relative wage rate changes are smaller than between-group variations. In common with the household taxonomy, an inverted tree-structure may be built. A classification by industry of employment is less relevant, because this is already shown in the SAM by the cross-classification of value added. If, for example, employees in establishments belonging to a corporate enterprise are separated from those working in unincorporated firms, and the industries are tabulated by ISIC-class, the value-added submatrix would show labour income in plantations separately from labour income in small-holdings growing fruit, nuts, beverages or spice crops.

20.77. As explained in paragraph 20.53 above, resident persons employed in non-resident enterprises should constitute a separate group. If one wants to arrive at an estimate of employment by counting the number of employed person units, non-resident persons working for resident enterprises and employees working temporarily abroad should also be set apart. In this case the group of employed persons should evidently incorporate the self-employed for whose labour input an imputed remuneration should then be isolated from the rest of net mixed income in the SAM (see paragraph 20.102 below).

20.78. Ideally, the residual net mixed income and net operating surplus are broken down into various more specific categories of primary inputs, like the services derived from using various types of land and various types of subsoil assets. However, such a breakdown is only feasible if sufficient data on the own-account input of an asset type are available and if a reasonable imputation for the price thereof can be found. For instance, if a well-developed market exists for the rental of farmland of various qualities and if the (own-account) input of these types of land is regularly surveyed, part of agricultural mixed income and operating surplus could in fact be assigned to the services derived from using land. A similar procedure may be followed for some subsoil assets, for R&D assets like patents, etc. In this way, several categories of property income payable, including an imputation for self-earned property incomes, would be distinguished as sub-components of mixed incomes and operating surplus by industry. This serves to yield more insights into (a) which (primary) inputs have produced the outputs of a certain industry, and (b) which sub-sectors have provided these inputs, wihout pretending that a complete enumeration is feasible; a renumeration for the use of some assets, like the organization of production or the external environment, cannot usually be isolated. The "unexpected" value added may then be classified by sub-sector to which the establishments in each industry belong (see paragraphs 20.52 and 20.76 above).

20.79. The value added category "other taxes on production" may be subdivided to single out dues which could in fact also be seen as a payment for the use of an input, like a levy on the discharge of oxygen-demanding materials into surface water. In this case it is the budget mechanism and not the market mechanism which determines the price.

20.80. Products may be distinguished by type, adapting the CPC to specific circumstances and needs, followed by a subdivision of some of these categories into domestic products and imports (see also chapter XV). Sometimes, products which are apparently very much alike ought not to be grouped in a single category, because they are traded in totally different markets, at very different prices. As a rule, an important consideration in a taxonomy of products should be that within-group variations in relative price changes are smaller than between-group variations.

20.81. For industries it is sometimes useful to supplement a local

Figure 20.1.   An example of a household taxonomy using a tree structure

1 All households are subdivided into institutional households
and non-institutional households (see paragraph 4.137 of chapter
IV for a definition of institutional households).
2 All non-institutional households are split into rural and urban.
3 Both rural and urban households are split into (a) recipients of
property or transfer income, (b) employees and (c) self-employed
(employers and own-account workers).
4 Recipients of property or transfer income are split into (a) recipients of property income, (b) recipients of pensions, and (c) recipients of other transfers.

5 In rural areas, the employee and the self-employed households
are subdivided into agricultural and non-agricultural.
6 Agricultural (rural) employees are not further broken down.
7 Non-agricultural rural and all urban employee households are
grouped according to occupational category of the reference person (three skill categories) and subsequently according to (main)
sub-sector of his or her employment: (a) unincorporated enterprise and NPISHs, (b) public corporations and government, (c)
national private corporations and (d) foreign-controlled corporations.

8 Rural, agricultural self-employed households are further partitioned into three size-classes of land owned.
9 Non-agricultural rural and all urban, self-employed households are bisected twice, (a) into own-account workers and employers, and (b) into informal and formal establishments,
whereby the former may be defined as, e. g., firms which involve
less than five (paid plus unpaid) full-time worker equivalents and
which belong to an ISIC-category with low skill- and (other)
capital-intensity; the rest of the establishments are then considered as formal.

variation of the ISIC by a classification by institutional sub-sector of the enterprise to which the establishment belongs; there may be informal household firms and foreign-controlled corporations which produce similar products, like clothing, but these establishments do not operate on the same output or input markets. Analogously, production for own consumption by households may be presented in one or more separate "industries". In addition, key industries could be set apart. In the fixed capital formation account, a different (more aggregated) taxonomy of industries can be applied.

2. Structure of a more detailed SAM

20.82. Table 20.5 serves to illustrate what kind of information can be derived from a more detailed SAM. The main orientation of this particular table is to show:

(a)   The circular flow of income, including a subdivision of labour income by a few categories of employed persons; this enables a more detailed analysis of the linkage between value added of industries and primary income of household subgroups;

(b)   The interdependence between the distribution of income and the structure of production; among other things, this is related to diverging demand patterns of various household groups;

(c)   The sub-sector allocation of saving, including a subdivision of fixed capital formation by investing industry; this enables a more detailed analysis of the linkage between fixed capital formation of sub-sectors and fixed capital formation by category of goods and services.

For purposes of presentation, the number of groups in each account is kept at a minimum. Obviously, a full-fledged SAM should distinguish more categories per account.

20.83. In table 20.5, each subaccount is labelled first according to its position in the aggregate SAM (table 20.4) and then according to a label specific to this table. Such a labelling system should be applied throughout the whole set of tables, in order to enable an easy linkage of (very) detailed figures to the overall state of affairs in the economy.

20.84. The discussion of this table focuses on elements which are less elaborated either in table 20.4 or in the set of supply and use tables plus sector accounts in the central framework. The figures in this table are also the same, or where supplementary details have been inserted, add up to the same as the concomitant figures in those data sets.

20.85. The submatrix in the top left-hand corner contains a specification of the trade and transport margins. In the row for (trade and transport) services, it shows the relevant margins on agricultural and industrial products, and records the sum of these as a negative entry in the column for (trade and transport) services, such that the figures in this block add up, row-wise, to

zero. Thus the valuation of uses (at purchasers' prices) in rows 1a-1c is not affected, while this method of recording ensures that the total of columns 1a-1c (total supply) is also valued at purchasers' prices. For some purposes, this may not be the ideal way of recording trade and transport margins. An alternative registration method is sketched in paragraph 20.105 below.

20.86. Due to the overlap of the use table and the use of income account (rows 1a-1c and columns 6a-6b), a SAM reveals the differences in demand patterns across socio-economic subgroups. This information is generally more reliable than that available from a household budget survey which has not been reconciled with the national accounts.

20.87. In rows 1a-1c, columns 7a-7d show the changes in inventories, while columns 8a-8c record in which industry one invests in what kind of produced asset. Intermediate inputs (columns 2a-2c), government consumption expenditure (column 6d), and exports (column 10) are the same as in the supply and use table. In columns 1a-1c, this also holds true for the (transposed) make-matrix (rows 2a-2c), for taxes on products less subsidies, which accrue to the government as primary income (row 4d) and for imports (row 10).

20.88. Columns 2a-2c contain various kinds of inputs by industry. The intersection between these columns and rows 3a-3g presents a decomposition of total net value added, at basic prices, by primary input category and by industry. In this submatrix, compensation of employees is shown separately for residents and non-residents, and the former is split into both sexes. This may point to an under-representation of female labour income in some industries. The block containing the consumption of fixed capital (rows 8a-8c) is a diagonal matrix.

20.89. In row 3d and column 10, compensation of residents working for non-resident enterprises is shown. Through a careful choice of the employed person unit (e.g., number of months worked in the reference year divided by 12), the number of national wage-earners equals the total number of units in accounts 3a, 3b and 3d. As stated above, an additional distinction of various categories of self-employed persons in this account would have been particularly relevant to an analysis of national total (un)employment on the basis of a SAM. In turn, these categories would then have received an imputed labour income, with a concomitant reduction of net mixed income.

20.90. In columns 3a-3g, generated income is allocated to institutional sectors (rows 4a-4d), and to the rest of the world (row 10). The sectors in this example are two household groups (employee households and other households), a category combining NPISHs and both corporations sectors, and the general government, including social security funds.

20.91. The data in rows 4a and 4b reveal to what extent both categories of households depend on female labour income. Most property income received by households originates from corporations (see rows 4a-4b and columns 4a-4d and 10). A small

Table 20.6. Detailed value added sub-matrix (table 20.4, cell 3.2)

Industries [by ISIC tabulation categories]

Classifications (Domestic)		Codes*	Agric., hunting and forestry 2aA	Fishing 2aB	Mining and quarrying 2bC	Manufacturing 2bD	Electricity, gas and water supply 2bE	Construction 2bF	Wholesale, retail trade and repair of motor vehicles households goods 2cG	Hotels and restaurants 2cH	Transport, storage, communication 2cI	Financial mediation 2cJ	Real estate and business services 2cK	Public admin., defence and other public services 2cL	Education 2cM	Health and social work 2cN	Other community, social, personal services 2cO	Total 2
Compensation of Employees																		
Resident male — Agricultural	Rural	3aA	6.2	0.5	0.0	0.0	0.0	0.0	0.0	0.0	0.0	0.0	0.0	0.1	0.0	0.0	0.0	6.8
	Urban	3aB	0.2	0.2	0.0	0.0	0.0	0.0	0.0	0.0	0.0	0.0	0.0	0.1	0.0	0.0	0.0	0.5
Manual	Rural	3aC	0.2	0.0	3.2	21.1	0.6	12.4	1.9	0.1	2.8	0.6	0.1	0.2	0.8	0.2	1.8	46.0
	Urban	3aD	0.0	0.0	1.8	105.3	9.8	27.4	4.0	0.4	7.9	1.5	0.4	0.9	1.0	0.8	4.7	165.9
Clerical, sales, service	Rural	3aE	0.2	0.0	0.5	5.9	0.0	0.9	3.0	0.2	0.5	3.7	0.6	1.5	0.6	0.0	2.4	20.1
	Urban	3aF	0.0	0.1	1.5	35.6	2.1	3.7	6.6	0.5	1.8	6.9	3.0	5.8	0.6	0.4	7.3	75.9
Professional, managerial, etc.	Rural	3aG	0.1	0.0	1.7	17.7	0.2	2.6	0.7	0.2	0.3	1.8	1.3	2.7	14.0	1.0	1.8	46.2
	Urban	3aH	0.0	0.0	2.5	47.7	2.7	4.4	1.3	0.4	1.0	5.6	5.9	10.6	20.1	4.1	4.7	110.8
Resident female — Agricultural	Rural	3bI	1.0	0.1	0.0	0.0	0.0	0.0	0.0	0.0	0.0	0.0	0.0	0.0	0.0	0.0	0.0	1.1
	Urban	3bJ	0.0	0.0	0.0	0.0	0.0	0.0	0.0	0.0	0.0	0.0	0.0	0.0	0.0	0.0	0.0	0.0
Manual	Rural	3bK	0.0	0.0	0.0	5.7	0.0	0.0	0.1	0.1	0.0	0.1	0.0	0.1	0.4	0.2	0.8	7.5
	Urban	3bL	0.0	0.0	0.4	13.6	0.1	0.1	0.2	0.2	0.1	0.3	0.2	0.3	0.4	0.8	2.6	18.9
Clerical, sales & service	Rural	3bM	0.0	0.0	1.2	5.6	0.0	1.3	6.2	0.6	0.4	1.6	0.8	1.8	4.3	0.6	24.2	47.8
	Urban	3bN	0.0	0.0	0.0	49.6	2.9	4.6	14.3	2.5	1.0	8.8	4.7	9.0	4.9	2.0	36.6	142.1
Professional, managerial, etc.	Rural	3bO	0.0	0.0	0.0	1.3	0.0	0.1	0.2	0.0	0.0	1.0	0.3	0.9	9.3	2.4	5.5	21.1
	Urban	3bP	0.0	0.0	0.1	7.3	0.1	0.3	0.3	0.1	0.0	3.6	1.1	4.8	10.6	9.8	11.2	49.4
Non-resident employees		3cQ	0.1	0.1	0.1	0.9	0.0	0.2	0.2	0.0	0.1	0.0	0.0	0.3	0.0	0.0	0.0	2.0
Resident employees in non-resident enterprises		3dR																
Net mixed income	Rural	3eS	12.3	1.4	0.0	65.4	0.0	9.4	10.7	0.5	0.5	3.0	32.9	0.0	0.0	3.4	2.1	141.6
	Urban	3eT	0.2	0.2	0.0	161.6	0.0	25.6	20.4	4.3	2.5	2.0	61.1	0.0	0.0	7.5	4.9	290.4
Net operating surplus																		
Households (owner-occupied housing) NPISHs and government unincorporated enterprises		3fU	0.0	0.0	0.0	0.0	0.0	0.0	0.0	0.0	0.0	0.0	60.0	0.0	0.0	0.0	0.0	60.0
Corporations: public		3fU	0.0	0.0	2.2	6.5	7.5	1.1	-12.6	0.1	3.6	1.5	0.0	0.0	0.0	5.2	9.1	21.0
national private		3fV	0.1	0.0	1.4	5.0	0.0	0.4	0.5	0.3	1.8	2.2	1.0	0.0	0.0	0.0	0.0	25.3
foreign		3fX	9.7	0.2	0.4	10.9	0.1	19.5	5.5	2.2	6.6	14.8	46.0	0.0	0.0	1.3	10.5	127.7
		3gZ											1.5					13.1
Other taxes less subsidies on production			-2.0	0.0	-2.0	41.1	4.9	5.0	0.0	0.0	-6.0	8.3	3.7	1.0	0.0	0.0	4.0	58.0
Subtotals:																		
Compensation of employees (paid by resident producers)			8.0	1.0	13.0	317.4	18.5	58.0	38.9	5.2	16.0	35.5	18.4	39.0	67.0	22.3	103.6	762.0
Resident male		3a	6.9	0.8	11.2	233.4	15.4	51.3	17.4	1.7	14.4	20.1	11.3	21.7	37.2	6.5	22.8	472.1
Resident female		3b	1.0	0.1	1.7	83.2	3.1	6.5	21.2	3.4	1.5	15.5	7.1	17.0	29.9	15.8	80.9	287.9
Non-resident		3c	0.1	0.1	0.1	0.8	0.0	0.2	0.3	0.1	0.1	0.0	0.0	0.3	0.0	0.0	0.0	2.0
Mixed income and operating surplus			22.2	1.8	4.0	249.4	7.6	56.0	24.5	7.4	15.0	23.5	202.5	0.0	0.0	17.5	47.6	679.1
Net mixed income		3e	12.4	1.6	0.0	227.0	0.0	35.0	31.1	4.8	3.0	5.0	94.0	0.0	0.0	10.9	7.0	432.0
Net operating surplus		3f	9.8	0.2	4.0	22.4	7.6	21.0	-6.6	2.6	12.0	18.5	108.5	0.0	0.0	6.6	40.6	247.1
Net value added, at basic prices		3	28.2	2.8	15.0	607.9	31.1	119.0	63.4	12.6	25.0	67.3	224.7	40.0	67.0	39.8	155.2	1 499.1

* Based on row and col. codes in table 20.5.

part concerns rent etc. directly received from other households (columns 4a-4b) and, for example, interest earned on foreign bank accounts (column 10).

20.92. A table like this reveals from whom all sub-sectors receive their property income and to whom they pay it. In this example the government pays property income to the corporate sector and, to a lesser extent, to the rest of the world (see rows 4a-4d and 10 and column 4d).

20.93. The diagonal submatrix in the crossing of rows 5a-5d and columns 4a-4d contains net primary income by sector. The next block (rows and columns 5a-5d) discloses from whom to whom current taxes on income, wealth, etc., social contributions and benefits and other current transfers are disbursed. In this SAM, these amounts include imputed social contributions and exclude social transfers in kind. Current transfer flows from and to abroad (rows 5a-5d, column 10 and row 10, columns 5a-5d, respectively) consist of migrant remittances (from and to the household sub-sectors), non-life insurance premiums and claims (here, both paid abroad, by non-financial and financial corporations respectively) and taxes and current transfers related to international cooperation (exchanged with the government).

20.94. The diagonal submatrix in the intersection of rows 6a-6d and columns 5a-5d gives net disposable income by sub-sector, used for final consumption expenditure and net saving in columns 6a-6d.

20.95. Rows 7a-7d show the sub-sector acquisition of funds, through saving (columns 6a-6d), capital transfers receivable and net sales of land and other non-produced assets (columns 7a-7d and 11) and increases in various types of liabilities (columns 9a-9c).

20.96. An allocation of these funds is specified in columns 7a-7d. Special attention should be paid to sector differences in the allocation of net fixed capital formation to industries (see rows 8a-8c). The industrial distribution of investments (by sub-sector) obviously provides an indication of the direction the economy is heading.

20.97. The elements in rows and columns 8a-11 have already been discussed above or are also shown in the central framework of the System.

20.98. A real, more detailed SAM cannot usually be presented on a single page, and even if this is technically feasible, showing much empty space on one, very large sheet of paper may not lead to an optimal absorption of information by the reader. Instead, the labelling system described above could be used to present one non-empty block (or a few small, adjacent blocks) at the time. This idea is illustrated in the next section.

3. A detailed value-added submatrix

20.99. Table 20.6 unveils part of the information contained in a full-fledged SAM. It looks at total net value added, i.e., cell (3,2)

of the aggregate table 20.4, through a magnifying glass. To facilitate cross-reference with the supply and use table, industries are only classified by ISIC-categories. Male and female labour incomes are broken down by category of occupation and place of residence of the employed person. Net mixed income is shown according to the location of the enterprise owned by a household, and net operating surplus according to the (sub)sector of the enterprise to which the establishment belongs. In this example, mixed income still includes an imputed remuneration for the labour of the self-employed. Obviously, the (stylized) figures in this table add up to the concomitant totals shown in tables 20.4 and 20.5. For instance, total net value added appears in the bottom right-hand corner.

20.100. The additional insights which can be obtained from such a table include the following:

> The share of female labour income by industry and region

> The degree of concentration of female labour income in a certain occupational category, by industry and region

> The composition of labour income by occupation in each industry and region, for both sexes

> The regional split of mixed income by industry

> The weight of public enterprise and foreign-controlled corporations in the operating surplus of each industry.

In table 20.6 the detailed information on compensation of employees comes from labour statistics; its integration into a national accounts framework will improve the relevance as well as the reliability of both this source and the national accounts.

20.101. Labour incomes as presented in this table should be decomposed into a volume and a price component by labour type and industry: full-time equivalent employment and (weighted, full-time equivalent) wage rates, respectively. Apart from that, a full-fledged SESAME also contains a table showing the allocation of these labour incomes and the concomitant employment to household groups (paragraph 20.29 above). Similar transactions might be shown for imputed labour income of the self-employed.

20.102. A data set which contains an estimate of imputed labour income of the self-employed person units as well as a split of all labour income into a volume and a price component, yields detailed labour data which are quite useful to all kinds of analysis and which are directly linked to all important macroeconomic aggregates, including employment (i.e., the total number of employed person units) and full-time equivalent employment (i.e, total labour input volume). For that purpose, it would be useful to break down mixed income in table 20.6 into an imputed compensation for work done by the self-employed, including unpaid helpers belonging to the same household, and a residual which has more in common with the operating surplus of other enterprises. The imputed compensation per self-employed person unit could be estimated as hours worked multiplied by the hourly wage of an employee with similar background and job characteristics in the same industry. On the basis of such a SESAME, "conventional" employment and full-time equivalent employment can be specified according to labour category, and as well according to industry and household group

F. Alternative social accounting frameworks

1. Alternative accounting structures

20.103. The SAM shown above stays fairly close to the sequence of flow accounts in the central framework. Most existing SAMs lead off with the generation of income account, while the goods and services account and the production account are placed lower and more to the right.

20.104. The following accounts are sometimes consolidated:

Goods and services account and production account

The primary and secondary distribution of income and use of income accounts

Capital account and fixed capital formation account

Capital account and financial account.

20.105. Depending on the purposes of the SAM and on data availability, separate accounts may be inserted for categories of transactions such as:

Taxes and subsidies on production and imports (classified by type; this facilitates a recording of taxes or subsidies which only apply to specific categories of use)

Trade and transport margins (possibly split up and classified by type of distributed product; due to this separate account, these margins are excluded from all use values and from total supply of goods)

Household final consumption expenditure (classified by purpose)

Government final consumption expenditure (classified by function).

In the case, for example, of household final consumption expenditure by purpose it is not really an "account" that is added. Instead, such extra rows and columns should be seen as a "mapping": a cross-classification of the same information from different points of view. A real account shows actual transactions between units or contains at least two cells in either the row or the column of the macro-matrix (see table 20.4). In general, an account ends up with a balancing item, while a mapping does not.

20.106. With regard to the redistribution of income in kind account and the use of adjusted disposable income account, two alternatives for their registration in the central framework could be considered. First, in a "monitoring" SAM, they may be consolidated with the distribution of income account and the use of income account. This implies that the balancing item dis-

as far as full-time equivalent employment is concerned. The distribution of "conventional" employment (by labour category) over household groups can then be shown in another satellite table.

posable income drops out; only adjusted disposable income is shown. Secondly, in an "analytical" SAM, these accounts may be relegated to the set of satellite tables; incorporating them in the SAM proper would complicate the estimation of average or marginal expenditure propensities.[10]

20.107. Satellite tables can also present a breakdown of several transactions shown in the SAM according to a third criterion. Examples of such three-dimensional tables are: (a) property incomes by type (rent, dividend, interest, etc.), as well as by paying and receiving sub-sector, (b) financial transactions both by type of financial asset and by creditor and debtor sector, and (c) all primary input categories by paying industry and by receiving sub-sector. Alternatively, this third aspect can be shown in the SAM proper, i.e., by inserting it (partly) in one or both classifications. Table 20.6 has illustrated this for the case of operating surplus, categorized by receiving sub-sector.

20.108. Conceptually, it is not difficult to incorporate in the SAM an other changes in assets account, classified by type of asset or by type of other change, and a changes between balance sheets account, classified by sub-sector or by type of asset. In such a framework it is advisable to subdivide the capital account such that each subaccount yields one balancing item: net lending on one hand and changes in net worth due to saving and net capital transfers on the other. The first subaccount (named generation of worth account), then receives net saving from the use of income account and settles the capital transfers to yield changes in net worth due to saving and net capital transfers, to be put on the changes between balance sheets account. In turn, the second capital subaccount (named other capital account) receives this balancing item from the changes between balance sheets account and adds purchases minus sales of land and other non-produced assets to yield net lending, to be put on the financial account. Alternatively, transactions in financial assets can be expressed in gross instead of net terms, while other, positive and negative, changes in assets can be inserted in the crossings of the other changes in assets account and this other capital account. This capital subaccount then yields changes in net worth due to other changes in assets as a balancing item. This balancing item is put on the changes between balance sheets account, which thus adds up to total changes in net worth. Finally, in the column of the changes between balance sheets account, changes in net worth due to other changes in assets are transferred to the other changes in assets account.

20.109. Like T accounts, SAMs can be extended to incorporate economic aspects which are not part of the SNA's central framework, such as environmental concerns, production of unpaid domestic and personal services for own consumption within households, or a broader concept of capital (see chapters XIX and XXI). In these information systems, non-monetary data have a crucial role to play (refer to the outline for a SESAME in section C.1 above). Since this often entails the introduction of additional units, a matrix format is particularly useful. Another extension refers to the incorporation of balance sheets within the SAM proper. Evidently, in many cases, the data required for such an extension are not available; yet, for the sake of completeness, a possible design of such a SAM is sketched in the following section.

2. An example of a SAM including balance sheets

20.110. Table 20.7 gives an example of a SAM which is oriented towards an analysis of the interrelationships between economic stocks and flows. It includes an other changes in assets account, a changes between balance sheets account, and balance sheets. The other changes in assets account is classified by institutional sub-sector, with a separate account for the rest of the world, the changes between balance sheets account is broken down by type of asset and the balance sheets are shown both by sub-sector (plus the rest of the world) and by type of asset. Apart from this, table 20.4 has been altered as follows:

(a) The primary and secondary distribution of income and use of income accounts have been combined;

(b) Current and capital accounts for the rest of the world have been combined;

(c) The separate fixed capital formation account has been consolidated;

(d) Purchases minus sales of land and other non-produced assets are shown in the other changes in assets account and not in the capital account;

(e) The financial account is subdivided by institutional sub-sector, plus an account for the rest of the world;

(f) A dummy account has been inserted to absorb the balances, for institutional sub-sectors and the rest of the world, of transactions in financial assets and in non-financial, non-produced assets; as in the column of this dummy account nothing is recorded, it has been deleted.

The first two changes of this list are optional; they were only made here in order to limit the size of table 20.7. The dummy account is a possible solution to the problem of incorporating in a SAM both balancing items of the System's capital account, that is, (a) net lending, and (b) changes in net worth due to saving and net capital transfers.

20.111. Otherwise, the current accounts (labelled 1–6) and all account codes in this table are analogous to those in table 20.4. The capital account (account 7) now records net saving and capital

transfers, resulting in the balancing item changes in net worth due to saving and net capital transfers (row 14 and column 7).

20.112. The financial account registers in the row, that is, in cell (9,18), acquisitions minus disposals of existing financial assets and (minus) liabilities plus the simultaneous creation or extinction of financial assets and counterpart liabilities. The balance, net lending of the nation, is put on the dummy account for the balance of transactions in financial and non-financial, non-produced assets; cell (12,9). A similar procedure is followed in the financial account for the rest of the world (account 19); in this case, the balancing item is net lending of the rest of the world, see cell (12,19).

20.113. The row of the dummy account for the balance of transactions in financial and non-financial, non-produced assets (account 12) records net lending of the nation (cell 12,9) and net lending of the rest of the world (cell 12,19), which always add up to zero, and acquisitions less disposals of non-financial, non-produced assets, by institutional sub-sectors (cell 12,13) and by the rest of the world (cell 12,20), and the sum of these transactions is also zero by definition. Hence, it is not necessary to insert a column for this account.

20.114. The row of the other changes in assets account (account 13) shows:

(a) Purchases minus sales of land and other non-produced assets in cell (13,17);

(b) Other changes in the volume and price of produced assets in cell (13,16);

(c) Other changes in the volume and price of non-financial, non-produced assets in cell (13,17);

(d) Other changes in the volume and price of financial assets and (minus) liabilities in cell (13,18).

Purchases minus sales of existing produced assets are not included in this list, since they are recorded as part of gross capital formation in cell (1,16) (see chapter X).

20.115. In the column of the other changes in assets account, the first item of the above list is put on the dummy account for the balance of transactions in financial and non-financial, non-produced assets; see cell (12,13). The balance of the other changes in assets, changes in net worth due to other changes in assets, is allocated to the changes between balance sheets account in cell (14,13). An analogous other changes in assets account is set up for the rest of the world (account 20); only in this case items (b) and (c) of the list in paragraph 20.114 are by definition excluded, while item (a) does not refer to land.

20.116. The changes between balance sheets account (account 14) adds several kinds of changes in net worth in the row and allocates these to the balance sheets of national sectors and the rest of the world in the column. Obviously, cells (14,7) and (14,13) add up to total changes in wealth held by national sectors—see cell (15,14), while cells (14,10&11) and (14,20) add

Table 20.7.   Example of a SAM with balance sheets

Account (classification)			0. Goods and services (products) 1	I. Production (industries) 2	II.1.1. Generation of income (value added components) 3	II.1.2-4. Income distribution and use (institutional sectors) 4&5&6	III.1. Capital (institutional sectors) 7	III.2. Financial (institutional sectors) 9	III.3. Other changes in assets (institutional sectors) 13
Goods and services (products)		1	Trade and transport margins 0	Intermediate consumption 1 883		Final consumption expenditure 1 399			
Production (industries)		2	Output 3 604						
Income generation (value added components)		3		*Net value added at basic prices* 1 499					
Distribution and use of income (institutional sectors)		4 5 6	Taxes on products less subsidies 133		*Net generated income at basic prices* 1 503	Property income and current taxes and current transfers to ROW [1] 1 230			
Capital (institutional sectors)		7				*Net saving* 233	Capital transfers 61		
Financial (institutional sectors)		9							
Balance of transactions, financial and non-prod. assets		12						Net lending of the total economy 38	Net purchases of non-produced assets 0
Other changes in assets (institutional sectors)		13							
Changes between balance sheets (asset types)		14					*Changes in net worth due to saving & capital transfers* 230		*Changes in net worth due to other changes in assets* 305
Balance sheets (institutional sectors)		15							
Balance sheets by type of assets	Produced assets (industries)	16		Consumption of fixed capital 222					
	Non-produced assets (types)	17							
	Financial assets (types)	18							
Rest of the world, current and capital		10 11	Imports of goods and services 499		Compensation of employees to ROW 2	Property income and current taxes and current transfers to ROW [1] 77	Capital transfers to ROW 4		
Rest of the world, financial		19							
Rest of the world, other changes in assets		20							
Rest of the World balance sheets		21							
Total			4 236	3 604	1 505	2 939	295	38	305

1 Including taxes on production and imports and adjustments to changes in the net equity of households with pension funds, from (cell 3&4&5, 10&11) and to (cell 10&11 and 3&4&5) ROW.

IV.2. Changes in balance sheets (asset types) 14	IV.1.1. and IV.3.1. Balance sheets (institutional sectors) 15	IV.1.2.-3.2. Asset type balance sheets — Produced assets (industries) 16	Non-produced assets (types) 17	Financial assets (types) 18	V. Rest of the world — I-III.1. Current and capital 10&11	III.2. Financial 19	III.3. Other changes in assets 20	IV.1 and IV.3. Balance sheets 21	Total
		Gross capital formation (in produced assets) 392	Gross capital formation (in non-produced assets) 22		Exports of goods and services 540				4 236
									3 604
					Compensation of employees from ROW 6				1 505
					Property income and current taxes and current transfers from ROW [1] 73				2 939
					Capital transfers from ROW 1				295
				Net acquisition of of assets (+) and incurrence of liabil. (−) 38					38
						Net lending of ROW −38	Net acquisition by ROW non-produced assets 0		0
		Net other changes in produced assets 119	Net other changes in non- produced assets 171	Net other changes in finan. assets (+) and liabilities (−) 15					305
					Net worth due to changes of current external balance and cap. transfers −38			*Changes in net worth of ROW due to other changes in assets* 4	501
Total changes in net worth due to other changes in assets 535		Opening stocks produced assets 6 047	Opening stocks non-produced assets 3 875	Opening stocks finan. assets (+) and liab. (−) 494					10 951
	Closing stocks produced assets 6 336								6 558
	Closing stocks non-prod. assets 4 068								4 068
	Closing stocks fin. assets (+) & liabilities (−) 547							*Closing stock of fin. assets (+) and liabil. (−) ROW* 242	789
									582
				Net acquisition of (+) finan. assets less incurr. liabil. (−) by ROW −38					−38
			Acquisitions (+) less disposals (−) of non-prod. assets by ROW 0	Net other changes in finan. assets (+) and liab. (−) of ROW 4					4
Total changes net worth ROW −34				Open. stocks fin. assets (+) and liab. (−) ROW 276					242
501	10 951	6 558	4 068	789	582	−38	4	242	

up to total changes in wealth held by the rest of the world, see cell (21,14). If this account is subdivided by type of asset and the category of produced assets is broken down by industry, a submatrix based on cell (14,7) would show, among other things, net capital formation by institutional sector of origin and by industry of destination.

20.117. The balance sheets are first presented for the national sectors (account 15). Row-wise, total changes in net worth of the nation are added to the (net) opening stocks. This gives the net closing stocks, which are transferred to the balance sheets by type of asset (accounts 16-18). In this aggregate table, net opening worth of the nation can be found as the total of cells (15,16), (15,17) and (15,18), while net closing worth of the nation agrees with the total of column (or row) 15.

20.118. The balance sheets by type of asset (accounts 16, 17 and 18) contain consumption of fixed capital and net closing stocks in the row, and gross capital formation, net transactions in finan-

cial assets, net transactions in non-financial, non-produced assets, other changes in assets and the opening stocks in the column.

20.119. The combined current and capital account for the rest of the world (accounts 10 and 11) ends with changes in net worth due to current external balance and net capital transfers (row 14 and column 10&11). Finally, the balance sheet for the rest of the world (account 21) resembles the one for the national sectors, except that it is limited to financial assets and liabilities.

20.120. Subsequent tables may disaggregate parts of this matrix to show, e.g., financial transactions by sub-sector and by type of financial asset, which then add up to cell (9,18) in table 20.7. In general, such a detailed set of tables would contain cross-classifications, by institutional sub-sector and by type of asset, of both opening and closing stocks and various changes in stocks. In any case the dummy account (account 12) is not sub-divided.

G. Applications of the SAM

1. More integration of available basic data

20.121. Chapter XV has outlined the suitability of a matrix framework to compile the goods and services account, the production account for industries and the generation of income account in the central framework. As a SAM integrates both income and expenditure flows and the supply and use table at a meso-level, it may serve as a format for the estimation of a wider set of accounts. The SAM-approach is particularly useful if one wants to reconcile detailed information on, for example, production and international trade with basic data from, for example, a labour force survey, a household budget survey and an investment survey for industries. In addition, casting accounts into a SAM-framework implies that matrix algebra can be applied to balance them. If a SAM is principally used for monitoring purposes, including comparisons with other economies, a large degree of international uniformity of these SAMs is important. Therefore, these SAMs may generally utilize concepts of the SNA's central framework. They can be considered as a unifying presentation of both the supply and use table and institutional sector accounts.

20.122. The abundance of data included in most SAMs may give the impression that it can only be constructed for countries with a wealth of statistical information. In practice, developing countries have taken the lead in compiling SAMs. Actually, it is in situations where basic information and other statistical resources are (very) scarce that it is all the more important to make the best possible use of whatever data are available. Integrating outcomes of all kinds of costly censuses and surveys into a consistent overall framework may increase both their relevance and their reliability. This applies in particular to household surveys and population censuses. Generally speaking, carefully acquired consistency at the meso-level leads to

a higher degree of accuracy at the macro-level. Naturally, if there are too many holes in the basic data, the reliability of (parts of) the SAM remains dubious. In this way, building a SAM will also pinpoint gaps in the available data set and discrepancies in the survey concepts. This should then have a streamlining feedback effect on both economic and social basic statistics.

20.123. As processing censuses and surveys is very time-consuming, and as the construction of a detailed SAM also tends to involve a substantial input of human resources, until recently SAMs have generally become available with a lag of several years. In fact, it is most practical to begin with building a full-fledged SAM only for years for which main surveys or censuses are held. It then serves as a benchmark data set, updated yearly or even quarterly, with the help of relevant indicators, to obtain the necessary timeliness without giving up too much in terms of reliability. A matrix framework is especially suitable in this regard, in view of the availability of various updating and reconciliation algorithms that apply matrix algebra. For the T accounts, other types of algorithms are available. Obviously, some computerization of the construction process of a SAM will prove quite useful in its updating as well.

20.124. Integration of more basic data entails the possibility of more policy issues being monitored and analysed interrelatedly. Above all, the linkage of employment and income distribution aspects to more macro-oriented objectives like NDP-growth, balance of payments equilibrium, stable price levels, etc., comes within reach with a SAM.

20.125. Since household surveys tend to underestimate not only total incomes or expenditures, but also inequality among households, a reconciliation of these sources with demographic statistics, an input-output table, wage surveys, profit and loss statements, government accounts, a balance of payments summary, financial data, etc., in a SAM will lead to a more reliable description of inequalities among household groups.

20.126. The applicability of a national accounts framework, like a SAM, to the measurement of poverty is less evident. In this case, households might be classified by income size-class, including a group with income below some pre-defined poverty-level. In practice, the limited capability of nationwide household surveys in covering the poor may pose a problem. Besides, underestimation of income and expenditure in such a survey is not equally spread across the whole range of incomes or expenditures. Relatively large errors frequently occur at the tail of the distribution. In fact, part of the within-subgroup heterogeneity in a SAM is caused by false outliers. All the same, if the households are classified according to socio-economic characteristics, it may more safely be assumed that errors are not concentrated in specific subgroups, so that some scaling cum reconciliation procedure of original subgroup average (per capita) values will not distort the inequality between subgroups. Summarizing, on one hand, it is rather hazardous to count the poor on the basis of national accounts, but on the other hand, a SAM which contains an elaborate classification of households may provide a dependable summary of "structural" poverty; it will identify subgroups in which the households are typically poor, it will show which needs cannot be properly met in these groups, and, above all, it allows for analyses concerning the causes and consequences of these circumstances.

20.127. Some of the above arguments apply to micro-macro links in general. A SAM may reveal the "structural" or average situation in the whole range of household groups. Again, a proper classification, resulting in fairly homogeneous categories qua behaviour, is crucial. In addition, micro-macro links are considerably facilitated if the concepts applied in the SAM are tuned to the perceptions at the micro-level.

20.128. Another application of SAMs refers to regional or supra-national accounting. In many instances it is neither necessary nor feasible to construct complete regional SAMs, or input-output tables for that matter. However, the SAM-feature of multiple sectoring implies that the regional dimension can be introduced into the classifications wherever this is considered relevant and as far as data availability allows. For example, a regional aspect can be introduced into the classifications of employed persons and households.

20.129. Interesting applications of a series of SAMs plus a set of commodity price and volume indices are, among other things: (a) tracing the relationship between changes in the terms of trade and productivity by industry and the income distribution, and (b) fixing weighting baskets for household group-specific consumer price indices (CPIs) which are consistent with the overall CPI.

2. SAMs as a tool for modelling and policy-analysis

20.130. The structure of each SAM already reflects the relationships represented in an economy-wide model. Tailoring this model to specific circumstances and needs thus has repercussions on the organization of data in the SAM. As a rule, the outlays in each column of such an "analytical" SAM should be directly related to total receipts in the concomitant row. This could imply, for instance, that taxes and social contributions are transferred to the secondary distribution of income account for the government in accordance with their incidence: product taxes from the goods and services account, other taxes on production from the production account, wage-related social contributions from the income generation account, taxes on primary incomes from the allocation of primary income account, capital gains taxes from the other changes in assets account, taxes on wealth from the balance sheets, etc. Another example refers to other changes in assets: if one thinks that some of these changes, such as capital gains, are directly and to a large extent reflected in final consumption expenditure, these values could be booked as an incoming on the (secondary) distribution of income account. Evidently, in such a SAM the stress lays on a representation of the economic structure. The other side of the picture is that some conventional balancing item(s) can then no longer be derived from a single cell of the aggregate SAM (see property (f) of matrix accounting, as shown in paragraph 20.23 above).

20.131. Analogous to an input-output table, a SAM provides a framework for a simple, linear model which is based on the inverse of the endogenous part of the matrix. In this case the multiplier model is closed, at least concerning the linkages between primary incomes and final expenditures. When compared with a fixed coefficient input-output model, a SAM-based inverse enables a more complete analysis of employment multipliers, the impact of exogenous changes in government expenditures and foreign trade, etc. Moreover, income distribution effects can be studied as well. In a SAM for use in multiplier analysis, accounts considered exogenous, like some or all accounts for the government sector, are singled out and shown at the end. In addition, the structure of the SAM should then be oriented towards obtaining the most realistic proportionality assumptions. Realism may be further increased by estimating coherent sets of relevant elasticities to arrive at marginal instead of average expenditure propensities. In any case, the (cross-) classifications selected in the SAM will have a dominant influence on the outcomes of the analysis. For some purposes, the relative simplicity of the multiplier approach is appealing. However, in several other applications the absence of supply constraints and of endogenous prices in this model is a serious limitation.

20.132. These shortcomings may be overcome in another important application of a SAM: its use in a so-called applied general equilibrium (AGE) model. These economy-wide models, which apply micro-economic insights at a meso-level, serve to simulate the effects on growth and income distribution of a range of policies, from trade liberalization measures to tax rate changes and structural adjustment packages. Minimal data requirements for AGE Models are: (a) a base-year SAM, (b) a decomposition of SAM-values per category of goods and services (preferably including various types of labour and asset services) into appropriate price and volume components, (c) data on various stocks, like population and production capacity and, possibly, (d) additional data required for a more realistic derivation of relevant elasticities. This may be supplemented by econometric estimation of some parameters, on the basis of time-series data which are scaled such that the base-year values are in conformity with the concomitant SAM-values. The output of such a modelling exercise typically consists of a reproduction of the base-year SAM, which validates the model, and of a series of SAMs for future periods.

20.133. A distinctive feature of all SAM-based models is their reliance on complete balances, at a multisector level, of incomes and outlays of institutions and of supply and use of goods and services, usually including labour services. Ideally, the supply and use balances are maintained for values and volumes separately and for some assets as well. Another feature is that the structure of the model and the structure of the SAM are closely interlinked. To a lesser extent, this also applies to the parameter values. This means a departure from a model specification which hinges on co-variations among time-series of considerable length. In turn, it implies that SAM-based models are less liable to the disadvantages of that approach, such as: (a) its use of proxy variables and independently estimated deflators for various transaction categories, which does not guarantee consistency; (b) its dependence on longer time-series, which in many cases are not available at a meso-level, and (c) its reliance on the constancy of relationships over a longer period, which is often questionable in view of various structural external shocks (energy crises) and continual institutional reforms (lifting trade barriers, large-scale privatizations, etc.).

20.134. The above examples illustrate that SAM-based models are particularly relevant to policy analyses in which the structural features of an economy play an important role. For instance, in a situation of structural adjustment one might use such models for simulating the macro-economic and distributional implications of price liberalization measures or, reversely, of proposals for a certain environmental levy. In analyses with a relatively short time-horizon, it can safely be assumed that many structural features can be represented by fixed coefficients. In longer-term models, feedbacks at the meso-level need to be incorporated more carefully. In both cases, a SAM, or preferably a more extended SESAME as sketched in section C.2 above, then serves as a framework to guarantee consistency, both in current and in constant prices. However, until more timely SAMs with well-articulated financial accounts become available, these models have only limited relevance to short-term, monetary stabilization policies.

20.135. Finally, SAMs are suitable for use in a macroeconomics teaching course, in view of their concise and conveniently arranged description of interrelationships between economic processes, their function as a systematic database for the joint derivation of monetary and non-monetary aggregate indicators and their close connection to flexible, economy-wide models of varying degrees of complexity.

Note

1 As redistributed income in kind is by definition fully spent on certain goods and services, its size influences neither saving nor the final consumption of other products. Note, though, that the same applies to income imputed as a consequence of valuing output for own final consumption at equivalent market prices (subsistence production, services of owner-occupied dwellings, etc.), and to wages in kind.

XXI. Satellite analysis and accounts

A. Introduction

21.1. The central framework of the SNA presents a number of characteristics which give it the advantages of an integrated accounting structure. It is exhaustive and consistent within the boundary of the economic activities it covers; that is to say, each unit, transaction, product and purpose is given a place, and only one, in the classifications and accounts of the System. Moreover, the set of concepts adopted by the System is fully coherent.

21.2. The counterpart of these benefits is that there are certain limitations as to what may be accommodated directly in the central framework. The central framework may be used in a flexible way, as explained in chapter XIX, in order to put greater or lesser emphasis on specific aspects of economic life, such as the public sector, households, or high inflation. However, the margins of flexibility allowed by the central conceptual framework do not permit conflicting approaches to be covered simultaneously.

21.3. As already indicated in several earlier chapters, the SNA does not claim that its categories and concepts are in all cases the only right ones. Additional or different requirements necessitate the development of complementary or alternative categories and concepts.

21.4. Satellite accounts or systems generally stress the need to expand the analytical capacity of national accounting for selected areas of social concern in a flexible manner, without overburdening or disrupting the central system. It is useful to preview in very summary form the characteristics of satellite accounts or systems, which will be elaborated throughout the chapter. Typically satellite accounts or systems allow for:

(a)   The provision of additional information on particular social concerns of a functional or cross-sector nature;

(b)   The use of complementary or alternative concepts, including the use of complementary and alternative classifications and accounting frameworks, when needed to introduce additional dimensions to the conceptual framework of national accounts;

(c)   Extended coverage of costs and benefits of human activities;

(d)   Further analysis of data by means of relevant indicators and aggregates;

(e)   Linkage of physical data sources and analysis to the monetary accounting system.

21.5. These characteristics, even in the summary form, point to important roles for satellite analysis and accounts. On the one hand, satellite accounts are linked with the central framework of national accounts (as will be spelled out at several points in the chapter) and through them to the main body of integrated economic statistics. On the other hand, as they are more specific to a given field or topic, they are also linked to the information system specific to this field or topic. They also call for better integration of monetary and physical data. Because they preserve close connections with the central accounts, they facilitate analyses of specific fields in the context of macro-economic accounts and analyses. Satellite accounts in various fields may, in addition, help to connect analyses between some of those fields. Satellite accounts are thus able to play a dual role, as tools for analyses and for statistical coordination.

21.6. The objectives of the present chapter are threefold. First, it indicates, in section B, what kind of variants are or could be thought of in general when allowing for additional degrees of freedom. The approaches referred to may lead to various types of solutions, from just introducing some additional figures to redesigning the main concepts of the central framework. Secondly, in section C, the chapter presents a framework for functionally oriented satellite accounts, the goal of which is somewhere in between these two extreme types of solutions. Thirdly, in section D, the chapter presents environmental accounting in a SNA satellite accounting framework. Environmental accounting, which is of such importance as to deserve special consideration, is explained by reference to a generalized and extended version of the system of environmental economic accounts.

B. Satellite analysis

21.7. In this section, a step-by-step approach is followed in order to illustrate by example various means of broadening the analyses. Production and products, primary incomes and transfers, uses of goods and services, assets and liabilities, purposes as well as aggregates are considered in turn.

1. Production and products

21.8. Within the production boundary of the central framework of the SNA, producer units are establishments or, in a more refined analysis, units of homogeneous production, classified according to their principal economic activity. Both kinds of units are classified according to the International Standard Industrial Classification (ISIC).

21.9. When establishments, and consequently industries, are not homogeneous at a given level of the ISIC, they undertake both a principal activity and one or more secondary activities. The output of these secondary activities is identified according to its nature, following a product classification, but the inputs of secondary activities are not separated from the ones of the principal activities. Ancillary activities, on the other hand, are not analysed and classified according to their own nature, but as part of the activities of the establishment(s) they serve. This means that ancillary activities are not undertaken by distinct producer units and the related products do not appear as autonomous products.

21.10. When examining certain kinds of activity and products, it may be useful to separate secondary from principal activity, in order to get a full picture of the inputs (intermediate and factor inputs) corresponding to the activity being examined. This aspect is well-known in input-output analysis. In addition, it may be necessary to identify some ancillary activities and their output within the producer units.

21.11. Take the example of transportation. The output of transportation activities in the central framework covers only transport services rendered to third parties. Own-account transportation is treated as an ancillary activity; its inputs are unidentified components of the costs of the producing units it serves. If one wants a broader picture of transportation activity, own-account transportation of producing units has to be identified and measured. With regard to health activities, some of them also are treated as ancillary activities, such as the on-site medical facilities provided by employers to their employees. Thus the cost of many activities includes an unidentified health component.

21.12. More generally, inputs of producer units cover the direct cost of making the principal and secondary output and the cost of various internal functions which are, to varying degrees, indirect components of the total cost. In addition to the above-mentioned activities, we could mention training, electronic data processing, accountancy and trade.

21.13. Thus, for complete coverage of certain activities and products within the production boundary of the central framework, we have to deal with a number of elements:

(a) The establishments, or the units of homogeneous production, whose principal or single activity is the one we are interested in (the choice between these two types of units depending on the objectives pursued and the structure of the economy);

(b) If we are dealing with establishments, the relevant secondary output of other establishments, and the intra-establishment deliveries;

(c) The relevant ancillary activities and their output, presumably measured by their costs in general.

21.14. In many cases this process is straightforward, because the specified activities and products appear as such in the classifications of the central framework, although, of course, additional data are necessary as regards (c) above. Naturally the relative magnitude of (c) may differ from one activity to another, being more crucial for transportation or data processing than for education, for instance.

21.15. However, in some important cases, such as tourism and environmental protection activities, the process of identification is complex, because the relevant activities and products appear only to a small extent in the central framework classifications.

21.16. An output is usually identified according to a list of observable products, independent of the use that is made of them. This is possible for part of tourism: the services rendered by travel agencies or hotels are typically tourism products. More generally, however, tourism activities are defined by the fact that the goods and services they produce are delivered to tourists—i.e., people who spend at least one night away from home, whatever the purpose of their travel. So, long distance transportation is clearly a tourist activity; short distance transportation may or may not be, depending on who is using it. The same is true for shops in tourist areas. Some activities, though clearly tourist in nature, are isolated only at very detailed levels of classifications, for which national accounts are not commonly available, or not identified at all. Consequently, delineating tourism activities raises a lot of difficulties. The approach in most cases is an indirect one, starting from analysing the structure of tourist expenditure by product and looking at what activities deliver these goods and services.

21.17. The case of environmental protection activities and products is even more complex. Some establishments specialize in the production of environmental protection services for delivery to other units (e.g., waste disposal, sewage treatment) or goods which are used for environmental protection (e.g., filters). Others direct only part of their activity to delivering such goods and services to third parties. Moreover, an important part of environmental protection activities is internal to establishments. They are ancillary activities in the central framework and have to be externalized if one wants to measure the environmental activities more broadly. Again the purpose of the expenditure has to be considered in conjunction with the kind of activities undertaken and the goods and services used.

21.18. The above-mentioned re-analyses take place within the limits of the central framework's boundary of production. For certain objectives, however, the production boundary itself may be changed. This can be done in a rather global way, for example, by including services rendered by persons to other members of their household or/and voluntary work. It may also be done when trying to get a very broad picture of a given activity. For instance, to make an overall estimate of the transportation function in an economy, it might be useful to cover transport services rendered by households using their own cars and to try to value the time people spend using transport facilities. Generally speaking, the scope of non-market activities may be extended considerably.

2. Income

Primary incomes

21.19. When the production boundary is extended, as suggested above, the magnitude of primary incomes is increased, income being imputed for the additional activities which are inserted within the boundary of production.

21.20. Additional analyses are also possible. For example, one may try to separate the mixed income or entrepreneurial income of the household sector into an element of return to labour and an element of return to capital.

21.21. In conditions of inflation, nominal interest may be judged not to be a convenient measure of the return to lent funds. Nominal interest includes an implicit or explicit (in case of indexation) component as compensation for the change inflation occasions in the real value of monetary assets and liabilities. This component may be analysed as a holding gain for the borrower and a holding loss for the lender, rather than as an element of property income (see chapter XIX for a possible parallel treatment of interest suitable for countries experiencing significant inflation).

Transfers and disposable income

21.22. Several kinds of transfers in addition to those in the central framework may be delineated, if meaningful.

21.23. First, transfers may appear in relation to ancillary activities when these activities are externalized, especially when their output is allocated to final consumers. Transfers internal to

units may also cover the counterpart of the cost of production of non-market services produced by government when it is useful to distinguish the producing and the financing functions of government.

21.24. Secondly, implicit transfers may be made explicit. Implicit transfers change the situation between units without any flow being treated as an imputed transfer in the central framework. For instance, tax benefits refer to the advantages or disadvantages economic units incur as a consequence of tax legislation by reference to a kind of average situation. Another, simpler example is the case of non-market services provided free of charge by government units to market producers. In the central framework these services are a collective consumption of government. If a further analysis treats them as an addition to intermediate consumption of market producers, a counterpart should be introduced, preferably in subsidies on production. This approach may be undertaken systematically to measure all types of transfers between government and particular sectors, such as agriculture. The implicit benefits resulting from tax concessions, equity participation, soft loans, differential exchange rates, differential domestic prices, etc., may then be added to subsidies, other current transfers, or capital transfers embodied in the central framework data.

21.25. Externalities may give rise to a wide range of implicit transfers, when trying to depict and value advantages/disadvantages that are not accounted for in the value of monetary transactions between economic units or that result from actions of these units in the absence of any monetary transaction. The environment, of course, gives rise to many external effects (see section D). For example, pollution and nuisances created by producers may have negative effects on final consumers. These negative effects might be estimated, not very easily of course, and recorded as negative transfers from producers to households. In order to balance these negative transfers, one possibility might be to introduce a concept of production of externalities which would result in an output of negative or positive services and the corresponding final consumption.

21.26. Thirdly, flows in the other changes in volume of assets account and the revaluation account of the central framework are candidates for enlarged concepts of transfers and disposable income. One could treat all of them as within an enlarged class of current transfers. The balancing item of the other changes in volume of assets account, i.e., "changes in net worth due to other changes in volume of assets", and the balancing item "changes in net worth due to real holding gains/losses" in the revaluation account, would then appear as extraordinary (disposable) income, subsequently as extraordinary saving. In this hypothesis the resulting enlarged disposable income would approximate more closely the ex-post Hicksean income concept. Enlarged saving in effect would then become equal to changes in real net worth less net capital transfers received.

21.27. However, one may think of making only limited steps in this direction. For instance, a country engaged in a war might find it useful to estimate an additional concept of disposable income by taking into account the destruction due to war. In countries where holding gains or losses on financial assets/liabilities are significant, real holding gains and losses on financial assets and liabilities could be added to disposable income in order to derive a broader measure of income.

21.28. Naturally, changes in primary incomes of the type described above would also result in adjusted figures for disposable income. One possibility in that context would be to adjust the latter only for the component of nominal interest which compensates for inflation, or for the difference between nominal and real interest.

3. Uses of goods and services

21.29. The coverage of uses of goods and services, either for intermediate or final consumption or capital formation, obviously changes as a result of enlarging the concept of production. For example, if services rendered to each other by members of the same household are included in production, they are finally consumed.

21.30. The borderline between intermediate, final consumption and capital formation may also be modified in various ways. Two typical cases refer to human capital and consumer durables. When final consumption in education and health is, at least in part, treated as fixed capital formation, the corresponding central framework transactions are reclassified from consumption (mainly final, partly intermediate) to fixed capital formation which results in human capital assets. A less radical treatment is to capitalize only actual expenditures on education (and possibly part of expenditures on health) as intangible assets, so extending the scope of the latter. As an immediate consequence, the concept of consumption of fixed capital would be extended.

21.31 An alternative to the inclusion of expenditures on consumer durables such as cars and furniture in household final consumption is to treat them as fixed capital formation. Only that part of the resulting fixed asset that is estimated as consumption of fixed capital then enters final consumption. Strictly speaking, this procedure implies enlarging the concept of production to include household services.

21.32. As a consequence of the changes just considered, the concept of saving is extended.

4. Assets and liabilities

21.33. The scope of assets, either tangible or intangible, is modified as a consequence of extending the concept of production or modifying the borderline between consumption and capital formation, as indicated in the previous paragraphs.

21.34. The scope of financial assets and liabilities may also be broadened by including contingent assets and liabilities in the clas-

sification of financial instruments. In fact, this modification would be simply a formal one as presumably, following current corporate practice, equivalent amounts would be included in both the assets and liabilities of each sector involved, unless the present value of the net risk taken is estimated and recorded under other changes in volume of assets, for example.

21.35. The scope of non-produced assets recorded in the balance sheets might be extended to other naturally occurring assets. In the central framework, natural assets are included in balance sheets only to the extent that they are owned and capable of bringing economic benefits to their owners. Of course, these criteria would apply to some additional natural assets if the services they provided were to be included in an enlarged concept of production. Moreover, attempts might be made to cover natural assets more widely to account for natural assets in general. In most cases, however, measurement is then usually only feasible in non-monetary terms.

5. Purposes

21.36. In the central framework an analysis by purpose is applied to most transactions of general government and non-profit institutions serving households, to final consumption and some other transactions of households and to certain transactions of producers. (The classifications are described in chapter XVIII.) This approach may be extended in order to cover a broader range of transactions and transactors. Moreover, the functional approach may be more flexible than it is in the central framework.

21.37. In the classifications by purpose used in the central framework, headings at a given level are mutually exclusive. A transaction classified under education may not also be classified under health, for example. In some cases, the part of expenditure missing when focusing on a given purpose may be significant and, therefore, a problem. In particular cases, purposes of current interest hardly feature in the existing general classifications because, for historical or other reasons, priority is given to the analysis of other purposes. For example, besides the fact that tourism does not appear as such as a main category in the classification of household goods and services by object, it is not even possible to reassemble the necessary pieces because not all of them are shown in the classification. The case of environment is similar with respect to various classifications.

21.38. Consequently, when emphasis is given to a particular purpose, a reclassification of a number of transactions is often necessary. All programmes or transactions related to environmental protection, for example, may thus be identified and grouped into a specific purpose classification. Such specific classifications have to be designed to cover the various units concerned in a consistent way. Of course, once reorganized that way, transactions classified by purpose are no longer additive since some of them may appear simultaneously under education and health, defence and health, environment and agricultural or energy affairs, transport and tourism, etc.

6. Aggregates

Changes in the main aggregates shown in the central framework

21.39. A number of the complementary or alternative analyses mentioned above may modify the main aggregates as shown in the central framework either directly or indirectly. Examples of direct modifications are the increase in output, value added and final consumption when household internal services are included within the boundary of production, or the increase in fixed capital formation if human capital is considered an economic asset. Other aggregates are indirectly modified: saving in the latter case, disposable income in the former one.

21.40. Accounting for the use of natural resources and changes therein, such as subsoil mineral deposits, might also lead to the measurement of complementary or alternative aggregates (see section D). In fact, in these and similar cases, a new system of national accounts is explicitly or implicitly rebuilt, as the alternative aggregates might be introduced in a differently conceived central framework.

Introduction of aggregates by purpose

21.41. In some types of analysis the objective is to focus on one specific field of concern, such as education or tourism. Changes in some concepts and aggregates of the central framework may be introduced, but this is not the primary intention, nor is it intended to give a different picture of the overall economic process.

21.42. In this approach, one may wish to define and measure one or more aggregates to capture at a glance the magnitude of the resources an economy is devoting to the field of concern. In some cases the functional analysis of the central framework directly provides figures that are very close to those sought. For defence, for instance, the sum of collective consumption and capital formation corresponding to that purpose in general government accounts will normally give what we want to know. This means that national expenditure on defence is obtained directly as a part of national expenditure. Here the problem is easy to solve because only one institutional sector is involved and the object concerned appears as a specific heading in the classification of functions of government. Even in this simple case, one might argue that a full picture of defence expenditure would necessitate including other elements such as the opportunity cost of conscripts and volunteers, some expenditures related to internal order, research on military objectives carried out under non-defence heading, etc.

21.43. In most cases, however, more than one sector is involved and the classifications do not directly contain the items of interest. In addition, the required aggregate is not necessarily composed only of final consumption and capital formation. A broader concept has therefore to be specifically defined, in order to cover all aspects of the national expenditure in the field of concern. This is further elaborated in section C.

7. Other aspects

21.44. This section illustrated various ways and means of extending national accounts work. The examples given do not attempt to cover systematically all kinds of complementary or alternative solutions. For instance, different methods may be used to value economic flows, as well as assets and liabilities. Some of these methods are included in the central framework; others, such as opportunity cost or the net present value may be considered more broadly in satellite analyses. The labour content of flows of goods and services may also be studied. The underlying economic significance of certain arrangements such as, for instance, advertising expenditures by businesses that provide major support to newspapers and television programmes, might be examined.

8. From analyses to accounts

21.45. Broadly speaking, two types of satellite analysis may be distinguished in their relationship with the central framework of the SNA. One type involves some rearrangement of central classifications and the introduction of complementary elements that differ from the conceptual central framework (such as the identification of the output of ancillary activities) without drastically diverging from the concepts on which the central framework is built. These constructs are not based on nor emphasize alternative concepts, even when they use some on a complementary basis. This first type of analysis mostly covers accounts specific to given fields such as education, tourism and environmental protection expenditures. Introducing their content into the central framework would overburden it and would not be totally possible; doing it in a specific, satellite, accounting framework allows additional margins of flexibility.

21.46. The second type of satellite analysis is mainly based on concepts that are alternatives to the ones of the SNA. A different production boundary or enlarged concepts of consumption and capital formation may be introduced, or the scope of assets may be extended, the borderline between economic phenomena as covered by the central framework and natural phenomena may be altered, the links between income and wealth may be put in the context of a broader concept of wealth, including natural assets, etc. Often a number of alternative concepts are used at the same time. This second type of analysis may involve, like the first, changes in definitions or classifications, but in the second type the main emphasis is on the alternative concepts. Using those alternative concepts may give rise to partial complementary aggregates the purpose of which is to supplement the central system. Various efforts are also made to include some or all of them in an alternative system of national accounts.

21.47. The second type of research work is evidently more controversial than the first one, but it is important. It allows national accounts work to be extended beyond what is, or perhaps might be, included in the central system of the SNA. It provides useful results for economic analysis. It experiments with new concepts and methodologies, with of course a much wider margin of freedom than in current national accounts work. This research work may influence the development of the central national accounts themselves. The System does not make standardized recommendations as to this type of work, which by definition must remain open. Environmental accounting is considered in this context in section D. For explanatory purposes that section uses a version of an accounting framework called the system of environmental economic accounts, which should be considered work-in-progress and just one of the frameworks in which environmental account could be developed.

21.48. On the other hand, the work already done in functionally oriented satellite accounts—the type of research work referred to in paragraph 21.45 above—refers to a family of satellite accounts for which it is possible to propose an accounting framework which could be used as a reference by people intending to build such accounts.

C. Framework for functionally oriented satellite accounts

21.49. It is clear from the previous section, that satellite analysis may apply to various aspects of national accounts and pursue different objectives. One approach is to concentrate on one field to give a full picture of it, in a systematic way, by establishing a specific accounting framework, articulated with the central framework.

21.50. As regards its relations with the central framework, such a specific, satellite framework does not aim at covering all economic life; it is a self-consistent framework in a partial domain. Escaping from some constraints of the central framework, which is mainly institutional in nature, a satellite framework or account is by hypothesis more functional.

21.51. To put more emphasis on the functional point of view, such satellite accounts combine an extension of the kind of activity and product analysis and a generalization of the purpose approach. It is then possible to try to design an accounting framework to cover a wide variety of cases, all of them belonging to a family of functionally oriented satellite accounts. Such accounts are relevant for many fields, such as culture, education, health, social protection, tourism, environmental protection, research and development (R and D), development aid, transportation, data processing, housing and communications.

21.52. Most of the fields just mentioned refer to services; they generally spread over a number of activities and they correspond in many cases to subjects that very often are of social concern. It should be noted at the outset that because the fields of functionally oriented satellite accounts sometimes overlap, the shares of national expenditure in those fields in relation with gross domestic product (GDP), for example, may not be strictly additive. Some activities/products/purposes may be classified in several places. Thus, if shares of overlapping fields have to be calculated, the denominator will normally have to be modified.

1. Scope of a functionally oriented satellite account

21.53. To analyse a specific field in depth while preserving the possibility of calculating some significant aggregates such as national expenditure, the starting point is an analysis of the uses. This corresponds to the questions "how many resources are devoted to (education, transportation, tourism, environmental protection, data processing, etc.)?" or, identically, "how much is spent on (education, transportation, etc.)?". In order to answer these questions, we have to decide upon:

(a) The goods and services that we will consider specific to this field, where national expenditure includes the uses (current or capital) of these specific products;

(b) The activities for which we will record capital formation;

(c) The transfers that we will consider specific to this field, recognizing that they will be a separate component of national expenditure only to the extent that they are not already included in the value of the uses of the specific products (otherwise, they will be analysed only in relation to financing).

21.54. Depending on the field, the design of a given satellite account will emphasize:

(a) The detailed analysis of the production and uses of the specific goods and services (e.g., R and D or transportation);

(b) The detailed analysis of transfers (e.g., social protection);

(c) Both production/uses and transfers equally (e.g., education and health);

(d) Uses as such (e.g., tourism, environmental protection).

21.55. When units which are the users, as actual consumers or investors, and units which ultimately bear the expenses coincide, figures for users tell us who finally bears the expenditure. This is the normal case for data processing and to a large extent transportation or tourism. On the other hand, ultimate users and ultimate bearers of the expenses may often differ, as is the case for education and health. In these cases, analysing the way the uses are financed is very important. When transfers represent all, or the main part of, national expenditure in a given field, this analysis is even more crucial.

21.56. Analysing in detail who are the users, consumers, investors, or transfer recipients is thus an important part of what can be done in a satellite account. Even if the aggregate under study is called national expenditure, the users in this context are the units which actually acquire the goods or services (for actual final consumption, intermediate consumption or capital formation) or receive specific transfers which are not intended to finance these acquisitions of goods and services.

21.57. Finally, as we focus attention on one field, it is useful to associate non-monetary figures to the monetary ones. Non-monetary figures relate to producing units and factors of production (labour, various kinds of assets) and users/beneficiaries.

21.58. In short, a satellite account in a given field covers the analysis of uses or benefits out of the national expenditure, production and its factors, transfers and other ways of financing the uses, both in value terms and, when relevant, in physical quantities.

2. Uses/national expenditure

21.59. The field of a given satellite account is essentially delineated by defining the content of the various types of uses to be included in the specific aggregates relevant to this field.

21.60. Table 21.1 shows the components of national expenditure. It is convenient in the first instance to define and measure the uses of resident units. However, uses of resident units may be financed partly by non-resident units. This part has to be deducted in order to get a total that corresponds to the effort a nation is making in a given field out of its own resources.

3. Components of uses/national expenditure

21.61. The first step is to define the goods and services that are considered specific to this field. It is convenient to distinguish two types of specific goods and services in this context: characteristic goods and services and connected goods and services. The first category covers the products which are typical for the field under study. We are interested in studying the way these goods and services are produced, what kinds of producers are involved, what kinds of labour and fixed capital they use and the efficiency of the production process and, hence, of the allocation of resources. For example, for health, characteristic products are health services, public administration services, education and R and D services in health.

21.62. The second category, connected goods and services, includes products in whose uses we are interested because they are clearly covered by the concept of expenditure in a given field, without being typical, either by nature or because they are classified in broader categories of products. In health, for example, transportation of patients may be considered con-

nected services; also pharmaceutical products and other medical goods, such as glasses, are very often treated as connected goods and services. For these connected goods and services, we are not primarily interested, when studying a given field, in their conditions of production. If we were, these products would have to be treated as characteristic goods and services. For example, pharmaceutical products might be considered characteristic in the account for health of a country at a first stage of developing a domestic industry. The precise borderline between characteristic and connected products depends on the economic organization in a given country and the purpose of a satellite account.

21.63. The economic activities providing the two types of specific products are treated differently in a satellite account, as explained below.

21.64. Specific goods and services generally appear at various levels and/or in various headings of the product classification used in the central framework. The headings in question are regrouped and additional details are introduced in order to build up the classification specific to a given satellite account. However, in order not to conflict with the requirements of statistical coordination, this specific classification remains strictly linked to the central classification of reference.

21.65. Some services may appear in the specific classifications of two or more satellite accounts. For instance, research in health services in higher education institutions is a specific product of both R and D and education and health.

21.66. Items 1 and 2 of the uses/expenditure table 21.1 relate to uses of the specific goods and services. In this table, and in following tables except table 21.5, characteristic products and connected products are not shown separately. This has been done only for the sake of simplification in the presentation of the tables. In actual satellite accounts it is necessary for analytical purposes to show the uses of characteristic goods and services and the uses of connected goods and services separately. Item 1 is consumption of specific goods and services. It covers actual final consumption (defined as in the central framework) and intermediate consumption. Market and non-market products are distinguished and, for the latter, individual and collective consumption. For the sake of simplicity, products for own final use and other non-market products are not shown separately in this chapter; they are both covered under non-market products. Similarly, producers for own final use and other non-market producers are both covered under non-market producers. The amounts are the same as in the central framework, unless the boundary of production is changed (for example, by including voluntary work in education and health) or a different type of valuation is adopted (see paragraph 21.75 below on consumption subsidies). Intermediate consumption generally has a broader coverage than in the central framework, as the output of the relevant ancillary activities is identified (while intra-establishment deliveries must be recorded). As a consequence, it covers (actual) intermediate consump-

Table 21.1.   Components of uses/national expenditure

Components of uses/national expenditure	Total
1. Consumption of specific goods and services	
1.1 Actual final consumption	
1.1.1 Market products	
1.1.2 Non-market products	
1.1.2.1. Individual	
1.1.2.2. Collective	
1.2 Intermediate consumption	
1.2.1. Actual intermediate consumption	
1.2.2. Internal intermediate consumption	
2. Capital formation in specific goods and services	
3. Fixed capital formation of characteristic activities in non-specific products(*)	
4. Specific current transfers (not counterpart of item 1)	
5. Specific capital transfers (not counterpart or item 2 or 3)	
Total uses of resident units	
6. Current uses of resident units financed by the rest of the world (less)	
7. Capital uses of resident units financed by the rest of the world (less)	
National expenditure	

* And their acquisition less disposals of non-produced non-financial assets.

tion as defined in the central framework and internal intermediate consumption. In some cases, such as transport services, the last component may be important in size. Sometimes, it could be considered that this internal intermediate consumption is treated as final consumption and added to actual final consumption, as in the use of ancillary education and health services, thus broadening the scope of household actual final consumption. Also the scope of consumption may be narrowed, if the use of certain services is treated as fixed capital formation in a satellite account instead of intermediate or final consumption as in the central framework (see paragraph 21.67 below).

21.67. Item 2 of table 21.1 is capital formation in specific goods and services. In an account for housing, for example, it covers fixed capital formation in residential buildings. In R and D, education and health, item 2 is empty if the related services are all included under consumption as in the central framework. Of course, if all or part of these services were treated as capital formation in a satellite account, the corresponding uses would appear under item 2.

21.68. In addition to fixed capital formation, item 2 may cover changes in inventories. It may be so when specific goods are

involved. As far as specific services are concerned, changes in inventories may relate to work-in-progress, for instance in software or some tourism services such as input costs already incurred in the preparation of tours not yet sold.

21.69. In an account for culture, acquisitions less disposals of valuables, such as paintings, may be significant. In this case it is also a component of item 2.

21.70. The definition of item 3, fixed capital formation of characteristic activities in non-specific products and their acquisitions less disposals of non-produced non-financial assets is a bit more complex:

(a)   It does not cover the total fixed capital formation of these activities because that part consisting of specific products is already included in item 2;

(b)   Only the fixed capital formation of activities whose output consists of characteristic goods and services is covered in item 3. (If the exclusion of capital formation of activities whose output consists of connected goods and services proves important, the products and activities in question may have to be redefined to be characteristic.)

(c)   An analysis based on establishments may give a broader coverage than normal because they may cover some secondary activities;

(d) Item 3 includes acquisitions less disposals of non-produced non-financial assets, mainly land. The acquisition of land may be important in such cases as education, health, tourism and housing.

21.71. The fixed capital formation in item 3 may be studied using a classification adapted to a particular satellite account. For example, if considering education or health, fixed capital formation in schools or hospitals could be further classified by various kinds of educational structures, medical equipment goods, etc.

21.72. The approach followed thus far when defining the content of items 1 to 3 of table 21.1 is relevant for most of the fields satellite accounts may cover. A more delicate approach is necessary, however, for environmental protection. As already stated, in this field, only some goods, services and activities in the usual sense may be considered characteristic and the relationship between products, activities and purposes is much looser than in the other fields previously referred to. Environmental protection expenditure is generally defined in terms of objectives pursued through actions or programmes related, for instance, to waste disposal, preservation of air quality, protection of other natural media, public administration in environmental affairs, etc. However, classifications currently proposed for environmental protection activities cover both economic activities in the SNA and ISIC sense and functions. In this context the definition of characteristic activities and of items 1 to 3 necessitate a specific analysis.

21.73. Item 4—Specific current transfers (not the counterpart of item 1) and item 5—Specific capital transfers (not the counterpart of items 2 or 3) are the most important components of national expenditure in cases such as social protection or development aid. In the examples mentioned above, items 1 and 2 refer only to the administrative costs, both current and capital, of the agencies managing social protection or international aid. The core of the expenditure consists of transfers.

21.74. In other fields, such as education and health, the major part of transfers (most of them in kind) are means of financing the acquisition by users of goods and services included in items 1 to 3. These transfers should not be counted twice in the expenditure. However, some transfers or parts of transfers are not used to counterbalance acquisition of products included in items 1 to 3. For example, student grants may serve to finance various outlays in addition to tuition fees or school books. This additional component of students grants is included under item 4.

21.75. In some situations, there may be subsidies designed to reduce the prices paid by final consumers for certain goods or services, such as food, transport services, or housing services. They are commonly called consumption subsidies. In the central framework, when these goods and services are considered market products, they are included in final consumption at purchasers' prices. In a satellite account there are two options: either consumption (item 1) is valued differently from the central framework in order to include the value of consumption subsidies or consumption is valued as it is in the central framework and specific current transfers (item 4) must include consumption subsidies. Subsidies included in item 4 may also be directed toward reducing the prices of intermediate consumption. Item 4 may also include other subsidies on production.

21.76. In each field a classification of specific transfers has to be established. As it is used for analysing both uses and financing, this classification covers all specific transfers, independently of whether they are or are not counterparts of items 1 to 3.

21.77. The total uses of resident units are the sum of the five components above. It is convenient to distinguish between current and capital uses financed by the rest of the world, in order to facilitate later on the calculation of current and capital national expenditure which is derived from the uses of resident units by deducting that part which is financed by the rest of the world by means of transfers or lending. National expenditure is thus equal to total uses of resident units financed by resident units. Total uses of resident units or national expenditure may in most cases be calculated either gross or net or both.

21.78. National expenditure, as defined above, does not include transactions in financial instruments. However, for certain types of analysis, such as development aid, loans which are given or received at preferential conditions must be accounted for. Benefits or costs resulting from rates of interest lower than the market ones are clearly implicit transfers.

21.79. Uses/national expenditure may be shown by type of products and transfers or by type of purpose (programmes). The main emphasis may be put on one or the other of these two alternatives, or they might be used jointly, depending on the field covered or the aim of the analysis pursued. The approach by programme is particularly relevant in the case of environmental protection or social protection.

21.80. Table 21.2 indicates the usual coverage of national expenditure in various fields. As explained above, not all items are relevant in every case. Current uses of resident units include components 1 and 4, capital uses components 2, 3 and 5. Current national expenditure is equal to the sum of components 1 and 4, less item 6. Capital national expenditure is equal to the sum of components 2, 3 and 5, less item 7.

21.81. Some explanation of the table is needed. Collective consumption for social protection and development aid refers to the current costs of managing agencies in these fields. Specific current transfers for tourism, transportation, housing and possibly education, health and culture cover subsidies on the relevant products unless they are included under item 1. In many fields they refer also to transfers to international organizations. Since financing by the rest of the world depends on specific circumstances, no crosses have been entered in table 21.2. For R and D, a satellite account allows expenditure to be

Table 21.2.   Coverage of national expenditure in various fields

Components of uses/ national expenditure	Culture	Education	Health	Social protec- tion	Tourism	Environ- mental protection	Research and develop- ment	Aid for develop- ment	Transpor- tation	Data processing	Housing
1. Consumption of specific goods and services											
1.1. Actual final consumption											
1.1.1. Market products	X	X	X		X	X			X	X	X
1.1.2. Non-market products											
1.1.2.1. Individual	X	X	X		X	X	X		X	X	
1.1.2.2. Collective	X	X	X	X	X	X	X	X	X	X	X
1.2. Intermediate consumption											
1.2.1. Actual intermediate consumption		X	X								
1.2.2. Internal intermediate consumption	X	X	X			X	X		X	X	
2. Capital formation in specific goods and services						X	X			X	X
3. Fixed capital formation of characteristic activities in non-specific products (*)	X	X	X	X	X	X	X		X	X	X
4. Specific current transfers (not counterpart of item 1)	X	X	X	X	X	X	X	X	X		X
5. Specific capital transfers (not counterpart of items 2 or 3)				X				X	X		
Total uses of resident units											
6. Current uses of resident units financed by the rest of the world (less)											
7. Capital uses of resident units financed by the rest of the world (less)											
National expenditure											

*   And their acquisition less disposals of non-produced non-financial assets.

treated either as consumption or capital formation or both. In certain cases, other aggregates are relevant and should be calculated. For instance, in the case of tourism, expenditure by tourists, both resident and non-resident, in the domestic market, is a significant aggregate. It is obtained, starting from item 1, by deducting expenditure abroad by resident tourists (imports) and adding expenditure by non-resident tourists in the domestic market (exports).

4. Users/beneficiaries

21.82. For users or beneficiaries, the terminology used may differ from one satellite account to another. "Users" is more relevant to tourism or housing for example, "beneficiaries" to social protection or development aid, etc. In both cases, the terms refer to who is using the goods and services or benefiting from the transfers involved.

21.83. At the most aggregated level, the classification of users/beneficiaries is simply a rearrangement of the central framework classification of institutional sectors and types of producers, in which production aspect and consumption aspect are separated. It may be as follows:

(a) Market producers;

(b) Non-market producers (producers for own final use; and other non-market producers);

(c) Government as a collective consumer;

(d) Households as consumers;

(e) Rest of the world.

21.84. Various sub-categories of producers may be distinguished under each main group, either by industry and/or by institutional sub-sector in order to show explicitly the detailed links with the central framework as well as for analytical purposes. For actual consumption, general government is supposed to be the final consumer of collective services produced by itself, on behalf of society as a whole.

21.85. Households, even individuals, as consumers are the most important type of users/beneficiaries in many satellite accounts. In order to be useful for social analysis and policy, a further breakdown of households is necessary. In the first instance this may be according to the various sub-sectors that are distinguished in the central framework or may use a more detailed or especially adapted socio-economic classification. Moreover, various criteria may be used according to different purposes, such as size of income, age, sex, location, etc. For analysis and policy-purposes, knowledge of the number of people concerned in each category is essential in order to calculate, for instance, the average consumption or transfer, the number of people who benefit very little or not at all from national expenditure in the field under study, etc.

21.86. Cross-classifying components of national expenditure and

types of users/beneficiaries leads to table 21.3. Crosses indicate cells which may be filled in, if relevant in a given field.

5. Financing

21.87. Users do not always bear the expenses themselves so that it is necessary to analyse the financing units, i.e., the units which ultimately bear the expenses. For this purpose a classification derived from the central framework classification of institutional sectors, such as the following, may be used:

(a) Market producers;

(b) NPISHs;

(c) General government;

(d) Households;

(e) Financial enterprises;

(f) Rest of the world.

21.88. It can be seen from this list that non-market producers are never considered ultimate financing units. All their costs, net of any secondary sales and possible transfers, are covered by their parent institutional units or by borrowed funds. Market producers refer to all institutional sectors in their capacity as producers for the market, as in the classification of users/beneficiaries. A separate category is introduced for financial enterprises covering financial corporations and, if any, unincorporated financial enterprises. It refers only to their function of providing other units with funds they gather through financial intermediation.

21.89. Table 21.4 cross-classifies components of national expenditure and financing units.

21.90. The identification of the ultimate bearer of the expenses is not always obvious. As the principle of the ultimate bearer of the expense is used in the central framework when attributing consumption expenditure to institutional sectors, one might think that it is a simple matter to apply the same solution here. In fact, the problem is more complicated. First, we have to analyse the financing of capital formation and transfers, not only consumption. Secondly, we have to take into account financing through capital transfers and borrowing. Thirdly, some refinements are needed, even for expenses made out of disposable income. In table 21.4, the following treatments are used:

(a) Market producers finance their intermediate consumption through their sales. Self-financing of capital formation by owners of market unincorporated enterprises not classified as quasi-corporations is considered financing by the owners themselves out of their saving or sale of assets. It is recorded in columns 2, 3 and 4 respectively, whenever relevant;

(b) Non-profit institutions serving households (NPISHs)

Table 21.3.   National expenditure by components and by users/beneficiaries

Components of uses/ national expenditure	Total	Users/beneficiaries				
		1 Market producers	2 Non-market producers	3 Government as collective consumer	4 Households as consumers	5 Rest of the world
1. Consumption of specific goods and services						
1.1. Actual final consumption						
1.1.1 Market products					X	
1.1.2 Non-market products						
1.1.2.1. Individual					X	
1.1.2.2. Collective				X	X	
1.2 Intermediate consumption						
1.2.1. Actual intermediate consumption		X	X			
1.2.2. Internal intermediate consumption		X	X			
2. Capital formation in specific goods and services		X	X			
3. Fixed capital formation of characteristic activities in non-specific products(*)		X	X			
4. Specific current transfers (not counterpart of item 1)		X			X	X
5. Specific capital transfers (not counterpart of items 2 or 3)		X			X	X
Total uses of resident units						
6. Current uses of resident units financed by the rest of the world (less)						
7. Capital uses of resident units financed by the rest of the world (less)						
National expenditure						

* And their acquisition less disposals of non-produced non-financial assets.

Table 21.4.   National expenditure by components and financing units

Components of uses/ national expenditure	Financing units						
	Total	1 Market producers	2 NPISHs	3 General government	4 Households as consumers	5 Financial enterprises	6 Rest of the world
1. Consumption of specific goods and services							
1.1 Actual final consumption							
1.1.1 Market products		X	X	X	X	X	X
1.1.2 Non-market products							
1.1.2.1. Individual			X	X	X		X
1.1.2.2. Collective				X	X		
1.2 Intermediate consumption							
1.2.1. Actual inter-mediate consumption		X	X	X			
1.2.2. Internal inter-mediate consumption		X	X	X			
2. Capital formation in specific goods and services		X	X	X	X	X	X
3. Fixed capital formation of characteristic activities in non-specific products(*)		X	X	X	X	X	X
4. Specific current transfers (not counterpart of item 1)			X	X	X		
5. Specific capital transfers (not counterpart of items 2 or 3)			X	X			
Total uses of resident units							
6. Current uses of resident units financed by the rest of the world (less)							-X
7. Capital uses of resident units financed by the rest of the world (less)							-X
National expenditure							

* And their acquisition less disposals of non-produced non-financial assets.

are treated as ultimate financing units, not the households who pay contributions to them;

(c) In general, general government is treated as the ultimate financing unit, not the units which pay taxes to it. However, in certain cases, when specific taxes or fees treated as taxes are levied by Government in relation with special concerns, such as environmental protection, it is necessary for sake of a better analysis to consider that the units paying these taxes are the ultimate financing units, not Government. Social contributions represent means of financing by households;

(d) Households are considered to be the financing units for all expenses made out of their income, except for transfers in kind received from the rest of the world and non-government/NPISHs sectors. Components in kind of compensation of employees and entrepreneurial income are thus financed by households themselves. Social contributions, as part of compensation of employees, represent means of financing by households. As indicated above (see paragraphs 21.88 and 21.90 (a) above), households are the financing units for all current costs, less any receipts, of their non-market unincorporated enterprises, as well as for the part of the capital formation of their market or non-market unincorporated enterprises that they finance through their saving or sale of assets;

(e) Incurrence of liabilities is treated as a source of financing expenditure. When the counterpart of this incurrence of liabilities is a direct acquisition of assets by institutional units other than financial enterprises, the corresponding financing is recorded in the relevant columns 1 to 4 or 6. Acquisition of financial assets by financial enterprises through their intermediation function is considered financing by these enterprises, not the units that own the deposits, for example;

(f) Transfers in kind received from the rest of the world and possibly non-government/NPISHs sectors are treated as means of financing by the rest of the world (or non-government/NPISHs sectors).

21.91. In the table, actual final consumption of market products, which is always a use of households, may be financed by general government and NPISHs (transfers in kind), possibly the rest of the world and market producers (transfers in kind), financial enterprises (loans), or finally households themselves. Individual consumption of non-market products is financed by general government and NPISHs or households. Collective consumption is exceptionally financed by households (see paragraph 21.94 below).

21.92. The financing of capital formation is complex. First take market producers—a case such as the building of a hotel by an unincorporated enterprise. If the government tries to encourage tourism activities, there may be a capital transfer receivable by

the investor, or there may be capital transfers from the rest of the world. A second part may be financed by a loan made by bank, for example. The residual represents self-financing by the owner of the unincorporated enterprise, through saving or sale of assets. These three components will appear in row and columns 3 (possibly 6), 5 and 4 respectively. The problem is simplest when market producers in a given field correspond very closely to a set of institutional units whose economic activity is essentially a characteristic activity in this field. If big corporations involved in a lot of different activities are concerned, the problem is more difficult. At the limit, loans and self-financing may in some cases have to be grouped together, the total appearing as financed by market producers, either now or in the future, when repaying the loans. Repayments of previous loans raise a general problem. It seems relevant in most cases to consider only net loans (that is, new loans less repayments of loans) linked to the financing of a given field as financing provided by financial enterprises. Consequently self-financing covers present self-finance plus repayments of previous loans.

21.93. When capital formation by government units is involved, the analysis of the financing process may become even more complex, as a government may cover its overall deficit by issuing bonds, for example, which are not intended to finance specific programmes. However, especially in developing countries, loans given by the rest of the world are often specifically directed to identified investment programmes.

21.94. In table 21.4, households appear as financing units under item 4, that is, specific current transfers. This covers social contributions which households pay to government or other sectors out of compensation of employees. A detailed analysis of households as beneficiaries of social benefits and households as financing social protection through social contributions makes it possible to analyse the redistributional effect of social protection schemes. A part of social contributions covers current cost and possibly capital outlays of social protection institutions; it appears on rows 1.1.2.2 and 3. When tax benefits are estimated and included in social protection accounts as item 4, households are at the same time beneficiaries and financing units, as a redistribution process between various types of households is involved.

21.95. In table 21.4, financing units are the ultimate bearers of the expenses. In more detailed analyses, transfers between initial, intermediary (if any) and ultimate financing units have to be shown in order to build up a complete set of accounts for the relevant managing agencies (social protection schemes in the case of social protection accounts).

21.96. The table shows first how uses of resident units are financed. In some cases the rest of the world may be a source of finance (by means of transfers or net lending). This appears in the relevant rows and the column for the rest of the world. In order to get the financing of national expenditure, the corresponding amounts are deducted in rows 6 and 7.

21.97. National expenditure is thus equal to the total outlays of resident financing units in the field under study. This is identical to total uses of resident units financed by resident units. In addition, it may be useful to cross-classify the total uses of resident units by type of users/beneficiaries (table 21.3) and type of financing units (table 21.4).

6. Production and products

21.98. In a satellite account the main emphasis when looking at production is on the analysis of characteristic activities and producers. As explained earlier, characteristic goods and services are typical of the field under study. The activities in which they originate are called characteristic activities, and producers which carry out a characteristic activity are said to be characteristic producers.

21.99. The way production units may be analysed in a satellite account has been dealt with in section B and is not repeated here. In a given field a list of characteristic activities has to be established. This list may include some activities which are also considered characteristic of other fields. Characteristic producers may be defined in various ways. Ideally, they are units of homogeneous production belonging either to establishments whose principal activity is a characteristic activity or to establishments which carry out a characteristic activity only as a secondary activity or to ancillary activities. They may also refer to an extension of the production boundary. For the sake of convenience, establishments whose principal activity is a characteristic activity may be covered totally, including their non-characteristic secondary activities. Market and non-market producers are distinguished.

21.100. Production activity of characteristic producers is studied in detail. This covers the production and generation of income accounts, the analysis of output by kind of products and number of units produced, the destination of this output (consumption, capital formation, exports) and the labour and fixed assets used. As to labour, in addition to compensation of employees, which may be subdivided according to various criteria (such as skill and sex), the number of people employed is shown in detail, again according to various criteria. Fixed capital formation is covered. Stocks of fixed assets in monetary value and/or physical quantities (number of hospital beds, of primary schools, etc.) are essential.

21.101. When relevant, the analysis of supply and use of specific goods and services may be inserted in an input-output framework. In that case, classifications of characteristic producers, characteristic products and connected goods and services are detailed, while classifications of other producers and products are compacted.

21.102. Table 21.5, which is a re-arrangement of the supply and use table of the central framework, tentatively suggests how such a satellite analysis might be inserted in an input-output table. In principle, units of homogeneous production are considered

for the characteristic activities. Characteristic producers and other producers are separated. Among characteristic producers, market producers cover units of homogeneous production belonging to principal producers (establishments whose principal activity is a characteristic activity), secondary producers (establishments whose principal activity is not a characteristic activity) and ancillary activities (whose output and input must be externalized) separately. The same distinction is made for non-market producers; in addition, a column "Others" under non-market producers refers to a possible extension of the production boundary. Other producers, from which secondary and ancillary activities characteristic of the field under study have been excluded, are grouped altogether (unless it is useful to show the main providers of intermediate inputs or fixed capital to characteristic producers, or suppliers of certain connected goods and services, separately).

21.103. As indicated above, for convenience, the establishments whose principal activity is a characteristic activity may be included in their totality. In this case the column for principal producers would include establishments. The column for secondary producers, and of course ancillary activities, should continue to refer to units of homogeneous production in order to limit the degree of heterogeneity of the group of characteristic producers. When secondary and/or ancillary output of characteristic products is not significant in size, it could be treated as secondary output of other producers.

21.104. The supply of characteristic and connected products appears in the rows. The sources are imports and domestic output. The output corresponding to intra-establishment deliveries must be included. If some secondary producers are not included in the relevant column for characteristic producers, their output is shown in the column for other producers, where the output of connected goods and services also appears. Other products are grouped altogether (unless, again, it is useful to show some detail).

21.105. In the lower part of the table, the use part of the production account and the generation of income account of producers is shown. At the bottom, three rows show gross fixed capital formation, stocks of fixed assets and labour inputs. In certain satellite accounts, a row for acquisitions less disposals of valuables may also have to be shown (see paragraph 21.69 above). Final uses are depicted in the relevant columns without any modification of presentation. Alternatively, the columns can be re-arranged and actual final consumption presented first.

7. Full accounts for characteristic producers

21.106. When analysing a given field in a satellite account, it is generally worthwhile to establish complete accounts for characteristic producers. However, complete accounts may be established only for institutional units. This seeming impasse can be surmounted because in a given field many units of ho-

Table 21.5.   Satellite input-output table (supply and use table)

Resources	Total supply, purchasers' prices	Trade and transport margins	Taxes on products	Subsidies on products (–)	Characteristic producers												Other producers	Total economy	Imports of goods and services
					Total	Market producers			Non-market producers									
						Principal producers	Secondary producers	Ancillary activities	Principal producers	Secondary producers	Ancillary activities	Others							
					Output														
Goods and services supply:																			
Characteristic products																			
1.																			
2.																			
...																			
m.																			
Connected products																			
1.																			
2.																			
...																			
n.																			
Other products																			
Total																			

Table 21.3.   Satellite input-output table (supply and use table) [cont.]

Uses	Total uses in purchasers' prices	Characteristic producers — Total	Market producers — Principal producers	Market producers — Secondary producers	Market producers — Ancillary activities	Non-market producers — Principal Government	Non-market producers — Secondary producers	Non-market producers — Ancillary activities	Others	Other producers	Total economy	Exports of goods and services	Households	NPISHs individual	Government collective	Government individual	Gross fixed capital formation	Changes in inventories	Acquisit. less disposals of valuables
Goods and services uses:					Intermediate consumption														
Characteristic products																			
1.																			
2.																			
...																			
m.																			
Connected products																			
1.																			
2.																			
...																			
n.																			
Other products																			
Total																			
Total gross value added/GDP																			
Compensation of employees																			
Taxes on products																			
Other taxes on production																			
Subsidies on products (−)																			
Other subsidies on production (−)																			
Operating surplus, net																			
Mixed income, net																			
Consumption of fixed capital																			
Specific products																			
Non-specific products																			
Operating surplus, gross																			
Mixed income, gross																			
Total																			
Labour inputs																			
Gross fixed capital formation																			
Specific products																			
Non-specific products																			
Stock of fixed assets, net																			

505

mogeneous production or establishments belong to institutional units whose principal productive activity is a characteristic activity in the same field. In order to extend the analysis, all these institutional units may be regrouped in a sector of characteristic producers. Their accounts may be shown using a simplified presentation, as shown in the example below (balance sheets may or may not be included):

Production and generation of income account

Intermediate consumption	Output
—of characteristic activities	—characteristic output
—of other activities	—other output
Compensation of employees	
—of characteristic activities	
—of other activities	
Taxes on production and imports	
Subsidies (–)	
Consumption of fixed capital	
Operating surplus, net	
—of characteristic activities	
—of other activities	
Mixed income, net	
—of characteristic activities	
—of other activities	

Other current accounts

Property income	Operating surplus
	Mixed income
Current taxes on income wealth, etc.	Property income
Social contributions and benefits	Social contributions and benefits
	Other current transfers
Other current transfers	
Adjustment for the change in net equity of households in pension funds	
Collective consumption	
Saving, net	

Accumulation accounts

Gross fixed capital formation	Saving, net
—of characteristic activities	Capital transfers receivable
—of other activities	Capital transfers payable (–)
Consumption of fixed capital (–)	
Changes in inventories	
Acquisition less disposals of valuables	
Acquisition less disposals of non-produced non-financial assets	

Net acquisition of financial assets	Net incurrence of liabilities
	—for financing characteristic activities
	—others
Other accumulation entries	Other accumulation entries
	Other changes in net worth

21.107. As satellite accounts are functionally oriented, the sector of characteristic producers may also cover units which are characteristic producers in the field under study but belong to institutional units whose principal activity is not in this field. To balance the accounts, the operating surplus or mixed income, if any, of these producing units is transferred as property income to their parent institutional units. In the accumulation accounts, the capital formation of these producing units is balanced by an equivalent capital transfer coming from their parent institutional units.

21.108. In fields such as social protection where distributing transfers is the main economic function involved, the production of services playing only a marginal role, the analysis of units managing the distribution and redistribution processes predominates. It is then simpler to group together all current accounts, the production part of them being simplified by showing administrative costs directly as uses and secondary sales, if any, as resources. If social protection institutions act as producers of health or welfare services and if a satellite account covers both production and redistribution functions, the above presentation of accounts remains relevant. In both cases, the analysis of transfers and their financing is given great importance.

21.109. Transfers are analysed according to their nature (in cash, in kind, subdivided in various ways) and the type of risks (sickness, unemployment, etc.). A detailed classification of social protection schemes is also used (basic, complementary or supplementary schemes, subdivided between national, general, special or voluntary schemes for instance).

8. Non-monetary data

21.110. A satellite account allows for the linkage of physical data to the monetary accounting system. In the central framework this kind of link remains generally implicit, being done only for population and labour inputs where these figures are necessary for calculating a number of per-person indicators such as income or consumption and indicators of productivity. Such physical data have been mentioned when going through the functionally oriented satellite account framework. It is worth recalling this kind of link here.

21.111. As output is studied in much more detail than in the central framework, even when it includes a detailed supply and use/input-output table, it is generally possible to show meaningful data on the number of units produced or used: physician consultations by kind of physician, hotel-nights of various types, student years in various levels of education, etc. The labour force may be presented in detail: number of people employed in various categories, according to skill and sex, number of hours worked or equivalent person years, number of people in training, etc. Data on existing assets in physical terms are especially interesting in such fields as education, culture, health or housing. In conjunction with labour force data, they constitute well-known social indicators such as number of teachers, of hospital beds or of physicians per ten thousand inhabitants.

21.112. Another important dimension of non-monetary data refers to users/beneficiaries of the goods and services and recipients of the transfers in question. Those data are especially meaningful in the fields of social concern such as education, health and social protection. They require information that is generally less developed than the ones on labour force and assets mentioned above. However, they are indispensable to assess the standard of living of various parts of the population and to look in depth at redistribution policy.

21.113. Physical data are not to be considered a secondary part of a satellite account. They are essential components, both for the information they provide directly and in order to make the monetary data fully meaningful.

9. Links with the central framework.

21.114. The tentative framework presented in this section departs little from the central framework standards. This resemblance might be more apparent than real if the amounts related to the various items are different from the ones attached to the same flows in the central framework—for example, where a satellite account is established independently from the central accounts themselves. Normally the assumption is that the same items are represented by the same figures in the central framework and in a functionally oriented satellite account.

21.115. Many elements shown in a satellite account are invisible in the central accounts. Either they are explicitly estimated in the making of the central accounts, but they are merged for presentation in more aggregated figures, or they are only implicit components of transactions which are estimated globally. For each of the fields mentioned in paragraph 21.51 above, only a small number of figures appear in the central accounts, even when the latter are very detailed. Consequently the first role of a functionally oriented satellite account is to make explicit the implicit figures of the central framework.

21.116. However, even in a satellite accounting framework as close to the central framework as the one presented above, some degrees of freedom are introduced. In a number of cases, classifications of economic activities, products and purposes have to be adapted to the field under study. This is mostly a problem of presentation. As the coverage of a given field sometimes ex-

tends beyond the corresponding aggregated positions in the central classifications (e.g, education and health, health and R and D) or is widely diffused (e.g, tourism or environmental protection), some re-arrangement of the positions of the central classifications has to be made when elaborating classifications for a given field. As a rule, all the links with the central classifications must remain visible. As explained earlier, the proposed classifications of users/beneficiaries and financing units follow this rule.

21.117. Other degrees of freedom are used in this framework. For instance, the output and input of the relevant ancillary activities are externalized, which is a difference with the central framework. This element is always apparent in the list of components of uses (see item 1.2.2 internal intermediate consumption) and in the satellite supply and use table, table 21.5. The concept of national expenditure is broader—it may include intermediate consumption and transfers—and narrower—financing by the rest of the world is excluded—than in the central framework.

21.118. In addition, the framework introduces a number of elements which are not in the central framework as such, but do not conflict with it. Above all, this refers to the introduction of the concepts of characteristic goods and services and connected goods and services, the total of which constitute the specific goods and services. The concept of characteristic producers is also introduced. Also gross fixed capital formation and consumption of fixed capital make the distinction between specific and non-specific products. Finally, physical data are introduced.

21.119. A satellite account may use elements which have no equivalent in the central framework. Such elements have not been shown when presenting the satellite accounting framework, because they vary according to specific requirements of the fields. Examples of such elements are classifications of diseases (for consumption of health services and connected products) and of scientific disciplines (for R and D expenditures).

21.120. The kind of satellite accounts studied in this section may also have recourse to alternative concepts, as was touched upon. The boundary of production could be changed in order to include housework and voluntary work (see the column "Others" in the supply and use table), which would affect, for example, education, health and social protection. All or part of R and D expenditures may be treated as gross fixed capital formation instead of current outlays. The satellite accounting framework presented in this section as a general orientation does not prevent the extension of some satellite accounts in the directions mentioned in this paragraph. On the contrary, these additional dimensions represent valuable enrichments of the analytical power of the national accounting approach.

10. Perspective on the framework

21.121. The framework presented in this section may cover an important number of fields, as already seen from the illustrative list in paragraph 21.51 above. This framework for functional analyses may not fit all topics which one might like to study in connection with central national accounting. However, the general approach may give valuable inputs for other types of accounts. Specific parts of the functionally oriented satellite framework may also be relevant in other cases, even in the context of the central framework itself, such as the satellite supply and use table which is used, with terminological adjustments, for key activities and products.

D. Satellite system for integrated environmental and economic accounting

1. The scope of environmental accounting

21.122. In the previous section, environmental analysis was dealt with as one of several topics that could be pursued as a functionally oriented satellite account. In this section, environmental analysis is dealt with in the context of a broadened framework that amends several concepts of the SNA to respond to the growing concerns of incorporating environmental criteria in economic analysis.

21.123. This section deals with the general orientation, design, concepts and classifications of integrated economic and environmental satellite accounts. In these accounts, SNA aggregates are amended to treat natural resources as capital in the production of goods and services, to record the cost of using—i.e., depleting and degrading—those resources and to record the implicit transfers needed to account for the imputed cost and capital items. The explanations are based to a large extent on the system of environmental economic accounts (SEEA) that is presented in the handbook *Integrated Environmental and Economic Accounting*[1]. The presentation below should be considered as a description of the present state of the art of integrated economic and environmental accounting, which may evolve over time as a result of continuing discussions.

21.124. The section is included to guide countries in responding effectively to the current emphases in policy-making and analysis on environmentally sound and sustainable economic growth and development and to help national accountants in elaborating environmental satellite studies which take the national accounts as a point of departure. The section shows how amended accounts could deal in a compatible manner with economic and environmental concerns and thus make operational the concepts of sustainable growth and development. The satellite studies should respond effectively to the two major drawbacks of conventional national accounting that are often mentioned: the neglect of new scarcities of natural resources which threaten the sustained productivity of the economy and the degradation of environmental quality and consequential effects on human health and welfare.

21.125. Insofar as consensus has been reached, relevant parts of the central framework of the SNA take into account aspects of environmental accounting. In particular, many cost and capital items of accounting for natural resources are identified separately in the classifications and accounts dealing with stocks and other volume changes of assets. These features of the SNA facilitate the use of the System as a point of departure for environmental accounting. However, several elements of the SNA, particularly those in the account for other volume changes, need to be broken down further and reclassified, and other elements have to be added for the specific purposes of environmental accounting.

21.126. In the SNA, only produced assets, including inventories, are explicitly taken into account in the calculation of net value added. The cost of their use is reflected in intermediate consumption and consumption of fixed capital. Non-produced natural assets—such as land, mineral resources and forests—are included in the SNA asset boundary insofar as they are under the effective control of institutional units. However, the cost of their use is not explicitly accounted for in production cost. This may either imply that the price of the products does not reflect such cost or, if it does—as may be the case for some depletion cost—such cost is not separately identified but lumped together with other unidentified elements in the residual derivation of operating surplus.

2. Alternative approaches to environmental accounting

21.127. Most systems of environmental accounting now under discussion broaden SNA concepts of cost, capital formation and the stock of capital by supplementing these with additional data in physical terms in order to encompass environmental cost and the use of natural assets in production, or by amending them through the incorporation of these effects in monetary terms. However, within this general orientation, the several existing approaches differ considerably in terms of methodology and environmental concerns addressed. The SEEA synthesizes as far as possible the various approaches and integrates them into one comprehensive approach.

21.128. There are now three main approaches to environmental accounting, and they complement and overlap each other. The first one, generally referred to as natural resource accounting, focuses on accounts in physical terms. The second approach, which is linked to national accounts and is in monetary terms, is generally called monetary satellite accounting. It identifies the actual expenditures on environmental protection and deals with the treatment of environmental cost to natural and other assets caused by production activities in the calculation of net product. Monetary satellite accounting is generally more limited in coverage of environmental concerns than physical resource accounting. The third approach is a welfare-oriented one. It deals with the environmental effects borne by individuals and by producers other than the producers causing these effects. The latter effects may often be much larger than the cost caused and do not affect net product but rather net income through transfers of environmental services.

21.129. Of the three approaches, physical resource accounting is the most advanced in terms of practical implementation. Experience with monetary satellite accounting is much more recent, and many controversies still surround this approach, particularly with regard to valuation. The least consensus exists with regard to the welfare approach to environmental accounting.

Natural resource accounting in physical terms

21.130. Natural resource accounting focuses on physical asset balances—i.e., opening and closing stocks and changes therein—of materials, energy and natural resources. Where applicable (for selected pollutants), it may also include changes in environmental quality of natural assets in terms of environmental (quality) indices. Several examples, developed by individual countries or sponsored by international organizations, now exist. Also, the multipurpose *Framework for the Development of Environment Statistics*, developed by the United Nations, includes the environment statistics elements from which the physical asset balances can be constructed, although it does not include the balances themselves. The SEEA, which shows the links between physical and monetary accounts, includes natural resource accounts as a module.

Environmental accounts in monetary terms

21.131. Monetary environmental accounts in a restricted sense only separately identify within the national accounts the actual expenditures on environmental protection. In some instances, these expenditures are externalized by treating ancillary environmental protection activities as separate establishments. Monetary environmental accounts in this restricted sense would also include the functional approach to environmental accounting dealt with in the previous section.

21.132. A broader interpretation of monetary environmental accounting may include the sort of environmental adjustments developed in projects carried out in several resource-oriented developing countries. In these studies, GDP is adjusted for selected environmental costs, including the cost of oil depletion, deforestation, depletion of fishstock and the cost of soil erosion. While these studies are based on detailed analyses in physical terms, distinguishing between a variety of species of timber, fish, and different types of soil based on geographical location and agricultural use, the ultimate focus is on the adjustment of GDP. The studies do not deal with an explicit allocation of the environmental adjustments between activity and expenditure components of GDP.

21.133. A comprehensive approach to adjusting national accounts aggregates is followed in case studies based on the system of environmental economic accounts, which were carried out in two developing countries, and in another approach, using a SAM, prepared for a developed country. The comprehensive accounting approaches take the SNA as a point of departure and thus stay very close to the analytical orientation of economic analysis. At the same time, they emphasize the importance of recording physical flows and stocks in support of the monetary environmental economic analysis. The SEEA does not distinguish between depletion and degradation, but rather between quantitative and qualitative use of natural assets. In the first case reference is made to the use of environmental goods and in the second case to the use of environmental services. In order to be as close as possible to the concepts and terminology used in the SNA, it has been assumed in this section that depletion approximately coincides with the quantitative use and degradation with the qualitative use of natural assets. Even though the distinction between depletion and degradation is made, it should be understood that economic activities may result in depletion and degradation at the same time.

21.134. The comprehensive accounting approaches allocate the environmental impacts of depletion and degradation to the separate economic activities causing these environmental impacts and to expenditure components reflecting the immediate effects corresponding to quantitative and qualitative changes in natural assets. The SEEA and the case studies mainly consider the effects on production analysis, identifying the environmental cost of depletion and degradation caused by different economic activities and showing the corresponding effects on natural and other assets. The SEEA furthermore introduces an enlarged concept of capital accumulation, which not only allows incorporation of depletion and degradation effects but also the transfer of natural resources to economic uses. The environmental SAM-based study mentioned earlier, in addition, considers the effects of present and past degradation borne in a concept of environmentally adjusted national income.

Welfare and similar approaches

21.135. One welfare approach, instead of dealing with the cost caused by production activities and their effects on capital used in production, focuses on the environmental impacts of cost borne or, in a broader sense, on well-being. The approach considers the free environmental services provided by nature to producers and consumers and the subsequent damage borne by them. The environmental services provided free and the damage borne are implicitly considered as transfers by and to nature, which increase or decrease environmentally adjusted net national income.

21.136. Another approach is based on the concept of environmental sustainability standards and on estimating the necessary avoidance or restoration costs to meet these standards. The approach does not deal with the immediate environmental impacts of production during the present accounting period, but rather with those impacts incurred over an unspecified length of time. The approach suggests that the cost should be charged to those industries that are able to absorb such cost given the price of their products; these are not necessarily the industries which caused the degradation in the first place.

3. General framework of environmental accounts and the SNA

21.137. Table 21.6 shows SNA concepts together with the alternative concepts used in environmental accounts. For purposes of explanation, a generalized and simplified version of the SEEA is used to present environmental accounts. The use of the SEEA framework to present environmental accounting and the relationship to the SNA is convenient as the SEEA was developed in immediate relationship to the SNA so that its concepts and classifications are more closely linked to those of the SNA than is the case for any other environmental accounting system. Nevertheless, format, concepts and classifications of the SEEA should be considered as work-in-progress, as many of its elements continue to be discussed among national and environmental accountants.

21.138 As will be shown in the description of the SEEA framework below, environmental cost and capital elements included can be interpreted in physical terms as well as in monetary terms. However, in view of the controversial issues surrounding valuation of environmental cost and capital, much caution should be exercised in the use of these elements in monetary terms and in the corresponding derivation of environmentally adjusted aggregates. This does not reduce the usefulness of environmental accounting, however, as the approaches to environmental accounting described above have shown that analysis in physical terms is as useful as environmental accounting in monetary terms, as long as the analysis is carried out in the context of a well-defined framework of satellite accounts.

SNA framework

21.139. The flow and stock items of the SNA are shown in the shaded area of table 21.6. The columns of the table related to flows are a column (1) for production, covering output (P), intermediate consumption (Ci), consumption of fixed capital (CFC) and net domestic product (NDP); a column (2) for the rest of the world, which includes exports (X) minus imports (M) and a column (3) for final consumption (C). The rows of the table referring to the SNA flows are a row (ii) for supply, including output and imports; a row (iii) for economic uses, including elements for intermediate consumption, exports, final consumption and gross capital formation (Ig); a row (iv) for CFC and, finally, a row (v) for NDP, which presents the elements that define the national accounts identity between NDP and the expenditure categories. The SNA column (4) for asset bal-

ances of produced assets includes the opening and closing stocks of produced assets ($Ko_{p.ec}$ & $K1_{p.ec}$) and the elements explaining the change between the two, i.e., net capital formation ($I= Ig - CFC$), holding gains/losses on produced assets ($Rev_{p.ec}$) and other changes in volume of produced assets ($Vol_{p.ec}$).

21.140. The asset balances in the SNA area cover all economic assets, and therefore include the assets covered by column (5) for non-produced natural assets. The elements of this column, however, do not figure in the calculation of NDP as all changes in non-produced natural assets between opening and closing stocks ($Ko_{np.ec}$ & $K1_{np.ec}$) are "explained" in the SNA as holding gains/losses ($Rev_{np.ec}$) and as other changes in volume of assets ($Vol_{np.ec}$).

The SNA framework extended to environmental accounts

21.141. The non-shaded areas of table 21.6 include the additional elements that are needed to supplement the SNA concepts with data in physical terms on environmental cost and capital, or amend the SNA concepts by valuing the physical data and incorporating the values in environmentally adjusted concepts of cost and capital. There are two types of additional elements. The first group is included in an additional column (6) which records the effects of economic activities on non-produced natural assets such as air, water and virgin forests that are not included as economic assets in the SNA. The second group of elements is included in two additional rows (vi-vii) that include elements for the use of non-produced natural assets by depletion and degradation, and for other accumulation of non-produced natural assets, which covers the transfer of natural assets to and between economic uses. The SEEA elements in the additional column (6) and rows (vi) and (vii) can be interpreted in physical as well as monetary terms. Another row (viii) is included to derive an environmentally adjusted net domestic product (EDP) and other environmentally adjusted concepts. This row is only relevant in the case of monetary environmental accounting when additional SEEA elements are specified in value terms.

21.142. In row (vi) related to the use of non-produced natural assets, an additional element (Use_{np}) has been included in the column for production. This reflects the use of non-produced natural assets in production; it is the sum of the counterpart items in columns (5) and (6) representing, respectively, the use of non-produced natural assets that are economic assets in the SNA sense ($-Use_{np.ec}$) and the degradation of other natural assets that are not economic assets ($-Use_{np.env}$). The use of non-produced economic assets ($-Use_{np.ec}$) includes the depletion of minerals, the extraction of timber from forests that are economic assets and the effects on productivity of those forests and agricultural land of soil erosion, acid rain, etc. The deteriorating effects of air pollution on buildings and structures and the effects of soil erosion on roads and other degrading effects on produced assets are not included as they are assumed to be

Table 21.6.   Basic structure of the SEEA

	Economic activities					Environment
				Economic assets		
	Production 1	Rest of world 2	Final consumption 3	Produced assets 4	Non-produced natural assets 5	Other non-produced natural assets 6
Opening stock of assets i				$K0_{p.ec}$	$K0_{np.ec}$	
Supply ii	P	M				
Economic uses iii	Ci	X	C	Ig		
Consumption of fixed capital iv	CFC			$-CFC$		
Net domestic product v	NDP	X-M	C	I		
Use of non-produced natural assets vi	Use_{np}				$-Use_{np.ec}$	$-Use_{np.env}$
Other accumulation of non-produced natural assets vii					$I_{np.ec}$	$-I_{np.env}$
Environmentally adjusted aggregates in monetary environmental accounting viii	EDP	X-M	C	$A_{p.ec}$	$A_{np.ec}$	$-A_{np.env}$
Holding gains/losses ix				$Rev_{p.ec}$	$Rev_{np.ec}$	
Other changes in volume of assets x				$Vol_{p.ec}$	$Vol_{np.ec}$	
Closing stock of assets xi				$K1_{p.ec}$	$K1_{np.ec}$	

reflected in CFC. The use of natural assets that are not economic assets ($-Use_{np.env}$) covers the non-sustainable extraction of fishstock from oceans and rivers, extraction of firewood and lumber from tropical and other virgin forests or hunting of animals living in the wild and also the effects of emission of residuals on the quality of air, water, fishstocks, wild forests, and the effects of other economic activities (recreation, agriculture, transport, etc.) on eco-systems and species habitat.

21.143. Other accumulation in row (vii) records in physical or monetary terms the transfer of natural assets to economic uses as a change in the stock of non-produced economic assets ($I_{np.ec}$). The counterpart of this increase in economic assets is the reduction of natural assets other than economic assets ($-I_{np.env}$). $I_{np.ec}$ would include the transfer of land to economic uses, the net additions to proven mineral reserves, the conversion of wild forests to timber tracts or agricultural land, and the conversion of fishstocks to economic control. If deterioration takes place at the same time that natural assets are incorporated as economic assets, the deterioration is not recorded in the other accumulation row, but is included as part of uses of natural resources. If this deterioration takes place before the transfer, it is recorded as the use of an asset in the environment ($-Use_{np.env}$), and if deterioration takes place after, it is recorded as uses of natural resources that are economic assets ($-Use_{np.ec}$).

21.144 As the elements of row (vi) for use (i.e., depletion or degradation) of non-produced natural assets, and row (vii) for other accumulation are included in the SNA in other volume changes, the content of other volume changes is reduced in the SEEA as compared with the SNA.

21.145. If the additional SEEA elements are valued in monetary terms, the incorporation of the use of non-produced natural assets (Use_{np}) as additional cost in the column for production results in an EDP, presented in row (viii), which is lower than NDP. The elements in row (vii) for other accumulation do not affect EDP. If the additional SEEA elements are expressed in physical terms, row (viii) is not relevant; in that case the additional information in rows (vi) and (vii) is only used to supplement NDP with information on environmental cost caused by economic activities.

21.146. Corresponding to the monetary valuation of the additional SEEA elements, on the expenditure side a new concept called net accumulation is introduced in the SEEA to replace net capital formation in the SNA. It is presented in row (viii), separately for produced assets ($A_{p.ec}$), non-produced economic assets ($A_{np.ec}$) and other natural assets ($-A_{np.env}$). For produced assets, it is the same as net capital formation (i.e., $A_{p.ec} = I$). For non-produced economic assets, it reflects the net effects of negative depletion and degradation and positive additions of natural assets that are transferred to economic uses (i.e., $A_{np.ec} = -Use_{np.ec} + I_{np.ec}$). For natural assets other than economic assets, it could be considered as the economic val-

uation of the impact of economic activities on the environment and it is the sum of negative depletion and degradation effects ($-Use_{np.env}$) and negative effects of incorporating natural assets as economic assets (i.e., $-A_{np.env} = -Use_{np.env} - I_{np.env}$). If no monetary valuation is used, the additional elements (i.e., $-Use_{np.ec}$, $I_{np.ec}$, $-Use_{np.env}$ and $I_{np.env}$) would supplement the SNA information on investments in produced assets (I) with information in physical terms on changes in natural non-produced assets that together with investments (I) support the generation of economic activities.

21.147. If net accumulation replaces net capital formation when the additional SEEA elements are valued in monetary terms, the national accounts identity between NDP and final expenditures changes. In the SNA this identity, as reflected in row (v) of table 21.6, is:

$$NDP = C + I + (X - M).$$

If net capital accumulation in economic assets ($A_{p.ec} + A_{np.ec}$) replaces net capital formation (I), the identity as reflected in row (viii) becomes:

$$EDP = C + (A_{p.ec} + A_{np.ec}) - A_{np.env} + (X - M).$$

In order to maintain the identity, the negative element for the economic counterpart of changes in natural assets other than economic assets ($-A_{np.env}$) is added. This implies that expenditures and, in particular, net capital accumulation of economic assets are only partly derived from net product of economic activities reflected in EDP; an important part of the expenditures may reflect the transfer of environmental assets and/or their services to economic activities. This can be shown more clearly by re-arranging the terms in the above EDP identity as follows:

$$EDP + A_{np.env} = C + (A_{p.ec} + A_{np.ec}) + (X - M).$$

4. Details on environmental amendments to SNA framework, concepts and classifications

21.148. In the overview of the environmental accounting frameworks above and in the presentation of table 21.6, several new concepts were introduced. This section specifies these concepts more precisely, explains why they were introduced and presents alternatives used in the SEEA and other environmental accounting approaches. Where necessary, reference is made to the rows and columns of table 21.6.

Alternative frameworks for environmental accounts

21.149. Alternative accounting approaches described earlier are reflected in different versions of the SEEA. For instance, resource accounting focuses mainly on recording information reflected in the asset balances of non-produced natural assets included in columns (5) and (6) of table 21.6, without explicitly entering into the counterpart cost calculations included in column (1). One of the approaches to monetary accounting mentioned above, on the other hand, focuses on the calculation of EDP as recorded in column (1), mainly taking into account depletion concerns. All other approaches cover the same ground as the SEEA, though their formats may differ. The SAM-based study used a matrix presentation of the SEEA framework of supply and use and asset balances of table 21.6. The welfare approaches fall outside the framework, as they deal with environmentally adjusted national income, which reflects transfers in kind of free environmental services received and damage incurred (transfers paid).

Asset boundary and classification

21.150. The most important amendment introduced into environmental accounting as compared with the SNA is the extension of the asset boundary. In the SNA, natural assets are included only if they provide economic benefits to the owner, a characteristic that manifests itself through being controlled by an institutional unit. This often means explicit ownership, subject to government legislation in the case of natural forests, and/or availability of a market price. These assets are referred to in the SNA as economic assets. In the SEEA, the asset boundary is defined to be much wider. It includes in principle all natural assets; some may directly participate in production activities while others may be affected by environmental impacts of economic activities. (The SEEA does not include human capital.) The SNA asset boundary only includes economic assets as dealt with in columns (4) and (5) of table 21.6. The SEEA asset boundary comprises all natural assets including those that are economic assets and are covered in columns (4) and (5) and other natural assets that are represented by column (6) of the table. The SEEA, however, does not distinguish between natural assets that are economic assets and those that are not, focusing on environmental impacts irrespective of particular institutional arrangements of ownership and control.

21.151. The main headings of the classification of natural assets in the SNA and the SEEA are presented in table 21.7, where they are related to each other. The two classifications are compatible, as they were developed in close coordination with each other. However, as the SNA includes a lesser number of natural assets, their detail and structure differ. Nevertheless, the SNA classification of natural assets can be used as a point of departure to arrive at the extended coverage and classification of natural assets in the SEEA.

21.152. Table 21.7 shows that some asset categories in the SNA and the SEEA are identical, some others are closely related but have a different coverage and still others are not included in the SNA but are included in the SEEA. The asset categories that have identical coverage are cultivated assets such as orchards and plantations, which are treated as fixed assets, and work-in-progress on cultivated assets including agricultural crops and livestock, which are treated as inventories in both systems. Also, the subsoil assets category is identical in both classifications. The coverage is based on the definition of

proven reserves: "the estimated quantities at a specific date, which analysis of geological engineering data demonstrate, with reasonable certainty, to be recoverable in the future from known reservoirs under the economic and operational conditions at the same date". The coverage of subsoil assets implied by this definition is the same as that implied by the definition of economic assets in the SNA. On the other extreme, air is included in the SEEA because it is affected by economic activities, but it is not included at all in the SNA as it does not satisfy the SNA criteria of economic assets.

21.153. All other categories of non-produced natural assets, which are similar in the two systems but have different coverage fall between these two extremes. Land in the SNA includes associated water surfaces such as lakes and rivers, which are generally associated with recreational land, and in some instances also groundwater. As the SEEA deals with the effects of economic activities on the quality of water in rivers and lakes and on the quantity and quality of available groundwater, it excludes these categories from land and includes them as subcategories under the category of water. Consequently, the category of water in the SEEA is much broader than the SNA category AN.214 Water resources; the SEEA category includes (not shown in the table) sub-categories for groundwater, water of lakes, rivers, etc., coastal water, and ocean water. The SNA category is mainly restricted to aquifers that are controlled by human activities. On the other hand, in the SEEA land includes the eco-systems, which are not explicitly included as economic assets in SNA analysis, but which are aspects of land that are very important for environmental analysis as they deal with such effects as soil erosion and the effects of acid rain on the quality of forests and land in general. The coverage of non-cultivated biological resources in the SNA and wild biota in the SEEA is also different. Non-cultivated biological resources in the SNA would generally include forests, fishstocks and animal herds in the wild that are controlled by human activities. In the SEEA wild biota would, in principle, include all forests (including virgin forests), all fishstocks and all animal herds whether they are controlled by human activities or not, as all can be affected by human activities.

21.154. The classification of natural assets such as that in the SEEA, which is presented in table 21.7, is needed in environmental accounting in order to fully cover depletion, degradation, and other accumulation i.e., transfer of natural assets to economic activities. It is applicable whether physical units or monetary values are used in the elaboration of environmental accounts. A more restricted coverage may be selected if the analysis is limited to environmental impacts that only affect specific natural assets. For instance, some studies have dealt only with oil exploitation, deforestation, depletion of fishstocks and land erosion. On the other hand, the case studies based on the SEEA mentioned earlier dealt with a wider range of natural assets and the environmental impacts on them, including groundwater depletion and air and water pollution. Of course, more se-

Table 21.7. Classification of natural assets in the SNA and the SEEA

	SNA	SEEA
AN.1	Produced assets	
AN.11	*Fixed assets*	
AN.1114	Cultivated assets	
AN.12	*Inventories*	
AN.1221	Work-in-progress on cultivated assets	
AN.2	Non-produced assets	
AN.21	*Tangible non-produced assets*	*Tangible non-produced assets*
AN.211	Land, including associated surface water	Land, including ecosystems
AN.212	Subsoil assets	Subsoil assets
AN.213	Non-cultivated biological resources	Wild biota
AN.214	Water resources	Water
		Air

lective environmental accounting could focus on only those natural assets that are economic assets; in that case the natural asset boundary would be the same as that of the SNA. One version of the SEEA in monetary values, which applies a market valuation approach deals explicitly with this case.

Environmental cost

21.155. The SEEA identifies two types of environmental cost. The first is the imputed cost for degradation and depletion. The second is the actual cost incurred in the form of environmental protection expenses. The content and classification of both types are dealt with below.

Use of non-produced natural assets

21.156. The use of non-produced natural assets is introduced as an additional cost in the SEEA when extending the SNA to environmental accounting. The additional cost elements are shown as the use of natural resources in row (vi) in table 21.6. They represent depletion and degradation in physical terms—e.g. quantity of minerals extracted, quantity of timber cut, volume of solid, liquid or gaseous wastes generated—or alternatively, monetary allowances for depletion and degradation.

21.157. Before discussing the treatment of depletion and degradation, the reader should be reminded in this context that there is less consensus with regard to monetary approaches to environmental accounting than environmental accounting in physical terms, in view of difficulties of valuation. Within the monetary approaches, there is more consensus with regard to amendment of SNA concepts for depletion than degradation. The main reason for the latter is that depletion allowances already

have found their way into commercial accounting practices and are thus implicitly reflected in the market prices of depleted assets. Commercial accounting practices generally have not been developed for externalities and consequently there is less consensus on this further amendment of the SNA in monetary environmental accounting. Equally in monetary environmental accounting, there is also less consensus with regard to the coverage of the concept of capital accumulation to replace the capital formation concept in environmentally sustainable growth analysis.

21.158. Depletion and degradation of economic assets are recorded in the SNA in monetary terms in the items of other accumulation entries presented in the top panel of table 21.8. They refer to parts (which are separate building blocks in the SEEA) of SNA items K.3 Economic appearance of non-produced assets and K.62 Other economic disappearance of non-produced assets, and with regard to depletion, to the entire SNA item K.61 Depletion of natural assets. The extent to which these uses of natural economic assets—in particular, the degradation and quality effects included in items K.3 and K.62—are recorded in the SNA, depends on whether market prices of the assets identify these uses and whether they can be separated from other price changes in the assets. Uses of natural assets that are not economic assets are not recorded in the SNA. If the depletion and degradation elements included in row (vi) of table 21.6 are in physical terms, the values included in the SNA elements of other volume changes mentioned, should be eliminated in environmental accounting and replaced in row (vi) by the physical units in which depletion and degradation are expressed.

21.159. The depletion of natural assets included in row (vi) of table 21.6 covers mainly depletion of economic assets. The reason is that when an asset is being depleted to a major extent it would most probably satisfy either one or more of the SNA criteria concerning the asset boundary mentioned above—i.e., market prices would most probably develop, ownership would be enforced and consequently the asset might be considered as being controlled by human activities.

21.160. Depletion, however, is not restricted to economic assets only. It may also include depletion of uncontrolled forests in some countries for the purpose of firewood collection; the firewood is often not sold nor ownership of the forests enforced. The same may apply to uncontrolled depletion of fishstocks. Also, lumber extraction associated with uncontrolled land clearance to acquire land for agriculture or urban settlements would lead to depletion of non-produced assets that are not economic assets at the time the land clearance takes place. In all these instances the assets may not be considered as economic assets in the SNA sense as the exploitation of the assets is uncontrolled; even though exploitation may be on a large scale, those assets still would be dealt with as other natural assets. In those instances a depletion allowance is calculated in the SEEA, except if the depletion in the case of wild biota is within the bounds of natural growth and the depleted assets would be naturally replaced.

21.161. If expressed in monetary terms, the depletion allowances could be considered as payments for the extraction of non-produced assets (such as minerals) which are in stock either as economic assets or as natural assets outside the economic asset boundary. Depletion of non-produced natural assets is, therefore, considered in the SEEA as cost and at the same time treated as negative changes in inventories. Alternatively, it may be treated neither as cost nor output. The latter treatment is thought to be more appropriate by some as this treatment would result in an output value for extraction industries which would only include value of the extraction activity without including the value of the mineral being extracted.

21.162. If monetary valuations are applied to stock changes in economic assets, such as mineral reserves and timber tracts which are under human control, the SNA rules on changes in inventories apply. Any change in the value of minerals extracted during the accounting period is reflected in changes in inventories of non-produced assets, in the same way as holding gains and losses of produced goods. On the other hand, if the stock changes are in natural assets other than economic assets, such as fishstock in the ocean or timber in wild forests, no price changes will be reflected in changes in inventories in the SNA because natural assets other than economic assets are not valued in the SNA.

21.163. When depletion of non-produced economic assets such as minerals takes place, the mineral deposits are first transferred to economic uses (in row (vii) of table 21.6) before the use of non-produced natural assets is recorded. When natural assets that are not economic assets are depleted, such as catching of fish from rivers, lakes and oceans or collection of firewood from virgin forests, it is assumed that transfer to economic uses and depletion take place at the same time; the assets are incorporated as economic assets only for the amount of depletion and degradation at the moment of extraction or harvesting.

21.164. Degradation effects in physical or monetary terms are included as additional cost elements in physical or monetary terms, no matter whether these affect natural assets that are economic assets such as land under cultivation and controlled forests or other natural assets such as virgin forests, water, air and land other than cultivated land. The effects of degradation may include the deterioration of natural assets as a result of their use as a "sink" for residues or as a consequence of other degrading activities, such as recreational uses. The deterioration of produced assets due to degradation is assumed to be reflected in consumption of fixed capital (CFC) which is already accounted for in the SNA.

21.165. Degradation effects in table 21.6 have all been included as a cost of production in physical values or monetary terms in item Use_{np} in column (1). The justification for treating the disposal services of the environment as a cost of production is based on a number of specific treatments that are adopted in the SEEA.

21.166. One convention of the SEEA concerns environmental degradation related to final demand. Environmental degradation by households of land, water and air through the use of fossil fuels, generation of garbage and as a consequence of recreational activities is treated in the SEEA as a cost of internal household production activities, which for this purpose are treated as part of an extended production boundary. Environmental degradation caused by fixed assets abandoned in the environment at the end of their useful economic life is allocated as cost of degradation to the producers owning those fixed assets. Both adjustments reduce EDP as compared to NDP in monetary environmental accounting.

21.167. Another convention of the SEEA relates to environmental degradation "imported from" or "exported to" neighbouring countries. The net external degradation effect incurred by the country, resulting from the two flows, is treated in the SEEA as a further environmental cost element. An alternative method found, for example, in the SAM-based environmental study mentioned earlier, is to treat this net external environmental impact as the provision of free environmental disposal services to the rest of the world, which would only be deducted in the derivation of environmentally adjusted net (national) income aggregates. In this approach the net exports of environmental disposal services would be treated in a manner similar to the treatment in the central framework of the SNA of net imports of labour services, which are not deducted to arrive at NDP but taken into account in the derivation of national income.

Table 21.8. Other accumulation entries of the SNA related to use of non-produced natural assets

Code	Description
Entries related to use	
K.61	Depletion of natural assets
K.3 part K.62 part	Quality changes of land due to changes in economic uses (e.g., due to restructuring)(+,-)
K.62 part	Degradation of land (soil, landscape, ecosystems) due to economic uses, except discharge of residuals (-)
K.62 part	Degradation of non-produced natural assets due to discharge of residuals (-)
K.62 part	Restoration of the quality of non-produced natural assets (+)
Additional entries related to accumulation	
K.3 part K.62 part	Gross additions (less other reductions) to the level of exploitable subsoil resources (+,-)
K.3 part	Transfers of other natural assets to economic activity (+,-)
K.12.22 part	Changes in classification of natural assets due to economic activities (e.g., change of economic use, +, -)
Entries not related to accumulation	
K.5	Natural growth of non-cultivated biological resources
K.7	Catastrophic losses
K.8	Uncompensated seizures
K.9	Other volume changes in non-financial assets n.e.c.
K.12 part	Changes in classifications and structure (excluding K.12.22)

Environmental protection expenses

21.168. In addition to the disposal services provided by the environment "free of charge" in the case of degradation, actual expenses are incurred to avoid environmental degradation or eliminate the effects after degradation takes place. Increasingly, enterprises explicitly produce such services on a commercial basis. In many instances, however, the services are produced as the ancillary activities.

21.169. The scope of environmental protection services is defined in table 21.9, which identifies the specific ISIC categories that are related to environmental protection activities. ISIC, however, does not include sufficient detail for the analysis of envi-

ronmental protection and, therefore, a further tentative breakdown is proposed in the SEEA. Additional categories are included in the table and indicated with asterisks. More comprehensive classifications of environmental protection expenditures are being developed by international organizations and further modifications of the breakdown in table 21.9 may result.

21.170. Environmental protection expenses made in the context of ancillary activities carried out by producers are externalized in one version of the SEEA, in the same manner as this was done in the functionally oriented satellite approach described in section C. The ancillary activities are treated as separate establishments with an identifiable output and intermediate costs. The externalization of ancillary environmental activities is done in order to measure and evaluate more comprehensively the efforts that have actually been made to combat environmental degradation and its effects. In terms of table 21.6 this would be reflected in a further breakdown of the production activities in column (1), identifying environmental protection services, and recording output and subsequent use of environmental protection products separately in the rows of supply (i) and economic use (ii). As a result, total output and intermediate consumption of the producers which carry out environmental protection activities as ancillary activities are adjusted upwards as compared with the SNA; NDP, however, is not affected by this treatment.

21.171. In general, the SEEA only considers those environmental protection expenses which are in immediate response to the effects caused by production. It excludes environmental protection expenditures responding to other environmental effects. They would only be considered in welfare approaches which are not further elaborated in the SEEA. This is the reason why household expenses for environmental protection are not considered; they respond to impacts borne by households. They are dealt with in the SEEA in the same manner as in the SNA.

21.172. An exception is made for environmental protection services produced as ancillary activities by government, which are included in the SNA as part of non-market output. They are identified in the SEEA as separate establishments. Their output is treated as government consumption if the government cleans up the effects of its own pollution, or alternatively as capital formation if such activity is interpreted as helping producers to remove the effects of degradation caused by them. This treatment applies to government environmental protection activities such as cleaning of lakes and rivers; restoring land polluted by industry, affected by mining operations and affected by military activities; etc., independently of whether the activities are aimed at eliminating the effects of degradation caused by others or by the government itself.

Net capital accumulation

21.173. In the context of monetary environmental accounting, the SEEA introduces a capital accumulation concept as an alternative to capital formation in the SNA. Capital formation in the SNA includes changes in the stock of produced assets used in production that are caused by economic decisions. Capital accumulation in the SEEA includes not only capital formation but also changes in non-produced natural assets that are explicitly used in production which are thus also related to economic decisions. Such changes include the reductions in the capital stock as a result of depletion and degradation shown in the top panel of table 21.8, and in addition, the incorporation of natural assets as economic assets and the transfer of natural assets between economic uses as a result of economic decisions taken in connection with production activities.

21.174. The middle of table 21.8 identifies additional entries: additions minus reductions in the level of subsoil resources (part of K.3 minus part of K.62), transfer of other natural assets, such as forests, to economic activities (also part of K.3) and classification changes due to economic decisions (part of K.12). The last item covers changes such as in the use of land (for example, between agricultural land and land for urban and rural settlements).

21.175. The other accumulation entries not included in the SEEA concept of capital accumulation are in the lower panel of table 21.8. Catastrophic losses due to events such as wars and natural disasters are not included in the concept of net capital accumulation unless they are caused in connection with productive activities; as they are not related to economic decisions, they remain with other accumulation entries in the lower part of the table. Nor is natural growth of non-cultivated biological resources included in net capital accumulation.

Valuation

21.176. For purposes of monetary accounting, valuation of the additional SEEA elements in column (6) and rows (vi) and (vii) of table 21.6 is needed, the environmentally adjusted elements in row (viii) of the table become relevant only in this case.

21.177. While recognizing that valuation of environmental cost and capital is still a controversial issue, the SEEA deals in some detail with valuation principles. Three alternative valuation methods are distinguished: market prices, maintenance cost and contingent valuation. In the SEEA prices on the market are the central valuation and the principles of market valuation are the same as in the SNA. They are applied to stocks of non-produced natural assets that are economic assets in the SNA, to changes therein as a result of uses of natural assets, and also to the depletion of natural assets that are not economic assets, such as the extraction of fish from the oceans and firewood from virgin forests.

21.178. Even though market valuation is the same in the SNA as it is in the SEEA, it has been more extensively elaborated in the SEEA insofar as natural resources are concerned. In the context of discussing amendments to the SNA to arrive at environ-

mental accounts, it is worthwhile highlighting a number of selected aspects of the market valuation.

21.179. Market values are used in the SNA and the SEEA to value stocks of economic non-produced natural assets. The valuation of depletion and degradation of natural assets that are economic assets in the SNA using prices on the market is consistent with the valuation of the stocks of the corresponding non-produced (natural) economic assets in both systems. The only difference between the SNA and the SEEA is that the use of non-produced natural economic assets is recorded in the SNA as other volume changes, while in the SEEA the cost of depletion and degradation is reflected in capital accumulation and deducted in the derivation of EDP.

21.180. Opening and closing stocks of other non-produced natural assets that are not economic assets in the SNA are not valued in monetary terms in either system; they are recorded in the SEEA, but only in physical terms. Nor is degradation of air and water valued in either system, as these are uses of non-produced natural assets that are not economic assets. However, while the SNA excludes, the SEEA includes in its market valuation all uses of natural assets that are not economic assets. For instance, the depletion of fish stocks from the ocean or extraction of firewood from virgin forests as the fish and firewood have a market value. This implies that the item $-\text{Use}_{np.env}$ in column (6) of table 21.6 has limited coverage in the monetary version of the SEEA, as it includes only depletion of natural assets that are not economic assets, but not degradation.

21.181. In valuing the changes in the stock of non-produced assets at monetary terms, two valuation methods are utilized in practice, mainly in the context of depletion. One is the so-called net rent approach. It values the units extracted on the basis of the difference between output and all costs—including labour costs and a normal profit margin—incurred as a result of depletion. The other is the so-called user cost approach, which values the units extracted on the basis of only a part of net rent, i.e., that part which if reinvested would generate a permanent income stream equal to the loss of income generation capacity through depletion.

21.182. Since the cost of depletion is more often reflected in prices than the cost of degradation, the SNA and the market valuation version of the SEEA incorporate depletion cost more fully than they do degradation. Insofar as the market recognizes the cost of degradation when specifying different prices for degraded natural assets such as contaminated land, the degradation cost is treated as other volume changes in the SNA. As it may be difficult in practice to separate these changes in the quality of assets due to degradation from price changes, SNA accounting may not attempt such separation. However, the SEEA—given its different analytical focus—identifies these quality changes in assets separately, deducting this value in principle from value added generated and capital accumulation.

Table 21.9. Two digit ISIC categories that identify environmental protection services

Code	Category		
37	Recycling		
90	Sewage and refuse disposal, sanitation and similar activities		
90.1*		Collection, transport, treatment and disposal of waste	
90.2*		Collection and treatment of waste water	
90.3*		Cleaning of exhaust gases	
90.4*		Noise abatement	
90.5*		Other environmental protection services n.e.c.	
90.6*		Sanitation and similar services	

*Proposed SEEA breakdown.

21.183. The two other valuations used in the SEEA, i.e., maintenance cost and contingency valuation, are only applied to uses and not to stocks of non-produced natural resources. The uses that are valued in this manner include uses of natural resources that are economic assets in the SNA sense as well as uses of other natural resources, such as contamination of air and water and depletion of fish stocks in the ocean. The maintenance valuation in these instances is based on the cost which would have been necessary to maintain natural assets at their level prior to depletion or degradation. The contingency valuation is based on the willingness-to-pay principle. It is used in the SEEA to value the environmental cost borne by households, which is deducted in the derivation of one of the alternatives of EDP. This differs from some other approaches, which deduct this cost outside the framework of table 21.6 in the derivation of environmentally adjusted national income instead of EDP.

21.184. Use of other than market valuation leads to a number of valuation inconsistencies within the SEEA. To some extent these reflect potential disequilibria resulting from the use of prices that do not recognize environmental cost. One of these inconsistencies has been identified explicitly in the SEEA. It is the discrepancy caused by incompatibilities between the market valuation of opening and closing stocks of non-produced natural assets that are economic assets in the SNA sense and the valuation of the corresponding flows which include the non-market valuation of uses of these assets and other natural assets that are not economic assets, in terms of maintenance and contingency cost. The valuation discrepancy could be interpreted as the quality changes of all natural assets that are not taken into account in the market valuation of economic assets. The discrepancy will be less the better the quality changes in the assets due to degradation are reflected in sub-items of K.62 covering negative effects of degradation of land and other non-produced economic assets, as well as the positive effects due to restoration activities (see table 21.8).

21.185. Another inconsistency concerns the compatibility between the valuation of output that is based on market cost and the valuation of inputs that include not only economic uses but also environmental uses that are not taken into account in the valuation of output. Whether this incompatibility is important depends on whether some of the assumptions implicit in the SEEA treatment are realistic. The first assumption is that the additional environmental costs that are imputed would not affect the prices of output of the products concerned if these costs were explicitly taken into account in the prices charged to the purchaser. In the case of degradation, there is a further assumption that if restoration activities were actually carried out, the resources needed would be available in sufficient supply and would not compete with the resources available for the production of other goods and services. Based on these assumptions, additional expenditures imputed to account for the cost of depletion and degradation, therefore, reduce value added and EDP to the full extent without taking into account any effects resulting from changes in prices of output and intermediate inputs.

21.186. The two assumptions are probably more realistic for depletion than for degradation. Producers of minerals and other products of depletable reserves, when calculating their profits and the part they would have to reserve in order to secure future income streams, may already have taken the depletion allowance into account. Incorporation in environmental accounts of such allowances would thus merely adjust net value added of the production in question to a more realistic level. However, even in case of pollution many corporations may have made allowances in their costs for possible liability for environmental contamination.

Note

1 The present discussion is based on United Nations, "Integrated environmental and economic accounting (an interim report)", (New York, 1992). This report has subsequently been issued as a United Nations publication, Sales No. E.93.XVII.12. It was prepared by the United Nations Statistical Division with the assistance of a consultant and in close coordination with the SNA.

Annexes

Annex I

Changes from the 1968 System of National Accounts

A. Introduction

1. The *System of National Accounts 1993* (1993 SNA), retains the basic theoretical framework of its predecessor, *A System of National Accounts* (1968 SNA). However, in line with the mandate of the United Nations Statistical Commission, it contains clarifications and justifications of the concepts presented, it is harmonized with other related statistical systems and it introduces a number of features that reflect new analytical and policy concerns of countries and international organizations.

2. The classifications and concepts of the central framework are internally more closely linked up with each other and more fully harmonized externally with standards of related statistical systems than in the 1968 SNA. It more fully integrates production, income, capital and financial accounts and balance sheets, and in doing so, it draws upon the guidelines given in separate United Nations manuals on balance sheets and reconciliation accounts (Series M, No.60), on tangible assets (Series M, No.68), on income distribution (Series M, No.61) and on constant prices (Series M, No.64). Furthermore, the new System describes in detail the links between the SNA and the related statistical system on balance of payments prepared by the International Monetary Fund (IMF). Particular attention has been given to the delineation of the production boundary with regard to coverage of own-account production of goods and services. Also, more precise criteria have been established for the delineation and coverage of the financial sector and identification and classification of financial instruments in light of the many innovations in this field in recent years due to financial deregulation. The central framework retains input-output tables as an integral part of the System particularly as the basis for balancing supply and demand. It includes a detailed breakdown of the household sector by sub-sectors including all accounts which facilitate the links between SNA and social accounting matrices (SAMs). The System also describes and incorporates population and employment data. The System pays special attention to the conceptual implications of some of the structural features of economies in transition.

3. There are two important elements of flexibility built into the System. The first concerns the flexible use of classifications, which is based on a hierarchical structure of classifications of transactors, transactions and assets that permits adaptation of data detail to data availability and other specific circumstances of different countries. This flexible use of classifications, which is further developed in one of the chapters, does not change the concepts of the central framework. The second element of flexibility, which is described in chapter XXI, extends the System to so-called satellite accounts that use product and income concepts that are alternative to those of the central framework. A description of satellite accounts relating to the environment provides a notable example of this kind of flexibility.

4. These changes in the general features of the System are in addition to a number of specific changes in the 1993 SNA as compared to the 1968 SNA, which are grouped together below in nine sections (B.1 to B.9). The descriptions given only highlight the main differences between the two Systems while refraining from exhaustive comparison of definitions. The discussion of all changes contains cross-references to the corresponding chapters and tables.

B. SNA revisions

1. Revision of the accounting structure and new balancing items

Partitioning and further integration of the accounts and balance sheets, and creation of new balancing items
Reference: chapter II, paragraphs 2.97 to 2.151

5. In the 1993 SNA the overall sequence of accounts of institutional units and sectors is now subdivided into current accounts, accumulation accounts and balance sheets. Thus, the accounting structure of the System integrates the balance sheets as an additional group. The 1968 SNA did not specify balance sheets in detail; they were developed later in a separate publication (United Nations, M/60).

6. The 1993 SNA partitions the production account of the 1968 SNA into two accounts: a production account, where the balancing item is "value added" (B.1), and a generation of income account, with "operating surplus/mixed income" (B.2/B.3) as the balancing item. The generation of income account has been moved to the next group of accounts, i.e., distribution and use of income accounts.

7. The group of distribution and use of income accounts of the 1993 SNA includes the income and outlay account of the 1968 SNA together with the generation of income account, which was previously included as part of the production account. This second group of accounts is divided into the following accounts: (a) generation of income account, with "operating surplus/mixed income" (B.2/B.3) as the balancing item; (b) allocation of primary income account, with "balance of primary incomes" (B.5) as the balancing item; (c) secondary distribution of income account, with "disposable income" (B.6) as the balancing item; (d) redistribution of income in kind account, with "adjusted disposable income" (B.7) as the balancing item; and (e) use of income account, with "saving" (B.8) as the balancing item.

8. The 1993 SNA divides the capital finance account of the 1968 SNA in order to separate the acquisition of non-financial assets from the acquisition of financial assets and incurrence of liabilities. The two resulting accounts are (a) the capital account, with "net lending/borrowing" (B.9) as the balancing item; and (b) the financial account also with "net lending/borrowing" (B.9) as the balancing item. An additional entry called "changes in net worth due to saving and capital transfers" (B.10.1) is identified on the right-hand side of the capital account.

9. In the 1993 SNA the reconciliation account of the 1968 SNA has been integrated into a new set of accumulation accounts which cover all changes between two successive balance sheets. Two new accounts are introduced: (a) the other changes in volume of assets account, with "changes in net worth due to other changes in volume of assets" (B.10.2) as the balancing item; and (b) the revaluation ac-

count, with "changes in net worth due to nominal holding gains/losses" (B.10.3) as the balancing item. The latter account is further broken down into two sub-accounts in order to separate real holding gains/losses in both financial and non-financial assets/liabilities from neutral holding gains/losses that are merely proportionate to changes in the general price level. Consequently, the 1993 SNA incorporates a new balancing item, "changes in net worth" (B.10), which includes three sub-elements: (a) changes in net worth due to saving and capital transfers (B.10.1); (b) changes in net worth due to other changes in volume of assets (B.10.2) and (c) changes in net worth due to nominal holding gains/losses (B.10.3).

Introduction of production accounts for all sectors and cross-classification of value added by activities and institutional sectors
Reference: chapter II, paragraph 2.210; chapter VI, paragraphs 6.1 to 6.3; chapter XV, paragraphs 15.105 to 15.109

10. The 1993 SNA includes production accounts for all institutional sectors in addition to production accounts for the establishment-based industries of the 1968 SNA. In order to link these two types of production accounts, the 1993 SNA recommends a cross-classification output, intermediate consumption, gross value added and its components by type of sector and industry. It does not use the terminology "dual sectoring" sometimes used in connection with the 1968 SNA.

Introduction of a new concept, called "mixed income", for unincorporated enterprises
Reference: chapter VII, paragraphs 7.81 to 7.87

11. The 1993 SNA introduces a distinction, not made in the 1968 SNA, between the operating surplus of certain unincorporated enterprises owned by households and the operating surplus of other enterprises. For this purpose, it introduces a new name for the net operating surplus arising from the productive activities of unincorporated enterprises owned by households (except for the surplus arising from the production of housing services for own consumption by owner occupiers). The new category is called mixed income (B.3) because it usually reflects remuneration for work done by the owner of the enterprise as well as a return to entrepreneurship.

Introduction of balance of primary incomes and gross national income (GNI) concepts
Reference: chapter II, paragraphs 2.116 and 2.181; chapter VII, paragraphs 7.1 and 7.2 and 7.13 to 7.16

12. The 1993 SNA introduces a new concept called balance of primary incomes (B.5), which is the sector equivalent of

national income and is the balancing item of the allocation of primary income account. The balance of primary incomes results from the distribution of value added to labour (compensation of employees), capital (property income) and government (taxes, less subsidies, on production and imports) and operating surplus and mixed income. The sum of the balance of primary incomes across sectors is GNI (B.5*), which is the new term for what was called gross national product (GNP) in the 1953 SNA.

2. Further specifications of statistical units, revisions in the sectoring and introduction of multiple sub-sectoring

Definitions of institutional units and establishments
Reference: chapter II, paragraphs 2.19 to 2.21 and 2.43 to 2.45; chapter IV, paragraphs 4.1 to 4.5; chapter V, paragraphs 5.21 to 5.24; chapter VII, paragraphs 7.118 to 7.121; chapter XV, paragraphs 15.13 to 15.19

13. The 1993 SNA defines an institutional unit as an economic entity that is capable in its own right of owning assets, incurring liabilities and engaging in economic activities and in transactions with other units. Corporations providing ancillary-type services to a parent corporation are merged with the parent corporation into one single institutional unit. Also included in the corporate sectors as separate institutional units are quasi-corporations—i.e., unincorporated enterprises owned by households, government or non-resident units that behave like corporations and have complete sets of accounts, including information on withdrawals of entrepreneurial income analogous to the payments of dividends in the case of a corporation. In the 1993 SNA, the family of enterprises is not used as a statistical unit. The 1968 SNA did not include explicit definitions for institutional units but made reference to one criterion—availability of complete accounts. It did not make reference to the requirement that information on withdrawals of entrepreneurial income had to be available.

14. The 1993 SNA introduces a distinction between an analytical unit and an observable unit in the production accounts in the supply and use and input-output tables. The establishment is defined by reference to one activity and one location as in the 1968 SNA, but for practical reasons and harmonization with the International Standard Industrial Classification (ISIC) Rev. 3, the 1993 SNA recognizes an observable unit version of the establishment, which, in addition to its main activity, may also have one or more secondary activities. The analytical unit (unit of homogeneous production) is used in the construction of the input-output table.

Explicit definition of statistical unit and gross output in agriculture
Reference: chapter VI, paragraphs 6.103 to 6.107

15. The 1993 SNA recommends that in agriculture the statistical unit and the definition of output should be the same as for other market producers. The establishment in agricultural activities refers to the individual agricultural holding. As in the case of other activities, the output includes transactions between agricultural holdings but excludes products for intermediate consumption within the same agricultural holding. (Statistical information in agriculture is often not available in this form, and it may be necessary to use either the "gross-gross" measurement of output, which includes products used for intermediate consumption in the same agricultural holding, or the concept of the "national farm", in which agricultural products used either in the same or other agricultural holdings are entirely omitted.) The 1968 SNA did not deal explicitly with the definition of statistical unit and gross output in agriculture.

Introduction of three sub-sectors for non-financial and financial corporations, i.e., public, national private, and foreign controlled
Reference: chapter IV, paragraphs 4.71 to 4.76 and 4.84

16. The 1993 SNA recommends identifying the following sub-sectors for the non-financial and financial corporation sectors: public corporations, national private corporations and foreign controlled corporations.

17. A public corporation is one controlled by the government. The government may exercise control by owning more than 50 per cent of the equity or by other means such as special legislation or decree even if it holds less than 50 per cent of the equity. An enterprise is also regarded as a public corporation if it is subject to control by another public corporation.

18. Foreign-controlled enterprises are defined as enterprises subject to control by non-residents. Foreign enterprises in which non-resident investment is less than 50 per cent may be included or excluded by individual countries according to their qualitative assessment of foreign control. Foreign-controlled corporations include those direct investment enterprises that are subsidiaries and branches, as defined in the draft fifth edition of the IMF *Balance of Payments Manual* (BPM) and in the Organisation for Economic Cooperation and Development (OECD) *Detailed Benchmark Definition of Foreign Direct Investment*.

19. The 1968 SNA terms "corporate enterprises" and "quasi-corporate enterprises" have been shortened to "corporations" and "quasi-corporations" in the 1993 SNA. In sub-sectoring non-financial and financial corporate and quasi-corporate enterprises, the 1968 SNA distinguished between public and private enterprises but did not distinguish

between resident enterprises that are subject to foreign control and those that are not.

New definition of the financial sector to include financial auxiliaries and exclude holding companies that control mainly non-financial subsidiaries
Reference: chapter IV, paragraphs 4.79 to 4.81, 4.96, and 4.100

20. The 1993 SNA has enlarged the 1968 SNA financial sector to include, in addition to financial corporations that incur financial liabilities and acquire financial assets on their own account, auxiliaries engaged primarily in activities that facilitate financial intermediation or provide financial services without placing themselves at risk.

21. The 1993 SNA recommends that holding companies should be assigned to the institutional sector in which the main activity of the group of subsidiaries is concentrated. Consequently, although holding companies often play a primarily financial role, they should be classified as financial corporations only when the preponderant activity of the group of corporations they control is financial.

Revised sub-sectoring of the financial corporate sector to reflect new developments in financial corporations, markets and instruments
Reference: chapter IV, paragraphs 4.83 to 4.98; chapter XI, paragraphs 11.56 and 11.57

22. The 1993 SNA sub-sectors financial corporations as follows: (a) central bank (S.121); (b) other depository corporations (S.122); (c) other financial intermediaries except insurance corporations and pension funds (S.123); (d) financial auxiliaries (S.124); and (e) insurance corporations and pension funds (S.125). However, due to the substantial variations among countries in defining money, the 1993 SNA does not include a definition of money but provides a classification of financial corporations and instruments compatible with national money definitions. Thus, the sub-sector "Other depository corporations" has been established to include all financial corporations except the central bank whose principal activity is financial intermediation and which have liabilities in the form of deposits or other financial instruments that are close substitutes for deposits and which are included in measures of money broadly defined. Where the distinction between narrow and broad money concepts is important, countries are encouraged to disaggregate this sub-sector between "Deposit money corporations (S.1221)", which have any liabilities in the form of deposits (narrow money), and "Other depository corporations (S.1222)", which have liabilities in the form of deposits that are not readily transferable or in the form of financial instruments (such as

short-term certificates of deposit) which are close substitutes for deposits and which are included in measures of money broadly defined. The 1968 SNA used the concept of narrow money as the classification principle for financial sub-sectors and thus included in "other financial corporations" many financial corporations that had liabilities in the form of broad money instruments.

23. Since the word "bank" has a specific legal connotation in some countries that is different from the new interpretation in the System, the 1993 SNA has changed two 1968 SNA related terms as follows: "depository corporation" is used instead of "bank" and "financial intermediation services" instead of "banking services".

Separate identification of unincorporated financial enterprises as distinct from quasi-corporate financial enterprises
Reference: chapter IV, paragraph 4.82

24. The 1993 SNA has eliminated the 1968 SNA convention that treated all financial unincorporated enterprises as quasi-corporations. In the 1993 SNA, financial unincorporated enterprises owned by households, such as individuals engaged in financial intermediation or in services auxiliary to financial intermediation, are classified in the households sector.

25. In line with the above, the 1993 SNA treats money lenders who incur liabilities to mobilize funds as financial intermediaries included in the households sector and their output is measured the same way as that of other financial intermediaries. Money lenders who make loans from their own resources are also considered producers of financial services provided their services can be measured. Money lenders were not explicitly referred to in the 1968 SNA.

Classification of government employee pension schemes in the financial sector
Reference: chapter IV, paragraph 4.98

26. The 1993 SNA, like the 1968 SNA, classifies pension funds invested entirely with the employer as part of the employer's sector, rather than placing them with insurance corporations and pension funds in the financial corporations sector. An exception has been made for government employee pension funds that are separate institutional units; they are classified in the financial corporations sector, even if most of their funds are invested in government securities for reasons of prudence, whether by legal requirement or by choice. The rationale is that investment of government employee pension funds with the employer does not indicate the degree of employer control that investment of private employee pension funds with an employer does.

Alternative methods of sub-sectoring for general
government
Reference: chapter IV, paragraph 4.131

27. The 1993 SNA recommends with equal priority two ways
for sub-sectoring general government: include social security funds as part of each level of government at which they
operate (central government security funds (S.13212),
state government security funds (S.13222) and local government security funds (S.13232), or as a sub-sector
(S.1314) separate from the operations of all levels of government. The 1968 SNA recommended only the latter classification, i.e., social security funds were shown as a separate sub-sector.

Inclusion of an additional sub-sector for state government
Reference: chapter IV, paragraphs 4.123 to 4.127

28. The 1993 SNA introduces state government (S.1312) as an
additional level of government between central (S.1311)
and local (S.1313) government. This breakdown is only to
be applied in those countries where it is meaningful.

Presentation of consolidated public sector accounts in
supplementary tables
Reference: chapter XIX, paragraphs 19.37 to 19.42

29. The 1993 SNA recommends, for supplementary analysis,
consolidated presentations of the public sector, covering
general government and non-financial public corporations
in a manner consistent with GFS.

Revised sub-sectoring of households based on type of income and introduction of the distinction between formal
and informal production activities
Reference: chapter IV, paragraphs 4.153 to 4.162;
annex to chapter IV; chapter XIX, paragraphs 19.9
to 19.13

30. The 1993 SNA recommends sub-sectoring the households
sector on the basis of the nature of the household's largest
source of income (employers' mixed incomes, own-account workers' mixed incomes, compensation of employees, property and transfer incomes). Thus, households are
allocated to sub-sectors depending on which of the four
categories of income is the largest for the household as a
whole, even if it does not always account for more than half
of total household income. Consequently, the following
sub-sectors are distinguished: (a) employers (S.141); (b)
own-account workers (S.142); (c) employees (S.143); and
(d) recipients of property and transfer income (S.144). The
1993 SNA also suggests sub-sectoring households on the
basis of other criteria of an economic, socio-economic or
geographical nature. It should be noted that since the 1993
SNA introduces the full set of accounts (including production accounts) for the household sector and its sub-sectors,
it allows analysis of the distributional effects of income

generation and distribution. The 1968 SNA recommended
a similar socio-economic breakdown for the household
sector but did not carry it through in all accounts and tables.

31. Unlike the 1968 SNA, the 1993 SNA recognizes that the
distinction between formal and informal sectors of the
economy is particularly important for many developing
countries. The International Conference of Labour Statisticians has developed criteria for the identification of those
production units of the households sector which make up
the informal sector as "informal own-account enterprises"
or "enterprises of informal employers". It is recognized,
however, that depending on national circumstances, certain production units of the households sector may fall outside the distinction between formal and informal sectors
(i.e., units exclusively engaged in agricultural activities,
the production of goods for own final use, or the production
of services for own final consumption by employing paid
domestic workers.

3. Further specifications of the scope of transactions including the production boundary

Further specification of the production boundary for
household production activities
Reference: chapter VI, 6.14 to 6.29; chapter XXI,
paragraphs 21.19 and 21.40

32. The production boundary in the 1993 SNA is only slightly
different from the one in the 1968 SNA. In defining the production boundary, the 1993 SNA draws on the distinction
between goods and services. It includes the production of
all goods within the production boundary, and the production of all services except personal and domestic services
produced for own final consumption within households
(other than the services of owner occupiers and those produced by employing paid domestic staff).

33. With regard to own-account production of goods by households, the 1993 SNA has removed the 1968 SNA limitations which excluded the production of goods not made
from primary products, the processing of primary products
by those who do not produce them and the production of
other goods by households who do not sell any part of them
on the market.

34. The coverage of own-account production is clarified. The
storage of agricultural goods produced by households is included within the production boundary as an extension of
the goods producing process, as is supply of water (water-
carrying).

35. The 1993 SNA, like the 1968 SNA, excludes from the production boundary the production of services by households
for own final consumption. Included, however, is the production of services of owner-occupied dwellings and the
production of services for own final consumption by em-

ploying paid domestic staff. The 1993 SNA explains that in the central framework no values are recorded for unpaid domestic or personal services produced within households because the production of such services within households is a self-contained activity with limited repercussions on the rest of the economy, there are typically no prices that can be satisfactorily used to value such services, and the estimated values would not be equivalent to monetary values for analytic or policy purposes. The 1993 SNA does, however, suggest that in satellite accounts an alternative concept of gross domestic product (GDP) be elaborated which is based on an extended production boundary, including estimates for household production of services for own use.

Voluntary labour inputs are valued on the basis of actual compensation paid
Reference: chapter VII, paragraphs 7.20 and 7.23

36. In general, neither the 1993 SNA nor the 1968 SNA includes an estimate of the value of voluntary labour inputs. Labour inputs are valued at actual compensation paid even if this is very low or even zero. However, in the case of production of tangible fixed assets for own use resulting from communal household activities, an estimate of value of labour input is needed in order to calculate the total cost of the assets (if a market price is not available). This inclusion results in mixed income being generated by the production.

Allocation of financial intermediation services indirectly measured (FISIM)
Reference: chapter VI, paragraphs 6.128 to 6.140

37. The 1993 SNA calculates the output of financial intermediation services indirectly measured (FISIM) (this term replaces the term bank service charges used in the 1968 SNA; see paragraph 23 above) in the same way as the 1968 SNA, i.e., as the difference between property income received and interest paid. The property income received should exclude that part which is received from investment of own funds. However, contrary to the 1968 SNA, the 1993 SNA, in principle, recommends to allocate the consumption of these services between users—who could be lenders as well as borrowers—treating the allocated amounts either as intermediate consumption by enterprises or as final consumption or exports. The 1993 SNA suggests that the allocation between different uses could be made on the basis of the difference between interest paid or received by financial intermediaries and a "reference rate" that does not include the value of financial intermediation services, such as an inter-bank lending rate or a central bank loan rate, or some other appropriate method. However, the allocation could be made using different criteria or methods, when appropriate.

38. Nevertheless, the 1993 SNA recognizes that, in practice, it may be difficult to find any method of allocating financial intermediation services indirectly measured among differ-

ent users and, therefore, accepts that some countries may prefer to continue to use the convention proposed in the 1968 SNA whereby the whole of the services are allocated to intermediate consumption of a notional industry. But, it is recommended that these countries provide supplementary estimates, even if only approximate and very aggregative, of the allocation between intermediate consumption and the main categories of final demand and thus would make it possible to have some estimate of the effect allocation would have on GDP, GNI, and other relevant aggregates. Also, the 1993 SNA requests those countries that allocate financial intermediation services indirectly measured, to identify those allocations separately.

39. The 1993 SNA uses a new term "output of financial intermediation services indirectly measured" to replace the 1968 SNA term "imputed output of bank services".

Inclusion, in principle, of all illegal production and other transactions
Reference: chapter VI, paragraphs 6.30 to 6.36

40. The 1993 SNA makes it clear that the illegality of a productive activity or transaction is not a reason for excluding it from the System. Comprehensive coverage of illegal activities is, in principle, essential in order not to introduce errors and imbalances in the accounts. For example, failure to record expenditures by households on illegal products will lead to over estimates of their saving and inconsistencies with the financial accounts. The 1968 SNA did not give clear guidance on the coverage of illegal activities.

Identification of non-monetary flows and re-routings from other transactions
Reference: chapter III, paragraphs 3.34 to 3.49; chapter XIX, paragraphs 19.20 to 19.29

41. The 1993 SNA recommends the identification of non-monetary flows and re-routings wherever possible, especially when they are large and significant. In this way, analysts interested in identifying only the monetary transactions in the economy can do so. The 1968 SNA made no such recommendation.

4. Changes in valuation and in the treatment of product taxes

Distinction between basic, producers' and purchasers' prices in the valuation of outputs and inputs
Reference: chapter VI, paragraphs 6.210 to 6.238

42. The 1993 SNA clarifies the terminology used for the valuation of products. The System refers to output prices received by producers, which may be either basic prices or—if difficult to implement—producers' prices, and to purchasers' prices that apply to intermediate and final uses. The basic prices exclude all taxes less subsidies on products (D.21 less D.31) but the producer's prices only ex-

clude invoiced value added tax (VAT) (D.211). Purchasers' prices, which are paid by intermediate or final users, include trade and transport margins.

43. When using basic prices to value output and purchasers' prices to value intermediate consumption, there are no product taxes less subsidies payable out of value added. They are treated as taxes less subsidies on uses, payable by the purchasers of the products. On the other hand, when producers' prices are used to value output, some taxes on products have to be paid out of value added. VAT and taxes and duties on imports are treated as taxes on uses payable by the purchasers of the products and therefore are not payable out of value added.

44. A consequence of the above treatment is that the sum of the values added of all enterprises in the economy is not equal to GDP. In the case of valuation of output in basic prices, all taxes less subsidies on products including import taxes need to be added to the sum in order to derive GDP; in the case of valuation of output in producers' prices, only VAT and import taxes need to be added.

45. The 1993 SNA has eliminated the 1968 SNA distinction between true and approximate basic prices since the "true price" is a hypothetical concept which is not observable. The 1968 SNA used producers' prices as the main valuation method for output and input. Basic prices together with commodity taxes were treated as a further subdivision of producers' prices, which was applied to both output and intermediate inputs for the purposes of input-output analysis.

Revision of the classification and terminology of taxes; explicit treatment of VAT
Reference: chapter VII, paragraphs 7.49 to 7.51; chapter VIII, paragraph 8.41

46. The 1993 SNA replaces the 1968 SNA term "indirect taxes" by the term "taxes on production and imports" (D.2), and replaces the distinction between "commodity taxes" and "other indirect taxes and imports" by "taxes on products" (D.21) and "other taxes on production" (D.29). The taxes on products are further subdivided into: (a) VAT-type taxes (D.211); (b) taxes on imports excluding VAT (D.212); (c) export taxes (D.213); and (d) taxes on products, except VAT, import and export taxes (D.214). The 1968 SNA makes only a brief reference to VAT and gives no specific recommendation for its treatment in the accounts.

47. The 1993 SNA has also replaced the 1968 SNA term "direct taxes" by the term "current taxes on income, wealth, etc.," and the previous category of capital transfers to government, including estate and gift taxes and non-recurrent taxes on property are treated as capital taxes.

Alignment of SNA and GFS/OECD tax coverage
Reference: chapter VIII, paragraphs 8.44 and 8.45

48. The 1993 SNA recommends that breakdowns of taxes beyond the main categories should be in terms of the GFS and OECD Revenue Statistics tax classifications. While no calculation of total taxes is required within the 1993 SNA accounts, compulsory social contributions are summed with taxes to reach the concept of total taxes used by the GFS and OECD Revenue Statistics. For this purpose the 1993 SNA provides a breakdown of social security contributions so that compulsory contributions can be identified separately and added to taxes to match up with the GFS/OECD concept of total taxes.

5. Distinction between market and other kinds of production and introduction of alternative concepts of consumption and disposable income

Explicit identification, valuation and treatment of market, own-account and other non-market production
Reference: chapter VI, paragraphs 6.44 to 6.56 and 6.88 to 6.101

49. The 1993 SNA distinguishes three types of output: i.e. market output (P.11), output for own final use (P.12) and other non-market output (P.13). Market output is output that is sold at economically significant prices. Output for own final use such as subsistence output of agricultural products or own account produced capital goods, while not sold on the market, are valued at the average prices of similar products traded on the market. Other non-market output which includes goods and services produced by government and non-profit institutions serving households and provided free, or at prices that are not economically significant, to individual households or the community, is valued at cost.

50. The distinction between market producers, producers for own final use and other non-market producers replaces the distinction in the 1968 SNA between "industries" and "other producers". Producers for own final use which were included in the 1968 SNA in "industries" are now distinguished as a separate category.

51. The three-way split of products and producers is complementary to the ISIC and Central Product Classification (CPC). The ISIC and CPC breakdowns would apply in principle to all three categories of producers and products respectively.

52. The criterion in the 1993 SNA for making a distinction between market and other output makes it possible to include all heavily subsidized public enterprises as market producers provided their prices are considered economically significant from the point of view of cost and demand. The 1968 SNA made a distinction between government producing units that sold the kind of goods and services often pro-

duced by what is called "business establishments" (private market producers) and government departments engaged in the usual social and community activities of government. The required criterion for making the distinction in the 1968 SNA was simply the existence of a price, while in the 1993 SNA the distinction between market and non-market output depends on whether the price is economically significant from the point of view of cost and demand. Since it is very rare that the government departments of the 1968 SNA engaged in social and community activities charge significant prices in the 1993 SNA sense, they are treated generally in the same way in the 1993 SNA.

53. The 1993 SNA distinction between market output, output produced for own final use and other non-market output has simplified the principles of valuation. Valuation of products of market producers is always based on the prices for which they are sold in the market. Output produced for own final use is valued on the basis of prices of similar products made by market producers where these exist. Other non-market output is valued as the sum of costs.

54. The 1993 SNA, like the 1968 SNA, treats all current transfers made by government to producers as subsidies, even if they benefit specific groups of the population or all households. However, recognizing the importance of these "consumption" subsidies in some countries, the 1993 SNA recommends a supplementary presentation of subsidies by purpose where "consumption" subsidies can be identified. This presentation would make it possible to show, outside the System, actual final consumption with an alternative valuation that includes the value of consumption subsidies.

Introduction of new concepts called "actual consumption" and "adjusted disposable income" to supplement the concepts of consumption expenditure and disposable income
Reference: chapter IX, paragraphs 9.93 to 9.98

55. The 1993 SNA introduces the concept of actual final consumption (P.4) for households and government to supplement the 1968 SNA concept of final consumption expenditure (presently P.3). Actual final consumption of households covers goods and services which are actually supplied to households, irrespective of whether the ultimate bearers of the expense are government, non-profit institutions serving households or households themselves. The actual consumption concept utilizes the distinction between individual consumption (benefiting identifiable households) and collective consumption (benefiting society as a whole) within final consumption expenditure by government. For households it is equal to the sum of household final consumption expenditure plus individual consumption items identified within consumption expenditure of government and non-profit institutions serving households. For government, actual consumption consists only of collective consumption. Non-profit institutions serving households, by convention, have no actual consumption; their final consumption expenditures are all categorized as individual consumption and, therefore, included with actual consumption of households.

56. The difference between final consumption expenditure (P.3) and actual final consumption (P.4) of households is treated in the accounts of the 1993 SNA as (current) social transfers in kind (D.63) provided by government and non-profit institutions serving households to households. For households, the imputed transfers are added to disposable income (B.6) to derive the concept of adjusted disposable income (B.7); for government and NPISHs, they are deducted.

57. The 1968 SNA did not identify different concepts of final consumption and disposable income. It only included one concept of final consumption expenditure and one corresponding concept of disposable income. On the other hand, the 1968 SNA had a wider concept of final consumption expenditure of households than the 1993 SNA, as it included not only what households actually paid, but also health and other expenditures paid or reimbursed by government for services that households are free to select or not.

Treatment of pension and other social insurance contributions and benefits as current transfers affecting disposable income of households
Reference: chapter VIII, paragraphs 8.7 to 8.14; chapter IX, paragraphs 9.6, and 9.14 to 9.16, annex IV

58. The 1993 SNA identifies some insurance and pension funds as social insurance schemes. This affects the recording of contributions and benefits of these schemes, especially pensions. The 1993 SNA treats pension contributions and benefits in the secondary distribution of income accounts as current transfers, which affect the level of disposable income of households. In order not to change the value of saving of households and maintain consistency with the item in the financial accounts called "changes in the net equity of households in life insurance reserves and in pension funds" (F.61) in line with the 1968 SNA treatment, the 1993 SNA introduces an adjustment item in the use of income accounts called "adjustment for the change in net equity of households in pension funds" (D.8), which is recorded as "resources" for households and as "uses" for financial corporations (S.12) or other sectors if the funded pension schemes are not institutional units separate from the employers. In the case of pension funds belonging to the financial corporations sector the 1968 SNA only included an entry in the financial account, where the difference between pension contributions and benefits is recorded as part of the change in the net equity of households in pension funds.

Enlargement of the concept of social insurance to include arrangements with insurance enterprises and education grants
Reference: chapter VIII, paragraphs 8.7 and 8.8, and 8.53 to 8.80

59. In the 1993 SNA social contributions and benefits (D.6) are not restricted to transactions with government and employers as they are in the 1968 SNA. They also include arrangements with insurance schemes that satisfy the definition of "social". Social benefits in the System are current transfers received by households intended to provide for the needs that arise from certain events or circumstances, such as sickness, unemployment, retirement, housing, education or family circumstances. To qualify as social insurance benefits, the transfers must be provided under organized social insurance schemes. Social insurance benefits may be provided under general social security schemes, under private social insurance schemes or by unfunded schemes managed by the employers for the benefit of their existing or former employees without involving other institutional units. Education grants, which in the 1968 SNA were treated as social assistance grants, are treated in the 1993 SNA as social benefits.

Channelling of social transfers in kind by enterprises to households through "quasi-NPISHs", provisional treatment for countries in transition
Reference: chapter XIX, paragraphs 19.30 to 19.35

60. The 1993 SNA recommends an exceptional and provisional treatment for social transfers in kind (D.63) made by state controlled enterprises in countries in transition to their employees as an extension of government policy to provide health, education and recreational services to the population. As a transitional treatment, it is recommended to create "quasi-NPISHs" which receive a transfer from the parent enterprise and pass them on to households as social transfers in kind to be included in the redistribution of income in kind account. As a consequence of this treatment, these expenditures enter only actual final consumption (P.4) of households and not their final consumption expenditure (P.3), thus affecting adjusted disposable income (B.7) and not disposable income (B.6). The 1968 SNA would have treated these expenditures as compensation in kind, entering consumption expenditure and disposable income of households.

6. Extension and further specification of the concepts of assets, capital formation and consumption of fixed capital

Explicit definition of asset and asset boundary and revised classification of assets
Reference: chapter X, paragraphs 10.2 to 10.12; annex to chapter XIII

61. In the 1993 SNA the assets recorded in the balance sheets of the System are economic assets. These are defined as entities over which ownership rights are enforced by institutional units, individually or collectively, and from which economic benefits may be derived by their owners by holding or using them over a period of time. With regard to the classification of assets, the 1993 SNA distinguishes at the first level of the classification between non-financial assets (AN) and financial assets/liabilities (AF). Within non-financial assets, it distinguishes between produced and non-produced assets and within each of these between tangible and intangible assets.

62. Produced assets (AN.1) in the 1993 SNA include not only tangible fixed assets (AN.111), but also intangible fixed assets (AN.112) such as mineral exploration (AN.1121), computer software (AN.1122), and entertainment, literary or artistic originals (AN.1123).

63. Non-produced assets (AN.2) in the 1993 SNA also include tangible non-produced assets (AN.21) and intangible non-produced assets (AN.22). The tangible non-produced assets include land (AN.211), subsoil assets (AN.212), non-cultivated biological resources (AN.213) and water resources (AN.214). The intangible non-produced assets include patented entities (AN.221), leases and other transferable contracts (AN.222), purchased goodwill (AN.223) and other intangible non-produced assets (AN.229).

64. In determining the economic asset coverage of the 1993 SNA in the case of natural assets such as mineral reserves, forests, orchards, plantations and so on, the economic benefit criterion is considered to manifest itself in the form of control by an institutional unit. The 1993 SNA includes specific guidelines with regard to natural assets that are economic assets in the SNA sense. Two types are distinguished: i.e., assets whose growth is the result of human cultivation and are treated as produced assets (AN.1), and all other natural assets including land (AN.211), subsoil assets (AN.212), non-cultivated biological resources (AN.213) and water resources (AN.214) that are not cultivated but are under control of institutional units and are treated as non-produced assets (AN.2). The cultivated natural assets that are treated as produced assets (AN.1) are further broken down into two groups, i.e., (a) cultivated assets which are included in the classification under tangible fixed assets (AN.111) and cover livestock for breeding, dairy, draught, etc. (AN.11141) and vineyards, orchards and other plantations of trees yielding repeat products

(AN.11142); and (b) work-in-progress on natural growth products which is included in the classification under inventories (AN.12) as work-in-progress on cultivated assets (AN.1221) and includes the growth of products such as livestock for slaughter, timber, agricultural crops, and fruits that are the products of orchards and plantations.

65. The 1968 SNA did not include much guidance on the balance sheets of the system and consequently provided little information on the coverage of assets. In principle, however, the 1968 SNA included produced tangible and non-produced tangible and intangible assets within its asset boundary, but did not provide for the inclusion of produced intangible assets. As regards natural assets, the 1968 SNA included in principle natural assets in its asset boundary, although in a much less systematic manner. Only livestock growth was recorded as the addition to a produced asset (see paragraph 71 below), and agricultural crops and fruits from orchards and plantations were only recorded when harvested and, therefore, not reflected in additions to produced assets.

Extension of produced assets and gross fixed capital formation to include expenditure on mineral exploration, computer software and entertainment, literary or artistic originals
Reference: chapter X, paragraphs 10.33, and 10.96 to 10.101; chapter XXI, paragraph 21.68

66. The 1993 SNA treats expenditures on mineral exploration as gross fixed capital formation resulting in the creation of an intangible fixed asset (AN.1121) under produced assets. All expenditures are included, no matter whether the exploration is successful or not. The average service lives similar to those used by mining or oil corporations in their own assets are suggested as the appropriate guide for the amortization period. The 1968 SNA treated expenditures on mineral exploration as intermediate consumption.

67. The 1993 SNA treats systems and standard applications computer software that a producer expects to use in production for more than one year as an intangible fixed asset (AN.1122), no matter whether the computer software is purchased in the market—separately or together with the hardware—or developed in-house. It also includes databases which the enterprise expects to use for more than one year. The 1968 SNA was interpreted as treating expenditures on software which is bought as an integral part of a major hardware purchase as gross fixed capital formation, but software purchased or developed independently was treated as intermediate consumption.

68. The 1993 SNA includes in output literary or artistic works (i.e., the writing of books, composing music, etc.) which

are produced for sale whether they are produced by employees or by self-employed workers. Furthermore, it recognizes that these outputs can contribute to production in subsequent periods and, therefore, treats expenditures on these outputs as gross fixed capital formation resulting in the creation of an intangible fixed asset (AN.1123). Consequently, fees, commissions, royalties, etc. stemming from licensing others to make use of the works are treated as payments for services rendered. Accordingly, copyrights no longer appear as non-financial non-produced intangible assets giving rise to property income, as they did in the 1968 SNA.

69. Like the 1968 SNA, the 1993 SNA continues to treat expenditures on research and development as intermediate consumption, not gross fixed capital formation. However, it recommends that these expenditures be identified within intermediate consumption to facilitate the development of satellite accounts for research and development. Consequently, there are no produced fixed assets in the accounts to which the legal title of a patent can be linked. Thus, purchase/sale of patents continue to be treated, as in the 1968 SNA, as net purchases of intangible non-produced assets, where the assets to be recorded under "patented entities" (AN.221) are the patented inventions, discoveries or processes that are the result of research and development activity and not the legal titles themselves. It should be noted, however, that the 1993 SNA, by convention, does include licensing related services in output and, therefore, royalty and similar payments in respect of patent licences are considered payment for services and not property income as in the 1968 SNA. The same treatment is applied to payments for services of trademarks and franchising in respect of other non-produced intangible assets.

Extension of government gross fixed capital formation to include expenditure by the military on structures and equipment, except weapons
Reference: chapter X, paragraphs 10.71 to 10.74

70. The 1993 SNA treats as gross fixed capital formation all expenditures by the military on fixed assets of a kind that could be acquired by civilian users for purposes of production and that the military use in the same way; this would include airfields, docks, roads, hospitals and other buildings or structures. On the other hand, military weapons, and vehicles and equipment whose sole purpose is to launch or deliver such weapons, are not to be treated as gross fixed capital formation but as intermediate consumption. The 1968 SNA excluded from gross fixed capital formation almost all military expenditures except those on construction or alteration of family dwellings for personnel of the armed forces.

Treatment of cultivated natural growth as output
Reference: chapter X, paragraphs 10.89 to 10.94,
and 10.112 to 10.115

71. The 1993 SNA includes in output the growth of cultivated
assets including the growth of livestock and fishstock,
vineyards, orchards, plantations and timber tracts, as well
as the growth of agricultural crops and fruits which are
products of plantations and the like. Prior to the harvest or
use of the products, the growth of agricultural crops, livestock for slaughter, timber, etc., is to be recorded as work-
in-progress (part of changes in inventories). Cultivated
growth should be distinguished from growth of biological
resources, which are not cultivated but are under human
control (such as forests used in timber logging); such
growth is treated as other volume changes in the 1993 SNA.
Output based on controlled but not cultivated growth and
also output based on non-controlled natural assets (e.g.,
gathering of fuel wood, fruit gathering, hunting, etc.) continues to be recorded when the products are harvested. The
1968 SNA included in output (and subsequently in gross
fixed capital formation) only the natural growth of livestock and fishstock. Output of agricultural products, orchards and timber tracts was recorded only at the moment
of harvest.

Treatment of assets with a long production period as
changes in inventories (work-in-progress) until such time
as the owner is deemed to have taken ownership
Reference: chapter X, paragraphs 10.79 to 10.83;
and 10.87

72. The 1993 SNA clarifies that fixed assets with a long period of production should be recorded as gross fixed capital formation at the time when the ownership of the output produced is transferred to the eventual user of the asset. Output that is not transferred and continues to belong
to the builder or producing enterprise must be recorded
as either work-in-progress or as an addition to inventories of finished goods, depending on whether the asset is
finished or not. However, a user is deemed to assume
ownership of buildings and other structures prior to their
completion in two situations: under a contract for pur-
chase/sale agreed in advance, and own-account construction. In the case of large equipment goods, the
change of ownership does not occur until the users take
delivery of the goods. The 1968 SNA recommended that
fixed assets with a long production period should be recorded as gross fixed capital formation at the moment the
purchaser took legal possession of the assets.

Treatment of services output as work-in-progress
Reference: chapter VI, paragraph 6.77; chapter X,
paragraph 10.108

73. The 1993 SNA recognizes that certain kinds of services

take a long time to produce, e.g., architectural design,
software development, project development, writing of
books, etc. Work-in-progress in service industries is to
be recorded as change in inventories by the producers of
such services. The 1968 SNA did not include any work-
in-progress on services.

Extension of government inventories to include all goods
held in inventories
Reference: chapter VI, paragraph 6.106; annex to
chapter XIII

74. The 1993 SNA includes all goods held by the government
in inventories. This new treatment is symmetrical with the
treatment of goods stored by market producers. The 1968
SNA treated strategic materials, grains and other commodities of special importance to the nation as inventories;
in general, stores of other commodities were not included
in inventories.

Retain treatment of purchases of consumer durables as
final consumption expenditure but include stocks of
consumer durables as memoranda items in the balance
sheets
Reference: chapter XIII, paragraphs 13.85 and 13.86;
annex to chapter XIII

75. Like the 1968 SNA, the 1993 SNA treats expenditures by
households (excluding expenditures by unincorporated enterprises owned by households) on consumer durable
goods as final consumption. However, the 1993 SNA recognizes that information about stocks of consumer durables (defined as durable goods that are not used by households as stores of value or by unincorporated enterprises
owned by households for purposes of production), with detail by type of durable is of considerable interest and therefore should be presented as memoranda items to the balance sheets.

Gross fixed capital formation not resulting in a separate
identifiable produced asset is reflected as an increased
value of the produced or non-produced asset embodying it
Reference: chapter X, paragraphs 10.45 to 10.55

76. In the 1993 SNA not all gross fixed capital formation is reflected in a separate identifiable asset in the balance sheet.
In some instances there is not a one-to-one correspondence
between transactions in gross fixed capital formation by
type and fixed assets by type. Examples of such gross fixed
capital formation items include costs of ownership transfer
and major improvements to existing fixed assets, such as
buildings or computer software, or tangible non-produced
assets such as land, that increase their productive capacity,
extend their service lives or both. The relation between the
classification of changes in assets and assets was not explicitly dealt with in the 1968 SNA.

77. Consumption of fixed capital related to these capital formation elements is treated as an integral part of consumption of fixed capital of the produced assets to which these expenditures are applied. As in the case of other consumption of fixed capital, it is calculated over the life time of the asset to which the expenditures relate. By convention the consumption of fixed capital also includes the writing off of the elements of gross fixed capital formation that add to the value of non-produced assets.

Extension of capital formation to include expenditures on valuables
Reference: chapter X, paragraphs 10.7 and 10.122 and 10.123; chapter XII, paragraphs 12.22 and 12.23; annex to chapter XIII

78. The 1993 SNA includes a third category of capital formation called "acquisitions less disposals of valuables" (P.53), covering expenditures on produced assets that are not used primarily for production or consumption, but acquired and held as stores of value. Examples of valuables are precious metals (non-monetary gold if used as store of value) and stones, antiques and other art objects. When a valuable which was previously not included in the balance sheet of any sector becomes an economic asset in the 1993 SNA sense (see paragraph 61 to 65 above), it enters the balance sheet of the sector in question through the account for other volume changes (economic appearance of produced assets). The 1968 SNA treated these acquisitions less disposals in various ways. In the case of households they were dealt with as final consumption expenditure.

Treatment of historical monuments as produced assets
Reference: chapter X, paragraph 10.85; chapter XII, paragraphs 12.22 to 12.24; chapter XIII, paragraph 13.37

79. Historical monuments—which may include old as well as new historical monuments—are treated in the 1993 SNA as produced assets. They are not separately classified but included as part of the categories of produced assets that refer to dwellings (AN.1111) and other (non residential) buildings and structures (AN.1112). Sales and purchases of historical monuments are treated as positive gross fixed capital formation of the purchasing sector and as negative capital formation of the sector selling the asset. When a historical monument which was previously not included in the balance sheet of any sector becomes an economic asset in the 1993 SNA sense (see paragraphs 61 to 65 above), it enters the balance sheet of the sector in question through the other changes in the volume of assets account (economic appearance of produced assets). The 1968 SNA did not specifically deal with the treatment of historical monuments.

Treatment of fixed assets resulting from community activities as output of household production activities and as gross fixed capital formation of the sector responsible for their upkeep
Reference: chapter X, paragraph 10.85

80. The 1993 SNA treats construction activities carried out collectively by groups of volunteers as production carried out by the households involved. The fixed assets produced in this way are recorded as output and gross fixed capital formation of households first and then they are allocated to the balance sheet of the sector responsible for their upkeep (non-profit institutions serving households or government). The allocation is accomplished by making a capital transfer which involves a negative gross fixed capital formation of households and a positive gross fixed capital formation of the sectors non-profit institutions serving households or general government. While the 1968 SNA also treated the output as gross fixed capital formation, it did not provide explicit guidance on the sector to which such gross capital formation should be allocated.

Extension of consumption of fixed capital to assets such as roads, dams and breakwaters
Reference: chapter X, paragraph 10.78

81. The 1968 SNA suggested that consumption of fixed capital need not be calculated in respect of such assets as roads, dams and breakwaters because it was assumed that the maintenance and repair performed on these assets was sufficient to ensure that these assets had infinite service lives. In practice, most assets of this kind have finite lives even though proper repair and maintenance may result in long lifespans. For this reason, the 1993 SNA recommends that consumption of fixed capital should be calculated for assets such as roads, dams and breakwaters.

7. Further refinement of the treatment and definition of financial instruments and assets

Description of a broad range of financial assets and distinction between actual and contingent assets
Reference: chapter XI, paragraphs 11.16 to 11.19 and 11.25 to 11.28

82. The 1993 SNA includes a more precise and elaborate description of a broad range of financial assets and distinguishes them from non-financial assets and from financial "contingent positions". The distinction between a financial liability and a contingent liability is made on the basis of the conditionality of the relationship between the transactors. Where an unconditional relationship exists on the part of both debtor and creditor, there exists an actual financial asset and liability. Thus, bankers' acceptances are classified as actual assets but letters of credit are not. The 1968 SNA had limited descriptions

of financial assets and therefore also did not deal with contingent positions.

Distinction between monetary and non-monetary gold
Reference: chapter XI, paragraphs 11.63 to 11.66

83. The 1968 SNA recognized two kinds of gold: (a) gold held as a financial asset, including gold owned by the monetary authorities which was not separately identified; and (b) other gold used for industrial purposes. The 1993 SNA distinguishes three types of gold: (a) monetary gold owned by the monetary authorities as a component of international reserves; (b) gold held as a store of value; and (c) other gold used for industrial purposes. The last two types of gold may be owned by any kind of institutional unit or sector. Items of gold jewellery of relatively small value purchased by households are not treated as assets, but as part of household consumption expenditure. As was noted in paragraph 78 above, gold purchased as a store of value is treated as a valuable and included in gross capital formation.

Less emphasis on the distinction between different types of deposits
Reference: chapter XI, paragraphs 11.69 to 11.73

84. The 1968 SNA included a distinction between "currency and transferable deposits" and "other deposits". However, in view of the emphasis placed on broad money as opposed to narrow money, the 1993 SNA includes only the total of "currency and deposits" (AF.2) in the first level of classification of financial assets while suggesting that sub-elements should be compiled only if they are analytically useful.

Less emphasis on the short- versus long-term distinction with regard to loans and other financial assets
Reference: chapter XI, paragraphs 11.72 to 11.84

85. The 1968 SNA short-term/long-term maturity distinction has become less relevant because of the improved facilities available in financial markets to re-finance short-term financial assets. Therefore, the 1993 SNA retains this distinction but only as a secondary classification criterion.

Changes to the treatment of insurance
Reference: chapter VI, paragraphs 6.135 to 6.141; chapter VIII, paragraphs 8.69, 8.70, and 8.85 to 8.89; chapter XI, paragraphs 11.89 to 11.99; annex IV

86. The 1993 SNA has replaced the 1968 term "casualty insurance" by the term "non-life insurance".

87. The basis of measuring the output of insurance has been changed. Income from the investment of insurance technical reserves is now taken into account when measuring the value of the services provided to policyholders. The income is distributed to policyholders as a property income flow, "property income attributed to insurance policyholders (D.44)" and repaid to the insurance corporations as premium supplements. This treatment applies to both life and non-life insurance.

88. In the 1968 SNA non-life premiums and claims were recorded when payable. In the 1993 SNA non-life premiums are recorded on the basis of premiums earned and non-life claims on a claims due basis. The differences between premiums payable and earned and claims due and payable are included in a new financial asset, "Prepayments of premiums and reserves against outstanding claims (AF.62)".

Distinction between financial leasing and operating leasing
Reference: chapter VI, paragraphs 6.123 to 6.127; chapter VII, paragraph 7.109; chapter X, paragraph 10.44; chapter XI, paragraph 11.31; chapter XIII, paragraphs 13.23 and 13.24

89. The 1993 SNA recognizes financial leases as financial instruments. Financial leases are distinguished from operating leases in that the former cover leases where the intention is to transfer all risks and rewards incident to ownership to the user of the asset. Assets acquired under financial leasing arrangements are to be treated as assets of the lessees, and the lessors hold a corresponding financial asset which is the equivalent of a loan. Lease payments under financial leases must be divided between interest payments recorded under current transactions and repayment of the loan recorded in the financial account. The 1968 SNA did not recognize financial leases and, as a consequence, treated them in the same manner as operating leases.

Identification of new financial instruments: repurchase agreements, derivatives and secondary instruments, deep discounted bonds
Reference: chapter XI, paragraphs 11.32 to 11.43

90. The 1993 SNA identifies and provides descriptions of a number of new financial instruments which were not treated explicitly in the 1968 SNA, including repurchase agreements, derivatives and secondary instruments and deep discounted bonds.

91. Repurchase agreements include the simultaneous sale of securities with the agreement to repurchase those same securities at a later date; they are regarded as financial instruments that are similar to loans secured by securities.

92. The 1993 SNA recommends that the difference between the issue price and the value at maturity of zero-coupon and other deep-discounted bonds should be treated as interest and that this interest should be converted into a series of annual or quarterly payments over the full lifetime of the instruments. Deep discounted bonds were not dealt with explicitly in the 1968 SNA.

8. Harmonization between concepts and classifications of the 1993 SNA and the fifth edition of the *Balance of Payments Manual*

Centre of economic interest as basic criterion for determining residence or non-residence of entities and one-year rule as operational guideline
Reference: chapter XIV, paragraphs 14.12 to 14.34

93. The 1993 SNA and the fifth edition of the BPM use the "centre of economic interest" as the basic criterion for determining whether or not an entity is a resident. The 1993 SNA specifies that an institutional unit be normally deemed to have a centre of economic interest if it has already engaged in economic activities and transactions in the country for one year or more or if it intends to do so for one year or more. However, the 1993 SNA emphasizes that one year is suggested only as a guideline and not an inflexible rule.

94. With regard to the residence of individuals, the 1993 SNA, as well as the fifth edition of the BPM, recommends that students should be treated as residents of the country from which they originate however long they study abroad, provided they maintain an economic attachment with their country of origin. The rationale behind this change from the 1968 SNA is that most students studying abroad return to their country of origin upon completion of their studies. With regard to the residence of individuals working abroad under long-term contracts and of technical assistance personnel, the 1993 SNA recommends no changes, in principle, from the 1968 SNA, but introduces a number of clarifications. In particular, it specifies that technical assistance personnel under bilateral agreements are regarded as residents of the country where they are working if they are staying for more than one year. This treatment is consistent with the treatment of personnel operating in the commercial sector and through international organizations. The fifth edition of BPM, follows the same treatment as the 1993 SNA as concerns technical assistance personnel, constituting a change from the fourth edition.

95. With regard to the residence of enterprises, the 1993 SNA recommends little change from the 1968 SNA, except in the treatment of installation services and of enterprises engaged in construction. The 1993 SNA recommends flexible application of the one-year rule as a guideline in both instances. Enterprises engaged in installing equipment abroad are considered residents of their home country even if the installation takes more than one year to complete. As for enterprises (or site offices) engaged in construction, criteria in addition to the one-year rule are introduced to help determine their residence. Included are such factors as whether or not there are separate sets of accounts maintained, payment of taxes, substantial physical presence, etc. The fifth edition of BPM follows the same treatment.

Goods exported or imported for processing and re-imported or re-exported thereafter are recorded gross
Reference: chapter XIV, paragraphs 14.61 to 14.64

96. The fifth edition of the BPM as well as the 1993 SNA recommend that goods that are sent abroad for processing and later on re-imported should be recorded gross by the processing economy as well as by the economy that sent the goods for processing, if the processing involves a substantial physical change in the goods. The value of the good before and after processing should be shown as part of the trade in goods. This recommendation does not entail any change for the 1993 SNA from the 1968 SNA but does constitute a change between the fourth and fifth edition of the BPM. However, the BPM, while agreeing in concept, recommends on practical grounds that all processing transactions be recorded under goods on a gross basis.

Distinction between the treatment of investment goods exported/imported for repair
Reference: chapter XIV, paragraph 14.91

97. The 1993 SNA as well as the fifth edition of the BPM make a distinction between repairs performed on investment goods and repairs performed on other goods. The value of repairs on investment goods should be shown as part of trade in goods while other repairs should be classified as service items. The 1968 SNA did not make this distinction. The BPM, on practical grounds, however, includes the value of all repairs as part of trade in goods.

Refinement of the classification of international transactions in services in order to identify separately services, income flows, transfers
Reference: chapter XIV, paragraphs 14.94 to 14.124

98. The fifth edition of the BPM, includes an expanded classification of international transactions in services, including financial and communication services. This BPM classification of services is compatible with the distinction made in the SNA between services on the one hand and income and transfer flows on the other. The details of the expanded classification are generally consistent with the CPC, which is the product classification used in the SNA. This implies no change in the SNA, but does constitute a change between the fourth and fifth edition of the BPM.

Valuation of total imports of goods f.o.b. values and imports by product groups in c.i.f. values
Reference: chapter XIV, paragraphs 14.36 to 14.43

99. The 1993 SNA, in conformity with the fifth edition of the BPM, values total imports of goods on an f.o.b. basis, i.e., excluding the cost of insurance and freight after the goods have left the frontier of the exporting country. Thus, the 1993 SNA includes the transport and insurance services provided by non-residents after the goods have left the

frontier as imports of services. Since, as a rule, for the detailed analysis of imports of goods in supply and use and input-output tables it is not possible to obtain f.o.b. values for each category of imported goods, a global adjustment has to be made in the supply and disposition estimates in order to adjust the c.i.f. total of imports to a f.o.b. valuation. The 1968 SNA always valued imports of goods in c.i.f. values, i.e., including the cost of insurance and freight services provided by residents or non-residents. Consequently, the 1968 SNA did not record the transport and insurance services provided by non-residents on imported goods as imports of services, and imputed an export of services corresponding to transport and insurance services provided by residents on imported goods. These two distortions have disappeared in the 1993 SNA.

Sole use of the national concept of final consumption (expenditure)
Reference: chapter IX, paragraphs 9.70 and 9.71

100. The 1993 SNA no longer makes a distinction between final consumption on a domestic and national basis. As a consequence, in principle it would no longer separately identify direct purchases in the domestic market by non-resident households which are exports of goods and services and resident households expenditures abroad which are imports of goods and services within the classification of international transactions in services as did the 1968 SNA. Nevertheless, as these direct purchases cannot readily be identified as specific types of goods and services, they remain treated as separate adjustment items in the supply and use table or input-output tables which comprise various types of goods and services that are lumped together as "travel" in the BPM. The 1968 SNA showed private final consumption expenditure as derived from final consumption of households in the domestic market first, and then adjusted it to a national basis by deducting direct purchases in the domestic market by non-resident households and adding resident household expenditures abroad.

Separate identification of direct foreign investments and the recording of reinvested earnings on direct foreign investment
Reference: chapter VII, paragraphs 7.122 to 7.125; chapter XI, paragraph 11.101; chapter XIII, paragraph 13.87; chapter XIV, paragraphs 14.123 and 14.151 to 14.154

101. The 1993 SNA recommends that the total and major subcomponents of direct investment be shown as a memorandum item to the relevant financial instruments in the financial account and in the balance sheet.

102. The 1993 SNA, in conformity with the fifth edition of the *Balance of Payments Manual*, includes the international flows of reinvested earnings attributable to direct investors (D.43) as part of the property income flow (D.4) in the ex-

ternal and corresponding domestic sector accounts. A contra-entry, equal and with opposite sign, is included in the financial account, under the item called "shares and other equity" (AF.5). Direct investment is defined as in the fifth edition of the *Balance of Payments Manual* and in the OECD *Detailed Benchmark Definition of Foreign Direct Investment*.

Treatment of write-off of bad debts and expropriation of property without compensation as other changes in volume of assets
Reference: chapter XII, paragraphs 12.37 to 12.39; and 12.50

103. The 1993 SNA, in conformity with the fifth edition of the BPM, treats the write-off of bad debt and expropriation of property without compensation as "other volume changes". These actions affect outstanding claims in the balance sheets but they are not transactions to be included in the capital and financial accounts. In contrast, when the cancellation of a debt involves a voluntary, contractual arrangement (debt forgiveness) between the parties concerned, it is considered a financial transaction and the offsetting entry to the reduction in debt should be treated as a capital transfer. The 1968 SNA treated the write-off of bad debts, etc. as transactions recorded in the second part of the capital finance account with an offsetting entry reflected under current transfers.

Recording of reclassification of commodity gold to monetary gold and vice versa and the allocation/ cancellation of SDRs as other changes in volume of assets
Reference: chapter XI, paragraphs 11.63 to 11.68; chapter XII, paragraph 12.59

104. The 1993 SNA treats gold monetization/demonetization in the same way as the fifth edition of BPM, that is, as entries in the other changes in the Volume of Assets Account. The 1968 SNA treated these transactions as exports and imports in the merchandise trade account and did not deal with SDRs because, at that time, SDRs were not in existence. The fifth edition of the BPM incorporates the same treatment as the 1993 SNA, in contrast to the inclusion of monetization/demonetization of gold and the allocation and cancellation of SDRs among balance of payments transactions in the fourth edition.

Incorporation of explicit guidelines for exchange rate conversion
Reference: chapter XIV, paragraphs 14.77 to 14.84

105. According to both the 1993 SNA and the fifth edition of the *Balance of Payments Manual*, the exchange rate to be used for conversion from one currency into another is the rate prevailing at the transaction date, or if that is not available, the average rate for the shortest period applicable.

The midpoint between buying and selling rates should be used, and the difference between that rate and the buying or selling rate is to be classified as a financial auxiliary service charge. In the case of multiple exchange rates that are the result of official exchange rate policies, the net proceeds accruing to the authorities as a result of transactions involving these multiple rates should be treated as implicit taxes or subsidies. These taxes or subsidies are calculated for each transaction as the difference between the value of the transaction at the actual exchange rate and a "unitary rate" which is calculated as the weighted average of all transactions in the external account. The implicit taxes appear as global adjustments in the external accounts with counterpart items in the central bank or government accounts. The 1968 SNA did not provide any explicit guidelines for conversion of transactions and/or treatment of revenues obtained from the spread between buying and selling rates of foreign currency nor for the case of multiple exchange rates.

9. Price and volume measures and introduction of real income measures

Introduction of new concept of real national disposable income into the System
Reference: chapter XVI, paragraphs 16.151 to 16.161

106. The 1993 SNA incorporates the calculation of trading gains and losses from changes in the terms of trade as an integral part of the System. These gains and losses are added to GDP at constant prices to derive real GDP. In the calculation of gains and losses from changes in the terms of trade, the 1993 SNA suggests that, if there is uncertainty about what numeraire index to select to deflate the current trade balance, the arithmetic average of price indexes for exports and imports should be used.

107. The 1993 SNA includes net national disposable income in real terms and derives it sequentially from GDP in constant prices in two alternative ways. The recommended method is to calculate, first, real GDP as described above and then calculate real net national disposable income by using the price deflator for gross national final expenditures (final consumption expenditure plus gross capital formation) to convert net primary incomes and current transfers from abroad to real terms. However, the System recognizes that there is no unique way of defining income aggregates in real terms and, therefore, suggests an alternative method of deflation where all net current receipts from abroad including exports minus imports, primary incomes and current transfers are deflated by a single deflator, i.e., the implicit deflator for net national final expenditures.

Retain nominal interest as the SNA concept
Reference: chapter VII, paragraphs 7.109 to 7.111; chapter XII, paragraphs 12.77 to 12.81

108. The 1993 SNA, as did the 1968 SNA, measures interest flows in the allocation of primary income account of the System in nominal terms. However, as the revaluation accounts present holding gains/losses on all assets and liabilities that are denominated in monetary terms and make a distinction between nominal, neutral and real holding gains/losses, users can adjust nominal interest flows to arrive at real interest flows. (An annex to chapter XIX includes a parallel treatment of interest under significant inflation.)

Price and volume measurements
Reference: chapter XVI, paragraphs 16.14 to 16.59

109. The 1993 SNA is more flexible with regard to the choice of index number to calculate price and volume measures for GDP and other aggregates. The best single measure of changes in the volume of GDP is considered to be an annual volume chain index for GDP which can also be used to generate value series by extrapolating GDP in the base year. However, chain indices do not generate series for interrelated aggregates that are additively consistent, and it is, therefore, recommended that Laspeyres volume indices on a fixed base year should also be calculated so that additive time series of values at the constant prices of the base year can also be shown. Such Laspeyres volume indices have nevertheless to be rebased every five years or so, and at least every ten years. The 1968 SNA did not recommend the use of chain indices.

International comparisons of prices and volumes
Reference: chapter XVI, paragraphs 16.82 to 16.84

110. The 1993 SNA recommends that comparisons of the volume of GDP, or GDP per capita, between countries should be based on international volume indices that use the same kinds of methodology as intertemporal price and volume measures. For this purpose, currencies have to be converted at purchasing power parities (PPPs). However, it is recognized that it is more difficult to make reliable price comparisons between countries than between time periods in the same country, and that the construction of a set of transitive multilateral volume indices for a group of countries may create further problems. The 1968 SNA did not consider the use of PPPs to make international comparisons.

The treatment of quality differences
Reference: chapter XVI, paragraphs 16.105 to 16.117

111. The 1993 SNA recommends that most goods or services that are sold at different prices should be treated as different products or, at least, different qualities of the same product when compiling price indices. However, when purchasers are not free to choose because of rationing, lack of information or price discrimination, identical products sold at different prices must be recognized as having the same quality and their prices must be averaged to obtain a single price relative in calculating price indexes.

Use of representative structures in compiling price indices for unique products
Reference: chapter XVI, paragraph 16.125

112. The 1993 SNA recommends that price indexes for unique structures should be based on a limited number of representative structures that should be selected and carefully defined. Experts in the field are then requested to make estimates of what it would cost to build these structures in successive years. The 1968 SNA did not include any guidance on the calculation of price indices for unique products.

Measurement of the real output of non-market services should be based whenever possible on output indicators
Reference: chapter XVI, paragraphs 16.133 to 16.141

113. The 1993 SNA stresses that valuing the output of non-market producers as the sum of costs does not mean that their output cannot be distinguished from the inputs used to produce them. Volume movements for non-market output should therefore be based on output and not input indicators, whenever possible. Adjustments should also be made for changes in quality. The 1968 SNA gave very little guidance on the measurement of the real output of these non-market services.

Annex II

Relationship of the rest of the world account to the balance of payments accounts and the international investment position

1. Introduction

1. The balance of payments accounts and related data on the international investment position (stocks of external financial assets and liabilities) are closely linked to the overall System of National Accounts. This linkage is reinforced by the fact that, in most countries, data on the balance of payments and international investment position are compiled first, and subsequently incorporated in relevant external account components of the rest of the world account of the System. There is virtually complete concordance between the SNA and the *Balance of Payments Manual* (the *Manual*) with respect to such issues as the delineation of resident units (either producers or consumers), valuation of transactions and of the stock of external assets and liabilities, time of recording of transactions, conversion procedures, coverage of international transactions in goods and services, income flows, current transfers, capital transfers, foreign financial assets and liabilities, and coverage of the international investment position. There are, however, differences in classification or level of detail in the rest of the world account and the *Manual*. These reflect, *inter alia*, differences in analytical requirements and the need, in the SNA, to adopt a uniform classification scheme for all sectors of the economy. The bulk of the discussion in this annex will focus on the relationship between aggregates and details contained in the rest of the world account and corresponding items in the Manual.

2. Resident units

2. The SNA and the *Manual* identify resident producers and consumers in an identical fashion. In the *Manual*, chapter IV on residence is entirely consistent with chapter XIV of the SNA. Both systems identify resident units by invoking the concept of the centre of economic interest and the definition of economic territory. (These definitions are elaborated in earlier chapters.)

3. Valuation

3. The SNA and the *Manual* use market price as the primary basis of valuation. In transaction accounts, market price valuation refers to the actual price agreed upon by transactors (i.e., the amount that a willing buyer pays to acquire something from a willing seller when the exchange is one between independent parties and one into which nothing but commercial considerations enter). Chapter V of the *Manual* notes the need to apply market price proxies or equivalents in situations in which a market price in its literal sense cannot be determined (e.g., the possible case of transfer pricing that significantly distorts measurement in resource transfers between affiliated enterprises, barter transactions, grants in kind, etc.). In balance sheet accounts affecting external claims and liabilities, both systems advocate the use of end-of-period market (current) prices or proxies thereof.

4. Time of recording

4. In the SNA and the balance of payments, the "time of recording" for transactions is the same as that for accrual accounting (i.e., when economic value is created, transformed, exchanged, transferred, or extinguished). Claims and liabilities are deemed to arise when there is a change in ownership. Both systems essentially adopt an identical application of the accrual basis in the case of specific categories of transactions. Thus, for example, exports and imports of goods are, in principle, recorded on a change of ownership basis, although in both systems specific exceptions are noted with regard to goods under financial lease, goods shipped between affiliated enterprises, goods for processing, and goods underlying merchanting transactions. Services are recorded when actually rendered—a time that often coincides with the time at which the service is produced. Interest is recorded on an accrual basis; dividends are recorded as of the date they are payable. Reinvested earnings on direct investment are recorded in the period in which the earnings are generated. Transfers—taxes, fines, etc.—that are imposed by one party on another are recorded as of the date of occurrence of the transaction that gives rise to the liability to pay; other transfers are recorded at the time that the resources to which they are offsets change ownership. Transactions in financial claims and liabilities are recorded on a change of ownership basis (i.e., when both the creditor and debtor enter the claim and liability, respectively, on their books). Chapter VI of the *Manual* provides a full discussion of the application of the accrual basis underlying the balance of payments accounts.

5. Conversion procedures

5. Both systems employ consistent procedures for converting transactions denominated in a variety of currencies or units of account into the unit of account (usually the national currency) adopted for compiling the balance of payments statement or the national accounts. Under a single exchange rate system, the SNA and the *Manual* suggest the use of the market exchange rate prevailing at the time the transaction takes place. This rate is defined as the midpoint between buying and selling rates applicable to the transaction or, alternatively, the average rate for the shortest period applicable. When parallel markets are in existence, the appropriate conversion rate is the rate (i.e., midpoint spot rate) applying to foreign currencies purchased/sold in respective parallel markets.

6. A system of multiple official exchange rates gives rise to implicit taxes and subsidies. The SNA recommends that transactions be converted at the actual (multiple) rates applicable but that global adjustments—reflecting the amount of taxes or subsidies—be shown in the rest of the world account and counterpart entries be made under capital transfers. Taxes and subsidies are calculated as the difference between the values of transactions at the actual multiple rates applicable to specific transactions and their values at a unitary rate, which is calculated as a weighted average of all official rates used for external transactions. When multiple rates exist, the *Manual* suggests using either a unitary rate or a principal rate, that is, the actual (multiple) exchange rate that applies to the largest part of external transactions.

7. As far as balance sheet items (stocks of external financial assets and liabilities) are concerned, both systems suggest the use, for conversion, of actual market exchange rates applicable to specific assets and liabilities on the date to which the balance sheet relates.

6. Classification and linkages

8. Although harmonization—in terms of the coverage of major aggregates—has been attained between both systems, differences in levels of detail reflect differences in analytical requirements, the relative quantitative significance of some items in international transactions, and constraints imposed by the internal structures of the respective systems. Nonetheless, bridges can be constructed to derive relevant national accounting flows and stocks from balance of payments accounts and the international investment position.

9. In terms of transactions, the SNA distinguishes the following accounts in respect of the rest of the world account (external transactions account): V.I: External account of goods and services; V.II: External account of primary incomes and current transfers; V.III.1: Capital account, and V.III.2: Financial account, which are components of V.III: External accumulation accounts. In the *Manual*, the transactions reflected in Accounts V.I and V.II are contained in the current account component of the balance of payments accounts, while those reflected in Account V.III.1 are contained in the capital account component of the capital and financial account of the balance of payments. The flows reflected in V.III.2 are shown in the financial account component of the capital and financial account. Account V.III.3.1: Other changes in volume of assets, and Account V.III.3.2: Revaluation account, are contained as separate subdivisions of the international investment position statement in the *Manual*. Thus, account V.III.3.1 corresponds to the column for other adjustments in the international investment position, while Account V.III.3.2 corresponds to the columns for valuation changes (i.e., price changes and exchange rate changes) in the international investment position. Account V.IV: External assets and liabilities account, of the SNA is equivalent to the international investment position in the *Manual*; the international investment position is that part of the national wealth statement representing the stock of external financial assets and liabilities. Tables A.II.1 to A.II.6 in this annex provide a reconciliation between the categories shown in relevant external accounts of the SNA and corresponding items in balance of payments accounts and the international investment position. Tables A.II.7 to A.II.9 in this annex refer to the classification scheme underlying balance of payments accounts and the international investment position statement as they are reflected in the *Manual*. Items denoted with an asterisk[*] are identified as additional details needed to permit the derivation of relevant national accounting flows from balance of payments and international investment position data.

10. As indicated in table A.II.1, SNA coverage of exports and imports of goods and exports and imports of services is identical to coverage of corresponding items in the balance of payments with the exception of the item "financial intermediation charge indirectly measured". In the *Manual* this service charge is included, under investment income, as an indistinguishable part of interest income. Also in the *Manual* exports and imports of services are disaggregated in considerable detail to meet analytical and policy needs for such data—particularly in the context of international negotiations in international trade in services within the framework of the General Agreement on Tariffs and Trade (GATT). The categories of services identified in the balance of payments are consistent with the Central Product Classification (CPC) except for the items travel and government transactions, n.i.e., which have no counterparts in the CPC.

11. As for the external account for primary incomes and current transfers, the relevant transactions are shown under the categories 1.B (income) and 1.C (current transfers), in the balance of payments. The coverage of compensation of employees and property income in account V.II is virtually identical with item 1.B (income) of the *Manual*, except that the latter includes "financial intermediation charge indirectly measured" indistinguishably under investment income (interest). This treatment in the *Manual* is predicated on grounds of the practical difficulties inherent in deriving a multiplicity of "reference" rates of interest and appropriate asset/liability positions by sector, instrument, currency, and term structure in order to derive estimates of the imputed financial intermediary service charge.

12. The major elements of the SNA capital account of the external accumulation accounts (Account V.III.1) are identical with the capital account component of the capital and financial account of the balance of payments. Although the balancing item, net lending/net borrowing, in the capital account of the SNA is not explicitly identified in the balance of payments, it nonetheless can be derived by adding the current account balance and the balance of transactions reflected in the capital account of the *Manual*.

13. Coverage of the SNA financial account (Account V.III.2) is identical with the coverage of the financial account of the capital and financial account in the balance of payments (table A.II.4 of this annex), although the level of detail is different. In the SNA, financial assets are classified primarily by type of instrument. In the *Manual*, financial items are classified primarily by function (i.e., direct investment, portfolio investment, other investment—including loans—and reserve assets). In addition to identifying types of financial instruments (insurance technical reserves being an exception), the *Manual* includes an abbreviated sector breakdown (i.e., monetary authorities, general government, banks, and other sectors) to furnish links with other bodies of economic and financial statistics (e.g., money and banking, government finance, international banking, and external debt). Furthermore, to conform with the SNA, the *Manual* states that entries in the financial account of the balance of payments are recorded, in principle, on a net basis (i.e., increases less decreases in assets or liabilities). However, gross recording is provided as supplementary information (e.g., in the case of drawings and repayments on long-term loans).

Tables. Reconciliation of the rest of the world account with the balance of payments accounts

Table A.II.1. Account V.I External account of goods and services

SNA categories		Correspond to	Balance of payments standard components (items), additional details, and aggregates
Uses			**Credit**
P.6	Exports of goods and services		Item 1.A.a and 1.A.b.1-11, as noted below
P.61	Exports of goods		Item 1.A.a goods
P.62	Exports of services		Sum of items 1.A.b.1-11 services plus items 1.B.2.2.2.1.1 and 1.B.2.3.1 financial intermediation charge indirectly measured.
Resources			**Debit**
P.7	Imports of goods and services		Items 1.A.a and 1.A.b.1-11, as noted below
P.71	Imports of goods		Item 1.A.a goods
P.72	Imports of services		Sum of items 1.a.b.1-11 services plus items 1.B.2.2.2.1.1 and 1.B.2.3.1 financial intermediation charge indirectly measured.
B.11	*External balance of goods and services*		Item 1.A

Table A.II.2. Account V.II: External account of primary incomes and current transfers

SNA categories		Correspond to	Balance of payments standard components (items), additional details, and aggregates
Uses			**Credit**
D.1	Compensation of employees		Item 1.B.1 compensation of employees
D.29	Other taxes on production		Item 1.C.1.2 other taxes on production
D.39	Other subsidies on production		Item 1.C.1.3 other subsidies on production
D.4	Property income		Item 1.B.2 investment income minus items 1.B.2.2.2.1.1 and 1.B.2.3.1 financial intermediation charge indirectly measured.
D.5	Current taxes on income, wealth, etc.		Item 1.C.1.1 current taxes on income, wealth, etc.
D.61	Social contributions		Item 1.C.1.4 social contribution
D.62	Social benefits		Item 1.C.2.2.5 social benefits
D.7	Other current transfers		Item 1.C.2.1 workers' remittances plus item 1.C.1.6 other current transfers of general government plus item 1.C.2.2.6 other current transfers of other sectors.
D.8	Adjustment for the change in net equity of households in pension funds*		
Resources			**Debit**
D.1	Compensation of employees		Item 1.B.1 compensation of employees
D.29	Other taxes on production		Item 1.C.2.2.2 other taxes on production
D.39	Other subsidies on production		Item 1.C.2.2.3 other subsidies on production
D.4	Property income		Item 1.B.2 investment income minus items 1.B.2.2.2.1.1 and 1.B.2.3.1 financial intermediation charge indirectly measured.
D.5	Current taxes on income, wealth, etc.		Item 1.C.2.2.1 current taxes on income, wealth etc.
D.61	Social contributions		Item 1.C.2.2.4 social contributions
D.62	Social benefits		Item 1.C.1.5 social benefits
D.7	Other current transfers		Item 1.C.2.1 workers' remittances plus item 1.C.1.6 other current transfers of general government plus item 1.C.2.2.6 other current transfers of other sectors.
B.12	*Current external balance*		Item 1. current account

*Item D.8 is not included in the current account in the balance of payments, nor are the receipts of pensions from, or net contributions to, (funded) pension funds.

Table A. II.3. Account V.III.1: Capital account (of Account V.III: External accumulation accounts)

SNA categories		Correspond to	Balance of payment standard components (items), additional details, and aggregates
Changes in assets			Transactions in assets
K.2	Acquisitions less disposals of non-produced non-financial assets		Item 2.A.2 acquisition/disposal of non-produced non-financial assets
B.9	*Net lending (+)/net borrowing (-)*		Item 1. current account balance plus item 2.A capital account balance
Changes in liabilities and net worth			Transactions in liabilities
B.12	*Current external balance*		Item 1. current account
D.9	Capital transfers receivable		Item 2.A.1 capital transfers
D.9	Capital transfers payable		Item 2.A.1 capital transfers
B.10.1	*Changes in net worth due to saving and net capital transfers*		Item 1. current account balance plus item 2.A.1 net capital transfers

Table A.II.4. Account V.III.2: Financial account (of Account V.III: External accumulation accounts)

SNA categories	Correspond to	Balance of payments standard components (items), additional details, and aggregates
Changes in assets		Transactions in assets
F.1 Monetary gold and SDRs		Sum of items 2.B.4.1 monetary gold and 2.B.4.2 special drawing rights
F.2 Currency and deposits		Sum of items 2.B.3.1.3 currency and deposits (part of other investment) and 2.B.4.3.1 deposits (part of reserve position in the Fund), 2.B.4.4.1 currency and deposits (part of foreign exchange), and 2.B.4.5.1 currency and deposits (part of other reserve claims)
F.3 Securities other than shares		Sum of items 2.B.2.1.2 debt securities (part of portfolio investment), 2.B.4.4.2.2 bonds and notes (part of foreign exchange), 2.B.4.4.2.3 money market instruments and financial derivatives (part of foreign exchange), 2.B.4.5.2.2 debt securities (part of other reserve claims), 2.B.1.2.3.1.1 debt securities issued by direct investors (part of direct investment in the reporting economy), and 2.B.1.1.3.1.1 debt securities issued by affiliated enterprises (part of direct investment abroad)
F.4 Loans		Sum of items 2.B.3.1.2 loans (part of other investment) and 2.B.4.3.2 loans (part of reserve position in the Fund)
F.5 Shares and other equity		Sum of items 2.B.1.1.1.1 equity capital: claims on affiliated enterprises (part of direct investment abroad), 2.B.1.1.2 reinvested earnings (part of direct investment abroad), 2.B.1.2.1.1 equity capital: claims on direct investors (part of direct investment in the reporting economy), 2.B.2.1.1 equity securities (part of portfolio investment), and 2.B.4.4.2.1 and 2.B.4.5.2.1 equities (part of reserve assets, foreign exchange, and other claims)
F.6 Insurance technical reserves		Sum of items 2.B.3.1.4.4.1.1 net equity of households in life insurance reserves and in pension funds and 2.B.3.1.4.1.1.1, 2.B.3.1.4.2.1.1, 2.B.3.1.4.3.1.1, and 2.B.3.1.4.4.1.2 prepayments of premiums and reserves against outstanding claims (all part of other investment)
F.7 Other accounts receivable		Sum of items 2.B.1.1.3.1.2 other claims on affiliated enterprises (part of direct investment abroad), 2.B.1.2.3.1.2 other claims on direct investors (part of direct investment in the reporting economy), 2.B.3.1.1 trade credits (part of other investment) and 2.B.3.1.4, other assets minus items 2.B.3.1.4.4.1.1, net equity of households in life insurance reserves and in pension funds, and 2.B.3.1.4.1.1.1, 2.B.3.1.4.2.1.1, 2.B.3.1.4.2.1.1, 2.B.3.1.4.3.1.1, and 2.B.3.1.4.4.1.2 prepayments of premiums and reserves against outstanding claims (all part of other investment)

Table A.II.4. Account V.III.2: Financial account (of Account V.III: External accumulation accounts) (*cont.*)

SNA categories		Correspond to	Balance of payments standard components (items), additional details, and aggregates
Changes in liabilities and net worth			Transactions in liabilities
F.2	Currency and deposits		Item 2.B.3.2.3 currency and deposits
F.3	Securities other than shares		Item 2.B.1.1.3.2.1 debt securities issued by direct investor plus item 2.B.1.2.3.2.1 debt securities issued by affiliated enterprises plus item 2.B.2.2.2 debt securities (part of portfolio investment)
F.4	Loans		Item 2.B.3.2.2 loans
F.5	Shares and other equity		Sum of items 2.B.1.1.1.2 equity capital: liabilities to affiliated enterprises (part of direct investment abroad), item 2.B.1.2.1.2 equity capital: liabilities to direct investors (part of direct investment in the reporting economy), item 2.B.1.2.2.2 reinvested earnings (part of direct investment in the reporting economy), and item 2.B.2.2.1 equity securities (part of portfolio investment)
F.6	Insurance technical reserves		Sum of items 2.B.3.2.4.4.1.1 net equity of households in life insurance reserves and in pension funds and 2.B.3.2.4.4.1.2 prepayments of premiums and reserves against outstanding claims
F.7	Other accounts payable		Sum of items 2.B.1.1.3.2.2 other liabilities of direct investors (part of direct investment abroad), 2.B.1.2.3.2.2 other liabilities to direct investors (part of direct investment in the reporting economy), item 2.B.3.2.1 trade credits (part of other investment), and item 2.B.3.2.4 other liabilities minus items 2.B.3.2.4.4.1.1 net equity of households in life insurance reserves and in pension funds, and 2.B.3.2.4.4.1.2 prepayments of premiums and reserves against outstanding claims (all part of other investment)
B.9	*Net lending (+)/net borrowing (-)*		

Table A.II.5. Account V.III.3: Other changes in asset accounts

Account V.III.3.1: Other changes in volume of assets account

SNA Categories		Correspond to	International investment position standard components and additional details
Changes in assets			Changes in assets
K.7	Catastrophic losses		Catastrophic losses (part of other adjustments)
K.8	Uncompensated seizures		Uncompensated seizures (part of other adjustments)
K.10	Other volume changes in financial assets and liabilities, n.e.c.		Other volume changes (part of other adjustments)
K.12	Changes in classifications and structure		Change in classifications and structure (part of other adjustments)
Changes in liabilities and net worth			Changes in liabilities
K.7	Catastrophic losses		Catastrophic losses (part of other adjustments)
K.12	Changes in classifications and structure		Changes in classifications and structure (part of other adjustments)
B.10.2	*Changes in net worth due to other changes in volume of assets*		

Account V.III.3.2: Revaluation Account

SNA Categories		Correspond to	International investment position standard components and additional details
Changes in assets			Changes in assets
K.11	Nominal holding gains/ losses in financial assets		Sum of entries in the columns for price and exchange rate changes
K.11.1	Neutral holding gains/losses in financial assets		Sum of entries in the columns for neutral holding gains/losses
K.11.2	Real holding gains/losses in financial assets		Sum of entries in the columns for real holding gains/losses
Changes in liabilities and net worth			Changes in liabilities
K.11	Nominal holding gains/losses in liabilities		Sum of entries in the columns for price and exchange rate changes
K.11.1	Neutral holding gains/losses in liabilities		Sum of entries in the columns for neutral holding gains/losses in liabilities
K.11.2	Real holding gains/losses in liabilities		Sum of entries in the columns for real holding gains/losses in liabilities
B.10.3	*Changes in net worth due to nominal holding gains/losses*		Price and exchange rate changes in assets less price and exchange rate changes in liabilities
B.10.31	*Changes in net worth due to neutral holding gains/losses*		Neutral holding gains/losses in assets less neutral holding gains/losses in liabilities
B.10.32	*Changes in net worth due to real holdings gains/losses*		Real holding gains/losses in assets less real holding gains/losses in liabilities

Table A.II.6. Account V.IV: External assets and liabilities

Account V.IV.1: Opening balance sheet

SNA categories		Correspond to	International investment position standard components and additional details
			Assets
AF	Financial assets		Sum of items A.1.1.1 claims (equity capital and reinvested earnings) on affiliated enterprises (part of direct investment abroad), A.1.2.1 claims (other capital) on affiliated enterprises (part of direct investment abroad), B.1.1.1 claims (equity capital and reinvested earnings (part of direct investment in the reporting economy), B.1.2.1 claims (other capital) on direct investors (part of direct investment in the reporting economy), A.2 portfolio investment, A.3 other investment, and A.4 reserve assets
			Liabilities
AF	Liabilities		Sum of items B.1.1.2 liabilities (equity capital and reinvested earnings) to direct investors (part of direct investment in the reporting economy), B.1.2.2 liabilities (other capital) to direct investors (part of direct investment in the reporting economy), A.1.1.2 liabilities (equity capital and reinvested earnings) to affiliated enterprises (part of direct investment abroad), A.1.2.2 liabilities (other capital) to affiliated enterprises (part of direct investment abroad), B.2 portfolio investment, and B.3 other investment
B.90	*Net worth*		

Account V.IV.2: Changes in balance sheet

SNA categories		Correspond to	International investment position standard components and additional details
AF	Total changes in financial assets		Sum of transactions, price and exchange rate changes, and other adjustments in respect of the corresponding international investment position items identified in Account V.IV.1 of the SNA
AF	Total changes in liabilities		Sum of transactions, price and exchange rate changes, and other adjustments in respect of corresponding international investment position items identified in Account V.IV.1 of the SNA
B.10	*Changes in net worth, total*		Total changes in item A (assets) - total changes in item B (liabilities)

Account V.IV.3: Closing balance sheet

SNA categories		Correspond to	International investment position standard components and additional details
AF	Financial assets		Sum of end of period values of corresponding items in the international investment position and identified in Account V.IV.1 of the SNA
AF	Liabilities		Sum of end of period value of corresponding items in the international investment position and identified in Account VI.V.1 of the SNA

Table A.II.7. Balance of payments: standard components and additional details

	Credit	Debit
1. Current account		
A. Goods and services		
a. Goods		
1. General merchandise		
2. Goods for processing		
3. Repairs on goods		
4. Goods procured in ports by carriers		
5. Non-monetary gold		
5.1 Held as a store of value		
5.2 Other		
b. Services		
1. Transportation		
1.1 Sea transport		
1.1.1 Passenger		
1.1.2 Freight		
1.1.3 Other		
1.2 Air transport		
1.2.1 Passenger		
1.2.2 Freight		
1.2.3 Other		
1.3 Other transport		
1.3.1 Passenger		
1.3.2 Freight		
1.3.3 Other		
2. Travel		
2.1 Business		
2.2 Personal [1]		
3. Communications services		
4. Construction services		
5. Insurance services [2]		
6. Financial services		
7. Computer and information services		
8. Royalties and license fees		
9. Other business services		
9.1 Merchanting and other trade-related services		
9.2 Operational leasing services		
9.3 Miscellaneous business, professional, and technical services [1]		
10. Personal, cultural and recreational services		
10.1 Audio-visual and related services		
10.2 Other cultural and recreational services		
11. Government services, n.i.e.		
B. Income		
1. Compensation of employees		
2. Investment income		
2.1 Direct investment		
2.1.1 Income on equity		
2.1.1.1 Dividends and distributed branch profits [3]		
2.1.1.2 Reinvested earnings and undistributed branch profits [3]		
2.1.2 Income on debt (interest)		

Table A.II.7. Balance of payments: standard components and additional details (*cont.*)

				Credit	Debit
	2.2	Portfolio investment			
		2.2.1	Income on equity (dividends)		
		2.2.2	Income on debt (interest)		
			2.2.2.1 Bonds and notes		
			2.2.2.1.1 Financial intermediation charge indirectly measured*		
			2.2.2.1.2 Other interest		
			2.2.2.2 Money market instruments and financial derivatives		
	2.3	Other investment			
		2.3.1	Financial intermediation charge indirectly measured*		
		2.3.2	Other interest		
		2.3.3	Imputed income to households from net equity in life insurance reserves and in pension funds*		
C. Current transfers					
1.	General government				
	1.1	Current taxes on income, wealth etc.*		XXX	
	1.2	Other taxes on production*		XXX	
	1.3	Other subsidies on production*			XXX
	1.4	Social contributions*		XXX	
	1.5	Social benefits*			XXX
	1.6	Other current transfers of general government*			
2.	Other sectors				
	2.1	Workers' remittances			
	2.2	Other transfers			
		2.2.1	Current taxes on income, wealth, etc.*		XXX
		2.2.2	Other taxes on production*		XXX
		2.2.3	Other subsidies on production*	XXX	
		2.2.4	Social contributions*		XXX
		2.2.5	Social benefits*	XXX	
		2.2.6	Other current transfers of other sectors*		
2. Capital and financial account					
A. Capital account					
1.	Capital transfers				
	1.1	General government			
		1.1.1	Debt forgiveness		
		1.1.2	Other		
	1.2	Other			
		1.2.1	Migrants' transfers		
		1.2.2	Debt forgiveness		
		1.2.3	Other		
2.	Acquisition/disposal of non-produced non financial assets				
B. Financial account					
1.	Direct investment				
	1.1	Abroad			
		1.1.1	Equity capital		
			1.1.1.1 Claims on affiliated enterprises		
			1.1.1.2 Liabilities to affiliated enterprises		
		1.1.2	Reinvested earnings		

Table A.II.7. Balance of payments: standard components and additional details (cont.)

	Credit	Debit

1.1.3   Other capital
        1.1.3.1   Claims on affiliated enterprises
                1.1.3.1.1   Debt securities issued by affiliated
                          enterprises*
                1.1.3.1.2   Other claims on affiliated enterprises*
        1.1.3.2   Liabilities to affiliated enterprises
                1.1.3.2.1   Debt securities issued by direct investors*
                1.1.3.2.2   Other liabilities of direct investors
1.2   In reporting economy
    1.2.1   Equity capital
        1.2.1.1   Claims on direct investors
        1.2.1.2   Liabilities to direct investors
    1.2.2   Reinvested earnings
    1.2.3   Other capital
        1.2.3.1   Claims on direct investors
                1.2.3.1.1   Debt securities issued by
                          direct investors*
                1.2.3.1.2   Other claims on direct investors*
        1.2.3.2   Liabilities to direct investors
                1.2.3.2.1   Debt securities issued by affiliated
                          enterprises*
                1.2.3.2.2   Other liabilities to direct investors*
2.   Portfolio investment
    2.1   Assets
        2.1.1   Equity securities
            2.1.1.1   Monetary authorities
            2.1.1.2   General government
            2.1.1.3   Banks
            2.1.1.4   Other sectors
        2.1.2   Debt securities
            2.1.2.1   Bonds and notes
                 2.1.2.1.1   Monetary authorities
                 2.1.2.1.2   General government
                 2.1.2.1.3   Banks
                 2.1.1.1.4   Other sectors
            2.1.2.2   Money-market instruments
                 2.1.2.2.1   Monetary authorities
                 2.1.2.2.2   General government
                 2.1.2.2.3   Banks
                 2.1.2.2.4   Other sectors
            2.1.2.3   Financial derivatives
                 2.1.2.3.1   Monetary authorities
                 2.1.2.3.2   General government
                 2.1.2.3.3   Banks
                 2.1.2.3.4   Other sectors
    2.2   Liabilities
        2.2.1   Equity securities
            2.2.1.1   Banks
            2.2.1.2   Other sectors
        2.2.2   Debt securities
            2.2.2.1   Bonds and notes
                 2.2.2.1.1   Monetary authorities
                 2.2.2.1.2   General government
                 2.2.2.1.3   Banks
                 2.2.2.1.4   Other sectors

Table A.II.7. Balance of payments: standard components and additional details (cont.)

	Credit	Debit

2.2.2.2 Money-market instruments
    2.2.2.2.1 Monetary authorities
    2.2.2.2.2 General government
    2.2.2.2.3 Banks
    2.2.2.2.4 Other sectors
2.2.2.3 Financial derivatives
    2.2.2.3.1 Banks
    2.2.2.3.2 Other sectors

3. Other investment
  3.1 Assets
    3.1.1 Trade credits
      3.1.1.1 General government
        3.1.1.1.1 Long-term
        3.1.1.1.2 Short-term
      3.1.1.2 Other sectors
        3.1.1.2.1 Long-term
        3.1.1.2.2 Short-term
    3.1.2 Loans
      3.1.2.1 Monetary authorities
        3.1.2.1.1 Long-term
        3.1.2.1.2 Short-term
      3.1.2.2 General government
        3.1.2.2.1 Long-term
        3.1.2.2.2 Short-term
      3.1.2.3 Banks
        3.1.2.3.1 Long-term
        3.1.2.3.2 Short-term
      3.1.2.4 Other sectors
        3.1.2.4.1 Long-term
        3.1.2.4.2 Short-term
    3.1.3 Currency and deposits
      3.1.3.1 Monetary authorities
      3.1.3.2 General government
      3.1.3.3 Banks
      3.1.3.4 Other sectors
    3.1.4 Other assets
      3.1.4.1 Monetary authorities
        3.1.4.1.1 Long-term
          3.1.4.1.1.1 Prepayments of premiums and reserves against outstanding claims*
          3.1.4.1.1.2 Other assets*
        3.1.4.1.2 Short-term
      3.1.4.2 General government
        3.1.4.2.1 Long-term
          3.1.4.2.1.1 Prepayments of premiums and reserves against outstanding claims*
          3.1.4.2.1.2 Other assets*
        3.1.4.2.2 Short-term
      3.1.4.3 Banks
        3.1.4.3.1 Long-term
          3.1.4.3.1.1 Prepayments of premiums and reserves against outstanding claims*
          3.1.4.3.1.2 Other assets*
        3.1.4.3.2 Short-term

Table A.II.7. Balance of payments: standard components and additional details (cont.)

	Credit	Debit
3.1.4.4 Other sectors		
3.1.4.4.1 Long-term		
3.1.4.4.1.1 Net equity of households in life insurance reserves and in pension funds*		
3.1.4.4.1.2 Prepayments of premiums and reserves against outstanding claims*		
3.1.4.4.1.3 Other assets*		
3.1.4.4.2 Short-term		
3.2 Liabilities		
3.2.1 Trade credits		
3.2.1.1 General government		
3.2.1.1.1 Long-term		
3.2.1.1.2 Short-term		
3.2.1.2 Other sectors		
3.2.1.3.1 Long-term		
3.2.1.3.2 Short-term		
3.2.2 Loans		
3.2.2.1 Monetary authorities		
3.2.2.1.1 Use of Fund credit and loans from the Fund		
3.2.2.1.2 Other long-term		
3.2.2.1.3 Short-term		
3.2.2.2 General government		
3.2.2.2.1 Long-term		
3.2.2.2.2 Short-term		
3.2.2.3 Banks		
3.2.2.3.1 Long-term		
3.2.2.3.2 Short-term		
3.2.2.4 Other sectors		
3.2.2.4.1 Long-term		
3.2.2.4.2 Short-term		
3.2.3 Currency and deposits		
3.2.3.1 Monetary authorities		
3.2.3.2 Banks		
3.2.4 Other liabilities		
3.2.4.1 Monetary authorities		
3.2.4.1.1 Long-term		
3.2.4.1.2 Short-term		
3.2.4.2 General government		
3.2.4.2.1 Long-term		
3.2.4.2.2 Short-term		
3.2.4.3 Banks		
3.2.4.3.1 Long-term		
3.2.4.3.2 Short-term		
3.2.4.4 Other sectors		
3.2.4.4.1 Long-term		
3.2.4.4.1.1 Net equity of households in life insurance reserves and in pension funds*		
3.2.4.4.1.2 Prepayments of premiums and reserves against outstanding claims*		
3.2.4.4.1.3 Other liabilities*		
3.2.4.4.2 Short-term		

Table A.II.7. Balance of payments: standard components and additional details (cont.)

			Credit	Debit
4.	Reserve Assets			
	4.1	Monetary gold		
	4.2	Special drawing rights		
	4.3	Reserve position in the Fund		
		4.3.1 Deposits*		
		4.3.2 Loans*		
	4.4	Foreign Exchange		
		4.4.1 Currency and deposits		
		4.4.1.1 With monetary authorities		
		4.4.1.2 With banks		
		4.4.2 Securities		
		4.4.2.1 Equities		
		4.4.2.2 Bonds and notes		
		4.4.2.3 Money-market instruments and financial derivatives		
	4.5	Other claims		
		4.5.1 Currency and deposits*		
		4.5.2 Securities*		
		4.5.2.1 Equities*		
		4.5.2.2 Debt securities*		

* Details needed to reconcile with the classifications used in the rest of the world account of the SNA.

1 See table A.II.8 for components.

2 Memorandum items: 5.1 Gross premiums 5.2 Gross claims.

3 If distributed branch profits are not identified, all branch profits are considered to be distributed.

Table A.II.8. Selected supplementary information

1. Liabilities constituting foreign authorities' reserves
   - 1.1 Bonds and other securities
     - 1.1.1 Monetary authorities
     - 1.1.2 General government
     - 1.1.3 Banks
     - 1.1.4 Other sectors
   - 1.2 Deposits
     - 1.2.1 Monetary authorities
     - 1.2.2 Banks
   - 1.3 Other liabilities
     - 1.3.1 Monetary authorities
     - 1.3.2 General government
     - 1.3.3 Banks
     - 1.3.4 Other sectors

2. Exceptional financing transactions
   - 2.1 Transfers
     - 2.1.1 Debt forgiveness
     - 2.1.2 Other intergovernmental grants
     - 2.1.3 Grants received from Fund subsidy accounts
   - 2.2 Direct investment
     - 2.2.1 Investment associated with debt reduction
     - 2.2.2 Other
   - 2.3 Portfolio investment: borrowing by authorities or other sectors on authorities' behalf--liabilities [1]
   - 2.4 Other investment--liabilities [1]
     - 2.4.1 Drawings on new loans by authorities or other sectors on authorities' behalf
     - 2.4.2 Rescheduling of existing debt
     - 2.4.3 Accumulation of arrears
       - 2.4.3.1 Principal on short-term debt
       - 2.4.3.2 Principal on long-term debt
       - 2.4.3.3 Original interest
       - 2.4.3.4 Penalty interest
     - 2.4.4 Repayments of arrears
       - 2.4.4.1 Principal
       - 2.4.4.2 Interest
     - 2.4.5 Rescheduling of arrears
       - 2.4.5.1 Principal
       - 2.4.5.2 Interest
     - 2.4.6 Cancellation of arrears
       - 2.4.6.1 Principal
       - 2.4.6.2 Interest

Table A.II.8. Selected supplementary information (*cont.*)

3. Other transactions	

3. Other transactions
   3.1 Portfolio investment income
      3.1.1   Monetary authorities
      3.1.2   General government
      3.1.3   Banks
      3.1.4   Other sectors
   3.2 Other (than direct investment) income
      3.2.1   Monetary authorities
      3.2.2   General government
      3.2.3   Banks
      3.2.4   Other sectors
   3.3 Other investment (liabilities)
      3.3.1   Drawings on long-term trade credits
      3.3.2   Repayments of long-term trade credits
      3.3.3   Drawings on long-term loans
      3.3.4   Repayments of long-term loans

4. Services sub-items
   4.1 Travel (personal)
      4.1.1   Health-related
      4.1.2   Education-related
      4.1.3   Other
   4.2 Miscellaneous business, professional, and technical services
      4.2.1   Legal, accounting, management consulting, and public relations
      4.2.2   Advertising, market research, and public opinion polling
      4.2.3   Research and development
      4.2.4   Architectural, engineering, and other technical services
      4.2.5   Agricultural, mining, and on-site processing
      4.2.6   Other

1 Specify sector involved and standard component in which the item is included.

Table A.II.9. International investment position: standard components and additional details

	Position at beginning of year	Transactions	Changes in position due to:			Position at end of year
			Price changes *a *b	Exchange rate changes *a *b	Other adjust-ments	

A.   Assets
  1. Direct investment abroad [1]
     1.1 Equity capital and reinvested earnings
         1.1.1 Claims on affiliated enterprises
         1.1.2 Liabilities to affiliated enterprises
     1.2 Other capital
         1.2.1 Claims on affiliated enterprises
         1.2.2 Liabilities to affiliated enterprises
  2. Portfolio investment
     2.1 Equity securities
         2.1.1 Monetary authorities
         2.1.2 General government
         2.1.3 Banks
         2.1.4 Other sectors
     2.2 Debt securities
         2.2.1 Bonds and notes
             2.2.1.1 Monetary authorities
             2.2.1.2 General government
             2.2.1.3 Banks
             2.2.1.4 Other sectors
         2.2.2 Money-market instruments
             2.2.2.1 Monetary authorities
             2.2.2.2 General government
             2.2.2.3 Banks
             2.2.2.4 Other sectors
         2.2.3 Financial derivatives
             2.2.3.1 Monetary authorities
             2.2.3.2 General government
             2.2.3.3 Banks
             2.2.3.4 Other sectors
  3. Other investment
     3.1 Trade credits
         3.1.1 General government
             3.1.1.1 Long-term
             3.1.1.2 Short-term
          3.1.2 Other sectors
             3.1.2.1 Long-term
             3.1.2.2 Short-term
     3.2 Loans
         3.2.1 Monetary authorities
             3.2.1.1 Long-term
             3.2.1.2 Short-term
          3.2.2 General government
             3.2.2.1 Long-term
             3.2.2.2 Short-term

Table A.II.9. International investment position: standard components and additional details

	Position at beginning of year	Transactions	Price changes *a *b	Exchange rate changes *a *b	Other adjust-ments	Position at end of year
			Changes in position due to:			

3.2.3 Banks
    3.2.3.1 Long-term
    3.2.3.2 Short-term
3.2.4 Other sectors
    3.2.4.1 Long-term
    3.2.4.2 Short-term
3.3 Currency and deposits
  3.3.1 Monetary authorities
  3.3.2 General government
  3.3.3 Banks
  3.3.4 Other sectors
3.4 Other assets
  3.4.1 Monetary authorities
    3.4.1.1 Long-term
    3.4.1.2 Short-term
  3.4.2 General government
    3.4.2.1 Long-term
    3.4.2.2 Short-term
  3.4.3 Banks
    3.4.3.1 Long-term
    3.4.3.2 Short-term
  3.4.4 Other sectors
    3.4.4.1 Long-term
    3.4.4.2 Short-term
4. Reserve assets
  4.1 Monetary gold
  4.2 Special drawing rights
  4.3 Reserve position in the Fund
  4.4 Foreign exchange
    4.4.1 Currency and deposits
      4.4.1.1 With monetary authorities
      4.4.1.2 With banks
    4.4.2 Securities
      4.4.2.1 Equities
      4.4.2.2 Bonds and notes
      4.4.2.3 Money-market instruments and financial derivatives
  4.5 Other claims

B. Liabilities
  1. Direct investment in reporting economy [1]
    1.1 Equity capital and reinvested earnings
      1.1.1 Claims on direct investors
      1.1.2 Liabilities to direct investors
    1.2 Other Capital
      1.2.1 Claims on direct investors
      1.2.2 Liabilities to direct investors

Table A.II.9. International investment position: standard components and additional details (cont.)

	Position at beginning of year	Transactions	Changes in position due to:				Position at end of year
			Price changes *a *b	Exchange rate changes *a *b	Other adjust-ments		

2. Portfolio Investment
   2.1   Equity securities
        2.1.1   Banks
        2.1.2   Other sectors
   2.2   Debt securities
        2.2.1   Bonds and notes
            2.2.1.1   Monetary authorities
            2.2.1.2   General government
            2.2.1.3   Banks
            2.2.1.4   Other sectors
        2.2.2   Money-market instruments
            2.2.2.1   Monetary authorities
            2.2.2.2   General government
            2.2.2.3   Banks
            2.2.2.4   Other sectors
        2.2.3   Financial derivatives
            2.2.3.1   Monetary authorities
            2.2.3.2   General government
            2.2.3.3   Banks
            2.2.3.4   Other sectors
3. Other investment
   3.1   Trade credits
        3.1.1   General government
            3.1.1.1   Long-term
            3.1.1.2   Short-term
        3.1.2   Other sectors
            3.1.2.1   Long-term
            3.1.2.2   Short-term
   3.2   Loans
        3.2.1   Monetary authorities
            3.2.1.1   Use of Fund credit and loans from the Fund
            3.2.1.2   Other long-term
            3.2.1.3   Short-term
        3.2.2   General government
            3.2.2.1   Long-term
            3.2.2.2   Short-term
        3.2.3   Banks
            3.2.3.1   Long-term
            3.2.3.2   Short-term
        3.2.4   Other sectors
            3.2.4.1   Long-term
            3.2.4.2   Short term
   3.3   Currency and deposits
        3.3.1   Monetary authorities
        3.3.2   Banks

Table A.II.9. International investment position: standard components and additional details (cont.)

			Position at beginning of year	Changes in position due to:				Position at end of year
				Transactions	Price changes *a *b	Exchange rate changes *a *b	Other adjust-ments	
3.4	Other liabilities							
	3.4.1	Monetary authorities						
		3.4.1.1　Long-term						
		3.4.1.2　Short-term						
	3.4.2	General government						
		3.4.2.1　Long-term						
		3.4.2.2　Short-term						
	3.4.3	Banks						
		3.4.3.1　Long-term						
		3.4.3.2　Short-term						
	3.4.4	Other sectors						
		3.4.4.1　Long-term						
		3.4.4.2　Short-term						

*　Details needed to reconcile with the classifications used in the rest of the world account of the SNA (a = neutral holding gains/losses; b = real holding gains/losses).

1　Because direct investment is classified primarily on a directional basis— abroad under the heading "Assets" and in reporting economy under the heading "Liabilities"—claims/liabilities breakdowns are shown for the components of each, although these sub-items do not strictly conform to the overall heading of "Assets" and "Liabilities".

Annex III
Financial intermediation services indirectly measured (FISIM)

1. The System recommends a single method of estimating the value of the services provided by financial intermediaries for which no explicit charges are made, known as the financial intermediation services indirectly measured (FISIM). However two alternative methods of allocation of FISIM to users are permitted in the System; FISIM may either be allocated to the industries and sectors of the total economy or to a nominal industry and sector. The purpose of this annex is to give, by means of a worked example drawing on the same information included in the other tables in this manual, a description of the alternative methods of allocation and the consequences for the presentation of the accounts.

1. The value of FISIM

2. Interest is payable by borrowers and by lenders to resident financial intermediaries and to the rest of the world. The first part of table A.III.1 in this annex gives illustrative data for the flows involved. The value of FISIM is calculated as the value of the property income receivable by financial intermediaries less the interest payable by them. In this example it is assumed that all property income other than interest is earned on their own funds and no interest is earned on their own funds. Thus the value of FISIM for the financial corporations is equal to the interest receivable (125) less the interest payable (77), or 48.

3. In this example it is assumed that all financial intermediation by resident units is carried out by financial corporations. Though it is theoretically possible for unincorporated enterprises to undertake financial intermediation, the volume of this output is likely to be small relative to that undertaken by financial corporations.

4. If FISIM is allocated to the industries and sectors of the economy, an allocation should also be made to non-resident borrowers and lenders. These allocations together appear as exports of FISIM in the rest of the world account. Similarly, an element of FISIM should be shown as payable to non-resident financial corporations by resident borrowers and lenders. Together, these elements should appear as imports of FISIM in the rest of the world account. The value of FISIM in respect of interest payments and receipts with non-resident financial intermediaries cannot be calculated directly because information is not available on the totality of all interest transactions by non-resident intermediaries including borrowing from and lending to non-residents. If an allocation of FISIM by institutional sector is made, an estimate of imported FISIM should be made independently. If FISIM is allocated only to a nominal sector, it is not necessary to estimate imported FISIM.

2. The allocation of FISIM to institutional sectors

5. It is assumed that FISIM is purchased implicitly by borrowers paying higher interest than would be necessary if FISIM were charged for explicitly and by lenders receiving lower interest than would be necessary if FISIM were charged for explicitly. The purpose of allocation of FISIM by sectors and industries is to identify the purchase of these services explicitly and to classify them as intermediate consumption, final consumption expenditure or exports according to which sector incurs the expenditure.

6. The first stage in the allocation of FISIM to sectors is to determine the amount of FISIM earned by resident intermediaries payable by borrowers and the amount payable by lenders. In this example it is assumed that borrowers must pay 19 and lenders 29 (total 48). These amounts must be allocated to all institutional units borrowing from and lending to resident financial intermediaries. In this example it is assumed that different rates of interest are applied to different classes of borrowers and lenders since, for example, transactions with the household sector are assumed to be more costly than similar transactions with general government. The value of FISIM earned in relation to interest paid to the rest of the world (20) and interest earned from the rest of the world (3) is taken to be 2 and to relate only to borrowers. The second part of table A.III.1 shows the allocation of FISIM by sectors for both borrowers and lenders.

7. The third part of table A.III.1 shows interest payable and receivable after FISIM has been deducted from actual payables by borrowers and added to actual receivables by lenders. The amount of interest receivable by resident financial intermediaries is now by definition equal to the amount of interest payable by them. It is this set of interest receivables and payables that appears in the item "interest" in the allocation of primary income account.

Table A.III.1. Calculation arising from the allocation of FISIM to sectors

Uses								Transactions and balancing items	Resources							
Total	S.2 Rest of the world	S.1 Total economy	S.15 NPISHs	S.14 Households	S.13 General government	S.12 Financial corporations	S.11 Non-financial corporations		S.11 Non-financial corporations	S.12 Financial corporations	S.13 General government	S.14 Households	S.15 NPISHs	S.1 Total economy	S.2 Rest of the world	Total
125	13	112	7	17	22	0	66	Interest paid by borrowers to financial corporations		125				125		125
17		17			17			Interest paid by borrowers to the rest of the world							17	17
77		77				77		Interest paid by financial corporations to lenders	22		12	33	5	72	5	77
3	3							Interest paid by the rest of the world to lenders	3					3		3
222	16	206	7	17	39	77	66	Actual interest payments	25	125	12	33	5	200	22	222
19	3	16	1	3	2	0	10	Service charge paid by borrowers to financial corporations		19				19		19
2		2			2			Service charge paid by borrowers to the rest of the world							2	2
29	1	28	2	16	2	0	8	Service charge paid by lenders to financial corporations		29				29		29
0		0					0	Service charge paid by lenders to the rest of the world							0	0
106	10	96	6	14	20	0	56	Interest excluding service charge paid by borrowers to financial corporations		106				106		106
15		15			15			Interest excluding service charge paid by borrowers to the rest of the world							15	15
106		106				106		Interest paid by financial corporations to lenders including service charge paid by lenders to financial corporations	30		14	49	7	100	6	106
3	3	0						Interest paid by the rest of the world to lenders including service charge paid by lenders to the rest of the world	3					3	0	3
230	13	217	6	14	35	106	56	Interest paid when FISIM is allocated	33	106	14	49	7	209	21	230
								Attribution of expenditure on service charges								
								Imports							2	2
								Output		48	6		3	57		57
27		27	3	0	6	0	18	Intermediate consumption								
28		28	3	19	6			Final consumption								
4	4							Exports								
59	4	55	6	19	12	0	18	Total		48	6		3	57	2	59

8. The value of FISIM produced by resident financial inter-mediaries represents output (value 48) and that coming from the rest of the world (value 2) represents imports. The total supply of FISIM is thus 50.

9. The FISIM paid by non-resident borrowers (value 3) and lenders (value 1) to resident financial intermediaries represents exports (total value 4). Payments by non-financial corporations (value 18), NPISHs (value 3) and general government (value 6) represent intermediate consumption. In this example no FISIM is consumed by financial inter-mediaries themselves, though inter-bank lending could give rise to a non-zero allocation of FISIM to financial cor-porations. Further, it is assumed that no interest paid by households is in respect of their productive activities and so all their consumption of FISIM (value 19) is treated as fi-nal consumption expenditure.

10. At this point the total demand for FISIM of 50 balances the supply, but the calculations are not complete. Intermediate consumption of non-financial corporations (18), financial corporations (0) and households (0) subtract from the amount of value added to be calculated. However, because general government and NPISHs are non-market produc-ers whose output is valued at cost, their intermediate con-sumption increases the value of their output and also the value of their final consumption expenditures by the same amount (3 for NPISHs and 6 for general government). The fourth and last part of table A.III.1 shows the attribution of expenditures arising out of the allocation of FISIM, as fol-lows:

	Allocation of FISIM	Effects on non-market producers	Total
Output of FISIM	48		48
Output of general government		6	6
Output of NPISHs		3	3
Imports	2		2
Total supply	50	9	59
Intermediate consumption			
Non-financial corporations	18		18
Financial corporations	0		0
General government	6		6
Households	0		0
NPISHs	3		3
Final consumption expenditure			
General government		6	6
Households	19		19
NPISHs		3	3
Exports	4		4
Total demand	50	9	59

The effects on GDP are as follows:

Output of FISIM	48	Final consumption expenditure	
Output of general government	6	General government	6
Output of NPISHs	3	Households	19
Less		NPISHs	4
Intermediate consumption		Exports	4
Non-financial corporations	18	*less*	
Financial corporations	0	Imports	2
General government	6		
Households	0		
NPISHs	3		
GDP	30	GDP	30

11. Table A.III.2 shows these entries in the format of the integrated economic accounts. The entries for item D41, Interest correspond exactly to those shown in table 7.1 in chapter VII. Other entries in table 2 show only part of the matching entries in other tables in this manual and cannot be identified explicitly elsewhere.

3. The allocation of FISIM to industries

12. The principles underlying the allocation of FISIM to sectors generalize directly to an allocation to industries when production accounts are compiled by industries, for example, in a supply and use table. For industries with market output or output for own use valued at market prices, the allocation of FISIM to that industry increases intermediate consumption and decreases value added. For industries with non-market output, the allocation of FISIM increases both intermediate consumption and output but leaves value added unchanged.

4. The allocation of FISIM to nominal sectors

13. Sometimes it may not be appropriate to allocate FISIM to using sectors. In such a case the whole of the value of the output of FISIM is treated as the intermediate consumption of a nominal sector with zero output and negative value added equal in size but opposite in sign from the intermediate consumption. In total, the value added generated by

FISIM is exactly offset by the intermediate consumption of the nominal unit and GDP is invariant to the size of FISIM estimated. This device does, however, allow the output and value added, and thus the production and generation of income accounts, for the financial corporations sector to be correctly measured.

14. In the allocation of primary income account, the entries shown for interest are those of actual interest payable and receivable. In this way the values of FISIM previously identified as either intermediate consumption, final consumption expenditure or exports remain included in the entries for interest. Further, in this account an item consolidating the entry of negative value added (and thus operating surplus) in the nominal sector with that of financial corporations is shown so that the excess of interest receivable over interest payable enters the balance of primary income for that sector only once. For all sectors, the changes to the balancing items of balance of primary incomes, carry through to disposable income and saving and ensure that the values derived for saving are the same for each sector whether or not FISIM is allocated by sector.

15. Table A.III.3 shows the entries in the format of the integrated economic accounts when FISIM is allocated to a nominal sector. In the supply and use tables or other analyses of the production accounts by industries, a nominal industry is shown with similar treatment as the nominal sector.

Table A.III.2. Effect of allocating FISIM to institutional sectors, including changes for non-market producers

Accounts (Uses)	Total	Goods and service (res.)	S.2 Rest of the world	S.1 Total economy	S.15 NPISHs	S.14 Households	S.13 General government	S.12 Financial corporations	S.11 Non-financial corporations	Transactions and balancing items	S.11 Non-financial corporations	S.12 Financial corporations	S.13 General government	S.14 Households	S.15 NPISHs	S.1 Total economy	S.2 Rest of the world	Goods and service (uses)	Total	Accounts (Resources)
I. Production/external account	2	2								P.72 Imports of services							2		2	I. Production/external account
	4		4							P.62 Exports of services								4	4	
	27			27	3	0	6	0	18	P.1 Output		48	6		3	57			57	
	30			30				48	−18	P.2 Intermediate consumption										
	30		−2	30						B.1 *Value added/external balance*	−18	48				30			30	
II.1.1. Generation of income account	30			30				48	−18	B.2 *Operating surplus*	−18	48				30			30	II.1.1. Generation of income account
II.1.2. Allocation of primary income account	230		13	217	6	14	35	106	56	D.41 Interest	33	106	14	49	7	209	21		230	II.1.2. Allocation of primary income account
	22			22	1	35	−21	48	−41	B.5 *Balance of primary incomes*	−41	48	−21	35	1	22			22	
II.2. Secondary distribution of income account	22			22	1	35	−21	48	−41	B.6 *Disposable income*	−41	48	−21	35	1	22			22	II.2. Secondary distribution of income account
II.4. Use of income account	28			28	3	19	6			P.3 Final consumption expenditure										II.4. Use of income account
			6	−6	−2	16	−27	48	−41	B.8 *Saving, net/external balance*										

Table A.III.3.   Effect of allocating FISIM to nominal sector only

Uses / Resources

Accounts (Uses)	Total	Goods and service (res.)	S.2 Rest of the world	S.1 Total economy	S.15 NPISHs	S.1 Household	S.13 General government	S.12 Financial corporations	S.11 Non-financial corporations	Nominal	Transactions and balancing items	Nominal	S.11 Non-financial corporations	S.12 Financial corporations	S.13 General government	S.14 Households	S.15 NPISHs	S.1 Total economy	S.2 Rest of the world	Goods and service (uses)	Total	Accounts (Resources)
I. Production account	48										P.1 Output			48				48			48	I. Production account
				48						48	P.2 Intermediate consumption									48	48	
II.1.1. Generation of income account								48		−48	B.1 Value added/external balance	−48		48								II.1.1. Generation of income account
II.1.2. Allocation of primary income account								48		−48	B.2 Operating surplus	−48		48								II.1.2. Allocation of primary income account
	222		16	206	7	17	39	77	66		D.41 Interest		25	125	12	33	5	200	22		222	
								−48			Adjustment for FISIM	48		−48								
				−6	−2	16	−27	48	−41		B.5 Balance of primary incomes		−41	48	−27	16	−2	−6				
II.2. Secondary distribution of income account				−6	−2	16	−27	48	−41		B.6 Disposable income		−41	48	−27	16	−2	−6				II.2. Secondary distribution of income account
II.4. Use of income account			6	−6	−2	16	−27	48	−41		B.8n Saving, net/external balance											II.4. Use of income account

Annex IV
The treatment of insurance, social insurance and pensions

Introduction

1. There are two types of insurance; life and non-life insurance (see figure A.IV.1). Life insurance is an activity whereby a policyholder makes regular payments to an insurer in return for which the insurer guarantees to provide the policyholder with an agreed sum, or an annuity, at a given date or earlier if the policyholder dies beforehand. The sum may be fixed or may vary to reflect the income earned from the investment of premiums during the period for which the policy operates. In such cases, the terms "with-profits" life insurance or endowment policy are generally used. Although the date and sum may be variable, a claim is always paid in respect of a life policy. Non-life insurance covers all other risks; accidents, sickness, fire, etc. A policy that provides a benefit in the case of death within a given period but in no other circumstances, usually called term insurance, is regarded as non-life insurance because as with other non-life insurance, a claim is payable only if a specified contingency occurs and not otherwise. In practice, because of the way in which insurance corporations keep their accounts, it may not always be possible to separate term insurance from other life insurance. In these circumstances, term insurance may have to be treated in the same way as life insurance for purely practical reasons.

2. What the two types of insurance have in common is that they both involve spreading risk. Insurers receive many (relatively) small regular payments of premiums from policyholders and pay much larger sums to claimants when the contingencies covered by the policy occur. For non-life insurance, the risks are spread over the whole population which takes out the insurance policies. For example, an insurance corporation determines the premiums charged for vehicle insurance in a year by relating them to the amount of claims it expects to pay on vehicle insurance in the same year. Typically, the number of claimants is much smaller than the number of policyholders. For an individual policyholder there is no relationship between the premiums paid and the claims received, even in the long run, but the insurance corporation establishes such a relationship for every class of non-life insurance on a yearly basis. For life insurance, a relationship between premiums and claims over time is important both to the policyholders and to the insurance corporation. For someone taking out a life policy, the benefits to be received are expected to be at least as great as the premiums paid up till the benefit (claim) is due and can be seen as a form of saving. The insurance corporation must combine this aspect of a single policy with the actuarial calculations about the insured population concerning life expectancy and the risks of fatal accidents when determining the relationship between the levels of premiums and benefits. Further, in the interval between the receipt of premiums and the payment of claims, the insurance corporation earns investment income on the value of the premiums received. This investment income also affects the levels of premiums and benefits set by the insurance corporations.

3. Simply recording the actual premiums and claims paid in the accounts of the System would not reflect the links between premiums and claims. Instead, some actual transactions are decomposed and others are imputed in order to bring out the underlying economic processes actually taking place. This annex attempts to bring together all the entries in the accounts connected with insurance and explain their interconnection.

4. Despite the similarity of the activity of life and non-life insurance, there are significant differences between them which lead to different types of entries in the accounts of the System. Further, in the System an important distinction is made between social insurance schemes and other insurance schemes which affects both life and non-life insurance. Payments to social insurance schemes are described in the System as contributions, rather than premiums, and claims including pensions paid by the schemes are described as benefits.

Figure A.IV1. Insurance and social insurance schemes

Figure A.IV.2 Social contributions

5. A social insurance scheme is one where the policyholder is obliged or encouraged to insure against certain contingencies by the intervention of a third party. For example, government may oblige all employees to participate in a social security scheme; employers may make it a condition of employment that employees participate in an insurance scheme specified by the employer; an employer may encourage employees to join a scheme by making contributions on behalf of the employee; or a trade union may arrange advantageous insurance cover available only to the members of the trade union. Contributions to social insurance schemes are usually paid by, or on behalf of employees, though under certain conditions non-employed or self-employed persons may also be covered (see figure A.IV.2). An insurance scheme is designated as a social insurance scheme in the System:

(a) If the benefits received are conditional on participation in the scheme and are as described in the next paragraphs; and

(b) At least one of the three conditions following is met:

    (i) Participation in the scheme is compulsory either by law or by the conditions of employment; or

    (ii) The scheme is operated on behalf of a group and restricted to group members; or

    (iii) An employer makes a contribution to the scheme on behalf of an employee.

6. Not all social benefits are provided by social insurance schemes but however they are provided, the characteristics of all social benefits can be described in the following general terms. Social benefits may be provided in cash or in kind. They become payable when certain events occur, or certain conditions exist, that may adversely affect the welfare of the households concerned either by imposing additional demands on their resources or reducing their incomes. There are six kinds of circumstances in which social benefits may be payable:

(a) The beneficiaries, or their dependants, require medical, dental or other treatment, or hospital, convalescent or long-term care, as a result of sickness, injuries, maternity, chronic invalidity, old age, etc. The social benefits are usually provided in kind in the form of treatments or care provided free or at prices which are not economically significant, or by reimbursing expenditures made by households. Social benefits in cash may also be payable to beneficiaries needing health care;

(b) The beneficiaries have to support dependants of various kinds—spouses, children, elderly relatives, invalids, etc. The social benefits are usually paid in cash in the form of regular dependants' or family allow-

ances;

(c) The beneficiaries suffer a reduction in income as a result of not being able to work, or to work full-time. The social benefits are usually paid in cash regularly for the duration of the condition. In some instances a lump sum may be provided additionally or instead of the regular payment. People may be prevented from working for various different reasons, in particular:

    (i) Voluntary or compulsory retirement;

    (ii) Involuntary unemployment, including temporary lay-offs and short-time working;

    (iii) Sickness, accidental injury, the birth of a child, etc., that prevents a person from working, or working full time;

    (iv) The beneficiaries suffer a reduction in income because of the death of the main income earner;

    (v) The beneficiaries are provided with housing either free or at prices which are not economically significant or by reimbursing expenditure made by households. These are social benefits in kind;

    (vi) The beneficiaries are provided with allowances to cover education expenses incurred on behalf of themselves or their dependants: occasionally education services may be provided in kind.

7. The above are typical circumstances in which social benefits are payable. However, the list is illustrative rather than exhaustive. It is possible, for example, that under some social insurance schemes other benefits may be payable. Conversely, by no means all schemes provide benefits in all the circumstances listed above. In practice, the scope of social insurance schemes is liable to vary significantly from country to country, or from scheme to scheme within the same country.

8. It is convenient in this annex to refer to insurance other than social insurance as other life or non-life insurance.

1. The units involved

9. The institutional units involved in other insurance are preeminently insurance corporations. In principle it is possible for another type of enterprise to carry out insurance as a non-principal activity, but usually the legal regulations surrounding the conduct of insurance mean that a separate set of accounts covering all aspects of the insurance activity must be kept and thus in the System a separate institutional unit, classified to the insurance corporations and pension funds sub-sector, is identifiable. Sometimes government may conduct other insurance activities, but again it is likely that a separate unit can be identified. Having noted that exceptionally other sectors may be involved, in what follows

it is assumed that all other insurance is carried out by insurance corporations, either resident or non-resident.

10. Social insurance schemes can be operated in a number of ways. They are usually organized either by government for the population at large (social security schemes), by employers on behalf of their employees and their dependants or by others, for example a trade union, on behalf of a specified group (both these cases are here called private social insurance schemes).

11. Private social insurance schemes may be arranged with an insurance corporation as a group policy or series of policies or they may be managed by the insurance corporation in return for a fee. Alternatively, the schemes may be managed by an employer directly on his own behalf. Schemes arranged via an insurance corporation are always funded. Those managed by employers themselves may be funded or unfunded. An unfunded scheme is one where there are no identifiable reserves assigned for the payments of benefits. In such cases, benefits are paid from the receipts of contributions with any surplus or deficit going into, or being drawn from, the scheme manager's other resources.

12. Cover other than for pensions may be provided via an insurance scheme or from an unfunded scheme. If an employer manages his own scheme in respect of non-pension cover, it is treated as unfunded because no reserves have to be established as is the case for pensions. On the other hand, employers not infrequently manage their own pension schemes. These may be funded or unfunded. Funded schemes are divided into those that are autonomous, that is they constitute separate institutional units operating on their own behalf, classified in the insurance corporation and pension fund sub-sector, and those where the funds are segregated from the rest of the employers' own funds but are not autonomous. These remain classified in the same institutional sector as the employer. In both these cases, the funds are regarded in the System as being the property of the beneficiaries of the schemes and not of the employers. Schemes where the pension provisions are not even segregated from the employers' own funds are regarded as unfunded pension schemes. In this case there are no separately identified funds to which the beneficiaries can lay claim. Often an unfunded pension scheme will be non-contributory for the employees, but this is not invariably so.

13. Social security schemes may be either funded or unfunded. Even where separate funds are identified, they remain the property of the government and not of the beneficiaries of the schemes. Schemes set up by government in respect of their employees only are not included in social security schemes but are treated in the same way as other employers' social insurance schemes.

2. The measurement of output of insurance corporations

14. The output of insurance corporations covers the operation of other life and non-life policies as well as those life and non-life policies included in social insurance schemes operated by insurance corporations. The output represents the value of the service provided by insurance corporations in arranging payments of claims and benefits in exchange for the receipts of premiums and contributions.

15. For both life and non-life insurance, the total amount of claims paid often exceeds the premiums receivable. This is possible because the contingencies covered by the policies do not occur, even for the whole population covered, in the same period as the premiums are paid. Premiums are usually paid regularly, often at the start of an insurance period, whereas claims fall due later, in the case of life insurance many years later. In the time between the payment of premium being made and the claim being receivable, the sum involved is at the disposal of the insurance corporation to invest and earn income from it. The income thus earned allows the insurance corporations to charge lower premiums than would be the case otherwise. An adequate measure of the service provided must take account of the size of this income as well as the relative size of premiums and claims.

16. The income concerned comes from the investment of the technical reserves of the insurance corporations, which are assets of the policyholders, and does not include any income from the investment of the insurance corporations' own funds. The technical reserves of an insurance corporation consist of pre-paid premiums, reserves against outstanding claims, actuarial reserves for life insurance and reserves for with-profit insurance. For non-life insurance, it is common for a premium to be payable at the start of a period of cover although the premiums are only earned on a continuous basis as the period passes. At any point before the end of the period, the policyholder will have to pay to the insurance corporation an amount relating to services to be provided in the future. This is a form of credit extended by the policyholder to the insurance corporation described as pre-paid premiums. Similarly, although claims become due for payment by the insurance corporation when the contingency specified in the policy eventuates, they may not be actually payable until some time later, often because of negotiation about the amounts due. This is another similar form of credit, described as reserves against outstanding claims. The claims involved may relate to either life or non-life policies. The other two elements of insurance technical reserves, actuarial reserves for life insurance and reserves for with-profit insurance, relate only to life insurance. They represent amounts set aside for payments of claims and benefits in future which exceed the receipts of premiums and contributions received to the current date.

17. Usually the technical reserves are invested in financial assets and the income is in the form of property income (interest and dividends). Sometimes, however, they may be used to generate net operating surplus either in a separate establishment or as a secondary activity. The most common example is from real estate.

18. Some of the income from the investment of the technical life reserves is explicitly attributed by the insurance corporation to the policyholders. In the System, all the income from the investment of both life and non-life technical reserves, calculated separately, is shown as property income attributed to policyholders and again as imputed life or non-life premiums or contribution supplements, as appropriate, paid by the policyholder to the insurer. The output of the insurance activity, which represents the service provided to policyholders, is calculated separately for life and non-life insurance as:

   (a) Total actual premiums or contributions earned;

   (b) Plus total premium or contribution supplements;

   (c) Less claims or benefits due;

   (d) Less increases (plus decreases) in actuarial reserves and reserves for with-profits insurance.

   Each of these items should be measured excluding holding gains and losses. If the data sources available do not exclude these holding gains and losses, appropriate adjustments must be made in calculating the value of the output.

3. The output of pension funds

19. The output of autonomous pension funds is calculated in a manner analogous to that for life insurance. The fund generates income from the investment of its reserves which is attributed to the policyholders who then pay a similar sum back to the fund as an imputed contribution supplement. The output of the fund is taken to be a service charge to the beneficiaries equal to:

   (a) Total actual contributions earned;

   (b) Plus total imputed contribution supplements;

   (c) Less benefits due;

   (d) Less increases (plus decreases) in pension reserves.

   As in the case of the output of insurance corporations, the output of pension funds must exclude holding gains or losses.

20. For non-autonomous pension funds, the costs of managing the funds are included with the other elements of cost in the enterprise's production account in the same way as the costs of an ancillary activity. There is therefore no service charge applied in this case and thus no output of the funds.

The property income attributed to the beneficiaries in the System is the same as that recorded in the funds and this represents the size of the imputed contribution also.

21. Obviously there is no output in respect of an unfunded pension scheme.

4. Property income attributed to policyholders/ beneficiaries

22. The value of the premium or contribution supplements paid by the policyholders or beneficiaries is equal in total to the entirety of the income earned by the insurance corporations or pension funds by investing their technical or pension reserves. Although the income earned by the insurance corporation may not all have been earned as property income, when attributed to policyholders the whole amount is so regarded and appears as the item "property income attributed to policyholders".

23. For other life insurance policies and all social insurance, the beneficiaries are always households, though some may be non-resident households, i.e., in the rest of the world. For other non-life insurance, the property income must be distributed across all policyholders. In principle the distribution should be made according to the proportion of reserves attributed to the different classes of insurance and policyholders, but in practice the usual method is to distribute the property income in proportion to the actual premiums payable.

5. Net premiums/contributions and consumption of insurance services

24. The actual premiums or contributions payable and the premiums or contribution supplements are shown in the System divided between two types of transactions. The first is the consumption or export of insurance services which in total is equal to the value of the output of insurance (plus, if appropriate, the value of imported insurance services). The second is net premiums or contributions earned. Because of the way in which the value of the service output is defined, net premiums for non-life insurance are equal in total to claims. The relationship between net premiums and claims for life insurance is discussed below.

25. Insurance services are consumed by those sectors (and the rest of the world) that pay actual and imputed premiums and contributions. Estimates of the value of consumption by sector are made by allocating the total value of the service in proportion to the actual premiums or contributions payable. Estimates of net premiums and contributions are then made by deducting the consumption of services from the total actual premiums and contributions payable plus the value of the imputed premiums and contribution supplements.

6. Insurance services provided to and from the rest of the world

26. Resident insurance corporations frequently provide insurance cover to households and enterprises in the rest of the world, and resident households and enterprises may purchase cover from insurance corporations in the rest of the world. In principle, the property income attributed by resident insurance corporations to policyholders should include an allocation to policyholders in the rest of the world. These non-resident policyholders would then also pay premium supplements to the resident insurance corporation. Both these flows should in principle appear in the rest of the world account, but because they are of equal size and in opposite direction, there will be no net effect on the current external balance. Similar considerations also apply to the treatment of resident enterprises and households taking out policies with non-resident insurers. They should receive imputed property income from abroad and pay premiums and supplements to abroad. Estimation of the size of these flows is particularly difficult but again these items would cancel in calculating the current external balance.

7. Reinsurance

27. Insurance corporations undertake insurance in two different ways. The first of these is direct insurance with an institutional unit outside the insurance corporation and pension fund sub-sector. The second is reinsurance which is a form of insurance that involves only institutional units classified as insurance corporations and pension funds, though one party to a transaction may be non-resident. This practice somewhat complicates the recording of transactions for the sub-sector.

28. Rcinsurancc transactions between resident insurance corporations should be consolidated; non-life direct insurance with non-life reinsurance corporations and life direct insurance with life reinsurance corporations. In consequence, the System records transactions between policyholders and claimants on the one hand and the resident life and non-life industries on the other without regard to the division within the industry between direct insurance and reinsurance.

29. When reinsurance takes place between resident direct insurers and non-resident reinsurers or between non-resident direct insurers and resident reinsurers, a complete consolidation is inappropriate. However, rather than show all flows of premiums, claims, commissions, etc., between direct insurers and reinsurers, it is simpler and more comprehensible to consider that the reinsurers deliver a service to direct insurers measured as the balance of all flows occurring between the reinsurers and direct insurers. In principle, imports of reinsurance services are estimated as the balance of all flows occuring between resident direct insurers and non-resident reinsurers. These flows include premiums ceded, investment income from technical reserves

payable, commissions receivable, claims recovered and reinsurers' share in the addition to technical reserves if relevant. Exports of reinsurance services are similarly estimated as the balance of all flows between resident reinsurers and non-resident direct insurers. Apart from these two flows, all insurance transactions in the rest of the world account refer to direct transactions only.

30. Imported reinsurance services appear as intermediate consumption of resident direct insurers.

8. The recording of insurance transactions in the System

31. As explained above, the total of actual premiums (contributions) and the supplements payable by policyholders are decomposed into two elements, the part corresponding to the consumption of the service provided by the insurance corporations and net premiums. It follows that the entries for insurance in the accounts of the System consist of two types of transactions. The first set corresponds to the production and consumption of insurance services. The second set corresponds to the payments of net premiums (contributions) and claims (benefits). Except for other life insurance, an equality is established in the accounts between total net premiums and total claims for each type of insurance. These transactions are thus essentially redistributive and are mainly recorded in the secondary distribution of income account as transfers.

32. Because the interaction of these two sets of transactions can seem complicated, the entries associated with the different types of insurance schemes in the System are described in turn below in ascending order of complexity. The first two cases discussed are those of the social security schemes of government and employers' unfunded schemes where no insurance services are separately recorded. The next case considered is the most familiar case of insurance, other non-life insurance which covers accident, fire, vehicle, etc., insurance. The next case described is for other life insurance. Lastly, the two cases of social insurance under private funded schemes are described where more elaborate recording of contributions and benefits is required.

33. In each description the type of transactions and the sectors involved are specified. The only exception is for imported insurance services. Not to over-complicate the exposition, the possibility of transactions with non-resident insurers is not included explicitly below. It should be remembered however, that every transaction with an insurance corporation could in principle be with a non-resident rather than resident institutional unit in which case the transaction should be recorded in the accounts for the rest of the world rather than with the insurance corporation and pension fund sub-sector.

Social security schemes of government

34. Most governments operate a social security scheme where employees, the self-employed and occasionally non-employed persons make contributions. However, pensions and other benefits are payable not only to those who have contributed but also to others, for example, surviving spouses and non-employed persons who have not contributed to the scheme. Contributions to the social security scheme may be made directly by employees, the self- and non-employed or on behalf of employees by employers. The value of these latter payments are treated in the System as part of compensation of employees, i.e., payable by employers to employees and then by employees to government in addition to the contributions they make on their own behalf as employees.

35. In the System flows are recorded as follows:

    (a) Employers' social security contributions are shown as payable by the sector in which the employer is located and a receivable by households. The sector of the employer may be any of non-financial corporations, financial corporations, general government (as an employer), employer households, NPISHs or the rest of the world (when a resident works for a non-resident institutional unit). For resident employers the payables are shown in the generation of income account; payables by non-resident employers are shown in the external account of primary incomes and current transfers. Receivables by resident households are shown in the allocation of primary income account and by non-resident households in the external account of primary incomes and current transfers;

    (b) In the secondary distribution of income account, employers' social security contributions and social security contributions by employees, self- and non-employed persons are shown as payable by households and receivable by government. If the resident employee makes payment to a foreign government, the payment is recorded in the external account of primary incomes and current transfers. Further, social security benefits in cash payable to households are shown as payable by government (or the rest of the world if from a foreign government) and receivable by households. Where non-resident households are involved, the receivables are recorded in the external account of primary incomes and current transfers. Although not formally part of social insurance as defined in the System social assistance benefits in cash payable are also recorded in these accounts in a manner parallel to those of social security benefits.

An example of these flows is shown in table A.IV.1.

Unfunded schemes operated by employers

36. In this case, the flows are similar to those above but all flows are between households and employers. The entries to be recorded are the same whether the benefits involved are pensions or other social benefits.

37. In the System an employer operating an unfunded scheme is regarded as making an imputed social contribution to the scheme on behalf of the employees. This contribution should be determined taking into account the composition of the labour force of the employer and the commitment to provide benefits in the future. In practice, however, it is usually set equal in value to the benefits payable in the period under consideration. The imputed contribution forms part of the compensation of employees and is also shown as being payable by the employees to the scheme together with any actual payments by the employees. However, it is not uncommon for unfunded schemes to be non-contributory for the employees. In these cases the payment by the employees to the scheme exactly matches the imputed contribution payable to them by the employer:

    (a) Employers' imputed contributions to unfunded social insurance schemes are shown as a payable by the sector in which the employer is located in the generation of income account and a receivable by households in the allocation of primary income account;

    (b) In the secondary distribution of income account, employers' imputed contributions and actual contributions by employees are shown as payable by households and receivable by the employer. Further, pensions and other benefits payable to households by the employer are shown as payable by the employer and receivable by households.

An example of these flows is shown in table A.IV.2.

Other non-life insurance

38. Altogether six sets of transactions need to be recorded in respect of other non-life insurance; two relating to the measurement of the production and consumption of the insurance service, three relating to redistribution and one in the financial account. The value of the output of the activity, the property income to be attributed to the policyholders and the value of the service charge are calculated specifically for other non-life insurance in the manner described above.

39. The production and consumption transactions are as follows:

    (a) Since all such activity by resident institutional units is undertaken by insurance corporations, the output is recorded in the production account of the insurance corporations and pension funds sub-sector;

Table A.IV.1.   Accounts for social security schemes

Uses									Transactions and balancing items	Resources								
Total	Goods and service account	Rest of the world account	S.1 Total economy	S.15 NPISHs	S.14 House-holds	S.13 General govern-ment	S.12 Financial corpo-rations	S.11 Non-financial corpo-rations		S.11 Non-financial corpo-rations	S.12 Financial corpo-rations	S.13 General govern-ment	S.14 House-holds	S.15 NPISHs	S.1 Total eco-nomy	Rest of the world account	Goods and service account	Total
									Generation of income account									
155		0	155	8	0	45	4	98	D.12 Employers' social security contributions									
									Distribution of primary income account									
									D.12 Employers' social security contributions				155		155	0		155
									Secondary distribution of income account									
155		0	155		155				Employers' social security contributions			155			155	0		155
76		0	76		76				Employees' social security contributions			76			76	0		76
32			32		32				D.6113 Social contributions by self-employed and non-employed persons			32			32	0		32
232		0	232		232				D.621 Social security benefits in cash				232		232	0		232
52		0	52		52				D.624 Social assistance benefits in cash				52		52	0		52

Table A.IV.2.   Accounts for unfunded social insurance schemes

Uses									Transactions and balancing items	Resources								
Total	Goods and service account	Rest of the world account	S.1 Total economy	S.15 NPISHs	S.14 House-holds	S.13 General govern-ment	S.12 Financial corpo-rations	S.11 Non-financial corpo-rations		S.11 Non-financial corpo-rations	S.12 Financial corpo-rations	S.13 General govern-ment	S.14 House-holds	S.15 NPISHs	S.1 Total eco-nomy	Rest of the world account	Goods and service account	Total
									Generation of income account									
19		0	19	1	0	5	1	12	D.122 Employers' imputed social contributions									
									Distribution of primary income account									
									D.122 Employers' imputed social contributions				19		19	0		19
									Secondary distribution of income account									
19		0	19		19				D.612 Imputed social contributions		12	1	5	0	1	19	0		19
19		0	19	1	0	5	1	12	D.623 Unfunded employee social benefits					19		19	0		19

(b) The service may be consumed by any of the sectors of the economy or by the rest of the world; the value of the service is payable to the insurance corporations and pension fund sub-sector. Payments by non-financial corporations, financial corporations, general government or non-profit institutions constitute intermediate consumption, recorded in their production account. Insurance clearly associated with the productive activity of an unincorporated enterprise is also recorded as intermediate consumption in the production account of households. Other insurance payments by households are part of final consumption expenditure, recorded in the use of income account. Payments by the rest of the world are recorded as exports in the external account of goods and services.

40. The redistributive transactions cover property income attributed to policyholders in respect of other non-life insurance, net non-life insurance premiums, and insurance claims:

(a) Property income attributed to policyholders in respect of other non-life insurance is recorded as payable by insurance corporations and pensions funds. It is recorded as receivable by all sectors and the rest of the world. Both payable and receivables are recorded in the allocation of primary income account or in the external account of primary incomes and current transfers;

(b) Net non-life insurance premiums are calculated as premiums earned plus premium supplements (equal to the property income attributed to policyholders) less the value of the services consumed. These net premiums are payable by all sectors of the economy or the rest of the world and receivable by the insurance corporations and pension fund sub-sector;

(c) Insurance claims due are payable by the insurance corporations and pension fund sub-sector and receivable by all sectors of the economy and the rest of the world. Both net premiums and claims are recorded in the secondary distribution of income account or in the external account of primary incomes and current transfers.

41. Net non-life insurance premiums should be recorded on the basis of the amounts due to procure cover in the period of account, not the amounts due to be paid in the period. Insurance claims should be recorded on the basis of the amounts due at the date of the event concerned. An entry in the financial account records any difference between premiums payable and premiums earned and claims due and claims payable:

(a) By convention, prepayment of premiums and reserves against outstanding claims is shown as a change in liabilities of the insurance corporation and pension fund sub-sector (with a negative sign if necessary) and a change in assets of all sectors and the rest of the world.

An example of these flows is shown in table A.IV.3.

Other life insurance

42. Other life insurance transactions take place only between insurance corporations and households, resident and non-resident. The production of the insurance service is matched by the value of the services consumed by households as part of final consumption expenditure and exports. The property income attributed to insurance policyholders is treated as premium supplements, but premiums and claims are not shown separately in the case of other life insurance. Rather they constitute components of a net transaction recorded in the financial account, the financial asset involved being the net equity of households in life insurance reserves.

43. Four transactions are recorded in the account; one each relating to production and consumption of the insurance service, one showing the attribution of property income to the propertyholders and one showing the change in the net equity of households in life insurance reserves:

(a) The output of the life insurance activity is recorded in the production account for the insurance corporation and pension fund sub-sector;

(b) The value of the services consumed is recorded as final consumption expenditure payable by households in the use of disposable income account or as payable by the rest of the world (exports to non-resident households);

(c) Property income attributed to insurance policyholders in respect of other life insurance is recorded in the allocation of primary income account. It is recorded as payable by insurance corporations and pensions funds and receivable by resident households or non-resident households in the rest of the world;

(d) In the financial account the item net equity of households in life insurance reserves is shown as a change in assets of households and the rest of the world and a change in liabilities of insurance corporations. It is equal to actual premiums plus premium supplements (equal to the property income attributed to policyholders) less the value of the services consumed and less claims due.

An example of these flows is shown in table A.IV.4.

Table A.IV.3. Accounts for individual non-life insurance

Uses									Transactions and balancing items	Resources								
Total	Goods and service account	Rest of the world account	S.1 Total economy	S.15 NPISHs	S.14 House-holds	S.13 General govern-ment	S.12 Financial corpo-rations	S.11 Non-finan-cial corpo-rations		S.11 Non-finan-cial corpo-rations	S.12 Finan-cial corpo-rations	S.13 General govern-ment	S.14 House-holds	S.15 NPISHs	S.1 Total eco-nomy	Rest of the world account	Goods and service account	Total
									External account									
0	0	0							P.6 Exports of goods and services							0	0	0
0	0	0							P.7 Imports of goods and services							0	0	0
									Production account									
									P.1 Output		6				6			6
4	4	0	4	0	3	0	0	1	P.2 Intermediate consumption									
									Distribution of primary income account									
6		0	6				6		D.44 Property income attributable to insurance policyholders	5	0	0	1		6	0		6
									Secondary distribution of income account									
45		2	43	0	31	4	0	8	D.71 Net non-life insurance premiums		45	0		0	45	0		45
45		0	45				45		D.72 Non-life insurance claims	6	0	1	35	0	42	3		45
									Use of disposable income account									
2			2		2				P.3 Final consumption expenditure									
									Financial account									
2		0	2	0	2	0	0	0	F.62 Prepayment of premiums and reserves against outstanding claims		2				2			2

Table A.IV.4. Accounts for individual life insurance

Uses (left side) — Resources (right side). "Corresponding entries of the" sub-columns appear on the outer edges of each side.

Uses: Goods and service account	Uses: Rest of the world account	Uses: Total	Uses: S.1 Total economy	Uses: S.15 NPISHs	Uses: S.14 Households	Uses: S.13 General government	Uses: S.12 Financial corporations	Uses: S.11 Non-financial corporations	Transactions and balancing items	Res: S.11 Non-financial corporations	Res: S.12 Financial corporations	Res: S.13 General government	Res: S.14 Households	Res: S.15 NPISHs	Res: S.1 Total economy	Res: Total	Res: Rest of the world account	Res: Goods and service account
									External account									
0	0	0							P.6 Exports of goods and services							0		0
0		0							P.7 Imports of goods and services							0	0	
									Production account									
									P.1 Output		4				4	4		
									Distribution of primary income account									
		7	7				7		D.44 Property income attributable to insurance policyholders				7		7	7	0	
									Use of disposable income account									
		4	4		4				P.3 Final consumption expenditure									
									Financial account									
22	0	22	22		22				F.611 Net equity of households in life insurance reserves		22				22	22		0

Table A.IV.5.   Accounts for private funded social insurance other than pensions

Uses									Transactions and balancing items	Resources								
	Corresponding entries of the															Corresponding entries of the		
Total	Goods and service account	Rest of the world account	S.1 Total economy	S.15 NPISHs	S.14 Households	S.13 General government	S.12 Financial corporations	S.11 Non-financial corporations		S.11 Non-financial corporations	S.12 Financial corporations	S.13 General government	S.14 Households	S.15 NPISHs	S.1 Total economy	Rest of the world account	Goods and service account	Total
									External account									
0	0								P.6 Exports of goods and services								0	0
0	0								P.7 Imports of goods and services							0		0
									Production account									
									P.1 Output		1				1			1
									Generation of income account									
5			5	1	0	1	0	3	Employers' actual social contributions to private funded schemes									
									Distribution of primary income account									
									Employers' actual social contributions to private funded schemes				5		5	0		5
5		0	5				5		D.44 Property income attributable to insurance policyholders				5		5	0		5
									Secondary distribution of income account									
5			5		5				Employers' actual social contributions to private funded schemes (net) other than for pensions		5				5			5
8			8		8				Employees' net social contributions to private funded schemes other than for pensions		8				8			8
13			13				13		Private funded social benefits other than pensions				13		13			13
									Use of disposable income account									
1		0	1		1				P.3 Final consumption expenditure									
									Financial account									
1			1		1				F.62 Prepayment of premiums and reserves against outstanding claims		1				1			1

Private funded social insurance other than pensions

44. As explained above, all privately funded social insurance covering benefits other than pensions is carried out by insurance corporations. The output of this activity is measured in the same way as the output of other non-life insurance but the matching consumption of the services is payable only by the households of the beneficiaries. These will be resident households except where a resident producer employs non-residents. Similarly, the property income attributed to the beneficiaries of the social insurance schemes can only be receivable by the same households.

45. All contributions to the schemes are payable by the employee. The contributions include that part paid by the employer as part of compensation of employees in the generation of income account as payable by employers to employees. They also include contributions paid directly by the employee funded from wages and salaries. Further, the employee receives property income attributed to policyholders in respect of both these contributions and this is treated, in total, as contribution supplements. The two items of contributions appearing in the secondary distribution of income account are, first, the employers' actual social contributions which is exactly equal in value to the amount receivable by households from the employer in the generation of income account. The second item, called employees' social contributions includes the direct payment by the employees plus the contribution supplements less the service charge payable to the social insurance schemes.

46. Seven types of transactions must be recorded, one each relating to production and consumption of the insurance service, three relating to contributions and benefits, one to the property income attributable to policyholders and one to an adjustment in the financial account:

    (*a*) Since all such activity by resident units is undertaken by insurance corporations, the output is recorded in the production account of the insurance corporations and pension funds sub-sector;

    (*b*) Employers' actual social contributions to privately funded social insurance schemes are shown as a payable by the sector in which the employer is located in the generation of income account and a receivable by households in the allocation of primary income account;

    (*c*) Property income attributed to policyholders (beneficiaries) in respect of these schemes is payable by insurance corporations and pensions funds and receivable by employee households. Both payable and receivables amounts are recorded in the allocation of primary income account;

    (*d*) In the secondary distribution of income account, employers' actual social contributions and employees' social contributions by employees, including contribution supplements but excluding the value of the service consumed, are shown as payable by households and receivable by the insurance corporations and pension funds sub-sector;

    (*e*) Private funded social benefits other than pensions are also shown in the secondary distribution of income account as payable by the insurance corporations and pension funds sub-sector and receivable by households;

    (*f*) The value of the service is payable by households as part of final consumption expenditure, and is recorded in the use of income account, except for non-resident employee households where it is payable by the rest of the world;

    (*g*) The entry in the financial account, prepayment of premiums and reserves against outstanding claims, records any difference between contributions payable and contributions earned and benefits due and benefits payable. By convention this item is shown as a change in liabilities of the insurance corporation and pension fund sub-sector (with a negative sign if necessary) and a change in assets of employee households.

An example of these flows is shown in table A.IV.5.

Privately funded pensions

47. As compared with other privately funded benefits, the recording of transactions concerned with the provision of privately funded pensions contains two further complexities. The first of these concerns the treatment of non-autonomous pension funds. Although as explained above no separate output is recorded for these funds, net contributions are payable to these funds and pensions are payable by the funds. Since an employer in any sector may operate a non-autonomous pension fund, this means that any sector may in principle be the recipient of net contributions and the payer of pensions. In practice, however, since most privately funded pension schemes are operated by insurance corporations or autonomous pension funds, much the largest entries will still refer to the insurance corporation and pension fund sub-sector.

48. The second feature that affects pensions but not other privately funded social benefits is that only pension provision leads to the build-up of reserves that represent equity belonging to households. These reserves increase due to the payment of actual contributions and contribution supplements by households (excluding the cost of the services payable) and are decreased by the payment of pensions to households. Both these transactions are recorded in the secondary distribution of income account so any net addition to the reserves by households appear in the disposable income of the sectors operating the pension funds. If no

Table A.IV.6. Accounts for private funded pensions

Uses — Corresponding entries of the: Goods and service account	Uses — Corresponding entries of the: Rest of the world account	Uses — Total	Uses — S.1 Total economy	Uses — S.15 NPISHs	Uses — S.14 Households	Uses — S.13 General government	Uses — S.12 Financial corporations	Uses — S.11 Non-financial corporations	Transactions and balancing items	Resources — S.11 Non-financial corporations	Resources — S.12 Financial corporations	Resources — S.13 General government	Resources — S.14 Households	Resources — S.15 NPISHs	Resources — S.1 Total economy	Resources — Rest of the world account	Resources — Goods and service account	Resources — Total
									External account									
0		0							P.6 Exports of goods and services								0	0
0		0							P.7 Imports of goods and services							0		0
									Production account									
									P.1 Output		2				2			2
									Generation of income account									
	0	14	14	1	0	2		11	Employers' actual social contributions to private funded schemes									
									Distribution of primary income account									
									Employers' actual social contributions to private funded schemes				14		14	0	0	14
	0	7	7				7		D.44 Property income attributable to insurance policyholders				7		7	0	0	7
									Secondary distribution of income account									
	0	14	14		14				Employers' actual social contributions to private funded schemes (net) in respect of pensions	1	13	0	0	0	14	0		14
	0	13	13	0	13				Employees' net social contributions in respect of pensions	1	12	0	0	0	13	0		13
	0	16	16	0	0	0	15	1	Private funded pensions				16		16		0	16
									Use of disposable income account									
		2	2		2				P.3 Final consumption expenditure								0	0
	0	11	11	0		0	11	0	D.8 Adjustment for the change in net equity of households in pension funds				11		11		0	11
									Financial account									
		11	11		11				F.612 Net equity of households in pension fund reserves	0	11	0		0	11		0	11

adjustment were made, this element of disposable income would also enter the saving of those sectors. However, in keeping with the treatment of other life insurance, this element of saving is considered a part of household saving and the build-up of the reserves a change in assets of households in the financial account, specifically the acquisition of the financial asset net equity of households in pension fund reserves. To ensure the transactions are recorded in this way, an adjustment item is inserted in the use of disposable income (and use of adjusted disposable income account) showing the reattribution of this part of saving from insurance corporations and pension funds to households. Since again, non-autonomous pension funds are involved, all sectors may be affected by this adjustment.

49. Eight types of transactions must be recorded, one each relating to production and consumption of the insurance service, three relating to contributions and benefits, one to the property income attributable to policyholders, one to the adjustment item in the use of income accounts and one to the adjustment in the financial account:

(a) As explained above, output by resident units is recorded only in the production account of the insurance corporations and pension funds sub-sector;

(b) Employers' actual social contributions to privately funded social insurance schemes are shown as a payable by the sector in which the employer is located in the generation of income account and a receivable by households in the allocation of primary income account;

(c) Property income attributed to policyholders in respect of autonomous pension funds is payable by insurance corporations and pension funds and receivable by employee households. The property income attributable to policyholders payable in respect of non-autonomous pension funds is payable by the employers operating the schemes and receivable by employee households. Both payables and receivables are recorded in the allocation of primary income account;

(d) In the secondary distribution of income account, employers' actual social contributions and employees' social contributions are shown as payable by households and receivable either by the insurance corporations and pension funds sub-sector or by sectors operating a non-autonomous pension fund. The employers' actual contributions is exactly equal in value to the amount receivable by households from the employer in the generation of income account. The employees' social contributions include the direct payment by the employees plus the contribution supplements less any service charge payable to the social insurance schemes. For contributions to insurance corporations and to autonomous pension funds there is a cost of the associated service to exclude from the amount recorded in this account. There is no associated service in respect of contributions to non-autonomous funds;

(e) Privately funded pensions are also shown in the secondary distribution of income account as private funded social benefits payable by the sector operating the pension fund and receivable by households;

(f) The value of the insurance service is payable by households as part of final consumption expenditure, recorded in the use of income account, except for non-resident employee households where the payable is by the rest of the world and is recorded as an export of services;

(g) The adjustment for the change in net equity of households in pension funds is shown in the use of disposable income account (or use of adjusted disposable income account) as receivable by households and payable by any sector operating a pension fund. The entry is exactly equal to net contributions (as recorded in the secondary distribution of income account but only in respect of pensions) less pensions payable;

(h) An exactly matching item, of the opposite sign, is shown in the financial account, as net equity of households in pension fund reserves. It appears as a change in assets of households and the rest of the world and a change in liabilities of the sectors operating pension funds.

An example of these flows is shown in table A.IV.6.

Annex V
Classifications and accounts

Part I. Classifications

A. Classification of institutional sectors (S)

S.1 **Total economy**

S.11 Non-financial corporations

S.11001	Public non-financial corporations
S.11002	National private non-financial corporations
S.11003	Foreign controlled non-financial corporations

S.12 Financial corporations

S.121 Central bank
S.122 Other depository corporations

S.1221	*Deposit money corporations*
S.12211	Public
S.12212	National private
S.12213	Foreign controlled
S.1222	*Other depository corporations, except deposit money corporations*
S.12221	Public
S.12222	National private
S.12223	Foreign controlled

S.123 Other financial intermediaries, except insurance corporations and pension funds

S.12301	Public
S.12302	National private
S.12303	Foreign controlled

S.124 Financial auxiliaries

S.12401	Public
S.12402	National private
S.12403	Foreign controlled

S.125 Insurance corporations and pension funds

S.12501	Public
S.12502	National private
S.12503	Foreign controlled

S.13 General government

S.131 General government classification alternatives (1)

S.1311	*Central government*
S.1312	*State government*
S.1313	*Local government*
S.1314	*Social security funds*
S.13141	Central government social security funds
S.13142	State government social security funds
S.13143	Local government social security funds

S.132 General government classification alternatives (2)

S.1321	*Central government* [a]
S.13211	Central government
S.13212	Central government social security funds
S.1322	*State government* [a]
S.13221	State government
S.13222	State government social security funds
S.1323	*Local government* [a]
S.13231	Local government
S.13232	Local government social security funds

S.14 Households

S.141 Employers
S.142 Own account workers
S.143 Employees
S.144 Recipients of property and transfer income

S.1441	*Recipients of property income*
S.1442	*Recipients of pensions*
S.1443	*Recipients of other transfers*

S.15 Non-profit institutions serving households

S.2 **Rest of the world**

B. Classification of transactions and other flows

1.	**Transactions in goods and services (products) (P)**		**2.**	**Distributive transactions (D)**	

P.1	**Output**	
P.11	Market output	
P.12	Output for own final use	
P.13	Other non-market output	

P.2   **Intermediate consumption**

P.3   **Final consumption expenditure**

P.31   Individual consumption expenditure
P.32   Collective consumption expenditure

P.4   **Actual final consumption**

P.41   Actual individual consumption
P.42   Actual collective consumption

P.5   **Gross capital formation**

P.51   Gross fixed capital formation
      P.511   *Acquisitions less disposals of tangible fixed assets*
      P.5111   Acquisitions of new tangible fixed assets
      P.5112   Acquisitions of existing tangible fixed assets
      P.5113   Disposals of existing tangible fixed assets
      P.512   *Acquisitions less disposals of intangible fixed assets*
      P.5121   Acquisitions of new intangible fixed assets
      P.5122   Acquisitions of existing intangible fixed assets
      P.5123   Disposals of existing intangible fixed assets
      P.513   *Addition to the value of non-produced non-financial assets*
      P.5131   Major improvements to non-produced non-financial assets
      P.5132   Costs of ownership transfer on non-produced non-financial assets
P.52   Changes in inventories
P.53   Acquisitions less disposals of valuables

P.6   **Exports of goods and services**

P.61   Exports of goods
P.62   Exports of services

P.7   **Imports of goods and services**

P.71   Imports of goods
P.72   Imports of services

D.1   **Compensation of employees**

D.11   Wages and salaries
D.12   Employers' social contributions
      D.121   *Employers' actual social contributions*
      D.122   *Employers' imputed social contributions*

D.2   **Taxes on production and imports**

D.21   Taxes on products
      D.211   *Value added type taxes (VAT)*
      D.212   *Taxes and duties on imports excluding VAT*
      D.2121   Import duties
      D.2122   Taxes on imports excluding VAT and duties
      D.213   *Export taxes*
      D.214   *Taxes on products, except VAT, import and export taxes*
D.29   Other taxes on production

D.3   **Subsidies**

D.31   Subsidies on products
      D.311   *Import subsidies*
      D.312   *Export subsidies*
      D.319   *Other subsidies on products*
D.39   Other subsidies on production

D.4   **Property income**

D.41   Interest
D.42   Distributed income of corporations
      D.421   *Dividends*
      D.422   *Withdrawals from income of quasi-corporatic*
D.43   Reinvested earnings on direct foreign investment
D.44   Property income attributed to insurance policy holders
D.45   Rent

D.5   **Current taxes on income, wealth, etc.**

D.51   Taxes on income
D.59   Other current taxes

D.6   **Social contributions and benefits**

D.61   Social contributions
      D.611   *Actual social contributions*
      D.6111   Employers' actual social contributions
      D.61111   Compulsory employers' actual social contributions
      D.61112   Voluntary employers' actual social contributions
      D.6112   Employees' social contributions
      D.61121   Compulsory employees' social contributions
      D.61122   Voluntary employees' social contributions

D.6113 Social contributions by self- and non-employed persons

D.61131 Compulsory social contributions by self- and non-employed persons

D.61132 Voluntary social contributions by self- and non-employed persons

D.612 *Imputed social contributions*

D.62 Social benefits other than social transfers in kind

D.621 *Social security benefits in cash*

D.622 *Private funded social benefits*

D.623 *Unfunded employee social benefits*

D.624 *Social assistance benefits in cash*

D.63 Social transfers in kind

D.631 *Social benefits in kind*

D.6311 Social security benefits, reimbursements

D.6312 Other social security benefits in kind

D.6313 Social assistance benefits in kind

D.632 *Transfers of individual non-market goods and services*

D.7 Other current transfers

D.71 Net non-life insurance premiums

D.72 Non-life insurance claims

D.73 Current transfers within general government

D.74 Current international cooperation

D.75 Miscellaneous current transfers

D.8 Adjustment for the change in net equity of households in pension funds

D.9 Capital transfers

D.91 Capital taxes

D.92 Investment grants

D.99 Other capital transfers

3. Transactions in financial instruments (F) (net acquisition of financial assets/net incurrence of liabilities)

F.1 Monetary gold and SDRs

F.2 Currency and deposits [bc]

F.21 Currency

F.22 Transferable deposits

F.29 Other deposits

F.3 Securities other than shares [c]

F.31 Short-term

F.32 Long-term

F.4 Loans [cd]

F.41 Short-term

F.42 Long-term

F.5 Shares and other equity [d]

F.6 Insurance technical reserves

F.61 Net equity of households in life insurance reserves and in pension funds

F.611 *Net equity of households in life insurance reserves*

F.612 *Net equity of households in pension funds*

F.62 Prepayment of premiums and reserves against outstanding claims

F.7 Other accounts receivable/payable [d]

F.71 Trade credits and advances

F.79 Other accounts receivable/payable, except trade credits and advances

4. Other accumulation entries (K)

K.1 Consumption of fixed capital

K.2 Acquisitions less disposals of non-produced non-financial assets

K.21 Acquisitions less disposals of land and other tangible non-produced assets

K.211 *Acquisitions of land and other tangible non-produced assets*

K.212 *Disposals of land and other tangible non-produced assets*

K.22 Acquisitions less disposals of intangible non-produced assets

K.221 *Acquisitions of intangible non-produced assets*

K.222 *Disposals of intangible non-produced assets*

K.3 Economic appearance of non-produced assets

K.4 Economic appearance of produced assets

K.5 Natural growth of non-cultivated biological resources

K.6 Economic disappearance of non-produced assets

K.61 Depletion of natural assets

K.62 Other economic disappearance of non-produced assets

K.7 Catastrophic losses

K.8 Uncompensated seizures

K.9 Other volume changes in non-financial assets n.e.c.

K.10 Other volume changes in financial assets and liabilities n.e.c.

K.11 Nominal holding gains/losses

K.11.1 Neutral holding gains/losses

K.11.2 Real holding gains/losses

K.12 Changes in classifications and structure

K.12.1 Changes in sector classification and structure

K.12.2   Changes in classification of assets and liabilities
  K.12.21 Monetization/demonetization of gold
  K.12.22 Changes in classification of assets or
       liabilities other than monetization/
       demonetization of gold

C. Classification of balancing items [e] (B)

B.1 Value added / B.1[*] Domestic product

B.2 Operating surplus

B.3 Mixed income

B.4 Entrepreneurial income

B.5 Balance of primary incomes/ B.5[*] National income

B.6 Disposable income

B.7 Adjusted disposable income

B.8 Saving

B.9 Net lending/net borrowing

B.10 Changes in net worth

B.10.1 Changes in net worth due to saving and capital transfers [f,g]

B.10.2 Changes in net worth due to other changes in volume of assets

B.10.3 Changes in net worth due to nominal holding gains/losses

  B.10.31 Changes in net worth due to neutral holding gains/losses

  B.10.32 Changes in net worth due to real holding gains/losses

B.11 External balance of goods and services

B.12 Current external balance

B.90 Net worth

D. Classification of assets

1. Non-financial assets (AN)

AN.1 Produced assets

AN.11 Fixed assets [h]
  AN.111 *Tangible fixed assets*
  AN.1111 Dwellings
  AN.1112 Other buildings and structures
  AN.11121 Non-residential buildings
  AN.11122 Other structures
  AN.1113 Machinery and equipment
  AN.11131 Transport equipment
  AN.11132 Other machinery and equipment
  AN.1114 Cultivated assets
  AN.11141 Livestock for breeding, dairy, draught, etc.
  AN.11142 Vineyards, orchards and other plantations of trees yielding repeat products.
  AN.112 *Intangible fixed assets*
  AN.1121 Mineral exploration
  AN.1122 Computer software
  AN.1123 Entertainment, literary or artistic originals
  AN.1129 Other intangible fixed assets
AN.12 Inventories
  AN.121 *Materials and supplies*
  AN.122 *Work in progress*
  AN.1221 Work in progress on cultivated assets
  AN.1222 Other work in progress
  AN.123 *Finished goods*
  AN.124 *Goods for resale*
AN.13 Valuables
  AN.131 *Precious metals and stones*
  AN.132 *Antiques and other art objects*
  AN.139 *Other valuables*

AN.2 Non-produced assets

AN.21 Tangible non-produced assets
  AN.211 *Land*
  AN.2111 Land underlying buildings and structures
  AN.2112 Land under cultivation
  AN.2113 Recreational land and associated surface water
  AN.2119 Other land and associated surface water
  AN.212 *Subsoil assets*
  AN.2121 Coal, oil and natural gas reserves
  AN.2122 Metallic mineral reserves
  AN.2123 Non-metallic mineral reserves
  AN.213 *Non-cultivated biological resources*
  AN.214 *Water resources*
AN.22 Intangible non-produced assets
  AN.221 *Patented entities*
  AN.222 *Leases and other transferable contracts*
  AN.223 *Purchased goodwill*
  AN.229 *Other intangible non-produced assets*

2.   **Financial assets/liabilities (AF)**

AF.1   Monetary gold and SDRs

AF.2   Currency and deposits [ij]

AF.21   Currency
AF.22   Transferable deposits
AF.29   Other deposits

AF.3   Securities other than shares [j]

AF.31   Short-term
AF.32   Long-term

AF.4   Loans [jk]

AF.41   Short-term

AF.42   Long-term

AF.5   Shares and other equity [k]

AF.6   Insurance technical reserves

AF.61   Net equity of households on life insurance reserves and on pension funds
AF.62   Prepayment of premiums and reserves against outstanding claims

AF.7   Other accounts receivable/payable [k]

AF.71   Trade credits and advances
AF.79   Other accounts receivable/payable, except trade credits and advances

E. Elements of complementary classifications of transactions and other flows

These elements of complementary classifications are intended to meet various requirements:

(a) They show separately the estimated components of certain flows, when these components are not already isolated in the classifications of the System. The latter show separately, for instance, the reinvested earnings on direct foreign investment or the imputed social contributions. However, they do not isolate many flows whose value is not directly observed, such as the services of owner-occupied dwellings or barter transactions. These flows are shown separately in the elements of complementary classifications;

(b) They separately show, more generally, the various components of certain transactions, in terms of both monetary and non-monetary components. For example, under "Market output, except in trade", sales, barter transactions, payments in kind, etc., are shown separately. Or under "Household final consumption expenditure", purchases, bartered consumption goods and services, own final consumption and various components of it, certain transfers in kind, etc., are distinguished;

(c) They sometimes simply provide additional details to the classifications of the System. In certain cases, this detailing is made systematically, i.e., a given item is broken down exhaustively, among more detailed pieces. In other cases, only certain especially important details are suggested. In such cases, these details are introduced by saying "of which";

(d) They also include a number of transactions, adjustments and other elements which are used in the supply and use tables, such as trade and transport margins or direct purchases abroad by residents. In a sense, these items are directly part of the classifications of the System. However, they play an auxiliary role;

(e) A special set of complements shows the additional transactions that are needed in relation with the treatment of multiple exchange rates.

In a number of cases, showing separately various monetary and non-monetary components of certain transactions leads to showing the definition itself or one definition of these flows. Examples are provided by "Market output in trade" or "Changes in inventories of materials and supplies".

These elements of complementary classifications are provided to help countries if they want to show certain details, either directly in their accounts or in complementary tables. In a number of cases there is room for variants in practice. As their name indicates, these elements do not intend to be exhaustive. Other complements may be introduced if found meaningful, useful and feasible.

1.   Transactions and other flows, other elements on goods and services

Output
Principal output
Secondary output

Product
Principal product
Secondary product

Market output, except in trade
Sales, except sales of goods purchased for resale
Barter transactions
Payments in kind
    of which: Compensation of employees in kind

E. Elements of complementary classifications of transactions and other flows (*cont.*)

Deliveries between establishments belonging to the same market enterprise to be used as intermediate consumption
Changes in inventories of finished goods and work-in-progress intended for one of the above uses
Output of insurance services
    output of non-life insurance services
    output of life insurance services
Output of pension funds
Output of financial intermediation services
indirectly measured

Market output in trade
Sales of goods purchased for resale
plus Other uses of goods purchased for resale
    of which: Compensation of employees in kind
minus Purchases of goods for resale
plus   Changes in inventories of goods for resale

Non-market output
Own final consumption
    of which: services of owner-occupied dwellings
Own gross fixed capital formation
Goods and service supplied free, or at not economically significant prices, to other institutional units
Goods and services supplied by one non-market establishment to another
Changes in inventories of finished goods and work-in-progress intended for one of the above uses

Intermediate consumption
Purchases of materials and supplies
plus Other acquisitions of materials and supplies
    of which:
        Deliveries between establishments belonging to the same market enterprise to be used as intermediate consumption
minus Changes in inventories of materials and supplies

Household final consumption expenditure
Purchases of consumption goods and services
minus Sales of existing consumption goods and services
plus   Bartered consumption goods and services (net)
plus Own final consumption
    in subsistence economy
    services of owner-occupied dwellings
    domestic services produced by employing paid domestic servants
    other
plus *Compensation of employees in kind*
plus Transfers in kind (other than from government or non-profit institutions)
plus Insurance services
plus Pension funds services
plus Financial intermediation services indirectly measured

Household actual final consumption
Household final consumption expenditure
Social transfers in kind

Gross fixed capital formation
Acquisition less disposals of tangible fixed assets
    Acquisitions of new tangible fixed assets
      Purchases
      Barter transactions
      Own gross fixed capital formation
      Capital transfers in kind
    Acquisitions of existing tangible fixed assets
      Purchases
      Barter transactions
      Capital transfers in kind
    Disposals of existing tangible fixed assets
      Sales
      Barter transactions
      Capital transfers in kind
Acquisitions less disposals of intangible fixed assets
    Acquisitions of new intangible fixed assets
      Purchases
      Barter transactions
      Own gross fixed capital formation
      Capital transfers in kind
    Acquisitions of existing intangible fixed assets
      Purchases
      Barter transactions
      Capital transfers in kind
    Disposals of existing intangible fixed assets
      Sales
      Barter transactions
      Capital transfers in kind
Addition to the value of non-produced non-financial assets
    Major improvements to non-produced non-financial assets
      Purchases
      Barter transactions
      Own gross fixed capital formation
      Capital transfers in kind
    Cost of ownership transfer on non-produced non-financial assets

Own gross fixed capital formation
New tangible fixed assets
New intangible fixed assets
Major improvements to non-produced non-financial assets

Gross fixed capital formation
Consumption of fixed capital
Net fixed capital formation

Net addition to the stock of fixed assets
Net fixed capital formation
Other changes in volume of fixed assets
    Catastrophic losses

E. Elements of complementary classifications of transactions and other flows (*cont.*)

Uncompensated seizures
Other volume changes in non-financial assets n.e.c.

Changes in inventories
Additions to inventories
minus Withdrawals from inventories
minus Current losses in inventories

Changes in inventories of finished goods
and work-in-progress
Additions to inventories of finished goods and work-in-progress
minus Withdrawals from inventories of finished goods and work-in-progress
minus Current losses in inventories of finished goods and work-in-progress

Changes in inventories of goods for resale
Additions to inventories of goods for resale
minus Withdrawals from inventories of goods for resale
minus Current losses in inventories of goods for resale

Changes in inventories of materials and supplies
Additions to inventories of materials and supplies
minus Withdrawals from inventories of materials and supplies
minus Current losses in inventories of materials and supplies

Changes in inventories
Closing inventories
minus Opening inventories
minus Holding gains less losses on inventories
plus Exceptional losses in inventories

(Non-financial) net accumulation
Gross capital formation
minus Consumption of fixed capital
plus Other changes in volume of non-financial assets

Exports of goods
of which:
  Exports of goods for processing
  Exports of goods transformed from goods imported for processing
  Exports of repairs to fixed assets
  Exports of goods under financial leasing
  Exports of non-monetary gold
    for use as valuables
    for other uses
  Transfers in kind to the rest of the world
    current
    capital
  Direct purchases in the domestic market by non-residents

Exports of goods
of which:
  Barter transactions

Intra-company flows

Exports of services
of which:
  Transfers in kind to the rest of the world
  Exports of insurance services
  Exports of financial intermediation services indirectly measured
  Counterpart of transport and insurance services provided by residents to residents and included in the value of imports f.o.b.
  Direct purchases in the domestic market by non-residents

Imports of goods (Import of goods f.o.b.)
Imports of goods c.i.f.
minus c.i.f./f.o.b. adjustment on imports

Imports of goods
of which:
  Imports of goods for processing
  Imports of goods from goods exported for processing abroad
  Imports of repairs to fixed assets
  Imports of goods under financial leasing
  Imports of non-monetary gold
    for use as valuables
    for other uses
  Transfers in kind from the rest of the world
    current
    capital
  Direct purchases abroad by residents

Imports of goods
of which:
  Barter transactions
  Intra-company flows

Imports of services
of which:
  Transfers in kind from the rest of the world
  Imports of insurance services
  Imports of financial intermediation services indirectly measured
  Counterpart of transport and insurance services provided by non-residents to non-residents and included in the value of export f.o.b.
  Direct purchases abroad by residents

Transactions, adjustments and other elements used in the supply and use tables
  Trade and transport margins
  Trade margins
  Transport margins

C.i.f./f.o.b. adjustment on imports
Transport services on imports rendered by residents
Transport services on imports rendered by non-residents

E. Elements of complementary classifications of transactions and other flows (*cont.*)

Insurance services on imports rendered by residents
Insurance services on imports rendered by non-residents

Direct purchases abroad by residents

Direct purchases in the domestic market by non-residents

Labour inputs

Stocks of fixed assets, net

2. Distributive transactions

Wages and salaries
Wages and salaries in cash
Wages and salaries in kind

Interest
Nominal interest
plus Financial intermediation services indirectly measured, provided to depositors
less Financial intermediation services indirectly measured, provided to borrowers

Rent
on land
    in cash
    in kind
on subsoil assets
    in cash
    in kind

Insurance services

Non-life insurance services (total)
Non-life insurance total premiums earned
minus Non-life insurance claims

Life insurance services (total)
Life insurance total premiums earned
Plus Net income from the investment of all (both life and non-life) insurance technical reserves
minus (Life) claims due
minus Changes in (life) actuarial reserves and reserves for with-profits insurance *less* Holding gains/losses allocated to (life) insurance policy holders
Non-life insurance premiums less service charges
Non-life insurance total premiums earned
minus Non-life insurance services

Current international cooperation
    in cash
    in kind

Miscellaneous current transfers
of which:
    Transfers to non-profit institutions
    Transfers between resident households
        in cash
        in kind

Remittances from family members living abroad
    in cash
    in kind
Fines and penalties
Lotteries and gambling
Payments of compensation

Capital transfers
Capital taxes
Investment grants
    in cash
    in kind
Other capital transfers
    in cash
    in kind
    of which: Debt cancellation

3. Complements in relation with the treatment of multiple exchange rates

Taxes on production and imports
...
    ...
        ...
        Taxes on imports excl. VAT and duties
            Implicit taxes on imports resulting from multiple exchange rates
            Others
        Export taxes
            Implicit taxes on exports resulting from multiple exchange rates
            Others
        ...
    Other taxes on production
        Implicit taxes on primary incomes resulting from multiple exchange rates
        Others

Subsidies
...
    Import subsidies
        Implicit subsidies on imports resulting from multiple exchange rates
        Others
    Export subsidies
        Implicit subsidies on exports resulting from multiple exchange rates
        Others
    ...
    Other subsidies on production
        Implicit subsidies on primary incomes resulting from multiple exchange rates
        Others

E. Elements of complementary classifications of transactions and other flows (*cont.*)

Current taxes on income, wealth, etc.

...

Other current taxes

    Implicit other current taxes resulting from multiple exchange rates

    Others

Other current transfers

...

Miscellaneous current transfers

of which:

    ...

    ...

    Implicit other current transfers resulting from multiple exchange rates

    Implicit current transfers between monetary authorities inrelation with multiple exchange rates

Capital transfers

Capital taxes

    Implicit capital taxes resulting from multiple exchange rates

    Others

...

Other capital transfers

    Implicit other capital transfers resulting from multiple exchange rates

    Implicit capital transfers between monetary authorities in relation with multiple exchange rates

    Others

Transactions, adjustments and other elements used in the supply and use table

Implicit taxes/subsidies on imports resulting from multiple exchange rates

Implicit taxes/subsidies on exports resulting from multiple exchange rates

Implicit taxes resulting from multiple exchange rates [1]

Implicit subsidies resulting from multiple exchange rates [1]

F. International Standard Industrial Classification of all Economic Activities (ISIC), Rev. 3

Tabulation categories	Division	Description
A		Agriculture, hunting and forestry
	01	Agriculture, hunting and related service activities
	02	Forestry, logging and related service activities
B		Fishing
	05	Fishing, operation of fish hatcheries and fish farms; service activities incidental to fishing
C		Mining and quarrying
	10	Mining of coal and lignite; extraction of peat
	11	Extraction of crude petroleum and natural gas; service activities incidental to oil and gas extraction excluding surveying
	12	ining of uranium and thorium ores
	13	Mining of metal ores
	14	Other mining and quarrying
D		Manufacturing
	15	Manufacture of food products and beverages
	16	Manufacture of tobacco products
	17	Manufacture of textiles
	18	Manufacture of wearing apparel; dressing and dyeing of fur
	19	Tanning and dressing of leather; manufacture of luggage, handbags, saddlery, harness and footwear
	20	Manufacture of wood and of products of wood and cork, except furniture; manufacture of articles of straw and plaiting materials
	21	Manufacture of paper and paper products
	22	Publishing, printing and reproduction of recorded media
	23	Manufacture of coke, refined petroleum products and nuclear fuel
	24	Manufacture of chemicals and chemical products
	25	Manufacture of rubber and plastics products
	26	Manufacture of other non-metallic mineral products
	27	Manufacture of basic metals
	28	Manufacture of fabricated metal products, except machinery and equipment
	29	Manufacture of machinery and equipment n.e.c.
	30	Manufacture of office, accounting and computing machinery
	31	Manufacture of electrical machinery and apparatus n.e.c.
	32	Manufacture of radio, television and communication equipment and apparatus
	33	Manufacture of medical, precision and optical instruments, watches and clocks

Tabulation categories	Division	Description
	34	Manufacture of motor vehicles, trailers and semi-trailers
	35	Manufacture of other transport equipment
	36	Manufacture of furniture; manufacturing n.e.c.
	37	Recycling
E		Electricity, gas and water supply
	40	Electricity, gas, steam and hot water supply
	41	Collection, purification and distribution of water
F		Construction
	45	Construction
G		Wholesale and retail trade; repair of motor vehicles, motorcycles and personal and household goods
	50	Sale, maintenance and repair of motor vehicles and motorcycles; retail sale of automotive fuel
	51	Wholesale trade and commission trade, except of motor vehicles and motorcycles
	52	Retail trade, except of motor vehicles and motorcycles; repair of personal and household goods
H		Hotels and restaurants
	55	Hotels and restaurants
I		Transport, storage and communications
	60	Land transport; transport via pipelines
	61	Water transport
	62	Air transport
	63	Supporting and auxiliary transport activities; activities of travel agencies
	64	Post and telecommunications
J		Financial intermediation
	65	Financial intermediation, except insurance and pension funding
	66	Insurance and pension funding, except compulsory social security
	67	Activities auxiliary to financial intermediation
K		Real estate, renting and business activities
	70	Real estate activities
	71	Renting of machinery and equipment without operator and of personal and household goods
	72	Computer and related activities
	73	Research and development
	74	Other business activities

Tabulation categories	Division	Description
L		Public administration and defence; compulsory social security
	75	Public administration and defence; compulsory social security
M		Education
	80	Education
N		Health and social work
	85	Health and social work
O		Other community, social and personal service activities
	90	Sewage and refuse disposal, sanitation and similar activities
	91	Activities of membership organizations n.e.c.
	92	Recreational, cultural and sporting activities
	93	Other service activities
P		Private households with employed persons
	95	Private households with employed persons
Q		Extra-territorial organizations and bodies
	99	Extra-territorial organizations and bodies

G. Central Product Classification (CPC)

Section Division

0   Agriculture, forestry and fishery products

01   Products of agriculture, horticulture and market gardening
02   Live animals and animal products
03   Forestry and logging products
04   Fish and other fishing products

1   Ores and minerals; electricity, gas and water

11   Coal and lignite; peat
12   Crude petroleum and natural gas
13   Uranium and thorium ores
14   Metal ores
15   Stone, sand and clay
16   Other minerals
17   Electricity, town gas, steam and hot water
18   Water

2   Food products, beverages and tobacco; textiles, apparel and leather products

21   Meat, fish, fruit, vegetables, oils and fats
22   Dairy products
23   Grain mill products, starches and starch products; other food product
24   Beverages
25   Tobacco products
26   Yarn and thread; woven and tufted textile fabrics
27   Textile articles other than apparel
28   Knitted or crocheted fabrics; wearing apparel
29   Leather and leather products; footwear

3   Other transportable goods, except metal products, machinery and equipment

31   Products of wood, cork, straw and plaiting materials
32   Pulp, paper and paper products; printed matter and related articles
33   Coke oven products; refined petroleum products; nuclear fuel
34   Basic chemicals
35   Other chemical products; man-made fibres
36   Rubber and plastics products
37   Glass and glass products and other non-metallic products n.e.c.
38   Furniture; other transportable goods n.e.c.
39   Wastes or scraps

4   Metal products, machinery and equipment

41   Basic metals
42   Fabricated metal products, except machinery and equipment
43   General purpose machinery
44   Special purpose machinery
45   Office, accounting and computing machinery
46   Electrical machinery and apparatus
47   Radio, television and communication equipment and apparatus
48   Medical appliances, precision and optical instruments, watches and clocks
49   Transport equipment

5   Construction work and constructions; land

51   Construction work
52   Constructions
53   Land

6   Trade services; hotel and restaurant services

61   Sale, maintenance and repair services of motor vehicles and motorcycles
62   Commission agents' and wholesale trade services, except of motor vehicles and motorcycles
63   Retail trade services; repair services of personal and household goods
64   Hotel and restaurant services

7   Transport, storage and communications services

71   Land transport services
72   Water transport services
73   Air transport services
74   Supporting and auxiliary transport services
75   Post and telecommunications services

8   Business services; agricultural, mining and manufacturing services

81   Financial intermediation services and auxiliary services therefor
82   Real estate services
83   Leasing or rental services without operator
84   Computer and related services
85   Research and development services
86   Legal, accounting, auditing and book-keeping services; taxation services; market research and public opinion polling services; management and consulting services; architectural, engineering and other technical services
87   Business services n.e.c.
88   Agricultural, mining and manufacturing services
89   Intangible assets

9   Community, social and personal services

     91   Public administration and other services to the community as a whole; compulsory social security services

     92   Education services

     93   Health and social services

     94   Sewage and refuse disposal, sanitation and other environmental protection services

     95   Services of membership organizations

     96   Recreational, cultural and sporting services

     97   Other services

     98   Private households with employed persons

     99   Services provided by extraterritorial organizations and bodies

H. Classification of individual consumption by purpose (COICOP) (one- and two-digit levels)

1.   Food, beverages and tobacco

     1.1   Food

     1.2   Beverages

     1.3   Tobacco

2.   Clothing and footwear

     2.1   Clothing

     2.2   Footwear

3.   Housing, water, electricity, gas and other fuels

     3.1   Gross rents

     3.2   Regular maintenance and repair of dwelling

     3.3   Other services relating to the dwelling

     3.4   Electricity, gas and other fuels

4.   Furnishings, household equipment and routine maintenance of the house

     4.1   Furniture, furnishings and decorations, carpets and other floor coverings and repairs

     4.2   Household textiles

     4.3   Heating and cooking appliances; refrigerators, washing machines, similar major household appliances, including fittings and repairs

     4.4   Glassware, tableware and household utensils

     4.5   Tools and equipment for the house and garden

     4.6   Goods and services for routine household maintenance

5.   Health

     5.1   Medical and pharmaceutical products and therapeutic appliances and equipment

     5.2   Non-hospital medical and paramedical services

     5.3   Hospital services

     5.4   Sickness and accident insurance services

6.   Transport

     6.1   Purchase of vehicles

     6.2   Operation of personal transport equipment

     6.3   Transports services

7.   Leisure, entertainment and culture

     7.1   Equipment and accessories, including repairs

     7.2   Recreational and cultural services

     7.3   Newspapers, books and stationery

8.   Education

     8.1   Educational services

     8.2   Educational materials

     8.3   Ancillary educational services

9.   Hotels, cafés and restaurants

     9.1   Catering

     9.2   Accommodation services

10.   Miscellaneous goods and services

     10.1 Personal care

     10.2 Personal effects n.e.c.

     10.3 Communications

     10.4 Social services

     10.5 Financial services n.e.c.

     10.6 Other services n.e.c.

I. Classification of the Functions of the Government (COFOG)

01   General public services

01.1 Executive and legislative organs, financial and fiscal affairs, external affairs other than foreign aid
01.2 Foreign economic aid
01.3 Fundamental research affairs and services
01.4 General services
01.5 General public services n.e.c

02   Defence affairs and services

02.1 Military and civil defence administration and operation
02.2 Foreign military aid
02.3 Defence-related applied research and experimental development
02.4 Defence affairs n.e.c.

03   Public order and safety affairs

03.1 Police and fire protection
03.2 Law courts
03.3 Prison administration and operation
03.4 Public order and safety affairs n.e.c.
04   Education affairs and services
04.1 Pre-primary and primary education affairs and services (ISCED levels 0 and 1)
04.2 Secondary education affairs and services (ISCED levels 2 and 3)
04.3 Tertiary education affairs and services (ISCED levels 5, 6 and 7)
04.4 Education services not definable by level (ISCED level 9)
04.5 Subsidiary services to education
04.6 Education affairs and services n.e.c.

05   Health affairs and services

05.1 Hospital affairs and services
05.2 Clinics, and medical, dental and para-medical practitioners
05.3 Public health affairs and services
05.4 Medicaments, protheses, medical equipment and appliances or other prescribed health-related products
05.5 Applied research and experimental development related to the health and medical delivery system
05.6 Health affairs and services n.e.c.

06   Social security and welfare affairs and services

06.1 Social security affairs and services
06.2 Welfare affairs and services
06.3 Social security and welfare affairs n.e.c.

07   Housing and community amenity affairs and services

07.1 Housing and community development
07.2 Water supply affairs and services
07.3 Sanitary affairs and services including pollution abatement and control
07.4 Street lighting affairs and services
07.5 Housing and community amenity affairs and services n.e.c.

08   Recreational, cultural and religious affairs and services

08.0 Recreational, cultural and religious affairs and services

09   Fuel and energy affairs and services

09.1 Fuel affairs and services
09.2 Electricity and other energy sources
09.3 Fuel and energy affairs and services n.e.c.

10   Agriculture, forestry, fishing and hunting affairs and services

10.1 Agriculture affairs and services
10.2 Forestry affairs and services
10.3 Fishing and hunting affairs and services
10.4 Agricultural research and experimental development n.e.c.
10.5 Agriculture, forestry, fishing and hunting affairs and services n.e.c.

11   Mining and mineral resource affairs and services, other than fuels; manufacturing affairs and services; and construction affairs and services

11.1 Mining and mineral resource affairs and services, other than fuels
11.2 Manufacturing affairs and services
11.3 Construction affairs and services
11.4 Mining and mineral resource affairs and services n.e.c.; manufacturing affairs and services n.e.c.; and construction affairs and services n.e.c.

12   Transportation and communication affairs and services

12.1 Road transport affairs and services
12.2 Water transport affairs and services
12.3 Railway affairs and services
12.4 Air transport affairs and services
12.5 Pipeline transport and other transport system affairs and services
12.6 Transportation system affairs and services n.e.c.
12.7 Communication affairs and services
12.8 Transportation and communication affairs and services n.e.c

13   Other economic affairs and services

    13.1 Distribution trade affairs and services
       including storage and warehousing; hotel
       and restaurant affairs and services
    13.2 Tourism affairs and services
    13.3 Multipurpose development project affairs
       and services

13.4 General economic and commercial affairs
     other than general labour affairs
13.5 General labour affairs and services
13.6 Other economic affairs and services n.e.c.

14   Expenditures not classified by major group

    14.0 Expenditure not classified by major group

J. Classification of the purposes of the non-profit institutions serving households (COPNI)

1.   Research and scientific services
2.   Education services
3.   Health services
4.   Welfare services
5.   Recreational, cultural and related services
6.   Religious services
7.   Services of professional and labour organizations and civic associations
8.   Miscellaneous services not elsewhere classified

K. Classification of outlays of producers by purpose (COPP) (one - and two-digit levels)

1.   Outlays on current production programmes
2.   Outlays on repair and maintenance

    2.1   Outlays to make good breakage and to keep fixed assets in good working order
    2.2   Outlays on cleaning and general housekeeping

3.   Outlays on engineering and related technological work

    3.1   Outlays on engineering and technological work
    3.2   Outlays on fashion designing and other artistic design work

4.   Outlays on research and development

4.1   Outlays on basic research
4.2   Outlays on applied research
4.3   Outlays on experimental development

5.   Outlays on pollution abatement and control
6.   Outlays on sales promotion

6.1   Outlays on direct sales effort
6.2   Outlays on advertising
6.3   Outlays on sales promotion, not elsewhere classified

7.   Outlays on external transportation
8.   Outlays on employee training, welfare and morale
9.   Outlays on general administration

Notes

[a] Including social security funds of this level of government.

[b] The following memorandum items are related to the elements of the category F.2 "currency and deposits":
m11: denominated in national currency
m12: denominated in foreign currency
m21: liability of resident institutions
m22: liability of the rest of the world

[c] The suggested breakdown is optional.

[d] Memo item: F.m direct foreign investment.

[e] All balancing items can be measured gross or net of consumption of fixed capital. The code for gross balancing item is constituted of the code for the item plus the letter "g". Similarly, the letter "n" attached to a code indicates net values.

[f] "Changes in net worth due to saving and capital transfers" is not a balancing item in the structure of the System. It is the total of the right-hand side of the capital account. However, as a significant component of changes in net worth, it is coded with the other components of the latter.

[g] "Changes in net worth due to saving and capital transfers" for the rest of the world refers to changes in net worth due to current external balance and capital transfers.

[h] Memorandum item AN.m Consumer durables.

[i] The following memorandum items are related to the categories of the item AF.2 "currency and deposits":
m11: denominated in national currency
m12: denominated in foreign currency
m21: liability of resident institutions
m22: liability of the rest of the world

[j] The suggested breakdown is optional.

[k] memorandum item AF.m : direct foreign investment

[l] Also used in the integrated economic accounts.

Part II. Accounts

Table A.V.1. Account 0: Goods and services account

Resources				Uses			
P.1	Output [1]		3 604	P.2	Intermediate consumption		1 883
P.11	Market output		3 057				
P.12	Output for own use		171	P.3/P.4	Final consumption expenditure/Actual final consumption		1 399
P.13	Other non-market output		376	P.31/P.41	Individual consumption expenditure/Actual individual consumption		1 243
				P.32/P.42	Collective consumption expenditure/Actual collective consumption		156
D.21	Taxes on products [1]		141				
D.31	Subsidies on products [1]		− 8	P.51	Gross fixed capital formation		376
				P.511	Acquisitions less disposals of tangible fixed assets		303
P.7	Imports of goods and services		499	P.5111	Acquisitions of new tangible fixed assets		305
P.71	Imports of goods		392	P.5112	Acquisitions of existing tangible fixed assets		11
P.72	Imports of services		107	P.5113	Disposals of existing tangible fixed assets		− 13
				P.512	Acquisitions less disposals of intangible fixed assets		51
				P.5121	Acquisitions of new intangible fixed assets		53
				P.5122	Acquisitions of existing intangible fixed assets		6
				P.5123	Disposals of existing intangible fixed assets		− 8
				P.513	Additions to the value of non-produced non-financial assets		22
				P.5131	Major improvements to non-produced non-financial assets		5
				P.5132	Costs of ownership transfer on non-produced non-financial assets		17
				P.52	Changes in inventories		28
				P.53	Acquisitions less disposals of valuables		10
				P.6	Exports of goods and services		540
				P.61	Exports of goods		462
				P.62	Exports of services		78

1 For the valuation of output and the resulting contents of the items "Taxes on products" and "Subsidies on products", refer to chapter VI, paragraphs 6.210 to 6.227.

Table A.V.2. Full sequence of accounts for the total economy

I: Production account

Uses				Resources		
P.2	Intermediate consumption		1 883	P.1	Output [1]	3 604
				P.11	Market output	3 057
				P.12	Output for own final use	171
				P.13	Other non-market output	376
				D.31	Taxes less subsidies on products [1]	133
B.1*g	*Gross domestic product* [2]		1 854			
K.1	Consumption of fixed capital		222			
B.1*n	*Net domestic product* [2]		1 632			

1 For the valuation of output, refer to chapter VI, paragraphs 6.210 to 6.227.
2 Gross domestic product/net domestic product is equal to the value added of the institutional sectors plus taxes less subsidies on products.

II. Distribution and use of income accounts

II.1: Primary distribution of income account

II.1.1: Generation of income account

Uses			Resources	
D.1	Compensation of employees	762	B.1	*Domestic product* [2][3]	1 632
D.11	Wages and salaries	569		
D.12	Employers' social contributions	193		
D.121	Employers' actual social contributions	174		
D.122	Employers' imputed social contributions	19		
D.2	Taxes on production and imports	235		
D.21	Taxes on products [1]	141		
D.211	Value added type taxes (VAT)	121		
D.212	Taxes and duties on imports excluding VAT	17		
D.2121	Import duties	17		
D.2122	Taxes on imports excluding VAT and duties	0		
D.213	Export taxes	1		
D.214	Taxes on products except VAT, import and export taxes	2		
D.29	Other taxes on production	94		
D.3	Subsidies	− 44		
D.31	Subsidies on products [1]	− 8		
D.311	Import subsidies	0		
D.312	Export subsidies	0		
D.319	Other subsidies on products	− 8		
D.39	Other subsidies on production	− 36		
B.2	*Operating surplus* [2]	247		
B.3	*Mixed income* [2]	432		

1 For the contents of the items "Taxes on products" and "Subsidies on products", refer to chapter VI, paragraphs 6.210 to 6.227.
2 The opening and the closing balancing item of this account can be expressed in gross or in net terms. The amount presented refers to the net value.
3 Domestic product is equal to the value added of the institutional sectors plus taxes less subsidies on products.

able A.V.2. Full sequence of accounts for the total economy [cont.]

II.1.2: Allocation of primary income account

Uses				Resources		
D.4	Property income	391		B.2	*Operating surplus* [1]	247
D.41	Interest	217		B.3	*Mixed income* [1]	432
D.42	Distributed income of corporations	84				
D.421	Dividends	60		D.1	Compensation of employees	766
D.422	Withdrawals from income of quasi-corporations	24		D.11	Wages and salaries	573
D.43	Reinvested earnings on direct foreign investment	0		D.12	Employers' social contributions	193
D.44	Property income attributed to insurance policyholders	25		D.121	Employers' actual social contributions	174
D.45	Rent	65		D.122	Employers' imputed social contributions	19
				D.2	Taxes on production and imports	235
				D.21	Taxes on products	141
				D.211	Value added type taxes (VAT)	121
				D.212	Taxes and duties on imports excluding VAT	17
				D.2121	Import duties	17
				D.2122	Taxes on imports excluding VAT and duties	0
				D.213	Export taxes	1
				D.214	Taxes on products except VAT, import and export taxes	2
				D.29	Other taxes on production	94
				D.3	Subsidies	− 44
				D.31	Subsidies on products	− 8
				D.311	Import subsidies	0
				D.312	Export subsidies	0
				D.319	Other subsidies on products	− 8
				D.39	Other subsidies on production	− 36
				D.4	Property income	416
				D.41	Interest	209
				D.42	Distributed income of corporations	103
				D.421	Dividends	46
				D.422	Withdrawals from income of quasi-corporations	57
				D.43	Reinvested earnings on direct foreign investment	14
				D.44	Property income attributed to insurance policyholders	25
				D.45	Rent	65
B.5*	*National income* [1]	1 661				

1 The opening and the closing balancing item of this account can be expressed in gross or in net terms. The amount presented refers to the net value.

Table A.V.2. Full sequence of accounts for the total economy [cont.]

II.1.2.1: Entrepreneurial income account

Uses				Resources			
D.4	Property income [2]		236	B.2	*Operating surplus [1]*		24
D.41	Interest		166	B.3	*Mixed income [1]*		43
D.44	Property income attributed to insurance policyholders		25				
D.45	Rent		45	D.4	Property income [2]		23
				D.41	Interest		13
				D.42	Distributed income of corporations		3
				D.421	Dividends		3
				D.422	Withdrawals from income of quasi-corporations		0
				D.43	Reinvested earnings on direct foreign investment		1
				D.44	Property income attributed to insurance policyholders		
B.4	*Entrepreneurial income [1]*		679	D.45	Rent		44

1 The opening and the closing balancing item of this account can be expressed in gross or in net terms. The amount presented refers to the net value.
2 Including only property income connected with market activities.

II.1.2.2: Allocation of other primary income account

Uses				Resources			
D.4	Property income		155	B.4	*Entrepreneurial income [1]*		679
D.41	Interest [2]		51				
D.42	Distributed income of corporations		84	D.1	Compensation of employees		766
D.421	Dividends		60	D.11	Wages and salaries		573
D.422	Withdrawals from income of quasi-corporations		24	D.12	Employers' social contributions		193
D.43	Reinvested earnings on direct foreign investment		0	D.121	Employers' actual social contributions		174
D.45	Rent [2]		20	D.122	Employers' imputed social contributions		19
				D.2	Taxes on production and imports		235
				D.21	Taxes on products		141
				D.211	Value added type taxes (VAT)		121
				D.212	Taxes and duties on imports excluding VAT		17
				D.2121	Import duties		17
				D.2122	Taxes on imports excluding VAT and duties		0
				D.213	Export taxes		1
				D.214	Taxes on products except VAT, import and export taxes		2
				D.29	Other taxes on production		94
				D.3	Subsidies		– 44
				D.31	Subsidies on products		– 8
				D.311	Import subsidies		0
				D.312	Export subsidies		0
				D.319	Other subsidies on products		– 8
				D.39	Other subsidies on production		– 36
				D.4	Property income [3]		180
				D.41	Interest		70
				D.42	Distributed income of corporations		66
				D.421	Dividends		9
				D.422	Withdrawals from income of quasi-corporations		57
				D.43	Reinvested earnings on direct foreign investment		3
				D.44	Property income attributed to insurance policyholders		20
B.5*	*National income [1]*		1 661	D.45	Rent		21

1 The opening and the closing balancing item of this account can be expressed in gross or in net terms. The amount presented refers to the net value.
2 Not connected with market activities.

3 Including only property income not connected with market activities.

Table A.V.2. Full sequence of accounts for the total economy [cont.]

II.2: Secondary distribution of income account

Uses				Resources		
				B.5	*National income* [1]	1 661
D.5	Current taxes on income, wealth, etc.	212				
D.51	Taxes on income	203		D.5	Current taxes on income, wealth, etc.	213
D.59	Other current taxes	9		D.51	Taxes on income	204
				D.59	Other current taxes	9
D.61	Social contributions	322		D.61	Social contributions	322
D.611	Actual social contributions	303		D.611	Actual social contributions	303
D.6111	Employers' actual social contributions	174		D.6111	Employers' actual social contributions	174
D.61111	Compulsory employers' actual social contributions	160		D.61111	Compulsory employers' actual social contributions	160
D.61112	Voluntary employers' actual social contributions	14		D.61112	Voluntary employers' actual social contributions	14
D.6112	Employees' social contributions	97		D.6112	Employees' social contributions	97
D.61121	Compulsory employees' social contributions	85		D.61121	Compulsory employers' actual social contributions	85
D.61122	Voluntary employees' social contributions	12		D.61122	Voluntary employers' actual social contributions	12
D.6113	Social contributions by self- and non-employed persons	32		D.6113	Social contributions by self- and non-employed persons	32
D.61131	Compulsory social contributions by self- and non-employed persons	22		D.61131	Compulsory social contributions by self- and non-employed persons	22
D.61132	Voluntary social contributions by self- and non-employed persons	10		D.61132	Voluntary social contributions by self- and non-employed persons	10
D.612	Imputed social contributions	19		D.612	Imputed social contributions	19
D.62	Social benefits other than social transfers in kind	332		D.62	Social benefits other than social transfers in kind	332
D.621	Social security benefits in cash	232		D.621	Social security benefits in cash	232
D.622	Private funded social benefits	29		D.622	Private funded social benefits	29
D.623	Unfunded employee social benefits	19		D.623	Unfunded employee social benefits	19
D.624	Social assistance benefits in cash	52		D.624	Social assistance benefits in cash	52
D.7	Other current transfers	269		D.7	Other current transfers	239
D.71	Net non-life insurance premiums	43		D.71	Net non-life insurance premiums	45
D.72	Non-life insurance claims	45		D.72	Non-life insurance claims	42
D.73	Current transfers within general government	96		D.73	Current transfers within general government	96
D.74	Current international cooperation	31		D.74	Current international cooperation	1
D.75	Miscellaneous current transfers	54		D.75	Miscellaneous current transfers	55
B.6	*Disposable income* [1]	1 632				

1   The opening and the closing balancing item of this account can be expressed in gross or in net terms. The amount presented refers to the net value.

II.3: Redistribution of income in kind account

Uses				Resources		
				B.6	*Disposable income* [1]	1 632
D.63	Social transfers in kind	228				
D.631	Social benefits in kind	162		D.63	Social transfers in kind	228
D.6311	Social security benefits, reimbursements	78		D.631	Social benefits in kind	162
D.6312	Other social security benefits in kind	65		D.6311	Social security benefits, reimbursements	78
D.6313	Social assistance benefits in kind	19		D.6312	Other social security benefits in kind	65
D.632	Transfers of individual non-market goods and services	66		D.6313	Social assistance benefits in kind	19
				D.632	Transfers of individual non-market goods and services	66
B.7	*Adjusted disposable income* [1]	1 632				

1   The opening and the closing balancing item of this account can be expressed in gross or in net terms. The amount presented refers to the net value.

Table A.V.2.   Full sequence of accounts for the total economy [cont.]

II.4: Use of income account

II.4.1: Use of disposable income account

Uses			Resources		
P.3	Final consumption expenditure	1 399	B.6	*Disposable income* [1]	1 632
P.31	Individual consumption expenditure	1243			
P.32	Collective consumption expenditure	156	D.8	Adjustment for the change in net equity of households on pension funds	11
D.8	Adjustment for the change in net equity of households on pension funds	11			
B.8	*Saving* [1]	233			

1   The opening and the closing balancing item of this account can be expressed in gross or in net terms. The amount presented refers to the net value.

II.4.2: Use of adjusted disposable income account

Uses			Resources		
P.4	Actual final consumption	1 399	B.7	*Adjusted disposable income* [1]	1 632
P.41	Actual individual consumption	1 243			
P.42	Actual collective consumption	156	D.8	Adjustment for the change in net equity of households on pension funds	11
D.8	Adjustment for the change in net equity of households on pension funds	11			
B.8	*Saving* [1]	233			

1   The opening and the closing balancing item of this account can be expressed in gross or in net terms. The amount presented refers to the net value.

Table A.V.2. Full sequence of accounts for the total economy [cont.]

III. Accumulation accounts

III.1: Capital account

Changes in assets

P.51	Gross fixed capital formation	376
P.511	Acquisitions less disposals of tangible fixed assets	303
P.5111	Acquisitions of new tangible fixed assets	305
P.5112	Acquisitions of existing tangible fixed assets	11
P.5113	Disposals of existing tangible fixed assets	− 13
P.512	Acquisitions less disposals of intangible fixed assets	51
P.5121	Acquisitions of new intangible fixed assets	53
P.5122	Acquisitions of existing intangible fixed assets	6
P.5123	Disposals of existing intangible fixed assets	− 8
P.513	Additions to the value of non-produced non-financial assets	22
P.5131	Major improvements to non-produced non-financial assets	5
P.5132	Costs of ownership transfer on non-produced non-financial assets	17
K.1	Consumption of fixed capital	− 222
P.52	Changes in inventories	28
P.53	Acquisitions less disposals of valuables	10
K.2	Acquisitions less disposals of non-produced non-financial assets	0
K.21	Acquisitions less disposals of land and other tangible non-produced assets	0
K.22	Acquisitions less disposals of intangible non-produced assets	0
B.9	*Net lending (+) / Net borrowing (−)*	38

Changes in liabilities and net worth

B.8n	*Saving, net*	233
D.9	Capital transfers, receivable	62
D.91	Capital taxes	2
D.92	Investment grants	23
D.99	Other capital transfers	37
D.9	Capital transfers, payable	− 65
D.91	Capital taxes	− 2
D.92	Investment grants	27
D.99	Other capital transfers	− 36
B.10.1	*Changes in net worth due to saving and capital transfers* [1]	230

1 "Changes in net worth due to saving and capital transfers" is not a balancing item but corresponds to the total of the right-hand side of the capital account.

Table A.V.2. Full sequence of accounts for the total economy [cont.]

III.2: Financial account

Changes in assets			Changes in liabilities and net worth		
F	Net acquisition of financial assets	641	F	Net incurrence of liabilities	603
F.1	Monetary gold and SDRs	– 1			
F.2	Currency and deposits [1]	119	F.2	Currency and deposits [1]	132
F.21	Currency	34	F.21	Currency	35
F.22	Transferable deposits	62	F.22	Transferable deposits	65
F.23	Other deposits	23	F.23	Other deposits	32
F.3	Securities other than shares	138	F.3	Securities other than shares	123
F.31	Short-term	54	F.31	Short-term	51
F.32	Long-term	84	F.32	Long-term	72
F.4	Loans [2]	244	F.4	Loans [2]	217
F.41	Short-term	83	F.41	Short-term	76
F.42	Long-term	161	F.42	Long-term	141
F.5	Shares and other equity [2]	44	F.5	Shares and other equity [2]	43
F.6	Insurance technical reserves	36	F.6	Insurance technical reserves	36
F.61	Net equity of households on life insurance reserves and on pension funds	33	F.61	Net equity of households on life insurance reserves and on pension funds	33
F.611	Net equity of households on life insurance reserves	22	F.611	Net equity of households on life insurance reserves	22
F.612	Net equity of households on pension funds	11	F.612	Net equity of households on pension funds	11
F.62	Prepayment of premiums and reserves against outstanding claims	3	F.62	Prepayment of premiums and reserves against outstanding claims	3
F.7	Other accounts receivable [2]	61	F.7	Other accounts payable [2]	52
F.71	Trade credits and advances	18	F.71	Trade credits and advances	18
F.79	Other accounts payable, except trade credits and advances	43	F.79	Other accounts payable, except trade credits and advances	34
			B.9	*Net lending(+)/net borrowing(–)*	38

1 The following memorandum items related to the elements of the category
F.2 "Currency and deposits":
    m11   denominated in national currency
    m12   denominated in foreign currency
    m21   liability of resident institutions
    m22   liability of rest of the world.
2 Memorandum item: F.m. Direct foreign investment.

Table A.V.2. Full sequence of accounts for the total economy [cont.]

III.3: Other changes in assets accounts

III.3.1: Other changes in volume of assets account

Changes in assets

AN	Non-financial assets	10
AN.1	Produced assets	– 7
K.4	Economic appearance of produced assets	3
K.7	Catastrophic losses	– 9
K.8	Uncompensated seizures	0
K.9	Other volume changes in non-financial assets n.e.c.	1
K.12	Changes in classifications and structure	– 2
K.12.1	Changes in sector classification and structure	0
K.12.2	Changes in classification of assets and liabilities	– 2
K.12.21	Monetization/demonetization of gold	– 2
K.12.22	Changes in classification of assets or liabilities other than monetization/demonetization of gold	0
of which :		
AN.11	Fixed assets	– 4
AN.12	Inventories	– 1
AN.13	Valuables	– 2
AN.2	Non-produced assets	17
K.3	Economic appearance of non-produced assets	24
K.5	Natural growth of non-cultivated biological resources	4
K.6	Economic disappearance of non-produced assets	– 9
K.61	Depletion of natural assets	– 8
K.62	Other economic disappearance of non-produced assets	– 1
K.7	Catastrophic losses	– 2
K.8	Uncompensated seizures	0
K.9	Other volume changes in non-financial assets n.e.c.	0
K.12	Changes in classifications and structure	0
K.12.1	Changes in sector classification and structure	0
K.12.2	Changes in classification of assets and liabilities	0
K.12.22	Changes in classification of assets or liabilities other than monetization/demonetization of gold	0
of which :		
AN.21	Tangible non-produced assets	17
AN.22	Intangible non-produced assets	0
AF	Financial assets	5
K.7	Catastrophic losses	0
K.8	Uncompensated seizures	0
K.10	Other volume changes in financial assets and liabilities n.e.c.	3
K.12	Changes in classifications and structure	2
K.12.1	Changes in sector classification and structure	0
K.12.2	Changes in classification of assets and liabilities	2
K.12.21	Monetization/demonetization of gold	2
K.12.22	Changes in classification of assets or liabilities other than monetization/demonetization of gold	0
of which:		
AF.1	Monetary gold and SDRs	7
AF.2	Currency and deposits	0
AF.3	Securities other than shares	0
AF.4	Loans	– 4
AF.5	Shares and other equity	0
AF.6	Insurance technical reserves	2
AF.7	Other accounts receivable	0

Changes in liabilities and net worth

AF	Liabilities	– 2
K.7	Catastrophic losses	0
K.8	Uncompensated seizures	0
K.10	Other volume changes in financial assets and net liabilities n.e.c.	– 2
K.12	Changes in classifications and structure	0
K.12.1	Changes in sector classification and structure	0
K.12.2	Changes in classification of assets and liabilities	0
K.12.22	Changes in classification of assets or liabilities other than monetization/demonetization of gold	0
of which:		
AF.2	Currency and deposits	0
AF.3	Securities other than shares	0
AF.4	Loans	– 4
AF.5	Shares and other equity	0
AF.6	Insurance technical reserves	2
AF.7	Other accounts payable	0

B.10.2	*Changes in net worth due to other changes in volume of assets*	17

Table A.V.2. Full sequence of accounts for the total economy [cont.]

III.3.2: Revaluation account

Changes in assets		
K.11	Nominal holding gains(+)/losses(–) [1]:	
AN	Non-financial assets	280
AN.1	Produced assets	126
AN.11	Fixed assets	111
AN.12	Inventories	7
AN.13	Valuables	8
AN.2	Non-produced assets	154
AN.21	Tangible non-produced assets	152
AN.22	Intangible non-produced assets	2
AF	Financial assets	84
AF.1	Monetary gold and SDRs	12
AF.2	Currency and deposits	0
AF.3	Securities other than shares	40
AF.4	Loans	0
AF.5	Shares and other equity	31
AF.6	Insurance technical reserves	0
AF.7	Other accounts receivable	0

Changes in liabilities and net worth		
K.11	Nominal holding gains(–)/losses(+) [1]:	
AF	Liabilities	76
AF.2	Currency and deposits	0
AF.3	Securities other than shares	42
AF.4	Loans	0
AF.5	Shares and other equity	34
AF.6	Insurance technical reserves	0
AF.7	Other accounts payable	0
B.10.3	*Changes in net worth due to nominal holding gains/losses*	288

1 Differences between data on individual items and totals of holding gains/losses
may not be entirely consistent due to rounding errors.

Table A.V.2. Full sequence of accounts for the total economy [cont.]

III.3.2.1: Neutral holding gains/losses account

Changes in assets

K.11.1	Neutral holding gains (+)/losses (−) [1]:	
AN	Non-financial assets	198
AN.1	Produced assets	121
AN.11	Fixed assets	111
AN.12	Inventories	5
AN.13	Valuables	5
AN.2	Non-produced assets	78
AN.21	Tangible non-produced assets	76
AN.22	Intangible non-produced assets	1
AF	Financial assets	136
AF.1	Monetary gold and SDRs	15
AF.2	Currency and deposits	30
AF.3	Securities other than shares	25
AF.4	Loans	28
AF.5	Shares and other equity	26
AF.6	Insurance technical reserves	7
AF.7	Other accounts receivable	5

Changes in liabilities and net worth

K.11.1	Neutral holding gains (−)/losses (+) [1]:	
AF	Liabilities	126
AF.2	Currency and deposits	29
AF.3	Securities other than shares	26
AF.4	Loans	29
AF.5	Shares and other equity	28
AF.6	Insurance technical reserves	7
AF.7	Other accounts payable	6

B.10.31 *Changes in net worth due to neutral holding gains/losses* 208

1 Differences between data on individual items and totals of holding gains/losses may not be entirely consistent due to rounding errors.

III.3.2.2: Real holding gains/losses account

Changes in assets

K.11.2	Real holding gains(+)/losses(−) [1]:	
AN	Non-financial assets	81
AN.1	Produced assets	5
AN.11	Fixed assets	0
AN.12	Inventories	3
AN.13	Valuables	2
AN.2	Non-produced assets	77
AN.21	Tangible non-produced assets	76
AN.22	Intangible non-produced assets	1
AF	Financial assets	−52
AF.1	Monetary gold and SDRs	−3
AF.2	Currency and deposits	−30
AF.3	Securities other than shares	15
AF.4	Loans	−28
AF.5	Shares and other equity	5
AF.6	Insurance technical reserves	−7
AF.7	Other accounts receivable	−5

Changes in liabilities and net worth

K.11.2	Real holding gains(−)/losses(+) [1]:	
AF	Liabilities	−50
AF.2	Currency and deposits	−29
AF.3	Securities other than shares	16
AF.4	Loans	−29
AF.5	Shares and other equity	6
AF.6	Insurance technical reserves	−7
AF.7	Other accounts payable	−6

B.10.32 *Changes in net worth due to real holding gains/losses* 80

1 Differences between data on individual items and totals of holding gains/losses may not be entirely consistent due to rounding errors.

Table A.V.2. Full sequence of accounts for the total economy [cont.]

IV: Balance sheets

IV.1: Opening balance sheet

Assets			Liabilities and net worth		
AN	Non-financial assets	9 922	AF	Liabilities	6 298
AN.1	Produced assets	6 047	AF.2	Currency and deposits	1 471
AN.11	Fixed assets	5 544	AF.3	Securities other than shares	1 311
AN.12	Inventories	231	AF.4	Loans	1 437
AN.13	Valuables	272	AF.5	Shares and other equity	1 406
AN.2	Non-produced assets	3 875	AF.6	Insurance technical reserves	371
AN.21	Tangible non-produced assets	3 809	AF.7	Other accounts payable	302
AN.22	Intangible non-produced assets	66			
AF	Financial assets	6 792			
AF.1	Monetary gold and SDRs	770			
AF.2	Currency and deposits	1 482			
AF.3	Securities other than shares	1 263			
AF.4	Loans	1 384			
AF.5	Shares and other equity	1 296			
AF.6	Insurance technical reserves	370			
AF.7	Other accounts receivable	227			
			B.90	*Net worth*	10 416

IV.2: Changes in balance sheet [1]

Assets			Liabilities and net worth		
	Total changes in assets			**Total changes in liabilities**	
AN	Non-financial assets	482	AF	Liabilities	677
AN.1	Produced assets	289	AF.2	Currency and deposits	132
AN.11	Fixed assets	239	AF.3	Securities other than shares	165
AN.12	Inventories	34	AF.4	Loans	213
AN.13	Valuables	16	AF.5	Shares and other equity	77
AN.2	Non-produced assets	193	AF.6	Insurance technical reserves	38
AN.21	Tangible non-produced assets	191	AF.7	Other accounts payable	52
AN.22	Intangible non-produced assets	2			
AF	Financial assets	730			
AF.1	Monetary gold and SDRs	18			
AF.2	Currency and deposits	119			
AF.3	Securities other than shares	178			
AF.4	Loans	240			
AF.5	Shares and other equity	75			
AF.6	Insurance technical reserves	38			
AF.7	Other accounts receivable	61			
			B.10	*Changes in net worth, total* due to:	535
			B.10.1	*Saving and capital transfers*	230
			B.10.2	*Other changes in volume of assets*	17
			B.10.3	*Nominal holding gains/losses*	288
			B.10.31	Neutral holding gains/losses	208
			B.10.32	Real holding gains/losses	80

1 Differences between data on individual items and totals of holding gains/losses
may not be entirely consistent due to rounding errors.

Table A.V.2. Full sequence of accounts for the total economy [cont.]

IV.3: Closing balance sheet [1]

Assets

AN	Non-financial assets	10 404
AN.1	Produced assets	6 336
AN.11	Fixed assets	5 783
AN.12	Inventories	265
AN.13	Valuables	288
AN.2	Non-produced assets	4 068
AN.21	Tangible non-produced assets	4 000
AN.22	Intangible non-produced assets	68

AF	Financial assets	7 522
AF.1	Monetary gold and SDRs	788
AF.2	Currency and deposits	1 601
AF.3	Securities other than shares	1 441
AF.4	Loans	1 624
AF.5	Shares and other equity	1 371
AF.6	Insurance technical reserves	408
AF.7	Other accounts receivable	288

Liabilities
and net worth

AF	Liabilities	6 975
AF.2	Currency and deposits	1 603
AF.3	Securities other than shares	1 476
AF.4	Loans	1 650
AF.5	Shares and other equity	1 483
AF.6	Insurance technical reserves	409
AF.7	Other accounts payable	354

B.90	*Net worth*	10 951

1   Differences between data on individual items and totals of holding gains/losses
may not be entirely consistent due to rounding errors.

Table A.V.3. Full sequence of accounts for non-financial corporations

I: Production account

Uses				Resources		
P.2	Intermediate consumption	899	P.1	Output [1]	1 753
			P.11	Market output	1 722
			P.12	Output for own final use	31
B.1g	*Value added, gross*	854			
K.1	Consumption of fixed capital	137			
B.1n	*Value added, net*	717			

1 For the valuation of output, refer to chapter VI, paragraphs 6.210 to 6.227.

II. Distribution and use of income accounts

II.1: Primary distribution of income account

II.1.1: Generation of income account

Uses				Resources		
D.1	Compensation of employees	545	B.1	*Value added* [1]	717
D.11	Wages and salaries	421			
D.12	Employers' social contributions	124			
D.121	Employers' actual social contributions	112			
D.122	Employers' imputed social contributions	12			
D.29	Other taxes on production	86			
D.39	Other subsidies on production	− 35			
B.2	*Operating surplus* [1]	121			

1 The opening and the closing balancing item of this account can be expressed
in gross or in net terms. The amount presented refers to the net value.

Table A.V.3.   Full sequence of accounts for non-financial corporations [cont.]

II.1.2: Allocation of primary income account

Uses				Resources			
D.4	Property income		135	B.2	*Operating surplus* [1]		121
D.41	Interest		56				
D.42	Distributed income of corporations		48	D.4	Property income		86
D.421	Dividends		24	D.41	Interest		33
D.422	Withdrawals from income of quasi-corporations		24	D.42	Distributed income of corporations		3
D.43	Reinvested earnings on direct foreign investment		0	D.421	Dividends		3
D.45	Rent		31	D.422	Withdrawals from income of quasi-corporations		0
				D.43	Reinvested earnings on direct foreign investment		4
				D.44	Property income attributed to insurance policyholders		5
				D.45	Rent		41
B.5	*Balance of primary incomes* [1]		72				

1   The opening and the closing balancing item of this account can be expressed
in gross or in net terms. The amount presented refers to the net value.

II.1.2.1: Entrepreneurial income account

Uses				Resources			
D.4	Property income		87	B.2	*Operating surplus* [1]		121
D.41	Interest		56				
D.45	Rent		31	D.4	Property income		86
				D.41	Interest		33
				D.42	Distributed income of corporations		3
				D.421	Dividends		3
				D.422	Withdrawals from income of quasi-corporations		0
				D.43	Reinvested earnings on direct foreign investment		4
				D.44	Property income attributed to insurance policyholders		5
				D.45	Rent		41
B.4	*Entrepreneurial income* [1]		120				

1   The opening and the closing balancing item of this account can be expressed
in gross or in net terms. The amount presented refers to the net value.

II.1.2.2: Allocation of other primary income account

Uses				Resources			
D.4	Property income		48	B.4	*Entrepreneurial income* [1]		120
D.42	Distributed income of corporations		48				
D.421	Dividends		24				
D.422	Withdrawals from income of quasi-corporations		24				
D.43	Reinvested earnings on direct foreign investment		0				
B.5	*Balance of primary incomes* [1]		72				

1   The opening and the closing balancing item of this account can be expressed
in gross or in net terms. The amount presented refers to the net value.

Table A.V.3. Full sequence of accounts for non-financial corporations [cont.]

II.2: Secondary distribution of income account

Uses			Resources		
D.5	Current taxes on income, wealth, etc.	24	B.5	*Balance of primary incomes* [1]	72
D.51	Taxes on income	20			
D.59	Other current taxes	4	D.61	Social contributions	14
			D.611	Actual social contributions	2
D.62	Social benefits other than social transfers in kind	13	D.6111	Employers' actual social contributions	1
D.622	Private funded social benefits	1	D.61111	Compulsory employers' actual social contributions	1
D.623	Unfunded employee social benefits	12	D.61112	Voluntary employers' actual social contributions	0
			D.6112	Employees' social contributions	1
D.7	Other current transfers	11	D.61121	Compulsory employees' social contributions	1
D.71	Net non-life insurance premiums	8	D.61122	Voluntary employees' social contributions	0
D.75	Miscellaneous current transfers	3	D.612	Imputed social contributions	12
			D.7	Other current transfers	10
			D.72	Non-life insurance claims	6
			D.75	Miscellaneous current transfers	4
B.6	*Disposable income* [1]	48			

1   The opening and the closing balancing item of this account can be expressed
in gross or in net terms. The amount presented refers to the net value.

II.4: Use of income account

II.4.1: Use of disposable income account

Uses			Resources		
D.8	Adjustment for the change in net equity of households on pension funds	0	B.6	*Disposable income* [1]	48
B.8	*Saving* [1]	48			

1   The opening and the closing balancing item of this account can be expressed
in gross or in net terms. The amount presented refers to the net value.

Table A.V.3. Full sequence of accounts for non-financial corporations [cont.]

III. Accumulation accounts

III.1: Capital account

Changes in assets			Changes in liabilities and net worth		
P.51	Gross fixed capital formation	250	B.8n	*Saving, net*	48
P.511	Acquisitions less disposals of tangible fixed assets	209			
P.5111	Acquisitions of new tangible fixed assets	211	D.9	Capital transfers, receivable	33
P.5112	Acquisitions of existing tangible fixed assets	4	D.92	Investment grants	23
P.5113	Disposals of existing tangible fixed assets	− 6	D.99	Other capital transfers	10
P.512	Acquisitions less disposals of intangible fixed assets	21			
P.5121	Acquisitions of new intangible fixed assets	21	D.9	Capital transfers, payable	− 16
P.5122	Acquisitions of existing intangible fixed assets	1	D.91	Capital taxes	0
P.5123	Disposals of existing intangible fixed assets	− 1	D.99	Other capital transfers	− 16
P.513	Additions to the value of non-produced non-financial assets	20			
P.5131	Major improvements to non-produced non-financial assets	3			
P.5132	Costs of ownership transfer on non-produced non-financial assets	17			
K.1	Consumption of fixed capital	− 137			
P.52	Changes in inventories	26			
P.53	Acquisitions less disposals of valuables	2			
K.2	Acquisitions less disposals of non-produced non-financial assets	− 7			
K.21	Acquisitions less disposals of land and other tangible non-produced assets	− 6			
K.22	Acquisitions less disposals of intangible non-produced assets	− 1			
B.9	*Net lending (+) / net borrowing (−)*	− 69	B.10.1	*Changes in net worth due to saving and capital transfers* [1]	65

1   "Changes in net worth due to saving and capital transfers" is not a balancing item but corresponds to the total of the right-hand side of the capital account.

Table A.V.3.　Full sequence of accounts for non-financial corporations [cont.]

III.2:　Financial account

Changes in assets			Changes in liabilities and net worth		
F	Net acquisition of financial assets	71	F	Net incurrence of liabilities	140
F.2	Currency and deposits [1]	17	F.2	Currency and deposits [1]	0
F.21	Currency	5	F.22	Transferable deposits	0
F.22	Transferable deposits	10	F.23	Other deposits	0
F.23	Other deposits	2			
F.3	Securities other than shares	18	F.3	Securities other than shares	6
F.31	Short-term	15	F.31	Short-term	2
F.32	Long-term	3	F.32	Long-term	4
F.4	Loans [2]	27	F.4	Loans [2]	71
F.41	Short-term	16	F.41	Short-term	16
F.42	Long-term	11	F.42	Long-term	55
F.5	Shares and other equity [2]	2	F.5	Shares and other equity [2]	26
F.6	Insurance technical reserves	0	F.6	Insurance technical reserves	0
			F.61	Net equity of households on life insurance reserves and on pension funds	0
F.62	Prepayment of premiums and reserves against outstanding claims	0	F.612	Net equity of households on pension funds	0
F.7	Other accounts receivable [2]	7	F.7	Other accounts payable [2]	37
F.71	Trade credits and advances	6	F.71	Trade credits and advances	8
F.79	Other accounts receivable, except trade credits and advances	1	F.79	Other accounts payable, except trade credits and advances	29
			B.9	*Net lending(+)/net borowing(−)*	− 69

1　The following memorandum items related to the elements of the category

F.2 "Currency and deposits":
　　m11　denominated in national currency
　　m12　denominated in foreign currency
　　m21　liability of resident institutions
　　m22　liability of rest of the world.
2　Memorandum item: F.m. Direct foreign investment.

Table A.V.3. Full sequence of accounts for non-financial corporations [cont.]

III.3: Other changes in assets accounts

III.3.1: Other changes in volume of assets account

Changes in assets

AN	Non-financial assets	12
AN.1	Produced assets	– 2
K.4	Economic appearance of produced assets	0
K.7	Catastrophic losses	– 5
K.8	Uncompensated seizures	– 1
K.9	Other volume changes in non-financial assets n.e.c.	1
K.12	Changes in classifications and structure	3
K.12.1	Changes in sector classification and structure	3
K.12.2	Changes in classification of assets and liabilities	0
K.12.22	Changes in classification of assets or liabilities other than monetization/demonetization of gold	0
of which:		
AN.11	Fixed assets	– 1
AN.12	Inventories	– 1
AN.13	Valuables	0
AN.2	Non-produced assets	14
K.3	Economic appearance of non-produced assets	24
K.5	Natural growth of non-cultivated biological resources	0
K.6	Economic disappearance of non-produced assets	– 7
K.61	Depletion of natural assets	– 6
K.62	Other economic disappearance of non-produced assets	– 1
K.7	Catastrophic losses	0
K.8	Uncompensated seizures	– 4
K.9	Other volume changes in non-financial assets n.e.c.	0
K.12	Changes in classifications and structure	1
K.12.1	Changes in sector classification and structure	1
K.12.2	Changes in classification of assets and liabilities	0
K.12.22	Changes in classification of assets or liabilities other than monetization/demonetization of gold	0
of which:		
AN.21	Tangible non-produced assets	14
AN.22	Intangible non-produced assets	0
AF	Financial assets	2
K.7	Catastrophic losses	0
K.8	Uncompensated seizures	0
K.10	Other volume changes in financial assets and liabilities n.e.c.	0
K.12	Changes in classifications and structure	2
K.12.1	Changes in sector classification and structure	2
K.12.2	Changes in classification of assets and liabilities	0
K.12.22	Changes in classification of assets or liabilities other than monetization/demonetization of gold	0
of which:		
AF.2	Currency and deposits	0
AF.3	Securities other than shares	0
AF.4	Loans	0
AF.5	Shares and other equity	2
AF.6	Insurance technical reserves	0
AF.7	Other accounts receivable	0

Changes in liabilities and net worth

AF	Liabilities	– 3
K.7	Catastrophic losses	0
K.8	Uncompensated seizures	0
K.10	Other volume changes in financial assets and liabilities n.e.c.	– 4
K.12	Changes in classifications and structure	1
K.12.1	Changes in sector classification and structure	1
K.12.2	Changes in classification of assets and liabilities	0
K.12.22	Changes in classification of assets or liabilities other than monetization/demonetization of gold	0
of which:		
AF.2	Currency and deposits	0
AF.3	Securities other than shares	0
AF.4	Loans	– 3
AF.5	Shares and other equity	0
AF.6	Insurance technical reserves	0
AF.7	Other accounts payable	0

B.10.2	*Changes in net worth due to other changes in volume of assets*	17

Table A.V.3. Full sequence of accounts for non-financial corporations [cont.]

III.3.2: Revaluation account

Changes in assets			Changes in liabilities and net worth		
K.11	Nominal holding gains(+)/losses(−) [1]:		K.11	Nominal holding gains(−)/losses(+) [1]:	
AN	Non-financial assets	144	AF	Liabilities	18
AN.1	Produced assets	63	AF.2	Currency and deposits	0
AN.11	Fixed assets	58	AF.3	Securities other than shares	1
AN.12	Inventories	4	AF.4	Loans	0
AN.13	Valuables	1	AF.5	Shares and other equity	16
AN.2	Non-produced assets	81	AF.6	Insurance technical reserves	0
AN.21	Tangible non-produced assets	80	AF.7	Other accounts payable	0
AN.22	Intangible non-produced assets	1			
AF	Financial assets	8			
AF.2	Currency and deposits	0			
AF.3	Securities other than shares	3			
AF.4	Loans	0			
AF.5	Shares and other equity	5			
AF.6	Insurance technical reserves	0			
AF.7	Other accounts receivable	0			
			B.10.3	*Changes in net worth due to nominal holding gains/losses*	134

1   Differences between data on individual items and totals of holding
gains/losses may not be entirely consistent due to rounding errors.

Table A.V.3. Full sequence of accounts for non-financial corporations [cont.]

III.3.2.1: Neutral holding gains/losses account

Changes in assets			Changes in liabilities and net worth		
K.11.1	Neutral holding gains (+)/losses (−) [1]:		K.11.1	Neutral holding gains (−)/losses (+) [1]:	
AN	Non-financial assets	101	AF	Liabilities	36
AN.1	Produced assets	60	AF.2	Currency and deposits	1
AN.11	Fixed assets	58	AF.3	Securities other than shares	1
AN.12	Inventories	2	AF.4	Loans	18
AN.13	Valuables	1	AF.5	Shares and other equity	14
AN.2	Non-produced assets	41	AF.6	Insurance technical reserves	0
AN.21	Tangible non-produced assets	40	AF.7	Other accounts payable	3
AN.22	Intangible non-produced assets	1			
AF	Financial assets	18			
AF.2	Currency and deposits	8			
AF.3	Securities other than shares	2			
AF.4	Loans	1			
AF.5	Shares and other equity	4			
AF.6	Insurance technical reserves	1			
AF.7	Other accounts receivable	3			
			B.10.31	*Changes in net worth due to neutral holding gains/losses*	82

1 Differences between data on individual items and totals of holding gains/losses may not be entirely consistent due to rounding errors.

III.3.2.2: Real holding gains/losses account

Changes in assets			Changes in liabilities and net worth		
K.11.2	Real holding gains(+)/losses(−) [1]:		K.11.2	Real holding gains(−)/losses(+) [1]:	
AN	Non-financial assets	43	AF	Liabilities	− 18
AN.1	Produced assets	3	AF.2	Currency and deposits	− 1
AN.11	Fixed assets	0	AF.3	Securities other than shares	1
AN.12	Inventories	3	AF.4	Loans	− 18
AN.13	Valuables	0	AF.5	Shares and other equity	3
AN.2	Non-produced assets	40	AF.6	Insurance technical reserves	0
AN.21	Tangible non-produced assets	40	AF.7	Other accounts payable	− 3
AN.22	Intangible non-produced assets	0			
AF	Financial assets	− 10			
AF.2	Currency and deposits	− 8			
AF.3	Securities other than shares	1			
AF.4	Loans	− 1			
AF.5	Shares and other equity	1			
AF.6	Insurance technical reserves	− 1			
AF.7	Other accounts receivable	− 3			
			B.10.32	*Changes in net worth due to real holding gains/losses*	51

1 Differences between data on individual items and totals of holding gains/losses may not be entirely consistent due to rounding errors.

Table A.V.3. Full sequence of accounts for non-financial corporations [cont.]

IV: Balance sheets

IV.1: Opening balance sheet

Assets			Liabilities and net worth		
AN	Non-financial assets	5 041	AF	Liabilities	1 817
AN.1	Produced assets	3 001	AF.2	Currency and deposits	40
AN.11	Fixed assets	2 878	AF.3	Securities other than shares	44
AN.12	Inventories	85	AF.4	Loans	897
AN.13	Valuables	38	AF.5	Shares and other equity	687
AN.2	Non-produced assets	2 040	AF.6	Insurance technical reserves	12
AN.21	Tangible non-produced assets	1 989	AF.7	Other accounts payable	137
AN.22	Intangible non-produced assets	51			
AF	Financial assets	897			
AF.2	Currency and deposits	382			
AF.3	Securities other than shares	90			
AF.4	Loans	50			
AF.5	Shares and other equity	200			
AF.6	Insurance technical reserves	25			
AF.7	Other accounts receivable	150			
			B.90	*Net worth*	4 121

IV.2: Changes in balance sheet [1]

Assets			Liabilities and net worth		
	Total changes in assets			Total changes in liabilities	
AN	Non-financial assets	290	AF	Liabilities	155
AN.1	Produced assets	182	AF.2	Currency and deposits	0
AN.11	Fixed assets	150	AF.3	Securities other than shares	7
AN.12	Inventories	29	AF.4	Loans	68
AN.13	Valuables	3	AF.5	Shares and other equity	42
AN.2	Non-produced assets	108	AF.6	Insurance technical reserves	0
AN.21	Tangible non-produced assets	108	AF.7	Other accounts payable	37
AN.22	Intangible non-produced assets	0			
AF	Financial assets	81			
AF.2	Currency and deposits	17			
AF.3	Securities other than shares	21			
AF.4	Loans	27			
AF.5	Shares and other equity	9			
AF.6	Insurance technical reserves	0			
AF.7	Other accounts receivable	7			
			B.10	*Changes in net worth, total*	216
				due to:	
			B.10.1	*Saving and capital transfers*	65
			B.10.2	*Other changes in volume of assets*	17
			B.10.3	*Nominal holding gains/losses*	134
			B.10.31	Neutral holding gains/losses	82
			B.10.32	Real holding gains/losses	51

1 Differences between data on individual items and totals of holding gains/losses may not be entirely consistent due to rounding errors.

Table A.V.3. Full sequence of accounts for non-financial corporations [cont.]

IV.3. Closing balance sheet [1]

Assets				Liabilities and net worth		
AN	Non-financial assets		5 331	AF	Liabilities	1 972
				AF.2	Currency and deposits	40
AN.1	Produced assets		3 183	AF.3	Securities other than shares	51
AN.11	Fixed assets		3 028	AF.4	Loans	965
AN.12	Inventories		114	AF.5	Shares and other equity	729
AN.13	Valuables		41	AF.6	Insurance technical reserves	12
AN.2	Non-produced assets		2 148	AF.7	Other accounts payable	174
AN.21	Tangible non-produced assets		2 097			
AN.22	Intangible non-produced assets		51			
AF	Financial assets		978			
AF.2	Currency and deposits		399			
AF.3	Securities other than shares		111			
AF.4	Loans		77			
AF.5	Shares and other equity		209			
AF.6	Insurance technical reserves		25			
AF.7	Other accounts receivable		157			
				B.90	*Net worth*	4 337

1   Differences between data on individual items and totals of holding
gains/losses may not be entirely consistent due to rounding errors.

Table A.V.4. Full sequence of accounts for financial corporations

I: Production account

Uses				Resources			
P.2	Intermediate consumption		29	P.1	Output [1]		102
				P.11	Market output		102
				P.12	Output for own final use		0
B.1g	*Value added, gross*		73				
K.1	Consumption of fixed capital		10				
B.1n	*Value added, net*		63				

1 For the valuation of output, refer to chapter VI, paragraphs 6.210 to 6.227.

II. Distribution and use of income accounts

II.1: Primary distribution of income account

II.1.1: Generation of income account

Uses				Resources			
D.1	Compensation of employees		15	B.1	*Value added net* [1]		63
D.11	Wages and salaries		10				
D.12	Employers' social contributions		5				
D.121	Employers' actual social contributions		4				
D.122	Employers' imputed social contributions		1				
D.29	Other taxes on production		3				
D.39	Other subsidies on production		0				
B.2	*Operating surplus* [1]		45				

1 The opening and the closing balancing item of this account can be expressed
in gross or in net terms. The amount presented refers to the net value.

Table A.V.4. Full sequence of accounts for financial corporations [cont.]

II.1.2: Allocation of primary income account

Uses			Resources		
D.4	Property income	167	B.2	*Operating surplus* [1]	45
D.41	Interest	106			
D.42	Distributed income of corporations	36	D.4	Property income	141
D.421	Dividends	36	D.41	Interest	106
D.422	Withdrawals from income of quasi-corporations	0	D.42	Distributed income of corporations	25
D.43	Reinvested earnings on direct foreign investment	0	D.421	Dividends	25
D.44	Property income attributed to insurance policyholders	25	D.422	Withdrawals from income of quasi-corporations	0
D.45	Rent	0	D.43	Reinvested earnings on direct foreign investment	7
			D.44	Property income attributed to insurance policyholders	0
			D.45	Rent	3
B.5	*Balance of primary incomes* [1]	19			

1 The opening and the closing balancing item of this account can be expressed in gross or in net terms. The amount presented refers to the net value.

II.1.2.1: Entrepreneurial income account

Uses			Resources		
D.4	Property income	131	B.2	*Operating surplus* [1]	45
D.41	Interest	106			
D.44	Property income attributed to insurance policyholders	25	D.4	Property income	141
D.45	Rent	0	D.41	Interest	106
			D.42	Distributed income of corporations	25
			D.421	Dividends	25
			D.422	Withdrawals from income of quasi-corporations	0
			D.43	Reinvested earnings on direct foreign investment	7
			D.44	Property income attributed to insurance policyholders	0
			D.45	Rent	3
B.4	*Entrepreneurial income* [1]	55			

1 The opening and the closing balancing item of this account can be expressed in gross or in net terms. The amount presented refers to the net value.

II.1.2.2: Allocation of other primary income account

Uses			Resources		
D.4	Property income	36	B.4	*Entrepreneurial income* [1]	55
D.42	Distributed income of corporations	36			
D.421	Dividends	36			
D.422	Withdrawals from income of quasi-corporations	0			
D.43	Reinvested earnings on direct foreign investment	0			
B.5	*Balance of primary incomes* [1]	19			

1 The opening and the closing balancing item of this account can be expressed in gross or in net terms. The amount presented refers to the net value.

Table A.V.4. Full sequence of accounts for financial corporations [cont.]

II.2: Secondary distribution of income account

Uses			Resources		
D.5	Current taxes on income, wealth, etc.	10	B.5	*Balance of primary incomes* [1]	19
D.51	Taxes on income	7			
D.59	Other current taxes	3	D.61	Social contributions	39
			D.611	Actual social contributions	38
D.62	Social benefits other than social transfers in kind	29	D.6111	Employers' actual social contributions	18
D.622	Private funded social benefits	28	D.61111	Compulsory employers' actual social contributions	15
D.623	Unfunded employee social benefits	1	D.61112	Voluntary employers' actual social contributions	3
			D.6112	Employees' social contributions	20
D.7	Other current transfers	46	D.61121	Compulsory employees' social contributions	15
D.71	Net non-life insurance premiums	0	D.61122	Voluntary employees' social contributions	5
D.72	Non-life insurance claims	45	D.612	Imputed social contributions	1
D.75	Miscellaneous current transfers	1			
			D.7	Other current transfers	49
			D.71	Net non-life insurance premiums	45
			D.72	Non-life insurance claims	0
			D.75	Miscellaneous current transfers	4
B.6	*Disposable income* [1]	22			

1   The opening and the closing balancing item of this account can be expressed
in gross or in net terms. The amount presented refers to the net value.

II.4: Use of income account

II.4.1: Use of disposable income account

Uses			Resources		
D.8	Adjustment for the change in net equity of households on pension funds	11	B.6	*Disposable income* [1]	22
B.8	*Saving* [1]	11			

1   The opening and the closing balancing item of this account can be expressed
in gross or in net terms. The amount presented refers to the net value.

Table A.V.4. Full sequence of accounts for financial corporations [cont.]

III. Accumulation accounts

III.1: Capital account

Changes in assets				Changes in liabilities and net worth		
P.51	Gross fixed capital formation		9	B.8n	*Saving, net*	11
P.511	Acquisitons less disposals of tangible fixed assets		8			
P.5111	Acquisitions of new tangible fixed assets		7	D.9	Capital transfers, receivable	0
P.5112	Acquisitions of existing tangible fixed assets		1	D.92	Investment grants	0
P.5113	Disposals of existing tangible fixed assets		0	D.99	Other capital transfers	0
P.512	Acquisitions less disposals of intangible fixed assets		1			
P.5121	Acquisitions of new intangible fixed assets		1	D.9	Capital transfers, payable	– 7
P.5122	Acquisitions of existing intangible fixed assets		0	D.91	Capital taxes	0
P.5123	Disposals of existing intangible fixed assets		0	D.99	Other capital transfers	– 7
P.513	Additions to the value of non-produced non-financial assets		0			
P.5131	Major improvements to non-produced non-financial assets		0			
P.5132	Costs of ownership transfer on non-produced non-financial assets		0			
K.1	Consumption of fixed capital		– 10			
P.52	Changes in inventories		0			
P.53	Acquisitions less disposals of valuables		0			
K.2	Acquisitions less disposals of non-produced non-financial assets		0			
K.21	Acquisitions less disposals of land and other tangible non-produced assets		0			
K.22	Acquisitions less disposals of intangible non-produced assets		0			
B.9	*Net lending (+) / net borrowing (–)*		5	B.10.1	*Changes in net worth due to saving and capital transfers* [1]	4

1   "Changes in net worth due to saving and capital transfers" is not a balancing item but corresponds to the total of the right-hand side of the capital account.

Table A.V.4. Full sequence of accounts for financial corporations [cont.]

III.2: Financial account

Changes in assets		Changes in liabilities and net worth	
F Net acquisition of financial assets	237	F Net incurrence of liabilities	232
F.1 Monetary gold and SDRs	− 1		
F.2 Currency and deposits [1]	15	F.2 Currency and deposits [1]	130
F.21 Currency	15	F.21 Currency	35
F.22 Transferable deposits	0	F.22 Transferable deposits	63
F.23 Other deposits	0	F.23 Other deposits	32
F.3 Securities other than shares	53	F.3 Securities other than shares	53
F.31 Short-term	4	F.31 Short-term	34
F.32 Long-term	49	F.32 Long-term	19
F.4 Loans [2]	167	F.4 Loans [2]	0
F.41 Short-term	63	F.41 Short-term	0
F.42 Long-term	104	F.42 Long-term	0
F.5 Shares and other equity [2]	3	F.5 Shares and other equity [2]	13
F.6 Insurance technical reserves	0	F.6 Insurance technical reserves	36
F.62 Prepayment of premiums and reserves against outstanding claims	0	F.61 Net equity of households on life insurance reserves and on pension funds	33
		F.611 Net equity of households on life insurance reserves	22
F.7 Other accounts receivable [2]	0	F.612 Net equity of households on pension funds	11
F.71 Trade credits and advances	0	F.62 Prepayment of premiums and reserves against outstanding claims	3
F.79 Other accounts receivable, except trade credits and advances	0		
		F.7 Other accounts payable [2]	0
		F.71 Trade credits and advances	0
		F.79 Other accounts payable, except trade credits and advances	0
		B.9 Net lending(+)/net borowing(−)	5

1 The following memorandum items related to the elements of the category
F.2 "Currency and deposits":
    m11   denominated in national currency
    m12   denominated in foreign currency
    m21   liability of resident institutions
    m22   liability of rest of the world.
2 Memorandum item: F.m. Direct foreign investment.

Table A.V.4. Full sequence of accounts for financial corporations [cont.]

III.3: Other changes in assets accounts

III.3.1: Other changes in volume of assets account

Changes in assets				Changes in liabilities and net worth		
AN	Non-financial assets		− 2	AF	Liabilities	2
AN.1	Produced assets		− 2	K.7	Catastrophic losses	0
K.4	Economic appearance of produced assets		0	K.8	Uncompensated seizures	0
K.7	Catastrophic losses		0	K.10	Other volume changes in financial assets and liabilities n.e.c.	2
K.8	Uncompensated seizures		0	K.12	Changes in classifications and structure	0
K.9	Other volume changes in non-financial assets n.e.c.		0	K.12.1	Changes in sector classification and structure	0
K.12	Changes in classifications and structure		− 2	K.12.2	Changes in classification of assets and liabilities	0
K.12.1	Changes in sector classification and structure		0	K.12.22	Changes in classification of assets or liabilities other than monetization/demonetization of gold	0
K.12.2	Changes in classification of assets and liabilities		− 2	of which:		
K.12.21	Monetization/demonetization of gold		− 2	AF.2	Currency and deposits	0
K.12.22	Changes in classification of assets or liabilities other than monetization/demonetization of gold		0	AF.3	Securities other than shares	0
of which:				AF.4	Loans	0
AN.11	Fixed assets		0	AF.5	Shares and other equity	0
AN.12	Inventories		0	AF.6	Insurance technical reserves	2
AN.13	Valuables		− 2	AF.7	Other accounts payable	0
AN.2	Non-produced assets		0			
K.3	Economic appearance of non-produced assets		0			
K.5	Natural growth of non-cultivated biological resources		0			
K.6	Economic disappearance of non-produced assets		0			
K.61	Depletion of natural assets		0			
K.62	Other economic disappearance of non-produced assets		0			
K.7	Catastrophic losses		0			
K.8	Uncompensated seizures		0			
K.9	Other volume changes in non-financial assets n.e.c.		0			
K.12	Changes in classifications and structure		0			
K.12.1	Changes in sector classification and structure		0			
K.12.2	Changes in classification of assets and liabilities		0			
K.12.22	Changes in classification of assets or liabilities other than monetization/demonetization of gold		0			
of which:						
AN.21	Tangible non-produced assets		0			
AN.22	Intangible non-produced assets		0			
AF	Financial assets		0			
K.7	Catastrophic losses		0			
K.8	Uncompensated seizures		− 3			
K.10	Other volume changes in financial assets and liabilities n.e.c.		1			
K.12	Changes in classifications and structure		2			
K.12.1	Changes in sector classification and structure		0			
K.12.2	Changes in classification of assets and liabilities		2			
K.12.21	Monetization/demonetization of gold		2			
K.12.22	Changes in classification of assets or liabilities other than monetization/demonetization of gold		0			
of which:						
AF.1	Monetary gold and SDRs		7			
AF.2	Currency and deposits		0			
AF.3	Securities other than shares		− 3			
AF.4	Loans		− 4			
AF.5	Shares and other equity		0			
AF.6	Insurance technical reserves		0			
AF.7	Other accounts receivable		0			
				B.10.2	*Changes in net worth due to other changes in volume of assets*	− 4

Table A.V.4. Full sequence of accounts for financial corporations [cont.]

III.3.2: Revaluation account

Changes in assets

K.11	Nominal holding gains(+)/losses(–) [1]:	
AN	Non-financial assets	4
AN.1	Produced assets	2
AN.11	Fixed assets	2
AN.12	Inventories	0
AN.13	Valuables	0
AN.2	Non-produced assets	2
AN.21	Tangible non-produced assets	1
AN.22	Intangible non-produced assets	0
AF	Financial assets	57
AF.1	Monetary gold and SDRs	11
AF.2	Currency and deposits	0
AF.3	Securities other than shares	30
AF.4	Loans	0
AF.5	Shares and other equity	16
AF.6	Insurance technical reserves	0
AF.7	Other accounts receivable	0

Changes in liabilities and net worth

K.11	Nominal holding gains(–)/losses(+) [1]:	
AF	Liabilities	51
AF.2	Currency and deposits	0
AF.3	Securities other than shares	34
AF.4	Loans	0
AF.5	Shares and other equity	17
AF.6	Insurance technical reserves	0
AF.7	Other accounts payable	0
B.10.3	*Changes in net worth due to nominal holding gains/losses*	10

1   Differences between data on individual items and totals of holding gains/losses may not be entirely consistent due to rounding errors.

Table A.V.4. Full sequence of accounts for financial corporations [cont.]

III.3.2.1: Neutral holding gains/losses account

Changes in assets

K.11.1	Neutral holding gains (+)/losses (−) [1]:	
AN	Non-financial assets	3
AN.1	Produced assets	2
AN.11	Fixed assets	2
AN.12	Inventories	0
AN.13	Valuables	0
AN.2	Non-produced assets	1
AN.21	Tangible non-produced assets	1
AN.22	Intangible non-produced assets	0
AF	Financial assets	70
AF.1	Monetary gold and SDRs	14
AF.2	Currency and deposits	0
AF.3	Securities other than shares	19
AF.4	Loans	24
AF.5	Shares and other equity	13
AF.6	Insurance technical reserves	1
AF.7	Other accounts receivable	0

Changes in liabilities and net worth

K.11.1	Neutral holding gains (−)/losses (+) [1]:	
AF	Liabilities	68
AF.2	Currency and deposits	26
AF.3	Securities other than shares	21
AF.4	Loans	0
AF.5	Shares and other equity	14
AF.6	Insurance technical reserves	7
AF.7	Other accounts payable	0
B.10.31	*Changes in net worth due to neutral holding gains/losses*	5

1 Differences between data on individual items and totals of holding gains/losses may not be entirely consistent due to rounding errors.

III.3.2.2: Real holding gains/losses account

Changes in assets

K.11.2	Real holding gains(+)/losses(−) [1]:	
AN	Non-financial assets	1
AN.1	Produced assets	0
AN.11	Fixed assets	0
AN.12	Inventories	0
AN.13	Valuables	0
AN.2	Non-produced assets	1
AN.21	Tangible non-produced assets	1
AN.22	Intangible non-produced assets	0
AF	Financial assets	− 13
AF.1	Monetary gold and SDRs	− 3
AF.2	Currency and deposits	0
AF.3	Securities other than shares	11
AF.4	Loans	− 24
AF.5	Shares and other equity	3
AF.6	Insurance technical reserves	− 1
AF.7	Other accounts receivable	0

Changes in liabilities and net worth

K.11.2	Real holding gains(−)/losses(+) [1]:	
AF	Liabilities	− 17
AF.2	Currency and deposits	− 26
AF.3	Securities other than shares	13
AF.4	Loans	0
AF.5	Shares and other equity	3
AF.6	Insurance technical reserves	− 7
AF.7	Other accounts payable	0
B.10.32	*Changes in net worth due to real holding gains/losses*	5

1 Differences between data on individual items and totals of holding gains/losses may not be entirely consistent due to rounding errors.

Table A.V.4. Full sequence of accounts for financial corporations [cont.]

IV: Balance sheets

IV.1: Opening balance sheet

Assets				Liabilities and net worth		
AN	Non-financial assets		144	AF	Liabilities	3 384
AN.1	Produced assets		104	AF.2	Currency and deposits	1 281
AN.11	Fixed assets		99	AF.3	Securities other than shares	1 053
AN.12	Inventories		0	AF.4	Loans	0
AN.13	Valuables		5	AF.5	Shares and other equity	715
AN.2	Non-produced assets		40	AF.6	Insurance technical reserves	335
AN.21	Tangible non-produced assets		37	AF.7	Other accounts payable	0
AN.22	Intangible non-produced assets		3			
AF	Financial assets		3 508			
AF.1	Monetary gold and SDRs		690			
AF.2	Currency and deposits		0			
AF.3	Securities other than shares		950			
AF.4	Loans		1 187			
AF.5	Shares and other equity		651			
AF.6	Insurance technical reserves		30			
AF.7	Other accounts receivable		0			
				B.90	*Net worth*	268

IV.2: Changes in balance sheet [1]

Assets				Liabilities and net worth		
	Total changes in assets				Total changes in liabilities	
AN	Non-financial assets		1	AF	Liabilities	285
AN.1	Produced assets		− 1	AF.2	Currency and deposits	130
AN.11	Fixed assets		1	AF.3	Securities other than shares	87
AN.12	Inventories		0	AF.4	Loans	0
AN.13	Valuables		− 2	AF.5	Shares and other equity	30
AN.2	Non-produced assets		2	AF.6	Insurance technical reserves	38
AN.21	Tangible non-produced assets		1	AF.7	Other accounts payable	0
AN.22	Intangible non-produced assets		0			
AF	Financial assets		294			
AF.1	Monetary gold and SDRs		17			
AF.2	Currency and deposits		15			
AF.3	Securities other than shares		80			
AF.4	Loans		163			
AF.5	Shares and other equity		19			
AF.6	Insurance technical reserves		0			
AF.7	Other accounts receivable		0			
				B.10	*Changes in net worth, total* due to:	10
				B.10.1	*Saving and capital transfers*	4
				B.10.2	*Other changes in volume of assets*	− 4
				B.10.3	*Nominal holding gains/losses*	10
				B.10.31	*Neutral holding gains/losses*	5
				B.10.32	*Real holding gains/losses*	5

1 Differences between data on individual items and totals of holding
gains/losses may not be entirely consistent due to rounding errors.

Table A.V.4. Full sequence of accounts for financial corporations [cont.]

IV.3. Closing balance sheet [1]

Assets

AN	Non-financial assets	145
AN.1	Produced assets	103
AN.11	Fixed assets	100
AN.12	Inventories	0
AN.13	Valuables	3
AN.2	Non-produced assets	42
AN.21	Tangible non-produced assets	38
AN.22	Intangible non-produced assets	3
AF	Financial assets	3 802
AF.1	Monetary gold and SDRs	707
AF.2	Currency and deposits	15
AF.3	Securities other than shares	1 030
AF.4	Loans	1 350
AF.5	Shares and other equity	670
AF.6	Insurance technical reserves	30
AF.7	Other accounts receivable	0

Liabilities and net worth

AF	Liabilities	3 669
AF.2	Currency and deposits	1 411
AF.3	Securities other than shares	1 140
AF.4	Loans	0
AF.5	Shares and other equity	745
AF.6	Insurance technical reserves	373
AF.7	Other accounts payable	0
B.90	*Net worth*	278

1 Differences between data on individual items and totals of holding gains/losses may not be entirely consistent due to rounding errors.

Table A.V.5. Full sequence of accounts for general government

I: Production account

Uses			Resources		
P.2	Intermediate consumption	252	P.1	Output [1]	440
			P.11	Market output	80
			P.12	Output for own final use	0
			P.13	Other non-market output	360
B.1g	*Value added, gross*	188			
K.1	Consumption of fixed capital	30			
B.1n	*Value added, net*	158			

1   For the valuation of output, refer to chapter VI, paragraphs 6.210 to 6.227.

II. Distribution and use of income accounts

II.1: Primary distribution of income account

II.1.1: Generation of income account

Uses			Resources		
D.1	Compensation of employees	140	B.1	*Value added* [1]	158
D.11	Wages and salaries	87			
D.12	Employers' social contributions	53			
D.121	Employers' actual social contributions	48			
D.122	Employers' imputed social contributions	5			
D.29	Other taxes on production	2			
D.39	Other subsidies on production	0			
B.2	*Operating surplus* [1]	16			

1   The opening and the closing balancing item of this account can be expressed in gross or in net terms. The amount presented refers to the net value.

Table A.V.5. Full sequence of accounts for general government [cont.]

II.1.2: Allocation of primary income account

Uses				Resources			
D.4	Property income		42	B.2	*Operating surplus* [1]		16
D.41	Interest		35				
D.42	Distributed income of corporations		0	D.2	Taxes on production and imports		235
D.422	Withdrawals from income of quasi-corporations		0	D.21	Taxes on products		141
D.43	Reinvested earnings on direct foreign investment		0	D.211	Value added type taxes (VAT)		121
D.45	Rent		7	D.212	Taxes and duties on imports excluding VAT		17
				D.2121	Import duties		17
				D.2122	Taxes on imports excluding VAT and duties		0
				D.213	Export taxes		1
				D.214	Taxes on products except VAT, import and export taxes		2
				D.29	Other taxes on production		94
				D.3	Subsidies		− 44
				D.31	Subsidies on products		− 8
				D.311	Import subsidies		0
				D.312	Export subsidies		0
				D.319	Other subsidies on products		− 8
				D.39	Other subsidies on production		− 36
				D.4	Property income		32
				D.41	Interest		14
				D.42	Distributed income of corporations		18
				D.421	Dividends		5
				D.422	Withdrawals from income of quasi-corporations		13
				D.43	Reinvested earnings on direct foreign investment		0
				D.44	Property income attributed to insurance policyholders		0
				D.45	Rent		0
B.5	*Balance of primary incomes* [1]		197				

1 The opening and the closing balancing item of this account can be expressed in gross or in net terms. The amount presented refers to the net value.

Table A.V.5. Full sequence of accounts for general government [cont.]

II.1.2.1: Entrepreneurial income account

Uses			Resources		
D.4	Property income [2]	9	B.2	*Operating surplus* [1]	16
D.41	Interest	2			
D.45	Rent	7	D.4	Property income [2]	4
			D.41	Interest	0
			D.42	Distributed income of corporations	4
			D.421	Dividends	4
			D.422	Withdrawals from income of quasi-corporations	0
			D.43	Reinvested earnings on direct foreign investment	0
			D.44	Property income attributed to insurance policyholders	0
			D.45	Rent	0
B.4	*Entrepreneurial income* [1]	11			

1   The opening and the closing balancing item of this account can be expressed in gross or in net terms. The amount presented refers to the net value.
2   Including only property income connected with market activities.

II.1.2.2: Allocation of other primary income account

Uses			Resources		
D.4	Property income [2]	33	B.4	*Entrepreneurial income* [1]	11
D.41	Interest	33			
			D.2	Taxes on production and imports	235
			D.21	Taxes on products	141
			D.211	Value added type taxes (VAT)	121
			D.212	Taxes and duties on imports excluding VAT	17
			D.2121	Import duties	17
			D.2122	Taxes on imports excluding VAT and duties	0
			D.213	Export taxes	1
			D.214	Taxes on products except VAT, import and export taxes	2
			D.29	Other taxes on production	94
			D.3	Subsidies	− 44
			D.31	Subsidies on products	− 8
			D.311	Import subsidies	0
			D.312	Export subsidies	0
			D.319	Other subsidies on products	− 8
			D.39	Other subsidies on production	− 36
			D.4	Property income [2]	28
			D.41	Interest	14
			D.42	Distributed income of corporations	14
			D.421	Dividends	1
			D.422	Withdrawals from income of quasi-corporations	13
B.5	*Balance of primary incomes* [1]	197			

1   The opening and the closing balancing item of this account can be expressed in gross or in net terms. The amount presented refers to the net value.
2   Property income not connected with market activities.

Table A.V.5. Full sequence of accounts for general government [cont.]

II.2: Secondary distribution of income account

Uses				Resources			
D.5	Current taxes on income, wealth, etc.		0	B.5	*Balance of primary incomes* [1]		197
D.59	Other current taxes		0				
				D.5	Current taxes on income, wealth, etc.		213
D.62	Social benefits other than social transfers in kind		289	D.51	Taxes on income		204
D.621	Social security benefits in cash		232	D.59	Other current taxes		9
D.622	Private funded social benefits		0				
D.623	Unfunded employee social benefits		5	D.61	Social contributions		268
D.624	Social assistance benefits in cash		52	D.611	Actual social contributions		263
				D.6111	Employers' actual social contributions		155
D.7	Other current transfers		139	D.61111	Compulsory employers' actual social contributions		144
D.71	Net non-life insurance premiums		4	D.61112	Voluntary employers' actual social contributions		11
D.73	Current transfers within general government		96	D.6112	Employees' social contributions		76
D.74	Current international cooperation		31	D.61121	Compulsory employees' social contributions		69
D.75	Miscellaneous current transfers		8	D.61122	Voluntary employees' social contributions		7
				D.6113	Social contributions by self- and non-employed persons		32
				D.61131	Compulsory social contributions by self- and non-employed persons		22
				D.61132	Voluntary social contributions by self- and non-employed persons		10
				D.612	Imputed social contributions		5
				D.7	Other current transfers		108
				D.72	Non-life insurance claims		1
				D.73	Current transfers within general government		96
				D.74	Current international corporations		1
				D.75	Miscellaneous current transfers		10
B.6	*Disposable income* [1]		358				

1   The opening and the closing balancing item of this account can be expressed in gross or in net terms. The amount presented refers to the net value.

II.3: Redistribution of income in kind account

Uses				Resources		
D.63	Social transfers in kind		212	B.6	*Disposable income* [1]	358
D.631	Social benefits in kind		162			
D.6311	Social security benefits, reimbursements		78			
D.6312	Other social security benefits in kind		65			
D.6313	Social assistance benefits in kind		19			
D.632	Transfers of individual non-market goods and services		50			
B.7	*Adjusted disposable income* [1]		146			

1   The opening and the closing balancing item of this account can be expressed in gross or in net terms. The amount presented refers to the net value.

Table A.V.5.   Full sequence of accounts for general government [cont.]

II.4: Use of income account

II.4.1: Use of disposable income account

Uses				Resources		
P.3	Final consumption expenditure		368	B.6	*Disposable income* [1]	358
P.31	Individual consumption expenditure		212			
P.32	Collective consumption expenditure		156			
D.8	Adjustment for the change in net equity of households on pension funds		0			
B.8	*Saving* [1]		−10			

1   The opening and the closing balancing item of this account can be expressed in gross or in net terms. The amount presented refers to the net value.

II.4.2: Use of adjusted disposable income account

Uses				Resources		
P.4	Actual final consumption		156	B.7	*Adjusted disposable income* [1]	146
P.42	Actual collective consumption		156			
D.8	Adjustment for the change in net equity of households on pension funds		0			
B.8	*Saving* [1]		−10			

1   The opening and the closing balancing item of this account can be expressed in gross or in net terms. The amount presented refers to the net value.

Table A.V.5. Full sequence of accounts for general government [cont.]

III. Accumulation accounts

III.1: Capital account

Changes in assets			Changes in liabilities and net worth		
P.51	Gross fixed capital formation	37	B.8n	*Saving, net*	− 10
P.511	Acquisitions less disposals of tangible fixed assets	23			
P.5111	Acquisitions of new tangible fixed assets	24	D.9	Capital transfers, receivable	6
P.5112	Acquisitions of existing tangible fixed assets	1	D.91	Capital taxes	2
P.5113	Disposals of existing tangible fixed assets	− 2	D.92	Investment grants	0
P.512	Acquisitions less disposals of intangible fixed assets	12	D.99	Other capital transfers	4
P.5121	Acquisitions of new intangible fixed assets	12			
P.5122	Acquisitions of existing intangible fixed assets	2	D.9	Capital transfers, payable	− 34
P.5123	Disposals of existing intangible fixed assets	− 2	D.91	Capital taxes	0
P.513	Additions to the value of non-produced non-financial assets	2	D.92	Investment grants	− 27
P.5131	Major improvements to non-produced non-financial assets	2	D.99	Other capital transfers	− 7
P.5132	Costs of ownership transfer on non-produced non-financial assets	0			
K.1	Consumption of fixed capital	− 30			
P.52	Changes in inventories	0			
P.53	Acquisitions less disposals of valuables	3			
K.2	Acquisitions less disposals of non-produced non-financial assets	2			
K.21	Acquisitions less disposals of land and other tangible non-produced assets	2			
K.22	Acquisitions less disposals of intangible non-produced assets	0			
B.9	*Net lending (+) / net borrowing (−)*	− 50	B.10.1	*Changes in net worth due to saving and capital transfers* [1]	− 38

1   "Changes in net worth due to saving and capital transfers" is not a balancing item but corresponds to the total of the right-hand side of the capital account.

Table A.V.5. Full sequence of accounts for general government [cont.]

III.2: Financial account

Changes in assets			Changes in liabilities and net worth		
F	Net acquisition of financial assets	120	F	Net incurrence of liabilities	170
F.1	Monetary gold and SDRs	0			
F.2	Currency and deposits [1]	7	F.2	Currency and deposits [1]	2
F.21	Currency	2	F.21	Currency	0
F.22	Transferable deposits	4	F.22	Transferable deposits	2
F.23	Other deposits	1	F.23	Other deposits	0
F.3	Securities other than shares	26	F.3	Securities other than shares	64
F.31	Short-term	11	F.31	Short-term	15
F.32	Long-term	15	F.32	Long-term	49
F.4	Loans [2]	45	F.4	Loans [2]	94
F.41	Short-term	1	F.41	Short-term	32
F.42	Long-term	44	F.42	Long-term	62
F.5	Shares and other equity [2]	36	F.5	Shares and other equity [2]	0
F.6	Insurance technical reserves	0	F.6	Insurance technical reserves	0
F.62	Prepayment of premiums and reserves against outstanding claims	0	F.61	Net equity of households on life insurance reserves and on pension funds	0
			F.612	Net equity of households on pension funds	0
F.7	Other accounts receivable [2]	6	F.7	Other accounts payable [2]	10
F.71	Trade credits and advances	1	F.71	Trade credits and advances	6
F.79	Other accounts receivable, except trade credits and advances	5	F.79	Other accounts payable, except trade credits and advances	4
			B.9	*Net lending(+)/net borrowing(−)*	−50

1 The following memorandum items related to the elements of the category
F.2 "Currency and deposits":
    m11   denominated in national currency
    m12   denominated in foreign currency
    m21   liability of resident institutions
    m22   liability of rest of the world.
2 Memorandum item: F.m. Direct foreign investment.

Table A.V.5. Full sequence of accounts for general government [cont.]

III.3: Other changes in assets accounts

III.3.1: Other changes in volume of assets account

Changes in assets				Changes in liabilities and net worth		
AN	Non-financial assets	0		AF	Liabilities	– 1
AN.1	Produced assets	– 3		K.7	Catastrophic losses	0
K.4	Economic appearance of produced assets	3		K.8	Uncompensated seizures	0
K.7	Catastrophic losses	– 4		K.10	Other volume changes in financial assets and liabilities n.e.c.	0
K.8	Uncompensated seizures	1		K.12	Changes in classifications and structure	– 1
K.9	Other volume changes in non-financial assets n.e.c.	0		K.12.1	Changes in sector classification and structure	– 1
K.12	Changes in classifications and structure	– 3		K.12.2	Changes in classification of assets and liabilities	0
K.12.1	Changes in sector classification and structure	– 3		K.12.22	Changes in classification of assets or liabilities other than monetization/demonetization of gold	0
K.12.2	Changes in classification of assets and liabilities	0		of which:		
K.12.21	Monetization/demonetization of gold	0		AF.2	Currency and deposits	0
K.12.22	Changes in classification of assets or liabilities other than monetization/demonetization of gold	0		AF.3	Securities other than shares	0
of which:				AF.4	Loans	– 1
AN.11	Fixed assets	– 3		AF.5	Shares and other equity	0
AN.12	Inventories	0		AF.6	Insurance technical reserves	0
AN.13	Valuables	0		AF.7	Other accounts payable	0
AN.2	Non-produced assets	3				
K.3	Economic appearance of non-produced assets	0				
K.5	Natural growth of non-cultivated biological resources	4				
K.6	Economic disappearance of non-produced assets	– 2				
K.61	Depletion of natural assets	– 2				
K.62	Other economic disappearance of non-produced assets	0				
K.7	Catastrophic losses	– 2				
K.8	Uncompensated seizures	4				
K.9	Other volume changes in non-financial assets n.e.c.	0				
K.12	Changes in classifications and structure	– 1				
K.12.1	Changes in sector classification and structure	– 1				
K.12.2	Changes in classification of assets and liabilities	0				
K.12.22	Changes in classification of assets or liabilities other than monetization/demonetization of gold	0				
of which:						
AN.21	Tangible non-produced assets	3				
AN.22	Intangible non-produced assets	0				
AF	Financial assets	1				
K.7	Catastrophic losses	0				
K.8	Uncompensated seizures	3				
K.10	Other volume changes in financial assets and liabilities n.e.c.	0				
K.12	Changes in classifications and structure	– 2				
K.12.1	Changes in sector classification and structure	– 2				
K.12.2	Changes in classification of assets and liabilities	0				
K.12.21	Monetization/demonetization of gold	0				
K.12.22	Changes in classification of assets or liabilities other than monetization/demonetization of gold	0				
of which:						
AF.1	Monetary gold and SDRs	0				
AF.2	Currency and deposits	0				
AF.3	Securities other than shares	3				
AF.4	Loans	0				
AF.5	Shares and other equity	– 2				
AF.6	Insurance technical reserves	0				
AF.7	Other accounts receivable	0				
				B.10.2	*Changes in net worth due to other changes in volume of assets*	2

Table A.V.5. Full sequence of accounts for general government [cont.]

III.3.2: Revaluation account

Changes in assets			Changes in liabilities and net worth		
K.11	Nominal holding gains(+)/losses(−) [1]:		K.11	Nominal holding gains(−)/losses(+) [1]:	
AN	Non-financial assets	44	AF	Liabilities	7
AN.1	Produced assets	20	AF.2	Currency and deposits	0
AN.11	Fixed assets	18	AF.3	Securities other than shares	7
AN.12	Inventories	1	AF.4	Loans	0
AN.13	Valuables	1	AF.5	Shares and other equity	0
AN.2	Non-produced assets	23	AF.6	Insurance technical reserves	0
AN.21	Tangible non-produced assets	23	AF.7	Other accounts payable	0
AN.22	Intangible non-produced assets	0			
AF	Financial assets	2			
AF.1	Monetary gold and SDRs	1			
AF.2	Currency and deposits	0			
AF.3	Securities other than shares	0			
AF.4	Loans	0			
AF.5	Shares and other equity	0			
AF.6	Insurance technical reserves	0			
AF.7	Other accounts receivable	0			
			B.10.3	*Changes in net worth due to nominal holding gains/losses*	38

1   Differences between data on individual items and totals of holding
gains/losses may not be entirely consistent due to rounding errors.

III.3.2.1: Neutral holding gains/losses account

Changes in assets			Changes in liabilities and net worth		
K.11.1	Neutral holding gains (+)/losses (−) [1]:		K.11.1	Neutral holding gains (−)/losses (+) [1]:	
AN	Non-financial assets	32	AF	Liabilities	14
AN.1	Produced assets	20	AF.2	Currency and deposits	2
AN.11	Fixed assets	18	AF.3	Securities other than shares	4
AN.12	Inventories	1	AF.4	Loans	7
AN.13	Valuables	1	AF.5	Shares and other equity	0
AN.2	Non-produced assets	12	AF.6	Insurance technical reserves	0
AN.21	Tangible non-produced assets	12	AF.7	Other accounts payable	0
AN.22	Intangible non-produced assets	0			
AF	Financial assets	8			
AF.1	Monetary gold and SDRs	2			
AF.2	Currency and deposits	3			
AF.3	Securities other than shares	0			
AF.4	Loans	2			
AF.5	Shares and other equity	0			
AF.6	Insurance technical reserves	0			
AF.7	Other accounts receivable	0			
			B.10.31	*Changes in net worth due to neutral holding gains/losses*	26

1   Differences between data on individual items and totals of holding
gains/losses may not be entirely consistent due to rounding errors.

Table A.V.5. Full sequence of accounts for general government [cont.]

III.3.2.2: Real holding gains/losses account

Changes in assets		
K.11.2	**Real holding gains(+)/losses(−) [1]:**	
AN	Non-financial assets	12
AN.1	Produced assets	0
AN.11	Fixed assets	0
AN.12	Inventories	0
AN.13	Valuables	0
AN.2	Non-produced assets	12
AN.21	Tangible non-produced assets	12
AN.22	Intangible non-produced assets	0
AF	Financial assets	− 6
AF.1	Monetary gold and SDRs	− 0
AF.2	Currency and deposits	− 3
AF.3	Securities other than shares	0
AF.4	Loans	− 2
AF.5	Shares and other equity	0
AF.6	Insurance technical reserves	− 0
AF.7	Other accounts receivable	− 0

Changes in liabilities and net worth		
K.11.2	**Real holding gains(−)/losses(+) [1]:**	
AF	Liabilities	− 7
AF.2	Currency and deposits	− 2
AF.3	Securities other than shares	3
AF.4	Loans	− 7
AF.5	Shares and other equity	0
AF.6	Insurance technical reserves	− 0
AF.7	Other accounts payable	− 0
B.10.32	*Changes in net worth due to real holding gains/losses*	12

1 Differences between data on individual items and totals of holding gains/losses may not be entirely consistent due to rounding errors.

Table A.V.5. Full sequence of accounts for general government [cont.]

IV: Balance sheets

IV.1: Opening balance sheet

Assets			Liabilities and net worth		
AN	Non-financial assets	1 591	AF	Liabilities	687
AN.1	Produced assets	1 001	AF.2	Currency and deposits	102
AN.11	Fixed assets	913	AF.3	Securities other than shares	212
AN.12	Inventories	47	AF.4	Loans	328
AN.13	Valuables	41	AF.5	Shares and other equity	4
AN.2	Non-produced assets	590	AF.6	Insurance technical reserves	19
AN.21	Tangible non-produced assets	578	AF.7	Other accounts payable	22
AN.22	Intangible non-produced assets	12			
AF	Financial assets	396			
AF.1	Monetary gold and SDRs	80			
AF.2	Currency and deposits	150			
AF.3	Securities other than shares	0			
AF.4	Loans	115			
AF.5	Shares and other equity	12			
AF.6	Insurance technical reserves	20			
AF.7	Other accounts receivable	19			
			B.90	*Net worth*	1 300

IV.2: Changes in balance sheet [1]

Assets			Liabilities and net worth		
	Total changes in assets			Total changes in liabilities	
AN	Non-financial assets	56	AF	Liabilities	176
AN.1	Produced assets	25	AF.2	Currency and deposits	2
AN.11	Fixed assets	20	AF.3	Securities other than shares	71
AN.12	Inventories	1	AF.4	Loans	93
AN.13	Valuables	4	AF.5	Shares and other equity	0
AN.2	Non-produced assets	30	AF.6	Insurance technical reserves	0
AN.21	Tangible non-produced assets	30	AF.7	Other accounts payable	10
AN.22	Intangible non-produced assets	0			
AF	Financial assets	123			
AF.1	Monetary gold and SDRs	1			
AF.2	Currency and deposits	7			
AF.3	Securities other than shares	29			
AF.4	Loans	45			
AF.5	Shares and other equity	34			
AF.6	Insurance technical reserves	0			
AF.7	Other accounts receivable	6			
			B.10	*Changes in net worth, total* due to:	2
			B.10.1	*Saving and capital transfers*	– 38
			B.10.2	*Other changes in volume of assets*	2
			B.10.3	*Nominal holding gains/losses*	38
			B.10.31	Neutral holding gains/losses	26
			B.10.32	Real holding gains/losses	12

1 Differences between data on individual items and totals of holding gains/losses may not be entirely consistent due to rounding errors.

Table A.V.5. Full sequence of accounts for general government [cont.]

IV.3. Closing balance sheet [1]

Assets

AN	Non-financial assets	1 647
AN.1	Produced assets	1 026
AN.11	Fixed assets	933
AN.12	Inventories	48
AN.13	Valuables	45
AN.2	Non-produced assets	620
AN.21	Tangible non-produced assets	608
AN.22	Intangible non-produced assets	12

AF	Financial assets	519
AF.1	Monetary gold and SDRs	81
AF.2	Currency and deposits	157
AF.3	Securities other than shares	29
AF.4	Loans	160
AF.5	Shares and other equity	46
AF.6	Insurance technical reserves	20
AF.7	Other accounts receivable	25

Liabilities
and net worth

AF	Liabilities	863
AF.2	Currency and deposits	104
AF.3	Securities other than shares	283
AF.4	Loans	421
AF.5	Shares and other equity	4
AF.6	Insurance technical reserves	19
AF.7	Other accounts payable	32

B.90	*Net worth*	1 302

1 Differences between data on individual items and totals of holding gains/losses may not be entirely consistent due to rounding errors.

Table A.V.6. Full sequence of accounts for households

I: Production account

Uses			Resources		
P.2	Intermediate consumption	694	P.1	Output [1]	1 269
			P.11	Market output	1 129
			P.12	Output for own final use	140
B.1g	*Value added, gross*	575			
K.1	Consumption of fixed capital	42			
B.1n	*Value added, net*	533			

1 For the valuation of output, refer to chapter VI, paragraphs 6.210 to 6.227.

II. Distribution and use of income accounts

II.1: Primary distribution of income account

II.1.1: Generation of income account

Uses			Resources		
D.1	Compensation of employees	39	B.1	*Value added [1]*	533
D.11	Wages and salaries	39			
D.12	Employers' social contributions	0			
D.121	Employers' actual social contributions	0			
D.122	Employers' imputed social contributions	0			
D.29	Other taxes on production	3			
D.39	Other subsidies on production	− 1			
B.2	*Operating surplus [1]*	60			
B.3	*Mixed income [1]*	432			

1 The opening and the closing balancing item of this account can be expressed
in gross or in net terms. The amount presented refers to the net value.

Table A.V.6   Full sequence of accounts for households [cont.]

II.1.2:   Allocation of primary income account

Uses				Resources		
D.4	Property income		41	B.2	*Operating surplus* [1]	60
D.41	Interest		14	B.3	*Mixed income* [1]	432
D.45	Rent		27			
				D.1	Compensation of employees	766
				D.11	Wages and salaries	573
				D.12	Employers' social contributions	193
				D.121	Employers' actual social contributions	174
				D.122	Employers' imputed social contributions	19
				D.4	Property income	150
				D.41	Interest	49
				D.42	Distributed income of corporations	57
				D.421	Dividends	13
				D.422	Withdrawals from income of quasi-corporations	44
				D.43	Reinvested earnings on direct foreign investment	3
				D.44	Property income attributed to insurance policyholders	20
				D.45	Rent	21
B.5	*Balance of primary incomes* [1]		1 367			

1   The opening and the closing balancing item of this account can be expressed
in gross or in net terms. The amount presented refers to the net value.

II.1.2.1:   Entrepreneurial income account

Uses				Resources		
D.4	Property income [2]		7	B.2	*Operating surplus* [1]	60
D.41	Interest		0	B.3	*Mixed income* [1]	432
D.45	Rent		7			
				D.4	Property income [2]	5
				D.41	Interest	0
				D.42	Distributed income of corporations	5
				D.421	Dividends	5
				D.422	Withdrawals from income of quasi-corporations	0
				D.44	Property income attributed to insurance policyholders	0
B.4	*Entrepreneurial income* [1]		490			

1   The opening and the closing balancing item of this account can be expressed
in gross or in net terms. The amount presented refers to the net value.
2   Including only property income connected with market activities.

Table A.V.6 Full sequence of accounts for households [cont.]

II.1.2.2: Allocation of other primary income account

Uses			Resources		
D.4	Property income ²	34	B.4	*Entrepreneurial income ¹*	490
D.41	Interest	14			
D.45	Rent	20	D.1	Compensation of employees	766
			D.11	Wages and salaries	573
			D.12	Employers' social contributions	193
			D.121	Employers' actual social contributions	174
			D.122	Employers' imputed social contributions	19
			D.4	Property income ²	145
			D.41	Interest	49
			D.42	Distributed income of corporations	52
			D.421	Dividends	8
			D.422	Withdrawals from income of quasi-corporations	44
			D.43	Reinvested earnings on direct foreign investment	3
			D.44	Property income attributed to insurance policyholders	20
			D.45	Rent	21
B.5	*Balance of primary incomes ¹*	1 367			

1 The opening and the closing balancing item of this account can be expressed in gross or in net terms. The amount presented refers to the net value.
2 Property income not connected with market activities.

II.2: Secondary distribution of income account

Uses			Resources		
D.5	Current taxes on income, wealth, etc.	178	B.5	*Balance of primary incomes ¹*	1 367
D.51	Taxes on income	176			
D.59	Other current taxes	2	D.61	Social contributions	0
			D.611	Actual social contributions	0
D.61	Social contributions	322	D.6111	Employers' actual social contributions	0
D.611	Actual social contributions	303	D.61111	Compulsory employers' actual social contributions	0
D.6111	Employers' actual social contributions	174	D.61112	Voluntary employers' actual social contributions	0
D.61111	Compulsory employers' actual social contributions	160	D.6112	Employees' social contributions	0
D.61112	Voluntary employers' actual social contributions	14	D.61121	Compulsory employees' social contributions	0
D.6112	Employees' social contributions	97	D.61122	Voluntary employees' social contributions non-employed persons	0
D.61121	Compulsory employees' social contributions	85			
D.61122	Voluntary employees' social contributions	12	D.62	Social benefits other than social transfers in kind	332
D.6113	Social contributions by self- and non-employed persons	32	D.621	Social security benefits in cash	232
D.61131	Compulsory social contributions by self- and non-employed persons	22	D.622	Private funded social benefits	29
D.61132	Voluntary social contributions by self- and non-employed persons	10	D.623	Unfunded employee social benefits	19
D.612	Imputed social contributions	19	D.624	Social assistance benefits in cash	52
D.62	Social benefits other than social transfers in kind	0	D.7	Other current transfers	36
D.622	Private funded social benefits	0	D.72	Non-life insurance claims	35
			D.75	Miscellaneous current transfers	1
D.7	Other current transfers	71			
D.71	Net non-life insurance premiums	31			
D.75	Miscellaneous current transfers	40			
B.6	*Disposable income ¹*	1 164			

1 The opening and the closing balancing item of this account can be expressed in gross or in net terms. The amount presented refers to the net value.

Table A.V.6 Full sequence of accounts for households [cont.]

II.3: Redistribution of income in kind account

Uses			Resources		
			B.6	*Disposable income* [1]	1 164
			D.63	Social transfers in kind	228
			D.631	Social benefits in kind	162
			D.6311	Social security benefits, reimbursements	78
			D.6312	Other social security benefits in kind	65
			D.6313	Social assistance benefits in kind	19
			D.632	Transfers of individual non-market goods and services	66
B.7	*Adjusted disposable income* [1]	1 392			

1   The opening and the closing balancing item of this account can be expressed in gross or in net terms. The amount presented refers to the net value.

II.4: Use of income account

II.4.1: Use of disposable income account

Uses			Resources		
P.3	Final consumption expenditure	1 015	B.6	*Disposable income* [1]	1 164
P.31	Individual consumption expenditure	1 015			
			D.8	Adjustment for the change in net equity of households on pension funds	11
B.8	*Saving* [1]	160			

1   The opening and the closing balancing item of this account can be expressed in gross or in net terms. The amount presented refers to the net value.

II.4.2: Use of adjusted disposable income account

Uses			Resources		
P.4	Actual final consumption	1 243	B.7	*Adjusted disposable income* [1]	1 392
P.41	Actual individual consumption	1 243			
			D.8	Adjustment for the change in net equity of households on pension funds	11
B.8	*Saving* [1]	160			

1   The opening and the closing balancing item of this account can be expressed in gross or in net terms. The amount presented refers to the net value.

Table A.V.6   Full sequence of accounts for households [cont.]

III. Accumulation accounts

III.1: Capital account

Changes in assets			Changes in liabilities and net worth		
P.51	Gross fixed capital formation	61	B.8n	*Saving, net*	160
P.511	Acquisitions less disposals of tangible fixed assets	49			
P.5111	Acquisitions of new tangible fixed assets	50	D.9	Capital transfers, receivable	23
P.5112	Acquisitions of existing tangible fixed assets	4	D.92	Investment grants	0
P.5113	Disposals of existing tangible fixed assets	– 5	D.99	Other capital transfers	23
P.512	Acquisitions less disposals of intangible fixed assets	12			
P.5121	Acquisitions of new intangible fixed assets	9	D.9	Capital transfers, payable	– 5
P.5122	Acquisitions of existing intangible fixed assets	3	D.91	Capital taxes, payable	– 2
P.5123	Disposals of existing intangible fixed assets	0	D.99	Other capital transfers, payable	– 3
P.513	Additions to the value of non-produced non-financial assets	0			
P.5131	Major improvements to non-produced non-financial assets	0			
P.5132	Costs of ownership transfer on non-produced non-financial assets	0			
K.1	Consumption of fixed capital	– 42			
P.52	Changes in inventories	2			
P.53	Acquisitions less disposals of valuables	5			
K.2	Acquisitions less disposals of non-produced non-financial assets	4			
K.21	Acquisitions less disposals of land and other tangible non-produced assets	3			
K.22	Acquisitions less disposals of intangible non-produced assets	1			
B.9	*Net lending (+) / net borrowing (–)*	148	B.10.1	*Changes in net worth due to saving and capital transfers* [1]	178

1   "Changes in net worth due to saving and capital transfers" is not a balancing item but corresponds to the total of the right-hand side of the capital account.

Table A.V.6 Full sequence of accounts for households [cont.]

III.2: Financial account

Changes in assets				Changes in liabilities and net worth		
F	Net acquisition of financial assets		181	F	Net incurrence of liabilities	33
F.2	Currency and deposits [1]		68	F.2	Currency and deposits [1]	0
F.21	Currency		10	F.22	Transferable deposits	0
F.22	Transferable deposits		41	F.23	Other deposits	0
F.23	Other deposits		17			
				F.3	Securities other than shares	0
F.3	Securities other than shares		29	F.31	Short-term	0
F.31	Short-term		22	F.32	Long-term	0
F.32	Long-term		7			
				F.4	Loans [2]	28
F.4	Loans [2]		5	F.41	Short-term	11
F.41	Short-term		3	F.42	Long-term	17
F.42	Long-term		2			
				F.7	Other accounts payable [2]	5
F.5	Shares and other equity [2]		3	F.71	Trade credits and advances	4
				F.79	Other accounts payable, except trade credits and advances	1
F.6	Insurance technical reserves		36			
F.61	Net equity of households on life insurance reserves and on pension funds		33			
F.611	Net equity of households on life insurance reserves		22			
F.612	Net equity of households on pension funds		11			
F.62	Prepayment of premiums and reserves against outstanding claims		3			
F.7	Other accounts receivable [2]		40			
F.71	Trade credits and advances		11			
F.79	Other accounts receivable, except trade credits and advances		29			
				B.9	*Net lending(+)/net borrowing(–)*	148

1 The following memorandum items related to the elements of the category
F.2 "Currency and deposits":
    m11   denominated in national currency
    m12   denominated in foreign currency
    m21   liability of resident institutions
    m22   liability of rest of the world.
2 Memorandum item: F.m. Direct foreign investment.

Table A.V.6   Full sequence of accounts for households [cont.]

III.3:   Other changes in assets accounts

III.3.1:   Other changes in volume of assets account

Changes in assets			Changes in liabilities and net worth		
AN	Non-financial assets	0	AF	Liabilities	0
AN.1	Produced assets	0	K.7	Catastrophic losses	0
K.4	Economic appearance of produced assets	0	K.8	Uncompensated seizures	0
K.7	Catastrophic losses	0	K.10	Other volume changes in financial assets and liabilities n.e.c.	0
K.8	Uncompensated seizures	0	K.12	Changes in classifications and structure	0
K.9	Other volume changes in non-financial assets n.e.c.	0	K.12.1	Changes in sector classification and structure	0
K.12	Changes in classifications and structure	0	K.12.2	Changes in classification of assets and liabilities	0
K.12.1	Changes in sector classification and structure	0	K.12.22	Changes in classification of assets or liabilities other than monetization/demonetization of gold	0
K.12.2	Changes in classification of assets and liabilities	0	of which:		
K.12.21	Monetization/demonetization of gold	0	AF.2	Currency and deposits	0
K.12.22	Changes in classification of assets or liabilities other than monetization/demonetization of gold	0	AF.3	Securities other than shares	0
of which:			AF.4	Loans	0
AN.11	Fixed assets	0	AF.7	Other accounts payable	0
AN.12	Inventories	0			
AN.13	Valuables	0			
AN.2	Non-produced assets	0			
K.3	Economic appearance of non-produced assets	0			
K.5	Natural growth of non-cultivated biological resources	0			
K.6	Economic disappearance of non-produced assets	0			
K.61	Depletion of natural assets	0			
K.62	Other economic disappearance of non-produced assets	0			
K.7	Catastrophic losses	0			
K.8	Uncompensated seizures	0			
K.9	Other volume changes in non-financial assets n.e.c.	0			
K.12	Changes in classifications and structure	0			
K.12.1	Changes in sector classification and structure	0			
K.12.2	Changes in classification of assets and liabilities	0			
K.12.22	Changes in classification of assets or liabilities other than monetization/demonetization of gold	0			
of which:					
AN.21	Tangible non-produced assets	0			
AN.22	Intangible non-produced assets	0			
AF	Financial assets	2			
K.7	Catastrophic losses	0			
K.8	Uncompensated seizures	0			
K.10	Other volume changes in financial assets and liabilities n.e.c.	2			
K.12	Changes in classifications and structure	0			
K.12.1	Changes in sector classification and structure	0			
K.12.2	Changes in classification of assets and liabilities	0			
K.12.22	Changes in classification of assets or liabilities other than monetization/demonetization of gold	0			
of which:					
AF.2	Currency and deposits	0			
AF.3	Securities other than shares	0			
AF.4	Loans	0			
AF.5	Shares and other equity	0			
AF.6	Insurance technical reserves	2			
AF.7	Other accounts receivable	0			

B.10.2	*Changes in net worth due to other changes in volume of assets*	2

Table A.V.6   Full sequence of accounts for households [cont.]

III.3.2: Revaluation account

Changes in assets			Changes in liabilities and net worth		
K.11	Nominal holding gains(+)/losses(–) [1]:		K.11	Nominal holding gains(–)/losses(+) [1]:	
AN	Non-financial assets	80	AF	Liabilities	0
AN.1	Produced assets	35	AF.2	Currency and deposits	0
AN.11	Fixed assets	28	AF.3	Securities other than shares	0
AN.12	Inventories	2	AF.4	Loans	0
AN.13	Valuables	5	AF.7	Other accounts payable	0
AN.2	Non-produced assets	45			
AN.21	Tangible non-produced assets	45			
AN.22	Intangible non-produced assets	0			
AF	Financial assets	16			
AF.2	Currency and deposits	0			
AF.3	Securities other than shares	6			
AF.4	Loans	0			
AF.5	Shares and other equity	10			
AF.6	Insurance technical reserves	0			
AF.7	Other accounts receivable	0			
			B.10.3	*Changes in net worth due to nominal holding gains/losses*	96

1   Differences between data on individual items and totals of holding
gains/losses may not be entirely consistent due to rounding errors.

Table A.V.6   Full sequence of accounts for households [cont.]

III.3.2.1: Neutral holding gains/losses account

Changes in assets			Changes in liabilities and net worth		
K.11.1	Neutral holding gains (+)/losses (–) [1]:		K.11.1	Neutral holding gains (–)/losses (+) [1]:	
AN	Non-financial assets	56	AF	Liabilities	6
AN.1	Produced assets	34	AF.2	Currency and deposits	0
AN.11	Fixed assets	28	AF.3	Securities other than shares	0
AN.12	Inventories	2	AF.4	Loans	3
AN.13	Valuables	4	AF.5	Shares and other equity	0
AN.2	Non-produced assets	22	AF.6	Insurance technical reserves	0
AN.21	Tangible non-produced assets	22	AF.7	Other accounts payable	2
AN.22	Intangible non-produced assets	0			
AF	Financial assets	36			
AF.2	Currency and deposits	17			
AF.3	Securities other than shares	4			
AF.4	Loans	0			
AF.5	Shares and other equity	8			
AF.6	Insurance technical reserves	6			
AF.7	Other accounts receivable	1			
			B.10.31 *Changes in net worth due to neutral holding gains/losses*		87

1   Differences between data on individual items and totals of holding
gains/losses may not be entirely consistent due to rounding errors.

III.3.2.2: Real holding gains/losses account

Changes in assets			Changes in liabilities and net worth		
K.11.2	Real holding gains(+)/losses(–) [1]:		K.11.2	Real holding gains(–)/losses(+) [1]:	
AN	Non-financial assets	24	AF	Liabilities	– 6
AN.1	Produced assets	1	AF.2	Currency and deposits	– 0
AN.11	Fixed assets	0	AF.3	Securities other than shares	0
AN.12	Inventories	0	AF.4	Loans	– 3
AN.13	Valuables	1	AF.7	Other accounts payable	– 2
AN.2	Non-produced assets	22			
AN.21	Tangible non-produced assets	22			
AN.22	Intangible non-produced assets	0			
AF	Financial assets	– 20			
AF.2	Currency and deposits	– 17			
AF.3	Securities other than shares	2			
AF.4	Loans	– 0			
AF.5	Shares and other equity	2			
AF.6	Insurance technical reserves	– 6			
AF.7	Other accounts receivable	– 1			
			B.10.32 *Changes in net worth due to real holding gains/losses*		9

1   Differences between data on individual items and totals of holding
gains/losses may not be entirely consistent due to rounding errors.

Table A.V.6   Full sequence of accounts for households [cont.]

IV: Balance sheets

IV.1: Opening balance sheet

Assets			
AN	Non-financial assets		2 822
AN.1	Produced assets		1 698
AN.11	Fixed assets		1 423
AN.12	Inventories		97
AN.13	Valuables		178
AN.2	Non-produced assets		1 124
AN.21	Tangible non-produced assets		1 124
AN.22	Intangible non-produced assets		0
AF	Financial assets		1 819
AF.2	Currency and deposits		840
AF.3	Securities other than shares		198
AF.4	Loans		24
AF.5	Shares and other equity		411
AF.6	Insurance technical reserves		291
AF.7	Other accounts receivable		55

Liabilities and net worth		
AF	Liabilities	289
AF.2	Currency and deposits	10
AF.3	Securities other than shares	2
AF.4	Loans	169
AF.7	Other accounts payable	108
B.90	*Net worth*	4 352

IV.2: Changes in balance sheet [1]

Assets		
Total changes in assets		
AN	Non-financial assets	110
AN.1	Produced assets	61
AN.11	Fixed assets	47
AN.12	Inventories	4
AN.13	Valuables	10
AN.2	Non-produced assets	49
AN.21	Tangible non-produced assets	48
AN.22	Intangible non-produced assets	1
AF	Financial assets	199
AF.2	Currency and deposits	68
AF.3	Securities other than shares	35
AF.4	Loans	5
AF.5	Shares and other equity	13
AF.6	Insurance technical reserves	38
AF.7	Other accounts receivable	40

Liabilities and net worth		
Total changes in liabilities		
AF	Liabilities	33
AF.2	Currency and deposits	0
AF.3	Securities other than shares	0
AF.4	Loans	28
AF.7	Other accounts payable	5
B.10	*Changes in net worth, total* due to:	276
B.10.1	*Saving and capital transfers*	178
B.10.2	*Other changes in volume of assets*	2
B.10.3	*Nominal holding gains/losses*	96
B.10.31	*Neutral holding gains/losses*	87
B.10.32	*Real holding gains/losses*	9

1   Differences between data on individual items and totals of holding gains/losses may not be entirely consistent due to rounding errors.

Table A.V.6 Full sequence of accounts for households [cont.]

IV.3. Closing balance sheet [1]

Assets			Liabilities and net worth		
AN	Non-financial assets	2 932	AF	Liabilities	322
AN.1	Produced assets	1 759	AF.2	Currency and deposits	10
AN.11	Fixed assets	1 470	AF.3	Securities other than shares	2
AN.12	Inventories	101	AF.4	Loans	197
AN.13	Valuables	188	AF.7	Other accounts payable	113
AN.2	Non-produced assets	1 173			
AN.21	Tangible non-produced assets	1 172			
AN.22	Intangible non-produced assets	1			
AF	Financial assets	2 018			
AF.2	Currency and deposits	908			
AF.3	Securities other than shares	233			
AF.4	Loans	29			
AF.5	Shares and other equity	424			
AF.6	Insurance technical reserves	329			
AF.7	Other accounts receivable	95			
			B.90	*Net worth*	4 628

1 Differences between data on individual items and totals of holding
gains/losses may not be entirely consistent due to rounding errors.

Table A.V.7. Full sequence of accounts for non-profit institutions serving households

I: Production account

Uses			Resources			
P.2	Intermediate consumption	9	P.1	Output [1]		40
			P.11	Market output		24
			P.12	Output for own final use		0
			P.13	Other non-market output		16
B.1g	*Value added, gross*	31				
K.1	Consumption of fixed capital	3				
B.1n	*Value added, net*	28				

1 For the valuation of output, refer to chapter VI, paragraphs 6.210 to 6.227.

II. Distribution and use of income accounts

II.1: Primary distribution of income account

II.1.1: Generation of income account

Uses			Resources		
D.1	Compensation of employees	23	B.1	*Value added [1]*	28
D.11	Wages and salaries	12			
D.12	Employers' social contributions	11			
D.121	Employers' actual social contributions	10			
D.122	Employers' imputed social contributions	1			
D.29	Other taxes on production	0			
D.39	Other subsidies on production	0			
B.2	*Operating surplus [1]*	5			

1 The opening and the closing balancing item of this account can be expressed in gross or in net terms. The amount presented refers to the net value.

Table A.V.7 Full sequence of accounts for non-profit institutions serving households [cont.]

II.1.2: Allocation of primary income account

Uses			Resources		
D.4	Property income	6	B.2	*Operating surplus* [1]	
D.41	Interest	6			
D.42	Distributed income of corporations	0	D.4	Property income	
D.422	Withdrawals from income of quasi-corporations	0	D.41	Interest	
D.43	Reinvested earnings on direct foreign investment	0	D.42	Distributed income of corporations	
D.44	Property income attributed to insurance policyholders	0	D.421	Dividends	
D.45	Rent	0	D.422	Withdrawals from income of quasi-corporations	
			D.43	Reinvested earnings on direct foreign investment	
			D.44	Property income attributed to insurance policyholders	
			D.45	Rent	
B.5	*Balance of primary incomes* [1]	6			

1 The opening and the closing balancing item of this account can be expressed
in gross or in net terms. The amount presented refers to the net value.

II.1.2.1: Entrepreneurial income account

Uses			Resources		
D.4	Property income [2]	2	B.2	*Operating surplus* [1]	
D.41	Interest	2			
D.45	Rent	0	D.4	Property income [2]	
			D.41	Interest	
			D.42	Distributed income of corporations	
			D.421	Dividends	
			D.422	Withdrawals from income of quasi-corporations	
B.4	*Entrepreneurial income* [1]	3			

1 The opening and the closing balancing item of this account can be expressed
in gross or in net terms. The amount presented refers to the net value.
2 Including only property income connected with market activities.

II.1.2.2: Allocation of other primary income account

Uses			Resources		
D.4	Property income [2]	4	B.4	*Entrepreneurial income* [1]	
D.41	Interest	4			
D.45	Rent	0	D.4	Property income [2]	
			D.41	Interest	
			D.42	Distributed income of corporations	
			D.421	Dividends	
			D.422	Withdrawals from income of quasi-corporations	
			D.43	Reinvested earnings on direct foreign investment	
			D.44	Property income attributed to insurance policyholders	
			D.45	Rent	
B.5	*Balance of primary incomes* [1]	6			

1 The opening and the closing balancing item of this account can be expressed
in gross or in net terms. The amount presented refers to the net value.
2 Property income not connected with market activities.

Table A.V.7   Full sequence of accounts for non-profit institutions serving households [cont.]

II.2: Secondary distribution of income account

Uses			Resources		
D.5	Current taxes on income, wealth, etc.	0	B.5	*Balance of primary incomes* [1]	6
D.59	Other current taxes	0			
			D.61	Social contributions	1
D.62	Social benefits other than social transfers in kind	1	D.611	Actual social contributions	0
D.622	Private funded social benefits	0	D.6111	Employers' actual social contributions	0
D.623	Unfunded employee social benefits	1	D.61111	Compulsory employers' actual social contributions	0
			D.6112	Employees' social contributions	0
D.7	Other current transfers	2	D.61121	Compulsory employees' social contributions	0
D.71	Net non-life insurance premiums	0	D.61122	Voluntary employees' social contributions	0
D.75	Miscellaneous current transfers	2	D.612	Imputed social contributions	1
			D.7	Other current transfers	36
			D.72	Non-life insurance claims	0
			D.75	Miscellaneous current transfers	36
B.6	*Disposable income* [1]	40			

1   The opening and the closing balancing item of this account can be expressed
in gross or in net terms. The amount presented refers to the net value.

II.3: Redistribution of income in kind account

Uses			Resources		
D.63	Social transfers in kind	16	B.6	*Disposable income* [1]	40
D.631	Social benefits in kind	0			
D.6313	Social assistance benefits in kind	0			
D.632	Transfers of individual non-market goods and services	16			
B.7	*Adjusted disposable income* [1]	24			

1   The opening and the closing balancing item of this account can be expressed
in gross or in net terms. The amount presented refers to the net value.

II.4: Use of income account

II.4.1: Use of disposable income account

Uses			Resources		
P.3	Final consumption expenditure	16	B.6	*Disposable income* [1]	40
P.31	Individual consumption expenditure	16			
D.8	Adjustment for the change in net equity of households on pension funds	0			
B.8	*Saving* [1]	24			

1   The opening and the closing balancing item of this account can be expressed
in gross or in net terms. The amount presented refers to the net value.

II.4.2: Use of adjusted disposable income account

Uses			Resources		
D.8	Adjustment for the change in net equity of households on pension funds	0	B.7	*Adjusted disposable income* [1]	24
B.8	*Saving* [1]	24			

1   The opening and the closing balancing item of this account can be expressed
in gross or in net terms. The amount presented refers to the net value.

Table A.V.7 Full sequence of accounts for non-profit institutions serving households [cont.]

III. Accumulation accounts

III.1: Capital account

Changes in assets			Changes in liabilities and net worth		
P.51	Gross fixed capital formation	19	B.8n	*Saving, net*	24
P.511	Acquisitions less disposals of tangible fixed assets	14			
P.5111	Acquisitions of new tangible fixed assets	13	D.9	Capital transfers, receivable	0
P.5112	Acquisitions of existing tangible fixed assets	1	D.92	Investment grants	0
P.5113	Disposals of existing tangible fixed assets	0	D.99	Other capital transfers	0
P.512	Acquisitions less disposals of intangible fixed assets	5			
P.5121	Acquisitions of new intangible fixed assets	10	D.9	Capital transfers, payable	− 3
P.5122	Acquisitions of existing intangible fixed assets	0	D.91	Capital taxes	0
P.5123	Disposals of existing intangible fixed assets	− 5	D.99	Other capital transfers	− 3
P.513	Additions to the value of non-produced non-financial assets	0			
P.5131	Major improvements to non-produced non-financial assets	0			
P.5132	Costs of ownership transfer on non-produced non-financial assets	0			
K.1	Consumption of fixed capital	− 3			
P.52	Changes in inventories	0			
P.53	Acquisitions less disposals of valuables	0			
K.2	Acquisitions less disposals of non-produced non-financial assets	1			
K.21	Acquisitions less disposals of land and other tangible non-produced assets	1			
K.22	Acquisitions less disposals of intangible non-produced assets	0			
B.9	*Net lending (+) / net borrowing (−)*	4	B.10.1	*Changes in net worth due to saving and capital transfers* [1]	21

1 "Changes in net worth due to saving and capital transfers" is not a balancing item but corresponds to the total of the right-hand side of the capital account.

Table A.V.7   Full sequence of accounts for non-profit institutions serving households [cont.]

III.2: Financial account

Changes in assets				Changes in liabilities and net worth			
F		Net acquisition of financial assets	32	F		Net incurrence of liabilities	28
F.2		Currency and deposits [1]	12	F.2		Currency and deposits [1]	0
F.21		Currency	2	F.22		Transferable deposits	0
F.22		Transferable deposits	7	F.23		Other deposits	0
F.23		Other deposits	3				
				F.3		Securities other than shares	0
F.3		Securities other than shares	12	F.31		Short-term	0
F.31		Short-term	2	F.32		Long-term	0
F.32		Long-term	10				
				F.4		Loans [2]	24
F.4		Loans [2]	0	F.41		Short-term	17
F.41		Short-term	0	F.42		Long-term	7
F.42		Long-term	0				
				F.5		Shares and other equity [2]	4
F.5		Shares and other equity [2]	0				
				F.6		Insurance technical reserves	0
F.6		Insurance technical reserves	0	F.61		Net equity of households on life insurance reserves and on pension funds	0
F.62		Prepayment of premiums and reserves against outstanding claims	0	F.612		Net equity of households on pension funds	0
F.7		Other accounts receivable [2]	8	F.7		Other accounts payable [2]	0
F.71		Trade credits and advances	0	F.71		Trade credits and advances	0
F.79		Other accounts receivable, except trade credits and advances	8	F.79		Other accounts payable, except trade credits and advances	0
				B.9		*Net lending(+)/net borrowing(−)*	4

1   The following memorandum items related to the elements of the category

F.2 "Currency and deposits":
   m11   denominated in national currency
   m12   denominated in foreign currency
   m21   liability of resident institutions
   m22   liability of rest of the world.
2   Memorandum item: F.m. Direct foreign investment.

Table A.V.7 Full sequence of accounts for non-profit institutions serving households [cont.]

III.3: Other changes in assets accounts

III.3.1: Other changes in volume of assets account

Changes in assets				Changes in liabilities and net worth			
AN	Non-financial assets		0	AF	Liabilities		
AN.1	Produced assets		0	K.7	Catastrophic losses		
K.4	Economic appearance of produced assets		0	K.8	Uncompensated seizures		
K.7	Catastrophic losses		0	K.10	Other volume changes in financial assets and liabilities n.e.c.		
K.8	Uncompensated seizures		0	K.12	Changes in classifications and structure		
K.9	Other volume changes in non-financial assets n.e.c.		0	K.12.1	Changes in sector classification and structure		
K.12	Changes in classifications and structure		0	K.12.2	Changes in classification of assets and liabilities		
K.12.1	Changes in sector classification and structure		0	K.12.22	Changes in classification of assets or liabilities other than monetization/demonetization of gold		
K.12.2	Changes in classification of assets and liabilities		0	of which:			
K.12.22	Changes in classification of assets or liabilities other than monetization/demonetization of gold		0	AF.2	Currency and deposits		
of which:				AF.3	Securities other than shares		
AN.11	Fixed assets		0	AF.4	Loans		
AN.12	Inventories		0	AF.5	Shares and other equity		
AN.13	Valuables		0	AF.6	Insurance technical reserves		
AN.2	Non-produced assets		0	AF.7	Other accounts payable		
K.3	Economic appearance of non-produced assets		0				
K.5	Natural growth of non-cultivated biological resources		0				
K.6	Economic disappearance of non-produced assets		0				
K.61	Depletion of natural assets		0				
K.62	Other economic disappearance of non-produced assets		0				
K.7	Catastrophic losses		0				
K.8	Uncompensated seizures		0				
K.9	Other volume changes in non-financial assets n.e.c.		0				
K.12	Changes in classifications and structure		0				
K.12.1	Changes in sector classification and structure		0				
K.12.2	Changes in classification of assets and liabilities		0				
K.12.22	Changes in classification of assets or liabilities other than monetization/demonetization of gold		0				
of which:							
AN.21	Tangible non-produced assets		0				
AN.22	Intangible non-produced assets		0				
AF	Financial assets		0				
K.7	Catastrophic losses		0				
K.8	Uncompensated seizures		0				
K.10	Other volume changes in financial assets and liabilities n.e.c.		0				
K.12	Changes in classifications and structure		0				
K.12.1	Changes in sector classification and structure		0				
K.12.2	Changes in classification of assets and liabilities		0				
K.12.22	Changes in classification of assets or liabilities other than monetization/demonetization of gold		0				
of which:							
AF.2	Currency and deposits		0				
AF.3	Securities other than shares		0				
AF.4	Loans		0				
AF.5	Shares and other equity		0				
AF.6	Insurance technical reserves		0				
AF.7	Other accounts receivable		0				

B.10.2 *Changes in net worth due to other changes in volume of assets*

Table A.V.7 **Full sequence of accounts for non-profit institutions serving households [cont.]**

III.3.2: Revaluation account

Changes in assets			Changes in liabilities and net worth		
K.11	Nominal holding gains(+)/losses(−) [1]:		K.11	Nominal holding gains(−)/losses(+) [1]:	
AN	Non-financial assets	8	AF	Liabilities	0
AN.1	Produced assets	5	AF.2	Currency and deposits	0
AN.11	Fixed assets	5	AF.3	Securities other than shares	0
AN.12	Inventories	0	AF.4	Loans	0
AN.13	Valuables	0	AF.5	Shares and other equity	0
AN.2	Non-produced assets	3	AF.6	Insurance technical reserves	0
AN.21	Tangible non-produced assets	3	AF.7	Other accounts payable	0
AN.22	Intangible non-produced assets	0			
AF	Financial assets	1			
AF.2	Currency and deposits	0			
AF.3	Securities other than shares	1			
AF.4	Loans	0			
AF.5	Shares and other equity	1			
AF.6	Insurance technical reserves	0			
AF.7	Other accounts receivable	0			
			B.10.3	*Changes in net worth due to nominal holding gains/losses*	10

1   Differences between data on individual items and totals of holding
gains/losses may not be entirely consistent due to rounding errors.

Table A.V.7   Full sequence of accounts for non-profit institutions serving households [cont.]

III.3.2.1: Neutral holding gains/losses account

Changes in assets				Changes in liabilities and net worth		
K.11.1	Neutral holding gains (+)/losses (−) [1]:			K.11.1	Neutral holding gains (−)/losses (+) [1]:	
AN	Non-financial assets		6	AF	Liabilities	2
AN.1	Produced assets		5	AF.2	Currency and deposits	1
AN.11	Fixed assets		5	AF.3	Securities other than shares	0
AN.12	Inventories		0	AF.4	Loans	1
AN.13	Valuables		0	AF.5	Shares and other equity	0
AN.2	Non-produced assets		2	AF.6	Insurance technical reserves	0
AN.21	Tangible non-produced assets		2	AF.7	Other accounts payable	1
AN.22	Intangible non-produced assets		0			
AF	Financial assets		3			
AF.2	Currency and deposits		2			
AF.3	Securities other than shares		1			
AF.4	Loans		0			
AF.5	Shares and other equity		0			
AF.6	Insurance technical reserves		0			
AF.7	Other accounts receivable		0			
				B.10.31	*Changes in net worth due to neutral holding gains/losses*	8

1   Differences between data on individual items and totals of holding
gains/losses may not be entirely consistent due to rounding errors.

III.3.2.2: Real holding gains/losses account

Changes in assets				Changes in liabilities and net worth		
K.11.2	Real holding gains(+)/losses(−) [1]:			K.11.2	Real holding gains(−)/losses(+) [1]:	
AN	Non-financial assets		2	AF	Liabilities	−2
AN.1	Produced assets		0	AF.2	Currency and deposits	−1
AN.11	Fixed assets		0	AF.3	Securities other than shares	0
AN.12	Inventories		0	AF.4	Loans	−1
AN.13	Valuables		0	AF.5	Shares and other equity	0
AN.2	Non-produced assets		2	AF.6	Insurance technical reserves	−0
AN.21	Tangible non-produced assets		2	AF.7	Other accounts payable	−1
AN.22	Intangible non-produced assets		0			
AF	Financial assets		−2			
AF.2	Currency and deposits		−2			
AF.3	Securities other than shares		0			
AF.4	Loans		−0			
AF.5	Shares and other equity		0			
AF.6	Insurance technical reserves		−0			
AF.7	Other accounts receivable		−0			
				B.10.32	*Changes in net worth due to real holding gains/losses*	2

1   Differences between data on individual items and totals of holding
gains/losses may not be entirely consistent due to rounding errors.

Table A.V.7 Full sequence of accounts for non-profit institutions serving households [cont.]

IV: Balance sheets

IV.1: Opening balance sheet

Assets

AN	Non-financial assets	324
AN.1	Produced assets	243
AN.11	Fixed assets	231
AN.12	Inventories	2
AN.13	Valuables	10
AN.2	Non-produced assets	81
AN.21	Tangible non-produced assets	81
AN.22	Intangible non-produced assets	0

AF	Financial assets	172
AF.2	Currency and deposits	110
AF.3	Securities other than shares	25
AF.4	Loans	8
AF.5	Shares and other equity	22
AF.6	Insurance technical reserves	4
AF.7	Other accounts receivable	3

Liabilities and net worth

AF	Liabilities	121
AF.2	Currency and deposits	38
AF.3	Securities other than shares	0
AF.4	Loans	43
AF.5	Shares and other equity	0
AF.6	Insurance technical reserves	5
AF.7	Other accounts payable	35

B.90	*Net worth*	375

IV.2: Changes in balance sheet [1]

Assets

Total changes in assets

AN	Non-financial assets	25
AN.1	Produced assets	21
AN.11	Fixed assets	21
AN.12	Inventories	0
AN.13	Valuables	0
AN.2	Non-produced assets	4
AN.21	Tangible non-produced assets	4
AN.22	Intangible non-produced assets	0

AF	Financial assets	33
AF.2	Currency and deposits	12
AF.3	Securities other than shares	13
AF.4	Loans	0
AF.5	Shares and other equity	1
AF.6	Insurance technical reserves	0
AF.7	Other accounts receivable	8

Liabilities and net worth

Total changes in liabilities

AF	Liabilities	28
AF.2	Currency and deposits	0
AF.3	Securities other than shares	0
AF.4	Loans	24
AF.5	Shares and other equity	4
AF.6	Insurance technical reserves	0
AF.7	Other accounts payable	0

B.10	*Changes in net worth, total due to:*	31
B.10.1	*Saving and capital transfers*	21
B.10.2	*Other changes in volume of assets*	0
B.10.3	*Nominal holding gains/losses*	10
B.10.31	Neutral holding gains/losses	8
B.10.32	Real holding gains/losses	2

1 Differences between data on individual items and totals of holding gains/losses may not be entirely consistent due to rounding errors.

Table A.V.7   Full sequence of accounts for non-profit institutions serving households [cont.]

IV.3. Closing balance sheet [1]

Assets			Liabilities and net worth		
AN	Non-financial assets	349	AF	Liabilities	149
AN.1	Produced assets	264	AF.2	Currency and deposits	38
AN.11	Fixed assets	252	AF.3	Securities other than shares	0
AN.12	Inventories	2	AF.4	Loans	67
AN.13	Valuables	10	AF.5	Shares and other equity	4
AN.2	Non-produced assets	85	AF.6	Insurance technical reserves	5
AN.21	Tangible non-produced assets	85	AF.7	Other accounts payable	35
AN.22	Intangible non-produced assets	0			
AF	Financial assets	205			
AF.2	Currency and deposits	122			
AF.3	Securities other than shares	38			
AF.4	Loans	8			
AF.5	Shares and other equity	23			
AF.6	Insurance technical reserves	4			
AF.7	Other accounts receivable	11			
			B.90	*Net worth*	406

1   Differences between data on individual items and totals of holding
gains/losses may not be entirely consistent due to rounding errors.

Table A.V.8. Full sequence of accounts for rest of the world (external transactions account)

V.I: External account of goods and services

Uses			Resources		
P.6	Exports of goods and services	540	P.7	Imports of goods and services	499
P.61	Exports of goods	462	P.71	Imports of goods	392
P.62	Exports of services	78	P.72	Imports of services	107
B.11	*External balance of goods and services*	−41			

V.II: External account of primary incomes and current transfers

Uses			Resources		
D.1	Compensation of employees	6	B.11	*External balance of goods and services*	−41
D.11	Wages and salaries	6			
			D.1	Compensation of employees	2
D.2	Taxes on production and imports	0	D.11	Wages and salaries	2
D.21	Taxes on products	0	D.12	Employers' social contributions	0
D.211	Value added type taxes (VAT)	0	D.121	Employers' actual social contributions	0
D.212	Taxes and duties on imports excluding VAT	0	D.122	Employers' imputed social contributions	0
D.2121	Import duties	0			
D.2122	Taxes on imports excluding VAT and duties	0	D.2	Taxes on production and imports	0
D.213	Export taxes	0	D.21	Taxes on products	0
D.214	Taxes on products except VAT, import and export taxes	0	D.211	Value added type taxes (VAT)	0
D.29	Other taxes on production	0	D.212	Taxes and duties on imports excluding VAT	0
			D.2121	Import duties	0
D.3	Subsidies	0	D.2122	Taxes on imports excluding VAT and duties	0
D.31	Subsidies on products	0	D.213	Export taxes	0
D.311	Import subsidies	0	D.214	Taxes on products except VAT, import and export taxes	0
D.312	Export subsidies	0	D.29	Other taxes on production	0
D.319	Other subsidies on products	0			
D.39	Other subsidies on production	0	D.3	Subsidies	0
			D.31	Subsidies on products	0
D.4	Property income	63	D.311	Import subsidies	0
D.41	Interest	13	D.312	Export subsidies	0
D.42	Distributed income of corporations	36	D.319	Other subsidies on products	0
D.421	Dividends	0	D.39	Other subsidies on production	0
D.422	Withdrawals from income of quasi-corporations	36			
D.43	Reinvested earnings on direct foreign investment	14	D.4	Property income	38
			D.41	Interest	21
D.5	Current taxes on income, wealth, etc.	1	D.42	Distributed income of corporations	17
D.51	Taxes on income	1	D.421	Dividends	14
D.59	Other current taxes	0	D.422	Withdrawals from income of quasi-corporations	3
			D.43	Reinvested earnings on direct foreign investment	0
D.61	Social contributions	0	D.44	Property income attributed to insurance policyholders	0
D.611	Actual social contributions	0			
D.6111	Employers' actual social contributions	0	D.5	Current taxes on income, wealth, etc.	0
D.61111	Compulsory employers' actual social contributions	0	D.51	Taxes on income	0
D.61112	Voluntary employers' actual social contributions	0	D.59	Other current taxes	0
D.6112	Employees' social contributions	0			
D.61121	Compulsory employees' social contributions	0	D.61	Social contributions	0
D.61122	Voluntary employees' social contributions	0	D.611	Actual social contributions	0
D.612	Imputed social contributions	0	D.6111	Employers' actual social contributions	0
			D.61111	Compulsory employers' actual social contributions	0
D.62	Social benefits other than social transfers in kind	0	D.61112	Voluntary employers' actual social contributions	0
D.622	Private funded social benefits	0	D.6112	Employees' social contributions	0
D.623	Unfunded employee social benefits	0	D.61121	Compulsory employees' social contributions	0

Table A.V.8 Full sequence of accounts for rest of the world (external transactions account) [cont.]

V.II: External account of primary incomes and current transfers [cont.]

Uses				Resources		
D.7	Other current transfers		9	D.61122	Voluntary employees' social contributions	0
D.71	Net non-life insurance premiums		2	D.612	Imputed social contributions	0
D.73	Current transfers within general government		4			
D.74	Current international cooperation		1	D.62	Social benefits other than social transfers in kind	0
D.75	Miscellaneous current transfers		2	D.621	Social security benefits in cash	0
				D.622	Private funded social benefits	0
D.8	Adjustment for the change in net equity of households on pension funds		0	D.624	Social assistance benefits in cash	0
				D.7	Other current transfers	39
				D.72	Non-life insurance claims	3
				D.73	Current transfers within general government	4
				D.74	Current international cooperation	31
				D.75	Miscellaneous current transfers	1
				D.8	Adjustment for the change in net equity of households on pension funds	0
B.12	*Current external balance*		– 41			

V.III. Accumulation accounts

V.III.1: Capital account

Changes in assets			Changes in liabilities and net worth		
K.2	Acquisitions less disposals of non-produced non-financial assets	0	B.12	*Current external balance*	– 41
K.21	Acquisitions less disposals of land and other tangible non-produced assets	0	D.9	Capital transfers, receivable	4
K.22	Acquisitions less disposals of intangible non-produced assets	0	D.91	Capital taxes	0
			D.92	Investment grants	4
			D.99	Other capital transfers	0
			D.9	Capital transfers, payable	– 1
			D.91	Capital taxes	0
			D.92	Investment grants	0
			D.99	Other capital transfers	– 1
B.9	*Net lending (+) / net borrowing (–)*	– 38	B.10.1	*Changes in net worth due to saving and capital transfers* [1] [2]	– 38

1 "Changes in net worth due to saving and capital transfers" is not a balancing item but corresponds to the total of the right-hand side of the capital account.
2 "Changes in net worth due to saving and capital transfers" for the rest of the world refers to changes in net worth due to current external balance and capital transfers.

Table A.V.8   Full sequence of accounts for rest of the world (external transactions account) [cont.]

V.III.2: Financial account

Changes in assets			Changes in liabilities and net worth		
F	Net acquisition of financial assets	50	F	Net incurrence of liabilities	88
F.1	Monetary gold and SDRs	1			
F.2	Currency and deposits [1]	11	F.2	Currency and deposits [1]	−2
F.21	Currency	3	F.21	Currency	2
F.22	Transferable deposits	2	F.22	Transferable deposits	−1
F.23	Other deposits	6	F.23	Other deposits	−3
F.3	Securities other than shares	5	F.3	Securities other than shares	20
F.31	Short-term	2	F.31	Short-term	5
F.32	Long-term	3	F.32	Long-term	15
F.4	Loans [2]	10	F.4	Loans [2]	37
F.41	Short-term	3	F.41	Short-term	10
F.42	Long-term	7	F.42	Long-term	27
F.5	Shares and other equity [2]	2	F.5	Shares and other equity [2]	3
F.6	Insurance technical reserves	0	F.6	Insurance technical reserves	0
F.61	Net equity of households on life insurance reserves and on pension funds	0	F.61	Net equity of households on life insurance reserves and on pension funds	0
F.611	Net equity of households on life insurance reserves	0	F.612	Net equity of households on pension funds	0
F.62	Prepayment of premiums and reserves against outstanding claims	0			
			F.7	Other accounts payable [2]	30
F.7	Other accounts receivable [2]	21	F.71	Trade credits and advances	18
F.71	Trade credits and advances	18	F.79	Other accounts payable, except trade credits and advances	12
F.79	Other accounts receivable, except trade credits and advances	3			
			B.9	*Net lending(+)/net borrowing(−)*	−38

1 The following memorandum items related to the elements of the category
F.2 "Currency and deposits":
  m11   denominated in national currency
  m12   denominated in foreign currency
  m21   liability of resident institutions
  m22   liability of rest of the world.
2 Memorandum item: F.m. Direct foreign investment.

Table A.V.8   Full sequence of accounts for rest of the world (external transactions account) [cont.]

V.III.3:   Other changes in assets accounts

V.III.3.1: Other changes in volume of assets account

Changes in assets		
AN	Non-financial assets	0
AN.2	Non-produced assets	0
K.8	Uncompensated seizures	0
K.12	Changes in classifications and structure	0
K.12.2	Changes in classification of assets and liabilities	0
K.12.22	Changes in classification of assets or liabilities other than monetization/demonetization of gold	0
of which:		
AN.21	Tangible non-produced assets	0
AN.22	Intangible non-produced assets	0
AF	Financial assets	0
K.7	Catastrophic losses	0
K.8	Uncompensated seizures	0
K.10	Other volume changes in financial assets and liabilities n.e.c.	0
K.12	Changes in classifications and structure	0
K.12.2	Changes in classification of assets and liabilities	0
K.12.22	Changes in classification of assets or liabilities other than monetization/demonetization of gold	0
of which:		
AF.1	Monetary gold and SDRs	0
AF.2	Currency and deposits	0
AF.3	Securities other than shares	0
AF.4	Loans	0
AF.5	Shares and other equity	0
AF.6	Insurance technical reserves	0
AF.7	Other accounts receivable	0

Changes in liabilities and net worth		
AF	Liabilities	0
K.7	Catastrophic losses	0
K.8	Uncompensated seizures	0
K.10	Other volume changes in financial assets and liabilities n.e.c.	0
K.12	Changes in classifications and structure	0
K.12.1	Changes in sector classification and structure	0
K.12.2	Changes in classification of assets and liabilities	0
K.12.22	Changes in classification of assets or liabilities other than monetization/demonetization of gold	0
of which:		
AF.2	Currency and deposits	0
AF.3	Securities other than shares	0
AF.4	Loans	0
AF.5	Shares and other equity	0
AF.6	Insurance technical reserves	0
AF.7	Other accounts payable	0
B.10.2	*Changes in net worth due to other changes in volume of assets*	0

Table A.V.8 Full sequence of accounts for rest of the world (external transactions account) [cont.]

V.III.3.2: Revaluation account

Changes in assets

K.11	Nominal holding gains(+)/losses(–) [1]:	
AN.2	Non-produced assets	0
AN.21	Tangible non-produced assets	0
AN.22	Intangible non-produced assets	0
AF	Financial assets	7
AF.1	Monetary gold and SDRs	0
AF.2	Currency and deposits	0
AF.3	Securities other than shares	4
AF.4	Loans	0
AF.5	Shares and other equity	3
AF.6	Insurance technical reserves	0
AF.7	Other accounts receivable	0

Changes in liabilities and net worth

K.11	Nominal holding gains(–)/losses(+) [1]:	
AF	Liabilities	3
AF.2	Currency and deposits	0
AF.3	Securities other than shares	2
AF.4	Loans	0
AF.5	Shares and other equity	0
AF.6	Insurance technical reserves	0
AF.7	Other accounts payable	0
B.10.3	*Changes in net worth due to nominal holding gains/losses*	4

1   Differences between data on individual items and totals of holding
gains/losses may not be entirely consistent due to rounding errors.

Table A.V.8   Full sequence of accounts for rest of the world (external transactions account) [cont.]

V.III.3.2.1: Neutral holding gains/losses account

Changes in assets		
K.11.1	Neutral holding gains (+)/losses (−) [1]:	
AN.2	Non-produced assets	0
AN.21	Tangible non-produced assets	0
AN.22	Intangible non-produced assets	0
AF	Financial assets	11
AF.1	Monetary gold and SDRs	0
AF.2	Currency and deposits	2
AF.3	Securities other than shares	3
AF.4	Loans	1
AF.5	Shares and other equity	2
AF.6	Insurance technical reserves	1
AF.7	Other accounts receivable	3

Changes in liabilities and net worth		
K.11.1	Neutral holding gains (−)/losses (+) [1]:	
AF	Liabilities	6
AF.2	Currency and deposits	2
AF.3	Securities other than shares	2
AF.4	Loans	0
AF.5	Shares and other equity	0
AF.6	Insurance technical reserves	1
AF.7	Other accounts payable	1
B.10.31	*Changes in net worth due to neutral holding gains/losses*	6

1   Differences between data on individual items and totals of holding
gains/losses may not be entirely consistent due to rounding errors.

V.III.3.2.2: Real holding gains/losses account

Changes in assets		
K.11.2	Real holding gains(+)/losses(−) [1]:	
AN.2	Non-produced assets	0
AN.21	Tangible non-produced assets	0
AN.22	Intangible non-produced assets	0
AF	Financial assets	5
AF.1	Monetary gold and SDRs	0
AF.2	Currency and deposits	− 2
AF.3	Securities other than shares	1
AF.4	Loans	− 1
AF.5	Shares and other equity	0
AF.6	Insurance technical reserves	− 1
AF.7	Other accounts receivable	− 3

Changes in liabilities and net worth		
K.11.2	Real holding gains(−)/losses(+) [1]:	
AF	Liabilities	− 3
AF.2	Currency and deposits	− 2
AF.3	Securities other than shares	1
AF.4	Loans	− 0
AF.5	Shares and other equity	0
AF.6	Insurance technical reserves	− 1
AF.7	Other accounts payable	− 1
B.10.32	*Changes in net worth due to real holding gains/losses*	− 1

1   Differences between data on individual items and totals of holding
gains/losses may not be entirely consistent due to rounding errors.

Table A.V.8 Full sequence of accounts for rest of the world (external transactions account) [cont.]

V.IV: External assets and liabilities account

V.IV.1: Opening balance sheet

Assets				Liabilities and net worth		
AN	Non-financial assets		0	AF	Liabilities	297
AN.2	Non-produced assets		0	AF.2	Currency and deposits	116
AN.21	Tangible non-produced assets		0	AF.3	Securities other than shares	77
AN.22	Intangible non-produced assets		0	AF.4	Loans	17
				AF.5	Shares and other equity	3
AF	Financial assets		573	AF.6	Insurance technical reserves	25
AF.1	Monetary gold and SDRs		0	AF.7	Other accounts payable	59
AF.2	Currency and deposits		105			
AF.3	Securities other than shares		125			
AF.4	Loans		70			
AF.5	Shares and other equity		113			
AF.6	Insurance technical reserves		26			
AF.7	Other accounts receivable		134	B.90	*Net worth*	276

V.IV.2: Changes in balance sheet [1]

Assets				Liabilities and net worth		
	Total changes in assets				Total changes in liabilities	
AN	Non-financial assets		0	AF	Liabilities	91
AN.2	Non-produced assets		0	AF.2	Currency and deposits	− 2
AN.21	Tangible non-produced assets		0	AF.3	Securities other than shares	22
AN.22	Intangible non-produced assets		0	AF.4	Loans	37
				AF.5	Shares and other equity	3
AF	Financial assets		57	AF.6	Insurance technical reserves	0
AF.1	Monetary gold and SDRs		1	AF.7	Other accounts payable	30
AF.2	Currency and deposits		11			
AF.3	Securities other than shares		9			
AF.4	Loans		10			
AF.5	Shares and other equity		5			
AF.6	Insurance technical reserves		0	B.10	*Changes in net worth, total* due to:	− 34
AF.7	Other accounts receivable		21	B.10.1	*Saving and capital transfers*	− 38
				B.10.2	*Other changes in volume of assets*	0
				B.10.3	*Nominal holding gains/losses*	4
				B.10.31	Neutral holding gains/losses	6
				B.10.32	Real holding gains/losses	− 1

1 Differences between data on individual items and totals of holding gains/losses may not be entirely consistent due to rounding errors.

Table A.V.8 Full sequence of accounts for rest of the world (external transactions account) [cont.]

V.IV.3. Closing balance sheet [1]

Assets			Liabilities and net worth		
AN	Non-financial assets	0	AF	Liabilities	388
AN.2	Non-produced assets	0	AF.2	Currency and deposits	114
AN.21	Tangible non-produced assets	0	AF.3	Securities other than shares	99
AN.22	Intangible non-produced assets	0	AF.4	Loans	54
			AF.5	Shares and other equity	6
AF	Financial assets	630	AF.6	Insurance technical reserves	25
AF.1	Monetary gold and SDRs	0	AF.7	Other accounts payable	89
AF.2	Currency and deposits	116			
AF.3	Securities other than shares	134			
AF.4	Loans	80			
AF.5	Shares and other equity	118			
AF.6	Insurance technical reserves	26			
AF.7	Other accounts receivable	155			
			B.90	*Net worth*	242

1   Differences between data on individual items and totals of holding
gains/losses may not be entirely consistent due to rounding errors.

Annex VI
List of expert group meetings on the revision of the System of National Accounts

1.	SNA structure	23-27 June 1986	Geneva
2.	Prices and quantity comparisons	10-14 November 1986	Luxembourg
3.	External sector	23 March-2 April 1987	Washington, D.C.
4.	Household sector	30 August-4 September 1987	Florence
5.	Public sector	25-29 January 1988	Washington, D.C.
6.	Production accounts and input-output tables	21-30 March 1988	Vienna
7.	Financial flows and balances	6-15 September 1988	Washington, D.C.
8.	SNA coordination	23-27 January 1989	Luxembourg
9.	SNA coordination	12-21 July 1989	New York
10.	SNA coordination	13-22 September 1989	New York
11.	Reconciliation of SNA and MPS	4-9 December 1989	Moscow
12.	SNA coordination	3-7 December 1990	Washington, D.C.
13.	SNA coordination	8-17 April 1991	Harare, Zimbabwe
14.	SNA coordination	1, 2 and 10 October 1992	Aguascalientes, Mexico

Index

European ... ns
... able from the
Office of C ... *n Communities*
D-2980, Luxembourg

How to obtain
International Monetary Fund publications

Interna' ... okstores and
distr ... r fax to:

Publ ... 31 USA

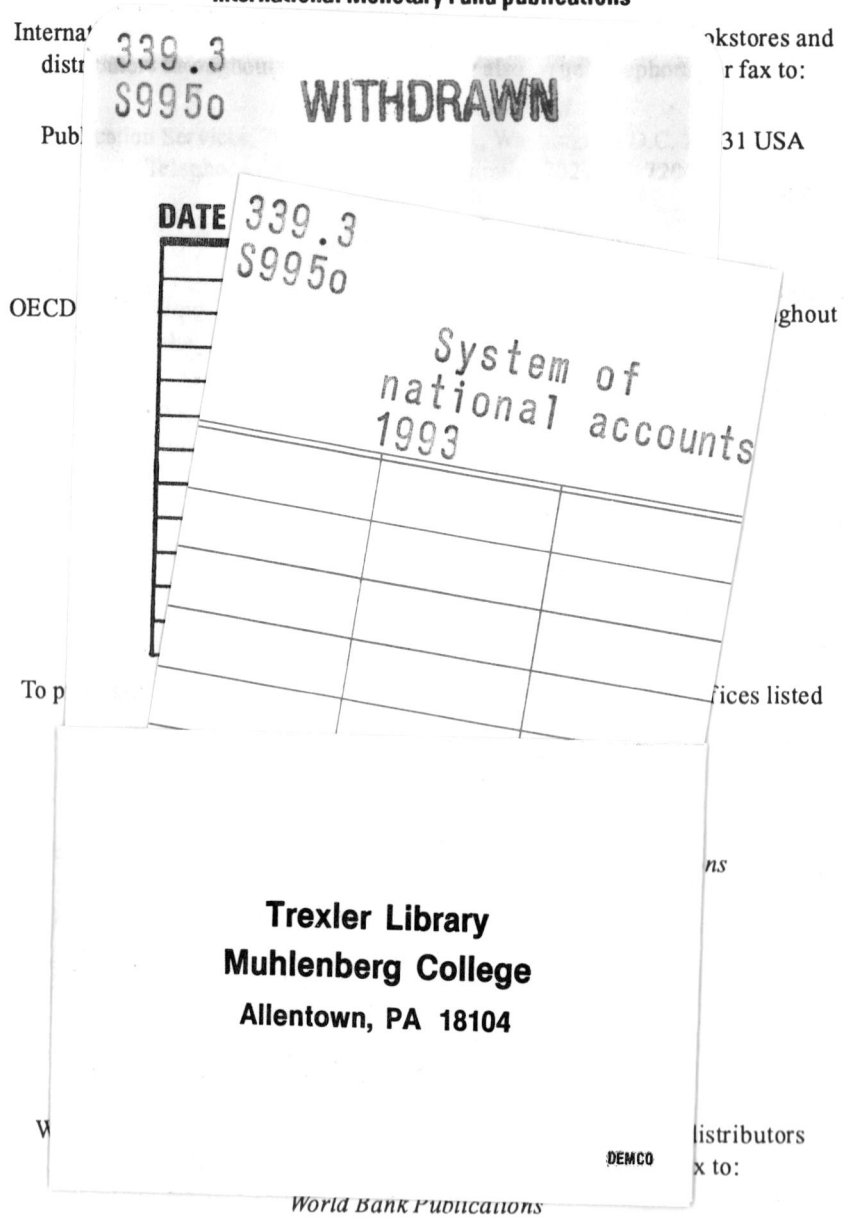

OECD ... ghout

To p ... ices listed

ns

W ... listributors
x to:

World Bank Publications
Box 7247-8619, Philadelphia, PA 19170-8619, USA
Telephone: (202) 473 1155 Facsimile (202) 676-0581